Andrew Mellow

Secretary of the Treasury Annual Report

1880

Andrew Mellow

Secretary of the Treasury Annual Report
1880

ISBN/EAN: 9783741135514

Manufactured in Europe, USA, Canada, Australia, Japa

Cover: Foto ©Thomas Meinert / pixelio.de

Manufactured and distributed by brebook publishing software
(www.brebook.com)

Anonymus

The Irish Ecclesiastical Record

THE IRISH

ECCLESIASTICAL RECORD

A Monthly Journal, under Episcopal Sanction

VOLUME XI.

JANUARY to JUNE, 1902

Fourth Series

DUBLIN
BROWNE & NOLAN, LIMITED, NASSAU-STREET
1902

Andrew Mellow

Secretary of the Treasury Annual Report

For miscellaneous expenditures, including public buildings, light-houses, and collecting the revenue. $34, 535, 691 0

For expenditures on account of the District of Columbia 3, 272, 384 63

For interest on the public debt.... ....   95, 757, 575 11

For premium on bonds purchased 2, 795, 320 42

    Total ordinary expenditures.................   267, 642, 957 78

Leaving a surplus revenue of............ .... $65, 883, 653 20

Which, with an amount drawn from cash balance in Treasury, of................................   8, 084, 434 21

    Making 73, 968, 087 41

Was applied to the redemption—

Of bonds for the sinking-fund.................   73, 652, 900 00

Of fractional currency for the sinking-fund.....   251, 717 41

Of the loan of 1858...........................   40, 000 00

Of temporary loan 100 00

Of bounty-land scrip 25 00

Of compound-interest notes...................   16, 500 00

Of 7.30 notes of 1864–'5.......................   2, 650 00

Of one and two-year notes 3, 700 00

Of old demand notes 495 00

                              73, 968, 087 41

The amount due the sinking-fund for this year was $37,931,643 55. There was applied thereto, from the redemption of bonds and fractional currency, as shown in the above statement, the sum of $73,904,617 41, an excess of $35,972,973 86 over the amount actually required for the year.

The requirements of the sinking-fund law have been substantially observed, and the principal of the public debt, less cash in the Treasury and exclusive of accruing interest, has been reduced from $2,756,431,571 43, its highest point, which it reached on August 31, 1865, to $1,890,025,740 89, on November 1, 1880—a reduction of $866,405,830 54.

Compared with the previous fiscal year, the receipts for 1880 have increased $62,629,438 23, in the following items: In customs revenue, $49,272,016 90; in internal revenue, $10,447,763 34; in sales of public lands, $91,725 54; in tax on circulation and deposits of national banks, $267,471 12; in proceeds of sales of Government property, $101,487 69;

in consular fees, $142,551 32; in custom-house fees, $92,403 63; in steamboat fees, $12,063 39; in marine-hospital tax, $27,183 29; in interest on Indian trust-funds, $640,901 59; in sales of Indian lands, $272,883 54; in deposits by individuals for surveying public lands, $380,062 33; and in miscellaneous items, $880,924 55. There was a decrease of $2,930,011 71, as follows: In premium on loans, $1,496,943 25; in repayment of interest by Pacific Railway Companies, $999,833 85; in profits on coinage, $132,751 89; in premium on sales of coin, $8,104 38; in customs fines, penalties, and forfeitures, $39,726 78; in customs-emolument fees, $4,748 35; and in unenumerated items, $247,903 21—making a net increase in the receipts, from all sources, for the year, of $59,699,426 52.

The expenditures show an increase over the previous year of $25,190,360 48, as follows: In the Interior Department, $22,395,040 06; (Indians, $739,348 01; and pensions, $21,655,692 05;) in premium on bonds purchased, $2,795,320 42. There was a decrease of $24,495,286 23, as follows: In the War Department, $2,308,744 51; in the Navy Department, $1,588,142 10; in the interest on public debt, $9,570,373 89; and in the civil and miscellaneous, $11,028,025 73—making a net increase in the expenditures, for the year, of $695,074 25.

FISCAL YEAR 1881.

For the present fiscal year the revenue, actual and estimated, is as follows:

Source.	For the quarter ended Sept. 30, 1880. Actual.	For the remaining three quarters of the year. Estimated.
From customs..............................	$56,395,143 44	$138,604,856 56
From internal revenue	32,496,422 38	97,503,577 62
From sales of public lands..................	434,590 66	765,409 34
From tax on circulation and deposits of national banks	3,933,346 37	3,190,653 63
From repayment of interest by Pacific Railway Companies	211,402 76	1,588,597 24
From customs fees, fines, penalties, &c.......	351,870 95	898,129 05
From fees—consular, letters-patent, and lands.	542,064 23	1,907,935 77
From proceeds of sales of Government property	56,311 23	193,688 77
From profits on coinage, &c..................	985,882 46	1,914,117 54
From revenues of the District of Columbia...	265,872 65	1,510,127 35
From miscellaneous sources.................	2,216,332 79	4,033,667 21
Total receipts......................	97,889,239 92	252,110,760 08

The expenditures for the same period, actual and estimated, are—

Source.	For the quarter ended Sept. 30, 1880. Actual.	For the remaining three quarters of the year. Estimated.
For civil and miscellaneous expenses, including public buildings, light-houses, and collecting the revenue	$16,363,841 35	$36,636,158 65
For Indians	2,800,661 99	3,849,338 01
For pensions	13,604,079 14	36,395,920 86
For military establishment, including fortifications, river and harbor improvements, and arsenals	12,640,602 13	28,359,397 87
For naval establishment, including vessels and machinery, and improvements at navy-yards	5,085,571 98	9,914,428 02
For expenditures on account of the District of Columbia	1,298,944 61	2,051,055 39
For interest on the public debt	25,224,830 58	65,775,169 42
Total ordinary expenditures	77,018,531 78	182,981,468 22

Total receipts, actual and estimated $350,000,000 00
Total expenditures, actual and estimated 260,000,000 00

                                                    90,000,000 00
Estimated amount due the sinking-fund 39,801,884 48

        Leaving a balance of 50,198,115 52

The act of February 25, 1862, amended by the act of July 14, 1870, providing for a sinking-fund for the payment of the public debt, is in conformity with the policy which has prevailed since the adoption of the Constitution, of regarding a public debt as a temporary burden, to be paid off as rapidly as the public interests will allow. The provisions of these acts have been substantially complied with. They were executed literally, until the panic of 1873, by largely decreasing the revenues of the Government, rendered it impossible to meet their requirements. The deficiency on the sinking-fund account is as follows:

In the fiscal year 1874 .... $16,305,421 96
In the fiscal year 1875 .... 5,996,039 62
In the fiscal year 1876 .... 1,143,769 82
In the fiscal year 1877 .... 9,225,146 63
In the fiscal year 1878 .... 18,415,557 31
In the fiscal year 1879 .... 36,231,632 87

Total amount due on sinking-fund 87,317,568 21

Less the payment made during the past fiscal year in excess of the amount required, as above set forth. $35,972,973 86

Leaving a balance still due on account of the sinking-fund, of....................................... 51,344,594 35

Or nearly the same amount as the balance of estimated receipts over the estimated expenditures, as shown above. Thus it is probable that there can be applied to the purchase of bonds for the sinking-fund during the present fiscal year an amount sufficient to cover the whole deficiency now existing on the account of that fund, thus making good the whole amount of the sinking-fund as required by law.

FISCAL YEAR 1882.

The revenues of the fiscal year ending June 30, 1882, estimated upon the basis of existing laws, will be—

From customs	$195,000,000 00
From internal revenue........................	130,000,000 00
From sales of public lands....................	1,000,000 00
From tax on circulation and deposits of national banks.	7,124,000 00
From repayment of interest by Pacific Railway Companies..........................	2,500,000 00
From sinking-fund for Pacific Railway Companies ..	1,500,000 00
From customs fees, fines, penalties, &c.............	1,150,000 00
From fees—consular, letters-patent, and lands......	2,350,000 00
From proceeds of sales of Government property....	200,000 00
From profits on coinage, &c.....................	2,800,000 00
From revenues of the District of Columbia.........	1,676,000 00
From miscellaneous sources.....................	4,700,000 00
Total ordinary receipts	350,000,000 00

The estimates of expenditures, for the same period, received from the several Executive Departments, are as follows:

Legislative	$3,038,643 26
Executive	14,536,404 23
Judicial	399,300 00
Foreign intercourse	1,257,035 00
Military establishment	30,240,790 04
Naval establishment............................	15,022,331 01
Indian affairs	4,858,866 80
Pensions	50,000,000 00

Public works:

Treasury Department	$3,583,022 56
War Department	9,896,050 00
Navy Department	931,421 05
Interior Department	605,042 07
Post-Office Department	36,000 00
Department of Agriculture	8,000 00
Postal service	3,630,757 90
Miscellaneous	16,794,646 91
District of Columbia	3,352,000 00

Permanent annual appropriations:

Interest on the public debt	88,877,410 00
Sinking-fund	41,639,840 20
Refunding—customs, internal revenue, lands, &c.	5,832,900 00
Collecting revenue from customs	5,500,000 00
Miscellaneous	1,514,261 25

Total estimated expenditures, including sinking-fund	301,554,722 28
Or, an estimated surplus of	$48,445,277 72

Excluding the sinking-fund, the estimated expenditures will be $259,914,882 08, showing a surplus of $90,085,117 92.

The Secretary respectfully renews his recommendation of last year that, with a view to promote economy in the public service, a permanent organization of an appropriation committee for each House be established, who shall have leave to sit during the recess of Congress, with power to send for persons and papers, and to examine all expenditures of the Government; that rules be adopted by the respective Houses limiting appropriation bills to items of appropriation and excluding legislative provisions; that all appropriations, except for the interest on the public debt, be limited to a period not exceeding two years, and that the expenditure of appropriations be strictly confined to the period of time for which they were appropriated.

REDUCTION OF TAXES.

It appears from the foregoing statements that the surplus revenue, actual and estimated, for the fiscal years 1880, 1881, and 1882, after providing for the sinking-fund for each year, is as follows:

For the year ended June 30, 1880	$27,952,009 65
For the year ending June 30, 1881	50,198,115 52
For the year ending June 30, 1882	48,445,277 72

This naturally presents to Congress the question whether the surplus revenue accruing after the present year should be applied to the
further reduction of the public debt, or whether taxes now imposed
should be repealed or modified to the extent of such surplus. The
many and sudden changes that have heretofore occurred in the
amounts realized from our system of taxation are a sufficient warning
that revenue should not be surrendered unless it satisfactorily appears
that the surplus is permanent, and not merely temporary. If the taxes
imposed by existing laws are not oppressive in their nature, it is perhaps better to bear with them than to endanger the ability of the
Government to meet the 'current appropriations and the sinking-
fund. A large portion of the surplus of revenue over expenditures is
caused by the reduction of the rate of interest and the payment of the
principal of the public debt. The reduction of annual interest caused
by refunding since March 1, 1877, is $14,290,453 50, and the saving
of annual interest resulting from the payment of $109,489,850 of the
principal of the public debt, since that date, is $6,144,737 50. The
interest is likely to be still further reduced during the next year
in an amount estimated at $12,101,429 50, by the refunding of bonds
as hereinafter proposed. To the extent of this annual saving,
amounting to $32,539,620 50, the public expenditures will be perma-
nently diminished. The large increase of revenue from customs on a
few articles during the last year may be somewhat abnormal, and the
estimates based upon it may not be realized. It is a question for
Congress to determine whether any material reduction should be made
at a time when the whole surplus revenue may be with great advantage applied directly to the payment of accruing debt, and when such
surplus is an important element in aid of refunding. If it should be
determined by Congress to reduce taxes, it is respectfully recommended
that all the taxes imposed by the internal-revenue law other than
those on bank-circulation and on spirits, tobacco, and fermented liquors
be repealed. The tax on the circulation of national banks is levied
partly in the nature of a moderate charge for a franchise conferred by
the Government, and partly to furnish means to pay the expense of
printing and issuing national-bank notes. It is easily collected by the
Treasurer of the United States, and is a just and proper tax, whether
regarded as a charge for the franchise or as a means of reimbursing
the Government the cost of printing the notes. The tax on State banks
is of the gravest importance, not for purposes of revenue, but as a
check upon the renewal of a system of local State paper money
which, as it would be issued under varying State laws, would neces-

sarily differ as to conditions, terms, and security, and could not, from its diversity, be guarded against counterfeiting, and would, at best, have but limited circulation.

REFUNDING.

A large portion of the public debt becomes payable or redeemable on or before July 1, next, as follows:

Title of loan.	Rate.	Payable.	Redeemable.	Amount.
Loan of February, 1861...	6 per cent .	Dec. 31, 1880	....	$13,414,000
Oregon-War debt	6 per cent .	July 1, 1881	....	711,800
Loan July and Aug., 1861.	6 per cent .	....	June 30, 1881	145,786,500
Loan of 1863, (1881's).....	6 per cent .	....	June 30, 1881	57,787,250
Funded Loan of 1881	5 per cent .	....	May 1, 1881	469,651,050
Outstanding Nov. 1, 1880..	....	....	....	687,350,600

The bonds maturing December 31, 1880, will be paid from accruing revenue. The surplus revenue accruing prior to July 1, 1881, estimated at about fifty million dollars, ($50,000,000,) will be applied under existing law to the purchase or payment of the bonds above described, thus leaving the sum of $637,350,600 to be provided for. The third section of the act approved July 14, 1870, for refunding the national debt, under which the five per cent. bonds, maturing May 1, 1880, are redeemable, requires the Secretary of the Treasury to give public notice three months in advance of their payment. To enable the Department to avail itself of the option of redeeming these bonds at their maturity, the necessary legislation for that purpose should be passed prior to February 1, next. The five and six per cent. bonds are not, by their terms, payable at a specific date, but they are redeemable at the pleasure of the United States after the dates above named. They bear a much higher rate of interest than the rate at which new bonds can be sold. Any delay in providing for their redemption will compel the continued payment of high rates of interest; it will make necessary the issue of a new series of coupons to the holders of coupon bonds, and may postpone to a less favorable period the completion of the operations of refunding. Under existing law, there is still available for this purpose four per cent. bonds authorized by the acts of July 14, 1870, and January 20, 1871, to the amount of $104,652,200. These could now be sold at a large premium, and, in the absence of legislation, it would be the duty of the Secretary, when any bonds became redeemable, to sell the four per cents and apply the proceeds to the

redemption of such bonds; but the amount of four per cents authorized
is inadequate to the purpose stated. It is therefore advisable, by new
and comprehensive legislation, to authorize the sale of other securities
sufficient to redeem the whole sum soon to be redeemable. The terms
and conditions of the securities to be authorized for this purpose have
received the careful attention of this Department. Hitherto the policy
has been to sell bonds bearing as low a rate of interest as possible,
running a number of years; but, in view of the requirements of the
sinking-fund, it is believed that a large portion of the public debt to be
redeemed can be provided for by Treasury notes, running from one to
ten years, issued in such sums as can, by the application of the sinking-
fund, be paid as they mature. The purchase of bonds not due has
heretofore involved the payment of premiums, which it is believed can,
in future, be avoided by the issue of such Treasury notes. The large
accumulation of money now seeking investment affords a favorable
opportunity for selling such notes bearing a low rate of interest. It
is believed that they will form a popular security, always available
to the holder, and readily convertible into money when needed for
other investment or business. They should be in such form and
denominations as to furnish a convenient investment for the small
savings of the people, and fill the place designed by the ten-dollar
refunding certificates authorized by the act of February 26, 1879. No
other United States bonds than those stated become redeemable prior
to the 1st of September, 1891, the date of maturity of the four-and-a-
half per cent. bonds. The requirements of the sinking-fund prior to
the maturity of the four-and-a-half per cent. bonds, for a period of ten
years, from 1882 to 1891, both inclusive, are estimated as follows:

For the fiscal year ending June 30, 1882 .... $43,386,645 00
For the fiscal year ending June 30, 1883........... 45,122,110 80
For the fiscal year ending June 30, 1884 .... 46,926,995 24
For the fiscal year ending June 30, 1885........... 48,804,075 04
For the fiscal year ending June 30, 1886........... 50,756,238 04
For the fiscal year ending June 30, 1887........... 52,786,487 56
For the fiscal year ending June 30, 1888 .... 54,897,947 07
For the fiscal year ending June 30, 1889........... 57,093,864 95
For the fiscal year ending June 30, 1890........... 59,377,619 55
For the fiscal year ending June 30, 1891 .... 61,752,724 33

520,904,707 58

It may be that during this period, by the change of our financial condition, or from unforeseen events, the Government will not be able, as in times past, to apply sums so large to the reduction of the debt; but it is probable that any temporary deficiency would soon be made good by increased revenue. This contingency may be provided for by the terms of the bonds.

The Secretary, therefore, recommends that provision be made for the issue of an amount not exceeding $400,000,000 of Treasury notes in denominations not less than ten dollars, bearing interest not exceeding four per cent. per annum, and running from one to ten years, to be sold at not less than par, the amount maturing during any year not to exceed the sinking-fund for that year, and the proceeds to be applied to the payment of five and six per cent. bonds, maturing in 1881. It is believed that, with the present favorable state of the money-market, a sufficient amount of such Treasury notes, bearing an annual interest of three per cent., can be sold to meet a considerable portion of the maturing bonds; but it is better to confer upon the Department a discretionary power to stipulate for a higher maximum rate, to avoid the possibility of failure. Such a discretion is not likely to be abused, while a power too carefully restricted may defeat the beneficial object of the law.

It is also recommended that authority be given to sell at par an amount not exceeding $400,000,000 of bonds of the character and description of the four per cent. bonds of the United States now outstanding, but bearing a rate of interest not exceeding three and sixty-five one-hundredths per cent. per annum, and redeemable at the pleasure of the United States after fifteen years, the proceeds to be applied to the payment of bonds redeemable on or before July 1, 1881. Though the amount of the two classes of securities recommended exceeds the amount of bonds to be redeemed, no more can be sold than the bonds to be redeemed, while the alternative authorized will permit a limited discretion to sell the securities most favorable to the Government. With the authority thus recommended, it is believed that the Department can within a year redeem all the five and six per cent. bonds now outstanding, and thus reduce the interest of the public debt $12,000,000 per annum, and leave the debt in a form most favorable for gradual payment by the application of the sinking-fund without cost or premium.

RESUMPTION.

Nothing has occurred since my last annual report to disturb or embarrass the easy maintenance of specie payments. United States notes are readily taken at par with coin in all parts of this country and in the chief commercial marts of the world. The balance of coin in the Treasury available for their redemption on the first day of November last was $141,597,013 61, and the average during the year has not materially varied from that sum. The only noticeable change in the reserve is the gradual increase of silver coin caused by the coinage of the silver dollar and the redemption of fractional silver coin, more fully stated hereinafter.

The amount of notes presented for redemption for one year prior to November 1, 1880, was $706,658. The amount of coin or bullion deposited in the Treasury, assay office, and the mints, during the same period was $71,396,535 67. These deposits have usually been paid for in coin, through the clearing house, but at times, when the currency in the Treasury would allow, and at the request of the depositors, they have been paid for in United States notes and silver certificates. Gold coin now enters largely into general circulation. Of the revenue from customs collected in New York for one year ending November 1, 1880, .57,475 per cent. was paid in gold coin, .00,125 per cent. in silver coin, .31,087, in silver certificates, and .11,313 per cent. in United States notes. While no distinction as to value is made between coin and notes in business transactions, a marked preference is shown for notes, owing to their superior convenience in counting and carrying. Many of the current payments from the Treasury are necessarily made in coin, and much of the funds held for the redemption of national-bank notes and of notes of banks that have failed or suspended is in coin. The total coin in the Treasury, at the close of business, November 1, was $218,710,154, of which $141,597,013 61 constituted the reserve fund for the redemption of United States notes, as above stated.

All the requirements of the resumption act have thus far been executed, and its wisdom has been fully demonstrated. It only remains to inquire whether any further measures are necessary or expedient to secure the maintenance of resumption. The Secretary expresses the utmost confidence that without new legislation the entire amount of United States notes now authorized and outstanding can be easily maintained at par in coin even if the present favorable financial condition should change; but, in order to accomplish this, the coin reserve must be kept unimpaired except by such payments as may be made from it in redemption of notes. Notes redeemed should be temporarily held in place of the coin paid out, especially if it appears that the call for coin is greater in amount than the coin coming in due course into the

Treasury or the mints. Ordinarily the superior convenience of notes will, as at present, make a greater demand for them than for coin ; but in case of an adverse balance of trade or a sudden panic, or other unforeseen circumstances, the ample reserve of coin on hand becomes the sure safeguard of resumption, dispelling not only imaginary fears, but meeting any demand for coin that is likely to arise. In a supreme emergency, the power granted to sell bonds will supply any possible deficiency.

It is suggested that Congress might define and set apart the coin reserve as a special fund for resumption purposes. The general available balance is now treated as such a fund, but, as this balance may, at the discretion of the Secretary of the Treasury, be unduly drawn upon for the purchase or payment of bonds, it would appear advisable that Congress prescribe the maximum and minimum of the fund.

United States notes are now, in form, security, and convenience, the best circulating medium known. The objection is made that they are issued by the Government, and that it is not the business of the Government to furnish paper money, but only to coin money. The answer is, that the Government had to borrow money, and is still in debt. The United States note, to the extent that it is willingly taken by the people, and can, beyond question, be maintained at par in coin, is the least burdensome form of debt. The loss of interest in maintaining the resumption-fund, and the cost of printing and engraving the present amount of United States notes, is less than one-half the interest on an equal sum of four per cent. bonds. The public thus saves over seven million dollars of annual interest, and secures a safe and convenient medium of exchange, and has the assurance that a sufficient reserve in coin will be retained in the Treasury beyond the temptation of diminution, such as always attends reserves held by banks.

Another objection to the issue of United States notes is, that they are made a legal-tender in the payment of debts. The question of the constitutional power of Congress to make them such, is one for another branch of the Government. The Secretary of the Treasury is still of the opinion that this quality of legal-tender does not add to the usefulness, safety, or circulation of United States notes. So far as it excites distrust and opposition to this form of circulating-notes it is a detriment. The fear that a withdrawal of this attribute will contract the currency is as delusive as was the fear that resumption would have a like effect. The notes would still be received and paid out by the Government, and, like bank-notes, would not be refused in payment for debts while they were redeemable and promptly redeemed in coin on presentation. As the quality of legal tender was attached to these notes when first issued, and was then essential to their value and circulation, the public mind is sensitive when any proposition is made that by possibility might impair their value, but it is their redemption in coin that makes them now equal to coin and of ready circulation in all the marts of the world. While this is maintained it becomes comparatively immaterial whether they are a legal-tender or not, and if by the action of Congress or the courts they are deprived of this quality they will still be the favorite money of the people.

Another objection to United States notes is, that the amount of the issue may be enlarged by Congress, and that this power is liable to abuse. This objection may be made to all the great essential powers of the Government. A sufficient answer is that, since their first issue, they have been carefully limited in amount, and invested with every quality to improve their value and circulation. Every effort to increase the amount, made during a period of great depression, failed. Now that they are redeemable in coin there is no temptation for over-issue.

These objections will, no doubt, in due time receive the careful consideration of Congress, and any practical difficulties in maintaining resumption will be met by new legislation. But the Secretary ventures to express the opinion that the present system of currency, the substantial features of which are a limited amount of United States notes, (with or without the legal-tender quality,) promptly redeemable in coin, with ample reserves in coin and ample power if necessary to purchase coin with bonds, supplemented by the circulating-notes of national banks issued upon conditions that guarantee their absolute security and prompt redemption, and all based on coin of equal value, generally distributed throughout the country, is the best system ever devised, and more free from objection than any other, combining the only safe standard with convenience for circulation and security and equality of value.

COINS AND COINAGE.

The coinage executed at the mints during the fiscal year has exceeded in value that of any previous year since the organization of the Government. Its total amount, not including the minor coinage, was $84,100,172 50, of which it is estimated $62,000,000 was probably from domestic, and $21,000,000 from imported bullion.

The annual report of the Director of the Mint furnishes detailed statements of the coinage of gold and silver, the amount deposited, parted, refined, or made into bars, the earnings, receipts, and expenditures, and other transactions and business operations of the mints and assay offices during the year, and contains valuable statistics and careful estimates of the production, consumption, and circulation of the precious metals in the United States and many other countries.

The inquiries as to the production, use in arts, coinage, and circulation of the precious metals, and the collection of other monetary statistics in our own and foreign countries, have been continued by the Mint Bureau, and much valuable information on these subjects has been obtained, and will be found in the report of the Director.

. The deposits of gold during the last fiscal year amounted to $98,835,096 85, being $56,580,940 05 in excess of that in the previous year, notwithstanding a probable slightly diminished domestic production. Out of a total import at the port of New York of $60,947,672 of foreign-gold coin and bullion, $60,584,395 13 were deposited at the New York assay office, and there exchanged for United States coin or bars, or for current money. Nearly all of this coin and bullion, being at or above the United States standard, is excepted from a melting-charge under present regulations, and is transported at Government expense to the mint for coinage. The coinage law makes no provision for any charges for melting gold bullion which is not below the United States standard, when deposited for coin, and requires such deposits to be transported from the New York assay office to the Philadelphia mint at the expense of the Government. As nearly all the imported bullion deposited is in such a form that it is necessary to melt it, in order to ascertain its fineness and value, a modification of the law so as to authorize a charge for melting is recommended.

The gold imported at New York, during the earlier part of the last fiscal year, exceeded the capacity of the Philadelphia mint for coinage, with its ordinary working-force, without incurring expenses much above the specific appropriations for its support. The coinage of gold at Philadelphia had to be made subordinate to that of silver, in order to comply with the requirements of the law directing the purchase and coinage of $2,000,000 worth of silver bullion in each month, and to satisfy the demand for minor coins authorized to be struck only at that mint. The mint was able, with its other work, to coin in gold an amount little exceeding on the average $2,000,000 per month, but this was found sufficient to satisfy the immediate demands upon it for coin. At the close of the year there remained in the mints and New York assay office $40,724,337 91, in gold bullion uncoined, nearly all of it imported.

The amount of coinage executed at the mints of the United States, during the fiscal year, was—

Gold	$56,157,735 00
Standard-silver dollars	27,933,750 00
Fractional silver coins	8,687 50
Minor coins	269,971 50
Total	84,370,144 00

Of the gold coinage $18,836,320 was in eagles, $15,790,860 in half-eagles, and $21,515,360 in double-eagles. Five-eighths of the coinage was in denominations which were less than $20. This was not only a larger proportion than in any preceding year, but was in amount nearly equal to the total coinage in those denominations during the preceding thirty years.

The coin circulation of the country on January 1, 1879, the date fixed for resumption, is estimated from the statistics of coinage and excess of imports of coin over exports, to have been—

United States gold coin	$273,271,707
United States gold bullion	5,038,419
United States silver coin	95,516,712
United States silver bullion	11,057,091
Total	384,883,929

This had increased, on the 30th of June last, by coinage and imports of coin, to—

United States gold coin	$358,958,691
United States silver coin	142,597,020
Total	501,555,711

This was further increased from coinage and imports, during the four months, to November 1, by—

Coinage of gold	$14,544,599
Excess of imports over exports of United States gold coin	1,820,591
Total	16,365,190

Coinage of silver	$9,113,000
Excess of imports over exports of United States silver coin	567,524
Total	9,680,524

There was in the mints and assay offices on the 1st of November, bullion held for coinage amounting to $78,553,811 55 of gold, and $6,043,367 37 of silver, making the total coin circulation and bullion available for coinage in the country of—

Gold $453,882,692
Silver 158,320,911

    Total 612,203,603

STANDARD-SILVER DOLLAR.

In compliance with the provisions of the act of February 28, 1878, during the last fiscal year 24,262,571.38 standard ounces of silver bullion, costing $24,972,161 81, (an average of $2,081,013 48 per month,) were purchased, of which 24,005,566.41 ounces were coined into 27,933,750 standard-silver dollars. The total coinage of standard-silver dollars since the passage of the act, up to November 1, 1880, has been $72,847,750, at which date $47,084,450 were in the Treasury. Of the latter amount $19,780,241 were represented by outstanding silver certificates, the amount in actual circulation at that date being $25,763,291.

Since the passage of that act, the Department has issued numerous circulars and notices to the public in which it has offered every inducement which it could under the law, to facilitate the general distribution and circulation of these coins. It has required United States disbursing officers to pay them out in payment for salaries and for other current obligations, and it has offered to place the silver in the hands of the people throughout the United States without expense for transportation, when sent by express, and at an expense for registration-fee only, when sent by registered mail.

Notwithstanding these efforts, it is found to be difficult to maintain in circulation more than 35 per cent. of the amount coined. While at special seasons of the year, and for special purposes, this coin is in demand, mainly in the South, it returns again to the Treasury, and its reissue involves an expense for transportation at an average rate of one-third of one per cent. each time. Unlike gold coin or United States notes, it does not, to the same extent, form a part of the permanent circulation, everywhere acceptable, and, when flowing into the Treasury, easily paid out with little or no cost of transportation. The reasons for this popular discrimination against the silver dollar are:

1st. It is too bulky for large transactions, and its use is confined mainly to payments for manual labor and for market purposes or for change. The amount needed for these purposes is already in excess of the probable demand.

2d. It is known to contain a quantity of silver of less market value than the gold in gold coin. This fact would not impair the circulation of such limited amount as experience shows to be convenient for use, but it does prevent its being held or hoarded as reserves, or exported, and pushes it into active circulation, until it returns to the Treasury, as the least valuable and desirable money in use.

For these reasons the Secretary respectfully but earnestly recommends that the further compulsory coinage of the silver dollar be suspended, or, as an alternative, that the number of grains of silver in the dollar be increased so as to make it equal in market value to the gold dollar, and that its coinage be left as other coinage to the Secretary of the Treasury or the Director of the Mint, to depend upon the demand for it by the public for convenient circulation.

The continued coinage of the silver dollar necessarily involves the expenditure of two million dollars per month of the current revenue, the proceeds of which must, as experience shows, mainly lie idle in the Treasury, involving a large expense for storage and custody. When issued, a considerable expense for its transportation is involved, it is taken reluctantly by the people, and is soon returned to the vaults of the Treasury. The tendency of this process is to convert into silver coin the reserve of gold coin held in the Treasury to maintain United States notes at par. The inevitable effect of the continuance of this coinage for a few years more will be to compel the Department to maintain its specie reserve in gold coin, irrespective of the silver on hand, or to adopt the single silver standard for all Government purposes. The object manifestly designed by the passage of the act for the coinage of the silver dollar was to secure to the people of the United States the benefits of a bimetallic standard of value. It was forcibly urged that to demonetize silver would increase the burden of debts, and rest the value of all property upon the quantity on hand of a single metal. It was not the intention of the framers of the act to demonetize gold, but to maintain both gold and silver as standards of value. This has been done for thousands of years; but only by adopting, as nearly as possible, the relative market value of the two metals as the ratio for coinage, and by changing the ratio adopted whenever for a period of years it was demonstrated that the market ratio had changed. The United States has conformed to this custom of civilized nations, and the Constitution recognized it by authorizing Congress to coin money, and to regulate its value.

Under this authority Congress provided, in 1793, that the ratio should be one ounce of gold to fifteen ounces of silver; and on the 28th of June, 1834, it changed the ratio to one ounce of gold to sixteen ounces of silver.

It would appear that Congress somewhat overrated silver in 1793, and underrated it in 1834, but it is now certain that sixteen ounces of silver are not worth one ounce of gold, and if silver were coined without limit on that basis, it would eventually bring us to a single silver standard, and reduce gold' to a commodity, or drive it to foreign countries—a result not intended by the act of February 28, 1878.

The average cost of the silver in a standard dollar, as shown by the purchases for the Government from the date of the resumption act to this time, measured by the gold standard, is $0.906, or in a ratio of 1 to 17.64. Upon this ratio a silver dollar, in order to be of equal value to a gold dollar, should contain 455.3 grains. As the expense of coining a silver dollar is equal to the value of about five grains of standard silver bullion, it is confidently believed that a silver dollar containing 450 grains, based upon a ratio of one of gold to about 17.5 of silver, could be safely coined, as demanded for use or exportation, without demonetizing gold or disturbing contracts or business, and with great advantage to the silver-mining interests of our country. Upon the facts stated, it would seem to be wise policy now, in the spirit of the Constitution, to regulate by law the coin-value of the two metals so as to conform to the market ratio.

The cost of recoining the silver dollars already issued into dollars of the weight suggested is estimated at about one per cent., or $728,477 50. Much confusion and delusion have arisen from treating as a profit the difference between the cost of the silver bullion coined into silver dollars and the face-value of the dollars coined therefrom. This difference, from February 28, 1878, the date of the act authorizing their coinage, to November, 1880, is $8,520,871 45. From this should be deducted the expense already incurred in distributing the coin and by wastage, which amounts to $262,008 01, leaving as the net nominal profit the sum of $8,258,863 44, of which $7,198,294 56 have been deposited in the Treasury, and $1,060,568 88 remain in the mints. This nominal profit is burdened with the necessity of receiving, and thus practically redeeming, these dollars at their nominal value in gold coin, and of reissuing, transporting, and maintaining them in circulation. This burden will soon exhaust the nominal profit. When held by the Government the coins are of no more real value than an equal weight of standard-silver bullion. To the extent of the difference between their bullion and nominal value, they are purely fiat money. This nominal profit applied to the purchase of silver bullion would be sufficient to meet the entire cost of converting the present dollars into an equal number of the. proposed dollars; or, in other words, if the present dollars were converted into the less number of the proposed dollars, the nominal loss would be fully covered by the nominal profit now in the Treasury and the mints.

It may be better for Congress at the present time to confine its action to the suspension of the coinage of the silver dollar, and to await negotiations with foreign powers for the adoption of an international ratio; but, compelled by official duty to report upon this subject, the Secretary feels bound to express his conviction that it is for the interest of the United States now, as the chief producer of silver, to recognize the great change that has occurred in the relative market value of silver and gold in the chief marts of the world, to adopt a ratio for coinage based upon market value, and to conform all existing coinage to that ratio, while maintaining the gold eagle of our coinage at its present weight and fineness. He confidently believes that the effect of this measure would be to make our gold and silver coins the best international standards of value known. Already the double-eagle, issued without cost for coinage, and in greater sums than any other gold coin, and of equal value to any other coin, whether measured by weight or tale, is received without question in all commercial countries as the most convenient medium of exchange. It is believed that a silver dollar of the weight and ratio of the proposed coinage would be the best silver standard for international exchange, and that it would tend to fix the market value of silver bullion at the ratio proposed, and would thus, as far as practicable, avoid the changing relative value of the two metals, while giving a steady market for the silver product of our country.

In this connection, the attention of Congress is respectfully invited to the operation of the act approved June 9, 1879, requiring the redemption in lawful money, at the office of the Treasurer or any assistant treasurer of the United States, of the silver coins of the United States of smaller denominations than one dollar.

When fractional silver coins were authorized by the act approved February 21, 1853, they were made to contain 384 grains of standard silver to the dollar. This was subsequently changed by the coinage act of 1873 to 25 grammes or 385.8 grains. They thus contain 26.7 grains, or nearly $6\frac{1}{2}$ per cent., less than the standard dollar. Prior to 1853, by reason of the large production of gold in California, the standard-

silver dollar and its fractional parts had risen in market value above
par in gold, and were largely exported. To prevent their exportation,
and in accordance with the example of Great Britain, the policy was
adopted, by that act, of reducing the weight of the minor silver coin,
and this policy operated well until, in the spring of 1862, both gold
and silver ceased to circulate as money. During the suspension of
specie payments a remarkable decrease in the value of silver occurred,
and now the market value of the silver in a dollar of the fractional coin is
only 82¼ cents.

The amount coined prior to November 1, 1880, under the provisions
of the resumption act, which substituted silver coin for fractional currency, was $42,974,931. To this has been added a very large sum issued
before the war, and again introduced into circulation since the resumption of specie payments. It is difficult to determine the amount of
such old coinage in circulation, but it is believed to exceed $22,000,000.
Prior to the act of June 9, 1879, this fractional coin filled the channels
of circulation, especially in commercial cities, and gave rise to the
passage of that act. At that date there was in the Treasury $6,813,589
fractional coin; on the 1st of November, 1880, the amount was
$24,629,489, from which it appears that $17,815,900 has been redeemed
with lawful money. The whole amount in the Treasury is counted
as a part of its reserve, although it is a legal-tender only in sums
not exceeding ten dollars, and is, therefore, not available as cash
for general purposes. It would seem wise that the excess not needed
for change should be coined into standard dollars, and that any further fractional coin, hereafter needed, should contain silver of approximate relative value to the standard coin. The nominal profit heretofore derived from this coinage is quite sufficient to cover the cost of
this change. It is also respectfully suggested that the act of July 9,
1879, should be repealed. When fractional coin is issued as money, it
should be treated like other coin, to be received by the Government
upon the same conditions as by the people, but not, like paper money,
to be redeemed. If it must be classed as money to be redeemed, it
should be supported by a reserve, like other redeemable money.

NATIONAL BANKS.

The report of the Comptroller of the Currency contains much information in reference to the national-banking system, and gives tables
showing the resources and liabilities of the national banks from the
date of their organization to the present time, and also tables showing
the number, capital, and deposits of the State banks, savings-banks,

and private bankers of the country, by States and geographical divisions, for a series of years.

The capital stock of the national banks on October 1, 1880, was $457,553,850; surplus, $120,518,583; and the total circulation outstanding, $343,949,893.

National banks are organized in every State of the Union except Mississippi, and in every Territory except Arizona; and the total number in operation is 2,095, which is the greatest number that has been in operation at any one time.

The Comptroller devotes considerable space to the discussion of the operations of the national banks since the date of resumption of specie payments, and the evils as well as the benefits which are likely to arise from the large addition of coin to the circulating medium made since that date.

The capital stock of the national banks is $47,000,000 less and the surplus nearly $14,000,000 less than at the corresponding date in 1875. The loans of the banks at the date of their last returns were $1,037,000,000, and the individual deposits $873,000,000, the highest points reached since the organization of the system, the loans being $207,000,000 greater and the individual deposits $253,000,000 greater than in October, 1878, while the capital and surplus at the previous date were $5,000,000 in excess of their present amounts.

The individual deposits and the public, private, and bank deposits, not deducting the amount due from banks and the amount of the clearing-house exchanges, have increased more than $322,000,000, and amount to the unprecedented sum of $1,155,000,000.

The Comptroller states that the abundance of money, and the low rates of interest, have made it difficult for capitalists to find satisfactory investments, and that he has, therefore, examined the statements of the banks for a series of years to ascertain if the banks have found use for their increased deposits. The amount of the loans of the banks in New York city, in October, 1879 and 1880, was 70.8 per cent. of the capital, surplus, and net deposits; while in 1878, it was 65.4 per cent.; in 1877, 68 per cent.; and in 1876, 65.1 per cent.; and the loans are now proportionally higher than at any time since 1873. The resources of the banks in the other principal cities of the country are shown by their reports for October 1, last, to have been then more fully employed than they were at the corresponding dates for the two previous years, although their business was not so much extended as it was during the four years following the crisis of 1873. The ratio of the loans of the banks in the country districts to their capital, surplus, and net deposits was, on October 1, 7.3 per cent. less than it was at the corresponding date in 1875, and 5.2 per cent. less than in 1877. The opportunities for using money in this group of banks is not in proportion to the increase of their deposits, and their balances in other banks have by no means diminished.

The tables given by the Comptroller show that, during the past two years, the loans of the banks in the city of New York have been extended to a much greater degree proportionably than the loans in other parts of the country, and that the cash reserves of the banks in New York have been unprecedentedly low. While the aggregate lawful-money reserve has, as far as is known, always been held by this class of banks, it has frequently been very close, some of the banks expanding their loans beyond reasonable limits, and relying upon imports of gold and purchases of bonds by the Treasury to replenish their deficient reserves.

The act of June 20, 1874, repealed the law requiring reserves to be held upon circulation, thus largely reducing the amount of legal reserve required. The enormous increase of individual and bank deposits during the last year should not be accompanied with a proportional increase of loans, since such increase would, it is believed, have the effect, indirectly, of increasing the market prices of many railroad and other stocks and bonds largely beyond their actual value. The banks in New York city hold more than $100,000,000 of the funds of other banks, which are payable on demand, and it is of the greatest importance that they should at all times exhibit great strength if they would keep themselves in condition for an adverse balance of trade, and for the legitimate demands of those dealers who confide in them.

The Comptroller gives some interesting tables showing the amount of coin and currency in the country on the day of resumption of coin payments, and on November 1 of the present year, together with the amount of coin and currency in the Treasury and in the banks, and the amount in the hands of the people outside of these depositories, from which it will be seen that while the amount in the Treasury and in the banks has increased more than $50,000,000 during that period, the amount in the hands of the people has also increased more than $195,000,000.

The most gratifying exhibit in the condition of the national banks is, that they are now doing business upon a specie basis, the amount of gold coin held by the national banks having increased since the day of resumption from $35,039,201 to $102,851,032, which is but about $18,000,000 less than the whole cash reserve required by law.

The national banks hold nearly $200,000,000 of United States bonds, which will mature on or before July next.

The whole amount of United States bonds held by the national banks as security for circulation and for other purposes is $403,369,350, and the average amount of capital invested by the State banks, savings-banks, and private bankers for the six months ending May 31, 1880, as shown by the returns to this Department for purposes of taxation, is $228,053,104, making a total of $631,422,454.

The profit upon circulation, to the national banks, at the present price of bonds in the market is estimated not to exceed one and one-half per cent. upon the capital invested, and the amount of State and National taxes is more than four per cent. upon the amount of circulation.

The banks and bankers of the country have complained that the taxes upon bank deposits and bank capital since the passage of the first internal-revenue act, have been greatly disproportioned to the amount paid by other classes of property, and it would seem that the time has now arrived, as hereinbefore recommended, when Congress might properly repeal all taxes on capital and deposits, retaining the present tax on circulation.

The national-banking system has fully realized all the expectations of its founders. It has furnished a safe currency, of uniform circulation, carefully guarded against counterfeiting, protected by ample reserves, and promptly redeemed both at the banks and the Treasury. No other legislation in respect to these important corporations seems to be required at the present session.

PUBLIC MONEYS.

The monetary transactions of the Government have been conducted through the offices of the United States Treasurer, nine assistant treasurers, one depositary, and one hundred and thirty national-bank depositaries.

The receipts of the Government, amounting, during the fiscal year, as shown by warrants, to $545,340,713 98, were deposited as follows: In independent-treasury offices, $404,301,155 37; in national-bank depositories, $141,039,558 61.

As far as accounts have been adjusted for the last fiscal year there appear to be no losses to the Government by public officers engaged either in the receipt, safe-keeping, or disbursement of the public moneys. It is to be regretted, however, that the apprehension of loss through the issue of duplicates of coupon bonds, expressed by the First Comptroller, in his report for last year, has proven too well founded.   Upon what seemed to be sufficient evidence of the destruction of a $500 coupon bond, a duplicate was issued several years since, and subsequently redeemed, as required by law. Sometime after this redemption the original bond was presented intact by an innocent holder, and, upon the recommendation of the Comptroller, it was redeemed. While there seemed to be no alternative but to pay this bond, the availability of any existing appropriation for the purpose may be questioned, and Congress will be asked for some needed legislation to meet such cases.

Additional legislation to authorize the refund of moneys paid into the Treasury, in excess, by receivers of public moneys, is recommended by the First Comptroller and meets with my approval.

The coinage of the silver three-cent and five-cent pieces was discontinued by the coinage act of 1873, and that of the silver twenty-cent piece by the act of May 2, 1878. Since the act of June 9, 1879, providing for the exchange of subsidiary coins for lawful money of the United States, a large amount of silver coins of the above-mentioned denominations has accumulated in the several sub-treasury offices. These coins constitute a portion of the Treasury balance, and, as they are not again paid out after being received in exchange for lawful money, they become practically unavailable for current use. The necessary legislation for their proper disposition is recommended.

By reference to the tables accompanying this report, it will be seen that, since the organization of the Government, there has been paid into the Treasury to the close of the last fiscal year .. $18,570,348,647 05
And that there has been paid out upon warrants in
  consequence of appropriations made by law, to the
  same date, the sum of 18,334,854,201 62

Leaving unexpended, charged to the Treasury, the
  sum of 235,494,445 43

This amount, however, is not all in actual cash, but is made up of items as follows:

Amount deposited with the States under act of Congress approved June 23, 1836 .... $28,101,644 91
Amount arising from defalcations, irredeemable
  bills, &c. 2,708,964 18
Cash 204,683,836 34

    Total 235,494,445 43

As the first two items are not available for disbursement, it would seem unnecessary to carry them longer as part of the balance; but neither of them can be disposed of without authority of law, though the amounts represented have passed beyond the control of the Department, or entirely disappeared.

The first amount was by law deposited with the States, not paid to them, and the Department cannot withdraw it without further authority. The second item mentioned arose many years ago from the failure of State banks to redeem their notes which the Government held, and of public officers to properly account for moneys received by them for the credit of the Treasury. These items, for convenience, have already been informally omitted from the current cash books and the monthly debt statements of the Department. There are also a few other items of like character, still treated as cash, on which no such action has yet been taken. To their amount they would further reduce the available balance on hand. A full statement of these unavailable amounts has been published for several years in the annual reports of the Treasurer of the United States.

It is recommended that authority be given to reimburse the Treasurer for these unavailable amounts, they being no longer under his control, though he is charged therewith, and to charge the amounts to the parties from whom they are respectively due. Such a course would take no money from the Treasury, would relieve no public debtor from any legal liability, while it would greatly simplify the accounts of the Treasury, and would cause the books of the Department to show always the real instead of the apparent balance of cash on hand available for disbursement.

It will be understood that the apparent discrepancies which have arisen from these unavailable amounts are due to no fault of accounting or book-keeping. On the contrary, it is worthy of note that the amount of these unavailable items, together with the actual money in the Treasury, makes precisely the amount of the moneys received by the Treasury and not expended, as shown by the books of the several bureaus of the Department. No better proof of the accuracy with which the accounts of the great fiscal operations of the Government have been kept could be asked for or obtained.

The amount of money reported on hand to the credit of the Treasurer is not, however, the entire amount of public moneys held by independent-treasury officers and depositary banks. As fiscal agents of the Government these officers and banks have held the funds advanced for disbursement to public officers, and also other funds in trust for the redemption of national-bank notes and for other purposes, aggregating a monthly average during the past year of over sixty millions of dollars. Under the existing system, by which the Government practically holds and disburses its own money and that of its officers, the fiscal operations are conducted without disturbance, embarrassment or favoritism, and with satisfaction to all concerned.

CUSTOMS.

The revenue from customs for the year ended June 30, 1880, was $186,522,064 60; the revenue for the preceding year was $137,250,047 70, an increase of $49,272,016 90. This large gain was due in part to an exceptional demand for certain classes of foreign merchandise, principally iron and steel and their manufactures, which is not likely to be maintained during the present year. Of this sum, about $42,000,000 was collected on sugar; $18,500,000, on manufactures of silk; $19,000,000, on manufactures of iron and steel; $10,000,000, on manufactures of cotton; $29,000,000, on wool and manufactures of wool; and $6,000,000, on wines and spirits, making a total of nearly $125,000,000 collected on these six classes of articles. The precise amounts, however, cannot be given, because the statistics are based, to a certain extent, on unliquidated entries.

The expenses for collection for the past year were $5,995,878 06, an increase over the preceding year of $510,099 03, occasioned to a large extent by the increase in the importation of bulky articles.

The expenses of collection and percentage of cost for the past four years were as follows:

	Expenses.	Percentage.
1877	$6,501,037 57	4.90
1878	5,826,974 32	4.41
1879	5,485,779 03	3.94
1880	5,995,878 06	3.18

It is believed that, by reason of the vigilance of the customs officers, frauds upon the customs revenue have not during the past year been so extensive as formerly. The measures referred to in the last report of the Secretary for a more faithful collection of the duties on sugar have been continued in force, but they are and should be regarded as but temporary, and not as justifying longer delay in the legislation necessary to place this most important feature of our commerce upon a foundation which will enable the Government and the importers to conduct their business with greater certainty than at present. It is earnestly hoped that a settlement of this much-vexed question may be made by Congress at its present session.

The present tariff is but a compilation of laws passed during many succeeding years, and to meet the necessities of the Government from time to time. These laws have furnished the greater part of our revenue, and have incidentally protected and diversified home manufactures. The general principle upon which they are founded is believed to be wise and salutary. No marked or sudden change, which would tend to destroy or injure domestic industries built upon faith in the stability of existing laws, should be made in them. Changes, however, have occurred in the value of some articles, caused mainly by important inventions and improvements in the mode of manufacture. These have produced irregularities and incongruities in the rates of taxation, so that on some articles the duties have become prohibitory, while on others the rate of taxation is too low. Some duties ad valorem might, with the experience acquired under existing laws, be converted into specific duties. Many articles which do not compete with domestic industry, and yield but a small amount of revenue, might be added to the free list. The changes suggested would tend to simplify the work of appraisement, remove the irritations among business men, which so often arise in an enforcement of the laws imposing duties ad valorem, and reduce the cost of collection. Former reports of the Secretary exhibit many facts, showing in detail the necessity of such modifications.

By section 2501 of the Revised Statutes, an additional duty of 10 per cent. ad valorem is imposed on all goods (except wool, raw cotton, and raw silk) the growth or production of countries east of the Cape of Good Hope, when imported into the United States from places west of the cape. Coffee produced in the Dutch Colonial possessions beyond the cape, and imported from places this side of the cape, has been charged with this additional duty. The fifth article of the Treaty with the Netherlands, of February 26, 1853, provides that discriminating duties against tea and coffee, the products of the possessions of the Netherlands, shall be removed by the United States whenever the discriminating export-duties imposed by the government of the Netherlands in favor of direct shipments to Holland of the products of its colonial possessions are removed. The discriminating export-duties were sometime since removed by the Netherlands government, and it is, therefore, incumbent upon the United States, under the treaty, to remove the discriminating import-duties on tea and coffee produced in the possessions of the Netherlands. It is recommended that early action be taken by Congress in the matter.

In this connection it may be questioned whether the discriminating duties imposed by section 2501 of the Revised Statutes, should not be altogether repealed. The provision of law now embodied in that section was originally passed to encourage the direct shipment to the United States of goods around the Cape of Good Hope, as against the shipment of such goods to Europe and their transshipment thence to the United States.

The Suez Canal has, however, so changed the course of trade, that most of the goods which are produced beyond the cape and imported into the United States are sent to European ports and transshipped thence for the United States. It therefore often becomes difficult to decide whether such goods, when shipped from the country of production, were destined for the American or European markets, the shipments being rarely made on through-bills of lading. The total revenue derived from this source for the past year was only $167,436 31. It is recommended that the provision of law in question be repealed.

INTERNAL REVENUE.

From the various sources of taxation under the internal-revenue laws, the receipts for the fiscal year ending June 30, 1880, were as follows:

From spirits	$61,185,508 79
From tobacco....................................	38,870,140 08
From fermented liquors	12,829,802 84
From banks and bankers	3,350,985 28
From penalties, &c	383,755 08
From adhesive-stamps...........................	7,668,394 22
From arrears of taxes under repealed laws	228,027 73
Total	124,516,614 02

The foregoing statement does not include the tax collected by the Treasurer of the United States from national banks, which amounts to $7,014,971 44.

The amount of collections exhibited in the foregoing table includes commissions on sales of stamps, paid in kind, as well as amounts collected in 1879, but not deposited till within the last fiscal year. An apparent variation consequently arises between the amounts of collections given in the tables and those shown by the covering warrants of the Treasury.

The increase of the revenue from spirits during the last fiscal year was $8,615,224 10. But there was a decrease in the revenue from to-

bacco in its various forms of manufacture, for the same period, of
$1,264,862 57, which was to be expected on account of the reduction
in the rate of taxation upon that commodity. The increase of income
from the tax on fermented liquors was $2,100,482 76. The total in-
crease of revenue from spirits and fermented liquors was $11,934,075 99.
The increase of revenue from taxes on banks and bankers was but
$152,101 69 over the income for 1879. The total increase of internal
revenue, after deduction of the decrease of income from tobacco and the
decrease from collections on the arrears of taxes, was $10,598,147 15.

The Secretary cannot too strongly urge the importance of stability
in the rates imposed on spirits, tobacco, and fermented liquors. These
articles are regarded by all Governments as proper objects of taxation.
Any reduction in the rates imposes a heavy loss to the owner of the
stock on hand, while an increase operates as a bounty to such owner.
When the rate is fixed, the trade adapts itself to it. A change dis-
turbs the collection of the tax and the manufacture of the article. As
already suggested, the time is opportune for reducing the subjects of
internal taxation to the articles named and the taxes on circulating-
notes of banks. The taxes proposed to be repealed yielded during the
last fiscal year as follows:

From banks and bankers other than national	$3,350,985 28
From national banks other than on circulation	4,438,134 80
From adhesive stamps	7,668,394 22
In all	15,457,514 30

In case of such repeal, ample time should be given to exhaust the
tax-paid stamps without loss to the manufacturer.

EXPORTS AND IMPORTS.

The exports and imports during the last fiscal year have been as
follows:

Exports of domestic merchandise	$823,946 353
Exports of foreign merchandise	11,692,305
Total	835,638,658
Imports of merchandise	667,954,746
Excess of exports over imports of merchandise	$167,683,912
Aggregate of exports and imports	1,503,593,404

Compared with the previous year, there was an increase of $125,199,217
in the value of exports of merchandise, and an increase of $222,176,971
in the value of imports. The annual average of the excess of such

imports over exports for ten years previous to June 30, 1873, was $104,706,922, but for the last five years there has been an excess of exports over imports of merchandise amounting to $920,955,387—an annual average of $184,191,077. The specie value of the exports of domestic merchandise increased from $376,616,473 in 1870, to $823,946,353 in 1880—an increase of $447,329,880, or 119 per cent. The imports of merchandise increased from $435,958,408 in 1870, to $667,954,746 in 1880—an increase of $231,996,338, or 53 per cent.

There was an increase in the value of the exports of wheat, wheat-flour, and corn, as compared with similar exports of the preceding year, of $78,253,837, or 39 per cent.; an increase in the value of the exports of cotton of $49,231,655, or 30.3 per cent.; an increase in the value of the exports of provisions of $10,184,592, or 8.7 per cent.; and an increase in the exports of live animals of $4,394,366, or 38.3 per cent. There has also been a noticeable increase in the value of the exports of tallow, oil-cake, vegetable-oils, seeds, clocks and watches, hops, wool, and a few other commodities. During the last fiscal year breadstuffs constituted 35 per cent. of the value of our exports of domestic merchandise, cotton 27 per cent., and provisions 15 per cent.

The imports of merchandise for the past year exceeded such imports during any previous year in the history of the country. The leading articles, showing marked increase in quantity or value imported, are coffee, hides and skins, raw silk, and tea, all of which are free of duty, and copper, manufactures of cotton, silk, and wool, fruits, glass, iron and steel, lead, leather, precious stones, leaf tobacco, wool, and zinc. The imports of unmanufactured wool increased from 39,000,000 pounds in 1879 to over 128,000,000 pounds in 1880. The value of the imports of railroad-bars of iron and steel increased from $70,071 in 1879, to $4,952,286 in 1880.

During each year from 1862 to 1879, inclusive, the exports of specie exceeded the imports thereof. The largest excess of such exports over imports was reached during the year 1864, when it amounted to $92,280,919. But during the year ended June 30, 1880, the imports of coin and bullion exceeded the exports thereof by $75,891,391. During July, August, September, and October of the current fiscal year the imports of specie were $47,940,805, and the exports were $4,721,828, making an excess of imports over exports of $43,218,977.

The large and continued excess of the value of the exports of merchandise over the imports of merchandise appears to render it probable that we shall see a continuation of, and, perhaps, a large increase in, the flow of specie into this country.

EXPORTATION AND IMPORTATION OF CATTLE.

In a letter of February 19, 1880, from this Department to the Speaker of the House of Representatives, the attention of Congress was called to the prevalence of the disease known as pleuro-pneumonia, or lung-plague, in neat-cattle, and some recommendations were made as to the proper legislation on the subject.

It may be assumed that this disease has never existed in this country west of the Alleghany mountains; and that it has not for a long time existed in Canada, or in this country near the line of Canada. The exportation of live horned cattle from the United States is very large, and is rapidly increasing, the cattle going mostly to Great Britain. For the eight months ended August 31, 1880, the value of such animals exported was $12,462,837, which is nearly double the value of the exportation for the same period in 1879.

By an order of the Privy Council of Great Britain, all American cattle must be slaughtered at the port of arrival within ten days. The effect of this order is to prevent the shipment of any but fat cattle; and it entails great loss as to that class of animals, by compelling the immediate slaughter of such as are injured, or become sick upon the voyage, and therefore of little value for food. It also prevents the owners from driving the cattle from the port of importation to a better market, or from keeping them until the market improves. Furthermore, there is a large demand in England for store or stock-cattle, to be fed and fattened in that country for its own markets, a demand which this country could supply to an unlimited extent. It is believed that this trade, if unrestricted, might far exceed the trade in fat cattle. The losses and embarrassments by reason of the order for immediate slaughter are, commercially considered, very great. The British government, however, is ready to rescind it when it may be done without danger of spreading pleuro-pneumonia in their country through importations from the United States.

The question of the rescission of the order has been the subject of official discussion between this Government and the Government of Great Britain, as well as in Parliament. It is believed that whenever Congress makes provision for the extinction or prevention of the disease, or for such security of the great routes of travel from the West to the seaboard as will make it reasonably certain that the cattle shipped from our ports, or any of them, will not carry infection with them, the order of Council requiring immediate slaughter will be rescinded.

The recommendation that a commission be created, whose duty it shall be to investigate reports of the existence of the disease, and to collect information respecting it, reporting the results to some Department for official publication, is renewed. It is further recommended that such commission be authorized to co-operate with State and municipal authorities, and corporations and persons engaged in the transportation of neat-cattle, and establish regulations for the safe conveyance of such cattle from the interior to the seaboard, and the shipment of them, so that they may not be exposed to the disease; and that such commission, also, may establish such quarantine stations and regulations as may be deemed necessary to prevent the spread of the disease by importations from abroad. It is believed that the legislation thus indicated, properly executed, will induce the Government of Great Britain to rescind its order for immediate slaughter, and thus promote a very large increase in the exportation of neat-cattle from this country. Whether Congress should go further, and undertake the extirpation of the disease in the States where it now exists, is a question of more difficulty, and it is deemed best to leave that part of the subject for independent consideration.

COMMERCE AND NAVIGATION.

The records of the Register of the Treasury show that the total tonnage of vessels of the United States, at the close of the fiscal year ended June 30, 1880, was 4,068,034 tons. Of this amount 1,352,810 tons were comprised in 2,378 vessels registered for the foreign trade, and 2,715,224 tons in 22,334 vessels enrolled and licensed for the coasting trade and fisheries. There has been a decrease of 138,723 tons in vessels employed in the foreign trade, and a decrease of 37,157 tons in such as were engaged in the domestic trade.

The vessels built during the last fiscal year, with their tonnage, are exhibited in the following table:

	Number.	Tonnage.
Sailing-vessels	460	59,057
Steam-vessels	348	78,854
Canal-boats enrolled	17	1,887
Barges	77	17,612
Total	902	157,410

The decrease in the tonnage built during the last fiscal year, as compared with that of the preceding year, was 35,620 tons.

TRADE IN AMERICAN AND FOREIGN BOTTOMS.

The total tonnage of vessels entered at the seaboard ports from foreign countries was 13,768,137 tons during the year ended June 30, 1879, and 15,240,534 tons during the last fiscal year, showing an increase

of 1,472,397 tons, or about 10½ per cent. The American tonnage entered
exhibited an increase of only 78,631 tons, or 2½ per cent., while the
foreign showed an increase of 1,393,766 tons, or about 13 per cent. The
tonnage in these cases is computed on the basis of the number of entries of vessels and not on the number of vessels, and is restricted to
the seaboard ports. Of the merchandise brought in at seaboard, lake,
and river ports during the last fiscal year, an amount of the value of
$149,317,368, was imported in American vessels, and $503,494,913 in
foreign; of the exports of merchandise an amount of the value of
$109,028,860 was shipped in American and $720,770,521 in foreign
vessels. Of the combined imports and exports of merchandise 17 per
cent. only of the total value was conveyed in American vessels.

In 1856 over 75 per cent. of the total value of the imports and exports
was carried in American vessels, while last year but 17 per cent. was
carried in such vessels, though the total volume of commerce has risen
from a value of $724,000,000, to over $1,500,000,000.

The disproportion between the commodities carried in American and
those carried in foreign vessels still continues, and is even greater than
during the fiscal year 1879, the amount of merchandise transported
in our vessels during the fiscal year 1880, estimated on the basis of
value, being five per cent. less than that transported during the former
year.

The foreign carrying-trade in American bottoms is more than 50 per
cent. less than it has been, or than it might be, and if it is desirable to
save to the country the annual freightage on merchandise of the value
of twelve hundred millions of dollars, the only course to reach that result would seem to be to increase our registered shipping. But while
the ordinary demand for increased tonnage causes no annual increase
in the building of vessels, the only method available, as a measure of
public policy, of effecting such an increase, is either to allow American
citizens the privilege of purchasing vessels of foreign build, to give a
bounty on home-built vessels, or to await the increase of American-built
vessels and their tardy substitution in the foreign trade for those of other
nationalities. Doubtless the number of vessels of home-build will be
adequate in time to take up the freightage lost to American bottoms
in consequence of the war of the rebellion. At present, however, the
demand for vessels to carry on our immense import and export trade
does not seem to so stimulate the ship-building industry as to prevent
an annual decrease in the number of ships built. The present facilities for freighting in foreign vessels appear to be a greater discour-
agement to that industry than would be the privilege of purchasing
such vessels.

PREVENTION OF COLLISIONS AT SEA.

In 1864, Congress established certain rules and regulations for preventing collisions on the water which are still in force. The principal maritime nations of the world have recently concurred in adopting a new code of regulations for the same purpose. These regulations went into operation on the first of September last. In many points they differ materially from those adopted in 1864 which govern our own mercantile and naval marine. The result is, that our vessels are subject, in certain contingencies, to one set of rules for navigation in foreign waters and to different ones when sailing in our own. In cases of collision accordingly, they are subject to liabilities, which vary with the waters in which they are employed, most foreign maritime courts conforming in their decrees to the new regulations, while our own adhere to the regulations of 1864.

I would recommend that this uncertain status of our vessels be removed by the prompt acceptance by statute of the regulations already adopted by other nations, leaving the correction or amendment of the regulations to international arrangement if Congress should consider such amendment imperatively required.

INTERNAL COMMERCE.

The reports of tonnage moved on the principal trunk-railroad lines of the country, and the more recent data in regard to traffic on inland water lines and coastwise upon the ocean, indicate that the internal commerce of the United States has rapidly increased during the past year. Railroads now constitute the principal avenues of our internal trade. The traffic over the four east and west trunk lines greatly exceeds in value both the commerce of the Mississippi river and its tributaries and the commerce on the Great Lakes.

Through the facilities afforded for continuous traffic by means of combinations entered into between connecting railroads and between railroads and ocean-steamer lines at the principal seaports of the country, the interior cities are now able to carry on a direct trade not only with all parts of the country, but are also able to engage in direct foreign commerce, both as to the exportation of American products to other countries and to the importation of foreign merchandise into the United States. Through these facilities all the principal cities of the country have been brought into direct competition with each other. The sphere of the commercial operations of each city has been greatly extended, while competition has become sharper and profits have been reduced to a narrower margin. The varied productions and industries of the different States and sections of our country present highly favorable conditions for the development of internal trade. Already our internal commerce many times exceeds in value our foreign commerce. Its rapidly-increasing importance seems to justify a more liberal appropriation than has heretofore been made for the purpose of collecting and presenting annually information in regard to it, especially such information as may be of service for the use of Congress.

CLAIMS.

§ §The necessity of legislation for the adjudication of claims now within the jurisdiction of this Department has been called to the attention of Congress in several former reports. It is deemed unnecessary to repeat in detail the reasons which exist for the enactment of the measures which have heretofore been recommended. It will be sufficient to call the attention of Congress, in a condensed statement, to the objects which it is proposed to accomplish.

As suggested in a former report, the great object of legislation on the subject of claims is, to render their adjustment speedy and final and to discourage the allowance of old demands, or the re-examination of those already settled. A general provision of law by which all important disputed questions of law or fact may be referred to the Court of Claims for trial, would greatly relieve the officers of this Department, and tend to promote the ends of justice. That tribunal adopts the methods used by all courts of justice for ascertaining the truth, which include the requirement of the best evidence of which the nature of the case admits; the cross-examination of witnesses, instead of *ex parte* statements; and public hearings, and a public record of proceedings. In such legislation express provision should be made against the rehearing of claims which have been once adjudicated in any court, or by Congress, or by the accounting officers of the Treasury, or that have been barred by any statute of limitations.

The former recommendation that some limitation of time within which claims against the Government shall be prosecuted, or, for want of such prosecution, be forever barred, is renewed. For the reasons which have introduced statutes of limitation into the codes of all civilized nations, it is again recommended that it be provided by law that no claim pending in any of the Executive Departments shall be allowed unless presented for payment within six years after such claim has accrued, with the usual exception in the case of those prevented by infancy or otherwise from presenting their claims within such time, and that provisions of a similar character in favor of those against whom the Government holds claims may be enacted. The Department is well organized for the investigation of claims accruing in the ordinary course of current business, and decisions thereon by the accounting officers made final by existing laws should not be referred to the Court of Claims or any other tribunal for examination.

TRIBUNAL FOR TRIAL OF REVENUE CASES.

About two-thirds of the customs business of the country is transacted at the port of New York. The multiplicity of suits growing out of the vast amount of business constantly crowds the dockets of the courts, so that there is great delay in the decision of cases. The speedy decision of customs cases is of great importance both to the Government and to the importers, and great embarrassment ensues in the administration of the customs laws from the usual delay of three or four years before a final decision can be reached.

The Secretary renews his recommendation that a special tribunal be created by law for the trial of customs-revenue cases at the port of New York.

He also repeats his recommendation that the Secretary of the Treasury be authorized, in cases of variance between the appraised value, or classification for duty, of similar merchandise at two or more ports of the United States, to prescribe regulations under which the board of general appraisers, or a majority of them, may decide upon the true dutiable value or classification of such imports; and that authority be given for the appointment of three additional general appraisers.

BUREAU OF ENGRAVING AND PRINTING.

During the year the building for the Bureau of Engraving and Printing, authorized by the act of June 20, 1878, has been completed, and the bureau has been removed from the Treasury-Department building, without occasioning any material delay in its business, and successfully established in its new quarters.

The bureau now has superior facilities for executing the work pertaining to it; and, as it has been demonstrated that such work can be executed therein more safely and more economically, all things considered, than elsewhere, the necessary steps have been taken to have all the work of engraving and plate-printing, required by the Treasury Department, to be performed in the bureau.

PRINTING INTERNAL-REVENUE STAMPS.

In making the appropriation for "dies, paper, and stamps" for the present fiscal year, Congress required that the engraving and printing of internal-revenue stamps should be done in the Bureau of Engraving and Printing of the Treasury Department, provided the cost did not exceed the price paid under existing contracts. In accordance with this requirement, an estimate was procured from the bureau for the printing of certain internal-revenue stamps, then being done under contract with the American Bank-Note Company of New York, and, as the rates proposed in the estimate appeared to be lower than those paid to the company, the contract with the company was annulled as soon as practicable, and, in the month of October, the printing of the stamps was transferred to the Bureau of Engraving and Printing, where it is now being done with advantage to the Government.

DISTINCTIVE PAPER.

The new distinctive paper, the adoption and manufacture of which was mentioned in the last annual report, has been used for printing notes, certificates, checks, and other obligations since January last, and has been found to answer the requirements of the Government in all respects. It is believed that the special features of this paper will afford increased protection against counterfeiting, while its superior quality, and consequent longer life while in circulation, renders its adoption a measure of economy as well as safety.

It is estimated that the saving on account of the reduction in its price below that paid for the paper heretofore used will be not less than $50,000 for the present fiscal year. If a large supply of paper should be required for an issue of bonds during the year, the saving will be correspondingly greater.

LIGHT-HOUSE ESTABLISHMENT.

The Light-house Establishment continues in its usual satisfactory condition. During the fiscal year it has put into operation twenty-five new light-houses, eighty-two new river-lights, one new fog-signal, eleven new automatic whistling-buoys, and fifteen new buoys of the ordinary kind. It has discontinued eight lights, which were no longer needed, and has changed the characteristics of twelve others, so that they will be more useful than heretofore to commerce and navigation.

The board has continued the work of changing the burners of the smaller lights in the several light-house districts, so as to substitute mineral oil for lard-oil as an illuminant, until mineral-oil is now used in all its lights, with the exception of about one hundred and twenty-five of the first, second, and third orders. The board has also, by careful and long-continued experiment, been enabled to use mineral-oil as an illuminant on light-ships and in screw-pile light-houses, as it is believed, without danger to these isolated stations. In so doing it has, in each instance, increased the power of the light, while it has at the same time decreased its cost.

The board has continued its experiments with the electric light as far as was possible in the laboratory. It will be unable to determine its practical value until it has a working-test in a light-house. It has again submitted an estimate for this purpose, which is commended to the attention of Congress.

The curious and interesting experiments of the board, to ascertain the laws of sound when acting through fog and snow, have been continued, and seem to be tending to practical results of importance to commerce.

COAST AND GEODETIC SURVEY.

In the coast and geodetic survey, the work of its several branches has advanced steadily. For public uses essential in engineering and in local development generally, information is gathered by a comprehensive system, which gives results of great exactness. Relative positions along the coast and on the continent are ascertained by final measurements. Permanent dangers to navigation are carefully marked on the charts of the survey, as well as their relation to light-houses, buoys, beacons, and sailing-lines. The publication of a third volume of the Atlantic Coast Pilot, with sailing directions and descriptions of the local dangers, is in progress, and good advance has been made in a compilation of the same kind for the Pacific coast. For the principal ports of the eastern and western coasts of the United States, tide-tables are computed one year in advance, and printed for the use of navigators. All the publications of the survey are in great request. The demand for its charts has greatly increased. Of upwards of eighteen thousand points determined in latitude and longitude along the coast, and in parts of the interior, the intervening distances and bearings of the junction-lines are recorded in the office, with descriptions of the ground-marks; and thus, what was indispensable for the coast development avails for State surveys. The requisitions for such data increase in number yearly. The annual reports of the survey show that the Engineer department, the Light-house Board, harbor commissions, and State authorities have drawn largely from this source for information necessary in connection with proposed improvements. Calls are frequent in regard to the variation of the compass for the past as well as for the present time. For the present era the variation in all parts of the United States is shown by a map published within the year. Deep-sea soundings made within the year have incidentally added subjects of special interest for the study of naturalists. Within the year the survey has co-operated with the Mississippi River Commission.

THE MARINE-HOSPITAL SERVICE.

The Supervising Surgeon-General of the Marine-Hospital Service reports that 24,860 seamen were afforded relief during the fiscal year ended June 30, 1880, and 290,501 days' relief in hospital were furnished; 13,697 patients were treated at the dispensaries; 795 persons were examined physically as a preliminary to shipping them; 2,870 pilots were examined for color-blindness, of whom 64 were found to be color-blind; and 25 seamen, hopelessly diseased, have been furnished transportation from hospitals to their own homes. The number of patients treated shows an increase of nearly 4,000 over the previous year, and the cost *per capita* has been reduced to $16 18, the lowest rate yet reached. The ordinary expenses of the service have been $370,744 64, and the extraordinary expenses $31,440 85, making a total of $402,185 49, the details of which will be found in the report of the Surgeon-General.

The first section of the act approved March 3, 1875, directed the Secretary to "cause to be prepared a schedule of the average number of seamen required in the safe and ordinary navigation of registered, enrolled, and licensed vessels of the United States, basing such schedule upon the differences in rig, tonnage, and kind of traffic;" and, after its preparation, to assess and collect hospital-dues from the master or owner of the vessel upon the average number of seamen as set forth in the schedule. The Department has made every effort to prepare such a schedule as would meet the requirements of the law, but has found it to be impossible. It is therefore recommended that the provision be repealed. The details of the subject will be found in the report of the Surgeon-General.

The recommendations made in the last annual report relative to statutory provisions for appointments and promotions in the medical corps of this service, and for the compulsory physical examination of seamen, are respectfully renewed.

Provision should be made for the return to the marine-hospital fund of the proceeds of sale of all property originally purchased for or produced from it, such proceeds being now covered into the Treasury. There is now in the Department, as a special deposit, $1,309 14, unclaimed money of deceased seamen, and there are in the several custom-houses and marine-hospitals unclaimed effects, such as watches, jewelry, and clothing, of considerable value. It is recommended that the sale of such effects be authorized, and that the proceeds thereof, and the unclaimed money referred to, be permitted to be carried to the credit of the marine-hospital fund.

The Secretary recommends that a National Snug Harbor or Sailors'

Home be established by law for the reception of destitute American seamen incurably diseased or permanently disabled in the line of duty, and placed under the direction of the Marine-Hospital Service. After provision is made for a site and buildings, it is believed that the ordinary expenses could be met from the marine-hospital fund. The physical examination of seamen, before allowing them to be shipped, would, by keeping disabled men out of the merchant service, rid the hospitals of hundreds, and thus leave a surplus for this purpose. The number of American seamen in our vessels is diminishing from year to year, and their places are filled by foreigners. A provision for the support of seamen in disease and old age, it is believed, will greatly increase the enlistment of native citizens in the merchant marine.

As a measure in the interest of American commerce, it is also recommended that the "advance wages," authorized by section 4532 of the Revised Statutes, be abolished; and the form of "articles of agreement," in section 4612, be amended accordingly.

It is recommended that section 4569, Revised Statutes, which requires a medicine-chest to be kept on merchant vessels, be amended by providing that each vessel, before clearance, shall present, to the collector of customs, a certificate of an officer of the Marine-Hospital Service that the medicine-chest is properly supplied.

It is also recommended that an appropriation be made, to be expended under the direction of this service, for the relief of seamen shipwrecked in places beyond the reach of the Life-Saving Service.

LIFE-SAVING SERVICE.

The past year appears to have been remarkable in the operations of the Life-Saving Service. The season was marked by numerous storms of great severity, resulting in disaster to a larger number of vessels upon our shores than in any previous year since the organization of the service, and severely testing the ability and fidelity of its crews, and the methods employed for the saving of life. The gales upon the lakes were especially violent, the consequent casualties to shipping within the reach of this service being one hundred and thirty-six, but of the nine hundred and seven lives endangered in these disasters only a single one was lost.

On the Atlantic coast, also, the storms were very destructive to shipping. The number of lives imperilled in disasters within reach of the service was one thousand and forty-nine, of which only eight were lost.

The whole number of disasters to vessels during the year, reported by the district officers, is three hundred. The number of persons on board these vessels was nineteen hundred and eighty-nine, of whom nineteen hundred and eighty were saved, and nine lost. Succor was given at the stations to four hundred and fifty persons. The number of days' relief afforded was twelve hundred. The estimated value of property involved was $3,811,708, of which $2,619,807 was saved, and $1,191,901 was lost. The number of vessels totally lost was sixty-seven.

It may be proper to call special attention to the loss of six men of the crew at the Point aux Barques station, a crew distinguished for many brilliant rescues, the members of which, after having this year saved nearly a hundred lives, all perished, except one, in a gallant effort to reach a distressed vessel.

Six new stations have been completed and put in operation during the year upon the Gulf coast, involving the organization of a new life-saving district, designated the eighth. For the remaining stations authorized by Congress to be erected, plans and specifications are ready, and they will be constructed as soon as practicable.

The advance of wages in some localities renders it difficult to retain in the service the trained men, who now render it so efficient, and who cannot easily be replaced. It is recommended, therefore, that the General Superintendent be allowed to fix the compensation of the surfmen, employed at the several stations within defined limits.

Attention is invited to the recommendations of the Superintendent, in his annual report, in relation to increasing the number of stations, to supplying draught-horses for stations where they cannot be readily obtained in emergencies, for the employment of an additional man in each crew, and for additional apparatus at the stations. A bill, in which provision is made for most of these objects, is now pending, and deserves the attention of Congress.

It is worthy of remark that the successes of the service have, during the past year, excited attention abroad, and that the Department has been solicited for aid in introducing the American system into foreign countries.

NATIONAL BOARD OF HEALTH.

The National Board of Health has submitted to the Secretary of the Treasury its annual report of operations, for transmission to Congress, according to the requirement of the act of June 8, 1879.

It appears that the expenditures of the board for the year ended September 30, 1880, amounted to $266,762 16. While the act provides that the appropriation made by said act shall be disbursed under the direction of the Secretary of the Treasury, on estimates made by the National Board of Health, to be approved by him, no further duty devolves upon the Secretary as to such disbursements than to decide whether the requisitions made by the board are for purposes within the provisions of law making the appropriation. A large proportion of the amount expended appears to have been used by the board under section third of said act, in co-operating with and aiding State and municipal boards of health in the execution and enforcement of the rules and regulations of such boards to prevent the introduction of contagious or infectious diseases into the United States from foreign countries or into one State from another.

The several amounts for these and other purposes, and for the general expenditures of the board, having been drawn by the board upon requisitions specifying in general the legal and proper purposes for which the funds were to be used, neither the Secretary nor the accounting officers of the Treasury have deemed it their duty to exercise any supervision over the details of the various expenditures of the amounts thus drawn from the Treasury. The Secretary has no reason to believe, however, that the funds have not been properly expended.

PUBLIC BUILDINGS.

The Supervising Architect reports the progress of work on the public buildings as generally satisfactory, but, in several instances, suspension of work has been caused by insufficient appropriations.

It appears that twenty-one buildings are now in process of construction, of which nine are approaching completion. The estimated amount of the appropriations available for their completion is $217,000. The buildings in the cities of Albany, N. Y., Boston, Cincinnati, New York, (barge office,) Philadelphia, St. Louis, and Topeka, are so advanced that it is estimated that a further appropriation of $3,700,000 will complete them. Comparatively little progress has been made on the remaining buildings.

It is respectfully recommended that Congress, having fixed upon such an amount as it may deem best to expend on public buildings, shall, out of that sum, appropriate sufficient to complete the nine buildings above referred to, and make liberal appropriations for the work on the buildings in the cities named. It is also recommended that, in authorizing the erection of new buildings, consideration be given only to those for localities where the rental paid for accommodations for Government offices, represents a fair percentage on the cost of the construction of suitable buildings. It would seem to be better, and it is certainly more economical, to appropriate freely for buildings in process of construction, than to commence too great a number for the amount appropriated.

The accompanying report of the Supervising Architect will furnish full details of the progress made in the buildings now in process of erection.

The Revenue Marine has performed efficient service during the past year. Its vessels have cruised an aggregate of 265,763 miles, and its officers have boarded and examined 36,318 vessels, of which 23,243 were American, and 13,075 foreign. Of the number examined, 3,556 were found to have violated the law in some particular, and were seized or reported to the proper authorities.

The expenses of the service for the year were $845,333 74.

Under the provisions of section 1536 of the Revised Statutes, vessels of the Revenue Marine, in addition to their regular duties, are yearly charged with cruising during the inclement season, for the relief of distressed mariners. In.the performance of this duty one hundred and fourteen distressed merchant-vessels, representing with their cargoes a value of $2,011,509, and having on board nine hundred and thirty-five persons, have been assisted during the past year, and sixty-five persons have been rescued from drowning.

Besides the regular duties which officers of the Revenue Marine have performed under the law, in connection with the Life-Saving Service, its vessels have rendered frequent assistance in transporting persons and supplies for that service. They have also rendered special services to the Light-house Establishment and to the United States Commissioner of Fish and Fisheries.

It is recommended that an appropriation be made for the construction of two revenue-vessels to be stationed on the southern coast, and for the rebuilding of the revenue-steamer "Fessenden," now laid up as unseaworthy at Detroit. For these purposes the sum of $225,000 has been included in the estimates.

Under the provisions of the acts of May 31 and June 16, last, the revenue-steamer "Corwin" was dispatched from San Francisco to cruise within the Arctic ocean and on the northern coasts of Alaska, to assist in the enforcement of the laws governing that Territory, and to relieve the officers and crews of the whaling-barks "Mount Wollaston" and "Vigilant," which are supposed to have been shipwrecked in that region. The cruise of the "Corwin" has resulted in the seizure of two vessels engaged in illicit traffic, the discovery and location of important coal deposits on the coast of Alaska within the Arctic ocean, the collection of valuable ethnological statistics, and the making of useful hydrographic surveys and soundings, but no trace was found of the missing whalers.

STEAMBOAT INSPECTION.

During the past year 4,536 steam-vessels have been inspected, of an aggregate tonnage of 1,121,808 tons, and licenses have been issued to 16,661 officers—an increase over last year of 248 vessels, of 29,454 tons, and of 1,449 officers.

The total receipts, from the inspection of vessels and licensing of officers, were $282,468 96, and the total disbursements for salaries, and travelling and other expenses, were $212,849 88, leaving a surplus of receipts over expenditures of $69,619 08.

There were carried during the year some 220,000,000 passengers, of which number 103 lost their lives by various casualties.

The Board of Supervising Inspectors, at its meeting in January last, adopted a rule relative to the examination of pilots for color-blindness, which requires that, before granting or renewing a license to any person to act as a pilot, inspectors shall satisfy themselves that the applicant can properly distinguish the colored lights used as signals on steam-vessels. To carry this rule into effect, it was deemed advisable that such examinations should be made by the surgeons of the Marine-Hospital Service, and free of charge.

Considerable opposition to this rule was at first manifested, but as every pilot who successfully passed the required examination became its advocate, its opponents now consist of a portion only of the rejected applicants, some, even of these, admitting its propriety, and their own defective vision in regard to colors.

It is believed that the rule referred to will have a tendency to decrease night-collisions between steamers and other vessels.

The Supervising Inspector-General, in his annual report, suggests several amendments to the steamboat laws, deemed by him necessary to further increase their efficiency, which are commended to the consideration of Congress.

ALASKA.

In the last report of this Department attention was called to the necessity of establishing some form of government for Alaska. A form of bill to accomplish this end was subsequently prepared in this Department and transmitted to the House of Representatives for consideration, but thus far no final action on the subject has been taken. The adoption of some simple form of government to protect persons and property, to provide for the record of wills and transfers of property, and possibly to extend the land laws of the United States over the main-land, would encourage immigration and tend to develop the resources of the Territory. A peaceful condition of affairs has, however, prevailed in Alaska during the past year, owing largely to the presence of a naval vessel at Sitka, and the cruise, already referred to, of the revenue-cutter "Corwin" to its northern and western waters. The inhabitants, except those of the Seal Islands, depend to a large extent for a livelihood upon the traffic in furs obtained from the sea-otter and other valuable fur-bearing animals; and the oft-repeated visits of white men to the haunts of these animals, using fire-arms in hunting them, must soon result in their extermination and the reduction of the natives to extreme poverty.   The commander of the "Corwin," who visited St. Lawrence Island, reports the death by starvation of over four hundred of the natives, from neglect to make proper provision for the winter, owing to their use of rum, furnished them by the illicit traders.

To protect the sea-otter hunting-grounds and suppress illicit traffic in fire-arms and whiskey, as well as to guard the extensive coast-line against smuggling, there should be provided a steam-vessel especially adapted to cruising in Alaskan waters.   The recommendation heretofore made for legislative action to that end is accordingly renewed.

The captain of the revenue-cutter reports the presence of an increased number of seals at the Seal Islands the past season.

The Alaska Commercial Company have taken during the past year the maximum number of seals allowed by law under their lease.

DISTRICT OF COLUMBIA.

The net expenditures on account of the District of Columbia for the fiscal year 1880, were $3,272,384 63.   The revenues deposited in the Treasury for the same period were $1,809,469 70.

From December 1, 1879, to June 30, 1880, the bonded indebtedness has been reduced, by operation of the sinking-fund, $200,423 33; and the annual interest-charge upon the District debt has been reduced $8,827 66.   Since the offices of the commissioners of the sinking-fund of the District of Columbia were abolished, and their duties and powers transferred to the Treasurer of the United States by the act of Congress of June 11, 1878, the principal of the funded debt has been reduced $618,750, and the annual interest-charge has been reduced $38,981 77.

Under existing law the sinking-fund of the three-sixty-five loan of the District must be invested in bonds of that loan, which do not mature until August 1, 1924; while District bonds bearing higher rates of interest, in which investments can more profitably be made, mature at earlier dates, from time to time.   It is recommended, therefore, that authority of law be given for the investment of that sinking-fund in any bonds of the District of Columbia.

PUBLIC SERVICE.

In closing his annual report the Secretary takes pleasure in bearing testimony to the general fidelity and ability of the officers and employés of this Department. As a rule they have by experience and attention to duty become almost indispensable to the public service. The larger portion of them have been in the Department more than ten years, and several have risen by their efficiency from the lowest-grade clerks to high positions. In some cases their duties are technical and difficult, requiring the utmost accuracy; in others, they must be trusted with great sums, where the slightest ground for suspicion would involve their ruin; in others, they must act judicially upon legal questions affecting large private and public interests, as to which their decisions are practically final. It is a just subject of congratulation that, during the last year, there has been among these officers no instance of fraud, defalcation, or gross neglect of duty. The Department is a well-organized and well-conducted business office, depending mainly for its success upon the integrity and fidelity of the heads of bureaus and chiefs of divisions. The Secretary has therefore deemed it both wise and just to retain and reward the services of tried and faithful officers and clerks.

During the last twenty years the business of this Department has been greatly increased, and its efficiency and stability greatly improved. This improvement is due to the continuance during that period of the same general policy, and the consequent absence of sweeping changes in the public service; to the fostering of merit by the retention and promotion of trained and capable men; and to the growth of the wholesome conviction in all quarters that training, no less than intelligence, is indispensable to good service. Great harm would come to the public interests should the fruits of this experience be lost, by whatever means the loss occurred. To protect not only the public service, but the people from such a disaster, the Secretary renews the recommendation made in a former report, that provision be made for a tenure of office for a fixed period, for removal only for cause, and for some increase of pay for long and faithful service.

The several reports of the heads of offices and bureaus are herewith respectfully transmitted.

JOHN SHERMAN,
Secretary.

To Hon. S. J. RANDALL,
 Speaker of the House of Representatives.

TABLES ACCOMPANYING THE REPORT.

TABLE A.—*STATEMENT of the NET RECEIPTS (by warrants) during the fiscal year ended June 30, 1880.*

CUSTOMS.

Quarter ended September 30, 1879	$44, 083, 497 93	
Quarter ended December 31, 1879	40, 816, 906 82	
Quarter ended March 31, 1880	53, 537, 903 72	
Quarter ended June 30, 1880	48, 083, 756 13	
		$186, 522, 064 60

SALES OF PUBLIC LANDS.

Quarter ended September 30, 1879	117, 383 61	
Quarter ended December 31, 1879	185, 573 28	
Quarter ended March 31, 1880	347, 403 61	
Quarter ended June 30, 1880	366, 146 10	
		1, 016, 506 60

INTERNAL REVENUE.

Quarter ended September 30, 1879	29, 400, 691 81	
Quarter ended December 31, 1879	31, 286, 903 96	
Quarter ended March 31, 1880	28, 501, 040 74	
Quarter ended June 30, 1880	34, 751, 677 39	
		124, 009, 373 92

TAX ON CIRCULATION, DEPOSITS, ETC., OF NATIONAL BANKS.

Quarter ended September 30, 1879	3, 360, 569 60	
Quarter ended December 31, 1879	7, 181 42	
Quarter ended March 31, 1880	3, 634, 130 70	
Quarter ended June 30, 1880	13, 089 72	
		7, 014, 971 44

REPAYMENT OF INTEREST BY PACIFIC RAILROAD COMPANIES.

Quarter ended September 30, 1879	252, 427 46	
Quarter ended December 31, 1879	671, 993 34	
Quarter ended March 31, 1880	151, 361 49	
Quarter ended June 30, 1880	631, 594 69	
		1, 707, 387 18

CUSTOMS FEES, FINES, PENALTIES, AND FORFEITURES.

Quarter ended September 30, 1879	321, 370 06	
Quarter ended December 31, 1879	389, 645 39	
Quarter ended March 31, 1880	306, 974 05	
Quarter ended June 30, 1880	413, 279 62	
		1, 431, 269 12

FEES, CONSULAR, LETTERS PATENT, AND LAND.

Quarter ended September 30, 1879	506, 864 29	
Quarter ended December 31, 1879	586, 090 84	
Quarter ended March 31, 1880	539, 962 99	
Quarter ended June 30, 1880	704, 110 88	
		2, 337, 029 00

PROCEEDS OF SALES OF GOVERNMENT PROPERTY.

Quarter ended September 30, 1879	55, 965 33	
Quarter ended December 31, 1879	60, 806 23	
Quarter ended March 31, 1880	135, 573 48	
Quarter ended June 30, 1880	30, 271 46	
		282, 616 50

PROFITS ON COINAGE.

Quarter ended September 30, 1879	409, 486 09	
Quarter ended December 31, 1879	504, 566 56	
Quarter ended March 31, 1880	814, 733 74	
Quarter ended June 30, 1880	853, 380 37	
		2, 792, 186 76

REVENUES OF DISTRICT OF COLUMBIA.

Quarter ended September 30, 1879	238, 864 06	
Quarter ended December 31, 1879	969, 900 01	
Quarter ended March 31, 1880	168, 392 25	
Quarter ended June 30, 1880	432, 304 38	
		1, 809, 460 70

MISCELLANEOUS.

Quarter ended September 30, 1879	1, 067, 543 37	
Quarter ended December 31, 1879	812, 281 07	
Quarter ended March 31, 1880	729, 094 75	
Quarter ended June 30, 1880	2, 034, 836 95	
		4, 603, 756 14

Total ordinary receipts	333, 526, 610 68
Cash in Treasury June 30, 1879	358, 730, 943 74
Total	692, 257, 554 72

TABLE B.—*STATEMENT of the NET DISBURSEMENTS (by warrants) during the fiscal year ended June 30, 1880.*

CIVIL.

Congress	$4, 993, 470 32	
Executive	6, 374, 913 52	
Judiciary	2, 888, 430 97	
Government of Territories	160, 360 07	
Subtreasuries	336, 660 04	
Public land offices	541, 203 45	
Inspection of steam-vessels	213, 509 47	
Mint and assay-offices	174, 346 81	
Total civil		$15, 693, 963 55

FOREIGN INTERCOURSE.

Diplomatic salaries	325, 155 01	
Consular salaries	463, 041 95	
Contingencies of consulates	164, 061 33	
Relief and protection of American seamen	50, 123 15	
Rescuing American seamen from shipwreck	1, 922 02	
American and Spanish Claims Commission	7, 068 13	
Contingent expenses of foreign missions	91, 734 05	
Tribunal of Arbitration at Geneva	3, 952 21	
Prisons for American convicts	12, 169 84	
International Exhibition at Paris	5, 000 00	
International Bureau of Weights and Measures	1, 500 00	
Berlin Fishery Exhibition	18, 366 50	
International Exhibition at Sidney and Melbourne, Australia	15, 786 40	
International remonetization of silver	9, 060 00	
Shipping and discharging seamen	5, 295 08	
Contingent and miscellaneous	28, 234 91	
Total foreign intercourse		1, 211, 490 58

MISCELLANEOUS.

Mint establishment	1, 105, 411 12
Coast Survey	550, 469 58
Light-House Establishment	1, 868, 039 74
Building and repairs of light-houses	558, 230 87
Refunding excess of deposits for unascertained duties	2, 632, 104 44
Revenue-cutter service	845, 333 74
Life-saving service	518, 497 43
Custom-houses, court-houses, post-offices, &c	2, 451, 994 37
Furniture, fuel, &c., for public buildings under Treasury Department.	470, 861 32
Repairs and preservation of buildings under Treasury Department	191, 156 07
Collecting customs revenue	6, 023, 253 53
Debentures and drawbacks under customs laws	1, 831, 197 67
Marine-Hospital Establishment	492, 665 76
Compensation in lieu of moieties	92, 186 30
Assessing and collecting internal revenue	3, 657, 195 10
Punishing violations of internal revenue laws	95, 568 69
Internal-revenue stamps, papers, and dies	410, 512 01
Refunding duties erroneously or illegally collected	44, 382 05
Internal-revenue allowances and drawbacks	57, 012 27
Redemption of internal-revenue stamps	24, 072 71
Deficiencies of revenue of Post-Office Department	3, 071, 000 00
Return of proceeds of captured and abandoned property	75, 454 50
Expenses of national loan, salaries	190, 201 38
Expenses refunding national debt	515, 922 48
Expenses national currency	100, 398 63
Suppressing counterfeiting and fraud	58, 530 05
Contingent expenses, Independent Treasury	42, 840 75
Survey of public lands	567, 270 29
Repayment for lands erroneously sold	18, 651 25
Five per cent. funds, &c., to States	8, 529 74
Payments under relief acts	64, 216 35
Southern Claims Commission	28, 146 71
Reissuing of national currency	158, 939 06
Postage	163, 437 48
Purchase and management of Louisville and Portland Canal	71, 910 00
Vaults, safes, and locks for public buildings	57, 694 44
Indemnity for swamp lands	4, 552 60
Propagation, &c., of food-fishes	136, 288 53
Collecting statistics relating to commerce	8, 799 57
Geological survey of Territories	99, 990 63
Deposits by individuals for surveys of public lands	275, 080 26
Defending suits and claims for seizure of contraband and abandoned property	23, 441 36
Sinking-fund of Pacific railroads	480, 011 12
Education of the blind	5, 775 00
Transportation of United States securities	49, 288 86
National Board of Health	204, 182 05
Expenses of eighth, ninth, and tenth census	270, 396 86
Improvement of Yellowstone National Park	10, 000 00
Miscellaneous	98, 034 44
Payment of judgments, Court of Claims	137, 062 24

TABLE B.—*STATEMENT of the NET DISBURSEMENTS (by warrants), &c.*— Continued.

Purchase of stereotype plates	8, 600 00
Mail transportation. Pacific Railroads	938, 357 28
Department of Agriculture	128, 100 00
Patent Office	92, 296 16
Expenses of Bureau of Engraving and Printing	321, 002 81
Removal of Bureau of Engraving and Printing	46, 076 80
Smithsonian Institution	100, 500 00
Completion of Washington Monument	124, 016 93
Public buildings and grounds in Washington	701, 610 46
Annual repairs of the Capitol	81, 000 00
Improving and lighting Capitol grounds	114, 517 31
State, War, and Navy Departments building	544, 150 00
Columbian Institute for Deaf and Dumb	50, 000 00
Government Hospital for the Insane	204, 868 91
Freedmen's Hospital	41, 736 00
Support and treatment of transient paupers	15, 000 00
Redemption of District of Columbia securities	20, 126 83
Refunding taxes District of Columbia	5, 753 31
Water fund, District of Columbia	180, 088 90
Expenses of District of Columbia	3, 192, 880 35
Washington Aqueduct	20, 000 00
Charitable institutions	129, 504 28

Total miscellaneous... $37, 808, 075 63

INTERIOR DEPARTMENT.

Indians	5, 945, 457 09
Pensions	56, 777, 174 44

Total Interior Department... 62, 722, 631 53

MILITARY ESTABLISHMENT.

Pay Department	11, 064, 910 69
Commissary Department	2, 273, 288 62
Quartermaster's Department	10, 518, 600 86
Medical Department	300, 080 96
Ordnance Department	1, 524, 331 09
Military Academy	107, 442 62
Improving rivers and harbors	8, 012, 758 26
Survey of Territories west of the one hundredth meridian	14, 000 00
Contingencies	38, 592 43
Expenses of recruiting	66, 455 33
Signal Service	385, 422 10
Expenses of military convicts	11, 854 05
Publishing the official records of the rebellion	40, 490 00
Support of National Home for Disabled Volunteers	880, 000 00
Support of Soldiers' Home	117, 920 33
Horses and other property lost in service	117, 742 22
Payments under relief acts	25, 517 18
Construction of military posts and roads	136, 494 08
Fortifications	204, 600 58
Miscellaneous	109, 225 38
National cemeteries	196, 470 16
Fifty per cent. arrears of Army transportation due certain railroads	285, 884 09
Construction of military bridges	65, 000 00
Construction of military telegraphs	104, 310 58
Bounty to soldiers, act July 28, 1866	129, 469 57
Transportation, Army and supplies, Pacific Railroads	800, 719 06
Survey of northern and northwestern lakes	85, 000 00

Total military establishment.. 38, 110, 616 22

NAVAL ESTABLISHMENT.

Pay and contingencies of the Navy	5, 916, 908 20
Marine Corps	732, 090 33
Navigation	245, 342 27
Ordnance	331, 309 04
Equipment and Recruiting	1, 068, 484 23
Yards and Docks	685, 118 07
Medicine and Surgery	150, 696 84
Provisions and Clothing	1, 171, 037 69
Construction and Repair	1, 502, 926 63
Steam Engineering	994, 430 07

TABLE C.—*STATEMENT of the ISSUE and REDEMPTION of LOANS and TREASURY NOTES (by warrants) for the fiscal year ended June 30, 1880.*

	Issues.	Redemptions.	Excess of issues.	Excess of redemptions.
Bounty land scrip, act of February 11, 1847	....	$25 00	....	$25 00
Loan of 1858, act of June 14, 1858	....	40,000 00	....	40,000 00
Loan of February, 1861, act of February 8, 1861	....	2,837,000 00	....	2,837,000 00
Loan of July and August, 1861, acts of July 17 and August, 1861	....	32,004,250 00	....	32,004,250 00
Oregon war debt, act of March 2, 1861	....	202,550 00	....	202,550 00
Old demand notes, acts of July 17 and August 5, 1861, and July 12, 1862	....	495 00	....	495 00
Five-twenties of 1862, act of February 25, 1862	....	9,100 00	....	9,100 00
Legal-tender notes, acts of February 25 and July 11, 1862, January 7 and March 3, 1863	$81,302,563 00	81,302,563 00	....	....
Temporary loan, acts of February 25, March 17, and July 11, 1862, and June 30, 1864	....	100 00	....	100 00
Fractional currency, acts of July 17, 1862, March 3, 1863, and June 30, 1864	....	251,717 41	....	251,717 41
Loan of 1863, act of March 3, 1863, and June 30, 1864	....	12,797,150 00	....	12,797,150 00
One year notes of 1863, act of March 3, 1863	....	2,150 00	....	2,150 00
Two year notes of 1863, act of March 3, 1863	....	1,550 00	....	1,550 00
Coin certificates, act of March 3, 1863	....	7,400,100 00	....	7,400,100 00
Compound interest notes, acts of March 3, 1863, and June 30, 1864	....	16,500 00	....	16,500 00
Ten-forties of 1864, act of March 3, 1864	....	135,709,750 00	....	135,709,750 00
Seven-thirties of 1864 and 1865, acts of June 30, 1864, and March 3, 1865	....	2,650 00	....	2,650 00
Five-twenties of June, 1864, act of June 30, 1864	....	3,550 00	....	3,550 00
Five-twenties of 1865, act of March 3, 1865	....	31,100 00	....	31,100 00
Consols of 1865, act of March 3, 1865	....	988,500 00	....	988,500 00
Consols of 1867, act of March 3, 1865	....	36,894,250 00	....	36,894,250 00
Consols of 1868, act of March 3, 1865	....	19,351,250 00	....	19,351,250 00
Certificates of deposit, act of June 8, 1872	47,355,000 00	63,260,000 00	....	15,905,000 00
Silver certificates, act of February 28, 1878	10,091,000 00	163,680 00	$9,907,320 00	....
Refunding certificates, act of February 26, 1879	614,040 00	12,095,850 00	....	11,481,210 00
Funded loan of 1881, acts of July 14, 1870, July 20, 1871, and January 14, 1875	....	23,575,450 00	....	23,575,450 00
Funded loan of 1907, acts of July 14, 1870, July 20, 1871, and January 14, 1875	72,450,900 00	1,500,000 00	70,950,900 00	....
Total	211,814,103 00	432,590,280 41	80,858,220 00	301,634,397 41
Excess of issues	....	....	....	301,634,397 41
Excess of redemptions	....	....	....	80,858,220 00
Net excess of redemptions charged in receipts and expenditures	....	....	....	220,776,177 41

TABLE D.—*STATEMENT of the NET RECEIPTS and DISBURSEMENTS (by warrants) for the quarter ended September 30, 1880.*

RECEIPTS.

Customs	$56, 295, 143 44
Sales of public lands	434, 800 60
Internal revenue	22, 436, 422 38
Tax on circulation, deposits, &c., of national banks	3, 933, 346 37
Repayment of interest by Pacific Railroad Companies	211, 402 70
Customs fees, fines, penalties, and forfeitures	333, 870 95
Consular, letters patent, homestead, &c., fees	542, 054 23
Proceeds of sales government property	56, 311 23
Profits on coinage	965, 582 40
Miscellaneous	2, 482, 205 44
Total net ordinary receipts	97, 689, 239 92
Balance in Treasury June 30, 1880	203, 638, 419 53
Total	301, 727, 659 45

DISBURSEMENTS.

Customs	$5, 027, 406 26
Internal revenue	4, 624, 028 58
Diplomatic service	240, 239 53
Judiciary	1, 256, 703 22
Interior (civil)	2, 212, 277 37
Treasury proper	7, 040, 421 48
Quarterly salaries	132, 874 14
Total civil and miscellaneous	10, 968, 950 58
Indians	2, 800, 891 99
Pensions	13, 604, 070 14
Military establishment	12, 940, 602 13
Naval establishment	5, 083, 571 98
Interest on public debt	25, 234, 830 58
Premium on bonds purchased	75, 324, 896 40
Redemption of the public debt	663, 515 38
Balance in Treasury September 30, 1880	23, 782, 554 00
	209, 926, 263 67
Total	301, 727, 659 45

TABLE E.—*STATEMENT of OUTSTANDING PRINCIPAL of the PUBLIC DEBT of the UNITED STATES on the 1st of January of each year from 1791 to 1843, inclusive, and on the 1st of July of each year from 1844 to 1880, inclusive.*

Year.	Amount.
Jan. 1, 1791	$75,463,476 52
1792	77,227,924 66
1793	80,352,634 04
1794	78,427,404 77
1795	80,747,587 39
1796	83,762,172 07
1797	82,064,479 33
1798	79,228,520 12
1799	78,408,669 77
1800	82,976,294 35
1801	83,038,050 80
1802	80,712,632 25
1803	77,054,686 30
1804	86,427,120 88
1805	82,312,150 50
1806	75,723,270 66
1807	69,218,398 64
1808	65,196,317 97
1809	57,023,192 09
1810	53,173,217 52
1811	48,005,587 76
1812	45,209,737 90
1813	55,962,827 57
1814	81,487,846 24
1815	99,833,660 15
1816	127,334,933 74
1817	123,491,965 16
1818	103,466,633 83
1819	95,529,648 28
1820	91,015,566 15
1821	89,987,427 66
1822	93,546,676 98
1823	90,875,877 28
1824	90,269,777 77
1825	83,788,432 71
1826	81,054,059 99
1827	73,987,357 20
1828	67,475,043 87
1829	58,421,413 67
1830	48,565,406 50
1831	39,123,191 68
1832	24,322,235 18
1833	7,001,698 83
1834	4,760,082 08
1835	37,733 05
1836	37,513 05
1837	336,957 83
1838	3,308,124 07
1839	10,434,221 14
1840	3,573,343 82
1841	5,250,875 54
1842	13,594,480 73
1843	20,601,226 28
July 1, 1843	32,742,922 00
1844	23,461,652 50
1845	15,925,303 01
1846	15,550,202 97
1847	38,826,534 77
1848	47,044,862 23
1849	63,061,858 69
1850	63,452,773 55
1851	68,304,796 02
1852	66,199,341 71
1853	59,803,117 70
1854	42,242,222 42
1855	35,586,956 56
1856	31,972,537 00
1857	28,699,831 85
1858	44,911,881 03
1859	58,496,837 88
1860	64,842,287 88
1861	90,580,873 72
1862	524,176,412 13
1863	1,119,772,138 63
1864	1,815,784,370 57
1865	2,680,647,869 74
1866	2,773,236,173 69
1867	2,678,126,103 87
1868	2,611,687,851 19

TABLE E.—*STATEMENT of OUTSTANDING PRINCIPAL of the PUBLIC DEBT, &c.*—Continued.

Year.	Amount.
July 1, 1869	\$2, 588, 452, 213 04
1870	2, 480, 672, 427 81
1871	2, 353, 211, 332 32
1872	2, 253, 251, 328 78
1873	*2, 234, 482, 993 20
1874	*2, 251, 690, 468 43
1875	*2, 232, 284, 531 95
1876	*2, 180, 395, 667 15
1877	*2, 205, 301, 392 10
1878	*2, 256, 205, 892 53
1879	*2, 349, 567, 482 04
1880	*2, 120, 415, 370 63

* In the amount here stated as the outstanding principal of the public debt are included the certificates of deposit outstanding on the 30th of June, issued under act of June 8, 1872, amounting to \$31,730,000, in 1873; \$33,760,000, in 1874; \$58,415,000, in 1875; \$32,840,000, in 1876; \$54,060,000, in 1877; \$46,755,000, in 1878; \$30,370,000 in 1879, and \$14,465,000, in 1880, for which a like amount in United States notes was on special deposit in the Treasury for their redemption, and added to the cash balance in the Treasury. These certificates, as a matter of accounts, are treated as a part of the public debt, but, being offset by notes held on deposit for their redemption should properly be deducted from the principal of the public debt in making comparison with former years.

STATEMENT of the PUBLIC DEBT, including ACCRUED INTEREST thereon, less cash in the Treasury on the 1st day of July of each year, from July 1, 1869, to July 1, 1880, compiled from the published monthly debt-statements of those dates.

Years.	Outstanding principal.	Accrued interest.	Cash in the Treasury.	Debt less cash in the Treasury.
July 1, 1869	*\$2, 597, 722, 983 37	\$47, 447, 910 70	\$150, 167, 813 58	\$2, 489, 002, 480 58
1870	*2, 601, 675, 127 83	50, 607, 556 52	265, 924, 084 61	2, 386, 358, 599 74
1871	2, 353, 211, 332 32	45, 036, 766 23	106, 217, 263 65	2, 292, 030, 834 90
1872	2, 253, 251, 328 78	41, 705, 813 27	103, 470, 798 43	2, 191, 486, 343 62
1873	2, 234, 482, 993 20	42, 856, 652 82	129, 020, 922 45	2, 147, 318, 713 57
1874	2, 251, 690, 468 43	38, 939, 987 47	147, 541, 914 74	2, 143, 088, 341 16
1875	2, 232, 284, 531 95	38, 047, 556 19	142, 243, 361 82	2, 128, 088, 726 32
1876	2, 180, 395, 667 15	38, 514, 994 54	119, 469, 726 70	2, 099, 436, 344 99
1877	2, 205, 301, 392 10	40, 882, 701 89	186, 025, 960 73	2, 060, 158, 229 26
1878	2, 256, 205, 892 53	36, 404, 551 37	*256, 823, 612 08	2, 035, 786, 831 82
1879	2, 349, 567, 482 04	39, 792, 351 34	353, 152, 577 01	2, 027, 207, 256 37
1880	2, 120, 415, 370 63	22, 845, 547 59	-201, 088, 622 88	1, 942, 172, 295 34

* It will be noticed that there is a difference in the amounts represented by these two statements as the principal of the debt July 1, 1869, and July 1, 1870. This difference is explained thus: In the principal of the debt as shown by the monthly debt-statements of these dates, the bonds purchased for the sinking-fund and paid for from money in the Treasury, were included as a part of the outstanding debt and were also treated in the cash as a cash item, or asset, for the reason that at that time there was no authority or law for deducting them from the outstanding debt. Congress, by the sixth section of the act of July 14, 1870, directed that these bonds should be canceled and destroyed and deducted from the amount of each class of the outstanding debt to which they respectively belonged, and such deductions were accordingly made on the books of the department and in the table of the debt in the annual report.

TABLE F.—*ANALYSIS of the PRINCIPAL of the PUBLIC DEBT of the UNITED STATES, from July 1, 1856, to July 1, 1880.*

Year.	3 per cents.	4 per cents.	4½ per cents.	5 per cents.	6 per cents.	7 3-10 per cents.	Total interest-bearing debt.
1856				$3,632,000 00	$26,130,701 77		$31,762,701 77
1857				3,480,000 00	24,971,958 93		28,400,958 93
1858				23,538,000 00	21,162,838 11		44,700,838 11
1859				37,127,800 00	21,162,838 11		58,290,738 11
1860				43,476,300 00	21,154,538 11		64,640,838 11
1861				33,022,200 00	57,358,673 95		90,380,873 95
1862		$57,926,116 57		30,483,000 00	154,313,225 01	$122,582,485 34	363,304,826 92
1863		105,629,385 20		30,483,000 00	431,444,813 83	139,574,435 34	707,531,684 47
1864		77,547,696 07		300,213,480 00	842,882,652 09	139,286,935 34	1,350,930,783 50
1865		90,496,930 74		245,709,420 03	1,213,495,169 90	671,610,307 62	2,221,311,918 29
1865—Aug. 31		618,127 98		269,375,727 65	1,281,736,439 33	830,000,000 00	2,381,530,294 96
1866		121,343,879 62		201,982,655 01	1,195,546,041 02	813,460,621 95	2,332,331,207 60
1867		17,737,925 68		198,533,435 01	1,543,452,080 02	488,344,846 95	2,248,067,387 66
1868	$64,000,000 00	801,961 23		221,586,185 01	1,878,303,984 50	37,397,196 96	2,202,088,727 69
1869	66,125,000 00			221,588,300 00	1,874,347,222 39		2,162,060,522 39
1870	59,550,000 00			221,588,300 00	1,765,317,422 39		2,046,455,722 39
1871	45,685,000 00	678,000 00		274,236,450 00	1,613,897,300 00		1,934,606,750 00
1872	24,665,000 00	678,000 00		414,567,300 00	1,374,883,800 00		1,814,794,100 00
1873	14,000,000 00	678,000 00		414,567,300 00	1,281,238,650 00		1,710,483,950 00
1874	14,000,000 00	678,000 00		510,028,050 00	1,213,624,700 00		1,738,030,750 00
1875	14,000,000 00	678,000 00		607,132,750 00	1,100,865,550 00		1,722,676,300 00
1876	14,000,000 00			711,685,800 00	984,999,650 00		1,710,685,450 00
1877	14,000,000 00		$140,000,000 00	703,266,650 00	854,621,850 00		1,711,888,580 00
1878	14,000,000 00	98,850,000 00	240,000,000 00	703,266,650 00	738,619,000 00		1,794,735,650 00
1879	14,000,000 00	741,522,000 00	250,000,000 00	508,440,350 00	283,681,350 00		1,797,643,700 00
1880	14,000,000 00	738,347,800 00	250,000,000 00	484,864,000 00	235,780,400 00		1,723,093,100 00

[Continued on next page.]

TABLE F.—ANALYSIS of the PRINCIPAL of the PUBLIC DEBT of the UNITED STATES, &c.—Continued.

Year.	Debt on which interest has ceased.	Debt bearing no interest.	Outstanding principal.	Cash in the Treasury July 1.	Total debt, less cash in Treasury.	Annual interest charge.
1856—July 1	$209,776 13		$31,972,537 90	$31,005,584 89	$16,965,953 01	$1,809,445 70
1857	208,872 02		28,699,831 85	18,701,216 09	9,028,621 76	1,672,767 53
1858	211,042 03		44,011,881 03	7,011,689 31	37,900,191 72	2,446,670 28
1859	200,090 77		58,496,837 88	5,001,603 60	53,405,234 19	3,126,166 28
1860	201,449 77		64,842,287 88	4,877,885 87	59,964,402 01	3,443,687 29
1861	199,999 77		90,580,873 72	2,862,212 92	87,718,660 80	5,092,630 43
1862	280,195 21	$158,591,390 00	524,176,412 13	18,863,659 96	505,312,732 17	22,048,509 50
1863	473,048 16	411,767,456 00	1,119,772,138 63	8,421,401 72	1,111,350,737 41	41,854,148 91
1864	415,335 86	455,437,271 21	1,815,784,370 57	100,332,203 53	1,702,452,277 04	78,853,487 24
1865—August 31	1,245,771 20	458,090,180 25	2,680,647,869 74	5,832,012 08	2,674,815,650 76	137,742,617 43
1865—July 1	1,503,020 09	461,616,311 51	2,844,649,626 56	88,218,055 13	2,756,431,571 43	150,977,697 87
1866—July 1	935,092 05	430,909,874 04	2,773,236,173 69	137,200,009 85	2,636,036,163 84	146,068,196 29
1867	1,840,615 01	428,218,101 20	2,678,126,103 87	102,974,802 18	2,508,151,211 69	138,892,451 39
1868	1,197,340 80	408,401,782 61	2,611,687,851 19	130,834,437 96	2,480,853,413 23	128,459,598 14
1869	5,203,161 00	421,131,510 55	2,588,452,213 94	155,680,340 85	2,432,771,873 09	125,523,998 34
1870	3,708,641 00	430,508,064 42	2,480,672,427 81	149,502,471 60	2,331,160,956 21	118,784,960 34
1871	1,948,902 20	416,565,660 00	2,353,211,332 32	105,217,263 65	2,246,994,068 07	111,049,330 50
1872	7,926,797 26	430,530,431 52	2,253,251,328 78	103,470,798 43	2,149,780,530 35	103,363,403 00
1873	51,929,710 20	472,069,332 94	2,234,482,993 20	120,020,923 45	2,105,402,069 75	98,049,804 00
1874	3,216,590 26	509,543,128 17	2,251,690,468 43	147,541,314 74	2,104,149,153 69	98,796,604 50
1875	11,425,820 26	498,182,411 69	2,232,284,531 95	142,243,361 82	2,090,041,170 13	96,855,690 50
1876	3,902,420 26	455,807,196 89	2,180,395,067 15	110,460,726 70	2,069,925,340 45	93,104,269 00
1877	16,648,860 26	470,764,031 84	2,205,301,392 10	180,025,960 73	2,019,275,431 37	93,160,643 50
1878	5,594,560 26	455,875,682 27	2,256,205,892 53	256,823,612 08	1,990,382,280 45	94,654,472 50
1879	37,015,639 26	410,835,741 78	2,345,405,072 04	349,080,167 01	1,996,414,905 03	83,773,778 50
1880	7,621,455 26	388,800,815 37	2,120,415,370 63	201,088,622 88	1,919,326,747 75	79,633,981 00

NOTE 1.—The annual interest charge is computed upon the amount of outstanding principal at the close of the fiscal year, and is exclusive of interest charge on Pacific Railway bonds.

NOTE 2.—The figures for July 1, 1879, were made up, assuming pending funding operations to have been completed.

NOTE 3.—The temporary loan, per act of July 11, 1862, is included in the 4 per cents. from 1862 to 1866, inclusive, with the exception of the amount outstanding for August 31, 1865, this being the date at which the public debt reached its highest point. This loan bore interest from 4 per cent. to 6 per cent., and was redeemable on ten days' notice after thirty days; but being constantly changing, it has been considered more equitable to include the whole amount outstanding as bearing 4 per cent. interest on an average for the year.

NOTE 4.—In the recent monthly statements of the public debt, the interest accrued has been added to the principal, making the net debt larger in that amount than the amount herein stated for each year.

TABLE G.—*STATEMENT of RECEIPTS of UNITED STATES from March 4, 1789,*

Year	Balance in the Treasury at commencement of year.	Customs.	Internal revenue.	Direct tax.	Public lands.	Miscellaneous.
1791		$4,399,478 09	$208,942 81			$10,478 10
1792	$073,905 75	3,443,070 85	337,705 70			9,918 65
1793	763,444 51	4,255,306 56	274,089 62			21,410 88
1794	753,661 69	4,801,065 28	337,755 36			53,277 97
1795	1,151,924 17	5,588,461 26	475,289 60			24,317 97
1796	516,442 61	6,567,987 94	575,491 45		$4,836 13	1,169,415 98
1797	888,995 42	7,549,649 65	644,357 95		83,540 60	399,189 29
1798	1,021,899 04	7,106,061 93	779,136 44		11,963 11	58,192 81
1799	617,451 43	6,610,449 31	809,396 55			86,187 56
1800	2,161,867 77	9,080,932 73	1,048,033 43	$734,223 97	443 75	152,712 10
1801	2,623,311 99	10,750,778 93	621,898 89	534,343 38	167,726 06	345,649 15
1802	3,205,391 00	12,438,235 74	215,179 69	206,565 44	188,628 02	1,500,505 88
1803	3,020,697 04	10,479,417 61	50,941 29	71,879 20	165,675 69	131,945 44
1804	4,825,811 00	11,098,565 33	21,747 15	50,198 44	487,526 79	139,075 53
1805	4,037,005 20	12,936,487 04	20,101 45	21,882 91	540,193 80	40,382 30
1806	3,999,368 99	14,667,698 17	13,051 40	55,763 86	765,245 73	51,121 86
1807	4,538,123 80	15,845,521 61	8,190 23	34,732 56	466,163 27	38,550 42
1808	9,643,850 07	16,363,550 58	4,034 29	10,159 21	647,939 06	21,822 85
1809	9,941,809 95	7,257,500 02	7,430 63	7,517 31	442,252 33	62,162 57
1810	3,848,056 78	8,583,309 31	2,295 05	12,448 68	696,548 82	84,476 84
1811	2,672,276 57	13,313,222 73	4,903 06	7,666 66	1,040,237 53	59,211 22
1812	2,502,305 80	8,958,777 53	4,755 04	859 22	710,427 78	126,165 17
1813	3,862,217 41	13,224,623 25	1,662,984 82	3,805 52	835,655 14	271,571 00
1814	3,196,542 00	5,598,772 08	4,678,059 07	2,219,497 36	1,135,971 09	164,399 81
1815	1,727,848 03	7,282,942 22	5,124,708 31	2,162,673 41	1,287,959 28	285,282 84
1816	13,106,592 88	36,306,874 88	2,678,100 77	4,253,635 09	1,717,985 03	273,782 35
1817	22,033,519 19	26,283,348 49	955,270 20	1,834,187 04	1,991,226 06	109,761 08
1818	14,989,465 48	17,176,385 00	229,593 63	264,333 36	2,606,564 77	57,617 71
1819	1,478,526 74	20,283,608 76	106,260 53	83,650 78	3,274,422 78	57,098 43
1820	2,079,992 24	15,005,612 15	69,027 63	31,586 82	1,635,871 61	61,338 44
1821	1,198,461 21	13,004,447 15	67,665 71	29,349 05	1,212,966 46	152,569 43
1822	1,031,592 24	17,589,761 94	34,242 17	20,961 56	1,803,581 54	452,957 10
1823	4,237,427 55	19,088,433 44	34,033 37	10,337 71	916,523 10	141,129 84
1824	9,463,922 81	17,878,325 71	25,771 35	6,201 96	984,418 15	127,603 60
1825	1,946,597 13	20,098,713 45	21,589 93	2,330 85	1,216,090 56	130,451 61
1826	5,201,650 43	23,341,331 77	19,885 68	6,638 76	1,393,785 09	94,588 66
1827	6,358,686 18	19,712,283 29	17,451 54	2,626 90	1,495,845 26	1,315,722 83
1828	6,668,268 10	23,205,523 04	14,603 74	2,218 81	1,018,308 75	65,126 49
1829	5,972,435 81	22,681,965 91	12,160 02	11,335 05	1,517,175 13	112,648 55
1830	5,755,704 79	21,922,391 39	6,933 51	10,909 59	2,329,356 14	73,227 77
1831	6,014,539 75	24,224,441 77	11,630 65	10,506 01	3,210,815 48	584,124 05
1832	4,502,914 45	28,465,237 24	2,759 00	6,791 13	2,623,381 30	270,410 61
1833	2,011,777 50	29,032,508 91	4,196 09	394 12	3,967,682 55	470,096 67
1834	11,702,905 31	16,214,957 15	10,450 48	19 80	4,857,600 69	480,812 32
1835	8,892,858 42	19,391,310 59	970 00	4,203 35	14,757,600 75	750,972 13
1836	26,749,803 96	23,409,940 53	5,498 84	728 79	24,877,179 86	2,245,902 29
1837	46,708,436 00	11,169,290 89	2,467 27	1,087 70	6,776,236 52	7,001,444 59
1838	37,327,252 09	16,158,800 36	2,553 82	755 22	3,730,945 66	6,410,348 45
1839	36,891,196 94	23,137,924 81	1,682 25		7,361,576 40	976,909 86
1840	33,157,503 68	13,499,502 17	3,261 36		3,411,818 63	2,567,112 28
1841	29,963,163 46	14,487,216 74	495 00		1,365,627 42	1,004,054 75
1842	28,685,111 08	18,187,908 76	103 25		1,335,797 52	451,995 97
1843*	30,521,979 44	7,046,843 91	1,777 34		898,158 18	285,895 92
1844	30,186,284 74	26,183,570 94	3,517 12		2,059,939 80	1,075,419 70
1845	36,742,829 02	27,528,112 70	2,897 26		2,077,022 30	361,433 68
1846	36,194,274 81	26,712,667 87	375 00		2,694,452 48	289,950 13
1847	38,261,959 35	23,747,864 66	375 00		2,498,355 20	220,808 30
1848	33,079,276 43	31,757,070 96			3,328,642 56	612,610 09
1849	29,416,012 45	28,346,738 82			1,688,959 55	683,379 10
1850	32,827,082 69	39,668,686 42			1,859,894 25	2,064,306 31
1851	35,871,753 31	49,017,567 92			2,352,305 30	1,185,166 11
1852	40,158,353 25	47,339,326 62			2,043,239 58	464,249 40
1853	43,338,860 02	58,931,865 52			1,667,084 99	968,981 17
1854	50,261,901 09	64,224,190 27			8,470,798 39	1,105,352 74
1855	46,591,079 41	53,025,794 21			11,497,049 07	827,731 40
1856	47,777,072 13	64,022,863 50			8,917,644 93	1,116,190 81
1857	49,108,229 80	63,875,905 05			3,829,486 64	1,259,920 88
1858	46,802,855 00	41,789,620 96			3,513,715 87	1,352,029 13
1859	35,113,334 22	49,565,824 38			1,756,687 30	1,454,596 24
1860	33,193,248 60	53,187,511 87			1,778,557 71	1,088,530 25
1861	32,979,530 78	39,582,125 64		1,795,331 73	870,658 54	1,023,515 31
1862	46,965,304 87	49,056,397 62	37,640,787 95	1,485,103 61	152,203 77	915,327 97
1863	36,523,046 13	69,059,642 40	109,741,134 10	475,648 96	167,617 17	3,741,794 38
1864	46,965,304 87	102,316,152 99	209,464,215 25	1,200,973 03	588,333 29	30,291,701 86
1865	134,433,738 44	84,928,260 60	209,464,215 25	1,200,973 03	996,553 31	25,441,550 00

* For the half-year from Jan

to June 30, 1880, by calendar years to 1843 and by fiscal years (ended June 30) from that time.

Year.	Dividends.	Net ordinary receipts.	Interest.	Premiums.	Receipts from loans and Treasury notes.	Gross receipts.	Unavailable.
1791	....	$4,409,951 19	....	....	$361,391 34	$4,771,342 53	....
1792	$8,028 00	3,669,960 31	....	....	5,102,498 45	8,772,458 70	....
1793	38,500 00	4,652,923 14	....	....	1,797,272 01	6,450,195 15	....
1794	303,472 00	5,431,904 87	....	....	4,007,950 78	9,439,855 65	....
1795	160,000 00	6,114,534 59	$4,800 00	....	3,396,424 00	9,515,758 59	....
1796	160,000 00	8,377,529 65	42,800 00	....	320,000 00	8,740,329 65	....
1797	80,960 00	8,688,780 99	....	....	70,000 00	8,758,780 99	....
1798	79,920 00	7,900,495 80	78,675 00	....	200,000 00	8,179,170 80	....
1799	71,040 00	7,546,813 31	....	....	5,000,000 00	12,546,813 31	....
1800	71,040 00	10,848,749 10	....	....	1,565,229 24	12,413,978 34	....
1801	88,800 00	12,935,330 95	10,125 00	....	....	12,945,455 95	....
1802	39,960 00	14,995,793 95	....	....	....	14,995,793 95	....
1803	....	11,064,097 63	....	....	....	11,064,097 63	....
1804	....	11,826,307 38	....	....	....	11,826,307 38	....
1805	....	13,560,693 20	....	....	....	13,560,693 20	....
1806	....	15,559,931 07	....	....	....	15,559,931 07	....
1807	....	16,398,019 26	....	....	....	16,398,019 26	....
1808	....	17,060,661 93	....	....	....	17,060,661 93	....
1809	....	7,773,473 12	....	....	....	7,773,473 12	....
1810	....	9,384,214 28	....	....	2,750,000 00	12,134,214 28	....
1811	....	14,422,634 09	....	....	....	14,422,634 09	....
1812	....	9,801,132 76	....	....	12,837,900 00	22,639,032 76	....
1813	....	14,340,409 95	300 00	....	26,184,135 00	40,524,844 95	....
1814	....	11,181,625 16	85 79	....	23,377,826 00	34,550,530 93	....
1815	....	15,696,916 82	11,541 74	$32,107 64	35,230,071 40	50,901,327 60	....
1816	....	47,676,985 06	68,665 10	686 09	9,425,084 91	57,171,421 82	....
1817	202,426 30	33,099,049 74	267,819 14	....	466,723 45	33,833,592 33	....
1818	525,000 00	21,585,171 04	412 62	....	8,353 00	21,593,936 56	....
1819	675,000 00	24,603,374 37	....	....	2,291 00	24,605,665 37	....
1820	1,000,000 00	17,840,669 55	....	....	3,000,824 13	20,681,493 68	....
1821	105,000 00	14,573,379 72	....	46,000 00	5,000,324 00	19,573,703 72	....
1822	297,500 00	20,232,427 94	....	....	....	20,232,427 94	....
1823	350,000 00	20,540,666 26	....	....	....	20,540,666 26	....
1824	350,000 00	19,381,212 79	....	....	5,000,000 00	24,381,212 79	....
1825	307,500 00	21,840,858 02	....	....	5,000,000 00	26,840,858 02	....
1826	402,500 00	25,290,434 21	....	....	....	25,290,434 21	....
1827	420,000 00	22,966,363 96	....	....	....	22,966,363 96	....
1828	455,000 00	24,763,629 23	....	....	....	24,763,629 23	....
1829	490,000 00	24,827,627 38	....	....	....	24,827,627 38	....
1830	490,000 00	24,844,116 51	....	....	....	24,844,116 51	....
1831	490,000 00	28,526,820 82	....	....	....	28,526,820 82	....
1832	490,000 00	31,867,450 66	....	....	....	31,867,450 66	$1,889 50
1833	474,985 00	33,948,426 25	....	....	....	33,948,426 25	....
1834	234,349 50	21,791,935 55	....	....	....	21,791,935 55	....
1835	505,460 82	35,430,087 10	....	....	....	35,430,087 10	....
1836	292,074 67	50,826,796 08	....	....	....	50,826,796 08	....
1837	....	24,954,153 04	....	....	2,992,989 15	27,947,142 19	68,286 35
1838	....	26,302,561 74	....	....	12,716,820 86	39,019,382 60	....
1839	....	31,482,749 61	....	....	3,857,276 21	35,340,025 82	1,458,782 93
1840	....	19,480,115 33	....	....	5,589,547 51	25,069,662 84	37,469 25
1841	....	16,860,160 27	....	....	13,659,317 38	30,519,477 65	....
1842	....	19,976,197 25	....	....	14,808,735 64	34,784,932 89	11,188 00
1843	....	8,231,001 26	....	71,700 83	12,473,708 36	20,782,410 45	....
1844	....	29,320,707 78	....	666 60	1,877,181 35	31,198,555 73	....
1845	....	29,970,105 80	....	....	....	29,970,105 80	28,251 90
1846	....	29,699,967 74	....	....	....	29,699,967 74	....
1847	....	26,467,403 10	....	26,365 91	28,872,399 45	55,366,168 52	30,000 00
1848	....	35,698,699 21	....	37,080 00	21,256,700 00	56,992,479 21	....
1849	....	30,721,077 50	....	487,065 48	28,588,750 00	59,796,892 98	....
1850	....	43,592,888 88	....	10,550 00	4,045,950 00	47,640,388 88	....
1851	....	52,555,039 33	....	4,264 92	203,400 00	52,762,704 25	....
1852	....	49,846,815 60	....	....	46,300 00	49,893,115 60	....
1853	....	61,587,031 68	....	22 50	16,350 00	61,603,404 18	103,501 97
1854	....	73,800,341 40	....	....	2,001 67	73,802,343 07	....
1855	....	65,356,574 68	....	....	800 00	65,351,374 68	....
1856	....	74,056,699 24	....	....	200 00	74,056,899 24	....
1857	....	68,965,312 57	....	....	3,900 00	68,969,312 57	....
1858	....	46,655,365 96	....	....	23,717,300 00	70,372,665 96	15,408 34
1859	....	52,777,107 92	....	709,357 72	28,287,500 00	81,773,965 64	....
1860	....	56,054,599 83	....	10,008 00	20,776,800 00	76,841,407 83	....
1861	....	41,476,299 49	....	33,630 90	41,861,709 74	83,371,640 13	....
1862	....	51,919,261 09	....	96,400 00	529,692,460 50	581,680,121 50	11,110 81
1863	....	112,094,945 51	....	602,845 44	776,682,361 57	889,379,952 52	6,000 01
1864	....	243,412,971 20	....	21,174,101 01	1,128,873,945 98	1,393,461,017 57	9,210 40
1865	....	322,031,158 19	....	11,683,446 89	1,472,224,740 85	1,805,939,345 93	6,085 11

nary 1, 1843, to June 30, 1843.

TABLE G.—*STATEMENT of the RECEIPTS of the UNITED*

Year.	Balance in the Treasury at commencement of year.	Customs.	Internal revenue.	Direct tax.	Public lands.	Miscellaneous.
1866	$33,009,657 89	$179,046,651 56	$309,226,813 42	$1,974,754 12	$665,031 03	$29,036,314 23
1867	160,817,099 73	176,417,810 88	266,027,537 43	4,200,233 70	1,163,575 76	15,037,522 15
1868	198,076,537 09	164,464,599 56	191,087,589 41	1,788,145 85	1,348,715 41	17,745,403 59
1869	158,936,082 87	180,048,426 63	158,356,460 86	765,685 61	4,020,344 34	13,997,338 65
1870	183,781,985 76	194,538,374 44	184,899,756 49	229,102 88	3,350,481 76	12,942,118 30
1871	177,604,116 51	206,270,408 05	143,098,153 63	580,355 37	2,388,646 68	22,093,541 21
1872	138,019,122 15	216,370,286 77	130,642,177 72	....	2,575,714 19	15,106,051 23
1873	134,666,001 85	188,089,522 70	113,729,314 14	315,254 51	2,882,312 38	17,161,270 05
1874	150,293,073 41	163,103,833 69	102,409,784 90	....	1,852,428 98	32,575,043 32
1875	178,833,339 54	157,167,722 35	110,007,493 58	....	1,413,640 17	15,431,915 31
1876	172,804,061 32	148,071,984 61	116,700,732 03	93,798 80	1,129,466 95	24,070,602 81
1877	140,909,377 21	130,956,493 07	118,630,407 83	....	976,253 68	30,437,487 42
1878	214,887,645 88	130,170,680 20	110,581,624 74	....	1,079,743 37	15,614,728 09
1879	286,591,453 88	137,250,047 70	113,561,610 58	....	924,781 06	20,585,097 49
1880	396,872,582 65	186,522,064 60	124,009,373 92	30 85	1,016,506 00	21,078,525 01
	....	4,438,963,426 40	2,972,993,960 77	27,648,756 58	205,564,310 41	323,428,350 02

* Amounts heretofore credited to the Treasurer as

STATES from March 4, 1789, to June 30, 1880, &c.—Continued.

Year.	Dividends.	Net ordinary receipts.	Interest.	Premiums.	Receipts from loans and Treasury notes.	Gross receipts.	Unavailable.
1866	....	$519,949,584 38	....	$38,083,055 68	$712,851,553 05	$1,278,884,173 11	$172,094 29
1867	....	462,846,679 92	....	27,787,330 35	640,426,910 29	1,131,060,920 56	721,827 93
							2,675,918 19
1868	....	376,434,453 82	....	29,283,629 50	625,111,433 20	1,030,749,516 52	....
1869	....	357,188,256 09	....	13,755,491 12	238,678,081 06	609,621,828 27	*2,070 73
1870	....	395,959,833 87	....	15,295,643 76	285,474,496 00	696,729,973 63	....
1871	....	374,431,104 94	....	8,892,839 95	268,768,523 47	652,092,468 36	*3,396 18
1872	....	364,894,229 91	....	9,412,637 65	305,047,054 00	679,153,921 56	*18,228 35
1873	....	322,177,073 78	....	11,560,530 89	214,931,017 00	548,669,221 67	*3,047 80
1874	....	299,941,090 84	....	5,037,665 22	439,272,535 48	744,251,291 52	12,091 40
1875	....	284,020,771 41	....	3,979,279 69	387,971,556 00	675,971,607 10	....
1876	....	290,066,584 70	....	4,029,280 58	397,455,808 00	691,551,673 28	....
1877	....	281,000,642 00	....	405,776 58	348,871,749 90	630,278,167 58	....
1878	....	257,446,776 40	....	317,102 30	404,581,201 00	662,345,079 70	....
1879	....	273,322,186 83	....	1,505,047 63	792,807,048 00	1,066,634,827 46	....
1880	....	333,526,500 96	....	110 00	211,814,183 00	545,340,713 98	....
	$9,729,136 29	7,767,417,979 47	465,224 45	204,259,226 83	10,507,293,707 84	18,569,456,132 59	2,061,866 53

unavailable, and since recovered and charged to his account.

TABLE II.—*STATEMENT of EXPENDITURES of UNITED STATES from Mar. 4,*

Year.	War.	Navy.	Indians.	Pensions.	Miscellaneous.
1791	$632, 804 03		$27, 000 00	$175, 813 88	$1, 083, 971 61
1792	1, 100, 702 09		13, 648 85	100, 243 15	4, 672, 664 38
1793	1, 130, 249 08		27, 282 83	80, 087 81	511, 451 01
1794	2, 639, 097 59	$61, 408 97	13, 042 46	81, 399 24	750, 350 74
1795	2, 480, 910 13	410, 562 03	23, 475 68	68, 673 22	1, 378, 920 66
1796	1, 280, 203 84	274, 784 04	113, 563 98	100, 843 71	801, 847 58
1797	1, 039, 402 46	382, 631 89	62, 306 58	92, 256 97	1, 250, 422 62
1798	2, 009, 522 30	1, 381, 347 76	16, 470 09	104, 845 33	1, 130, 524 94
1799	2, 466, 040 98	2, 858, 081 84	20, 302 13	95, 444 03	1, 920, 391 68
1800	2, 560, 878 77	3, 448, 716 03	31 22	64, 130 73	1, 337, 613 22
1801	1, 672, 944 08	2, 111, 424 00	9, 000 00	73, 533 37	1, 114, 768 45
1802	1, 179, 148 25	915, 561 87	94, 000 00	85, 440 39	1, 462, 929 40
1803	822, 055 85	1, 215, 230 53	60, 000 00	62, 902 10	1, 842, 635 76
1804	875, 423 93	1, 189, 832 75	116, 500 00	80, 092 80	2, 101, 009 42
1805	712, 781 28	1, 597, 500 00	100, 500 00	81, 854 59	3, 768, 306 75
1806	1, 224, 355 38	1, 649, 641 44	234, 200 00	81, 875 53	2, 890, 137 01
1807	1, 288, 685 91	1, 722, 064 47	205, 425 00	70, 500 00	1, 697, 897 51
1808	2, 900, 834 40	1, 884, 067 80	213, 575 00	82, 576 04	1, 433, 285 61
1809	3, 345, 772 17	2, 427, 758 80	337, 503 84	87, 833 54	1, 215, 803 79
1810	2, 294, 323 94	1, 054, 244 20	177, 625 00	83, 744 16	1, 101, 144 98
1811	2, 032, 828 19	1, 965, 566 39	151, 875 00	75, 043 88	1, 367, 291 40
1812	11, 817, 798 24	3, 959, 365 15	277, 845 00	91, 402 10	1, 683, 088 21
1813	19, 652, 013 02	6, 446, 600 10	167, 358 28	86, 989 91	1, 729, 435 61
1814	20, 350, 806 86	7, 311, 290 60	167, 394 86	90, 164 36	2, 208, 020 70
1815	14, 794, 294 22	8, 660, 000 25	530, 750 00	69, 656 06	2, 898, 870 47
1816	16, 012, 096 80	3, 908, 278 30	274, 512 16	188, 804 15	2, 989, 741 17
1817	8, 004, 236 53	3, 314, 598 49	319, 463 71	297, 374 43	3, 518, 936 76
1818	5, 622, 715 10	2, 953, 695 00	505, 704 27	890, 719 90	3, 835, 839 51
1819	6, 506, 300 37	3, 847, 640 42	463, 181 39	2, 415, 939 85	3, 067, 211 41
1820	2, 630, 392 31	4, 387, 990 00	315, 750 01	3, 208, 376 31	2, 592, 031 94
1821	4, 461, 291 78	3, 319, 243 06	477, 005 44	242, 817 25	2, 223, 121 54
1822	3, 111, 981 48	2, 224, 458 98	575, 007 41	1, 948, 199 40	1, 967, 996 24
1823	3, 096, 924 43	2, 503, 765 83	380, 781 82	1, 780, 588 52	2, 022, 093 00
1824	3, 340, 939 85	2, 904, 581 56	429, 987 90	1, 499, 326 59	7, 155, 308 81
1825	3, 659, 914 18	3, 049, 083 86	724, 106 44	1, 308, 810 57	2, 748, 544 89
1826	3, 943, 194 37	4, 218, 902 45	743, 447 83	1, 556, 593 83	2, 600, 177 79
1827	3, 948, 977 88	4, 263, 877 45	750, 624 88	976, 138 86	2, 713, 476 58
1828	4, 145, 544 56	3, 918, 786 44	705, 084 24	850, 573 57	3, 676, 052 64
1829	4, 724, 291 07	3, 308, 745 47	576, 344 74	945, 594 47	3, 082, 234 65
1830	4, 767, 128 88	3, 239, 428 63	622, 262 47	1, 368, 267 31	3, 237, 416 04
1831	4, 841, 835 55	3, 856, 183 07	980, 738 04	1, 170, 665 14	3, 064, 646 10
1832	5, 446, 034 88	3, 956, 370 29	1, 352, 419 75	1, 184, 422 40	4, 577, 141 45
1833	6, 704, 019 10	3, 901, 356 75	1, 802, 980 93	4, 580, 152 40	5, 716, 245 08
1834	5, 696, 189 38	3, 956, 290 42	1, 003, 053 20	3, 364, 285 30	4, 404, 728 05
1835	5, 759, 156 89	3, 864, 930 06	1, 706, 444 48	1, 954, 711 32	4, 229, 698 53
1836	11, 747, 345 25	5, 807, 718 23	5, 037, 022 88	2, 882, 797 00	5, 399, 279 72
1837	13, 682, 730 80	6, 646, 914 53	4, 348, 080 14	2, 672, 162 45	9, 898, 370 27
1838	12, 897, 224 16	6, 131, 580 58	5, 504, 191 34	2, 156, 057 29	7, 100, 664 76
1839	8, 916, 995 80	6, 182, 294 25	2, 528, 917 28	3, 142, 750 51	5, 725, 990 89
1840	7, 095, 267 23	6, 113, 896 89	2, 331, 794 86	2, 603, 562 17	5, 996, 398 96
1841	8, 801, 610 24	6, 001, 076 97	2, 514, 837 12	2, 388, 434 51	6, 490, 881 45
1842	6, 610, 438 02	8, 397, 242 95	1, 199, 099 68	1, 378, 931 33	6, 775, 624 61
1843*	2, 908, 671 95	3, 727, 711 53	578, 371 00	830, 041 12	3, 202, 713 00
1844	5, 218, 183 66	6, 498, 199 11	1, 280, 582 20	2, 032, 008 99	5, 645, 180 66
1845	6, 740, 361 28	6, 297, 177 89	1, 530, 381 35	2, 400, 788 21	5, 911, 760 98
1846	10, 413, 970 58	6, 455, 013 92	1, 027, 693 64	1, 811, 097 56	6, 711, 283 89
1847	35, 840, 030 33	7, 900, 635 76	1, 430, 411 30	1, 744, 883 63	6, 885, 698 35
1848	27, 688, 334 21	9, 408, 476 02	1, 252, 296 81	1, 227, 496 48	5, 650, 831 25
1849	14, 558, 473 26	9, 786, 705 92	1, 374, 161 55	1, 328, 867 04	12, 883, 334 24
1850	9, 687, 024 58	7, 904, 724 66	1, 668, 591 47	1, 866, 886 02	16, 043, 763 38
1851	12, 161, 965 11	8, 880, 581 38	2, 870, 801 77	2, 293, 377 23	17, 888, 992 18
1852	8, 521, 506 19	8, 918, 842 10	3, 043, 576 04	2, 401, 858 78	17, 504, 171 45
1853	9, 910, 498 49	11, 067, 789 53	3, 880, 494 12	1, 756, 306 20	17, 463, 068 01
1854	11, 722, 282 87	10, 790, 096 32	1, 550, 399 85	1, 332, 663 08	26, 672, 144 68
1855	14, 648, 074 07	13, 327, 095 11	2, 772, 990 78	1, 477, 612 33	24, 090, 425 43
1856	16, 963, 160 51	14, 074, 834 64	2, 644, 263 97	1, 296, 229 65	31, 794, 038 87
1857	10, 150, 150 87	12, 651, 694 61	4, 354, 418 87	1, 310, 380 58	26, 565, 428 77
1858	25, 679, 121 63	14, 053, 264 64	4, 078, 266 18	1, 219, 768 30	26, 400, 016 42
1859	23, 154, 720 53	14, 690, 927 90	3, 490, 534 53	1, 222, 222 71	29, 797, 544 40
1860	16, 472, 202 72	11, 514, 649 83	2, 991, 121 54	1, 100, 802 32	27, 077, 078 30
1861	23, 001, 530 07	12, 387, 156 02	2, 865, 481 17	* 1, 034, 599 73	23, 327, 287 69
1862	389, 173, 562 29	42, 640, 353 09	2, 327, 948 27	852, 170 47	21, 385, 862 50
1863	603, 314, 411 82	63, 261, 235 31	3, 152, 032 70	1, 078, 513 36	23, 196, 382 57
1864	690, 391, 048 66	85, 704, 003 74	2, 029, 075 07	4, 985, 473, 90	27, 572, 216 87

* For the half year from Jan-

1789, to June 30, 1880, by cal. years to 1843 and by fiscal years (ended June 30) from that time.

Year.	Net ordinary expenditures.	Premiums.	Interest.	Public debt.	Gross expenditures.	Balance in Treasury at the end of the year.
1791	$1,919,589 52		$1,177,863 03	$699,984 23	$3,797,436 78	$973,905 75
1792	5,896,238 47		2,373,611 28	693,050 25	8,962,920 00	783,444 51
1793	1,749,070 73		2,097,859 17	2,633,048 07	6,479,977 97	753,661 69
1794	3,545,299 00		2,752,523 04	2,743,771 13	9,041,593 17	1,151,924 17
1795	4,362,541 73		2,947,059 06	2,841,639 37	10,151,240 15	516,442 01
1796	2,551,303 15		3,239,347 68	2,577,126 01	8,367,776 84	888,995 46
1797	2,836,110 52		3,172,516 73	2,617,250 12	8,625,877 37	1,021,899 04
1798	4,651,710 42		2,955,875 90	976,032 68	8,584,618 41	617,451 43
1799	6,480,166 72		2,815,651 41	1,706,578 84	11,002,396 97	2,161,867 77
1800	7,411,369 97		3,402,601 04	1,138,563 11	11,952,534 12	2,623,311 99
1801	4,981,669 90		4,411,830 06	2,870,876 98	12,273,376 94	3,295,391 00
1802	3,737,079 91		4,230,172 16	5,294,235 24	13,270,487 31	5,020,697 64
1803	4,002,824 24		3,949,462 36	3,306,697 07	11,258,983 67	4,825,811 60
1804	4,452,858 91		4,185,048 74	3,977,206 07	12,615,113 72	4,037,005 26
1805	6,357,234 62		2,657,114 22	4,583,960 63	13,598,309 47	3,999,388 99
1806	6,080,209 36		3,368,968 26	5,572,018 64	15,021,196 26	4,538,123 80
1807	4,984,572 89		3,369,578 48	2,938,141 62	11,292,292 99	9,643,850 07
1808	6,504,338 85		2,557,074 23	7,701,288 96	16,762,702 04	9,941,809 96
1809	7,414,672 14		2,866,074 90	3,586,479 26	13,867,226 30	3,848,056 78
1810	5,311,082 28		3,163,671 09	4,835,241 12	13,309,994 49	2,672,276 57
1811	5,592,604 86		2,585,435 57	5,414,564 43	13,593,604 86	3,502,305 80
1812	17,829,498 70		2,451,272 57	1,998,349 88	22,279,121 15	3,862,217 41
1813	28,082,396 92		3,599,455 22	7,508,668 22	39,190,520 36	5,196,542 90
1814	30,127,686 38		4,593,239 04	3,307,304 90	38,028,230 32	1,727,848 63
1815	26,953,571 00		5,990,090 24	6,638,832 11	39,582,493 35	13,106,592 88
1816	23,373,432 58		7,822,923 34	17,048,139 59	48,244,495 51	22,033,519 19
1817	15,454,609 92		4,536,282 55	20,886,753 57	40,877,646 04	14,989,465 48
1818	13,808,673 78		6,209,954 03	15,086,247 59	35,104,875 40	1,478,526 74
1819	16,300,273 44		5,211,730 56	2,492,195 73	24,004,199 73	2,079,992 38
1820	13,134,530 57		5,151,004 32	3,477,489 96	21,763,024 85	1,198,461 21
1821	10,723,479 07		5,126,073 79	3,241,019 83	19,090,572 69	1,681,592 24
1822	9,827,643 51		5,172,788 79	2,676,160 33	17,676,592 63	4,237,427 55
1823	9,784,154 59		4,922,475 40	607,541 01	15,314,171 00	9,463,922 81
1824	15,330,144 71		4,943,557 93	11,624,835 83	31,898,538 47	1,946,597 13
1825	11,490,459 94		4,366,757 40	7,728,587 38	23,585,804 72	5,201,650 43
1826	13,062,316 27		3,975,542 95	7,065,530 24	24,103,388 46	6,358,686 18
1827	12,653,005 65		3,486,071 51	6,517,596 88	22,656,764 04	6,668,286 10
1828	13,296,041 45		3,098,800 60	9,064,637 47	25,459,479 52	5,972,435 81
1829	12,041,210 40		2,542,843 23	9,860,304 77	26,044,358 40	5,755,704 70
1830	13,229,533 33		1,912,574 93	9,443,173 29	24,585,281 55	6,014,539 75
1831	13,864,067 90		1,373,748 74	14,800,629 48	30,038,446 12	4,502,914 45
1832	16,516,388 77		772,561 50	17,067,747 79	34,356,698 06	2,011,777 55
1833	22,713,755 11		303,796 87	1,239,746 51	24,257,298 49	11,702,905 31
1834	18,425,417 25		202,152 98	5,974,412 21	24,601,982 44	8,892,858 42
1835	17,514,950 28		57,863 08	328 20	17,573,141 56	26,749,803 06
1836	30,868,164 04				30,868,164 04	46,708,436 00
1837	37,243,214 24			21,822 91	37,265,037 15	37,327,252 69
1838	33,849,718 08		14,996 48	5,590,723 79	39,455,438 35	36,891,196 94
1839	20,496,948 73		399,833 89	10,718,153 53	37,014,936 15	33,157,503 68
1840	24,139,920 11		174,598 08	3,912,015 62	28,226,533 81	29,963,163 46
1841	26,196,840 29		284,977 55	5,315,712 19	31,797,530 03	28,685,111 08
1842	24,361,336 59		773,549 85	7,801,990 09	32,936,876 53	30,521,979 44
1843	11,256,508 60		523,583 91	338,012 64	12,118,105 15	35,186,284 74
1844	20,650,108 01		1,833,452 13	11,158,450 71	35,042,010 86	36,742,829 62
1845	21,895,369 61	$18,231 43	1,040,458 18	7,536,349 49	30,490,408 71	36,194,274 81
1846	26,418,459 59		842,723 27	371,100 04	27,632,282 90	38,261,959 65
1847	53,801,569 37		1,119,214 72	5,600,067 65	60,520,851 74	33,079,276 43
1848	45,227,454 77		2,390,765 88	13,036,922 54	60,655,143 19	29,416,612 45
1849	39,933,542 61	$82,805 81	3,565,535 78	12,804,478 54	56,386,422 74	32,827,082 69
1850	37,165,990 09		3,782,393 03	3,956,305 14	44,604,718 26	35,871,753 31
1851	44,054,717 66	69,713 19	3,696,760 75	654,912 71	48,476,104 31	40,158,353 25
1852	40,389,954 56	170,063 42	4,000,297 80	2,152,293 05	46,712,608 82	43,338,860 02
1853	44,078,156 35	420,498 64	3,665,832 74	6,412,574 01	54,577,061 74	56,261,901 09*
1854	51,087,528 42	2,877,818 09	3,070,926 69	17,556,896 95	75,473,170 75	48,591,073 41
1855	56,316,197 72	873,047 39	2,314,464 90	6,662,065 86	66,164,775 96	47,777,672 13
1856	66,772,527 84	385,372 90	1,953,822 37	3,614,618 66	72,726,341 57	49,108,229 80
1857	66,041,143 79	363,572 39	1,808,205 23	3,276,606 05	71,274,587 47	46,802,855 00
1858	72,390,437 17	574,443 08	1,652,055 67	7,505,250 82	82,062,186 74	35,113,334 22
1859	66,355,950 07		2,637,649 70	14,685,043 15	83,678,642 92	33,193,248 60
1860	60,056,754 71		3,144,120 94	13,854,250 00	77,055,125 65	32,979,530 78
1861	62,616,055 78		4,034,157 30	18,737,100 00	85,387,313 08	30,963,857 83
1862	456,379,896 81		13,190,344 84	96,097,322 09	565,667,563 74	46,965,304 87
1863	694,004,575 56		24,729,700 62	181,081,635 07	890,815,911 25	36,523,046 13
1864	811,283,076 24		53,685,421 69	430,572,014 03	1,295,541,114 86	134,433,738 44

nary 1, 1843, to June 30, 1843.

2 F

REPORT OF THE SECRETARY OF THE TREASURY.

TABLE H.—*STATEMENT of the EXPENDITURES of the UNITED*

Year.	War.	Navy.	Indians.	Pensions.	Miscellaneous.
1865	$1,030,690,400 06	$122,617,434 07	$5,050,360 71	$16,347,621 34	$42,989,383 10
1866	283,154,676 06	43,285,662 00	3,295,729 32	15,605,549 88	40,613,114 17
	3,508,698,312 28	717,551,816 83	103,369,211 42	119,607,656 01	648,004,854 33
	*3,621,780 07	*77,992 17	*53,286 61	*9,737 87	*716,709 52
	2,372,260,092 35	717,629,808 50	103,422,408 03	119,617,393 88	644,323,323 85
1867	95,224,415 63	31,034,011 04	4,642,531 77	20,936,551 71	51,110,223 72
1868	123,246,648 62	25,775,502 72	4,100,682 32	23,782,386 78	53,009,867 67
1869	78,501,990 61	20,000,757 07	7,042,923 06	28,476,621 78	56,474,061 53
1870	57,655,675 40	21,780,229 87	3,407,938 15	28,340,202 17	53,237,461 56
1871	35,799,991 82	19,431,927 21	7,426,997 44	34,443,894 88	60,481,916 23
1872	35,372,157 20	21,249,809 99	7,061,728 82	28,533,402 76	60,984,757 42
1873	46,323,138 31	23,526,256 79	7,951,704 88	29,359,426 86	73,328,110 06
1874	42,313,927 22	30,932,587 42	6,692,462 09	29,038,414 60	85,141,503 61
1875	41,120,645 98	21,497,626 27	8,384,656 82	29,456,216 22	71,070,702 98
1876	38,070,868 64	18,963,309 82	5,966,558 17	28,257,395 69	73,599,661 04
1877	37,082,735 90	14,959,935 36	5,277,007 22	27,963,752 27	58,926,532 53
1878	32,154,147 85	17,365,301 37	4,629,280 28	27,137,019 08	53,177,703 57
1879	40,425,660 73	15,125,126 84	5,206,100 08	35,121,482 39	65,741,555 49
1880	38,116,916 22	13,536,984 74	5,945,457 09	50,777,174 44	54,713,529 76
	4,313,669,032 48	1,012,808,275 97	187,158,035 22	547,241,335 57	1,515,321,001 02

* Outstanding

NOTE.—This statement is made from warrants *paid* by the Treasurer up to June 30, 1866. The outstanding balance reported in the Treasury at the end of 1879 and 1880 are included the amounts of $28,101,644.91 on the books of the Register's Office, which amounts have been deducted by the Treasurer of the United

STATES from March 4, 1879, to June 30, 1880, &c.—Continued.

Year.	Net ordinary expenditures.	Premiums.	Interest.	Public debt.	Gross expenditures.	Balance in Treasury at the end of the year.
1865	$1,217,704,109 28	$1,717,000 11	$77,395,090 30	$609,616,141 68	$1,906,433,831 37	$33,933,657 89
1866	385,954,731 43	58,476 51	133,067,624 91	620,263,249 10	1,139,344,081 95	165,301,654 76
	5,152,771,550 43	7,011,003 56	502,680,519 27	2,374,677,103 12	8,037,740,176 38	....
	*4,481,566 24	....	*2,888 48	*100 91	*4,484,555 03	*4,484,555 03
	5,157,253,116 07	7,011,003 56	502,692,407 75	5,874,677,203 43	8,042,283,731 41	160,817,090 73
1867	202,947,733 87	10,813,340 38	148,781,501 01	735,536,980 11	1,098,079,655 27	158,076,537 09
1868	229,915,088 11	7,001,151 04	140,424,045 71	692,549,685 88	1,069,889,970 74	158,936,082 87
1869	190,496,354 95	1,674,680 05	130,694,242 80	261,912,718 31	584,777,996 11	183,781,985 76
1870	164,421,507 15	15,996,555 90	120,235,498 00	303,254,282 13	702,907,842 88	177,604,110 51
1871	157,583,827 58	9,016,794 74	125,576,565 93	309,503,070 65	601,680,858 90	138,019,122 15
1872	153,201,856 19	6,958,266 76	117,357,839 72	405,007,307 54	682,525,270 21	134,666,001 85
1873	180,488,636 90	5,105,919 90	104,750,688 44	233,699,352 58	524,044,597 91	159,293,673 41
1874	194,118,985 60	1,395,073 55	107,119,815 21	422,065,060 23	724,698,933 99	178,833,339 54
1875	171,529,848 27	....	103,093,544 57	407,377,492 48	682,000,885 32	172,804,061 32
1876	164,857,813 39	....	100,243,271 23	449,345,272 80	714,446,357 89	149,909,377 21
1877	144,209,963 28	....	97,124,511 58	343,965,424 05	585,299,898 91	214,887,645 88
1878	134,463,452 15	....	102,500,874 65	358,676,944 03	595,641,271 70	286,591,453 88
1879	161,610,994 59	....	105,327,949 00	699,445,809 16	966,308,693 69	386,522,586 05
1880	169,090,062 23	2,795,320 42	95,757,575 11	432,500,280 41	700,233,238 19	231,940,064 44
	7,576,108,180 20	68,368,115 09	2,105,080,421 01	8,584,607,484 60	18,334,854,201 62	....

warrants.

standing warrants are then added, and the statement is by warrants *issued* from that date. In the
deposited with the States and $47,607.65 arising from deficiency in the Treasurer's Office, transferred to
States, leaving a net balance of covered moneys, as per his books, of $203,701,221.88.

TABLE I.—*STATEMENT showing the CONDITION of the SINKING-FUND from its institution in May, 1869, to and including June 30, 1880.*

THE SECRETARY OF THE TREASURY IN ACCOUNT WITH SINKING-FUND.

Dr.			Cr.		
July 1, 1868	To ¼ of 1 per cent. on the principal of the public debt, being for the three months from April 1 to June 30, 1868..	$6,529,219 63	June 30, 1869	By amount of principal purchased, $6,691,000, including $1,000 donation, estimated in gold..................	$7,261,437 30
June 30, 1869	To interest on $6,691,000, being amount of principal of public debt purchased during fiscal year 1869 on this account..	196,590 00		By accrued interest on the amount of purchases in 1869.	136,392 50
	Balance to new account..................................	672,020 23			
		7,397,829 86			7,397,829 80
July 1, 1869	To 1 per cent. on the principal of the public debt on June 30, 1869, $2,588,452,213.94	25,884,522 14	July 1, 1869	By balance from last year..............................	672,020 23
June 30, 1870	To interest on $4,691,000, amount of redemption in 1869..	521,460 00	June 30, 1870	By amount of principal purchased, $28,151,900, estimated in gold..	25,893,143 57
	To interest on $28,151,900, amount of principal of public debt purchased during fiscal year 1870 on this account.	1,254,897 00		By accrued interest on account of purchases in 1870....	351,003 54
				By balance to new account..............................	744,711 80
		27,600,879 14			27,000,870 14
July 1, 1870	To balance from last year..............................	744,711 80	June 30, 1871	By amount of principal purchased, $20,096,250, estimated in gold..	28,694,017 73
June 30, 1871	To 1 per cent. on the principal of the public debt on June 30, 1870, $2,480,672,427.81......................	24,806,724 28		By accrued interest on account of purchases in 1871 ...	307,782 53
	To interest on redemption of 1869, $6,691,000	521,460 00		By balance to new account	257,474 32
	To interest on redemption of 1870, $28,151,900.........	1,680,114 00			
	To interest on $20,936,250, amount of principal of public debt purchased during fiscal year 1871 on this account.	1,537,364 50			
		29,310,274 58			29,319,274 58
July 1, 1871	To balance from last year..............................	257,474 32	June 30, 1872	By amount of principal purchased, $32,618,450, estimated in gold..	32,248,645 22
June 30, 1872	To 1 per cent. on the principal of the public debt on June 30, 1871, $2,353,211,332.32......................	23,532,113 32		By accrued interest on account of purchases in 1872 ...	430,998 38
	To interest on redemption of 1869, $6,691,000	521,460 00			
	To interest on redemption of 1870, $28,151,900.........	1,680,114 00			
	To interest on redemption of 1871, $20,936,250	1,796,175 00			
	To interest on redemption of 1871, $22,018,450, amount of principal of public debt purchased during fiscal year	....			

Date	Debit	Amount	Date	Credit	Amount
July 1, 1872	To 1 per cent. on the principal of the public debt on June 30, 1872, $2,283,351,328.78	22,532,513 20	July 1, 1872	By balance from last year	2,823,591 46
June 30, 1873	To interest on redemption of 1860, $8,651,000	521,460 00	June 30, 1873	By amount of principal purchased, $28,678,000, estimated in gold	28,457,562 83
	To interest on redemption of 1870, $28,151,900	1,689,114 00		By accrued interest on account of purchases in 1873	392,385 45
	To interest on redemption of 1871, $20,036,250	1,790,175 00			
	To interest on redemption of 1872, $39,618,450	3,957,167 00			
	To interest on redemption of $28,078,000, amount of principal of public debt purchased during fiscal year 1873 on this account	1,725,861 50			
	To balance to new account	1,451,588 95			
		31,673,839 74			31,673,839 74
July 1, 1873	To 1 per cent. on the principal of the public debt on June 30, 1873, $2,234,482,993.20	22,344,829 93	July 1, 1873	By balance from last year	1,451,588 95
June 30, 1874	To interest on redemption of 1860, $8,691,000	521,460 00	June 30, 1874	By amount of principal purchased, $12,936,450, estimated in gold	12,872,850 74
	To interest on redemption of 1870, $28,151,900	1,689,114 00		By accrued interest on account of purchases in 1874	222,589 28
	To interest on redemption of 1871, $20,036,250	1,790,175 00		By balance	16,365,421 96
	To interest on redemption of 1872, $32,018,450	1,957,167 00			
	To interest on redemption of 1873, $26,078,000	1,720,680 00			
	To interest on redemption of $12,936,450, amount of principal of public debt purchased during fiscal year 1874 on this account	823,082 00			
		30,682,447 93			30,682,447 93
July 1, 1874	To 1 per cent. on the principal of the public debt on June 30, 1874, $2,251,090,468.43	22,516,904 68	June 30, 1875	By amount of principal redeemed, estimated in gold	25,170,400 00
June 30, 1875	To interest on redemption of 1860, $8,691,000	521,460 00		By accrued interest on account of redemption in 1875	353,061 56
	To interest on redemption of 1870, $28,151,900	1,689,114 00		By balance	5,996,039 62
	To interest on redemption of 1871, $20,036,250	1,790,175 00			
	To interest on redemption of 1872, $42,618,450	1,957,167 00			
	To interest on redemption of 1873, $3,678,000	1,720,680 00			
	To interest on redemption of 1874, $12,936,450	776,087 00			
	To interest on redemption of $25,170,400, amount of principal of public debt "paid" during fiscal year 1875 on this account	541,973 50			
		31,519,561 18			31,519,561 18

TABLE I.—STATEMENT showing the CONDITION of the SINKING-FUND, &c.—Continued.

THE SECRETARY OF THE TREASURY IN ACCOUNT WITH SINKING-FUND.

Dr.

July 1, 1875	To 1 per cent. on the principal of the public debt on June 30, 1875, $2,232,284,531.95.........................	$22,322,845 32
June 30, 1876	To interest on redemption of 1860, $8,601,000...........	521,460 00
	To interest on redemption of 1870, $28,151,900.........	1,689,114 00
	To interest on redemption of 1871, $29,936,250.........	1,796,175 00
	To interest on redemption of 1872, $32,618,450.........	1,957,107 00
	To interest on redemption of 1873, $28,678,000.........	1,720,680 00
	To interest on redemption of 1874, $12,936,450.........	776,087 00
	To interest on redemption of 1875, $25,170,400.........	1,510,224 00
	To interest on redemption of $32,183,488.09, amount of principal of public debt "paid" during fiscal year 1876 on this account.................................	1,291,083 50
		33,584,775 82
July 1, 1876	To 1 per cent. on the principal of the public debt on June 30, 1876, $3,180,305,067.15	21,803,950 07
June 30, 1877	To interest on redemption of 1860, $8,601,000...........	521,460 00
	To interest on redemption of 1870, $26,151,900.........	1,689,114 00
	To interest on redemption of 1871, $29,936,250.........	1,796,175 00
	To interest on redemption of 1872, $32,618,450.........	1,957,107 00
	To interest on redemption of 1873, $28,678,000.........	1,720,680 00
	To interest on redemption of 1874, $12,936,450.........	776,087 00
	To interest on redemption of 1875, $25,170,400.........	1,510,224 00
	To interest on redemption of 1876, $32,183,488.09	931,000 28
	To interest on redemption of $24,498,919.95, amount of principal of public debt "paid" during fiscal year 1877 on this account.................................	24,026 25
		33,729,833 20
July 1, 1877	To 1 per cent. on the principal of the public debt on June 30, 1877, $2,205,301,392.10...........·........	22,053,013 92
June 30, 1878	To interest on redemption of 1860, $8,601,000...........	521,460 00
	To interest on redemption of 1870, $26,151,900.........	1,580,114 00
	To interest on redemption of 1871, $29,936,250.........	1,796,175 00
	To interest on redemption of 1872, $32,618,450.........	1,957,107 00
	To interest on redemption of 1873, $28,678,000	1,720,680 00
	To interest on redemption of 1874, $12,936,450.........	776,087 00
	To interest on redemption of 1875, $25,170,400.........	1,510,224 00
	To interest on redemption of 1876, $32,183,488.09.......	931,000 28

Cr.

June 30, 1876	By amount of principal redeemed, estimated in gold ...	$18,444,050 00
	By accrued interest on account of redemption in 1876 ..	257,517 01
	By amount of fractional currency redeemed............	7,062,142 09
	By amount of legal-tenders redeemed	5,999,296 00
	By amount of certificates of indebtedness redeemed....	678,000 00
	By balance...	1,143,769 82
		33,584,775 82
June 30, 1877	By amount of principal redeemed, estimated in gold ...	467,500 00
	By accrued interest on account of redemption in 1877 ..	5,776 52
	By amount of fractional currency redeemed............	14,043,458 05
	By amount of legal-tenders redeemed	10,007,982 00
	By balance...	9,225,146 63
		33,729,833 20
June 30, 1878	By amount of principal redeemed, estimated in gold ...	73,950 00
	By accrued interest on account of redemption in 1878 ..	809 02
	By amount of fractional currency redeemed............	3,835,368 57
	By amount of legal-tenders redeemed	10,083,316 00
	By balance...	18,415,557 31

July 1, 1878	To 1 per cent. on the principal of the public debt on June 30, 1878 $2,250,205,892.53	22,562,058 93	June 30, 1879	By amount of principal redeemed, estimated in gold ...	18,500 00
June 30, 1879	To interest on redemption of 1869, $8,691,000	521,460 00		By accrued interest on account of redemption in 1879 ..	308 77
	To interest on redemption of 1870, $28,151,900	1,985,114 00		By amount of fractional currency redeemed............	705,162 99
	To interest on redemption of 1871, $20,936,250	1,796,175 00		By balance....................................	36,231,632 87
	To interest on redemption of 1872, $32,618,450	1,957,107 00			
	To interest on redemption of 1873, $28,079,000	1,720,580 00			
	To interest on redemption of 1874, $12,936,450	776,087 00			
	To interest on redemption of 1875, $25,170,400	1,510,224 00			
	To interest on redemption of 1876, $32,183,488.09.......	1,931,009 28			
	To interest on redemption of 1877, $24,498,910.05.......	1,469,934 60			
	To interest on redemption of 1878, $17,012,634.57.......	1,020,758 07			
	To interest on redemption of $723,602.99, amount of principal of public debt "paid" during fiscal year 1879 on this account...............................	966 75			
		36,955,604 63			36,955,604 63
July 1, 1879	To 1 per cent. on the principal of the public debt on June 30, 1879, $2,349,567,482.04.....................	23,495,674 82	June 30, 1880	By amount of principal redeemed in 1880.............	73,652,900 00
June 30, 1880	To balance from fiscal year 1874....... $16,305,421 96			By accrued interest on account of redemption in 1880 ..	935,031 60
	To balance from fiscal year 1875....... 5,990,039 82			By amount of premium paid	2,795,320 42
	To balance from fiscal year 1876 ...... 1,143,780 82			By amount of fractional currency redeemed............	231,737 41
	To balance from fiscal year 1877....... 9,225,146 63			By balance....................................	49,817,128 78
	To balance from fiscal year 1878....... 18,415,557 31				
	To balance from fiscal year 1879....... 36,231,632 87				
		87,317,568 21			
	To interest on redemption of 1869, $8,691,000	521,460 00			
	To interest on redemption of 1870, $28,151,900	1,680,114 00			
	To interest on redemption of 1871, $20,936,250	1,796,175 00			
	To interest on redemption of 1872, $32,618,450	1,957,107 00			
	To interest on redemption of 1873, $28,678,000	1,720,680 00			
	To interest on redemption of 1874, $12,936,450	776,087 00			
	To interest on redemption of 1875, $25,170,400	1,510,224 00			
	To interest on redemption of 1876, $32,183,488.09	1,931,009 28			
	To interest on redemption of 1877, $24,498,910.05.......	1,469,934 80			
	To interest on redemption of 1878, $17,012,634.97.......	1,020,758 97			
	To interest on redemption of 1879, $723,602.99	43,419 78			
	To interest on redemption of $73,004,617.41, amount of principal of public debt "paid" during fiscal year 1880 on this account...............................	2,203,806 45			
		127,453,018 21			127,453,018 21

TABLE K.—*STATEMENT showing the PURCHASE of BONDS on account of the SINKING-FUND during each fiscal year from its institution in May, 1869, to and including June 30, 1880.*

Year ended—	Principal redeemed.	Premium paid.	Net cost in currency.	Net cost estimated in gold.	Interest due at close of fiscal year.	Accrued interest paid in coin.	Balance of interest due at close of fiscal year.
JUNE 30, 1869.							
Five-twenties of 1862	$1,021,000 00	$253,822 84	$1,874,822 84	$1,349,070 02	$16,210 00	$7,354 60	$8,825 40
Five-twenties of March, 1864	70,000 00	11,725 00	81,725 00	57,552 42	700 00	218 03	481 37
Five-twenties of June, 1864	1,051,000 00	161,946 45	1,212,946 45	873,205 61	10,510 00	1,470 42	9,039 58
Five-twenties of 1865	465,000 00	74,969 00	539,969 00	387,566 28	4,650 00	2,683 54	1,966 46
Consols, 1865	491,000 00	73,736 80	534,736 80	367,903 26	13,830 00	429 01	13,400 06
Consols, 1867	4,718,000 00	749,208 08	5,467,208 08	3,046,555 11	141,540 00	116,042 35	25,507 65
Consols, 1868	305,000 00	49,442 50	354,442 50	256,653 20	9,150 00	8,173 98	976 02
Total	8,691,000 00	1,374,850 67	10,065,850 67	7,261,437 30	196,590 00	136,392 56	60,197 44
JUNE 30, 1870.							
Five-twenties of 1862	3,542,050 00	493,479 42	4,035,529 42	3,263,099 51	100,919 50	45,994 49	114,925 01
Five-twenties of March, 1864	85,000 00	15,742 87	100,742 87	75,638 54	5,350 00	1,060 99	4,269 01
Five-twenties of June, 1864	3,971,400 00	506,189 91	4,477,589 91	3,647,628 29	165,834 00	49,946 00	115,888 00
Five-twenties of 1865	2,790,250 00	361,735 43	3,151,985 43	2,606,636 20	105,257 50	37,113 53	68,143 97
Consols, 1865	11,532,150 00	1,454,778 37	12,986,928 37	10,681,736 97	495,421 50	145,518 29	349,903 21
Consols, 1867	5,682,550 00	861,763 73	6,744,313 73	5,300,810 90	302,784 50	66,111 51	236,672 09
Consols, 1868	348,500 00	53,363 95	401,863 95	308,573 16	19,380 00	5,238 73	14,141 27
Total	28,151,900 00	3,747,053 68	31,898,953 68	25,893,143 57	1,254,897 00	351,903 54	903,893 46
JUNE 30, 1871.							
Five-twenties of 1862	2,792,850 00	227,607 56	3,020,557 56	2,680,269 05	145,975 00	36,657 80	109,317 20
Five-twenties of March, 1864	29,500 00	2,277 20	31,777 20	28,590 88	1,240 00	388 35	851 65
Five-twenties of June, 1864	3,967,350 00	340,529 63	4,307,879 63	3,847,182 42	201,375 00	51,703 46	149,671 54
Five-twenties of 1865	6,768,000 00	574,923 00	7,343,523 00	6,525,291 42	331,933 50	92,259 58	239,673 92
Consols, 1865	10,223,200 00	850,949 79	11,073,149 79	9,762,387 78	522,117 00	109,455 28	412,661 72
Consols, 1867	6,103,050 00	541,559 41	6,644,609 41	5,806,018 37	351,528 00	76,745 93	274,782 07
Consols, 1868	52,600 00	4,784 61	57,384 61	49,707 81	3,096 00	572 13	2,523 87

JUNE 30, 1872.

Five-twenties of 1862	6,417,850 00	764,055 21	7,181,905 21	6,345,391 98	427,849 00	75,179 43	352,660 57
Five-twenties of March, 1864	127,100 00	14,359 03	142,059 03	126,123 46	8,834 00	1,336 70	7,555 36
Five-twenties of June, 1864	3,604,650 00	438,656 16	4,043,306 16	3,573,223 63	246,001 50	57,449 80	188,551 70
Five-twenties of 1865	3,635,200 00	438,838 70	4,074,038 70	3,504,747 85	246,502 00	37,817 37	208,744 63
Consols, 1865	11,788,900 00	1,436,989 46	13,225,889 46	11,666,785 89	707,334 00	149,248 21	558,085 79
Consols, 1867	6,958,900 00	832,600 15	7,782,500 15	6,863,777 39	417,534 00	108,487 92	309,046 08
Consols, 1868	85,850 00	9,951 63	95,801 63	84,595 02	5,151 00	1,386 95	3,764 05
Total	**32,618,450 00**	**3,935,050 34**	**36,553,500 34**	**32,248,645 22**	**2,059,325 50**	**430,908 38**	**1,628,417 12**

JUNE 30, 1873.

Five-twenties of 1862	7,137,100 00	925,783 87	8,062,883 87	7,089,542 58	431,450 50	101,960 57	329,489 93
Five-twenties of March, 1864	59,900 00	7,372 50	67,372 50	49,786 91	3,500 00	813 70	2,686 30
Five-twenties of June, 1864	3,741,150 00	480,684 37	4,221,834 37	3,715,211 22	223,270 50	42,216 46	181,054 04
Five-twenties of 1865	1,959,850 00	250,635 93	2,210,485 93	1,943,488 03	120,260 50	23,744 47	96,522 03
Consols, 1865	10,768,250 00	1,371,187 17	12,139,437 17	10,668,617 09	646,095 00	145,069 34	501,025 66
Consols, 1867	4,462,100 00	553,610 89	4,955,710 89	4,373,781 76	294,126 00	69,632 51	194,493 49
Consols, 1868	619,550 00	81,983 44	701,533 44	617,146 34	37,173 00	8,948 40	28,224 60
Total	**28,078,000 00**	**3,671,258 17**	**32,349,258 17**	**28,457,562 53**	**1,725,881 50**	**392,385 45**	**1,333,496 05**

JUNE 30, 1874.

Five-twenties of 1862	1,421,700 00	161,219 79	1,582,919 79	1,415,301 05	99,519 00	31,743 95	67,775 05
Five-twenties of June, 1864	2,026,550 00	218,457 39	2,230,007 39	2,012,651 32	141,438 50	48,013 40	93,425 04
Five-twenties of 1865	1,247,250 00	135,577 95	1,382,827 95	1,241,571 09	87,307 50	29,348 19	57,959 31
Consols, 1865	3,303,650 00	390,964 62	3,754,614 62	3,374,934 42	203,619 00	46,489 33	157,129 67
Consols, 1867	4,051,000 00	432,348 18	4,483,348 18	4,029,975 86	243,060 00	55,976 97	187,083 03
Consols, 1868	862,300 00	86,505 62	688,805 62	798,926 40	48,138 00	11,014 38	37,123 62
Total	**12,906,450 00**	**1,395,073 55**	**14,331,523 55**	**12,872,850 74**	**823,082 00**	**222,586 26**	**600,495 72**

JUNE 30, 1875.

Five-twenties of 1862	25,170,400 00			25,170,400 00	541,973 50	353,061 56	188,911 94

JUNE 30, 1876.

Five-twenties of 1862	5,785,200 00			5,785,200 00	404,964 00	54,745 72	350,218 28
Five-twenties of June, 1864	10,860,600 00			10,860,600 00	760,872 00	171,966 33	588,905 67
Five-twenties of 1865	1,789,250 00			1,789,250 00	125,247 50	30,805 86	94,441 64
Total	**18,444,050 00**			**18,444,050 00**	**1,291,083 50**	**257,517 91**	**1,033,565 59**

TABLE K.—STATEMENT showing the PURCHASE of BONDS on account of the SINKING-FUND, &c.—Continued.

Year ended—	Principal redeemed.	Premium paid.	Net cost in currency.	Net cost estimated in gold.	Interest due at close of fiscal year.	Accrued interest paid in coin.	Balance of interest due at close of fiscal year.
JUNE 30, 1877.							
Five-twenties of 1862	$81,200 00			$81,200 00	$4,352 25	$1,161 07	$3,170 58
Five-twenties of June,1864	178,900 00			178,900 00	9,045 50	1,329 60	8,610 00
Five-twenties of 1865	180,350 00			180,350 00	9,510 00	3,141 08	6,377 92
Consols, 1865	6,050 00			6,050 00	181 50	108 97	72 53
Consols, 1867	1,000 00			1,000 00	30 00	21 20	!' 00
Total	447,500 00			447,500 00	24,026 25	5,776 52	18,249 73
JUNE 30, 1878.							
Five-twenties of 1862	17,900 00			17,900 00	996 00	102 65	773 35
Five-twenties of June,1864	15,900 00			15,900 00	834 00	78 41	755 59
Five-twenties of 1865	2,350 00			2,350 00	129 00	40 92	88 08
Consols, 1865	23,600 00			25,600 00	1,416 00	273 35	1,142 65
Consols, 1867	5,700 00			5,700 00	342 00	134 76	207 24
Consols, 1868	8,500 00			8,500 00	510 00	89 83	420 17
Total	73,950 00			73,950 00	4,197 00	809 92	3,387 08
JUNE 30, 1879.							
Five-twenties of 1862	2,650 00			2,650 00	165 75	40 35	125 40
Five-twenties of June,1864	3,150 00			3,150 00	94 50	18 53	75 97
Five-twenties of 1865	1,850 00			1,850 00	83 50	41 22	44 28
Consols, 1865	1,700 00			1,700 00	102 00	41 49	60 51
Consols, 1867	9,050 00			9,050 00	543 00	106 02	370 38
Consols, 1868	100 00			100 00	6 00	56 00	5 44
Total	18,500 00			18,500 00	996 75	308 77	687 98
JUNE 30, 1880.							
Five-twenties of 1862	100 00			100 00	4 00	67	3 33
Five-twenties of June,1864	100 00			100 00	4 00	49	3 51
Five-twenties of 1865	250 00			250 00	14 50	5 85	8 65
Ten-forties of 1864	676,050 00			676,050 00	28,168 75	12,872 65	15,296 10
Loan of February, 1861	2,637,000 00	$74,161 95		2,911,161 95	85,110 00	47,540 20	37,569 80
Loan of July and August, 1861	32,064,250 00	1,376,085 04		33,440,335 04	1,165,807 50	518,148 79	647,658 71
Loan of March, 1863	12,797,150 00	548,035 18		13,346,185 18	484,747 50	213,179 29	271,568 21
Oregon war debt	202,550 00	8,273 02		210,823 02	9,787 50	3,662 56	6,124 94
Funded loan of 1881	23,575,450 00	662,206 97		24,237,656 97	415,162.70	130,349 36	284,813 34

TABLE L.—*STATEMENT SHOWING the PURCHASES of BONDS on ACCOUNT of the SINKING FUND, from November, 1879, to October 31, 1880.*

Date of purchase.	Title of loan.	Authorizing act.	Rate.	When redeemable.	When payable.	Interest payable.	Amount purchased.	Net premium paid.	Accrued interest paid.	Total.
1879.			*Pr. ct.*							
Nov. 8	Oregon war debt	March 2, 1861	6	....	July 1, 1881	Jan. and July	$121, 200 00	$4, 642 13	$2, 629 87	$128, 472 00
8	Loan of July and Aug., 1861.	July 17 and Aug. 5, 1861	6	June 30, 4881	....	...do	6, 715, 800 00	257, 158 74	145, 789 26	7, 118, 748 00
8	Loan of 1863 (1881s)	March 3, 1863	6	.... do	....	...do	3, 213, 000 00	123, 062 25	69, 717 75	3, 405, 780 00
Dec. 6	Oregon war debt	March 2, 1861	6	....	July 1, 1881	...do	2, 500 00	93 00	65 75	2, 658 75
6	Loan of July and Aug., 1861.	July 17 and Aug. 5, 1861	6	June 30, 1881	....	...do	80, 300 00	2, 983 32	2, 109 38	85, 292 70
6	Loan of 1863 (1881s)	March 3, 1863	6	.... do	....	...do	148, 100 00	5, 509, 12	3, 805 23	157, 504 35
1880.										
Jan. 7	Oregon war debt	March 2, 1861	6	....	July 1, 1881	...do	7, 000 00	289 05	8 05	7, 296 10
7	Loan of July and Aug., 1861.	July 17 and Aug. 5, 1861.	6	June 30, 1881	....	...do	2, 007, 600 00	82, 555 24	2, 310 10	2, 092, 465 34
7	Loan of 1863 (1881s)	March 3, 1863	6	.... do	....	...do	1, 040, 400 00	42, 791 39	1, 197 17	1, 084. 388 56
7	Funded loan of 1881	July 14, 1870, and Jan. 20, 1871.	5	May 1, 1881	....	Feb., May, Aug., and Nov.	1, 945, 000 00	47, 906 09	17, 851 41	2, 010, 157 50
Feb. 11	Loan of Feb., 1861....	Feb. 8, 1861	6	....	Dec. 31, 1880	Jan. and July	186, 000 00	5, 651 02	1, 253 58	192, 904 60
11	Oregon war debt	March 2, 1861	6	....	July 1, 1881	...do	27. 000 00	1, 241 33	181 97	28, 423 30
11	Loan of July and Aug., 1861.	July 17 and Aug. 5, 1861.	6	June 30, 1881	....	...do	4, 675, 800 00	217, 616 52	31, 513 60	4, 924, 923 12
11	Loan of 1863 (1881s)	March 3, 1863	6	.... do	....	...do	1, 508, 750 00	70, 899 74	10, 106 58	1, 589, 818 32
11	Funded loan of 1881	July 14, 1870, and Jan. 20, 1871.	5	May 1, 1881	....	Feb., May, Aug., and Nov.	5, 076, 450 00	160, 872 38	6, 954 18	5, 244, 276 56
18	Loan of Feb., 1861....	Feb. 8, 1861	6	....	Dec. 31, 1880	Jan. and July	57, 000 00	1, 810 75	449 75	59, 260 50
18	Oregon war debt	March 2, 1861	6	....	July 1, 1881	...do	7, 000 00	338 52	55 23	7, 393 75
18	Loan of July and Aug., 1861.	July 17 and Aug. 5, 1861.	6	June 30, 1881	....	...do	390, 050 00	19, 323 46	3, 155 76	422, 429 22
18	Loan of 1863 (1881s)	March 3, 1863	6	.... do	....	...do	125, 050 00	6, 056 02	986 71	132, 092 73
18	Funded loan of 1881	July 14, 1870, and Jan. 20, 1871.	5	May 1, 1881	....	Feb., May, Aug., and Nov.	411, 000 00	14, 007 80	957 13	425, 964 93
25	Loan of Feb., 1861....	Feb. 8, 1861	6	....	Dec. 31, 1880	Jan. and July	154, 000 00	4, 050 28	1, 302 32	160, 651 50
25	Oregon war debt	March 2, 1861	6	....	July 1, 1881	...do	2, 500 00	121 46	23 05	2, 604 51
25	Loan of July and Aug., 1861.	July 17 and Aug. 5, 1861.	6	June 30, 1881	....	...do	1, 518, 600 00	72, 592 01	13, 729 78	1, 604, 921 79
25	Loan of 1863 (1881s)	March 3, 1863	6	.... do	....	...do	325, 150 00	15, 497 14	2, 939 70	343, 586 84
Mar. 3	Oregon war debt	March 2, 1861	6	....	Dec. 31, 1880	...do	14, 000 00	417 32	142 68	14, 500 00
3	Loan of July and Aug., 1861.	July 17 and Aug. 5, 1861.	6	June 30, 1881	....	...do	6, 500 00	315 62	66 25	6, 881 87
3	Loan of 1863 (1881s)	March 3, 1863	6	.... do	....	...do	1, 536, 450 00	74, 273 61	15, 679 56	1, 626, 403 17
3	Loan of 1863 (1881s)	March 3, 1863	6	.... do	....	...do	957, 050 00	46, 227 02	9, 754 06	1, 013, 031 08
10	Loan of Feb., 1861....	Feb. 8, 1861	6	....	Dec. 31, 1880	...do	718, 000 00	20, 509 10	8, 143 90	746, 653 00
10	Funded loan of 1881	July 14, 1870, and Jan. 20, 1871.	5	May 1, 1881	....	Feb., May, Aug., and Nov.	1, 282, 000 00	37, 274 37	6, 673 43	1, 325, 947 80

TABLE L.—*STATEMENT SHOWING the PURCHASES of BONDS on ACCOUNT of the SINKING FUND, &c.*—Continued.

Date of purchase.	Title of loan.	Authorizing act.	Rate.	When redeemable.	When payable.	Interest payable.	Amount purchased.	Net premium paid.	Accrued interest paid.	Total.
1880.			Pr. ct.							
Mar. 17	Oregon war debt.......	March 2, 1861..........	6	....	July 1, 1881	Jan. and July.........	$6,000 00	$247 54	$74 96	$6,322 50
17	Loan of July and Aug., 1861.	July 17 and Aug. 5, 1861.	6	June 30, 1881	....	......do	925,450 00	38,765 55	11,561 80	975,777 35
17	Loan of 1863 (1881s)	March 3, 1863..........	6	....do	....	......do	305,550 00	12,729 67	3,817 28	322,106 95
17	Funded loan of 1881....	July 14, 1870, and Jan. 20, 1871.	5	May 1, 1881	....	Feb., May, Aug., and Nov.	763,000 00	10,278 97	4,703 43	780,982 40
24	Loan of Feb., 1861......	Feb. 8, 1861...........	6	....	Dec. 31, 1880	Jan. and July.........	86,000 00	2,050 24	1,173 36	89,223 60
24	Oregon war debt.......	March 3, 1861..........	6	....	July 1, 1881	......do	500 00	19 98	6 82	526 80
24	Loan of July and Aug., 1861.	July 17 and Aug. 5, 1861.	6	June 30, 1881	....	......do	1,355,490 00	53,599 39	18,462 84	1,427,402 23
24	Loan of 1863 (1881s)	March 3, 1863..........	6	....do	....	......do	357,300 00	14,170 02	4,874 01	376,344 03
24	Funded loan of 1881....	July 14, 1870, and Jan. 20, 1871.	5	May 1, 1881	....	Feb., May, Aug., and Nov.	200,800 00	4,781 04	1,430 36	207,012 30
31	Loan of Feb., 1861......	Feb. 8, 1861...........	6	....	Dec. 31, 1880	Jan. and July.........	30,000 00	722 60	443 83	31,166 43
31	Loan of July and Aug., 1861.	July 17 and Aug. 5, 1861.	6	June 30, 1881	....	......do	1,497,150 00	61,143 34	22,140 61	1,580,442 05
31	Loan of 1863 (1881s)	March 3, 1863..........	6	....do	....	......do	377,350 00	15,427 96	5,582 72	398,360 67
31	Funded loan of 1881....	July 14, 1870, and Jan. 20, 1871.	5	May 1, 1881	....	Feb., May, Aug., and Nov.	3,005,500 00	77,502 20	25,018 44	3,108,029 70
Apr. 7	Loan of Feb., 1861......	Feb. 8, 1861...........	6	....	Dec. 31, 1880	Jan. and July.........	20,000 00	495 99	318 01	20,814 00
7	Oregon war debt.......	March 2, 1861..........	6	....	July 1, 1881	......do	5,000 00	213 27	79 73	5,293 00
7	Loan of July and Aug., 1861.	July 17 and Aug. 5, 1861.	6	June 30, 1881	....	......do	551,150 00	23,675 25	8,788 19	583,613 44
7	Loan of 1863 (1881s)	March 3, 1863..........	6	....do	....	......do	212,550 00	9,192 28	3,389 14	225,131 42
7	Funded loan of 1881....	July 14, 1870, and Jan. 20, 1871.	5	May 1, 1881	....	Feb., May, Aug., and Nov.	711,300 00	19,748 67	6,430 92	737,479 59
14	Loan of Feb., 1861......	Feb. 8, 1861...........	6	....	Dec. 31, 1880	Jan. and July.........	220,000 00	5,430 91	3,761 09	229,192 00
14	Oregon war debt.......	March 2, 1861..........	6	....	July 1, 1881	......do	5,800 00	243 70	99 16	6,142 86
14	Loan of July and Aug., 1861.	July 17 and Aug. 5, 1861.	6	June 30, 1881	....	......do	975,700 00	40,589 60	15,646 27	1,031,335 87
14	Loan of 1863 (1881s)	March 3, 1863..........	6	....do	....	......do	305,500 00	12,050 45	5,137 32	318,287 77
21	Loan of Feb., 1861......	Feb. 8, 1861...........	6	....	Dec. 31, 1880	......do	217,000 00	5,293 78	3,960 52	226,163 30
21	Loan of July and Aug., 1861.	July 17 and Aug. 5, 1861.	6	June 30, 1881	....	......do	699,900 00	28,054 06	12,661 30	735,515 36
21	Loan of 1863 (1881s)	March 3, 1863..........	6	....do	....	......do	23,100 00	958 24	421 49	24,479 73
21	Funded loan of 1881....	July 14, 1870, and Jan. 20, 1871.	5	May 1, 1881	....	Feb., May, Aug., and Nov.	2,066,000 00	53,077 90	22,641 10	2,141,019 00

Date	Loan	Act authorizing	Rate	Redeemable	Matured	Interest payable	Principal	Interest	Premium	Total
May 5	Loan of Feb., 1861	Feb. 8, 1861	6		Dec. 31, 1880	Jan. and July	20,000 00	507 04	410 96	20,918 00
5	Oregon war debt	March 2, 1861	6		July 1, 1881	...do	600 00	26 60	12 32	638 92
5	Loan of July and Aug., 1861	July 17 and Aug. 5, 1861	6	June 30, 1881		...do	1,318,600 00	58,781 45	27,094 46	1,404,475 91
5	Loan of 1863 (1881s)	March 3, 1863	6	...do		...do	710,800 00	32,604 45	14,605 45	757,439 90
5	Funded loan of 1881	July 14, 1870, and Jan. 20, 1871	5	May 1, 1881		Feb., May, Aug., and Nov.	950,000 00	26,787 98	520 52	977,308 50
13	Loan of Feb., 1861	Feb. 8, 1861	6		Dec. 31, 1880	Jan. and July	327,000 00	8,209 02	7,095 45	342,304 47
12	Loan of July and Aug., 1861	July 17 and Aug. 5, 1861	6	June 30, 1881		Jan. and July	1,126,150 00	49,770 31	24,435 87	1,200,356 18
12	Loan of 1863 (1881s)	March 3, 1863	6	...do		...do	244,850 00	10,633 83	5,312 89	260,998 72
12	Funded loan of 1881	July 14, 1870, and Jan. 20, 1871	5	May 1, 1881		Feb., May, Aug., and Nov.	1,302,000 00	36,577 63	1,901 87	1,340,539 50
19	Loan of Feb., 1861	Feb. 8, 1861	6		Dec. 31, 1880	Jan. and July	60,000 00	1,514 04	1,370 96	62,885 00
19	Oregon war debt	March 2, 1861	6		July 1, 1881	...do	6,300 00	280 63	148 95	6,733 57
19	Loan of July and Aug., 1861	July 17 and Aug. 5, 1861	6	June 30, 1881		...do	1,314,650 00	60,088 48	30,036 56	1,404,075 04
19	Loan of 1863 (1881s)	March 3, 1863	6	...do		...do	970,150 00	45,102 87	22,372 89	1,046,025 76
19	Funded loan of 1881	July 14, 1870, and Jan. 20, 1871	5	May 1, 1881		Feb., May, Aug., and Nov.	640,000 00	18,857 66	1,578 09	660,435 75
20	Loan of July and Aug., 1861	July 17 and Aug. 5, 1861	6	June 30, 1881		Jan. and July	622,800 00	28,957 80	14,947 20	666,704 80
26	Loan of 1863 (1881s)	March 3, 1863	6	...do		...do	327,200 00	15,213 40	7,853 80	350,295 20
26	Funded loan of 1881	July 14, 1870, and Jan. 20, 1871	5	May 1, 1881		Feb., May, Aug., and Nov.	2,050,000 00	61,241 88	7,020 02	2,118,262 50
June 2	Loan of July and Aug., 1861	July 17 and Aug. 5, 1861	6	June 30, 1881		Jan. and July	1,100,550 00	48,069 82	27,905 94	1,185,525 76
2	Loan of 1863 (1881s)	March 3, 1863	6	...do		...do	373,150 00	16,162 03	9,384 06	398,696 09
2	Funded loan of 1881	July 14, 1870, and Jan. 20, 1871	5	May 1, 1881		Feb., May, Aug., and Nov.	17,300 00	407 02	73 84	17,843 76
2	Consols of 1907	...do	4	July 1, 1907		Jan., April, July, and Oct.	1,500,000 00	125,558 26	10,191 74	1,635,750 00
9	Loan of Feb., 1861	Feb. 8, 1861	6		Dec. 31, 1880	Jan. and July	244,900 00	5,513 26	6,417 54	255,930 80
9	Oregon war debt	March 2, 1861	6		July 1, 1881	...do	700 00	30 03	18 41	748 44
9	Loan of July and Aug., 1861	July 17 and Aug. 5, 1861	6	June 30, 1881		...do	1,352,250 00	57,750 89	35,505 06	1,445,506 95
9	Loan of 1863 (1881s)	March 3, 1863	6	...do		...do	403,650 00	17,279 65	10,600 76	430,930 41
16	Loan of Feb., 1861	Feb. 8, 1861	6		Dec. 31, 1880	...do	108,000 00	2,304 29	2,904 81	113,209 10
16	Loan of July and Aug., 1861	July 17 and Aug. 5, 1861	6	June 30, 1881		...do	580,250 00	24,222 07	15,929 07	620,401 14
16	Loan of 1863 (1881s)	March 3, 1863	6	...do		...do	194,750 00	8,133 07	5,346 29	208,229 36
16	Funded loan of 1881	July 14, 1870, and Jan. 20, 1871	5	May 1, 1881		Feb., May, Aug., and Nov.	1,117,000 00	29,065 86	7,038 64	1,153,104 50
23	Loan of Feb., 1861	Feb. 8, 1861	6		Dec. 31, 1880	Jan. and July	103,000 00	2,226 00	2,946 07	108,172 10
23	Oregon war debt	March 2, 1861	6		July 1, 1881	...do	3,900 00	162 17	111 54	4,173 71
23	Loan of July and Aug., 1861	July 17 and Aug. 5, 1861	6	June 30, 1881		...do	688,550 00	29,091 63	19,604 41	737,336 04
23	Loan of 1863 (1881s)	March 3, 1863	6	...do		...do	405,650 00	17,147 82	11,583 59	433,763 95
23	Funded loan of 1881	July 14, 1870, and Jan. 20, 1871	5	May 1, 1881		Feb., May, Aug., and Nov.	799,500 00	21,793 46	5,804 58	827,098 04
30	Loan of Feb., 1861	Feb. 8, 1861	6		Dec. 31, 1880	Jan. and July	21,000 00	447 38	624 82	22,072 20
30	Oregon war debt	March 2, 1861	6		July 1, 1881	...do	600 00	25 65	17 85	643 50

TABLE L.—*STATEMENT SHOWING the PURCHASES of BONDS on ACCOUNT of the SINKING FUND, &c.*—Continued.

Date of purchase.	Title of loan.	Authorizing act.	Rate.	When redeemable.	When payable.	Interest payable.	Amount purchased.	Net premium paid.	Accrued interest paid.	Total.
1880. June 30	Loan of July and Aug., 1861.	July 17 and Aug. 5, 1861	Pr. ct. 6	June 30, 1881	....	Jan. and July..........	$146,700 00	$6,290 09	$4,364 81	$157,354 90
30	Loan of 1863 (1881s)...	March 3, 1853..........	6	....do	....	....do	96,350 00	4,664 31	2,866 74	103,311 05
30	Funded loan of 1681....	July 14, 1870, and Jan. 20, 1871.	5	May 1, 1881	....	Feb., May, Aug., and Nov.	735,350 00	21,047 73	6,043 96	762,441 69
July 28	Loan of Feb., 1861....	Feb. 8, 1861	6	....	Dec. 31, 1880	Jan. and July.........	433,000 00	7,756 55	1,017 35	441,673 90
28	Oregon war debt	March 2, 1861..........	6	....	July 1, 1881	......do	6,250 00	244 81	27 74	6,522 55
28	Loan of July and Aug., 1861.	July 17 and Aug. 5, 1861	6	June 30, 1881	....	......do	658,500 00	25,986 33	2,922 64	687,408 97
28	Loan of 1863 (1881s)...	March 3, 1863..........	6	....do	....	......do	308,250 00	12,205 85	1,368 12	321,824 97
28	Funded loan of 1681....	July 14, 1870, and Jan. 20, 1871.	5	May 1, 1881	....	Feb., May, Aug., and Nov.	595,000 00	14,801 65	7,172 60	616,974 25
Aug. 4	Loan of Feb., 1861......	Feb. 8, 1861	6	....	Dec. 31, 1880	Jan. and July.........	96,000 00	1,729 05	536 55	96,265 60
4	Loan of July and Aug., 1861.	July 17 and Aug. 5, 1861	6	June 30, 1881	....	......do	1,811,800 00	73,183 48	10,126 16	1,895,109 64
4	Loan of 1803 (1881s)...	March 3, 1863..........	6	....do	....	......do	592,200 00	23,910 51	3,306 80	619,426 31
11	Loan of Feb., 1861....	Feb. 8, 1861..........	6	....	Dec. 31, 1880	......do	113,090 00	1,068 41	761 59	115,750 00
11	Oregon war debt	March 2, 1861..........	6	....	July 1, 1881	......do	10,000 00	400 60	67 40	10,468 00
11	Loan of July and Aug., 1861.	July 17 and Aug. 5, 1861	6	June 30, 1881	....	......do	720,700 00	29,171 12	4,857 34	754,728 46
11	Loan of 1863 (1881s)...	March 3, 1863..........	6	....do	....	......do	576,300 00	23,314 18	3,884 10	603,498 28
11	Funded loan of 1881....	July 14, 1870, and Jan. 20, 1871.	5	May 1, 1881	....	Feb., May, Aug., and Nov.	1,080,000 00	27,543 02	1,479 48	1,109,022 50
18	Loan of Feb., 1861......	Feb. 8, 1861 ;	6	....	Dec. 31, 1880	Jan. and July.........	50,000 00	979 97	465 53	66,445 50
18	Oregon war debt	March 2, 1861..........	6	....	July 1, 1881	......do	650 00	20 07	5 12	681 19
18	Loan of July and Aug., 1861.	July 17 and Aug. 5, 1861	6	June 30, 1881	....	......do	330,500 00	13,236 17	2,607 79	346,343 96
18	Loan of 1863 (1881s)...	March 3, 1863..........	6	....do	....	......do	65,750 00	2,029 17	518 78	68,897 95
18	Funded loan of 1881....	July 14, 1870, and Jan. 20, 1871.	5	May 1, 1881	....	Feb., May, Aug., and Nov.	2,044,100 00	51,182 51	4,700 28	2,100,042 79
25	Loan of Feb., 1861.....	Feb. 8, 1861..........	6	....	Dec. 31, 1880	Jan. and July.........	34,000 00	533 37	307 38	34,840 95
25	Oregon war debt	March 2, 1861..........	6	....	July 1, 1881	......do	1,000 00	38 96	9 04	1,048 00
25	Loan of July and Aug., 1861.	July 17 and Aug. 5, 1861	6	June 30, 1881	....	......do	1,769,100 00	69,005 67	16,175 44	1,874,071 11
25	Loan of 1863 (1881s)....	March 3, 1863..........	6	....do	....	......do	492,000 00	19,150 38	4,448 22	515,507 60

	Loan	Act	Rate	Date	Date	Interest periods				
1	Funded loan of 1881...	July 14, 1870, and Jan. 20, 1871.	5	May 1, 1881	....	Feb., May, Aug., and Nov.	801,000 00	26,980 69	3,783 71	915,769 80
8	Oregon war debt......	March 2, 1861......	6	....	July 1, 1881	Jan. and July......	10,000 00	355 58	113 42	10,469 00
8	Loan of July and Aug., 1861.	July 17 and Aug. 5, 1861	6	June 30, 1881	....	...do......	965,900 00	35,095 97	11,182 56	1,032,178 53
8	Loan of 1863 (1881s)...	March 3, 1863......	6	...do......	....	...do......	827,600 00	29,482 78	9,387 04	806,460 82
8	Funded loan of 1881...	July 14, 1870, and Jan. 20, 1871.	5	May 1, 1881	....	Feb., May, Aug., and Nov.	676,500 00	14,832 34	3,521 51	694,853 85
15	Loan of Feb., 1861......	Feb. 8, 1861......	6	....	Dec. 31, 1880	Jan. and July......	103,000 00	2,343 43	2,411 17	197,054 60
15	Oregon war debt......	March 2, 1661......	6	....	July 1, 1881	...do......	1,500 00	50 11	18 74	1,568 85
15	Loan of July and Aug., 1861.	July 17 and Aug. 5, 1861	6	June 30, 1881	....	...do......	435,950 00	14,281 10	5,446 39	455,677 49
15	Loan of 1863 (1881s)...	March 3, 1863......	6	...do......	....	...do......	194,050 00	6,373 24	2,424 29	202,847 53
15	Funded loan of 1881...	July 14, 1870, and Jan. 20, 1871.	5	May 1, 1881	....	Feb., May, Aug., and Nov.	1,675,500 00	33,508 05	10,328 44	1,719,337 39
22	Loan of Feb., 1861......	Feb. 8, 1861......	6	....	Dec. 31, 1880	Jan. and July......	48,000 00	564 00	654 90	49,210 80
22	Funded loan of 1881...	July 14, 1870, and Jan. 20, 1871.	5	May 1, 1881	....	Feb., May, Aug., and Nov.	2,452,000 00	49,103 07	17,466 33	2,518,569 40
29	Loan of Feb., 1861......	Feb. 8, 1861......	6	....	Dec. 31, 1880	Jan. and July......	2,000 00	19 61	20 50	2,040 40
29	Loan of July and Aug., 1861.	July 17 and Aug. 5, 1861	6	June 30, 1881	....	...do......	1,692,500 00	51,590 63	25,039 70	1,769,130 53
29	Loan of 1863 (1881s)...	March 3, 1863......	6	....	...do......	...do......	264,700 00	8,172 26	3,016 10	276,768 36
29	Funded loan of 1881...	July 14, 1870, and Jan. 20, 1871.	5	May 1, 1881	....	Feb., May, Aug., and Nov.	540,800 00	9,753 19	4,370 84	554,924 03
Oct. 6	Loan of Feb., 1861......	Feb. 8, 1861......	6	....	Dec. 31, 1880	Jan. and July......	140,000 00	1,255 68	2,232 32	143,488 20
6	Oregon war debt......	March 2, 1861......	6	....	July 1, 1881	...do......	650 00	18 89	10 36	679 25
6	Loan of July and Aug., 1861.	July 17 and Aug. 5, 1861	6	June 30, 1881	....	...do......	648,800 00	18,911 51	10,345 23	678,056 74
6	Loan of 1863 (1881s)...	March 3, 1863......	6	...do......	....	...do......	218,200 00	6,386 62	3,479 22	228,065 84
6	Funded loan of 1881...	July 14, 1870, and Jan. 20, 1871.	5	May 1, 1881	....	Feb., May, Aug., and Nov.	1,402,350 00	25,331 34	13,492 49	1,331,173 83
13	Loan of Feb., 1861......	Feb. 8, 1861......	6	....	Dec. 31, 1880	Jan. and July......	21,000 00	170 68	350 02	21,538 70
13	Loan of July and Aug., 1861.	July 17 and Aug. 5, 1861	6	June 30, 1881	....	...do......	418,050 00	11,874 34	7,146 04	437,071 28
13	Loan of 1863 (1881s)...	March 3, 1863......	6	...do......	....	...do......	81,050 00	2,327 71	1,401 01	85,678 72
13	Funded loan of 1881...	July 14, 1870, and Jan. 20, 1871.	5	May 1, 1881	....	Feb., May, Aug., and Nov.	1,979,000 00	32,104 30	19,790 00	2,030,894 30
20	Loan of Feb., 1861......	Feb. 8, 1861......	6	....	Dec. 31, 1880	Jan. and July......	29,000 00	229 45	529 15	29,758 60
20	Loan of July and Aug., 1861.	July 17 and Aug. 5, 1861	6	June 30, 1881	....	...do......	1,123,500 00	34,081 56	20,500 03	1,178,081 59
20	Loan of 1863 (1881s)...	March 3, 1863......	6	...do......	....	...do......	479,150 00	14,596 23	8,742 84	502,489 07
20	Funded loan of 1881...	July 14, 1870, and Jan. 20, 1871.	5	May 1, 1881	....	Feb., May, Aug., and Nov.	808,350 00	15,483 20	9,516 18	803,349 38
27	Loan of Feb., 1861......	Feb. 8, 1861......	6	....	Dec. 31, 1880	Jan. and July......	466,000 00	3,680 44	9,077 92	480,767 36
27	Oregon war debt......	March 2, 1861......	6	....	July 1, 1881	...do......	1,250 00	36 48	24 25	1,312 73
27	Loan of July and Aug., 1861.	July 17 and Aug. 5, 1861	6	June 30, 1881	....	...do......	1,446,600 00	43,823 63	28,060 12	1,518,483 75
27	Loan of 1863 (1881s)...	March 3, 1863......	6	...do......	....	...do......	571,150 00	17,495 86	11,078 73	599,724 61
	Total						108,758,100 00	3,786,520 01	1,275,046 00	113,820,566 04

TABLE L.—*STATEMENT SHOWING the PURCHASES of BONDS on ACCOUNT of the SINKING FUND, &c.*—Continued.

RECAPITULATION.

Title of loan.	Authorizing act.	Rate.	When redeemable.	When payable.	Interest payable.	Amount purchased.	Net premium paid.	Accrued interest paid.	Total.
		Pr. ct.							
Loan of Feb., 1861	Feb. 8, 1861	6	....	Dec. 31, 1880	Jan. and July	$5,460,000 00	$110,319 19	$77,394 67	$5,056,713 86
Oregon war debt	March 2, 1861	6	....	July 1, 1881	......do	234,450 00	9,472 17	3,870 98	247,793 15
Loan of July and Aug., 1861	July 17 and Aug. 5, 1861	6	June 30, 1881	....	......do	44,981,450 00	1,830,865 72	677,750 70	47,490,064 42
Loan of 1863 (1881s)	March 3, 1863	6	.....do	....	......do	17,783,900 00	727,897 88	274,058 16	18,785,856 04
Funded loan of 1881	July 14, 1870, and Jan. 20, 1871.	5	May 1, 1881	....	Feb., May, Aug., and Nov.	38,789,300 00	982,378 79	232,679 78	40,004,358 57
Consols of 1907	......do	4	July 1, 1907	....	Jan., April, July, and Oct.	1,500,000 00	125,558 26	10,191 74	1,635,750 00
Total			....	....		108,753,100 00	3,786,520 01	1,275,946 03	113,820,566 04

NOTE.—The purchase of October 27, 1880 ($2,487,000) was not redeemed until the following month.

TABLE M.—*STATEMENT of the OUTSTANDING PRINCIPAL of the PUBLIC DEBT of the UNITED STATES, June 30, 1880.*

	Length of loan.	When redeemable.	Rates of interest.	Price at which sold.	Amount authorized.	Amount issued.	Amount outstanding.
OLD DEBT.							
Unclaimed dividends upon debt created prior to 1800, and the principal and interest of the outstanding debt created during the war of 1812, and up to 1837. (For detailed information in regard to earlier loans see Finance Report for 1876.)		On demand....	5 and 6 per cent.				$57,665 00
TREASURY NOTES PRIOR TO 1846.							
The acts of October 12, 1837 (5 Statutes, 201); May 21, 1838 (5 Statutes, 228); March 31, 1840 (5 Statutes, 370); February 15, 1841 (5 Statutes, 411); January 31, 1842 (5 Statutes, 469); August 31, 1842 (5 Statutes, 581); and March 3, 1843 (5 Statutes, 614), authorized the issue of Treasury notes in various amounts, and with interest at rates named therein, from 1 mill to 6 per centum per annum.	1 and 2 years.	1 and 2 years from date.	1 mill to 6 per cent.	Par.....			83,825 85
TREASURY NOTES OF 1846.							
The act of July 22, 1846 (9 Statutes, 39), authorized the issue of Treasury notes in such sums as the exigencies of the government might require, the amount outstanding at any one time not to exceed $10,000,000, to bear interest at not exceeding 6 per centum per annum, redeemable one year from date. These notes were receivable in payment of all debts due the United States, including customs duties.	1 year	One year from date.	1 mill and 5½ per cent.	Par.....	$10,000,000 00	$7,687,800 00	5,000 00
MEXICAN INDEMNITY.							
A proviso in the civil and diplomatic appropriation act of August 10, 1846 (9 Statutes, 94), authorized the payment of the principal and interest of the fourth and fifth installments of the Mexican indemnities, due April and July, 1844, by the issue of stock, with interest at 5 per centum, payable in five years.	5 years	April and July, 1849.	5 per cent...	Par.....	350,000 00	303,573 92	1,104 91
TREASURY NOTES OF 1847.							
The act of January 28, 1847 (9 Statutes, 118), authorized the issue of $23,000,000 Treasury notes, with interest at not exceeding 6 per centum per annum, or the issue of stock for any portion of the amount, with interest at 6 per centum per annum. The Treasury notes under this act were redeemable at the expiration of one or two years; and the interest was to cease at the expiration of sixty days' notice. These notes were receivable in payment of all debts due the United States, including customs duties.	1 and 2 years.	After 60 days' notice.	5½ and 6 per cent.	Par.....	23,000,000 00	*26,122,100 00	950 00

* Including reissues.

TABLE M.—*STATEMENT of the OUTSTANDING PRINCIPAL of the PUBLIC DEBT, &c.*—Continued.

	Length of loan.	When redeemable.	Rates of interest.	Price at which sold.	Amount authorized.	Amount issued.	Amount outstanding.
LOAN OF 1847.							
The act of January 28, 1847 (9 Statutes, 118), authorized the issue of $23,00,000 Treasury notes, with interest at not exceeding 6 per centum per annum, or the issue of stock for any portion of the amount, with interest at 6 per cent. per annum, reimbursable after December 31, 1867. Section 14 authorized the conversion of Treasury notes under this or any preceding act into like stock, which accounts for the apparent overissue.	20 years.....	January 1, 1868	6 per cent...	.0125 to .02 per cent. premium.	$23,000,000 00	*$28,207,000 00	$1,250 00
BOUNTY-LAND SCRIP.							
The 9th section of the act of February 11, 1847 (9 Statutes, 125), authorized the issue of land-warrants to soldiers of the Mexican war, or scrip, at the option of the soldier, to bear 6 per centum interest per annum, redeemable at the pleasure of the government, by notice from the Treasury Department. Interest ceased July 1, 1849.	Indefinite ...	July 1, 1849....	6 per cent...	Par.....	Indefinite	233,075 00	3,275 00
TEXAN INDEMNITY STOCK.							
The act of September 9, 1850 (9 Statutes, 447), authorized the issue of $10,000,000 stock, with interest at 5 per centum per annum, to the State of Texas, in satisfaction of all claims against the United States arising out of the annexation of the said State. The stock was to be redeemable at the end of fourteen years.	14 years.....	January 1, 1865	5 per cent...	Par.....	10,000,000 00	5,000,000 00	21,000 00
TREASURY NOTES OF 1857.							
The act of December 23, 1857 (11 Statutes, 257), authorized the issue of $20,000,000 in Treasury notes, $6,000,000 with interest at not exceeding 6 per centum per annum, and the remainder with interest at the lowest rates offered by bidders, but not exceeding 6 per centum per annum. These notes were redeemable at the expiration of one year, and interest was to cease at the expiration of sixty days' notice after maturity. They were receivable in payment of all debts due the United States, including customs duties.	1 year......	60 days' notice.	5 and 5½ per cent.	Par.....	20,000,000 00	20,000,000 00	1,700 00
LOAN OF 1858.							
The act of June 14, 1858 (11 Statutes, 365), authorized a loan of $20,000,000, with interest at not exceeding 5 per centum per annum, and redeemable any time after January 1, 1874.	15 years.....	January 1, 1874	5 per cent...	.0205 to .0703 premium.	20,000,000 00	20,000,000 00	8,000 00
LOAN OF 1860.							

LOAN OF FEBRUARY, 1861 (1881s.—

The act of February 8, 1861 (12 Statutes, 129), authorized a loan of $25,000,000, with interest at not exceeding 6 per centum per annum, reimbursable in not less than ten nor more than twenty years from the date of the act.

| 10 or 20 years. | Dec. 31, 1880.. | 6 per cent... | (Av.)89.03 | 25,000,000 00 | 18,415,000 00 | 15,578,000 00 |

TREASURY NOTES OF 1861.

The act of March 2, 1861 (12 Statutes, 178), authorized a loan of $10,000,000, with interest at not exceeding 6 per centum per annum, redeemable on three months' notice after July 1, 1871, and payable July 1, 1881. If proposals for the loan were not satisfactory, authority was given to issue the whole amount in Treasury notes, with interest at not exceeding 6 per centum per annum. The same act gave authority to substitute Treasury notes for the whole or any part of loans authorized at the time of the passage of this act. These notes were to be received in payment of all debts due the United States, including customs duties, and were redeemable at any time within two years from the date of the act.

| 2 years.... / 60 days..... | 2 years after date. / 60 days after date. | 6 per cent... | Par.... | { 32,468,100 00 / 12,896,350 00 } 35,364,450 00 | 3,000 00 |

OREGON WAR DEST.

The act of March 2, 1861 (12 Statutes, 198), appropriated $2,800,000 for the payment of expenses incurred by the Territories of Washington and Oregon in the suppression of Indian hostilities in the years 1855 and 1856. Section 4 of the act authorized the payment of these claims in bonds redeemable in twenty years, with interest at 6 per centum per annum.

| 20 years..... | July 1, 1881.... | 6 per cent... | Par..... | 2,800,000 00 | 1,090,850 00 | 742,450 00 |

LOAN OF JULY AND AUGUST, 1861 (1881s.)

The act of July 17, 1861 (12 Statutes, 259), authorized the issue of $250,000,000 bonds with interest at not exceeding 7 per centum per annum, redeemable after twenty years. The act of August 5, 1861 (12 Statutes, 313), authorized the issue of bonds, with interest at 6 per centum per annum, payable after twenty years from date, in exchange for 7.30 notes issued under the act of July 17, 1861. None of such bonds were to be issued for a sum less than $500, and the whole amount of them was not to exceed the whole amount of 7.30 notes issued under the above act of July 17. The amount issued in exchange for 7.30s was $139,321,350.

| 20 years.... | July 1, 1881.... | 6 per cent... | Par*... | 250,000,000'00 | { 50,000,000 00 / 139,321,350 00 } 157,237,100 00 |

OLD DEMAND-NOTES.

The act of July 17, 1861 (12 Statutes, 259), authorized the issue of $50,000,000 Treasury notes, not bearing interest, of a less denomination than fifty dollars and not less than ten dollars, and payable on demand by the assistant treasurers at Philadelphia, New York, or Boston. The act of August 5, 1861 (12 Statutes, 313), authorized the issue of these notes in denomination of five dollars; it also added the offices of assistant treasurer at Saint Louis and the designated depositary at Cincinnati to the places where these notes were made payable. The act of February 12, 1862 (12 Statutes, 338), increased the amount of demand-notes authorized $10,000,000.

| .... | On demand... | None........ | Par..... | 60,000,000 00 | 60,000,000 00 | 60,975 00 |

* $50,000,000 6 per cent. bonds issued at a discount of $5,338,768.09, being equivalent to par for 7 per cent. bonds authorized by the act.

TABLE M.—*STATEMENT of the OUTSTANDING PRINCIPAL of the PUBLIC DEBT, &c.*—Continued.

	Length of loan.	When redeemable.	Rate of interest.	Price at which sold.	Amount authorized.	Amount issued.	Amount outstanding.
SEVEN-THIRTIES OF 1861.							
The act of July 17, 1861 (12 Statutes, 259), authorized a loan of $250,000,000, part of which was to be in Treasury notes, with interest at 7⅓₀ per centum per annum, payable three years after date.	3 years......	August 19 and October 1, 1864.	7₃₀ per cent,..	Par	$140,094,750 00	$140,094,750 00	$16,600 00
FIVE-TWENTIES OF 1862.							
The act of February 25, 1862 (12 Statutes, 345), authorized a loan of $500,000,000 for the purpose of funding the Treasury notes and floating debt of the United States, and the issue of bonds therefor, with interest at 6 per centum per annum. These bonds were redeemable after five and payable twenty years from date. The act of March 3, 1864 (13 Statutes, 13), authorized an additional issue of $11,000,000 of bonds to persons who subscribed for the loan on or before January 21, 1864. The act of January 28, 1865 (13 Statutes, 425), authorized an additional issue of $4,000,000 of these bonds and their sale in the United States or Europe.	5 or 20 years.	May 1, 1867....	6 per cent ...	Par	515,000,000 00	514,771,600 00	393,406 00
LEGAL-TENDER NOTES.							
The act of February 25, 1862 (12 Statutes, 345), authorized the issue of $150,000,000 United States notes, not bearing interest, payable to bearer, at the Treasury of the United States, and of such denominations, not less than five dollars, as the Secretary of the Treasury might deem expedient, $50,000,000 to be in lieu of demand-notes authorized by the act of July 17, 1861; these notes to be a legal tender. The act of July 11, 1862 (12 Statutes, 532), authorized an additional issue of $150,000,000 United States Treasury notes, of such denominations as the Secretary of the Treasury might deem expedient, but no such note should be for a fractional part of a dollar, and not more than $35,000,000 of a lower denomination than five dollars; these notes to be a legal tender. The act of March 3, 1863 (12 Statutes, 710), authorized an additional issue of $150,000,000 United States notes, payable to bearer, of such denominations, not less than one dollar, as the Secretary of the Treasury might prescribe; which notes were made a legal tender. The	....	On demand....	None.......	Par	450,000,000 00	....	346,681,016 00

TEMPORARY LOAN.

The act of February 25, 1862 (12 Statutes, 346), authorized temporary loan deposits of $25,000,000, for not less than thirty days, with interest at 5 per centum per annum, payable after ten days' notice. The act of March 17, 1862 (12 Statutes, 370), authorized the increase of temporary-loan deposits to $50,000,000. The act of July 11, 1862 (12 Statutes, 532), authorized a further increase of temporary loan deposits to $100,000,000. The act of June 30, 1864 (13 Statutes, 218), authorized a further increase of temporary-loan deposits to not exceeding $150,000,000, and an increase of the rate of interest to not exceeding 6 per centum per annum, or a decrease of the rate of interest on ten days' notice, as the public interest might require.	Not less than 30 days.	After ten days' notice.	4, 5, and 6 per cent.	Par	150,000,000 00	....	2,960 00

CERTIFICATES OF INDEBTEDNESS.

The act of March 1, 1862 (12 Statutes, 352), authorized the issue of certificates of indebtedness to public creditors who might elect to receive them, to bear interest at the rate of 6 per centum per annum, and payable one year from date, or earlier, at the option of the government. The act of May 17, 1862 (12 Statutes, 370), authorized the issue of these certificates in payment of disbursing officers' checks. The act of March 3, 1863 (12 Statutes, 710), made the interest payable in lawful money.	1 year.......	1 year after date.	6 per cent...	Par	No limit	561,753,241 65	4,000 00

FRACTIONAL CURRENCY.

The act of July 17, 1862 (12 Statutes, 592), authorized the use of postal and other stamps as currency, and made them receivable in payment of all dues to the United States less than five dollars. The fourth section of the act of March 3, 1863 (12 Statutes, 711), authorized the issue of fractional notes in lieu of postal and other stamps and postal currency; made them exchangeable in sums not less than three dollars for United States notes, and receivable for postage and revenue stamps, and in payment of dues to the United States, except duties on imports, less than five dollars; and limited the amount to $50,000,000. The fifth section of the act of June 30, 1864 (13 Statutes, 220), authorized an issue of $50,000,000 in fractional currency, and provided that the whole amount of these notes outstanding at any one time should not exceed this sum.	....	On presentation.	None........	Par	50,000,000 00	40,102,660 27	7,214,954 37

LOAN OF 1863.

The act of March 3, 1863 (12 Statutes, 709), authorized a loan of $900,000,000, and the ... .se of bonds, wit'i interest at not exceeding 6 per centum per annum, and redeemable in not less than ten nor more than forty years, principal and interest payable in coin. The act of June 30, 1864 (13 Statutes, 219), repeals so much of the preceding act as limits the authority thereunder to the current fiscal year, and also repeals the authority altogether except as relates to $75,000,000 of bonds already advertised for.	17 years.....	July 1, 1881....	6 per cent...	Average premium of 4.13.	75,000,000 00	75,000,000 00	62,202,850 00

	Length of loan.	When redeemable.	Rate of interest.	Price at which sold.	Amount authorized.	Amount issued.	Amount outstanding.
ONE-YEAR NOTES OF 1863.							
The act of March 3, 1863 (12 Statutes, 710), authorized the issue of $400,000,000 Treasury notes, with interest at not exceeding 6 per centum per annum, redeemable in not more than three years, principal and interest payable in lawful money, to be a legal tender for their face value.	1 year.......	1 year after date.	5 per cent...	Par	$400,000,000 00	$44,520,000 00	$46,535 00
TWO-YEAR NOTES OF 1863.							
The act of March 3, 1863 (12 Statutes, 710), authorized the issue of $400,000,000 Treasury notes, with interest at not exceeding 6 per centum per annum, redeemable in not more than three years, principal and interest payable in lawful money, to be a legal tender for their face value.	2 years......	2 years after date.	5 per cent...	Par	$400,000,000 00	166,480,000 00	35,950 00
COIN-CERTIFICATES.							
The fifth section of the act of March 3, 1863 (12 Statutes, 711), authorized the deposit of gold coin and bullion with the Treasurer or any assistant treasurer, in sums not less than $20, and the issue of certificates therefor in denominations the same as United States notes; also authorized the issue of these certificates in payment of interest on the public debt. It limits the amount of them to not more than 20 per centum of the amount of coin and bullion in the Treasury, and directs their receipt in payment for duties on imports.	....	On demand ...	None	Par	Indefinite.....	57,883,400 00	8,004,600 00
COMPOUND-INTEREST NOTES.							
The act of March 3, 1863 (12 Statutes, 709), authorized the issue of $400,000,000 Treasury notes, with interest at not exceeding 6 per centum per annum, in lawful money, payable not more than three years from date, and to be a legal tender for their face value. The act of June 30, 1864 (13 Statutes, 218), authorized the issue of $200,000,000 Treasury notes, of any denomination not less than $10, payable not more than three years from date, or redeemable at any	3 years	June 10, 1867, and May 15, 1868.	6 per cent. compound.	Par	400,000,000 00	266,595,440 00	242,590 00

TEN-FORTIES OF 1864.

The act of March 3, 1864 (13 Statutes, 13), authorized the issue of $200,000,000 bonds, at not exceeding 6 per centum per annum, redeemable after five and payable not more than forty years from date, in coin.

10 or 40 years.	March 1, 1874..	5 per cent...	Par to 7 per c't prem.	200,000,000 00	196,117,300 00	2,655,400 00

FIVE-TWENTIES OF JUNE, 1864.

The act of June 30, 1864 (13 Statutes, 218), authorized a loan of $400,000,000, and the issue therefor of bonds redeemable not less than five nor more than thirty (or forty, if deemed expedient) years from date, with interest at not exceeding 6 per centum per annum, payable semi-annually in coin.

5 or 20 years.	Nov. 1, 1869...	6 per cent...	Par	400,000,000 00	125,561,300 00	68,250 00

SEVEN-THIRTIES OF 1864 AND 1865.

The act of June 30, 1864 (13 Statutes, 218), authorized the issue of $200,000,000 Treasury notes, of not less than $10 each, payable at not more than three years from date, or redeemable at any time after three years, with interest at not exceeding $7\frac{3}{10}$ per centum per annum. The act of March 3, 1865 (13 Statutes, 468), authorized a loan of $600,000,000, and the issue therefor of bonds or Treasury notes; the notes to be of denominations of not less than $50, with interest in lawful money at not more than $7\frac{3}{10}$ per centum per annum. See also act January 28, 1865 (13 Statutes, 425).

3 years ...	Aug. 15, 1867 / June 15, 1868 / July 15, 1868	$7\frac{3}{10}$ per cent.	Par	830,000,000 00	830,000,000 00	144,900 00

NAVY PENSION FUND.

The act of July 1, 1864 (13 Statutes, 414), authorized the Secretary of the Navy to invest in registered securities of the United States so much of the Navy pension fund in the Treasury January 1 and July 1 in each year as would not be required for the payment of naval pensions. Section 2 of the act of July 23, 1868 (15 Statutes, 170), makes the interest on this fund 3 per centum per annum in lawful money, and confines its use to the payment of naval pensions exclusively.

Indefinite...	....	3 per cent...	Par	Indefinite.....	14,000,000 00	14,000,000 00

FIVE-TWENTIES OF 1865.

The act of March 3, 1865 (13 Statutes, 468), authorized the issue of $600,000,000 of bonds or Treasury notes, in addition to amounts previously authorized; the bonds to be for not less than $50, payable not more than forty years from date of issue, or after any period not less than five years; interest payable semi-annually, at not exceeding 6 per centum per annum when in coin, or $7\frac{3}{10}$ per centum per annum when in currency. In addition to the amount of bonds authorized by this act, authority was also given to convert Treasury notes or other interest-bearing obligations into bonds authorized by it. The act of April 12, 1866 (14 Statutes, 31), construed the above act to authorize the Secretary of the Treasury to receive any obligations of the United States, whether bearing interest or not, in exchange for any bonds authorized by it, or to sell any of such bonds, provided the public debt is not increased thereby.

5 or 20 years.	Nov. 1, 1870 ...	6 per cent...	Par	203,327,250 00	203,327,250 00	114,550 00

TABLE M.—*STATEMENT of the OUTSTANDING PRINCIPAL of the PUBLIC DEBT, &c.*—Continued.

	Length of loan.	When redeemable.	Rate of interest.	Price at which sold.	Amount authorized.	Amount issued.	Amount outstanding.
CONSOLS OF 1865.							
The act of March 3, 1865 (13 Statutes, 468), authorized the issue of $600,000,000 of bonds or Treasury notes, in addition to amounts previously authorized; the bonds to be for not less than $50, payable not more than forty years from date of issue or after any period not less than five years, interest payable semi-annually, at not exceeding 6 per centum per annum when in currency, or 7¾ per centum per annum when in currency. In addition to the amount of bonds authorized by this act, authority was also given to convert Treasury notes or other interest-bearing obligations into bonds authorized by it. The act of April 12, 1866 (14 Statutes, 31), construed the above act to authorize the Secretary of the Treasury to receive any obligations of the United States, whether bearing interest or not, in exchange for any bonds authorized by it, or to sell any of such bonds, provided the public debt is not increased thereby.	5 or 20 years	July 1, 1870 ..	6 per cent...	Par ...	$332,998,950 00	$332,998,950 00	$612,400 00
CONSOLS OF 1867.							
The act of March 3, 1865 (13 Statutes, 468), authorized the issue of $600,000,000 of bonds or Treasury notes, in addition to amounts previously authorized; the bonds to be for not less than $50, payable not more than forty years from date of issue or after any period not less than five years, interest payable semi-annually, at not exceeding 6 per centum per annum when in coin, or 7¾ per centum per annum when in currency. In addition to the amount of bonds authorized by this act, authority was also given to convert Treasury notes or other interest-bearing obligations into bonds authorized by it. The act of April 12, 1866 (14 Statutes, 31), construed the above act to authorize the Secretary of the Treasury to receive any obligations of the United States, whether bearing interest or not, in exchange for any bonds authorized by it, or to sell any of such bonds, provided the public debt is not increased thereby.	5 or 20 years.	July 1, 1872 ..	6 per cent...	Par	379,618,000 00	379,618,000 00	2,330,150 00
CONSOLS OF 1868.							
The act of March 3, 1865 (13 Statutes, 468), authorized the issue of $600,000,000 of bonds or Treasury notes, in addition to amounts pre-	5 or 20 years	July 1, 1873 ..	6 per cent...	Par	42,539,350 00	42,539,350 00	752,300 00

notes or other interest-bearing obligations into bonds authorized by it. The act of April 12, 1866 (14 Statutes, 31), construed the above act to authorize the Secretary of the Treasury to receive any obligations of the United States, whether bearing interest or not, in exchange for any bonds authorized by it, and to sell any such bonds, provided the public debt is not increased thereby.

THREE-PER-CENT. CERTIFICATES.

The act of March 3, 1867 (14 Statutes, 558), authorized the issue of $50,000,000 in temporary-loan certificates of deposit, with interest at 3 per centum per annum, payable in lawful money, on demand, to be used in redemption of compound-interest notes. The act of July 25, 1868 (15 Statutes, 183), authorized $25,000,000 additional of these certificates, for the sole purpose of redeeming compound-interest notes.	Indefinite...	On demand...	3 per cent...	Par.....	85, 155, 000 00	85, 155, 000 00	5, 000 00

FIVE-PER-CENT. LOAN OF 1881. (FOR SILVER.)

The act of January 14, 1875 (18 Statutes, 296), authorizes the Secretary of the Treasury to use any surplus revenues from time to time in the Treasury not otherwise appropriated, and to issue, sell, dispose of, at not less than par, in coin, either of the description of bonds of the United States described in the act of July 14, 1870 (16 Statutes, 272), to the extent necessary for the redemption of fractional currency in silver coins of the denominations of ten, twenty-five, and fifty cents of standard value.	10 years ..	May 1, 1881 ..	5 per cent...	Par......	Indefinite....	17, 494, 150 00	

FIVE-PER-CENT. LOAN OF 1881. (TO PAY J. B. EADS.)

The act of March 3, 1875 (18 Statutes, 460), directs the Secretary of the Treasury to issue bonds of the character and description set out in the act of July 14, 1870 (16 Statutes, 272), to James B. Eads or his legal representatives in payment at par of the warrants of the Secretary of War for the construction of jetties and auxiliary works to maintain a wide and deep channel between the South Pass of the Mississippi River and the Gulf of Mexico, unless Congress shall have previously provided for the payment of the same by the necessary appropriation of money.	10 years.....	May 1, 1881 ...	5 per cent...	Par	Indefinite.....	500, 000 00	

FIVE-PER-CENT. LOAN OF 1881. (REFUNDING.)

The act of July 14, 1870 (16 Statutes, 272), authorizes the issue of $200,000,000 of 5 per centum, principal and interest payable in coin of the present standard value, at the pleasure of the United States Government, after ten years; these bonds to be exempt from the payment of all taxes or duties of the United States, as well as from taxation in any form by or under State, municipal, or local authority. Bonds and coupons payable at the Treasury of the United States. This act not to authorize an increase of the bonded debt of the United States. Bonds to be sold at not less than par in coin, and the proceeds to be applied to the redemption of outstanding 5-20s, or to	10 years ...	May 1, 1881....	5 per cent...	Par.....	....	486, 043, 000 00	484, 864, 900 00

TABLE M.—*STATEMENT of the OUTSTANDING PRINCIPAL of the PUBLIC DEBT, &c.*—Continued.

42

REPORT OF THE SECRETARY OF THE TREASURY.

	Length of loan.	When redeemable.	Rate of interest.	Price at which sold.	Amount authorized.	Amount issued.	Amount outstanding
be exchanged for said 5-20s, par for par. Payment of those bonds, when due, to be made in order of dates and numbers, beginning with each class last dated and numbered. Interest to cease at the end of three months from notice of intention to redeem. The act of January 20, 1871 (16 Statutes, 399), increases the amount of 5 per cents to $500,000,000, provided the total amount of bonds issued shall not exceed the amount originally authorized, and authorizes the interest on any of these bonds to be paid quarterly. The act of December 17, 1873 (18 Statutes, 1), authorized the issue of an equal amount of bonds of the loan of 1858, which the holders thereof may, on or before February 1, 1874, elect to exchange for the bonds of this loan						$13,957,000 00	
FOUR-AND-ONE-HALF-PER-CENT. LOAN OF 1891. (REFUNDING.)							
The act of July 14, 1870 (16 Statutes, 272), authorizes the issue of $300,000,000 at 4½ per centum, payable in coin of the present standard value, at the pleasure of the United States Government, after fifteen years; these bonds to be exempt from the payment of all taxes or duties of the United States, as well as from taxation in any form by or under State, municipal, or local authority. Bonds and coupons payable at the Treasury of the United States. This act not to authorize an increase of the bonded debt of the United States. Bonds to be sold at not less than par in coin, and the proceeds to be applied to the redemption of outstanding 5-20s, or to be exchanged for said 5-20s, par for par. Payment of these bonds, when due, to be made in order of dates and numbers, beginning with each class last dated and numbered. Interest to cease at the end of three months from notice of intention to redeem. Under the act of January 20, 1871 (16 Statutes, 399), which authorized the increase of 5 per cent. bonds to $500,000,000, the amount of the 4½ per cents were reduced to $200,000,000.	15 years	Sept. 1, 1891	4½ per cent.	Par		185,000,000 00	$185,000,000 00
FOUR-PER-CENT. LOAN OF 1907. (REFUNDING.)					$1,500,000,000 00		
The act of July 14, 1870 (16 Statutes, 272), authorizes the issue of $1,000,000,000 at 4 per centum, payable in coin of the present standard value, at the pleasure of the United States Government, after thirty years; these bonds to be exempt from the payment of all taxes or duties of the United States, as well as from taxation in any form by or under State, municipal, or local authority. Bonds and coupons payable at the Treasury of the United States. This act not to au-	30 years	July 1, 1907	4 per cent.	Par to one-half per cent. premium.		708,980,800 00	707,480,800 00

to the redemption of outstanding 5-20s, or to be exchanged for said 5-20s, par for par. Payment of these bonds, when due, to be made in order of dates and numbers, beginning with each class last dated and numbered. Interest to cease at the end of three months from notice of intention to redeem. See Refunding Certificates, page 36.

FOUR-AND-ONE-HALF PER CENT. LOAN OF 1891. (RESUMPTION.)

The act of January 14, 1875 (18 Statutes, 296), authorizes the Secretary of the Treasury to use any surplus revenues from time to time in the Treasury not otherwise appropriated, and to issue, sell, dispose of, at not less than par, in coin, either of the description of bonds of the United States described in the act of July 14, 1870 (16 Statutes, 272), for the purpose of redeeming, on and after January 1, 1879, in coin, at the office of the assistant treasurer of the United States in New York, the outstanding United States legal-tender notes when presented in sums of not less than fifty dollars.	15 years	Sept. 1, 1891	4½ per cent	Par to one and one-half per cent. premium.	Indefinite	65,000,000 00	65,000,000 00

FOUR-PER-CENT. LOAN OF 1907. (RESUMPTION.)

The act of January 14, 1875 (18 Statutes, 296), authorizes the Secretary of the Treasury to use any surplus revenues from time to time in the Treasury not otherwise appropriated, and to issue, sell, dispose of, at not less than par, in coin, either of the description of bonds of the United States described in the act of July 14, 1870 (16 Statutes, 272), for the purpose of redeeming, on and after January 1, 1879, in coin, at the office of the assistant treasurer of the United States in New York, the outstanding United States legal-tender notes when presented in sums of not less than fifty dollars.	30 years	July 1, 1907	4 per cent	Par	Indefinite	30,500,000 00	30,500,000 00

CERTIFICATES OF DEPOSIT.

The act of June 8, 1872 (17 Statutes, 336), authorizes the deposit of United States notes without interest by banking associations in sums not less than $10,000, and the issue of certificates therefor in denominations of not less than $5,000; which certificates shall be payable on demand in United States notes at the place where the deposits were made. It provides that the notes so deposited in the Treasury shall not be counted as a part of the legal reserve, but that the certificates issued therefor may be held and counted by the national banks as part of their legal reserve, and may be accepted in the settlement of clearing-house balances at the places where the deposits therefor were made, and that the United States notes for which such certificates were issued, or other United States notes of like amount, shall be held as special deposits in the Treasury, and used only for the redemption of such certificates.	Indefinite	On demand	None	Par	No limit	64,780,000 00	14,465,000 00

SILVER CERTIFICATES.

The act of February 28, 1878 (20 Statutes, 26, sec. 3), provides that any holder of the coin authorized by this act may deposit the same with the Treasurer or any assistant treasurer of the United States, in	Indefinite	On demand	None	Par	No limit		12,874,270 60

	Length of loan.	When redeemable.	Rate of interest.	Price at which sold.	Amount authorised.	Amount issued.	Amount outstanding.
sums not less than ten dollars, and receive therefor certificates of not less than ten dollars each, corresponding with the denominations of the United States notes. The coin deposited for or representing the certificates shall be retained in the Treasury for the payment of the same on demand. Said certificates shall be receivable for customs, taxes, and all public dues, and, when so received, may be reissued.							
REFUNDING CERTIFICATES.							
The act of February 26, 1879 (20 Statutes, 321), authorizes the Secretary of the Treasury to issue, in exchange for lawful money of the United States, certificates of deposit, of the denomination of ten dollars, bearing interest at the rate of four per centum per annum, and convertible at any time, with accrued interest, into the four per centum bonds described in the refunding act; the money so received to be applied only to the payment of the bonds bearing interest at a rate not less than five per centum, in the mode prescribed by said act.	Indefinite	Convertible into 4 per cent. bonds.	4 per cent.	Par	No limit	$40,012,750 00	$1,367,000 00
							2,120,415,370 63

TABLE N.—*STATEMENT of 30-YEAR 6 PER CENT. BONDS (interest payable January and July) ISSUED to the several PACIFIC RAILWAY COMPANIES under the acts of July 1, 1862 (12 Statutes, 492), and July 2, 1864 (13 Statutes, 359).*

Railway companies.	Amount of bonds outstanding.	Amount of interest accrued and paid to date, as per preceding statement.	Amount of interest due as per Register's schedule.	Total interest paid by the United States.	Repayment of interest by transportation of mails, troops, &c.	Balance due the United States on interest account, deducting repayments.	Balance of accrued interest due the United States on interest account.	Total amount of interest due the United States from Pacific railway companies.
On January 1, 1876:								
Central Pacific	$25,885,120 00	$13,027,697 67	$776,553 60	$11,804,251 27	$1,191,765 86	$10,612,485 41	$2,712,527 92	$13,325,013 33
Kansas Pacific	6,303,000 00	3,103,893 09	189,090 00	3,292,983 09	1,440,664 84	1,852,318 25	456,846 99	2,308,165 24
Union Pacific	27,236,512 00	11,884,324 65	817,095 36	12,701,420 01	3,943,715 65	8,757,704 36	2,170,415 23	10,928,119 59
Central Branch Union Pacific	1,600,000 00	781,808 26	48,000 00	829,808 26	44,408 05	785,400 21	230,955 19	1,016,355 40
Western Pacific	1,970,560 00	722,380 14	59,116 80	781,496 94	9,367 00	772,129 94	163,069 89	935,199 83
Sioux City and Pacific	1,628,320 00	683,703 89	48,849 60	731,553 49	39,005 96	692,547 53	174,873 65	867,421 18
	64,623,512 00	28,202,807 70	1,938,705 36	30,141,513 06	6,668,927 36	23,472,585 70	5,907,688 87	29,380,274 57
On July 1, 1876:								
Central Pacific	25,885,120 00	11,804,251 27	776,553 60	12,580,804 87	1,331,213 76	11,349,591 11	3,112,076 38	14,461,667 49
Kansas Pacific	6,303,000 00	3,292,983 09	189,090 00	3,482,073 09	1,448,327 39	2,033,745 70	525,021 79	2,558,767 49
Union Pacific	27,236,512 00	12,701,420 01	817,095 36	13,518,515 37	4,079,704 77	9,438,810 60	2,496,152 67	11,934,963 27
Central Branch Union Pacific	1,600,000 00	829,808 26	48,000 00	877,808 26	44,408 05	833,400 21	261,445 84	1,094,846 05
Western Pacific	1,970,560 00	781,496 94	59,116 80	840,613 74	9,367 00	831,246 74	201,125 89	1,032,372 03
Sioux City and Pacific	1,628,320 00	731,553 49	48,849 60	780,403 09	39,470 28	740,932 81	200,898 52	941,826 33
	64,623,512 00	30,141,513 06	1,938,705 36	32,080,218 42	6,652,491 25	26,227,727 17	6,786,716 09	32,014,443 26
On January 1, 1877:								
Central Pacific	25,885,120 00	12,580,804 87	776,553 60	13,357,358 47	1,286,672 12	12,088,686 35	3,544,981 77	15,633,668 12
Kansas Pacific	6,303,000 00	3,482,073 09	189,090 00	3,671,163 09	1,515,718 49	2,155,444 60	601,026 62	2,756,471 22
Union Pacific	27,236,512 00	13,518,515 37	817,095 36	14,335,610 73	4,126,871 52	10,208,739 21	2,853,345 13	13,062,084 34
Central Branch Union Pacific	1,600,000 00	877,808 26	48,000 00	925,808 26	44,408 05	881,400 21	294,291 22	1,175,691 43
Western Pacific	1,970,560 00	840,613 74	59,116 80	899,730 54	9,367 00	890,363 54	221,797 08	1,112,160 62
Sioux City and Pacific	1,628,320 00	780,403 09	48,849 60	829,252 69	39,440 28	789,782 41	229,148 30	1,018,930 71
	64,623,512 00	32,080,218 42	1,938,705 36	34,018,923 78	7,004,597 46	27,014,416 32	7,744,590 12	34,759,006 44

TABLE N.—*STATEMENT of 30-YEAR 6 PER CENT. BONDS, &c.*—Continued.

Railway companies.	Amount of bonds outstanding.	Amount of interest accrued and paid to date, as per preceding statement.	Amount of interest due as per Register's schedule.	Total interest paid by the United States.	Repayment of interest by transportation of mails, troops, &c.	Balance due the United States on interest account, deducting repayments.	Balance of accrued interest on the United States interest account.	Total amount of interest due the United States from the Pacific railway companies.
On July 1, 1877:								
Central Pacific	$25,685,120 00	$13,357,358 47	$776,553 60	$14,133,912 07	$2,065,324 01	$12,068,586 06	$4,004,003 32	$16,072,591 38
Kansas Pacific	6,303,000 00	3,671,163 09	189,090 00	3,860,253 09	1,531,680 06	2,328,573 03	683,507 94	3,012,080 97
Union Pacific	27,236,512 00	14,335,610 78	817,095 36	15,152,706 09	4,787,041 07	10,365,664 42	3,237,456 77	13,603,121 19
Central Branch Union Pacific	1,600,000 00	925,808 26	48,000 00	973,808 26	58,498 35	915,309 91	329,369 47	1,244,679 38
Western Pacific	1,970,560 00	828,730 54	50,116 80	878,847 34	9,367 00	949,480 34	255,161 91	1,204,642 25
Sioux City and Pacific	1,628,320 00	820,252 69	57,849 60	878,102 29	62,578 80	815,523 49	259,414 61	1,074,938 10
	64,623,512 00	34,016,023 78	1,938,705 36	35,957,629 14	8,514,489 80	27,443,139 25	8,768,914 02	36,212,053 27
On January 1, 1878:								
Central Pacific	25,685,120 00	14,133,912 07	776,553 60	14,910,465 67	2,108,960 71	12,711,504 96	4,484,140 29	17,195,645 25
Kansas Pacific	6,303,000 00	3,860,253 09	189,090 00	4,049,343 09	1,532,350 07	2,516,903 02	772,863 85	3,290,859 87
Union Pacific	27,236,512 00	15,152,706 09	817,095 36	15,969,801 45	5,134,103 84	10,835,697 61	3,641,300 88	14,476,998 49
Central Branch Union Pacific	1,600,000 00	973,808 26	48,000 00	1,021,808 26	62,298 35	958,809 91	306,641 04	1,325,450 95
Western Pacific	1,970,560 00	958,847 34	50,116 80	1,017,064 14	9,367 00	1,008,597 14	291,301 17	1,299,898 31
Sioux City and Pacific	1,628,320 00	878,102 29	45,849 50	920,951 80	68,409 65	858,542 24	291,575 23	1,150,117 47
	64,623,512 00	35,957,629 14	1,938,705 36	37,896,334 50	9,006,180 62	28,890,144 88	9,848,825 46	38,738,970 34
On July 1, 1878:								
Central Pacific	25,685,120 00	14,910,465 67	776,553 60	15,687,019 27	2,343,659 54	13,343,359 73	4,996,311 56	18,341,671 29
Kansas Pacific	6,303,000 00	4,049,343 09	189,090 00	4,238,433 09	1,532,530 42	2,705,902 67	872,589 09	3,578,491 76
Union Pacific	27,236,512 00	15,969,801 45	817,095 36	16,786,896 81	5,852,870 95	10,934,025 86	4,072,654 57	15,006,680 43
Central Branch Union Pacific	1,600,000 00	1,021,808 26	48,000 00	1,069,808 26	67,498 35	1,002,309 91	406,347 61	1,408,657 52
Western Pacific	1,970,560 00	1,017,064 14	50,116 80	1,077,080 94	9,367 00	1,067,713 94	330,298 11	1,398,012 05
Sioux City and Pacific	1,628,320 00	920,951 89	45,849 50	975,801 49	75,517 90	900,283 50	326,013 09	1,226,296 59
	64,623,512 00	37,896,334 50	1,938,705 36	39,835,039 86	9,881,444 25	29,953,595 61	11,006,214 03	40,959,809 64
On January 1, 1879:								

Western Pacific	1,970,560 00	1,077,080 94	50,116 80	1,136,197 74	9,367 00	1,126,830 74	330,298 11	1,457,128 85
Sioux City and Pacific	1,628,320 00	975,801 49	48,849 60	1,024,651 09	83,648 56	941,002 53	326,013 09	1,367,015 62
	64,623,512 00	39,535,039 86	1,938,705 36	41,773,745 22	10,571,102 71	31,202,642 51	11,006,214 03	42,208,856 54
On July 1, 1879:								
Central Pacific	25,885,130 00	16,463,572 87	776,553 60	17,240,126 47	2,771,419 23	14,468,707 24	4,998,311 56	19,467,018 80
Kansas Pacific	6,303,000 00	4,427,523 09	189,090 00	4,616,613 09	3,324,910 55	2,291,702 54	872,589 09	3,164,291 63
Union Pacific	27,236,512 00	17,603,992 17	817,095 36	18,421,087 53	7,325,466 49	11,095,621 04	4,072,654 57	15,168,275 61
Central Branch Union Pacific	1,600,000 00	1,117,508 26	48,000 00	1,165,508 26	73,142 73	1,092,365 53	406,347 61	1,499,013 14
Western Pacific	1,970,560 00	1,136,197 74	50,116 80	1,195,314 54	9,367 00	1,185,947 54	330,298 11	1,516,245 65
Sioux City and Pacific	1,628,320 00	1,024,651 09	48,849 60	1,073,500 69	91,747 39	981,753 30	326,013 09	1,307,766 39
	64,623,512 00	41,773,745 22	1,938,705 36	43,712,450 58	13,590,053 39	31,116,397 19	11,006,214 03	42,122,611 22
On January 1, 1880:								
Central Pacific	25,885,120 00	17,240,126 47	776,553 60	18,016,680 07	3,552,135 70	14,464,544 37	4,998,311 56	19,462,855 93
Kansas Pacific	6,303,000 00	4,616,613 09	189,090 00	4,805,703 09	2,370,109 88	2,435,503 21	872,589 09	3,308,192 30
Union Pacific	27,236,512 00	18,421,087 53	817,095 36	19,236,182 89	7,421,734 97	11,816,447 92	4,072,654 57	15,889,102 49
Central Branch Union Pacific	1,600,000 00	1,105,808 26	48,000 00	1,213,808 26	73,142 73	1,140,665 53	406,347 61	1,547,013 14
Western Pacific	1,970,560 00	1,195,314 54	50,116 80	1,254,431 34	9,367 00	1,245,064 34	330,298 11	1,575,362 45
Sioux City and Pacific	1,628,320 00	1,073,500 69	48,849 60	1,122,350 29	93,983 91	1,028,366 38	326,013 09	1,354,379 47
	64,623,512 00	43,712,450 58	1,938,705 36	45,651,155 94	13,920,474 19	32,130,681 75	11,006,214 03	43,136,895 78
On July 1, 1880:								
Central Pacific	25,885,120 00	18,016,680 07	776,553 60	18,793,233 67	3,200,380 64	15,592,844 03	4,998,311 56	20,591,155 59
Kansas Pacific	6,303,000 00	4,805,703 09	180,090 00	4,994,793 09	2,447,397 26	2,547,395 81	872,589 09	3,419,964 90
Union Pacific	27,236,512 00	19,238,182 89	817,095 36	20,055,278 25	7,804,484 27	12,250,793 88	4,072,654 57	16,323,448 45
Central Branch Union Pacific	1,600,000 00	1,213,808 26	48,000 00	1,261,808 26	47,621 09	1,214,186 57	406,347 61	1,620,534 18
Western Pacific	1,970,560 00	1,254,431 34	50,116 80	1,313,648 14	9,367 00	1,304,181 14	330,298 11	1,634,479 25
Sioux City and Pacific	1,628,320 00	1,122,350 29	48,849 60	1,171,199 89	106,032 57	1,065,167 32	326,013 09	1,391,180 41
	64,623,512 00	45,051,155 94	1,938,705 36	47,589,861 30	13,015,292 55	33,974,568 75	11,006,214 03	44,980,782 78

TABLE O.—STATEMENT showing the AMOUNT of NOTES, SILVER CERTIFICATES, and FRACTIONAL SILVER COIN OUTSTANDING at the CLOSE of EACH FISCAL YEAR from 1860 to 1880, inclusive.

Year ended June 30.	State-bank circulation.	National-bank circulation.	Demand notes.	Legal-tender notes.	One and two year notes of 1863. (See Note 3.)	Compound-interest notes. (See Note 3.)	Silver certificates.	Fractional currency, paper.	Fractional currency, silver. (See Note 4.)	Total amount in currency.	Value of paper dollar as compared with coin July 1 of each year.	Value of currency in gold.
1860	$207,102,477 00									$207,102,477 00		
1861	202,005,767 00									202,005,767 00		
1862	183,792,079 00		$53,040,000 00	$96,620,000 00						333,452,079 00	86.6	$288,769,500 41
1863	238,677,218 00		3,351,019 75	297,767,114 00	$189,979,475 00		$20,192,456 00			649,807,282 75	76.6	497,706,338 50
1864	179,157,717 00	$31,335,270 00	780,999 25	431,178,670 84	153,471,450 00	$315,000,000 00		22,894,877 25		833,718,964 34	38.7	322,649,246 94
1865	142,919,638 00	146,137,860 00	472,603 00	432,987,966 00	42,338,710 00	193,756,680 00		35,006,828 76		983,818,685 76	70.4	692,256,354 77
1866	19,996,163 00	281,479,908 00	272,162 00	400,619,206 00	3,454,230 00	159,012,140 00		27,070,878 96		891,904,685 96	66.0	588,657,092 73
1867	4,484,112 00	298,625,379 00	206,432 00	371,783,597 00	1,133,630 00	122,394,480 00		28,307,523 52		826,927,153 52	71.7	502,906,769 07
1868	3,163,771 00	299,762,855 00	141,723 00	356,000,000 00	555,492 00	28,161,810 00		32,626,951 75		720,412,602 75	70.1	505,009,234 53
1869	2,558,874 00	299,629,624 00	123,739 25	356,000,000 00	347,772 00	2,873,410 00		32,114,637 38		693,946,056 61	73.5	510,050,351 61
1870	2,222,793 00	299,766,984 00	106,256 00	356,000,000 00	248,272 00	2,152,910 00		39,878,684 48		700,375,899 48	85.0	590,521,709 95
1871	1,968,058 00	318,261,241 00	96,505 50	356,000,000 00	198,572 00	768,500 00		40,582,874 56		717,675,751 06	89.0	638,906,418 44
1872	1,700,935 00	337,664,795 00	88,296 25	357,500,000 00	167,522 00	598,520 00		40,855,835 27		738,576,903 52	87.5	644,240,540 58
1873	1,294,470 00	347,267,061 00	79,907 50	356,000,000 00	142,105 00	479,400 00		44,799,365 44		750,062,358 94	86.4	648,053,886 76
1874	1,009,021 00	351,861,032 00	76,732 50	382,000,000 00	127,625 00	415,210 00		45,881,295 07		781,490,916 17	91.2	711,156,733 71
1875	786,544 00	354,408,008 00	70,107 50	375,771,580 00	113,375 00	367,390 00		42,129,424 19		773,646,728 69	87.2	674,619,947 42
1876	658,938 00	332,998,336 00	56,017 50	369,772,284 00	104,705 00	328,780 00		34,446,595 39	$10,926,938 00	749,303,473 89	89.5	671,773,937 62
1877	521,611 00	317,048,872 00	63,902 50	359,764,332 00	95,725 00	296,630 00		20,403,137 34	33,185,273 00	731,379,542 84	94.7	694,375,246 54
1878	426,504 00	324,514,284 00	62,297 50	346,681,016 00	90,485 00	274,920 00	$1,462,500 00	16,547,768 77	39,155,633 00	729,215,508 27	99.4	725,085,924 62
1879	352,452 00	329,691,697 00	61,470 00	346,681,016 00	86,185 00	259,090 00	2,466,950 00	15,842,095 78	39,360,529 00	734,801,994 78	100.0	734,801,994 78
1880	299,790 00	344,505,427 00	60,975 00	346,681,016 00	82,485 00	242,590 00	12,374,270 00	*7,214,954 37	24,061,449 00	735,522,956 37	100.0	735,522,956 37

NOTE 1.—The amount of State and national bank circulation is compiled from the reports of the Comptroller of the Currency at the nearest dates obtainable to the end of each fiscal year; the other amounts are taken from the official printed reports of the Secretary of the Treasury.

*NOTE 2.—Exclusive of $3,375,934, amount estimated as lost or destroyed, act June 21, 1879.

NOTE 3.—The one and two year notes of 1863, and the compound-interest notes, though having a legal-tender quality for their face-values, were in fact interest-bearing securities, payable at certain times, as stated on the notes. They entered into circulation for but a few days, if at all, and since maturity, those presented have been converted into other interest-bearing bonds, or paid for in cash, interest included.

NOTE 4.—The amount of fractional silver in circulation in 1880, 1861, and 1862, cannot be stated. The amounts stated for 1876, and subsequent years, are the amounts coined and issued since January, 1876. To these amounts should be added the amount of silver previously coined which has come into circulation.

TABLE P.—*STATEMENT showing the ANNUAL APPROPRIATIONS made by CONGRESS for EACH FISCAL YEAR from 1873 to 1881, inclusive, together with the COIN VALUE of such APPROPRIATIONS computed upon the average price of gold for each year in question.*

	2d session 42d Congress. Fiscal year 1873.	3d session 42d Congress. Fiscal year 1874.	1st session 43d Congress. Fiscal year 1875.	2d session 43d Congress. Fiscal year 1876.	1st session 44th Congress. Fiscal year 1877.	2d session 44th Congress. Fiscal year 1878.	1st and 2d sessions 45th Congress. Fiscal year 1879.	3d session 45th Congress, and 1st session 46th Congress. Fiscal year 1880.	2d session 46th Congress. Fiscal year 1881.
To supply deficiencies for the service of the various branches of the government	$6,596,677 39	$11,143,239 96	$4,053,812 39	$2,387,372 38	$834,695 66	$2,547,186 31	$15,213,259 21	$4,633,924 55	$6,118,065 10
For legislative, executive, and judicial expenses of the government	18,624,972 74	18,170,441 18	20,758,255 50	16,938,609 49	16,057,020 82	15,756,774 05	15,868,684 60	16,136,230 31	16,785,308 93
For sundry civil expenses of the government	30,134,660 33	62,173,257 90	26,924,746 88	29,450,853 02	15,895,065 58	17,079,256 19	24,968,589 68	17,634,808 56	24,216,136 90
For support of the army	28,683,615 32	31,796,608 81	27,788,300 00	27,933,830 00	27,621,867 90	....	51,279,679 39	26,797,900 00	26,425,800 00
For the naval service	18,231,065 95	22,278,707 65	20,813,946 70	17,001,306 90	12,741,790 90	13,539,982 90	14,153,431 70	14,028,468 95	14,405,797 70
For the Indian service	6,196,362 91	5,505,218 00	5,528,774 87	5,425,627 00	4,567,017 63	4,827,665 69	4,734,675 72	4,713,478 58	4,687,262 72
For rivers and harbors	5,588,000 00	7,352,900 00	5,228,000 00	6,648,517 50	5,015,000 00	....	8,322,700 00	9,577,494 61	8,976,500 00
For forts and fortifications	2,037,000 00	1,899,000 00	964,000 00	850,000 00	315,000 00	275,000 00	275,000 00	275,000 00	550,000 00
For support of Military Academy	326,101 32	344,317 56	339,835 00	364,740 00	290,065 00	286,604 00	292,805 00	310,547 33	316,234 28
For service of Post Office Department	6,425,970 00	6,498,602 00	7,175,542 00	8,376,205 00	5,927,498 00	2,939,725 00	4,222,274 72	5,872,376 10	3,883,420 00
For invalid and other pensions	30,480,000 00	30,480,000 00	29,980,000 00	30,900,000 00	29,533,500 00	28,533,000 00	29,371,574 00	56,233,200 00	41,644,000 00
For consular and diplomatic service	1,268,819 00	1,311,359 00	3,404,804 00	1,374,985 00	1,188,797 50	1,146,747 50	1,067,535 00	1,097,735 00	1,160,335 00
For miscellaneous	9,623,477 36	3,342,647 86	2,108,040 86	1,853,804 52	4,134,691 93	1,425,091 49	2,226,390 29	5,065,123 77	4,999,332 01
Total	154,216,751 92	173,290,700 82	155,017,756 20	147,714,040 81	124,122,010 92	88,350,983 13	172,016,809 21	162,404,647 76	154,118,212 04
Coin value of one dollar paper currency	87.3	89.3	88.8	87.8	92.7	97.6	99.8	100	100
Coin value of amount appropriated	134,631,223 90	153,855,595 83	137,055,769 28	129,693,718 03	115,061,104 12	86,236,415 53	171,672,775 59	162,464,647 76	154,118,212 64

TABLE Q.—*RETURNS, by JUDGMENTS, of the UNITED STATES COURT of CLAIMS, of PROCEEDS of, PROPERTY SEIZED as CAPTURED or ABANDONED, under the act of March 12, 1863, PAID from July 1, 1879, to June 30, 1880.*

Date.	To whom paid.	Amount.
July 2, 1879	John C. Calhoun, administrator of A. P. Calhoun	$1, 526 89
July 21, 1879	Calhoun Fluker, administrator of Isabella Ann Fluker	8, 650 00
September 3, 1879	Frederick L. Meyer, administrator of Henry Jager	2, 881 39
September 17, 1879	Cunningham Boyle, administrator of John Murphy	2, 501 86
September 23, 1879	Robert M. and Stephen A. Douglass	58, 419 20
October 27, 1879	Benjamin F. Grafton, administrator of John C. Murphy	1, 473 16
Total		75, 454 50

TABLE R.—*JUDGMENTS of the UNITED STATES COURT of CLAIMS for PROCEEDS of PROPERTY SEIZED as CAPTURED or ABANDONED under the act of March 12, 1863, RENDERED, but NOT PAID, during the fiscal year ended June 30, 1880.*

Date of judgment.	Name of claimant.	Amount awarded.
April 26, 1880	George Patten	$1, 753 33

TABLE S.—*RECEIPTS and DISBURSEMENTS of UNITED STATES ASSISTANT TREASURERS, and DESIGNATED DEPOSITARY at TUCSON, ARIZONA, during the fiscal year ended June 30, 1880.*

BALTIMORE.

Balance June 30, 1879 .... $4, 637, 991 43

RECEIPTS.

On account of customs	$2, 969, 773 92	
On account of internal revenue	274, 576 91	
On account of currency redemption	484, 024 21	
On account of semi-annual duty	123, 501 29	
On account of certificates of deposit, act June 8, 1872	5, 350, 000 00	
On account of Post-Office Department	214, 290 32	
On account of transfers	6, 089, 875 60	
On account of patent fees	430 00	
On account of disbursing officers	2, 156, 445 65	
On account of interest in currency, 6 per cent	542, 010 00	
On account of miscellaneous	10, 299 17	
		18, 236, 147 07
		22, 874, 138 50

DISBURSEMENTS.

On account of Treasury drafts	3, 436, 749 53	
On account of Post-Office drafts	165, 199 40	
On account of disbursing accounts	2, 102, 222 82	
On account of currency redemption	500, 694 11	
On account of miscellaneous	30 42	
On account of interest, funded loans	1, 054, 084 39	
On account of interest in currency	542, 010 00	
On account of transfers	5, 692, 595 97	
On account of certificates of deposit, act June 8, 1872	5, 100, 000 00	
		18, 593, 586 64

Balance June 30, 1880 .... 4, 280, 551 86

TABLE S.—*RECEIPTS and DISBURSEMENTS, &c.*—Continued.

BOSTON.

Balance June 30, 1879 .... $7,504,805 51

RECEIPTS.

On account of customs	$22,038,971 71	
On account of internal revenue	1,147,802 64	
On account of certificates of deposit, act June 8, 1872	5,070,000 00	
On account of Post-Office Department	703,127 77	
On account of transfers	14,566,272 85	
On account of patent fees	7,035 00	
On account of disbursing officers	19,919,031 18	
On account of interest, in coin $4,928,290 24		
On account of interest, in currency 385,830 72		
	5,314,120 96	
On account of miscellaneous	1,324,635 16	
		70,261,894 27
		77,796,700 78

DISBURSEMENTS.

On account of Treasury drafts	16,843,596 78	
On account of Post-Office drafts	582,952 43	
On account of disbursing accounts	10,677,652 86	
On account of interest, in coin $10,945,815 17		
On account of interest, in currency 384,960 72		
	11,330,775 89	
On account of transfers	12,668,895 74	
On account of certificates of deposit, act June 8, 1872	5,665,000 00	
On account of fractional silver and currency redeemed	1,098,542 10	
On account of miscellaneous	13,990 60	
		67,981,406 40
Balance June 30, 1880		9,815,294 38

CHICAGO.

Balance June 30, 1879 .... $6,344,651 62

RECEIPTS.

On account of customs	$2,818,281 21	
On account of internal revenue	2,028,790 74	
On account of sale of lands	113,806 53	
On account of redemption account	194,830 00	
On account of certificates of deposit, act June 8, 1872	2,170,000 00	
On account of Post-Office Department	983,286 64	
On account of transfers	17,907,388 39	
On account of patent fees	11,021 00	
On account of disbursing officers	11,661,688 03	
On account of interest in currency	107,817 00	
On account of miscellaneous	110,747 16	
		38,128,656 70
		44,473,308 32

DISBURSEMENTS.

On account of Treasury drafts	11,066,749 24	
On account of Post-Office drafts	763,753 47	
On account of disbursing accounts	11,869,263 06	
On account of interest in currency	107,920 50	
On account of transfers	10,305,347 29	
On account of certificates of deposit, act June 8, 1872	1,920,000 00	
On account of redemption account	194,830 00	
		36,226,883 56
Balance June 30, 1880		8,246,444 76

TABLE S.—*RECEIPTS* and *DISBURSEMENTS, &c.*—Continued.

CINCINNATI.

Balance June 30, 1879 .... $2,900,736 13

RECEIPTS.

On account of customs..	$729,145 28	
On account of internal revenue...................................	365,550 10	
On account of semi-annual duty..................................	75,089 97	
On account of Secretary's special deposit account No. 1.............	930 89	
On account of Secretary...	3 45	
On account of certificates of deposit, act June 8, 1872.............	2,665,300 00	
On account of Post-Office Department............................	289,547 62	
On account of transfers..	6,881,856 16	
On account of patent fees..	4,486 20	
On account of disbursing officers.................................	1,518,725 53	
On account of interest, in coin...................................	1,789,272 45	
On account of interest, in currency...............................	3,180 00	
On account of miscellaneous......................................	50,728 47	
		14,373,516 12
		17,364,252 30

DISBURSEMENTS.

On account of Treasury drafts....................................	1,853,064 03	
On account of Post-Office drafts..................................	275,318 29	
On account of disbursing accounts................................	1,514,272 32	
On account of interest, in coin...................................	1,789,272 45	
On account of interest, in currency...............................	3,180 00	
On account of transfers..	6,508,572 34	
On account of certificates of deposit, act June 8, 1872.............	2,535,000 00	
On account of fractional currency redeemed.......................	5,654 09	
		14,484,334 23
Balance June 30, 1880		2,879,918 07

NEW ORLEANS.

Balance June 30, 1879 .... $4,080,037 19

RECEIPTS.

On account of customs...	$2,332,096 21	
On account of internal revenue...................................	1,182,576 40	
On account of sale of lands......................................	17,102 86	
On account of Post-Office Department............................	786,751 48	
On account of transfers..	3,215,752 42	
On account of patent fees..	834 00	
On account of disbursing officers.................................	3,762,023 54	
On account of interest...	5,904 00	
On account of miscellaneous......................................	1,272,612 79	
		12,576,620 70
		17,256,657 89

DISBURSEMENTS.

On account of Treasury drafts....................................	2,765,056 72	
On account of Post-Office drafts..................................	705,227 69	
On account of disbursing accounts................................	4,716,637 65	
On account of interest...	5,889 00	
On account of transfers..	5,414,700 00	
On account of fractional currency redeemed.......................	1,800 00	
		13,609,311 06
Balance June 30, 1880		3,647,346 83

TABLE S.—*RECEIPTS and DISBURSEMENTS, &c.*—Continued.

NEW YORK.

Balance June 30, 1879 .... $159, 674, 686 54

RECEIPTS.

On account of customs	$135, 263, 589 77	
On account of internal revenue....................................	2, 619, 086 24	
On account of silver notes issued.................................	904, 000 00	
On account of certificates of deposit, act June 8, 1872	10, 270, 000 00	
On account of Post-Office Department	5, 964, 662 50	
On account of transfers..	296, 134, 619 30	
On account of patent fees..	5, 321 50	
On account of disbursing officers	284, 613, 444 76	
On account of bullion account superintendent assay office	69, 175, 443 35	
On account of miscellaneous..	118, 470, 970 34	
On account of interest accounts	60, 824, 344 46	
		991, 945, 082 22
		1, 151, 619, 768 76

DISBURSEMENTS.

On account of Treasury drafts......................................	518, 229, 775 09	
On account of Post-Office drafts	6, 668, 726 51	
On account of disbursing accounts	284, 337, 054 72	
On account of bullion account superintendent assay office	63, 679, 129 84	
On account of certificates, act June 8, 1872, sent to department.	33, 785, 000 00	
On account of gold certificates sent to department..............	7, 449, 100 00	
On account of silver certificates sent to department	49, 850 00	
On account of fractional currency sent to department	79, 000 00	
On account of United States bonds, account sinking fund, sent to department	76, 957, 416 06	
On account of interest accounts sent to department	60, 321, 388 71	
		1, 051, 557, 040 87

Balance June 30, 1880 .... 100, 062, 727 89

PHILADELPHIA.

Balance June 30, 1879 .... $16, 022, 184 58

RECEIPTS.

On account of customs	$12, 600, 817 38	
On account of internal-revenue stamps	496, 741 86	
On account of fractional currency for redemption	19, 179 90	
On account of fractional silver coin for exchange.............	8, 050, 140 00	
On account of semi-annual duty	442, 500 00	
On account of certificates of deposit, act June 8, 1872	11, 065, 900 00	
On account of Post-Office Department.........................	607, 754 69	
On account of transfers..	13, 494, 575 37	
On account of patent fees...	4, 892 96	
On account of disbursing officers	12, 087, 532 76	
On account of interest..	1, 107, 766 50	
On account of miscellaneous.......................................	1, 069, 912 00	
		55, 730, 818 13
		71, 753, 997 71

DISBURSEMENTS.

On account of Treasury drafts	12, 047, 554 12	
On account of Post-Office drafts	590, 643 29	
On account of disbursing accounts	12, 120, 304 08	
On account of fractional silver coin exchanged	8, 402, 820 00	
On account of interest..	5, 119, 563 18	
On account of transfers..	6, 929, 285 00	
On account of certificates of deposit, act June 8, 1872	13, 110, 000 00	
On account of fractional currency redeemed	19, 233 60	
		58, 339, 343 17

Balance June 30, 1880 .... 18, 413, 654 54

TABLE S.—*RECEIPTS and DISBURSEMENTS, &c.*—Continued.

SAINT LOUIS.

Balance June 30, 1879.. $3, 817, 447 00

RECEIPTS.

On account of customs	1, 468, 954 33	
On account of internal revenue...........................	813, 115 02	
On account of sale of lands....................................	20, 448 95	
On account of certificates of deposit, act June 8, 1872..................	700, 000 00	
On account of Post-Office Department..............................	1, 240, 760 75	
On account of transfers.......................................	16, 057, 412 40	
On account of patent fees....................................	4, 602 20	
On account of disbursing officers	6, 950, 296 65	
On account of 5 per cent. redemption..........................	856, 597 17	
On account of miscellaneous..................................	244, 705 63	
		21, 836, 956 10
		25, 654, 403 10

DISBURSEMENTS.

On account of Treasury drafts..................................	7, 260, 184 29	
On account of Post-Office drafts	1, 462, 143 39	
On account of disbursing accounts	6, 510, 926 96	
On account of Treasurer's transfer account...................	454, 860 21	
On account of interest, in coin...............................	642, 302 31	
On account of transfers	4, 910, 477 85	
On account of certificates of deposit, act June 8, 1872........	1, 035, 000 00	
On account of fractional currency redeemed....................	1, 660 00	
		22, 278, 555 00
Balance June 30, 1880		3, 375, 848 10

SAN FRANCISCO.

Balance June 30, 1879.. *$23, 394, 396 99

RECEIPTS.

On account of customs..	$5, 925, 336 24	
On account of internal revenue	2, 860, 596 29	
On account of sale of lands...................................	209, 280 02	
On account of refund certificates, 4 per cent. loan 1907.......	202 80	
On account of silver dollars for silver certificates	3, 001, 000 00	
On account of Post-Office Department..........................	586, 311 47	
On account of transfers......................................	13, 763, 197 22	
On account of patent fees....................................	13, 228 00	
On account of disbursing officers.............................	11, 644, 057 90	
On account of miscellaneous..................................	1, 024, 608 19	
		39, 121, 318 53
		62, 515, 715 52

DISBURSEMENTS.

On account of Treasury drafts.................................	7, 226, 579 53	
On account of Post-Office drafts	640, 144 55	
On account of disbursing accounts............................	12, 272, 121 82	
On account of bullion account	1, 025, 000 00	
On account of interest, in coin...............................	363, 514 73	
On account of transfers......................................	15, 648, 729 75	
		37, 176, 090 38
Balance June 30, 1880		25, 339, 625 14

* The reserve fund, amounting to $2,240,000, is included in this amount.

TABLE S.—*RECEIPTS and DISBURSEMENTS, &c.*—Continued.

TUCSON.

Balance June 30, 1879	$280, 761 58

RECEIPTS.

On account of customs	$10, 232 67	
On account of internal revenue	24, 815 40	
On account of sale of lands	13, 602 47	
On account of transfers	742, 660 18	
On account of disbursing officers	608, 788 92	
On account of miscellaneous	34, 880 42	
		1, 432, 900 06
		1, 722, 701 64

DISBURSEMENTS.

On account of Treasury drafts	26, 652 78	
On account of disbursing accounts	992, 405 80	
On account of transfers	468, 047 11	
		1, 408, 095 73
Balance June 30, 1880		224, 655 91

REPORT OF COMMISSIONER OF INTERNAL REVENUE.

REPORT

OF

THE COMMISSIONER OF INTERNAL REVENUE.

TREASURY DEPARTMENT,
OFFICE OF INTERNAL REVENUE,
Washington, November 24, 1880. .

SIR: I have the honor to submit the report of the Bureau of Internal Revenue for the fiscal year ended June 30, 1880, with accompanying tables, exhibiting in detail the receipts from each specific source of revenue by years and collection districts, together with additional facts and figures, showing the operations of the bureau during the months of July, August, September, and October, being the first four months of the current fiscal year.

I am glad to be able to bring to your attention the fact that since my last annual report still further improvement has been made in the condition of the internal-revenue service.

The efforts of the past four years for the suppression of the illicit manufacture and sale of spirits and tobacco have been substantially crowned with success. The frauds upon the revenue and the resistance to authority still existing are confined to a few localities, and I am of opinion that the hearty co-operation of all officers charged with the enforcement of the laws will, before the close of the present administration, have established the authority of the government for the collection of the taxes and the equal enforcement of its laws in all parts of the country.

The discipline, efficiency, and fidelity to duty of the officers of internal revenue have steadily improved; the manner in which they have enforced the laws has promoted the relations of harmony which should subsist between the tax-payer and the government, and I take pleasure in noting the fact of an almost universal disposition on the part of tax-payers to observe the laws and see them faithfully executed.

REDUCTION OF TAXATION.

The receipts of internal revenue for the fiscal year 1879 were $113,449,621.38, showing an increase of $2,795,458.01 upon the previous year. The receipts for the fiscal year 1880, in the face of the reduction of the tax on tobacco, were $123,981,916.10, showing an increase of $10,532,294.72. The receipts for the first four months of the present fiscal year amount to $43,789,318.30, showing an increase over the corresponding period of last year of $3,658,213.48. I know of no reason why this increase should not be maintained during the fiscal year, so that the total collections for the year from internal revenue taxes at the present rates would be $135,000,000.

While the receipts from taxes are thus increasing in amount, the demands upon the Treasury are being lessened by the reduction of the public debt, and of the annual interest charge. It is probable, therefore, that Congress will be disposed to relieve the people from some of the internal-revenue taxes, and if such a reduction is to be made, I respectfully suggest the following list of taxes collected during the fiscal year 1880 for the consideration of the law-making power:

Bank checks	$2,270,421 00
Friction matches	3,561,300 00
Patent medicines or preparations, perfumery, cosmetics, &c.	1,836,673 22
Bank deposits	2,347,568 07
Savings-banks deposits	163,207 36
Bank capital	811,436 48
Total	10,990,606 13

In the event it is deemed advisable to take the tax off matches, patent medicines, perfumery, &c., due consideration should be had to the fact that large stocks of these articles, tax paid, are now in the hands of the trade, and that a very serious reduction in their value, especially of matches, would result if the tax were taken off suddenly, and articles manufactured free of tax were brought into competition with those upon which the existing taxes had been paid. In my opinion an act abolishing these taxes should not go into effect earlier than, say three months from its passage.

The same may be said in regard to check stamps. Considerable stocks of stamped checks are now in the hands of individuals, banks, and bankers, upon which the stamps have been imprinted. I think it would be wise that the operation of the repeal should be delayed at least three months, so as to give time for the use of these stamps.

Whenever the interests of the government will allow it, I think it will be wise to confine internal-revenue taxation to spirits, malt liquors, tobacco, snuff, cigars, and special taxes upon the manufacturers and dealers in these articles. I am of opinion that reliance can be placed upon receiving the sum of $124,000,000 annually from these sources, which sum would gradually increase with the increase of population, but which would probably be subjected to diminution upon a recurrence of hard times.

In considering the question of relieving patent medicines from internal revenue taxes, it should be understood that many of the articles put upon the market and taxed as medicinal bitters are used as a beverage. Persons engaged in the sale of such articles are not required to pay special taxes as retail dealers in liquors, so that if the articles were relieved from taxation medicinal bitters would be sold everywhere without paying any internal-revenue tax whatever.

In passing upon the right of these various medicated bitters to be taxed as such, and sold without payment of the special tax as retail liquor dealers, the office is often seriously embarrassed to find the exact line between a medicinal bitter liable to stamp tax and a compound liquor subject to be sold only as a beverage. In my opinion it would be wise to continue the stamp tax upon all medical bitters containing more than 20 per cent. of proof spirits.

The tax upon savings banks, in my judgment, should be removed, or the whole legislation upon the subject of taxing savings banks should be modified and made more equitable; and there would seem to be no just ground for continuing the tax upon the capital and deposits of banks and bankers if it is found that the revenues are sufficient without it.

ASSESSMENTS ON CIRCULATING NOTES.

The assessments on circulating notes of corporations and individuals under sections 3412 and 3413 United States Revised Statutes, and sections 19 and 20 of the act of February, 8, 1875, amounted, during the year ended June 30, 1880, to $461,597.82, an increase of $452,355.20 over those made during the preceding year. The chief motive for issuing the notes upon which these assessments were made was unquestionably to supplement an insufficient capital or to bolster up the waning credit of the firms or corporations making the issues. The large increase in these assessments clearly indicates the disposition of individuals and corporations to flood the country with an insecure "shinplaster" circulation. The existing laws of the United States seem to constitute the only breakwater for the protection of the people against an inundation of every imaginable character of individual and corporate circulating notes designed to take the place of money. In my judgment those laws should be maintained upon the statute book.

RESISTANCE TO ENFORCEMENT OF THE LAWS.

By reference to the table on page 24, it will be seen that during the last four years and four months, 4,061 illicit distilleries have been seized, 7,339 persons have been arrested for illicit distilling, 26 officers and employés have been killed and 57 wounded, in the enforcement of the internal-revenue laws. During the past sixteen months 1,120 stills have been seized, 1,265 persons arrested, and 10 officers wounded in the enforcement of the laws. While the number of stills seized and persons arrested since my last annual report is very large, I am satisfied that there will be a decrease henceforward in the number of such seizures and arrests.

In January of the present year a combined movement was made, by armed bodies of internal-revenue officers, from West Virginia southward through the mountains and foothills infested by illicit distillers, which resulted in the seizure of a number of illicit distilleries, and the arrest of many persons engaged therein. The effect of this movement was to convince violators of the law that it was the determination of the government to put an end to frauds and resistance to authority, and since that time it has been manifest to all well-meaning men in those regions of country that the day of the illicit distiller is past. Public sentiment has been gradually setting in against these frauds, and I feel assured that if continued efforts are made for the enforcement of the laws the taxes upon whisky and tobacco can soon be collected in the districts where frauds have been so rife without the use of armed posses of men.

For the purpose of preventing old offenders from resuming the business of illicit distilling, I have deemed it advisable to maintain a special force of deputies in many of the districts to police the districts and seize illicit distilleries. These officers are armed and move in small posses so as to deter resistance. They are instructed to establish friendly relations with the people and to encourage the observance of the laws. This system has worked satisfactorily and beneficially, and except in the second district of Georgia there has been very little disturbance during the past few months.

ENCOURAGEMENT OF LEGAL DISTILLERIES.

It has been the policy of this office to encourage the establishment of legal distilleries in those collection districts where illicit distillation has heretofore prevailed, and there are now 469 licensed grain distilleries in those districts against 380 in 1879, and 177 in 1878. I have felt that if the manufacture of whisky was to be carried on at all in this section of country it was much better that it should be done openly and in full compliance with the requirements of law rather than secretly in violation and defiance of law, and with the demoralizing influences of dishonesty, turbulence, outlawry, and murder, which invariably prevail in a community where illicit distilling is carried on unchecked. The policy thus adopted has worked well. In every county where legal distilleries have been established in any number, illicit distilling has almost entirely ceased, violent resistance to law has become almost unknown, and there has been a large increase of revenue.

It must be understood that many of the legal distilleries thus established have no greater capacity than ten gallons per day, and that it is necessary for the protection of the rights of the government to have a storekeeper and gauger assigned to each distillery. It is thus obvious that the expense of collecting the taxes upon the spirits so made is very heavy, and necessarily increases the estimates for this year for the pay of storekeepers and gaugers. It is, however, unquestionable that it is far preferable to incur this expenditure to secure the collection of the revenue and an orderly observance of the laws than to spend large sums of money in the employment of raiding parties for the seizure of illicit distilleries and the arrest of illicit distillers. So long as the government looks to the tax upon distilled spirits for a large proportion of its revenues, it is just and right that every producer of distilled spirits shall be held to the payment of his legal tax, and such appropriations should be made as will enable the executive branch of the government to enforce the tax law so as to collect the revenues justly from all alike.

I have the honor to earnestly recommend that the appropriation asked for for this service be granted.

PROTECTION OF REVENUE OFFICERS.

I again recommend additional legislation for the protection of the lives and persons of officers of the United States from the unlawful assaults of those who resist their authority, and refer to the remarks on this subject in my last annual report, page v.

FRAUDS IN THE MANUFACTURE OF VINEGAR.

I respectfully direct attention to House bill No. 6460, entitled "A bill to regulate the manufacture of vinegar by the alcoholic vaporizing process," now pending in Congress, and urgently request that the same be taken up and passed into law at the earliest practicable moment. I state without hesitation that the provisions of section 5 of the act of March 1, 1879, authorizing the use of a process for the vaporizing of alcohol in the manufacture of vinegar, has opened the door to frauds upon the revenue which cannot be guarded against successfully under existing laws. While the great majority of manufacturers of vinegar by this process are, no doubt, following a legitimate and honest business, I am convinced that there are many who have engaged in the business for the express purpose of defrauding the government out of its tax upon distilled spirits. As was shown before the Committee on Ways and Means of the House of Representatives, at its last session, it is easy for a manufacturer of vinegar by this process to produce low-wines of 50 or 60 per cent. strength. As there are no storekeepers or other government officers connected with these establishments, it is obvious that these low-wines may be removed and sold as distilled spirits without the payment of the tax if the vinegar manufacturer sees fit to do so. The law authorizing the vaporizing of alcohol by vinegar manufacturers should either be repealed, or else a government storekeeper should be stationed at each vinegar factory using this process, the expense of such storekeeper to be borne by the manufacturer.

EMPLOYÉS ON THE STAMP ROLL.

Sections 321, 3238, 3312, 3328, 3330, 3341, 3369, 3395, 3445, and 3446 of the United States Revised Statutes charge the Commissioner of Internal Revenue with the duty of procuring and issuing appropriate stamps for all internal-revenue taxes imposed by law. Most of these stamps are now being produced by the Bureau of Engraving and Printing. They are delivered to the Commissioner of Internal Revenue, and are by him issued to collectors of internal revenue, and sold to tax-payers.

The work of issuing all stamps, except stamps on bank checks and tin-foil tobacco wrappers, directly from the Internal Revenue Bureau, was commenced in September, 1877, since which time nearly $334,000,000 worth of stamps have been sent out. The accounting officers of the Treasury Department charge to the Commissioner the stamps delivered to him by the Bureau of Engraving and Printing, and credit him with all stamps properly issued and sold. The honorable First Comptroller, who passes upon these accounts, has expressed to the Commissioner the opinion that he (the Commissioner) is personally liable to the government for the safe-keeping and proper issue of these stamps.

When it became necessary to employ a force to perform the work of receiving and issuing these stamps the question arose as to who should exercise that power, the law making the appropriation for dies, paper, and stamps requiring that the sum appropriated should be expended " under the direction of the Secretary of the Treasury." Upon consultation between the Secretary of the Treasury and the Commissioner of Internal Revenue it was then decided that the Commissioner was the proper officer to employ that force. The number of persons to be employed and the salaries to be paid them were fixed by the direction and with the approval of the honorable Secretary. The Commissioner then proceeded to employ the necessary force, and from month to month the pay-rolls for the persons so employed were passed by the accounting officers and paid without question.

On the 28th of June last, the following letter was received:

TREASURY DEPARTMENT, OFFICE OF THE SECRETARY,
Washington, D. C., June 28, 1880.

SIR: I am in receipt of the letters of the acting Commissioner of the 24th and 26th instant, informing me of the employment of a messenger in your office, and of certain persons to be employed at East Pepperell, Mass., all to be paid from the appropriation for dies, paper, and stamps.

The legislative bill approved the 15th instant, provides that the appropriation for that purpose for the next fiscal year shall be expended under the direction of the Secretary of the Treasury. You will, therefore, please transmit to this office any recommendations which you may have for the employment of the persons named in the two above-mentioned letters, or for the employment of any other persons paid out of the above appropriations, and will notify them that their services will not be required on and after the first proximo, unless previously authorized by the Secretary.

Very respectfully,

JOHN SHERMAN, *Secretary.*

Hon. GREEN B. RAUM,
Commissioner of Internal Revenue.

Under the instructions of this letter the persons employed upon the stamp-roll by authority of the Commissioner were discharged, and a majority of them were subsequently re-employed by direction of the Secretary of the Treasury. The effect of this letter was to divest the Commissioner of an authority which had been exercised by him for nearly three years under the sanction of the Secretary.

The principle seems to me well established that no officer shall be held pecuniarily responsible for the neglect or dishonesty of an employé in whose appointment he has no voice, and I respectfully submit that the sections of law above referred to impose such duties and confer such powers upon the Commissioner of Internal Revenue, taken in connection with his pecuniary responsibility for the custody of these stamps, as should carry with them authority to select and employ the persons engaged in the work of receiving, counting, caring for, and issuing said stamps. In coming to this conclusion I have duly considered the constitutional provision which authorizes Congress to empower the heads of departments to appoint inferior officers, and that section of the act above alluded to appropriating money for dies, paper, and stamps, which provides that the same " shall be expended under the direction of the Secretary of the Treasury." The persons employed upon this work are not " officers "; they are clerks, book keepers, counters, and messengers. And the statutory provision is, in my opinion, fully met by the Secretary directing the number of persons to be employed and fixing their pay, thus controlling the expenditure of the appropriation. Under the changed system persons who were regarded by the Commissioner as competent and experienced in their work and were satisfactory to him have been removed, and others without experience and unknown to the Commissioner have been substituted.

With the utmost respect to the honorable Secretary I will say that in my opinion this action is erroneous in principle and in law, and in my judgment should be revoked. The Commissioner of Internal Revenue should not be chargeable with the shortcomings of persons employed in the business of handling $150,000,000 worth of stamps per annum without having the selection of such persons, and I respectfully recommend that if upon a further consideration of this question the honorable Secretary entertains a doubt as to the correctness of the positions above stated, legislation should be asked for to place the authority of selection and employment in the hands of the officer on whom rests the pecuniary responsibility for the conduct of the persons employed.

APPOINTMENT OF STOREKEEPERS, GAUGERS, AND TOBACCO INSPECTORS.

For about twelve years preceding June 30 last, under a plan adopted by Hon. Hugh McCulloch, Secretary of the Treasury, the correspondence with collectors of internal revenue and others in respect to the appointment and removal of storekeepers, gaugers, and tobacco inspectors was conducted by the Commissioner of Internal Revenue, and the appointments were made on his recommendation. This system was changed by the following circular:

TREASURY DEPARTMENT,
OFFICE OF THE SECRETARY,
Washington, D. C., June 30, 1880.

To Collectors of Internal Revenue and others :

On and after July 1, 1880, any application for appointment to the office of gauger storekeeper, storekeeper and gauger, or inspector of tobacco in the internal-revenue service will be made to the Secretary of the Treasury, and in each case will be in the handwriting of the applicant, and signed by him, stating his age, legal residence, where born, and service in the Army or Navy, if any. The application must be accompanied by testimonials as to character for sobriety, industry, and business habits.

Collectors of internal revenue will report to the Secretary of the Treasury whenever the necessities of the service require new appointments or removals of incumbents, giving the reasons therefor, and forwarding to this office the papers in each case.

Removals from office of any of the above-named officers will hereafter be made only by the Secretary of the Treasury.

JOHN SHERMAN,
Secretary.

The correspondence in respect to these appointments and removals is now carried on by the Secretary of the Treasury through the Appointment Division of his office. Having observed the workings of the new system since its inauguration, I deem it my duty in the interest of the public service, to point out the reasons why, in my judgment, this work can be better done by the Commissioner of Internal Revenue.

By existing laws all the officers enumerated in this circular perform their duties under the general instruction of the Commissioner of Internal Revenue, to whom they make return of work done upon forms prescribed by him. In the case of storekeepers, they are assigned to duty by the Commissioner, and in the case of gaugers, their accounts are audited by him. Revenue agents, under the instructions of the Commissioner, constantly supervise the work of these officers and report upon the same, and periodically inspect them and report as to their capacity and fidelity to duty. No new distillery can be started without the approval of the Commissioner of Internal Revenue, and reports of the closing of distilleries are promptly made to him ; a record is kept in his office of the assignment of all storekeepers and gaugers. There are in the Internal Revenue Bureau persons who are experts in the work of gaugers and storekeepers, and who are able to and do criticise their work so as to keep the Commissioner advised upon these matters. This condition of things enables the Commissioner of Internal Revenue to decide when it is proper to appoint new officers in a district, and also when an officer in consequence of neglect of duty or incapacity should be removed. These means of information are not in the Secretary's office.

It may be proper to say that the appointment clerk and his assistants frequently obtain verbal information from this office in regard to matters connected with the appointment and removal of officers of this class. This, however, is always in an informal way, no record being made of the matter on either hand.

I have not questioned and do not question the right of the Secretary to obtain information from such sources as he may deem proper upon which to make these appointments and removals, but it occurs to me that the officer who by law has charge of the general superintendence of the collection of the revenues and who has so much to do with the officers in question should be consulted as to the necessity of making appointments and the propriety of making removals.

The plan adopted by the foregoing circular was tried for a short time by Secretary McCulloch, with this exception, that he expressly invited the aid of the Commissioner in regard to removing incompetent persons from office, but the system was not found to work well and was abandoned.

I claim that the storekeepers and gaugers have during the past four years steadily improved in their knowledge of law and regulations, in diligence and fidelity in the performance of their duties, and in their pride in the service. This corps of officers for efficiency and discipline is

5 F

not excelled by any branch of the civil service, and this state of things is the outgrowth for the most part of the measures set on foot at this office for the improvement of the service. The same system of examination and inspection adopted for collectors' offices, with a similar grading according to a scale of merit, has been applied in the case of storekeepers and gaugers, and the result has been a laudable ambition on their part to excel in intelligence and efficiency in the discharge of their duties. It is obvious that the effect of this system will be lost, and that officers will be made indifferent to or independent of criticism or commendation by this office when it is understood that only on the recommendation of a collector will a removal be made.

In my judgment it would be wise for the honorable Secretary of the Treasury to reconsider this subject with a view to a modification of his present order.

IMPROVEMENTS IN THE PUBLIC SERVICE.

In administering the Internal Revenue Office during the past four years I have directed my efforts—

1st. To popularizing the internal revenue system of taxation, so that tax-payers everywhere would cheerfully observe the laws, and a healthy public sentiment would be aroused favorable to their enforcement.

2d. To break up frauds of every kind, especially the illicit manufacture and sale of spirits and tobacco, and thoroughly establish and maintain the supremacy of the laws of the United States.

3d. To correct abuses of administration, especially the institution of suits and prosecutions for trivial and technical violations of law.

4th. To bring into the public service honest, capable, and efficient men, to increase them in the knowledge of their duty as prescribed by law and regulations, and to stimulate a just spirit of emulation amongst officers in the performance of duty.

5th. To establish a more perfect and uniform system for the transaction of the public business by collectors in their offices and by their deputies in their divisions, and to insure strict accountability for the public funds.

6th. To secure a prompt and careful transaction of the public business in the Bureau of Internal Revenue, and so to dispose of such business as had accumulated during past years that the labor of the office might be directed to current work.

Some of the leading improvements in the public service which have been effected are hereinafter recapitulated.

RELATIVES IN OFFICE.

Upon an examination of the *personnel* of the internal revenue service, I deemed it advisable to issue to each collector the following circular, known as Circular Letter 44, which was approved by Hon. R. C. McCormick, Acting Secretary:

TREASURY DEPARTMENT,
OFFICE OF INTERNAL REVENUE.
Washington, August 17, 1877.

The reports of collectors, in reply to Circular No. 42, dated June 19, 1877, disclose the fact that in a number of districts the officers and employés appointed by collectors or upon their recommendation, are, to a large extent, related by blood or marriage to such collectors; or, if not so related, are related to each other, so that, in fact, the selection of officers and employés in many instances is confined to a few families, upon whom alone fall the responsibilities and emoluments of office.

I regard this condition of affairs as an abuse in administration, the continuance of which is incompatible with the best interests of the public service, as greatly tending to a lax discipline, and to the condonation of irregularities.

For the purpose of rectifying this condition of things, collectors will observe the following rules in respect to the officers and employés of their respective districts:

First. Of persons related to a collector by blood or marriage, but one shall be retained in office.

Second. Of persons not related to a collector, but related to each other by blood or marriage, but one shall be retained in office.

Collectors will make the necessary recommendations for the appointment of gaugers, storekeepers, and storekeepers and gaugers, and change their force of deputies and clerks so as to have their respective forces conform to the foregoing rules.

All changes under this circular will take effect on or before the 1st day of October, 1877.

GREEN B. RAUM,
Commissioner.

The principle of this circular has, I think, received the approbation of the public, and its enforcement has been beneficial to the service.

EX PARTE DEPOSITIONS.

In my annual report for the year 1876, I recommended the passage of a law in regard to the taking of depositions for use in internal-revenue cases. No such act having been passed by Congress, and believing that the system which had long prevailed of deciding cases upon *ex parte* evidence should be changed, I issued the following circular:

TREASURY DEPARTMENT,
OFFICE OF INTERNAL REVENUE,
Washington, D. C., October 30, 1877.

In all claims for abatement, refunding, drawback, or reward for information, all applications for compromise, all contested questions as to claims of the government for taxes not assessed, and generally in all matters wherein additional testimony is required to be taken, no *ex parte* affidavit or deposition will be considered unless the same shall have been taken after due notice to the Commissioner as herein prescribed.

Such notice must state the time and place at which, and the officer before whom, the testimony will be taken; the name, age, residence, and business of the proposed witness, with the questions to be propounded to the witness, or a brief statement of the substance of the testimony he is expected to give.

The notice shall be delivered or mailed to the Commissioner a sufficient number of days previous to the day fixed for taking the testimony, to allow him, after its receipt, at least five days, exclusive of the period required for mail-communication with the place at which the testimony is to be taken, in which to give, should he so desire, instructions as to the cross-examination of the proposed witness.

Whenever practicable the affidavit or deposition should be taken before a collector or deputy collector of internal revenue, in which case reasonable notice should be given to the collector or deputy collector of the time fixed for taking the deposition or affidavit.

It will be observed that these regulations relate to affidavits and depositions *additional* to those presented with the claim or matter in question as now provided for under existing regulations.

The foregoing regulations are not intended to preclude the examination of witnesses before the Commissioner; and he also reserves to himself the right to receive and consider affidavits as to which previous notice has not been given where the reason for failure to give such notice shall appear to him to be sufficient, and also in other cases in which, from their exceptional character, or the character of the affidavit, he shall be satisfied that the rule should not be enforced.

These regulations shall apply to all matters of the character first above mentioned pending in this office on and after the first day of December next.

GREEN B. RAUM,
Commissioner.

Approved:
    R. C. McCORMICK,
      Acting Secretary.

The enforcement of this circular has rendered the evidence upon which action is had in internal-revenue cases very much more definite and satisfactory than was practicable under the system previously prevailing.

PROSECUTIONS FOR TECHNICAL VIOLATIONS OF LAW.

For the purpose of preventing the institution of suits and prosecutions for technical and trivial causes, I addressed to collectors of internal revenue the following letter:

> TREASURY DEPARTMENT,
> OFFICE OF INTERNAL REVENUE,
> *Washington, April 25, 1878.*
>
> SIR: The number of cases for violations of the internal-revenue laws that are placed upon the dockets of the courts throughout the country is so great, and the expenditure for the trial of these cases is so large, and in many courts, in consequence of the great number of cases, the delay in bringing cases to trial is so great, that it becomes a matter of great importance that the officers of the government should observe the utmost degree of care in bringing cases into court in view of the facts above stated, as well as the rights of the citizens accused.
>
> You are therefore instructed, before reporting a case to the district attorney for prosecution, to examine into the same with the utmost degree of care, with a view of giving the district attorney such definite information in regard to the case as will enable him to determine the question of the propriety of instituting proceedings. It is not the wish of this office that trivial cases, or cases of a mere technical character, involving no loss to the government, and where no fraud has been committed or intended, should be dignified by being brought into court for prosecution.
>
> On the other hand, where persons have knowingly and willfully violated the law with the evident intention of defrauding the government of its revenues, vigorous measures should be taken to bring the parties to trial and punishment.
>
> Very respectfully,
>
> GREEN B. RAUM,
> *Commissioner.*

Collectors have, for the most part, been guided by the spirit of this letter, and the number of improper suits and prosecutions, instituted apparently for the creation of costs only, has been very greatly diminished. The principles of this letter have recently been embodied in instructions to district attorneys and United States marshals with the approval of the honorable Secretary.

EXAMINATION OF COLLECTORS' OFFICES.

In March, 1877, I adopted a plan of making quarterly examinations of the accounts of collectors with a view of establishing a more uniform system of transacting the public business, of requiring all the books and accounts to be properly written up to date, of securing rigid accountability for the public funds, and by these means of promoting the efficiency of the collectors and their subordinates. An official standard of a first-class office was established, as follows:

First. Where the officers are honest, capable, and faithful.

Second. Where the collector devotes his best energies to the proper organization and discipline of his clerical and division force, and uses every endeavor to collect all the taxes due the government.

Third. Where every subordinate manifests pride in his position, and ambition to excel in his line of duty.

Fourth. Where no errors or discrepancies are found in the cash or stamp account.

Fifth. Where all the entries are made before the close of each day's business, cash balanced, and books and packages of stamps sold from during the day verified.

Sixth. Where every possible effort is made to promptly dispose of each item on the lists.

Seventh. Where all bonds are properly executed, approved, recorded, and filed.

Eighth. Where the penalties are collected, compromise cases promptly reported, and money properly deposited.

Ninth. Where the office is furnished with a view to the preservation of public records, the facilitating of business, and in a manner suitable and becoming the purpose for which it is used.

Tenth. Where every record is completed to date, and is without erasures, blots, or any defacement.

Eleventh. Where the Internal-Revenue Record and the lists are bound, and letter-books and circulars indexed.

Twelfth. Where everything presents the appearance of a first-class business office.

Thirteenth. Where the deputies in charge of stamps are supplied with the proper records, their books, accounts, and stamps in perfect order, and *stamp* and *cash* account verified by the collector at least once each quarter.

The following requirement has recently been added :

Fourteenth. Where all required reports and returns are made to the office at Washington, and where there is no unnecessary delay in correspondence with that office.

An office in which all of these requirements are fulfilled is graded as No. 1. Failure to come up to the official standard in any one of these particulars results in the office being marked down at a lower grade. Experience has shown that these examinations have created a splendid *esprit de corps* in the service; and to-day, out of 126 collectors' offices, 119 are graded as first-class according to the official standard.

INSPECTION OF OFFICERS.

The system of inspecting officers established in 1877 was intended to more thoroughly create and diffuse a knowledge of internal-revenue laws and regulations amongst both officers and tax-payers, to establish a greater uniformity in the enforcement of the laws, and to place upon the files of this office the record of every officer connected with the service. It was believed that this system would prove an efficient school for the officers, and I am glad to say that my expectations have been more than realized.

The inspections of deputy collectors, taken in connection with their diary reports attached to their monthly accounts, give the collectors and this office an insight into the manner in which they perform their duties, and so with the storekeepers and gaugers the inspection reports taken in connection with their reports of work done enable the collectors and this office to form a proper estimate of the value of these officers to the service. The incompetent officer is soon discovered and the government is enabled to properly dispense with his services, while the diligent and faithful officer has a record in this office which can always be invoked in his behalf.

In connection with the reports of examinations and inspections the officers have been subjected to just criticism for shortcomings and have received commendation for diligence and efficiency.

An important part of the work of the internal-revenue service is the policing by deputy collectors of their respective divisions. To promote efficiency in this work the great majority of policing deputies have been relieved from the sale of stamps. A system has been introduced of making an annual allowance for traveling expenses to be accounted for by the deputy in his accounts. With the approval of the honorable First Comptroller deputy collectors have been required to render monthly pay accounts instead of quarterly, rendering with said accounts a diary report setting forth the work performed by them. These measures have secured a more thorough system of work on the part of division deputies.

GAUGING.

To secure greater efficiency and uniformity in the work of gaugers, competent experts have, from time to time, been detailed to visit the leading spirit-producing districts and inspect the gaugers and correct any errors of work into which they might have fallen. Gaugers have also been required in their reports of work done to give the length and mean diameter of each package gauged, so that their work and calculations can be easily verified. This, added to certain improvements which

have been made in the gauging instruments, has resulted in greatly increased accuracy in the work of gauging.

STOREKEEPERS.

The storekeepers have been greatly improved in diligence and efficiency by periodical inspections and by frequent visits from collectors
and revenue agents.

CONDITION OF THE OFFICE.

It is gratifying to be able to state that the work of this office is now
thoroughly in hand, and that the time of almost the entire force is exclusively devoted to the transaction of current business. The correspondence of the office receives prompt attention; accounts are adjusted
without delay and forwarded to the accounting officers for audit and
payment. The redemption of stamps and settlement of drawback claims
are part of the current business. Claims for the abatement and refunding of taxes and offers in compromise receive the consideration of the
office as soon as the proper proofs are filed. The books containing the
accounts with the Bureau of Engraving and Printing, with collectors,
and with tax-payers who purchase stamps directly from the office, are
kept written up to date and the account of stamps on hand is daily carefully verified and balanced. The work in connection with the establishment and operation of distilleries, breweries, and tobacco and cigar
manufactories is promptly and diligently performed.

For this satisfactory condition of the office, I desire to return my sin-
cere thanks to the officers, clerks, and employés for their diligence, fidelity, and zeal in the performance of duty.

AMOUNTS COLLECTED AND ACCOUNTED FOR BY COLLECTION DIS-
TRICTS.

Soon after the close of the fiscal year ended June 30, last, I caused
the customary annual examination to be made of the records and accounts of each collector of internal revenue throughout the United
States, for the purpose of ascertaining whether the public moneys collected had been duly accounted for. This examination disclosed the
gratifying fact that during the past fiscal year $123,981,916.10 of inter-
nal revenue taxes had been collected, and that every dollar had been
paid into the Treasury. During the past four fiscal years, $467,080,885 of
taxes have been received by collectors of internal revenue, and the entire sum has been paid into the Treasury. All deficiencies which have
occurred in the accounts of collectors during that period have been
made good by payments into the Treasury. Fidelity in accounting for
the public funds being one of the highest tests of the efficiency of officers intrusted with the collection of revenue and the disbursement of
public money, the officers of internal revenue, judged by this rule, are
entitled to a high rank in the public service; and I take pleasure in
bearing testimony to the fact that, as a body of officers, it will be difficult to improve upon them in respect to integrity, intelligence, fidelity,
and zeal in the performance of duty.

I append a statement of the collections made, by districts, during the
past fiscal year, with the name of each collector and the amount collected and paid into the Treasury by him.

Collection districts.	Names of collectors.	Aggregate collections.
First Alabama	Louis H. Mayer	$63, 250 41
Second Alabama	James T. Rapier	72, 633 97
Arizona	Thomas Cordis	26, 384 10
Arkansas	Edward Wheeler	126, 089 12
First California	William Higby	2, 437, 650 82
Fourth California	Amos L. Frost	345, 583 82
Colorado	James S. Wolfe	168, 259 54
First Connecticut	Joseph Selden	212, 856 32
Second Connecticut	David F. Hollister	248, 322 80
Dakota	John L. Pennington	41, 653 29
Delaware	James McIntire	304, 398 21
Florida	Dennis Eagan	204, 590 53
Second Georgia	Andrew Clarke	223, 543 92
Third Georgia	Edward C. Wade	98, 530 26
Idaho	Austin Savage	22, 665 54
First Illinois	Joel D. Harvey	8, 396, 614 85
Second Illinois	William R. Allen (late)	45, 260 58
Do	W. S. Beaupre (acting)	35, 293 96
Do	Lucien B. Crooker (present)	152, 606 39
Third Illinois	Adam Nase (late)	175, 920 91
Do	A. H. Hershey (acting)	41, 995 41
Do	Alfred M. Jones (present)	487, 448 96
Fourth Illinois	John Tillson	983, 112 88
Fifth Illinois	Howard Knowles	10, 394, 576 75
Seventh Illinois	John W. Hill	57, 203 47
Eighth Illinois	Jonathan Merriam	815, 000 92
Thirteenth Illinois	Jonathan C. Willis	980, 581 46
First Indiana	James C. Veatch	271, 781 89
Fourth Indiana	Will Cumback	3, 283, 992 01
Sixth Indiana	Frederick Bagge	377, 927 99
Seventh Indiana	Delos W. Minshall	1, 531, 283 31
Tenth Indiana	George Moon	162, 978 54
Eleventh Indiana	John F. Wildman	85, 973 86
Second Iowa	Sewall S. Farwell	303, 114 74
Third Iowa	James E. Simpson	287, 818 99
Fourth Iowa	John Connell	165, 050 34
Fifth Iowa	Lampson P. Sherman	118, 875 71
Kansas	John C. Carpenter	282, 734 01
Second Kentucky	William A. Stuart	620, 133 04
Fifth Kentucky	James F. Buckner	3, 563, 114 63
Sixth Kentucky	Winfield S. Holden	3, 298, 244 82
Seventh Kentucky	Armsted M. Swope	1, 013, 072 33
Eighth Kentucky	William J. Landram	236, 342 19
Ninth Kentucky	John E. Blaine	149, 687 89
Louisiana	Morris Marks	712, 049 65
Maine	Franklin J. Rollins	76, 767 87
Third Maryland	Robert M. Proud	2, 293, 283 80
Fourth Maryland	Daniel C. Bruce	130, 073 21
Third Massachusetts	Charles W. Slack	1, 398, 963 60
Fifth Massachusetts	Charles C. Dame	850, 147 57
Tenth Massachusetts	Edward R. Tinker	386, 521 93
First Michigan	Luther S. Trowbridge	1, 099, 764 17
Third Michigan	Harvey B. Rowlson	926, 719 99
Fourth Michigan	Simean S. Bailey	131, 769 28
Sixth Michigan	Charles V. De Land	153, 505 15
First Minnesota	Andrew C. Smith	107, 369 53
Second Minnesota	William Bickel	257, 390 11
Mississippi	James Hill	91, 233 50
First Missouri	Isaac H. Sturgeon	4, 680, 205 14
Second Missouri	Alonzo B. Carroll	61, 635 57
Fourth Missouri	Arthur C. Stewart (late)	390, 484 63
Do	Rynd E. Lauder (present)	72, 511 95
Fifth Missouri	David H. Budlong	118, 826 94
Sixth Missouri	Robert T. Van Horn	255, 949 55
Montana	Thomas P. Fuller	38, 714 17
Nebraska	Lorenzo Crounse	912, 734 86
Nevada	Frederick C. Lord	60, 455 19
New Hampshire	Andrew H. Young	278, 139 08
First New Jersey	William P. Tatem	314, 590 06
Third New Jersey	Culver Barcalow	260, 338 62
Fifth New Jersey	Robert B. Hathorn	3, 726, 969 19
New Mexico	Gustavus A. Smith	31, 850 93
First New York	James Freeland (late)	784, 940 00
Do	Silas J. Boone (acting)	847, 806 19
Do	Rodney C. Ward (present)	1, 631, 606 17
Second New York	Marshall B. Blake	3, 199, 960 87
Third New York	Max Weber	5, 064, 296 32
Eleventh New York	Moses D. Stivers	182, 026 24
Twelfth New York	Jason M. Johnson	519, 719 96
Fourteenth New York	Ralph T. Lathrop	571, 102 97
Fifteenth New York	Thomas Stevenson	289, 023 63
Twenty-first New York	James C. P. Kincaid	309, 412 51
Twenty-fourth New York	John B. Strong	472, 403 27
Twenty-sixth New York	Benjamin De Voe	273, 483 82

Collection districts.	Names of collectors.	Aggregate collections.
Twenty-eighth New York	Burt Van Horn	$946, 711 55
Thirtieth New York	Frederick Buell	1, 287, 401 54
Second North Carolina	Thomas Powers (late)	3, 705 87
Do	Elihu A. White (present)	54, 989 85
Fourth North Carolina	Isaac J. Young	925, 483 18
Fifth North Carolina	William H. Wheeler	911, 998 83
Sixth North Carolina	John J. Mott	457, 918 98
First Ohio	Amor Smith, jr	11, 556, 640 75
Third Ohio	Robert Williams, jr	1, 255, 043 19
Fourth Ohio	Robert P. Kennedy	512, 184 48
Sixth Ohio	James Pursell	633, 678 60
Seventh Ohio	Charles C. Walcutt	475, 976 33
Tenth Ohio	Clark Waggoner	1, 092, 852 40
Eleventh Ohio	Benjamin F. Coates	1, 425, 831 06
Fifteenth Ohio	Jewett Palmer	210, 324 75
Eighteenth Ohio	Charles B. Pettengill (late)	483, 327 97
Do	Worthy S. Streator (present)	233, 479 46
Oregon	John C. Cartwright	76, 981 70
First Pennsylvania	James Ashworth	2, 523, 444 87
Eighth Pennsylvania	Joseph T. Valentine	553, 173 93
Ninth Pennsylvania	Thomas A. Wiley	1, 664, 642 47
Twelfth Pennsylvania	Edward H. Chase	326, 321 92
Fourteenth Pennsylvania	Charles J. Bruner	190, 145 19
Sixteenth Pennsylvania	Edward Scull	191, 065 09
Nineteenth Pennsylvania	Charles M. Lynch	115, 337 59
Twentieth Pennsylvania	James C. Brown	86, 989 28
Twenty-second Pennsylvania	Thomas W. Davis	1, 184, 418 98
Twenty-third Pennsylvania	John M. Sullivan	692, 361 33
Rhode Island	Elisha H. Rhodes	230, 383 98
South Carolina	Ellery M. Brayton	111, 960 78
Second Tennessee	Joseph A. Cooper (late)	1, 788 72
Do	James M. Melton (present)	86, 309 99
Fifth Tennessee	William M. Woodcock	805, 308 60
Eighth Tennessee	Robert F. Patterson	110, 328 55
First Texas	William H. Sinclair	99, 255 52
Third Texas	Benjamin C. Ludlow	72, 722 29
Fourth Texas	Adam G. Malloy	61, 124 74
Utah	Ovando J. Hollister	74, 352 48
Vermont	Charles S. Dana	50, 545 74
Second Virginia	James D. Brady	866, 292 51
Third Virginia	Otis H. Russell	2, 054, 557 71
Fourth Virginia	William L. Fernald	1, 002, 952 34
Fifth Virginia	J. Henry Rives	1, 602, 624 13
Sixth Virginia	Beverly B. Botts	234, 962 89
Washington	James R. Hayden	27, 013 34
First West Virginia	Isaac H. Duval	308, 824 72
Second West Virginia	George W. Brown	51, 847 43
First Wisconsin	Irving M. Bean	2, 214, 102 88
Second Wisconsin	Henry Harnden	155, 605 99
Third Wisconsin	Albert K. Osborn (late)	23, 421 16
Do	Howard M. Kutchin (acting)	181, 194 80
Do	Charles A. Galloway (present)	8, 108 53
Sixth Wisconsin	Hiram R. Kelley	116, 083 43
Wyoming	Edgar P. Snow	15, 947 95
Total from collectors		116, 848, 219 80
Cash receipts from sale of adhesive stamps		7, 133, 696 30
Total receipts from all sources		123, 981, 916 10

COST OF COLLECTION.

The total cost of collecting internal revenue in the United States for he fiscal year ended June 30, 1880, was as follows:

'or salaries and expenses of collectors, including pay of deputy collectors, clerks, &c	$1,798,954 61
For salaries and expenses of revenue agents, surveyors of distilleries, gaugers, storekeepers, and miscellaneous expenses	1,955,000 00
'or stamps, paper, and dies	423,558 15
'or expenses of detecting and punishing violations of internal revenue laws	74,797 97
'or salaries of officers, clerks, and employés in the office of Commissioner of Internal Revenue	253,330 00
Total	4,505,640 73

Being 3.63 per cent. of the total amount collected.

ESTIMATED EXPENSES FOR NEXT FISCAL YEAR.

I estimate the expenses of the Internal Revenue Service for the fiscal 'ear ending June 30, 1882, as follows:

'or salaries and expenses of collectors	$2,000,000
'or salaries and expenses of thirty-five revenue agents, for surveyors, for fees and expenses of gaugers, for salaries of storekeepers, and for miscellaneous expenses	2,100,000
'or dies, paper, and stamps	442,000
'or detecting and bringing to trial and punishment persons guilty of violating the internal revenue laws, including payment for information and detection	100,000
'or salaries of officers, clerks, and employés in the office of the Commissioner of Internal Revenue	253,330
Total	4,895,330

SCALE OF SALARIES OF COLLECTORS.

The recommendations made for the salaries of collectors for the fiscal 'ear ending June 30, 1881, are based upon an estimate of their probable ollections according to the following scale, with the qualification that f the actual collections should vary from the amounts estimated, the ialaries would be readjusted at the end of the fiscal year:

For collection of—		
$25,000 or less		$2,000
25,000 to	$37,500—$12,500	2,125
37,500 to	50,000— 12,500	2,250
50,000 to	75,000— 25,000	2,375
75,000 to	100,000— 25,000	2,500
100,000 to	125,000— 25,000	2,625
125,000 to	175,000— 50,000	2,750
175,000 to	225,000— 50,000	2,875
225,000 to	275,000— 50,000	3,000
275,000 to	325,000— 50,000	3,125
325,000 to	375,000— 50,000	3,350
375,000 to	425,000— 50,000	3,375
425,000 to	475,000— 50,000	3,500
475,000 to	550,000— 75,000	3,625
550,000 to	625,000— 75,000	3,750
625,000 to	700,000— 75,000	3,875
700,000 to	775,000— 75,000	4,000

* This includes an estimated deficiency of $135,000, being the expenses in excess of the imount appropriated.

$775,000 to $850,000—$75,000..$4,125
850,000 to 925,000— 75,000.. 4,250
925,000 to 1,000,000— 75,000.. 4,375
1,000,000 and upward.. 4,500

OFFICIAL FORCE FOR FISCAL YEAR 1881.

The force connected with this bureau in the various districts throughout the United States is as follows :

One hundred and twenty-six collectors, who receive salaries as follows :

Twenty-nine	$4,500	Four	$3,125
Two	4,375	Seventeen	3,000
Five	4,250	Eight	2,875
Five	4,125	Nine	2,750
Two	4,000	Eight	2,625
One	3,875	Eleven	2,500
Three	3,750	Four	2,375
Two	3,625	Five	2,250
Four	3,500	One	2,125
Two	3,375	Two	2,000
Two	3,250		

There are also employed nine hundred and forty-nine deputy collectors, who receive salaries as follows :

One	$2,100	One	$1,025
Fourteen	2,000	Thirty	1,000
One	1,950	Six	950
Nine	1,900	Thirty-six	900
One	1,850	Two	850
Twenty-seven	1,800	Eight	800
Five	1,750	Two	775
Twenty-six	1,700	Two	750
Eight	1,650	Three	720
Fifty-four	1,600	Eight	700
Ten	1,550	Two	650
Eighty-six	1,500	One	640
Sixteen	1,450	Fifteen	600
One	1,425	Two	550
Two hundred and fifty-seven	1,400	Four	500
Twenty-six	1,350	One	475
One	1,325	One	450
Forty-nine	1,300	Three	400
Seventeen	1,250	Twenty	300
One	1,225	Five	250
Ninety-three	1,200	One	240
One	1,175	Thirteen	200
Twenty-one	1,150	Two	150
Thirty-eight	1,100	One	120
Four	1,075	One	100
Ten	1,050	Two	60

Also one hundred and seventy-nine clerks, messengers, and janitors, who receive salaries as follows :

One clerk	$1,600	Fourteen	$600
Eight clerks	1,500	One	550
Seven clerks	1,400	Five	500
Two clerks	1,350	One	480
Four clerks	1,300	Two	400
Twenty-six clerks	1,200	Two	300
Five clerks	1,150	One messenger	450
Sixteen clerks	1,100	Two messengers	300
Seventeen clerks	1,000	Four janitors	300
Twenty-seven clerks	900	One janitor	125
Eighteen clerks	800	Four janitors	100
Two clerks	720	One janitor	75
Five clerks	700	One janitor	52
Two clerks	670		

There are also employed 648 gaugers, who receive fees not to exceed $5 per diem ; 945 storekeepers and gaugers, who receive not to exceed $4 per diem ; 543 storekeepers, who receive not to exceed $4 per diem (all of the foregoing officers are paid only when actually employed); and 56 tobacco inspectors, who receive fees to be paid by the manufacturers.

SALARIES.

I have the honor to recommend that Congress appropriate, for the fiscal year ending June 30, 1882, the sum of $254,880, as salaries for the following officers, clerks, and employés in this bureau :

One Commissioner, at	$6,000
One deputy commissioner, at	3,500
Seven heads of division, at	2,500
One stenographer, at	1,800
Twenty-three clerks, class four, at	1,800
Twenty-six clerks, class three, at	1,600
Thirty-six clerks, class two, at	1,400
Twenty-one clerks, class one, at	1,200
Thirteen clerks, at	1,000
Fifty clerks, at	900
Four assistant messengers, at	720
Ten laborers, at	660

An aggregate of one hundred and ninety-three persons.

An increase in the salary of the deputy commissioner, and of the five heads of division, is recommended for the following reasons:

The law creating the office of deputy commissioner fixed his salary at $3,500. The duties of the office are of great importance, and their faithful performance fully entitles the officer to that pay.

The law, creating the office of head of division states that there shall be seven heads of division, who shall receive each a salary of $2,500. The appropriations for the years ending June 30, 1878, June 30, 1879, June 30, 1880, and June 30, 1881, allowed two heads of division at a salary of $2,500 each, and five heads of division at a salary of $2,250 each. There is no just ground for this discrimination; the officers fully earn $2,500 each, and, in my judgment, should receive that amount.

An increase of $1,550 over the appropriation for the present year will give the above-named officers the salaries to which they are entitled under the law.

REPORT OF WORK PERFORMED DURING THE FISCAL YEAR ENDED JUNE 30, 1880.

Division of Law.

Offers in compromise received and briefed	1,097
Opinions prepared	1,062
Offers in compromise acted upon	1,121
Reward claims received and acted upon	494
Railroad cases adjusted	20
Orders for abatement of taxes issued	617
Claims for abatement of taxes disposed of	4,498
Amount of abatement claims allowed (uncollectible)	$194,923 38
Amount of abatement claims allowed (erroneous assessment)	$227,169 00
Amount of abatement claims rejected (uncollectible)	$40,220 08
Amount of abatement claims rejected (assessment claimed to be erronous).	$538,599 81
Claims for refunding of taxes disposed of	620
Amount of refunding claims allowed	$64,246 61
Amount of refunding claims rejected	$141,673 29

Division of Distilled Spirits.

Returns and reports relating to distilled spirits received, examined, and disposed of... 205,665

Returns and reports relating to fermented liquors received, examined, and disposed of... 34,080

Computations of capacities of distilleries made, and data for assessment furnished... 14,498

Locks examined and issued.. 3,926

Hydrometer sets, stems, cups, and thermometers tested and issued...... 2,589

Gauging-rods examined and issued.. 259

Wantage-rods examined and issued.. 822

Division of Tobacco.

Reports relating to tobacco received, examined, and disposed of..... 4,575

Reports relating to cigars received, examined, and disposed of...... 24,519

Abatement and refunding claims audited................................... 332

Division of Stamps.

Value of stamps received and counted............................... $132,479,680 00

Value of stamps counted and transmitted to the Secretary of the Treasury for destruction.. $1,073,839 16

Number of stubs examined.. 10,881,630

Number of stamps and coupons received for credit and counted..... 46,264,775

Number of reports received, examined, and disposed of............. 167,185

Division of Assessments.

Reports relating to assessments received, examined, and disposed of. 51,172

Reports relating to bonded accounts received, examined, and disposed of... 314,986

Reports and vouchers covering exportations received, examined, and disposed of... 445,714

Claims for drawback disposed of.. 873

Division of Accounts.

Weekly reports received, examined, and disposed of 5,171

Monthly reports received, examined, and disposed of 21,641

Quarterly reports received, examined, and disposed of 533

Certificates of deposit received and recorded 33,115

Final accounts of collectors referred for settlement............... 32

Drafts mailed to collectors for expenses of office 1,575

Drafts mailed to collectors for gaugers' fees and expenses 6,028

Drafts mailed to collectors, transfer of special deposits 361

Collectors' monthly reports of taxes, &c., consolidated into yearly statements... 1,626

Division of Revenue Agents.

Reports of revenue agents received and disposed of................. 2,278

Reports of collectors relative to illicit distilleries received and disposed of... 364

Accounts of revenue agents received and examined.................. 843

Miscellaneous expense accounts received and examined.............. 301

Railroad and income cases examined and reported on................ 38

Transcripts of books of leaf-tobacco dealers examined and abstracted. 2,514

Division of Appointments, Records, and Files.

Commissions of storekeepers, storekeepers and gaugers, gaugers and tobacco inspectors prepared and bonds examined................... 62

Collectors' bonds recorded.. 2

Reports of inspecting officers as to condition of collection districts received, examined, and acted upon.................................. 10

Reports of examining officers as to condition of collectors' offices received, examined, and acted upon.................................. 3

Pages of letters recorded 23,566
Press copies of letters briefed, registered, and arranged for reference.. 58,086
Pages of miscellaneous copying...... 16,476
Letters for the entire bureau received and registered 45,806
Letters indorsed, briefed, and filed................................. 42,686
Aggregate number of letters mailed by the bureau 65,576
Blank forms prepared and issued 6,824,133
Blank books prepared and issued ....: 12,019

MANUFACTURE OF PAPER.

During the fiscal year, all paper for internal-revenue stamps has been made by Messrs. S. D. Warren & Co., of Boston, under the contract entered into with said firm, which was referred to in my last annual report, and a new contract was made with them May 24, 1880. The prices paid under the new contract are for vegetable-sized paper, $11\frac{1}{2}$ cents per pound, and for animal-sized paper, $12\frac{1}{2}$ cents per pound, as against $9\frac{3}{4}$ cents and $10\frac{3}{4}$ cents paid under the previous contract. The paper furnished has been satisfactory as to quality, and all orders have been promptly executed.

PRODUCTION OF STAMPS.

Since the close of the fiscal year, viz, on the 15th October, the work of printing documentary and proprietary stamps, which had been done by the American Bank Note Company of New York City, was transferred to the Bureau of Engraving and Printing. At this time all internal-revenue stamps are produced by said bureau except stamps imprinted upon bank-checks, which are supplied by the Graphic Company of New York City, and stamps upon foil wrappers for tobacco, which are printed by John J. Crooke & Co., of New York, both under the superintendence of this office.

NUMBER AND VALUE OF STAMPS ISSUED.

During the fiscal year stamps were received by the stamp division of this office from the printers named, and issued to collectors, agents, and purchasers, as follows, viz:

Kind.	Number.	Value.
Stamps for distilled spirits..	5,107,550	$62,733,675 00
Stamps for tobacco and snuff..	219,862,792	26,410,511 52
Stamps for cigars and cigarettes......................................	61,743,548	15,136,078 25
Stamps for fermented liquors and brewers' permits	44,896,240	13,172,936 00
Stamps for special taxes	716,620	9,715,300 00
Stamps for documents and proprietary articles........................	579,275,864	7,780,360 40
Total	911,602,614	134,942,860 17

The stamps delivered to this office by the Bureau of Engraving and Printing were, on their receipt, counted, and their issue involved the preparation of 18,547 packages, all of which were transmitted to collectors of internal revenue by registered mail. This business was conducted without the loss of a stamp, either while in the hands of the printers, in the custody of this office, or in the course of transmission. Thanks are due to the officers of the Washington City post-office for the promptness and fidelity manifested in the handling of this large amount of registered matter.

ABOLITION OF THE CHARGE OF TEN CENTS EACH FOR "OTHER THAN TAX-PAID SPIRIT-STAMPS."

By act of Congress approved May 28, 1880, the charge of 10 cents each for distillery-warehouse stamps, stamps for rectified spirits, wholesale liquor dealers' stamps, stamps for imported spirits, and warehousing and rewarehousing stamps for grape brandy was abolished. The change in account was made by inventorying the stamps in collectors' hands and giving them credit for the value of the same, and did not necessitate the return of the stamps or any alteration in the form or style of them.

Collectors have been allowed credit for the stamps in their hands when the act took effect, with one exception, and this account will probably be settled at an early date.

REDEMPTION OF STAMPS.

I renew the recommendation made in my last report that that portion of section 17 of the act of March 1, 1879, which prohibits the redemption of stamps unless the same are presented within three years after their purchase from the government or a government agent for the sale of stamps, be repealed.

STAMPS REDEEMED AND EXCHANGED.

Number of claims for redemption of stamps allowed	590
Amount of claims for redemption of stamps allowed	$32,361 67
Number of claims for exchange of stamps allowed	292
Amount of claims for exchange of stamps allowed	$30,988 29

MATCH STAMPS SOLD.

Amount of stamps sold to match manufacturers during the following fiscal years, commissions not deducted.

1876	$2,849,524
1877	2,982,275
1878	3,064,574
1879	3,357,251
1880	3,561,300

A limited number of general proprietary stamps has, no doubt, been purchased by match manufacturers, and are not included in the above statement. Nearly all the stamps sold to match manufacturers are sold on sixty days' credit, under the provisions of section 3425, United States Revised Statutes. There are now pending thirteen suits upon stamp-agents' and match manufacturers' bonds for the recovery of $117,413.01 due on the sale of stamps during the past five years.

REVENUE AGENTS.

During the fiscal year ended June 30, 1880, thirty-five revenue agents were employed, and this force has been brought to the discharge of its duties a high order of intelligence, experience, and zeal.

Aggregate salary of agents	$82,411 00
Aggregate amount for traveling expenses	46,774 46
Stationery furnished agents	383 54
Total amount of expenses of revenue agents for fiscal year	129,569 00

Revenue agents have been employed as follows:

As chief of division in this office	
Assigned to divisions	
Employed in examining collectors' accounts	
Assistants to agents in charge of divisions	
Special duty	

WORK OF REVENUE AGENTS.

Number of persons arrested for violating internal-revenue laws on information of revenue agents.. 504
Violations of law reported... 1,901
Value of property reported for seizure by revenue agents.............. $194,593 76
Amount of uncollected taxes and penalties reported to collectors by revenue agents.. 95,109 28

STATISTICS OF OPERATIONS AGAINST ILLICIT DISTILLERS.

The following table shows the number of illicit stills seized, persons arrested, and casualties to officers and employés during the last fiscal year, and from July 1 to October 31 this year, inclusive:

Districts.	Stills seized.			Persons arrested.			Officers and employés killed and wounded.	
	During fiscal year.	Since June 30.	Total.	During fiscal year.	Since June 30.	Total.	Killed.	Wounded.
First Alabama..........................	1	....	1	2	....	2	....	....
Second Alabama........................	44	1	45	....	....	....	....	2
First California........................	2	....	2	3	....	3	....	....
First Connecticut......................	1	....	1	3	....	3	....	....
Dakota................................	1	....	1	3	....	3	....	....
Florida................................	1	....	1	....	....	....	....	....
Second Georgia........................	180	45	225	310	137	447	....	5
Third Georgia.........................	17	3	20	6	....	6	....	....
Thirteenth Illinois....................	3	....	3	3	....	3	....	....
First Indiana..........................	1	....	1	....	....	....	....	....
Second Iowa...........................	4	....	4	4	....	4	....	....
Third Iowa............................	1	....	1	2	....	2	....	....
Kansas................................	1	....	1	3	....	3	....	....
Second Kentucky.......................	32	9	41	15	5	20	....	....
Fifth Kentucky........................	14	9	23	23	....	23	....	....
Eighth Kentucky.......................	55	....	55	9	4	13	....	....
Ninth Kentucky........................	9	....	9	37	1	38	....	....
Louisiana..............................	9	....	9	3	....	3	....	....
Third Maryland........................	1	....	1	7	....	7	....	....
Fifth Massachusetts...................	1	....	1	2	....	2	....	....
Tenth Massachusetts...................	1	....	1	2	....	2	....	....
First Mississippi......................	1	....	1	1	....	1	....	....
Second Missouri.......................	3	....	3	9	....	9	....	....
Sixth Michigan........................	1	....	1	3	....	3	....	....
First New Jersey.......................	1	....	1	1	....	1	....	....
First New York........................	1	....	1	....	....	....	....	....
Third New York........................	2	....	2	4	....	4	....	....
Twelfth New York......................	1	1	2	....	....	....	....	....
Twenty-sixth New York.................	1	....	1	....	....	....	....	....
Second North Carolina.................	1	....	1	....	....	....	....	....
Fourth North Carolina.................	44	3	47	11	....	11	....	....
Fifth North Carolina..................	63	9	72	6	....	6	....	....
Sixth North Carolina..................	268	47	315	97	....	97	....	1
Tenth Ohio............................	1	....	1	2	....	2	....	....
Fifteenth Ohio.........................	1	....	1	1	....	1	....	....
Eighth Pennsylvania...................	1	....	1	....	....	....	....	....
Twelfth Pennsylvania..................	2	....	2	3	....	3	....	....
Fourteenth Pennsylvania...............	3	....	3	2	....	2	....	....
South Carolina........................	54	3	57	15	1	16	....	1
Second Tennessee......................	32	3	35	26	....	26	....	....
Fifth Tennessee........................	61	6	67	223	49	272	....	1
Eighth Tennessee......................	4	2	6	4	1	5	....	....
Third Texas...........................	2	....	2	16	....	16	....	....
Fourth Texas..........................	....	....	....	1	....	1	....	....
Vermont...............................	3	....	3	4	....	4	....	....
Third Virginia.........................	....	....	....	1	....	1	....	....
Fourth Virginia........................	5	....	5	42	35	77	....	....
Fifth Virginia.........................	24	3	27	118	....	118	....	....
Sixth Virginia.........................	1	....	1	....	....	....	....	....
First West Virginia....................	8	5	13	3	....	3	....	....
Second West Virginia..................	1	1	2	1	....	1	....	....
Washington Territory..................	....	1	1	....	1	1	....	....
Total............................	969	151	1,120	1,031	234	1,265	....	10

The following table shows the number of illicit stills seized, persons arrested operating the same, and casualties to officers and employés in the suppression of illicit distillation, during the last four fiscal years, and from June 30 to November 1, 1880:

	1877.	1878.	1879.	1880.	June 30, 1880, to November 1, 1880.	Total.
Stills seized	598	1,024	1,319	969	151	4,061
Persons arrested	1,174	1,976	2,924	1,031	234	7,339
Officers and employés killed	12	10	4	......	......	26
Officers and employés wounded	8	17	22	8	2	57

PROSECUTIONS OF REVENUE OFFICERS IN STATE COURTS.

The number of officers and employés of the government who have been proceeded against in State courts for acts committed while in discharge of their official duties during the present year is as follows:

Arkansas 4
Second district of Georgia 38
Third district of Georgia 1
Second district of Kentucky 2
Fifth district of Kentucky 1
Fourth district of North Carolina 2
Number of prosecutions previously reported during last four fiscal years ... 165

    Total 213

EXPENDITURES FOR THE DISCOVERY OF AND PUNISHMENT FOR FRAUDS UPON THE INTERNAL REVENUE.

In accordance with the provisions of the act making the appropriation, the following detailed statement of expenditures from the appropriation for detecting and bringing to trial and punishment persons guilty of violating the internal-revenue laws is submitted.

Amount expended through collectors of internal revenue in the employment of persons for the detection of frauds, and for information leading to the discovery of frauds, and punishment of guilty persons, as follows:

Brayton, E. M., South Carolina $1,311 10
Bean, I. M., First Wisconsin 20 00
Brown, G. W., Second West Virginia 266 74
Brown, J. C., Twentieth Pennsylvania 22 00
Buckner, J. F., Fifth Kentucky 1,265 00
Blaine, Jno. G., Ninth Kentucky 431 00
Clark, A., Second Georgia 8,479 35
Carroll, A. B., Second Missouri 111 00
Cooper, J. A., Second Tennessee 20 00
Dana, C. S., Vermont 33 75
Duval, I. H., First West Virginia 746 90
Eagan, D., Florida 26 88
Fernald, W. L., Fourth Virginia 83 00
Harvey, J. D., First Illinois 135 75
Hill, James, Mississippi 0 00
Hollister, D. F., Second Connecticut 150 00
Landram, W. J., Eighth Kentucky 1,673 00
Ludlow, B. C., Third Texas 12 00

Mayer, L. H., First Alabama $73 00
Marks, M., Louisiana 20 00
Melton, J. M., Second Tennessee 438 16
Mott, J. J., Sixth North Carolina 1,446 50
Patterson, R. F., Eighth Tennessee 539 45
Proud, R. M., Third Maryland 160 08
Rapier, J. T., Second Alabama 919 50
Rives, J. H., Fifth Virginia 1,188 16
Stuart, W. A., Second Kentucky 839 00
Wade, E. C., Third Georgia 741 16
Wheeler, E., Arkansas 56 00
White, E. A., Second North Carolina 264 50
Woodcock, W. M., Fifth Tennessee 1,402 00
Wheeler, W. H., Fifth North Carolina 337 50
Young, I. J., Fourth North Carolina 377 03

Total disbursed by collectors 23,594 61

Amount expended through internal-revenue agents in the employment of persons for the discovery of violations of the internal-revenue
law, and the punishment of guilty persons, as follows:

Atkinson, G. W $20 00
Brown, C. P. 240 00
Brooks, A. H 5,173 64
Blocker, O. H 907 00
Crane, A. M 4,510 31
Chapman, W. H 1,128 12
Eldridge, C. W 50 00
Gavett, W. A 561 10
Grimeson, T. J 2,014 14
Hale, J. H 36 00
Kinney, T. J 270 00
Kellogg, H 442 15
Latham, E 157 25
McLeer, E 529 50
Meyer, F 2,791 31
Montrose, H. L 8 00
Spencer, D. A 15 00
Somerville, W 2,027 66
Trumbull, J. L 4,680 85
Tracie, T. C 50 00
Wheeler, J. C 1,506 58
Wagner, Jacob 119 30
Whitfield, S. A 2,614 93
Webster, E. D 1,374 71

Total disbursed by revenue agents 30,627 55

For information leading to the discovery of unpaid taxes and penalties under
  Circular No. 99 .... 15,901 64
For rewards for illicit distilleries, under circular of March 10, 1875 .... 100 00
Amount paid for extra work in the examination of abstracts of the books of
  leaf-tobacco dealers, for the discovery of violations of law by manufactu-
  rers 4,286 87
Miscellaneous expenditures 287 30

Grand total 74,797 97

The accounts for expenditures under this appropriation are rendered
monthly with an itemized statement, and in all cases supported by sub-
vouchers duly sworn to. These accounts pass through all the accounting offices of the Treasury Department, and are filed in the Register's
office.

TAXES COLLECTED FROM RAILROAD COMPANIES.

The following is a statement of unpaid internal revenue taxes, which accrued under former laws, collected from railroad companies during the last four fiscal years:

Fiscal year ended June 30, 1877	$55,590 30
Fiscal year ended June 30, 1878	218,302 73
Fiscal year ended June 30, 1879	101,340 96
Fiscal year ended June 30, 1880	118,907 12
Total	494,141 11

The amount collected during the past fiscal year was received from twenty different railroad companies.

SUITS AGAINST EX-COLLECTORS.

Subjoined is a list of suits against late collectors of internal revenue in which judgments have been rendered during the fiscal year ended June 30, 1880, furnished by the courtesy of the Solicitor of the Treasury:

United States vs. Jarrard O. Rawlins, late collector of internal revenue for the first collection district of California. Judgment for $28,409.53.

United States vs. James B. Maupin, late collector of internal revenue for the second collection district of Missouri. Judgment for $2,666.84.

United States vs. Frederick A. Sawyer, late collector of internal revenue for the second collection district of South Carolina. Judgment for amount of offer of compromise, $5,219.15.

United States vs. Milton Stapp, late collector of internal revenue for the first collection district of Texas. Judgment for $565.52.

COMPROMISES AFTER JUDGMENT.

The records of the Solicitor of the Treasury show that for the fiscal year ending June 30, 1880, thirteen internal-revenue cases were compromised after judgment, the amount accepted being $12,566.01, besides costs. Thirty-one offers of compromise after judgment were rejected, the amount involved being $8,025.83. Twenty offers of compromise were pending July 1, 1880, the amount involved being $6,554.28.

SALE OF REAL ESTATE.

The United States has acquired title to about $500,000 worth of real estate under the internal-revenue laws. Efforts are constantly made, through collectors and revenue agents and by correspondence, to make sale of this property, but with slight progress. Much of this property has been owned by the government for a number of years, and there seems to be no immediate prospect of being able to sell it at a fair valuation, especially in view of the fact that only quit-claim deeds are given upon the sale of said property.

It has occurred to me that it would be wise after the United States has held real estate so acquired for a period of eight or ten years without being able to sell it at a fair cash valuation that it should be put up and sold for whatever it would bring, and as no officer would probably desire to take the responsibility of ordering such a sale it seems to me the provision of law might well be made for the same.

RECEIPTS FOR FIRST FOUR MONTHS OF PRESENT FISCAL YEAR.

The following table shows the receipts from the several sources of revenue for the first four months of the current fiscal year. The receipts for the corresponding period in the last fiscal year and a comparison of the receipts for the two periods are also given :

Sources of revenue.	Receipts from July 1, 1879, to October 31, 1879.	Receipts from July 1, 1880, to October 31, 1880.	Increase.	Decrease.
SPIRITS.				
Brandy distilled from apples, peaches, or grapes	$269,975 05	$389,440 74	$119,465 69	....
Spirits distilled from materials other than apples, peaches, or grapes	18,242,981 09	20,361,947 31	2,118,966 22	....
Rectifiers' special tax	12,012 53	9,586 03	....	$2,426 50
Dealers, retail liquor	343,021 18	355,990 96	12,969 78	....
Dealers, wholesale liquor	27,720 58	22,866 77	....	4,853 81
Manufacturers of stills, and stills and worms manufactured	1,235 02	3,370 84	2,135 82	....
Stamps for distilled spirits intended for export	3,942 20	4,334 40	392 20	....
Stamps, warehouse, rectifiers', dealers', &c.	100,792 20	1,001 60	....	99,790 70
Interest on tax upon spirits	51,721 54	31 87	....	51,689 67
Total	19,053,401 49	21,148,570 52	2,095,169 03	....
TOBACCO.				
Cigars and cheroots	4,758,928 89	5,476,026 05	717,097 16	....
Cigarettes	225,921 76	410,892 12	184,970 36	....
Manufacturers of cigars	7,854 24	6,607 04	....	1,247 20
Snuff	233,185 56	241,098 28	8,812 72	....
Tobacco of all descriptions	7,824,981 03	7,819,753 79	....	5,227 24
Stamps for tobacco or snuff intended for export	2,081 30	2,432 30	351 00	....
Dealers in leaf tobacco	5,346 96	4,847 63	....	499 33
Retail dealers in leaf tobacco	520 83	859 34	338 51	....
Dealers in manufactured tobacco	166,388 52	173,113 16	6,724 64	....
Manufacturers of tobacco	712 13	540 85	....	171 28
Peddlers of tobacco	4,082 80	3,565 75	....	516 85
Total	13,230,003 82	14,140,636 31	910,632 49	....
FERMENTED LIQUORS.				
Fermented liquors, tax of $1 per barrel on.	4,477,362 07	5,051,650 12	574,293 45	....
Brewers' special tax	7,345 86	6,133 47	....	1,112 39
Dealers in malt liquors' special tax	42,871 80	39,449 42	....	3,422 38
Total	4,527,480 33	5,097,239 01	569,758 68	....
BANKS AND BANKERS.				
Bank deposits	541,106 75	493,822 71	....	47,384 04
Bank deposits, savings, &c	24,433 56	17,460 29	....	6,973 27
Bank capital	221,005 58	192,731 45	....	28,274 13
Bank circulation	25,743 94	544 32	....	25,199 62
Total	812,289 83	704,558 77	....	107,731 06
MISCELLANEOUS.				
Adhesive stamps	2,403,163 68	2,571,536 43	168,372 75	....
Penalties	60,370 39	90,970 00	30,599 61	....
Articles and occupations formerly taxed but now exempt	44,395 28	35,807 26	....	8,588 02
Total	2,507,929 35	2,698,313 69	190,384 34	....
Aggregate receipts	40,131,104 82	43,789,318 30	3,658,213 48	....

TOBACCO.

The total amount of collections from tobacco for the fiscal year ended June 30, 1880, was $38,370,140.08. This amount includes the collections of internal revenue taxes imposed upon imported manufactured tobacco, snuff, and cigars, and the special taxes paid by manufacturers of and dealers in leaf and manufactured tobacco, and is less than the receipts from the same source for the fiscal year immediately preceding by $1,264,862.57.

The following exhibit will show the several amounts collected from the different sources of the tobacco tax, and the relative increase or decrease, in each case, as compared with the collections from the same sources for the fiscal year ended June 30, 1879.

TOBACCO AND SNUFF.

Manufactured tobacco at 16 cents per pound	$21,168,766 28
Manufactured tobacco at 20 cents per pound	244 32
Manufactured tobacco at 24 cents per pound	1,743 80
Snuff, taxed at 16 cents per pound	634,609 34
Total for the year ended June 30, 1880	21,804,763 74
Total for the year ended June 30, 1879	25,606,010 25
Decrease of collections on tobacco and snuff	3,801,246 51

Of this decrease $3,533,720.50 was on chewing and smoking tobacco, and $267,526.01 on snuff.

CIGARS AND CIGARETTES.

Cigars, taxed at $6 per thousand	$14,206,819 49
Cigarettes, taxed at $1.75 per thousand	715,227 39
Cigarettes, taxed at $6 per thousand	42 00
Total collections for year ended June 30, 1880	14,922,088 88
Total collections for year ended June 30, 1879	12,532,452 72
Increase in collections from cigars and cigarettes	2,389,636 16

OTHER COLLECTIONS.

Export stamps, year ended June 30, 1880	$6,622 40
Export stamps, year ended June 30, 1879	7,863 90
Decrease in sale of export stamps	1,241 50
Dealers in manufactured tobacco, year ended June 30, 1880	1,864,422 41
Dealers in manufactured tobacco, year ended June 30, 1879	1,705,720 20
Increase in collections from dealers in manufactured tobacco	158,702 21
Special taxes, manufacturers of tobacco and cigars, in 1880	153,132 71
Special taxes, manufacturers of tobacco and cigars, in 1879	161,435 23
Decrease in special taxes, manufacturers of tobacco and cigars	8,302 52
Special taxes, peddlers of tobacco, year ended June 30, 1880	28,700 46
Special taxes, peddlers of tobacco, year ended June 30, 1879	31,247 67
Decrease in collections from peddlers of tobacco	2,547 1
Dealers in leaf tobacco, year ended June 30, 1880	90,409 7
Dealers in leaf tobacco, year ended June 30, 1879	90,272 7
Increase in collections from dealers in leaf tobacco	136

PRODUCTION OF MANUFACTURED TOBACCO, CIGARS, ETC.

Adding to the several quantities of tobacco, snuff, and cigars removed for consumption during the fiscal year ended June 30, 1880, as computed from the amount of revenue derived therefrom, the quantities removed in bond for export, we have the following results, which show the entire production for the last fiscal year:

	Pounds.
Tobacco, taxed at 16 cents per pound	132,301,039
Tobacco, taxed at 20 cents per pound	1,222
Tobacco, taxed at 24 cents per pound	7,266
Total quantity removed for consumption	132,309,527
Snuff, taxed at 16 cents per pound, removed for consumption	3,966,308
Tobacco and snuff removed for exportation	9,807,050
Total product of tobacco and snuff, 1880	146,082,885
Total production for year ended June 30, 1879	131,433,409
Increase of production	14,649,476

PRODUCTION OF CIGARS AND CIGARETTES.

	Number.
Cigars, cheroots, &c., taxed at $6 per thousand	2,367,803,250
Cigarettes, taxed at $1.75 per thousand	408,701,365
Cigarettes, taxed at $6 per thousand	7,000
Cigars removed for exportation	2,540,925
Cigarettes removed for exportation	41,107,380
Total product for fiscal year 1880	2,820,159,920
Total product for fiscal year 1879	2,276,534,081
Increase during fiscal year 1880 of	543,625,739

APPARENT EFFECTS OF REDUCTION OF TAX RATE.

From the foregoing statement it will be seen that the entire receipts from manufactured tobacco, including snuff, for the fiscal year ended June 30, 1880, were $21,804,763.74. This is $3,801,246.51 less than the receipts from the same sources during the fiscal year ended June 30, 1879, and $4,579,108.56 less than the receipts from the same sources during the fiscal year ended June 30, 1878, when the taxes on snuff were collected at the rate of 32 cents per pound, and on manufactured tobacco at 24 cents per pound. These collections were made from 3,966,308 pounds of snuff and 132,309,527 pounds of smoking and chewing tobacco.

Had there been no reduction in the rate of tax on snuff and tobacco, the number of pounds which reached taxation during the last fiscal year would have yielded a revenue of $33,023,505.04, or $11,218,741.30 more than was collected.

The total collections from cigars, cheroots, and cigarettes for the fiscal year ended June 30, 1880, were $14,922,088.88. This is $2,389,636.16 more than the receipts from the same sources during the previous fiscal year.

Owing to the large increase in the collections from cigars and cigarettes, the total collections from tobacco, snuff, cigars, and cigarettes amount to $36,726,852.62, which is only $1,411,610.35 less than the collections from the same sources for the previous fiscal year.

To fairly determine the effects of the reduction of the rate of tax on manufactured tobacco, including snuff, made by the act of March 1, 1879, a comparison should be made of the receipts of the two entire fiscal years—1878, when the rate of tax on snuff was 32 cents per pound, and the rate of tax on chewing and smoking tobacco was 24 cents per pound, and 1880, when the tax was uniformly collected on all classes of manufactured tobacco, including snuff, at 16 cents per pound—leaving out all collections made from cigars and cigarettes, as no change was made in the rate of tax on cigars and cigarettes by the act of March 1, 1879. .

This comparison shows a falling off in the receipts from chewing and smoking tobacco and snuff, due to the reduction of rates of $4,579,108.56.

The apparent increase in the consumption of manufactured tobacco, or in the quantity placed on the market tax paid, is not thought to be due to a reduction of the cost of tobacco to consumers as has been claimed, for the reason that there has been no reduction of the price of tobacco paid by consumers, excepting, perhaps, a slight reduction on the very lowest grades of smoking and chewing tobacco.

The true cause of the increase in consumption is to be found in the general revival of business within the last two years, more and better pay to laborers, and increased means to purchase with.

The natural increase in population, and the large influx into the country of foreigners during the last two years, nearly all of whom are consumers of tobacco, have also tended to increase consumption. The presumption is by no means a violent one that the increased consumption would have been about equal if there had been no reduction of rate, and that the collections, instead of being less than $22,000,000 during the last fiscal year, would have been more than $33,000,000 from chewing and smoking tobacco and snuff, and the total collections from all tobacco sources would have reached the round sum of $50,000,000.

IMPORTED CIGARS.

The cigars imported during the fiscal year ended June 30, 1880, as given by the Bureau of Statistics—

	Pounds.
Aggregated in weight	652,402
Of this quantity there were exported	41,329
Leaving to be withdrawn for consumption	611,073
Allowing 13½ pounds to the thousand as the weight of imported cigars, the number of imported cigars included in the above table would be.	45,264,667
Number withdrawn in 1879 was	40,666,518
Increase during fiscal year 1880 was	4,598,149

LEAF TOBACCO.

Assuming that for every one hundred pounds of leaf tobacco used in the manufacture of tobacco and snuff eighty-five pounds of manufactured products have resulted, and that for every one thousand cigars manufactured twenty-five pounds of leaf tobacco were used, and that for every thousand cigarettes made five pounds of leaf tobacco were required, the leaf tobacco used during the fiscal year ended June 30,

SUGGESTED CHANGE IN CIGAR STAMPS.

? The attention of the Secretary of the Treasury and of the Commissioner of Internal Revenue, as well as of both Houses of Congress, has been called to suggested changes in the present mode of collecting the tax on cigars by placing the stamp upon the box, and the question arose whether the penal provisions of the law would still apply if for the present mode of affixing the stamp some plan were substituted which contemplated the destruction of portions of the stamp piecemeal as the cigars were sold from the box. The question was submitted to the Attorney-General, who held that the penal provisions of the law would not so apply. As this subject has been considered by appropriate committees of Congress, I respectfully submit whether it would not be proper to have the law so modified as to allow such changes in the form of the stamps as the Secretary of the Treasury and the Commissioner of Internal Revenue might deem would best protect the interests of the government.

DISTILLED SPIRITS.

In my report for the fiscal year ended June 30, 1879, attention was called to the collection of the taxes on the spirits withdrawn from distillery warehouses for exportation and lost in transportation between the distillery and the port of exportation, and to the complaint made by distillers and others engaged in the export trade as to the hardship of such collections. In accordance with my recommendation in the matter, exporters were relieved from this tax by an act of Congress passed December 20, 1879. Pursuant to the provisions of the act allowance was made during the year for loss by leakage in transportation amounting to 8,484 gallons.

EXPORTATION OF ALCOHOL IN METALLIC CANS.

In connection with the subject of deficiency taxes on spirits withdrawn for exportation I had the honor to recommend in my last annual report that provision be made by law for the exportation of alcohol in metallic cans of ten gallons and upward. In accordance with this recommendation certain changes were made in sections 3287 and 3330 Revised Statutes; by sections 6 and 11 of the internal-revenue act of May 28, 1880, providing for the withdrawal of spirits from receiving cisterns into casks or *packages* of not less capacity than ten gallons, wine measure, and providing for the exportation of spirits in original *packages*. No exports of alcohol in tin cans have, however, been made under these privileges, as it appears that there is no foreign demand for packages of alcohol in cans of larger size than five gallons. As it also appears that exporters are willing to encase two five-gallon tin cans in one wooden inclosure, and as I believe such a package may be properly protected by stamps, I would recommend that the law be so amended as to provide for the exportation of alcohol in metallic cans of five gallons and upward, provided the quantity contained in the wooden inclosure is not less than ten gallons.

PRODUCTION OF SPIRITS DURING THE YEAR.

The quantity of spirits (90,355,270 gallons) produced and deposited in distillery warehouses during the fiscal year ended June 30, 1880, exceeded the production of the previous year by 18,462,649 gallons, the product for 1879, as was shown in my report for that year, having been greater than for any previous year.

The increase in production for the fiscal year 1880 over the production for the fiscal year 1879 is distributed among the different varieties known to the trade, as follows:

Increase in production of—

	Gallons.
Bourbon whisky	6, 827, 067
Rye whisky	2, 340, 943
Alcohol	2, 036, 726
Rum	185, 846
Gin	21, 892
Pure, neutral, or cologne spirits	7, 198, 489
Miscellaneous	2, 684, 949
Total	21, 285, 912

Decrease in production of—

High wines	2, 823, 263
Net increase	18, 462, 649

The causes which, in addition to the improvement of the times, have led to this great increase in the production of distilled spirits, are the amendments of the internal-revenue laws, which have secured—

1. The increase in the bonded period from one year to three years;
2. The allowance for loss by leakage while in warehouse;
3. Relief from the payment of interest on taxes while in bonded warehouse; and
4. The allowance for leakage of spirits while in transportation for export or to manufacturing warehouse.

APPARENT OVER-PRODUCTION OF SPIRITS.

I take the liberty of calling especial attention of distillers and the trade to the fact that on the 1st July, 1879, there were on hand in distillery warehouses 19,212,000 gallons of spirits, which was an increase of about 5,000,000 of gallons over the stock on hand at the same period of the previous year, and that on the 1st day of November, 1880, the amount of spirits on hand was 32,640,000, being an increase of 13,400,000 gallons over the amount on hand on the 1st July, 1879. The steady increase in the number and capacity of distilleries in operation, suggests the probability of the continued enlargement of the stock on hand. It has occurred to me that this business was on the eve of being overdone, and that in the event of a recurrence of the agitation for a reduction of the tax, the holders of these spirits would be in danger of loss.

RECEIPTS FROM DISTILLED SPIRITS.

The following statement shows the receipts from the several articles or occupations relating to distilled spirits subject to tax under internal-revenue laws now in force, for the fiscal years ended June 30, 1879 and

1880, together with the increase or decrease on each article or occupation:

Articles or occupations.	Receipts for fiscal year ended June 30—		Increase.	Decrease.
	1879.	1880.		
Spirits distilled from apples, peaches, or grapes	$919,099 74	$905,201 75	....	$13,897 99
Spirits distilled from materials other than apples, peaches, or grapes	46,790,364 50	55,013,917 43	$8,223,552 93	....
Wine made in imitation of champagne	....	....	....	....
Rectifiers (special tax)	160,123 21	172,004 60	11,881 39	....
Retail liquor dealers (special tax)	3,903,036 24	4,172,283 85	269,247 61	....
Wholesale liquor dealers (special tax)	409,115 56	406,526 72	....	2,588 94
Manufacturers of stills (special tax)	1,315 86	1,787 53	471 67	....
Stills or worms manufactured (special tax)	2,210 00	4,360 06	2,150 06	....
Stamps for distilled spirits intended for export	17,212 20	19,748 60	2,581 40	....
Stamps, distillery warehouse	126,374 50	149,505 00	23,130 56	....
Stamps for rectified spirits	122,503 20	133,193 70	10,690 50	....
Stamps, wholesale liquor dealers'	43,804 90	47,339 10	3,534 20	....
Stamps, special bonded warehouse	225 30	364 90	139 60	....
Stamps, special bonded warehouse (re-warehousing)	....	1 00	1 00	....
Stamps for imported spirits	....	285 20	285 20	....
Interest on tax upon spirits	74,899 48	158,994 41	84,094 93	....
Total	52,370,284 69	61,185,508 79	8,615,224 10	....

* * * * * * *

NOTE.—Many tabular statements are omitted for want of space, but they can all be found in the bound volume of the Commissioner's report.

SPIRITS AND TOBACCO REMOVED IN BOND FOR EXPORT.

The following statement shows the quantity and percentage of production of distilled spirits and manufactured tobacco (including snuff) removed in bond for export during each fiscal year since the passage of the act of June 6, 1872:

Year.	Distilled spirits.		Year.	Manufactured tobacco.	
	Taxable (proof) gallons exported.	Percentage of production.		Pounds of tobacco exported.	Percentage of production.
1873	2,358,630	3.45+	1873	10,116,045	8.59+
1874	4,960,100	5.90+	1874	10,806,927	9.11+
1875	587,413	0.96+	1875	9,179,316	7.13+
1876	1,308,900	2.23+	1876	9,434,485	7.87+
1877	2,529,528	4.22+	1877	11,335,046	8.88+
1878	5,499,252	9.80+	1878	10,581,744	8.89+
1879	14,837,581	20.03+	1879	11,934,951	8.62+
1880	16,765,686	18.55+	1880	9,808,409	6.71+
Total	47,947,130		Total	82,284,923	

EXPORTATION OF DISTILLED SPIRITS.

The following figures show the increase or decrease as to the various kinds of spirits exported in the year 1880, as compared with the year 1879:

	Gallons.
Increase in alcohol	1,313,993
Increase in rum	85,861
Increase in pure, neutral, or cologne spirits	548,908
Increase in high wines	3,128
Total increase	1,951,890

	Gallons.
Decrease in bourbon whisky	17,563
Decrease in rye whisky	5,013
Decrease in miscellaneous	1,229
Total decrease	23,805

Net increase	1,928,085

As was the case in the fiscal years 1878 and 1879, the bulk of the spirits exported during the fiscal year 1880 was alcohol produced in the northern part of Illinois, shipped on foreign-bound vessels at New York, and consigned to Marseilles, France. During the year 1880 the exportations to Genoa, Gibraltar, and Valencia have in each case exceeded one million gallons, and the quantity exported to each of the ports of Bilboa and Palma, Spain, has nearly reached one million gallons.

The number of ports to which alcohol was exported in 1879 was forty-four, and during 1880, fifty-three. During the fiscal year 1879 the total number of ports to which spirits were exported was sixty-four, and during the fiscal year 1880 was seventy-one.

It will be observed that the foreign demand for American spirits is still increasing, and that the quantity exported during each fiscal year continues to be greater than during the preceding year.

Realizing the importance of placing the legitimate distilling interests of the country on a sound business basis, and thus discouraging the production of illicit spirits, this office has encouraged the exportation of spirits, affording such facilities as was consistent with the due protection of the interests of the government from time to time as occasion required.

Those features of the act passed during last session of Congress, providing for the allowance for actual loss during transportation and for removing the restriction as to size of exported packages and to the thousand gallons limitation, were passed upon my recommendation.

Railroads and other transportation companies have also been authorized by regulations of the department to become sureties for exporters where it has been shown that such corporations have legal ability to act in that capacity. This measure has been found to operate satisfactorily. Under this system the security of the United States has been of the best character, and the exporters have been enabled to land spirits at foreign ports at quite a saving in brokerage charges incurred in obtaining sureties who were not jointly interested with them in the due delivery of the goods.

SPIRITS WITHDRAWN FROM DISTILLERY WAREHOUSES UPON PAYMENT OF TAX.

	Gallons.
The quantity of spirits withdrawn from distillery warehouses upon payment of tax was in 1880	61,100,362
And was in 1879	51,885,939
Increase	9,214,423

This increase is distributed, except as to the kind known as high wines, as follows:

	Gallons.
Bourbon whisky	1,601,020
Rye whisky	750,206
Alcohol	537,089
Rum	108,792
Gin	36,507
Pure, neutral, or cologne spirits	6,866,998
Miscellaneous	1,829,791
Total increase	11,730,405
Decrease in withdrawals of high wines	2,515,982
Net increase in withdrawals, tax-paid	9,214,423

The amount of interest tax collected during the fiscal year to May 28, 1880, the date of the repealing act, was $158,994.41.

The quantity of each month's product of spirits in warehouse July 1, 1879, which was withdrawn during the year ended June 30, 1880, is shown in the following tabular statement:

Product of the month of—	In warehouse July 1, 1879.	Withdrawn during year ended June 30, 1880.	Remaining in warehouse June 30, 1880.
1877.	*Gallons.*	*Gallons.*	*Gallons.*
March	263,183	} 1,095,558	8,008
April	399,062		
May	440,481		
June	350,848	238,865	111,983
July	96,450	65,731	30,719
August	30,933	26,184	4,749
September	43,706	37,407	6,299
October	34,313	22,436	11,887
November	82,066	57,495	24,571
December	171,162	122,186	48,976
1878.			
January	401,470	271,186	130,313
February	498,412	348,782	149,630
March	649,542	469,608	179,436
April	888,379	622,600	265,779
May	846,344	538,208	308,136
June	521,126	374,865	146,321
July	240,363	167,087	73,276
August	127,394	84,630	43,255
September	123,474	86,867	35,607
October	208,487	166,612	79,876
November	496,549	291,684	198,865
December	947,705	594,716	352,989
1879.			
January	1,236,742	652,077	584,665
February	1,514,341	741,387	772,954
March	2,036,418	1,062,471	973,947
April	2,271,892	996,847	1,275,045
May	2,298,061	976,461	1,321,600
June	1,942,328	1,026,756	915,572
Total	19,219,470	11,160,983	8,051,487

TRANSFER OF SPIRITS TO MANUFACTURING WAREHOUSES.

Section 20 of the internal-revenue act of March 1, 1879, providing for transfers of spirits from distillery warehouses to manufacturing warehouses, was amended by section 14 of the act of May 28, 1880, so as to read as follows:

That under such regulations and requirements as to stamps, bonds, and other security as shall be prescribed by the Commissioner of Internal Revenue, any manufacturer

of medicines, preparations, compositions, perfumeries, cosmetics, cordials, and othe
liquors, for export, manufacturing the same in a duly constituted manufacturing ware
house, shall be authorized to withdraw, in original packages, from any distillery ware
house, so much distilled spirits as he may require for the said purpose, without th
payment of the internal-revenue tax thereon.

The amendment made by the act of May 28, 1880, enlarged the scop
of the act of March 1, 1879, so as to provide for the withdrawal of any
kind of distilled spirits from distillery warehouses, the articles to b
withdrawn having theretofore been limited to alcohol.

The section as amended also provides for the use of the spirits in man
ufacturing warehouses in all of the articles authorized by law to b
made in such warehouses. The effect of the amendment has been t
make a new outlet for the exportation of American spirits.

Section 15 of the act of May 28, 1880, also makes provision, in case o
transfers of spirits to manufacturing warehouses, for an allowance for
loss by unavoidable accident, without fraud or negligence, as in the
case of spirits shipped in bond for exportation.

The transfers during the fiscal year 1879 were 13,213 gallons, and
during the fiscal year 1880 were 218,212 gallons. Attention, however
is called to the fact, that inasmuch as the original act was passed March
1, 1879, and the amendatory act May 28, 1880, the transactions of the
respective fiscal years are not fair indications of the quantity that wil
probably be annually withdrawn under said acts.

SPIRITS WITHDRAWN FROM WAREHOUSE FOR SCIENTIFIC PURPOSES
AND FOR USE OF THE UNITED STATES.

The quantity of alcohol withdrawn free of tax from distillery ware
houses for the use of colleges and other institutions of learning in the
preservation of specimens of natural history in their several museums,
or for use in their chemical laboratories, and of spirits of various kinds
for use of the United States, amounted during the year to 23,048 gallons,
an increase of 5,362 gallons over the quantity withdrawn during the
previous year.

SPIRITS LOST BY CASUALTY DURING THE YEAR.

	Gallons.
The quantity of spirits on deposit in distillery warehouses at commencement of fiscal year was	19,212,47(
The quantity deposited during the year was	90,355,27(
Total	109,567,74(

Of this quantity, 14,231 gallons were lost by casualty, being about
one-seventy-seventh of one per cent., or one gallon of each 7,696 + gal
lons was so lost.

It was my pleasure, in my report of last year, during which the loss of
spirits was less than one-fiftieth of one per cent. of the quantity stored in
warehouses, to call attention to the care exercised by the distillers and
storekeepers in the preservation of this inflammable material. As the
loss this year is much less than that occurring during the year 1879, it
is deemed proper to call renewed attention to the diligence exercised by
the distillers and government officers in the preservation of this class of
property.

It is quite evident, from the slight loss for the past four years, that
the fire insurance on spirits in distillery warehouses might with safety
be fixed at the very lowest rate.

The quantity of spirits lost by casualty, on which the tax was abated,
during the year, under sections 3221, 3222, and 3223, Revised Statutes,
was 4,276 gallons.

DISTILLED SPIRITS ALLOWED FOR LOSS BY LEAKAGE OR EVAPORA-
TION IN WAREHOUSES.

The quantity of distilled spirits allowed under the provisions of section 17 of the act of May 28, 1880, for loss by leakages or evaporation
in warehouses during June, 1880 (the only month of the fiscal year in
which the act was in force), was 75,834 gallons.
The quantity allowed during the first four months of the current fiscal
year was 271,169 gallons.

SPIRITS REMAINING IN WAREHOUSES AT THE CLOSE OF THE YEAR.

In my report for the year ended June 30, 1879, it was shown that the
quantity (19,212,470 gallons) in warehouses June 30, 1879, exceeded the
quantity in warehouse at the close of any preceding fiscal year. This
quantity, however, is greatly exceeded by the quantity (31,363,869 gallons) remaining in warehouses June 30, 1880.
The following table shows the quantity remaining in distillery warehouses at the close of each of the twelve fiscal years during which spirits
have been stored in such warehouses:

	Gallons.
Quantity remaining June 30, 1869	16,685,166
Quantity remaining June 30, 1870	11,671,886
Quantity remaining June 30, 1871	6,744,360
Quantity remaining June 30, 1872	10,103,392
Quantity remaining June 30, 1873	14,650,148
Quantity remaining June 30, 1874	15,575,224
Quantity remaining June 30, 1875	13,179,596
Quantity remaining June 30, 1876	12,595,850
Quantity remaining June 30, 1877	13,091,773
Quantity remaining June 30, 1878	14,088,773
Quantity remaining June 30, 1879	19,212,470
Quantity remaining June 30, 1880	31,363,869

It is understood from leading distillers that since the extension of the
bonded period the business of selling spirits in bond has largely increased, and that the greater portion of goods now in bond is owned by
dealers in various parts of the country who have assumed to the distiller the payment of the taxes as they fall due.
It is evident that the causes adverted to in my last year's report as
leading to this great increase in the stock of spirits remaining in distillery warehouses, and as indicating the growing ability on the part of
distillers to discharge their obligations to the government, have been
in full operation the past fiscal year.
The case of the sixth district of North Carolina was then cited as
illustrating the great increase in the number of the legally authorized
distilleries in sections of the country recently infested by illicit distillers. The same district can be again used as illustrating this fact, the
number of distillery warehouses in that district having increased from
184 July 1, 1879, to 229 June 30, 1880.
In my last year's report reference was made to the building of the
largest distillery in the United States at the close of the fiscal year. I have
now to report that this distillery has been in successful operation during
the year, and that others of its class have been greatly enlarged and
fitted up with the latest improvements, thus enabling them to materially
reduce the cost of production and to improve the character of their products. By the use of the latest improved purifying, refining, and redis-
tilling apparatus, and the employment of experts, fine grades of alcohol,

and pure, neutral, or cologne spirits are produced in distilleries ready for use in the arts and sciences without additional manipulation.

The decrease in the production and withdrawal of high wines, and the increase in the production and withdrawal of all other and finer kinds of spirits, are facts satisfactorily showing the improvement in the methods of producing distilled spirits.

Nearly nine-tenths of the spirits remaining in warehouse June 30, 1880 (27,311,138 gallons out of 31,363,869 gallons), were bourbon and rye whiskies, and the increase in the quantity in warehouse that day over that in warehouse June 30, 1879, was mainly the increase in these two varieties.

There was an increase in all varieties except high wines, as follows:

Increased quantity in warehouse, of—

	Gallons.
Bourbon whisky	7,747,856
Rye whisky	3,482,525
Alcohol	56,056
Rum	54,164
Miscellaneous	1,222,860
Total increase	12,563,461

Decreased quantity in warehouse, of—

	Gallons.	Gallons.
High wines	224,713	
Pure, neutral, or cologne spirits	158,061	
Gin	29,288	
		412,062
Net increase of spirits in warehouse		12,151,399

FERMENTED LIQUORS.

The receipts from fermented liquors for the fiscal years ended June 30, 1879 and 1880, are shown in the following statement:

Sources.	Receipts for fiscal year ended June 30—		Increase.	Decrease.
	1879.	1880.		
Fermented liquors, tax of $1 per barrel on	$10,270,352 83	$12,346,077 26	$2,075,724 43	
Brewers' special tax	202,779 61	201,395 97		$1,383 64
Dealers in malt liquors' special tax	256,187 64	282,329 61	26,141 97	
Total	10,729,320 08	12,829,802 84	2,100,482 76	

The following statement shows, by fiscal years, the aggregate production of fermented liquors from September 1, 1862, to June 30, 1880:

Fiscal years ended June 30—	Barrels of not more than 31 gallons each.	Fiscal years ended June 30—	Barrels of not more than 31 gallons each.

Prior to September 1, 1866, the tax on fermented liquors was paid in currency and the full amount of tax was returned by collectors. From and after that date the tax was paid by stamps on which a deduction of 7½ per cent. was allowed to brewers using them. Of the 6,207,401 barrels produced during the fiscal year 1866, the tax on 1,033,319 barrels was paid in money, and the tax on 5,174,082 barrels was paid by stamps.

The foreign demand for American malt liquors is still increasing, the applications for drawback during the fiscal year ended June 30, 1880, upon exports made to foreign ports having more than quadrupled those made for the fiscal year ended June 30, 1879. I take this occasion to renew my recommendation that provision be made in internal revenue laws for the exportation of this article in bond.

EXPORTATION OF MANUFACTURED TOBACCO AND SNUFF IN BOND.

The subjoined table shows, as removed and unaccounted for July 1, 1879, and July 1, 1880, the quantity in pounds of manufactured tobacco and snuff which had been removed for exportation in bond, and concerning which the proofs of landing at a foreign port had not been furnished prior to the dates named.

1. *Removed and unaccounted for July 1, 1879.*

	Pounds.	Pounds.
Tobacco, at 20 cents tax	39,575.00	
Bonds in the hands of district attorneys	17,094.00	
Tobacco, at 24 cents, removed under exportation bonds	3,047,262.50	
Tobacco, at 24 cents, removed under transportation bonds.	474,336.50	
Tobacco, at 16 cents, removed under exportation bonds	1,673,900.00	
Tobacco, at 16 cents, removed under transportation bonds.	104,750.50	
Snuff, at 32 cents, removed under exportation bonds	1,642.00	
Snuff, at 32 cents, removed under transportation bonds	84.00	
		5,358,644.50

2. *Removed during the year ended June 30, 1880.*

Tobacco, at 24 cents tax (excess)	487.00	
Tobacco and snuff, at 16 cents tax	9,807,050.25	
Tobacco, at 16 cents tax (excess)	871.50	
		9,808,408.75
		15,167,053.25

3. *Exported and during the year accounted for.*

Tobacco, at 20 cents tax	10,573.00	
Tobacco, at 24 cents tax	2,778,006.00	
Tobacco, at 16 cents tax	7,330,787.50	
Tobacco, at 24 cents tax paid on deficiencies	3,207.50	
Tobacco, at 16 cents tax paid on deficiencies	1,049.00	
Snuff, at 32 cents tax	1,726.00	
		10,125,349.00

4. *Remaining unaccounted for June 30, 1880.*

Tobacco, at 20 cents tax	29,002.00	
Bonds in the hands of district attorneys	17,094.00	
Tobacco, at 24 cents, removed under exportation bonds	533,212.00	
Tobacco, at 24 cents, removed under transportation bonds.	207,660.50	
Tobacco, at 16 cents, removed under exportation bonds	3,946,809.25	
Tobacco, at 16 cents, removed under transportation bonds.	307,926.50	
		5,041,704.25
		15,167,053.25

The quantity removed from manufactories for exportation during the fiscal year ended June 30, 1880, is 1,226,542.75 pounds less than that removed during the fiscal year ended June 30, 1879.

EXPORTATION OF CIGARS AND CIGARETTES IN BOND.

1. *Removed and unaccounted for July 1, 1879.*

	Number.	Number.
Cigars, at $6 per M tax	1,019,375	
Cigarettes, at $1.75 per M tax	7,184,500	
		8,203,875

2. *Removed during the year ended June 30, 1880.*

Cigars, at $6 per M tax	2,540,825	
Cigarettes, at $1.75 per M tax	41,107,380	
		43,648,205
		51,852,080

3. *Exported and accounted for during the year ended June 30, 1880.*

Cigars, at $6 per M tax	2,436,600	
Cigarettes, at $1.75 per M tax	27,935,600	
		30,372,200

4. *Remaining unaccounted for June 30, 1880.*

Cigars, at $6 per M tax	1,123,600	
Cigarettes, at $1.75 per M tax	20,356,280	
		21,479,880
		51,852,080

DATE OF BONDS REMAINING UNACCOUNTED FOR JUNE 30, 1880.

The years in which the bonds were given for the exportation of the tobacco, snuff, cigars, and cigarettes remaining unaccounted for by evidence of landing June 30, 1880:

Year.	Tobacco.	Snuff.	Cigars.	Cigarettes.
	Pounds.	Pounds.	Number.	Number.
1872	17,094.00			
1873				
1874	25,562.00			
1875	74,704.00			
1876	178,275.00			36,000
1877	275,118.00			
1878	150,470.00		47,000	119,000
1879	1,050,300.00		137,625	2,904,500
1880	3,270,241.25		938,975	17,331,780
Total	5,041,704.25		1,123,600	20,356,280

AMENDATORY ACT REGULATING THE EXPORTATION OF TOBACCO, SNUFF, AND CIGARS IN BOND.

By an act of Congress passed during the latter part of the fiscal year, namely, on the 9th of June, 1880, section 3385 of the Revised Statutes, governing the exportation of manufactured tobacco, snuff, and cigars in bond, was amended so as to provide that export bonds which had been given or which should thereafter be given under the provisions of that section should be canceled upon the presentation to the collector of internal revenue of the detailed report from the inspector of customs and a certificate of the collector of customs at the port from which the goods are exported, that the goods removed from the manufactory under bond and described in the permit of the collector of internal revenue had been received by the said collector of customs, and that said goods were duly laden on a foreign-bound vessel, naming the vessel, and that the said merchandise was entered on the outward manifest of said vessel, and that said vessel and cargo were duly cleared from said port, and on the payment of the taxes on the deficiency, if any.

The effect of the amendment is to relieve exporters of tobacco, snuff, and cigars, exporting under the provisions of the law as amended, from the production of evidence showing landing of the goods at a foreign port. The law has not yet been sufficiently long in operation to show whether the release from the obligation to produce a landing certificate will be accompanied by a corresponding large increase of exportations. It, however, appears that in striking out a portion of section 3385, Revised Statutes, and substituting for the portion stricken out the amendatory provisions of the new law, the language of that part of section 3385 relied upon as authorizing the exportation of tobacco, snuff, and cigars by railroad cars or other land conveyances was, through inadvertence, not restored. I see no good reasons why the exportation of these articles under section 3385, as amended, should be confined to vessels, and I would therefore recommend that as early as possible in the next session of Congress the law be amended so as to clearly provide for the exportation of tobacco, snuff, and cigars by railroad or other land conveyances.

Exportation of friction matches and proprietary articles under section 19 of the act of March 1, 1879.

	Amount of tax.	Amount of tax.
1. Remaining unaccounted for June 30, 1879	$10,146 24	
2. Bonded during the year ended June 30, 1880	235,512 46	
		$245,658 70
		245,658 70
3. Accounted for as exported during the year	236,412 94	
4. Remaining unaccounted for June 30, 1880	9,245 76	
		245,658 70
		245,658 70

OPERATIONS AT SPECIAL BONDED WAREHOUSES FOR STORAGE OF GRAPE BRANDY.

The following statement shows the quantity of grape brandy placed in special bonded warehouses, withdrawn therefrom, and remaining

7 F

therein at the beginning and close of the fiscal year ended June 30, 1880, in taxable gallons:

	Gallons.	Gallons.	Gallons.
Remaining in warehouse July 1, 1879:			
First district of California	72, 561		
Fourth district of California	34, 523		
		107, 084	
Removed for exportation and unaccounted for July 1, 1879:			
First district of California		1, 974	
			109, 058
Produced and bonded during the year:			
First district of California	50, 229		
Fourth district of California	78, 857		
		129, 086	
Received in first district from fourth district of California		1, 151	
			130, 237
			239, 295
Exported and accounted for during the year:			
First district of California		2, 293	
Removed tax-paid during the year:			
First district of California	59, 982		
Fourth district of California	51, 738		
		111, 720	
Loss by regauge, act of May 28, 1880:			
First district of California	44		
Fourth district of California	35		
		79	
Removed from fourth district to first district of California		1, 151	
			115, 243
Removed for exportation and unaccounted for June 30, 1880:			
First district of California		439	
Remaining in warehouse June 30, 1880:			
First district of California	63, 157		
Fourth district of California	60, 456		
		123, 613	
			124, 052
			239, 295

The amount produced and bonded during the fiscal year ended June 30, 1880, was 59,746 gallons more than in the previous year, while the amount removed tax-paid was 15,430 gallons larger than in 1879.

Of the quantity in warehouse June 30, 1880, 63,157 gallons were in the following-named warehouses in the first district of California:

                                                      Gallons.

No. 1. Bode & Danforth, at San Francisco 39, 697
No. 2. Juan Bernard, at Los Angeles 15, 811
No. 3. G. C. Carlon, at Stockton 7, 649

and 60,456 gallons were in the following-named warehouses in the fourth district of California:

                                                      Gallons.

No. 1. George Lichthardt, at Sacramento 26, 655
No. 2. J. F. Boyce, at Santa Rosa 15, 327
No. 3. R. A. Haskins, at Saint Helena...................................... 12, 704
No. 4. John Tivnen, at Sonoma... 5, 770

DRAWBACK.

STATEMENT of DRAWBACK of INTERNAL REVENUE TAXES ALLOWED on EXPORTED MERCHANDISE during the fiscal year 1880.

Port of export.	No. of claims.	Proprietary articles.	Tobacco.	Cigars.	Fermented liquors.	Stills.	Machinery.	Total.
Baltimore	23	$110 16	$11,791 58	$899 47		$20 00		$12,801 21
Boston	31	1,134 90	352 80		$82 31	$20 00		1,590 01
Charleston	1		6 00	48 00				54 00
New York	708	33,033 68	1,680 00		558 05	60 00	$888 00	96,219 73
Philadelphia	13	809 60	154 88	60 00				1,024 48
San Francisco	24	52 56	7,997 56	87 50				8,137 62
Saint Louis	70				1,565 06			1,565 06
Suspension Bridge	1	12 96						12 96
Portland	1		331 20					331 20
Total	872	35,153 86	22,314 62	1,094 97	2,205 42	80 00	888 00	61,736 27
Allowed, 1879	744	43,184 71	12,113 86	230 20	533 69	*1,426 92		57,509 38

* Distilled spirits.

In connection with the foregoing statement I have to call attention to the fact that while a drawback of tax on exported stills is authorized by section 3244, Revised Statutes, as amended by section 16 of the act of March 1, 1879, no provision has been made for the allowance of drawback on exported worms belonging to stills, which, like stills, are subject to a tax of $20 each.

I have, therefore, to renew the recommendation made in my last annual report, that section 3244 named be amended so as to include such worms exported subsequent to March 1, 1879, the date above referred to. I have also to call attention to the fact that no appropriation for the payment of drawback authorized by sections 3244 and 3329, Revised Statutes, has been made, and I would therefore further recommend that section 3689, Revised Statutes, making appropriation for the payment of internal-revenue drawback be also amended so as to include all articles exported under the provisions of said sections.

REPORT ON THE FINANCES.

F The following table shows the number of persons who paid special taxes during the special-tax year ended April 30, 1880:

States and Territories.	Rectifiers.	Retail liquor dealers.	Wholesale liquor dealers.	Manufacturers of stills.	Manufacturers of cigars.	Dealers in leaf tobacco.	Retail dealers in leaf tobacco.	Dealers in manufactured tobacco.	Manufacturers of tobacco.	Peddlers of tobacco.	Brewers.	Dealers in malt liquors.
Alabama	4	1,386	50		26			5,240	1		1	18
Arizona	3	414	20		2			490	5		15	5
Arkansas		1,136	22		7	6	1	3,845	5	2		13
California	118	8,084	258	2	322	30		10,726	5	24	223	219
Colorado	5	1,777	67		14	2		3,174	11	1	36	113
Connecticut	15	2,472	49		290	96		5,043	2	17	20	317
Dakota	1	592	21		20	1		1,319		4	19	19
Delaware	3	653	9	1	67	2		2,761	3	6	7	8
Dist. of Columbia*												
Florida		560	4		76	7		1,929				19
Georgia	17	2,200	54	1	19			6,803	6	4	2	44
Idaho	1	305	12					386			11	4
Illinois	87	10,442	201	6	891	63		24,006	23	78	130	404
Indiana	19	5,352	84	1	491	68		14,011	12	26	96	181
Iowa	10	3,965	58	1	264	5		11,929	5	10	130	478
Kansas	4	1,821	25		96	1		6,451	1	5	39	117
Kentucky	43	3,581	188	4	240	1,004		7,194	59	17	42	162
Louisiana	14	3,972	155		141	31		6,062	07	30	11	28
Maine		757	9		46	1		4,763		50		87
Maryland	73	4,931	165	4	678	139	1	9,144	14	13	73	131
Massachusetts	54	6,403	196	1	477	61		13,670	10	110	37	796
Michigan	7	4,751	46	1	433	16		12,853	14	70	141	590
Minnesota	11	2,355	36		89	1		5,395		10	132	137
Mississippi		1,335	27					4,565	2			50
Missouri	62	6,372	202	1	596	124	1	13,813	79	20	88	172
Montana	3	545	39					692		1	24	16
Nebraska	3	1,044	19		47	1		3,150		6	24	45
Nevada	2	874	19		3			1,168			35	13
New Hampshire		747	13		46			2,303		20	6	270
New Jersey	39	6,260	56	1	726	9		12,733	14	82	56	669
New Mexico		503	19		1			796		1	3	13
New York	279	24,672	745	7	3,713	374	1	47,947	79	379	397	4,082
North Carolina	6	1,805	29		23	140		6,328	264	191	2	18
Ohio	98	14,338	358	1	1,381	314		27,170	42	164	214	453
Oregon	5	930	19		10	4		1,761	1	2	32	40
Pennsylvania	225	16,550	420	2	3,348	272		40,637	32	212	372	1,026
Rhode Island	5	1,326	38		80	2		2,894		23	7	158
South Carolina	2	1,200	20		20	2		4,857	8		4	10
Tennessee	12	2,946	93	1	27	202	I	6,190	37	23	4	52
Texas	8	2,741	97		51	28	2	9,516	5	5	28	314
Utah	4	387	18		3			664			3	14
Vermont		508	3		23	2		2,326		13		94
Virginia	15	2,533	60		106	488		5,400	295	14	3	30
Washington		231	8		4			630			15	38
West Virginia	3	724	11		99	35		2,655	13		12	35
Wisconsin	40	5,158	74		390	25		10,394	7	47	225	200
Wyoming		218	9					325			9	1
Total	1,291	163,529	4,122	35	15,206	3,568	7	365,499	1,026	1,080	2,741	11,610

* Since October 2, 1876, part of the third district of Maryland.

AVERAGE CAPITAL AND DEPOSITS IN 1879.

STATEMENT of the AVERAGE CAPITAL and DEPOSITS of BANKS and BANKERS for the twelve months ended May 31, 1879.

States and Territories.	Average capital and deposits of banks and bankers.—Form 67.			Average capital and deposits of savings-banks.—Form 106.			
	Average capital.	Average taxable capital.	Average deposits.	Average capital.	Average taxable capital.	Average deposits.	Average taxable deposits.
Alabama	$1,055,694	$1,042,506	$1,822,241				
Arizona	67,935	67,935	58,090				
Arkansas	213,167	144,112	307,518				
California	26,729,123	24,243,462	45,020,068	$2,152,068	$1,998,038	$48,106,844	$21,263,826
Colorado	589,722	588,722	1,441,934				
Connecticut	2,405,319	2,057,386	3,809,066			71,373,322	5,913,150
Dakota	87,339	96,854	225,550				
Delaware	640,161	614,623	688,594			1,056,842	15,548
Florida	83,616	83,616	195,688				
Georgia	4,033,097	3,973,278	3,420,248			537,571	310,562
Idaho	32,166	32,166	39,236				
Illinois	7,596,927	4,205,094	18,964,662	65,700	65,451	584,294	58,202
Indiana	4,796,732	4,375,042	8,968,654			1,162,479	119,224
Iowa	5,058,772	4,855,598	8,756,374	20,750	15,000	51,175	5,262
Kansas	1,377,219	1,294,104	3,020,982				
Kentucky	12,052,297	11,370,222	11,539,840				
Louisiana	3,553,391	3,142,218	5,078,396	500,000	500,000	1,773,889	546,365
Maine	43,258	28,258	113,490			23,396,349	224,618
Maryland	4,974,312	3,674,568	6,701,344	16,458	16,458	20,522,343	1,154,036
Massachusetts	4,048,421	1,896,658	9,222,188			251,866,389	297,012
Michigan	3,400,568	2,972,574	10,352,708	37,500	37,500	272,324	9,924
Minnesota	1,638,575	1,600,310	3,451,536	6,643	6,144	146,680	15,564
Mississippi	1,232,892	1,029,436	1,518,956				
Missouri	10,361,779	8,594,178	26,171,462				
Montana	147,690	147,690	264,500				
Nebraska	428,579	417,092	1,253,374				
Nevada	396,491	396,491	1,780,520				
New Hampshire	61,000	61,000	160,432			20,623,751	999,116
New Jersey	1,502,218	1,196,542	2,805,124	20,000	5,250	18,495,615	2,163,246
New Mexico	5,000	5,000	79,682				
New York	52,469,184	31,328,590	114,064,142			268,339,187	9,046,476
North Carolina	643,766	643,766	779,214				
Ohio	8,437,985	6,706,784	24,765,154	68,916	6,428	8,310,923	1,800,630
Oregon	938,455	895,306	1,222,628	41,741	36,240	59,738	4,194
Pennsylvania	16,147,619	14,139,483	55,327,194	304,150	272,976	25,067,481	1,291,516
Rhode Island	3,382,116	3,011,603	3,442,656			40,112,520	7,997,616
South Carolina	772,969	712,218	817,012				
Tennessee	1,734,732	1,512,592	2,732,084				
Texas	3,590,689	3,326,810	4,964,792				
Utah	230,625	230,625	786,896				
Vermont	348,700	308,680	1,341,620			6,586,078	69,436
Virginia	2,806,219	2,142,692	6,313,004	361,466	361,466	287,474	122,198
Washington	206,500	206,500	303,656				
West Virginia	1,475,592	1,349,036	3,800,344				
Wisconsin	2,138,185	1,962,170	9,838,320				
Wyoming	101,583	101,583	179,628				
Total	193,781,219	153,267,838	407,661,079	3,597,392	3,322,951	629,912,178	53,419,589

AVERAGE CAPITAL AND DEPOSITS IN 1880.

STATEMENT of the AVERAGE CAPITAL and DEPOSITS of BANKS and BANK-ERS for the twelve months ended May 31, 1880.

States and Territories.	Average capital and deposits of banks and bankers.—Form 67.			Average capital and deposits of savings-banks.—Form 106.			
	Average capital.	Average taxable capital.	Average deposits.	Average capital.	Average taxable capital.	Average deposits.	Average taxable deposits.
Alabama	$1,037,541	$1,037,541	$2,914,806	....	....	....	....
Arizona	99,688	99,688	204,286	....	....	....	....
Arkansas	230,823	156,738	444,340	....	....	....	....
California......	21,556,404	19,046,300	36,726,052	$2,758,110	$2,362,480	$44,888,379	$15,189,078
Colorado	578,241	573,241	3,057,688	....	....	....	....
Connecticut ...	3,541,708	3,200,402	4,431,490	....	....	72,398,522	1,100,726
Dakota........	126,897	126,867	356,168	....	....	....	....
Delaware.......	626,397	616,927	791,500	....	....	1,162,104	8,720
Florida........	77,977	77,977	233,558	....	....	....	....
Georgia	3,708,344	3,672,778	3,678,374	....	....	848,773	405,668
Idaho	8,962	8,962	38,210	....	....	....	....
Illinois	8,323,244	4,769,700	27,030,242	67,400	67,400	522,500	15,860
Indiana	4,533,080	4,032,818	11,367,716	....	....	1,313,113	64,152
Iowa	5,005,604	4,701,328	11,867,800	44,833	42,918	191,090	21,560
Kansas	1,534,898	1,436,606	4,461,320	....	....	....	....
Kentucky	11,584,210	10,594,480	13,022,150	....	....	....	....
Louisiana	3,261,756	3,550,896	4,777,706	41,666	41,866	20,833	12,666
Maine	47,637	36,122	154,796	....	....	21,223,370	72,008
Maryland	4,286,746	3,337,018	7,511,212	30,118	30,118	21,584,253	80,680
Massachusetts .	4,229,315	2,369,672	9,641,443	....	....	190,541,100	115,926
Michigan........	3,242,540	2,750,460	11,911,454	150,000	150,000	1,784,898	168,848
Minnesota......	1,933,571	1,725,044	4,433,632	....	....	239,537	19,518
Mississippi....	1,134,153	920,166	2,005,284	....	....	....	....
Missouri	9,604,376	8,343,336	30,598,526	....	....	....	....
Montana	265,883	285,883	497,586	....	....	....	....
Nebraska......	601,526	524,556	1,764,456	....	....	....	....
Nevada	303,112	303,112	1,646,763	....	....	....	....
New Hampshire	56,009	51,690	184,294	2,063	2,063	25,098,662	312,392
New Jersey ...	1,301,883	965,786	2,795,798	45,006	5,000	16,868,209	121,460
New Mexico ...	5,833	5,833	196,744	....	....	....	....
New York......	50,430,688	39,199,858	140,196,414	....	....	310,782,302	1,093,552
North Carolina.	482,556	482,556	864,604	....	....	....	....
Ohio	8,069,345	6,296,594	27,948,784	65,000	27,386	5,364,939	27,496
Oregon	1,590,323	1,072,024	988,244	20,871	17,720	26,333	1,104
Pennsylvania ..	14,471,166	12,901,106	60,996,564	433,300	403,784	23,777,962	625,094
Rhode Island...	3,205,618	2,606,662	9,933,962	....	....	37,640,116	2,558,186
South Carolina.	520,828	469,912	623,962	....	....	....	....
Tennessee......	1,724,862	1,598,366	2,932,256	....	....	....	....
Texas	3,507,522	3,357,700	5,845,150	....	....	....	....
Utah	208,500	208,500	1,170,064	....	....	....	....
Vermont	353,700	315,174	1,552,842	....	....	6,770,695	17,542
Virginia........	2,759,924	2,476,758	7,170,372	346,440	346,440	107,126	107,126
Washington ...	232,000	232,000	454,070	....	....	....	....
West Virginia..	1,277,764	1,223,296	3,996,672	....	....	....	....
Wisconsin......	2,139,081	1,997,748	12,200,396	....	....	....	....
Wyoming......	121,717	121,717	254,636	....	....	....	....
Total....	192,173,565	151,801,690	469,124,384	4,004,821	3,496,945	796,704,336	22,141,192

AVERAGE CAPITAL AND DEPOSITS IN 1880.

STATEMENT of the AVERAGE CAPITAL and DEPOSITS of BANKS and BANKERS for the twelve months ended May 31, 1880.

States and Territories.	Total average and taxable average of capital and deposits.— Forms 67 and 106.			
	Average capital.	Average taxable capital.	Average deposits.	Average taxable deposits.
Alabama	$1,037,541	$1,037,541	$2,014,606	$2,014,606
Arizona	96,688	99,688	204,286	204,286
Arkansas	230,823	156,738	444,340	444,340
California	24,317,574	21,408,730	81,615,331	51,916,630
Colorado	373,241	373,241	3,057,638	3,057,638
Connecticut	2,641,768	2,200,403	76,880,012	5,582,212
Dakota	126,897	126,897	350,168	350,168
Delaware	626,927	616,927	1,953,604	800,230
Florida	77,977	77,977	233,558	233,558
Georgia	3,708,344	3,072,778	4,727,147	4,285,042
Idaho	8,902	8,902	38,110	38,110
Illinois	8,390,644	4,837,100	27,352,742	27,046,102
Indiana	4,583,080	4,032,818	12,706,820	11,451,868
Iowa	5,051,437	4,744,246	12,058,800	11,889,680
Kansas	1,594,888	1,436,606	4,461,820	4,461,820
Kentucky	11,584,219	10,594,439	13,022,150	13,022,150
Louisiana	3,303,424	2,592,472	4,798,539	4,790,372
Maine	47,637	36,122	21,376,166	228,804
Maryland	4,316,864	3,367,136	39,095,465	7,501,892
Massachusetts	4,229,915	2,369,672	209,082,602	9,657,398
Michigan	3,392,540	2,900,460	13,645,812	12,080,302
Minnesota	1,833,571	1,725,044	4,673,169	4,453,150
Mississippi	1,134,153	920,106	2,005,284	2,005,284
Missouri	9,804,376	8,343,336	30,598,526	30,598,526
Montana	265,883	265,883	497,536	497,536
Nebraska	601,596	524,558	1,764,456	1,764,456
Nevada	303,112	303,112	1,646,762	1,646,762
New Hampshire	58,083	53,773	25,882,956	495,686
New Jersey	1,346,882	970,786	19,064,097	2,917,258
New Mexico	5,833	5,833	196,744	196,744
New York	59,430,688	30,199,858	450,977,716	141,288,986
North Carolina	482,556	482,556	864,604	864,604
Ohio	8,134,345	6,323,980	37,313,723	27,978,279
Oregon	1,551,194	1,089,744	1,014,577	989,348
Pennsylvania	14,904,458	13,304,800	84,714,526	61,561,596
Rhode Island	3,205,618	2,606,662	41,574,078	6,492,146
South Carolina	520,628	469,912	623,962	623,962
Tennessee	1,724,882	1,596,906	2,852,256	2,852,256
Texas	3,597,522	3,357,700	5,845,150	5,845,150
Utah	208,500	208,500	1,170,064	1,170,064
Vermont	368,700	315,174	6,323,537	1,570,384
Virginia	3,106,384	2,823,198	7,286,498	7,286,498
Washington	232,000	232,000	454,079	454,079
West Virginia	1,277,764	1,223,396	3,995,672	3,995,672
Wisconsin	2,139,081	1,937,748	12,309,396	12,309,396
Wyoming	121,717	121,717	254,636	254,636
Total	190,176,376	155,298,635	1,265,826,720	491,265,576

REPORT ON THE FINANCES.

ASSESSMENTS ON CAPITAL AND DEPOSITS IN 1879.

STATEMENT of the AMOUNT of TAXES ASSESSED on the CAPITAL and DEPOS-
ITS of BANKS and BANKERS held during the twelve months ended May 31, 1879.

States and Territories.	Banks and bankers.		Savings-banks.		Total.
	On capital.	On deposits.	On capital.	On deposits.	
Alabama	$5,212 63	$9,111 21	....	....	$14,323 84
Arizona	339 07	200 00	....	....	639 07
Arkansas	720 56	1,537 59	....	....	2,258 15
California	131,217 81	225,145 94	$9,990 19	$106,444 13	462,796 97
Colorado	2,943 61	7,209 65	....	....	10,153 26
Connecticut	10,269 43	19,049 84	....	29,565 75	58,905 02
Dakota	434 27	1,129 25	....	....	1,563 52
Delaware	3,073 10	3,442 97	....	77 73	6,593 80
Florida	418 07	978 44	....	....	1,396 51
Georgia	10,886 99	17,146 54	....	1,552 81	38,565 44
Idaho	160 83	196 13	....	....	356 96
Illinois	24,529 67	95,223 31	327 26	291 01	120,971 25
Indiana	21,875 21	44,843 27	....	595 12	67,314 60
Iowa	24,267 99	43,701 87	75 00	41 31	68,176 17
Kansas	6,470 52	15,104 91	....	....	21,575 43
Kentucky	56,851 11	57,649 20	....	....	114,500 31
Louisiana	15,711 09	25,391 99	2,500 00	2,731 82	46,334 90
Maine	161 25	567 30	....	1,123 09	1,831 68
Maryland	16,372 94	33,506 22	82 29	5,770 18	57,731 63
Massachusetts	9,483 20	46,110 94	....	1,039 56	56,633 79
Michigan	14,662 87	51,763 54	187 50	49 62	66,863 53
Minnesota	8,001 55	17,257 05	80 72	77 82	25,367 74
Mississippi	5,147 18	7,594 78	....	....	12,741 96
Missouri	42,970 89	130,857 31	....	....	173,828 20
Montana	738 45	1,332 50	....	....	2,060 95
Nebraska	2,085 46	6,166 87	....	....	8,252 33
Nevada	1,982 44	8,902 60	....	....	10,885 04
New Hampshire	305 00	797 16	....	4,995 58	6,097 74
New Jersey	5,982 71	14,475 62	26 25	10,816 23	31,300 81
New Mexico	25 00	398 41	....	....	423 41
New York	156,642 95	570,320 71	....	45,247 88	772,211 54
North Carolina	2,218 83	3,896 07	....	....	6,114 90
Ohio	33,503 92	123,825 77	42 14	9,303 00	166,674 83
Oregon	4,476 03	6,160 14	181 20	20 97	10,838 34
Pennsylvania	70,697 41	276,635 97	1,364 88	6,457 58	355,155 84
Rhode Island	15,055 02	17,213 28	....	39,938 08	72,205 38
South Carolina	3,561 09	4,089 56	....	....	7,650 65
Tennessee	7,562 96	13,660 42	....	....	21,223 38
Texas	16,634 05	24,923 96	....	....	41,558 01
Utah	1,153 12	3,934 49	....	....	5,087 61
Vermont	1,543 42	6,708 13	....	347 18	8,598 74
Virginia	10,713 48	31,565 02	1,807 38	610 99	44,696 80
Washington	1,532 50	1,818 20	....	....	2,850 79
West Virginia	6,745 18	19,001 72	....	....	25,746 90
Wisconsin	9,810 85	46,691 60	....	....	56,502 45
Wyoming	507 92	898 14	....	....	1,406 06
	766,339 25	2,036,305 38	16,614 76	267,097 94	3,088,357 33

ASSESSMENTS ON CAPITAL AND DEPOSITS IN 1880.

STATEMENT of the AMOUNT of TAXES ASSESSED on the CAPITAL and DEPOSITS of BANKS and BANKERS held during the twelve months ended May 31, 1880.

States and Territories.	Banks and bankers.		Savings-banks.		Total.
	On capital.	On deposits.	On capital.	On deposits.	
Alabama	$5,187 70	$10,073 03			$15,260 73
Arizona	498 46	1,021 43			1,519 89
Arkansas	783 69	2,221 70			3,005 39
California	95,281 50	183,634 76	$11,812 15	$75,948 39	366,626 80
Colorado	2,866 22	15,288 19			18,154 41
Connecticut	11,002 01	22,407 45		5,503 63	38,913 09
Dakota	634 52	1,795 84			2,430 36
Delaware	3,054 04	3,957 50		43 60	7,055 74
Florida	389 85	1,167 79			1,557 64
Georgia	18,363 80	19,391 87		2,033 34	39,789 10
Idaho	44 82	190 55	387 00	79 30	651 66
Illinois	23,848 80	135,151 21			159,000 01
Indiana	20,164 00	56,938 58		320 76	77,423 43
Iowa	22,505 94	59,339 00	214 59	109 30	83,169 53
Kansas	7,183 03	22,309 10			29,492 13
Kentucky	52,972 15	65,110 75			118,082 90
Louisiana	12,756 03	23,685 53	208 33	63 33	36,914 22
Maine	180 91	773 98		360 04	1,314 63
Maryland	16,685 00	37,556 06	150 59	403 40	54,795 14
Massachusetts	11,848 36	47,707 21		579 63	60,135 20
Michigan	13,782 30	59,267 27	750 00	844 24	74,903 81
Minnesota	8,025 22	22,168 16		97 59	30,890 97
Mississippi	4,600 33	10,026 42			14,627 25
Missouri	41,716 98	152,992 63			194,709 31
Montana	1,329 42	2,487 68			3,817 10
Nebraska	2,622 79	6,822 28			11,445 07
Nevada	1,515 55	8,233 81			9,749 36
New Hampshire	258 45	991 47	10 42	1,501 96	2,752 30
New Jersey	4,828 93	13,078 99	25 00	607 30	19,440 22
New Mexico	29 16	983 72			1,012 88
New York	195,999 20	700,977 07		5,407 76	902,444 12
North Carolina	2,412 77	4,323 02			6,735 79
Ohio	31,482 97	139,743 92	136 93	137 43	171,501 25
Oregon	5,360 12	4,941 22	88 60	5 52	10,395 40
Pennsylvania	64,505 53	304,682 82	2,018 92	3,125 17	374,332 44
Rhode Island	13,083 31	10,609 81		12,790 03	45,494 05
South Carolina	2,349 56	8,119 81			5,469 37
Tennessee	7,991 03	14,261 28			22,252 31
Texas	16,788 50	20,225 75			46,014 25
Utah	1,042 50	5,850 32			6,892 82
Vermont	1,575 87	7,764 21		87 71	9,427 79
Virginia	12,363 70	35,896 86	1,782 20	535 63	50,548 48
Washington	1,160 00	2,270 35			3,430 35
West Virginia	6,118 48	19,978 36			26,094 84
Wisconsin	9,688 74	61,546 98			71,235 72
Wyoming	608 60	1,273 18			1,881 78
Total	750,008 48	2,345,621 92	17,484 73	110,705 06	3,232,821 09

AVERAGE CAPITAL AND DEPOSITS FOR LAST FOUR FISCAL YEARS.

STATEMENT of the GROSS AMOUNT of AVERAGE CAPITAL and DEPOSITS of SAVINGS-BANKS, BANKS, and BANKERS, other than NATIONAL BANKS, for the years ended May 31, 1877, 1878, 1879, and 1880.

	1877.	1878.	1879.	1880.
Capital of savings-banks	$4,965,500	$5,609,330	$3,507,392	$4,004,823
Capital of banks and bankers	217,215,388	206,897,732	193,781,219	192,173,555
Deposits of savings-banks	893,112,507	843,416,920	820,912,178	796,704,336
Deposits of banks and bankers	475,790,964	483,426,532	407,661,079	469,124,384
Total	1,591,083,519	1,539,350,514	1,434,951,868	1,462,007,096

AVERAGE CAPITAL AND DEPOSITS OF SAVINGS-BANKS AND CAPITAL
OF BANKS INVESTED IN UNITED STATES BONDS FOR LAST FOUR
YEARS.

*STATEMENT of AVERAGE CAPITAL and DEPOSITS of SAVINGS-BANKS, and
the CAPITAL of BANKS and BANKERS, other than NATIONAL BANKS, invested
in UNITED STATES BONDS, compiled from the returns of said banks and bankers for
the years ended May, 1877, 1878, 1879, and 1880.*

	1877.	1878.	1879.	1880.
Capital of savings-banks	$362, 095	$601, 872	$429, 791	$507, 876
Capital of banks and bankers	33, 027, 436	36, 425, 306	40, 013, 376	40, 374, 965
Deposits of savings-banks	102, 859, 674	121, 855, 022	154, 847, 346	182, 586, 893
Total......	136, 249, 205	158, 682, 800	195, 290, 513	223, 469, 634

ABSTRACT OF SEIZURES.

Seizures of property for violation of internal-revenue laws during the
fiscal year ended June 30, 1880, were as follows:

72,083 gallons of distilled spirits, valued at................................ $68,752 98
560,967 pounds of tobacco, valued at................................... 42,718 66
803,544 cigars, valued at... 9,392 46
Miscellaneous property, valued at...................................... 212,102 94

  Total value of seizures.. 332,967 04

ABSTRACT OF REPORTS OF DISTRICT ATTORNEYS.

The following is an abstract of reports of district attorneys for the
fiscal year 1880 of internal-revenue suits commenced, pending, and disposed of:

Suits pending July 1, 1879.

Number of criminal actions...................................... 8,137
Number of civil actions *in personam* 988
Number of actions *in rem*....................................... 351

  Whole number of suits pending July 1, 1879........................ 9,476

Suits commenced during fiscal year 1880.

Number of criminal actions 5,027
Number of civil actions *in personam* 651
Number of actions *in rem* 170

  Whole number commenced 5,848

Suits decided in favor of the United States.

Judgment and costs paid:
Number of criminal actions........:............................ 711
Number of civil actions *in personam* 117
Number of actions *in rem* 49
                                                                      877
Judgment and costs not paid:
Number of criminal actions.. 1,517
Number of civil actions *in personam*........................... 210
Number of actions *in rem* 17
                                                                    1,744

  Whole number of suits decided in favor of the United States............ 2,621

Suits settled by compromise.

Number of criminal actions..	280
Number of civil actions *in personam*	106
Number of actions *in rem*...	29

Whole number of suits settled by compromise	415

Suits decided against the United States.

Number of criminal actions..	499
Number of civil actions *in personam*	39
Number of actions *in rem*	33

Whole number of suits decided against the United States	571

Suits dismissed.

Number of criminal actions..	1,512
Number of civil actions *in personam*	99
Number of actions *in rem*...	42

Whole number of suits dismissed	1,653

Suits pending July 1, 1880.

Number of criminal actions	6,393
Number of civil actions *in personam*	1,060
Number of actions *in rem*	296

Whole number of suits pending July 1, 1880.............................	7,749

Suits wherein sentence is suspended.

Number of criminal actions...	2,259

Judgment of forfeiture and no returns of sales.

Number of actions *in rem*	56

Amount of judgments recovered and costs taxed in criminal actions.

Principal	$256,803 11
Costs	123,212 52

Total	379,015 63

Amount of judgments recovered and costs taxed in civil actions in personam.

Principal	$433,178 59
Costs	17,277 01

Total	450,455 60

Amount of judgments recovered and costs taxed in actions in rem.

Principal...	$20,828 46
Costs	8,470 68

Total	29,299 14

Amount paid to collectors in criminal actions.

Principal $32,465 44
Costs 42,428 97

　　Total 74,894 41

Amount paid to collectors in civil actions in personam.

Principal $109,408 38
Costs 9,119 23

　　Total 118,527 61

Amount paid to collectors in actions in rem.

Principal $32,030 20
Costs 5,487 92

　　Total 37,518 12

OFFERS IN COMPROMISE.

The following statement shows the number of offers received and accepted in compromise cases, for the fiscal year ended June 30, 1880, with amount of tax, assessed penalty, and specific penalty accepted, as provided under section 3229 Revised Statutes:

Months.	Compromise offers—		Amount of tax.	Assessed penalty.	Amount of specific penalty.	Total.
	Received.	Accepted.				
1879.						
July	74	99	$15,198 69	$50 00	$2,355 73	$17,604 42
August	53	15	51,700 99	100 00	645 00	52,445 99
September	65					
October	116	129	391 72	15 00	5,329 88	5,736 60
November	59	51	28,587 15	87 50	4,107 33	32,701 98
December	84	89	670 80	10 00	3,609 17	4,289 97
1880.						
January	91	85	52,094 06	83 75	4,922 55	57,110 36
February	125	71	1,341 51	68 75	2,648 58	4,058 84
March	159	86	11,337 91	65 00	6,389 90	17,792 81
April	54	93	32,587 80	91 25	3,456 63	36,134 88
May	61	98	24,310 99	37 50	5,048 25	29,396 74
June	69	75	532 20	48 33	1,510 40	2,090 93
Total	1,050	891	218,703 02	637 08	40,023 42	259,363 52

Whole number of offers received 1,050
Whole number of offers accepted 891
Amount of tax accepted $218,703 02
Amount of assessed penalty fixed by law 637 08
Amount of specific penalty, in lieu of fines, forfeitures, and penalties.... 40,023 42

　　Total 259,363 52

ASSESSMENTS.

The following table shows the assessments made by the Commissioner of Internal Revenue during the fiscal years ended June 30, 1879, and

June 30, 1880, respectively, and the increase or decrease on each article or occupation:

Article or occupation.	Amount assessed during fiscal year ended—		Fiscal year ended June 30, 1880.	
	June 30, 1879.	June 30, 1880.	Increase over 1879.	Decrease from 1879.
Tax on deficiencies in production of distilled spirits	$63, 574 50	$73, 158 63	$9, 584 13	
Tax on excess of materials used in the production of distilled spirits	5, 050 27	2, 829 97		$2, 220 30
Tax on deposits and capital of banks and bankers	3, 143, 302 64	3, 247, 998 90	104, 696 26	
Tax on circulation of banks and others	9, 242 62	461, 597 82	452, 355 20	
Tax on distilled spirits fraudulently removed or seized	126, 002 14	53, 312 18		72, 689 96
Tax on fermented liquors removed from brewery unstamped	6, 144 33	877 75		5, 266 58
Tax on tobacco, snuff, and cigars removed from factory unstamped	61, 917 45	88, 584 85	26, 667 40	
Tax on proprietary articles removed unstamped	2, 614 95	1, 529 86		1, 088 09
Assessed penalties	102, 285 72	93, 265 14		9, 020 58
Legacies and successions	182, 036 71	135, 532 80		46, 503 91
Unassessed and unassessable penalties, interest, taxes previously abated, conscience money, and deficiencies in bonded accounts which have been collected; interest tax on distilled spirits; also fines, penalties, and forfeitures, and costs paid to collectors by order of court, or by order of Secretary, and unassessable taxes recovered; also amount of penalties and interest received for validating unstamped instruments (Form 58)	401, 978 22	555, 315 50	153, 337 28	
Special taxes (licenses)	97, 068 91	50, 776 56		27, 292 35
Tax on income and dividends	34, 539 54	40, 614 60	6, 075 06	
Total	4, 235, 756 00	4, 814, 394 56	578, 638 56	

It will be observed that a decrease has occurred in the assessment of the following taxes, viz: On excess of materials used in the production of distilled spirits; on distilled spirits fraudulently removed; on fermented liquors removed from the brewery unstamped; on proprietary articles removed unstamped; on assessed penalties; and on occupations (special taxes).

This indicates a better observance of the laws on the part of taxpayers, and a more prompt payment of their taxes.

The assessment of taxes on legacies and successions is under a law long since repealed, and in the nature of things such assessments must naturally decrease.

There has been an increase in (1) the assessments on deficiencies in the production of distilled spirits; (2) of the tax on tobacco, snuff, and cigars removed from factories unstamped; (3) on the capital and deposits of banks and bankers; (4) on the circulating notes of individuals and corporations; (5) taxes recovered by suit, and (6) on incomes and dividends.

As to the first two classes named the slight increase is not regarded as significant of increased violations of law, as the assessments are below the average.

An increase in the third class is a gratifying evidence of increased prosperity in the business of the banks and bankers of the country.

The increase in the fifth class arises mainly from collections of taxes on net earnings and gross receipts of railroad and other State corporations.

The following statement shows the amount of assessments in each of the several States and Territories of the United States during the fiscal year ended June 30, 1880:

State	Amount	State	Amount
Alabama	$33,402 91	Montana	$4,129 60
Arizona	2,634 96	Nebraska	14,832 90
Arkansas	11,146 45	Nevada	11,485 22
California	392,448 72	New Hampshire	5,811 65
Colorado	25,787 56	New Jersey	55,709 17
Connecticut	59,620 93	New Mexico	1,211 21
Dakota	4,480 57	New York	1,132,572 61
Delaware	9,588 61	North Carolina	46,215 02
Florida	2,863 99	Ohio	224,013 65
Georgia	59,036 94	Oregon	11,091 96
Idaho	524 06	Pennsylvania	890,224 19
Illinois	214,091 02	Rhode Island	47,105 07
Indiana	114,086 33	South Carolina	11,840 52
Iowa	98,346 17	Tennessee	48,890 13
Kansas	32,280 53	Texas	55,534 95
Kentucky	290,072 52	Utah	33,078 75
Louisiana	112,912 06	Vermont	13,149 39
Maine	4,298 45	Virginia	79,233 66
Maryland	99,613 72	Washington	3,657 03
Massachusetts	77,710 14	West Virginia	32,789 66
Michigan	95,768 77	Wisconsin	84,750 29
Minnesota	35,036 89	Wyoming	2,463 88
Mississippi	17,648 64		
Missouri	211,202 91	Total	4,814,394 56

TABULAR STATEMENTS.*

I append tabular statements to accompany the bound volume, as follows:

Table A, showing the receipts from each specific source of revenue, and the amounts refunded in each collection district, State, and Territory of the United States, for the fiscal year ended June 30, 1880.

Table B, showing the number and value of internal-revenue stamps ordered monthly by the Commissioner and from the office of the Commissioner; the receipts from the sale of stamps and the commissions allowed thereon; also the number and value of stamps for special taxes, tobacco, cigars, cigarettes, snuff, distilled spirits, and fermented liquors, issued monthly to collectors during the fiscal year ended June 30, 1880.

Table C, showing the percentages of receipts from the several general sources of revenue in each State and Territory of the United States to the aggregate receipts from the same sources, by fiscal years, from July 1, 1863, to June 30, 1880.

Table D, showing the aggregate receipts from all sources in each collection district, State, and Territory of the United States, by fiscal years, from September 1, 1872, to June 30, 1880.

Table E, showing the receipts in the United States from each specific source of revenue, by fiscal years, from September 1, 1862, to June 30, 1880.

Table F, showing the ratio of receipts in the United States from specific sources of revenue to the aggregate receipts from all sources, by fiscal years, from July 1, 1863, to June 30, 1880.

Table G, showing the returns of distilled spirits, manufactured tobacco, snuff, cigars, and cigarettes, under the several acts of legislation and by fiscal years, from September 1, 1862, to June 30, 1880.

Table H, showing the receipts from special taxes in each collection district, State, and Territory for the special-tax year ended April 30, 1880.

Table I, Abstract of reports of district attorneys concerning suits and prosecutions under the internal-revenue laws during the fiscal year ended June 30, 1880.

Table K, Abstract of seizures of property for violation of internal-revenue laws during the fiscal year ended June 30, 1880.

Very respectfully,

GREEN B. RAUM,
Commissioner.

Hon. JOHN SHERMAN,
Secretary of the Treasury.

* These tabular statements are omitted for want of space, but they are printed in the bound volumes.

REPORT OF THE COMPTROLLER OF THE CURRENCY.

a

REPORT

OF

THE COMPTROLLER OF THE CURRENCY.

TREASURY DEPARTMENT,
OFFICE OF THE COMPTROLLER OF THE CURRENCY,
Washington, November 27, 1880.

I have the honor to submit for the consideration of Congress the eighteenth annual report of the Comptroller of the Currency, in compliance with section 333 of the Revised Statutes of the United States.

Fifty-seven national banks have been organized since November 1, 1879, with an aggregate authorized capital of $6,374,170, to which $3,662,200 in circulating notes have been issued.

Three banks, having a total capital of $700,000, have failed, and dividends amounting to sixty-five, eighty, and ninety per cent., respectively, have been paid to the creditors of these banks during the year and since the date of failure.

Ten banks, with an aggregate capital of $1,070,000 and an aggregate circulation of $928,800, have voluntarily discontinued business during the year; and one bank, which had formerly gone into liquidation, has been placed in the hands of a receiver for the purpose of enforcing the individual liability of the shareholders. The total number of national banks organized from the establishment of the national banking system, February 25, 1863, to November 1 of the present year, is 2,495. Of these, 314 have gone into voluntary liquidation by the vote of shareholders owning two-thirds of their respective capitals, and 86 have been placed in the hands of receivers for the purpose of closing up their affairs.

National banks are located in every State of the Union except Mississippi, and in every Territory except Arizona; and the total number in operation at the date last named was 2,095, which is the greatest number of banks that has been in operation at any one time.

The 13 States having the largest capital are Massachusetts, New York, Pennsylvania, Ohio, Connecticut, Rhode Island, Illinois, Indiana, Maryland, New Jersey, Maine, Kentucky, and Michigan, in the order named. The shares of the national banks which in the year 1876 numbered more than six and a half millions, and were held in average amounts of $2,400, were then distributed among more than 208,000 persons residing in every State and Territory of the Union, in eleven countries or provinces of this continent and adjacent islands, and in twenty-five countries in Europe, Asia, and Africa.[*]

Included in the aggregate number of national banks organized are ten national gold banks, three of which, still in operation, are located in the State of California, having an aggregate capital of two millions

---

[*] Interesting information in reference to the distribution of national-bank stock will be found on pp. 69 and 144 to 148 of Comptroller's Report for 1876.

8 F

113

of dollars and a total circulation of $840,000. Four of these banks have changed into other organizations under the act of February 14, 1880, which provided for such conversions.

A bill is now pending in Congress providing for the repeal of section 5176 of the Revised Statutes, which limited the amount of circulation to be issued to the national banks organized subsequently to July 12, 1870, to $500,000, and also authorizing all national banks to issue circulation not exceeding the amount of their capital, upon the deposit of the necessary amount of United States bonds. The passage of this act will entitle all national banks to the same proportion of circulation upon capital and bonds as is possessed by those organized prior to March 3, 1865, and the passage of this bill is recommended.

The following table exhibits the resources and liabilities of the national banks at the close of business on the first day of October, 1880, the returns from New York City, from Boston, Philadelphia, and Baltimore, from the other reserve cities, and from the remaining banks of the country, being tabulated separately:

	New York City.	Boston, Philadelphia, and Baltimore.	*Other reserve cities.	Country banks.	Aggregate.
	47 banks.	101 banks.	83 banks.	1,850 banks.	2,090 banks.
RESOURCES.					
Loans and discounts	$238,428,501	$191,312,159	$104,026,057	$503,294,724	$1,037,061,441
Overdrafts	66,825	95,770	314,797	3,438,474	3,915,826
Bonds for circulation	21,170,500	56,562,300	25,550,300	254,486,250	357,789,350
Bonds for deposits	820,000	550,000	8,309,500	5,947,500	14,827,000
U. S. bonds on hand	7,011,450	2,620,250	3,641,200	15,510,500	28,793,400
Other stocks and bonds	10,420,603	4,348,177	3,633,116	30,466,254	48,863,150
Due from reserve agents		26,278,079	21,913,471	86,371,229	134,562,779
Due from other national banks	14,191,525	13,145,804	9,374,611	26,311,857	63,023,797
Due from other banks and bankers	3,010,707	1,634,443	2,930,254	8,305,794	15,881,198
Real estate, furniture, and fixtures	10,048,431	6,989,071	4,798,064	26,210,247	48,045,833
Current expenses	1,045,085	769,375	679,264	3,892,458	6,386,182
Premiums	750,763	449,063	288,294	2,030,350	3,488,470
Checks and other cash items	2,444,390	1,075,684	882,536	8,326,392	12,729,002
Exchanges for clearing-house	94,520,216	19,939,292	6,132,142	503,690	121,095,250
Bills of other national banks	1,534,823	2,208,774	2,577,436	11,889,910	18,210,943
Fractional currency	48,388	28,996	52,974	236,814	367,172
Specie	59,783,555	18,368,959	10,001,177	21,192,818	109,346,509
Legal tender notes	9,726,303	6,937,458	12,303,367	27,613,370	56,640,458
U. S. certificates of deposit	1,310,000	3,655,000	2,050,000	640,000	7,655,000
Five per cent redemption fund	940,597	2,544,725	1,101,572	11,334,907	15,921,741
Due from U. S. Treasury	411,383	99,021	108,748	562,973	1,182,125
Totals	477,684,045	359,637,310	215,898,760	1,052,566,511	2,105,786,626
LIABILITIES.					
Capital stock	50,650,000	78,748,330	37,595,500	290,560,155	457,553,985
Surplus fund	18,185,383	20,099,979	11,353,641	70,279,580	120,518,583
Undivided profits	10,396,427	4,960,959	4,125,305	26,656,999	46,139,690
National-bank notes outstanding	18,594,918	50,102,858	22,270,608	226,381,652	317,350,036
State-bank notes outstanding	47,482	46,221		177,342	271,045
Dividends unpaid	188,702	1,272,861	155,813	1,835,128	3,452,504
Individual deposits	242,044,722	146,079,901	88,224,947	397,188,067	873,537,637
U. S. deposits	276,099	347,687	1,955,554	4,969,199	7,548,539
Deposits of U. S. disbursing officers	132,118	8,284	809,749	2,394,235	3,344,387
Due to national banks	105,933,844	40,811,064	27,933,758	17,446,040	192,124,705
Due to other banks and bankers	31,234,350	14,275,452	20,675,304	10,150,572	75,735,677
Notes and bills re-discounted		502,957	803,705	2,371,570	3,178,233
Bills payable		1,780,757	1,094,876	2,155,972	5,031,605
Totals	477,684,045	359,637,310	215,898,760	1,052,506,511	2,105,786,626

*The reserve cities, in addition to New York, Boston, Philadelphia, and Baltimore, are Albany, Pittsburgh, Washington, New Orleans, Louisville, Cincinnati, Cleveland, Chicago, Detroit, Milwaukee, Saint Louis, and San Francisco.

COMPARATIVE STATEMENTS OF THE NATIONAL BANKS FOR ELEVEN
YEARS.

The following table exhibits the resources and liabilities of the national banks for eleven years, at nearly corresponding dates from 1870 to 1880:

	Oct. 8, 1870.	Oct. 2, 1871.	Oct. 3, 1872.	Sept. 12, 1873.	Oct. 2, 1874.	Oct. 1, 1875.	Oct. 2, 1876.	Oct. 1, 1877.	Oct. 1, 1878.	Oct. 2, 1879.	Oct. 1, 1880.
	1,615 banks.	1,767 banks.	1,919 banks.	1,976 banks.	2,004 banks.	2,087 banks.	2,089 banks.	2,080 banks.	2,053 banks.	2,048 banks.	2,090 banks.
RESOURCES.	Millions	Millions	Millions	Millions	Millions	Millions	Millions	Millions	Millions	Millions	Millions
Loans	715.9	831.6	877.2	944.2	954.4	984.7	931.3	891.9	834.0	878.5	1,041.6
Bonds for circulation	340.9	364.5	382.0	386.3	383.3	370.3	337.2	336.8	347.6	357.3	357.8
Other U. S. bonds	37.7	45.8	27.6	23.6	28.6	28.1	47.8	45.0	94.7	71.2	43.8
Stocks, bonds, &c	23.6	24.5	23.5	23.7	27.8	33.5	34.4	34.5	36.9	39.7	48.9
Due from banks	109.4	143.2	128.2	149.5	134.8	144.7	140.9	129.9	138.9	167.3	213.5
Real estate	27.5	30.1	32.3	34.7	38.1	42.4	43.1	45.2	46.7	47.5	48.0
Specie	18.5	13.2	10.3	19.9	21.2	8.1	21.4	23.7	30.7	43.2	109.3
Legal-tender notes	79.3	107.0	102.1	92.4	86.0	76.5	84.2	66.9	64.4	69.2	56.6
Nat'l bank notes	12.5	14.3	15.8	16.1	18.5	16.5	15.9	15.6	16.9	16.7	18.2
C. H. exchanges	79.1	115.3	125.0	100.3	109.7	87.9	100.0	74.5	82.4	113.0	121.1
U. S. cert. of deposit			6.7	20.6	42.8	48.8	29.2	33.4	32.7	26.8	7.7
Due from U. S. Treas			1		30.3	19.6	16.7	16.0	16.5	17.0	17.1
Other resources	66.3	41.2	25.2	17.3	18.3	19.1	19.1	28.7	24.9	22.1	23.0
Totals	1,510.7	1,730.6	1,755.8	1,830.0	1,877.2	1,882.2	1,827.2	1,741.1	1,767.3	1,868.8	2,105.8
LIABILITIES.											
Capital stock	430.4	458.3	479.6	491.0	493.8	504.8	498.8	479.5	466.2	454.1	457.6
Surplus fund	94.1	101.1	110.3	120.3	129.0	134.4	132.2	122.6	116.9	114.8	120.5
Undivided profits	38.6	42.0	46.6	54.5	51.5	53.0	46.4	44.5	44.9	41.3	46.1
Circulation	293.9	317.4	335.1	340.3	334.2	319.1	292.2	291.9	301.9	313.8	317.3
Due to depositors	515.2	631.4	628.9	640.0	683.8	679.4	666.2	630.4	668.4	736.9	887.9
Due to banks	130.1	171.9	143.8	173.0	175.8	179.7	179.8	161.6	165.1	201.2	267.9
Other liabilities	8.4	8.5	11.5	11.5	9.1	11.8	10.6	10.4	7.9	6.7	8.5
Totals	1,510.7	1,730.6	1,755.8	1,830.6	1,877.2	1,882.2	1,827.2	1,741.1	1,767.3	1,868.8	2,105.8

THE BANKS SINCE RESUMPTION.

The movement of the currency and the operations of the banks have never been more interesting than during the months which have intervened since the resumption of specie payments. To most of the political economists of this and other countries the resumption of coin payments by the United States at the time fixed by law, and its successful maintenance, were deemed almost impossible. No country had ever before successfully maintained payments in coin with so large a volume of currency outstanding, or with an amount of currency greatly in excess of its coin. Even those who were known to be earnestly in favor of resumption, both in and out of Congress, doubted the ability of the government and of the banks to commence and continue coin payments without a preparatory reduction of the amount of notes in circulation. They said, truthfully, that no nation maintains at par a convertible paper currency which has not in its banks or among its people an equal amount of coin, and that, if successful, the United States would be an exception, and the only exception in this respect, among commercial nations. But the resumption act giving authority for the purchase of coin in the markets of the world with United States four, four and one-half, or five per cent. bonds made resumption certain, if the bonds for a sufficient amount could be readily marketed at not less than par, as authorized by law. Purchasers for the bonds were promptly found, and resumption came so easily that many persons now believe it could have been as well accomplished one year earlier, if Congress had fixed upon January 1, 1878, instead of upon the following New Year's day.

Since the date of resumption the country has been month by month growing richer in coin, not by the sales of bonds, which have been rapidly increasing in value, but by the production of the mines and the influx of specie in return payment for the excess of exports of our abundant products over our imports. The whole country has become so habituated to the use of paper money that the difficulty has been—not to provide means for its payment, for scarcely a dollar has been demanded—but to supply the people with Treasury and national-bank notes, which have been almost universally preferred.

For many years past, large amounts of currency have been annually drawn from the banks of the city of New York by the banks in the interior, for the purchase and shipment of grain and other products. The banks in the West and South supply the grain-buyers with money, who pay it to the farmers, and by them it is disbursed to the country merchants. It then goes to the wholesale merchants in the larger cities of the interior, by whom it is deposited in the banks and returned again to the money centers in the Eastern States. Thus the money which was paid out in the fall returns again to the city of New York long before midwinter, whereby much of the currency of the country, instead of continuing to circulate, accumulates in the New York banks both before and after the time for the large movements of produce.

This ebb and flow of the currency continued yearly up to the time of the great harvest of 1879. The drain of coin and currency from the large cities, amounting to more than 100 million dollars during the fall of that year, made currency scarce in New York notwithstanding the unprecedented influx of gold from abroad. The usual return of the currency in the winter was expected, but did not occur.

The experience of 1879 was considered exceptional, but another year has nearly passed and the experience of the former year has been, to a considerable extent, repeated. A large portion of the avails of produce has been retained, either for the liquidation of debts, for employment in trade and commerce at home, or in the many new and extensive enterprises for which the West is distinguished, where there would appear to be no limit for the safe and profitable employment of capital. The coin in the banks has increased from 41 millions on January 1, 1879, to 109 millions on October 1, 1880. The Treasury holds its immense hoard of gold, not surpassed in amount by any other depository in the world.

The merchant, the manufacturer, and the farmer are alike prosperous; the people have paid their debts to an unprecedented degree, and hold their earnings in the paper currency of the government and of the banks in larger amounts than have hitherto been known. The receipts of the government have been so large that, after refunding many millions of 5 and 6 per cent. bonds into 4 per cents., it has still been able during the year to purchase in the market at a premium more than 100 millions of its bonds for cancellation. The deposits of the banks have everywhere increased, and money has been abundant wherever business or investment has invited capital, and there has probably never been a period when it has generally commanded so low a rate of interest as during the last two years.

The rate at the Bank of England and the Bank of France has, for a considerable portion of this period been 2½ per cent. The English consols have for the first time in twenty-seven years advanced to par, while the rate for call loans in London has at times been at what may be termed the infinitesimal rate of from one-half to seven-eighths of one per cent.

per annum. Low rates have also prevailed in this country. In New York for some months past money at call, upon the best collaterals, could be obtained at from 2 to 3 per cent. The average rate upon first-class commercial paper during the fiscal year of 1879 was 4.4 per cent., while the average rate during the succeeding fiscal year has been 5.3 per cent., owing not to natural but to artificial causes. The rate, however, for first-class mercantile paper in the past four months has been from 4 to 4½ per cent. Low rates have prevailed, not only in New York City, where money is not unfrequently borrowed upon good collaterals for speculative purposes, but also throughout the country, including many places where money has heretofore been loaned, if at all, at usurious rates. The rates during the past year on large transactions in first-class commercial paper have been: In Philadelphia 3 to 5 per cent.; Boston and Baltimore, average 5; Washington, 7; Chicago, 4 to 7; Saint Louis, 5 to 7; Milwaukee, 6 to 8; Cincinnati, 6 to 7; Cleveland, 6 to 8; Saint Paul, 8 to 10; Omaha, 10; Denver, 10 to 15; San Francisco, 8; California (country), 9 to 12; Louisville, 6 to 7; Richmond, 7; Charleston, 7 to 8; Savannah, 8; Selma, average 9; Atlanta, 10; New Orleans, 4 to 6. Rates at nearly every point are less than for previous years.

The borrowing power of the government for a considerable portion of the year has been at 3½ per cent., and that of many of the leading States and cities 4 per cent. The legal rate in the State of New York has been reduced from 7 to 6 per cent. There has also been a large reduction in rates at remote points, which, until recently, have been considered upon the frontier. Many seven per cent. railroad bonds were until recently placed with difficulty, even at a discount; now six per cent. bonds, upon lines at more remote points, are, in many instances, sold at par. In portions of the country the rates for loans upon real estate are higher than for business paper. In some of the Southern States it is difficult to loan money upon real estate, on account of the legal obstacles in the way of collecting it. The highest prevailing rates are found in the country districts of the South, but it is now believed they will be gradually reduced, both by the increasing value of its productions and by the introduction of foreign capital to be employed in manufactures, which have already been introduced with great success. In large districts of the West, where formerly money could not be readily obtained upon real estate, the number of borrowers is much less, and the demand by no means equal to the supply of funds seeking investment in that class of securities. Such loans are now regarded not only as desirable investments, so far as security is concerned, but are made at a much less rate of interest than formerly. The rates in New York are subject to frequent changes, not only on account of the importation of coin, the drain in payment for produce from the interior, and the purchase of bonds by the government, but by the influx of foreign capital seeking employment in consequence of the prevailing depression in business elsewhere. If the rates are favorable, large amounts of money are placed by cable by residents in foreign countries, and by telegraph between remote points in our own country, with as much certainty and safety as by the use of bills of exchange or by the movement of coin itself. So reliable has this means of transfer become that not only are payments thus made at home and abroad, but large sales of breadstuffs and other products are accomplished by parties in the interior cities without the intervention of agents at the sea-ports, thus shortening the time of bills drawn upon shipments of

Many men who were formerly borrowers have become lenders; and numerous lenders now seek investment in government bonds and other securities which yield much less than the legal rate of interest.

The abundance of money and the low rates of interest have made it difficult for capitalists to find satisfactory investments and have led the Comptroller to examine the statements of the banks for a series of years in order to compare their ratios of loans to their means, and to ascertain if, during the past two years, they have found use for their increased deposits.

In order to show this, the following table is given, which exhibits concisely the ratios of the loans of the banks to their capital, surplus, and net deposits, and the ratios of specie and legal-tender notes to net deposits, in New York and in the group of other principal cities separately, at corresponding dates from 1870 to 1880, inclusive:

NEW YORK CITY.

Dates.	No. of banks.	Loans.	Capital.	Surplus.	Net deposits.	Specie.	Legal-tender notes and U. S. certificates.	Ratios of— Loans to capital, surplus, and net deposits.	Cash to net deposits.
		Millions.	Millions.	Millions.	Millions.	Millions.	Millions.	Per cent.	Per cent.
October 2, 1870	54	168.1	73.4	18.8	155.8	9.1	45.8	66.7	34.4
October 2, 1871	54	198.0	71.2	10.5	191.3	8.7	50.4	70.0	30.9
October 3, 1872	50	188.4	71.3	20.9	158.0	6.4	39.0	73.3	28.7
Septem. 12, 1873.....	48	199.3	70.3	21.0	172.7	14.0	39.3	75.3	27.3
October 2, 1874	48	202.2	68.5	22.7	204.6	14.4	52.4	66.4	32.6
October 1, 1875	48	202.4	68.5	22.5	202.3	5.0	54.5	69.0	29.4
October 2, 1876	47	184.3	66.4	15.0	197.9	14.6	45.3	65.1	30.3
October 1, 1877	47	169.3	57.4	16.6	174.9	15.9	34.3	68.0	27.0
October 1, 1878	47	169.7	53.8	15.9	189.8	13.3	36.5	65.4	26.2
October 2, 1879	47	196.0	50.7	16.0	210.2	19.4	32.6	70.8	24.7
October 1, 1880	47	238.5	50.7	18.2	268.1	59.8	11.0	70.8	26.4

OTHER RESERVE CITIES.

		Millions.	Millions.	Millions.	Millions.	Millions.	Millions.	Per cent.	Per cent.
October 6, 1870	159	194.1	112.0	28.5	147.5	3.0	38.5	67.9	28.1
October 2, 1871	174	230.7	119.0	28.3	167.5	1.5	42.5	68.7	23.5
October 3, 1872	180	242.0	124.9	29.8	179.6	1.9	36.7	73.4	21.5
Septem. 12, 1873.....	181	263.1	127.2	32.5	197.6	3.2	36.3	73.6	20.0
October 2, 1874	182	272.5	127.1	35.2	213.9	4.4	36.7	71.3	18.7
October 1, 1875	188	279.3	128.8	37.0	222.9	1.5	37.1	71.9	17.3
October 2, 1876	189	264.7	127.9	37.4	216.3	4.0	37.1	69.4	19.0
October 1, 1877	188	254.3	123.7	33.1	203.4	5.0	34.4	70.6	19.7
October 1, 1878	184	231.2	119.2	30.8	199.2	9.4	29.5	66.2	19.5
October 2, 1879	181	244.4	115.4	30.2	226.2	11.3	33.0	65.4	19.4
October 1, 1880	184	295.6	116.3	32.0	286.8	28.3	25.0	67.7	16.5

If the ratios of the loans of the banks in New York City to their capital, surplus, and net deposits be examined, it will be found that in October of 1879 and 1880 they were 70.8 per cent., in 1878 but 65.4 per cent., in 1877 but 68 per cent., and in 1876 65.1 per cent.; and that the loans are now proportionately higher than at any time since 1873. The means of the banks in Boston and the other reserve cities were more fully employed in October than they were at the corresponding dates for the two previous years, though the business of the banks was not as much extended as it was during the four years following the crisis of 1873.

It will surprise those whose attention has not heretofore been called to the subject to find how closely the means of the banks in the commercial cities have been employed during the last eleven years, notwithstanding the variations in rates of interest, and particularly during the last two years, when money has been so abundant and the deposits have so rapidly increased. It will be seen that prior to 1876, with the exception of a single year, the loans in New York exceeded the net deposits, while since that time, though there has been considerable variation, the net deposits have been somewhat in excess of the loans at the dates given. In the other principal cities, which continually keep large amounts of money in New York subject to demand, and thus diminish their own net deposits as given in the above table, the loans have always largely exceeded their deposits. The same remark is more emphatically true of the banks in the country districts which have in New York, as well as in other cities, large amounts of money on deposit subject to call. The capital of this class of banks is also much larger as compared with their deposits than is that of the banks in the large cities, and their loans therefore relatively greater.

The ratio of the loans of this group of banks to their capital, surplus, and net deposits will be seen in the statement below, which also includes a table showing the loans, capital, surplus deposits and cash reserves of all the national banks of the United States:

STATES AND TERRITORIES.

Dates.	No. of banks.	Loans.	Capital.	Surplus.	Net deposits.	Specie.	Legal-tender notes and U. S. certificates.	Ratios of—	
								Loans to capitol, surplus, and net deposits.	Cash to net deposits.
		Millions.	*Millions.*	*Millions.*	*Millions.*	*Millions.*	*Millions.*	*Per cent.*	*Per cent.*
October 8, 1870	1,402	353.7	245.0	48.8	216.2	2.4	36.4	68.4	18.9
October 2, 1871	1,539	402.0	265.1	53.3	237.8	1.8	41.6	69.8	16.2
October 3, 1872	1,689	451.8	282.4	59.6	282.1	1.9	43.3	72.3	16.0
Septem. 12, 1873	1,747	481.8	292.7	65.9	303.1	2.1	44.5	72.7	15.4
October 2, 1874	1,774	479.7	298.2	71.1	292.9	2.4	33.7	72.5	12.3
October 1, 1875	1,851	503.0	307.5	74.9	306.7	1.6	33.7	73.0	11.5
October 2, 1876	1,853	482.3	305.5	75.9	291.5	2.8	31.0	71.7	11.6
October 1, 1877	1,845	468.3	298.4	73.1	289.4	4.2	31.6	70.9	12.4
October 1, 1878	1,822	438.1	293.1	70.2	288.3	8.0	31.1	68.5	13.6
October 2, 1879	1,820	436.1	288.0	68.5	329.3	11.5	30.4	63.9	12.7
October 1, 1880	1,859	506.7	290.6	70.3	410.3	21.2	28.3	65.7	12.1

UNITED STATES.

Dates.	No. of banks.	Loans.	Capital.	Surplus.	Net deposits.	Specie.	Legal-tender notes and U. S. certificates.	Ratios of—	
		Millions.	*Millions.*	*Millions.*	*Millions.*	*Millions.*	*Millions.*	*Per cent.*	*Per cent.*
October 8, 1870	1,615	715.9	430.4	94.1	523.5	14.5	122.7	68.3	26.2
October 2, 1871	1,767	831.6	458.2	101.1	636.6	12.0	184.5	69.5	23.8
October 3, 1872	1,919	877.2	479.6	110.3	619.8	10.2	119.0	72.5	26.8
Septem. 12, 1873	1,976	944.2	491.1	120.3	673.4	19.9	113.1	73.5	19.8
October 2, 1874	2,004	954.4	493.8	129.0	717.3	21.2	192.8	71.2	20.0
October 1, 1875	2,097	984.7	504.8	134.4	731.9	8.1	125.3	71.8	18.2
October 2, 1876	2,089	931.3	499.8	132.2	705.7	21.4	113.4	69.6	19.1
October 1, 1877	2,080	891.9	479.5	122.8	667.7	22.7	100.3	70.2	18.4
October 1, 1878	2,053	834.0	466.1	116.9	677.3	30.7	97.1	66.2	18.9
October 2, 1879	2,048	878.5	454.1	114.8	767.7	42.2	96.0	65.7	18.0
October 1, 1880	2,090	1,041.0	457.6	120.5	967.2	109.3	64.3	69.3	17.9

The ratios of the loans of the banks in the country districts were, on October 1, last, 7.3 per cent. less than at the corresponding dates in 1875, and 5.2 per cent. less than in 1877. The opportunities for using money in this group of banks are not in proportion to the increase of deposits, and their balances in other banks have by no means diminished.

It will be seen that the loans of the banks now exceed 1,041 millions, which is 207 millions more than at the corresponding date in 1878, while the capital and surplus at the previous date was 5 millions in excess of the present amount. The net deposits in the same period increased nearly 290 millions, and the total individual and bank deposits,

not deducting the amount due from banks and the clearing-house ex·
changes, more than 322 millions, amounting to the large and unprecedented sum of 1,155 millions, as may be seen from a previous table.

The following table gives a classification of the loans of the banks in
the city of New York, in Boston, Philadelphia, and Baltimore, and in
the other reserve cities, for the last two years, at the dates of their reports in the month of October:

1879.

Classification.	New York City.	Boston, Philadelphia, and Baltimore.	Other reserve cities.	Country banks.	Aggregate.
	47 banks.	99 banks.	82 banks.	1,820 banks.	2,048 banks.
On U. S. bonds on demand.....	$8,286,525	$2,017,226	$4,360,523	....	$14,664,274
On other stocks, bonds, &c., on demand	78,062,085	22,605,795	11,445,079	....	112,112,969
On single-name paper without other security	22,491,926	13,136,911	7,150,239	....	42,779,076
All other loans	87,011,366	118,267,128	65,023,494	$435,154,810	705,456,798
Totals.................	195,851,902	156,027,060	87,979,335	435,154,810	875,013,107

1880.

	47 banks.	101 banks.	83 banks.	1,859 banks.	2,090 banks.
On U. S. bonds on demand	$8,015,077	$925,445	$1,378,168	....	$5,818,690
On other stocks, bonds, &c., on demand	92,636,982	30,835,692	16,558,260	....	140,027,934
On single-name paper without other security	27,755,152	22,542,776	10,402,295	....	60,700,223
All other loans.	114,127,290	137,405,246	75,987,334	$503,294,724	830,514,594
Totals	236,428,501	191,312,159	104,026,057	503,294,724	1,097,061,441

In this table will be seen—what would be expected from a large increase in the clearing-house exchanges, which are 38 millions more
than in 1878, and larger than at any time since 1873—a large increase
in loans upon stocks and bonds payable on demand. Much of this increase is due to operations at the stock board, which are always most
buoyant in prosperous times; but a considerable portion may be due to
loans made to banks and bankers in the interior upon collateral security,
at rates so low as to leave room for profit in reloaning to their own
dealers.

The amount invested by the banks in United States and other stocks
and bonds is more than 92 millions of dollars, as may be seen in a previous table, which fact is evidence either of a difficulty in obtaining
satisfactory loans or of a preference for such temporary investments.

When the rates of interest are low there is danger that bank managers, in their desire to use their available means, may be induced to loan
upon securities which are not of the best character, and thus in the end
diminish rather than increase their earnings. The loans were at the
highest point in the year 1875, and the two previous years, and the national banks were then enthusiastic over the high rates of interest,
their large deposits, and their large earnings and dividends; but the
delusion has been dispelled by the enormous losses which they have
been obliged to charge off during the past five years, reaching the extra-

ordinary sum of 100 millions, which were largely the result of overtrad-
ing during the period when gold coin was a commodity, and the legal
standard a promise to pay, unfulfilled and fluctuating in value for seventeen years. The great losses experienced during these years, which
will not soon be forgotten, enforce the principle that no legitimate business is safe which is conducted upon a varying standard of value; and
the crisis of 1873 will always be remembered as a striking example of the
evil results arising from business conducted during "good times" upon
a fictitious basis.

The amount of legal cash reserve required of the banks in New York
City is 25 per cent. of their deposits, of the banks in the other reserve
cities one-half of this ratio, and of the banks in the country districts six
per cent. of their deposits. The amount required has in the aggregate
always been held, except in a single instance in the city of New York,
during the last ten years (without including the redemption fund in the
Treasury), by the three different groups of national banks; but the
aggregate amount in the city of New York has been at times very close,
and particularly during the last three years, and some banks have frequently, if not habitually, expanded their loans beyond reasonable limits, relying upon imports of gold or purchases of bonds by the Treasury
to replenish their deficient reserves.

The banks in the interior, if we consider their large deposits elsewhere,
are as a rule found to be much stronger in available means than the
banks in New York City; while the reverse of this should always be true
when such large balances, amounting to more than 100 millions of the
funds of other banks, are constantly on deposit in the latter city subject
to demand.

The imports of gold in excess of exports, from the date of resumption
to November 1, 1880, have been $119,384,795,* and the estimated gold
production of the mines is $67,449,929; in all, $186,834,724. During
this period the gold in the Treasury has increased $20,976,007, and in
the banks $73,976,149, and the remainder, $91,882,568, has been dispersed throughout the country or used in the arts.

The amount of currency and coin in the country is known to be much
greater than at any former time, and its distribution, together with its
partial disappearance from the money-centers, has been an interesting
subject for discussion.

Tables are herewith given showing the amount of coin and currency
in the country on January 1 and November 1, 1879, and on November 1
of the present year; the amounts of silver and gold coin, which include
the bullion in the Treasury, being the estimates of the Director of the
Mint:

	January 1, 1879.	November 1, 1879.	November 1, 1880.
Legal-tender notes	$346, 681, 016	$346, 681, 016	$346, 681, 016
National-bank notes	323, 791, 674	337, 181, 418	343, 834, 107
Gold coin	278, 310, 126	355, 681, 532	454, 012, 030
Silver coin	106, 573, 803	126, 009, 537	158, 271, 327
Total	1, 055, 356, 619	1, 165, 553, 503	1, 302, 798, 480

The amount of Treasury notes has remained the same since January
1, 1879, as provided by law. There was an increase of bank notes for
the first ten months of 1879 of $13,389,744, and for the present year of

---

* Not including imports outside of New York City in October of this year.

$6,652,689. The total net increase of national-bank notes issued since resumption is $20,042,433, and the total increase of gold $175,701,90 and of silver $51,697,524. The statement below gives the amount of currency and coin in the Treasury at the same dates as in the previous tables, and the amount in the national banks, on the dates of their returns nearest thereto—namely, January 1 and October 2, 1879, and October 1, 1880, respectively. The amount given for the State banks and trust companies and the savings banks is at the nearest comparative dates of their official reports. The banks in the State of California report their coin and currency in the aggregate, and in this table the coin is estimated to be three-fourths of the total amount and the currency one-fourth.

	January 1, 1879.	November 1, 1879.	November 1, 1880.
Gold—In the Treasury, less certificates	$112,703,342	$156,907,986	$133,079,34
In National banks	35,039,201	37,187,238	102,851,03
In State banks	10,937,812	12,171,292	17,102,13
Total gold	158,680,355	206,266,516	253,632,51
Silver—In the Treasury, standard silver dollars	17,249,740	32,115,073	47,156,58
In the Treasury, bullion	9,121,417	3,824,931	6,185,00
In the Treasury, fractional coin	6,046,194	17,854,327	24,635,56
In National banks, including certificates	6,460,557	4,986,492	6,495,47
Total silver	38,870,908	58,780,823	84,472,62
Currency—In the Treasury	77,615,655	41,906,376	26,846,82
In National banks	126,491,720	118,546,369	86,439,92
In State banks	25,944,485	25,555,280	25,828,79
In savings banks	14,513,779	15,880,921	17,072,68
Total currency	244,565,639	201,888,946	156,188,22
Grand totals	442,125,902	466,936,285	494,293,36

The silver certificates, of which $1,165,120 was held by the national banks and the remaining $18,615,121 was in circulation on November 1, 1880, are not included in the above exhibit.

If from the amount of coin and currency in the country, as given in the first table, the amount in the Treasury and the banks be deducted, the remainder will give the amount of each kind then in the hands of the people outside of these depositories, as follows:

	January 1, 1879.	November 1, 1879.	November 1, 1880.
Gold	$119,629,771	$149,415,016	$200,379,51
Silver	67,699,895	67,228,714	73,798,70
Currency	425,907,051	481,973,488	534,326,89
Totals	613,236,717	698,617,218	808,505,11

The gold in the Treasury has increased $20,976,007, and in the banks $73,976,149, releasing $50,768,829 of paper currency in the Treasury and $37,608,585 in the banks. The increase of gold outside of the Treasury and the banks is 80.7 millions and of paper currency 108.4 millions. The amount of standard dollars coined is $72,847,750, of which $47,156,588 are in the Treasury and $25,691,162 in circulation. The remainder of the silver, $85,423,577, is subsidiary and trade dollars, and bullion, of which $30,820,561 is in the Treasury and $54,603,016, is in use in place of the previous fractional paper currency which, on March 23, 1874, was at its highest point, and amounted to $49,566,760. The additional amount of gold coin, of silver dollars, and paper currency outside of the Treasury and the banks is thus estimated to be $195,274,401, which amount has been dispersed among the people since the date of resumption.

The average prices and value of manufactured goods, of breadstuffs, of provisions, and of other products have largely increased. The laborer has been steadily employed at remunerative wages. The frontier has rapidly receded. All classes of people have been liquidating their debts, and much greater amounts of money have been held in the tills of country traders and at home for ready use. The hoarding of a small amount by each of fifty millions of people, or by ten millions of families, is of itself sufficient to account for the disappearance from the usual places of deposit of a large portion of the addition to the circulating medium since the date of resumption.

The most gratifying exhibit in the above statement is the fact that the national banks are now doing business upon a specie basis and with a true standard. For the ten years preceding the resumption of specie payments the average amount of coin held by the banks was but $26,303,309, and all but $8,540,252 of this amount was held by the banks in the city of New York. The amount of coin held has, of course, at times largely exceeded this average, as on January 20, 1877, when it was more than 49 millions. But this amount was soon reduced, and in the following April it had fallen to 27 millions, the previous increase having been due chiefly, not to deposits of dealers or payments on loans, but to disbursements of interest by the government. At other times the banks have held much less than the average amount stated. For instance, on October 1, 1875, they held but $8,050,329, of which the banks in the city of New York held but $4,955,-624, and on May 1 of the same year they held but $10,620,361, of which the banks in the city of New York held $6,683,325. This was at the time when both the paper issues of the government and the circulation of the banks were at their highest amounts, the former being 428 millions and the latter 354 millions, in all, 782 millions, while the proportion of coin to their circulation then held by the banks was only about three per cent.

One year ago it was urgently recommended "that all the national banks should take advantage of the present influx of gold to accumulate in their vaults an amount equal to the total cash reserve required by law," and the hope was then expressed "that the reports of another year might show them to be possessed of at least 100 millions in gold coin." On June 14 of the present year the banks reported 99 millions of specie, and on October 1 more than 109 millions of coin (including nearly six and one-half of silver), which more than equals one-third of the total circulation of the banks in operation. The amount of gold coin now held is but 18 millions less than the whole cash reserve required, and would undoubtedly have been still greater except for the high rates charged for the transportation of gold coin, which are greatly disproportioned to the cost of moving paper currency and which, it is to be hoped, will, by some means, be largely reduced.

Much newspaper criticism has appeared in the mean time, complaining of the comparatively small amount of legal-tender silver dollars held by the banks, and some of the banks have themselves encouraged this criticism. The arguments used in favor of the accumulation of silver under existing laws are unsound in principle and against all experience. No one prefers to put away for future use a product which will spoil by lapse of time, or which will deteriorate in value. The banks, if well managed, will transact business upon the same general principles as those on which an individual of superior judgment would conduct his own affairs, holding in reserve that coin which is known to be of uniform value everywhere in preference to that which, by the operation of the laws of trade or business, will be likely to become of less value. The law compels the citizen and the corporation to receive all legal-tender money in payment of debts; but it does not, and ought not to, require any one to receive on deposit that which will not as readily be received in turn by the depositor.

The Bank of France on January 1, 1877, as will be seen in a subsequent table, held 306 million dollars of gold and 127 millions of silver, or seventy-one per cent. of gold and twenty-nine per cent. of silver. On November 4, 1880, it held $113,855,000 of gold and $365,929,000 of silver, or twenty-four per cent. of the former and seventy-six per cent. of the latter, having lost in the interval 192 millions of gold and gained 239 millions of silver, thus very nearly reversing the percentage of each ; and it is said that about 70 millions of this amount is distributed among the 90 branches of the Bank, and adds but little to the strength of the reserve of the parent bank.* Since September 23 last, while its circulation was 475 million dollars, and its deposits 115 millions, it has lost $31,300,000 of gold. "During a part of this time it has endeavored to check the demand for export by various expedients, without raising the rate of discount. Gold was offered by the Bank in pieces of ten francs, in coins not of full weight, and other restrictive measures were adopted. Gradually the inutility of these expedients became obvious. The drain of gold still continued. The Bank then proceeded to employ the only efficacious method of protecting the reserve, and raised the rate of discount. At the same time it removed all restrictions on the issue of coin. This also had a good effect. * * * Confidence in fact was restored by following the ordinary rules of business, and the first of these rules is, that the price of an article should follow its demand."†

France is fast traveling the road open for all nations who try to maintain a double standard where the intrinsic value of gold and silver coin is widely at variance. Sooner or later the time will come when the creditors of the Bank will prefer payment in the dearer metal, and the refusal to pay the kind of coin asked for by the creditor who has the option will bring down the cheaper coin to its value in the markets of the world. Then the Bank must replenish its store by selling its bonds under disadvantageous circumstances or remain permanently upon the silver basis.

The United States is at the present time in a similar situation to the Bank of France, except that its liabilities are less and its store of gold somewhat greater. On September 30, 1877, the Treasury held 107 millions ($107,039,529) of gold and nearly seven and one-half millions of silver ($7,425,454), or ninety-three and one-half per cent. of the former and six and one-half per cent. of the latter. On November 1, 1880, it held in all 141 millions of gold ($141,133,849), including $7,454,500 held for the redemption of certificates outstanding, and 77 millions of silver ($77,977,149), or sixty-four per cent. of gold and thirty-six per cent. of silver. Everything is favorable at the present time, but the operation

* The Public, November 18, 1880.   † London Economist, Nov. 6, 1880.

of laws now in force will continue to reduce the gold and increase the silver. The government, by trying to force silver upon the holder of bonds matured, or in payment of legal-tender notes—thereby assuming that the silver dollar is not the equal of the gold dollar—and by taking the option away from the holder of the note, may any day bring the nation upon the silver standard, which will at once advance the price of all products, and place gold at such a premium that an investment in it at par would be at least twice as profitable as in United States bonds. Such a situation is not satisfactory to any intelligent business man, and no effort should be spared to enlighten the people upon the silver question and to effect the repeal of the present law. The banks as a class have no prejudice against silver coin other than that occasioned by its inconvenience. If Congress shall, by wise legislation, diminish the issue of small notes, and restrict the silver coinage within judicious limits, the standard silver dollar will do good service, and soon accumulate in bank vaults and find its way into general circulation. If not, it is wisdom on the part of bank officers, who act for the interest of their stockholders, to keep their reserves and all their ready means as nearly as possible in gold coin.

This brief outline of some of the transactions of the national banks covers the most important period of the financial history of the country, and shows the immense advantage experienced by this country from having, during the years following the great war, an excellent banking system. The system was established, not for the benefit of the stockholders of the banks, but for the benefit of all the people. Its ample basis of unimpaired capital, its large surplus, its large cash reserves, its secured circulation, its protection to depositors, and its general management, must commend it to every student of political economy; and it is among the most gratifying of political signs that during the late exciting campaign, while both parties have claimed the credit of having brought about a return to specie payments, neither party has urged the abolishment of the system. The national banks have now entered upon a new career. The machinery is in excellent working order, and but little legislation is needed to perfect it into a homogeneous system which will be part and parcel of the nation.

But it does not follow because the banks are transacting business upon a true standard that they will be exempt from further losses. The hazards of business are certainly much less on that account, but the rapid and unprecedented increase of the circulating medium, such as has been experienced during the last two years, may result in great injury as well as benefit to the country. The good harvests, the large products of the mines, the influx of specie from abroad, the increasing demand for produce and manufactures, the prosperous condition of trade and of the industries of the country, are sure to be followed by periods of depression which will seriously affect, not only the value of the collaterals upon which large amounts of call loans are based, but also the payment of commercial paper. The amount of legal reserve required to be held by the banks was largely reduced by the act of June 20, 1874, and the percentage held in the larger cities has been greatly diminished during the past few years. The sudden and enormous increase of individual and bank deposits in the commercial centers should be accompanied, not only by the reserve required by law, but by a much greater percentage of coin and a much smaller expansion of loans, if the banks would check unhealthy speculation, and keep themselves in condition for an adverse balance of trade and for the legitimate demands of the depositors and correspondents who confide in them.

DISTRIBUTION OF LOANS BY THE BANK OF FRANCE, THE NATIONAL
BANKS OF THE UNITED STATES, AND THE IMPERIAL BANK OF GER-
MANY.

The Bank of France.

The report of the transactions of the Bank of France for 1879, made
by the general council to the general meeting of the shareholders on the
29th of January, 1880, contains much interesting information in reference to its operations.*

The Bank of France has a capital of 182,500,000 francs, which, expressed in the currency of this country, at the rate of five francs to the
dollar, is equal to $36,500,000. It has ninety branches, as required by
law, forty-one of which were carried on in 1878 at a loss of $162,225,
and thirty in 1879 at a loss $95,840. The circulation of the bank on
November 4, 1880, was $473,805,793; its deposits $108,892,222, of which
$40,521,965 were government deposits; its coin, $113,850,000 of gold and
$249,400,000 of silver; and its loans $195,707,859.†

The amount of commercial paper discounted at the Bank of France
and its branches during the year 1879 reached its maximum on November 28, when it was $172,360,000, being nearly five times the amount of
its capital. The minimum amount of discounts was on March 20, being then $74,720,000, or about twice the amount of its capital. In ad-
dition to commercial paper, or trade bills, discounted, the bank makes
advances on collateral securities, such as bullion, railway shares, and
government bonds. The highest amount of such advances in 1878 was
$22,960,000, which was increased in 1879 to $31,100,000. The combined
amount of commercial paper, or trade bills, and of advances on securities, ranged from $190,000,000 to $200,000,000. In addition to its discounts and loans the bank usually holds about $54,500,000 in various
securities of the French Government.

About one-third of the commercial paper discounted at Paris ($209,-
888,385) was payable in towns where the bank had branches, the remaining two-thirds ($468,320,475) being payable in that city. The total
amount of commercial paper discounted during the entire year was more
than 1,452 millions of dollars ($1,452,175,260). The total number of
pieces of paper discounted during the year was 8,071,505, of which
number 4,169,292 were payable at the branches and 3,902,213 at Paris.

The reports for 1878 and 1879 give classifications of the Paris bills.
The discount of certain classes of these trade bills, which are for very
small amounts, is a characteristic of the Bank of France, and the statistics are both interesting and curious. The report gives a classification
of the bills on Paris for 1879, as follows :

Bills of 10 francs, or $2 each, and under	7,842
Bills of 11 francs to 50 francs each, or $2.20 to $10	392,845
Bills of 51 francs to 100 francs each, or $10.20 to $20	623,232
Bills of above 100 francs each, or $20	2,878,294
Total	3,902,213

It will be observed that the whole number of these bills was nearly four
millions, of which more than two-thirds (2,878,294) were for amounts above
twenty dollars. The remaining 1,023,919 bills were all for sums less than
twenty dollars, and, at the highest limit, could not much exceed 16
millions. There were 623,232 bills in amounts varying from $10.20 to $20.
There were also 392,845 bills varying in amount from $2.20 to $10; and

---

* L'Économiste Française, April 10, 1880.   † London Economist, November 6, 1880.

7,842 bills as low as two dollars each, or under. The number of trade bills in 1877 below $20 was 393,503; in 1878, 1,054,381; and in 1879, 1,023,919. The average amount of each of the Paris bills in 1879 was $171.80; the average of the bills at the branches was $185.60; and taking the whole number together the average was $180.

The number, classification, and amount of commercial bills discounted during the years 1878 and 1879 are stated below in tabular form:

1878.

Where discounted.	Classification.					Amount.	
	10 francs, or $2 and below.	11 francs to 50 francs, or $2.20 to $10.	51 francs to 100 francs, or $10.20 to $20.	Above 100 francs, or $20.	Total number.	In francs.	In dollars.
Paris	4,898	240,640	808,843	2,428,508	3,482,889	3,108,226,250	621,245,250
Branches					3,791,950	3,760,636,075	752,127,215
	4,898	240,640	808,843	2,428,508	7,274,839	6,868,862,325	1,373,372,466

1879.

Paris	7,842	392,845	623,232	2,878,294	3,902,213	3,391,044,344	678,208,869
Branches					4,169,262	3,869,832,100	773,966,420
	7,842	392,845	623,232	2,878,294	8,071,505	7,260,876,444	1,452,175,289

In 1878 the average amount of each bill discounted at Paris was $178.40, and at the branches $198.40, the average of the whole being $188.80.

The Bank of France receives these bills chiefly from bankers, who keep accounts with it, as it discounts only for its depositors. These bankers in turn discount them for small brokers, who receive them for this purpose from the working classes. The bills are presented to the bank for discount, with accompanying schedules. The rate of interest is the same on small bills as on large ones, and no charge is made beyond the discount or interest. The greater part of them are bills of exchange, and issue from small manufacturers, and also from workmen on their own account, known as makers of the "*Articles de Paris.*"

The National Banks of the United States.

The following table gives by geographical divisions a classification, similar to the foregoing, of the notes and bills discounted held by the national banks on October 2, 1879, when the total amount of loans was $875,013,107:

Geographical divisions.	No. of banks.	Number and classification of bills.						Total bills.		Average.
		$100 and less.	$100 to $500.	$500 to $1,000.	$1,000 to $5,000.	$5,000 to $10,000.	$10,000 and over.	No.	Amount.	
New England States	547	30,167	54,965	20,444	33,621	10,082	4,590	153,869	$240,552,898 63	$1,562 36
Middle States	641	115,285	132,032	39,484	50,854	11,453	5,276	354,384	416,600,230 30	1,175 56
Southern States	175	15,752	24,460	7,862	8,936	1,283	416	58,729	43,890,807 35	781 40
Western States and Territories	685	90,141	84,563	27,590	31,812	5,381	1,800	241,287	171,969,170 22	712 72
United States	2,048	251,345	296,040	95,380	125,223	28,199	12,082	808,269	875,013,107 10	1,082 58

The number of pieces of paper discounted, as will be seen, was 808,269, and the average of each discount, $1,082.59. If the average time of these bills was sixty days, and the banks held continuously the same amount, the number of discounts made during the year would be nearly five millious (4,849,614), the total discounts more than five thousand millions (5,250,000,000), which would be equal to a discount of $700 annually for each voter, or $500 for each family in the country. The number of notes and bills of $100 each, or less, at the date named was 251,345, or nearly one-third of the whole; the number of bills of less than $500 each was 547,385, or considerably more than two-thirds of the whole; while the number of bills of less than $1,000 each was 642,765, which is more than three-fourths of the whole number.

Every State and Territory, except Florida, Dakota and Washington, had single discounts of $10,000 and over, and every State, except Florida, had discounts of $5,000 and over. All the States had discounts in amounts varying from $100, or less, to $1,000, and over. The discounts of the banks in the State of New York amounted to 260 millions, the number of pieces of paper held being 170,137, which was more than was held by all of the New England banks combined. The discounts of the New England banks were 240 millions, which were represented by 153,869 pieces of paper. The amount of discounts in the New England States was considerably more than those of the Western and Southern States; but the number of loans in New England was only about one-half the number in the South and West. The banks in New York City held 2,907 pieces of paper of $10,000 each, and over, and those in the remainder of the State 451. Boston held 2,258 of such pieces, and the remainder of Massachusetts 995. Philadelphia held 809, and the remainder of Pennsylvania 558; Chicago held 322, and the remainder of Illinois 105. The total number of pieces held by the four cities here named was 6,296, which is more than one-half of the aggregate of this class of bills held by all the national banks in the United States. The bank examiner in the city of New York gives the following estimate of the average amount of loans in the city of New York:

41,598 loans, averaging $2,500 each, amounting to	$104,000,000
4,926 loans, averaging 7,500 each, amounting to	37,000,000
2,907 loans, averaging 19,000 each, amounting to	55,000,000

Of the loans exceeding $10,000 each he estimates as follows: 150 of $50,000, amounting to $7,500,000, and 80 of $100,000, amounting to $8,000,000. He says that the largest loan of any kind which ever passed through his hands was one for the sum of $1,000,000, secured by United States bonds, and that it was a legitimate loan, understood to have been principally employed in the erection of an enormous oil-refinery in New Jersey. He also says that he has frequently handled demand loans of $500,000 each.

In answer to an inquiry in reference to small loans, he replies that the tobacco manufacturers receive large numbers of promissory notes, of a small amount each, payable in almost every city, town, and village in the country, and running from thirty to fifty days' time. The sewing-machine companies and the manufacturers of billiard-tables, pianos, and farming implements also receive large numbers of notes of from $10 to $50 each, being monthly payments on articles sold by them. These small notes are usually received by the banks as collateral security for loans, and are forwarded by them for collection. A charge for collection of from 10 to 25 cents is made upon each small note.

The average amount of each loan in New York City was $3,962; in Boston, $3,083; Philadelphia, $1,688; Pittsburgh, $1,993; Chicago, $2,244; Baltimore, $1,593; Milwaukee, $2,086; Saint Louis, $1,575; Cincinnati, $1,231; Cleveland, $1,244; Detroit, $1,320; Louisville, $1,007; and New Orleans, $1,936.

Among the States having the smallest average loans were the following: New York, exclusive of the cities of New York and Albany, $499; Pennsylvania, exclusive of Philadelphia and Pittsburgh, $535; Maryland, exclusive of Baltimore, $505; Kansas, in which the average was $353; Iowa, with an average of $375; West Virginia, of $350; Delaware, $556; New Jersey, $566; Minnesota, $621; Vermont, $645; North Carolina, $662; Tennessee, $651; Maine, $740; Indiana, $711; New Hampshire, $815; South Carolina, $846; Georgia, $882.

A table will be found in the appendix giving the number of each class of discounts held, their average amount, and the total amount of money loaned in each of the States and principal cities of the Union. An examination of this table will give full and interesting information relative to the distribution of loans by the banks in the different sections of the country.

The Imperial Bank of Germany.

The Imperial Bank of Germany has a capital of 30 millions of dollars, and is situated in the city of Berlin.

The total number of bills of all kinds discounted during the year 1879 was 2,374,394, amounting to $852,175,650, the average amount of each bill being $358.90. The bills are classified as follows: There were 533,564 Berlin bills, amounting to $263,663,280—average $494.15 each; the number of inland bills was 1,834,351, amounting to $578,693,335, and averaging $315.47 each; and the number of foreign bills was 6,479, in amount $9,819,035, and averaging $1,515.52 each. The average amount of loans and discounts for the year was $82,073,500. The loans and discounts were highest on December 31, when they were as follows:

Berlin bills	83,157, amounting to $44,636,600, averaging	$536	77
Inland bills	164,844, amounting to 51,840,460, averaging	314	48
Foreign bills	1,442, amounting to 3,936,230, averaging	2,729	70
Total bills	249,443, amounting to 100,413,290, averaging	402	55

The discounts were lowest on March 23, their total amount being then $67,349,000.

The time of the Berlin bills varied from 16 to 76 days, their average being 55 days, and the time of the inland bills was from 14 to 63 days, their average being 26 days.

STATE BANKS, SAVINGS-BANKS, AND TRUST COMPANIES.

The first systematic effort to obtain annual statistics showing the condition of banks organized under State laws was commenced by the Treasury Department in 1834, in compliance with a resolution of the House of Representatives, passed July 10, 1832. These statistics were compiled from such returns as were required by the laws of various States to be made to their authorities. This compilation was continued for twenty-nine years, from 1834 to 1863, after which it was discontinued. The annual returns from this source were given for each State, in concise form, in the Comptroller's report for 1876, as were also such other data as could be obtained in regard to the two Banks of the United States, and other moneyed corporations of the country in operation prior to the year 1834. Those returns were incomplete and unsatisfactory.

9 F

In many of the States no reports were required from banks organized under their laws, in others reports were infrequently required, and in all there was an entire absence of uniformity as to the dates upon which reports were required to be made.

The act of Congress of February 19, 1873, section 333 of the Revised Statutes, requires the Comptroller to obtain from authentic sources, and to report to Congress, statements exhibiting under appropriate heads the resources and liabilities of such banks and savings banks as are organized under the laws of the several States and Territories. In compliance with this act he has presented annually in the appendices to his reports the resources and liabilities of these corporations, so far as it has been possible to obtain them.

Through the courtesy of State officers, returns of State banks, savings-banks, and trust and loan companies have during the past year been received from nineteen States. Twenty-seven of the States and Territories, including Illinois, Nebraska, Dakota, Oregon, Virginia, and Tennessee, do not require periodical returns of the condition of the different classes of banks organized under their laws. Statements showing the condition of the banks of each State from which returns could be obtained will, as usual, be found in the appendix. The returns received embrace 650 State banks and trust companies, and 629 savings banks.

Returns were made to the Commissioner of Internal Revenue, for purposes of taxation, showing the average capital and deposits for the six months ending May 31, 1880, by 996 State banks and trust companies, and 658 savings banks. Returns made to the Commissioner are supposed to cover all banks of this description in the United States, as well as private bankers. It can therefore be seen that, while the returns made to the different State authorities omit 346 State banks and trust companies, they are quite complete as to that class of savings-banks having no capital, the difference being only 29 banks.

State banks and trust companies.

From returns obtained by the Comptroller from State officers, the following abstract has been compiled, showing the resources and liabilities of 650 State banks and trust companies:

RESOURCES.

Loans and discounts	$281, 498, 741
Overdrafts	597, 669
United States bonds	26, 252, 182
Other stocks, bonds, &c	35, 661, 792
Due from banks	40, 340, 345
Real estate	19, 489, 056
Other assets	7, 274, 037
Expenses	979, 492
Cash Items	11, 176, 592
Specie	6, 905, 977
Legal tenders, bank notes, &c	51, 500, 226
Total	481, 774, 159

LIABILITIES.

Capital stock	$109, 318, 451
Circulation	283, 308
Surplus fund	25, 068, 431
Undivided profits	16, 774, 731
Dividends unpaid	486, 004
Deposits	298, 759, 619
Due to banks	18, 613, 336
Other liabilities	18, 530, 189
Total	481, 774, 150

The foregoing table was prepared from returns from five New England States, not including Maine, which has but one State bank in operation; from four Middle States, not including Delaware; and from the Western States, with the exception of Illinois, Kansas, and Nebraska. The only Southern States represented therein are Louisiana, Texas, and Kentucky. The only Pacific State is California. There is but one State bank in New Hampshire, five in Vermont, none in Massachusetts. There are, however, five trust and loan companies in the latter State and ten in Connecticut.

In comparing the capital and deposits reported to State authorities with the same items as reported to the Commissioner of Internal Revenue, it must be remembered that, in addition to the discrepancy in the number of banks reporting, there is an important difference in the character of the reports. The reports made to State authorities give the gross deposits at certain dates, while those made to the Commissioner give the average deposits for a period of six months.

The total number of banks of all classes which report to the State authorities, and from which reports have been received, is 1,279, having a total capital of $113,172,078, and total deposits of $1,117,866,592; the total number of incorporated banks reporting to the Commissioner of Internal Revenue is 1,654, having a total capital of $118,014,862, and deposits amounting to $1,136,427,338. It thus appears that 375 banks, with capital and deposits amounting to $4,842,784 and $18,560,746 respectively, either do not report to the Commissioner, or if such reports are made it is impossible to obtain them.

Of the 4,456 banks reporting to the Commissioner of Internal Revenue, there are 2,802 private banking institutions, with a total capital of $76,121,962, and deposits of $182,667,237, from which no reports have been received by the Comptroller through State authorities.

Savings banks.

The following table exhibits the aggregate resources and liabilities of 629 savings banks of the United States, whose returns, as made to the State authorities, have been obtained by the Comptroller. The aggregate of the resources and liabilities of these savings banks, for each State separately, is given in the appendix:

RESOURCES.	
Loans on real estate	$315,273,232
Loans on personal and collateral security	70,175,090
United States bonds	187,413,220
State, municipal, and other bonds and stocks	150,440,359
Railroad bonds and stocks	20,705,378
Bank stock	32,225,923
Real estate	39,038,502
Other assets	27,053,452
Expenses	216,433
Due from banks	23,083,091
Cash	17,072,580
Total	881,677,350

LIABILITIES.	
Deposits	819,106,973
Surplus fund	51,726,472
Undivided profits	4,740,861
Other liabilities	6,603,044
Total	881,677,350

The foregoing table includes the returns from the six New England States, from four Middle States, not including Delaware, from the State of California, and from five savings banks in the other States.

The aggregate of loans in the New England States is $295,700,696, and of deposits $378,848,429. In the Middle States the aggregate of loans is $114,277,627, and of deposits $380,666,166.

The amount of average deposits returned to the Commissioner of Internal Revenue by the savings banks of the New England States, for purposes of taxation, was $368,757,040 for the six months ending May 31, 1880, and by the savings banks of the Middle States the average deposits returned for the same period were $389,183,856, showing but a slight difference between the returns made by these banks to the State officers and those made by them to the Commissioner.

All but three of the savings banks in the State of California are organized with capital stock, and dividends are paid to stockholders as well as to depositors. The whole amount of deposits is $47,719,829. Of this amount, banks with capital stock amounting to $3,853,627 hold $32,177,037. The remaining three banks, which are without capital, hold $15,542,792 of deposits.

Some of the largest savings banks in the city of Philadelphia, organized under old charters, are not required to make reports to any State officer. Returns received directly from four of these banks, having deposits amounting to $23,956,285, are included in the returns for the State of Pennsylvania.

The reports to the Commissioner of Internal Revenue, which are made by all banks in the United States other than national, show that in the Southern States there are but five savings banks (including three with capital of $342,912.16), with deposits aggregating $1,457,924; and that in the Western States and Territories, exclusive of California, there are but 34 savings banks, with deposits amounting to $14,019,997; making, in the two sections named, 39 savings banks, out of the total in the United States of 658.

The savings bank deposits given in the foregoing table for 1880, based on reports made to the State authorities, are $819,106,973, and the deposits of the State banks and trust companies were $298,759,619. These deposits do not include bank deposits. The deposits of the national banks, exclusive of those due to banks on June 11, 1880, were $845,738,876 These deposits of the national banks bear to those of the savings banks the proportion nearly of 50.8 to 49.2, to those of the State banks and trust companies the proportion of 74 to 26, and to the combined deposits of both the proportion of 43 to 57.

The deposits of the savings banks of the six New England States alone, for the year 1880, were $378,848,429, while the deposits of the national banks of the same States on June 11, 1880, were $142,163,316. The former amount bears to the latter the proportion of 73 to 27.

The total population of New England is estimated to be 3,920,000, and the number of open deposit accounts in the savings banks is 1,165,653; which is equal to 30 accounts to each one hundred of the entire population. The average amount of each account is $325; and if the total deposits were divided among the entire population the average sum of $96.65 could be given to each individual.

The deposits of the savings banks in the State of New York were $319,258,501 in 1880, while the population is estimated to be 5,120,000; showing that an equal distribution of the savings-bank deposits among the entire population of the State would give $62.36 to each individual.

The loans and investments of the savings banks of the six New England States, in United States and other bonds and stocks, amounted in 1880 to $31,109,999, which is equal to 34.61 per cent. of deposits. In 1873 the amount invested in the same manner by the savings banks of

New England was $97,692,286, equal to 25.63 per cent. of their deposits, which were $381,207,058 at that date. The cash on hand in 1880 was $6,521,510, or say 1.72 per cent. of their liabilities to depositors, while in 1873 it was $4,290,121, or 1.13 per cent. of the same liability at that date. In the State of New York, in 1880, the amount invested in United States and other stocks and bonds by the savings banks was $212,103,-705,or 66.44 per cent. of deposits, while the cash on hand was $4,271,445, or 1.34 per cent. of deposits. In 1873 the savings banks in New York had $153,355,664 invested in this manner, or 53.71 per cent. of deposits, and the cash on hand was $6,714,404, or 2.35 per cent. of the deposits.

In California, in 1880, the investments of the savings banks in United States and other stocks and bonds were $4,228,001, or 8.8 per cent. of the deposits, against $1,294,600, or 4.2 per cent. of the deposits, in 1877. The cash reserve on hand in California savings banks was $2,897,471, or about 6 per cent. of the deposits, in 1880, and $1,965,600, or about the same percentage, in 1877. While, as has been seen, the amount invested in United States and other bonds and stocks by the savings banks of the six New England States was $131,109,999, or 34.61 per cent. of the aggregate deposits, the amount due from banks shown by the returns of the same savings banks was $6,348,135, or 1.67 per cent. of their deposits; showing that the resources of these savings banks consist largely of deposits in national or other banks, and of investments in United States and other bonds and stocks.

In New York State the amount invested in United States bonds was $119,985,590, and the amount in other stocks and bonds was $92,118,115, a total of $212,103,705, or 66 per cent. of the aggregate deposits, while the amount due from banks was $13,893,109.

The following statement, compiled from returns made to the Commissioner of Internal Revenue, gives by States and principal cities the average capital and deposits of the State banks, trust companies, private bankers, and savings banks, in each of the New England and Middle States, for the six months ending May 31, 1880, together with the average amount of capital invested in United States bonds:

| States and Territories. | No. of banks. | Capital. | Deposits. | Invested in United States bonds. | | Total. |
				By State banks, private bankers, and trust companies.	By savings banks.	
Maine	64	$47,319	$21,721,964	$8,313	$3,284,637	$3,292,950
New Hampshire	71	51,000	28,301,549	5,202	919,297	924,499
Vermont..................	22	353,780	8,531,140	36,984	653,862	690,846
Massachusetts	161	510,000	144,268,273	223,019	13,633,993	13,857,606
Boston	57	5,128,099	64,553,766	2 552,061	6,499,110	9,051,771
Rhode Island	56	3,305,504	43,134,708	637,588	4,570,369	5,207,937
Connecticut	105	2,616,896	78,457,961	272,732	8,131,932	8,404,664
New England States	536	12,015,518	388,969,361	3,737,093	37,693,200	41,430,293
New York	303	8,525,645	162,275,473	2,300,138	45,993,290	48,293,438
New York City	508	49,335,396	291,914,072	15,153,033	73,737,079	88,890,112
Albany	12	641,000	13,751,649	357,521	2,552,905	2,910,426
New Jersey	51	1,334,553	20,391,118	269,683	5,871,992	6,141,675
Pennsylvania	271	8,799,931	29,071,133	752,796	70,000	822,796
Philadelphia	61	2,108,904	51,490,370	198,403	6,472,097	6,671,500
Pittsburgh	31	4,053,579	14,651,589	661,363	1,679,366	2,340,729
Delaware	8	675,689	2,127,436	26,000	....	26,000
Maryland................	12	564,434	819,944	251,189	13,538	264,727
Baltimore............	36	3,134,842	25,814,319	309,900	9,890,353	10,200,253
Washington	7	357,060	3,305,875	389,758	20,535	310,293
Middle States	1,300	79,510,943	615,618,967	20,564,834	146,301,155	166,865,989

The following statement gives like information in reference to the same classes of banks in the Southern and Western States, and in the Pacific States and Territories:

States and Territories	No. of banks.	Capital.	Deposits.	Invested in United States bonds.		
				By State banks, private bankers, and trust companies.	By savings banks.	Total.
Virginia	76	$3,036,974	$7,757,202	$294,208	0	$294,208
West Virginia	20	1,247,128	4,034,743	137,486	0	137,486
North Carolina	13	790,321	1,596,692	0	0	0
South Carolina	13	511,499	658,812	52,333	0	52,333
Georgia	58	4,068,279	5,910,827	18,050	1,000	19,050
Florida	9	53,830	287,280	0	0	0
Alabama	26	1,640,241	2,269,647	742	0	742
Mississippi	33	1,089,690	2,634,915	209,358	0	209,358
Louisiana	3	126,263	87,343	45,000	0	45,000
New Orleans	11	2,777,031	4,632,122	643,013	0	643,013
Texas	105	3,701,080	6,332,751	163,132	0	163,132
Arkansas	15	245,110	577,626	75,102	0	75,102
Kentucky	71	6,090,866	7,698,114	306,979	0	306,979
Louisville	15	5,267,028	5,803,673	471,197	0	471,197
Tennessee	30	1,760,228	3,222,740	125,388	0	125,388
Southern States	498	31,847,370	53,504,438	2,541,991	1,000	2,542,991
Ohio	248	5,704,140	20,834,648	887,475	86,959	984,488
Cincinnati	12	1,403,341	4,302,711	275,671	0	275,671
Cleveland	9	1,045,924	13,965,571	678,379	2,151,270	2,829,649
Indiana	144	4,365,434	13,172,723	507,953	42,061	550,014
Illinois	316	4,092,314	17,061,786	675,606	60,000	735,606
Chicago	34	4,272,455	12,584,083	2,556,523	0	2,556,828
Michigan	135	2,346,799	7,105,952	154,894	0	154,894
Detroit	14	1,066,941	7,544,048	345,742	134,267	480,009
Wisconsin	109	1,578,843	5,964,028	184,761	0	184,761
Milwaukee	9	634,731	7,788,900	15,914	0	15,914
Iowa	300	5,153,906	13,326,191	319,876	0	319,876
Minnesota	95	1,906,375	5,000,150	119,968	0	119,968
Missouri	170	4,250,175	13,307,216	428,208	0	428,208
Saint Louis	28	5,705,555	13,688,690	873,395	0	873,395
Kansas	146	1,564,144	4,877,150	90,397	0	90,397
Nebraska	83	653,890	2,019,814	39,492	0	39,492
Western States	1,883	45,743,007	169,633,732	8,137,554	2,474,557	10,612,111
Oregon	15	1,245,208	1,038,108	112,423	6,300	118,723
California	85	9,430,629	14,926,718	197,341	0	197,341
San Francisco	25	12,104,546	67,407,294	3,449,052	2,711,604	6,160,656
Colorado	38	584,217	3,479,877	0	0	0
Nevada	13	364,457	834,548	100,000	0	100,000
Utah	11	208,000	1,293,952	0	0	0
New Mexico	5	6,867	161,926	0	0	0
Wyoming	4	126,054	271,301	0	0	0
Idaho	2	5,358	16,265	0	0	0
Dakota	18	127,511	396,279	0	0	0
Montana	13	446,708	724,031	0	0	0
Washington	4	257,000	526,109	0	0	0
Arizona	5	112,892	343,673	25,000	0	25,000
Pacific States and Territories	239	25,019,987	91,366,078	3,683,816	2,717,904	6,601,720

The total number of State and savings banks, trust companies and private bankers in the United States, with the average amount of their capital, deposits, and investments in United States bonds, for the six months named, were as follows:

Number of banks.. 4,456
Average capital $194,136,825
Average deposits 1,319,094,576
Average investments in United States bonds 228,053,104

COMPTROLLER OF THE CURRENCY. 135

The following table exhibits in a concise form, by geographical divisions, the total average capital and deposits of all State and savings banks and private bankers in the country, for the six months ending May 31, 1880:

Geographical divisions.	State banks and trust companies.			Private bankers.			Savings banks with capital.			Savings banks without capital.	
	No.	Capital.	Depos-its.	No.	Capital.	Depos-its.	No.	Capital.	Depos-its.	No.	Depos-its.
		Mill-ions.	*Mill-ions.*		*Mill-ions.*	*Mill-ions.*		*Mill-ions.*	*Mill-ions.*		*Mill-ions.*
New England States....	40	6.86	16.47	74	5.16	3.74	....	....	....	422	368.76
Middle States	294	38.98	154.89	885	40.01	71.54	6	0.53	3.19	175	386.00
Southern States	241	26.69	38.51	252	4.81	13.54	3	0.34	0.57	2	0.88
Western States and Territories..............	481	41.44	108.91	1,591	26.14	93.85	20	3.17	30.85	30	27.39
United States......	906	113.97	318.78	2,802	76.12	182.67	29	4.04	34.61	629	783.03

NUMBER, CAPITAL AND DEPOSITS OF NATIONAL BANKS, STATE AND SAVINGS-BANKS, AND PRIVATE BANKERS.

The capital of the 2,076 national banks in operation on June 11, 1880, as will be seen by a table in the appendix, was $455,909,565, not including surplus, which fund at that date amounted to 118 millions of dollars; while the average capital of all the State banks, private bankers, and savings banks for the six months ending May 31, 1880, was but $194,136,825; which amount is but little more than one-third of the combined capital and surplus of the national banks.

The net deposits of the national banks were $900,788,714, and the average deposits of all other banks, including savings banks, were $1,319,094,576, of which more than one-half, or $783,033,149, consisted of the deposits of the 629 savings banks having no capital-stock, which are included in the above aggregate.

The increase in the net deposits of the national banks during the year was $187,385,075; of the savings banks, $34,508,295; of the private bankers, $42,749,684; and of the State banks and trust companies $61,713,761, making a total increase in the bank deposits of the country of $326,356,815.

The table below exhibits the aggregate average capital and deposits for the six months ending May 31, 1880, of all classes of banks other than national, and the capital and net deposits of the national banks on June 11 following:

Geographical divisions.	State banks, savings banks, private bankers, &c.			National banks.			Total.		
	No.	Capital.	Deposits.	No.	Capital.	Net deposits.	No.	Capital.	Deposits.
		Millions.	*Millions.*		*Millions.*	*Millions.*		*Millions.*	*Millions.*
New England States....	536	12.02	388.97	548	165.60	161.96	1,084	177.62	550.93
Middle States	1,300	78.51	615.62	654	170.44	480.06	1,954	249.95	1,095.68
Southern States	498	31.85	53.50	177	30.79	45.90	675	62.64	99.40
Western States and Territories..............	2,122	78.76	261.00	697	89.08	212.87	2,819	150.84	473.87
United States......	4,456	194.14	1,319.09	2,076	455.91	900.79	6,532	650.05	2,219.88

From this table it will be seen that the total number of banks and bankers in the country at the dates named was 6,532, with a total banking capital of $650,049,390, and total deposits* of $2,219,883,290.

In the appendix will be found similar tables for various periods, from 1875 to 1880, where will also be found other tables giving the assets and liabilities of State institutions during the past year, so far as they could be obtained from the official reports of the several State officers.

A table arranged by States and principal cities, giving the number, capital and deposits, and the tax thereon, of all banking institutions other than national, for the six months ending May 31, 1880, and for previous years, will be found in the appendix.

The following table exhibits, for corresponding dates in each of the last five years, the aggregate amounts of the capital and deposits of each of the classes of banks given in the foregoing table:

Years	National banks.			State banks, private bankers, &c.			Savings banks with capital.			Savings banks without capital.		Total.		
	No.	Capital.	Deposits.	No.	Capital.	Deposits.	No.	Capital.	Deposits.	No.	Deposits.	No.	Capital.	Deposits.
		Mill. ions.	Mill. ions.		Mill. ions.	Mill. ions.		Mill. ions.	Mill. ions.		Mill. ions.		Mill. ions.	Mill. ions.
1876..	2,091	500.4	713.5	3,803	214.0	480.0	26	5.0	37.2	691	344.6	6,611	719.4	2,075.3
1877..	2,078	481.0	708.2	3,799	215.6	470.5	26	4.9	38.2	676	842.3	6,579	704.5	2,128.1
1878..	2,056	470.4	677.2	3,709	202.2	413.3	23	3.2	26.2	658	803.3	6,456	675.8	1,920.0
1879..	2,048	456.3	713.4	3,639	197.0	397.0	29	4.2	36.1	644	747.1	6,360	666.5	1,893.5
1880..	2,076	455.9	900.8	3,798	190.1	501.5	29	4.0	34.6	629	783.0	6,532	650.0	2,219.9

SECURITY OF CIRCULATING NOTES.

The following table exhibits the classes and amounts of United States bonds held by the Treasurer on the 1st day of November, 1880, to secure the redemption of the circulating notes of the national banks:

Class of bonds.	Authorizing act.	Rate of interest.	Amount.
Loan of February, 1861 (81s)	February 8, 1861	6 per cent	$2,040,000
Loan of July and August, 1861 (81s)	July 17 and August 5, 1861	...do	33,405,050
Loan of 1863 (81s)	March 3, 1863	...do	17,027,100
Consols of 1867	March 3, 1865	...do	3,000
Consols of 1868	......do	...do	5,000
Ten-forties of 1864	March 3, 1864	5 per cent	526,900
Funded loan of 1881	July 14, 1870, and January 20, 1871	...do	140,552,850
Funded loan of 1891	......do	4½ per cent	36,968,950
Funded loan of 1907	......do	4 per cent	110,075,100
Pacific Railway bonds	July 1, 1862, and July 2, 1864	6 per cent	4,119,000
Total			359,748,950

On October 1, 1865, the total amount of bonds held for this purpose was $276,250,550, of which $199,397,950 was in six per cents, and

---

* The terms "gross deposits," "individual deposits," and "net deposits" of national banks, as used in this report, are explained as follows:

The gross deposits of the national banks are the amounts reported by them to the credit of stockholders for dividends unpaid; to the credit of individuals, companies, and firms; to the credit of the United States and its disbursing officers; and to the credit of other banks. The individual deposits are the amounts reported under that head, consisting of amounts to the credit of individuals, companies, and firms only. The net deposits are arrived at by deducting from the sum of the items making up the gross deposits the amount of clearing-house exchanges reported, and the amount of balances due from banks (with the exception of that due from reserve agents) not exceeding the amount due to banks.

$76,852,600 in five per cents. On October 1, 1870, the banks held $246,891,300 of six per cents, and $95,942,550 of five per cents. Since that time there has been to November 1, 1880, a decrease of $190,286,150 in six per cent bonds, and an increase of $51,137,200 in five per cents.

The banks now hold $36,988,950 of four and a half per cents, all of which have been deposited in the Treasury since September 1, 1876, and $119,075,100 of four per cents, which have been deposited since July 1, 1877.

During the last year $19,243,300 of four per cents have been with-'drawn by the banks, chiefly for the purpose of realizing the large premiums thereon, and $22,370,750 of five per cents have been deposited, which will mature in a few months. The banks still hold $8,000 of six per cent. five-twenty bonds, and $526,900 of five per cent. ten-forty bonds, upon which interest has ceased. They also hold $146,552,350 of the fives of 1881, which are redeemable on the 1st. of next May; $2,046,000 of sixes of 1880, payable on the first day of January next; and $50,432,150 of sixes of 1881, which are redeemable on the 1st of July next.

NATIONAL-BANK AND LEGAL-TENDER NOTES, BY DENOMINATIONS. CIRCULATING NOTES OF THE BANK OF FRANCE AND IMPERIAL BANK OF GERMANY, BY DENOMINATIONS.

The following table exhibits by denominations the amount of national-bank and legal-tender notes outstanding on November 1, 1880, and the aggregate amounts of both kinds of notes for the same date in 1878 and 1879:

Denominations.	1880.			1879.	1878.
	Amount of national-bank notes.	Amount of legal-tender notes.	Aggregate.	Aggregate.	Aggregate.
Ones	$2,292,462	$21,954,900	$24,247,362	$22,887,502	$24,652,750
Twos	1,297,200	21,820,313	23,056,578	21,930,863	22,915,066
Fives	99,910,750	67,132,138	167,042,898	159,622,853	148,116,015
Tens	113,820,580	75,835,008	189,655,588	181,447,858	168,908,071
Twenties	75,631,550	72,088,277	147,719,837	141,445,933	181,753,709
Fifties	21,418,300	24,359,175	45,777,475	46,177,945	47,658,905
One hundreds	26,888,900	33,060,700	59,958,600	58,338,780	58,331,470
Five hundreds	639,500	16,126,000	16,765,500	23,068,000	31,150,000
One thousands	239,000	14,401,500	14,949,500	23,111,500	38,794,500
Five thousands		595,000	595,000	3,250,000	
Ten thousands		320,000	320,000	2,500,000	
Add for fractions of notes not presented or destroyed	15,129		15,129	13,586	11,561
Totals	342,063,451	347,681,016	689,744,467	682,815,520	667,333,137
Deduct for legal-tender notes destroyed in Chicago fire		1,000,000	1,000,000	1,000,000	1,000,000
Totals	342,063,451	346,681,016	688,744,467	681,815,520	666,333,127

The law provides that, after specie payments are resumed, national-banks shall not be furnished with notes of a less denomination than five dollars; and in accordance with this provision no notes of the denominations of one and two dollars have been issued since the first day of January, 1879. The amount of ones outstanding on that day was $4,793,817, and of twos, $2,924,930; total, $7,718,747. Since that date the ones have been reduced $2,501,355, and the twos, $1,717,670, making a total reduction of small bank notes of $4,219,025.

The amount of legal-tender notes of the denomination of one dollar outstanding on that date was $20,257,109, and of twos, $20,035,525;

total, $40,292,634. The increase since that date to November 1, 1880, has been $3,491,584. Thus it will be seen that while the small notes of the national banks have been reduced more than four millions ($4,219,025), in compliance with law, since the date of resumption, the legal-tender notes of the same denominations have been increased $3,491,584. The total amount, in these denominations, of both kinds of notes outstanding on November 1, 1880, was $47,283,940. The total increase during the year has been $3,365,575 ; the decrease during the year previous was $3,649,451. Of the entire amount of national-bank and legal-tender notes now outstanding, nearly seven per cent. consists of one and two dollar notes, and more than thirty-one per cent. of ones, twos, and fives, while more than fifty-eight per cent. is in the notes of a less denomination than twenty dollars, and about eighty per cent. is in notes of a lower denomination than fifty dollars. Of the entire issue, about twenty per cent. in amount is in denominations of fifty dollars and upwards.

The circulation of the Imperial Bank of Germany, on January 1, 1879, was $165,933,942 ; its circulation on January 1, 1880, was $198,201,144 ; showing an increase of $32,267,202 during the year.

The following table exhibits by denominations the circulation of the Imperial Bank of Germany, on January 1, 1880, in thalers and marks, which are here converted into our currency:

Thalers.				Marks.			
Number of pieces.	Denominations.	Value of each piece in dollars.	Amount in dollars. (Thaler = 75 cents.)	Number of pieces.	Denominations.	Value of each piece in dollars.	Amount in dollars. (Mark = 25 cents.)
183	500 thalers.	375.00	68,375	255,753	1,000 marks.	250	63,938,250
2,387	100 thalers.	75.00	179,775	218,384	500 marks.	125	26,073,000
1,716½	50 thalers.	37.50	64,369	4,281,731½	100 marks.	25	107,043,287
5,034	25 thalers.	18.75	167,512	....	....	....	....
9,143½	10 thalers.	7.50	68,576	....	....	....	....
22,336	....	....	546,607	4,750,868½	....	....	197,054,537

The following table* gives the circulation of the Bank of France and its branches, with the number of pieces, and the denominations in francs and in dollars, on January 29, 1880:

Number of pieces.	Denominations.	Value of each piece in dollars.	Amount in francs.	Amount in dollars. (Fr. = 20 cents.)
5	5,000 francs.	1,000	25,000	5,009
1,371,477	1,000 francs.	200	1,371,477,000	274,295,400
716,960	500 francs.	100	358,490,000	71,698,000
3,009	200 francs.	40	601,800	120,360
5,716,919	100 francs.	20	571,691,900	114,338,380
207,516	50 francs.	10	10,375,800	2,075,180
27,323	25 francs.	5	683,075	136,615
335,635	20 francs.	4	6,712,700	1,342,540
197,448	5 francs.	1	987,240	197,448
1,241	Forms out of date.	....	429,850	85,970
8,577,553	....	....	2,321,474,365	464,294,873

The amount of circulation of the Bank of France on January 30, 1879, was 2,290,970,830 francs, or say $458,194,166, showing an increase between that time and January 29, 1880, the date of the foregoing table, of 30,503,535 francs, or $6,100,707.

*London Bankers' Magazine for August, 1880, pp. 656 and 662.

It will be seen that the Imperial Bank of Germany issues no notes of a less denomination than $7.50, and that the Bank of France issues less than two millions of dollars in notes of a less denomination than five dollars. The Bank of England issues no notes of less than twenty-five dollars, and the Banks of Ireland and Scotland none less than five dollars.

The amount of circulation in this country in denominations of five dollars and under on November 1, 1880, was $214,326,838. In the foreign countries named a large amount of silver and gold coin of the lower denominations enters into general circulation. It will be impossible to keep in circulation any large amount of small gold coins or silver dollars, unless the coinage of the latter is restricted and the small notes withdrawn.

Section 5182 of the Revised Statutes requires that the circulating notes of the national banks shall be signed by the president or vice-president and by the cashier of the association issuing the same. The written signature of at least one bank officer is necessary as a check between this office and the issuing banks, for if an illegal issue should occur the signature of such officer would be a means of determining the genuineness of the note. The written signatures of the officers of the banks are also necessary as an additional precaution against counterfeiting. A number of the banks, however, issue their notes with printed signatures, and in some cases with badly executed lithographed ones. A bill is now pending in one of the bank committees of Congress, imposing a fine of twenty dollars for every circulating note issued by any national bank without the written signature thereon of at least one of its officers; and the Comptroller respectfully repeats his previous recommendation for the passage of such an act, which act should also impose a fine upon any engraver or lithographer who shall print the signatures of bank officers upon such circulating notes.

UNITED STATES BONDS OUTSTANDING, AND THE AMOUNT HELD BY THE NATIONAL BANKS, STATE BANKS, AND PRIVATE BANKERS.

The following table exhibits the classification of the unmatured, interest-bearing, bonded debt of the United States on August 31, 1865, when the public debt reached its maximum, and on the 1st day of July in each year thereafter, together with the amount outstanding on November 1 of the present year:*

Date.	6 per cent. bonds.	5 per cent. bonds.	4½ per cent. bonds.	4 per cent. bonds.	Total.
August 31, 1865	$996, 518, 001	$199, 792, 100			$1, 106, 310, 101
July 1, 1866	1, 008, 386, 460	108, 528, 433			1, 206, 916, 904
July 1, 1867	1, 421, 110, 719	198, 533, 435			1, 619, 644, 154
July 1, 1868	1, 841, 521, 800	221, 586, 400			2, 063, 110, 200
July 1, 1869	1, 886, 341, 300	221, 589, 300			2, 107, 930, 600
July 1, 1870	1, 764, 932, 300	221, 589, 300			1, 986, 521, 600
July 1, 1871	1, 613, 897, 300	274, 236, 450			1, 888, 133, 750
July 1, 1872	1, 374, 883, 800	414, 567, 300			1, 789, 451, 100
July 1, 1873	1, 281, 238, 650	414, 567, 300			1, 695, 805, 950
July 1, 1874	1, 213, 624, 700	510, 628, 050			1, 724, 252, 750
July 1, 1875	1, 100, 865, 550	607, 132, 750			1, 707, 998, 300
July 1, 1876	984, 999, 650	711, 685, 800			1, 696, 685, 450
July 1, 1877	854, 621, 850	703, 266, 650	$140, 000, 000		1, 696, 888, 500
July 1, 1878	738, 619, 000	703, 266, 650	240, 000, 000	$98, 850, 000	1, 780, 735, 650
July 1, 1879	310, 932, 500	646, 905, 500	250, 000, 000	679, 878, 110	1, 887, 716, 110
July 1, 1880	235, 780, 400	484, 864, 900	250, 000, 000	739, 347, 800	1, 709, 993, 100
November 1, 1880	217, 699, 550	409, 861, 050	250, 000, 000	739, 347, 800	1, 676, 908, 400

* The Navy pension fund, amounting to $14,000,000 in 3 per cents., the interest upon which is applied to the payment of naval pensions exclusively, is not included in the table.

Since the year 1865, the national banks have held an average of more than one-fifth, and now nearly one-fourth, of the interest-bearing debt of the United States. Previous to the year 1872 much the larger portion of these bonds bore interest at the rate of 6 per cent., and until the year 1877 all of the bonds bore interest at either five or six per cent. These classes of bonds have since been greatly reduced, and are now less than three-fifths of the amount pledged for circulation, while more than two-fifths of the amount consists of bonds bearing interest at 4 and 4½ per cent. only. This will be seen from the following table, which exhibits the amounts and classes of United States bonds owned by the banks, including those pledged as security for circulation and for public deposits, on the first day of July in each year since 1865, and upon November 1 of the present year:

Date.	United States bonds held as security for circulation.					U. S. bonds held for other purposes at nearest date.	Grand total.
	6 per cent. bonds.	5 per cent. bonds.	4½ per cent. bonds.	4 per cent. bonds.	Total.		
July 1, 1865....	$170,382,500	$65,576,600	....	....	$235,959,100	$155,785,750	$391,744,850
July 1, 1866....	241,088,500	86,226,850	....	....	327,310,350	121,152,950	448,463,300
July 1, 1867....	251,430,400	89,177,100	....	....	340,607,500	84,002,650	424,610,150
July 1, 1868....	250,726,350	90,766,950	....	....	341,495,900	83,922,500	425,418,400
July 1, 1869....	255,190,350	87,661,250	....	....	342,851,000	55,102,000	397,996,600
July 1, 1870....	247,355,350	94,923,200	....	....	342,278,550	43,980,600	386,259,150
July 1, 1871....	220,497,750	139,387,800	....	....	359,885,550	39,450,800	399,336,350
July 1, 1872....	173,251,450	207,189,250	....	....	380,440,700	31,868,200	412,308,900
July 1, 1873....	160,923,500	229,487,050	....	....	390,410,550	25,724,400	416,134,950
July 1, 1874....	154,370,700	236,800,600	....	....	391,171,300	25,347,100	416,518,300
July 1, 1875....	136,955,100	239,359,400	....	....	376,314,500	26,900,200	403,214,700
July 1, 1876....	109,313,450	232,081,300	....	....	341,394,750	45,170,300	386,565,050
July 1, 1877....	87,690,300	206,051,050	$44,372,250	....	338,713,600	47,315,050	386,028,650
July 1, 1878....	82,421,300	199,514,550	48,448,630	$13,182,000	343,566,400	68,850,900	418,397,300
July 1, 1879....	56,042,800	144,610,300	35,056,550	118,538,050	354,254,600	78,603,520	430,858,120
July 1, 1880....	58,056,150	139,758,650	37,760,950	126,078,300	361,653,050	42,831,300	404,483,350
Nov. 1, 1880....	56,605,150	147,079,750	30,968,950	119,075,100	359,748,950	43,620,400	403,369,350

All of the five and six per cent. bonds now held by the national banks, with the exception of Pacific Railway bonds, will mature on or before July 1, 1881, and will probably be replaced by bonds bearing interest at 4 or 4½ per cent., or by new bonds hereafter to be issued by authority of Congress bearing a less rate of interest.

The amount of United States bonds held by State and savings-banks cannot be accurately ascertained, for the reason that banks in seventeen of the States do not make reports of their condition to State authorities. From such reports as have been received through the courtesy of State officers, it is found that the State banks and trust companies and the savings banks held the following amount of United States bonds, at different dates during the year 1880:

State banks in twenty States	$7,142,532
Trust companies in five States..	19,109,650
Savings banks in fourteen States..	187,413,220
Total	213,665,402

The Commissioner of Internal Revenue receives semi-annual reports from all banks organized under State laws, and also reports from private bankers, giving their average capital and deposits, and the amount of such capital invested in United States bonds; and from these returns the following table has been compiled, showing, by geographical divisions, the average amount of capital invested in United States bonds for the six months ending May 31, in the years 1878, 1879, and 1880:

Six months ending—	By State banks, private bankers, and trust companies.	By savings banks.	Total.
May 31, 1878:			
New England States	$8,079,738	$26,597,718	$39,626,456
Middle States	23,915,787	102,163,965	126,079,742
Southern States	1,523,882	66,667	1,590,549
Western States	6,062,265	1,172,598	7,234,863
Pacific States and Territories	3,356,369	1,082,620	4,438,989
United States	37,887,011	131,083,588	168,970,599
May 31, 1879:			
New England States................................	3,669,967	34,941,378	38,611,345
Middle States	25,686,469	123,818,148	149,504,617
Southern States	3,593,179	86,021	3,679,200
Western States	8,326,402	2,164,668	10,491,070
Pacific States and Territories	5,015,948	1,372,845	6,388,798
United States	46,291,965	162,383,060	208,675,025
May 31, 1880:			
New England States................................	3,737,093	37,693,200	41,430,293
Middle States	20,564,834	146,301,155	166,865,989
Southern States	2,541,991	1,000	2,542,991
Western States	8,137,554	2,474,557	10,612,111
Pacific States and Territories	3,883,816	2,717,904	6,601,720
United States	38,865,288	189,187,816	228,053,104

The above table gives the average amount of capital invested in United States bonds, from which should be deducted the amount of premium paid at the time of purchase, which cannot be ascertained.

The amount of United States bonds held by the national banks on November 1, 1880, as above shown, was $403,369,350, and the average amount held by the other banks and bankers of the country, during the six months ending May 31 last, was $228,053,104. The total amount held by all the banks and bankers is thus shown to be considerably more than one-third of the whole interest-bearing, funded debt of the United States, as follows:

```
Savings banks................................................$189,187,816
State banks and trust companies.............................  24,498,604
Private bankers.............................................  14,366,684
National banks..............................................  403,369,350
                                                            _____
    Total...................................................  631,422,454
```

If the amount of bonds held by national banks and private bankers be deducted from the last total, the remainder will agree very nearly with the amount of bonds held by State and savings banks as returned by State officers, and shown on the preceding page. These amounts, therefore, seem to be very nearly correct, and to comprise the whole amount of United States bonds held by all the banks and bankers of the country.

A table will be found in the appendix giving the number of each class of banks and of private bankers in each State, together with the amount of their capital, deposits, and United States bonds held.

CLEARING-HOUSE CERTIFICATES.

Section 5192 Revised Statutes provides that clearing-house certificates, representing specie or lawful money specially deposited for the purpose of any Clearing House association, shall also be deemed to be lawful money in the possession of any association belonging to such

Clearing House holding and owning such certificate; and section 5193 provides that the Secretary of the Treasury may receive United States notes on deposit, without interest, from any national banking associations, in sums not less than ten thousand dollars, and issue certificates therefor in denominations of not less than five thousand dollars, which certificates may be counted as part of the lawful money reserve, and may be accepted in the settlement of clearing-house balances at the places where the deposits therefor were made.

The legal-tender note certificates were first issued in the fiscal year 1873. On June 30, 1875, there were outstanding $59,045,000 of these certificates, of which the national banks held $47,310,000. On June 30, 1876, the amount outstanding was $33,140,000, of which the banks held $27,955,000. On June 30, 1879, the amount had been reduced to $29,330,000, and the banks held on June 14 of the same year $25,180,000. The amount outstanding on October 1 was $9,885,000, and the national banks held on that day $7,655,000, they having surrendered a large portion of these certificates for the purpose of supplying the demand for United States notes.

The issue of the gold certificates was authorized by the fifth section of the act March 3, 1863, and they were used for clearing-house purposes soon after the passage of the national-bank act. The first issue was made on November 13, 1865. On June 30, 1875, there were outstanding $21,796,300, of which the national banks in New York City held $12,642,180. The issue of these certificates was discontinued on December 1, 1878, and the amount outstanding had decreased on June 30, 1879, to $15,413,700, and on October 1, 1880, to $7,480,100. The issue of gold certificates having been discontinued by the government, and the amount of gold coin having rapidly increased, the banks in New York found it necessary to establish a depository of gold coin for the convenience of the Clearing House. This depository at the present time is the Bank of America, by which bank certificates of deposit were first issued on October 14, 1879. The amount of such certificates outstanding on November 1, 1879, was $9,155,000, on January 1, 1880, $25,610,000, and on June 1, and since that time, $39,550,000, which is the full capacity of the vault. Of this amount the national banks of New York City held on June 11, 1880, $33,337,000; on October 1, $36,189,000.

The Clearing Houses of Boston, Philadelphia, and Baltimore have organized similar depositories in order to utilize their gold coin and save the risk and inconvenience of handling and transporting the coin itself. The total amount of such certificates issued to the national banks in New York up to October 1 was $36,189,000, in Philadelphia, $6,040,000, in Boston, $5,908,000, and in Baltimore, $30,000; total, $48,167,000.

TRANSACTIONS OF THE NEW YORK CLEARING HOUSE.

The New York Clearing House Association is composed of forty-five national and twelve State banks, and the assistant treasurer of the United States at New York. The exchanges at the Clearing House for the year ending October 1, 1880, obtained through the courtesy of Mr. W. A. Camp, its manager, were more than thirty-seven thousand millions, and the balances paid in money were more than fifteen hundred millions. The average daily exchanges were more than one hundred and twenty-one millions, and the average daily balances paid in money were but about four and nine-tenths millions, or only four and one-tenth per cent. of the amount of the settlements.

The New York Clearing House was organized in 1853, and the following table exhibits its transactions yearly, and the amount and ratio of currency required for the payment of daily balances, for the last twenty-seven years:

Years.	No. of banks.	*Capital.	Exchanges.	Balances paid in money.	Average daily exchanges.	Average daily balances paid in money.	Ratios.
							Pr. ct.
1854	50	$47,044,900	$5,750,455,987	$297,411,494	$19,104,505	$968,078	5.2
1855	48	48,884,180	5,362,912,098	289,694,137	17,412,052	940,505	5.4
1856	50	52,883,700	6,906,213,328	334,714,489	22,278,108	1,079,794	4.8
1857	50	64,420,200	8,333,226,718	365,313,902	26,963,271	1,182,346	4.4
1858	46	67,146,018	4,756,664,386	314,238,911	15,393,736	1,016,954	6.6
1859	47	67,921,714	6,443,005,956	363,984,683	20,807,333	1,177,944	5.6
1860	50	69,907,435	7,231,143,057	380,693,438	23,401,757	1,233,018	5.3
1861	50	68,900,605	5,915,742,758	353,383,944	19,269,520	1,151,088	6.0
1862	50	68,375,870	6,871,443,591	415,530,331	22,237,682	1,344,758	6.0
1863	50	68,972,568	14,867,597,849	677,626,483	48,428,658	2,207,252	4.6
1864	49	68,586,763	24,097,196,656	885,719,205	77,984,455	2,866,405	3.7
1865	55	80,363,013	26,032,384,342	1,035,765,108	84,790,040	3,373,923	4.0
1866	58	82,370,200	28,717,146,914	1,066,135,106	93,541,195	3,472,753	3.7
1867	58	81,770,300	28,675,159,472	1,144,963,451	93,101,167	3,717,414	4.0
1868	60	82,270,200	28,484,288,637	1,125,455,237	92,182,164	3,642,250	4.0
1869	59	82,776,200	37,407,028,987	1,130,318,308	121,451,393	3,637,207	3.0
1870	61	83,620,200	27,904,539,406	1,036,484,822	90,274,478	3,365,210	3.7
1871	62	84,420,200	29,300,986,682	1,209,721,029	95,133,074	3,927,666	4.1
1872	61	84,420,200	32,636,097,404	1,213,293,827	105,964,277	3,999,266	3.7
1873	59	83,370,200	33,972,773,943	1,152,372,108	111,022,137	3,765,922	3.4
1874	59	81,635,200	20,850,681,963	971,231,281	68,139,484	3,173,958	4.7
1875	59	80,435,200	23,042,276,858	1,104,346,345	75,301,558	3,608,977	4.8
1876	59	81,731,200	19,874,815,361	1,009,533,037	64,738,813	3,298,361	5.1
1877	58	71,934,200	20,376,555,937	1,015,256,483	68,447,794	3,928,710	4.9
1878	57	63,611,900	19,932,733,547	951,970,454	65,106,974	3,111,015	4.8
1879	59	60,800,200	24,558,196,689	1,321,119,398	79,977,839	4,303,320	5.4
1880	57	60,475,200	37,182,128,621	1,516,538,631	121,510,234	4,956,009	4.1
....		†71,783,043	‡535,874,207,547	‡22,672,815,042	†164,503,878	†2,733,300	4.2

* The capital is for various dates, the amount at a uniform date in each year not being obtainable.
† Yearly averages for twenty-seven years. ‡ Totals for twenty-seven years.

The Clearing House transactions of the assistant treasurer of the United States at New York, for the year ending November 1, 1880, were as follows:

Exchanges received from Clearing House $343,622,365
Exchanges delivered to Clearing House   78,193,328
Balances paid to Clearing House 266,387,853
Balances received from Clearing House   958,819
Showing that the amount paid by the assistant treasurer to the Clearing
  House was in excess of the amount received by him.................. 265,429,034

The amount of clearings during the last year exceeded any previous year's transactions since the organization of the Clearing House. The average amount per day for the year was $126,466,232.85. The maximum was on November 3, when it reached $202,558,252.11. The largest amount of balances in any one day was on November 11, when it was $11,208,025.20, and $8,300,000 of this amount, weighing about 15½ tons, was paid in gold coin.

The total amount of transactions in the twenty-seven years since the organization of the Clearing House is $574,849,719,103, and the average for each year is $21,290,734,040. The amount of gold coin actually paid in settlement of balances in the last year is $340,538,000; of Clearing House gold certificates $1,056,462,000; of United States Clearing House certificates $34,260,000; and of legal-tenders $85,218,000. Of the legal-tenders, $46,852,000 were received in October, 1879, and only $38,366,000 during the remaining eleven months.

A table compiled, for purposes of comparison, from returns made to the New York Clearing House, will be found in the appendix, giving the clearings and balances weekly, for the months of September, October, and November of various years, from 1872 to 1880.

SPECIE IN BANK AND IN THE TREASURY OF THE UNITED STATES,
AND ESTIMATED AMOUNT IN THE COUNTRY—SPECIE IN THE BANK
OF ENGLAND AND IN THE BANK OF FRANCE.

The table below exhibits the amount of specie held by the national
banks at the dates of their reports for the last eleven years; the coin,
coin-certificates, and checks payable in coin held by the New York City
banks being stated separately:

Dates.	Held by national banks in New York City.				Held by other national banks.	Aggregate.
	Coin.	U. S. coin-certificates.	Checks payable in coin.	Total.		
Oct. 5, 1868..	$1,696,023 24	$6,390,140	$1,536,353 06	$9,625,116 90	$3,378,596 49	$13,003,713 39
Jan. 4, 1869..	1,602,769 46	18,095,520	2,346,140 48	22,269,439 97	7,337,320 29	29,626,750 26
Apr. 17, 1869..	1,653,575 21	3,720,048	1,469,828 64	6,842,441 85	3,102,090 30	9,944,532 15
June 12, 1869..	2,542,533 93	11,953,880	975,015 82	15,471,229 76	2,983,860 70	18,455,090 48
Oct. 9, 1869..	1,792,740 73	10,467,900	1,013,943 72	13,704,589 45	3,297,816 37	23,002,405 63
Jan. 22, 1870..	6,196,036 20	28,501,460	2,190,644 74	36,886,141 03	11,457,242 69	48,345,383 73
Mar. 24, 1870..	2,647,908 89	21,872,480	1,069,094 30	25,589,482 69	11,507,060 75	37,096,543 44
June 9, 1870..	3,842,400 24	18,660,250	1,163,905 88	22,767,236 13	8,332,201 66	31,099,437 73
Oct. 8, 1870..	1,607,742 91	7,593,900	3,994,008 42	13,195,649 33	5,378,362 14	18,400,011 47
Dec. 28, 1870..	2,268,561 96	14,063,540	3,746,126 87	30,060,348 83	6,227,002 76	26,307,251 59
Mar. 18, 1871..	2,982,155 01	13,090,720	3,829,361 64	19,911,737 25	5,857,409 39	25,769,166 64
Apr. 29, 1871..	2,947,930 71	9,645,080	4,382,307 24	16,975,117 95	6,456,909 07	22,732,027 02
June 10, 1871..	2,349,402 06	9,161,160	3,680,854 02	15,001,422 98	4,933,532 18	19,934,955 16
Oct. 2, 1871..	1,121,869 40	7,590,260	1,163,628 44	9,875,757 84	3,377,240 33	13,252,996 17
Dec. 16, 1871..	1,454,980 73	17,354,740	4,255,681 39	23,066,302 12	6,579,997 44	29,076,299 56
Feb. 27, 1872..	1,490,417 70	12,341,960	3,117,100 90	16,948,578 60	8,589,246 72	25,507,825 32
Apr. 19, 1872..	7,838,650 74	10,102,400	4,715,364 25	16,046,423 99	7,787,475 47	24,433,699 46
June 10, 1872..	8,782,909 64	11,411,160	4,219,419 52	16,414,489 16	4,842,154 98	24,256,644 14
Oct. 3, 1872..	920,767 37	5,454,580		6,375,347 37	3,854,409 42	10,229,756 79
Dec. 27, 1872..	1,306,091 05	12,471,940		13,778,031 05	5,309,305 40	19,047,336 45
Feb. 28, 1873..	1,956,769 90	11,539,780		13,496,549 80	4,279,123 67	17,777,673 53
Apr. 25, 1873..	1,344,250 93	11,743,320		13,088,260 93	3,780,537 81	16,868,808 74
June 13, 1873..	1,445,097 71	22,139,080		23,581,177 71	4,368,909 01	27,950,086 72
Sept. 12, 1873..	1,063,210 55	13,522,600		14,585,810 55	5,282,658 90	19,865,469 45
Dec. 26, 1873..	1,376,170 50	18,325,760		19,701,930 50	7,205,107 08	26,907,037 58
Feb. 27, 1874..	1,167,820 09	22,518,640		24,686,460 09	8,679,403 49	33,365,863 58
May 1, 1874..	1,530,282 10	23,454,660		34,964,942 10	7,585,027 16	32,569,969 26
June 26, 1874..	1,542,525 00	13,671,660		15,514,185 00	6,812,622 27	22,326,807 27
Oct. 2, 1874..	1,291,786 56	13,114,480		14,406,266 56	6,834,878 67	21,240,945 23
Dec. 31, 1874..	1,443,215 42	14,410,940		15,854,155 42	6,582,608 63	22,436,761 04
Mar. 1, 1875..	1,084,555 54	10,622,160		11,706,715 54	4,960,390 63	16,667,106 17
May 1, 1875..	930,105 70	5,753,220		6,683,325 76	3,937,035 88	10,620,361 64
June 30, 1875..	1,922,015 86	12,642,180		13,665,195 86	5,294,386 44	18,958,582 30
Oct. 1, 1875..	753,904 90	4,201,720		4,955,624 90	3,094,704 83	8,050,329 73
Dec. 17, 1875..	869,436 72	12,532,810		13,402,246 72	3,668,659 18	17,070,905 90
Mar. 10, 1876..	3,261,131 36	10,080,920		23,346,051 36	6,720,294 49	20,077,345 85
May 12, 1876..	832,313 70	15,183,760		16,016,073 70	5,608,520 66	21,714,594 36
June 30, 1876..	1,214,522 02	16,672,780		16,087,302 92	7,131,167 00	25,218,469 92
Oct. 2, 1876..	1,120,814 34	13,446,760		14,576,574 34	6,785,079 09	21,361,654 63
Dec. 22, 1876..	1,434,721 83	21,605,900		23,037,601 83	9,903,046 06	32,999,647 89
Jan. 20, 1877..	1,609,284 94	38,029,660		36,295,944 94	14,410,322 61	49,709,267 55
Apr. 14, 1877..	1,990,726 59	13,809,180		15,829,905 59	11,240,132 19	27,070,037 78
June 22, 1877..	1,423,258 17	10,324,920		11,747,578 17	9,588,417 59	21,335,996 06
Oct. 1, 1877..	1,538,486 47	11,409,920		12,948,406 47	9,710,413 84	22,658,820 31
Dec. 28, 1877..	1,955,746 20	19,119,080		21,074,826 20	11,832,924 50	32,907,750 70
Mar. 15, 1878..	2,428,707 44	35,003,020		37,432,017 44	17,290,040 58	54,722,058 02
May 1, 1878..	2,688,092 06	26,897,640		28,085,732 06	17,938,024 00	46,023,756 06
June 29, 1878..	1,905,705 22	11,954,500		13,860,205 23	15,391,264 55	29,251,469 77
Oct. 1, 1878..	1,779,792 43	13,514,610		15,294,402 43	17,304,604 16	32,598,606 59
Dec. 6, 1878..	4,509,200 01	12,277,180		16,286,479 01	18,068,771 35	34,355,250 36
Jan. 1, 1879..	5,421,552 49	12,739,544		18,161,092 49	23,338,664 83	41,499,757 32
Apr. 4, 1879..	5,312,906 90	12,220,940		17,533,906 90	23,614,656 51	41,148,563 41
June 14, 1879..	6,058,472 34	12,291,270		18,349,743 34	23,993,545 10	42,333,357 44
Oct. 2, 1879..	7,216,967 69	12,130,900		19,349,867 69	22,822,873 54	42,173,731 23
Dec. 12, 1879..	20,096,240 64	8,366,140	*21,568,000 00	50,031,380 04	28,081,651 96	79,013,041 99
Feb. 21, 1880..	13,262,541 44	7,464,650	*35,855,000 00	50,573,191 44	23,860,800 31	80,442,951 76
Apr. 23, 1880..	12,505,720 49	6,914,250	*26,458,000 00	44,967,970 49	41,461,761 72	86,429,732 21
June 11, 1880..	16,682,226 40	7,816,200	*33,337,000 00	57,829,420 40	41,677,078 86	99,506,505 26
Oct. 1, 1880..	16,104,855 28	7,489,700	*30,188,000 00	59,783,555 38	49,562,954 11	109,346,509 49

*Gold clearing-house certificates.

The amount of silver coin held by the national banks on October 1, 1877,
was $3,700,703, and on October 1, 1878, $5,392,628. The amount held on

October 2, 1879, was $4,986,493, and on October 1, 1880, $6,495,477, including $1,165,120 in silver treasury certificates. The aggregate amount· of specie held by the State banks in New England, New York, New Jersey, Pennsylvania, Maryland, Louisiana, Kentucky, Ohio, Iowa, Wisconsin, and Minnesota, as shown by their official reports for 1880, was $6,201,617, of which the banks in New York City held $4,968,722. In the returns from California the amount of coin is not given separately, but it is estimated to be three-fourths of the amount returned as currency, which was $13,785,015.

The Director of the Mint, in his report for 1879, estimated the amount of coin in the country on June 30, 1879, at $398,541,683, of which $286,490,698 was gold and $112,050,985 was silver.

His estimate for the fiscal year ending June 30, 1880, is as follows :

Amount of coin in the country June 30, 1879	$398,541,683
Net gold coinage for the year	55,948,407
Net silver coinage for the year	27,903,139
Net importation of gold for the year	16,519,586
Net importation of silver for the year	2,642,896
Total coin circulation June 30, 1880	501,555,711

Of this amount it is estimated that $358,958,691 consists of gold coin, and $142,597,020 of silver coin. The Director estimates that from the close of the last fiscal year to November 1 there has been added to the coin $6,494,528 of gold and $9,630,940 of silver, making the stock of coin in the country at the latter date $517,681,179, and consisting of $365,-453,219 of gold coin and $152,227,960 of silver. The amount of bullion in the mints and New York assay office on November 1 is stated to have been $78,558,811 of gold and $6,043,367 of silver, making in all $84,602,178; which, added to the estimated amount of coin stated above, gives $602,283,357 as the total estimate of coin and bullion in the country on November 1, of which amount $444,012,030 was gold and $158,271,327 was silver.

The amount of gold and silver, and the percentage of each, in the Treasury of the United States, on September 30 in each year from 1876 to 1880, and on November 1, 1880, is shown in the following table :

Period.	Silver.			Gold coin and bullion.	Total coin and bullion.	Per cent. of—	
	Standard dollars.	Other coin and bullion.	Total silver.			Silver.	Gold.
September 30, 1876 ...	....	$6,029,387	$6,029,387	$55,423,069	$61,452,426	9.8	90.2
September 30, 1877 ...	....	7,425,454	7,425,454	107,039,529	114,464,983	6.5	93.5
September 30, 1878 ...	$12,155,205	15,777,937	27,933,142	136,036,302	163,969,444	17.0	83.0
September 30, 1879 ...	31,805,774	21,173,023	52,979,797	169,827,571	222,807,368	23.8	76.2
September 30, 1880 ...	47,784,744	30,878,286	78,663,030	135,641,450	214,304,480	36.7	63.3
November 1, 1880	47,156,588	30,820,561	77,977,149	141,127,049	219,104,198	35.6	64.4

The following table shows the amount of bullion held by the Bank of England in each year from 1870 to 1880, the pound sterling being estimated at five dollars :

1870	$103,900,000	1876	$143,500,000
1871	117,950,000	1877	126,650,000
1872	112,900,000	1878	119,200,000
1873	113,500,000	1879*	150,942,980
1874	111,450,000	1880†	141,637,000
1875	119,600,000		

* London Economist, November 8, 1879.
† London Bankers' Magazine, October 1880.

The amount of gold and silver, and percentage of each, held by the Bank of France on December 31 of each year from 1870 to 1879, and on October 21, 1880, is shown in the following table, five francs being taken for one dollar : *

Years.	Silver coin and bullion.	Gold coin and bullion.	Total.	Per cent of—	
				Silver.	Gold.
December 31, 1870	$13, 700, 000	$85, 740, 000	$99, 440, 000	13. 8	86. 2
December 31, 1871	16, 240, 000	110, 680, 000	126, 920, 000	12. 8	87. 2
December 31, 1872	26, 520, 000	131, 740, 000	158, 260, 000	16. 8	83. 2
December 31, 1873	31, 260, 000	122, 260, 000	153, 520, 000	20. 4	79. 6
December 31, 1874	62, 640, 000	204, 220, 000	266, 860, 000	23. 5	76. 5
December 31, 1875	101, 000, 000	234, 600, 000	335, 560, 000	30. 1	69. 9
December 31, 1876	127, 720, 000	306, 080, 000	433, 800, 000	29. 4	70. 6
December 31, 1877	173, 080, 000	235, 420, 000	408, 500, 000	42. 4	57. 6
December 31, 1878	211, 620, 000	196, 720, 000	408, 340, 000	51. 8	48. 2
December 31, 1879	245, 520, 000	148, 320, 000	393, 840, 000	62. 3	37. 7
October 21, 1880	249, 789, 000	116, 140, 000	365, 929, 000	68. 3	31. 7

STATE TAXATION OF NATIONAL BANKS.

Section 5219 of the Revised Statutes of the United States provides that nothing in the national-bank act shall prevent all the shares in any national association from being included in the valuation of the personal property of the owner or holder of such shares in assessing taxes imposed by the authority of the State in which the association is located, but that the legislature of each State may determine and direct the manner and place of taxing all the shares of national banking associations located within the State, subject only to two restrictions: first, that the taxation shall not be at a greater rate than is assessed upon other moneyed capital in the hands of the individual citizens of such State; and, second, that the shares of any national banking association owned by non-residents of any State shall be taxed in the city or town where the bank is located, and not elsewhere. The same section provides that nothing herein contained shall be held or construed to exempt the real property of associations from either State, county, or municipal taxes, to the same extent, according to its value, as other real property is taxed.

In the decision of the United States Supreme Court, in the case of *Williams vs. The Board of Assessors of the City of Albany*, at the October term in 1879, Mr. Justice Miller, who delivered the opinion, commenting on this provision in reference to State taxation of national-bank shares, said:

That the provision was necessary, to authorize the States to impose any tax whatever on national-bank shares, is abundantly established by former decisions of the United States Supreme Court. As Congress was conferring a power on the States which they would not otherwise have had—to tax these shares—it undertook to impose a restriction on the exercise of that power, manifestly designed to prevent taxation which should discriminate against this class of property as compared with other moneyed capital. In permitting the States to tax these shares it was foreseen—the cases we have cited from our former decisions of the United States Supreme Court showed too clearly—that the State authorities might be disposed to tax the capital invested in these banks oppressively. This might have been prevented by fixing a precise limit in amount; but Congress, with due regard to the dignity of the States, and with a desire to interfere only so far as was necessary to protect the banks from any-

* The Bulletin de Statistique, as quoted in the Bankers' Magazine, New York, vol. XIII, page 740; except the items for 1879 and 1880, which were obtained from the London Bankers' Magazine for August, 1880, page 661, and New York Bankers' Magazine for November, 1880, page 335.

thing beyond their equal share of the public burdens, said you may tax the real estate of the bank as other real estate is taxed, and you may tax the shares of the bank as the personal property of the owner to the same extent you tax other moneyed capital invested in your State. It was conceived that by this qualification of the power of taxation equality would be secured and injustice prevented.

Prior to this decision of the Supreme Court, the intent of Congress in providing for the taxation of national-bank shares by the States, had been overlooked or evaded, in collecting taxes on such shares under the laws of many of the States. As a consequence, capital invested in national banks has, in the assessment and collection of taxes, been subjected to unjust and severe discrimination in different ways in these States.

In New York the law permits the deduction of the just debts of an individual from his personal property, including his moneyed capital, excepting only from his bank shares. In Ohio the law provides certain State boards for equalizing the taxation on real estate, on railroad capital, and on capital invested in bank shares; but there is no State board for equalizing the taxation on personal property other than bank shares, railroad stock or other moneyed capital. The equalizing process as to all other personal property ceases with the county boards. But the county boards throughout the State fixed the valuation of moneyed capital for purposes of taxation at six-tenths of its true value, while the State board fixed the value of bank shares at their actual cash value. Thus while the rates of taxation were the same, yet, the valuation being different, bank shares were discriminated against to the extent of four-tenths of their value.

The States have a right to impose whatever tax they choose upon the shares of banks organized under their own laws, but they have no right to impose a greater valuation on national bank shares than on other moneyed capital in the hands of individuals, since thereby the tax becomes heavier on the bank shares than on the moneyed capital, while the law, rightly construed, says it shall be the same.

The decisions of the United States Supreme Court delivered March 2, 1880, in cases arising under the laws of the two States mentioned, protect national banks from these forms of discrimination, and indirectly protect the State banks, as these States will doubtless so modify their laws as to place State banks within their borders on at least as good a footing in respect to taxation as the national banks. By these decisions also the Supreme Court pointed out the appropriate mode of relief for national banks, when taxes are assessed upon them at a greater rate than upon other moneyed capital in the same State. This mode is to pay such portion of the unjustly imposed tax as is equal to the tax paid on other moneyed capital, and to enjoin the collection of the excess.

But these decisions do not point out any satisfactory method for the recovery of taxes which have been heretofore illegally assessed on national-bank shares and collected by the State authorities. On this point it was decided that the question of the recovery from the assessors of taxes overpaid, through errors in assessments arising from misconstructions of the law of the United States relative to the taxation of national-bank shares by the States, is not one to be decided by the Federal courts, but must be governed by the common law or the statute law of the State.

As it is in the power of the States, under the present law of Congress, so to legislate that, through mistaken construction of said law by the assessors, bank shares may be discriminated against as compared with other moneyed capital, and as redress for such mistakes depends on the action of the State courts; and as, further, to secure a true construction of the

federal law by the assessors in each State may require protracted litigation, before the question of the legality of the form of taxation in each
particular State can be finally decided; it becomes a question whether
Congress may not better settle the whole matter by fixing more precisely the amount of taxation which may be imposed by the States on
national-bank shares.

The decision of the Supreme Court, heretofore quoted, states that this
oppressive taxation "might have been prevented by fixing a precise limit
in amount," and it is respectfully suggested to Congress whether it would
not be advisable, in order to avoid the expense and annoyance of long-
continued litigation, to pass a law fixing the maximum amount of taxation which may be imposed upon national banks by State authorities.
It is true that if this should be done the States so disposed might discriminate in favor of banks of their own creation, or in favor of other
moneyed capital, by making the weight of taxation on such property
less oppressive than that fixed on national-bank shares by Congress;
but such action would be so manifestly unjust that it is more likely that
legislation would follow in the more important States, the object of which
would be to impose just and equitable assessments upon every class of
moneyed corporations. It is also true that if the maximum rate of taxation were fixed by law, the courts and the board of assessors could yet, by
construction, discriminate in favor of other moneyed corporations by
requiring the tax to be at a uniform rate, while the valuation of the
assessors is unequal.

The Supreme Court, in the decision already referred to upon this point,
quotes from the law as follows:

Taxation shall not be at a greater rate than is assessed upon other moneyed capital
in the hands of individuals.

The Court then proceeds to say:

Seizing upon the word *rate* in this sentence as if disconnected from the word assessment, and construing it to mean percentage on *any* valuation that might be made, the
Court of Appeals arrives at the conclusion that since that percentage is the same in all
cases the act of Congress is not infringed. If this philological criticism were perfectly
just, we still think the manifest purpose of Congress in passing this law should prevail. We have already shown what that was. But the criticism is not sound. The
section to be construed begins by declaring that these shares may be "included in the
valuation of the personal property of the owner in assessing taxes imposed by authority of the State within which the association is located." This *valuation*, then, is part
of the *assessment* of taxes. It is a necessary part of every assessment of taxes which
is governed by a ratio or percentage. There can be no rate or percentage without a
valuation. This taxation, says the act, shall not be at a greater rate than is assessed on other moneyed capital. What is it that shall not be greater? The answer
is taxation. In what respect shall it not be greater than the *rate assessed* upon other
capital? We see that Congress had in its mind an assessment, a *rate* of assessment,
and a valuation, and taking all these together the taxation on these shares was not to
be greater than on other moneyed capital.

If section 5219 of the Revised Statutes were to be so amended as to
read as follows, it would cover the two points under consideration:

But the legislature of each State may determine and direct the manner and place of
taxing all the shares of national banking associations located within the State, subject
only to the two restrictions, that the maximum rate of taxation shall not exceed ——
per cent., and that the valuation shall not be at a greater rate than upon other moneyed
capital in the hands of individual citizens of such State, and that the shares of any
national banking association owned by non-residents of any State shall be taxed in
the city or town where the bank is located, and not elsewhere.

TABLES OF NATIONAL AND STATE TAXATION.

The Comptroller herewith presents his usual annual tables, giving, as far as can be ascertained, the amount of taxes imposed upon the banking capital of the country, and respectfully repeats his previous recommendation for the repeal of the law imposing a tax upon capital and deposits, and of the two-cent stamp tax upon bank checks.

The amount collected by the Commissioner of Internal Revenue during the last fiscal year was $123,981,916, and the whole of this amount, with the exception of $11,096,464.39, was derived from the tax on spirits, beer, and tobacco. Were the entire tax upon banks and bankers of the country, including the two-cent check tax, as well as the tax upon matches and patent medicines, removed, the amount of revenue received by the government from the tax on spirits, beer and tobacco, and from customs duties, would alone be sufficient to meet its expenses and reduce the public debt at the rate of at least seventy millions annually.

The principal reason heretofore urged against the repeal of these taxes has been that the amount produced was necessary for the support of the government; but this reason has ceased to exist. The repeal of the laws imposing taxes, not only upon the national banks, but also upon the State and private banks and savings-banks of the country—which institutions hold, as has been seen, one-third of the whole public debt of the United States—will indirectly aid the government in refunding the remainder of the debt at a low rate of interest, by increasing the demand and extending the market for its bonds, thus to a considerable extent saving to the government in interest what may be lost to it in revenue from taxes.

The enormous State taxes which the banks and bankers of the country have paid for a series of years, and still pay, and which are in a much greater ratio to values than are those imposed on any other species of property, are as much as should be imposed upon this great interest, and particularly at a time when the rates of interest throughout the country are being greatly reduced.

The following table for the year 1879, similar to the one for the year 1878, which was given in the last annual report of the Comptroller, shows the amount of United States and State taxes, and the rate of taxation paid by the national banks, in every State and principal city of the Union for that year. Similar tables for the years 1867 and 1869, and for the years from 1874 to 1878 inclusive, may be found in the appendix.

TAXATION of NATIONAL BANKS.

States and Territories.	Capital.*	Amount of taxes.			Ratios to capital.		
		United States.	State.	Total.	United States.	State.	Total.
					Per ct.	*Per ct.*	*Per ct.*
Maine	$10,507,115	$114,855	$228,030	$342,885	1.1	2.2	3.3
New Hampshire	5,666,257	65,138	97,950	163,088	1.2	1.7	2.9
Vermont	8,528,353	89,863	100,699	259,562	1.0	2.1	3.1
Massachusetts	44,302,447	517,410	719,629	1,237,039	1.2	1.6	2.8
Boston	50,445,725	678,371	675,691	1,354,062	1.3	1.3	2.6
Rhode Island	20,009,800	195,509	251,079	446,588	1.0	1.2	2.2
Connecticut	20,572,815	281,063	389,926	670,989	1.1	1.5	2.6
New England States	165,032,512	1,942,209	2,532,004	4,474,213	1.2	1.5	2.7

* The capital of the banks that reported State, county, and municipal taxes on stock and real estate
$452,868,712.

REPORT ON THE FINANCES.

TAXATION of NATIONAL BANKS—Continued.

States and Territories.	Capital.	Amount of taxes.			Ratios to capital.		
		United States.	State.	Total.	United States.	State.	Total.
					Per ct.	Per ct.	Per ct.
New York.................	82,973,060	511,243	637,489	1,148,732	1.5	2.0	3.5
New York City......	50,813,657	1,299,166	1,466,570	2,765,736	2.6	2.9	5.5
Albany..............	1,920,220	56,177	50,532	106,709	2.9	2.5	5.4
New Jersey..............	13,553,308	205,856	241,379	447,235	1.5	1.8	3.3
Pennsylvania...........	26,513,098	408,310	191,626	599,936	1.4	0.7	2.1
Philadelphia.......	16,818,000	358,023	109,508	467,531	2.1	0.7	2.8
Pittsburgh..........	9,897,077	143,056	59,834	202,890	1.4	0.6	2.0
Delaware...............	1,763,985	25,527	6,215	31,742	1.4	0.4	1.8
Maryland...............	2,265,125	32,841	30,522	63,363	1.5	1.3	2.8
Baltimore...........	10,585,760	129,781	138,415	268,196	1.2	1.3	2.5
District of Columbia.....	262,000	4,509	130	4,639	1.8	0.1	1.9
Washington........	1,128,000	15,624	4,049	19,673	1.4	0.4	1.8
Middle States	170,431,205	3,190,113	2,936,269	6,126,382	1.9	1.7	3.6
Virginia................	2,947,500	49,380	53,710	103,090	1.7	1.9	3.6
West Virginia...........	1,606,000	21,523	26,915	48,438	1.8	1.6	2.9
North Carolina.........	2,500,684	31,586	38,356	69,942	1.3	1.6	2.9
South Carolina.........	2,450,000	28,705	49,787	78,496	1.3	2.0	3.2
Georgia................	2,119,216	27,807	36,037	63,844	1.3	1.7	3.0
Florida................	50,000	794	815	1,609	1.6	1.6	3.2
Alabama................	1,662,000	20,367	31,530	51,797	1.2	2.0	3.2
New Orleans	2,875,000	50,212	13,144	63,356	1.7	0.5	2.2
Texas..................	1,950,000	15,439	19,596	35,035	1.5	1.9	3.4
Arkansas...............	205,000	3,217	2,870	6,087	1.6	1.4	3.0
Kentucky...............	7,037,974	82,347	39,814	122,161	1.2	0.6	1.8
Louisville............	2,995,500	44,606	19,285	63,891	1.5	0.6	2.1
Tennessee..............	3,005,884	50,110	52,068	102,178	1.7	1.8	3.5
Southern States	30,555,018	425,907	383,927	809,924	1.4	1.3	2.7
Ohio...................	18,451,403	264,013	368,946	632,959	1.4	2.0	3.4
Cincinnati..........	4,108,333	79,722	99,415	179,137	1.9	2.4	4.3
Cleveland...........	3,887,500	50,530	78,862	120,392	1.3	2.0	3.8
Indiana................	13,828,674	196,213	289,043	486,155	1.4	2.1	3.5
Illinois...............	11,068,214	169,594	194,416	364,010	1.5	1.8	3.3
Chicago.............	4,020,054	137,681	94,288	231,969	3.4	2.4	5.8
Michigan...............	7,263,673	96,743	118,018	214,761	1.3	1.6	2.9
Detroit.............	2,100,000	38,391	46,687	85,078	1.8	2.2	4.0
Wisconsin..............	2,530,000	41,295	44,425	85,720	1.6	1.8	3.4
Milwaukee...........	650,000	18,190	16,236	34,426	2.8	2.5	5.3
Iowa...................	5,900,832	86,537	118,066	204,603	1.5	2.1	3.6
Minnesota..............	4,662,307	95,598	85,475	181,073	1.4	1.8	3.2
Missouri...............	1,282,065	18,740	28,637	47,377	1.5	2.4	3.9
Saint Louis.........	2,850,000	47,910	55,642	103,552	1.8	2.1	3.9
Kansas.................	816,394	17,006	21,783	38,829	2.1	2.7	4.8
Nebraska...............	927,141	24,321	28,814	48,135	2.6	2.6	5.2
Colorado...............	1,050,000	34,545	35,412	68,957	3.3	3.4	6.7
Oregon.................	250,000	6,836	3,900	9,736	2.7	1.2	3.9
California*	1,559,045	19,645	4,229	23,874	1.3	0.3	1.6
San Francisco*	2,750,000	21,543	122	21,665	0.8	0.0	0.8
New Mexico	325,000	4,598	4,264	8,862	1.4	1.4	2.8
Utah	200,000	3,098	3,350	6,448	1.5	1.7	3.2
Idaho	100,000	1,434	3,478	4,912	1.4	3.5	4.9
Montana	200,000	5,416	4,477	9,893	2.7	3.0	5.7
Wyoming	125,000	2,403	2,731	5,134	1.9	2.2	4.1
Dakota.................	185,041	4,206	3,509	7,715	2.3	2.0	4.3
Washington.............	150,000	1,544	1,987	3,481	1.0	1.3	2.3
Western States and Territories	90,949,769	1,457,812	1,751,032	3,208,844	1.6	2.0	3.6
Totals..............	456,968,504	7,016,131	7,603,232	14,619,363	1.5	1.7	3.2

* California banks pay no State taxes on capital, except on such as is invested in real estate.

The following table exhibits the amount of taxes annually paid by the national banks to the United States, from the establishment of the system to July 1, 1880, the rate of taxation being one per cent. annually upon the average amount of notes in circulation, one-half of one per cent. annually upon the average amount of deposits, and the same rate upon the average amount of capital not invested in United States bonds:

Years.	On circulation.	On deposits.	On capital.	Total.
1864	$853,198 32	$905,911 87	$16,432 07	$107,537 26
1865	733,247 59	1,087,530 66	133,251 15	1,954,029 60
1866	2,106,785 30	2,633,102 77	406,947 74	5,146,835 81
1867	2,868,636 78	2,550,180 09	321,881 36	5,840,698 23
1868	2,946,343 07	2,564,143 44	306,781 07	5,817,268 18
1869	2,957,416 73	2,014,558 58	312,913 68	5,684,888 99
1870	2,949,744 13	2,514,787 61	375,952 26	5,940,474 00
1871	2,987,021 69	2,802,840 85	385,292 13	6,175,154 67
1872	3,193,570 08	3,120,984 37	380,356 27	6,703,910 67
1873	3,353,186 13	3,190,569 29	454,891 51	7,004,646 93
1874	3,404,483 11	3,209,907 72	469,048 03	7,083,498 85
1875	3,283,450 89	3,514,205 39	507,417 76	7,305,134 04
1876	3,091,795 76	3,505,129 54	632,296 16	7,729,221 56
1877	2,900,957 53	3,451,965 38	660,784 90	7,013,707 81
1878	2,948,047 08	3,273,111 74	560,296 83	6,781,455 65
1879	3,009,647 10	3,309,668 90	401,920 61	6,721,230 67
1880	3,153,635 63	4,058,710 61	379,424 19	7,591,770 43
Aggregates	45,941,101 93	47,703,404 11	6,718,903 31	100,361,409 35

The table below gives the taxes annually paid under the United States laws, by banks other than national, to the Commissioner of Internal Revenue, on deposits, on circulation, and on capital, for the years from 1864 to 1880, inclusive. The rate of taxation imposed by United States laws on these banks, on account of their circulation, deposits and capital, is precisely the same as that imposed upon national banks. The present duties on their circulation, however, are derived mainly from the tax of ten per cent. imposed upon the amount of such circulation paid out by them:

Years.	On circulation.	On deposits.	On capital.	Totals.
1864	$2,056,996 30	$780,723 52		$2,837,719 82
1865	1,993,661 84	2,043,841 08	$903,367 98	4,940,870 90
1866	990,278 11	2,099,835 83	374,074 11	3,463,988 05
1867	214,298 75	1,355,395 98	476,807 73	2,046,502 46
1868	38,609 86	1,438,512 77	399,562 90	1,866,745 55
1869	16,505 05	1,734,417 63	445,071 49	2,196,054 17
1870	15,419 94	2,177,576 46	827,087 21	3,020,083 61
1871	22,781 92	2,702,196 54	919,262 77	3,644,241 83
1872	8,919 82	3,643,251 71	976,057 61	4,628,229 14
1873	24,778 62	3,009,302 79	736,950 05	3,771,031 46
1874	16,738 26	2,453,544 26	916,878 15	3,387,160 67
1875	22,740 27	2,972,260 27	1,102,241 58	4,097,248 12
1876	17,047 67	2,999,530 75	989,319 61	4,006,698 03
1877	5,430 16	2,896,637 93	927,661 24	3,829,729 33
1878	1,118 72	2,569,087 29	897,225 84	3,492,031 85
1879	13,903 29	2,354,911 74	830,068 56	3,198,883 50
1880	26,773 37	2,510,775 43	811,435 48	3,350,985 28
Aggregates	5,470,027 97	39,706,202 28	12,533,033 31	57,778,263 56

It will be seen that of the whole amount of taxes paid to the United States, during the years given in the foregoing tables, by all the banks and bankers of the country, the national banks alone have paid nearly two-thirds. The amount of tax upon circulation has been $45,941,162, while the cost to the government of the national system since its inauguration in 1863 has been but $4,934,530.51.

From tables similar to the one first given herein for 1879, the following condensed table has been prepared, which shows the taxes, national and State, paid by the national banks during each year from 1866 to 1879, inclusive. The figures given for the year 1868, and for the years from 1870 to 1873, inclusive, are estimated. With these exceptions the amounts of the taxes shown by this table are from complete data obtained by this Office.

Years.	Capital stock.	Amount of taxes.			Ratio of tax to capital.		
		United States.	State.	Total.	United States.	State.	Total.
					Per ct.	Per ct.	Per ct.
1866	$410,503,435	$7,949,451	$8,069,938	$16,019,389	1.9	2.0	3.9
1867	432,894,668	9,525,607	8,813,127	18,338,734	2.2	2.1	4.3
1868	420,143,491	9,465,652	8,757,656	18,223,308	2.2	2.1	4.3
1869	419,619,860	10,061,244	7,297,096	17,378,340	2.4	1.7	4.0
1870	429,314,041	10,190,682	7,465,675	17,656,357	2.4	1.7	4.1
1871	451,994,133	10,649,895	7,860,078	18,509,973	2.4	1.7	4.1
1872	472,096,958	6,703,910	8,343,772	15,047,682	1.4	1.8	3.2
1873	488,778,418	7,004,040	8,496,748	15,504,394	1.4	1.8	3.2
1874	493,751,679	7,396,083	9,020,326	16,876,409	1.5	2.0	3.5
1875	503,687,911	7,317,531	10,058,122	17,375,653	1.5	2.0	3.5
1876	501,788,079	7,076,087	9,701,732	16,777,819	1.4	2.0	3.4
1877	485,250,694	6,902,573	8,829,304	15,731,877	1.4	1.9	3.3
1878	471,064,238	6,727,332	8,056,533	14,783,765	1.4	1.7	3.1
1879	456,908,504	7,016,131	7,603,232	14,619,363	1.5	1.7	3.2

In order that the great inequality of the percentage of these United States and State taxes to the capital of national banks in different geographical divisions of the country may be seen, the following tables have been prepared, giving for the years from 1875 to 1879, inclusive, the capital stock invested, and the percentage thereto of taxes paid, in each of such geographical divisions:

TAXATION of NATIONAL BANKS.

1875.

Geographical divisions.	Capital.*	Amount of taxes.			Ratios to capital.		
		United States.	State.	Total.	United States.	State.	Total.
					Per ct.	Per ct.	Per ct.
New England States......	$164,316,333	$1,937,016	$3,016,537	$4,953,553	1.2	1.8	3.0
Middle States	198,585,507	3,300,408	4,062,459	7,362,957	1.7	2.1	3.8
Southern States	34,485,483	445,948	476,396	921,284	1.3	1.4	2.7
Western States and Terr's	111,300,582	1,634,969	2,502,890	4,137,859	1.5	2.4	3.9
United States	503,687,911	7,317,531	10,058,122	17,375,653	1.5	2.0	3.5

1876.

New England States......	$158,068,379	$1,947,970	$2,914,808	$4,862,778	1.2	1.7	2.8
Middle States	192,163,773	3,190,247	4,025,316	7,215,563	1.7	2.2	3.9
Southern States	33,430,193	423,781	431,164	854,945	1.3	1.3	2.6
Western States and Terr's.	108,116,734	1,514,089	2,330,444	3,844,533	1.4	2.3	3.7
United States	501,788,079	7,076,087	9,701,732	16,777,819	1.4	2.0	3.4

1877

New England States......	$167,758,475	$1,907,776	$2,864,119	$4,771,895	1.1	1.7	2.8
Middle States	182,885,502	3,129,090	3,544,862	6,674,852	1.7	1.9	3.6
Southern States	32,212,286	411,486	429,149	840,635	1.3	1.4	2.7
Western States and Terr's.	102,364,369	1,453,321	1,991,174	3,444,495	1.4	2.1	3.5
United States	485,250,694	6,902,573	8,820,304	15,731,877	1.4	1.9	3.3

* The capital of the banks which reported State taxes in 1875 was $499,738,408; in 1876, $488,272,783;

TAXATION of NATIONAL BANKS—Continued.

1878.

Geographical divisions.	Capital.	Amount of taxes.			Ratios to capital.		
		United States.	State.	Total.	United States.	State.	Total.
					Per ct.	Per ct.	Per ct.
New England States......	$166,737,504	$1,900,735	$2,508,043	$4,403,778	1.1	1.6	2.7
Middle States	176,786,399	3,054,576	3,217,485	6,272,061	1.7	1.8	3.5
Southern States	31,583,348	409,839	406,076	815,915	1.3	1.3	2.6
Western States and Terr's.	95,974,897	1,362,082	1,839,929	3,202,011	1.4	2.0	3.4
United States	471,064,238	6,727,232	8,056,533	14,783,765	1.4	1.7	3.1

1879.

New England States......	$165,632,512	$1,942,209	$2,532,004	$4,474,213	1.2	1.5	2.7
Middle States	170,431,205	3,190,113	2,936,269	6,126,382	1.0	1.7	3.6
Southern States	30,555,018	425,997	383,927	809,924	1.4	1.3	2.7
Western States and Terr's.	90,949,769	1,457,812	1,751,032	3,208,844	1.6	2.0	3.6
United States	456,968,504	7,016,131	7,603,232	14,619,363	1.5	1.7	3.2

In the foregoing tables there appears to be an inequality in the percentages of national taxation as well as in those of State taxation; but this inequality as to national taxation is in appearance only, and arises from the fact that while the rate of United States tax imposed on circulation, deposits, and capital is uniform as to all banks and in all parts of the country, yet in the tables there is given the percentage of the total tax to the *capital* only. Therefore, in those States where the deposits and circulation are large in proportion to capital the percentage of United States tax in the table is greater. In States where the deposits and circulation are proportionately smaller the percentage of such tax is less. In the case of State taxation the inequality is a real one, and represents very nearly the difference in the rates, as the only tax which can be laid by the States on national banks under the law must be laid directly on the shares of capital stock. It will be seen that the heaviest taxes are paid in the Western and Middle States, and the lightest in the Southern and Eastern.

The table below shows for three different years the great inequality in the rates of State taxation paid in the principal cities of the country:

Cities.	Rates of taxation.								
	1877.			1878.			1879.		
	United States.	State.	Total.	United States.	State.	Total.	United States.	State.	Total.
	Per ct.	Per ct.	Per ct.	Per ct.	Per ct.	Per ct.	Per ct.	Per ct.	Per ct.
Boston	1.3	1.6	2.9	1.3	1.3	2.6	1.3	1.3	2.6
New York................	2.1	2.9	5.0	2.2	2.9	5.1	2.6	2.9	5.5
Albany....................	3.0	3.2	6.2	2.8	2.8	5.6	2.9	2.5	5.4
Philadelphia	2.1	0.7	2.8	2.0	0.7	2.7	2.1	0.7	2.8
Pittsburgh	1.4	0.5	1.9	1.3	0.5	1.8	1.4	0.6	2.0
Baltimore................	1.2	1.9	3.1	1.2	1.8	3.0	1.2	1.3	2.5
Washington	1.3	0.7	2.0	1.4	0.6	2.0	1.4	0.4	1.8
New Orleans.............	1.5	0.9	2.4	1.5	1.0	2.5	1.7	0.5	2.2
Louisville	1.4	0.5	1.9	1.4	0.5	1.9	1.5	0.5	2.1
Cincinnati................	1.7	2.9	4.6	1.5	2.7	4.2	1.9	2.4	4.3
Cleveland................	1.1	2.2	3.3	1.1	2.0	3.1	1.3	2.0	3.3
Chicago..................	2.2	2.9	5.8	2.5	2.6	5.1	3.4	2.4	5.8
Detroit...................	1.6	1.7	3.3	1.7	1.5	3.2	1.8	2.2	4.0
Milwaukee...............	2.4	2.6	5.0	2.4	2.6	5.0	2.8	2.5	5.3
Saint Louis...............	1.4	2.5	3.9	1.6	2.4	4.0	1.8	2.1	3.9
Saint Paul................	1.3	1.7	3.0	1.3	1.5	2.8	1.5	1.5	3.0

All of the foregoing tables indicate the necessity of securing some uniform rule of State taxation, to which reference has already been made. The States in which the rates of State taxation were most excessive during the years 1877, 1878, and 1879 are shown in the table below:

States.	1877.			1878.			1879.		
	United States.	State.	Total.	United States.	State.	Total.	United States.	State.	Total.
	Per ct.	Per ct.	Per ct.	Per ct.	Per ct.	Per ct.	Per ct.	Per ct.	Per ct.
New York	1.9	2.7	4.6	2.0	2.6	4.6	1.5	2.0	3.5
New Jersey	1.4	1.9	3.3	1.4	1.8	3.2	1.5	1.9	3.3
Ohio	1.4	2.4	3.8	1.3	2.2	3.5	1.4	2.0	3.4
Indiana	1.2	2.3	3.5	1.3	2.1	3.4	1.4	2.1	3.5
Illinois	1.7	2.2	3.9	1.7	2.1	3.8	1.5	1.8	3.3
Wisconsin	1.7	2.1	3.8	1.7	2.2	3.9	1.6	1.8	3.4
Kansas	1.7	2.6	4.3	1.6	2.6	4.2	2.1	2.7	4.8
Nebraska	2.3	2.3	4.6	2.3	2.6	4.9	2.6	2.6	5.2
South Carolina	1.0	2.6	3.6	1.0	2.1	3.1	1.2	2.0	3.2
Tennessee	1.6	2.2	3.8	1.6	2.1	3.7	1.7	1.8	3.5

The statistics given show that, year by year, the States collect more from the national banks in taxes than does the United States; that on an average, during the past twelve years, the total annual amount paid to both State and national governments by such banks has been about sixteen millions of dollars, or nearly four per cent. upon the capital stock; and that during the past year it was $14,619,363, or more than four and one-half per cent. upon the amount of circulation issued to the banks then in operation.

THE LOSSES, SURPLUS, EARNINGS AND DIVIDENDS OF THE NATIONAL BANKS.

Section 5204 of the Revised Statutes provides that no association, or any member thereof, shall, during the time it shall continue its banking operations, withdraw, or permit to be withdrawn, either in the form of dividends or otherwise, any portion of its capital. If losses have, at any time, been sustained by any such association, equal to or exceeding its undivided profits then on hand, no dividend shall be made; and no dividend shall ever be made by any association, while it continues its banking operations, to an amount greater than its net profits then on hand, deducting therefrom its losses and bad debts. And section 5212 requires that each association shall report to the Comptroller of the Currency, within ten days after declaring any dividend, the amount of such dividend, and the amount of net earnings in excess of such dividend.

These reports, which are made semi-annually, give full information from each bank of its dividends, earnings, and losses for the period named; and from these reports tables have been prepared in this Office for a series of years, containing items of great interest, and of a kind never before regularly given to the public in reference to the gains and losses of any class of corporations. The following table exhibits by States and reserve cities the number of banks which have charged off losses, and the amount of losses charged off by them, in each of the two periods of six months, ending on March 1 and September 1, 1880,

together with the total amount for the year; to which have been added
the amounts charged off in each of the four preceding years:

States and Territories.	March 1, 1880.		September 1, 1880.		Total losses.
	No. of banks.	Losses.	No. of banks.	Losses.	
Maine	41	$130,010 53	34	$69,539 69	$199,550 22
New Hampshire	20	41,876 46	18	71,442 47	113,318 93
Vermont	31	79,400 77	27	118,218 52	197,619 29
Massachusetts	140	728,231 40	134	817,486 42	1,546,717 82
Boston	42	648,327 16	44	462,504 56	1,110,831 72
Rhode Island	38	409,957 46	23	107,723 02	517,680 48
Connecticut	50	204,124 51	56	219,743 28	423,867 79
New York	156	807,652 59	147	615,797 81	1,423,450 40
New York City	42	1,254,820 30	42	799,561 32	2,054,381 62
Albany	5	84,808 40	5	137,604 52	222,412 92
New Jersey	51	167,075 14	52	194,659 42	362,684 56
Pennsylvania	118	354,603 98	120	578,669 19	933,273 17
Philadelphia	25	151,638 53	26	248,305 21	399,943 74
Pittsburgh	18	146,404 90	17	111,723 25	258,128 15
Delaware	2	1,499 67	5	1,448 96	2,948 63
Maryland	13	16,335 22	8	34,007 98	50,343 20
Baltimore	12	142,318 89	12	69,010 12	211,329 01
District of Columbia			1	2,675 85	2,675 85
Washington	4	24,259 28	5	24,405 99	48,665 27
Virginia	14	32,377 06	18	58,088 88	90,465 94
West Virginia	5	8,526 48	7	5,276 56	13,803 04
North Carolina	8	10,532 59	10	114,227 87	124,760 46
South Carolina	8	74,413 21	7	211,985 00	286,398 21
Georgia	8	58,452 91	9	50,511 05	108,964 56
Florida	1	7,398 05	1	5,039 33	12,437 38
Alabama	7	27,782 38	6	20,433 19	48,215 57
New Orleans	7	43,970 39	7	74,109 99	118,080 38
Texas	9	40,692 59	9	68,714 77	109,407 36
Arkansas	1	505 05	2	3,879 67	4,384 72
Kentucky	33	124,578 02	26	94,903 29	219,481 31
Louisville	7	59,588 63	7	23,651 44	83,240 07
Tennessee	13	36,951 78	17	61,224 48	98,176 26
Ohio	88	262,896 12	98	311,625 14	574,021 26
Cincinnati	3	43,877 37	4	45,274 42	89,151 79
Cleveland	3	48,854 56	4	72,486 88	121,341 80
Indiana	56	211,193 66	59	280,377 16	491,570 82
Illinois	74	251,963 13	73	187,150 79	439,113 92
Chicago	6	73,098 40	7	37,977 46	111,075 86
Michigan	57	101,473 26	59	127,574 72	229,049 98
Detroit	3	5,050 87	2	8,381 00	13,434 87
Wisconsin	20	27,168 62	16	27,133 47	54,302 09
Milwaukee	3	30,092 55	2	33,779 52	63,872 07
Iowa	39	64,735 99	38	96,864 86	161,600 85
Minnesota	23	201,930 44	20	38,035 14	239,965 58
Missouri	9	40,628 58	9	10,594 55	51,223 13
Saint Louis	9	80,930 44	5	121,416 43	202,346 87
Kansas	8	20,281 86	7	39,479 52	59,761 38
Nebraska	8	14,004 18	8	88,243 87	102,248 05
Colorado	12	44,305 66	12	107,296 40	151,472 46
Oregon	1	2,372 60	1	2,975 00	5,347 60
California	7	47,263 87	3	12,558 30	59,822 17
San Francisco	3	19,456 21	1	9,363 73	28,829 94
New Mexico	2	28,241 57	2	7,076 85	35,318 42
Utah	1	1,918 75	1	1,504 27	3,423 02
Montana	2	8,552 30	2	1,805 20	10,357 50
Wyoming	2	4,192 51	2	529 71	4,722 22
Dakota	2	9,992 79	1	1,441 97	11,434 76
Totals for 1880	1,360	7,663,886 04	1,321	7,142,519 06	14,700,400 00
Add for 1879	1,421	10,338,334 98	1,442	11,487,330 17	21,725,665 15
Add for 1878	1,304	10,903,145 04	1,430	13,563,654 85	24,466,799 89
Add for 1877	980	8,175,960 56	1,108	11,797,627 43	19,933,587 99
Add for 1876	806	6,561,169 82	1,034	13,217,856 60	19,719,026 42
Aggregate losses for five years		43,382,486 44		57,168,989 01	100,551,475 45

Similar tables for the years 1876, 1877, 1878, and 1879 are given in the appendix. In the following table the total losses charged off in each geographical division of the country during the last five years are shown, with the number of banks reporting losses:

Six months end- ing—	New England States.		Middle States.		Southern States.		Western States and Territories.		United States.	
	No.	Amount.	No.	Amount.	No.	Amount.	No.	Amount.	No.	Amount.
March 1, 1876	201	$1,485,532	268	$3,553,129	67	$308,561	270	$1,152,648	806	$6,501,178
September 1, 1876	282	3,074,128	344	7,156,349	90	896,891	318	2,090,480	1,034	13,217,857
Total, 1876	.....	4,559,660	.....	10,709,478	.....	1,205,752	.....	3,244,127	......	19,719,097
March 1, 1877	289	2,465,328	314	3,462,684	80	478,252	297	1,769,697	980	8,175,961
September 1, 1877	312	4,825,040	353	3,945,806	86	511,841	357	2,474,940	1,108	11,797,627
Total, 1877	.....	7,290,368	.....	7,408,490	.....	990,093	.....	4,244,637	......	19,933,588
March 1, 1878	327	3,344,012	417	4,506,813	124	672,022	436	2,380,298	1,304	10,903,145
September 1, 1878	399	4,016,814	449	5,502,770	140	1,225,602	442	2,818,469	1,430	13,563,655
Total, 1878	.....	7,360,826	.....	10,009,583	.....	1,897,634	.....	5,198,757	......	24,466,800
March 1, 1879	379	3,612,128	459	3,592,950	125	696,646	458	2,336,600	1,421	10,238,324
September 1, 1879	384	3,388,394	463	4,360,440	139	1,235,784	456	2,502,712	1,442	11,487,330
Total, 1879	.....	7,000,522	.....	7,953,390	.....	1,932,430	.....	4,839,312	......	21,725,654
March 1, 1880	362	2,236,928	446	3,152,317	121	530,769	431	1,643,872	1,360	7,563,886
September 1, 1880	326	1,866,658	440	2,817,870	124	787,046	431	1,670,946	1,321	7,142,520
Total, 1880	.....	4,103,586	.....	5,970,187	.....	1,317,815	.....	3,314,818	......	14,706,406
Total for five years	.....	30,314,962	.....	42,051,128	.....	7,343,724	.....	20,841,661	......	100,551,475

It will be seen from the foregoing table that the total losses charged off by the banks during the current year were $14,706,406, and for the four previous years $85,845,069, making an aggregate of more than one hundred millions of dollars of losses which the banks have sustained during the five years named. Of the $72,656,488 of losses charged off within the last three and a half years, $10,835,760 was on account of depreciation in the premium on United States bonds held by the banks. The amount of premium thus charged off during the past year was $2,196,353. The total losses charged off during the last five years are more than 21 per cent. of the entire capital of the banks.

The amount of losses sustained during the last five years by the national banks in several of the principal cities of the United States is shown in the following table:

Cities.	1876.	1877.	1878.	1879.	1880.	Total.
New York	$6,873,750 97	$4,247,941 66	$5,147,319 98	$3,135,557 37	$2,054,361 52	$21,456,960 50
Boston	1,598,722 68	2,192,053 81	2,489,197 46	2,655,390 58	1,110,831 72	10,047,196 25
Philadelphia	152,976 14	333,248 47	561,676 30	491,556 36	399,043 74	1,939,493 01
Pittsburgh	333,851 56	289,466 59	419,036 51	333,022 99	258,126 15	1,633,505 80
Baltimore	876,207 32	200,597 74	368,915 99	294,507 60	211,329 01	1,951,557 06
New Orleans	519,781 41	286,259 47	338,496 90	272,889 87	118,080 38	1,535,428 03

These losses have to a considerable extent been charged to the current profits of the banks. In some instances, however, where the losses were large, they have been partly met from the accumulated profits and partly from the surplus account. In extreme cases they have been met, either by assessment upon the shareholders, or by a reduction of the capital stock under section 5143 Revised Statutes. The law requiring losses to be charged off before dividends are paid is rigidly enforced, in order that the reports of the banks may show as far as possible their true condition. These enormous losses are largely attributable to the general depression which, from 1873 to 1879, affected all branches of trade and industry, and it is a gratifying fact to know that the losses for the present year are considerably less than for any of the four years preceding, being $7,019,249 less than for 1879, and $9,760,394 less than for 1878.

Surplus.

The law provides that a surplus fund shall be accumulated, by setting aside, before the usual semi-annual dividend is declared, one-tenth part of the semi-annual net profits of the bank. In some cases this legal surplus now exceeds the capital of the bank. The capital and the surplus together form the working fund of the bank, each contributing to its ultimate profits ; and the banks which make the largest dividends in proportion to their capital are those which have accumulated a large surplus, such dividends being really earned by capital and surplus combined.

The following table shows the growth of surplus from the commencement of the system to the present time, as nearly as possible by semi-annual periods, with the increase or decrease for each period :

Dates.	Surplus.		Dates.	Surplus.	
	Amount.	Semi-annual increase or decrease.		Amount.	Semi-annual increase or decrease.
		Increase.			*Increase.*
July 4, 1864	$1,129,910		June 13, 1873	$116,847,455	$5,437,300
January 2, 1865	8,663,311	$7,533,401	December 26, 1873	120,961,208	4,113,813
July 3, 1865	31,303,566	22,640,255	June 26, 1874	126,239,308	5,278,040
January 1, 1866	43,000,371	11,696,805	December 31, 1874	130,485,641	4,340,333
July 2, 1866	50,151,992	7,151,621	June 36, 1875	133,169,095	2,083,454
January 7, 1867	59,992,875	9,840,883			*Decrease.*
July 1, 1867	63,232,511	3,239,936	December 17, 1875	133,085,422	$83,073
January 6, 1868	70,586,126	7,253,315	June 30, 1876	131,897,197	1,188,225
July 6, 1868	75,840,119	5,253,993	December 22, 1876	131,390,605	506,582
January 4, 1869	81,160,937	5,320,818	June 22, 1877	124,714,073	6,676,592
June 12, 1869	82,218,576	1,048,639	December 28, 1877	121,568,455	3,145,618
January 22, 1870	90,174,281	7,955,705	June 29, 1878	118,178,531	3,389,924
June 9, 1870	91,689,834	1,515,553	January 1, 1879	116,200,864	1,977,667
December 28, 1870	94,705,740	3,015,906	June 14, 1879	114,321,376	1,879,488
June 10, 1871	98,322,204	3,616,464			*Increase.*
December 16, 1871	101,573,154	3,250,950	December 12, 1879	115,428,032	$1,107,656
June 10, 1872	105,181,943	3,608,789	June 11, 1880	118,102,014	2,673,982
December 27, 1872	111,410,249	6,228,306			

Dividends and earnings.

Since the year 1869, the banks have been required to make semi-annual returns of their dividends and earnings. From these reports tables have been prepared, showing their profits and dividends, and the ratio of such profits, not alone to capital, but to capital and surplus combined, since the surplus contributes proportionately as much to the semi-annual profits from which dividends are derived as does the capital. The following table shows the capital, surplus, dividends, and total earnings of all the national banks for each half year, from March 1, 1869, to September 1, 1880, together with the ratio of dividends to capital and to capital and surplus, and of earnings to capital and surplus:

Period of six months ending—	No. of banks.	Capital.	Surplus.	Total dividends.	Total net earnings.	RATIOS.		
						Dividends to capital.	Dividends to capital and surplus.	Earnings to capital and surplus.
						Per cent.	Per cent.	Per cent.
Sept. 1, 1869	1,481	$401,650,802	$82,105,848	$21,767,831	$29,321,184	5.42	4.50	6.04
Mar. 1, 1870	1,571	415,366,991	86,118,210	21,479,095	28,996,994	5.16	4.27	5.77
Sept. 1, 1870	1,601	425,317,104	91,636,620	21,660,342	26,613,885	4.96	4.08	5.19
Mar. 1, 1871	1,605	428,699,165	94,672,401	22,905,150	27,342,162	5.18	4.24	5.21
Sept. 1, 1871	1,693	445,999,264	98,286,591	22,125,279	27,315,311	4.96	4.07	5.02
Mar. 1, 1872	1,750	450,693,706	99,431,242	22,859,626	27,592,539	5.07	4.16	5.08
Sept. 1, 1872	1,852	465,676,023	105,181,045	23,827,269	30,572,891	5.12	4.17	5.36
Mar. 1, 1873	1,912	475,918,683	114,257,288	24,896,061	31,926,478	5.22	4.21	5.41
Sept. 1, 1873	1,955	488,100,951	118,113,848	24,823,029	33,125,000	5.09	4.09	5.46
Mar. 1, 1874	1,967	489,510,323	123,460,859	25,529,998	29,544,120	4.81	3.94	4.82
Sept. 1, 1874	1,974	489,936,284	128,364,039	24,929,307	30,036,811	5.09	4.03	4.86
Mar. 1, 1875	2,007	492,566,831	131,960,037	24,750,816	29,136,007	5.01	3.96	4.66
Sept. 1, 1875	2,047	497,864,838	134,133,649	24,317,785	28,800,217	4.88	3.85	4.56
Mar. 1, 1876	2,076	504,500,491	134,407,665	24,811,681	23,097,921	4.92	3.86	3.62
Sept. 1, 1876	2,081	500,482,271	132,251,078	22,563,829	20,540,231	4.50	3.57	3.26
Mar. 1, 1877	2,089	496,651,580	130,872,155	21,803,969	19,592,962	4.39	3.47	3.12
Sept. 1, 1877	2,072	486,324,860	134,949,254	22,117,116	15,374,028	4.54	3.62	2.56
Mar. 1, 1878	2,074	475,609,751	122,973,561	18,982,390	16,940,696	3.99	3.17	2.83
Sept. 1, 1878	2,047	470,231,806	118,687,194	17,959,223	13,658,893	3.81	3.04	2.31
Mar. 1, 1879	2,043	464,413,996	116,744,135	17,541,054	14,678,660	3.78	3.02	2.53
Sept. 1, 1879	2,045	455,132,056	115,149,951	17,401,867	16,873,200	3.82	3.05	2.96
Mar. 1, 1880	2,046	454,080,090	117,226,501	18,121,273	21,152,784	3.99	3.17	3.70
Sept. 1, 1880	2,072	454,215,062	120,145,640	18,290,200	24,033,250	4.03	3.18	4.18

The following statement shows by geographical divisions the number of national banks, with their capital, which have paid no dividends to their stockholders during the two semi-annual periods of 1880, together with the totals for each semi-annual period in the four preceding years:

Geographical divisions.	Six months ending—				Average for the year.	
	March 1, 1880.		September 1, 1880.			
	No. of banks.	Capital.	No. of banks.	Capital.	No. of banks.	Capital.
New England States	20	$6,965,000	15	$3,025,000	23	$4,995,000
Middle States	68	9,950,000	73	9,138,000	70	9,548,500
Southern States	29	4,129,000	27	3,945,900	28	4,037,450
Western States and Territories	99	9,354,200	118	10,225,250	109	9,788,725
Totals for 1880	226	30,407,200	233	26,334,150	230	28,370,675
Totals for 1879	309	53,843,700	299	44,576,300	304	49,210,000
Totals for 1878	328	48,797,900	357	58,736,950	343	53,767,425
Totals for 1877	245	40,452,000	288	41,166,200	266	40,809,100
Totals for 1876	235	34,290,320	273	44,057,725	254	39,174,022
Average for five years	269	41,558,224	290	42,974,265	279	42,266,244

The number of banks passing dividends in the first dividend period of 1880 was 226, with a total capital of $30,407,200; in the second period the number was 233, with a capital of $26,334,150; while during the last five years the average number of banks semi-annually passing dividends on account of losses has been 279. The average amount of capital upon which no dividends have been paid during that time is $42,266,244. From these facts it follows that, for a continuous period of five years, about one-seventh of the whole number of banks in operation have paid no dividends, and that nearly one-tenth of the total capital has been unremunerative.

The percentage to capital of dividends paid, and of dividends and earnings to combined capital and surplus, is given by similar divisions in the following table, for the years 1878, 1879, and 1880:

Geographical divisions.	1878.			1879.			1880.		
	Divi-dends to capital.	Divi-dends to capital and sur-plus.	Earnings to capital and sur-plus.	Divi-dends to capital.	Divi-dends to capital and sur-plus.	Earnings to capital and sur-plus.	Divi-dends to capital.	Divi-dends to capital and sur-plus.	Earnings to capital and sur-plus.
	Per ct.	Per ct.	Per ct.	Per ct.	Per ct.	Per ct.	Per ct.	Per ct.	Per ct.
New England States	6.9	5.5	4.3	6.4	5.2	4.2	6.8	5.5	6.4
Middle States	7.9	6.1	4.9	7.9	6.1	5.8	8.4	6.5	8.6
Southern States	7.3	6.2	5.7	7.0	6.0	5.4	7.8	6.7	7.6
Western States and Territories	9.6	7.8	6.9	9.4	7.5	7.1	9.5	7.6	9.3
United States	7.8	6.2	5.1	7.6	6.1	5.5	8.0	6.4	7.9

UNITED STATES LEGAL-TENDER NOTES AND NATIONAL BANK CIRCULATION.

The acts of February 25, 1862, July 11, 1862, and March 3, 1863, each authorized the issue of 150 millions of dollars of legal-tender notes, making an aggregate of 450 millions of dollars. On January 30, 1864, the amount of such notes outstanding was $449,338,902, which was the highest amount outstanding at any one time.

The act of June 30, 1864, provided that the total amount of United States notes issued or to be issued should not exceed 400 millions of dollars, and such additional sum, not exceeding 50 millions, as may be temporarily required for the redemption of temporary loans.

The act of April 12, 1866, authorized the retiring and cancellation of not more than 10 millions of legal-tender notes, within six months from the passage of the act, and thereafter not more than 4 millions in any one month; and under this act the amount outstanding was so far reduced that on December 31, 1867, the amount was 356 millions. On February 4, 1868, the further reduction of the volume of legal-tender notes was prohibited, leaving the last-named amount outstanding until October 1, 1872. Between that date and January 15, 1874, the amount was increased to $382,979,815, and on June 20, 1874, the maximum amount was fixed at $382,000,000; section 6 of the act of that date providing that "the amount of United States notes outstanding and to be used as a part of the circulating medium shall not exceed the sum of 382 millions, which said sum shall appear in each monthly statement of the public debt, and no part thereof shall be held or used as a reserve."

Section 3 of the act of January 14, 1875, authorized an increase of the circulation of national banks in accordance with existing law, without respect to the limit previously existing, and required the Secretary of the Treasury to retire legal-tender notes to an amount equal to 80 per cent. of the national bank notes thereafter issued, until the amount of such legal-tender notes outstanding should be 300 millions, and no more. Under the operation of this act $35,318,984 of legal tender notes were retired, leaving the amount in circulation on May 31, 1878, the date of the repeal of the act, $346,681,016, which is the amount now outstanding. The act of February 25, 1863, and the subsequent act of June 3, 1864, authorized the issue of 300 millions of dollars of national bank circulation, which amount was increased by the act of July 12, 1870, to 354 millions. The act of June 20, 1874, authorized any national bank desiring to withdraw its circulating notes, in whole or in part, to deposit lawful money with the Treasurer of the United States in sums of not less than nine thousand dollars, and to withdraw a proportionate amount of bonds held as security for such notes; and the act of January 14, 1875, repealed all previous provisions restricting the aggregate amount of national bank circulation. Subsequent to the passage of the acts of June 20, 1874, and of January 14, 1875, which authorized the retirement and reissue of national bank notes at the pleasure of the banks the circulation steadily decreased in volume until the year 1877, the total decrease in this interval being $30,869,655. During the year ending November 1, 1878, there was an increase of $4,216,684, and during the year ending November 1, 1879, an increase of $14,742,503, the total amount now outstanding being $9,343,288 less than on January 14, 1875.

The act of March 3, 1865 (section 5171 Revised Statutes), which was passed at a time when the legal limit of bank circulation was 300 millions of dollars, proportioned the amount to be issued by each bank to the amount of its capital. Banks having a capital of less than 500 thousand dollars were limited to 90 per cent. of such capital; those whose capital was between 500 thousand dollars and one million to 80 per cent.; those whose capital exceeded one million and was less than three millions, to 75 per cent.; and that class of banks whose capital exceeded three millions, to 60 per cent. of their capital.

The increase in the issue of circulating notes during the present year has been but $6,783,864, of which more than one-half was issued to banks recently organized. The profit upon circulation does not exceed one and one-half per cent. per annum, and many banks have reduced their bonds, thus retiring a part of their circulation, in order to avail themselves of the existing high rates of premium, which premium is now equal to the profits upon circulation for six years. While the present small profit upon circulation continues, but little elasticity in the currency can be expected. The New York free-banking act authorized the banks of that State to issue currency without regard to capital, upon the deposit of the necessary amount of bonds. Such legislation by Congress would undoubtedly give elasticity to the national currency, but it would also stimulate a desire to organize banks of circulation only, and it is not recommended.

The bill now pending in Congress authorizes all banks to receive circulation equal to the full amount of their capital, as was the case in the original bank act. The passage of this bill would give the banks the privilege of increasing their circulation up to the limit of their capital, if at certain seasons of the year such an increase should be desirable. This increase would not probably be great, for the amount of circulation outstanding is now much less than that authorized by law, as may be seen in the following table:

Geographical divisions.	Banks having capital not exceeding $500,000.		Banks having capital exceeding $500,000.		Total.	
	Issued.	Uncalled for.	Issued.	Uncalled for.	Issued.	Uncalled for.
New England States	$79,322,430	$7,046,763	$43,014,500	$11,485,238	$122,336,930	$18,532,001
Middle States	82,940,955	9,291,590	29,681,740	21,094,833	112,622,695	30,386,423
Southern States	23,162,985	2,620,845	1,370,000	510,000	24,532,985	3,130,845
Western States	52,284,710	11,620,690	5,707,380	4,552,620	57,992,090	16,173,310
Pacific States and Territories	3,244,700	935,800	640,000	560,000	3,884,700	1,495,800
United States	240,955,780	31,515,688	80,413,620	38,202,691	321,369,400	69,718,379

It will be seen that the banks already organized and in operation are entitled to receive nearly 70 millions of additional circulation, whenever they may see fit to deposit United States bonds to secure it. This table also shows that the profit upon circulation is, as has been already stated, very small, otherwise the banks would avail themselves of the privilege of issuing additional notes. There is, however, a certain class of banks, with capital exceeding 500 thousand dollars, that would find it convenient during the fall season of the year, when currency is in demand, to increase their circulation, notwithstanding the high price of bonds; to the amount of their capital if authorized to do so, and the passage of the bill now pending is recommended.

Since the passage of the act of June 20, 1874, $104,075,752 of legal-tender notes have been deposited in the Treasury by the national banks, for the purpose of reducing their circulation, and $87,329,415 of bank notes have been redeemed, destroyed and retired.

The following table exhibits the amount and kinds of outstanding paper currency of the United States and of the national banks, on August 31, 1865, when the public debt reached its maximum, and annually thereafter at the dates named, with the currency price of gold and the gold price of currency at the same dates:

Date.	United States issues.			Notes of national banks including gold notes.	Aggregate.	Currency price of $100 gold.	Gold price of $100 currency.
	Legal tender notes.	Old demand notes.	Fractional currency.				
August 31, 1865...	$432,553,912	$402,905	$26,344,742	$176,218,955	$635,515,574	$144 25	$69 32
January 1, 1866...	425,839,319	392,070	26,906,429	298,588,419	750,820,228	144 50	69 20
January 1, 1867...	380,276,160	221,632	28,732,812	299,846,206	709,076,860	133 00	75 18
January 1, 1868	356,000,000	159,127	31,597,583	299,747,569	687,504,279	137 25	75 04
January 1, 1869...	356,000,000	128,098	34,215,715	299,629,322	689,973,135	135 00	74 07
January 1, 1870	356,000,000	113,098	39,762,664	299,904,029	695,779,791	120 00	83 33
January 1, 1871...	356,000,000	101,086	39,995,089	306,307,672	702,403,847	110 75	90 29
January 1, 1872...	357,500,000	92,801	40,767,877	328,465,431	726,826,109	109 50	91 32
January 1, 1873	356,557,907	84,387	45,722,061	344,582,812	748,947,167	112 00	89 28
January 1, 1874...	378,401,702	79,537	48,544,792	350,848,236	777,874,367	110 25	90 70
January 1, 1875...	382,000,000	72,317	46,390,598	354,128,250	782,591,165	112 50	88 89
January 1, 1876...	371,827,220	69,642	44,147,072	346,479,756	792,523,690	112 75	88 69
January 1, 1877...	366,055,084	65,462	26,348,206	321,595,606	714,064,358	107 00	93 46
January 3, 1878...	349,943,776	63,532	17,764,109	321,673,505	689,443,922	102 87	97 21
January 1, 1879...	346,681,016	62,035	16,108,159	323,781,674	686,642,884	100 00	100 00
January 1, 1880...	346,681,016	61,350	15,674,304	342,387,536	704,804,006	100 00	100 00
November 1, 1880	346,681,016	60,825	7,181,861	343,834,187	697,737,809	100 00	100 00

The amount of additional circulation issued for the year ending November 1, 1880, was $13,402,215; the amount issued to banks organized during the year was $3,662,200; the amount retired was $6,618,351, the actual increase for the year being $6,783,864. During the year ending November 1, 1880, lawful money to the amount of $13,845,866 was deposited with the Treasurer to retire circulation, of which amount $947,326 was deposited by banks in liquidation. The amount previously deposited under the act of June 20, 1874, was $72,786,458, and by banks in liquidation $17,443,428, to which is to be added a balance of $3,813,675 remaining from deposits made by liquidating banks prior to the passage of that act. Deducting from the total, $107,889,427, the amount of circulating notes redeemed and destroyed without reissue ($87,329,415), there remained in the hands of the Treasurer on November 1, 1880, $20,560,012 of lawful money for the redemption and retirement of bank circulation.

11 F

The following table exhibits by States the issue and retirement of circulation during the year ending November 1, 1880, and the total amount issued and retired since June 20, 1874:

States and Territories.	Circulation issued.	Circulation retired.		
		Under act of June 20, 1874.	Of liquidating banks.	Total.
Maine		$8, 565	$25, 554	$34, 119
New Hampshire	$127, 500	1, 869	6, 350	8, 219
Vermont	127, 350	30, 537	21, 947	52, 484
Massachusetts	3, 693, 685	493, 667	9, 397	503, 064
Rhode Island	404, 770	102, 279	2, 164	104, 443
Connecticut	74, 110	229, 155	2, 885	232, 030
New York	1, 896, 160	1, 699, 880	162, 211	1, 862, 092
New Jersey	10, 500	141, 452	46, 301	187, 753
Pennsylvania	2, 036, 890	376, 685	90, 789	461, 474
Delaware	59, 000			
Maryland	278, 750	62, 041	3, 307	65, 348
District of Columbia	1, 000	15, 260	15, 452	30, 712
Virginia	126, 000	43, 550	38, 200	81, 750
West Virginia	103, 440	28, 140	15, 126	43, 566
North Carolina	18, 000	52, 486	13, 080	65, 566
South Carolina	40, 500	16, 304		16, 304
Georgia	49, 500	7, 505	12, 128	19, 633
Florida	27, 000			
Alabama		36, 235	7, 783	44, 018
Mississippi			75	75
Louisiana	1, 000	98, 920	13, 770	112, 690
Texas	252, 000		3, 655	3, 655
Arkansas	27, 000	8, 722	130	8, 852
Kentucky	211, 500	65, 398	34, 896	100, 294
Tennessee	112, 370	13, 155	28, 077	41, 232
Missouri	153, 000	83, 316	102, 674	185, 890
Ohio	704, 600	245, 521	115, 674	361, 195
Indiana	365, 890	560, 747	111, 879	672, 626
Illinois	488, 790	196, 949	154, 551	351, 500
Michigan	522, 600	125, 946	35, 934	161, 880
Wisconsin	152, 000	50, 786	52, 555	103, 341
Iowa	243, 000	26, 490	66, 207	92, 697
Minnesota		49, 150	31, 385	80, 535
Kansas			49, 435	49, 435
Nebraska		9, 274	2, 701	11, 975
Nevada	30, 000		230	230
Oregon				
Colorado	117, 000		12, 165	12, 165
Utah	45, 000		3, 829	3, 829
Idaho				
Montana	67, 500		26, 687	26, 687
Wyoming	3, 600			
New Mexico	45, 000			
Dakota	76, 500			
Washington				
California	480, 000			
Surrendered to this office and retired				425, 299
Total	13, 402, 215	4, 873, 890	1, 319, 163	6, 618, 351
Totals from June 20, 1874, to October 31, 1879..	78, 344, 060	66, 261, 458	14, 874, 904	81, 136, 362
Surrendered to this office between same dates.				11, 369, 582
Total issued and retired from June 20, 1874, to October 31, 1880	91, 746, 275	71, 135, 348	16, 194, 067	99, 124, 295

LOST OR UNREDEEMED BANK NOTES.

In his report for 1875 the Comptroller gave some statistics in relation to the percentage of bank notes not presented for redemption under State laws. Returns were given for 286 banks in the State of New York, which included thirty banks now in operation in the city of New York, either as State or national institutions. The maximum amount of circulation issued to the 286 banks was $50,754,515, and the total circulation then outstanding was $1,336,337, showing that the proportion of unredeemed circulation was 2.63 per cent. only of the amount issued. The maximum amount of circulation issued to the thirty banks in the city of New York was $7,763,010, and the amount remaining unredeemed in October, 1875, was $142,365. The percentage of that unredeemed to that issued was 1.83. The lowest percentage of unredeemed circulation was 0.58, upon an issue of $241,174. The highest was 4.81, upon an issue of $123,974, seventeen banks of the thirty reporting the percentage of unredeemed notes outstanding at less than two per cent. In his report for 1876 the following table was given, showing the greatest amount of circulation issued to 707 banks organized under the laws of twelve different States, the amount outstanding, and the percentage unredeemed, which was 2.35 only.

States.	Number of banks.	Greatest circulation.	Circulation outstanding.	Percentage unredeemed.
Maine	29	$3,375,130	$53,102	1.6
New Hampshire	27	2,520,339	35,860	1.4
Vermont	16	3,143,348	37,027	1.2
Massachusetts	41	10,086,357	254,954	2.3
Rhode Island	44	6,369,652	156,834	2.5
Connecticut	53	12,850,554	253,190	2.0
New York	286	50,754,515	1,336,337	2.6
New Jersey	35	7,111,047	162,961	2.3
Delaware	5	950,770	36,461	3.7
Maryland	16	6,847,844	172,669	2.5
Ohio	25	2,196,381	61,340	2.8
Wisconsin	140	7,565,409	134,747	1.8
Totals	707	114,871,348	2,696,282	2.4

The following table gives similar information in reference to the national banks which failed prior to the year 1870, to the year 1873, and to the year 1874:

Name and location of bank.	Receiver appointed.	Circulation issued.	Circulation outstanding.	Percentage unredeemed.
First National Bank, Attica, N. Y.	Apr. 14, 1865	$44,000	$334	.74
Venango National Bank, Franklin, Pa.	May 1, 1866	85,000	397	.47
Merchants' National Bank, Washington, D. C.	May 8, 1866	180,000	1,226	.68
First National Bank, Medina, N. Y.	Mar. 13, 1867	40,000	398	.75
Tennessee National Bank, Memphis, Tenn.	Mar. 21, 1867	90,000	526	.58
First National Bank, Selma, Ala.	Apr. 30, 1867	85,000	608	.72
First National Bank, New Orleans, La.	May 20, 1867	180,000	1,845	1.03
National Unadilla Bank, Unadilla, N. Y.	Aug. 20, 1867	100,000	386	.38
Farmers and Citizens' National Bank, Brooklyn, N.Y	Sept. 6, 1867	253,900	1,905	.75
Croton National Bank, New York, N. Y.	Oct. 1, 1867	180,000	729	.41
First National Bank, Bethel, Conn	Feb. 28, 1868	26,300	346	.04
First National Bank, Keokuk, Iowa	Mar. 3, 1868	90,000	586	.65
National Bank, Vicksburg, Miss	Apr. 24, 1868	25,500	151	.60
First National Bank, Rockford, Ill	Mar. 15, 1869	45,000	512	1.12
First National Bank of Nevada, Austin, Nev	Oct. 14, 1869	129,700	1,879	1.45
Totals and average percentage to 1870		1,554,400	11,028	.78
Ocean National Bank, New York, N. Y	Dec. 13, 1871	800,000	16,268	2.03
Union Square National Bank, New York, N. Y.	Dec. 15, 1871	50,000	689	1.38
Eighth National Bank, New York, N. Y.	Dec. 15, 1871	243,293	4,877	2.00
Fourth National Bank, Philadelphia, Pa	Dec. 20, 1871	179,000	3,805	2.13
Waverly National Bank, Waverly, N. Y	Apr. 23, 1872	71,000	1,797	2.53
First National Bank, Fort Smith, Ark	May 2, 1872	45,000	860	1.91
Scandinavian National Bank, Chicago, Ill	Dec. 12, 1872	135,000	2,208	1.79
Wallkill National Bank, Middletown, N. Y.	Dec. 31, 1872	118,900	3,442	2.89
Totals and average percentage to 1873		3,196,693	45,644	1.43
Crescent City National Bank, New Orleans, La	Mar. 18, 1873	450,000	16,120	3.58
Atlantic National Bank, New York, N. Y.	Apr. 28, 1873	100,000	2,743	2.74
First National Bank, Washington, D. C.	Sept. 19, 1873	450,000	24,637	5.47
National Bank of the Commonwealth, New York, N.Y	Sept. 22, 1873	234,000	11,713	5.01
Merchants' National Bank, Petersburg, Va	Sept. 25, 1873	360,000	28,250	7.85
First National Bank, Petersburg, Va	Sept. 25, 1873	179,200	13,790	7.69
First National Bank, Mansfield, Ohio	Oct. 18, 1873	90,000	5,330	6.92
New Orleans National Banking Association, New Orleans, La	Oct. 23, 1873	360,000	17,500	4.86
First National Bank, Carlisle, Pa	Oct. 24, 1873	45,000	2,700	6.00
First National Bank, Anderson, Ind	Nov. 23, 1873	45,000	2,586	5.68
First National Bank, Topeka, Kans	Dec. 16, 1873	90,000	6,466	7.18
Totals and average percentage to 1874		5,599,893	177,449	3.17

From this table it will be seen that the highest amount of circulation issued to fifteen national banks which failed previous to 1870 was $1,554,400, and the amount outstanding on November 1, 1880, was $11,628, the proportion of notes remaining unredeemed being only 0.75 per cent. of the amount issued. The percentage of notes unredeemed of the same banks on November 1, 1875, was 1.39, in 1876, 1.35, in 1878, 0.86, and in 1880, as has been seen, it is 0.75; showing a rapid increase in the redemption of the notes of these banks. The total amount issued to twenty-three national banks, in which are included the fifteen banks, already mentioned, which failed previous to the year 1873, was $3,196,693, and the amount outstanding on November 1, 1880, was $45,644, the proportion of notes remaining unredeemed being but 1.43 per cent. of the amount issued. The total amount outstanding of the notes of these banks has been reduced $11,430 since November 1, 1878, and the percentage reduced from 1.78 to 1.43. The total amount issued to thirty-four national banks which failed prior to 1874 was $5,599,893, and the amount outstanding on November 1, 1880, was $177,449, the proportion of notes unredeemed being 3.17 per cent. of the amount issued.

Of the circulation of fifty-one national banks in voluntary liquidation previous to 1870, amounting to $5,832,940, there yet remains outstanding $117,467, or 2.01 per cent. only of the amount issued; of the circulation of seventy-five banks in liquidation prior to 1872, amounting to $8,648,980, there remains outstanding $177,075, which is equal to a percentage of 2.05; of a circulation of eighty-nine banks in liquidation prior to 1873, in amount $10,764,080, there remains outstanding $232,879, or 2.17 per cent. of the amount issued; and of the circulation of one hundred and five banks in liquidation prior to 1874, in amount $12,709,100, there remains outstanding $326,568, or 2.58 per cent. of the amount issued.

The percentage of the fifty-one national banks in voluntary liquidation previous to 1870, which is now 2.01, in 1878 was 2.59; the percentage of seventy-five banks in liquidation prior to 1872, which is now 2.05, in 1878 was 2.63; and the percentage of eighty-nine banks in liquidation prior to 1873 is now 2.17, which in 1878 was 2.82.

These statistics show a rapid reduction during the last two years in the amount of outstanding circulation of banks which have ceased to do business, and they indicate that the final loss upon the notes of national banks will not exceed one or one and a half per cent.

The amount of demand Treasury notes, payable in gold coin, issued from July 17, 1861, to December 31, 1862, was $60,000,000, in denominations of five, ten, and twenty dollars, and the amount outstanding on November 1 last, was $60,825, the proportion unredeemed being but little more than one tenth of one per cent.—$8,882 having been redeemed within the last five years.

The highest outstanding amount of legal-tender notes of the first issue was $449,479,222, on February 3, 1864. The amount of these notes outstanding on November 1, 1880, was $14,947,895, or 3.33 per cent. of the highest amount issued. The issues of Treasury notes of the series of 1869 and 1874 have not been as largely reduced. This is accounted for by the fact that large amounts of the legal-tender notes have been held for years by the national banks as reserve, and have not therefore been returned to the Treasury for destruction and replacement by subsequent issues. As the amount of legal-tender notes held by the national banks as reserves has been recently largely displaced by coin, it is probable that the amount of the early issues of these notes will be speedily reduced.

These tables are given somewhat in detail, for the purpose of correcting the belief, very generally entertained, that the proportion of circulating notes outstanding which will ultimately be lost or destroyed is much greater than is shown therein. It is also believed by many that the loss of such notes is a gain to the bank which issues them. The Comptroller receives frequent letters of inquiry upon this subject, and therefore repeats the following paragraph, which was given in a former report:

"Section 5222 of the Revised Statutes requires that all national banks which go into voluntary liquidation shall, within six months thereafter, deposit in the Treasury an amount of lawful money equal to the amount of their circulating notes outstanding. The law also requires that full provision shall be made for the redemption of the circulating notes of any insolvent bank before a dividend is made to its creditors. Thus it will be seen that no association can close up its business without first providing for the payment of all its circulating notes, and that the amount deposited for their redemption must remain in the Treasury until the last outstanding note shall have been presented. It is therefore plain that the government, and not the bank, receives all the benefit arising from lost or unredeemed circulating notes."

LOANS AND RATES OF INTEREST OF NEW YORK CITY BANKS.

The following table contains a classification of the loans of the national banks in New York City for the last five years:

Loans and discounts.	October 2, 1876.	October 1, 1877.	October 1, 1878.	October 2, 1879.	October 1, 1880.
	47 banks.	47 banks.	47 banks.	47 banks.	47 banks.
On endorsed paper	$95,510,311	$92,618,776	$83,934,338	$81,520,129	$107,058,860
On single-name paper	16,634,532	15,860,546	17,297,475	22,491,936	27,755,152
On U. S. bonds on demand	6,277,492	4,763,448	7,063,085	8,286,525	3,915,077
On other stock, &c., on demand	58,749,574	48,376,633	51,152,021	78,062,085	92,630,982
On real-estate security	536,802	407,524	785,514	670,021	1,336,513
Payable in gold	4,681,570	4,319,014	6,752,181		
All other loans	1,852,944	2,786,456	2,670,371	4,821,216	5,731,917
Totals	184,243,225	169,162,391	169,585,980	195,851,902	238,428,501

The average rate of interest in New York City for each of the fiscal years from 1874 to 1880, as ascertained from data derived from the Journal of Commerce and The Commercial and Financial Chronicle, was as follows:

1874, call loans, 3.8 per cent.; commercial paper, 6.4 per cent.
1875, call loans, 3.0 per cent.; commercial paper, 5.6 per cent.
1876, call loans, 3.3 per cent.; commercial paper, 5.3 per cent.
1877, call loans, 3.0 per cent.; commercial paper, 5.2 per cent.
1878, call loans, 4.4 per cent.; commercial paper, 5.1 per cent.
1879, call loans, 4.4 per cent.; commercial paper, 4.4 per cent.
1880, call loans, 4.9 per cent.; commercial paper, 5.3 per cent.

The average rate of discount of the Bank of England for the same years was as follows:

During the calendar year ending December 31, 1874, 3.69 per cent.
During the calendar year ending December 31, 1875, 3.23 per cent.
During the calendar year ending December 31, 1876, 2.61 per cent.
During the calendar year ending December 31, 1877, 2.91 per cent.
During the calendar year ending December 31, 1878, 3.78 per cent.
During the calendar year ending December 31, 1879, 2.50 per cent.
During the fiscal year ending June 30, 1880, 2.63 per cent.

The rate of interest in the city of New York on November 26 of the
present year, as quoted in the Daily Bulletin, was, on call loans, 6 per
cent., and on commercial paper of the best grade, from 5 to 5½ per cent.

The rate of interest of the Bank of England on November 29, 1877,
was 4 per cent. On January 30, 1878, it was 2 per cent., from which
date to October 14, 1878, there were seven changes, and, with a single
exception, on May 29, a gradual increase. The rate was fixed at the
date last named at 6 per cent., and reduced on November 21, 1878, to
5 per cent., since which time there have been changes in the rate as follows: On January 15, 1879, 4 per cent.; on the 29th of the same month
3 per cent.; on March 12 it was reduced to 2½ per cent., and again on
April 9 to 2 per cent., at which rate it remained until November 7, 1879,
when it was increased to 3 per cent., which was, also, at that time, the
rate of the Bank of France.

On June 17, 1880, the rate of the Bank of England was reduced to
2½ per cent., which is the present rate. The London rate of interest,
outside of the Bank of England, was, on October 25, on call loans, 1½ per
cent., on three months' time, 1¾, and on six months' time, 2½; the best
bills having actually been placed ⅞ per cent. below the rate of the Bank
of England.

The rate of discount at the Bank of France, which on October 16, 1878,
was raised from 2 per cent. to 3 per cent., was reduced to 2 per cent. on the
23d of May, 1879, and then raised to 3 per cent. on the 23d of the following
October. The rate was reduced to 2½ per cent. on April 2, 1880, and
advanced on October 14 to 3½ per cent., which is the present rate. The
average rate of discount during the year 1879 was 2.58 per cent.

The rate of the Imperial Bank of Germany was reduced from 5½ per
cent. to 5 per cent. on October 6, and to 4½ per cent. on October 18 last.

The market discount rates in Berlin, Hamburg and Frankfort, during
the month of October, were about 4 per cent.

REDEMPTION OF NATIONAL-BANK CURRENCY.

The expense of redeeming the national-bank currency bears oppressively in one respect upon the banks in operation, as they are obliged to
pay a proportionate share of the cost of redeeming the notes of associations which are either reducing their circulation, have gone into liquidation, or have become insolvent; the banks continuing business having of
course no interest whatever in the circulation thus redeemed.

The Treasury has for a long time had the use of a permanent fund
belonging to the assets of banks which are insolvent. It has also a
large fund deposited by banks which have gone into voluntary liquidation, or have deposited legal-tender notes for the purpose of reducing
their circulation. According to the statement of the Treasurer for November 1 last, the sum of these two funds then amounted to $20,942,032,
the whole of the currency balance at that date being but $26,846,826.
In addition to the use of these funds, which is a great convenience to
the Treasury when the currency balance is at a low point, the government, under existing law, receives the whole gain arising from lost or
unredeemed notes of the national banks, which gain will ultimately
amount to a very large sum—certainly, with no more than the present
amount of circulation, to not less than $3,500,000. Any large national
bank in New York City would, on these terms, gladly undertake the
redemption of all the notes presented for that purpose at the commercial center—which is the only appropriate place for the redemption of

bank notes—without any charge therefor to the banks whose notes are redeemed. It is recommended that the law now in force on this subject be amended, and that the cost of redemption shall be assessed in such manner as that the banks in operation shall pay for the redemption of their own notes only, the remaining cost being borne by the government. Moreover, the government has for fifteen years received annually an average sum of more than three millions of dollars in taxes upon deposits, under a system unknown elsewhere in any country; and it is certainly only just that it should bear the expense of the redemption of those circulating notes from which it alone receives the entire benefit.

Section 3 of the act of June 20, 1874, provides that every national bank "shall, at all times, keep and have on deposit in the Treasury of the United States, in lawful money of the United States, a sum equal to five per centum of its circulation, to be held and used for the redemption of such circulation." Since the passage of this act the banks have, as a rule, maintained their redemption fund, and their circulating notes have been promptly redeemed at the Treasury without expense to the government.

The following table exhibits the amount of national-bank notes received for redemption monthly, by the Comptroller of the Currency, for the year ending November 1, 1880, and the amount received for the same period at the redemption agency of the Treasury, together with the total amount received since the passage of the act of June 20, 1874:

Months.	Received by Comptroller.				Total.	Received at the redemption agency.
	From national banks for reissue or surrender.	From redemption agency for reissue.	Notes of national banks in liquidation.	Under act of June 20, 1874.		
1879.						
November	$8,620	$1,502,700	$75,510	$218,090	$1,804,920	$3,251,634
December	10,725	1,717,900	86,690	144,492	1,958,907	2,922,490
1880.						
January	9,620	2,134,100	53,545	898,142	2,535,407	5,641,102
February	50,240	2,478,500	189,846	388,099	3,106,595	3,960,505
March	18,160	2,322,500	88,735	322,485	2,751,880	3,144,811
April	31,300	2,057,200	105,234	429,570	2,623,310	4,005,205
May	17,690	3,654,600	151,877	711,987	4,535,494	7,554,660
June	22,300	4,435,600	276,899	962,297	5,696,866	7,808,961
July	25,460	2,732,400	70,607	500,614	3,329,081	4,709,894
August	14,915	2,522,500	129,790	302,742	2,969,947	3,469,894
September	24,800	2,461,000	99,630	541,528	3,117,958	3,348,638
October	10,200	2,406,800	....	149,153	2,566,153	3,708,448
Total	243,970	30,424,300	1,319,163	5,009,085	36,996,518	53,526,722
Received from June 20, 1874, to October 31, 1879	12,423,225	356,889,855	14,749,912	65,336,423	450,399,415	984,486,292
Grand total	12,667,195	387,314,155	16,069,075	71,345,508	487,395,933	1,038,013,014

From the passage of the act of June 20, 1874, to November 1, 1880, there was received at the redemption agency of the Treasury $1,038,013,014 of national-bank currency. The receipts reached the highest point during the year ending November 1, 1877, when they amounted to $229,308,507, since which date they have steadily decreased; being for the year 1878, $202,499,740, for 1879, $117,191,999, and for 1880, but $53,526,722.

At this Office, the maximum yearly receipts of currency for redemption was reached during the year ending November 1, 1875, when the amount was $140,577,505. There has been a decrease in each succeeding year, but the percentage has been much less as compared with the decrease at the redemption agency.

During the year ending November 1, 1880, there was received at the redemption agency of the Treasury $53,526,000 of national-bank notes, of which amount, $24,312,000, or about 45 per cent., was received from the banks in New York City, and $5,682,000, or about 10 per cent., from Boston. The amount received from Philadelphia was $3,531,000; from Baltimore, $499,000; Pittsburgh, $597,000; Cincinnati, $864,000; Chicago, $1,937,000; Saint Louis, $446,000; Providence, $1,229,000. The amount of circulating notes fit for circulation returned by the agency to the banks of issue during the year was $15,010,700. The total amount received by the Comptroller for destruction, from the redemption agency and from the national banks direct, was $35,677,355. Of this amount, $2,966,700 were issues of banks in the city of New York; $3,088,611, of Boston; $1,398,800, of Philadelphia; $1,207,489, of Providence; $556,550, of Baltimore; $661,738, of Pittsburgh; and of each of the other principal cities less than $500,000.

The following table exhibits the number and amount of national-bank notes, of each denomination, which have been issued and redeemed since the organization of the system, and the number and amount outstanding on November 1, 1880:

Denominations.	Number.			Amount.		
	Issued.	Redeemed.	Outstanding.	Issued.	Redeemed.	Outstanding.
Ones............	23, 167, 677	20, 875, 215	2, 292, 462	$23, 167, 677	$20, 875, 215	$2, 292, 462
Twos	7, 747, 519	7, 143, 889	603, 630	15, 495, 038	14, 287, 778	1, 207, 260
Fives............	89, 131, 976	49, 149, 824	19, 982, 152	345, 659, 880	245, 749, 120	99, 910, 760
Tens............	27, 203, 168	15, 821, 110	11, 382, 058	272, 031, 680	158, 211, 100	113, 820, 580
Twenties	8, 266, 398	4, 484, 820	3, 781, 578	165, 327, 960	89, 696, 400	75, 631, 560
Fifties	1, 253, 865	825, 499	428, 366	62, 693, 250	41, 274, 950	21, 418, 300
One hundreds ...	879, 490	610, 601	268, 889	87, 949, 000	61, 080, 100	26, 868, 900
Five hundreds..	20, 763	19, 484	1, 279	10, 381, 500	9, 742, 000	639, 500
One thousands..	6, 363	6, 124	239	6, 363, 000	6, 124, 000	239, 000
					*—15, 129	*+15, 129
Total	137, 677, 219	98, 936, 566	38, 740, 653	989, 068, 985	647, 005, 534	342, 063, 451

* Portions of notes lost or destroyed.

A table showing the number and denominations of the national-bank notes issued and redeemed, and the number of each denomination outstanding on November 1, for the last twelve years, will be found in the appendix.

The following table shows the amount of national-bank notes received at this Office and destroyed yearly, since the establishment of the system:

Prior to November 1, 1865 .... $175, 490
During the year ending October 31, 1866 .... 1, 050, 382
During the year ending October 31, 1867 .... 3, 401, 423
During the year ending October 31, 1868 .... 4, 602, 825
During the year ending October 31, 1869 .... 6, 603, 729
During the year ending October 31, 1870 .... 14, 305, 689
During the year ending October 31, 1871 .... 24, 344, 047
During the year ending October 31, 1872 .... 36, 211, 729
During the year ending October 31, 1873 .... 36, 433, 171
During the year ending October 31, 1874 .... 49, 939, 741
During the year ending October 31, 1875 .... 137, 607, 696
During the year ending October 31, 1876 .... 98, 672, 716
During the year ending October 31, 1877 .... 76, 918, 963
During the year ending October 31, 1878 .... 57, 361, 249
During the year ending October 31, 1879 .... 41, 101, 839
During the year ending October 31, 1880 .... 35, 539, 660
Additional amount destroyed of notes of banks in liquidation 26, 696, 663

Total 647, 676, 993

NATIONAL BANK FAILURES.

Three banks have failed during the year ending November 1, 1880, and have been placed in the hands of receivers, as follows:

	Capital.
First National Bank of Meadville, Pa	$100,000
First National Bank of Newark, N. J	300,000
First National Bank of Brattleboro', Vt	300,000

The Manufacturers' National Bank of Chicago, Ill., which went into voluntary liquidation on September 25, 1873, has been placed in the hands of a receiver for the purpose of enforcing the individual liability of shareholders.

Dividends have been paid to the creditors of these banks during the present year, as follows:

	Per cent.
First National Bank of Meadville, Pa	65
First National Bank of Newark, N. J	80
First National Bank of Brattleboro', Vt	90

The aggregate amount of these dividends is $580,656.70, and their average per cent. to claims proved is 77.4.

Dividends have also been paid to the creditors of banks which had failed prior to November 1, 1879, as follows:

Atlantic National Bank, New York, N. Y .... 5 per cent.; total, 95 per cent.
New Orleans National Banking Association, New Orleans,
  La.. 5 per cent.; total, 55 per cent.
Charlottesville National Bank, Charlottesville, Va...10 per cent.; total, 50 per cent.
First National Bank, Duluth, Minn.,................28 per cent.; total, 100 per cent.
First National Bank, La Crosse, Wis.................10 per cent.; total, 45 per cent.
First National Bank, Wichita, Kans................10 per cent.; total, 70 per cent.
National Bank of Fishkill, N. Y.....................30 per cent.; total, 85 per cent.
First National Bank, Franklin, Ind ....25 per cent.; total, 90 per cent.
Northumberland County National Bank, Shamokin, Pa.12¼ per cent.; total, 75 per cent.
National Exchange Bank, Minneapolis, Minn.....13⅘ per cent.; total, 88⅘ per cent.
National Bank of the State of Missouri, Saint Louis, Mo. 20 per cent.; total, 90 per cent.
First National Bank, Georgetown, Colo...............10 per cent.; total, 22½ per cent.
Lock Haven National Bank, Lock Haven, Pa........20 per cent.; total, 80 per cent.
Central National Bank, Chicago, Ill.................. 5 per cent.; total, 60 per cent.
First National Bank, Kansas City, Mo................10 per cent.; total, 40 per cent.
First National Bank, Tarrytown, N. Y................. 5 per cent.; total, 85 per cent.
First National Bank, Dallas, Tex....................27 per cent.; total, 37 per cent.
First National Bank, Bozeman, Mon................ ...30 per cent.; total, 70 per cent.
Merchants' National Bank, Fort Scott, Kans..........30 per cent.; total, 45 per cent.
First National Bank, Warrensburg, Mo ....65 per cent.; total, 75 per cent.
German American National Bank, Washington, D. C..10 per cent.; total, 20 per cent.
German National Bank, Chicago, Ill.................30 per cent.; total, 55 per cent.
Commercial National Bank, Saratoga Springs, N. Y...25 per cent.; total, 85 per cent.
National Bank of Poultney, Vt.......................35 per cent.; total, 60 per cent.
First National Bank, Monticello, Ind.................30 per cent.; total, 30 per cent.
First National Bank, Butler, Pa.....................15 per cent.; total, 30 per cent.

The total amount of dividends paid by the Comptroller to creditors of insolvent national banks during the year ending November 1, 1880, was $1,712,731.16. The total dividends paid since the organization of the system is $17,632,639, upon proved claims amounting to $25,786,261. The dividends paid equal 68.4 per cent. of the amount of the claims.

Assessments amounting to $7,176,750 have been made upon the shareholders of insolvent banks, for the purpose of enforcing their individual liability, of which amount $2,617,571 has been collected in all, and $801,563 of it during the past year.

A table showing the national banks which have been placed in the hands of receivers, the amount of their capital, and of claims proved, and the rates of dividends paid, and also one showing the amount of circulation of such banks, issued, redeemed, and outstanding, will be found in the appendix.

In the case of the Ocean National Bank of New York, there are dividend checks amounting to $4,189.70 which have never been called for by the creditors, although every effort has been made to find them. Small amounts are also held belonging to creditors of other national banks which are insolvent, and the Comptroller respectfully recommends the passage of a bill, authorizing him to divide these balances among the other creditors at the time of the final closing of such banks.

RESERVE.

The following table exhibits the amount of net deposits, and the reserve required thereon by the act of June 20, 1874, together with the amount and classification of reserve held by the national banks in New York City, in the other reserve cities, and by the remaining banks, at the dates of their reports in October of each year from 1875 to 1880 :

NEW YORK CITY.

	Number of banks	Net deposits.	Reserve required.	Reserve held.		Classification of reserve.			
				Amount.	Ratio to deposits.	Specie.	Other law-ful money.	Due from agents.	Redemption fund.
		Millions.	Millions.	Millions.	Per cent.	Millions.	Millions.	Millions.	Millions.
October 1, 1875.	48	202.3	50.6	60.5	29.9	5.0	54.4	....	1.1
October 2, 1876.	47	197.9	49.5	60.7	30.7	14.6	45.3	....	0.8
October 1, 1877.	47	174.9	43.7	48.1	27.5	13.0	34.3	....	0.8
October 1, 1878.	47	189.8	47.4	50.9	26.8	13.3	36.5	....	1.1
October 2, 1879.	47	210.2	52.6	53.1	25.3	19.4	32.6	....	1.1
October 1, 1880.	47	268.1	67.0	70.6	26.4	58.7	11.0	....	0.9

OTHER RESERVE CITIES.

	Number of banks	Net deposits.	Reserve required.	Amount.	Ratio to deposits.	Specie.	Other law-ful money.	Due from agents.	Redemption fund.
October 1, 1875.	188	223.9	56.0	74.5	33.3	1.5	37.1	32.3	3.6
October 2, 1876.	189	217.0	54.2	76.1	35.1	4.6	37.1	32.0	3.0
October 1, 1877.	188	204.1	51.0	67.3	33.0	5.6	34.3	24.4	3.0
October 1, 1878.	184	199.0	50.0	71.1	35.6	9.4	29.4	29.1	3.2
October 2, 1879.	181	228.8	57.2	83.5	36.5	11.3	33.0	35.7	3.5
October 1, 1880.	184	289.4	72.4	105.2	36.3	28.3	25.0	48.2	3.7

STATES AND TERRITORIES.

	Number of banks	Net deposits.	Reserve required.	Amount.	Ratio to deposits.	Specie.	Other law-ful money.	Due from agents.	Redemption fund.
October 1, 1875.	1,851	307.9	46.3	100.1	32.5	1.6	33.7	53.3	11.5
October 2, 1876.	1,853	291.7	43.8	99.9	34.3	2.7	31.0	55.4	10.8
October 1, 1877.	1,845	290.1	43.0	95.4	32.9	4.2	31.6	48.9	10.7
October 1, 1878.	1,822	280.1	43.4	105.1	36.7	8.9	31.1	56.0	11.0
October 2, 1879.	1,820	329.9	49.5	124.3	37.7	11.5	30.3	71.3	11.3
October 1, 1880.	1,850	410.5	61.6	147.2	35.8	21.2	28.3	86.4	11.3

SUMMARY.

	Number of banks	Net deposits.	Reserve required.	Amount.	Ratio to deposits.	Specie.	Other law-ful money.	Due from agents.	Redemption fund.
October 1, 1875.	2,087	734.1	152.2	285.1	32.0	8.1	125.2	85.6	16.2
October 2, 1876.	2,089	706.6	147.5	236.7	33.5	21.3	113.4	87.4	14.6
October 1, 1877.	2,080	669.1	138.3	210.8	31.5	22.8	100.2	73.3	14.5
October 1, 1878.	2,053	678.3	140.8	228.1	33.6	30.7	97.0	85.1	15.3
October 2, 1879.	2,048	766.0	155.3	269.9	33.9	42.2	95.9	107.0	15.8
October 1, 1880.	2,090	968.0	201.0	323.0	33.4	108.3	64.3	134.6	15.9

A table showing the average weekly deposits, circulation and reserve of the national banks in New York City, in September and October of each year since 1873, will be found in the appendix.

¶ The following table, compiled from returns made to the Clearing House by the national banks in New York City, exhibits the movement of their reserve, weekly, during October, for the last eight years:

Week ending—	Specie.	Legal-tenders.	Total.	Ratio of reserve to—	
				Circulation and deposits.	Deposits.
				Per cent.	Per cent.
October 4, 1873	$9, 240, 300	$9, 251, 900	$18, 492, 200	11. 6	14. 0
October 11, 1873	10, 506, 900	8, 049, 300	18, 556, 200	11. 6	14. 1
October 18, 1873	11, 650, 100	5, 179, 800	16, 829, 900	10. 7	13. 0
October 25, 1873	11, 433, 500	7, 187, 300	18, 620, 800	12. 2	14. 8
October 3, 1874	15, 373, 400	53, 297, 600	68, 671, 000	30. 0	33. 9
October 10, 1874	14, 517, 700	52, 152, 000	66, 669, 700	29. 6	33. 3
October 17, 1874	12, 691, 400	51, 855, 100	64, 546, 500	29. 0	32. 7
October 24, 1874	11, 457, 900	49, 893, 900	61, 351, 800	28. 8	31. 7
October 31, 1874	10, 324, 900	50, 773, 000	61, 097, 900	27. 9	31. 6
October 2, 1875	5, 438, 900	56, 181, 500	61, 620, 400	28. 1	30. 6
October 9, 1875	5, 716, 200	51, 342, 300	57, 058, 500	26. 5	28. 9
October 16, 1875	5, 528, 500	48, 582, 700	54, 111, 200	25. 4	27. 7
October 23, 1875	5, 735, 000	47, 300, 900	53, 035, 900	25. 3	27. 7
October 30, 1875	8, 975, 600	45, 762, 800	54, 738, 400	26. 5	29. 0
October 7, 1876	17, 682, 600	45, 535, 600	63, 218, 200	30. 5	32. 4
October 14, 1876	16, 233, 600	43, 004, 600	59, 238, 200	28. 8	31. 1
October 21, 1876	15, 577, 500	41, 421, 700	56, 999, 200	27. 8	30. 0
October 28, 1876	14, 011, 600	41, 645, 600	55, 657, 200	28. 0	30. 3
October 6, 1877	14, 665, 600	36, 168, 300	50, 833, 900	27. 0	29. 5
October 13, 1877	14, 726, 500	35, 178, 900	49, 905, 400	26. 7	29. 2
October 20, 1877	14, 087, 400	35, 101, 700	40, 189, 100	26. 5	29. 0
October 27, 1877	15, 209, 000	34, 367, 800	49, 576, 800	26. 6	29. 4
October 5, 1878	14, 965, 800	38, 334, 900	53, 300, 700	25. 7	28. 4
October 12, 1878	12, 184, 600	37, 685, 100	49, 869, 700	24. 4	27. 0
October 19, 1878	13, 531, 400	36, 576, 000	50, 107, 400	24. 7	27. 3
October 26, 1878	17, 384, 200	35, 690, 500	53, 074, 700	25. 8	28. 5
October 4, 1879	18, 979, 600	34, 368, 000	53, 347, 600	23. 3	25. 8
October 11, 1879	20, 901, 800	32, 830, 300	53, 732, 100	23. 4	25. 9
October 18, 1879	24, 686, 500	29, 305, 200	53, 991, 700	23. 5	26. 1
October 25, 1879	25, 635, 900	26, 713, 900	52, 349, 900	23. 0	25. 5
October 2, 1880	59, 823, 700	11, 129, 100	70, 952, 800	25. 4	26. 4
October 9, 1880	62, 521, 300	10, 785, 000	73, 306, 300	25. 4	27. 2
October 16, 1880	63, 780, 600	10, 920, 200	73, 699, 800	25. 4	27. 1
October 23, 1880	60, 888, 200	10, 968, 200	71, 676, 400	24. 9	26. 6
October 30, 1880	61, 471, 600	10, 925, 000	72, 396, 600	25. 0	26. 7

APPENDIX.*

Tables will be found in the appendix, exhibiting the reserve of the national banks as shown by their reports, from October 2, 1874, to October 1, 1880; the reserve by States and principal cities for October 1, 1880; and in the States and Territories, in New York City, and in the other reserve cities, separately, at three dates in each year, from 1877 to 1880.

Special attention is called to the synopsis of judicial decisions contained in the appendix, to the numerous and carefully prepared tables in both report and appendix, and to the index of subjects and list of tables to be found at the close of the appendix. At the end of the full volume of more than seven hundred pages is an alphabetical list of the cities and villages in which the national banks are situated.

In concluding this report the Comptroller performs a pleasant duty in acknowledging the zeal and efficiency of the officers and clerks associated with him in the discharge of official duties.

JOHN JAY KNOX,
Comptroller of the Currency.

Hon. SAMUEL J. RANDALL,
Speaker of the House of Representatives.

---

* The appendix, which is omitted for want of space, may be found in the bound volume of the Comptroller's report.

REPORT OF THE DIRECTOR OF THE MINT.

REPORT

OF

THE DIRECTOR OF THE MINT.

TREASURY DEPARTMENT,
BUREAU OF THE MINT,
November 23, 1880.

SIR: I have the honor to submit the following report of the operations of the mints and assay offices of the United States for the fiscal year ended June 30, 1880, being my second and the eighth annual report of the Director since the organization of the Bureau of the Mint:

DEPOSITS AND PURCHASES.

The deposits of gold and silver bullion at the mints and assay offices, including deliveries upon purchases for silver coinage, have been in number and value far greater than in any previous year since the establishment of the Mint. Of gold, besides the deposit of $35,821,705.40 of domestic production, and $1,385,834.59 of plate, jewelry, and worn coin, $61,627,556.86 of foreign coin and bullion, out of a total import of $62,550,837, was brought to the mints and assay offices during the year, and its value paid to depositors in gold coin and bars.

The aggregate of the gold deposits was $98,835,096.85, and exceeded by $29,750,567.11 the amount of gold deposited at the mints and assay offices in 1861, which was the greatest amount received in any previous year.

The total deposits of silver, including deliveries upon purchases, were in excess of those of the previous year, and only surpassed during the coinage of fractional silver and trade dollars in 1877 and 1878.

The total deposits and purchases of silver bullion were, of domestic bullion $32,132,756.95, foreign coin and bullion $2,219,105.83, plate, jewelry and American coin $288,660.01, a total of $34,640,522.79.

The forms in which the above amounts were brought to the mints and assay offices were as follows:

	Gold.	Silver.	Total.
Domestic production	$35,821,705 40	$32,132,756 95	$67,954,462 35
United States coin	209,328 82	39,298 28	248,627 10
Foreign bullion	21,260,907 23	1,154,859 57	22,355,956 80
Foreign coin	40,426,559 63	1,064,746 26	41,491,305 89
Old jewelry, plate, and jewelers' bars	1,176,505 77	249,361 73	1,425,867 50
Total	98,895,096 85	34,640,522 79	133,475,619 64

In addition to the above net amount of deposits, bars amounting to $36,141,366.83 in gold, and $2,574,235.35 in silver, made at one institu-
175

tion were subsequently received and operated upon at another, making the total amounts received and worked $134,976,463.68 in gold and $37,214,758.14 in silver.

These amounts were distributed among the mints and assay offices as follows:

Mint or assay office.	Gold.	Silver.	Total.
Philadelphia	$36,637,651 39	$16,671,599 21	$53,309,250 60
San Francisco	28,545,544 46	10,842,390 58	39,387,935 04
Carson	368,174 51	622,291 88	990,406 39
Denver	344,900 86	4,443 77	349,353 63
New Orleans	97,620 40	4,502,275 24	4,599,895 64
New York	68,273,627 74	4,508,067 20	72,781,694 94
Boise	147,619 16	2,052 83	149,671 99
Helena	473,532 06	61,068 23	534,601 19
Charlotte	87,783 20	569 20	88,352 40
Total	134,976,463 68	37,214,758 14	172,191,221 82

COINAGE.

The unusual imports of foreign gold coin and bullion brought to the New York assay office and mints during the first half of the last fiscal year gold bullion beyond the capacity of the mints for immediate coinage. Fortunately the condition of the Treasury and slight demand for coin in redemption of government obligations did not require the immediate conversion of this bullion into coin.

It was deemed advisable to increase the work at the Philadelphia Mint to a monthly coinage, besides the coinage of silver and minor coins, of from $3,000,000 to $5,000,000 of gold. This Mint was able with existing facilities, and the employment of additional labor, to coin during the year $27,639,445 of gold, leaving at the close $38,348,874 of gold bullion in that Mint and the New York assay office uncoined.

For the first time a successful effort has been made to obtain a large portion of the coinage of gold pieces in denominations less than twenty dollars. To do this has required positive instructions from this office, in accordance with your views. As was said by James Ross Snowden, Director of the Mint in 1860, "The chief design of a national mint is to subserve the interests of the people at large, preferably to a few large owners of bullion or coin. The interests of the public and of depositors are not always concurrent in the matter under discussion. Depositors of large amounts call for coin in a form which gives the least trouble to count; and banking institutions, in addition to that, may prefer it in a form not likely to be drawn out. Many who present their checks at these institutions would doubtless ask for specie, but are deterred from doing so by the expectation of receiving double eagles, instead of half or quarter eagles. In a word, the plain effect of issuing gold coin of a large size is to keep down the circulation of specie and increase the use of paper money."

In Great Britain the gold coinage consists almost wholly of sovereigns and half-sovereigns; in France, of twenty and ten franc pieces; and in Germany, of ten-mark pieces, all of these coins being of less value than five dollars. The absorption by France of $1,100,000,000 of gold imports into her circulation during the thirty years, from 1850 to 1880, may in part be accounted for by the coinage of nearly all this gold into denominations of less than two and four dollars' value.

Let the people have gold and silver coins for their use, for the ordinary and smaller business transactions, and the best secured redeemable paper circulation for the larger transactions of trade and commerce.

While the law gives the depositor the option into what denominations his bullion shall be coined, if, in lieu of waiting for such coins to be struck, he asserts his right to be paid the value out of the bullion funds kept by the Secretary of the Treasury at the Mint for such payment, he must take such funds and denominations as are lawfully provided, and loses all claim to the bullion he has deposited or power to control its future disposition. However, while asserting the right to direct the coinage of gold belonging to the United States, as seemed to be for the interests of the community, the wishes and conveniences of depositors and those using large sums of money in their transactions have not been overlooked, and a limited coinage of double eagles has been permitted.

The total coinage during the year amounted to $84,370,144, of which $56,157,735 was gold, $27,942,437.50 silver, and $269,971.50 minor coins. The number of pieces of each denomination struck, were as follows, viz, of double eagles, 1,075,768; eagles, 1,883,632; half eagles, 3,158,172; three dollars, 3,030; quarter eagles, 1,230; gold dollars, 3,030; standard silver dollars, 27,933,750; half-dollars, 6,550; quarter dollars, 15,350; dimes, 15,750; five cents, 24,950; three cents, 32,750; and cents, 26,774,150; a total number of pieces of 60,928,112.

Notwithstanding the large number of cents struck, the demand for this denomination of coin has been so great that the Mint at Philadelphia—the only mint at which minor coins are struck—has been unable to manufacture a sufficient supply to promptly fill the orders received, although the bronze alloy has been purchased in the form of manufactured blanks or planchets ready for striking, and thus greatly lessened the amount of labor required.

The coinage of the last three calendar years has been:

	1877.	1878.	1879.
Gold	$43,999,864 00	$49,786,052 00	$39,080,080 00
Silver	28,393,045 50	28,518,850 00	27,568,235 00
Minor	8,525 00	58,186 50	165,003 00
Total	72,401,434 50	78,363,088 50	66,813,318 00

Detailed statements of the coinage executed are presented in the appendix.

BARS.

During the year the mints and assay offices manufactured bars to the amount of $69,949,778.05 in gold and $6,924,501.17 in silver.

Of the gold bars, $57,368,761.15 were made at the New York assay office for transmission to the Mint at Philadelphia for coinage, $11,524,181.83 were fine bars, and $1,056,835.07 were unparted.

Of the silver bars made, $6,811,645.76 were fine, $24,347.93 sterling, and $88,507.48 unparted.

PARTING AND REFINING.

The refineries of the coinage mints and of the assay office at New York operated upon 10,537,106.42 ounces gross of bullion, and separated therefrom 1,241,137.981 ounces of standard gold and 8,577,111.12 ounces of standard silver.

12 F

The following statement shows in detail the quantities and value of gold and silver operated upon at the respective refineries during the year.

OUNCES.

Mint or assay office.	Gross.	Standard gold.	Standard silver.
Philadelphia	130,879.38	78,414.164	51,897.97
San Francisco	6,072,432.80	524,229.418	4,587,291.16
Carson	418,912.65	18,998.260	428,841.57
New Orleans	3,227.59	1,844.139	827.42
New York	9,911,654.00	617,652.000	3,208,253.00
Total	10,537,106.42	1,241,137.981	8,577,111.12

VALUE.

Mint or assay office.	Gold.	Silver.	Total.
Philadelphia	$1,458,868.16	680,390.36	$1,519,258.52
San Francisco	9,753,105.45	5,687,029.71	15,440,135.16
Carson	353,456.00	499,015.64	852,471.64
New Orleans	34,309.56	962.81	35,272.37
New York	11,491,200.00	3,733,239.85	15,224,439.85
Total	23,090,939.17	9,980,638.37	33,071,577.54

DIES AND MEDALS.

The engraving department of the mint at Philadelphia prepared during the year 1,092 coinage and medal dies. The number of medals struck was 1,347, of which 43 were in gold, 446 in silver, and 858 in bronze. A medal of fine gold was prepared for presentation to Bendix Koppel in recognition of his services as arbitrator in the "Montijo" arbitration. Fourteen medals of fine gold and three of fine silver were made for award to various persons who had exhibited special heroism in saving life from the perils of the sea.

PURCHASES OF SILVER BULLION.

Purchases of silver bullion for delivery at the mints at Philadelphia, San Francisco, Carson, and New Orleans have been made in the manner described in the last annual report, with the exception that the day for receiving offers was changed January 3, 1880, from Wednesday, three o'clock p. m., to Thursday, two o'clock p. m.

The superior facilities at San Francisco for filling with dispatch orders for speedy delivery of silver bullion in China, and the diminished production of silver in the States and Territories contiguous to the Pacific coast, have frequently operated to carry the price of silver bullion at San Francisco above the prices at New York and London, and to render it difficult at times to purchase at market rates silver bullion for delivery at the Pacific Coast Mints. During the year the department was able to procure for those mints bullion only sufficient to coin 8,318,000 standard silver dollars. This inability compelled the suspension of coinage at the Carson Mint from November 1, 1879, to May 1, 1880, the stock of silver bullion at the former date having become reduced to 12,342.41 standard ounces. The purchase and reception of silver bullion was, however, in the mean time continued, and a stock accumulated by the

6th of April, 1880, of 227,087.54 standard ounces. This amount, with he prospect of additional supplies, justified the resumption of coinage, ut the whole amount of silver bullion obtained for the Carson Mint uring the year amounted at its coining value to $597,624.28 only.

In preference to purchasing bullion for delivery at the New Orleans lint at figures regarded as in excess of the market price, it was at first eemed advisable to transfer from the New York assay office 1,798,167.82 andard ounces purchased prior to June 30, 1879. This was insufficient) supply that mint with an amount of bullion equal to its capacity and ie demand upon it for silver coinage; it therefore became necessary to urchase additional bullion at such rates as were offered or to suspend)inage at that mint.

The rates, though at first above the New York price, were less than ie cost to the department to purchase and transfer from Philadelphia · New York. Offers were accepted during the year for the delivery at ew Orleans of 1,684,158 standard ounces at the lowest rates attaina- le, but above the New York price.

Treasury and public demands for coin in exchange for the heavy im-)rtation of foreign gold, and the urgent and increasing demand for one int bronze coins, rendered it impossible to increase the coinage of andard silver dollars at the Philadelphia Mint. It was also found ore advantageous to purchase and coin silver bullion at New Orleans an at San Francisco, as the resulting coin could be far more rapidly id economically distributed from the former than the latter. No diffi- lty was experienced in procuring at market rates during the year all e silver bullion necessary for the Philadelphia Mint. At no time dur- g the year was that institution without an ample stock of bullion.

The purchases during the year, as will be seen from the accompany- g table, were 24,069,134.02 standard ounces, at a cost of $24,778,724.45, iile the silver parted from gold deposits and purchased in pursuance section 3527, Revised Statutes, at a price fixed by the Director of the int, and which during the year was $1. per standard ounce, amounted 193,437.36 standard ounces, costing $193,437.36, making the total quan- y purchased 24,262,571.38 standard ounces, at a cost of $24,972,161.81, d an average per month of $2,081,013.48 worth of bullion.

The average London price of silver during the year was 52$\frac{7}{16}$ pence, th exchange at par ($4.8665) equivalent to $1.14436 per ounce fine, d at the average monthly price at New York, of exchange on London, .8634, equivalent to $1.14397 per ounce fine. The average New York ice of silver during the year was $1.14162 per ounce fine.

. SILVER PURCHASES, 1880.

lint or assay ice at which delivered.	Purchases.		Partings purchased.		Total purchased.	
	Standard ounces.	Cost.	Standard ounces.	Cost.	Standard ounces.	Cost.
ladelphia	14,224,005 64	$14,614,490 49	20,254 78	$20,254 78	14,244,260 42	$14,634,745 27
Francisco	7,264,591 05	7,499,069 11	67,261 95	67,261 95	7,331,853 00	7,566,331 06
Orleans	2,070,351 88	2,141,329 00	623 08	623 08	2,070,974 96	2,141,952 08
on City	510,185 45	523,835 85	3,397 93	3,397 93	513,583 38	527,233 78
York			101,899 62	101,899 62	101,899 62	101,899 62
Total	24,069,134 02	24,778,724 45	193,437 36	193,437 36	24,262,571 38	24,972,161 81

On the first of July, 1879, the amount of standard silver dollars in circulation was 7,653,649, and on the first of July, 1880, 19,309,435, showing an increase in the circulation during the year of 11,645,786.

Up to November 1, 1880, there had been coined 72,847,750 standard silver dollars, of which 19,780,241 were held by the Treasury for the redemption of silver-certificates and $27,304,218 for distribution, $12,918,505 of the latter being in the mints, making the total amount in the Treasury $47,084,459, and in circulation $25,763,291, an increase of $6,453,856 in the circulation from July 1 to November 1, 1880.

The authority for the issue and distribution of standard silver dollars at the mints other than in payment for purchases of silver bullion, and other expenses is contained in the coinage act of 1873, and the act of February 28, 1878, providing for the coinage of the standard silver dollar.

Section 28 of the coinage act of 1873 provides "that silver coins other than the trade dollar shall be paid out at the several mints and the assay office in New York City, in exchange for gold coins at par, in sums not less than one hundred dollars; and it shall be lawful, also, to transmit parcels of the same, from time to time, to the assistant treasurers, depositaries, and other officers of the United States, under general regulations proposed by the Director of the Mint and approved by the Secretary of the Treasury."

Under the provisions of these acts the issue and paying out of silver dollars has been effected.

First. By payment in standard silver dollars for all silver bullion purchased for coinage and delivered at the mints during the year, amounting to $24,972,161.81.

Second. By exchange for gold coin.

Third. Under general regulations prescribed by the Director of the Mint, and approved by the Secretary of the Treasury September 3, 1878, directing that the superintendents of the coinage mints "upon the receipt of a written request of the Treasurer of the United States, forward by express standard silver dollars in the sum of one thousand dollars, or a multiple thereof, to such party or parties as he may designate. The expense of transportation to be paid by the mint from the silver profit fund."

Section 27 of the coinage act of 1873 provides that the expense of distributing the subsidiary silver coins shall be paid from the silver profit fund. In the act directing the coinage of the standard silver dollar the gain arising from such coinage is required to be accounted for and paid into the Treasury as provided under existing laws relative to the subsidiary coinage.

Under these provisions and the regulation referred to, standard silver dollars are transported from the mints not only to assistant treasurers, depositaries, and other officers of the United States, but to such point as the Treasurer of the United States may designate, and the expense is charged to the silver profit fund.

If there is any doubt as to this construction of the law, or of the propriety of such method of distribution, and the payment of expenses thereof, I respectfully suggest that additional legislation be requested conferring any needed authority, or more specifically defining the proper cases for its application.

Section 28 of the coinage act of 1873 provides that the subsidiary silver coins shall only be paid out at the mints in sums of not less than $100 at par in exchange for gold coins.

The propriety of limiting such exchange to gold coin at the present time is not apparent, and if any exchange for United States notes is not authorized I respectfully suggest that the existing laws ought to be amended.

I append herewith a table exhibiting the movement, circulation, and coinage of standard silver dollars on July 1, 1878, and each six months thereafter to July 1, 1880, and for the four months ending November 1, 1880, as shown by the books of this office and the Treasurer's monthly statement of assets and liabilities:

COMPARATIVE STATEMENT of the MOVEMENT, CIRCULATION, and COIN-AGE of STANDARD SILVER DOLLARS at the end of each six months, from July 1, 1878, to July 1, 1880, and for the four months ending November 1, 1880.

Period.	In the Treasury.			In circula-tion.	Total coin-age.
	Held for pay-ment of cer-tificates out-standing.	For distri-bution.	Total.		
July 1, 1878	$7,080	$5,273,964	$5,281,044	$3,292,456	$8,573,500
January 1, 1879	413,360	16,283,970	16,697,390	5,796,220	22,495,560
July 1, 1879	412,480	27,733,871	28,147,351	7,653,649	35,801,000
January 1, 1880	3,824,252	29,343,813	33,168,064	16,897,586	50,065,650
July 1, 1880	5,780,560	38,635,746	44,426,315	19,309,435	63,734,750
November 1, 1880	19,780,241	27,304,218	47,084,459	25,763,291	72,847,790

APPROPRIATIONS, EARNINGS, AND EXPENDITURES.

The amount appropriated for the support of the respective mints and assay offices during the fiscal year ended June 30, 1880, was $1,228,800, out of which the sum of $1,085,482.91 was expended. In addition the sum of $92,033.46 was expended on account of the mints, and $13,558.62 at the Treasury Department, a total of $105,592.06 from the appropri-ation contained in the act of February 28, 1878, authorizing the coinage of the standard silver dollar.

The use of this appropriation to meet the expenditures at the Phila-delphia and New Orleans mints became necessary on account of the large coinage of standard silver dollars executed at those mints, which unavoidably carried the expenses above the specific appropriations for their support. This, however, was offset by reduced expenses result-ing from correspondingly diminished coinage at other mints.

The total expenditures at all the mints and assay offices were $51,283.63 less than the amount specifically appropriated.

The appropriations and expenditures were distributed as shown in the following table:

Appropriations, 1880.

Institution.	Salaries.	Wages.	Contingent.	Coinage of stand-ard silver dol-lars (act of Feb-ruary 28, 1879), *indefinite*	Total.
Philadelphia mint	$34,850 00	$300,000 00	$87,500 00	....	$422,350 00
San Francisco mint	24,900 00	275,000 00	87,500 00	....	387,400 00
Carson mint	23,550 00	80,000 00	42,500 00	....	146,050 00
New Orleans mint...............	21,400 00	80,000 00	*35,000 00	....	136,400 00
Denver mint	10,750 00	10,000 00	6,000 00	....	26,750 00
New York assay-office	33,150 00	22,500 00	9,000 00	....	64,650 00
Helena assay-office	5,700 00	12,000 00	15,000 00	....	32,700 00
Boise City assay-office	3,000 00	....	6,000 00	....	9,000 00
Charlotte assay-office...........	2,500 00	....	1,000 00	....	3,500 00
Total	159,800 00	779,500 00	289,500 00	....	1,228,800 00

* Contains $5,000 for repairs and machinery.

Expenditures, 1880.

Institution.	Salaries.	Wages.	Contingent.	Coinage of standard silver dollars (act of February 28, 1878), indefinite.	Total.
Philadelphia mint	$33,632 87	$287,645 92	$37,468 13	$86,221 43	$494,998 3
San Francisco mint	24,900 00	232,235 75	46,525 75	....	323,661 5
Carson mint	28,550 00	62,294 62	11,312 73	....	97,157 3
New Orleans mint	20,961 89	77,278 91	*34,928 39	5,812 03	138,981 1
Denver mint	10,620 70	10,000 00	4,118 95	....	24,739 6
New York assay office	33,150 00	20,765 88	8,750 12	....	62,666 0
Helena assay office	5,769 00	8,656 24	9,960 19	....	24,316 4
Boise City assay office	2,959 28	3,525 97	1,095 22	....	7,580 4
Charlotte assay office	2,500 00	....	915 46	....	3,415 4
Total	157,974 74	722,403 29	205,104 88	92,033 46	1,177,516 3

*Contains $4,994.06 for "Repairs and machinery."

The charges collected from depositors for parting and refining bullion are used as provided by law for paying in full the expenses thereof, including labor, material, and wastage.

The total amount collected from depositors and paid into the Treasury on account of parting and refining bullion during the year ended June 30, 1880, was $257,771.37, of which the sum of $249,479.23 has been expended.

The following statement shows the amount of charges and expenditures, including the proper portion of the operative wastages and loss on sale of sweeps, on account of parting and refining bullion at the mints at Philadelphia, San Francisco, and Carson, and the assay-office at New York, during the fiscal year ended June 30, 1880.

Refinery earnings and expenditures.

Institution.	Charges collected.	Expenses.
Philadelphia mint	$6,773 47	$11,382 57
San Francisco mint	158,477 34	151,014 48
Carson City mint	9,864 42	4,537 59
New York assay office	80,656 14	82,544 59
Total	257,771 37	249,479 23

ANNUAL ASSAY.

The commission appointed by the President to make the annual test of the fineness and weight of the coins reserved from each delivery at the mints, met at the mint at Philadelphia, pursuant to law for that purpose.

The following extracts from the reports of the committees on weighing and assaying show that the examination was in all respects satisfactory. The committee on weighing report:

That from the tabular statement submitted it appears that the weights of the reserved coin from the several mints, both in masses and in single pieces, are in all cases within the limits of legal tolerance, and are therefore entirely satisfactory. The result also of the examination of the weights ordinarily employed in the mint is entirely satisfactory to the committee.

The Committee on Assaying beg leave to present the following report: That they have taken the gold and silver coins reserved from the several mints, viz, Philadelphia, San Francisco, Carson City, and New Orleans, and have assayed the same either in mass or in individual coins and have found in all cases the coins to be in conformity with law of Congress, and all safely within the limits of tolerance.

ESTIMATION OF THE VALUE OF FOREIGN COINS.

Pursuant to the provisions of section 3564 of the Revised Statutes, on the 1st day of January last estimation was made by the Director of the Mint and proclamation by the Secretary of the Treasury, of the values of the standard coins in circulation of the various nations of the world.

The basis of comparison for estimating the values of certain silver coins was changed from that taken in preceding years, for the reason stated in the correspondence relating thereto, copies of which are submitted herewith.

The values of foreign gold coins of full standard weight and fineness are readily computed and expressed in the money of account of the United States, the gold-dollar piece at the standard weight of twenty-five and eight-tenths grains having been established by section 3511 of the Revised Statutes as the unit of value.

The weight and fineness of foreign gold coins in comparison with that of such gold dollar readily determines their value.

But as to foreign silver coins, while standard dollars and fractions of dollar of given weight and fineness have been authorized and made legal tender, the standard of value legally provided has not been changed.

When gold and silver coins of the same denomination are in circulation with like actual purchasing power, the comparative values of the gold coin and gold dollar measured by their weight and fineness can still be taken as the basis for estimating the value of both coins. But where the coinage of silver is unrestricted, and the actual circulation consists chiefly of silver coins, must the value of such coins be estimated by comparing their weight and fineness with United States silver coins, or by ascertaining their commercial value compared with the standard gold dollar?

The latter was taken as the proper construction of the law, and the values of foreign silver coins in countries where silver is the sole standard, or coined without limitation, were estimated for 1880 at their commercial gold value.

A different rule having been heretofore followed, the estimation for 1880 will show changes in the valuations of several foreign silver coins, other than would have been occasioned simply by variations in the price of silver bullion.

EXAMINATIONS AND ANNUAL SETTLEMENTS.

During the year personal examinations were made by the Director or his representatives of all the mints and assay-offices except those at Boise City and Charlotte.

They were generally found to be in an efficient and satisfactory condition, and the officers and employés attentive to their duties. But few errors appeared to have occurred in their transactions with individuals or in keeping their books and records and rendering their accounts to the government.

The wastage of the operative officers at the annual settlement was found in each case to be within the legal limits and appeared to have been actually incurred, and was therefore, with my approval, credited to their respective accounts.

The total wastage during the year at the coinage mints was $18,369.14 gold, and $26,617.93 silver.

The amount operated upon in the melting and refining departments of the mints was of gold bullion 6,905,941.191 standard ounces, upon which the legal limit for wastage was 6,905.941 standard ounces, the actual wastage only 866.174 standard ounces; and of silver bullion 51,313,811.72 standard ounces, on which the legal limit for wastage was 76,970.71 standard ounces, and the wastage 18,789.53 ounces.

The amount operated upon in the coining departments of the mints was of gold bullion 6,653,791.119 standard ounces, on which the legal limit for wastage was 3,326.895 ounces, the actual 121.164 ounces; and of silver bullion 48,302,083.84 standard ounces, on which the legal limit for wastage was 48,302.08 ounces, and the actual wastage only 4,085.23 ounces.

In the appendix will be found a statement showing in detail the wastage of the operative officers and the loss on sale of sweeps at the coinage mints and the manner in which the bullion fund was reimbursed for the same.

PRESENT CONDITION OF THE MINTS AND ASSAY OFFICES.

United States Mint at Philadelphia.—The coinage at the parent mint has been unusually heavy, having in number and value of pieces coined been double that executed in the preceding year.

The increase was chiefly in the gold and minor coinage. The yearly coinage of standard silver dollars, however, was one-quarter greater than in 1879.

The comparative deposits and coinage of the two years have been as follows:

Deposits and coinage.	1879.	1880.
Deposits, value	$19,340,176	$51,388,973
Gold coinage, pieces	936,564	3,789,820
Silver coinage, pieces	12,125,850	15,223,400
Minor coinage, pieces	9,620,200	26,831,850
Total coinage, pieces	22,682,614	45,845,070
Total coinage, value	$23,552,032	$43,168,854

It is a gratification to report that this increased coinage did not cause a proportionate increase of expenditures.

The regular and specific appropriations were, however, inadequate to meet all the expenses of the mint in accomplishing this unusual amount of work, and it became necessary to make use of the appropriations contained in the act of February 28, 1878, for the coinage of the standard silver dollar. On account of the large amount of imported gold bullion yet uncoined and the lower rates at which silver bullion can be procured for delivery at this mint, its coinage, so long as silver dollars are coined and the excessive importation of gold continues, will be unusually heavy, and increased facilities will be needed to perform the work required.

United States Mint at San Francisco.—The diminished production of gold and silver on the Pacific coast has sensibly affected both the amount of deposits and coinage.

The coinage at this mint was, in 1880, $13,000,000 less of gold and $6,000,000 of silver than in 1878.

The comparative values of the deposits and number of pieces coined for the last and preceding years, are:

Deposits and coinage.	1879.	1680.
Deposits, value	$43,920,884	$39,387,949
Gold coinage, pieces	1,798,500	2,284,950
Silver coinage, pieces	12,732,000	7,910,000
Total coinage, pieces	14,530,500	10,194,950
Total coinage value	$42,051,250	$36,053,000

A large number of eagles and half eagles have been coined, and consequently the number of gold pieces struck has been increased instead of diminished. Improvements in refining bullion, in the appliances used and arrangement of apparatus have been made, and experiments instituted to ascertain the most economical and desirable processes for parting and refining the precious metals. I made careful inquiry into the unusual wastage of the melter and refiner, and found upon examination of the character of the deposits and a comparison of the fineness of the bullion of the last with the preceding years, that the amount of low-grade and refractory bullion had largely increased without any deduction having been made from the weight of the deposit for the protection of the government, as authorized by the instructions.

I directed that thereafter deductions should be made on unusually base deposits of gold or silver sufficient to cover the probable and unavoidable loss on such bullion.

United States Mint at Carson City.—The stock of bullion at the mint having become reduced in October, 1879, to $107,023 of gold, and $14,362 of silver, being an insufficient supply for a single month's work, coinage was temporarily suspended, but the mint was kept open for the purchase of silver, and deposit and refining of gold and silver.

So small an amount, however, came to the mint that, up to April 16, 1880, only $228,177 gold, and $258,427 silver, had accumulated. This, however, was deemed sufficient to authorize the resumption of coinage operations, which were thereafter continued to the close of the year.

The deposits and coinage of 1879 and 1880 compare as follows:

Deposits and coinage.	1879.	1880.
Deposits, value	$1,339,513	$553,885
Gold coinage, pieces	24,357	20,567
Silver coinage, pieces	1,644,000	408,000
Total coinage, pieces	1,668,357	447,567
Total coinage, value	$1,972,310	$654,790

United States Mint at New Orleans.—The difficulty alluded to in my previous report of procuring silver bullion for this mint, which seemed likely to cripple if not destroy its usefulness, has but in part been removed. A considerable demand in the Gulf States for silver coins for circulation has necessitated monthly allotments at this mint for the coinage of 400,000 standard dollars, which is about equal to its ordinary coinage capacity with the present force and appropriations.

The deposits and coinage for the last two years have been :

Deposits and coinage.	1879.	1880.
Deposits, value..	$1,195,907	$4,344,284
Gold coinage, pieces	....	10,525
Silver coinage, pieces	787,000	4,430,000
Total coinage, pieces ....?	787,000	4,440,525
Total coinage, value..	$787,000	$4,558,500

During the year it became my painful duty to report the death of
Henry S. Foote, who had been superintendent of the mint from December, 1878, until the date of his death on the 19th day of May, 1880.
A representative of this bureau was instructed to proceed to New
Orleans, examine the condition of the mint, and superintend the deliveries
and transfers to be made upon the appointment of a successor. Mr.
Foote's continued ill health and inability to give the necessary attention
to the business of the mint occasioned some neglect and laxity in keeping records and supervision of mint transactions. Upon a transfer of
the funds and bullion and property belonging to the mint to M. V. Davis,
who, on the 11th day of June, 1880, was promoted from coiner to superintendent, the amount of coin charged to the cashier on the books of the
mint and required to be delivered was found to lack 1,000 standard dollars, which remains to be accounted for on final settlement of the account
of the late superintendent.

The discrepancy was apparently a surprise to the cashier and officers
of the mint. There had previously been frequent urgent demands for
the shipment of standard dollars and the error was supposed to have
occurred from an undiscovered mistake in the report or count of the
sacks at some delivery for distribution.

New York assay office.—The unusual import of gold has correspondingly increased the usefulness of this office, as will be seen by comparing
the value of the deposits and of the bars manufactured in the last two
years as follows :

Deposits and bars.	1879.	1880.
Gold deposits, value	$11,345,563	$68,273,628
Silver deposits, value	7,019,698	4,491,416
Total deposits, value...	18,365,261	72,765,044
Gold, fine bars, manufactured	6,639,213	11,378,960
Gold, mint bars, manufactured	5,309,001	57,368,781
Silver, fine bars, manufactured................................	7,006,828	4,372,705
Silver, sterling bars, manufactured............................	....	24,347
Total bars manufactured, value	18,955,042	73,144,795

Sixty-eight million two hundred and eleven thousand nine hundred
and eighty-five dollars were paid in coin and bars to depositors. Of the
deposits $28,355,070 were during the year transported to Philadelphia
for conversion into gold coin.

At the annual settlement the melter and refiner returned a surplus of
861.616 standard ounces gold above amount charged him, which had
been recovered from gold not credited to the depositors contained in
silver deposits.

This value, $16,030.06 was covered into the Treasury as a miscellaneous receipt.

The *U. S. mint at Denver, U. S. assay offices at Helena, Boise, and Charlotte* have been open during the whole year for the receipt, assaying and stamping of bullion, and for the payment of coin for gold bullion, affording the miners in the vicinity opportunities for the immediate conversion of gold bullion into coin at the coinage value less the cost of transportation and mint charges. They have made and forwarded to the United States Mint unparted bars of the following value:

Name of assay office.	Year.	
	1879.	1880.
Denver...value..	$415,268	$346,222
Helena..do...	730,178	534,001
Boise...do...	71,171	147,730
Charlotte...do...	54,344	88,952

LEGISLATION SUGGESTED.

Melting charge.

I respectfully suggest the propriety of imposing a melting charge in all cases on deposits of bullion either for coin or bars. Prior to 1873 a charge for refining was authorized on bullion below standard but none for melting bullion. The coinage act of that date amended the existing provision by inserting the words "melting and" before the word refining so as to permit a charge for melting and refining when bullion is below standard.

It may have been intended that the melting charge should be imposed in all cases where the value of a deposit could not be accurately ascertained without melting. But the language of the act limits the charge to "bullion below standard" and makes no provision for a melting charge when bullion is at or above standard.

Scarcely any imported gold bullion or coin is below the United States standard of fineness and liable to a charge for melting. During the last year the mints and New York assay office were required, at considerable expense, to melt free of charge not only many millions of domestic refined gold, but over $60,000,000 of imported gold coin and bullion.

It does not seem reasonable that bullion which must be melted before assay should be exempt from paying the expense of the operation.

Coinage charge.

From 1853 to 1873 a coinage charge on gold was imposed of $\frac{1}{2}$ of 1 per cent. During the time $540,736,349.50 in gold was coined and the coinage charges amounted to $2,703,681, the average yearly coinage being $27,368,175, upon which the coinage charge amounted annually to about $137,000.

The coinage act of 1873 reduced the charge to $\frac{1}{5}$ of 1 per cent., and the resumption act of 1875 repealed it. Had it been continued at the latter rate on the gold coinage of the last five years which has amounted to $232,200,788.50, the sum of $480,000 would have been collected.

While it was uncertain whether sufficient gold could be attracted to the mints to supply the coin necessary to maintain the redemption of United States notes in gold, it may have been prudent and advisable to remove every charge that might hamper the conversion of gold into coin. And now, if our supply of metallic circulation depended upon the amount of foreign bullion brought to the mints for coinage an exemption from charge either for melting or coinage might, for similar reasons appear to be defensible. But the amount of domestic production is more than sufficient to supply the increasing annual needs of this country for the coinage of either gold or silver and a large part of the domestic gold as well as silver, like other surplus products, must at some time in the future again be exported. It can be of no national advantage to export gold or silver in the form of coin if those coins abroad do not pass into circulation, but are there again melted and recoined. The coinage of countries not producing the precious metals is composed chiefly of remelted foreign coins, for the latter cannot well circulate in countries having different monetary units of value.

It has been said that the remission of such charge enables a country to invite and secure gold for circulation.

The experience of the United States, France, and Great Britain shows that, other circumstances being favorable, a coinage charge does not prevent a country from securing the coinage of all the coin the condition of its foreign trade will permit it to retain.

In the United States, although from 1863 to 1873, on account of the suspension of specie payments, there was no demand for gold for circulation, $242,416,377.50 of gold was brought to the mints and coined, notwithstanding the coinage charge of $\frac{1}{5}$ of 1 per cent.

France imposing a charge for assay melting and coinage exceeding $\frac{1}{4}$ of 1 per cent. (= .00216), coined in the last 30 years over $1,300,000,000 of gold.

It is believed that no country really coins bullion free of expense to the public. In Great Britain no bullion fund is provided as in the United States for the immediate payment of the value of a deposit, and it is found more profitable to the public and even to importers, in preference to waiting for coinage at the mint, to exchange their bullion at the Bank of England for its notes at $1\frac{1}{2}$ pence per ounce less than the coining rate. This is $\frac{1}{8}$ of 1 per cent. (= .0016), and with other deduction for assay and melting exceeds the former United States coinage of $\frac{1}{5}$ of 1 per cent. (.002).* Should it be deemed advisable to reinstate the coinage charge the present is the most favorable time, as the supply of gold bullion now in the mints is sufficient to employ them at their ordinary rate of coinage for more than a year and a half, and so long as a bullion fund is kept at the mints and assay offices out of which to pay depositors coin on the delivery of their bullion, all the gold not needed for export undoubtedly will as heretofore come to the mints regardless of the charge.

Reynold's Patent.

A suit has been commenced and is now pending in the circuit court of the United States, District of California, by John Reynolds against the superintendent and melter and refiner of the San Francisco mint, for an alleged infringement of a patent issued to him on March 20, 1866, for "new and useful improvements in refining bullion."

The process of parting at the mint has been in use since its organiza-

---

* Report Silver Com. vol. 1, page 229-230.

tion, and was continued by the present superintendent solely for the benefit of the United States, and if any advantage has accrued it has been to the United States and not these officers.

They ought not to be required either to pay or even be called upon to defend themselves at their own expense in this suit.

The plaintiff justifies his personal suit for the alleged reason that no court has jurisdiction of any suit he could bring against the United States.

I respectfully recommend, that the jurisdiction of the Court of Claims be extended to enable it to hear this case, or that such other legislation be obtained as will enable the patentee to test the validity of his claim, and make the government and not the officers responsible for the benefit (if any) it may have derived from the use of the process in case he substantiates his patent, and its infringement at the mint.

Indebtedness of the San Francisco Mint to the Treasury.

There is charged against the San Francisco mint upon the books of the Treasury several deficits of officers, the first occurring in 1857, in the accounts of the melter and refiner, amounting to $152,227.03, the second, $20,000 in 1866, in the accounts between the coiner and treasurer, the third, $10,665.28 in 1867, in the accounts of the melter and refiner, and the last, $16,373.93, in 1869, in the accounts of the coiner, the total being $199,366.24.

A deficit of $21,962.85 exists by reason of the pyx coins of 1865, 1866, and 1867, sent to the Philadelphia mint for trial at the annual assay, being used in paying for supplies purchased and shipped the San Francisco mint, instead of being restored to the accounts. Besides these sums the loss on sale of sweeps and the wastage of the operative officers for a number of years prior to 1871 (although within the legal limit of allowance), amounting to $195,158.81, were not paid as they should have been out of the annual appropriations, and it therefore appears as a deficit in the accounts. These losses all occurred prior to the organization of the mint bureau and to the appointment of the present officers of the San Francisco mint.

Their accounts have been annually satisfactorily adjusted, and as there is no hope of collecting the amount from the former officers or their sureties, I recommend that legislation be procured to authorize the cancellation of the indebtedness by an appropriation of the necessary amount from the profit on the coinage of silver or from moneys in the Treasury of the United States.

STATISTICS OF THE PRODUCTION, CONSUMPTION, COINAGE, AND CIRCULATION OF THE PRECIOUS METALS.

The investigations and inquiries heretofore instituted for procuring the latest and most reliable and valuable information upon these subjects have been continued, and are presented in detail in the tables and communications accompanying this report.

MONETARY STATISTICS OF THE UNITED STATES.

Production of gold and silver.

As there are thousands of mines, yielding annually more or less gold and silver, scattered over an area embracing more than half of the territory of the United States, to obtain accurate and complete statistics of their aggregate production is evidently a work of great difficulty; and to make annual personal examination of each is physically impossible, without employing a large number of assistants, and expending annually an amount disproportionate to the value of the information to be obtained.

The appropriation for the collection during the present fiscal year of the statistics of the production of the precious metals in the United States became available on the 1st of July last, and the work was assigned to this bureau. Considerable progress has been made in procuring the necessary information, especially for the Pacific Coast; and the data already obtained have been found of great advantage in ascertaining the locality from which gold and silver have been obtained, as well as in estimating the total production for the last fiscal year.

Through the mints and assay offices, to which nearly all the gold and a large proportion of the silver production come yearly, and the custom-house returns, which record the movement from and into the country, the domestic product is readily ascertained. By adding to the amounts thus reported, the gold and silver of domestic production used in the arts and manufactures, other than that deposited in the mints, I estimate the production of the United States to have been, during the last fiscal year—

In gold $36,000,000
In silver (coining value) 37,700,000

    Total.. 73,700,000

To make an intelligent estimate of the production of different States and Territories is a more difficult task, from the fact that a large portion of the deposits of both gold and silver at the mints and assay offices comes in the form of fine bars from various refineries on both sides of the continent.

The time that has elapsed since the appropriation for the collection of mining statistics became available has been so short, and returns and information from distant localities have come in so slowly, that I find it impossible to present in this report, in proper shape, the data already obtained.

It seems therefore preferable to submit at a later date the statistics of the production of the precious metals in the various States during the last fiscal year, and when complete data shall have been received.

Consumption of the precious metals.

The investigation of the annual use and consumption of the precious metals in ornamental manufactures and the arts was prosecuted in the same manner as in the previous year. A greater number of persons were addressed, and replies received, the latter showing a much greater quantity of gold and silver consumed than previously reported.

Seven thousand two hundred and ninety circular letters were addressed to parties using gold and silver in the arts and manufactures; two thousand seven hundred and ninety-one replies were received; and of the latter, one thousand three hundred and eighty-one were manufacturing.

A table is submitted showing the respective amounts of the different manufactures using gold and silver.

The amounts reported as consumed are—

	United States coin.	Fine bars.	Old articles and foreign coin.	Total.
Gold..........................	$2, 408, 768	$5, 511, 047	$714, 378	$8, 634, 193
Silver.......................	541, 894	2, 749, 190	173, 145	3, 464, 169
Total	2, 950, 602	8, 260, 237	887, 523	12, 098, 362

The New York assay office reports the value of bars made and delivered during the year for use in the arts and manufacturing, from description of bullion, as follows:

Bars manufactured from—	Gold.	Silver.	Total.
United States coin (defaced)......................	$4, 929	$982	$5, 911
Foreign coin	260, 222	72, 668	332, 890
Foreign bullion	1, 007, 400	278, 622	1, 286, 022
Domestic bullion	2, 988, 422	3, 883, 126	6, 851, 548
Plate, &c......................................	394, 871	144, 992	539, 863
Total	4, 655, 844	4, 360, 390	9, 016, 234

The replies made to the circulars from the Mint Bureau show a consumption of about $1,000,000 greater of fine gold bars, and $1,600,000 less silver bars, than reported by the New York assay office.

Doubtless both statements are below the amount of gold as well as silver actually appropriated during the year for use in the arts, ornamentation, and manufactures.

The estimate of last year that in the form of bullion, coin, or plate, &c., $5,000,000 of silver and $7,000,000 of gold were during the present year appropriated for purposes other than coin circulation, is sustained as to silver and increased as to gold to $10,000,000, if not more.

An examination and comparison of these statements and of the value of the fine bars issued from all the mints lead to the conclusion that probably $5,500,000 of gold and $4,000,000 of silver of domestic bullion produced during the year, together with $2,500,000 gold and $600,000 silver United States coin, were thus consumed. .

The estimated disposition made of the amount of gold and silver bullion in the mints and New York assay office at the commencement and deposited during the year, and amounts held by each at the close of the year, are presented in tabulated statements in the appendix.

Coin circulation of the United States.

The coinage and net imports of United States gold and silver coin were shown in my last annual report (p. 22) to have increased the coin circulation in six years prior to the 1st of July, 1879, $151,490,698 in gold, and $107,050,985 in silver, being a total gain of $258,541,683.

The coinage and imports during the last fiscal year have further augmented the metallic circulation as follows:

United States coin.	Gold.	Silver.	Total.
Amount June 30, 1879	$286, 490, 698	$112, 050, 985	$398, 541, 683
Coinage less recoinage.......................	55, 948, 407	27, 903, 139	83, 851, 546
Net import	16, 519, 586	2, 642, 896	19, 162, 482
Circulation June 30, 1880	358, 958, 691	142, 597, 020	501, 555, 711

During the first four months of the present fiscal year there has been a further increase by the coinage of $14,544,599 gold and $9,113,000 silver, and a net import of $1,820,591 United States gold coin and $567,524 United States silver coin, making the amount of United States coin— not including minor coins—in the country on the 1st of November, 1880, $527,601,425, of which $375,323,881 consisted of gold, 72,847,750 standard dollars, and $79,429,794 of fractional coin and trade dollars, the latter probably amounting to $7,000,000.

Besides the above amounts of United States coin the Treasury held on the 1st of November, in the mints and assay offices, $78,558,811 of gold bullion, and $6,043,367 of silver bullion, making an aggregate of coin in circulation and bullion in the Treasury of $612,203,603, of which $453,882,692 consists of gold coin and bullion.

The coin circulation on the 1st day of January, 1879 and 1880, based upon the estimate for June 30, 1878,* and the subsequent net coinage and import of United States coin is as follows.

United States coin.	Gold.	Silver.	Total.
Amount June 30, 1878	$247,429,570	$80,352,328	$327,781,898
Net coinage to January 1, 1879	24,189,858	13,916,814	38,106,672
Net import to January 1, 1879	1,652,279	1,247,570	2,899,849
Total January 1, 1879	273,271,707	95,516,712	368,788,419
Net coinage to January 1, 1880	38,874,789	27,524,639	66,399,428
Net import to January 1, 1880	14,727,586	4,756,343	19,483,929
Total January 1, 1880	326,874,082	127,797,604	454,671,776

The gain in coin circulation during the calendar year 1879 was $53,602,375 in gold and $32,280,982 in silver, a total of $85,883,357, and the increase in coin circulation from the date fixed for resumption, January 1, 1879, to November 1, 1880, was gold coin $102,329,718, silver coin $56,760,832.

This computation is exclusive of the stock of gold and silver bullion in the mints and assay offices, which held for coinage January 1, 1879, $5,038,419 in gold and $11,057,091 in silver bullion, showing a gain of coin and bullion from that date to November 1, 1880, of $175,701,904 in gold and $51,697,524 in silver coin and bullion available for coinage.

In this foregoing estimates the amount of United States coin consumed in the arts and manufactures reported at about $2,500,000 in gold and $500,000 in silver, is not deducted for the reason that it is estimated that an equal amount of United States coin is probably brought into the country by immigrants and not reported by the custom-houses.

From the reports of the Treasurer and the Comptroller of the Currency the coin in the Treasury on the 1st of November, and in national and State banks on the 1st of October, 1880, and the estimated circulation not in the banks and Treasury appears to have been—

	Gold.	Silver.		Total.
		Legal tender.	Subsidiary.	
Treasury	$62,107,141	$47,064,458	$24,629,489	$133,581,089
National banks	95,675,472	*2,500,000	*2,839,357	101,005,829
Other banks	17,102,130	} 23,263,291	51,960,948	292,714,507
Private hands	200,379,138			
Total	375,323,881	72,847,750	79,429,794	527,601,425

* Director's Report, 1879, p. 22.
† Not distinguished; total silver reported, $5,330,357.

MONETARY STATISTICS OF FOREIGN COUNTRIES.

The effort to gather and present in convenient form for reference statistics of the production, coinage and use of the precious metals in other countries and the amount and character of their circulation was continued with advantage during the year, and much valuable information has been obtained in reply to the inquiries transmitted by the Secretary of State at your request.

Our ministers and consuls abroad have displayed commendable zeal and activity in securing the desired statistics, and grateful acknowledgements are due to the officials of foreign governments, from whom replies have been received, for their prompt and satisfactory responses.

The information in relation to coinage, circulation, production and specie reserves has been collated from these dispatches and other sources into tables, which will be found in the appendix.*

A brief review of some of the most useful facts contained in the papers received is herewith presented :

Great Britain.—From the papers received it would appear the net specie exports of Great Britain were, during the year 1879, gold £2,937,000, silver £500,000. Mr. Freemantle estimates the specie circulation at the close of 1879 to have been as follows :

Gold coin, £122,474,000 =	$596,019,721
Silver coin, £19,017,000 =	92,546,231
A total of	688,565,952

which shows the circulation to be about $23,500,000 less than my estimation for last year. It can hardly be said that there is any stock of silver bullion in the United Kingdom, the imports and exports being about equal. The coinage of gold at the royal mint was very small, being only £35,050, while the total value of silver coined was £549,054, and the amount of worn silver coin withdrawn from circulation during the year was £495,944. The report of the deputy master of the mint shows that the average price at which silver (British standard) was purchased during the year was 52$\frac{5}{8}$d. per ounce, the seigniorage accruing to the state being at the rate of 13$\frac{1}{8}$d. per ounce, or 24$\frac{11}{16}$ per cent. The rate of seigniorage was nearly 7 per cent. less than during the previous year.

Australia.—The dispatches of O. M. Spencer, consul-general at Melbourne, contain seriatim replies to the circular of the Secretary relative to monetary statistics, and also inclose interesting papers from J. W. Smith, consular agent at Port Adelaide, and from V. Delves Broughton, deputy master of Melbourne branch mint: the first giving the history of the discovery of gold in 1851 and the exodus to South Australia in consequence, and the business crises occasioned thereby, and the second an instructive account of the discovery of the " chlorine process " for separating and refining gold. Both these papers will be found well worthy of perusal.

The production of gold in the province of Victoria amounted in 1879 to 758,947 ounces, valued at $15,000,000, and the average annual production for the past ten years has been 1,063,148 ounces, valued at $20,000,000. No silver is mined, but a small quantity is parted from gold. The coinage at the Melbourne mint during 1879 was the largest since its establishment, amounting to £2,740,000, all in sovereigns.

India.—Information in regard to the paper and specie circulation of India has of late years been sought for with more than usual eagerness

---

* The documents here referred to are omitted for want of space, but they are printed in the pamphlet copies of the Director's report.

on account of the important relation sustained by that country to the future of silver. Two papers have been received from Consul-General Litchfield, one transmitting information from the Hon. R. B. Chapman, secretary of the government of India, together with tabular statements showing the imports, exports, and coinage of gold and silver in India, and the paper money issued by the Bengal, Madras, and Bombay presidencies from 1835 to 1879 inclusive. These tables are especially valuable as showing the immense quantity of silver absorbed by India in the last half century. The net imports of silver during 1879 were £3,970,694. The other paper contains a *résumé* of the mint laws and regulations of India.

No banks or other private corporations are allowed to issue paper money—the only notes in circulation being those of the State, for which the government holds a reserve of specie and bonds equal to the entire paper issue.

These government notes are received everywhere at their nominal value, and amount at present to $48,060,176.

Silver is the standard of value of the country; gold is not rated a legal tender, but is received in payment of debts. The coins of other countries, or of native Indian States, do not circulate.

Canada.—The response of the deputy minister of finance of the Dominion of Canada, with documents, transmitted through the Hon. J. Q. Smith, consul-general of the United States, show the following facts:

There is no mint in Canada, its coin being supplied from the home government. The system of paper money of Canada is similar to that of the United States, consisting of Dominion notes to the amount of $12,000,000 and bank notes to the amount of $20,000,000. The issue of Dominion notes is limited to $20,000,000, for which specie and government securities are held.

Germany.—Valuable documents have been received from Germany, together with a communication from the Hon. Andrew D. White, United States minister at Berlin, commenting upon the efforts being made for the remonetization of silver by Germany, which it would appear is under consideration. The principal item of information in this paper is that the annual production of the mines (silver) of Freiberg has fallen off about $250,000 since the demonetization of silver.

The quantity of silver remaining in Germany to be sold amounted at the close of 1879 to 3,932,353 fine pounds (63,212,574 fine ounces), which at the average price of former sales (79.824 marks per fine pound) would realize 313,896,000 marks = $74,707,248. The loss on the sale of this silver at the rates previously realized would amount to about $17,000,000 (an average of 21 per cent.)

France.—The documents received from Mr. Noyes, United States minister at Paris, show the coinage of France from 1795 to 1879 to have been—

	Francs.
Gold	8,716,438,200
Silver	5,511,952,863

The amount of specie imported in 1879 was 339,170,000 francs, and exported during the same year 424,543,000 francs. No coinage of silver was executed at the Paris mint in 1879. The gold coinage consisted of 3,860,100 francs in 100-franc and 24,610,540 francs in 20-franc pieces; in all, 28,470,640 francs, besides the coinage of a million francs in 20-franc pieces, for the principality of Servia.

The new agreement of the Latin Monetary Union went into effect on the first of the present year. A law was passed July 31, 1879, by the French legislature abolishing the contract system of coinage and creating a bureau for the management of the mint, and placing the coinage, as in this country and Great Britain, under the control of a responsible officer—called there, also, a Director—and subject to the direction of the minister of finance.

In my last report (page 28), in stating the metallic circulation of France, I said " While doubting the accuracy of the exhibit, in default of better data the estimates given are accepted." Among the documents since received are the reports made to their respective governments by the delegates to the monetary convention of the states of the Latin Union held November 5, 1878, from which valuable information has been obtained in revising the table of circulation found in this report.

The specie-circulation of France is given as—

Gold	$927,000,000
Silver (full legal tender)	540,786,000
Silver (limited tender)	57,900,000
Total	$1,525,686,000

The statement of the gold circulation is based upon the estimate for 1878 of M. Folville, adopted by Dr. Soetbeer, 5,000 million francs, from which is deducted the loss by export and use in the arts for 1879, 203,000,000 francs.

The five-franc silver circulation is stated at a mean of three estimates made by the following distinguished statisticians, after adding subsequent importation and subtracting exports and consumption in the arts, viz:

1st. Report made 1878 by a committee of French Chamber of Deputies through M. Guyot, five-franc pieces, close of 1877, 2,530,000,000 francs.

2d. Herr de Folville (quoted by Dr. Soetbeer), close of 1878, 2,-880,000,000 francs.

3d. Ernest Seyd's estimate in 1870, with subsequent importation given in tables (less fractional silver and payment to Germany, 539,000,000 francs), close of 1879, 2,747,000,000 francs.

The circulation of five-franc pieces at the close of 1879 would be, taking the mean of these estimates, 2,802,000,000 francs.

Austria.—Minister Kasson transmits, under date of July 6, 1880, interesting statistics in relation to the coinage laws of Servia and a communication from the Austro-Hungarian minister of finance, giving the laws regulating the coinage of money in Austria and tables of coinage and circulation. Silver is the standard of value in Austria and Hungary. Gold as well as silver coins are struck at the mints at Vienna and Kremnitz, but the principal circulating medium is paper money, the total issue of which amounted on the 31st of December, 1879, to $259,682,597, being about equally divided between state and bank notes.

Since the suspension of specie payments in 1848, private debts and internal taxes have been paid in bank and government notes. Customs dues are paid in gold and silver. The value of the paper money has enhanced as the value of silver became depreciated, and since the 1st of January last the paper and silver florin have been of equal value.

A dispatch is printed in the appendix from Mr. J. F. Delaplaine, of the legation at Vienna, to the effect that intelligence has been received there that the principality of Bulgaria intends coining money, the monetary unit of which will be the franc, and the total silver coinage has been fixed at 9,500,000 francs. The largest gold piece will be the "Alexander," of the value of 20 francs. The amount of the gold coinage has not been fixed. The coinage will be executed at Paris.

Netherlands.—The papers forwarded by our minister at The Hague show that no coinage was executed at the mint of Holland during the year 1879. The silver standard prevailed in the Netherlands up to 1875, when the double standard was adopted. The metallic money in circulation is principally silver, which is coined only on government account, and the coinage is at present restricted. The paper circulation consists of bank-notes, issued by the Bank of Netherlands, and is not a legal tender, but is received by the government and preferred by individuals, and is secured by a deposit of government interest-bearing bonds.

The Scandinavian countries—Denmark, Norway, and Sweden.—The documents and communications received through our ministers in relation to the monetary statistics of these countries, contain especially full and valuable information. These States still adhere to the single gold standard adopted in 1873, silver being subsidiary and for change purposes only.

The imports of gold into Norway in the year 1878 exceeded the exports by $556,904. The imports of specie into Sweden during the two years 1878 and 1879 exceeded the exports by $6,135,367, nearly all of this amount being gold.

The paper circulation of both countries consists of bank-notes, the governments issuing no paper money. In Denmark the National Bank of Copenhagen, a private corporation, has the sole monopoly of issuing bank-notes possessing the quality of legal tender. The bank is authorized to issue as much as may be required by the necessities of trade, but is required to keep a metallic reserve of not less than three-eighths of the volume of bank-notes, and bonds of an actual value, one and one-half times as great as the portion of the bank-notes in circulation not covered by the metallic reserve.

Switzerland.—The papers transmitted by Minister Fish contain, in addition to statistics of coinage and circulation, the laws governing the organization and coinage of the Federal mint.

Switzerland, being one of the States of the Latin Union, does not depend upon its own coinage for its circulation, as the coins of the States composing the Union circulate freely in all. No gold is coined in the confederation. The coinage of silver from the year 1850 to December, 31, 1879, was 50,052,828 francs = $10,000,000, nearly. No government paper is issued, and bank-notes are not a legal tender. The amount of this currency is about $17,000,000.

Italy.—The dispatch and inclosures from our minister at Rome show the coinage of the Italian mint from 1862 to 1878, inclusive, to have been gold, $43,175,695; silver, $96,621,945, and the production of the mines for the years 1875, 1876, 1877: Gold, $143,013; silver, $60,988.

The paper circulation is reported by the minister of finance to have been September 30, 1879, $315,788,724.

The specie circulation was estimated at $57,900,000, of which about $38,000,000 are held as a reserve by the treasury and banks.

Portugal.—The dispatch of Minister Moran, under date of June 26, 1880, contains very desirable and complete information in relation to the monetary affairs of Portugal, including tables showing the amount of gold and silver coined in Lisbon from 1855 to 1879, inclusive, and the imports of coin and bullion from 1869 to 1878, inclusive.

Portugal has the single gold standard, and the English sovereign and half sovereign are almost the only gold coin in circulation. Silver is a legal tender to the amount of 5 milreis ($5.40). The Bank of Portugal is the financial agent and depository of the government; its outstanding paper circulation amounts to about $5,000,000.

Russia.—The papers received through our legation at St. Petersburg will be found valuable as containing the production of the mines of this country, one of the largest producers of the precious metals.

The production of gold· in Russia from 1751 to the present time has been 80,000 poods = $793,760,000. .During the ten years from 1868 to 1877 the production was—

Gold, 21,230 poods... $210,635,570
Silver, 8,630 poods.. 5,354,045

The net exports of gold and silver coin, and bullion for ten years from 1869 to 1878, inclusive, was $107,106,900.

Russia has a large paper circulation, amounting to about $775,000,000, while the amount of coin in the State banks is about $115,000,000, of which about $8,000,000 is silver.

Turkey.—Very interesting dispatches from the Hon. Horace Maynard, late United States minister to Turkey, together with official papers from the officers of the Ottoman Empire in relation to the money and finances of that country have been received, also a copy of official decrees in relation to the issue of paper money.

The government of Turkey coins both gold and silver on its own account; that is, buys the bullion at the imperial mint at Constantinople at the rate of 48 piasters per drachm of pure gold, and 3.12½ piasters per drachm of pure silver of standard fineness, and lower rates for bullion below standard.

The proportion of gold to silver in the Turkish coinage is as 1 to 15.0909.

The coin circulation of Turkey is reported as about $15,000,000. The British pound and French franc pieces also circulate freely. The principal circulating medium of Turkey has been paper money, but it has become so enormously depreciated that its circulation is almost abandoned, and the government is making efforts to replace it with silver.

The amount of paper outstanding March 31, 1880, was estimated to be in the neighborhood of $21,000,000. The relative value of Ottoman moneys is shown by the following statement, furnished by Mr. Maynard, giving the rate of exchange between the different kinds:

Date.	Gold.	Silver.	Beshlix (heavily alloyed silver).	Copper.	Paper.
December 2, 1879	100	106½	117.⁴⁴⁄₁₀₀	370	880

To those interested in Turkish finance, the papers in the appendix will be found worthy of perusal.

Mexico.—The dispatches from Mexico show that the production of the mines during the year 1879 was, gold $989,161, silver $25,167,763, and that the circulation of coins of other countries has been considerably reduced by exportation. The standard of value is the silver dollar.

Central American States.—The communications from our minister at Guatemala show the amount of gold and silver in circulation in Costa Rica to be about $2,500,000, in addition to a considerable amount of foreign coins, the values of which are fixed by law. The gold coined from 1829 to 1877 was $2,318,381, silver $373,919. Notwithstanding the rich minerals which abound in the republic, lack of capital and intelligent labor prevents the mines from being worked on the large scale their value merits.

The laws of Nicaragua, promulgated under date of May 29, 1880, provide for the coinage to the extent of $100,000 of silver pieces of 20, 10, and 5 cents, eight-tenths fine, to be a legal tender in the State. A one-cent coin has also been made by decree of 1878 a legal tender in any quantity. No information with regard to the circulation of Nicaragua has been obtained.

The State of Salvador uses principally coins of other nations and paper as its circulating medium. The coins of the United States, Mexico, and England are preferred and command a premium. The paper circulation is placed at $60,000.

South American States.—Dispatches have been received from only three of the South American countries, Venezuela, Peru, and Argentine Republic. In Peru gold is the legal standard of value and the Inca is the monetary unit. Silver is limited as legal tender to 25 pesetas. The pound sterling of England has been provisionally adopted as legal money. No statistics in regard to the amount of circulation of either coin or paper are furnished.

The circulation of gold and silver in the Argentine Republic is about $7,000,000, a little over a million of which is held by the First National Bank; about two-thirds of this amount is gold. The paper circulation is very large, amounting to $364,000,000, and in addition $9,470,000 of metallic notes. The production of the mines is calculated at 3,800 ounces of gold and 325,000 ounces of silver, during 1879. The gold is obtained from the copper mines and is exported to England. The exportation of specie is chiefly carried on with that country, and amounted in the last year to about $2,000,000.

Venezuela coins no money; but the French franc, under the name of *bolivar*, is the monetary unit, and all laws relating to finance are adopted from the French. Its silver mines are not worked. The production of the gold mines in the year 1875–76 amounted to $1,324,000. Paper money is not issued by the government, but the notes of the Bank of Carracas are in circulation to the extent of $250,000.

Cuba and Hayti.—The dispatch from our consul-general at Havana states that the amount of gold and silver coin in the treasury is nominal only, and that the amount of gold coin in the Bank of Havana, April 30, 1880, was $10,522,000. The gold in circulation in the island is estimated at $32,500,000 and silver $1,000,000. The legal standard of value is the gold dollar (peso).

There is no gold or silver mined and no mint, its coins being imported from Spain. The bills of the Spanish Bank of Havana constitute the paper currency, and amounted on the 30th of April last to $57,857,000, of which $44,900,000 had been issued on account of the government. The dollar of this paper circulation is worth about 41 cents in United States gold coin. The imports and exports are about equal.

Two dispatches from Hon. John M. Langston, minister to Hayti, have been received. There is no bank or paper currency of any kind in Hayti. Prior to 1872 it had a paper currency estimated as high as $800,000,000, of which $544,675,404 was redeemed at the rate of 300 paper for one of silver, $2,154,266 in American silver having been provided therefor. The present coin circulation is estimated at about $5,000,000, consisting chiefly of American and Mexican coins. United States gold and silver coins are held in especial favor, the former selling generally for a considerable premium, and the latter, as against Mexican dollars, being held preferable, sometimes selling as high as 7 per cent. premium. A million Mexican silver dollars have recently been imported into the island, and a decree was issued compelling merchants to receive them at par.

Japan.—Hon. John A. Bingham transmits under date of April 14, 1880, very complete information in relation to the monetary statistics of Japan. He also notifies this country of the establishment of a branch of the imperial mint at Tokio, and incloses a copy of the regulations governing it. The production of the mines of Japan during the fiscal years of 1878 and 1879 was gold 36,870 ounces, silver 1,272,515 ounces. The net exports for the same years were gold 661,787 ounces, silver 3,973,673 ounces. The minister of foreign affairs reports the total paper circulation at $147,288,681, nearly all of government issue, while the coin and bullion in circulation and reserve amount to nearly $150,000,000, about one-third being silver.

Egypt.—The communication from our consul general at Cairo states that the gold piaster is the unit of account in Egypt, and that gold is generally the circulating medium, silver being only used for purposes of change. Of the gold coins English sovereigns constitute the larger part. There is no paper currency. The treasury reserve is limited. No gold or silver is produced in the country.

African States.—Dispatches have been received from United States consuls at Algiers, Morocco, and Cape of Good Hope, which state that there are no gold mines in any of those countries, and that the production of silver is insignificant. Algiers has no mint and uses French coins as its principal metallic medium, which amounts to about $8,500,000 in gold, and $5,500,000 in silver. The Bank of Algeria is authorized to issue currency, of which there is outstanding between eight and nine millions of dollars.

The circulation of Morocco consists principally of French and Spanish gold and silver coin, the amount of which is not known. Moorish gold coins have disappeared from circulation, having been exported to Europe on account of their high standard. Gold dust and trinkets brought by caravans are exported in small quantities. Morocco has no banks and no paper circulation.

British coin constitutes the circulating medium of the Cape of Good Hope, the amount of which is not known.

THE WORLD'S PRODUCTION OF GOLD AND SILVER.

No new facts have been obtained which would materially change the estimates and conclusions presented in my last report of the annual supply and appropriation of the precious metals.

A valuable table is presented in the appendix showing the production of the principal producing countries of the world for the years 1877, 1878, and 1879, and estimating the small amount produced from the mines of other countries.

The reported production of Russia and Australia, next to this country, the largest gold-producing countries, somewhat exceeds the estimate in my report for last year.

The total gold product for the calendar year 1879 (the United States and Japan alone being for the fiscal year, which would not materially alter the total) was $105,365,697, and silver $81,037,220, which is 8 millions of gold and one-half million of silver less than the annual average given by Dr. Soetbeer for 1871–1875.

THE COINAGE OF FOREIGN COUNTRIES.

The drain of gold during the last calendar year from Europe to the United States has had a marked effect upon the gold coinage of several countries, not only from the export of our own gold having ceased to supply them with material for new coinage, but because the United States has appropriated the stock of bullion from other gold-producing countries, as well as large amounts of foreign gold coins, and absorbed almost the entire world's production for the year.

The British mint was occupied with the coinage of gold only during a part of the month of December, and coined but $170,571. Less than $5,000,000 was coined at the French, and about $11,000,000 at the German mints in 1879, which present a striking contrast to the coinage of $39,080,000 gold at the United States mints, and an accumulation of gold bullion by the 1st of January amounting to $60,734,318 beyond the capacity of the mints for coinage. A table of coinages for the years 1877, 1878, 1879, to be found in the appendix, shows the total coinages of 19 countries to have been for the

Years—	Gold.	Silver.	Total.
1877	$201,616,466	$114,359,332	$315,975,798
1878	188,386,611	161,191,913	349,578,524
1879	89,969,091	117,318,293	207,287,384

COIN AND PAPER CIRCULATION OF THE PRINCIPAL COUNTRIES OF THE WORLD.

The papers forwarded through the State Department contain recent and authentic information in regard to the paper currency, as well as the specie circulation and bank reserves of foreign countries.

Tables have therefore been prepared presenting both the coin and paper circulation of nearly every commercial nation, giving the *per capita* amount of each.

The figures given for each of the 31 countries embraced in the table are believed to approximate their actual coin and paper circulation.

The aggregates are, of paper $4,021,721,853, gold $2,819,301,004, silver full legal-tender $2,060,697,480, and limited tender $422,252,541; total paper and specie $9,470,564,706; total specie $5,488,842,853. The statement of the amount of gold and silver in circulation in the world at the present time is below the usual estimate, and is less than half of the production since the discovery of America, which was estimated in the report of the Silver Commission, page 78, to have been, gold $5,841,000,000, silver $7,072,000,000; total $12,913,000,000.

As bearing upon the question of the proper specie reserve to paper circulation, the amounts of coin and bullion in banks and national treasuries available for the redemption of their outstanding paper issues, as far as could be ascertained from the dispatches and latest reliable authorities, are, for convenient reference, tabulated and submitted with this report.

COURSE OF PRICES.

The past fiscal year has exhibited monetary phenomena unusual and unexpected. The deficient harvests in Europe, and our unusual bounteous supply of exportable food, produced an importation of gold unchecked by advancing prices or the amount of existing circulation, already seemingly abundant. The heavy importation of foreign coin and bullion which commenced in August, 1879, continued until the close of the calendar year, and has been again resumed within the last three months. The remarkable increase of metallic circulation has been largely absorbed by the business community.

The speculative advance in prices first in the United States and then abroad subsided in part before the close of the year. Comparisons of the prices of 1880 with those of former years have been made similar to those in my last report. The table of the prices of exported commodities at different periods and for the whole of the last fiscal year shows an advance of $8\frac{1}{2}$ per cent. on the average prices of the same commodities during the fiscal year 1879, and but 6 per cent. below the gold prices of the same commodities in 1870.

In this connection an examination will be interesting of a table in the appendix compiled from official data contained in this and the preceding report, showing the increase of the net gain in specie in France from 1850 to 1878, and the outstanding bank circulation, and the comparative prices of exports and imports for a corresponding period.

It has been a gratification to find at every institution, and among those connected with the Mint Bureau, a commendable desire to secure the highest efficiency for every branch of the Mint service. During the year over $133,000,000 of gold and silver bullion received on deposits or silver purchases, and, in addition, nearly $40,000,000 received on transfers from other institutions, have been faithfully accounted for.

In the preparation of the statistical information embraced in this report, as well as in the discharge of the routine duties of the office, I have had the ready co-operation of the clerks in the Mint Bureau, for whose valuable assistance I desire to make acknowledgments.

I am, very respectfully,

HORATIO C. BURCHARD,
Director of the Mint.

Hon. JOHN SHERMAN,
    Secretary of the Treasury.

APPENDIX.

I.—DEPOSITS and PURCHASES of GOLD and SILVER BULLION during the fiscal year ended June 30, 1880.

Description.	Mints.					Assay offices.				Total.
	Philadelphia.	San Francisco.	Carson.	Denver.	New Orleans.	New York.	Boise.	Helena.	Charlotte.	
GOLD.										
Redeposits... { Fine bars	$35, 027, 097 76					$25, 312 93				$35, 052, 910 69
Redeposits... { Unparted bars	906, 501 41	$116, 111 22				55, 669 02		$6, 996 36	$3, 178 13	1, 082, 456 14
United States bullion (domestic production)	125, 584 80	27, 546, 640 57	$368, 174 51	$344, 909 86	$2, 350 43	6, 737, 404 27	$147, 619 16	466, 431 79	82, 590 61	35, 821, 705 40
United States coin	76, 332 74	55 00			5, 371 63	127, 327 04		40 00	202 41	209, 328 62
Foreign bullion	38, 109 31	264, 785 86			2, 062 74	20, 895, 974 51		64 81		21, 200, 997 23
Foreign coin	75, 871 19	599, 739 45			62, 338 96	39, 686, 420 62			189 41	40, 426, 559 63
Jewelers' bars, old plate, &c	388, 154 18	18, 212 36			25, 496 64	743, 019 35			1, 623 24	1, 176, 505 77
Total gold	36, 637, 551 39	28, 545, 544 46	368, 174 51	344, 909 86	97, 620 40	68, 273, 627 74	147, 619 16	473, 532 96	87, 783 20	134, 976, 463 62
SILVER.										
Redeposits... { Fine bars	406, 568 28				2, 092, 413 47	17, 189 98				2, 518, 171 72
Redeposits... { Unparted bars	44 56					55, 578 97		437 26	4 83	56, 063 62
United States bullion (domestic production)	15, 597, 582 96	9, 987, 566 59	622, 291 88	4, 443 77	1, 942, 936 12	3, 934, 708 56	2, 052 83	60, 639 49	443 75	32, 132, 756 95
United States coin	36, 508 72	6 00			1, 783 09	988 11			12 36	39, 298 28
Foreign bullion		861, 488 68			12, 370 21	280, 500 20		48		1, 154, 359 57
Foreign coin	547, 062 67	13, 222 21			431, 190 20	73, 245 68			5 60	1, 064, 746 26
Jewelers' bars, old plate, &c	81, 712 02	167 10			21, 582 15	145, 857 70			102 76	249, 361 73
Total silver	16, 671, 599 21	10, 842, 390 58	622, 291 88	4, 443 77	4, 502, 275 24	4, 508, 067 20	2, 052 83	61, 068 23	569 30	37, 214, 758 14
Gold and silver received and operated upon	53, 309, 250 60	39, 387, 935 04	996, 466 39	349, 353 63	4, 599, 895 64	72, 781, 694 94	149, 671 99	534, 601 19	88, 352 40	172, 191, 221 82
Less redeposits:										
Gold	35, 933, 599 17	116, 111 22				81, 481 95		6, 996 36	3, 178 13	36, 141, 366 83
Silver	406, 612 84				2, 092, 413 47	72, 768 95		437 26	4 83	2, 574, 235 35
Total redeposits	36, 342, 212 01	116, 111 22			2, 092, 413 47	154, 248 90		7, 433 62	3, 182 96	38, 715, 602 18

II.—DEPOSITS of GOLD of DOMESTIC PRODUCTION during the fiscal year ended June 30, 1880.

Locality.	Mints.					Assay offices.				Total.
	Philadelphia.	San Francisco.	Carson.	Denver.	New Orleans.	New York.	Boisé.	Helena.	Charlotte.	
Alabama	$665 94					$86 85				$752 79
Alaska		$5,950 90								5,950 90
Arizona	4,070 85	152,967 26	$367 91			1,513 73				158,919 75
California	8,752 54	7,033,656 05		25,369 85	$2,350 43	48,687 55				7,118,816 42
Colorado	1,430 39	338 72			$344,756 91	1,897,553 72				2,244,069 74
Dakota	971 58	64,350 06				2,684,700 45				2,750,022 09
Georgia	28,923 24					44,733 69			$16,174 15	89,831 08
Idaho	4,565 31	365,570 55	1,374 84			20,919 54	$116,309 37	$1,807 62		510,546 73
Montana	656 41	16,441 84				1,324,982 19		463,587 56		1,805,768 00
Nevada		38,119 81		340,837 45		139,304 69				518,261 95
New Mexico	607 82					90,429 46				91,037 28
North Carolina	14,159 73					14,542 55			58,956 29	85,659 37
Oregon		552,280 41					31,064 93			583,365 34
South Carolina	2,493 26								9,368 44	11,861 70
Tennessee	1,907 95					90 35				1,998 30
Utah	401 22	13,295 30		204 66		13,128 01				27,029 19
Virginia	7,851 24					1,470 83				9,322 07
Washington Territory		34,529 34								34,529 24
Wyoming	11,174 63	928 84		152 95		5,664 28				17,320 70
Refined bullion		18,161,943 52								18,161,943 52
Parted from silver	24,041 43	1,106,868 07				318,615 04				1,449,524 54
Contained in silver							224 86	936 61		1,161 47
Other sources	12,921 26					131,000 74			91 13	144,013 13
Total	125,584 80	27,546,640 57	368,174 51	344,909 86	2,350 43	6,737,404 27	147,619 16	466,431 79	82,590 01	35,821,705 40

DIRECTOR OF THE MINT.

III.—DEPOSITS and PURCHASES of SILVER of DOMESTIC PRODUCTION during the fiscal year ended June 30, 1880.

Locality.	Mints.					Assay offices.				Total.
	Philadelphia.	San Francisco.	Carson.	Denver.	New Orleans.	New York.	Boisé.	Helena.	Charlotte.	
Arizona	$121,438 31	$831,016 67	$12 58			$38,855 82				$991,323 38
California		263,734 46				781 40				303,846 91
Colorado			19,331 05			1,253,346 64				1,257,790 41
Dakota				4,443 77		21,104 54				21,104 54
Georgia									48 73	48 73
Idaho		86,724 16	24 72			14,152 85	41 29	856 74		102,999 86
Michigan (Lake Superior)	3,230 96					126,455 98				129,686 94
Montana	6,813 52	252,086 30				937,475 44		59,607 96		1,262,982 32
Nevada		4,123,732 53	602,920 00			360,589 65				5,087,242 18
New Mexico						424,907 91				434,907 31
North Carolina									379 18	379 18
Oregon		1,174 26								1,174 26
South Carolina									15 52	15 52
Utah	3,373 41	11,827 38	3 53			612,499 53				627,703 85
Refined bullion		2,970,757 92								2,970,787 92
Parted from gold	22,357 99	76,278 43				118,550 84	2,011 54	965 69		219,387 26
Contained in gold										2,978 23
Other sources	15,440,268 77	1,319,234 48			$1,942,936 12	25,928 46			32	18,728,368 15
Total	15,597,682 96	9,967,566 59	622,291 88	4,443 77	1,942,936 12	3,934,708 56	2,052 83	60,630 49	443 75	32,193,766 95

IV.—*COINAGE EXECUTED during the fiscal year ended June 30, 1880.*

Denomination.	Mint at Philadelphia.		Mint at San Francisco.		Mint at Carson.		Mint at New Orleans.		Total.	
	Pieces.	Value.	Pieces.	Value.	Pieces.	Value.	Pieces.	Value.	Pieces.	Value.
GOLD.										
Double-eagles	110,870	$2,217,400 00	960,800	$19,216,000 00	1,773	$35,460 00	2,325	$46,500 00	1,075,768	$21,515,360 00
Eagles	1,409,710	14,097,100 00	461,250	4,612,500 00	4,472	44,720 00	8,200	82,000 00	1,883,632	18,836,320 00
Half-eagles	2,261,950	11,309,750 00	862,900	4,314,500 00	33,322	166,610 00			3,158,172	15,790,860 00
Three dollars	3,030	9,090 00							3,030	9,090 00
Quarter-eagles	1,230	3,075 00							1,230	3,075 00
Dollars	3,030	3,030 00							3,030	3,030 00
Total gold	3,789,820	27,639,445 00	2,284,950	28,143,000 00	39,567	246,790 00	10,525	128,500 00	6,124,862	56,157,735 00
SILVER.										
Dollars	15,185,750	15,185,750 00	7,910,000	7,910,000 00	408,000	408,000 00	4,430,000	4,430,000 00	27,933,750	27,933,750 00
Half-dollars	6,550	3,275 00							6,550	3,275 00
Quarter-dollars	15,350	3,837 50							15,350	3,837 50
Dimes	15,750	1,575 00							15,750	1,575 00
Total silver	15,223,400	15,194,437 50	7,910,000	7,910,000 00	408,000	408,000 00	4,430,000	4,430,000 00	27,971,400	27,942,437 50
MINOR.										
Five cents	24,950	1,247 50							24,950	1,247 50
Three cents	32,750	962 50							32,750	962 50
One cent	26,774,150	267,741 50							26,774,150	267,741 50
Total minor	26,831,850	269,971 50							26,831,850	269,971 50
Total coinage	45,845,070	43,103,854 00	10,194,950	36,053,000 00	447,567	654,790 00	4,440,525	4,558,500 00	60,928,112	84,370,144 00

V.—BARS MANUFACTURED *during the fiscal year ended June 30, 1880.*

Description.	Mints.					Assay offices.				Total.
	Philadelphia.	San Francisco.	Carson.	Denver.	New Orleans.	New York.	Boisé.	Helena.	Charlotte.	
GOLD.										
Fine bars	$145,200 85					$11,378,980 98				$11,524,181 83
Mint bars						57,368,761 15				57,368,761 15
Unparted bars			$1,980 84	$346,072 72			$147,465 35	$473,532 96	$87,783 20	1,056,835 07
Total gold	145,200 85		1,980 84	346,072 72		63,747,742 13	147,465 35	473,532 96	87,783 20	69,949,778 05
SILVER.										
Fine bars	83,668 67	$2,355,252 07				4,372,705 02				6,811,645 76
Sterling bars						24,347 93				24,347 93
Unparted bars			24,455 37	2,149 73			264 95	61,068 23	569 20	88,507 48
Total silver	83,668 67	2,355,252 07	24,455 37	2,149 73		4,397,052 95	264 95	61,068 23	569 20	6,934,501 17
Total gold and silver	228,889 52	2,355,252 07	26,436 21	348,222 45		73,144,795 08	147,730 30	534,601 19	88,352 40	76,874,279 22

VI.—*COINAGE and MEDAL DIES MANUFACTURED at the MINT at PHILA-DELPHIA during the fiscal year ended June 30, 1880.*

Denomination.	Philadel-phia.	San Fran-cisco.	Carson.	New Or-leans.	Total.
For gold coinage:					
Double-eagle	11	65	....	....	76
Eagle	57	52	15	5	129
Half-eagle	111	49	20	10	190
Three-dollar	2	....	....	....	2
Quarter-eagle	....	8	....	....	8
Dollar	2	....	....	....	2
Total	183	174	35	15	407
For silver coinage:					
Standard dollar	199	110	25	80	414
Half-dollar	2	5	....	....	7
Quarter-dollar	....	5	....	....	5
Dime	13	5	....	....	18
Total	214	125	25	80	444
For minor coinage:					
Five-cent	12	....	....	....	12
Three-cent	8	....	....	....	8
One-cent	182	....	....	....	182
Total	202	....	....	....	202

Total NUMBER of DIES.

Gold coinage	407
Silver coinage	444
Minor coinage	202
Experimental dies	6
Proof coinage	24
Bendix Koppel medal	2
D. De Fleury, Stony Point, medal (reproduction)	2
Horatio Gates reverse die (reproduction)	1
Annual assay	4
Total	1,092

VII.—*MEDALS MANUFACTURED at the MINT at PHILADELPHIA during the fiscal year ended June 30, 1880.*

Name.	Gold.	Silver.	Bronze.
Adams Academy	1		
Adams, J. Q.		1	
Agricultural and Industrial Society		6	
Allegiance			26
American University	1		
Amidon	1		
Baltimore Female College		8	
Brown, Major-General			17
Brown Memorial		8	
Cabinet		1	
College of Pharmacy	2		
Croghan, Col. George			14
Davis Prize			4
Denman School	3	20	
Dodd, H. M	1		
Franklin		17	
Gaines, Major-General			18
Gates, Major-General			18
Georgetown College	1		
Grant, Indian Peace		8	
Harrison, Major-General			18
Hodge, Dr	1		
Honor, Medals of			75
Howard, J. E			18
Jackson, Major-General			8
Jones, Capt. Jacob		5	
Ketchum, Jesse (large)		25	
Ketchum, Jesse (small)		30	
Knight Templar			40
Koppel, Bendix	1		7
Life Saving (first class)	14		
Life Saving (second class)		8	
McKee	1		
Macomb, Major-General	1		36
Maine State Agricultural Society	1	16	
Michigan State Agricultural Society		25	
Mighty Dollar		80	
Miller, Brigadier-General			15
Morgan, General			15
New England Agricultural Society		70	80
New Hampshire Agricultural Society		60	22
Norman	1		8
Patterson, Robert			10
Peabody		6	1
Pennsylvania Marksmen Badge			300
Philadelphia Rifle Club		20	5
Pomological Society		10	
Porter, Major-General			17
Ripley, Brigadier-General			14
Robinson Prize			
Sagadahoc	2	6	18
Santini	1		
Scott, John			
Scott, Major-General			18
Shakespeare	1		
Shelby, Gov. Isaac			10
Stoddard Prize	1		2
Union League	3		
Valley Forge		20	
Vanderbilt	7		
Washington before Boston			18
Washington, Col. William			16
Wisconsin State Agricultural Society		6	
Total	43	446	858

VIII.—*MEDALS and PROOF SETS SOLD during the fiscal year ended June 30, 1880.*

Description.	Number sold.	Value.
MEDALS.		
Gold	43	$1,808 50
Silver	480	983 85
Bronze	646	435 75
Total	1,169	3,228 10
PROOF SETS.		
Gold	31	1,333 00
Silver	1,606	6,432 00
Total	1,639	7,765 00
Trade dollars (sold singly)	872	1,090 00

IX.—*MINOR COINS REDEEMED, REISSUED, EXCHANGED, and MELTED during the fiscal year ended June 30, 1880.*

Denomination.	Pieces.	Value.
REDEEMED.		
Copper, one-cent pieces	344,525	$3,445 25
Nickel, one-cent pieces	657,125	6,571 25
Bronze, one-cent pieces	3,159,162	31,591 62
Bronze, two-cent pieces	707,664	14,153 28
Nickel, three-cent pieces	822,040	24,661 20
Nickel, five-cent pieces	10,111,630	505,576 50
Total	15,802,046	585,999 10
REISSUED.		
Bronze, one-cent pieces	2,362,500	23,625 00
Nickel, three-cent pieces	1,766,800	53,004 00
Nickel, five-cent pieces	10,949,700	547,485 00
Total	15,079,000	624,114 00
EXCHANGED.		
Copper, one-cent pieces	475	4 75
Nickel, one-cent pieces	8	8
Bronze, one-cent pieces	22	22
Bronze, two-cent pieces	25	50
Nickel, three-cent pieces	1,445	43 35
Total	1,975	48 90
MELTED.		
Bronze, two-cent pieces	500,000	10,000 00

14 F

X.—STATEMENT of EARNINGS and EXPENDITURES of UNITED STATES MINTS and ASSAY OFFICES for fiscal year ended June 30, 1880.

EARNINGS.

	Mints.					Assay offices.				Totals.
	Philadelphia.	San Francisco.	New Orleans.	Carson.	Denver.	New York.	Boisé.	Charlotte.	Helena.	
Charges collected for parting and refining bullion	$8,773 47	$158,477 94	$722 52	$9,864 42		$80,656 14				$258,493 89
Charges collected for alloying gold coins	163 73	2,743 24	6 19	88 60		1,951 83				4,953 59
Charges collected for assaying, melting, and stamping bars					$356 01		$164 53	$118 10	$549 97	1,188 61
Seigniorage on standard silver dollars coined	1,829,314 78	965,279 71	512,252 12	47,830 29						3,354,676 90
Seigniorage on subsidiary silver coined	1,541 18									1,541 18
Profit on the manufacture of minor coins	198,178 16									198,178 16
Amount received for medals and proof coins	12,414 54									12,414 54
Amount received for assays of ores	308 00	90 00	18 50		1,107 00	559 00	105 00	398 05	989 00	3,673 55
Grains, fluxes, and sweepings from deposit melting room	2,020 38	1,303 70			560 53	8,983 34	250 75	40 05	1,264 54	14,513 29
Surplus bullion returned by the melter and refiner in settlement	347 92		1,060 27			16,454 58				18,762 77
Gain from assays and collection, and transportation charges on bullion shipped the Mint for coinage					66 20		713 02	158 43		937 84
Proceeds of sale of old material	1,141 64	1,455 75	411 97	915 00						3,924 36
Totals	2,054,203 80	1,129,448 74	515,371 57	58,698 31	2,089 03	108,604 89	1,323 36	714 63	2,803 51	3,873,258 68

EXPENDITURES.

	Philadelphia.	San Francisco.	New Orleans.	Carson.	Denver.	New York.	Boisé.	Charlotte.	Helena.	Totals.
Salaries of officers and clerks	33,632 87	24,900 00	20,961 89	23,550 00	10,620 70	33,150 00	2,959 28	2,500 00	5,700 00	157,974 74
Wages of workmen	287,645 92	252,235 75	77,278 91	62,294 62	10,000 00	20,765 88	3,525 97		8,656 24	722,403 29
Contingent expenses, not including wastage and loss on sweeps	75,333 43	41,313 81	29,934 27	11,312 73	4,118 95	8,750 12	1,095 22	915 46	9,960 19	182,734 18
Parting and refining expenses, not including wastage and loss on sweeps	10,994 41	137,671 98		4,402 08		82,544 59				235,043 06
Expenses paid from the appropriation for the coinage of the standard silver dollar, act of February 28, 1878	86,221 43		5,812 03							92,033 46
Repairs and new machinery			4,994 06							4,994 06
Expenses of distributing standard silver dollars	62,189 05	210 18	2,829 19	108 00						65,336 42
Expenses of distributing minor coins	12,592 83									12,592 83
Amount paid for medals and proof coins	9,470 84									9,470 84
Value of the gold and silver wastage of the operative officers	14,281 71	29,273 07	955 63	476 66						44,987 07
Minor coinage wastage	416 49									416 49
Loss on sale of sweeps	8,127 08	16,973 88				5,758 28				30,859 24

XI.—*WASTAGES and LOSS on SALE of SWEEPS*, 1880.

Losses.	Philadelphia mint.	San Francisco mint.	Carson mint.	New Orleans mint.	New York assay office.	Totals.
Melter and refiner's gold wastage.	$10,726 12	$5,258 82	$124 50	$5 49	....	$16,114 93
Coiner's gold wastage	9 12	2,188 32	45 51	11 26	....	2,254 21
Melter and refiner's silver wastage...	....	21,706 69	197 47	....	....	21,884 16
Coiner's silver wastage	3,546 47	119 24	149 18	938 88	....	4,753 77
Loss on sale of sweeps	8,127 08	16,973 88	....	....	$5,758 28	30,859 24
Totals	22,408 79	46,246 95	476 66	955 63	5,758 28	75,846 31
Paid as follows :						
From contingent appropriation ...	12,164 70	5,211 94	....	....	....	17,376 64
From parting and refining appropriation.	448 16	13,342 50	124 50	....	....	13,915 16
From profit and loss	1,470 39	1,303 76	45 51	16 75	5,758 28	8,084 69
From silver profit fund	8,325 54	26,298 75	306 65	938 88	....	35,869 82
Totals	22,408 79	46,246 95	476 66	955 63	5,758 28	75,846 31

XII.—*GOLD and SILVER of DOMESTIC PRODUCTION DEPOSITED at the MINTS and ASSAY OFFICES from their ORGANIZATION to the close of the fiscal year ended June 30, 1880.*

Locality.	Gold.	Silver.	Total.
Alabama	$219,872 95	....	$219,872 95
Alaska	29,972 47	....	29,972 47
Arizona	2,256,742 06	$2,116,717 64	4,373,459 70
California	702,058,970 35	1,677,550 45	703,736,520 80
Colorado	35,417,517 54	20,182,889 56	55,601,407 10
Dakota	7,235,112 89	21,121 54	7,256,234 43
Georgia	7,698,082 03	458 20	7,698,540 23
Idaho	24,137,417 11	727,295 50	24,864,712 61
Maryland	402 12	....	402 12
Massachusetts	....	917 56	917 56
Michigan (Lake Superior)..................	123 99	3,433,074 78	3,433,198 77
Montana	48,689,006 09	4,371,384 12	53,060,390 21
Nevada	14,432,322 55	72,107,030 69	86,539,353 24
New Hampshire............................	11,020 55	....	11,020 55
New Mexico	1,569,472 14	2,221,484 63	3,790,956 77
North Carolina............................	10,613,351 10	45,581 33	10,658,932 43
Oregon	15,414,509 57	4,406 38	15,418,915 95
South Carolina............................	1,461,845 30	30 44	1,461,875 74
Tennessee	84,266 25	....	84,266 25
Utah	445,133 61	9,036,957 01	9,482,090 62
Vermont	10,981 27	....	10,981 27
Virginia	1,672,667 70	....	1,672,667 70
Washington Territory	208,959 37	....	208,959 37
Wyoming	716,966 47	11,793 86	728,760 33
Refined bullion............................	201,055,915 26	42,790,012 87	243,845,928 13
Parted from silver	13,974,774 89	....	13,974,774 89
Contained in silver	9,322,268 97	....	9,322,268 97
Parted from gold	....	6,813,476 84	6,813,476 84
Contained in gold	....	520,623 81	520,623 81
Other sources	10,242,731 33	31,337,203 76	41,579,935 09
Total.....................	1,108,920,405 93	197,421,612 97	1,306,342,018 90

XIII.—*STATEMENT of COINAGE from the ORGANIZATION of the MINT to the close of the fiscal year ended June 30, 1860.*

GOLD COINAGE.

Period.	Double-eagles.	Eagles.	Half-eagles.	Three-dollars.	Quarter-eagles.	Dollars.
1793 to 1795		$27, 950	$43, 535			
1796		60, 340	20, 960		$2, 407 50	
1797		88, 280	18, 045		2, 147 50	
1798		70, 740	124, 335		1, 535 00	
1799		174, 830	37, 255		1, 200 00	
1800		250, 650	58, 110			
1801		292, 540	130, 030			
1802		150, 900	265, 880		6, 530 00	
1803		89, 790	167, 530		1, 057 50	
1804		97, 050	152, 375		6, 317 50	
1805			165, 915		4, 452 50	
1806			320, 465		4, 040 00	
1807			420, 465		17, 630 00	
1808			277, 890		6, 775 00	
1809			169, 375			
1810			501, 435			
1811			497, 905			
1812			290, 435			
1813			477, 140			
1814			77, 270			
1815			3, 175			
1816						
1817						
1818			242, 940			
1819			258, 615			
1820			1, 319, 030			
1821			173, 205		16, 120 00	
1822			88, 980			
1823			72, 425			
1824			80, 700		6, 500 00	
1825			145, 300		11, 085 00	
1826			90, 345		1, 800 00	
1827			124, 565		7, 000 00	
1828			140, 145			
1829			287, 210		8, 507 50	
1830			631, 755		11, 350 00	
1831			702, 270		11, 800 00	
1832			787, 435		11, 000 00	
1833			968, 150		10, 400 00	
1834			3, 660, 845		293, 425 00	
1835			1, 887, 670		322, 505 00	
1836			3, 765, 735		1, 369, 985 00	
1837			1, 085, 605		112, 700 00	
1838		72, 090	1, 900, 285		137, 310 00	
1839		382, 480	802, 745		170, 660 00	
1840		473, 380	1, 048, 380		153, 502 50	
1841		856, 310	380, 725		54, 562 50	
1842		1, 089, 070	653, 330		89, 770 00	
1843		2, 506, 340	4, 275, 425		1, 327, 132 50	
1844		1, 260, 810	4, 088, 275		89, 345 00	
1845		736, 530	2, 743, 640		276, 277 50	
1846		1, 018, 780	2, 736, 155		279, 272 50	
1847		14, 307, 640	5, 461, 688		462, 060 00	
1848		1, 813, 340	1, 863, 560		98, 612 50	
1849		6, 775, 180	1, 184, 645		111, 147 50	$936, 789
1850	$26, 225, 220	3, 489, 510	860, 180		605, 547 50	511, 301
1851	48, 643, 100	4, 393, 280	2, 051, 256		3, 297, 897 50	3, 056, 820
1852	44, 860, 520	2, 811, 060	3, 089, 636		3, 283, 827 50	2, 201, 145
1853	26, 646, 520	2, 522, 580	2, 305, 096		3, 519, 615 00	4, 384, 149
1854	18, 052, 340	2, 305, 760	1, 513, 198	$491, 214	1, 896, 397 50	1, 657, 013
1855	24, 636, 820	1, 487, 010	1, 257, 090	171, 465	600, 700 00	824, 883
1856	30, 277, 560	1, 484, 900	1, 751, 665	181, 530	1, 213, 117 50	1, 788, 996
1857	14, 058, 900	129, 100	673, 610	38, 496	320, 465 00	595, 532
1858	20, 058, 880	620, 900	772, 775	66, 177	515, 632 50	230, 361
1859	16, 236, 730	146, 000	406, 710	34, 572	213, 010 00	259, 065
1860	15, 458, 800	342, 130	361, 145	61, 206	138, 580 00	63, 215
1861	59, 316, 430	552, 050	453, 590	18, 216	338, 440 00	15, 521
1862	36, 247, 500	072, 000	3, 287, 100	17, 355	3, 208, 122 50	1, 799, 259
1863	20, 387, 720	126, 580	117, 010	117	62, 475 00	1, 950
1864	21, 465, 640	85, 800	51, 500	16, 470	23, 185 00	5, 750
1865	24, 876, 600	93, 750	88, 075	10, 065	30, 502 50	7, 225
1866	27, 404, 900	376, 100	300, 750	12, 090	122, 975 00	7, 130
1867	27, 925, 400	51, 150	154, 475	7, 875	73, 062 50	5, 325
1868	17, 705, 800	156, 500	153, 750	14, 700	74, 125 00	10, 550
1869	21, 276, 500	209, 850	228, 925	7, 575	108, 862 50	5, 925
1870	22, 018, 480	80, 130	94, 625	10, 605	35, 137 50	9, 335

XIII.—*STATEMENT of COINAGE, &c.*—Continued.

GOLD COINAGE—Continued.

Period.	Double-eagles.	Eagles.	Half-eagles.	Three-dollars.	Quarter-eagles.	Dollars.
1871	20, 919, 240	163, 250	158, 625	4, 020	53, 400 00	3, 940
1872	19, 798, 500	254, 600	243, 700	6, 090	72, 575 00	1, 030
1873	34, 785, 500	204, 650	237, 525	75	39, 062 50	2, 525
1874	48, 363, 900	383, 430	809, 780	125, 460	516, 150 00	323, 920
1875	32, 748, 140	599, 840	203, 655	60	2, 250 00	20
1876	37, 896, 720	153, 610	71, 800	135	53, 052 50	3, 645
1877	43, 941, 700	56, 200	67, 835	4, 464	5, 780 00	2, 220
1878	51, 406, 340	155, 490	688, 680	137, 850	406, 900 00	1, 720
1879	97, 234, 340	1, 031, 440	1, 442, 130	109, 182	1, 166, 800 00	3, 020
1880	21, 515, 960	18, 836, 320	15, 790, 860	9, 090	3, 075 00	3, 030
Total	919, 754, 480	76, 730, 470	87, 334, 485	1, 556, 154	26, 374, 525 00	19, 353, 208

XIII.—*STATEMENT of COINAGE from the ORGANIZATION of the MINT, &c.*—Continued.

SILVER COINAGE.

Period.	Trade-dollars.	Dollars.	Half-dollars.	Quarter-dollars.	Twenty-cents.	Dimes.
1793 to 1795		$204,791	$161,572 00			
1796		72,920	1,959 00	$1,473 50		$2,213 50
1797		7,776		63 00		2,526 10
1798		327,536				2,755 00
1799		423,515				
1800		220,920				2,176 00
1801		54,454	15,144 50			3,464 00
1802		41,650	14,945 00			1,097 50
1803		66,064	15,857 50			3,304 00
1804		19,570	78,259 50	1,684 50		826 50
1805		321	105,861 00	30,348 50		12,078 00
1806			419,788 00	51,521 00		
1807			525,788 00	55,160 75		16,500 00
1808			684,300 00			
1809			702,905 00			4,471 00
1810			633,136 00			635 50
1811			601,822 00			6,518 00
1812			814,029 50			
1813			620,951 50			
1814			519,587 50			42,150 00
1815				17,308 00		
1816			23,575 00	5,000 75		
1817			607,783 50			
1818			980,161 00	90,283 50		
1819			1,104,000 00	36,000 00		
1820			375,561 00	31,861 00		94,258 70
1821			652,898 50	54,212 75		118,651 20
1822			779,786 50	16,020 00		10,000 00
1823			847,100 00	4,450 00		44,000 00
1824			1,752,477 00			
1825			1,471,583 00	42,000 00		51,000 00
1826			2,002,090 00			
1827			2,746,700 00	1,000 00		121,500 00
1828			1,537,600 00	25,500 00		12,500 00
1829			1,856,078 00			77,000 00
1830			2,382,400 00			51,000 00
1831			2,936,830 00	99,500 00		77,135 00
1832			2,398,500 00	80,000 00		52,250 00
1833			2,603,000 00	39,000 00		48,500 00
1834			3,206,002 00	71,500 00		63,500 00

Year							
1838			1,773,000 00	208,000 00		239,493 00	112,750 00	
1839		300	1,717,280 50	122,786 50		229,471 50	106,487 50	
1840		61,005	1,145,054 00	153,331 75		253,358 00	113,954 25	
1841		173,000	356,500 00	148,000 00		363,000 00	98,250 00	
1842		184,618	1,484,882 00	214,250,00		390,750 00	58,250 00	
1843		165,100	3,056,000 00	403,400 00		152,000 00	58,250 00	
1844		20,000	1,885,500 00	290,300 00		7,250 00	32,500 00	
1845		24,500	1,341,500 00	230,500 00		198,500 00	78,200 00	
1846		169,000	2,257,000 00	127,500 00		3,130 00	1,350 00	
1847		140,750	1,270,000 00	280,500 00		24,500 00	63,700 00	
1848		15,000	1,880,000 00	36,500 00		45,150 00	63,400 00	
1849		62,600	1,781,000 00	85,000 00		113,900 00	72,450 00	
1850		47,500	1,341,500 00	150,700 00		944,150 00	82,250 00	
1851		1,300	301,375 00	62,000 00		142,650 00	82,050 00	$185,022 00
1852		1,100	110,565 00	68,265 00		196,550 00	63,025 00	569,905 00
1853		46,110	2,430,354 00	4,146,555 00		1,327,361 00	785,251 00	342,000 00
1854		33,140	4,111,000 00	3,466,000 00		624,000 00	365,000 00	20,130 00
1855		26,000	2,284,725 00	861,350 00		207,500 00	117,500 00	4,170 00
1856		63,800	1,903,500 00	2,129,500 00		696,000 00	299,000 00	43,740 00
1857		94,000	114,000 00	583,000 00		489,000 00	197,000 00	
1858			4,430,000 00	3,019,750 00		226,000 00	327,000 00	37,980 00
1859		288,500	4,005,500 00	1,428,000 00		229,000 00	195,000 00	41,400 00
1860		600,530	1,627,400 00	330,430 00		98,600 00	96,500 00	16,440 00
1861		559,900	959,850 00	771,550 00		107,300 00	130,350 00	7,950 00
1862		1,750	1,785,425 00	730,937 50		156,405 00	177,627 50	18,256 50
1863		31,400	963,630 00	113,965 00		34,071 00	8,223 00	2,803 80
1864		23,170	483,985 00	22,492 50		14,037 00	4,518 50	11 10
1865		32,900	558,100 00	27,950 00		17,180 00	4,880 00	618 00
1866		58,550	579,525 00	9,712 50		21,065 00	10,732 50	679 50
1867		57,000	897,450 00	18,175 00		13,670 00	435 00	141 00
1868		54,800	946,750 00	37,475 00		73,315 00	24,290 00	120 00
1869		231,350	561,675 00	23,137 50		23,895 00	527 50	151 50
1870		586,308	1,009,375 00	28,047 50		98,185 00	46,222 50	115 50
1871		857,929	1,242,771 00	29,971 75		10,707 50	14,396 25	129 75
1872		1,112,961	1,486,492 50	55,096 25		222,471 50	152,751 75	61 05
1873		977,150	1,199,775 00	174,362 50		416,040 00	175,442 50	25 50
1874	$3,588,900		1,438,930 00	458,515 50		497,255 80		
1875	5,697,500		2,853,560 00	623,850 00	$5,858 00	880,560 00		
1876	6,132,050		4,985,525 00	4,106,262 50	263,560 00	3,636,105 00		
1877	9,162,900		9,746,350 00	7,584,175 00	1,440 00	2,055,070 00		
1878	11,378,010	8,573,500	3,875,255 00	3,703,027 50	142 00	760,891 00		
1879		27,227,500	225 00	113 50		45 00		
1880		27,933,750	3,275 00	3,897 50		1,575 00		
Total	35,959,360	71,780,588	122,748,295 50	38,481,099 00	271,000 00	16,904,297 30	4,806,946 90	1,281,859 20

XIII.—*STATEMENT of COINAGE from the ORGANIZATION of the MINT, &c.—Continued.*

Period.	Minor coinage.					Total coinage.			
	Five-cents.	Three-cents.	Two-cents.	Cents.	Half-cents.	Gold.	Silver.	Minor.	Total.
1793 to 1795				$10,660 33	$712 97	$71,485 00	$370,683 80	$11,373 00	$453,541 80
1796				9,747 00	977 40	102,727 50	79,077 50	10,324 40	192,129 40
1797				8,975 10	535 24	103,422 50	12,591 45	9,510 34	125,524 29
1798				9,797 00		205,610 00	330,291 00	9,797 00	545,698 00
1799				9,045 85	60 83	213,285 00	423,515 00	9,106 68	645,906 68
1800				28,221 75	1,057 65	317,760 00	224,296 00	29,279 40	571,335 40
1801				13,628 37		422,570 00	74,758 00	13,628 37	510,956 37
1802				34,351 00	71 83	423,310 00	58,343 00	34,422 83	516,075 83
1803				24,713 53	489 50	258,377 50	87,118 00	25,203 03	370,698 53
1804				7,568 38	5,276 56	258,642 50	100,340 50	12,844 94	371,827 94
1805				9,411 16	4,072 32	170,367 50	149,388 50	13,483 48	333,239 48
1806				3,480 00	1,780 80	324,505 00	471,319 00	5,260 00	801,084 00
1807				7,272 21	2,380 00	437,495 00	597,448 75	9,652 21	1,044,595 96
1808				11,090 00	2,000 00	284,665 00	684,300 00	13,090 00	982,055 00
1809				2,228 67	5,772 86	169,375 00	707,376 00	8,001 53	884,752 53
1810				14,685 00	1,075 00	501,435 00	638,773 50	15,660 00	1,155,868 50
1811				2,180 25	315 70	497,905 00	608,340 00	2,495 95	1,108,740 95
1812				10,755 00		290,435 00	814,029 50	10,755 00	1,115,219 50
1813				4,180 00		477,140 00	620,951 50	4,180 00	1,102,271 50
1814				3,578 30		77,270 00	561,687 50	3,578 30	642,535 80
1815						3,175 00	17,308 00		20,483 00
1816				28,209 82			28,575 75	28,209 82	56,785 57
1817				39,484 00			607,783 50	39,484 00	647,267 50
1818				31,870 00		242,940 00	1,070,454 50	31,870 00	1,345,064 50
1819				26,710 00		258,615 00	1,140,000 00	26,710 00	1,425,325 00
1820				44,075 50		1,319,030 00	501,680 70	44,075 50	1,864,786 20
1821				3,890 00		189,325 00	825,762 45	3,890 00	1,018,977 45
1822				20,723 39		88,980 00	805,806 50	20,723 39	915,509 89
1823						72,425 00	895,550 00		967,975 00
1824				12,620 00		93,200 00	1,752,477 00	12,620 00	1,858,297 00
1825				14,611 00	315 00	156,385 00	1,564,583 00	14,926 00	1,735,894 00
1826				15,174 25	1,170 00	92,245 00	2,002,090 00	16,344 25	2,110,679 25
1827				23,577 32		131,565 00	2,869,200 00	23,577 32	3,024,342 32
1828				22,606 24	3,030 00	140,145 00	1,575,600 00	25,636 34	1,741,381 34
1829				14,145 00	2,435 00	295,717 50	1,994,578 00	16,580 00	2,306,875 50
1830				17,115 00		643,105 00	2,495,400 00	17,115 00	3,155,620 00
1831				33,592 60	11 00	714,270 00	3,175,600 00	33,603 60	3,923,473 60
1832				23,620 00		798,435 00	2,579,000 00	23,620 00	3,401,055 00
1833				27,390 00	770 00	978,550 00	2,759,000 00	28,160 00	3,765,710 00
1834				18,551 00	600 00	3,954,270 00	3,415,002 00	19,151 00	7,388,423 00

Year									
1837				55,583 00		1,146,305 00	2,098,010 00	55,583 00	3,299,898 00
1838				63,702 00		1,809,595 00	2,833,248 00	63,702 00	4,206,540 00
1839				31,286 61		1,355,885 00	2,176,296 00	31,286 61	3,563,467 61
1840				24,627 60		1,675,302 50	1,726,703 00	24,627 00	3,426,632 50
1841				15,973 67		1,091,597 50	1,132,750 00	15,973 67	2,240,321 17
1842				23,833 90		1,834,170 00	2,332,750 00	23,833 90	4,190,753 00
1843				24,283 20		8,108,797 50	3,834,750 00	24,283 20	11,967,830 70
1844				23,987 62		5,426,230 60	2,335,550 00	23,987 52	7,687,767 52
1845				38,948 04		3,756,447 50	1,873,200 00	38,948 04	5,668,595 54
1846				41,208 00		4,034,177 50	2,558,580 00	41,208 00	6,633,965 50
1847				61,836 69		20,221,385 00	2,379,450 00	61,836 69	22,662,671 89
1848				64,157 99		3,775,512 50	2,040,050 00	64,157 99	5,879,720 49
1849				41,785 00	199 32	9,007,761 50	2,114,950 00	41,984 32	11,164,695 82
1850				44,268 44	199 08	31,981,738 50	1,866,100 00	44,467 50	33,892,306 00
1851				98,897 07	738 36	62,614,492 50	774,397 00	99,635 43	63,488,534 93
1852				50,630 94		56,846,187 50	999,410 00	50,630 94	57,896,228 44
1853				66,411 31	648 47	39,377,909 00	9,077,571 00	67,059 78	48,522,539 78
1854				42,361 56	276 79	25,915,018 50	8,619,270 00	42,638 35	34,577,826 85
1855				15,748 29	282 50	28,977,968 00	3,501,245 00	16,030 79	32,495,243 79
1856				26,904 63	202 15	36,697,768 50	5,135,240 00	27,106 78	41,860,115 28
1857				68,334 56	175 90	15,811,586 00	1,477,000 00	68,510 46	17,352,073 46
1858				234,000 00		30,258,726 50	8,040,730 00	234,000 00	38,528,455 50
1859				307,000 00		17,296,077 00	6,187,400 00	307,000 00	23,790,477 00
1860				342,000 00		16,445,476 00	2,769,920 00	342,000 00	19,557,396 00
1861				101,660 00		60,693,237 00	2,605,700 00	101,660 00	63,400,597 00
1862				116,000 00		45,532,386 50	2,812,401 50	116,000 00	48,560,788 00
1863				478,450 00		20,595,852 00	1,174,092 80	478,450 00	22,348,394 80
1864			$381,450 00	427,350 00		21,649,345 00	548,214 10	463,800 00	22,661,359 10
1865			535,600 00	541,800 00		25,107,217 50	686,308 00	1,163,330 00	26,936,855 50
1866	$866,240 00	$105,080 00	122,980 00	187,080 00		24,313,945 00	680,264 50	646,970 00	29,540,779 50
1867	1,562,500 00	270,270 00	80,880 00	113,750 00		28,217,187 50	986,871 00	1,879,540 00	31,088,698 50
1868	1,445,100 00	133,410 00	61,330 00	98,565 00		18,114,425 00	1,138,750 00	1,713,385 00	20,944,360 00
1869	1,101,250 00	106,390 00	34,615 00	78,810 00		21,828,037 50	840,746 50	1,279,055 00	23,948,439 00
1870	487,500 00	64,380 00	22,890 00	58,365 00		22,297,312 50	1,737,253 50	611,445 00	24,636,011 00
1871	171,950 00	43,690 00	22,105 00	63,075 00		21,302,475 00	1,955,905 25	283,760 00	23,542,149 25
1872	89,200 00	27,630 00	6,170 00	9,320 00		20,376,495 00	3,029,834 05	123,030 00	33,529,349 05
1873	392,400 00	18,330 00		107,330 00		35,249,337 50	2,945,795 50	494,050 00	38,689,183 00
1874	244,350 00	34,320 00		137,935 00		50,442,690 00	5,982,601 30	411,925 00	56,838,216 30
1875	94,650 00	29,640 00		123,185 00		33,553,965 00	10,070,368 00	230,375 00	43,854,708 00
1876	132,700 00	12,540 00		130,090 00		38,178,963 50	19,126,502 50	260,350 00	57,565,815 00
1877	25,250 00	7,500 00		36,915 00		44,078,199 00	28,549,985 00	62,165 00	72,890,299 00
1878	80 00	68 00		30,566 00		52,798,980 00	28,290,825 50	30,699 00	81,120,490 50
1879	1,175 00	984 00		95,639 00		40,986,912 00	27,227,882 50	97,798 00	68,312,592 50
1880	1,247 50	982 50		267,741 50		56,157,735 00	27,942,437 50	269,971 50	84,370,144 00
Total	5,775,592 50	857,104 50	912,020 00	5,696,523 94	3,926 11	1,133,103,322 00	292,333,436 90	13,283,167 05	1,438,719,925 95

XIV.—*COINAGE EXECUTED during the Calendar Years 1877, 1878, and 1879.*

Denomination.	1877.	1878.	1879.
GOLD.			
Double-eagles	$43, 529, 700 00	$45, 916, 500 00	$28, 889, 260 00
Eagles	211, 490 00	1, 031, 440 00	6, 120, 320 00
Half-eagles	177, 660 00	1, 427, 470 00	3, 727, 155 00
Three-dollars	4, 464 00	248, 970 00	9, 090 00
Quarter-eagles	72, 630 00	1, 160, 650 00	331, 225 00
Dollars	3, 920 00	3, 020 00	3, 030 00
Total gold	43, 990, 864 00	49, 786, 052 00	39, 080, 080 00
SILVER.			
Trade-dollars	13, 092, 710 00	4, 259, 906 00	*1, 541 00
Standard-dollars		22, 495, 550 00	27, 560, 100 00
Half-dollars	7, 540, 255 00	726, 200 00	2, 950 00
Quarter-dollars	6, 024, 927 50	849, 200 00	3, 675 00
Twenty-cents	102 00	120 00	
Dimes	1, 735, 051 00	187, 880 00	1, 510 00
Total silver	28, 393, 045 50	28, 518, 850 00	27, 569, 776 00
MINOR.			
Five-cents		117 50	1, 465 00
Three-cents		70 50	1, 236 00
One-cent	8, 525 00	57, 998 50	162, 312 00
Total minor	8, 525 00	58, 186 50	165, 008 00
Total coinage	72, 401, 434 50	73, 363, 088 50	66, 814, 859 00

* Proof pieces.

XV.—*GENERAL REGULATIONS for the DISTRIBUTION of STANDARD SILVER DOLLARS.*

No. 1.

TREASURY DEPARTMENT,
OFFICE OF THE DIRECTOR OF THE MINT,
Washington, D. C., September 3, 1878.

In conformity with sections 3526 and 3527, Revised Statutes, and with the first section of the act authorizing the coinage of the standard silver dollar and restoring its legal-tender character, passed February 28, 1878, it is hereby ordered and directed that the superintendents of the mints at Philadelphia, San Francisco, Carson, and New Orleans will, upon the receipt of a written request of the Treasurer of the United States, forward, by express, standard silver dollars in the sum of one thousand dollars, or a multiple thereof, to such party or parties as he may designate.

The expense of transportation to be paid by the Mint from the "silver-profit fund."

Shipments will, however, be made only to parties reached through established express lines.

R. E. PRESTON,
Acting Director.

Approved:
JOHN SHERMAN,
Secretary of the Treasury.

No. 2.

TREASURY DEPARTMENT,
OFFICE OF THE DIRECTOR OF THE MINT,
Washington, D. C., August 21, 1880.

In order to facilitate the distribution of standard silver dollars from the mints at Philadelphia, San Francisco, and New Orleans, the following regulations for the government of the superintendents thereof are prescribed:

Upon the receipt from an Assistant Treasurer of the United States of an original certificate of deposit on account of standard silver dollars, giving the name and address of the party or parties to whom the coin is to be sent, the superintendent of the mint in the same city as the Assistant Treasurer issuing the certificate will ship a like amount of standard silver dollars, and pay the charges for transportation from the "silver-profit fund."

The superintendent of the mint will report to the Treasurer of the United States and the Assistant Treasurer, at the close of business each day, the amount of standard silver dollars shipped upon such certificates, giving the number and date of each certificate.

All shipments of standard silver dollars under the foregoing regulations will be treated as a transfer to the Treasurer of the United States.

R. E. PRESTON,
Acting Director.

Approved:
JOHN SHERMAN,
Secretary of the Treasury.

XVI.—ESTIMATION OF VALUE OF FOREIGN COINS.

BUREAU OF THE MINT,
Washington, D. C., December 29, 1879.

Hon. JOHN SHERMAN,
Secretary of the Treasury:

SIR: The money of account of the United States is required by the act of April 2, 1792 (Revised Statutes, section 3563), to "be expressed in dollars or units, dimes or tenths," &c., "a dime being the tenth part of a dollar."

The coinage act of February 12, 1873 (Revised Statutes, section 3511), provides "that the gold coins of the United States shall be a one-dollar piece, which, at the standard weight of twenty-five and eight-tenths grains, shall be the unit of value," &c.

The act of March 3, 1873 (Revised Statutes, section 3564), provides "that the value of foreign coins as expressed in the money of account of the United States shall be that of the pure metal in such coin, of standard value, and the values of the standard coins in circulation of the various nations of the world shall be estimated annually by the Director of the Mint, and be proclaimed on the first day of January by the Secretary of the Treasury."

In estimating the value of coins of foreign countries where gold is the standard of value no difficulty is experienced; the value is readily ascertained by comparing the amount of pure gold contained with that in the gold dollar, but in silver coins the law does not definitely state what shall be the basis of comparison in estimating the value of the pure metal of such coins when silver is the standard of the country.

The coinage act of 1873 discontinued the coinage of the silver dollar of 412½ grains, and also failed to make provision that it should be a unit of value as in case of the one-dollar gold piece, but it still remained an existing coin and a legal tender to the amount of five dollars in any one payment.

The trade-dollar of 420 grains and subsidiary coins of 25 grammes to the dollar were authorized by the same act, and also constituted a legal tender to a like amount, but none of these coins were declared units or standards of value. If it had been intended that the value of foreign silver coins should be ascertained by comparing the pure metal contained with that in the United States silver coins, the law failed to specify what silver coin or what quantity of silver should be the standard for valuation.

I therefore have the honor to request that you will furnish this office with your opinion as to whether under the provisions of the act of March 3, 1873, referred to, the value of foreign silver coins should be estimated by comparing their weight and fineness with that of the silver dollar or other silver coins of the United States, of the nominal value of one dollar, or by taking the commercial bullion value of the pure silver in such foreign silver coins valued in gold dollars as units.

If computed by the former method, what silver coin should be the basis of comparison; and if by the latter method, in what manner should the gold value of the pure silver in such foreign silver coin be ascertained?

Very respectfully,

HORATIO C. BURCHARD, *Director.*

TREASURY DEPARTMENT, OFFICE OF THE SECRETARY,
Washington, D. C., December 30, 1879.

Hon. H. C. BURCHARD,
Director of the Mint:

SIR: I am in receipt of your letter of this date, asking my opinion as to the basis on which estimates of the values of foreign silver coin should be made under the provisions of section 3564, Revised Statutes.

In reply I have to inform you that in my opinion the law clearly contemplates that the estimates should be based on the commercial value of the pure silver contained in the coin of full weight, expressed in terms of the standard unit of value of the United States, which, under the law, is declared to be the gold dollar of the standard weight of 25 ${}^{8}_{10}$ grains. In estimating the commercial value of the pure silver in question, as required by law, a proper basis would seem to be the London quotations of such silver for a period immediately preceding the year for which the estimate is made, and I would suggest that a period of three months be taken for this purpose.

Very respectfully,

JOHN SHERMAN, *Secretary.*

CIRCULAR ESTIMATING AND PROCLAIMING, IN UNITED STATES MONEY OF ACCOUNT, THE VALUES OF THE STANDARD COINS IN CIRCULATION OF THE VARIOUS NATIONS OF THE WORLD.

1880.
DEPARTMENT No. 1. }
SECRETARY'S OFFICE. }

TREASURY DEPARTMENT,
BUREAU OF THE MINT,
Washington, D. C., January 1, 1880.

Hon. JOHN SHERMAN,
    Secretary of the Treasury:

SIR: In pursuance of the provisions of section 3564 of the Revised Statutes of the United States, I have estimated the values of the standard coins in circulation of the various nations of the world, and submit the same in the accompanying table.

Very respectfully,

HORATIO C. BURCHARD,
Director of the Mint.

ESTIMATE of VALUES of FOREIGN COINS.

Country.	Monetary unit.	Standard.	Value in United States money.	Standard coin.
Austria	Florin	Silver..........	$0 41.3	
Belgium	Franc	Gold and silver .	19.3	5, 10, and 20 francs.
Bolivia	Boliviano	Silver..........	83.6	Boliviano.
Brazil	Milreis of 1,000 reis ...	Gold	54.5	
British Possessions in North America.	Dollar	....do	1 00	
Central America.........	Peso	Silver..........	83.6	Peso.
Chili...................	... do	Gold..........	91.2	Condor, doubloon, and escudo.
Denmark	Crown	...do	26.8	10 and 20 crowns.
Ecuador	Peso	Silver..........	83.6	Peso.
Egypt	Pound of 100 piasters .	Gold	4 97.4	5, 10, 25, and 50 piasters.
France.................	Franc................	Gold and silver .	19.3	5, 10, and 20 francs.
Great Britain	Pound sterling........	Gold	4 86.6½	½ sovereign and sovereign.
Greece..................	Drachma	Gold and silver .	19.3	5, 10, 20, 50, and 100 drachmas.
German Empire	Mark	Gold..........	23.8	5, 10, and 20 marks.
India	Rupee of 16 annas ...	Silver..........	39.7	
Italy...................	Lira	Gold and silver .	19.3	5, 10, 20, 50, and 100 lire.
Japan	Yen (gold)...........	....do	99.7	1, 2, 5, 10, and 20 yen.
Liberia	Dollar	Gold	1 00	
Mexico	... do	Silver..........	90.9	Peso or dollar, 5, 10, 25, and 50 centavos.
Netherlands	Florin	Gold and silver .	40.2	
Norway.................	Crown	Gold..........	26.8	10 and 20 crowns.
Peru	Sol..................	Silver..........	83.6	Sol.
Portugal...............	Milreis of 1,000 reis ...	Gold..........	1 08	2, 5, and 10 milreis.
Russia.................	Rouble of 100 copecks.	Silver..........	66.9	¼, ½, and 1 rouble.
Sandwich Islands	Dollar	Gold..........	1 00	
Spain..................	Peseta of 100 centimes.	Gold and silver .	19.3	5, 10, 20, 50, and 100 pesetas.
Sweden.................	Crown	Gold..........	26.8	10 and 20 crowns.
Switzerland.............	Franc................	Gold and silver .	19.3	5, 10, and 20 francs.
Tripoli.................	Mahbub of 20 piasters.	Silver..........	74.8	
Turkey	Piaster	Gold..........	04.4	25, 50, 100, 250, and 500 piasters.
United States of Colombia	Peso.................	Silver..........	83.6	Peso.

TREASURY DEPARTMENT,
Washington, D. C., January 1, 1880.

The foregoing estimation, made by the Director of the Mint, of the value of the foreign coins above mentioned, I hereby proclaim to be the values of such coins expressed in the money of account of the United States, and to be taken in estimating the values of all foreign merchandise, made out in any of said currencies, imported on or after January 1, 1880.

JOHN SHERMAN,
Secretary of the Treasury.

XVII.—*AVERAGE MONTHLY PRICE of FINE SILVER BARS at LONDON and the EQUIVALENT per OUNCE FINE in UNITED STATES MONEY with EXCHANGE at PAR, and the AVERAGE MONTHLY PRICE at NEW YORK of EXCHANGE on LONDON and the AVERAGE MONTHLY PRICE of FINE SILVER BARS at NEW YORK during the fiscal year ended June 30, 1880.*

Date.	Price per ounce British standard, .925 thousandths fine.	Equivalent in United States money per ounce fine with exchange at par, $4, 86, 65.	Average monthly price at New York of exchange on London.	Equivalent in United States money of fine bar silver, 1,000 fine, based on average monthly London quotation with exchange at average monthly rate.	Average monthly New York price of fine bar silver.
1879.	*Pence.*				
July	51⅜	$1 13. 167	$4 87. 7	$1 13. 412	$1 13. 468
August	51⅜	1 13. 030	4 84. 5	1 12. 534	1 12. 600
September	51 7/16	1 13. 030	4 84. 1	1 12. 430	1 12. 192
October	52 1/16	1 14. 674	4 83. 7	1 13. 98	1 13. 810
November	53⅜	1 17. 003	4 83. 8	1 16. 319	1 15. 815
December	52 7/16	1 15. 222	4 84. 7	1 14. 761	1 14. 404
1880.					
January	52⅜	1 15. 085	4 85	1 14. 700	1 14. 394
February	52 7/16	1 14. 674	4 86. 5	1 14. 594	1 14. 840
March	52 1/16	1 14. 126	4 88. 5	1 14. 511	1 14. 479
April	52	1 13. 989	4 88. 4	1 14. 953	1 14. 403
May	52 1/16	1 14. 126	4 89. 4	1 14. 726	1 14. 726
June	52⅜	1 15. 085	4 88. 3	1 15. 712	1 15. 308
Average	52 7/16	1 14. 436	4 86. 34	1 14. 397	1 14. 162

XVIII.—*TABLE showing the RELATIVE MARKET VALUE of GOLD to SILVER, from the date of the PASSAGE of the RESUMPTION ACT (by monthly and yearly averages).*

[Based on London price of silver bullion.]

Date.	1875.	1876.	1877.	1878.	1879.	1880.
January	1 to 16. 38	1 to 16. 10	1 to 16. 95	1 to 17. 51	1 to 18. 81	1 to 17. 90
February	16. 41	17. 48	16. 61	17. 31	18. 90	18. 02
March	16. 38	17. 66	17. 14	17. 35	19. 02	18. 11
April	16. 47	17. 54	17. 86	17. 44	18. 98	18. 13
May	16. 61	17. 79	17. 42	17. 63	18. 71	18. 11
June	16. 93	18. 46	17. 55	17. 73	18. 13	17. 96
July	16. 91	19. 46	17. 42	17. 91	18. 26	17. 90
August	16. 74	18. 00	17. 40	17. 91	18. 28	17. 91
September	16. 62	18. 25	17. 33	18. 22	18. 28	18. 00
October	16. 56	17. 95	17. 11	18. 60	18. 02	18. 08
November	16. 60	17. 43	17. 30	18. 65	17. 66	......
December	16. 72	16. 59	17. 46	18. 86	17. 94	......
Average	16. 606	17. 739	17. 204	17. 904	18. 411	18. 018

XIX.—*STATEMENT of IMPORTS and EXPORTS of GOLD and SILVER during the fiscal year ended June 30, 1880.* (*Reported by Chief of Bureau of Statistics.*)

IMPORTS.

Ports.	Gold.			Silver.				Total.
	Bullion.	Coin.		Bullion.	Coin.			
		American.	Foreign.		American.		Foreign.	
					Trade-dollars.	Other.		
NEW YORK.								
July, 1879	$20,467	$22,690	$71,843	$10,274	$265,078	$180,092	$192,252	$729,686
August, 1879	3,466,940	602,612	2,091,384	6,847	43,638	256,864	244,037	6,712,520
September, 1879	5,145,857	3,965,886	18,126,926	5,950	275	178,969	275,931	27,599,847
October, 1879	3,568,353	3,118,307	12,278,384	4,531	132,358	312,820	130,434	19,564,197
November, 1879	4,737,904	6,553,026	5,766,541	16,020	99,588	81,836	357,394	17,614,909
December, 1879	1,591,009	1,981,578	2,425,960	4,960	54,361	107,591	715,027	6,830,566
January, 1880	459,360	13,905	51,608	1,245	94	174,072	181,136	561,507
February, 1880	13,879	64,374	199,006	....	22,296	162,719	500,107	972,041
March, 1880	154,758	13,332	135,700	695	899	146,148	347,310	792,905
April, 1880	46,762	15,925	16,464	3,580	9,737	146,791	167,131	405,690
May, 1880	8,747	18,069	11,158	90,564	53,517	130,218	230,304	542,577
June, 1880	55,492	27,359	470,433	494	17,041	160,888	280,208	1,020,910
Total	19,298,538	16,245,053	41,649,144	145,163	699,080	3,050,951	3,570,326	83,658,245
SAN FRANCISCO.								
July, 1879	80,862	11,994	....	128,698	....	20,210	191,721	428,485
August, 1879	127,484	6,467	1,700	122,878	3,420	17,036	290,592	479,971
September, 1879	147,125	10,689	4,895	101,653	....	9,896	159,380	433,576
October, 1879	400,222	16,601	620	153,374	....	13,414	213,579	497,810
November, 1879	237,451	15,257	71,240	86,211	25,015	12,853	120,873	577,900
December, 1879	83,921	8,596	140,555	76,698	40,560	15,467	345,270	711,013
January, 1880	7,054	9,900	115,900	83,309	....	5,853	261,922	473,398
February, 1880	46,650	3,929	15,500	238,000	15,000	7,517	98,781	420,377
March, 1880	37,932	6,809	32,412	120,064	....	28,104	401,751	627,152
April, 1880	....	35,833	21,521	198,991	....	11,509	354,695	502,529
May, 1880	20,601	40,553	....	123,370	....	116,368	122,851	423,563
June, 1880	52,976	27,926	....	107,070	....	9,119	180,489	378,180
Total	942,278	194,404	404,283	1,505,905	83,935	267,429	2,645,310	6,043,566
ALL OTHER PORTS.								
July, 1879	4,888	18,872	10,765	47,372	....	30,401	21,022	133,960
August, 1879	1,890	401,080	23,747	66,730	....	13,918	66,352	573,736
September, 1879	50	203,920	22,794	3,936	43	13,685	83,734	228,162
October, 1879	16,400	50,291	16,453	30,640	....	47,311	4,700	150,795
November, 1879	2,890	18,123	23,832	16,306	....	28,922	117,998	203,041
December, 1879	60,583	205,827	14,601	1,667	....	15,191	120,293	518,192
January, 1880	756	130,205	6,793	300	....	3,300	87,805	229,159
February, 1880	790	110,573	9,103	1,300	....	6,678	28,897	157,410
March, 1880	4,306	502,537	4,334	110,784	4	11,017	61,793	695,275
April, 1880	1,581	26,145	2,851	38,997	....	6,011	58,212	143,797
May, 1880	8,055	6,465	11,132	....	....	10,847	107,754	156,097
June, 1880	462	64	13,560	....	....	13,512	6,107	33,765
Total	96,630	1,768,102	159,965	336,326	47	201,453	775,967	3,322,490
Total imports	20,337,445	18,207,559	42,213,392	1,981,425	783,062	3,519,824	6,991,603	93,034,310

EXPORTS (DOMESTIC).

Ports.	Gold.		Silver.			Total.
	Bullion.	Coin.	Bullion.	Coin.		
				Trade dollars.	Other.	
NEW YORK.						
July, 1879	649	5,000	307,451			313,100
August, 1879	971	3,325	182,600			186,896
September, 1879	500	108,400	155,612		65,660	330,172
October, 1879		5,650	196,415		82,885	284,950
November, 1879		7,000	135,000		48,053	190,053
December, 1879		381	305,315		67,100	372,796
January, 1880		112,700	245,000		9,350	367,050
February, 1880		12,400	192,000		7,515	211,915
March, 1880	43,667	14,025	108,000		22,525	188,217
April, 1880		15,000	15,000			30,000
May, 1880		8,000	95,000		5,900	108,900
June, 1880		25,413	311,500		15,000	351,913
Total	45,787	317,294	2,248,893		323,088	2,935,062
SAN FRANCISCO.						
July, 1879	1,280	39,360	155,009	7,962	21,400	225,011
August, 1879	3,080	26,788	804,622	7,390		841,880
September, 1879	2,645	11,398	529,838	13,325		557,206
October, 1879	13,635	40,230	347,804	11,900	240	413,809
November, 1879	8,615	53,872	192,718	1,406		256,611
December, 1879	8,861	91,800	1,154,738	400	1,000	1,256,739
January, 1880		11,915	419,665		500	432,080
February, 1880	1,367	18,207	269,125	1,000	19,226	308,925
March, 1880	286	14,373	17,700		102,600	134,959
April, 1880	550	31,042	72,001		500	104,093
May, 1880		48,513	666,299		9,000	728,812
June, 1880	1,020	55,534	84,452		21,600	112,606
Total	41,279	443,032	4,663,971	43,383	176,066	5,367,731
ALL OTHER PORTS.						
July, 1879		300,000			1,641	301,641
August, 1879		316,500			670	317,170
September, 1879		8,500			725	9,225
October, 1879		226,311			3,857	230,168
November, 1879		34,762			1,800	36,562
December, 1879		30,822			315	31,137
January, 1880		4,600			20,336	24,936
February, 1880		838			29,368	30,206
March, 1880		2,314			14,426	16,740
April, 1880		500			6,857	7,357
May, 1880		2,500			12,703	15,203
June, 1880					24,755	24,755
Total		927,647			117,453	1,045,100
Total domestic exports	87,066	1,687,973	6,912,864	43,383	616,607	9,347,893

EXPORTS (FOREIGN)

Ports.	Gold.		Silver.		Total.
	Bullion.	Coin.	Bullion.	Coin.	
NEW YORK.					
July, 1879	$1,500	....	$46,703	$102,493	$210,696
August, 1879	....	....	199,725	70,923	270,648
September, 1879	....	$1,000	40,000	144,069	185,069
October, 1879	....	....	....	239,803	239,803
November, 1879	....	1,750	17,681	456,424	477,855
December, 1879	....	300	....	267,058	267,358
January, 1880	....	96,990	4,500	352,729	454,219
February, 1880	....	116,800	2,000	274,307	393,107
March, 1880	102,704	982,310	....	249,481	1,441,495
April, 1880	....	42,100	....	122,533	164,633
May, 1880	....	47,484	....	323,285	370,769
June, 1880	....	459,394	....	203,508	662,902
Total	104,204	1,755,128	310,609	2,968,633	5,138,574
SAN FRANCISCO.					
July, 1879	....	1,990	13,900	157,490	173,380
August, 1879	....	....	....	212,421	212,421
September, 1879	....	....	....	149,308	149,308
October, 1879	....	....	....	324,730	324,730
November, 1879	....	....	....	146,205	146,205
December, 1879	....	2,452	....	251,522	253,974
January, 1880	....	....	....	140,214	140,214
February, 1880	....	....	....	325,913	325,913
March, 1880	....	....	....	205,231	205,231
April, 1880	....	....	....	110,300	110,300
May, 1880	....	....	....	487,747	487,747
June, 1880	....	....	....	102,819	102,819
Total	....	4,442	13,900	2,613,900	2,632,242
ALL OTHER PORTS.					
July, 1879	....	....	....	1,325	1,325
August, 1879	....	....	....	....	....
September, 1879	....	....	....	....	....
October, 1879	....	....	....	....	....
November, 1879	....	....	....	....	....
December, 1879	....	212	....	173	385
January, 1880	....	....	....	....	....
February, 1880	....	....	....	....	....
March, 1880	....	....	....	22,500	22,500
April, 1880	....	....	....	....	....
May, 1880	....	....	....	....	....
June, 1880	....	....	....	....	....
Total	....	212	....	23,998	24,210
Total foreign exports	104,204	1,750,782	324,509	5,606,531	7,795,026

XX.—*STATEMENT by COUNTRIES of the NET IMPORTS of AMERICAN SILVER COIN for the fiscal years ended June 30, 1878, 1879, and 1880.*

[From the reports of the Bureau of Statistics.]

Countries.	1878.	1879.	1880.
Argentine Republic		$1,000	
Brazil	$1,300	6,693	$10,531
Central American States	77,063	224,310	122,489
China	65	1,400	90,991
Danish West Indies	475,170	343,339	96,690
France	1,200	231,325	844
French Possessions in Africa	500	150	
French Possessions, all other		132	2,349
Germany	4,268	43,799	15,465
England	193,969	2,492,061	907,021
Gibraltar		687	169
Nova Scotia, New Brunswick, and Prince Edward's Island			918
Quebec, Ontario, Manitoba, Rupert's Land, and the Northwest Territory	6,979	7,458	3,565
British Columbia			1,492
British West Indies and British Honduras	102,887	80,982	156,741
British Possessions in Africa and adjacent islands	30,564	20,899	32,796
British Possessions in Australasia		4	508
Hawaiian Islands	300		4,161
Hayti	769,255	785,398	739,338
Japan	785	950	16,621
Mexico	475,043	423,000	306,649
Dutch West Indies	20,715	28,005	33,150
Dutch Guiana			2,530
Peru			8,623
Azores, Madeira, and Cape Verde Islands	35	8	215,423
San Domingo	181,365	222,678	
Spain			804
Cuba	28,674	192,237	143,748
Porto Rico	205,848	392,431	180,985
United States of Colombia	182,933	368,270	184,354
Venezuela		4,341	20,604
Total imports	2,764,858	5,873,151	*3,291,463
Total exports	†5,394,270	†11,526,886	§659,990
Net imports	‖2,629,412	4,346,265	2,631,473

* Includes 783,062 trade dollars.   † Includes 228,264 trade dollars.   ‡ Includes 288,137 trade dollars.
§ Includes 43,383 trade dollars.   ‖ Excess of exports.

15 F

XXI.—*TABLE exhibiting the VALUE and CHARACTER of the GOLD and SILVER USED in MANUFACTURES and the ARTS in the UNITED STATES during the fiscal year ended June 30, 1880, as REPORTED by PERSONS and FIRMS ENGAGED in the MANUFACTURES NAMED, in response to circular inquiries addressed from the BUREAU of the MINT.*

Manufactures of—	Number of letters sent.	Answers.	Number manufacturing.	Not replying.	Gold. United States coins melted and worked up.	Fine bars used.	Foreign coins and old manufactured articles made into new work.	Total.	Silver. United States coins melted and worked up.	Fine bars used.	Foreign coins and old manufactured articles made into new work.	Total.	Grand total.
Watches and jewelry	6,444	2,451	1,172	2,821	$2,005,983	$3,901,352	$610,651	$6,517,986	$104,460 00	$777,483	$77,699 00	$959,642	$7,477,628
Watch cases and manufactures	309	110	77	122	203,180	947,641	52,051	1,202,872	420,032 50	1,351,901	44,434 50	1,817,248	3,020,120
Gold leaf and plate	333	153	103	77	183,520	623,360	44,040	850,920	14,745 00	541,696	49,887 00	606,320	1,457,255
Chemicals	84	35	9	40	14,575	34,635	6,200	55,410	25 00	76,494	....	76,519	131,929
Instruments	120	42	20	58	1,510	4,050	3,430	8,998	1,601 00	1,616	1,125 00	4,432	11,428
Totals	7,290	2,791	1,381	3,118	2,408,768	5,511,047	714,378	8,634,193	541,834 50	2,749,100	173,145 50	3,464,170	12,098,363

XXII.—*STATEMENT of the ESTIMATED DISPOSITION made of the GOLD and SILVER BULLION in the COINAGE MINTS and NEW YORK ASSAY OFFICE DEPOSITED during and on hand at the commencement of the fiscal year ended June 30, 1880.*

Disposition.	On hand June 30, 1879.	Source obtained.		Total.
		Deposited.		
		Domestic.	Coin, plate, jewelry, and foreign bullion.	
GOLD.				
Coinage....................................	$5,275,424	$28,178,359	$22,803,952	$56,157,735
Arts		5,358,739	1,812,623	7,141,362
Exports...................................		87,068	....	87,068
On hand at close of the year	....	2,297,541	38,496,817	40,724,358
Total......................	5,275,424	35,921,705	63,113,392	104,310,521
SILVER.				
Coinage....................................	5,226,819	20,706,116	2,010,502	27,943,437
Arts...	....	3,593,645	497,264	4,090,909
Exports...................................	....	2,322,092	....	2,322,092
On hand at close of the year	752,709	5,510,904	....	6,263,613
Total......................	5,979,528	32,132,757	2,507,766	40,620,051

XXIII.—*STATEMENT of GOLD and SILVER BULLION and COIN on hand at the UNITED STATES MINTS and NEW YORK ASSAY OFFICE, years ending June 30, 1879, and June 30, 1880.*

June 30, 1879.	Philadelphia.	San Francisco.	Carson.	New Orleans.	New York.	Total.
Gold bullion	$1,054,729 29	$1,557,700 82	$45,216 32	$967,520 62	$2,530,257 40	$5,275,424 45
Gold coin	1,601,540 32	1,945,725 00	296,010 00	52,466 04	1,899,758 33	5,795,394 39
Silver bullion ...	1,909,487 30	371,984 26	87,553 42	546,701 08	3,063,801 57	5,979,527 63
Silver coin	996,375 16	351,219 22	1,031,468 35	669,555 51	136,026 14	3,184,648 38
Total	5,562,132 27	4,226,629 30	1,461,148 09	1,336,237 75	7,638,845 44	20,234,992 85

June 30, 1880.	Philadelphia.	San Francisco.	Carson.	New Orleans.	New York.	Total.
Gold bullion ...	$9,887,445 94	$2,042,450 73	$135,260 98	$27,723 17	$28,581,428 09	$40,724,337 91
Gold coin	3,419,347 50	749,134 18	297,784 57	67,319 67	7,503,642 08	12,037,228 55
Silver bullion ...	3,304,258 80	969,168 25	276,381 93	619,997 07	1,113,866 47	6,283,613 12
Silver coin	1,378,345 19	6,266,004 72	1,442,430 96	3,056,417 34	30,862 62	12,174,050 83
Total	17,989,397 43	10,026,727 88	2,301,857 44	3,771,457 65	37,229,799 81	71,219,230 41

XXIV.—AVERAGE and COMPARATIVE PRICE of the PRINCIPAL DOMESTIC COMMODITIES EXPORTED from the UNITED STATES.

Commodities.	Average prices during month of—			Average price during year ended—		Comparative rates of 1880.	
	June, 1879.	December, 1879.	June, 1880.	June 30, 1879.	June 30, 1880.	Assuming prices of 1879 as 100.	Assuming prices of 1879 as 100.
						Per ct.	Per ct.
Acids ....pound..	$0 3.5	$0 2.8	$0 2.8	$0 2.6	$0 2.9	54.7	111.5
Hogs ....piece..	8 09.3	5 07.5	5 80.7	9 32.0	5 04.6	32.0	54.1
Horned cattle ....do....	56 33.1	61 96.8	72 34.6	61 28.7	73 01.6	21.8	119.1
Horses.......................do....	100 35.0	121 27.3	144 51.6	196 86.8	220 63.3	263.6	112.0
Mules........................do....	100 98.3	115 70.6	90 00.0	127 85.6	102 41.6	72.6	80.1
Sheep........................do	7 16.3	3 72.2	2 56.4	5 02.1	4 26.8	177.4	85.0
Ashes, pot and pearl ....pound..	5.5	6.0	7.6	5.6	8.9	123.6	158.9
Beer:							
In bottles ....dozen..	1 83.1	1 76.5	1 74.8	1 62.2	1 76.8	85.5	110.3
In casks ....gallon..	39.0	33.8	37.8	37.6	32.6	91.3	86.7
Bones and bone-dust ....cwt..	63.1	5 10.1	2 d8.6	1 66.9	1 42.0	86.3	85.0
Bone-black, lamp-black ....pound..	20.9	5.4	7.4	4.7	5.2	118.6	110.6
Barley....................bushel..	39.8	64.9	46.5	58.0	69.5	120.6	134.1
Bread and biscuit ....pound..	4.2	4.5	4.2	4.3	4.6	59.7	107.0
Indian corn ....bushel..	46.1	61.0	51.5	47.1	54.2	58.0	115.0
Indian-corn meal ....barrel..	2 37.6	3 03.9	2 78.1	2 64.9	2 79.8	56.9	105.6
Oats......................bushel..	44.3	51.9	42.2	29.6	40.2	63.9	135.8
Rye........................do	65.2	94.9	83.6	63.9	81.1	71.7	126.9
Rye-flour ....barrel..	2 01.8	5 25.0	4 26.0	3 61.3	4 76.4	86.3	156.0
Wheat.....................bushel..	1 07.8	1 36.0	1 27.3	1 06.8	1 34.3	96.4	116.3
Wheat-flour................barrel..	5 25.6	6 13.3	5 69.9	5 25.2	5 97.6	96.1	111.8
Bricks........................M.	6 39.2	10 42.4	8 01.0	6 60.7	7 78.4	70.0	117.8
Candles ....pound..	11.5	12.2	12.1	12.3	12.1	73.8	98.3
Coal:							
Anthracite................ton..	2 92.6	3 82.8	4 33.0	3 23.0	3 47.1	52.3	107.4
Bituminous...............do....	2 38.1	3 48.3	3 67.2	3 62.0	3 12.2	66.2	86.2
Copper, pigs, bars.........pound..	14.9	20.1	20.3	15.9	15.8	90.8	93.6
Cordage, rope, twine.........do....	8.8	10.7	14.3	9.8	11.0	58.6	112.2
Cotton:							
Sea-island............pound..	26.3	35.0	25.2	27.4	33.2	61.8	121.1
Other ....do....	11.5	11.5	11.6	9.2	11.5	48.9	125.0
Colored ....yard..	6.6	8.2	8.0	7.1	7.8	45.8	109.8
Uncolored ....do....	7.1	7.7	8.6	7.4	8.4	51.8	113.5
Ginseng ....pound..	1 23.2	1 45.7	1 35.8	1 19.0	1 36.2	142.3	114.4
Glue......................do....	10.1	11.0	15.7	11.1	15.0	66.0	136.3
Hay ....ton..	16 10.9	14 26.5	18 05.4	15 02.6	15 95.3	96.4	106.1
Hemp cables, cordage.......cwt..	9 77.7	10 72.4	11 01.9	10 51.6	10 91.4	71.5	103.7
Hops ....pound..	10.3	34.4	25.3	12.8	26.4	172.5	206.2
Ice.........................ton..	4 05.5	2 86.2	2 97.5	3 40.0	2 90.3	73.5	88.0
Apples, dried ....pound..	4.8	6.6	7.1	4.0	6.0	63.8	150.0
India-rubber boots, &c......pair..	1 87.3	1 49.1	1 95.3	1 56.1	2 00.8	61.8	128.6
Iron:							
Pig ....pound..	1.5	1.4	1.1	1.2	1.8	112.5	150.0
Bar ....do....	2.2	5.6	3.9	2.6	3.4	68.0	130.7
Boiler-plate ....do....	4.8	4.0	3.5	3.1	3.5	76.0	112.9
Railroad bars ....do....	1.0	1.3	1.6	1.5	2.1	58.3	140.0
Sheet, band, &c..........do....	4.2	3.7	5.4	3.1	5.2	96.3	167.7
Car-wheels ....piece..	8 95.7	5 84.6	9 96.8	8 78.7	7 92.5	39.7	90.1
Nails and spikes ....pound..	2.7	4.1	3.6	2.7	3.9	68.4	144.4
Steel:							
Ingots...................pound..	13.7	19.5	14.4	8.3	11.5	96.6	138.5
Railroad bars...........do....				2.1	2.1		100.0
Leather, sole and upper.....do....	19.6	27.2	22.1	20.3	23.2	81.7	114.2
Boots and shoes ....pair..	1 06.4	1 26.7	1 17.7	1 22.2	1 16.6	76.7	95.4
Lime and cement..........barrel..	1 16.1	1 14.1	1 30.5	1 22.1	1 25.2	63.4	102.5
Rosin and turpentine.......do....	1 07.1	2 05.4	2 70.5	1 94.0	2 27.6	74.7	117.3
Tar and pitch.............do....	1 93.7	2 30.7	2 15.9	1 93.7	2 05.5	67.9	106.0
Oil cake....................pound..	1.3	1.4	1.3	1.2	1.3	61.9	108.3
Mineral-oil, crude ....gallon..	7.6	7.7	6.5	8.4	6.8	31.6	80.9
Naphthae, benzine &c......do....	7.6	6.2	6.5	8.3	6.4	69.6	77.1
Illuminating oil ....do....	8.9	8.9	9.3	10.8	8.6	28.4	79.6
Lubricating oil ....do....	22.1	18.2	21.0	26.3	20.1	...	76.4
Lard-oil..................do....	44.7	58.6	54.0	52.8	54.1	39.3	102.4
Neat's-foot oil.............do....	70.5	90.7	79.2	92.5	77.4	50.7	83.6

XXIV.—*AVERAGE and COMPARATIVE PRICE, &c.*—Continued.

Commodities.	Average prices during month of—			Average price during year ended—		Comparative rates of 1880.	
	June, 1879.	December, 1879.	June, 1880.	June 30, 1879.	June 30, 1880.	Assuming prices of 1879 as 100.	Assuming prices of 1879 as 100.
						Per ct.	Per ct.
Sperm-oil ....gallon..	$0 82.8	$1 00.6	$1 02.2	$0 86.5	$1 01.0	63.5	114.1
Whale-oil ....do....	29.5	35.8	35.9	33.8	34.1	46.4	100.9
Cotton-seed oil.............do....	41.6	46.8	44.6	41.7	46.0	....	110.3
Linseed-oil.................do....	72.6	86.5	78.0	73.3	81.2	76.7	110.7
Gunpowder ....pound..	13.5	11.0	13.4	13.2	14.7	93.6	111.3
Bacon and hams ....do....	6.7	6.5	6.8	6.9	6.7	42.6	97.1
Fresh beef ....do....	9.3	9.8	8.6	9.6	8.7	....	90.6
Salted beef ....do....	5.8	6.7	6.4	6.8	6.3	87.5	100.0
Butter ....do....	12.9	21.1	17.5	14.1	17.0	56.0	120.5
Cheese ....do....	7.8	11.7	11.4	8.6	9.5	62.0	107.9
Eggs ....dozen..	12.3	22.8	11.8	15.5	16.4	41.5	105.8
Fish:							
Dried ....cwt..	4 07.2	3 98.0	3 96.9	3 79.8	4 11.9	79.4	108.4
Pickled ....barrel.	5 23.4	5 04.1	5 29.7	6 98.9	5 23.1	63.9	88.9
Lard ....pound..	6.6	8.7	7.4	6.9	7.4	44.8	107.2
Mutton, fresh ....do....	9.5	7.3	6.9	8.5	7.5	....	88.2
Pork ....do....	5.8	6.7	6.3	5.6	6.1	44.8	106.9
Onions ....bushel.	90.3	97.6	1 43.9	92.7	96.7	54.1	97.6
Potatoes ....do....	97.3	69.5	76.5	87.1	74.9	108.5	85.9
Quicksilver ....pound..	33.4	40.7	38.3	39.1	38.0	93.6	97.1
Rags ....do....	1.0	4.1	1.4	2.0	1.8	20.2	90.0
Rice ....do....	8.6	8.1	7.0	4.8	7.2	122.0	150.0
Salt ....bushel.	56.2	20.8	41.0	31.1	29.8	74.3	95.8
Cotton-seed ....pound..	.9	.9	.5	.6	1.1	....	137.5
Soap ....do....	4.8	4.7	4.4	5.0	4.7	55.7	90.4
Sperm aceti ....do....	23.1	22.4	20.1	24.0	22.7	69.0	94.5
Spirits:							
Grain ....gallon..	28.9	35.8	20.0	32.0	25.5	12.5	79.6
Molasses ....do....	29.9	32.8	33.1	32.1	30.9	41.3	96.2
Spirits of turpentine........do....	25.4	39.7	27.4	27.0	30.0	71.7	111.1
Starch ....pound..	3.7	4.9	4.8	4.2	4.3	52.4	102.3
Sugar:							
Brown ....pound..	7.2	....	6.8	7.2	6.3	56.2	87.5
Refined ....do....	8.0	9.1	9.2	8.5	9.0	72.0	105.8
Molasses................gallon..	11.7	16.6	20.1	19.4	15.9	50.0	77.3
Tallow ....pound..	6.3	7.1	6.7	6.9	6.2	61.3	89.8
Tobacco, leaf ....do....	7.6	7.4	8.9	7.8	7.5	68.2	96.1
Varnish..................gallon..	1 96.9	1 55.9	2 61.8	1 57.4	2 11.6	133.3	164.4
Wax, bees'..............pound..	21.7	23.7	33.1	27.1	25.2	63.6	92.9
Boards, planks ....M feet..	14 12.1	14 87.4	15 84.3	14 44.6	14.80.8	71.4	102.5
Timber, sawed ....cubic foot..	12.0	12.4	14.1	13.1	13.5	76.9	103.9
Wool, raw ....pound..	29.8	....	16.7	29.0	37.5	104.4	120.3
Zinc:							
Ore ....cwt..	3 33.1	3 08.5	3 60.0	37.8	3 22.7	60.5	85.8
Plates, bars...........pound..	7.3	8.8	8.9	8.0	8.7	90.6	108.7
Average	....	....	....	....	....	74.0	108.5

XXV.—*TABLE SHOWING the MOVEMENT of SPECIE in FRANCE, PRODUC-TION and CONSUMPTION, and the INCREASE PER ANNUM, from 1850 to 1878.*

GOLD.

Year.	Excess of imports over exports.	Excess of exports over imports.	Production of metallurgical works.	Consumed in arts and manufactures.	Gain during the year.	Loss during the year.	Total increase.
	Francs.	*Francs.*	*Francs.*	*Francs.*	*Francs.*	*Francs.*	*Francs.*
1850	16, 989, 000				16, 969, 000		16, 969, 000
1851	84, 602, 000				84, 902, 000		101, 591, 000
1852	16, 908, 000				16, 908, 000		118, 499, 000
1853	289, 059, 000				289, 059, 000		407, 558, 000
1854	416, 122, 000				416, 122, 000		823, 680, 000
1855	218, 243, 000		822, 000	35, 390, 000	183, 736, 000		1, 007, 416, 000
1856	375, 253, 000		247, 000	35, 450, 000	340, 050, 000		1, 347, 466, 000
1857	445, 822, 000		260, 000	48, 485, 000	397, 597, 000		1, 745, 063, 000
1858	487, 105, 000		326, 000	45, 960, 000	441, 471, 000		2, 186, 534, 000
1859	539, 343, 000		963, 000	40, 815, 000	498, 751, 000		2, 685, 335, 000
1860	311, 690, 000		1, 755, 000	45, 050, 000	265, 404, 800		2, 950, 789, 900
1861		22, 734, 000	1, 590, 000	46, 505, 000		68, 640, 000	2, 882, 080, 000
1862	165, 036, 000		1, 783, 000	51, 130, 000	115, 661, 000		2, 997, 731, 000
1863	11, 976, 000		1, 700, 000	54, 615, 000		40, 920, 000	2, 956, 792, 000
1864	125, 142, 000		2, 603, 000	53, 870, 000	74, 964, 000		3, 031, 656, 000
1865	150, 824, 000		2, 728, 000	51, 225, 000	102, 322, 000		3, 133, 978, 000
1866	465, 252, 000		2, 447, 000	50, 626, 000	417, 074, 000		3, 551, 052, 000
1867	408, 674, 000		2, 531, 000	49, 920, 000	361, 285, 000		3, 912, 337, 000
1868	212, 863, 000		2, 603, 000	49, 735, 000	165, 731, 000		4, 078, 068, 000
1869	274, 354, 000		2, 591, 000	49, 500, 000	227, 445, 000		4, 305, 513, 000
1870	119, 706, 000		1, 178, 000	36, 975, 000	84, 869, 000		4, 390, 382, 000
1871		213, 814, 000	1, 513, 000	31, 245, 000		243, 846, 000	4, 146, 536, 000
1872		52, 592, 000	1, 408, 000	49, 720, 000		101, 204, 000	4, 045, 332, 000
1873		108, 630, 000	3, 091, 000	43, 418, 000		149, 053, 000	3, 896, 279, 000
1874	431, 250, 000		2, 913, 000	47, 105, 000	386, 908, 000		4, 283, 277, 000
1875	470, 320, 000		3, 288, 000	49, 550, 000	424, 058, 000		4, 707, 335, 000
1876	503, 650, 000			44, 545, 000	459, 107, 000		5, 166, 443, 000
1877	456, 736, 000			44, 628, 000	411, 111, 000		5, 577, 553, 000
1878	236, 404, 900			54, 085, 000	182, 319, 000		5, 759, 872, 000

SILVER.

Year.	Excess of imports over exports.	Excess of exports over imports.	Production of metallurgical works.	Consumed in arts and manufactures.	Gain during the year.	Loss during the year.	Decrease.
	Francs.	*Francs.*	*Francs.*	*Francs.*	*Francs.*	*Francs.*	*Francs.*
1850	72, 584, 000				72, 584, 000		
1851	77, 980, 000				77, 980, 000		
1852		2, 447, 000				2, 447, 000	
1853		116, 885, 000				116, 885, 000	
1854		163, 694, 000				163, 694, 000	
1855		197, 160, 000	1, 920, 000	16, 395, 000		212, 573, 000	
1856		288, 623, 000	7, 013, 000	20, 970, 000		297, 580, 000	
1857		359, 820, 000	10, 197, 000	18, 690, 000		368, 313, 000	
1858		14, 940, 000	11, 716, 000	18, 205, 000		21, 429, 000	
1859		171, 523, 000	10, 902, 000	18, 350, 000		178, 914, 000	
1860		157, 343, 000	10, 991, 000	19, 615, 000		165, 967, 000	
1861		61, 513, 000	9, 140, 000	19, 380, 000		72, 093, 000	
1862		85, 181, 000	4, 931, 000	19, 110, 000		101, 200, 000	
1863		68, 341, 000	9, 796, 000	18, 655, 000		77, 290, 000	
1864		42, 474, 000	7, 441, 000	15, 550, 000		50, 583, 000	
1865	72, 586, 000		7, 073, 000	15, 235, 000	64, 423, 000		
1866	44, 905, 000		7, 006, 000	15, 515, 000	36, 546, 000		
1867	189, 840, 000		6, 096, 000	15, 245, 000	181, 480, 000		
1868	109, 275, 000		9, 585, 000	15, 875, 000	102, 985, 000		
1869	111, 423, 000		10, 113, 000	14, 815, 000	106, 722, 000		
1870	35, 467, 000		8, 070, 000	9, 910, 000	33, 627, 000		
1871	15, 516, 000		6, 290, 000	11, 585, 000	10, 140, 000		
1872	102, 256, 000		7, 877, 000	19, 065, 000	90, 782, 000		
1873	181, 406, 000		7, 095, 000	22, 005, 000	166, 588, 000		
1874	360, 934, 000		10, 155, 000	15, 250, 000	355, 839, 000		
1875	185, 343, 000		3, 787, 000	10, 965, 000	178, 165, 000		
1876	140, 355, 000			16, 435, 000	123, 920, 000		
1877	105, 960, 000			15, 800, 000	90, 160, 000		
1878	118, 834, 000			16, 250, 000	102, 584, 000		35, 404, 000

XXVI.—*TABLE SHOWING the SPECIE and PAPER CIRCULATION in FRANCE from 1850 to 1878, together with COMPARATIVE PRICE of EXPORTS and IMPORTS for the years stated on the BASIS of PRICES for the same commodities in the year 1862.*

Year	Gold circulation	Silver circulation	Paper circulation	Specie (gold and silver) circulation	Total specie and paper circulation	Fluctuation in price of imports. a	Fluctuation in price of exports. a	Average of imports and exports.
	Francs.	*Francs.*	*Francs.*	*-Francs.*	*Francs.*			
1850	2, 126, 607, 000	3, 326, 146, 000	511, 900, 000	5, 452, 753, 000	5, 964, 653, 000	82	91	86.5
1851	2, 111, 209, 000	3, 404, 105, 000	802, 900, 000	5, 615, 314, 000	6, 218, 214, 000	80	90	85
1852	2, 228, 117, 000	3, 401, 658, 000	672, 000, 000	5, 629, 775, 000	6, 301, 775, 000	81	98	89.5
1853	2, 517, 176, 000	3, 284, 773, 000	632, 000, 000	5, 801, 949, 000	6, 433, 949, 000	88	109	98.5
1854	2, 933, 298, 000	3, 121, 079, 000	628, 300, 000	6, 054, 377, 000	6, 682, 677, 000	91	108	99.5
1855	3, 117, 034, 000	2, 907, 506, 000	592, 800, 000	6, 024, 540, 000	6, 617, 340, 000	95	104	99.5
1856*	3, 457, 084, 000	2, 609, 926, 000	583, 100, 000	6, 067, 010, 000	6, 650, 110, 000	106.5	111.5	109
1857	3, 854, 681, 000	2, 241, 613, 000	532, 300, 000	6, 096, 294, 000	6, 628, 594, 000	105	110	107.5
1858	4, 296, 152, 000	2, 220, 184, 000	687, 300, 000	6, 516, 336, 000	7, 203, 636, 000	92	102	97
1859	4, 794, 943, 000	2, 041, 270, 000	678, 500, 000	6, 836, 213, 000	7, 514, 713, 000	95	109	102
1860	5, 060, 347, 000	1, 875, 403, 000	747, 200, 000	6, 935, 750, 000	7, 682, 950, 000	98	105	101.5
1861	4, 991, 698, 000	1, 803, 370, 000	715, 800, 000	6, 795, 068, 000	7, 510, 868, 000	99	99	99
1862	5, 107, 349, 000	1, 702, 110, 000	781, 500, 000	6, 809, 459, 000	7, 591, 059, 000	†100	†100	†100
1863	5, 066, 410, 000	1, 624, 860, 000	754, 900, 000	6, 691, 290, 000	7, 446, 190, 000	102.5	100.8	101.6
1864	5, 141, 274, 000	1, 574, 297, 000	722, 300, 000	6, 715, 571, 000	7, 437, 871, 000	104.5	101.3	102.6
1865	5, 243, 596, 000	1, 638, 720, 000	879, 700, 000	6, 882, 316, 000	7, 762, 016, 000	99.2	97.8	98.5
1866	5, 860, 670, 000	1, 675, 266, 000	938, 900, 000	7, 335, 936, 000	8, 272, 836, 000	93.5	91.5	92.5
1867	6, 021, 955, 000	1, 856, 666, 000	1, 122, 500, 000	7, 878, 621, 000	9, 001, 221, 000	89.7	87	88.3
1868	6, 187, 586, 000	1, 959, 651, 000	1, 382, 600, 000	8, 147, 237, 000	9, 530, 137, 000	87.2	83.5	85.3
1869	6, 415, 131, 000	2, 066, 373, 000	1, 398, 600, 000	8, 481, 504, 000	9, 880, 104, 000	86.6	82.9	84.7
1870	‡6, 500, 000, 000	‡2, 100, 000, 000	‡3, 100, 000, 000	8, 600, 000, 000	....	84.3	81.2	85.2
1871	6, 256, 154, 000	2, 110, 140, 000	3, 325, 400, 000	8, 366, 294, 000	10, 091, 694, 000	93.9	81.4	87.6
1872	6, 154, 950, 000	2, 200, 902, 000	3, 656, 300, 000	8, 355, 852, 000	11, 012, 152, 000	97.3	83.3	90.3
1873	6, 005, 897, 000	2, 367, 490, 000	2, 807, 700, 000	8, 373, 387, 000	11, 181, 087, 000	96.1	80.3	88.2
1874	6, 392, 895, 000	2, 723, 329, 000	2, 644, 800, 000	9, 116, 224, 000	11, 761, 024, 000	89.9	76.6	83.2
1875	6, 816, 953, 000	2, 901, 494, 000	2, 438, 000, 000	9, 718, 447, 000	12, 156, 447, 000	86.7	73.8	80.2
1876	7, 276, 060, 000	3, 025, 414, 000	2, 562, 700, 000	10, 301, 474, 000	12, 864, 174, 000	87.5	75.9	81.7
1877	7, 587, 171, 000	3, 215, 574, 000	2, 468, 300, 000	10, 802, 745, 000	13, 271, 045, 000	85.2	72.9	79
1878	7, 860, 490, 000	3, 218, 158, 000	2, 207, 300, 000	11, 087, 648, 000	13, 294, 948, 000	78.8	67.3	73

*a*Journal of the Statistical Society, December, 1879, p. 853.   *War with Russia.   † Comparison made on basis of 100 in 1862.
‡ Mr. Ernest Seyd in his testimony before the Select Committee of Parliament on Depreciation of Silver, estimated the quantity of gold money present before 1871 at £260,000,000; full legal-tender silver £70,000,000, and subsidiary change £14,000,000. (Report of Committee, p. 56.)

REPORT OF THE FIRST COMPTROLLER.

REPORT

OF

THE FIRST COMPTROLLER OF THE TREASURY.

TREASURY DEPARTMENT,
FIRST COMPTROLLER'S OFFICE,
Washington, November 10, 1880.

SIR: In compliance with the request contained in your letter of September 14, 1880, I have the honor to submit the following report of the transactions of this office during the fiscal year which ended June 30, 1880.

The following warrants were received, examined, countersigned, entered into blotters, and posted into ledgers under their proper heads of appropriations:

Kind.	Number.	Amounts covered thereby.
APPROPRIATION.		
Treasury proper	30	$93, 171, 207 53
Public debt	1	531, 144, 303 40
Diplomatic and consular	1	1, 064, 735 00
Customs	6	14, 735, 488 29
Internal revenue	5	4, 308, 422 96
Interior civil	9	2, 753, 882 81
Interior proper	43	65, 745, 019 86
War	19	99, 864, 026 92
Navy	15	14, 570, 435 98
	129	737, 399, 814 75
ACCOUNTABLE AND SETTLEMENT.		
Treasury proper	2, 950	27, 903, 075 97
Public debt	100	531, 883, 450 04
Quarterly salaries	1, 301	561, 404 33
Diplomatic and consular	2, 661	1, 251, 787 52
Customs	4, 766	17, 415, 959 73
Internal revenue	4, 482	5, 451, 119 61
Judiciary	2, 537	2, 721, 993 87
Interior civil	1, 710	3, 531, 890 60
Interior proper	3, 574	64, 541, 953 00
War	3, 574	59, 656, 690 65
Navy	2, 069	26, 077, 949 75
	29, 733	714, 986, 297 97
COVERING.		
Customs	1, 352	186, 522, 064 60
Internal revenue	1, 718	124, 009, 373 92
Public lands	1, 085	1, 916, 506 60
Miscellaneous revenue	7, 579	233, 792, 768 88
Interior proper repay	566	1, 819, 321 47
War repay	1, 066	1, 373, 711 93
Navy repay	399	6, 540, 965 01
Miscellaneous repay	1, 925	3, 795, 224 97
	16, 440	558, 869, 937 36
Total	46, 302	2, 011, 258, 050 08

Accounts have been received from the auditing offices, revised, recorded, and the balances thereon certified to the Register of the Treasury, as follows:

Kind.	Number.	Vouchers.	Amount involved.
FROM THE FIRST AUDITOR.			
1. *Judiciary.*			
Accounts of United States marshals for their fees, and expenses of United States courts, and accounts of United States district attorneys, United States commissioners, and clerks of the United States courts	2, 697	....	$3, 067, 157 19
Judgments by Court of Claims examined and ordered paid....	36	....	212, 516 74
Total....................................	2, 733	60, 008	3, 279, 673 93
2. *Public Debt.*			
Accounts of the Treasurer of the United States:			
For coupons paid in coin	68	3, 066, 715	29, 083, 604 18
For coupons of Treasury notes, Louisville and Portland Canal stock, and the water stock and old funded debt of the District of Columbia..	26	59, 428	766, 641 07
For registered stock of the District of Columbia redeemed	3	1, 040	941, 165 88
For District of Columbia 3.05 bonds purchased for sinking fund	2	454	236, 745 56
For United States called bonds redeemed	29	520, 776	558, 991, 228 97
For United States bonds purchased for sinking fund	5	20, 212	38, 058, 256 69
For sinking fund Union and Central Pacific Railroad stock	2	2	88, 500 00
For interest on United States registered stock (paid on schedules)	35	28, 859	17, 139, 017 75
For interest on Pacific Railroad stock	22	1, 629	2, 122, 960 36
For interest checks, funded loan of 1881, 1891, and consols of 1907	5	50, 890	13, 254, 753 06
For commissions on 4 per cent. bonds	2	2	68, 500 00
For redemption of gold, silver, and refunding certificates	36	2, 723, 163	37, 994, 152 27
For redemption of certificates of deposit, act of June 8, 1872	14	12, 480	115, 690, 000 00
For redemption of legal-tender notes and fractional currency ...	25	1, 542	88, 790, 294 66
For redemption of old demand notes and old Treasury notes ...	56	834	28, 380 83
For interest on Navy pension fund	1	1	420, 000 00
Total.......................................	351	6, 494, 113	903, 654, 199 33
3. *Public Buildings.*			
Embracing accounts for the construction of public buildings throughout the United States; accounts of the geological, geographical, and coast surveys; accounts in relation to charitable institutions and public buildings and grounds in the District of Columbia; accounts for the Smithsonian Institution and museums; for the United States Fish Commission; for incidental expenses of the Patent Office; for repairs of the Capitol and improvement of the Capitol grounds; for the construction of the Washington Monument, and for salaries and contingent expenses of the State Department in Washington..	412	37, 943	4, 943, 466 80
4. *Steamboats.*			
Accounts for salaries and incidental expenses of inspectors of hulls and boilers	691	6, 991	250, 040 00
5. *Territorial.*			
Accounts for salaries of Territorial officers and for the legislative and contingent expenses incidental to the government of the Territories	251	2, 147	222, 302 81
6. *Mint and Assay.*			
Accounts for gold, silver, and nickel coinage; for bullion; for salaries of the officers and employés of the several mints, and for the general expenses of the same	222	106, 087	1, 193, 616 91
Bullion deposits and transfers.............................	....	....	225, 091, 645 96
7. *Transportation.*			
Accounts for the transportation of gold and silver coin and bullion, minor and base coins, United States currency, national-bank notes, complete and incomplete coin certificates, registered and coupon bonds, mutilated currency, canceled and incomplete securities, national-bank notes for redemption, stamp-paper, stationery, boxes, parcels, &c...................	160	54, 274	206, 515 00

Kind.	Number.	Vouchers.	Amount involved.
8. *Congressional.*			
Accounts for salaries of the officers and employés and for contingent and other expenses of the United States Senate and House of Representatives	138	5,006	$816,602 21
9. *Outstanding Liabilities.*			
Accounts arising from demands for the payment of checks, the amounts of which have been covered into the Treasury...	104	139	13,760 61
10. *District of Columbia.*			
Accounts for the payment of claims of workingmen, filed under the act of Congress approved June 20, 1878, and accounts of the Commissioners of the District of Columbia.	127	*1,970	67,479 78
11. *Public Printing.*			
Accounts of the Public Printer for the salaries and wages of the employés of the Government Printing Office, for the purchase of materials for printing, and for contingent expenses of the Government Printing Office	159	630	456,000 00
12. *Treasurer's General Accounts.*			
Quarterly accounts of the Treasurer of the United States for receipts and expenditures, including receipts from all sources covered into the Treasury, and all payments made from the Treasury	3	37,805	936,717,280 17
13. *Assistant Treasurers' Accounts.*			
Accounts of the several assistant treasurers of the United States for the salaries of their employés and the incidental expenses of their offices	102	1,020	320,967 85
14. *Miscellaneous.*			
Such as accounts with the disbursing officers of the Executive Departments for salaries of officers and employés, and contingent expenses of the same; accounts for salaries of Senators and Representatives in Congress; for salaries of the judges of the United States Supreme Court, United States circuit and district judges, district attorneys, and marshals; for salaries and contingent expenses of the National Board of Health; for the expenses of the tenth census, and of the International exhibitions of 1875, 1876, and 1878...........................	3,185	96,357	17,299,030 82
Total from First Auditor	6,638	6,904,390	2,094,530,985 24
FROM THE FIFTH AUDITOR.			
15. *Internal Revenue.*			
Accounts of collectors of internal revenue......................	584		
Accounts of the same acting as disbursing agents	968		
Accounts of internal-revenue stamp agents	266		
Miscellaneous internal-revenue accounts, such as direct-tax accounts with commissioners and with the States; six different monthly accounts with the Commissioner of Internal Revenue for revenue stamps; accounts with the disbursing clerk of the Treasury Department for salaries of officers and employés in the office of the Commissioner of Internal Revenue, and for the payment of internal-revenue gaugers; with the Secretary of the Treasury for fines, penalties, and forfeitures; with the Treasury Department for stationery; with revenue agents and distillery surveyors; drawback accounts; accounts for refunding taxes illegally collected; for the redemption of internal-revenue stamps; for the collection of legacy and succession taxes; for expenses of detecting and suppressing violations of internal-revenue laws, including rewards therefor, &c	2,450		
	4,217	134,820	703,780,450 60
16. *Diplomatic and Consular.*			
Accounts for the salaries of ministers, charges d'affaires, consuls, commercial agents, interpreters, secretaries to legations and marshals of consular courts; accounts for the relief and protection of American seamen; for expenses of prisons in China and Japan; for contingent expenses of legations and consulates; for salaries and expenses of mixed commissions; accounts of United States bankers in London; accounts of the disbursing clerk Department of State for miscellaneous diplomatic expenses, &c	2,533	29,114	4,503,443 92

Kind.	Number.	Vouchers.	Amount involved.
17. *Transportation.*			
Accounts for the transportation of internal-revenue moneys to the sub-treasuries and designated depositaries, and for the transportation of stationery, &c., to internal-revenue officers.	59	8, 737	$5, 850 89
Total from Fifth Auditor.................................	6, 809	172, 680	768, 389, 744 69
FROM THE COMMISSIONER OF THE GENERAL LAND OFFICE.			
18. *Public Lands.*			
Accounts of surveyors-general and the employés in their offices	138	302	40, 458 07
Accounts of surveyors-general acting as disbursing agents	138	1, 932	166, 995 49
Accounts of deputy surveyors	402	1, 138	589, 005 13
Accounts of receivers of public moneys	481	5, 097	2, 790, 913 90
Accounts of same acting as disbursing agents.................	658	3, 209	1, 508, 085 33
Accounts for the refunding of purchase-money paid for lands erroneously sold..............................	129	819	22, 345 18
Accounts of timber agents......................................	11	34	20, 733 74
Adams Express accounts	5	1, 096	636 15
Miscellaneous accounts, such as accounts with the several States for indemnity for swamp and overflowed lands erroneously sold, and for 2 per cent., 3 per cent., and 5 per cent. upon the proceeds of sales of public lands; accounts of surveyors-general for the contingent expenses of their offices; accounts for the salaries and commissions of registers of local land offices not paid by the receivers; accounts with the Kansas, Denver, Central, Northern, and Union Pacific Railroads for the transportation of special agents of the General Land Office; accounts for printing and stationery furnished the several surveyors-general, registers, and receivers; accounts of special agents of the Interior Department; accounts for the transportation of public moneys from the local land offices to designated depositaries; accounts for salaries and incidental expenses of agents employed to examine and verify public surveys; for the return of deposits in excess of the amount required for the survey of private land claims; for the transportation of stationery to the several district land offices, &c.	242	2, 296	94, 663 44
Total from Commissioner of General Land Office........	2, 204	15, 803	5, 243, 997 03

RECAPITULATION.

From—	Number.	Vouchers.	Amount involved.
First Auditor..	8, 638	6, 904, 390	$2, 094, 539, 965 24
Fifth Auditor..	6, 809	172, 680	768, 389, 744 69
Commissioner of the General Land Office	2, 204	15, 803	5, 243, 997 03
Total..	17, 651	7, 092, 873	2, 868, 073, 606 96

Requisitions have been examined and advances thereon recommended as follows:

Internal revenue	1, 544
Diplomatic and consular..	1, 145
Judiciary..	489
Public buildings	210
Mint and assay..	173
District of Columbia..	76
Territorial	30
Public printing	120
Miscellaneous	302
Total..	4, 089

The following number of suits have been instituted against defaulting officers:

Collectors of internal revenue	7
United States marshals..	3
Receivers of public moneys	13

Internal revenue stamp agents	7
Disbursing agents	1
United States consuls	1
Total	32

Official letters written	12,256
Letters received, briefed, and registered	4,406
Powers of attorney recorded	710
Official bonds registered and filed	3,629
Miscellaneous contracts and bonds received and registered	466
Internal-revenue collectors' tax-list receipts recorded, scheduled, and referred	1,503
Orders for special allowances to collectors of internal revenue, recorded, scheduled, and referred	280
Internal-revenue special-tax stamp-books counted and certified	5,189
Internal-revenue tobacco-stamp-books counted and certified	11,065
Internal-revenue spirit-stamp-books counted and certified	8,386
Pages copied	4,560

Copies of accounts made, compared, and transmitted:

Internal revenue	1,662
Public lands	1,181
	2,843

I will here repeat what my predecessor said in his last annual report, that—

The foregoing statement omits mention of a great deal of labor which cannot easily be reported, but which has required much time and care, such as the examination in place of securities lost and destroyed; the examination of powers of attorney for collection of money due to creditors of the United States; decisions upon the right of persons claiming to be executors, administrators, or heirs of deceased claimants, to receive money due from the United States to said decedents; the examination, registry, and filing of official bonds; the copying of letters forwarded; answering calls for information made by Congress, the departments, and private persons; the investigation of legal points arising in the adjustment of accounts, and other work of a miscellaneous character.

INVESTIGATIONS.

The Secretary of the Treasury is authorized by general laws and appropriation acts to make investigations in many cases of the official transactions and accounts of officers in the public service under the Treasury Department. The exercise of this power in proper cases has a most salutary effect.

These investigations have generally been made by clerks in the Treasury Department detailed for the purpose, and have been attended with considerable expense, especially when conducted at long distances from the capital. It is believed that it would contribute to the efficiency of the public service, and aid in securing fidelity and economy, if the Secretary should be authorized to require any officer connected with this Department whom he might designate to make the requisite investigations, especially if the officers so deputed could be invested with power in some form to secure the presence of witnesses, evidence under oath, and the production of books and papers.

If, upon the request of the Secretary of the Treasury, the heads of other Departments respectively should be authorized to require officers connected therewith to make similar investigations for the Treasury Department, it might be found of great practical value.

Investigations could thus be made by officers not now subject to the direction of the Secretary of the Treasury, and in the vicinity of the transactions requiring examination. This would be attended with advantage in the means of local knowledge, and in facilities for acquiring information, by affording ample time for ascertaining all material facts, and with the least possible expense.

. It has sometimes been found necessary to ascertain facts and procure information on questions of law in foreign countries. Thus, government bonds have been held by citizens or subjects of foreign governments, and upon the death of the owners, controverted questions of fact and of law, as to the proper parties entitled to the bonds, have arisen, requiring determination in this office. If the Secretary of the Treasury should be invested with power to call upon any representative or agent of our government abroad to make investigations and report the result, and if such representatives and agents should be given ample authority to require evidence and the production of papers by citizens of the United States in foreign countries, and by citizens or subjects of foreign governments, so far as by them permitted, it is believed it would be found a salutary means of securing justice, of facilitating the operations of the Treasury Department, and a protection to the Treasury.

LOST AND DESTROYED BONDS.

Section 3702 of the Revised Statutes enacts that whenever it appears to the Secretary of the Treasury, by clear and unequivocal proof, that any interest-bearing bond of the United States has, without bad faith upon the part of the owner, been destroyed wholly or in part, or so defaced as to impair its value to the owner, and the bond is identified by number and description, the Secretary shall, under such regulations and with such restrictions as to time and retention for security or otherwise, as he may prescribe, issue a duplicate thereof, etc.; or, if the bonds have been called in for redemption, instead of issuing a duplicate, it shall be paid.

The next section enacts that the owner shall file in the Treasury a bond, in a sum prescribed, with two good and sufficient sureties, residents of the United States, to be approved by the Secretary, with condition to indemnify and save harmless the United States from any claim upon such destroyed or defaced bond.

Applications for duplicates, or for the redemption of "called lost" bonds, are referred under regulations prescribed by the Secretary of the Treasury to the First Comptroller, to be decided upon by him.

My predecessor, Hon. A. G. Porter, in the report of the office for the last fiscal year, made the following statement and recommendation:

It will be perceived that bonds payable to bearer come within the terms of this statute; and the practice has been to issue duplicates for, or to redeem, bonds of this character alleged to have been destroyed, upon evidence furnished by affidavits taken before certain prescribed officers of the United States. The redemption of such bonds and the issuing of duplicates have always been refused until after the lapse of six months from the filing of an application; but even with this precaution the statute is fraught with great danger to the Treasury. In practice it has been found that in fully half the cases where evidence has been offered to establish the fact of destruction, the bonds have not been destroyed, but have passed either by theft or collusion into the hands of other holders. When a bond of this kind is lost or stolen, the owner who has been deprived of it is apt soon to persuade himself that it has been destroyed, as only in case of its having been destroyed can he entertain reasonable hope of ever receiving payment. Instances also have occurred of persons offering most impressive evidence of the destruction of bonds alleged to have been owned by them, who, subsequent events have shown, had no title to them whatever. Great vigilance has been practiced by the Treasury by the invocation, even when very slight doubt has been excited, of the aid of the secret-service division; but it is believed that no vigilance can be sufficient to guard against the ingenious methods by which fraudulent applications may occasionally be made successful. If no radical change is made in the existing statute, authority ought at least to be given to require more than two sureties to the bond of indemnity.

I concur in this recommendation.

The greatest danger of loss to the Treasury arises from the possibility that the sureties upon the bonds of indemnity may prove to be worthless in the event of a suit against them. The regulations of the Department provide that the sufficiency of the sureties must be approved by some one of several prescribed officers. Most of these officers have performed the duty imposed upon them with the utmost fidelity, but in many cases such approval is made without any knowledge whatever of the parties, the officers feeling that such duties are extra-official, and that they are not required to make an examination into the condition of the sureties. A wise caution would dictate that the Secretary be empowered to require each officer to make a thorough examination into the financial status of the parties to bonds before appending his approval of the same, and that such officers be invested with authority to require evidence under oath.

It may also be found proper to make some regulations by statute in relation to the payment of lost government bonds.

LAW CLERK AND STENOGRAPHER.

A law clerk and a stenographer are deemed necessary for the efficiency of the service in this office. The First Comptroller is the law officer of the Treasury Department. He is charged with the duty of ultimately deciding all questions of law arising upon warrants for the payment of money from the Treasury, and the accounts of the Treasurer of the United States. This includes all the agencies by which money may be paid from the Treasury. The decisions so made are generally final, subject only to the revision of Congress, and in certain cases, not frequent in practice, by the Court of Claims. (Winnisimmet Company v. United States, 12 Court of Claims Reports, 326.)

It must be apparent that questions of great magnitude and difficulty are frequently presented for decision. Counsel of great ability are often retained by claimants to present oral and written or printed arguments against the government, which is not represented by counsel. It is therefore important that every reasonable aid should be furnished to this office to protect the interests of the government.

DECISIONS OF FIRST COMPTROLLER.

It is so important that the leading general principles of law applicable to the business of the Department should, so far as practicable, be settled, and in an accessible form, that it has been deemed proper, in order to secure these objects, to prepare and cause to be printed formal decisions in a considerable number of cases. A copy of these is herewith transmitted. None of the decisions made by my predecessors have been printed, except in rare instances.

The work of preparing decisions in the form now adopted involves much research and labor, but it is hoped the result may be found acceptable, and of such utility as to justify it.

STATUTE AS TO PERJURY.

There may be some doubt whether the existing statute defining perjury is sufficiently broad to include all cases of corrupt false swearing in affidavits used for various purposes in the Treasury Department. Affidavits are necessarily used for a great variety of purposes, and it is of the utmost importance that all who make them should be amenable

16 F

to punishment in cases deserving it. A comprehensive provision on this subject was included in a bill introduced in the Forty-fourth Congress, on which no final action was taken (H. R. 451, first session Forty-fourth Congress, January 5, 1876).

I respectfully submit that the subject is worthy of consideration by Congress.

UNPAID BALANCES.

In the adjustment of the accounts of receivers of public moneys, and other officers whose duty it is to collect the revenues of the government, such officers are charged with the amount of their collections and credited with the amount of money deposited by them in the Treasury. In many cases officers have deposited by mistake more money than they have collected, thus creating a balance in their favor.

The seventh clause of the ninth section of Article 1 of the Constitution prohibits the payment of any money from the Treasury, except in consequence of appropriations made by law. The above accounts come under no appropriation now existing, for the money deposited and covered into the Treasury constitutes an unappropriated fund, and the accounts of such officers under appropriations for the payment of their compensation and the expenses of their offices are kept entirely distinct from their accounts for the collection of revenues. In the absence of a provision for the payment of balances upon the latter class of accounts they have accumulated from year to year until quite a number now stand upon the books of the Department. It would be a great convenience if means for their payment should be provided.

I respectfully call attention to, and renew, the recommendations made by my predecessor in his last annual report.

The deputy comptroller, chiefs of division, clerks, and other persons employed in this bureau, deserve commendation for the intelligence, ability, and fidelity with which they have performed their respective duties.

I am, very respectfully, your obedient servant,
WILLIAM LAWRENCE,
First Comptroller.

Hon. JOHN SHERMAN,
Secretary of the Treasury.

REPORT OF THE SECOND COMPTROLLER.

REPORT

OF

THE SECOND COMPTROLLER OF THE TREASURY.

TREASURY DEPARTMENT,
SECOND COMPTROLLER'S OFFICE,
Washington, October 29, 1880.

SIR: In compliance with your direction, by letter of the 14th ultimo, I submit a report, in two tabular statements, of the transactions of this office during the fiscal year which ended on the 30th day of June 1880. The first tabular statement shows the total number of accounts, claims, and cases of every kind settled and adjusted, and the amounts allowed thereon. The second table furnishes a more detailed statement of the same accounts, claims, and cases; showing the character of the accounts, the source from which received, the number of each kind, and the amounts allowed. A still more detailed statement is prepared and filed for preservation in this office, but it is deemed too voluminous for publication.

From—	Number revised.	Amounts.
Second Auditor	9, 354	$17, 788, 881
Third Auditor	5, 273	50, 860, 845
Fourth Auditor	1, 862	15, 986, 825
	16, 489	84, 664, 351
Various sources not involving present expenditure	2, 494	462, 862
Total number accounts and claims and amounts settled	18, 983	85, 127, 213

ACCOUNTS REVISED during the year.

Character of accounts.	Number revised.	Amounts.
FROM THE SECOND AUDITOR.		
1. Of recruiting officers, for regular recruiting service	273	$145, 821
2. Of paymasters, for pay of the Army	433	9, 296, 679
3. Of disbursing officers of the Ordnance Department, for ordnance, ordnance stores, supplies, armories, and arsenals	200	885, 591
4. Of disbursing officers of the Medical Department, for medical and hospital supplies and services	10	8, 101
5. Of disbursements for the contingent expenses of War Department	153	80, 516
6. Special accounts settled by the Pay Division	1, 134	315, 551
7. Of Indian agents' current and contingent expenses, annuities, and installments	2, 631	6, 630, 648
	4, 834	17, 364, 907
FROM THE THIRD AUDITOR.		
1. Of disbursing officers of the Quartermaster's Department, for regular supplies and incidental expenses	1, 014	11, 698, 244
2. Of disbursing officers of the Subsistence Department	669	2, 811, 904
3. Of disbursing officers of the Engineer Department, for military surveys, construction of fortifications, river and harbor surveys and improvements.	84	4, 820, 225
4. Of pension agents, for payment of Army pensions	176	28, 625, 487
	1, 943	47, 955, 860

ACCOUNTS REVISED during the year—Continued.

Character of accounts.	Number revised.	Amounts.
FROM THE FOURTH AUDITOR.		
1. Of disbursing agents of the Marine Corps	9	$717,979
2. Of paymasters of the Navy proper	94	4,584,446
3. Of paymasters of the navy-yards	82	6,675,719
4. Of paymasters of the Navy as Navy agents and disbursing officers	14	2,806,091
5. Of Navy pension agents, for payment of pensions of Navy and Marine Corps	94	947,164
6. Of miscellaneous naval accounts	37	138,197
	330	15,871,596

CLAIMS ALLOWED during the year.

Character of claims.	Number.	Amounts.
FROM THE SECOND AUDITOR.		
1. Soldiers' pay and bounty	4,520	$421,974
FROM THE THIRD AUDITOR.		
1. Property lost under the act of March 3, 1849	577	101,400
2. Quartermasters' and commissary stores and supplies, act of July 4, 1864, transportation and miscellaneous	2,711	2,696,701
3. Oregon and Washington Indian war claims	34	6,096
4. State war claims	8	130,788
FROM THE FOURTH AUDITOR.		
1. Sailors' pay and bounty	1,307	104,992
2. Prize money	225	10,037
	9,382	3,471,988

CASES NOT INVOLVING PRESENT EXPENDITURE.

	Number.	Amounts.
1. Duplicate checks approved	428	$30,868
2. Financial agents' accounts	4	431,994
3. Referred cases adjusted	2,062	
	2,494	462,862

	Number.
Bonds filed during the year	92
Contracts filed during the year	1,597
Official letters written	1,495
Requisitions recorded	11,708
Settlements recorded	7,785
Differences recorded, pages	4,987
Clerks, average during year	52.8

All the public business intrusted to my charge is, I believe, promptly and properly attended to by the officers and clerks of the office, and has progressed with reasonable dispatch.

    Very respectfully,

W. W. UPTON,
Comptroller.

Hon. JOHN SHERMAN,
   Secretary of the Treasury.

REPORT OF THE COMMISSIONER OF CUSTOMS.

REPORT

OF

THE COMMISSIONER OF CUSTOMS.

TREASURY DEPARTMENT,
OFFICE OF COMMISSIONER OF CUSTOMS,
Washington, October 21, 1880.

SIR: I have the honor to submit herewith, for your information, a statement of the work performed in this office during the fiscal year ending June 30, 1880:

Number of accounts on hand July 1, 1879	299	
Number of accounts received from the First Auditor during the year	6,430	
		6,729
Number of accounts adjusted during the year	6,576	
Number of accounts returned to the First Auditor	13	
		6,589
Number of accounts on hand June 30, 1880		140

There was paid into the Treasury from sources the accounts relating to which are settled in this office—

On account of customs	$186,522,064 60
On account of marine-hospital tax	386,973 33
On account of steamboat fees	282,468 96
On account of fines, penalties, and forfeitures	123,786 28
On account of storage, fees, &c.	840,780 27
On account of deceased passengers	170 00
On account of emolument fees	183,150 91
On account of mileage of examiners	1,082 70
On account of interest on debts due	9,381 14
On account of rent of public buildings	12,560 30
On account of relief of sick and disabled seamen	1,619 54
On account of proceeds of government property	14,573 52
Aggregate	188,378,611 55

And there was paid out of the Treasury on the following accounts, viz:

Expenses of collection	$6,023,253 53
Excess of deposits	2,632,164 44
Debentures	1,831,060 76
Public buildings	2,290,511 73
Construction and maintenance of lights	2,426,370 61
Construction and maintenance of revenue-cutters	843,989 57
Marine-hospital service	402,917 49
Life-saving stations	518,407 43
Compensation in lieu of moieties	32,186 30
Seal-fisheries in Alaska	9,571 02
Metric standard weights and measures	6,316 90
Debentures and other charges	136 91
Detection and prevention of frauds upon the customs revenue	19,994 32
Unclaimed merchandise	1,750 41

Refunding moneys erroneously received and covered into the Treasury... $127 50
Refunding duties to University of Notre Dame du Lac..............   2,334 07
Protection of sea-otter hunting grounds and seal-fisheries in Alaska..   22,902 88

      Aggregate..   17,063,995 87

The number of estimates received and examined...../..............   3,505
The number of requisitions issued...............................   3,505
The amount involved in requisitions $15,062,080 75
The number of letters received   10,452
The number of letters written...................................   10,378
The number of letters recorded   10,342
The number of stubs of receipts for duties and fees returned by collectors...   205,009
The number of stubs examined....................................   215,306
The number of stubs of certificates of payment of tonnage dues received and entered   10,481
The number of returns received and examined.....................   11,941
The number of oaths examined and registered   3,992
The number of appointments registered   3,227
The average number of clerks employed...........................   30

I inclose herewith a statement of the transactions in bonded goods during the year ending June 30, 1880, as shown by the adjusted accounts.

I am, very respectfully, your obedient servant,

                  H. C. JOHNSON,
                  Commissioner of Customs.

Hon. JOHN SHERMAN,
   Secretary of the Treasury.

STATEMENT of WAREHOUSE TRANSACTIONS at the several DISTRICTS and PORTS of the UNITED STATES, for the year ending June 30, 1880.

Districts.	Balance on bonds to secure duties on goods remaining in warehouse on July 1, 1879.	Warehoused and bonded.	Rewarehoused and bonded.	Constructively warehoused.	Increase of duties ascertained on liquidation.	Withdrawal duty paid.	Withdrawal for transportation.	Withdrawal for exportation.	Allowances and deficiencies.	Balance on bonds to secure duties on goods remaining in warehouse on June 30, 1880.
Albany				$141, 736 00		$143, 736 00				
Alexandria	$90 76		$155 00	119 04	$9 98	383 78				
Baltimore	68, 007 08	$701, 407 98	8, 297 08	488, 171 86	7, 070 24	436, 076 98	$396, 051 90	$117, 089 46	$13, 110 82	$320, 615 08
Bangor		1, 906 20	439 00			1, 483 08				861 52
Barnstable	522 95		4, 696 65	3, 279 34		90 41		7, 627 19		783 34
Bath	1, 909 96	31, 116 18	22, 218 59	1, 109 47	161 56	9, 269 05	483 98	480 59	4, 123 40	42, 156 75
Beaufort, S. C				56 00		56 00				
Boston and Charlestown (May 31, 1880)	3, 046, 747 99	10, 963, 736 93	115, 219 27	725, 508 67	165, 104 75	8, 516, 685 27	186, 611 84	914, 810 32	328, 866 99	4, 869, 632 49
Brazos de Santiago	7, 451 98	879, 509 13	135, 018 23	1, 050 80	25 10	748 08	711, 363 61			10, 982 80
Buffalo Creek	2, 645 90	39, 772 40	2, 220 39	550, 746 68	103 53	30, 312 46	138, 326 50	425, 307 22		1, 642 72
Belfast	1, 333 18		1, 556 04	7 40	22 07	456 49		1, 568 40	206 32	746 48
Cape Vincent				5, 494 38			5, 445 58	48 80		
Castine	54 40		132 00	906 36		46 80		1, 013 04		33 12
Champlain		9, 859 64		232, 182 78		3, 589 90	203, 990 61	28, 232 17		5, 769 74
Charleston	1, 274 41	1, 004 40	353 96	1, 026 20	113 68	3, 494 62				278 03
Chicago	120, 023 34	790, 161 23	72, 897 16	207, 528 13	18, 765 72	832, 885 40	25, 834 10	6, 632 93	10, 539 37	344, 002 76
Cincinnati	14, 886 05	44, 340 45	22, 402 02	30, 989 69	132 19	86, 648 50	132 65		60 75	25, 988 50
Corpus Christi		1, 052 65	44, 588, 08		88	408 80	1, 052 65	44, 478 18		
Cuyahoga	2, 849 44	10, 945 12	3, 054 61	16, 714 15	9 21	14, 897 72	10, 656 00	55 25		7, 703 56
Delaware	2, 163 77		15, 520 43			17, 684 20				
Detroit	22, 222 95	18, 630 73	41, 704 61	600, 017 24	635 93	46, 594 90	25, 908 70	588, 792 60	286 23	22, 729 03
Duluth			4, 490 02	822, 849 64		9 50	85 00	826, 813 50		432 66
Dubuque			1, 078 74			219 35				859 39
Erie				21 60		21 60				
Fall River			12, 464 20	2, 774 36		2, 774 36				
Fernandina			1, 067 12	21 60		2, 647 75				9, 816 45
Frenchman's Bay	336 87		1, 927 75	296 23	2 77	76 31	1, 350 70			296 98
Galveston	4, 540 63	97, 304 55	7, 857 87	28, 441 83	482 69	38, 782 45	4, 802 67	10, 512 97	1, 427 58	68, 145 80
Genesee	10, 408 06	2, 381 54	4, 727 44	10, 893 27	124 58	17, 525 72	6, 036 15	18 00		8, 091 23
Gloucester	9, 812 90	32, 477 82	1, 563 05	27 84	559 84	1, 735 06	544 56	35, 075 20	1, 211 48	9, 038 64
Georgetown, D. C	527 20			4, 682 24	21 34	4, 103 91			2, 099 02	590 90
Huron				1, 137, 620 94		130 80	121, 752 87	1, 015, 737 27		
Kennebunk				217 28				217 28		
Key West	50, 049 04	200, 046 40	2, 201 85	16, 500 33	3, 373 60	166, 144 05	34, 145 57	1, 218 88	252 76	71, 009 96
Louisville	3, 383 62	8, 920 46	17, 333 67	4, 598 15	161 17	15, 543 00	676 20		26 65	13, 152 22
Memphis	1, 441 52			1, 818 54	4 96	2, 630 02				635 00
Miami	219 68			7, 726 39	7 64	1, 520 19		6, 433 52		

STATEMENT of WAREHOUSE TRANSACTIONS at the several DISTRICTS and PORTS of the UNITED STATES, &c.—Continued.

Districts.	Balance on bonds to secure duties on goods remaining in warehouse on July 1, 1879.	Warehoused and bonded.	Rewarehoused and bonded.	Constructively warehoused.	Increase of duties ascertained on liquidation.	Withdrawal duty paid.	Withdrawal for transportation.	Withdrawal for exportation.	Allowances and deficiencies.	Balance on bonds to secure duties on goods remaining in warehouse on June 30, 1880.
Middletown	$3,118 41	$352 00	$68,574 99	$7,936 86		$47,265 05	$540 00			$32,176 21
Milwaukee	542 58	15,136 34	15,063 89	121,253 13		85,086 00		$52,938 75		14,871 19
Minnesota	1,009 81	4,843 40	2,269 53	46,285 06	$34 35	9,028 84	8,197 34	35,261 05		1,455 52
Mobile (to November 30, 1879)				588 65				588 85		
Montana and Idaho				448 39			11 69	436 70		
Nashville			339 71	345 70		550 21			$135 20	
Newburyport	106 72			420 42		52 09		243 82	231 30	
New Haven	15,017 79	458,164 95	2,274 08			368,649 14	90,066 36		52 09	16,689 33
New Bedford		175 60	3,922 34	9,096 08		8,016 72	226 40	1,104 40		3,247 50
New Orleans	182,505 40	648,802 59	7,079 85	647,860 90	9,870 13	445,287 36	669,169 29	140,359 02	31,771 73	200,580*57
New York (to February 29, 1880)	12,714,913 96	27,890,293 64	281,873 56	5,867,199 08	576,954 94	27,419,143 22	523,714 93	6,710,839 32	1,339,935 97	11,345,432 36
Niagara (to February 29, 1880)				1,271,002 66		4,301 11	169,114 46	1,101,888 24		
Newark				4,301 11		24,878 31				201 94
New Loudon	2,782 09	23,450 55		864 97			1,624 98	962 38		335 73
Omaha	275 00		77 10	1,747 40	1 63	1,765 40				
Oswegatchie	1,390 74	8,104 07		15,773 43	26 49	1,874 23	10,228 03	5,400 33		1,792 15
Oswego	6,772 45	626,774 75		51,334 76	61	256,061 20	410,240 58	1,828 90	601 05	14,133 45
Passamaquoddy	283 48	5,855 39	2,536 00	21,634 66		2,820 70	15,974 54	9,617 02		1,872 27
Pensacola				308 25				308 25		
Philadelphia	978,962 84	3,805,850 22	46,237 94	140,003 10	265,984 25	3,740,437 39	80,111 06	18,162 58	128,236 14	1,270,076 68
Pittsburgh	14,649 13	33,553 04	4,131 80	248,644 95	1,008 05	275,025 24				31,961 73
Plymouth	4,549 39		23,096 15	419 84		9,187 39		417 60		18,452 39
Portland and Falmouth	50,873 23	161,830 35	61,270 36	2,791,064 80	656 10	154,132 77	71,631 28	2,775,876 02	5,673 60	58,387 17

Willamette	19,959 42	15,229 56	....	....	100 66	27,643 12	....	44 52	....	7,602 02
Wiscasset	240 66	....	3,875 68	....	....	....	....	2,531 96	....	584 38
Wilmington, Del	526 49	2,937 79	....	....	11 02	121 23	....	2,937 79	....	415 98
York	....	....	23 28	....	....	....	....	23 28	....	....
	18,600,073 37	50,353,336 83	1,405,852 71	17,750,808 17	1,092,104 57	47,003,129 09	3,560,606 08	16,421,402 65	2,177,437 96	20,039,597 87
* New York (for April, May, and June, 1879)	10,112,027 97	12,110,727 58	184,518 62	985,533 33	374,359 88	8,902,408 67	182,949 60	1,485,426 78	431,468 86	12,714,913 66

* Not included in report for fiscal year ended June 30, 1879.

RECAPITULATION.

Balance July 1, 1879	$18,600,073 37		Withdrawal duty paid	$47,003,129 09
Warehoused and bonded	50,353,336 83		Withdrawals for transportation	3,560,606 08
Rewarehoused and bonded	1,405,852 71		Withdrawals for exportation	16,421,402 65
Constructively warehoused	17,750,808 17		Allowances and deficiencies	2,177,437 96
Increase of duties ascertained on liquidation	1,092,104 57		Balance June 30, 1880	20,039,597 87
Total	89,202,175 65		Total	89,202,175 65

TREASURY DEPARTMENT, OFFICE COMMISSIONER OF CUSTOMS, *October 21, 1880.*

H. C. JOHNSON,
Commissioner of Customs.

Balance taken up in this statement	$18,600,073 37
Balance reported by last statement	15,997,187 68
Difference	2,602,885 69
Arising from—	
Increase in balance in New York (from March 31 to June 30, 1879)	2,602,885 69

REPORT OF THE FIRST AUDITOR.

REPORT

OF

THE FIRST AUDITOR OF THE TREASURY.

TREASURY DEPARTMENT,
FIRST AUDITOR'S OFFICE,
Washington, October 21, 1880.

SIR: In compliance with your letter of the 14th ultimo, I have the honor to submit the following exhibit of the business transacted in this office during the fiscal year ending June 30, 1880:

Accounts adjusted.	Number of accounts.	Amount.
RECEIPTS.		
Duties on merchandise and tonnage..	1,355	$163,998,486 68
Steamboat fees...	1,136	293,255 48
Fines, penalties, and forfeitures...	608	126,445 02
Marine-hospital money collected...	1,582	379,285 51
Official emoluments of collectors, naval officers, and surveyors...........	1,276	616,569 70
Moneys received from sales of old materials, rents, &c.....................	171	155,694 87
Moneys received on account of deceased passengers.........................	33	480 00
Miscellaneous receipts...	593	804,380 96
Treasurer of the United States, for moneys received.......................	3	906,351,686 31
Mints and Assay Offices..	31	133,289,717 55
Water rents, Hot Springs, Arkansas.......................................	9	1,903 36
Receipts on counter warrants...	298	280,504 32
Total...	7,035	1,206,298,429 71
DISBURSEMENTS.		
Expense of collecting the revenue from customs............................	1,486	5,464,960 40
Debentures, drawbacks, &c..	178	3,952,260 83
Excess of deposits refunded..	403	2,261,691 22
Revenue-cutter service...	507	767,352 41
Duties refunded, fines remitted, judgments satisfied, &c..................	1,747	328,455 09
Marine-hospital service..	1,247	416,040 17
Official emoluments of collectors, naval officers, and surveyors..........	1,256	639,539 08
Awards of compensation..	108	36,630 95
Light-house Establishment, miscellaneous.................................	67	61,776 99
Salaries of light-house keepers..	437	611,341 07
Supplies of light-houses...	163	565,363 73
Repairs of light-houses..	112	370,787 59
Expenses of light-vessels..	121	304,652 45
Expenses of buoyage..	158	496,183 26
Expenses of fog-signals..	87	81,999 53
Expenses of lighting and buoyage of the Mississippi, Missouri, and Ohio rivers...	88	179,581 54
Expenses of inspection of lights...	12	3,099 37
Steam-tenders for the Light-House Service.................................	19	106,172 56
Commissions on light-house disbursements.................................	124	8,582 58
Salaries and mileage of Senators...	1	125,803 71
Salaries, officers and employés, Senate...................................	5	190,498 86
Salaries and mileage, members and delegates House of Representatives......	1	1,200,622 42
Salaries, officers and employés, House of Representatives.................	12	246,649 34
Salaries of employés, Executive Mansion..................................	6	47,626 80
Salaries paid by disbursing clerks of the Departments....................	322	5,499,672 62
Salaries, officers and employés, Independent Treasury.....................	38	319,686 95
Salaries of the civil list paid directly from the Treasury...............	1,285	563,691 84

17 F   257

Accounts adjusted.	Number of accounts.	Amount.
DISBURSEMENTS—Continued.		
Salaries, office of the Public Printer	4	$13,600 00
Salaries, Bureau of Engraving and Printing	13	25,925 71
Salaries, Congressional Library	6	52,038 93
Salaries, standard weights and measures	5	5,353 40
Salaries, Steamboat Inspection Service	4	180,012 46
Salaries, special agents, Independent Treasury	4	3,690 85
Salaries, custodians and janitors	7	75,594 51
Salaries, Botanic Garden	3	7,549 10
Salaries and expenses, Hot Springs Commission	5	26,065 02
Salaries and expenses, Southern Claims Commission	13	6,427 93
Salaries of employés, public buildings and grounds	5	34,963 22
Salaries and expenses of National Board of Health	13	190,826 60
Salary of Director of Geological Survey	5	5,126 37
Contingent expenses, Executive Mansion	5	7,064 29
Contingent expenses, United States Senate	48	170,443 62
Contingent expenses, House of Representatives	72	221,190 93
Contingent expenses, Departments, Washington	678	396,986 68
Contingent expenses, Independent Treasury	154	42,491 92
Contingent expenses, Steamboat Inspection Service	788	34,922 02
Contingent expenses, public buildings and grounds	4	462 46
Contingent expenses, office of Public Printer	6	1,313 09
Contingent expenses, Southern Claims Commission	14	5,264 93
Contingent expenses, National Currency, reimbursable	42	55,226 39
Contingent expenses, Court of Claims	3	1,839 68
Contingent expenses, Library of Congress	5	509 95
Contingent expenses of the Executive offices, Territories	13	4,186 87
Stationery, Interior Department	10	43,809 27
Treasurer of the United States, for general expenditures	3	833,118,463 88
Treasurer of the United States, for sinking-fund, Pacific railroads	4	366,506 71
Gold and silver bullion accounts	81	131,817,754 56
Ordinary expenses, Mints and Assay Offices	146	932,725 44
Parting and refining bullion	18	216,726 87
Coinage of standard silver dollars	15	55,947 89
Freight on bullion	5	9,345 75
Recoinage of gold and silver coins	3	5,090 94
Transportation of coin and bullion	10	21,341 39
Storage of silver dollars	3	2,685 61
Manufacture of medals	1	2,348 69
Legislative expenses, Territories of the United States	20	87,775 17
Captured and abandoned property	1	4,576 92
Defending suits and claims for seizure of captured and abandoned property	7	23,138 84
Examination of rebel archives and records of captured and abandoned property	3	3,599 09
Coast and geodétic survey of the United States	23	651,694 71
Geological survey of the Territories	32	125,173 70
Lands and other property of the United States	12	2,405 81
Protection and improvement of Hot Springs, Arkansas	1	961 70
Expenses of collecting rents, Hot Springs, Arkansas	9	377 09
Reproducing plats of surveys, General Land Office	9	15,624 00
Adjusting claims for indemnity for swamp lands	5	12,280 55
Protection and improvement of Yellow Stone National Park	8	18,131 51
Commission to classify land and codify land laws	1	3,695 67
Depredations on public timber	13	35,310 25
Judicial expenses, embracing accounts of United States marshals, district attorneys, clerks, and commissioners, rent of court-houses, support of prisoners, &c	3,906	3,267,574 36
Prosecution of crimes	7	11,624 45
Suppressing counterfeiting and crime	27	69,308 15
Detection and prevention of frauds upon the customs revenue	4	22,008 13
Investigation of frauds, Office of Commissioner of Pensions	10	31,218 80
INTEREST ACCOUNT.		
Registered stock	48	42,586,352 04
Coin coupons	97	32,237,218 65
District of Columbia 3-65 bonds and water stock	8	740,115 18
Pacific Railroad bonds	25	3,665,255 35
Navy pension fund	1	420,000 00
Louisville and Portland Canal Company's bonds	4	47,490 00
REDEMPTION ACCOUNT.		
United States 5-20 bonds, called:		
Principal	17	497,310,850 00
Interest		10,226,170 63
United States bonds, purchased for sinking-fund:		
Principal	14	49,949,100 00
Interest		558,490 51
Premium		1,837,539 35
United States bonds, 10-40's for conversion:		
Principal	2	2,090,000 00
Interest		14,404 73
Premium		10,447 50

Accounts adjusted.	Number of accounts.	Amount.
DISBURSEMENTS—Continued.		
REDEMPTION ACCOUNT—Continued.		
Refunding certificates, converted into 4-per cent. bonds:		
Principal	21	$20, 116, 450 00
Interest		258, 754 29
Coin certificates of deposit	13	8, 771, 200 00
Silver certificates of deposit	7	734, 810 00
Currency certificates of deposit	14	115, 890, 000 00
Bonds of District of Columbia (Washington and Georgetown)...........	5	1, 126, 780 00
Notes, one and two years, compound interest and 7-30's:		
Principal	47	24, 320 00
Interest		4, 449 82
War-bounty scrip, certificate of deposit:		
Principal	2	225 00
Interest		12 20
Legal-tender notes destroyed	13	90, 631, 624 00
Fractional currency destroyed	13	321, 075 14
Old demand notes destroyed	13	835 00
Refunding the national debt	52	850, 514 13
Expenses of national currency	16	15, 166 71
Examination of national banks and bank-plates	5	408 77
Transportation of United States securities	98	79, 384 07
Judgments of the Court of Claims	32	232, 043 53
Reporting decisions of the Court of Claims	1	1, 000 00
Post Office Department requisitions	30	2, 476, 255 24
Outstanding drafts and checks	109	10, 730 21
Life-saving Service	99	485, 490 02
Life-saving Service, contingent expenses	115	59, 941 86
Establishing life-saving stations	74	94, 082 62
Rebuilding and improving life-saving stations	1	75 00
Public printing and binding	162	1, 472, 084 69
Labor and expenses of engraving and printing	15	886, 252 04
Propagation of food-fishes	28	69, 695 46
Illustrations for report on food-fishes	9	1, 000 00
Inquiry respecting food-fishes	2	3, 500 00
Steam-vessel (food-fishes)	2	33, 373 33
Increase of Library of Congress	5	7, 597 14
Works of art for the Capitol	3	6, 225 00
Portraits of the Presidents	3	872 00
Library, Treasury Department	10	905 30
Pedestal for the statue of Gen. George H. Thomas	2	1, 881 62
Construction of custom-houses	346	2, 398, 799 62
Construction of court-houses and post-offices	345	1, 193, 562 85
Construction of appraisers' stores	13	91, 334 44
Construction of sub-treasury building, New York	6	10, 366 28
Construction of National Museum	12	188, 452 60
Construction of building for State, War, and Navy Departments.........	8	618, 726 63
Construction of barge office, New York	9	47, 236 98
Construction of jail for District of Columbia	2	431 80
Construction of assay office building	15	5, 667 99
Construction of light-houses	307	435, 730 03
Construction of extension of Government Printing Office	7	37, 389 29
Construction of building for Bureau of Engraving and Printing..........	14	195, 941 38
Fixtures, &c., new building, for Bureau of Engraving and Printing.........	1	4, 994 63
Plans for public buildings	5	3, 326 98
Completion of Washington Monument........................	4	91, 887 54
Reconstruction of Interior Department building	5	120, 542 57
Repairs, fuel, lighting, &c., Executive Mansion	10	25, 903 14
Annual repairs of the Capitol	10	57, 770 86
Annual repairs of the Treasury building	9	22, 912 96
Repairs and preservation of public buildings	84	132, 861 15
Repairs of Interior Department building	7	3, 356 76
Repairs of building on Tenth street	1	4, 641 43
Rent of buildings in Washington	43	65, 773 73
Lighting the Capitol and grounds	8	27, 916 71
Fuel, lights, and water for public buildings	53	407, 379 57
Fuel, lights, &c., Interior Department	9	5, 953 27
Furniture and repairs of same, public buildings	31	207, 970 65
Furniture, contingencies, &c., Pension Office	8	3, 190 83
Furniture for new War Department building	8	42, 498 51
Furniture for new Navy Department building	3	44, 236 84
Vaults, safes, and locks for public buildings	6	40, 735 87
Heating apparatus for public buildings	30	91, 213 90
Heating apparatus for Senate	8	3, 414 41
Ventilation of House of Representatives	8	29, 924 79
Fire-escape ladders, Government Printing Office..............	4	2, 004 55
Telephonic connection between the Capitol and Government Printing Office.	9	147 96
Telegraph between the Capitol, Departments, and Government Printing Office.	5	1, 318 20
Improvement and care of public grounds	5	35, 994 65
Improving Capitol grounds ....&.........	10	91, 478 96
Improving Botanic Gardens and buildings	7	8, 526 05

Accounts adjusted.	Number of accounts.	Amount.
DISBURSEMENTS—Continued.		
REDEMPTION ACCOUNT—Continued.		
Improving grounds, Agricultural Department	4	6, 129 12
Washington Aqueduct	4	17, 182 12
Repairs of water-pipes and fire-plugs	5	2, 893 56
Constructing, repairing, and maintaining bridges, District of Columbia	4	4, 971 40
Removal of Bureau of Education	2	312 00
Distributing documents, Bureau of Education	7	738 50
Rearranging Court of Claims rooms in Capitol	3	1, 737 18
Postage, Executive Departments	8	2, 362 06
Postage, Agricultural Department	4	4, 123 40
Building, Agricultural Department	3	1, 500 00
Laboratory, Agricultural Department	3	1, 393 43
Library, Agricultural Department	5	1, 064 32
Museum, Agricultural Department	4	1, 213 66
Furniture, cases, &c	4	4, 448 25
Experimental garden	4	5, 634 70
Purchase and distribution of valuable seeds	5	73, 263 16
Collecting agricultural statistics	4	8, 143 35
Investigating diseases of swine and other domestic animals	5	5, 890 10
Commission to report on depredations of Rocky Mountain locusts	8	21, 444 88
Investigating the habits of insects injurious to cotton-plant and agriculture	3	2, 417 49
Investigating the history of insects injurious to agriculture	5	6, 573 25
Investigation of epidemic diseases	1	7, 993 07
Reform school, District of Columbia	4	33, 445 99
Government Hospital for the Insane, buildings, &c	7	39, 414 38
Government Hospital for the Insane, current expenses	4	185, 340 23
Columbia Institution for the Deaf and Dumb, buildings, &c	1	284 57
Columbia Institution for the Deaf and Dumb, current expenses	4	37, 111 07
Columbia Hospital for Women, grounds	1	1, 970 10
Columbia Hospital for Women, current expenses	7	17, 985 12
Howard University	2	4, 129 66
Freedmen's Hospital and Asylum	10	39, 398 10
Penny Lunch House	1	1, 500 00
Saint Ann's Infant Asylum	2	2, 494 69
Children's Hospital	5	7, 307 49
National Association for the Relief of Colored Women and Children	3	2, 993 18
Women's Christian Association	6	2, 475 79
Industrial Home School	2	4, 671 81
Maryland Institution for the Instruction of the Blind	4	5, 775 00
Miscellaneous	210	204, 309 96
Disbursements on transfer-warrants	238	280, 524 32
DISTRICT OF COLUMBIA ACCOUNTS.		
Salaries and contingent expenses	202	171, 965 47
Improvement and repairs	66	430, 402 79
Constructing, repairing, and maintaining bridges	7	1, 000 00
Transportation of paupers and prisoners	15	2, 975 04
Public schools	16	366, 353 17
Metropolitan police	17	396, 919 33
Fire department	31	127, 486 52
Courts, expenses of	29	17, 564 32
Streets	106	294, 240 13
Health department	16	23, 889 67
Miscellaneous and contingent expenses	68	27, 967 44
Water fund	20	82, 110 61
Judgments	3	32, 404 92
Support and medical treatment of the infirm poor	9	3, 322 97
Reform School	8	17, 637 11
Washington Asylum	24	43, 740 48
Georgetown Almshouse	11	1, 583 00
Hospital for the Insane	4	10, 369 47
Children's Hospital	1	10, 000 00
Saint Ann's Infant Asylum	1	5, 000 00
Industrial Home School	1	5, 000 00
National Association for Relief of Colored Women and Children	1	5, 000 00
Workingmen's claims allowed	29	3, 830 20
Treasurer of the United States for amount allowed to workingmen	1	21, 155 77
Total	20, 046	1, 893, 413, 341 53

Number of certificates recorded 13, 768

Number of letters recorded 3, 443

Judiciary emolument accounts registered and referred 516

Number of powers of attorney for collection of interest on the public debt, examined, registered, and filed 3, 691

Requisitions answered 1, 023

SUMMARY STATEMENT of the WORK of the OFFICE as shown by the REPORTS of the various DIVISIONS and MISCELLANEOUS DESKS.

CUSTOMS DIVISION.

Accounts of Collectors of Customs for Receipts of Customs Revenue and Disbursements for the Expenses of Collecting the same, and also including Accounts of Collectors for Receipts and Disbursements in connection with the Revenue cutter, Steamboat, Pines, Light-house, and Marine Hospital Services, with Accounts for Official Emoluments, Debentures, Refunds of Duties, Sales of Old Materials, and Miscellaneous Disbursements.

	No. of accounts.	Amount.
Receipts	6,735	$166,258,823 96
Disbursements	7,173	14,162,131 32
	13,908	180,420,955 28

JUDICIARY DIVISION.

Accounts of District Attorneys, Marshals, Clerks, and Commissioners, Rents, and Miscellaneous Court Accounts.

	No. of accounts.	Amount.
Disbursements	3,906	$3,267,574 36

PUBLIC DEBT DIVISION.

Accounts for Payment of Interest on the Public Debt, both Registered Stock and Coupon Bonds, Interest on District of Columbia Bonds, Pacific Railroad Bonds, Louisville and Portland Canal Bonds, Navy Pension Fund, Redemption of United States and District of Columbia Bonds, Redemption of Coin and Currency Certificates, Old Notes and Bounty Scrip, and Accounts for Notes and Fractional Currency Destroyed.

	No. of accounts.	Amount.
Interest accounts	178	$79,699,431 23
Redemption accounts	181	799,661,448 17
	359	879,360,879 40

WAREHOUSE AND BOND DIVISION.

STATEMENT of TRANSACTIONS in BONDED MERCHANDISE, as shown by WAREHOUSE and BOND ACCOUNTS ADJUSTED during the fiscal year ending June 30, 1880.

Number of accounts adjusted	813
Number of reports of "no transactions" received, examined, and referred	529

Balance of duties on merchandise in warehouse per last report	$13,711,864 28
Duties on merchandise warehoused	54,203,099 40
Duties on merchandise rewarehoused	1,396,477 00
Duties on merchandise constructively warehoused	12,513,146 66
Increased and additional duties, &c	1,400,728 61
Total	83,225,315 95

Contra :

Duties on merchandise withdrawn for consumption	$49,833,561 36
Duties on merchandise withdrawn for transportation	3,310,275 67
Duties on merchandise withdrawn for exportation	11,997,258 41
Allowances for deficiencies; damage, &c	2,208,194 36
Duties on withdrawals for construction and repair of vessels	86,491 94
Duties on bonds delivered to district attorneys for prosecution	34,403 64
Balance of duties on merchandise in warehouse	15,755,130 57
Total	83,225,315 95

MISCELLANEOUS DESKS.

No. 1.—*Accounts of Disbursing Clerks of the Departments for Salaries, Salary Accounts of the various Assistant Treasurers, and of the Congressional Library, Public Printer, and Executive Office, Accounts for Salaries of the Officers and Employés, House of Representatives, and the Accounts relating to the Coast Survey.*

	No. of accounts.	Amount.
Disbursements	411	$6,768,937 91

No. 2.—*Accounts of the Disbursing Clerks of the Departments for Contingent Expenses, Contingent Expenses of the House of Representatives and Assistant Treasurers, Accounts of the Bureau of Engraving and Printing, Geological Survey, National Board of Health, Reform School, New Building for State, War, and Navy Departments, and a very great number of Miscellaneous Accounts. The Accounts on this desk during the last fiscal year covered one hundred and seventy different appropriations.*

	No. of accounts.	Amount.
Receipts..	9	$1,903 36
Disbursements..	1,133	4,976,076 24
	1,142	4,977,979 60

No. 3.—*Accounts for Construction of Custom-Houses, Post-Offices, Court-Houses, and other Public Buildings; Accounts of Light-House Engineers and Inspectors; Accounts of the Public Printer; Steamboat Inspection and Life-Saving Service; the Accounts of the Government Hospital for the Insane, Columbia Hospital for Deaf and Dumb, and many charitable institutions.*

	No. of accounts.	Amount.
Receipts..	19	$115,774 21
Disbursements..	3,379	10,664,079 25
	3,398	10,779,853 46

No. 4.—*Account of the Treasurer of the United States for General Expenditures; the Salary and Mileage Accounts for the Senate and House of Representatives, and the Accounts for Contingent Expenses of the United States Senate.*

	No. of accounts.	Amount.
Receipts..	3	$906,351,686 81
Disbursements..	58	834,814,832 49
	61	1,741,166,518 80

No. 5.—*Accounts of Mints and Assay Offices; Salaries of the Civil List paid directly from the Treasury on First Auditor's Certificates, Captured and Abandoned Property Accounts, and Accounts for the Legislative and Contingent Expenses of the United States Territories.*

	No. of accounts.	Amount.
Receipts..	31	$133,289,717 55
Disbursements..	1,558	133,750,060 17
	1,589	267,039,777 72

No. 6.—*Accounts of the District of Columbia, and Accounts under the act for the Relief of Workingmen under the late Board of Public Works.*

	No. of accounts.	Amount.
Disbursements..	686	$1,991,237 81

No. 7.—*Under the Chief of the Warehouse and Bond Division, and comprising Judgments of the Court of Claims, Outstanding Liabilities, Postal Requisitions, Transportation of United States Securities, Transfer of Appropriations, &c.*

	No. of accounts.	Amount.
Receipts	238	$280,524 32
Disbursements	1,383	3,656,132 58
	1,621	3,936,656 90

In submitting the foregoing exhibits, showing the official labor performed in this office during the last fiscal year, I desire to call attention to the fact that the number of accounts examined and adjusted, and the amount of money involved in their settlement, are without precedent in the history of this bureau.

It will be observed that the number of accounts adjusted for the year was 27,081, and the amount of money involved, as per vouchers examined, was $3,099,712,371.24, which is over one thousand millions of dollars in excess of the national debt during the same time.

The amounts of accounts examined during the last four years are over nine thousand millions of dollars, making an average of more than two thousand millions of dollars in yearly settlements made in this office.

The following table, showing the comparative labor performed annually in the First Auditor's Office since 1860, will more fully illustrate what is here stated relating to the present labor and official responsibility compared with former years.

COMPARATIVE STATEMENT, by FISCAL YEARS, of TRANSACTIONS in the FIRST AUDITOR'S OFFICE, from 1861 to 1880, inclusive.

Fiscal year.	Number of accounts examined and adjusted.		Total.	Amount.		Total amount.	Number of certificates recorded.	Number of letters written.	Number of postage or stamp accounts filed.
	Receipts.	Disbursements.		Receipts.	Disbursements.				
1861	1,744	7,461	9,205	$40,092,704 08	$201,800,753 25	$341,893,457 28	7,249	727	....
1862	1,477	7,906	9,383	47,225,611 94	352,564,687 88	399,790,299 82	7,997	1,065	....
1863	1,407	8,543	9,950	67,417,405 95	890,917,695 77	958,335,101 72	7,486	1,389	....
1864	1,342	9,560	10,902	81,540,726 80	1,447,668,825 90	1,529,209,552 70	7,580	1,316	1,646
1865	1,972	10,520	12,492	90,763,695 52	1,755,151,626 75	1,845,915,262 27	8,524	1,834	2,454
1866	2,122	13,329	15,451	221,445,243 71	1,972,713,889 06	2,194,159,132 77	12,635	1,909	2,326
1867	2,055	10,812	12,867	218,884,931 81	2,339,633,571 08	2,558,518,502 89	10,823	1,735	2,973
1868	2,364	11,396	13,760	215,497,965 23	1,949,304,287 09	2,164,802,212 32	10,160	1,737	3,022
1869	2,547	13,352	15,899	231,762,318 23	1,808,644,481 50	2,040,406,799 73	10,859	1,900	4,295
1870	2,441	12,630	15,071	240,196,398 97	1,344,512,789 41	1,584,709,088 38	10,572	2,295	7,680
1871	2,864	14,101	16,965	239,338,078 13	1,773,277,492 08	2,012,615,570 21	11,436	2,239	6,856
1872	4,511	15,293	19,804	912,200,147 78	1,339,778,632 45	2,251,978,780 23	12,900	2,356	5,672
1873	5,522	14,474	19,996	1,202,869,370 18	1,416,193,007 42	2,619,062,377 60	12,433	2,339	5,138
1874	6,586	17,237	23,823	875,692,671 71	1,283,786,750 33	2,159,479,422 04	13,766	1,905	5,362
1875	7,065	17,994	25,059	1,144,320,298 80	1,491,427,101 07	2,635,747,399 87	12,860	2,282	4,149
1876	6,615	16,847	23,462	1,139,847,330 52	1,746,678,602 58	2,886,525,933 10	12,162	2,048	2,948
1877	7,016	17,544	24,560	696,493,650 61	986,401,191 96	1,682,894,851 57	13,059	2,058	4,505
1878	7,038	16,381	23,419	959,620,393 82	1,287,812,745 00	2,346,833,138 82	12,729	2,473	4,626
1879	7,207	17,618	24,825	917,547,049 73	1,147,581,192 79	2,065,128,242 52	13,824	3,219	5,891
1880	7,035	20,046	27,081	1,206,298,429 71	1,893,413,941 53	3,099,712,371 24	13,768	3,443	3,891
	....	....	....	....	....	....	....	....	75,414

An examination of the foregoing table will show that the labor and official responsibility has increased in this office three hundred per cent. since 1861. This increase will doubtless continue in the future, yet in a less ratio perhaps, growing out of the fact that all public accounts, except those specially assigned by statutes to other accounting officers, are referred to this office for examination and adjustment; and for the further reason that, with the increase of population, and of organized States and Territories, the Treasury Department will of necessity be required to adjust and pay a larger number of accounts that will be filed for settlement. This table clearly shows the necessity for the additional clerical force in this bureau heretofore recommended by me, and which was granted by act of Congress approved June 15, 1880.

While the labor required of the office had increased three hundred per cent. over that of 1861, the clerical force had not been increased over one hundred per cent., and this compelled a constant detail of clerks for special duty in the office in order that the public business might be dispatched without embarrassment.

Attention is called to the number of accounts and the amounts involved in the settlement of what are known as "miscellaneous accounts," under the designation of "miscellaneous desks," from No. 1 to 7 inclusive. These embrace the largest part of the disbursements from the United States Treasury during the year, yet their examination is not under the supervision of a chief of division, as they do not belong to any class pertaining to divisions of the First Auditor's Office as now organized.

I would respectfully recommend that a new division be organized, to be known as the Division of Miscellaneous Accounts, to which should be referred all accounts not now assignable to existing divisions in this office.

While the accounts settled upon these desks are now carefully and critically examined by clerks in charge who would be a credit and honor to any office, for I except none, as to diligence, efficiency, and integrity, this will secure a supervision of the accounts stated by them, which will be an additional guarantee of their correct adjustment. In cases of enforced absence of clerks from duty on account of sickness or otherwise, the work of the new division will proceed with less embarrassment under the charge of an efficient chief.

Renewing my former commendations of the deputy auditor, chiefs of divisions, and clerks and employés of the office for faithful and intelligent performance of duty,

I am, sir, most respectfully, your obedient servant,

R. M. REYNOLDS,
First Auditor.

Hon. JOHN SHERMAN,
  Secretary of the Treasury.

REPORT OF THE SECOND AUDITOR.

REPORT

OF

THE SECOND AUDITOR OF THE TREASURY.

TREASURY DEPARTMENT,
SECOND AUDITOR'S OFFICE,
Washington, September 30, 1880.

SIR: In accordance with section 283 of the Revised Statutes, and your request of the 13th instant, I have the honor to submit my report of the business assigned to this office for the fiscal year ending June 30, 1880.

BOOKKEEPERS' DIVISION.

The application of money appropriated for the War Department and Indian service is shown by the following condensed balance sheet of appropriations:

	War.	Indian.
CREDITS.		
Balance to the credit of all appropriations on the books of this office, July 1, 1879	$1,904,873 55	$5,018,999 73
Amount of repayments during the year	1,012,259 91	325,114 55
Amount repaid through the Third Auditor's Office to the appropriation for "Clothing, Camp and Garrison Equipage"	86,155 40	....
Amount credited by warrants issued to adjust appropriations under section 5, act March 3, 1875, and by other counter warrants	1,081 60	1,349,016 89
Amount of annual, permanent, and specific appropriations made by law	16,613,396 22	6,910,577 07
Total credits	19,524,766 68	13,603,708 02
DEBITS.		
Amounts paid out on requisitions issued by the Secretary of War, and charged as follows:		
To appropriations of the Pay Department	12,680,861 29	....
To appropriations of the Ordnance Department	1,586,538 64	....
To appropriations of the Medical Department	276,861 91	....
To appropriations of the Adjutant-General's Department	71,748 95	....
To appropriations under the immediate control of the Secretary of War	86,051 52	....
To the appropriation for the Commanding General's Office	3,622 53	....
To the Soldiers' Home	103,987 18	....
To the National Home for Disabled Volunteer Soldiers	880,090 00	....
To special acts of relief	5,452 64	....
Amount drawn through the Third Auditor's Office from the appropriation for "Clothing, Camp and Garrison Equipage"	1,068,537 29	....
Amount paid out on requisitions issued by the Secretary of the Interior	....	6,271,506 15
Amount charged by warrants issued to adjust appropriations and by other transfer warrants	1,313 96	1,349,016 69
Amount carried to the surplus fund under section 3691, Revised Statutes	963,371 23	527,466 55
Total debits	17,740,337 14	8,147,989 39
Balance remaining to the credit of all appropriations on the books of this office June 30, 1880	1,784,369 54	5,455,718 63

269

The number of requisitions registered, journalized, and posted was 5,119, namely: War, 1,260 debit and 508 credit; Interior, 3,135 debit and 216 credit. Twenty-nine miscellaneous settlements, involving $224,403.10, were made in this division; 1,170 certificates of deposit were listed; 546 repay requisitions were prepared for the War and Interior Departments; 53 official bonds of disbursing officers were recorded; 370 certificates of non-indebtedness were issued, and 26 special reports were made in reply to inquiries from committees of Congress and individual Senators and Representatives. A statement was prepared, showing the expenditures on account of the War of the Rebellion chargeable to appropriations on the books of this office. The amount disbursed on account of said war up to June 30, 1879, was ascertained to be $1,558,138,343.88.

The following settlements confirmed by the Second Comptroller were entered and posted:

Disbursing accounts: Army officers', 243; Indian agents', 227	470
Claims: War, 331; Indian, 2,337	2,668
Special settlements connected with overpayments, refundments, removal of suspensions, &c	426
Miscellaneous	148
Total	3,712

PAYMASTERS' DIVISION.

Paymasters' accounts on hand unexamined July 1, 1879	154
Received during the year	516
Total	670
Audited and reported to the Second Comptroller	540
On hand, unexamined, June 30, 1880	130

The amount involved in the 540 audited accounts, and in 294 miscellaneous settlements, was $12,110,035.15, as follows:

Disbursements by paymasters	$11,854,187 21
Fines and stoppages paid to the Soldiers' Home	110,386 20
Transfers to the Third Auditor's books on account of tobacco sold to soldiers, $118,156.55; and on account of stoppages for subsistence and quartermaster's stores, $5,371.52	123,528 07
Charges to officers and men of the Army and late volunteer forces on account of overpayments	7,726 38
Amount of overpayments refunded	5,245 59
Sundry charges and credits	8,961 70
Total	12,110,035 15

The accounts of seventeen paymasters were finally adjusted during the year, showing balances due the United States amounting to $12,645.10; of which $9,622.46 has been collected and deposited in the Treasury. From the record of deposits by enlisted men under the act of May 15, 1872, kept in this division, it appears that the sum of $343,381.95 was deposited with paymasters whose accounts have been audited during the year; and that $250,725.78 was returned to the depositors. Under the act of June 18, 1878, which authorizes officers of the Army to count service as enlisted men in making up their longevity record, one hundred and ten records have been examined and revised, in order to determine from what date the officers interested are entitled to increased pay for length of service.

MISCELLANEOUS DIVISION.

There were 1,865 accounts examined in this division during the year, in which disbursements aggregating $3,890,788.07 were passed to the credit of the officers concerned, under the following heads of appropriations:

Ordnance, ordnance stores and supplies, armament of fortifications, manufacture of arms, arming and equipping the militia, ordnance service, repairs of arsenals, and other appropriations of the Ordnance Department	$1,484,230 92
Medical and hospital department, artificial limbs and appliances, Medical and Surgical History of the War of the Rebellion, Army medical museum, and other appropriations of the Medical Department	142,670 24
Recruiting, including $159,126.88 allowed on the adjustment of volunteer recruiting accounts	235,555 07
National Home for Disabled Volunteer Soldiers	1,819,416 84
Contingencies of the Army, expenses of military convicts, publication of official records of the War of the Rebellion, and other appropriations under the control of the Secretary of War	87,837 83
Arrears of pay and bounty due colored soldiers	87,855 50
Miscellaneous	33,221 67
Total disbursements	3,890,788 07
Accounts on hand July 1, 1879	481
Received during the year	1,830
Total	2,311
Accounts examined during the year	1,865
Remaining on hand June 30, 1880	446

The clerks engaged in recording payments to officers of the Regular Army and volunteer forces have examined and entered 100,247 vouchers, discovering, incidentally, thirty cases of double payment, which have been reported for appropriate action.

It is suggested that Congress be asked to amend the act of March 3, 1875 (18 Statutes, 360), so as to require the fiscal officer of the National Home for Disabled Volunteer Soldiers to give a bond to the United States in such sum as the President of the United States may deem proper, said bond to be approved by the Secretary of War, and be subject to the provisions of sections 1192 and 3639, Revised Statutes. Under existing laws the moneys appropriated for the support of the National Home are placed to the credit of the fiscal officer of that institution with a designated depositary of the United States, in the same manner that other public moneys are advanced to disbursing officers of the War Department. The act of March 3, 1875, requires that the managers of the Home shall render to the Secretary of War accounts of all their receipts and expenditures, and that such accounts shall be audited and allowed, as required by law for the general appropriations and expenditures of the War Department. Until the accounts are so audited and allowed the fiscal officer is a debtor to the United States on the books of this office for advances made to him without the security ordinarily demanded of officers who are intrusted with the disbursement of public funds. For this reason I think he should give a bond to the United States. At the same time I disclaim any reflection on the past or present officers of the National Home.

INDIAN DIVISION.

Last year's report showed that, in consequence of a large increase in the number of accounts and claims presented for adjustment, the work of this division had fallen in arrear. Additional clerical force was assigned·to it as early as practicable, and the number of accounts on hand has been materially lessened.

The greater portion of the money appropriated by Congress for the Indian service is now paid directly from the Treasury, on requisitions issued by the Secretary of the Interior, based upon accounts stated by the Second Auditor and certified by the Second Comptroller. Formerly the bulk of the money was advanced to Indian agents for disbursement. Accounts for Indian supplies, &c., were then paid first and audited afterwards. Now they are audited prior to payment. This method undoubtedly has its advantages, but it is also open to objections, one of which is that it throws upon the Treasury Department the labor of paying by draft numerous claims for comparatively insignificant amounts that might be paid more promptly and with less expense to the government by the bonded disbursing officers of the Indian service. During the last fiscal year one hundred and six claims of $5 each or less, and four hundred and thirty-five for sums varying from $5 to $25, have been paid by draft. The weight of the objection here suggested will be appreciated when it is stated that a claim for 50 cents must pass through the same channels and undergo the same manipulation as one for $50,000, and, in its progress through the Interior and Treasury Departments, must pass through the hands of nearly fifty persons, including two heads of departments, one Assistant Secretary, two members of the Board of Indian Commissioners, six heads of bureaus, and eight chief clerks and chiefs of division.

To show how the business of this office has been affected by the change in the method of disbursing Indian appropriations, I append a statement of the number of claims settled and requisitions issued since July 1, 1869, from which it will be seen that, while in 1880 there were five and one-half times as many claims and six times as many requisitions as in 1869, the increase in the amount involved is only 50 per cent.

Fiscal year.	Claims settled.	Requisitions issued.	Amount.
1869	584	560	$2,750,539 75
1870	635	625	1,307,683 96
1871	962	1,606	2,973,705 72
1872	966	977	3,108,160 49
1873	984	1,386	4,730,749 34
1874	1,161	1,462	3,050,552 94
1875	1,678	1,867	4,422,865 55
1876	1,236	1,488	3,556,269 38
1877	2,248	2,194	3,575,641 22
1878	2,966	2,873	3,395,813 00
1879	2,937	3,019	3,795,896 05
1880	3,220	3,351	4,146,681 39

The accounts and claims received, adjusted, and remaining on hand during the last fiscal year are shown by the following statement:

	On hand July 1, 1879.	Received during the year.	Examined and disposed of.	Remaining on hand June 30, 1880.	Amount of disbursements.
Money accounts of Indian agents	451	673	781	343	$1,513,548 27
Property accounts of Indian agents	352	330	333	349	....
Claims of contractors, employés, &c.	393	2,975	3,220	148	4,146,681 39
Total disbursements	......	......	......	......	5,660,229 66

It is proper to remark that the 148 claims remaining unexamined belong to a large class of outstanding claims that accrued between 1873 and 1876, chargeable to appropriations that have been exhausted or carried to the surplus fund, and that they cannot be paid until Congress shall have provided the necessary funds.

Forty one transcripts of accounts of Indian agents, no longer in the service, have been prepared for suit, and the sum of $25,556.82 has been recovered by suit and otherwise and covered into the Treasury.

PAY AND BOUNTY DIVISION.

The work of this division is exhibited in the subjoined tabular statements of claims examined and claims settled. When claims for arrears of pay and bounty are presented to the office, it is the duty of the "Examining Branch" of this division to ascertain whether or not they have already been paid or rejected, and to see that all the evidence required by law and regulation is filed by the claimant or his attorney. The "Settling Branch" deals only with claims that have been reported by the Examining Branch as technically correct and ready for adjustment.

Examining Branch.

Class of claims.	Original claims.					Suspended claims.					Letters written.
	Number examined.	Number found correct.	Number found incomplete and suspended.	Number rejected.	Number of duplicate applications found.	Number examined.	Number completed by additional evidence.	Number again suspended—additional evidence insufficient.	Number rejected.	Total number examined.	
White soldiers.											
Arrears of pay, original bounty, and bounty under act of April 22, 1872.......	10, 810	4	10, 691	109	6	17, 821	1, 170	11, 704	4, 947	28, 631	$1, 233
Additional bounty, act July 28, 1866........	3, 599	......	3, 506	32	61	6, 178	595	4, 354	1, 229	8, 777	13, 599
Mexican war claims, three months' extra pay, act February 19, 1879.............	781	......	391	390	......	840	33	496	311	1, 621	4, 464
Colored soldiers.											
Arrears of pay and all bounties	2, 114	1	2, 099	9	5	12, 084	396	10, 368	1, 320	14, 198	21, 277
Total..........	16, 304	5	15, 687	540	72	36, 923	2, 194	26, 922	7, 807	53, 227	90, 563

18 F

Settling Branch.

Class of claims.	Number of claims.				Letters written.	Certificates issued.	Amount involved.
	Received.	Allowed.	Rejected.	Total disposed of.			
White soldiers.							
Arrears of pay, original bounty and bounty under act April 22, 1872	15,830	1,642	6,824	8,466	....	....	$178,991 91
Additional bounty, act July 28, 1866	1,658	975	996	1,971	....	....	99,629 10
Mexican war claims, three months' extra pay, act February 19, 1879	1,300	167	1,565	1,732	....	....	4,860 56
Colored soldiers.							
Arrears of pay and all bounties	6,329	1,529	2,119	3,648	....	....	139,551 68
Total..............................	25,117	4,313	11,504	15,817	17,939	3,602	423,033 25

In addition to the settlements reported above, one was made for $5,006.13 in favor of the Soldiers' Home, under section 4818, Revised Statutes, on account of unclaimed arrears of pay due deceased soldiers of the United States Army.

The total number of claims remaining on hand June 30, 1880, was 29,470, namely:

Arrears of pay and bounty to white soldiers.................................. 17,164
Additional bounty, under the act of July 28, 1866............................ 2,625
Arrears of pay and bounty to colored soldiers 9,523
Three months' extra pay to soldiers who served in the war with Mexico, act February 19, 1879... 158

Total 29,470

It will be observed that comparatively few of the claims for three months' extra pay to soldiers of the Mexican war, so far presented, have been allowed. The whole number filed up to June 30, 1880, was 3,963, of which only 167 have been paid, while 3,638 were rejected, and 158 remain on hand for adjustment. The time for filing claims for additional bounty, under the act of July 28, 1866, expired on June 30th last. Many claimants do not appear to be aware of this, although the fact has been repeatedly published. Claims continue to be presented, but as the accounting officers cannot entertain them, they are at once returned to the claimants. Unless the time for filing this class of claims be further extended by Congress, I anticipate that the next annual report will show that all have been disposed of.

DIVISION FOR THE INVESTIGATION OF FRAUD.

During the year, 8,722 cases were before this division for examination and investigation. Of these, 4,639 were examined and partially investigated, 332 were finally disposed of, and 8,390 cases remain on hand for further consideration. Abstracts of facts were made in 547 cases; 69 were transmitted to the Department of Justice for suit and criminal prosecution, and 4,900 letters were written. These cases comprise such claims presented on account of military service to the United States as involve apparent, alleged, and suspected fraud in their prosecution and collection, unlawful withholding of money from claimants, forgery, criminal personation of soldiers and their heirs, difficult identification, overpayments and double payments of officers and enlisted men, conflicting testimony, contested heirship, &c., and are as follows :

Unsettled cases of 1,000 white and 1,574 colored soldiers, and cases of 1,900 white and 3,517 colored soldiers in which notice of fraud or wrong was not presented until after settlement of the claims.

The amount recovered by suit and otherwise and returned to the Treasury was $4,696.17; amount of judgments recovered, but not yet satisfied, $375.22; amount secured to claimants from parties unlawfully withholding, $1,741.22; and amount returned to the Treasury by the paymaster having charge of the business of the late freedmen's branch of the Adjutant General's Office, $27,219.41.

I respectfully invite your attention to the urgent necessity of some action on the part of Congress with regard to the claims of colored soldiers and their heirs, to which special reference was made in the annual reports for 1875, 1876, 1877, 1878, and 1879. The case was succinctly stated in last year's report as follows:

> Many colored soldiers now living, and the heirs of others who were killed in the military service, are clamorous for the pay and bounty which they claim to have been defrauded of under the *regime* of the Freedmen's Bureau. The accounting officers of the Treasury Department, to whom their reiterated applications are made, are powerless to afford them any satisfaction.

PROPERTY DIVISION.

Property returns (clothing, camp and garrison equipage) on hand July 1, 1879	7,776
Received during the year	3,817
	11,593
Settled during the year	4,032
Property returns unsettled June 30, 1880	7,561

The sum of $1,204.89 has been charged to officers for property not accounted for, $365.36 has been recovered, and 342 certificates of non-indebtedness have been issued to officers no longer in the service.

DIVISION OF INQUIRIES AND REPLIES.

The records of this division show that 5,467 inquiries remained unanswered on July 1, 1879; that 9,665 have been received since that date; and that 10,360 replies, containing information of a varied character, have been made to inquiries from the Adjutant-General, Quartermaster-General, Commissary-General, Chief of Ordnance, Commissioner of Pensions, and the Third and Fourth Auditors. There are 4,772 inquiries awaiting attention, the major part of which are from the Adjutant-General. The following miscellaneous work has been performed:

Rolls and vouchers copied for the Adjutant-General (414) and for the Department of Justice (50)	464
Miscellaneous papers copied, namely, affidavits, final statements, certificates of disability, letters, furloughs, &c	2,367
Signatures on claims, &c., compared with signatures on muster and pay rolls, vouchers, &c	3,831
Descriptive lists briefed and filed away	13,965
Overpayments and double payments discovered, amounting to	$22,436 48
Amount recovered in satisfaction of charges raised against officers and enlisted men at the instance of this division	2,066 18

DIVISION OF CORRESPONDENCE AND RECORDS.

Letters received, 37,116; written, 32,258; referred to other offices, having been sent here in error, 2,145; recorded and indexed, 984; dead letters received and registered, 1,824; claims received, briefed, and registered, 30,602; miscellaneous vouchers received, stamped, and distributed, 49,743; letters containing additional evidence to perfect suspended claims briefed and registered, 18,080; pay and bounty certificates examined, registered, and mailed, 4,591; pay and bounty certificates examined, registered, and sent to the pay department, 3,692; reports calling for requisitions sent to the Secretary of War, 452; miscellaneous cases disposed of, 3,864.

ARCHIVES DIVISION.

Paymasters' accounts received from the Pay Department to be audited	516
Confirmed settlements received from the Second Comptroller, entered, indexed, and placed in permanent files: Paymasters', 161; Indian, 2,591; miscellaneous, 608	3,360
Miscellaneous accounts withdrawn and returned to files	1,807
Vouchers withdrawn from files for reference in the settlement of accounts and claims	31,929
Vouchers returned to files	49,338
Vouchers briefed	127,976
Mutilated rolls repaired	21,365

RECAPITULATION.

Number of accounts and claims, of all kinds, on hand unexamined July 1, 1879	29,777
Number received during the year	35,258
Total	65,035
Number adjusted during the year	26,588
Number of accounts and claims, of all kinds, remaining on hand June 30, 1880	38,447

Amount drawn out of the Treasury by requisitions on account of claims allowed, and advances made to disbursing officers, $20,633,746.37.

Amount involved in claims and disbursing accounts audited and adjusted during the year, $22,057,617.42.

Total number of letters written, 162,828.

Average number of clerks employed, 136.

As will be seen by the foregoing recapitulation, there were 38,447 unsettled accounts on hand June 30, 1880, against 29,777 on July 1, 1879, an increase of 8,670, as follows:

Increase in number of unsettled claims for back pay and bounty	9,300
Decrease in number of unsettled accounts of all other classes	630
Net increase in number of unsettled cases	8,670

The accumulation of unsettled claims for arrears of pay and bounty is due to insufficient clerical force and peculiarities in the character of the claims presented. The first of these causes has been in a measure removed by an addition to the force of the office, which has enabled me to place more clerks in the Bounty Division, with a view of bringing the work up to date as early as possible; but the difficulties attending the adjustment of these claims increase rather than diminish. Questions of law and fact, heirship, identity, &c., now arise that were comparatively unknown when the claims accrued, and call for an amount of careful investigation and tedious correspondence not required ten years ago.

Very respectfully,

O. FERRISS, *Auditor.*

Hon. JOHN SHERMAN,
   Secretary of the Treasury.

REPORT OF THE THIRD AUDITOR.

REPORT

OF

THE THIRD AUDITOR OF THE TREASURY.

TREASURY DEPARTMENT,
THIRD AUDITOR'S OFFICE,
Washington, October 25, 1880.

SIR: I have the honor to transmit herewith report of the operations of this office for the fiscal year ended June 30, 1880. The following statement shows, in tabular form, the number and amount of accounts and claims received and audited, and the number and amount of accounts and claims remaining unsettled at that date, viz:

Description of accounts.	Number of accounts remaining on hand June 30, 1879.	Number of accounts received in fiscal year ended June 30, 1880.	Number of accounts settled in fiscal year ended June 30, 1880.		Number of accounts unsettled June 30, 1880.	
	Monthly and quarterly.	Monthly and quarterly.	Monthly and quarterly.	Amount involved.	Monthly and quarterly.	Amount involved.
Quartermasters' money.....	556	3,017	2,739	$11,824,068 66	836	$2,144,673 26
Quartermasters' property...	220	4,094	3,762	....	552	....
Commissaries' money.......	625	1,687	1,872	2,790,182 60	440	543,774 26
Pension agents' money......	89	547	277	31,160,748 01	359	42,115,488 37
Engineers' money..........	33	189	186	7,014,215 22	36	2,470,226 88
Signal officers' money......	50	155	89	160,903 94	116	571,655 73
Signal officers' property....	179	701	758	....	122	....
Claims for horses lost.......	5,196	323	617	125,114 57	4,902	891,715 12
Claims for steamboats destroyed..................	73	1	1	1,500 00	73	727,378 87
Oregon war claims.........	710	56	59	7,466 75	707	882 44
Miscellaneous claims	12,674	2,946	2,807	3,349,000 96	13,013	8,175,232 09
State war claims............	9	2	3	687,131 22	8	4,096,750 88
Total	20,416	13,718	12,970	56,922,333 93	21,164	61,737,777 40

BOOKKEEPERS' DIVISION.

	Advances to officers and agents during the fiscal year.	Claims paid during the fiscal year.	Transfers not involving an expenditure from the Treasury.	Special relief acts.	Total.
Number of requisitions drawn by the Secretaries of War and Interior on the Secretary of the Treasury in favor of sundry persons, 2,894, amounting to $75,448,629.86, paid out of the following appropriations:					
Regular supplies, Q. M. D	$3, 321, 030 87	$21, 969 81	$503 04	....	$3, 343, 503
Incidental expenses, Q. M. D	957, 160 09	4, 364 24	29, 740 53	....	991, 264
Barracks and quarters, Q. M. D	871, 759 09	4, 219 42	7, 212 39	....	883, 190
Army transportation	4, 203, 546 11	896, 107 36	3, 964 61	....	5, 103, 618
Clothing, camp, and garrison equipage	1, 064, 157 41	4, 379 88	....	....	1, 068, 537
National cemeteries	109, 029 08	48 74	....	....	109, 077
Pay of superintendents of national cemeteries	58, 775 64	....	....	....	58, 775
Construction and repair of hospitals	75, 540 27	....	....	....	75, 540
Observation and report of storms	375, 039 06	....	....	....	375, 039
Claims for quartermasters' stores and commissary supplies, &c	....	2, 231 92	....	....	2, 231
Cavalry and artillery horses	198, 965 72	625 00	....	....	199, 590
Miscellaneous claims audited by Third Auditor	....	989 54	....	....	989
Constructing jetties, &c., at South Pass, Mississippi River	....	1, 100, 000 00	....	....	1, 100, 000
Repair of road between Fortress Monroe and Mill Creek	6, 500 00	....	....	....	6, 500
Telegraphic cable from main land, in Rhode Island, to Block Island	15, 000 00	....	....	....	15, 000
Fifty per cent. of arrears of Army transportation due land-grant railroads, act March 3, 1879	....	285, 554 09	....	....	285, 554
Claims of loyal citizens for supplies furnished, &c	....	645 40	....	....	645
Buildings for military quarters at Fort Snelling, Minn	25, 000 00	....	....	....	25, 000
Rebuilding officers' quarters at Madison barracks, Sacket's Harbor	25, 000 00	....	....	....	25, 000
Headstones for graves of soldiers in private cemeteries	30, 000 00	....	....	....	30, 000
Military road from Alamosa, Colo., to Pagosa Springs	10, 000 00	....	....	....	10, 000
Military post near Niobrara River, Northern Nebraska or Dakota	50, 000 00	....	....	....	50, 000
Signal Service	10, 501 06	....	....	....	10, 501
Construction, maintenance, and repair of military telegraph lines	50, 000 00	....	....	....	50, 000
Erection of barracks at Fortress Monroe, Va	34, 000 00	....	....	....	34, 000
Extension of military telegraph lines from Fort Elliott	20, 000 00	....	....	....	20, 000
Extension of military telegraph lines, via Newport, on Mill Creek	20, 000 00	....	....	....	20, 000
Military road from Ojo Caliente, New Mexico, to Pagosa Springs	5, 000 00	....	....	....	5, 000
Military road from Scottsburg to Camp Stewart, Oreg	5, 000 00	....	....	....	5, 000
Military post at El Paso, Tex	40, 000 00	....	....	....	40, 000
Military post near Pagosa Springs, Colo	40, 000 00	....	....	....	40, 000
Removing remains of officers to national cemeteries	300 00	....	....	....	300
Refunding to States for expenses incurred, &c	....	8, 513 06	....	....	8, 513
Removing remains of W. E. English, lieutenant Seventh Infantry, U. S. A.	300 00	....	....	....	300
Payment to State of Tennessee for keeping, &c., United States prisoners	....	5, 400 69	....	....	5, 400
Engineer appropriations	7, 249, 809 25	101, 596 01	....	....	7, 351, 405
Subsistence of the Army	2, 389, 481 86	3, 985 36	2, 697 39	....	2, 396, 164
Support of military prison at Fort Leavenworth, Kans	67, 440 00	....	....	....	67, 440
Lost horses, &c., act March 3, 1849	....	111, 225 51	6, 976 71	....	118, 202
Army pensions	54, 481, 808 02	2, 533 94	9, 212 50	....	54, 493, 553
Commutation of rations to prisoners of war, &c	....	7 88	....	....	7

	Advances to officers and agents during the fiscal year.	Claims paid during the fiscal year.	Transfers not involving an expenditure from the Treasury.	Special relief acts.	Total.
Relief of board of trustees of Antietam national cemetery				$13, 223 41	$13, 223 41
Relief of John N. Reed				4, 124 50	4, 124 50
Relief of personal representative of M. G. Harman				354 00	354 00
Relief of the families of the men who perished on the United States dredge-boat McAllister				1, 080 00	1, 080 00
Relief of Michael Granery, Nicholas Wax, and Molere Lange				1, 500 00	1, 500 00
Purchase of cemetery grounds near Columbus, Ohio		$500 00			500 00
Total	$75, 810, 143 53	2, 554, 897 25	$60, 307 17	20, 281 91	78, 445, 929 86

The number of credit and counter requisitions drawn by the Secretaries of War and Interior on sundry persons in favor of the Treasurer of the United States is 1,170, on which repayments into the Treasury have been made through the Third Auditor's Office, during the fiscal year ended June 30, 1880:

Deposits $1, 811, 469 28
Transfer accounts 127, 200 40

Total 1, 938, 669 68

QUARTERMASTERS' DIVISION.

	Money accounts.		Property returns.	Supplemental settlements.	
	Number.	Amount involved.		Money.	Amount involved.
On hand per last report	558	$1, 800, 668 67	220		
Received during the fiscal year	3, 017	12, 168, 073 25	4, 094	300	$105, 909 39
Total	3, 575	13, 968, 741 92	4, 314	300	105, 909 39
Reported during the fiscal year	2, 739	11, 824, 068 66	3, 762	300	105, 909 39
Remaining unsettled	836	2, 144, 673 26	552		
Total	3, 575	13, 968, 741 92	4, 314	300	105, 909 39

	Signal accounts.			Total.	
	Property.	Money.	Amount involved.	Number.	Amount involved.
On hand per last report	179	50	$143, 772 13	1, 007	$1, 943, 840 80
Received during the fiscal year	701	155	588, 787 59	8, 267	12, 863, 370 23
Total	880	205	732, 559 72	9, 274	14, 807, 211 03
Reported during the fiscal year	758	89	160, 903 94	7, 648	12, 090, 881 99
Remaining unsettled	122	116	571, 655 78	1, 626	2, 716, 329 04
Total	880	205	732, 559 72	9, 274	14, 807, 211 03

Number of letters written, 5,417; number of clerks employed, 18; number of vouchers examined, 239,767; number of pages of manuscript written, 10,012.

SUBSISTENCE DIVISION.

The transactions of the subsistence and engineer branches for the fiscal year are shown by the following statement, viz:

	Subsistence accounts.		Engineer accounts.	
	Number.	Amount involved.	Number.	Amount involved.
On hand per last report, June 30, 1879............	625	8823, 183 14	33	$2, 342, 074 34
Received during the fiscal year..................	1, 687	2, 510, 773 72	189	7, 142, 367 76
Total......	2, 312	3, 333, 956 86	222	9, 484, 442 10
Reported during the fiscal year..................	1, 872	2, 790, 182 60	186	7, 014, 215 22
Remaining on hand June 36, 1880........:.........	440	543, 774 26	36	2, 470, 226 88

Number of vouchers examined, 138,851; number of letters written, 1,873; number of difference sheets written, 1,021; number of calls answered, 642; number of clerks employed, 9.

MISCELLANEOUS CLAIMS DIVISION.

	Number.	Amount claimed.	Amount allowed.
On hand July 1, 1879...............................	12, 674	a$8, 427, 840 54	....
Received during the year...........................	2, 946	b3, 096, 392 51	....
Total........................	15, 620	11, 524, 233 05	....
Disposed of during the year........................	2, 607	c3, 349, 000 96	$2, 690, 525 89.
On hand July 1, 1880...............................	13, 013	d8, 175, 232 09	....

	Oregon and Washington Indian war claims 1855-'56.			Lost vessels, &c., act of March 3, 1849.		
	Number.	Amount claimed.	Amount allowed.	Number.	Amount claimed.	Amount allowed.
On hand July 1, 1879......................	710	e$5, 499 69	....	73	f$727, 378 87	....
Received during the year...................	56	f3, 351 50	....	1	1, 500 00	....
Total........................	766	8, 851 19	....	74	728, 878 87	....
Disposed of during the year	59	g7, 968 75	$5, 484 18	1	1, 500 00	$800 00
On hand July 1, 1880......................	707	h862 44	....	73	727, 378 87	....

a This is the amount claimed in 11,142 cases, the amount claimed in the other 1,532 cases not being stated.
b This is the amount claimed in 2,701 cases, the amount claimed in the other 245 cases not being stated.
c This is the amount claimed in 2,433 cases, the amount claimed in the other 174 cases not being stated.
d This is the amount claimed in 11,410 cases, the amount claimed in the other 1,603 cases not being stated.
e This is the amount claimed in 345 cases, the amount claimed in the other 365 cases not being stated.
f This is the amount claimed in 21 cases, the amount claimed in the other 35 cases not being stated.
g This is the amount claimed in 28 cases, the amount claimed in the other 31 cases not being stated.
h This is the amount claimed in 398 cases, the amount claimed in the other 369 cases not being stated.

Number of letters written during the year, 2,373.

STATE AND HORSE CLAIMS DIVISION.

State claims.	Original account.		Suspended account.	
	Number.	Amount.	Number.	Amount.
On hand June 30, 1879.................................	9	$4, 247, 868 07	21	$4, 385, 151 41
Received during the fiscal year ended June 30, 1880..........	2	336, 013 48	14	710, 813 05
Total.................................	11	4, 583, 881 55	35	5, 095, 964 46
Reported during the fiscal year ended June 30, 1880	3	487, 131 22	4	67, 320 91
On hand June 30, 1880.................................	8	4, 096, 750 33	31	5, 028, 643 55

Horse claims.	Num-ber.	Amount.	Num-ber.	Amount.
On hand June 30, 1879.	.....	....	5, 196	$941, 316 51
Received during the fiscal year ended June 30, 1880.	.....	....	256	66, 315 92
Reconsidered during the fiscal year ended June 30, 1880.	.....	....	67	9, 197 26
Total.	.....	....	5, 519	1, 016, 829 69
Claims allowed during the fiscal year ended June 30, 1880.	581	$105, 720 99	.....	
Amount disallowed on same.	.....	13, 706 78	.....	
Amount claimed.	.....	119, 427 77	.....	
Claims rejected during the fiscal year ended June 30, 1880.	36	5, 686 80	.....	
Total.	617	125, 114 57	.....	
Deduct as finally disposed of.	.....	....	617	125, 114 57
On hand June 30, 1880.	.....	....	4, 902	891, 715 12

Number of briefs made, 881. Number of claims examined and suspended, 1,893. Number of letters written, 5,500. Number of letters received and recorded, 5,230. Number of clerks employed, 5.

COLLECTION DIVISION.

	Entries on registers	Number of special cases.	Accounts referred to.	Bounty-land and pension cases examined.	Letters written.	Names of soldiers of war of 1812 abstracted.	Days comparing.	Cases prepared for suit.
July, 1879.	1, 206	307	3, 693	578	253	2, 691	5	....
August, 1879.	1, 120	254	2, 988	428	234	708	6	....
September, 1879.	939	401	4, 044	65	387	1, 913	54	1
October, 1879.	884	191	1, 425	297	158	3, 517	......	....
November, 1879.	960	204	2, 391	253	192	3, 589	56	2
December, 1879.	823	210	1, 488.	855	189	5, 626	57	3
January, 1880.	311	139	1, 272	965	82	5, 763	50	1
February, 1880.	257	139	971	549	113	8, 732	8	....
March, 1880.	1, 079	275	1, 520	682	211	12, 950	......	....
April, 1880.	906	207	1, 656	327	183	11, 464	......	....
May, 1880.	792	222	1, 953	260	195	11, 297	......	1
June, 1880.	795	198	5, 872	322	178	7, 036	......	1
Total.	10, 066	2, 747	29, 273	5, 591	2, 365	75, 198	238	9

Work has been continued during the fiscal year in abstracting the names of soldiers of the war of 1812, for the purpose of arrangement in alphabetical registers, with all the clerical force available. Up to date three hundred and forty-six thousand four hundred and thirty-two payments have been abstracted, which is probably one-half of the payments made for services in that war. In order to complete these registers within a period of time that will be available to the old soldiers and their widows, whose applications for pension are now pending in the office of the Commissioner of Pensions, but whose service cannot be traced for lack of data to base a search upon, an increase in the clerical force in this division will be necessary. In many cases, of widows, especially, who know the fact by tradition that their former husbands served in the war of 1812, the claimants do not know or have forgotten the names of the officers under whom they served. Until these alphabetical registers are completed this office is unable to trace the service of any soldier without the name of the captain or colonel under whom the soldier served. When these registers shall be completed a knowledge of the name of the soldier will be a sufficient clue to trace his military service. When the abstract slips are entered upon registers they may be sent to the States from which the soldiers enlisted to become a part of the records of the State. The current work of the collection division has largely increased during the fiscal year, and if the same ratio of increase continues additional clerical force will be required to keep it up.

ARMY PENSION DIVISION.

Amounts refunded to the credit of the following appropriations, during the fiscal year ended June 30, 1880:

Army pensions 1877 and prior years	$23, 628 45
Army pensions 1878	2, 077 68
Army pensions 1878, being amount to credit of appropriation June 30, 1879	1, 339, 582 06

The above amounts were carried to the surplus fund.

Balance on hand June 30, 1879, appropriation 1879, being the unexpended part of the $1,500,000 appropriated	736, 173 34
Amount refunded and deposited, appropriation 1879	596, 365 67
	1, 332, 539 01
Amount paid on settlement of accounts, appropriation 1879	89, 562 36
Balance to credit of appropriation June 30, 1880	1, 242, 976 65

	Army pensions.	Pay and allowances.	Fees to surgeons.	Total.
Amount appropriated for Army pensions, fiscal year 1880; act January 27, 1879	$28, 400, 000 00	$225, 000 00	$202, 500 00	$28, 827, 500 00
Amount appropriated for Army pensions, fiscal year 1880; act May 31, 1880	8, 500, 000 00	15, 000 00		8, 515, 000 00
Total	36, 900, 000 00	240, 000 00	202, 500 00	37, 342, 500 00
Amount to credit of appropriation undrawn June 30, 1880	357 53	6, 587 64	111, 340 00	118, 285 17
Amount drawn to be accounted for	36, 899, 642 47	233, 412 36	91, 160 00	37, 224, 214 83
Amount disbursed by pension agents	36, 291, 814 64	211, 391 66	73, 161 00	36, 576, 367 30
Amount unexpended on change of bond deposited but not yet credited	80, 892 43	368 28	1, 579 00	82, 839 71
Amount of unexpended balance in hands of agents June 30, 1880, to be deposited	526, 912 47	20, 652 42	15, 920 00	563, 484 89
Amount transferred from Army to Navy pensions by Treasury warrant		1, 000 00	500 00	1, 500 00
Amount erroneously deposited by agent to be repaid	22 93			22 93
Total	36, 899, 642 47	233, 412 36	91, 160 00	37, 224, 214 83

ARREARS of PENSIONS.

	Arrears of pensions.	Fees on vouchers.	Total.
Amount appropriated, acts January 29 and March 3, 1879.	$25, 000, 000 00	$15, 000 00	$25, 015, 000 00
Amount appropriated, act May 31, 1880	500, 000 00		500, 000 00
Total	25, 500, 000 00	15, 000 00	25, 515, 000 00
Amount disbursed by pension agents, fiscal year 1879, "Army"	4, 019, 527 33	1, 884 00	4, 021, 411 33
Amount disbursed by pension agents, fiscal year 1880, "Army"	19, 609, 855 78	10, 535 10	19, 620, 390 88
Total	23, 629, 383 11	12, 419 10	23, 641, 802 21

The following tabular statement shows the number of accounts received and audited during the fiscal year :

	Army pensions.		Arrears of pensions.		Total.	
	Num-ber.	Amount.	Num-ber.	Amount.	Num-ber.	Amount.
Accounts on hand June 30, 1879 ..	89	$12, 275, 103 43	.....	....	89	$12, 375, 103 43
Accounts received during the year.	316	37, 490, 642 83	231	$23, 519, 490 12	547	61, 010, 132 95
Total	405	49, 765, 746 26	231	23, 519, 490 12	636	73, 285, 236 38
Accounts reported to the Second Comptroller	265	29, 639, 695 23	12	1, 530, 052 78	277	31, 169, 748 01
Accounts on hand unsettled......	140	20, 126, 051 03	219	21, 989, 437 34	359	42, 115, 488 37
Total ......,............	405	49, 765, 746 26	231	23, 519, 490 12	636	73, 285, 236 38

Pensioners recorded	19, 235
Pensioners transferred	942
Pensioners increased	7, 355
Pensioners restored	1, 258
Certificates reissued	1, 811
Changes noted	695
Corrections made..	3, 711
Arrears notifications recorded..	2, 836
Pension vouchers examined...	832, 890
Payments entered	777, 964
Pages of abstract added	26, 801
Pages of miscellaneous copied	933
Payments corrected	451
Copies of surgeons' certificates sent to Commissioner....................	220
Vouchers withdrawn from files	6, 525
Letters received and registered	3, 624
Letters written	4, 414
Letters copied in record	3, 635
Letters indexed	3, 603
Pension checks verified before payment, 65, amounting to	$2, 605 75
Settlements for lost checks made, 53, amounting to.....................	2, 021 84
Amount appropriated for printing pension checks, act March 3, 1879, "1879".	8, 500 00
Amount appropriated for printing pension checks, act March 3, 1879, "1880".	9, 000 00
Amount paid on settlement of accounts, "1879"........................	8, 500 00
Amount paid on settlement of accounts, "1880"........................	8, 336 00

The following tabular statement exhibits the number and amount of accounts on hand and unsettled July 1, 1869, together with those received and audited each fiscal year since.

	Received.		Audited.	
	Number.	Amount	Number.	Amount.
On hand July 1, 1869	637	$34, 811, 593 83	....	....
Received during fiscal year 1870	714	27, 743, 819 29	631	$25, 596, 876 39
Received during fiscal year 1871	930	28, 513, 262 44	789	32, 813, 334 28
Received during fiscal year 1872	684	28, 661, 597 26	900	40, 000, 205 68
Received during fiscal year 1873	711	28, 756, 792 92	795	33, 926, 556 19
Received during fiscal year 1874	864	29, 708, 332 26	786	26, 431, 956 71
Received during fiscal year 1875	798	29, 572, 855 54	619	19, 888, 428 52
Received during fiscal year 1876	741	28, 348, 161 99	1, 150	48, 433, 036 92
Received during fiscal year 1877	834	27, 899, 359 30	952	34, 067, 985 43
Received during fiscal year 1878	538	33, 194, 149 18	715	24, 133, 591 52
Received during fiscal year 1879	256	26, 129, 111 64	281	35, 765, 870 58
Received during fiscal year 1880	547	61, 010, 132 95	277	31, 169, 748 01
On hand and received.........................	8, 254	384, 343, 078 60	7, 895	342, 227, 590 23
Amount audited	7, 895	342, 227, 590 23		
Balance on hand June 30, 1880	359	42, 115, 488 37		

The force employed in this division during the last year numbered 36 clerks and 1 copyist. The consolidation of agencies, together with the granting of pensions by acts of March 9, 1878, and "arrears of pension," have caused the vast accumulation of work now on hand. There are over 40,000 notifications of "arrears" received not yet recorded. Large numbers of cases are referred to this office for verification of records and calculation of amount due before payment can be made by the agent. This current work requires prompt attention. The force heretofore employed has been insufficient to keep up the work, but the clerks have all been faithful and energetic in the discharge of their duties, the pro rata of labor performed being larger. The following tabular statements exhibit the amount disbursed by the several agents, and the unexpended balances in hand June 30, 1880:

AMOUNT DISBURSED by PENSION AGENTS, during the fiscal year ended June 30, 1880, as shown by their ACCOUNTS-CURRENT.

State.	Agency.	Agent.	Invalids.	Widows.	Minors.	Dependent relatives.	War of 1812. Survivors.	War of 1812. Widows.	Surgeons.	Salaries.	Voucher fees.	Contingent.	Total.
California	San Francisco	W. H. Payne	$159,702 87	$28,236 88	$7,734 85	$12,062 00	$4,908 81	$12,877 73	$287 00	$3,999 99	$175 29	$740 71	$230,719 84
Dist. Columbia	Washington	J. S. Witcher	1,978,483 07	408,488 37	75,121 80	232,198 19	39,501 60	141,224 13	4,325 00	4,000 00	8,727 75	1,164 19	2,893,234 10
Indiana	Indianapolis	F. Kuefler	1,286,561 39	359,569 21	151,664 62	175,099 02	27,027 21	94,909 75	4,409 80	4,000 00	8,157 00	79 26	2,113,566 46
Illinois	Chicago	Ada C. Sweet	1,979,718 83	532,272 25	187,231 77	377,890 26	32,758 59	106,858 68	5,421 00	4,000 00	9,870 00	1,406 39	3,236,427 77
Iowa	Des Moines	B. F. Gue	1,352,427 30	210,853 35	68,909 96	194,130 57	18,827 77	49,729 30	4,183 00	4,000 00	5,512 35	1,037 82	1,909,420 02
Kentucky	Louisville	R. M. Kelly	353,240 55	259,160 42	51,610 13	136,051 10	25,113 63	105,144 74	1,415 00	3,999 96	2,950 50	226 78	968,913 81
Massachusetts	Boston	D. W. Gooch	1,278,505 22	538,588 70	90,064 16	416,073 99	60,992 98	204,112 92	5,873 00	4,000 00	6,608 85	103 46	2,577,922 36
Missouri	Saint Louis	R. Campion	1,290,779 99	322,147 05	143,565 41	137,970 88	25,795 47	85,631 59	4,212 50	4,000 00	6,278 55	574 78	2,030,056 22
Michigan	Detroit	S. Post	931,258 72	197,909 66	67,413 53	143,850 81	29,051 23	75,671 20	3,184 05	4,000 00	5,432 05	873 54	1,458,674 64
New Hampshire	Concord	E. L. Whitford	1,286,967 31	351,261 21	61,609 76	550,921 70	167,683 79	306,242 01	4,800 00	4,000 00	10,632 10	1,762 54	2,686,080 42
New York	Syracuse	T. L. Poole	1,362,000 94	416,677 33	76,026 24	457,211 11	92,153 93	229,307 09	4,915 50	4,000 00	9,763 80	1,037 36	2,653,093 32
Do	New York City	C. R. Coster	1,005,090 31	445,047 37	71,585 61	301,379 49	42,958 50	139,116 33	3,676 00	4,000 00	7,274 78	4,774 96	2,025,903 27
Ohio	Columbus	A. T. Wikoff	1,798,022 51	626,444 30	131,867 00	380,573 00	62,025 42	214,415 60	9,569 00	4,000 00	12,472 80	869 87	3,249,279 50
Pennsylvania	Pittsburgh	W. A. Herron	1,157,465 12	265,882 92	79,582 95	314,183 53	24,729 02	87,598 40	4,618 00	3,999 98	6,396 60	722 74	1,945,179 25
Do	Philadelphia	H. G. Sickel	1,334,845 48	454,529 12	65,799 02	381,275 97	19,936 95	95,680 70	5,957 00	4,000 00	8,425 65	1,869 05	2,372,298 94
Tennessee	Knoxville	D. T. Boynton	648,751 10	476,114 64	133,221 92	165,064 32	154,934 72	668,154 96	3,571 00	4,000 00	8,818 70	803 15	2,262,944 45
Wisconsin	Milwaukee	E. Ferguson	1,308,842 31	234,861 07	92,756 77	251,577 64	20,710 79	41,303 01	3,744 00	4,000 00	5,084 85	25 50	1,961,887 94
Total			20,524,672 89	6,127,417 85	1,555,867 10	4,636,521 38	790,710 39	2,656,054 14	73,161 00	67,999 91	125,301 45	18,092 20	36,577,802 31
Deduct amount of credits on account of overpayments			916 08	302 16	92 20	26 67	....	96 00	....	....	90	1 00	1,435 01
Total			20,523,756 81	6,127,115 69	1,555,774 90	4,636,494 71	790,710 39	2,657,962 14	73,161 00	67,999 91	125,300 55	18,091 20	36,576,367 30

THIRD AUDITOR.

AMOUNT of "ARMY ARREARS of PENSION" DISBURSED, *during the fiscal year ended June 30, 1880.*

State.	Agency.	Agent.	Invalids.	Widows, &c.	Voucher fees.	Total.
California	San Francisco	William H. Payne	$112,109 51	$9,278 32	$61 80	$121,449 63
District of Columbia	Washington	J. S. Witcher	946,410 91	227,301 23	612 90	1,174,325 04
Indiana	Indianapolis	F. Knefler	1,310,736 70	226,249 85	846 00	1,537,832 55
Illinois	Chicago	Ada C. Sweet	1,573,226 61	301,062 14	998 70	1,875,286 85
Iowa	Des Moines	B. F. Gue	976,740 67	143,152 48	624 90	1,120,518 05
Kentucky	Louisville	R. M. Kelly	360,961 81	230,223 47	287 10	591,473 38
Massachusetts	Boston	D. W. Gooch	691,326 37	298,454 57	528 60	990,309 54
Missouri	Saint Louis	R. Campion	1,156,121 18	184,184 08	698 10	1,341,003 36
Michigan	Detroit	S. Post	711,583 36	188,504 71	502 50	900,590 57
New Hampshire	Concord	E. L. Whitford	644,980 55	559,245 39	594 30	1,204,820 24
New York	Syracuse	T. L. Poole	791,141 75	383,192 93	624 30	1,174,958 98
Do	New York City	C. R. Coster	931,124 81	298,216 98	668 70	1,230,010 48
Ohio	Columbus	A. T. Wikoff	1,509,715 28	394,601 44	1,090 80	1,905,407 52
Pennsylvania	Pittsburgh	W. A. Herron	801,896 27	260,346 90	600 00	1,062,643 17
Do	Philadelphia	H. G. Sickel	1,034,038 61	271,559 09	777 30	1,306,375 00
Tennessee	Knoxville	D. T. Boynton	519,010 69	446,525 98	445 50	965,982 17
Wisconsin	Milwaukee	E. Ferguson	877,722 79	240,353 01	573 60	1,118,649 40
Total			14,948,647 27	4,662,452 57	10,535 10	19,621,634 94
Deduct amount of credits on account of overpayments			668 33	575 73	....	1,244 06
Total			14,947,978 94	4,661,876 84	10,535 10	19,620,390 88

AMOUNT of UNEXPENDED BALANCES in HANDS of PENSION AGENTS June 30, 1880.

State.	Agency.	Agent.	Army pensions.				Arrears of pensions.		
			Army.	Surgeons.	Pay, &c.	Total.	Arrears.	Fees.	Total.
California	San Francisco	William H. Payne	$1,494 06	$1,013 00	$284 10	$2,791 16	$14,864 00	$11 40	$14,875 40
District of Columbia	Washington	J. S. Witcher	14,109 13	2,248 00	1,508 21	17,865 34	86,155 94	130 00	86,285 94
Indiana	Indianapolis	F. Knefler	143,238 13	1,081 00	2,263 74	146,592 87	20,174 20	33 70	20,207 90
Illinois	Chicago	Ada C. Sweet	279 88	79 00	722 61	1,082 49	427 39	142 60	569 99
Iowa	Des Moines	B. F. Gue	161 15	317 00	49 83	527 98	15,260 34	92 20	15,353 54
Kentucky	Louisville	R. M. Kelly	88,793 61	505 00	2,155 08	91,453 69	17,019 54	20 80	17,040 34
Massachusetts	Boston	D. W. Gooch	(*)	627 00	2,787 69	3,414 69	102,685 62	131 90	102,817 52
Missouri	Saint Louis	R. Campion	16 28	287 50	146 67	450 45	25,908 71	(†)	25,908 71
Michigan	Detroit	S. Post	4,835 85	316 00	374 31	5,526 16	447 25	31 20	478 45
New Hampshire	Concord	E. L. Whitford	25,314 22	700 00	105 36	26,119 58	111,337 47	75 80	111,413 27
New York	Syracuse	T. L. Poole	41,623 34	594 50	1,698 84	43,906 68	42,665 32	25 70	42,691 02
Do	New York City	C. R. Coster	194,172 49	1,824 00	1,950 49	197,946 98	93,705 73	99 60	93,805 33
Ohio	Columbus	A. T. Wikoff	2,747 05	931 00	638 33	4,316 38	5,702 16	45 10	5,747 26
Pennsylvania	Pittsburgh	W. A. Herron	558 05	82 00	1,380 70	2,020 75	43,361 11	53 10	43,414 21
Do	Philadelphia	H. G. Sickel	8,509 04	3,130 00	3,817 51	15,456 55	23,313 85	245 40	23,559 25
Tennessee	Knoxville	D. T. Boynton	3,858 30	929 00	378 30	5,165 60	35,186 09	148 40	35,334 49
Wisconsin	Milwaukee	Ed. Ferguson	472 94	1,256 00	389 65	2,118 59	57,630 73	52 90	57,683 63
Total			530,183 52	15,920 00	20,652 42	566,755 94	695,855 45	1,330 90	697,186 25
Deduct amounts overdrawn by agents			*3,271 05			3,271 05		†6 10	6 10
Total			526,912 47	15,920 00	20,652 42	563,464 89	695,855 45	1,324 70	697,180 15

THE FILES.

The number of official money settlements filed during the year is 4,638, making the number since March, 1817, when this office was created, 183,380. In this number are included only the settlements for horses lost in the military service which were made since February, 1878. The pension settlements, which include all vouchers of army pensioners from 1818 to the present time, are in a good state of preservation, but many of the abstracts have been often handled and need repairing and binding.

These settlements are now numbered and kept in a separate series, and the papers are much greater in bulk than all the others. The settlements of accounts of officers of the quartermaster, commissary, and engineer departments are now filed in one series and are in good condition. The settlements of miscellaneous claims also form a separate series, and are rapidly increasing in number and bulk; they are well preserved. There are more than 50,000 property returns filed in this office not included in the above which are also well kept. Much inconvenience has been caused in the past few months by want of room for new settlements which were accumulating; but a large apartment recently vacated by the Bureau of Engraving and Printing has been assigned for the use of this bureau. This room, which is a large apartment, well lighted and ventilated, is quite suitable for files. It will probably soon be ready for occupancy, and when completed will suffice for several years to come.

There were nine lady copyists employed during the year. The number of pages copied and compared by them was 13,678, letters recorded 4,496, making a total of 18,174 pages. The number of names indexed was 25,555. Number of papers copied, 4,747.

It gives me pleasure to testify to the general faithfulness, industry, and fidelity displayed by the clerks employed in this office, and to commend them for the intelligent discharge of the duties assigned them.

E. W. KEIGHTLEY,
Third Auditor.

Hon. JOHN SHERMAN,
Secretary of the Treasury.

REPORT OF THE FOURTH AUDITOR.

v

REPORT

OF

THE FOURTH AUDITOR OF THE TREASURY.

TREASURY DEPARTMENT,
FOURTH AUDITOR'S OFFICE,
Washington, November 1, 1880.

SIR: In obedience to the law requiring the auditor charged with the examination of the accounts of the Department of the Navy to report annually on the first Monday in November to the Secretary of the Treasury the application of the money appropriated for the Navy Department, and in compliance with your request of September 13 last, for a statement showing the condition of the public business intrusted to my charge, for the fiscal year ending June 30, 1880, I respectfully submit the following:

APPLICATION OF MONEY.

The subjoined statement gives in a summary way the application of the money appropriated by Congress for the support of the Navy. It is desirable that this information should be given more in detail, which would require also more minuteness of specification in the appropriations themselves. Wise economy in the appropriation and expenditure of money requires an itemized account. A complete exhibit of this kind would show specifically the precise purpose for which every dollar was appropriated and how expended. If the expenditure had been greater or less than the specific appropriation, the reason would be stated. Such an exhibit, while furnishing desirable information for the people, would give the appropriating power the exact facts needed when grants for a subsequent year are under consideration.

The last column of the following table is made up from the sums named in the money requisitions passed during the fiscal year. It shows approximately the expenditures for the year; but, owing to the nature of the naval service which is performed in remote seas, it occurs unavoidably that bills made on account of accident or other unforeseen circumstances near the close of the year do not reach this office until a considerable time after the year has closed. It sometimes happens that a disbursing officer may charge a payment to a wrong appropriation, and the error, when discovered, is corrected by the accounting officers in the adjustment of his account. The discrepancy which appears in the aggregate amount of the drafts drawn on the Messrs. Seligman Bros., and the amount paid by them during the year, is explained by the fact that bills sold near the close of the year may not be paid until after the beginning of the succeeding fiscal year.

Title of appropriation.	Year.	Amount appropriated.	Amount expended.
Pay of the Navy	1880	$6, 768, 275 00	$5, 578, 184 81
Pay, miscellaneous	1880	475, 000 00	256, 463 41
Contingent of the Navy	1880	80, 000 00	79, 233 30
Marine Corps:			
Pay of the		646, 397 00	559, 673 35
Provisions	1880	75, 007 50	47, 538 11
Clothing	1880	60, 000 00	59, 738 23
Fuel	1880	20, 000 00	11, 731 07
Military stores	1880	9, 686 50	9, 686 50
Transportation and recruiting	1880	7, 000 00	7, 000 00
Repairs of barracks	1880	13, 000 00	13, 000 00
Forage for horses	1880	500 00	450 00
Contingent of	1880	20, 000 00	20, 000 00
Naval Academy:			
Pay of professors and others	1880	53, 126 00	52, 000 00
Pay of watchmen	1880	24, 455 00	24, 455 00
Pay of mechanics	1880	16, 835 95	16, 835 95
Pay of steam-employés	1880	8, 377 50	8, 377 50
Repairs	1880	21, 000 00	21, 000 00
Heating and lighting	1880	17, 000 00	16, 000 00
Library	1880	2, 000 00	2, 000 00
Stationery	1880	2, 000 00	2, 000 00
Chemistry	1880	2, 500 00	2, 500 00
Stores	1880	800 00	800 00
Materials	1880	1, 000 00	1, 000 00
Board of visitors	1880	2, 600 00	2, 600 00
Miscellaneous	1880	34, 600 00	34, 600 00
Navigation and navigation supplies	1880	104, 500 00	99, 628 15
Hydrographic work	1880	46, 000 00	37, 655 87
Navigation:			
Contingent	1880	2, 000 00	1, 980 22
Civil establishment	1880	10, 417 25	10, 417 25
Naval Observatory	1880	22, 100 00	21, 265 30
Nautical almanac	1880	22, 500 00	19, 298 47
Velocity of light, nautical almanac	1880	5, 000 00	413 00
Solar and stellar photography		1, 000 00	1, 000 00
Illustrations for Report on Solar Eclipse		1, 500 00	1, 373 36
Wood-cuts of nebula in Orion		350 00	350 00
Ordnance and ordnance stores	1880	225, 000 00	175, 322 30
Ordnance:			
Civil establishment	1880	11, 866 25	11, 885 24
Contingent of	1880	3, 000 00	2, 192 85
Torpedo corps	1880	45, 000 00	40, 557 88
Equipment of vessels	1880	806, 000 00	678, 890 10
Equipment and recruiting:			
Civil establishment	1880	18, 251 75	18, 251 75
Contingent of	1880	50, 000 00	47, 019 11
Yards and docks:			
Maintenance of	1880	440, 000 00	416, 372 69
Civil establishment	1880	37, 906 25	37, 113 75
Contingent of	1880	20, 000 00	13, 980 46
Naval Asylum, Philadelphia	1880	59, 300 00	18, 341 94
Medicine and surgery:			
Medical department	1880	45, 000 00	36, 102 26
Naval hospital fund	1880	50, 000 00	35, 917 21
Civil establishment	1880	40, 000 00	39, 425 00
Repairs	1880	20, 000 00	16, 293 82
Contingent of	1880	15, 000 00	13, 124 14
Provisions of Navy	1880	1, 025, 000 00	901, 784 02
Provisions and clothing:			
Civil establishment	1880	11, 304 25	11, 392 36
Contingent of	1880	60, 000 00	53, 516 97
Construction and repair	1880	1, 500, 000 00	1, 400, 089 32
Civil establishment, construction and repair	1880	40, 105 75	39, 721 00
Steam machinery	1880	800, 000 00	615, 127 50
Machine for testing iron	1880	3, 000 00	....
Steam engineering:			
Civil establishment	1880	20, 038 00	20, 037 99
Contingent of	1880	1, 000 00	999 80
Navy-yard, Mare Island	1880	75, 000 00	75, 000 00
Navy-yard, Boston	1880	20, 000 00	19, 997 33
Repairs and preservation, navy-yards	1880	300, 000 00	286, 353 51
Repairs of United States steamship Antietam	1880	7, 525 00	7, 517 13
New propeller for United States steamship Alarm		20, 000 00	11, 616 97
Extra pay to officers and men who served in the Mexican war		36, 179 26	18, 961 28
Transfer of lands in Florida not needed for naval purposes		3, 000 00	953 11
Total		14, 393, 323 23	12, 083, 725 43

Permanent and miscellaneous appropriations and funds.

Prize money to captors		$5,883 11
Medals of honor		55 50
Destruction of bedding and clothing for sanitary reasons	$1,200 00	258 59
Miscellaneous expenses, new Naval Academy	5,000 00	5,000 00
Clothing, Navy		178,545 36
Relief act for children of O. H. Berryman and others		289 31
Relief of the administrators of J. D. McGill	102 00	102 00
Relief of Peter Meagher	170 00	170 00
Relief of sufferers by wreck of Huron		504 00
Sale of small arms	46,401 00	33,837 10
Ordnance materials, proceeds of sales		26,342 23

The amount appropriated for officers of the active list was $3,822,875; for the retired list $645,400; total $4,468,275. The amount due and unpaid June 30, 1880, was $110,325.53. Net amount paid to officers $4,357,949.47. The amount appropriated for petty officers and men was $2,300,000. The amount due and unpaid June 30, 1880, was $608,652.85. Net amount paid to petty officers and men $1,691,347.15. The whole amount due and unpaid to officers and men at the close of the fiscal year was $718,978.38. This amount has doubtless been mostly paid by this time and the unexpended balance of the appropriation for pay of Navy correspondingly diminished. Vouchers for payments made during the year, but not included in the above table, will probably exhaust the balances as shown there.

ACCOUNT WITH SELIGMAN BROS.

The disbursements of the Department of the Navy, through the Messrs. Seligman Bros., temporary special agents in London, amount for the year to $1,724,746.79, being $213,592.80 less than the previous year. A commission of 1 per cent. was paid to these agents amounting to $17,246.02. By the terms of the contract they pay interest on balances in favor of the Department at the rate of 4 per cent. per annum, and for the advances made by them they receive 5 per cent. The interest paid to them during the year was $2,698.50; and the interest paid by them $2,925.44. For the previous year the interest account was $6,194.82 against the Department and $2,475.04 in its favor. The interest paid to Seligman Bros. for the first two months of the current fiscal year, July and August, 1880, was $2,372.42. For the twenty-six months closing with the date last named, the interest paid on advances made by them was $11,265.74, and the interest paid by them was $5,400.48, the balance of interest against the Department being $5,865.26. Money is transferred to London usually by the purchase in New York of sixty-day bills of exchange on London, resulting in almost all cases to the advantage of the Department. The net gain from this source during the year was $7,963.41, and for the previous year $10,764.99.

EXCHANGE.

Bills of exchange were sold by the pay officers of the Department of the Navy during the year to the amount of $1,935,478.30. These, with the exception of thirty in number drawn directly on the Secretary of the Navy, and amounting to $188,590.91, were sight drafts on Seligman Bros., London. The premiums amounted to $1,459.63, and the discount to $28,089.20—a net loss to the Department of $26,629.57. The net loss on the drafts drawn on the Secretary was $285.21. Pay officers are instructed to draw on the Secretary when practicable; but in the larger number of foreign ports at which our vessels touch, drafts on the United States are either not salable or cannot be negotiated so satisfactorily as those on London. On the Pacific coast of Mexico and South America, the Sandwich Islands and the West Indies, drafts on the Secretary have been sold to good advantage; but in the ports of China and Japan, the South Atlantic, and the Mediterranean, bills are not often wanted except on London.

During the past year more than usual attention has been given to this subject in this office. A circular was prepared showing in detail the drafts drawn on Seligman Bros. for the fiscal years ending June 30, 1878, and June 30, 1879. This was printed and sent to pay officers by the authority of the Secretary of the Navy, with the hope that it would result in an increase of diligence on their part and a consequent reduction of expense in converting drafts into money. It was shown that for the two years named the gains had been $30,699.91, and the losses $52,277.17—a net loss of $21,279.20. The gains resulted mainly from transactions in Mexican dollars, which were then valued according to the United States silver standard. It was suggested in the above-mentioned circular that the credit of the United States was so thoroughly established, and the demand for the best bills on London so general in the ports visited by the vessels of our Navy, that the drafts of pay officers, if carefully negotiated, should, in nearly all places, bring their face value, and often a premium, in gold or its equivalent.

On January 1, 1880, the value of the Mexican dollar, which had been for the year previous $1.015, was fixed by the annual circular of the Treasury Department at $0.909. Some question arose as to the effect this new valuation would have on the cost of maintaining the Navy of the United States in parts of the world where the Mexican dollar was one of the principal kinds of money in use. The first sale for Mexican dollars under the new valuation was at Shanghai, China, April 7, 1880. The bill was for £8,000, or $38,932, and the number of Mexican dollars received for it was $41,290.32. These, paid out at the new rate, amounted to $37,532.90, or $3,757.42 less than the face of the Mexicans. As the bill was sold, the loss to the Department in exchange was $1,399.10. At the former valuation this loss would have been changed into a gain of $1,358.32. The sale of bills for Mexican dollars from April 7 to June 30, 1880, all in China and Japan, amounted to $218,992.50, and the number of Mexican dollars received therefor was $234,052.72. The aggregate loss to the Department on these was $8,965.58. Had the Mexican dollars been paid out at their face value this loss would have been transformed into a gain of $15,060.22. During the first three quarters of the fiscal year bills were sold in China and Japan for gold, the Japanese "yen," a gold coin almost identical in weight and fineness with our gold dollar, being worth $0.997, serving as the unit of value. These transactions amounted in the aggregate to $433,118.50. The loss on exchange was $7,807.71, or $1,157.87 less than the loss in the silver transactions mentioned above, involving but a trifle over one-half the aggregate sum. Unless circumstances exist which have not been explained, it would have been a considerable saving to the Department if sales for gold had been continued.

The embarrassing feature connected with this subject, so far as this office is concerned, is an almost total lack of means necessary for any intelligent supervision of the sales of bills of exchange. The regulations of the Navy require that the account of sale forwarded to this office must include the certificate of two respectable merchants resident at the place where the bill was sold, stating the current rates of exchange at that time on London and New York, and in what money payable. Such certificates, however, are considered of very little value, if not actually worthless, in a majority of cases. It is in evidence that these certificates can easily be obtained, signed in blank, at the instance of an interested broker or banker, and that sometimes instead of being a help to a proper dispatch of business they may become a convenient cloak to cover improper transactions. Careful pay officers do not esteem such certificates as evidence of due diligence on their part, but protect their reputation by other and better means.

While, during the last year, bills have been sold in more than fifty different ports, full three-fourths of the sales in amount have been made in one-fifth of that number of places. Thus the aggregate sales in Callao, Constantinople, Gibraltar, Hong-Kong, Honolulu, Montevideo, Nice, Rio Janeiro, Shanghai, and Yokohama amounted to $1,462,846.60. If this office were furnished with the financial reports contained in the newspapers of these ten places, it would have a basis for intelligent judgment concerning the bulk of the sales of exchange. These could be supplied at a comparatively small cost. It may also be added that financial reports giving the rates of exchange taken from newspapers of even date with the account of sales and attached thereto would be of much more value than the certificates of any number of resident merchants, the most of whom would not be engaged in foreign trade nor have any special knowledge of the current rates of exchange.

WORK OF THE OFFICE.

The following tables give a brief exhibit of the work of the office for the year. The whole number of accounts and claims received was 2,531. The number settled was 2,829, and the amount involved $18,244,321.01. The number of letters received was 17,741, and the number written 18,862. The number of letters recorded was 26,458; indexed, 39,298. Cash requisitions issued, 2,145, amounting to $19,482,638.33. Refunding requisitions, 347, amounting to $6,617,068.39. Unsettled accounts on hand June 30, 1879, 949. The same June 30, 1880, 651; a decrease of 298.

PAYMASTERS' AND MARINE ACCOUNTS DIVISION.

Date.	Accounts received.	Accounts settled.	Letters received.	Letters written.	Cash vouchers.	Cash disbursements.
1879.						
July	32	36	121	96	978	$883,957 04.
August	39	27	102	83	445	548,584 25
September	23	21	100	112	762	510,451 66
October	29	32	148	116	687	1,264,062 94
November	42	33	115	102	527	918,745 58
December	19	29	101	104	1,149	677,471 15
1880.						
January	26	31	138	92	515	835,897 98
February	34	40	127	112	619	1,017,429 06
March	27	31	110	141	1,935	1,829,883 27
April	27	37	130	98	817	1,116,722 86
May	37	31	121	134	486	1,514,948 44
June	24	36	105	118	570	1,180,586 24
Total	359	386	1,428	1,308	9,430	12,295,740 49

Accounts on hand July 1, 1879, 70.
Accounts on hand June 30, 1880, 43.

PURCHASING PAYMASTERS' AND ALLOTMENT ACCOUNTS DIVISION.

Date.	Accounts received.	Accounts settled.	Letters received.	Letters written.	Amount involved.
1879.					
July	9	4	193	202	$110, 537 36
August	11	8	189	177	597, 028 79
September	2	24	209	207	56, 261 39
October	7	32	209	200	506, 898 36
November	5	30	200	171	485, 722 60
December	13	67	266	252	547, 079 38
1880.					
January	9	44	203	181	473, 621 11
February	7	20	232	220	117, 156 63
March	9	50	225	221	216, 175 74
April	9	6	210	210	226, 482 91
May	6	11	240	205	573, 062 33
June	10	11	209	215	1, 232, 353 40
Total	97	297	2, 585	2, 461	5, 132, 381 90

ALLOTMENT ACCOUNTS.

Date.	Allotments registered.	Allotments discontinued.
1879.		
July	81	118
August	62	101
September	83	72
October	188	140
November	111	105
December	130	206
1880.		
January	187	69
February	138	109
March	84	104
April	131	105
May	92	119
June	65	100
Total	1, 332	1, 339

AMOUNTS PAID for ALLOTMENTS at NAVY PAY OFFICES, during the year 1879.

New York	$141, 716 00
Boston	105, 329 00
Philadelphia	88, 292 00
Washington	83, 963 00
Baltimore	30, 599 00
San Francisco	27, 640 00
Norfolk	23, 892 00
Total	501, 431 00

Accounts remaining on hand June 30, 1879, 507.
Accounts remaining on hand June 30, 1880, 307.
Number of vouchers examined, 32,400.

BOOKKEEPERS' DIVISION.

Date.	Number of pay requisitions.	Amount of pay requisitions.	Number of repay requisitions.	Amount of repay requisitions.	Letters received.	Letters written.	Accounts journalized and entered.	Ledger extracts for settlements.	Answers to inquiries for accounts on ledgers.	Accounts received.	Accounts settled.	Summary statements entered.
1879.												
July	187	$1,395,520 76	34	$40,132 63	106	333	25	25	117	....	....	166
August	195	1,636,173 60	33	564,512 12	160	306	19	32	221	....	....	70
September...	193	2,062,471 10	19	257,026 55	181	317	10	30	103	....	....	50
October......	174	1,583,289 64	39	372,650 15	198	307	98	40	98	1	1	112
November ...	166	1,826,345 83	30	217,010 25	136	257	137	35	76	2	2	117
December ...	184	2,091,475 41	21	929,546 78	110	251	112	36	101	....	....	77
1880.												
January	184	587,189 50	33	345,304 71	168	307	72	27	114	....	....	74
February ...	149	1,859,108 29	32	933,684 15	129	234	116	30	78	....	....	66
March	178	1,447,877 77	16	343,818 98	139	276	60	40	114	....	....	72
April	179	2,102,141 63	48	1,511,097 48	200	250	29	44	113	2	2	75
May	169	1,301,197 13	16	207,134 19	140	221	30	37	114	1	1	67
June.........	187	1,811,847 68	26	994,530 39	175	317	26	41	111	....	....	89
Total ...	2,145	19,482,638 33	347	6,617,058 39	1,902	3,370	754	417	1,360	6	6	1,026

PRIZE-MONEY AND RECORD DIVISION.

Date.	Letters.		Claims.			Amount paid, prize-money.	Records.				Dead letters registered.
	Received.	Written.	Received.	Settled.	Rejected.		Letters keyed in.	Letters keyed out.	Letters recorded.	Letters indexed.	
1879.											
July...............	176	199	40	12	16	$1,407 61	1,598	1,757	1,824	2,326	8
August	161	199	39	27	11	1,289 92	1,460	1,535	1,766	1,766	5
September	243	180	40	23	16	999 34	1,394	1,544	756	2,160	12
October	179	181	29	16	13	467 04	1,417	1,617	2,024	3,476	10
November..........	134	163	36	19	17	557 52	1,358	1,387	2,120	2,120	13
December	156	184	22	11	8	265 74	1,415	1,452	1,087	2,608	6
1880.											
January............	184	224	31	21	10	532 80	1,574	1,677	2,466	3,628	13
February...........	165	186	33	19	12	1,125 01	1,437	1,448	2,577	4,095	22
March	183	250	51	26	25	665 83	1,438	1,768	2,722	4,721	11
April	186	237	30	19	11	1,039 72	1,612	1,635	2,061	4,579	10
May................	121	156	22	12	10	981 45	1,479	1,415	2,598	3,773	5
June	169	249	53	28	18	787 38	1,571	1,927	3,283	3,981	9
Total	1,961	2,408	426	233	167	10,069 36	17,741	18,862	26,458	39,298	124

This division is charged also with the preparation of all reports and tabular statements called for by Congress and the Secretary of the Treasury, keeping a record of appointments, resignations, removals, and absences, the care and issuing of stationery used in the office, and the payment of salaries to employés.

NEW ORLEANS AND OTHER PRIZE-MONEY.

Prize-money amounting to nearly fifteen millions of dollars has been awarded for captures made during the rebellion. The apportionment to the captors of the proceeds of each prize has been made upon the books of this office, and all claims presented in due form have been settled up to date. There is yet remaining a considerable sum uncalled for, but claims are constantly being received, presented by seamen who have been abroad, or for other reasons have not been informed of the adjudication of prizes in which they are interested. Claims of heirs of deceased officers and seamen are also being presented, and these require very careful scrutiny to avoid erroneous payments.

Claims have been presented during the year for prize-money accruing during the war with Mexico, the war of 1812, the war with Algiers, and even the Revolutionary War. Most of them have been rejected on account of lack of evidence.

A balance of bounty for the destruction of vessels at New Orleans has not yet been distributed on account of the failure of Congress to appropriate the money required. Besides the vessels captured by the fleet under the command of Admiral Farragut during the engagements near Forts Jackson and Saint Philip, a large number of vessels were destroyed, for which the court in 1873 awarded the sum of $268,600. At the date of the award there was in the Treasury, after paying fees, &c., but $93,865.20 to the credit of the appropriation "Bounty for the destruction of enemies' vessels." This amount was distributed to all the captors. There remains to be appropriated by Congress the sum of $143,644.47.

Forty-four vessels were admitted to share in this award, and the number of persons entitled to share is more than five thousand.

BOUNTY, ARREARS OF PAY, AND GENERAL CLAIMS DIVISION.

Date.	Claims received.	Claims adjusted.	Amount involved.	Letters received.	Letters written.	Reports on applications for pension.	Reports on admission to Naval Asylum.
1879.							
On hand June 30	352	......					
July	192	119	$16,759 48	856	895	78	2
August	145	158	8,871 72	704	733	167	3
September	111	177	8,863 03	690	696	173	......
October	144	128	6,230 28	641	775	135	1
November	185	125	4,106 71	579	654	265	2
December	75	118	7,436 75	582	612	92	1
1880.							
January	87	124	9,297 76	752	774	201	1
February	61	78	7,487 08	685	643	202	3
March	68	127	7,349 75	681	837	285	......
April	138	103	6,768 16	782	801	193	2
May	136	134	9,404 97	706	642	141	1
June	185	172	7,082 39	815	681	31	......
Total	1,829	1,563	99,587 09	8,473	8,742	1,963	16

THE THREE MONTHS' EXTRA PAY.

Of the number of claims settled in this division, 824 were for the three months' extra pay authorized by the act of February 19, 1879, for services in the war with Mexico, and amount to the sum of $34,800.33 in the aggregate.

Complaint has been made in some instances, originating, no doubt, from a misapprehension of the facts, that the construction placed upon this law has, to a very great extent, defeated the intention of Congress. The act provides that the gratuity is to be paid subject to the limitations contained in the act of July 18, 1848. That law was passed for the exclusive benefit of persons who were employed in the military service during the Mexican war, and limited the payment to those who " served out their term of engagement, or have been or may be honorably discharged," and to the widows, children, &c., of those " who have been killed in battle, or who died in service, or who *having been honorably discharged* have since died, or may hereafter die, without receiving the three months' pay." The term honorably discharged, as used in the law, applied to the enlisted men, and to the volunteer officers of the army who received an honorable discharge when mustered out at the close of the war, or when their services were no longer required. It will be seen, therefore, that the " limitations " of the law of 1848 necessarily excluded those officers of the Navy and Marine Corps who resigned their positions or remained in the service, and also the heirs of those who resigned or died in the service after the 19th of July, 1848.

A bill amending the act of February, 1879, is now before Congress, and if it should become a law it is presumed that all officers and men of the Navy and Marine Corps who were employed in the prosecution of the war with Mexico, and who have not been dishonorably discharged, will become entitled to the gratuity.

NAVY PENSION ACCOUNTS DIVISION.

Date.	Accounts received.	Accounts settled.	Letters received.	Letters written.	Amount involved.
1879.					
July	6	10	64	32	$58,609 62
August	18	15	144	44	27,258 59
September	13	4	71	32	28,914 26
October	7	18	42	39	84,420 28
November	13	20	190	39	30,581 67
December	14	18	200	49	84,188 96
1880.					
January	14	11	129	09	66,201 25
February	19	8	96	53	30,749 79
March	4	10	100	43	120,639 54
April	30	14	104	39	13,858 38
May	18	22	151	57	93,389 06
June	10	18	98	47	47,749 77
Total	166	177	1,392	578	686,542 17

ARREARS of PENSION PAID Under Acts of January 25 and March 4, 1879.

Date.	Accounts received.	Accounts settled.	Amount involved.
1879.			
July	10	....	....
August	11	....	....
September	4	....	....
October	1	....	....
November	16	....	....
December	3	....	....
1880.			
January	1	7	$54,084 03
February	9	15	79,016 02
March	2	11	30,444 15
April	21	30	61,056 61
May	8	2	1,910 94
June	....	15	28,690 86
Total	86	80	255,182 .81

Pension agencies.	Number of Navy pension-ers.	Number of widow pensioners and de-pendent relatives.	Total number of Navy pensioners.	Disbursements at each agency for the year ending June 30, 1880.
Boston, Mass	480	464	944	$168,551 96
Columbus, Ohio	46	96	142	24,922 23
Chicago, Ill	72	52	124	29,677 66
Concord, N. H	147	164	311	56,994 96
Detroit, Mich	22	28	50	8,326 32
Knoxville, Tenn	64	108	172	28,118 30
Louisville, Ky	11	23	34	3,536 48
Milwaukee, Wis	34	30	64	6,214 62
New York City	479	438	917	146,462 49
Pittsburgh, Pa	32	43	75	21,543 64
Philadelphia, Pa	270	421	691	104,109 20
San Francisco, Cal	45	18	63	8,384 21
Saint Louis, Mo	24	37	61	8,033 38
Washington, D. C	350	447	797	144,041 03
Total	2,076	2,369	4,445	758,916 48

Number of accounts on hand June 30, 1880, 9; vouchers examined, 14,675.

NAVY PENSION FUND.

At a very early period of the government Congress enacted that all money accruing to the United States from the sale of prizes shall be and remain forever a fund for the payment of pensions to the officers, seamen, and marines who may be entitled to receive the same. The aggregate amount of this fund now on deposit in the Treasury of the United States is $14,000,000, on which the government pays interest at the rate of 3 per cent., amounting to $420,000 a year. If the interest paid on this fund were 4 per cent., the lowest rate at which the government has yet sold any of its bonds, the amount realized would be $560,000, a sum sufficient to meet the annual pension claims.

Notwithstanding the sacredness of this fund, there are annually bills introduced into Congress designed to make inroads upon it, and to divert it from the righteous purpose to which it has been so justly appropriated. It is to be sincerely hoped that all such designs will fail, and that the principal shall remain intact, while the interest is annually devoted to the just and worthy purpose of compensating officers and men, their widows and children, who have so freely given their services to the government. Instead of dissipating this fund it ought, if possible, to be still more carefully guarded, and secured beyond all peradventure of loss or diminution.

I take pleasure in expressing my obligations to William B. Moore, the long-time faithful and efficient deputy auditor, to the chiefs of divisions, and to the clerks and employés generally, for their devoted and capable service and close attention to their respective duties. While there may be and probably is room for improvement in the condition of the public business committed to my charge, I am glad to believe and to report that it has been carefully attended to during the year, and so conducted as to merit your approval and commendation.

I have the honor to be, very respectfully, your obedient servant,

CHARLES BEARDSLEY,
Auditor.

Hon. JOHN SHERMAN,
Secretary of the Treasury.

٢

REPORT OF THE FIFTH AUDITOR.

REPORT

OF

THE FIFTH AUDITOR OF THE TREASURY.

TREASURY DEPARTMENT,
FIFTH AUDITOR'S OFFICE,
Washington, D. C., November 1, 1880.

SIR: I have the honor to submit herewith the operations of this office for the fiscal year ended June 30, 1880.

* * * * * * *

The adjustments required the examination of one hundred and eighty-six thousand seven hundred and seventy vouchers, amounting to eight hundred and six millions, five hundred and twenty-nine thousand, seven hundred and ninety-five dollars and eighty-three cents ($806,529,795.83).

The several clerks engaged in the examination and adjustment of accounts, and keeping the records, and the copyists employed, have been faithful and industrious, and have given great satisfaction by the manner their respective duties have been performed.

J. B. MANN,
Acting Auditor.

Hon. JOHN SHERMAN,
Secretary of the Treasury.

NOTE.—The tables pertaining to this report are omitted for want of space, but they will be found in the pamphlet edition of the Auditor's report.

REPORT OF THE SIXTH AUDITOR.

REPORT

OF THE

AUDITOR OF THE TREASURY FOR THE POST-OFFICE DEPARTMENT.

—————

OFFICE OF THE AUDITOR
OF THE TREASURY FOR THE
POST-OFFICE DEPARTMENT,
Washington, D. C., October 26, 1880.

SIR : I have the honor to submit the following report of the business operations of this office for the fiscal year ended June 30, 1880. My annual report to the Postmaster-General, now in course of preparation, will exhibit in detail the financial transactions of the Post-Office Department during the past fiscal year.

*   *   *   *   *   *   *

NECESSITY FOR THE INCREASED APPROPRIATION FOR WHICH ESTIMATES HAVE BEEN SUBMITTED.

I have the honor to invite your attention to the large increase of business in this office over last fiscal year, as shown by the reports of the several chiefs of division, especially of the Money-Order Division.

The general average of the increase of work in the various divisions is as follows:

Examining Division, six per cent.
Registering Division, ten per cent.
Bookkeeping Division, thirteen per cent.
Stating Division, nine per cent.
Collecting Division, seven per cent.
Foreign Mail Division, eleven per cent.
Pay Division, ten per cent.
Money-Order Division, thirty-two per cent.

In my estimates for the service of this bureau for the fiscal year ending June 30, 1882, I have asked for an appropriation for fifteen additional clerks, and I refer to the foregoing statement as conclusive evidence of the necessity for that increase.

There was also submitted an estimate for one chief clerk, at $2,100 per annum, and, in support thereof, I have to offer the following reasons:

The force now employed in this bureau is greater than that of any of the other bureaus of the Department, and the details of business probably more numerous. Much of the time of the Auditor and Deputy Auditor is occupied with routine office affairs which could very properly be disposed of by a chief clerk.

_____

NOTE.—A summary of the principal labors performed by the several divisions of this office will be found in the pamphlet copies of the Auditor's report.

Under the present organization, no provision is made for filling the place of the Deputy Auditor during his absence or sickness, or that of the Auditor. The appointment of a chief clerk would supply an officer upon whom this duty could devolve.

By the last reorganization of the clerical force of this office, the position of principal clerk of the Law Division was abolished, and it is intended that the duties formerly discharged by that officer—namely, the preparation of cases for suit and the conduct of the correspondence arising therein—shall be performed by the chief clerk.

I have fixed the compensation at $2,100 for the reason that the duties and responsibilities proposed to be assigned to the chief clerk would, in my opinion, fully justify such a salary, and in order that the rank of the position may be superior to that of the chiefs of division, over whom he would be called to exercise authority.

This additional appropriation is earnestly recommended as much needed, and in the confident belief that it would materially facilitate the transaction of the business of the office and advance the public interest.

I am pleased to report, in conclusion, that the work of the bureau, in all its branches, is in excellent condition. The accounts of the Post-Office Department, numbering over four hundred thousand, and involving over two hundred million dollars, have been promptly settled, collections made, and liabilities paid, with a loss so slight as to be scarcely appreciable. Never, since the organization of the government, have the accounts of the Post-Office Department been in so satisfactory a condition as at the present time.

To my efficient and faithful Deputy Auditor, Mr. F. B. Lilley, the chiefs of the various divisions, and to the conscientious and untiring efforts of the clerks and other employés of this office, I am indebted for this very favorable condition of the work, and I commend them all to your special favor and confidence.

I am, sir, very respectfully,

J. M. McGREW,
Auditor.

Hon. JOHN SHERMAN,
Secretary of the Treasury,
Washington, D. C.

REPORT OF THE TREASURER OF THE UNITED STATES.

REPORT

OF

THE TREASURER OF THE UNITED STATES.

TREASURY OF THE UNITED STATES,
Washington, November 1, 1880.

SIR: The following statement of the transactions of this office and of the condition of the public business therein, during the fiscal year 1880, is respectfully submitted.

From the tables in the appendix the following facts appear: .

The receipts of the government compare very favorably with those of the previous fiscal year, and show an increase from customs, internal revenue, and sales of public lands, of $59,811,505.78, and a decrease in those from miscellaneous sources of only $112,079.26. The expenditures show a slight increase of $695,074.25 in the aggregate as compared with the previous fiscal year, caused by an increase of $22,395,040.06 in the payments on account of the Interior Department, but show a decrease of $21,699,965.81 in the expenditures for interest and premium on the public debt, on civil and miscellaneous accounts, and for the War and Navy Departments.

The balance of public money on deposit in the Treasury and subject to draft at the close of business June 30, 1879, was $417,223,787.08; the receipts during the year from all sources amounted to $494,578,241.20 and the drafts paid to $708,190,900.76. After deducting receipts properly refunded and outstanding drafts, there was subject to draft, at the close of business June 30, 1880, $204,683,836.34, which differs from the debt statement balance by $3,595,213.46, as explained in the appendix.

The business of the government involved the transfer during the year of $1,053,357,082.22, the greater portion through the medium of the accounts of this office, and the remainder by actual transportation of the funds.

At the close of the year $28,581,290.93 stood to the credit of disbursing agents of the United States upon the books of the Treasury.

The amount subject to draft June 30, 1879, on account of the postal service was $2,660,412.29; the receipts during the year, including the amount paid from the Treasury for the deficiency in the postal revenues, were $35,691,810.29, of which amount $26,048,562.16 was received and disbursed by postmasters without having been deposited in the Treasury. After deducting deposits refunded and outstanding drafts, there remained subject to draft June 30, 1880, $2,375,727.04.

The total unavailable funds have not increased during the year by loss or defalcation, but remain unchanged at $29,512,206.85 for the Treasury, and at $40,078.06 for the Post-Office Department.

Fifty-eight national banks were organized during the year, five failed,

315

and twenty-one went into voluntary liquidation, leaving two thousand, one hundred and two doing business at the close of the year.

The amount collected from national banks by the Treasurer of the United States for semi-annual duty accruing during the year was $7,591,770.43. The total amount collected during the existence of the national banking system is $100,361,469.35.

There were on deposit in this office, at the close of the year, for the security of the circulating notes of national banking associations, United States bonds to the amount of $361,652,050, and to secure public deposits therein $14,777,000.

At the close of the year the United States notes and paper currency outstanding amounted to $362,659,008.70. The total face value of currency redeemed from the date of the first issue is $2,229,368,462.17, from which the deductions for mutilations under the regulations amounted to $297,363.76.

The total amount of United States bonds retired by purchase, redemption, conversion, and exchange, from March 11, 1869, to June 30, 1880, is $1,898,040,750.

The coupons from United States bonds paid during the year amounted to $31,479,603.86, and there were 296,936 quarterly checks issued in payment of $40,719,376.04 interest on registered bonds.

There was redeemed during the year $61,585,675 in national bank notes, making the aggregate amount redeemed under the act of June 20, 1874, $1,039,838,889.

THE STATE OF THE TREASURY.

The resources and liabilities of the Treasury on the 30th day of September, 1877, 1878, 1879, and 1880, are exhibited in the following statement:

STATEMENT of LIABILITIES and ASSETS of the TREASURY of the UNITED STATES, September 30, 1877, 1878, 1879, and 1880.

	September 30, 1877.	September 30, 1878.	September 30, 1879.	September 30, 1880.
LIABILITIES.				
Fund for redemption of Certificates of Deposit (Act June 8, 1872)	$41,675,000 00	$40,890,000 00	$31,335,000 00	$9,975,000 00
Post-Office Department Account......	1,672,707 96	2,151,693 76	2,187,891 50	2,600,489 19
Disbursing Officers' Balances........	13,733,913 59	17,049,019 89	26,007,876 95	22,189,236 49
Fund for redemption of Notes of National Banks "failed," "in liquidation," and "reducing circulation"..	13,602,238 00	9,182,400 90	12,939,880 75	19,746,955 25
Undistributed Assets of failed National Banks......................	856,379 42	775,814 12	642,314 33	616,560 21
Five-per-cent. Fund for redemption of National-Bank Notes	14,109,294 60	12,974,232 75	15,082,482 99	15,428,016 82
Fund for redemption of National Bank Gold-Notes	1,720 00	1,720 00	219,940 00	475,965 00
Currency and Minor-Coin Redemption-Account	23,104 41	5,987 00	4,213 15	3,075 60
Fractional Silver-Coin Redemption-Account	....	....	152,604 10	74,681 75
Interest Account	595,662 25	670,593 00	101,514 75	99,585 00
Interest Account, Pacific Railroads, and Louisville and Portland Canal Company	32,280 00	15,650 40	6,270 00	8,400 00
Treasurer United States, Agent for paying interest on District of Columbia Bonds	27,558 80	40,811 27	298,435 54	366,532 59
Treasurer's Transfer-Checks outstanding........................	2,520,702 79	2,482,885 05	3,053,101 29	2,667,773 97

STATEMENT of LIABILITIES and ASSETS of the TREASURY, &c.—Continued.

	September 30, 1877.	September 30, 1878.	September 30, 1879.	September 30, 1880.
Treasurer's General Account.				
Old Debt	$617,885 58	$677,864 26	$840,608 41	$916,585 07
Interest due and unpaid	8,447,864 77	9,345,289 13	11,561,093 77	9,784,449 42
Called Bonds and Interest	19,064,191 25	12,013,016 78	31,033,519 63	5,959,436 43
Gold Certificates	37,997,580 00	32,826,660 00	14,910,990 06	7,511,709 00
Silver Certificates		2,028,070 00	4,571,850 00	18,521,960 00
Special Fund for redemption of Fractional Currency	8,265,412 00	10,000,000 00		
Drafts Outstanding	1,319,793 05	1,258,709 91	3,979,232 69	1,540,071 97
Balance, including Bullion Fund	78,724,902 78	182,845,615 52	143,977,096 20	149,281,443 97
Total	243,681,111 25	337,434,964 74	303,485,995 07	267,676,912 40
ASSETS.				
Gold Coin and Bullion	$107,039,526 85	$136,030,392 20	$169,827,571 29	$135,640,185 77
Standard Silver Dollars		12,155,295 00	31,896,774 00	47,784,744 00
Fractional Silver Coin	*7,425,453 04	6,143,903 02	16,873,696 47	24,723,692 08
Silver Bullion		9,634,634 48	4,290,124 25	6,154,392 93
Gold Certificates	18,994,000 00	9,392,920 00	70,790 00	31,000 00
Silver Certificates		1,316,470 00	3,131,180 00	6,692,579 00
United States Notes	74,558,308 23	63,049,399 67	48,762,728 01	27,901,504 07
United States Notes, Special Fund for redemption of Fractional Currency	8,265,412 00	10,000,000 00		
National-Bank Notes	14,109,541 51	9,230,043 81	4,278,958 76	3,288,404 57
National-Bank Gold-Notes	1,720 00	1,720 00	183,640 00	220,125 00
Fractional Currency	237,203 64	161,681 86	90,978 15	60,712 08
Deposits held by National-Bank Depositaries	10,731,025 90	75,661,403 15	17,836,816 48	11,212,315 94
Nickel and Minor Coin	870,140 54	1,416,898 50	1,924,790 87	1,063,665 22
New York and San Francisco Exchange	333,500 00	367,000 00	1,799,734 51	1,453,000 00
One and Two Year Notes, &c	503 70	8,016 51	400 40	325 50
Redeemed Certificates of Deposit (Act June 8, 1872)		1,345,000 00	2,025,000 00	90,000 00
Quarterly Interest Checks and Coin Coupons paid	90,012 01	256,900 46	189,579 73	141,517 91
Registered and Unclaimed Interest paid	383,907 50	370,482 80	22,355 00	10,203 50
United States Bonds and Interest			567 64	297,343 81
Interest on District of Columbia Bonds	6,562 48	1,345 64	516 97	3,047 12
Refunding Certificates and Interest			34,119 74	
Pacific Railroads Sinking Fund			45,212 75	
Speaker's Certificates	6,235 00	120,802 00		126,315 00
Deficits, unavailable Funds	737,345 93	729,195 64	690,848 50	690,848 90
Total	243,681,111 25	337,434,964 74	303,485,995 07	267,676,912 40

* Fractional Silver Coin, and Silver Bullion.

It appears from the above table that the gold and silver coin and bullion ranged from $114,464,982.79 in 1877 to $163,969,444.70 in 1878, to $222,807,368.01 in 1879, and to $214,303,215.38 in 1880. The decrease of $8,500,000 between 1879 and 1880 is represented by a reduction in the gold balance of $34,000,000 and an increase in the silver coin and bullion on hand. The influences tending to the decrease of the gold balance have been, primarily, the scarcity of notes, compelling payments of the daily balance to the New York Clearing-House in gold coin. There has been but a small amount of United States notes and gold certificates presented for redemption in gold coin. There has been during the year an increase in silver coin of $15,977,970 in standard dollars and of $7,849,994.21 in fractional silver coin.

The note assets, including balances due from depositary banks, have decreased from $107,664,287.64 in 1877 to $93,417,282.91 in 1878, to $33,926,653.25 in 1879, and to $42,402,314.58 in 1880. The steady decrease is due in great measure to the withdrawal of notes, caused by the presentation of clearing-house certificates for redemption, the amount

of these certificates outstanding having been reduced from $31,335,000
1879 to $9,975,000 in 1880. Another reason for the smallness of the n(
balance may be found in the falling off in note receipts, the revenues
the government being now largely paid in coin and in silver certificat

From the following tables of assets and liabilities for November
1879, and 1880, the changes in the funds can more readily be seen. Th
also show the excess of assets, constituting the reserve available i
resumption purposes.

*STATEMENT of the ASSETS and LIABILITIES of the GOVERNMENT, Novem
1, 1879.*

ASSETS.

Gold Coin in Treasury and Mints...	$121,355,448 90	
Gold Bullion	50,358,464 75	
Silver Bullion	3,537,224 31	
Standard Silver Dollars	32,322,634 00	
Fractional Silver Coin..............	17,755,986 76	
		$225,329,758 72
United States Notes		49,537,815 74
Total		$274,867,574

LIABILITIES.

Called Bonds matured	$24,271,506 95		
Less amount on hand..............	762 93		
		$24,270,744 02	
Interest due	9,704,299 49		
Less amount on hand..............	277,706 29		
		9,426,593 20	
Gold Certificates	14,591,000 00		
Less amount on hand..............	213,400 00		
		14,377,600 00	
Silver Certificates	6,135,850 00		
Less amount on hand..............	4,531,480 00		
		1,604,370 00	
Certificates of Deposit (Act of June			
8, 1872)	22,510,000 00		
Less amount on hand	2,315,000 00		
		20,195,000 00	
Disbursing Officers' Balances.......................		18,337,397 01	
Outstanding Drafts and Checks....................		5,020,764 96	
Five per cent. Redemption Fund....................		15,742,887 52	
Fund for redemption of Notes of National Banks—			
failed, liquidating, and reducing circulation......		13,052,124 25	
Post-Office Department Account		1,793,049 26	
			123,820,530
Available for Resumption..			151,047,044

*STATEMENT of the ASSETS and LIABILITIES of the GOVERNMENT, Novem
1, 1880.*

ASSETS.

Gold Coin in Treasury and Mints...................	$60,210,179 75	
Gold Bullion..	80,742,657 99	
Silver Bullion......................................	6,043,367 37	
Standard Silver Dollars............................	47,084,459 00	
Fractional Silver Coin..............................	24,629,429 89	
Deposits with National Bank Deposi-		
taries	$8,550,467 82	
United States Notes	26,389,331 51	
		34,939,799 33
Total..		$253,649,953

LIABILITIES.

Old Debt...........................	$816,585 07	
Less amount on hand............,...	2,298 96	
		$814,286 11
Called Bonds Matured...............	5,550,742 04	
Less amount on hand...............	507 64	
		5,550,234 40
Interest due	8,871,464 54	
Less amount on hand..............	323,755 46	
		8,547,709 08
Gold Certificates..................	7,454,500 00	
Less amount on hand...............	6,800 00	
		7,447,700 00
Silver Certificates................	27,113,960 00	
Less amount on hand...............	7,333,719 00	
		19,780,241 00
Certificates of Deposit (Act of June 8, 1872)...........................	8,775,000 00	
Less amount on hand...............	150,000 00	
		8,625,000 00
Disbursing Officers' Balances......................		20,170,794 19
Outstanding Drafts and Checks....................		3,106,882 65
Five per cent. Redemption Fund..................		15,369,491 18
Fund for Redemption of Notes of National Banks—failed, liquidating, and reducing circulation......		20,825,767 25
Post-Office Department Account..................		1,814,833 86
		112,052,939 72

Available for Resumption..................................141,597,013 61

The amount of gold coin and bullion in the Treasury January 1, 1879, the date of resumption of specie payments, was $135,382,639.42, and at this date it is $140,952,837.74, a gain of $5,570,198.32; and, in addition, there have accumulated in the Treasury $47,084,459 in standard silver dollars.

The redemptions of United States notes in gold since the resumption of specie payments have aggregated $11,963,336, as follows:

	1879.	1880.
January...	$1,571,725	$71,500
February..	909,249	72,080
March...	952,766	43,020
April..	699,773	16,000
May...	1,339,883	51,000
June..	2,503,302	47,200
July..	954,800	25,000
August..	981,400	22,000
September...	603,485	150,000
October...	740,295	9,000
November...	77,499	....
December...	122,359	....

Since the order of the Department of January 1, 1879, authorizing the receipt of United States notes for customs duties, there have been received on that account $142,323,601, as follows:

	1879.	1880.
January...	$6,864,889	$4,126,450
February..	9,340,452	4,477,161
March...	11,919,876	3,702,727
April..	10,562,006	3,231,697
May...	9,703,566	2,888,138
June..	9,336,778	3,951,568
July..	10,588,145	4,029,892
August..	11,961,307	2,844,658
September...	12,506,018	2,241,305
October...	9,281,243	1,802,288
November...	4,612,198	....
December...	3,051,219	....

REFUNDING.

The refunding operations virtually ceased in September, 1879, by the closing of the loan accounts with depositary banks, though the conversion of ten-dollar refunding certificates into 4 per cent. consols of 1907 still continues. The receipts into the Treasury on account of the 5 per cent. funded loan of 1881, of the 4½ per cent. funded loan of 1891, and of the 4 per cent. consols of 1907, to October 31, 1880, aggregate, principal and interest, $1,514,084,180.03, which was deposited in depositary banks and at the various subtreasury offices as set forth in the following table:

With whom deposited.	Funded Loan of 1881 (5 per cent.).	Funded Loan of 1891 (4½ per cent.).	Funded Loan of 1907 (4 per cent.).
Treasurer U. S., Washington, D. C...............	$270, 327, 152 73	$178, 852, 831 21	$100, 935, 498 21
Assistant Treasurer U. S., New York, N. Y.....	47, 914, 175 65	71, 258, 010 33	38, 526, 829 47
Assistant Treasurer U. S., Boston, Mass	1, 067, 003 37	1, 648, 000 00	847, 116 31
Assistant Treasurer U. S., Philadelphia, Pa	17, 104 69	....	358, 426 77
Assistant Treasurer U. S., Baltimore, Md	....	....	322, 505 84
Assistant Treasurer U. S., Cincinnati, Ohio.....	16, 659 91	....	2, 349, 448 89
Assistant Treasurer U. S., Chicago, Ill	618 30	....	4, 562, 457 22
Assistant Treasurer U. S., Saint Louis, Mo	94, 806 71	....	467, 447 94
Assistant Treasurer U. S., New Orleans, La	....	....	293, 791 67
Assistant Treasurer U. S., San Francisco, Cal ..	142, 000 00	....	8, 756, 106 75
Depositary U. S., Pittsburgh, Pa	1, 850 00	....	....
Depositary U. S., Santa Fé, N. Mex	10, 550 00	....	....
National Bank Depositaries	200, 958, 362 23	49, 590, 000 00	575, 744, 304 83
Total..........................	520, 551, 342 59	251, 348, 841 54	742, 183, 995 90

The conversions of refunding certificates, amounting to $39,367,857.69, are included in the sum of $109,935,498.21, received by the Treasurer of the United States on account of the funded loan of 1907.

REFUNDING CERTIFICATES.

The amount of refunding certificates of the denomination of $10 issued under the act of February 26, 1879, was $40,012,750, including registered certificates. Up to this date there have been received for conversion into 4 per cent. bonds $39,033,550 from 8,534 depositors, the average amount presented by each depositor being $4,574. The amount outstanding at this date is $979,200.

RETIREMENT OF BONDS.

There were redeemed and paid for by this office from November 1, 1879, to date, $17,444,800 in called bonds upon which the interest had ceased, the proceeds of which, including interest, amounted to $17,774,333.94.

There were also purchased on account of the sinking fund during the same period $106,271,100 in United States bonds, the total cost of which, including interest and premium, was $111,220,366.09.

UNITED STATES NOTES.

The following table shows the total amount of United States note outstanding at the close of the fiscal years 1877, 1878, 1879, and 1880, b denominations. The fractional parts of a dollar and the odd amoun appearing therein arise from the discounting under the rules of the Department of mutilated notes redeemed.

Denomination.	1877.	1878.	1879.	1880.
One dollar	$25,160,287 80	$20,929,874 30	$18,209,980 80	$20,322,332 00
Two dollars	25,369,826 20	20,910,948 20	18,092,653 20	20,352,813 00
Five dollars	49,338,224 90	54,669,856 50	54,107,113 00	65,432,548 00
Ten dollars	64,495,717 00	65,551,644 00	64,638,562 00	74,916,751 00
Twenty dollars	62,607,197 00	62,720,643 00	60,470,887 00	72,143,207 00
Fifty dollars	35,912,910 00	27,182,680 00	26,523,340 00	24,808,995 00
One hundred dollars	29,410,170 00	31,624,670 00	32,038,480 00	32,797,870 00
Five hundred dollars	33,884,500 00	30,878,500 00	32,586,500 00	19,224,000 00
One thousand dollars	34,585,500 00	33,212,500 00	35,070,500 00	16,532,500 00
Five thousand dollars			4,000,000 00	680,000 00
Ten thousand dollars			2,960,000 00	460,000 00
Total	360,764,332 00	347,681,016 00	347,681,016 00	347,681,016 00
Destroyed in subtreasury in Chicago fire, denominations unknown	1,000,000 00	1,000,000 00	1,000,000 00	1,000,000 00
Outstanding	359,764,332 00	346,681,016 00	346,681,016 00	346,681,016 00

From the above it appears that, while the aggregate amount of notes outstanding has not changed, there has been an increase of $2,122,351 in one dollar notes, $2,260,160 in two dollar notes, $11,325,435 in five dollar notes, $10,278,189 in ten dollar notes, $11,672,320 in twenty dollar notes, and $759,390 in one hundred dollar notes; and a decrease of $714,345 in fifty dollar notes, $13,345,500 in five hundred dollar notes, $18,538,000 in one thousand dollar notes, $3,320,000 in five thousand dollar notes, and $2,500,000 in ten thousand dollar notes; showing an increase of $37,658,455 in notes of a less denomination than fifty dollars, and a corresponding decrease in the higher denominations. The notes of the denomination of five thousand and ten thousand dollars issued at the time of the suspension of the issue of gold notes are disappearing from circulation by being presented for redemption, and no more are being issued, the demand for them having virtually ceased.

The following table of issues and redemptions of United States notes during the fiscal years 1878, 1879, and 1880, shows the total redemption during those years, and the manner in which the changes in the denominations of outstanding notes were brought about:

Denomination.	1878.		1879.		1880.	
	Issued.	Redeemed.	Issued.	Redeemed.	Issued.	Redeemed.
One dollar	$7,562,851	$11,792,775	$6,508,133	$9,223,026 50	$9,057,863 00	$6,935,511 80
Two dollars	6,286,000	10,746,878	5,892,000	8,710,295 00	8,232,000 00	5,971,840 20
Five dollars	15,820,000	16,111,867	11,060,000	11,622,443 50	19,680,000 00	8,354,565 00
Ten dollars	11,380,000	13,763,963	9,280,000	10,193,082 00	16,520,000 00	6,241,811 00
Twenty dollars	9,200,000	9,086,554	7,400,000	8,649,755 00	17,360,000 00	5,687,680 00
Fifty dollars	3,200,000	6,367,030	2,400,000	4,058,340 00	1,400,000 00	2,114,345 00
One hundred dollars	6,408,600	4,194,100	5,007,700	4,583,890 00	3,052,700 00	2,293,310 00
Five hundred dollars	4,817,000	4,424,000	5,650,000	3,959,000 00	2,300,000 00	15,645,500 00
One thousand dollars	2,600,000	3,973,000	3,900,000	3,042,000 00	700,000 00	18,238,000 00
Five thousand dollars			4,005,000	5,000 00	1,000,000 00	4,320,000 00
Ten thousand dollars			3,010,000	50,000 00	2,000,000 00	4,500,000 00
Total	67,275,951	80,359,267	64,107,833	64,107,833 00	81,302,563 00	81,302,563 00

There will be a decrease in the issues and redemptions during the current fiscal year, for the reason that there is so much difficulty in obtaining notes for redemption and exchange for other denominations that the amount of such exchanges now being made is much less than during

21 F

the last fiscal year. The demand for notes is to a great extent being supplied by the issue of silver certificates of the denominations of ten and twenty dollars.

STANDARD SILVER DOLLARS.

The total coinage of standard silver dollars under the act of February 28, 1878, is $72,847,750. Of this amount $47,588,106 are in the Treasury and the mints, and $25,259,644, being more than thirty-four and two-thirds per cent. of the coinage, are in circulation. The amount in circulation November 1, 1878, was $4,922,623, or twenty-six and nine-tenths per cent. of $18,282,500 coined; at the same date in 1879 the amount in circulation was $13,002,842, or twenty-eight and three-fourths per cent. of $45,206,200 coined. Of the total amount coined to date $47,602,932, or more than sixty-five per cent., has been paid out from the Treasury offices and mints. Of the amount paid out nearly forty-seven per cent., or $22,343,288, has been returned to the Treasury in payment of dues or on account of silver certificates. While the amount distributed is only about one-third of the amount coined, there were placed permanently in circulation, during the first seven full months of coinage, 4,731,684 standard silver dollars, or 675,955 each month, and for the succeeding twelve months ending October 31, 1879, there were absorbed into the circulation of the country 8,080,219 standard silver dollars, or 673,351 per month. During the twelve months just ended 12,256,802 standard silver dollars and $18,175,871 in silver certificates entered into the circulation of the country, or an average of 1,021,400 standard silver dollars and $1,514,656 in silver certificates each month.

The following table shows the amount coined, on hand, and outstanding at the close of each month since the coinage began:

Month.	Monthly coinage.	Coined to the end of the month.	Balance on hand at the close of the month.	Net distribution during the month.	Outstanding at the close of the month.
1878.					
March	$1,001,500	$1,001,500	$810,561	$190,939	$190,939
April...........................	2,470,000	3,471,500	3,159,681	110,880	301,819
May.............................	3,015,000	6,486,500	5,950,401	234,230	536,049
June.............................	2,087,000	8,573,500	7,718,357	319,094	855,143
July	1,847,000	10,420,500	9,550,236	15,121	870,264
August...........................	3,028,000	13,448,500	11,292,849	1,285,387	2,155,651
September	2,764,000	16,212,500	12,155,205	1,901,644	4,057,295
October	2,070,000	18,282,500	13,359,877	865,328	4,922,623
November	2,156,050	20,438,550	14,843,319	672,708	5,595,331
December	2,057,000	22,495,550	16,704,829	195,390	5,790,721
1879.					
January..........................	2,060,200	24,555,750	18,625,223	130,806	5,930,527
February.........................	2,132,000	26,687,750	20,049,181	708,042	6,638,569
March............................	2,087,200	28,774,950	21,799,206	337,175	6,975,744
April............................	2,381,000	31,155,950	23,969,047	181,159	7,156,903
May..............................	2,330,000	33,485,950	26,386,154	....	7,099,796
June.............................	2,315,050	35,801,000	28,358,589	285,508	7,442,411
July.............................	1,650,000	37,451,000	29,347,201	661,398	8,103,799
August...........................	2,787,050	40,238,050	30,962,254	1,171,997	9,275,796
September	2,396,050	42,634,100	31,806,774	1,551,530	10,827,326
October	2,572,100	45,206,200	32,203,358	2,175,518	13,002,842
November	2,499,000	47,705,200	33,503,836	1,198,470	14,201,312
December	2,350,450	50,055,650	33,327,552	2,526,786	16,728,098
1880.					
January..........................	2,450,000	52,505,650	35,548,808	228,684	16,956,782
February.........................	2,300,400	54,806,050	37,513,420	335,843	17,292,680
March............................	2,350,200	57,156,250	39,057,856	805,782	18,098,397
April............................	2,300,000	59,456,250	41,052,639	305,219	18,403,49?
May..............................	2,267,000	61,723,250	43,356,807	....	18,366,4??
June.............................	2,011,500	63,734,750	45,108,296	229,843	18,826,4??
July.............................	2,280,000	66,014,750	47,073,470	314,826	18,941,?
August...........................	2,253,000	68,267,750	48,290,477	1,095,993	20,037,?
September	2,301,000	70,566,750	47,784,744	2,746,733	22,784,?
October	2,279,000	72,847,750	47,588,106	2,475,638	25,258,?

In addition to the ordinary influences which facilitate the distribution of standard silver dollars, the demonetization by the people of the Southwest of the Mexican silver dollar has created an extensive demand for the new dollar in that quarter. Were the trade-dollar withdrawn from circulation or everywhere rated at its bullion value, many more standard silver dollars would be required for circulation in the cities of New York and Philadelphia, and in other places in which the trade-dollar is now in use as a circulating medium, much to the advantage of the bullion dealers, who purchase trade-dollars at points where they are rated at 90 cents and sell them at an advance to parties in places where they circulate at their face value.

SILVER CERTIFICATES.

The total amount of silver certificates issued under the act of Congress of February 28, 1878, to September 30, 1880, is $27,308,000; of which there were issued at Washington, $10,080,000; at New York, $4,428,000; and at San Francisco, $12,800,000. There were in actual circulation at the latter date $12,429,381, which amount does not include $6,092,579 held in the cash of the various offices. The demand for silver certificates under the circular of the Department dated September 18, 1880, authorizing their exchange for gold coin or bullion has been quite extensive at New Orleans, Saint Louis, Chicago, and Cincinnati, and there were paid out at those points during the month of October $3,485,000 in silver certificates for an equal amount of gold coin deposited in the subtreasury at New York. The demand was stimulated by the scarcity of other circulating notes, and because, the certificates being furnished at the various subtreasuries without expense for transportation to the person desiring them, they became an inexpensive means of obtaining exchange, which was really of great advantage in the Southwest.

The following table shows the amount of silver certificates outstanding June 30, 1879, issued and redeemed during the fiscal year and outstanding at its close:

Denomination.	Outstanding June 30, 1879.	Issued.		Redeemed.		Outstanding June 30, 1880.
		During fiscal year.	To June 30, 1880.	During fiscal year.	To June 30, 1880.	
Ten dollars	$163,830	$2,007,000	$3,174,000	$23,490	$26,660	$2,147,340
Twenty dollars	95,420	1,890,000	1,986,000	10,540	11,120	1,974,880
Fifty dollars	145,000	1,195,000	1,340,000	11,050	11,050	1,328,950
One hundred dollars	475,700	1,449,000	1,930,000	20,100	25,400	1,904,600
Five hundred dollars	500,000	750,000	3,018,000	20,500	1,788,500	1,229,500
One thousand dollars	1,160,000	2,727,000	10,570,000	98,000	6,781,000	3,789,000
Total	2,539,950	10,018,000	21,015,000	183,680	8,643,730	12,374,270

FRACTIONAL CURRENCY AND FRACTIONAL SILVER COIN.

The total amount of fractional silver issued under the act of April 17, 1876, was $42,983,618.50; to which should be added at least 25 per cent. more represented by coins of dates prior to 1875 which have found their way into circulation since the resumption of specie payments. Of this in there is in the Treasury at this date $24,629,489.89, of which 7,296,671.13 has been withdrawn from circulation since the passage the act of June 9, 1879, providing for the exchange of fractional ver for lawful money. Since July 31, 1880, the amount in the Treasury decreased about $500,000, that amount in excess of redemptions having been reissued under a demand which has sprung up by reason of reduced transportation charges and an improved condition of business.

Under Department regulation of August 26, 1880, fractional silver coin has been sent at the risk and expense of the applicant by registered mail in four-pound packages, each containing $70. Under this arrangement 796 packages have been sent.

At the date of the act of April 17, 1876, authorizing the exchange of fractional silver coin for fractional currency, there was in circulation $41,508,737.48 of fractional currency, which, up to October 31, 1879, had been decreased by redemption to $15,710,964.24. Since that date there has been a further redemption, as shown by the following table, of $153,164.54, or an average of $12,763.71 per month, leaving the amount outstanding at this date $15,557,799.70.

Month.	Fractional currency outstanding at close of each month.	Fractional currency redeemed during each month.	Total redeemed to the end of each month.
1879.			
November	$15, 704, 353 12	36, 611 12	$25, 804, 384 36
December	15, 674, 308 11	30, 045 01	25, 894, 429 37
1880.			
January	15, 668, 734 29	5, 573 82	25, 840, 003 19
February	15, 631, 315 41	37, 418 88	25, 877, 422 07
March	15, 625, 301 33	6, 014 08	25, 883, 436 15
April	15, 604, 591 33	20, 710 00	25, 904, 146 15
May	15, 592, 938 70	11, 652 63	25, 915, 798 78
June	15, 590, 892 70	2, 046 00	25, 917, 844 78
July	15, 581, 648 70	9, 244 00	25, 927, 068 78
August	15, 557, 933 70	23, 715 00	25, 950, 803 78
September	15, 557, 878 70	55 00	25, 950, 858 78
October	15, 557, 799 70	79 00	25, 950, 937 78

MINOR COIN.

The Minor Coin in the vaults of the various offices September 30, 1880, amounted to $1,063,665.22, having decreased to that amount from $1,524,700.57 in the Treasury at the same date in 1879. The demand for five-cent nickels, which has amounted to $455,810.80 during the year in excess of redemptions, has been supplied from the amount on hand; but the demand for bronze one-cent pieces still continues, and the Mint has been unable to fill the orders for that denomination promptly. The following table shows the distribution of the Minor Coin on hand in the Treasury September 30, 1880:

Office by which held.	Five-cent nickel.	Three-cent nickel.	Two-cent bronze.	One cent, bronze, copper-nickel, and copper.	Mixed.	Total.

DEPOSITARY BANKS.

The total receipts of public money during the fiscal year by Depositary Banks were $119,493,171.94, the average daily balance therein being $8,000,000, secured by the deposit in this office of $14,777,000 United States bonds and personal bonds to the amount of $330,000. The receipts of public money by Depositary Banks from 1864 to 1880 aggregate $3,537,641,044.41. There were at the close of the fiscal year one hundred and thirty-one National Bank depositaries.

The following statement gives the receipts, disbursements, and balances of public money, as shown by the Treasurer's accounts with Depositary Banks, during the fiscal years from 1864 to 1880:

Fiscal year.	Receipts.	Funds transferred to depositary banks.	Funds transferred to the Treasury by depositary banks.	Drafts drawn on depositary banks.	Balance at close of the year.
1864	$153,395,108 71	$816,000 00	$85,507,674 06	$28,726,695 88	$39,976,738 75
1865	987,564,639 14	8,110,294 70	583,697,912 72	415,887,787 81	36,065,992 06
1866	497,566,670 42	13,523,972 62	363,065,565 65	149,772,756 11	34,298,319 34
1867	351,737,083 83	8,405,903 63	331,039,872 57	37,218,612 76	26,182,821 47
1868	225,244,144 75	9,404,392 00	215,311,460 69	22,218,187 92	23,301,709 61
1869	105,160,573 67	10,952,199 44	114,748,877 24	14,890,463 75	8,875,141 73
1870	120,084,041 79	2,466,521 06	111,123,926 18	11,818,228 61	8,483,549 79
1871	99,299,840 85	2,633,129 45	89,428,544 04	13,796,961 01	7,197,015 04
1872	106,104,855 16	3,050,444 95	94,936,603 76	13,935,837 49	7,777,873 00
1873	169,802,743 98	9,004,642 49	108,089,786 76	16,110,519 07	62,185,133 64
1874	91,108,846 70	2,729,958 81	134,869,112 57	13,364,554 52	7,790,292 06
1875	98,228,249 58	1,737,445 60	82,184,304 05	13,657,678 25	11,814,904 89
1876	97,402,227 57	2,443,451 49	89,961,146 99	13,909,616 83	7,870,920 12
1877	106,470,261 22	2,353,196 29	94,276,400 35	14,862,200 88	7,586,776 41
1878	99,781,053 48	2,385,920 38	90,177,963 35	12,606,870 60	6,937,916 32
1879	109,397,525 67	6,890,489 06	100,498,469 29	15,544,058 34	7,183,403 42
1880	119,493,171 94	6,489,634 17	109,641,233 64	15,535,023 03	7,960,953 86
Total......	3,537,641,044 41	92,499,795 24	2,796,600,852 93	823,540,032 86	....

CLEARING-HOUSE CERTIFICATES.

The following table shows the amount of Clearing-House Certificates issued, redeemed and outstanding for the fiscal years 1873 to 1880, inclusive. The total amount issued is $601,785,000, of which amount there was outstanding at the close of the year only $13,125,000, being by far the smallest amount outstanding since their first issue in 1873, and indicating the demand for United States notes by the banks and the increased use by them of coin for their reserves.

Fiscal year.	Total amount issued.	Total amount redeemed.	Outstanding, as shown by the Treasurer's books.
1873	$57,240,000	$25,430,000	$31,810,000
1874	137,905,000	78,915,000	58,990,000
1875	219,000,000	159,955,000	59,045,000
1876	301,400,000	268,260,000	33,140,000
1877	378,285,000	324,305,000	53,980,000
1878	464,965,000	418,720,000	46,245,000
1879	554,730,000	525,400,000	29,330,000
1880	601,785,000	588,660,000	13,125,000

SALES OF EXCHANGE.

For the purpose of supplying those offices with funds, there was sold the New Orleans subtreasury, $250,000 of New York exchange; at the San Francisco subtreasury, $6,690,000 of New York exchange, and by the depositary at Tucson, $123,500 of New York and San Francisco exchange, which was furnished to them from this office, by the Treasurer's checks on New York and San Francisco.

GOLD CERTIFICATES.

The issue of Gold Certificates was suspended by the Department December 1, 1878, at which time there had been issued $981,134,880.46. Of that amount there was outstanding at the close of the fiscal year but $8,004,600. The following table shows the amount issued and redeemed during each fiscal year from 1866 to 1880, inclusive, the total issued and redeemed, and the amount outstanding at the close of each year:

Period.	Issued during the fiscal year.	Total issued.	Redeemed during the fiscal year.	Total redeemed.	Outstanding at the close of the fiscal year.
From November 13, 1865, to June 30, 1866	$98,493,680 00	$98,493,680 00	$87,545,800 00	$87,545,800 00	$10,947,865 00
Fiscal year 1867	109,121,680 00	207,615,380 00	101,295,900 00	188,841,700 00	18,773,580 00
Fiscal year 1868	77,960,400 00	285,575,680 00	78,055,340 00	267,897,040 00	17,678,649 00
Fiscal year 1869	80,663,180 00	366,238,840 00	65,255,620 00	333,152,660 00	33,086,180 00
Fiscal year 1870	76,731,060 00	442,969,900 00	76,270,120 00	409,422,780 00	34,547,120 00
Fiscal year 1871	56,577,000 00	499,546,900 00	71,237,820 00	479,660,600 00	19,886,300 00
Fiscal year 1872	63,229,500 00	562,776,400 00	51,029,500 00	530,690,100 00	32,086,300 00
Fiscal year 1873	55,570,500 00	618,346,900 00	48,196,800 00	578,886,900 00	39,460,000 00
Fiscal year 1874	81,117,780 46	699,464,680 46	97,755,680 46	676,639,580 46	22,825,100 00
Fiscal year 1875	70,250,100 00	769,714,780 46	71,278,900 06	747,918,480 46	21,796,300 00
Fiscal year 1876	90,619,100 00	860,333,820 46	83,734,000 00	831,652,480 46	28,681,400 00
Fiscal year 1877	58,141,200 00	918,475,080 46	45,250,000 00	876,902,480 46	41,572,600 00
Fiscal year 1878	50,342,400 00	968,817,480 46	47,563,000 00	924,450,480 46	44,367,000 00
Fiscal year 1879	12,317,400 00	981,134,880 46	41,270,700 00	965,721,180 46	15,413,700 00
Fiscal year 1880	....	981,134,880 46	7,409,100 00	973,130,280 46	8,004,600 00

DRAFTS AND CHECKS.

There were drawn during the year 296,936 checks in payment of quarterly interest on registered stock of the United States, 31,385 drafts on warrants of the Secretary of the Treasury, 13,945 drafts on warrants of the Postmaster-General, and 66,059 transfer checks on assistant treasurers, making in all 408,325.

MUTILATED, STOLEN, AND COUNTERFEIT CURRENCY.

There were rejected, branded, and returned to the owners during the fiscal year $3,610 in counterfeit United States notes, $3,842 in counterfeit national-bank notes, and $770.10 in counterfeit fractional currency. Of the counterfeit bank-notes rejected $1,200 was in notes of the denomination of $100, purporting to be of the issue of the following national banks: First National Bank of Boston, $300; Central National Bank of New York, $100; National Revere Bank of Boston, $300; and Pittsburgh National Bank of Commerce of Pittsburgh, Pa., $500. The two last-mentioned counterfeits are printed from the same original plate and are by far the most difficult of detection of any which have yet appeared. Fortunately, the person by whom the plate was engraved has been recently arrested, and it is hoped that the further printing or putting in circulation of counterfeits printed from it will be prevented. There were also rejected $7,870.23 in stolen, pieced, and fragmentary national-bank notes. There was deducted on account of mutilation from the face value of United States notes redeemed during the fiscal year $10,157; from fractional currency, $430.73; and from notes of failed liquidating, and reducing banks, $80; making the total deductions to the close of the fiscal year $297,363.76 on notes of the face value of $2,229,368,462.17 redeemed. The deductions made prior to May 11, 1875, amounting to $229,824.09, have been covered into the Treasury, increasing by that amount the redemptions, as shown by the cash statements, and decreasing the outstanding, as shown by the public debt statements.

PACIFIC RAILROAD SINKING FUNDS.

There are held at this date on account of the Pacific Railroad Sinking Funds, established by the act approved May 7, 1878 (20 Statutes, 56), bonds as follows:

For the Union Pacific Railroad Company:

Pacific Railway bonds, currency sixes	$192,000	
Funded Loan of 1881, 5 per cent	256,450	
Funded Loan of 1907, 4 per cent	31,950	
		$480,400

For the Central Pacific Railroad Company:

Pacific Railway bonds, currency sixes	$119,000	
Funded Loan of 1881, 5 per cent	194,900	
Funded Loan of 1907, 4 per cent	198,300	
		$512,200

The third section of the act provides that in making investments for these funds, the Secretary of the Treasury "shall prefer the five per centum bonds of the United States, unless, for good reasons appearing to him, and which he shall report to Congress, he shall at any time deem it advisable to invest in other bonds of the United States."

Attention is invited to the disadvantage of investing these sinking funds in the bonds of the United States at the present high market rates, and it is suggested that the consent of Congress, by joint resolution, be obtained to the purchase for the purpose of any bonds of the United States, or of the first-mortgage bonds of the two railroad companies, authorized by section 10 of the act of Congress of July 2, 1864 (13 Statutes, 356), and section 1 of the act of Congress of March 3, 1865 (13 Statutes, 504), which are the only liens upon the property of those companies prior and paramount to that of the United States.

TRUST FUNDS.

The Indian Trust Fund.

The bonds and stocks of the Indian Trust Fund, at the close of the fiscal year, in the custody of this office in conformity with the act of Congress of June 10, 1876 (19 Statutes, 58), amounted to $4,580,216.83¾. Of this amount $2,469,400 was in United States bonds, as follows:

Loan of July and August, 1861	$500
Pacific Railway bonds, currency sixes	280,000
Funded loan of 1881, 5 per cent	2,188,900
Total	2,469,400

United States four per cent. bonds, of the face value of $496,350, held for the Indian Trust Fund were sold on April 8, 1880, and the proceeds, amounting to $531,349.47, deposited in the Treasury of the United States to the credit of the Secretary of the Interior as trustee of various Indian tribes, in accordance with the act of Congress approved April 1, 1880, authorizing that officer to deposit certain funds in the United States Treasury in lieu of investment.

Bonds of the Richmond and Danville Railroad Company belonging to this fund, amounting to $103,500, were redeemed by that company on the 28th day of February, 1880, and the amount, together with $946 accrued interest, was deposited in the Treasury to the credit of the Secretary of the Interior, trustee of various Indian tribes.

American Printing-House for the Blind.

Under the act of March 3, 1879 (20 Statutes, 467), $250,000 United States four per cent. bonds are held in the name of the Secretary of the Treasury, trustee, "to promote the education of the blind," the interest on which is paid to the trustees of the American Printing-House for the Blind, in Louisville, Ky., in conformity with'that act.

Pennsylvania Company.

Under the provisions of Department Circular No. 146, dated November 29, 1876, $200,000 in registered bonds of the funded loan of 1891 are held in trust for the Pennsylvania Company for the security of unappraised dutiable merchandise and dutiable merchandise in bond.

Manhattan Savings Institution.

Duplicates of United States bonds alleged to have been stolen from the vaults of the Manhattan Savings Institution are held in this office to the amount of $250,000 to protect the United States from loss, as provided by the act of December 19, 1878 (20 Statutes, 589).

SEMI-ANNUAL DUTY.

The semi-annual duty assessed upon, and collected from, the national banks by the Treasurer of the United States for the fiscal year 1880 is as follows:

On circulation $3,153,635 63
On deposits 4,058,710 61
On capital 379,424 19

Total 7,591,770 43

This is the largest amount of semi-annual duty that has been assessed and collected for any year since the establishment of the national banking system, and exceeds the amount for the fiscal year 1879 by $870,533.76.

The total amount of semi-annual duty collected by this office from the national banks for the fiscal years 1864 to 1880, as more fully set forth in the appendix, is—

On circulation $45,941,161 93
On deposits 47,703,404 11
On capital 6,716,903 31

Total 100,361,469 35

THE REDEMPTION OF NATIONAL-BANK NOTES.

The redemptions of national-bank notes fell off greatly during the fiscal year, the gross amount received for redemption having been only $61,585,675.68, as compared with $157,656,644.96 in 1879. The redemptions under the present system reached the highest point yet attained in 1877, when the amount redeemed was $242,885,375.14, or nearly four times as great as in 1880. The amount of notes fit for circulation redeemed fell off from $112,293,000 in 1879 to $24,977,600 in 1880; of notes unfit for circulation from $40,162,000 to $29,860,000, and of notes of failed, liquidating, and reducing national banks from $8,281,550 to $6,500,800. The chief part of the reduction took place in the notes fit for circulation, the amount for the first time since 1875 being less than that of the unfit notes redeemed. On the other hand, the redemptions of notes of failed, liquidating, and reducing banks—the expense of which is chiefly borne by the other national banks—show a relatively small falling off. The number of notes assorted was 7,576,175 against 18,295,558 in 1879. Of these 2,435,663 were fit, and 5,140,512 unfit for circulation, the average denomination of the former being $10.25 and of the latter $5.81. In accordance with the requirements of section 5175 of the Revised Statutes, no incomplete notes of a less denomination than five dollars have been furnished to national banks by the Comptroller of the Currency since the resumption of specie payments, although all one and two dollar notes fit for circulation redeemed by the Treasurer have been returned to the banks of issue as heretofore. The proportion of such notes returned during the last year was, however, very small, only $132,740 out of $1,337,860 in ones and $90,120 out of $919,370 in twos redeemed having been found to be fit for circulation.

The great decrease in bank-note redemptions during the last two years is, in the Treasurer's opinion, due to two causes—the general revival of business, and the changes in the regulations requiring the charges for the transportation of all notes other than those clearly unfit for circulation to be paid by the senders. The former is probably the more potent influence. The redemptions of bank notes under the act of 1874 have always been in inverse proportion to the activity of business, being heavy when business is dull, and light when business is active. Prior to the resumption of specie payments, great accumulations of bank notes took place in the principal cities—especially in New York and Boston—during the winter and summer months, when business in the interior was dullest. The interior banks having no other use for the bank notes which flowed into their vaults sent them to their city correspondents for their credit, interest being paid in most cases on the current balances. These notes, being unavailable for the national-bank reserves or for the settlement of balances at the clearing-house, were at once forwarded by the city banks to this office for redemption in legal-tenders, the conversion under the regulations then in force being made without any expense to the holders. Recently, however, there has been an almost complete cessation of the accumulation of bank notes in the money centers, and there has been a dearth rather than a plethora of both legal-tenders and bank notes in the principal cities. They have been absorbed by the demands of business and are in active circulation throughout the country. The consequence has been a great falling off in the receipts of bank notes for redemption from those sources. The receipts of bank notes from New York fell off from $66,273,000 in the fiscal year 1878 to $54,170,000 in 1879 and to $26,460,000 in 1880. The decrease in the amount received from Boston was much greater. The receipts from that city in 1880 were only $11,701,000, against $80,527,000 in 1878, and $59,375,000 in 1879. The aggregate receipts from the two cities in 1880 were but a little more than one-fourth of the receipts from those sources in 1877 and in 1878. But while the revival of business and the increased activity of the circulation have been the chief cause of the decrease in redemptions, the changes in the regulations have not been without their effect. Prior to October 1, 1878, all of the charges for transportation incurred in the redemption of bank notes, under the act of 1874, were defrayed out of the five per cent. redemption fund, and afterwards assessed upon the several national banks in proportion to the circulation of each redeemed. The charges thus assessed were those for the transportation of national-bank notes to the Treasurer for redemption in sums of $1,000 or its multiples, and of legal-tender notes returned for them, as well as of the redeemed and assorted notes fit for circulation forwarded to the several banks by which they were issued. On and after October 1, 1878, by direction of the Secretary, the express charges on all national-bank notes forwarded to the Treasurer for redemption were required to be paid by the senders. This requirement was subsequently so modified as to permit the payment out of the five per cent. fund of the charges on notes unfit for circulation received for redemption after December 1, 1879. This modification was made in the expectation that it would cause an increase in the redemption of unfit notes, and thus improve the condition of the currency; but it has wholly failed of its intended effect, the redemptions under the modified order being for ten months only $26,651,000, against redemptions of $31,487,400 for the corresponding ten months of the previous year, under the rule requiring all the charges to be defrayed by the senders. Whatever the cause, there is no doubt that the condition of the bank circulation has deteriorated within the last two years. Most of the notes received for redemption are badly worn, and ought to have been redeemed much earlier. The labor and annoyance of assorting the notes unfit for circulation from the currency coming into their hands, and of holding them until an amount accumulates sufficient to be forwarded to the Treasurer, seems to deter many banks from returning them for redemption. The notes, consequently, remain in circulation long after they have become unfit for use, to the great inconvenience of all persons handling them.

In view of this condition of the currency, a return to the system under which all of the charges for transportation incurred in the redemption of national-bank notes were defrayed out of the five per cent. fund and assessed upon the banks might be advisable as the only way in which the circulation can be kept in good condition. Such a course, it is believed, would not be in conflict with the law.

Although every endeavor has been made to reduce the costs of redemption, and although every item of expense has been curtailed, it was impossible, for manifest reasons, to reduce the cost in the same proportion in which the work fell off. Among these reasons are the greater proportion of mutilated notes received, which are much more difficult to handle than new notes; the smaller size of the packages, the number of packages received during the last year having been nearly three-fourths as great as in the preceding year, although the amount contained in them was less than two-fifths as much; the great fluctuations in the amounts received from month to month; the increase in the proportion of notes of failed, liquidating, and reducing banks, on which no assessment can be levied, constituting as they did 10.6 per cent. of the redemptions in 1880, against a little more than five per cent. in 1879; the fact that the clerical and bookkeeping work has not decreased to anything like the extent to which the amount redeemed has fallen off, and, generally, the impossibility of doing a small business as economically as a large one. Notwithstanding these drawbacks, the amount paid for salaries in the office of the Treasurer was reduced from $111,736.30 in 1879 to $82,144.88 in 1880. The amount paid on this account in the office of the Comptroller of the Currency was $22,205.20, making a total of $104,350.0

paid for salaries in the year 1880. The amount appropriated for "the force employed in redeeming the national currency" in the Treasurer's office was $101,584, of which $19,439.12, or more than 19 per cent. was unexpended. In every year since appropriations began to be made for this force in the Treasurer's Office a part of the amount appropriated has been returned to the Treasury. The amounts so returned were $12,238.62 in 1876, $1,955.52 in 1877, $3,453.25 in 1878, $5,447.70 in 1879, and $19,439.12 in 1880, making a total saving on this account alone of $42,534.21 in five years. The amount appropriated for this purpose for both offices for the fiscal year 1881 is $90,872, being $32,932 less than the amount appropriated for 1880, and $13,478.68 less than the amount expended in that year. The number of persons now actually employed on this work in the Treasurer's office is 59, as compared with 152 so employed in 1876.

The total "costs for assorting" were $108,964.15, against $142,651.20 in 1879, a reduction having been made in every item. The "charges for transportation" were $34,764.24, against $98,298.75 in 1879. The total expenses of redemption were $143,728.39, being $97,221.56 less than in the preceding year—a reduction of more that 40 per cent. The "costs for assorting" when assessed as heretofore on the net number of notes assorted, were 14.38\frac{1}{4}$ for each thousand notes, and the "charges for transportation" 63$\frac{316}{1000}$ cents for each $1,000 assorted. The latter rate shows a slight reduction as compared with the previous year, notwithstanding the large proportion of unfit notes, the charges on which were paid out of the five per cent. fund. The total expenses were about $\frac{11}{24}$ of 1 per cent. on the amount redeemed and charged to the banks of issue, and but a little more than $\frac{1}{40}$ of 1 per cent. on the total circulation of the national banks. The latter percentage properly expresses the cost of the redemption system to the national banks. It is, on an average, $37.69 for banks of $90,000 circulation—a burden so slight as to be scarcely appreciable.

THE REDUCTION AND INCREASE OF NATIONAL-BANK CIRCULATION.

Attention is invited to the practical bearing on the question of bank-note redemption of the construction heretofore placed by the Department on the various provisions of law authorizing the reduction and increase of the circulation of national banks. The fourth section of the act approved June 20, 1874 (18 Statutes, 124), authorizes any national bank, desiring to withdraw its circulating notes, to take up the bonds deposited for the security of such notes, upon the deposit of lawful money with the Treasurer of the United States, and provides that an equal amount of the outstanding notes of the bank shall be redeemed at the Treasury of the United States. The banks have availed themselves of the privilege accorded by this provision to a very large extent, more than $85,000,000 of circulation having been surrendered in the manner prescribed, and nearly $71,000,000 having been redeemed at this office. The notes are received at the Treasury mixed with other bank notes, and if they come from assistant treasurers, or in packages marked "unfit," the express charges on them are defrayed out of the five per cent. redemption fund. They necessarily pass through the various stages of counting and assorting before they can be separated from the other notes, so that almost the entire expense of the redemption of the whole $71,000,000 has been borne by the other national banks, there being no means of charging the "reducing" banks with the expenses of redeeming their notes until their deposits of legal-tender notes are exhausted. This provision was adopted in the expectation that it would act as a regulator of the volume of the bank circulation. It was expected that when the circulation became redundant, the surplus would be retired, and that when a demand for more circulation should spring up, the banks would increase their issues to meet it. This expectation has not been realized. The almost invariable answer to inquiries made of officers of banks which have reduced their circulation has been, that the reduction was made solely to enable the bank to avail itself of the ruling premium on the bonds withdrawn, either because the bonds were exceptionally high, or because the bank needed the premium to enable it to meet losses sustained, or to reduce its premium account. It is plain that the action of the banks would not be affected by the fact that the volume of the circulation was redundant, for the simple reason that a bank has more money at its disposal after reducing its circulation than before. A bank which deposits $45,000 to reduce its circulation and takes up $50,000 of its bonds, which it sells for ten per cent. premium, has $10,000 more to lend than it had before. While, therefore, the retirement of the bank circulation diminishes the aggregate volume of the circulation, it increases the loanable funds of the particular bank whose circulation is reduced.

Under the construction placed upon the law, banks which have thus reduced their circulation have been permitted to increase it again as often and as largely as they chose, whether their legal-tender deposits were exhausted or not. Although the exact amount cannot be ascertained, it is safe to say that many millions of dollars of additional circulation have been issued under the general provisions of the national currency act to banks which were still reducing their circulation under the act of June 20, 1874. The consequence has been that the new notes thus issued have, to a large extent, speedily been presented to the Treasury for redemption out of the legal-tender deposit. Banks which have applied in vain to the Treasurer for the surrender of their legal-tender deposits, have accomplished the same object by obtaining new circulation. The cost of printing the new notes thus issued is borne by the United States, so that the government, though not deriving the remotest benefit from the transaction, has been obliged to bear the whole expense of their issue, and a part of the expense of their redemption, simply to enable a bank to do by indirection what it was not permitted to do directly. In several instances banks have repeated the operation of reducing and increasing their circulation several times within a brief period, taking up their bonds and selling them, it would appear, whenever the premium constituted a sufficient inducement, and increasing their circulation again whenever bonds could be bought at better rates, the United States all the while redeeming their notes at its own expense or that of the other banks, and issuing others, also at its own expense, whenever called upon by them.

An example will better illustrate these operations. In January and February, 1875, a certain bank reduced its circulation from $308,490 to $45,000 by deposits of legal-tender notes. Between September 26, 1876, and May 26, 1877, and before that deposit was exhausted, it increased its circulation to $450,000. Between August 14 and September 10, 1877, it again reduced its circulation to $45,000. On September 19, 1877, nine days after completing the deposits for this reduction, it again began to take out additional circulation, although $402,550 of prior deposits remained in the Treasury, and by the 26th of that month its circulation had again been increased to $450,000. July 22, 1878, it, for the third time, reduced its circulation to $45,000, and in August and September, 1879, again increased it to $450,000, at which it now remains, the balance of its former legal-tender deposit then in the Treasury being $112,615. From January 13, 1875, to the date of this report, $778,275 of its notes have been redeemed, of which only $40,700 were redeemed at the expense of the bank, although, during more than one-third of that period, it had outstanding and was deriving the benefit from the full amount of circulation which its capital authorized. The only assessments which have been made on the bank for the expenses of redeeming its notes were $24.74 in 1875, and $4.39 in 1878. At one time there were in actual circulation $852,550 of its notes, although the highest amount ever borne on its books was $450,000.

Other banks have reduced and forthwith increased their circulation to its former amount, with the avowed object of relieving themselves from the trouble and expense of redeeming their notes through the five per cent. redemption fund. For example, a bank deposited $45,000 in legal-tender notes for the reduction of its circulation on April 3, 1878, and on April 5, 1878, two days afterwards, without having touched the bonds deposited as security, took out $45,000 of additional circulation. In like manner on July 11, 1879, it deposited $9,000 for the same purpose, and on the very same day, without disturbing its bonds, it took out $9,000 of additional circulation.

It is plain that such transactions as these are not within the spirit of the act of June 20, 1874. That act authorizes the deposit of legal-tender notes by any national bank "desiring to withdraw its circulation, in whole or in part." A wish to surrender circulation, with the reserved intention of taking out more at once, or as soon as a fall in the price of bonds shall make the transaction profitable, is not, it is submitted, such a desire to withdraw circulation as the law contemplates. The reduction of circulation therein authorized is a *bona fide* reduction, based on a well-settled intention of the bank to curtail its note issues. It could neither have been intended nor expected that the law would become the means of enabling banks to operate in the securities of the government deposited to secure the redemption of their notes, or to throw upon the United States, or the other banks of the country, the expense of redeeming their notes, while maintaining and enjoying the full circulation to which the law entitles them. Such a construction utterly perverts the original intention of the act. Instead of the volume of the circulation being regulated by the business needs of the country, it is governed by the price of United States bonds. The price of bonds may be such as to induce banks to surrender their circulation at the very time when there is a legitimate demand for more circulation. The profit to be derived from taking up and selling their bonds may be greater than that derivable from their circulation. Within the last year a large reduction of bank circulation has taken place in the face of an active demand for money, simply because a good profit could be made by withdrawing and selling the four per cents. deposited as security for circulation. Nearly twenty-five million dollars in four per cent. bonds were thus withdrawn during the last fiscal year. Banks can afford to forego the profit on their circulation for a few months, in order to realize more from the premium on their bonds. Such operations should not, in the Treasurer's opinion, be permitted. A bank, having signified an intention to reduce its circulation, and having acted on that intention by depositing legal-tenders for the purpose, should be held to its determination until the deposit is exhausted. It should not be permitted to increase its circulation until it had disappeared from the category of "reducing" banks on the books of the Department, or to extend its note issues through one branch of the

Department at the same time that they are being redeemed and destroyed through another. The adoption of this construction, while it would work no injustice to any legitimate interest, would confine the operation of the fourth section of the act of June 20, 1874, to cases where banks had formed a well-considered intention to permanently curtail their circulation, and would relieve the United States from the expense of issuing notes to banks, only to have them forthwith returned for destruction.

It is equally clear that where additional circulation has been issued to reducing banks the new notes ought not to be redeemed out of the legal-tender deposits previously made. The law provides for the redemption out of those deposits of the "outstanding notes" of the association, plainly meaning the notes outstanding at the time the deposit is made. The deposit has relation only to the notes then outstanding. It would be absurd to suppose that the law intended to permit a bank to deposit legal-tenders to-day to redeem new notes issued to it to-morrow on a fresh deposit of bonds, or on the self-same bonds. The additional notes issued stand by themselves. They are properly subject to the same provisions as to their redeemability as the notes of a bank which has made no legal-tender deposit. The United States has no concern with them, and should, if practicable, refuse to redeem them when presented for redemption out of the bank's legal-tender deposit. All "reducing" banks are required to maintain a five per cent. deposit under section 3 of the act of June 20, 1874, on the circulation borne on their books—that is, the circulation for the redemption of which no legal-tender deposit has been made. Any part of the additional circulation of such a bank presented for redemption should be charged to its five per cent. account, and be reimbursed for and disposed of in the same manner as the notes of banks not reducing their circulation.

THE PROPORTION OF BONDS OF NATIONAL BANKS TO CAPITAL.

An important question was raised by the Treasurer during the year concerning the surrender to national banks of the bonds deposited by them with him to secure the redemption of their circulating notes, and as the reasons for his action do not appear to have been fully understood, a brief statement of them may not be out of place here. Section 5159 of the Revised Statutes requires that "every [national banking] association * * * shall transfer and deliver to the Treasurer of the United States any United States registered bonds, bearing interest to an amount not less than thirty thousand dollars and *not less than one-third of the capital stock paid in*." Section 5160 provides that "the deposit of bonds made by each association shall be increased as its capital stock may be paid up or increased, so that every association shall at all times have on deposit with the Treasurer United States bonds to the amount of *at least one-third of its capital stock actually paid in*."

Section 4 of the act of June 20, 1874, provides "that any association * * * desiring to withdraw its circulating notes, in whole or in part, may, upon the deposit of lawful money with the Treasurer of the United States in sums of not less than nine thousand dollars, take up the bonds which said association has on deposit with the Treasurer for the security of such circulating notes; * * * *Provided*, That the amount of the bonds on deposit for circulation shall not be reduced below fifty thousand dollars." It was assumed immediately upon the passage of this act, apparently without any thorough consideration of the question, that it virtually repealed the above-quoted provisions of the Revised Statutes requiring the amount of bonds on deposit for each bank to be equal to one-third of its capital stock, and that any bank, however large its capital, might reduce its bond deposit to $50,000. Under this construction of the law there were surrendered to banks bonds to a considerable amount which they would not have been permitted to withdraw had the provisions of the Revised Statutes been treated as being in force. The present Treasurer's attention having been called to the various provisions above quoted, he came to the conclusion, upon the fullest consideration and after taking the best advice available to him, that the practice that had been followed was erroneous; that the provisions of the Revised Statutes were still in full force, and that the only effect of the proviso to section 4 was to prevent national banks having a less capital than $150,000 from reducing their deposit below $50,000, as they might have done had there been no limitation other than that fixed by the Revised Statutes.

Having come to this conclusion, the Treasurer deemed it his duty to obtain an authoritative decision of this question, which concerned the administration of his office. The contemplated loan by the government, at a low rate, for the purposes of funding, coupled with the provision in the bill then pending that national banks should hold and use the proposed bonds as security, made it important that the decision should be obtained at that time in order to determine to what extent the bonds might be so used. With this view he declined to allow the withdrawal of bonds on an application of a bank in an instance in which the withdrawal would have reduced its bond deposit below one-third of its capital stock; and with the concurrence, and at the suggestion of the Secretary, the point was at once submitted to the Attorney-General for his construction of the law.

The conclusion reached by the Attorney-General was that, as sections 7, 8, and 9 of the act of 1874 "treated the one-third policy as no longer existing," in that they provided for a compulsory withdrawal of circulation and a surrender of bonds which, in certain cases, might reduce the deposits below one-third of the capital stock, section 4 of that act is therefore "repugnant to section 5160 of the Revised Statutes and all other previous legislation that requires national banks to have and maintain in the Treasury of the United States a bond deposit equal to the amount of one-third of their capital stock."

This decision has of course governed the Treasurer's action, and no attempt has since been made to enforce the requirements of section 5160.

Very respectfully,

JAS. GILFILLAN,
Treasurer of the United States.

Hon. JOHN SHERMAN,
Secretary of the Treasury.

APPENDIX.

No. 1.—*RECEIPTS and EXPENDITURES, as shown by WARRANTS, for the FISCAL YEAR 1880.*

Receipts, covered in to the credit of—	Issue of notes and bonds.	Net receipts.	Repayments to appropriations.	Counter-credits to appropriations.	Total.
Customs		$186,522,064 60	$298,951 46	$52,112 40	$186,873,128 46
Internal Revenue		124,009,373 92	14,102 99	550 00	124,024,026 91
Lands		1,016,506 60			1,016,506 60
Miscellaneous Sources		21,978,665 86			21,978,665 86
Total Net Revenue		333,526,610 98			
Public Debt—					
Funded Loan of 1907	$72,450,900 00				
Silver Certificates	10,091,000 00				
Certificates of Deposit (act of June 8, 1872)	47,355,000 00				
Refunding Certificates	614,640 00				
United States Notes	81,302,563 00				2)1,814,103 00
		211,814,103 00			
Interest on the Public Debt			720,274 10		720,274 10
War Department Appropriations			1,351,195 45	190,578 99	1,541,774 44
Navy Department Appropriations			716,741 42	5,824,223 59	6,540,965 01
Interior Department Appropriations			1,792,125 30	27,196 17	1,819,321 47
Interior Civil Appropriations			43,675 44	12,928 54	56,603 98
Treasury Proper Appropriations			1,694,944 72	810,339 69	2,505,284 41
Diplomatic Appropriations			12,319 76	37,897 18	50,216 94
Quarterly Salaries Appropriations					
Judiciary Appropriations			76,555 94	20,572 75	97,128 69
Total Receipts		545,340,713 98	6,720,886 58	6,976,399 31	559,037,999 87
Balance, as shown by warrant ledger, June 30, 1879					358,683,846 09
Total					917,721,845 96

Expenditures, authorized by warrants from appropriations on account of—	Net expenditures.	Repayments of amounts unexpended.	Amounts re-credited to appropriations.	Total.
Customs, Light-houses, Public Buildings, &c.	$17,063,995 87		$298,951 46	$52,112 40	$17,415,059 73
Internal Revenue	4,950,075 63		14,102 99	550 00	4,964,728 62
Interior Civil	4,503,802 83		43,675 44	12,928 54	4,560,407 61
Treasury Proper	24,397,791 96		1,694,944 72	810,339 69	26,903,076 37
Diplomatic	1,211,490 58		12,319 76	37,897 18	1,261,707 52

Quarterly Salaries		561, 504 89		76, 555 94	20, 972 75	561, 504 89
Judiciary		2, 624, 867 56				2, 721, 996 25
Net Civil and Miscellaneous Expenditures			$54, 753, 529 76			
War Department			38, 116, 916 22	1, 351, 195 45	190, 578 99	39, 658, 690 66
Navy Department			13, 536, 984 74	716, 741 42	5, 824, 223 59	20, 077, 949 75
Interior Department			62, 752, 631 53	1, 792, 125 30	27, 196 17	64, 541, 953 00
Interest on the Public Debt			96, 757, 675 11	720, 274 10		96, 477, 849 21
Premium on Bonds Purchased			2, 795, 320 42			2, 795, 320 42
Total Net Expenditures			267, 642, 957 78			
Redemption of the Public Debt—						
Gold Certificates	7, 409, 100 00					
Silver Certificates	189, 680 00					
Certificates of Deposit (act of June 8, 1872)	63, 280, 000 00					
Refunding Certificates	12, 095, 850 00					
United States Notes	81, 302, 563 00					
Fractional Currency	251, 717 41					
Old Demand Notes	495 00					
Oregon War Debt	202, 550 00					
One-year Notes of 1863	2, 150 00					
Two-year Notes of 1863	1, 550 00					
Compound Interest Notes	16, 500 00					
Loan of 1858	40, 000 00					
Loan of February, 1861	2, 837, 000 00					
Loan of July and August, 1861	32, 064, 250 00					
Loan of 1863 (81a)	12, 797, 150 00					
7.30s of 1864 and 1865	2, 650 00					
5-20s of 1862	9, 100 00					
5-20s of June, 1864	3, 550 00					
5-20s of 1865	31, 100 00					
10-40s of 1864	135, 769, 750 00					
Consols of 1865	988, 500 00					
Consols of 1867	38, 894, 250 00					
Consols of 1898	19, 351, 250 00					
Funded Loan of 1881	23, 575, 450 00					
Funded Loan of 1907	1, 560, 800 00					
Bounty Land Scrip	25 00					
Temporary Loan	100 00					
		432, 590, 280 41				432, 590, 280 41
Total Expenditure		700, 233, 238 19		6, 720, 886 58	6, 976, 899 31	713, 930, 524 08
Balance, as shown by Warrant Ledger, June 30, 1886						203, 791, 321 88
Total						917, 721, 845 96

No. 2.—BALANCES and MOVEMENT of MONEYS of the GENERAL

Office.	Balances June 30, 1879.			Movement
	On deposit.	Outstanding drafts.	Subject to draft.	Receipts proper.
Treasury U. S., Washington, D. C.	$8, 252, 856 61	$368, 638 47	$7, 885, 218 14	$117, 245, 393 36
Sub-Treasury U. S., Baltimore, Md	3, 293, 034 75	20, 725 43	3, 272, 309 32	6, 748, 927 58
Sub-Treasury U. S., New York, N. Y	134, 950, 077 64	1, 040, 249 15	133, 909, 828 49	162, 943, 843 84
Sub-Treasury U. S., Philadelphia, Pa	13, 640, 715 46	156, 929 13	13, 483, 786 33	26, 396, 654 46
Sub-Treasury U. S., Boston, Mass	5, 700, 515 38	165, 410 96	5, 535, 104 42	28, 092, 796 41
Sub-Treasury U. S., Cincinnati, Ohio	2, 027, 003 33	104, 294 97	1, 922, 708 36	3, 686, 739 77
Sub-Treasury U. S., Chicago, Ill	4, 449, 610 77	169, 921 12	4, 279, 689 05	7, 327, 206 05
Sub-Treasury U. S., Saint Louis, Mo	3, 024, 636 88	43, 898 37	2, 980, 738 51	3, 262, 952 29
Sub-Treasury U. S., New Orleans, La	2, 482, 484 95	120, 179 16	2, 362, 305 79	3, 459, 789 23
Sub-Treasury U. S., San Francisco, Cal	18, 846, 269 35	75, 398 78	18, 770, 870 57	13, 137, 229 33
Depository U. S., Tucson, Ariz	254, 021 84	1, 650 40	252, 371 44	83, 540 96
Depository U. S., Pittsburgh, Pa	2, 126 11		2, 126 11	
Depository U. S., Santa Fé, N. Mex	249 90		249 90	
Depository U. S., Galveston, Tex. (old acc't)	778 66		778 66	
National Bank Depositaries	7, 266, 349 07	311, 665 61	6, 954, 683 46	119, 493, 171 96
National Banks, Special Designated Depositaries, Funded Loan of 1907	200, 004, 359 50		200, 004, 359 50	
National Banks, Refunding Certificates	1, 074, 797 28		1, 074, 797 28	
First National Bank, Selma, Ala. (old acc't)	34, 787 29		34, 787 29	
Venango National Bank, Franklin, Pa. (old account)	193, 932 67		193, 932 67	...6...
Special Designated Depositaries, Refunding Certificates	57, 632 14		57, 632 14	
Mint U. S., Philadelphia, Pa., Bullion Fund	4, 903, 362 96		4, 903, 362 96	
Mint U. S., San Francisco, Cal., Bullion Fund	4, 535, 290 36		4, 535, 290 36	
Mint U. S., New Orleans, La., Bullion Fund	1, 200, 737 94		1, 200, 737 94	
Mint U. S., Carson, Nev., Bullion Fund	1, 419, 540 86		1, 419, 540 86	
Mint U. S., Denver, Colo., Bullion Fund	11, 316 80		11, 316 80	
Branch Mint U. S., Dahlonega, Ga., Bullion Fund (old account)	27, 956 03		27, 956 03	
Assay Office U. S., New York, N. Y., Bullion Fund	7, 281, 948 61		7, 281, 948 61	
Assay Office U. S., Boisé City, Idaho, Bullion Fund	44, 656 59		44, 656 59	
Assay Office U. S., Charlotte, N. C., Bullion Fund	6, 316 34		6, 316 34	
Assay Office U. S., Charlotte, N. C., Bullion Fund (old account)	32, 000 00		32, 000 00	
Assay Office U. S., Helena, Mont., Bullion Fund	150, 500 00		150, 500 00	
Mint U. S., Philadelphia, Pa., Bullion Fund, Recoinage Account				
Mint U. S., San Francisco, Cal., Bullion Fund, Recoinage Account	90 94		90 94	
Mint U. S., Philadelphia, Pa., Minor Coin Redemption Account	228, 409 12		228, 409 12	
Mint U. S., Philadelphia, Pa., Minor Coin Metal Fund	50, 000 00		50, 000 00	
Less amounts "overdrawn" and "overpaid" Treasury U. S., Washington, D. C.				
	425, 440, 360 13	2, 580, 961 55	422, 862, 398 58	
Balance of moneys in transitu		5, 644, 611 50	5, 644, 611 50	
General Treasury balances and totals	425, 449, 360 13	8, 225, 573 05	417, 223, 787 08	494, 578, 241 20

TREASURY of the UNITED STATES for the fiscal year 1880.

during the fiscal year.				Balances June 30, 1880.		
Received by transfers from other offices.	Transferred to other offices.	Drafts paid.	Receipts refunded.	On deposit.	Outstanding drafts.	Subject to draft.
$504,049,450 14	$89,824,385 38	$549,077,771 50	$57,398 72	(Overpaid.)	(Below.)	(Overdrawn.)
5,482,449 54	10,534,976 50	3,282,988 89	230 42	$5,736,636 19	$30,510 37	$3,706,125 82
328,413,001 08	471,031,180 71	53,198,491 19	10,126 98	70,067,123 70	275,836 74	69,701,266 96
13,404,709 37	25,231,742 03	10,865,306 44	3,833 91	16,341,196 29	43,613 91	16,297,582 38
14,582,995 65	25,350,960 02	15,843,506 13	3,886 50	7,777,854 79	89,057 96	7,668,796 83
5,500,868 35	7,161,857 94	1,802,474 03	1,469 29	2,446,810 47	15,594 99	2,433,215 48
17,132,133 11	11,025,684 20	10,650,980 57	4,495 43	6,627,829 73	124,986 28	6,502,843 45
9,737,506 08	6,704,365 73	7,155,016 89	576 52	2,165,136 10	94,406 67	2,070,729 43
4,831,047 52	5,836,607 21	2,611,115 08	1,295 44	2,324,303 96	80,374 38	2,243,929 58
13,763,197 22	17,103,404 09	7,123,494 23	1,431 10	21,508,362 50	91,667 12	21,416,695 38
301,527 00		505,599 84		133,489 98	2,500 49	130,989 47
				2,126 11		2,126 11
				249 90		249 90
				778 66		778 66
5,472,209 78	109,044,243 90	16,104,576 00	90,654 61	7,992,316 28	221,082 38	7,771,233 90
422,885 17	200,427,244 67					
877 60	1,075,675 08					
				34,787 29		34,787 29
...6...				193,932 67		193,932 67
11,431 73	69,063 87					
43,549,422 17	31,290,836 41			17,161,948 72		17,161,948 72
9,018,942 95	3,688,535 00			9,865,608 31		9,865,608 31
8,275,320 57	5,426,471 73			4,049,588 78		4,049,588 78
452,000 00	8,738 00			1,862,902 88		1,862,902 88
440,507 48	330,855 96			120,968 32		120,968 32
				27,950 03		27,950 03
60,000,000 00	30,226,804 46			37,053,144 15		37,053,144 15
177,323 67	117,692 07			104,288 19		104,288 19
96,000 00	83,324 14			20,992 20		20,992 20
				32,000 00		32,000 00
541,505 22	487,602 41			204,402 81		204,402 81
47,788 96	47,289 47			499 49		499 49
	90 94					
565,999 10	625,500 00			188,908 22		188,908 22
				50,000 00		50,000 00
				212,098,124 68		211,028,493 49
				9,410,855 49	274,554 37	9,685,409 86
				202,687,269 19	1,344,185 56	201,343,083 63
				3,340,752 71		3,340,752 71
1,044,983,149 74	1,058,357,082 22	708,190,900 76	175,498 90	202,687,269 19	1,996,557 15	204,683,836 34

No. 3.—*COMPARATIVE STATEMENT of RECEIPTS, as shown by WARRANTS, for the fiscal years 1879 and 1880.*

Fiscal year.	Customs.	Internal revenue.	Lands.	Miscellaneous sources.	Total net revenues.
1879	$137, 250, 047 70	$113, 561, 610 58	$924, 781 06	$22, 090, 745 12	$273, 827, 184 46
1880	186, 522, 034 60	124, 009, 373 92	1, 016, 506 60	21, 978, 665 86	333, 526, 610 98
Decrease in 1880	....	....	....	112, 079 26	....
Increase in 1880	49, 272, 016 90	10, 447, 763 34	91, 725 54	....	59, 699, 426 52

No. 4.—*COMPARATIVE STATEMENT of EXPENDITURES, as shown by WARRANTS, for the fiscal years 1879 and 1880.*

Fiscal year.	Interest and premium on public debt.	Civil and miscellaneous.	War Department.	Navy Department.	Interior Department.	Total net expenditures.
1879......	$105, 327, 949 00	$65, 741, 555 49	$40, 425, 660 73	$15, 125, 126 84	$40, 327, 591 47	$266, 947, 883 58
1880......	98, 552, 895 53	54, 713, 529 76	38, 118, 916 22	13, 536, 984 74	62, 725, 631 53	267, 642, 957 76
Decr. 1880	6, 775, 053 47	11, 028, 025 73	2, 306, 744 51	1, 588, 142 10	....	695, 074 25
Incr. 1880	....	....	....	....	22, 398, 040 06	....

No. 5.—*COMPARATIVE STATEMENT of BALANCES in the TREASURY at the close of the fiscal years 1879 and 1880.*

Balance June 30, 1879, as shown by Warrant Ledger	....	$358, 063, 945 09
Net Revenues 1880..	$333, 526, 610 98	
Net Expenditures 1880...	267, 642, 957 78	
Increase of funds	....	65, 883, 653 20
		424, 567, 499 29

Public debt.	Issues during fiscal year.	Redemptions during fiscal year.	Excess of issues over redemptions.	Excess of redemptions over issues.	
Bonds and Securities	....	$268, 087, 370 00	....	$268, 087, 370 00	
Funded Loan of 1907	$72, 450, 000 00	....	$72, 450, 000 00	....	
Gold Certificates ...	....	7, 469, 100 00	....	7, 469, 100 00	
Silver Certificates...	10, 091, 000 00	183, 680 00	9, 907, 320 00	....	
Certificates of Deposit	47, 355, 000 00	63, 260, 000 00	....	15, 905, 000 00	
Refund'g Certificates	614, 640 00	12, 095, 850 00	....	11, 481, 210 00	
United States Notes.	81, 302, 563 00	81, 302, 563 00	....	....	
Fractional Currency	....	251, 717 41	....	251, 717 41	
Total............	211, 814, 103 00	432, 590, 280 41	82, 356, 320 00	303, 134, 397 41	
Net excess of Redemptions over Issue					220, 776, 177 41
Balance June 30, 1880, as shown by Warrant Ledger					203, 791, 321 89

No. 6.—*EXPLANATORY STATEMENT of DIFFERENCES between the BALANCES of June 30, 1880, as shown by the Treasurer's books and by the Public Debt Statement.*

The General Treasury balance subject to draft June 30, 1880, as shown by Statement No. 2, was $204, 683, 836 34
The cash in the Treasury June 30, 1880, as shown by the Public Debt Statement of July 1, 1880, was....................................... 201, 688, 622 88

The difference, amounting to $3, 595, 213 48
is explained in part by the fact that transcripts of the general account, containing reports of receipts into the Treasury prior to July 1, 1880, were not received by the Treasurer until after that date from the following offices, viz :

Sub-Treasury U. S., Boston, Mass	219, 743 51
Sub-Treasury U. S., Cincinnati, Ohio	63, 403 70
Sub-Treasury U. S., Chicago, Ill	90, 168 53
Sub-Treasury U. S., Saint Louis, Mo	11, 512 39
Sub-Treasury U. S., New Orleans, La	23, 115 84
Sub-Treasury U. S., San Francisco, Cal	276, 574 92
Depository U. S., Tucson, Ariz	6, 415 65
National Bank Depositaries	1, 869, 500 05

The remainder of the difference consists of the following items, viz :
Certificates of deposit (act of June 8, 1872) in the Treasurer's balance but not in that of the Public Debt Statement.................. 130, 000 00
Unavailable cash included in the Treasurer's balance but not in that of the Public Debt Statement 964, 773 87
_____
3, 595, 213 46

No. 7.—*BALANCES standing to the credit of DISBURSING OFFICERS and AGENTS of the UNITED STATES June 30, 1880.*

Office in which deposited.	Amount.
Treasury U. S., Washington, D. C	$1, 644, 169 27
Sub-Treasury U. S., New York, N. Y	18, 828, 545 37
Sub-Treasury U. S., Baltimore, Md	210, 758 34
Sub-Treasury U. S., Philadelphia, Pa	693, 411 78
Sub-Treasury U. S., Boston, Mass	757, 107 90
Sub-Treasury U. S., Cincinnati, Ohio	129, 128 29
Sub-Treasury U. S., Chicago, Ill	1, 104, 670 50
Sub-Treasury U. S., Saint Louis, Mo	365, 527 78
Sub-Treasury U. S., New Orleans, La	307, 674 98
Sub-Treasury U. S., San Francisco, Cal	726, 635 19
Depository U. S., Tucson, Ariz	91, 165 95
National Bank Depositaries	3, 222, 496 38
	28, 581, 290 93

No. 8.—*SUMMARY of the TREASURER'S QUARTERLY ACCOUNTS for the service of the POST-OFFICE DEPARTMENT for the fiscal year 1880.*

Expenditures by the Treasurer on Warrants... $9, 813, 688 03
Expenditures by Postmasters.. 25, 048, 862 16
_____
Total expenditures 35, 862, 450 19
Balance due the United States June 30, 1880... 2, 540, 591 43
_____
Total 38, 403, 041 62

Receipts covered into the Treasury by Warrants 9, 641, 583 04
Receipts by Postmasters.. 26, 048, 562 16
_____
Total net receipts... 35, 690, 145 20
Balance due the United States June 30, 1879... 2, 712, 896 42
_____
Total 38, 403, 041 62

No. 9.—*SUMMARY of the TREASURER'S QUARTERLY ACCOUNTS for the fiscal year 1880, as RENDERED to the FIRST AUDITOR of the TREASURY.*

Dr. | The United States in account with James Gilfillan, Treasurer of the United States, for the fiscal year 1880. | Cr.

To payments on current Quarters' Warrants on account of—				Balances of July 1, 1879:		
Treasury	$26,879,442 76			General Treasury	$417,223,787 08	
Quarterly Salaries	548,580 96			Less amount not covered by Warrants	58,539,940 99	
Judiciary	2,690,415 16					
Diplomatic	1,259,058 15			Balance of Warrant Ledger		$358,683,846 09
Customs	17,335,031 70			Amount on deposit with the States		28,101,644 91
Interior Civil	4,541,277 59			Amount of unpaid Warrants		339,159 35
Internal Revenue	4,337,196 31					
Public Debt	531,863,450 04			By balance of covered moneys		$387,124,650 35
Interior	64,517,987 98			By receipts covered in during the fiscal year by Warrants on account of—		
War	39,592,476 05			Miscellaneous Revenues and Revenue Counter Warrants	233,792,768 86	
Navy	20,076,502 29	$718,641,418 94		Customs	186,522,064 60	
				Lands	1,016,506 60	
To payments on previous Quarters' Warrants on account of—				Internal Revenue	124,009,373 92	
Treasury	62,414 03			Miscellaneous Repayments and Counter Warrants	3,795,224 97	
Quarterly Salaries	9,614 56			Interior Repayments and Counter Warrants	1,819,321 47	
Judiciary	20,596 21			War Repayments and Counter Warrants	1,541,774 44	
Diplomatic	3,326 41			Navy Repayments and Counter Warrants	6,540,965 01	559,037,999 87
Customs	60,478 83					
Interior Civil	26,598 08			By amount of War Warrant No. 1304, of first Quarter, 1879, in favor of Fountain Fullen, charged again to the Treasurer on account of defective voucher		108 00
Internal Revenue	64,374 92					
Interior	14,364 62					
War	116,437 84					
Navy	3,119 38	381,424 66	$714,022,943 62			
Balances:						
General Treasury (see Statement No. 2)	204,663,836 34					
Less amount not covered by warrants	892,514 46					

No. 10.—BALANCES and MOVEMENT OF MONEYS of the POST-OFFICE DEPARTMENT for the fiscal year 1880.

Office.	Balances June 30, 1879.			Movement during the fiscal year.					Balances June 30, 1880.		
	On deposit.	Outstanding drafts.	Subject to draft.	Received by transfers from other offices.	Receipts proper.	Expenditures.	Transferred to other offices.	Receipts refunded.	On deposit.	Outstanding drafts.	Subject to draft.
Treasury U. S., Washington, D. C.	$99,341 25	$1,136 77	$98,204 48	$456,403 25	$79,505 02	$519,434 30	....	$1,254 29	$114,560 93	$16,853 40	$97,707 53
Sub-Treasury U. S., Baltimore, Md	78,896 54	518 55	78,367 99	....	216,214 60	163,375 60	....	....	131,725 54	1,100 39	130,625 15
Sub-Treasury U. S., Boston, Mass	181,995 66	62 97	181,932 69	....	703,127 77	357,652 43	$325,000 00	....	202,471 00	142 20	202,328 80
Sub-Treasury U. S., Chicago, Ill	81,340 25	538 36	80,801 89	400,000 00	577,512 40	753,006 64	....	....	305,848 21	23,835 45	282,010 76
Sub-Treasury U. S., Cincinnati, Ohio	83,055 50	3,088 45	79,967 05	50,000 00	239,547 62	275,207 98	....	110 31	97,284 63	3,811 99	93,472 24
Sub-Treasury U. S., New Orleans, La	65,897 76	3,354 65	62,543 11	600,000 00	117,601 11	636,077 32	....	....	147,421 55	12,555 39	134,866 16
Sub-Treasury U. S., New York, N. Y	1,640,856 89	19,151 79	1,621,705 10	....	5,904,497 93	4,618,561 94	2,050,000 00	....	936,792 83	85,702 80	851,090 08
Sub-Treasury U. S., Philadelphia, Pa	124,581 75	65 44	124,516 31	....	667,727 19	590,591 40	....	24 39	201,693 15	2,203 69	199,489 46
Sub-Treasury U. S., San Francisco, Cal	205,126 32	18,908 45	186,217 87	....	586,211 47	440,144 55	200,000 00	....	151,193 24	11,884 26	139,308 98
Sub-Treasury U. S., Saint Louis, Mo	92,533 94	5,658 70	86,875 24	1,200,000 00	344,075 47	1,450,836 07	....	....	176,773 34	6,774 82	169,998 52
Sub-Treasury U. S., New Orleans, La. (old account)	31,164 44	....	31,164 44	....	....	....	....	....	31,164 44	....	31,164 44
Depository U. S., Little Rock, Ark. (old account)	5,823 50	....	5,823 50	....	....	....	....	....	5,823 50	....	5,823 50
Depository U. S., Galveston, Tex. (old account)	83 36	....	83 36	....	....	....	....	....	83 36	....	83 36
Depository U. S., Savannah, Ga. (old account)	205 76	....	205 76	....	....	....	....	....	205 76	....	205 76
National Bank Depositaries	19,202 50	....	19,202 50	....	147,227 55	....	131,403 25	276 10	34,750 70	....	34,750 70
Merchants' National Bank, Washington, D. C. (old account)	2,801 00	....	2,801 00	....	....	....	....	....	2,801 00	....	2,801 00
Total	2,712,896 42	52,484 13	2,660,412 29	2,706,403 25	9,643,248 13	9,813,688 03	2,706,403 25	1,665 09	2,540,591 43	164,864 39	2,375,727 04

Add revenues collected and expended by Postmasters as shown by Warrants of the Postmaster-General—

For the Quarter ended September 30, 1879					6,221,094 39	6,221,094 39
For the Quarter ended December 31, 1879					6,513,589 45	6,513,589 45
For the Quarter ended March 31, 1880					6,911,688 26	6,911,688 26
For the Quarter ended June 30, 1880					6,402,200 06	6,402,200 06
Aggregate Receipts and Expenditures					35,691,810 29	35,862,450 19

No. 11.—*UNAVAILABLE FUNDS of the GENERAL TREASURY and of the POST-OFFICE DEPARTMENT, June 30, 1880.*

The following items were unavailable on June 30, 1880, viz:
On deposit with the following States under the act of June 23, 1836:—

Maine	$956, 638 25
Vermont	669, 086 79
New Hampshire	609, 066 79
Massachusetts	1, 338, 173 58
Connecticut	764, 670 60
Rhode Island	382, 335 30
New York	4, 014, 520 71
Pennsylvania	2, 867, 514 78
New Jersey	764, 670 60
Ohio	2, 007, 260 34
Indiana	860, 254 44
Illinois	477, 919 14
Michigan	286, 751 49
Delaware	286, 751 49
Maryland	955, 838 25
Virginia	2, 198, 427 30
North Carolina	1, 433, 787 39
South Carolina	1, 051, 422 09
Georgia	1, 051, 422 09
Alabama	669, 086 79
Louisiana	477, 919 14
Mississippi	382, 335 30
Tennessee	1, 433, 757 39
Kentucky	1, 433, 757 39
Missouri	382, 335 30
Arkansas	286, 751 49

Total on deposit with the States	$28, 101, 644 91
Deficits and Defaults, Branch Mint, U. S., San Francisco, Cal., 1857 to 1860	419, 243 84
Default, Branch Mint U. S., Dahlonega, Ga., 1861, at the outbreak of the Rebellion	27, 950 03
Branch Mint U. S., Charlotte, N. C., 1861, at the outbreak of the Rebellion	32, 000 00
Depository U. S., Galveston, Tex., 1861, at the outbreak of the Rebellion	778 66
Depository U. S., Baltimore, Md., 1866	547 50
Deficit, Depository, U. S., Santa Fe, N. Mex., 1866, short in Remittance	249 90
Failure, Venango National Bank of Franklin, Pa., 1866	193, 932 67
First National Bank of Selma, Ala., 1867	34, 787 29
Default, Sub-Treasury U. S., New Orleans, La., 1867, May and Whitaker	675, 325 22
Sub-Treasury U. S., New Orleans, La., 1867, May property	5, 566 31
Deficit, Sub-Treasury U. S., New York, 1867, counterfeit 7.30s	8, 750 31
Default, Depository U. S., Pittsburgh, Pa., 1867	2, 126 11
Depository U. S., Baltimore, Md., 1867	6, 900 77
Depository U. S., Baltimore, Md., 1870	1, 126 87
Deficit, Treasury U. S., Washington, D. C., 1875	650 61
Treasury U. S., Washington, D. C., 1876	555 83
	1, 410, 561 94
Total	29, 512, 206 85

The Post-Office Department Balance "subject to draft" is $2,375.727.04, of which the following items were unavailable on June 30, 1880, viz:

Default, Sub-Treasury U. S., New Orleans, La., 1861, at the outbreak of the Rebellion	$31, 164 44
Depository U. S., Savannah, Ga., 1861, at the outbreak of the Rebellion	205 76
Depository U. S., Galveston, Tex., 1861, at the outbreak of the Rebellion	83 36
Depository U. S., Little Rock, Ark., 1861, at the outbreak of the Rebellion	5, 823 50
Failure, Merchants' National Bank of Washington, D. C., 1866	2, 801 00
Total	$40, 078 06

RECAPITULATION.

General Treasury Moneys unavailable June 30, 1880	$29, 512, 206 85
Post-Office Department Moneys unavailable June 30, 1880	40, 078 06
Total unavailable	29, 552, 284 91

No. 12.—*NUMBER of NATIONAL BANKS ORGANIZED, FAILED, and in VOLUNTARY LIQUIDATION to June 30, 1880.*

The number of National Banks which had deposited securities for their circulation to June 30, 1879, was 2,427
Organized during the fiscal year 1880 58

Total number of National Banks organized to June 30, 1880 2,485

Failed prior to July 1, 1879 81
Failed during the fiscal year 1880 5

Total number of failed National Banks June 30, 1880 86
In voluntary liquidation prior to July 1, 1879 276
Went into voluntary liquidation during the fiscal year 1880 21

Total number of National Banks in voluntary liquidation June 20, 1880 297
Number of National Banks doing business June 30, 1880 2,102

Total 2,485

No. 13.—*NATIONAL BANKS which FAILED during the fiscal year 1880.*

Place.	State.	Title.
Brattleboro'	Vermont	First National Bank.
Butler	Pennsylvania	First National Bank.
Meadville	Pennsylvania	First National Bank.
Monticello	Indiana	First National Bank.
Newark	New Jersey	First National Bank.

No. 14.—*NATIONAL BANKS which went into VOLUNTARY LIQUIDATION during the fiscal year 1880.*

Place.	State.	Title.
Afton	Iowa	First National Bank.
Auburn	New York	Auburn City National Bank.
Aurora	Illinois	Union National Bank.
Batavia	Illinois	First National Bank.
Bedford	Indiana	Bedford National Bank.
Centerville	Iowa	Farmers' National Bank.
Clyde	New York	First National Bank.
Deer Lodge	Montana Territory	First National Bank.
Delavan	Wisconsin	The National Bank.
Franklin	Kentucky	First National Bank.
Gainesville	Alabama	Gainesville National Bank.
Hackensack	New Jersey	First National Bank.
Keithsburg	Illinois	Farmers' National Bank.
Manchester	Ohio	Manchester National Bank.
Memphis	Tennessee	Fourth National Bank.
Meyersdale	Pennsylvania	First National Bank.
Mifflinburg	Pennsylvania	First National Bank.
Nashville	Tennessee	Mechanics' National Bank.
Salem	Indiana	The National Bank.
San Francisco	California	The National Gold Bank and Trust Co.
Winona	Minnesota	Mechanics' National Bank.

No. 15.—*SEMI-ANNUAL DUTY assessed upon and collected from NATIONAL BANKS by the TREASURER OF THE UNITED STATES for the fiscal years from 1864 to 1880, inclusive.*

Fiscal year.	On circulation.	On deposits.	On capital.	Total.
1864	$53, 193 32	$05, 911 87	$18, 432 07	$167, 537 26
1865	733, 247 59	1, 087, 530 88	133, 251 15	1, 954, 029 60
1866	2, 106, 785 30	2, 633, 102 77	406, 947 74	5, 146, 835 81
1867	2, 868, 698 78	2, 650, 180 09	321, 881 36	5, 840, 696 23
1868	2, 946, 343 07	2, 564, 143 44	306, 781 67	5, 817, 268 18
1869	2, 957, 416 73	2, 614, 353 58	312, 918 68	5, 884, 888 99
1870	2, 949, 744 13	2, 614, 767 61	375, 962 26	5, 940, 474 00
1871	2, 987, 021 69	2, 802, 840 85	385, 292 13	6, 175, 154 67
1872	3, 193, 570 03	3, 120, 984 37	389, 356 27	6, 703, 910 07
1873	3, 353, 186 13	3, 196, 569 29	454, 891 51	7, 004, 646 93
1874	3, 404, 483 11	3, 209, 967 72	469, 048 02	7, 083, 498 85
1875	3, 283, 450 59	3, 514, 265 39	507, 417 76	7, 305, 134 04
1876	3, 091, 795 70	3, 505, 129 64	632, 296 16	7, 229, 221 56
1877	2, 900, 957 53	3, 451, 965 33	660, 784 90	7, 013, 707 81
1878	2, 948, 047 08	3, 273, 111 74	560, 296 83	6, 781, 455 66
1879	3, 009, 647 16	3, 309, 668 90	401, 920 61	6, 721, 236 67
1880	3, 153, 635 63	4, 058, 710 61	379, 424 19	7, 591, 770 43
Total	45, 941, 161 93	47, 703, 404 11	6, 716, 903 31	100, 361, 469 36

No. 16.—*BONDS and STOCKS of the INDIAN TRUST FUND in CUSTODY of the TREASURER OF THE UNITED STATES June 30, 1880, under the act of June 10, 1876.*

Class of Bonds.	Registered.	Coupon.	Total.
State, Railway, and Canal Bonds.			
Arkansas : Funded Debt		$168, 000 00	$168, 000 00
Florida: State Stocks		132, 000 00	132, 000 00
Indiana: Wabash and Erie Canal Bonds		6, 000 00	6, 000 00
Louisiana: State Stocks		37, 000 00	37, 000 00
Maryland: State Stocks	$8, 350 17		8, 350 17
North Carolina: State Stocks		192, 000 00	192, 000 00
South Carolina: State Stocks		125, 000 00	125, 000 00
Tennessee: State Stocks	191, 666 66½	164, 000 00	355, 666 66½
Tennessee: Nashville and Chattanooga Railroad Bonds		512, 000 00	512, 000 00
Virginia : State Stocks		581, 800 00	581, 800 00
Virginia: Chesapeake and Ohio Canal Bonds		13, 000 00	13, 000 00
United States Bonds.			
Loan of July and August, 1861	500 00		500 00
Pacific Railway Bonds, sixes	280, 000 00		280, 000 00
Funded Loan of 1881, 5 per cent	2, 188, 900 00		2, 188, 900 00
Total	2, 669, 416, 83½	1, 916, 800 00	4, 580, 216 83½

o

No. 17.—*STATEMENT by LOANS of UNITED STATES BONDS held in TRUST for NATIONAL BANKS June 30, 1880, and of CHANGES during the FISCAL YEAR 1880 in CHARACTER of BONDS HELD.*

Title of Loan.	Bonds held in trust June 30, 1879.			Deposits and Withdrawals during fiscal year.				Bonds held in trust June 30, 1880.		
	For circulation.	For public deposits.	Total.	For circulation.		For public deposits.		For circulation.	For public deposits.	Total.
				Deposited.	Withdrawn.	Deposited.	Withdrawn.			
6 PER CENT. COIN.										
Loan of February, 1861	$2,176,000	$68,000	$2,244,000	$382,000	$466,000	....	$80,000	$2,092,000	$38,000	$2,130,000
Loan of July and August, 1861	31,739,100	880,800	32,619,900	5,923,850	3,413,900	$110,000	15,000	34,249,050	975,800	35,224,850
Loan of 1863 (81s)	17,077,100	696,500	17,773,600	2,330,550	2,078,550	35,000	4,000	17,329,100	727,500	18,056,600
Oregon War Debt	....	38,700	38,700	....	....	....	....	....	38,700	38,700
Consols of 1867	145,100	3,500	148,600	....	142,100	....	3,500	3,000	....	3,000
Consols of 1868	381,500	26,500	408,000	....	366,500	....	26,500	15,000	....	15,000
5 PER CENT. COIN.										
Ten-Forties of 1864	27,604,350	1,049,500	28,653,850	....	26,224,450	....	1,049,500	1,379,900	....	1,379,900
Funded Loan of 1881	117,011,950	3,452,400	120,464,350	28,303,450	6,936,650	994,500	196,000	138,373,760	4,250,900	142,629,650
4½ PER CENT. COIN.										
Funded Loan of 1891	35,056,550	1,230,000	36,286,550	5,909,480	3,205,000	100,000	385,000	37,760,950	945,000	38,705,950
4 PER CENT. COIN.										
Funded Loan of 1907	118,538,950	6,962,500	125,501,450	32,511,300	24,973,950	1,546,000	740,400	126,076,300	7,768,100	133,844,400
6 PER CENT. CURRENCY.										
Pacific Railway Bonds	4,524,000	13,000	4,537,000	353,000	509,000	20,000	....	4,368,000	33,000	4,401,000
Personal Bonds	....	330,000	330,000	....	....	....	....	....	330,000	330,000
Total	354,254,600	14,751,400	369,006,000	75,713,550	63,326,100	2,805,500	2,449,900	361,052,050	15,107,000	376,759,050

No. 18.—*UNITED STATES CURRENCY, of each issue, OUTSTANDING at the close of EACH FISCAL YEAR from 1862 to 1880, inclusive.*

Issue.	1862.	1863.	1864.	1865.	1866.	1867.	1868.	1869.	1870.	1871.
Old Demand Notes	$51,105,235 00	$3,384,000 00	$789,037 50	$472,603 80	$272,162 75	$208,432 50	$143,912 00	$123,739 25	$106,256 00	$96,505 50
United States Notes	96,620,000 00	387,646,580 00	447,300,203 10	431,066,427 99	400,780,305 85	371,783,597 00	356,000,000 00	356,000,000 00	356,000,000 00	356,000,000 00
One and two year Notes of 1863			172,620,550 00	50,625,170 00	8,439,540 50	1,325,889 50	716,212 00	347,772 00	253,952 00	205,922 00
Compound Interest Notes			6,060,000 00	191,721,470 00	172,369,941 00	134,774,981 00	54,968,230 00	3,063,410 00	2,191,670 00	814,280 00
Fractional Currency		20,192,456 00	22,324,283 10	25,033,128 76	27,008,875 26	26,474,623 02	33,727,908 47	32,114,037 36	39,878,684 48	40,582,874 56
Total	147,725,235 00	411,223,045 00	649,094,073 70	698,918,800 25	808,876,825 46	536,567,523 02	444,196,262 47	391,649,558 81	398,430,562 48	397,690,632 06

Issue.	1872.	1873.	1874.	1875.	1876.	1877.	1878.	1879.	1880.
Old Demand Notes	$68,296 25	$79,967 50	$75,732 50	$70,107 50	$66,917 50	$63,962 50	$62,297 50	$61,470 00	$60,975 00
United States Notes	357,500,000 00	356,000,000 00	381,999,073 00	375,771,580 00	369,772,284 00	359,764,332 00	346,681,016 00	346,681,016 00	346,681,016 00
One and two year Notes of 1863	178,222 00	148,135 00	130,805 00	114,175 00	105,405 00	96,285 00	90,475 00	86,845 00	82,515 00
Compound Interest Notes	623,010 00	499,780 00	429,080 00	371,470 00	331,290 00	300,360 00	274,780 00	260,660 00	243,310 00
Fractional Currency	40,855,835 27	44,799,365 44	45,912,009 84	43,129,424 19	34,446,595 39	20,403,137 84	16,547,768 77	15,843,610 11	16,590,892 70
Total	399,245,363 80	401,527,267 94	428,547,693 84	418,456,756 69	404,722,461 89	380,627,976 84	363,656,337 27	362,932,591 11	362,639,908 70

No. 19.—*REDEMPTIONS for the FISCAL YEAR 1880, and TOTAL REDEMPTIONS to June 30, 1880, of UNITED STATES CURRENCY and of NOTES of FAILED, LIQUIDATING, and REDUCING NATIONAL BANKS.*

Issue.	Redemptions (net value).			Deductions on account of mutilations.			Total face value of notes redeemed.
	To June 30, 1879	In fiscal year	To June 30, 1880	To June 30, 1879	In fiscal year	To June 30, 1880	

No. 20.—*UNITED STATES CURRENCY of each ISSUE and DENOMINATION ISSUED, REDEEMED, and OUTSTANDING at the CLOSE of the FISCAL YEARS 1879 and 1880.*

OLD DEMAND NOTES.

[Issue began August 26, 1861, and ceased March 5, 1862.]

Denomination.	Total issued.	Redeemed to June 30, 1879.	Outstanding June 30, 1879.	Redeemed to June 30, 1880.	Outstanding June 30, 1880.
5s	$21,800,000 00	$21,775,725 00	$24,275 00	$21,775,880 00	$24,120 00
10s	20,030,000 00	20,007,425 00	22,575 00	20,007,665 00	22,335 00
20s	18,200,000 00	18,185,380 00	14,620 00	18,185,480 00	14,520 00
Total	60,030,000 00	59,968,530 00	61,470 00	59,969,025 00	60,975 00

UNITED STATES NOTES, NEW ISSUE.

[Issue began April 2, 1862, and ceased April 19, 1869.]

Denomination.	Total issued.	Redeemed to June 30, 1879.	Outstanding June 30, 1879.	Redeemed to June 30, 1880.	Outstanding June 30, 1880.
1s	$28,351,348 00	$27,492,697 85	$858,650 15	$27,510,430 45	$840,917 55
2s	34,071,128 00	33,360,161 40	710,966 60	33,386,228 80	684,899 20
5s	101,000,000 00	99,106,196 75	1,893,803 25	99,374,070 75	1,625,929 25
10s	118,010,000 00	112,053,503 00	5,956,497 00	112,468,029 00	5,541,971 00
20s	102,920,000 00	98,285,667 00	4,634,333 00	98,702,481 00	4,217,519 00
50s	30,055,200 00	29,441,590 00	613,610 00	29,497,485 08	557,715 00
100s	40,000,000 00	39,078,990 00	921,010 00	39,175,190 00	824,810 00
500s	58,982,000 00	58,367,500 00	618,500 00	58,480,009 00	506,000 00
1,000s	155,928,000 00	155,115,500 00	812,500 00	155,258,500 00	669,500 00
Unknown	....	135,000 00	....	135,000 00	....
			17,019,870 00		15,468,361 00
Deduct for unknown denominations destroyed in the Chicago fire	....	....	135,000 00	....	135,000 00
Total	659,321,676 00	652,486,806 00	16,884,870 00	653,988,315 00	15,333,361 00

UNITED STATES NOTES, ISSUE OF 1869.

[Issue began October 19, 1869, and ceased July 25, 1874.]

Denomination.	Total issued.	Redeemed to June 30, 1879.	Outstanding June 30, 1879.	Redeemed to June 30, 1880.	Outstanding June 30, 1880.
1s	$42,456,812 00	$41,217,701 75	$1,239,110 25	$41,539,144 05	$917,667 95
2s	50,511,920 00	48,767,121 00	1,744,799 00	49,331,892 20	1,180,027 80
5s	50,581,780 00	37,828,435 25	12,753,344 75	39,998,845 75	10,582,914 25
10s	85,221,240 00	54,696,916 00	30,524,324 00	58,053,655 00	27,167,585 00
20s	73,162,400 00	43,776,050 00	29,386,350 00	46,774,294 00	26,388,106 00
50s	30,200,000 00	24,960,110 00	5,230,890 00	25,743,180 00	4,456,820 00
100s	37,104,080 00	26,314,130 00	10,780,870 00	27,609,580 00	9,494,420 00
500s	44,890,000 00	44,249,500 00	640,500 00	44,341,500 00	548,500 00
1,000s	79,700,000 00	51,749,000 00	27,951,000 00	68,028,000 00	11,672,000 00
Unknown	....	865,000 00	....	865,000 00	....
			120,209,178 00		92,408,041 00
Deduct for unknown denominations destroyed in the Chicago fire	....	....	865,000 00	....	865,000 00
Total	493,828,132 00	374,423,954 00	119,404,178 00	402,285,091 00	91,543,041 00

No. 20.—*UNITED STATES CURRENCY, &c.*—Continued.

UNITED STATES NOTES, ISSUE OF 1874.

[Issue began July 13, 1874, and ceased September 13, 1875.]

Denomination.	Total issued.	Redeemed to June 30, 1879.	Outstanding June 30, 1879.	Redeemed to June 30, 1880.	Outstanding June 30, 1880.
1s	$18, 968, 000 00	$17, 649, 050 80	$1, 338, 949 20	$18, 274, 808 00	$713, 192 00
2s	16, 520, 000 00	14, 668, 974 20	1, 851, 025 80	15, 584, 283 00	935, 767 00
50s	24, 460, 000 00	9, 844, 960 00	14, 615, 040 00	10, 873, 645 00	13, 586, 355 00
500s	28, 000, 000 00	14, 908, 000 00	13, 092, 000 00	21, 294, 000 00	6, 706, 000 00
Total	87, 968, 000 00	57, 130, 985 00	30, 837, 015 00	66, 026, 686 00	21, 941, 314 00

UNITED STATES NOTES, ISSUE OF 1875.

[Issue began July 20, 1875, and ceased June 20, 1879.]

Denomination.	Total issued.	Redeemed to June 30, 1879.	Outstanding June 30, 1879.	Redeemed to June 30, 1880.	Outstanding June 30, 1880.
1s	$26, 213, 000 00	$16, 960, 233 80	$9, 251, 766 20	$20, 834, 054 20	$5, 377, 945 80
2s	23, 036, 000 00	10, 800, 138 20	12, 235, 861 80	14, 756, 657 80	8, 279, 342 20
5s	46, 180, 000 00	14, 340, 483 00	31, 839, 517 00	18, 985, 190 00	27, 194, 810 00
10s	23, 660, 000 00	4, 608, 184 00	19, 051, 816 00	6, 225, 950 00	17, 434, 050 00
20s	25, 000, 000 00	4, 877, 760 00	20, 122, 240 00	6, 305, 798 00	18, 694, 202 00
50s	2, 000, 000 00	175, 450 00	1, 824, 550 00	294, 250 00	1, 705, 750 00
100s	16, 200, 000 00	3, 034, 000 00	13, 166, 000 00	3, 703, 180 00	12, 496, 820 00
500s	28, 400, 000 00	10, 121, 500 00	18, 278, 500 00	19, 100, 500 00	9, 299, 500 00
Total	190, 688, 000 00	64, 917, 749 00	125, 770, 251 00	90, 311, 580 00	100, 478, 420 00

UNITED STATES NOTES, ISSUE OF 1878.

[Issue began February 14, 1878, and still continues.]

Denomination.	Issued to June 30, 1879.	Redeemed to June 30, 1879.	Outstanding June 30, 1879.	Issued to June 30, 1880.	Redeemed to June 30, 1880.	Outstanding June 30, 1880.
1s	$6, 171, 076 00	$649, 571 00	$5, 521, 505 00	$12, 512, 000 00	$2, 740, 330 30	$9, 765, 669 70
2s	1, 560, 000 00	10, 000 00	1, 550, 000 00	9, 352, 000 00	519, 223 30	8, 832, 776 80
5s	7, 840, 000 00	219, 542 00	7, 620, 458 00	27, 520, 000 00	1, 491, 105 50	26, 028, 894 50
10s	9, 480, 000 00	374, 075 00	9, 105, 925 00	26, 000, 000 00	1, 225, 955 00	24, 774, 045 00
20s	6, 800, 000 00	672, 036 00	6, 327, 964 00	34, 150, 000 00	1, 316, 620 00	32, 843, 380 00
50s	3, 400, 000 00	169, 750 00	3, 230, 250 00	4, 800, 000 00	297, 645 00	4, 502, 355 00
100s	7, 681, 500 00	519, 900 00	7, 161, 600 00	10, 734, 200 00	746, 380 00	9, 987, 820 00
500s				2, 300, 000 00	136, 000 00	2, 164, 000 00
1,000s	6, 500, 000 00	193, 000 00	6, 307, 000 00	7, 300, 000 00	3, 000, 000 00	4, 191, 000 00
5,000s	4, 605, 000 00	5, 000 00	4, 000, 000 00	5, 000, 000 00	4, 325, 000 00	680, 000 00
10,000s	3, 010, 000 00	50, 000 00	2, 960, 000 00	5, 010, 000 00	4, 550, 000 00	460, 000 00
Total	56, 447, 576 00	2, 662, 874 00	53, 784, 702 00	134, 593, 200 00	20, 363, 259 00	114, 229, 941 00

UNITED STATES NOTES, ISSUE OF 1880.

[Issue began March 16, 1880, and still continues.]

Denomination.	Issued to June 30, 1880.	Redeemed to June 30, 1880.	Outstanding June 30, 1880.
1s	$2, 716, 939 00		$2, 716, 939 00
2s	440, 000 00		440, 000 00
Total	3, 156, 939 00		3, 156, 939 00

No. 20.—*UNITED STATES CURRENCY, &c.*—Continued.

ONE-YEAR NOTES OF 1863.

[Issue began February 4, 1864, and ceased June 1, 1864.]

Denomination.	Total issued.	Redeemed to June 30, 1879.	Outstanding June 30, 1879.	Redeemed to June 30, 1880.	Outstanding June 30, 1880.
10s	$6, 200, 000	$6, 190, 105	$9, 895	$6, 190, 685	$9, 315
20s	16, 440, 000	16, 418, 560	21, 440	16, 419, 760	20, 240
50s	8, 240, 000	8, 231, 300	8, 700	8, 231, 500	8, 500
100s	13, 640, 000	13, 630, 800	9, 200	13, 631, 200	8, 800
Unknown	....	90	....	90	....
			49, 235		46, 855
Deduct for unknown denominations destroyed	....	....	90	....	90
Total	44, 520, 000	44, 470, 855	49, 145	44, 473, 235	46, 765

TWO-YEAR NOTES OF 1863.

[Issue began March 16, 1864, and ceased May 30, 1864.]

Denomination.	Total issued.	Redeemed to June 30, 1879.	Outstanding June 30, 1879.	Redeemed to June 30, 1880.	Outstanding June 30, 1880.
50s	$6, 800, 000	$6, 791, 400	$8, 600	$6, 792, 200	$7, 800
100s	9, 680, 000	9, 674, 600	5, 400	9, 675, 100	4, 900
Total	16, 480, 000	10, 466, 000	14, 000	16, 467, 300	12, 700

TWO-YEAR COUPON NOTES OF 1863.

[Issue began January 12, 1864, and ceased April 20, 1864.]

Denomination.	Total issued.	Redeemed to June 30, 1879.	Outstanding June 30, 1879.	Redeemed to June 30, 1880.	Outstanding June 30, 1880.
50s	$5, 905, 600	$5, 903, 000	$2, 600	$5, 903, 050	$2, 550
100s	14, 484, 400	14, 475, 300	9, 100	14, 475, 600	8, 800
500s	40, 302, 000	40, 300, 500	1, 500	40, 300, 500	1, 500
1, 000s	89, 308, 000	89, 287, 000	21, 000	89, 287, 000	21, 000
Unknown	....	10, 500	....	10, 500	....
			34, 200		33, 850
Deduct for unknown denominations destroyed	....	....	10, 500	....	10, 500
Total	150, 000, 000	149, 976, 300	23, 700	149, 976, 650	23, 350

COMPOUND-INTEREST NOTES.

[Issue began June 9, 1864, and ceased July 24, 1865.]

Denomination.	Total issued.	Redeemed to June 30, 1879.	Outstanding June 30, 1879.	Redeemed to June 30, 1880.	Outstanding June 30, 1880.
10s	$23, 285, 200	$23, 247, 050	$38, 150	$23, 249, 700	$35, 440
20s	30, 125, 840	30, 066, 990	58, 850	30, 071, 270	54, 570
50s	60, 824, 000	60, 732, 850	91, 150	60, 737, 700	86, 300
100s	45, 094, 400	45, 044, 900	49, 500	45, 049, 400	45, 000
500s	67, 846, 000	67, 830, 000	16, 000	67, 831, 000	15, 000
1, 000s	39, 420, 000	39, 413, 000	7, 000	39, 413, 000	7, 000
Total	266, 595, 440	266, 334, 790	260, 650	266, 352, 130	243, 310

No. 20.—*UNITED STATES CURRENCY, &c.*—Continued.

FRACTIONAL CURRENCY, FIRST ISSUE.

[Issue began August 21, 1862, and ceased May 27, 1863.*]

Denomination.	Total issued.	Redeemed to June 30, 1879.	Outstanding June 30, 1879.	Redeemed to June 30, 1880.	Outstanding June 30, 1880.
5 cents	$2,242,889 00	$1,214,047 90	$1,028,841 10	$1,214,370 20	$1,028,509 80
10 cents	4,115,378 00	2,870,501 96	1,244,876 04	2,871,053 25	1,244,324 75
25 cents	5,225,696 00	4,185,321 21	1,040,374 79	4,185,898 56	1,039,797 44
50 cents	8,631,672 00	7,659,182 60	972,480 31	7,660,135 99	971,536 01
Total	20,215,635 00	15,929,053 76	4,286,581 24	15,931,467 00	4,284,168 00

* From June 4, 1866, to September 21, 1866, there were issued and sold as specimens of this issue $23,175.

FRACTIONAL CURRENCY, SECOND ISSUE.

[Issue began October 10, 1863, and ceased February 23, 1867.]

Denomination.	Total issued.	Redeemed to June 30, 1879.	Outstanding June 30, 1879.	Redeemed to June 30, 1880.	Outstanding June 30, 1880.
5 cents	$2,794,826 10	$2,095,552 61	$699,273 49	$2,095,883 60	$698,942 50
10 cents	6,176,084 30	5,263,017 69	913,066 61	5,263,409 67	912,074 63
25 cents	7,648,841 25	6,901,702 43	746,638 82	6,902,140 78	746,200 47
50 cents	6,545,232 00	5,793,438 10	751,793 90	5,793,990 95	751,241 05
Total	23,164,483 65	20,053,710 83	3,110,772 82	20,055,425 00	3,109,058 65

FRACTIONAL CURRENCY, THIRD ISSUE.

[Issue began December 5, 1864, and ceased April 16, 1869.]

Denomination.	Total issued.	Redeemed to June 30, 1879.	Outstanding June 30, 1879.	Redeemed to June 30, 1880.	Outstanding June 30, 1880.
3 cents	$601,923 90	$511,440 52	$90,483 38	$511,503 78	$90,420 12
5 cents	657,002 75	524,322 03	132,680 72	524,417 51	182,585 34
10 cents	16,976,134 50	15,920,430 48	1,055,704 02	15,922,430 58	1,053,723 92
15 cents	1,352 40	75 22	1,277 18	75 22	1,277 18
25 cents	31,143,188 75	30,235,395 98	907,792 77	30,237,649 76	905,538 99
50 cents	36,735,426 50	35,917,353 55	818,072 95	35,923,220 15	812,206 35
Total	86,115,028 80	83,109,017 78	3,006,011 92	83,119,277 00	2,995,751 60

FRACTIONAL CURRENCY, FOURTH ISSUE.

[Issue began July 14, 1869, and ceased February 16, 1875.]

Denomination.	Total issued.	Redeemed to June 30, 1879.	Outstanding June 30, 1879.	Redeemed to June 30, 1880.	Outstanding June 30, 1880.
10 cents	$34,940,060 00	$33,542,118 82	$1,398,841 18	$33,553,017 86	$1,387,942 14
15 cents	5,304,218 00	5,053,282 00	250,934 00	5,059,734 17	244,481 83
25 cents	58,922,256 00	57,856,050 75	1,066,205 25	57,873,810 92	1,048,445 08
50 cents	77,399,500 00	76,247,075 90	1,152,524 10	76,285,271 45	1,114,228 55
Unknown	....	....	32,000 00	....	32,000 00
			3,668,504 53		3,795,107 60
Deduct for unknown denominations destroyed.............	....	....	32,000 00	....	32,000 00
Total	176,567,032 00	172,730,527 47	3,636,504 53	172,893,834 40	3,763,197 60

No. 20.—*UNITED STATES CURRENCY, &c.*—Concluded.

FRACTIONAL CURRENCY, FIFTH ISSUE.

[Issue began February 26, 1874, and ceased February 15, 1876.]

Denomination.	Total issued.	Redeemed to June 30, 1879.	Outstanding June 30, 1879.	Redeemed to June 30, 1880.	Outstanding June 30, 1880.
10 cents	$19,969,906 00	$19,427,060 39	$542,839 61	$19,462,905 22	$526,994 78
25 cents	36,692,000 00	35,332,607 56	759,392 44	35,415,329 88	676,670 12
50 cents	6,560,000 00	6,299,491 55	280,508 45	6,344,948 25	235,051 75
Total	62,661,900 00	61,059,159 50	1,602,740 50	61,223,183 35	1,438,716 65

RECAPITULATION.

Issue.	Total issued.	Face value of notes redeemed to June 30, 1880 (see Statement No. 19).	Less deductions for mutilations since May 11, 1875, not covered into Treasury.	Redeemed to June 30, 1880, as shown by cash statements.	Outstanding June 30, 1880.
Old Demand Notes	$60,030,000 00	$59,969,927 50	$2 50	$59,969,925 00	$60,075 00
United States Notes...	1,579,555,947 00	1,232,924,894 00	49,963 00	1,232,874,931 00	346,681,016 00
One and two year Notes of 1863	211,000,000 00	210,917,185 00	....	210,917,185 00	82,815 00
Compound Interest Notes	266,595,440 00	266,352,130 00	....	266,352,130 00	243,310 00
Fractional Currency ...	368,724,079 45	353,149,374 67	16,187 92	353,133,186 75	15,590,892 70
Total	2,485,905,466 45	2,123,312,611 17	68,153 42	2,123,246,457 75	362,659,008 70

No. 21.—*SILVER CERTIFICATES, ISSUED, REDEEMED, and OUTSTANDING, by SERIES and DENOMINATIONS.*

Series and denomination.	Issued.		Redeemed.		Outstanding June 30, 1880.
	During fiscal year.	To June 30, 1880.	During fiscal year.	To June 30, 1880.	
Series of 1878.					
10s	$1,927,000	$3,094,000	$33,490	$26,660	$2,067,340
20s	1,890,000	1,986,000	10,540	11,120	1,974,880
50s	1,195,000	1,340,000	11,050	11,050	1,328,950
100s	1,449,000	1,930,000	20,100	25,400	1,904,600
500s	750,000	5,018,000	20,500	1,788,500	1,229,500
1,000s	2,727,000	10,570,000	98,000	6,781,000	3,789,000
Series of 1880.					
10s	80,000	80,000	....	....	80,000
Total	10,018,000	21,018,000	183,680	8,643,730	12,374,270

No. 22.—*SILVER CERTIFICATES, ISSUED, REDEEMED, and OUTSTANDING, at the several OFFICES of ISSUE.*

Office by which issued.	Issued.		Redeemed.		Outstanding.
	During fiscal year.	To June 30, 1880.	During fiscal year.	To June 30, 1880.	
Treasury United States, Washington	$5,905,000	$6,850,000	$65,080	$65,220	$6,784,780
Sub-Treasury United States, New York	1,022,000	1,368,000	12,550	79,300	1,288,700
Sub-Treasury United States, San Francisco	3,091,000	12,800,000	106,050	8,499,210	4,300,790
Total	10,018,000	21,018,000	183,680	8,643,730	12,374,270

23 T

No. 23.—*SEVEN-THIRTY NOTES, ISSUED, REDEEMED, and OUTSTANDING.*

Issue.	Total issued.	Redeemed to June 30, 1879.	Redeemed during fiscal year.	Redeemed to June 30, 1880.	Outstanding June 30, 1880.
July 17, 1861	$140,094,750	$140,078,150	....	$140,078,150	$16,600
August 15, 1864	299,992,500	299,933,800	$1,150	299,934,950	57,550
June 15, 1865	381,000,000	330,963,050	400	330,963,450	36,550
July 15, 1865	199,000,000	198,943,100	1,100	198,944,200	55,800
Total	970,087,250	969,918,100	2,650	969,920,750	166,500

NOTE:—The public debt statement shows $144,900 7.30s of 1864 and 1865 outstanding on June 30, 1880, being $5,000 less than the above, an error having occurred whereby an amount of $5,000, deducted as redeemed in August, 1868, the settlement of which was afterwards suspended, was again deducted when the suspension was removed.

No. 24.—*COUPONS from UNITED STATES BONDS PAID during the fiscal year 1880, classified by LOANS.*

Title of Loan.	Amount.
Loan of February, 1861	$299,847 00
Oregon War Debt	57,060 00
Loan of July and August, 1861	3,260,808 00
5-20s of 1862	1,40 00
Loan of 1863 (81s)	1,004,162 50
10-40s of 1864	89,972 50
5-20s of June, 1864	1,100 50
5-20s of 1865	1,804 50
Consols of 1865	37,519 50
Consols of 1867	265,953 00
Consols of 1868	207,688 50
Funded Loan of 1881	12,267,496 45
Funded Loan of 1891	3,978,595 56
Funded Loan of 1907	10,006,413 85
Total	31,479,603 96

No. 25.—*CHECKS for QUARTERLY INTEREST on the FUNDED LOANS of the UNITED STATES ISSUED, PAID, and OUTSTANDING.*

	Funded Loan of 1881; 86,937 Checks issued.	Funded Loan of 1891; 45,449 Checks issued.	Funded Loan of 1907; 214,550 Checks issued.
Amount of Checks outstanding July 1, 1879	$124,339 22	$129,887 67	$28,930 07
Amount of Checks issued during the fiscal year	14,016,454 37	7,557,039 00	19,145,882 67
	14,140,793 50	7,686,926 67	19,174,813 34
Paid by Treasurer United States, Washington	327,667 95	54,417 43	243,965 61
Paid by Assistant Treasurers United States—New York	9,653,368 88	4,825,003 31	13,158,243 50
Boston	1,676,924 24	1,667,043 94	2,472,529 00
Philadelphia	1,419,575 89	462,554 68	1,077,530 50
Baltimore	279,477 37	199,900 29	212,586 00
Cincinnati	319,279 92	127,064 95	467,653 50
Chicago	94,608 11	189,313 65	794,542 00
Saint Louis	45,300 60	37,917 39	197,620 00
New Orleans	6,085 62	75,226 98	292,079 00
San Francisco	26,622 50	5,436 50	125,168 00
Total paid	14,053,011 08	7,564,509 03	19,041,317 61
Amount outstanding June 30, 1880	88,782 51	122,417 64	133,495 73

No. 26.—*UNITED STATES BONDS purchased for the SINKING FUND during the fiscal year 1880, showing the AMOUNT PAID for PRINCIPAL, INTEREST, AND PREMIUM.*

Title of loan.	Coupon.	Registered.	Principal.	Interest accrued to date of purchase.	Net premium.
Loan of February, 1861	$621,000	$2,216,000	$2,837,000	$47,540 20	$74,161 95
Oregon War Debt	202,550	....	202,550	3,662 56	8,273 02
Loan of July and August, 1861	12,465,700	19,598,550	32,064,250	518,148 79	1,376,085 04
Loan of 1863 (81s)	5,152,450	7,644,700	12,797,150	213,179 29	549,035 13
Funded Loan of 1881	20,845,050	2,730,400	23,575,450	130,349 36	662,205 97
Funded Loan of 1907	950,000	550,000	1,500,000	10,191 74	125,558 26
Total.............	40,236,750	33,739,650	72,976,400	923,071 94	2,795,329 42

No. 27.—*TOTAL amount of UNITED STATES BONDS RETIRED for the SINKING FUND.*

Title of Loan.	How retired.	To June 30, 1879.	During fiscal year.	To June 30, 1880.
Loan of February, 1861	Purchased	....	$2,837,000	$2,837,000
Oregon War Debt	do	....	202,550	202,550
Loan of July and August, 1861	do	....	32,064,250	32,064,250
5-20s of 1862	Purchased	$24,029,150	....	24,029,150
	Redeemed	29,960,850	100	29,960,950
	Total	53,990,000	100	53,990,100
Loan of 1863 (81s)	Purchased	....	12,797,150	12,797,150
10-40s of 1864	Redeemed	....	676,050	676,050
5-20s of March, 1864..........	do	361,600	....	361,600
5-20s of June, 1864	Purchased	18,356,100	....	18,356,100
	Redeemed	11,067,550	150	11,067,700
	Total	29,423,650	150	29,423,800
5-20s of 1865...............	Purchased	18,866,150	....	18,866,150
	Redeemed	1,973,850	350	1,974,200
	Total	18,840,000	350	18,840,350
Consols of 1865	Purchased	48,166,150	....	48,166,150
	Redeemed	31,350	....	31,350
	Total	48,197,500	....	48,197,500
Consols of 1867	Purchased	32,115,600	....	32,115,600
	Redeemed	15,750	....	15,750
	Total	32,131,350	....	32,131,350
Consols of 1868..............	Purchased	2,213,800	....	2,213,800
	Redeemed	8,600	....	8,600
	Total	2,222,400	....	2,222,400
Funded Loan of 1881	Purchased	....	23,575,450	23,575,450
Funded Loan of 1907.........	do	....	1,500,000	1,500,000
	Total purchased	142,108,550	72,976,400	215,084,950
	Total redeemed	43,057,900	676,650	43,734,550
Aggregate.............	....	185,166,450	73,653,050	258,819,500

No. 28.—*TOTAL amount of UNITED STATES BONDS RETIRED from March 11, 1869, to June 30, 1880.*

Title of Loan.	How retired.	Rate of interest.	From March 11, 1869, to June 30, 1879.	During fiscal year.	To June 30, 1880.
		Per ct.			
Loan of February, 1861	Purchased	6	....	$2,837,000	$2,837,000
Oregon War Debt	Purchased	6	....	202,550	202,550
	Redeemed	6	$200,750	....	200,750
Total			200,750	202,550	403,300
Loan of July and August, 1861	Purchased	6	....	32,064,250	32,064,250
5-20s of 1862	Purchased	6	57,156,850	....	57,156,850
	Redeemed	6	430,122,250	9,100	430,131,350
	Converted	6	27,091,000	....	27,091,000
Total			514,369,100	9,100	514,378,200
Loan of 1863 (81s)	Purchased	6	....	12,797,150	12,797,150
5-20s of March, 1864	Purchased	6	1,119,800	....	1,119,800
	Redeemed	6	2,382,200	....	2,382,200
	Converted	6	380,500	....	380,500
Total			3,882,500	....	3,882,500
5-20s of June, 1864	Purchased	6	43,459,750	....	43,459,750
	Redeemed	6	69,811,100	3,550	69,814,650
	Converted	6	12,218,650	....	12,218,650
Total			125,480,500	3,550	125,493,050
5-20s of 1865	Purchased	6	36,023,350	....	36,023,350
	Redeemed	6	157,371,650	31,100	157,602,750
	Converted	6	9,586,600	....	9,586,600
Total			203,181,600	31,100	203,212,700
Consols of 1865	Purchased	6	118,950,550	....	118,950,550
	Redeemed	6	203,744,900	987,500	204,732,400
	Converted	6	8,703,600	....	8,703,600
Total			331,399,050	987,500	332,386,550
Consols of 1867	Purchased	6	62,846,950	....	62,846,950
	Redeemed	6	268,977,050	38,894,250	307,871,300
	Converted	6	5,807,500	....	5,807,500
	Exchanged	6	761,100	....	761,100
Total			338,392,600	38,894,250	377,286,850
Consols of 1868	Purchased	6	4,794,050	....	4,794,050
	Redeemed	6	17,385,100	19,351,250	36,736,350
	Converted	6	311,750	....	311,750
	Exchanged	6	44,900	....	44,900
Total			22,435,800	19,351,250	41,787,050
Total of six per cents			1,539,850,900	107,177,700	1,646,528,600
Texas indemnity	Redeemed	5	*4,979,000	....	4,979,000
Loan of 1858	Redeemed	5	5,995,000	40,000	6,035,000
	Converted	5	13,957,000	....	13,957,000
Total			19,952,000	40,000	19,992,000
10-40s of 1864	Redeemed	5	54,052,650	135,769,750	189,822,400
	Exchanged	5	2,089,500	....	2,089,500
Total			56,142,150	135,769,750	191,911,900
Funded Loan of 1881	Purchased	5	....	23,575,450	23,575,450
	Redeemed	5	9,553,800	....	9,553,800
Total			9,553,800	23,575,450	33,129,250
Total of five per cents			90,626,950	159,385,200	250,012,150
Funded Loan of 1907	Purchased	4	....	1,500,000	1,500,000

No. 28.—*TOTAL amount of UNITED STATES BONDS RETIRED, &c.*—Concluded.

RECAPITULATION.

	From March 11, 1869, to June 30, 1879.	During fiscal year.	To June 30, 1880.
Purchased	$324, 350, 300	$72, 976, 400	$397, 326, 700
Redeemed	1, 224, 775, 450	195, 086, 500	1, 419, 861, 950
Converted	77, 956, 600	....	77, 956, 600
Exchanged	2, 895, 500	....	2, 895, 500
Aggregate	1, 629, 977, 850	268, 062, 900	1, 898, 040, 750

No. 29.—*INTEREST on 3.65 BONDS of the DISTRICT of COLUMBIA PAID during the fiscal year 1880.*

Where paid.	Coupons.	Registered interest.		Total paid.
		Checks issued.	Checks paid.	
Treasury United States, Washington	$45, 462 68	$249, 514 60	$39, 310 50	$84, 773 18
Sub-Treasury United States, New York	198, 085 50	....	209, 491 75	407, 577 25
Total	243, 548 18	249, 514 60	248, 802 25	492, 350 43

No. 30.—*NUMBER of PACKAGES and AMOUNT of NATIONAL-BANK NOTES RECEIVED for REDEMPTION during each MONTH of the FISCAL YEAR 1880.*

Month.	Number of packages.	Amount.
1879.		
July	1, 468	$9, 123, 424 75
August	1, 283	6, 314, 586 01
September	1, 201	4, 508, 040 72
October	1, 197	3, 340, 766 35
November	1, 104	3, 251, 533 76
December	1, 219	2, 923, 489 87
1880.		
January	1, 376	5, 541, 192 27
February	1, 188	3, 960, 505 05
March	1, 347	3, 144, 810 88
April	1, 368	4, 908, 204 91
May	1, 434	7, 554, 659 92
June	1, 422	7, 808, 361 18
Total	15, 607	61, 585, 875 68

No. 31.—*MODE of PAYMENT for NATIONAL-BANK NOTES REDEEMED during the fiscal year 1880.*

By Transfer Checks on Assistant Treasurers of the United States	$10, 852, 505 53
By United States Notes forwarded by express	21, 174, 826 86
By Subsidiary Silver Coin forwarded by express	28, 290 59
By Standard Silver Dollars forwarded by express	174, 831 85
By Redemptions at the Counter	3, 883, 417 60
By Credits to Assistant Treasurers and Depositaries of the United States in general account	18, 218, 070 97
By Credits to National Banks in their five per cent. accounts	6, 924, 097 88
Total	61, 255, 980 48

No. 32.—*NATIONAL-BANK NOTES RECEIVED for REDEMPTION during each MONTH of the FISCAL YEAR 1880, from the PRINCIPAL CITIES and other places.*

City from which received.	1879.						1880.						Total.	Per Cent.
	July.	August.	September.	October.	November.	December.	January.	February.	March.	April.	May.	June.		
New York	$3,536,000	$2,047,000	$1,121,000	$946,000	$905,000	$927,000	$3,169,000	$1,709,000	$1,923,000	$1,761,000	$4,675,000	$4,541,000	$26,460,000	42.96
Boston	3,332,000	2,463,000	1,251,000	636,000	730,000	358,000	552,000	549,000	296,000	246,000	553,000	735,000	11,701,000	19.00
Philadelphia	416,000	241,000	262,000	241,000	216,000	213,000	245,000	210,000	171,000	326,000	378,000	439,000	3,358,000	5.45
Chicago	100,000	26,000	155,000	134,000	122,000	131,000	139,000	142,000	164,000	163,000	154,000	170,000	1,673,000	2.72
Cincinnati	55,000	40,000	69,000	53,000	48,000	54,000	72,000	61,000	71,000	60,000	145,000	91,000	819,000	1.33
Saint Louis	22,000	25,000	31,000	22,000	20,000	19,000	37,000	38,000	41,000	51,000	44,000	42,000	392,000	.64
Baltimore	22,000	18,000	18,000	17,000	21,000	16,000	34,000	22,000	27,000	32,000	66,000	122,000	415,000	.67
Providence	194,000	191,000	139,000	132,000	100,000	71,000	109,000	68,000	100,000	97,000	122,000	131,000	1,454,000	2.36
Pittsburgh	31,000	31,000	39,000	60,000	31,000	46,000	48,000	41,000	44,000	56,000	64,000	56,000	547,000	.89
Other places	1,415,000	1,160,000	1,423,000	1,109,000	1,059,000	1,087,000	1,236,000	1,121,000	1,208,000	1,214,000	1,354,000	1,381,000	14,767,000	23.98
Total	9,123,000	6,315,000	4,508,000	3,350,000	3,252,000	2,922,000	5,641,000	3,961,000	3,145,000	4,006,000	7,555,000	7,808,000	61,586,000	100.00

No. 33.—*NUMBER and AMOUNT of NATIONAL-BANK NOTES of each denomination, FIT and UNFIT for CIRCULATION, ASSORTED during the fiscal year 1880.*

Denomination.	Fit for circulation.		Unfit for circulation.		Aggregate.	
	Number.	Amount.	Number.	Amount.	Number.	Amount.
One Dollar	132,740	$132,740	1,205,120	$1,205,120	1,337,860	$1,337,860
Two Dollars	45,060	90,120	414,625	829,250	459,685	919,370
Five Dollars	1,140,012	5,700,060	2,565,730	12,828,650	3,705,742	18,528,710
Ten Dollars	766,891	7,668,910	705,837	7,058,370	1,472,728	14,727,280
Twenty Dollars	272,396	5,447,920	193,293	3,865,880	465,689	9,313,780
Fifty Dollars	42,765	2,138,250	32,437	1,621,850	75,202	3,760,100
One hundred Dollars	35,496	3,549,600	23,279	2,327,900	58,775	5,877,500
Five hundred Dollars	106	53,000	136	68,000	242	121,000
One thousand Dollars	197	197,000	55	55,000	252	252,000
Total	2,435,663	24,977,600	5,140,512	29,860,000	7,576,175	54,837,600

Average denomination of national-bank notes assorted during the fiscal year 1880.

No. 34.—*BALANCED STATEMENT of RECEIPTS and DELIVERIES of MONEYS by the NATIONAL-BANK REDEMPTION AGENCY from JULY 1, 1874, to JUNE 30, 1880.*

Dr.	Amount.	Cr.	Amount.
To National-Bank Notes received for redemption.........	$1,022,776,157 76	By packages referred to other offices and returned by mail..	$4,983,591 15
To United States Notes drawn from the Treasury for redemption of National-Bank Notes at the counter	17,062,732 00	By "Shorts" reported in National-Bank Notes received for redemption	102,273 11
To "Overs" reported in National-Bank Notes received for redemption	132,391 77	By counterfeit National-Bank Notes rejected and returned..	25,433 75
		By stolen, pieced, and rejected National-Bank Notes returned	45,643 19
		By express charges deducted from remittances of National-Bank Notes.................	35,780 56
		By United States Notes deposited in the Treasury......	1,387,818 90
		By Notes of National Gold Banks deposited in the Treasury......................	243,600 00
		By National-Bank Notes fit for circulation deposited in the Treasury	15,952,791 00
		By Notes of failed, liquidating, and reducing National Banks deposited in the Treasury...	82,581,367 00
		By assorted National-Bank Notes fit for circulation forwarded by express to the several National Banks......	553,592,100 00
		By assorted National-Bank Notes unfit for circulation delivered to the Comptroller of the Currency for destruction and replacement with new Notes...................	377,923,000 00
		By Cash Balance June 30, 1880..	3,097,983 77
Total..................	1,039,971,281 53	Total..................	1,039,971,281 53

No. 35.—*BALANCED STATEMENT of RECEIPTS and DELIVERIES of MONEYS by the NATIONAL-BANK REDEMPTION AGENCY for the FISCAL YEAR 1880.*

Dr.	Amount.	Cr.	Amount.
To Cash Balance June 30, 1879...	$3,784,589 29	By packages referred to other offices and returned by mail..	$305,432 14
To uncounted package on hand with unbroken seals, June 30, 1879.................	800 00	By "Shorts" reported in National-Bank Notes received for redemption	9,866 97
To National-Bank Notes received for redemption.......	61,586,675 68	By counterfeit National-Bank Notes rejected and returned..	3,846 75
To "Overs" reported in National-Bank Notes received for redemption	8,461 30	By stolen, pieced, and rejected National-Bank Notes returned	7,870 23
		By express charges deducted from remittances of National-Bank Notes.................	9,938 41
		By United States Notes deposited in the Treasury......	426,686 00
		By Notes of National Gold Banks deposited in the Treasury......................	176,900 00
		By Notes of failed, liquidating, and reducing National Banks	

No. 36.—*DISPOSITION made of NATIONAL-BANK NOTES REDEEMED during the fiscal year 1880.*

Notes, fit for circulation, assorted and forwarded by express to the several National Banks by which they were issued	$34,980,500 00
Notes, unfit for circulation, assorted and delivered to the Comptroller of the Currency for destruction and replacement with new Notes	29,861,700 00
Notes of failed, liquidating, and reducing National Banks, deposited in the Treasury of the United States	6,500,800 00
Notes of National Gold Banks deposited in the Treasury of the United States	170,900 00
Total	61,513,900 00

No. 37.—*CREDITS given to NATIONAL BANKS in their FIVE PER CENT. ACCOUNTS during the fiscal year 1880.*

For United States Notes deposited by them with Assistant Treasurers of the United States	$46,960,242 06
For United States Notes received from them by express	2,627,861 16
For National-Bank Notes received from them by express	6,924,097 88
Total	56,512,201 10

No. 38.—*NUMBER of PACKAGES of NATIONAL-BANK NOTES RECEIVED and DELIVERED during the fiscal year 1880.*

Packages of unassorted National-Bank Notes received for redemption	15,607
Packages of assorted National-Bank Notes, fit for circulation, forwarded by express to the several banks of issue	18,752
Packages of assorted National-Bank Notes, unfit for circulation, delivered to the Comptroller of the Currency	27,104

No. 39.—*COMPARATIVE STATEMENT of the EXPENSES incurred in the REDEMPTION of NATIONAL-BANK NOTES during the fiscal years 1879 and 1880.*

Nature of expenditure.	Amount expended in 1879.		Amount expended in 1880.		Decrease in 1880.	
Charges for transportation		$98,298 75		$34,764 24		$63,534 51
Costs for assorting:						
Salaries	$133,256 27		$104,350 08		$29,606 19	
Printing and binding	2,894 60		2,632 69		261 91	
Stationery	2,597 22		1,034 29		1,562 93	
Contingent expenses	3,203 11	142,651 20	947 09	108,964 15	2,256 02	33,687 05
Total		240,949 95		143,728 39		97,221 56

No. 40.—*LETTERS, TELEGRAMS, and MONEY PACKAGES RECEIVED and TRANSMITTED during the fiscal year 1880.*

Received by mail:

Letters containing money, registered	5,744
Letters containing money, not registered	5,179
	10,923
Letters not containing money	107,860
Total	118,783

Transmitted by mail:

Manuscript letters	6,491
Registered letters containing money	5,874
Printed forms filled in (inclosing checks)	37,818
Printed notices (inclosing interest checks)	296,936
Printed forms filled in (without inclosure)	145,405
Printed forms filled in (inclosing drafts)	26,578
Total	519,102

Telegrams received	284
Telegrams sent	458

No. 41.—*CHANGES during the fiscal year 1880 in the FORCE EMPLOYED in the TREASURER'S OFFICE.*

Total force of the Treasurer's Office June 30, 1879 324
Died 4
Resigned 5
Removed 46
Transferred from the Treasurer's Office 19
Appointments expired 12
　　　　　　　　　　　　　　　　　　　　　　　　　　　　　　　　　　　　　　—— 86
Appointed 34
Transferred to the Treasurer's Office 18
　　　　　　　　　　　　　　　　　　　　　　　　　　　　　　　　　　　　　　—— 52
　　　　　　　　　　　　　　　　　　　　　　　　　　　　　　　　　　　　　　　—— 34

Total force of the Treasurer's Office June 30, 1880 290

No. 42.—*APPROPRIATIONS made for, and SALARIES paid to, the FORCE EMPLOYED in the TREASURER'S OFFICE during the fiscal year 1880.*

Roll on which paid.	Appropriated.	Expended.	Balance unexpended.
Regular roll	$273,600 00	$273,586 93	$11 07
Reimbursable:			
Force employed in redemption of National Currency	101,584 00	82,144 88	19,439 12
Total	375,184 00	355,733 81	19,450 19

REPORT OF THE REGISTER OF THE TREASURY.

REPORT

OF

THE REGISTER OF THE TREASURY

TREASURY DEPARTMENT,
REGISTER'S OFFICE,
Washington, November 1, 1880.

SIR: I have the honor to submit herewith a report in detail of the work performed in the several divisions of this bureau during the year ended June 30, 1880.

LOAN DIVISION.

Total number of coupon and registered bonds issued	214,502
Total number of coupon and registered bonds canceled	676,715

Amount issued:

Original issue, coupon	$56,299,600 00
Original issue, registered	21,364,100 00
Coupon bonds issued on transfer Oregon war debt	8,400 00
Registered bonds issued on transfer (including Spanish indemnity)	289,637,979 00
Registered bonds issued in exchange for coupon	129,207,600 00
Total	496,517,679 00

Amount canceled:

Coupon bonds converted into registered	$129,207,600 00
Coupon bonds transferred (Oregon war debt)	8,400 00
Registered bonds transferred (including Spanish indemnity)	289,637,979 00
Registered bonds redeemed	277,070,200 00
Coupon bonds redeemed	188,657,250 00
Total	884,581,429 00

A synopsis of the vault account shows that the amount of bonds on hand July 1, 1879, including those held by Treasury agent abroad was

	$1,013,866,200 00
Received during the present year, coupon bonds	31,500,000 00
Received during the present year, registered bonds	127,172,000 00
District of Columbia 3.65 per cent. and 5 per cent. funding bonds	8,010,000 00
Total	1,180,548,200 00

Amount disposed of:

Coupon bonds issued		$56,308,000 00
Registered bonds issued (exclusive of Spanish indemnity)		440,162,900 00
Amount on hand June 30, 1880:		
Coupon bonds	$38,118,950 00	
Registered bonds	642,699,650 00	
District of Columbia 3.65 per cent. and 5 per cent. funding bonds	3,258,700 00	
		684,077,300 00
Total		1,180,548,200 00

Amount of canceled coupon bonds turned over to the committee for destruction	$333,106,600 00
In addition to above delivery were 643,677 canceled coupons representing value of	$4,384,213 50
being the coupons past due detached from bonds at the time of issue.	
The amount of actual redemptions, being for called bonds and purchases on account of sinking funds received during the year, was	$598,689,000 00
Number of bonds for same	708,256
Amount recorded for final disposition	$465,727,450 00
Number of bonds	445,139

365

STATEMENT showing the NUMBER and AMOUNT of REGISTERED and COUPON BONDS ISSUED during the fiscal year ending June 30, 1880.

Loans.		Bonds issued.				
		Original amount.	Exchanges, amount.	Transfers, amount.	Total amount issued.	Total number bonds issued.
Oregon war	C			$8,400	$8,400	24
February 8, 1861 (81s)	R		$786,000	2,935,000	3,721,000	653
July and August, 1861 (81s)	R		2,605,950	14,831,850	17,437,800	3,796
March 3, 1863 (81s)	R		447,450	7,474,600	7,922,050	1,992
Pacific Railroads	R			6,281,000	6,281,000	1,321
5 per cent. funded, 1881	R		30,716,000	50,444,850	81,160,850	12,980
4½ per cent. funded, 1891	R		5,106,600	29,160,350	34,356,950	9,522
4 per cent. consols, 1907	C	$55,316,300			55,316,300	80,938
	R	21,255,100	87,547,600	176,266,550	285,069,250	100,886
Spanish indemnity	R			46,779	46,779	9
3.65 per cent. District of Columbia, funded	R		1,908,000	2,152,000	4,060,000	1,168
5 per cent. District of Colum- bia, funded	C	983,300			983,300	1,067
	R	109,000		45,000	154,000	154
Total		77,663,700	129,207,600	289,646,379	496,517,679	214,502

STATEMENT showing the NUMBER and AMOUNT of REGISTERED and COUPON BONDS CANCELED during the fiscal year ending June 30, 1880.

Loans.		Bonds canceled.				
		Redemptions, amount.	Exchanges, amount.	Transfers, amount.	Total amount canceled.	Total number bonds canceled.
Oregon war debt	C	$179,750		$8,400	$188,150	412
February 8, 1861 (81s)	C	110,000	$786,000		896,000	896
	R	1,916,000		2,935,000	4,851,000	1,396
July and August, 1861 (81s)	C	7,292,300	2,605,950		9,898,250	13,876
	R	17,329,700		14,831,850	32,161,550	8,143
March 3, 1863 (81s)	C	3,153,050	447,450		3,600,500	5,033
	R	7,000,050		7,474,600	14,474,650	3,796
Pacific Railroads	R			6,281,000	6,281,000	1,398
5 per cent. funded, 1881	C	7,897,800	30,716,000		38,613,800	45,868
	R	2,867,100		50,444,850	53,311,950	12,150
4½ per cent. funded, 1891	C		5,106,600		5,106,600	6,649
	R			29,160,350	29,160,350	7,455
4 per cent. consols, 1907	C		87,547,600		87,547,600	117,541
	R			176,266,550	176,266,550	56,598
Spanish indemnity	R			46,779	46,779	19
3.65 per cent. District of Colum- bia, funded	C	221,450	1,908,000		2,129,450	4,321
	R	15,000		2,152,000	2,167,000	615
5 per cent. District of Columbia, funded	R			45,000	45,000	45
5 per cent. 1858	R	260,000			260,000	52
	C	17,500			17,500	102
1862—February 25	R	200			200	2
1864—March 3	C	28,902,800			28,902,800	41,293
	R	141,887,150			141,887,150	26,471
1864—June 30	C	9,300			9,300	37
	R	800			800	4
1865—March 3	C	60,300			60,300	129
	R	5,900			5,900	11
1865—Consols	C	46,985,100			46,985,100	100,192
	R	238,950			238,950	245
1867—Consols	C	77,199,300			77,199,300	156,638
	R	90,950,850			90,950,850	29,214
1868—Consols	C	16,627,600			16,627,600	34,438
	R	14,599,500			14,599,500	5,082
Total		465,727,450	129,207,600	289,646,379	884,581,429	676,715

NOTE AND COUPON DIVISION.

REDEEMED, EXCHANGED, and TRANSFERRED UNITED STATES BONDS, with COUPONS ATTACHED, EXAMINED, REGISTERED, and SCHEDULED.

Authorizing act.	Number of bonds.	Amount.	Number coupons attached.
March 3, 1865 (consols, '65)	80,423	$41,435,500	1,206,416
Funded loan, 1881, 5 per cent........................	46,573	39,250,000	335,225
Consols, 1907, 4 per cent	93,213	78,215,300	10,397,229
District of Columbia funded, 1924	5,308	2,330,000	486,473
Total...	225,517	161,232,800	12,425,343

THREE YEARS' 7 3-10 PER CENT. TREASURY NOTES.

Authorizing act.	Number of notes.	Amount.
June 30, 1864, and March 3, 1865	39	$2,850

INTEREST COIN-CHECKS.

Authorizing act.	Number of checks.	Amount.
Funded loan, 1881, 5 per cent	23,869	$9,157,853 21
Funded loan, 1891, 4½ per cent	9,292	1,760,850 08
Consols, 1907, 4 per cent	10,595	689,293 19
District of Columbia funded loan (old)	1,185	48,461 20
Total	44,841	11,656,457 68

CURRENCY CERTIFICATES of DEPOSIT.

Authorizing act.	Number of certificates.	Amount.
June 8, 1872	12,486	$115,690,000

GOLD CERTIFICATES.

Authorizing act.	Number of certificates.	Amount.
March 3, 1863	8,337	$8,771,200

ONE and TWO YEARS' 5 PER CENT. NOTES.

Authorizing act.	Number of notes.	Amount.
March 3, 1863	151	$4,030

THREE YEARS' 6 PER CENT. COMPOUND-INTEREST NOTES.

Authorizing acts.	Number of notes.	Amount.
March 3, 1863, and June 30, 1864	629	$17,340

Redeemed coupons detached from bonds and notes, assorted, arranged numerically, and counted, 2,684,137; registered, 2,824,757; examined and compared, 2,706,836.

NOTE AND FRACTIONAL CURRENCY DIVISION.

STATEMENT showing the NUMBER of NOTES and AMOUNT of UNITED STATES NOTES, REFUNDING CERTIFICATES, and FRACTIONAL CURRENCY EX-AMINED, COUNTED, CANCELED, and DESTROYED for the fiscal year ending June 30, 1880.

United States notes, &c.	Number of notes.	Amount.
New issue	151,087	$1,585,150
Series 1869	1,609,564	27,658,250
Series 1874	1,139,624	8,046,650
Series 1875	7,157,379	34,435,950
Series 1878	4,762,637	15,714,100
Demand notes	67	496
Refunding certificates	3,889,325	38,893,250
Fractional currency, first issue	15,400	2,315
Fractional currency, second issue	12,700	1,590
Fractional currency, third issue	41,500	10,521
Fractional currency, fourth issue	237,700	44,230
Fractional currency, fourth issue, second series	23,800	11,900
Fractional currency, fourth issue, third series	47,100	23,550
Fractional currency, fifth issue	812,400	175,585
Total	19,900,783	117,503,536

REGISTERED REFUNDING CERTIFICATES.

Amount issued, 5,850 .... $58,500
Amount funded, 5,207 52,070

TONNAGE DIVISION.

The total tonnage of the country exhibits a decrease of 101,566 tons, the enrolled tonnage having increased 37,751 tons, while the registered tonnage has decreased 138,723 tons, and the licensed, under 20 tons, 594 tons.

The barge tonnage has decreased 83,250 tons under the operation of the act of Congress approved June 30, 1879, leaving 18,316 tons as the estimated decrease in the tonnage during the past year.

Below are given the totals for the last two years:

	1879.		1880.	
	Vessels.	Tons.	Vessels.	Tons.
Registered	2,717	1,491,533	2,378	1,352,810
Enrolled and licensed	22,494	2,678,067	22,334	2,715,234
Total	25,211	4,169,601	24,712	4,068,034

The comparison of the different classes of vessels is as follows :

Class.	1879.		1880.	
	Vessels.	Tons.	Vessels.	Tons.
Sailing vessels	17,042	2,422,813	16,830	2,366,258
Steam vessels	4,509	1,176,172	4,717	1,211,558
Canal boats	1,266	103,738	1,235	106,590
Barges	2,394	466,878	1,930	383,628
Total	25,211	4,169,601	24,712	4,068,034

It may be seen from the foregoing that the steam tonnage has increased 35,386 tons, the canal-boat tonnage 2,852 tons, while the sailing tonnage has decreased 56,555 tons, and the barge tonnage 83,250 tons.

The proportion of the sailing tonnage registered is 42 per centum and the steam tonnage registered 12 per centum.

SHIP-BUILDING.

The following table exhibits the class, number, and tonnage of the vessels built during the last two years :

Class.	1879.		1880.	
	Vessels.	Tons.	Vessels.	Tons.
Sailing vessels	468	66,867	460	59,057
Steam vessels	335	86,361	348	78,854
Canal boats	36	4,069	17	1,887
Barges	293	35,733	77	17,612
Total	1,132	193,030	902	157,410

From the foregoing it appears that the amount built during the past year was less by 35,620 tons than that of the preceding year.

The tonnage built during the last two years in the several grand divisions of the country is shown below :

Division.	1879.		1880.	
	Vessels.	Tons.	Vessels.	Tons.
Atlantic and Gulf coasts	592	104,475	589	92,777
Pacific coast	65	11,207	41	8,843
Northern lakes	95	15,135	137	22,890
Western rivers	380	62,213	135	32,791
Total	1,132	193,030	902	157,410

The following table exhibits the iron tonnage built in the country since 1868 :

Class.	1868.	1869.	1870.	1871.	1872.	1873.	1874.
Sailing vessels		1,039	679	2,067			44
Steam vessels	2,801	3,545	7,502	13,412	12,766	26,548	33,097
Total	2,801	4,584	8,281	15,479	12,766	26,548	33,097

	1875.	1876.	1877.	1878.	1879.	1880.
Sailing vessels						44
Steam vessels	21,632	21,346	5,927	26,960	22,008	25,538
Total	21,632	21,346	5,927	26,960	22,008	25,582

Tables showing the amount of iron tonnage outstanding may be found in the Report on Commerce and Navigation.

THE FISHERIES.

The tonnage engaged in the fisheries during the last two years is as follows:

Fisheries.	1879.		1880.	
	Vessels.	Tons.	Vessels.	Tons.
Cod and mackerel fisheries	2,571	79,885	2,323	77,530
Whale fisheries	185	40,028	174	38,408

Below is shown the amount of tonnage employed in the cod and mackerel fisheries, with the per centum of each State:

States.	Tonnage.	Per cent.
Maine	18,785	24.2
New Hampshire	1,138	1.5
Massachusetts	39,766	51.3
Rhode Island	2,306	3.0
Connecticut	4,564	5.9
New York	8,636	11.1
New Jersey	25	0.0
Virginia	127	0.2
California	2,101	2.7
Oregon	70	0.1
Total	77,538	100.0

This shows a decrease of about 3 per cent. during the year.
The tonnage employed in the whale fisheries is given below:

Customs districts.	1879.		1880.	
	Vessels.	Tons.	Vessels.	Tons.
Boston, Mass	5	531	5	531
Barnstable, Mass	20	1,940	19	1,817
Edgartown, Mass	4	720	6	1,124
New Bedford, Mass	144	35,208	134	33,337
New London, Conn	12	1,629	10	1,599
Total	185	40,028	174	38,408

Of the above nearly 90 per cent. belongs at New Bedford.
Complete tables showing the various classes of tonnage may be found in the appendix to this report.

DIVISION OF RECEIPTS AND EXPENDITURES.

The following statement exhibits the work of this division for the year ending June 30, 1880:

The number of warrants registered during the year for civil, diplomatic, miscellaneous, internal revenue, and public-debt expenditures and repayments was 20,839

In the preceding year 24,025

Decrease 3,186

The number of warrants registered for receipts from customs, lands, internal revenue, direct tax, and miscellaneous sources was 6,183
In the preceding year 11,220

Decrease... 5,037

The number of warrants registered for payments and repayments in the War, Navy, and Interior (pension and Indian) Departments was 11,833
In the preceding year 16,797

Decrease..... ..../.............. 4,964

The number of draughts registered was 32,179
In the preceding year 40,760

Decrease... 8,581

The number of journal pages required for the entry of accounts relating to the civil, diplomatic, internal revenue, miscellaneous, and public debt receipts and expenditures was.. 5,437
In the preceding year 5,432

Increase ....'... 5

The number of certificates furnished for settlement of accounts was.......... 13,489
In the preceding year 12,759

Increase 730

The number of accounts received from the First and Fifth Auditors and Commissioner of the General Land Office was 22,390
In the preceding year 22,862

Decrease.. 572

In the appendix will be found a statement of the receipts and expenditures of the government, as required by the standing order of the House of Representatives of December 30, 1791, and section 237 of the Revised Statutes; also, statements of the money expended and the number of persons employed, and the occupation and salary of each person at each custom-house, as required by section 258 of the Revised Statutes.

Very respectfully, your obedient servant,

G. W. SCOFIELD,
Register.

Hon. JOHN SHERMAN,
Secretary of the Treasury.

APPENDIX.

STATEMENT of the RECEIPTS of the UNITED STATES for the fiscal year ending June
30, 1880.

FROM CUSTOMS.

A. Vandine, collector, Aroostook, Me.	$18,770 55
J. S. Smith, collector, Bangor, Me.	7,487 03
E. S. J. Nealley, collector, Bath, Me.	17,075 92
W. C. Marshall, collector, Belfast, Me	1,384 01
J. A. Hall, collector, Waldoborough, Me	415 76
N. B. Nutt, Passamaquoddy, Me	86,076 42
L. M. Morrill, collector, Portland, Me	304,825 85
George Leavctt, collector, Machias, Me	153 02
O. McFadden, collector, Wiscasset, Me	191 70
J. D. Hopkins, collector, Frenchman's Bay, Me	82 53
I. Lord, collector, Saco, Me	56 22
W. H. Sargent, collector, Castine, Mo	257 66
A. F. Howard, collector, Portsmouth, N. H	8,557 75
Wm. Wells, collector, Vermont, Vt	754,937 09
A. W. Beard, collector, Boston, Mass	20,674,444 97
J. Brady, jr., collector, Fall River, Mass	8,586 00
S. Dodge, collector, Marblehead, Mass	723 12
J. A. P. Allen, collector, New Bedford, Mass	17,005 95
W. H. Huse, collector, Newburyport, Mass	1,018 48
S. H. Doten, collector, Plymouth, Mass	9,278 15
C. H. Odell, collector, Salem, Mass	10,346 44
T. B. Goss, collector, Barnstable, Mass	1,400 25
F. J. Babson, collector, Gloucester, Mass	7,968 00
C. B. Marchant, collector, Edgartown, Mass	1,080 51
C. Harris, collector, Providence, R I	308,381 22
F. A. Pratt, collector, Newport, R. I	376 93
J. S. Hanover, collector, Fairfield, Conn	1,231 42
A. Putnam, collector, Middletown, Conn	47,403 73
C. Northrop, collector, New Haven, Conn	453,241 91
Geo. Hubbard, collector, Stonington, Conn	199 53
J. A. Tibbetts, collector, New London, Conn	45,913 21
E. A. Merritt, collector, New York, N. Y.	131,146,630 80
W. N. S. Sanders, collector, Albany, N. Y	141,736 00
J. Tyler, collector, Buffalo, N. Y	616,483 76
G. W. Warren, collector, Cape Vincent, N. Y	55,147 56
W. S. Simpson, collector, Geneseo, N. Y	103,323 71
B. Flagler, collector, Niagara, N. Y	521,211 57
S. P. Remington, collector, Oswegatchie, N. Y	147,293 73
W. H. Daniels, collector, Oswegatchie, N. Y	36,998 47
D. G. Fort, collector, Oswego, N. Y	738,752 68
S. Moffett, collector, Champlain, N. Y	266,295 56
P. F. Kidder, collector, Dunkirk, N. Y	33 54
W. A. Baldwin, collector, Newark, N. J	5,955 61
J. H. Bartlett, collector, Little Egg Harbor, N. J	130 00
J. S. Adams, collector, Great Egg Harbor, N. J	25 50
C. H. Houghton, collector, Perth Amboy, N. J	16,282 35
A. P. Tutton, collector, Philadelphia, Pa	12,665,576 79
J. S. Rutan, collector, Pittsburgh, Pa	811,377 84
H. L. Brown, collector, Erie, Pa	1,773 09
L. Thompson, collector, Wilmington, Del	21,145 94
J. L. Thomas, collector, Baltimore, Md	3,057,480 34
T. Ireland, collector, Annapolis, Md	194 40
F. Dodge, collector, Georgetown, D. C	9,486 37
A. A. Warfield, collector, Alexandria, Va	759 78
C. S. Mills, collector, Richmond, Va.	17,905 24
J. S. Braxton, late collector, Norfolk, Va	666 50
G. E. Bowden, collector, Norfolk, Va	34,619 87
T. A. Henry, collector, Pamlico, N. C	1,840 22
W. P. Canaday, collector, Wilmington, N. C	45,004 03
C. G. Manning, collector, Albemarle, N. C.	5 50
G. Gage, collector, Beaufort, S. C	9 05
G. Holmes, collector, Beaufort, S. C	6,070 73
C. H. Baldwin, collector, Charleston, S. C	62,711 61
H. F. Heriot, collector, Georgetown, S. C	242 88
J. Atkins, collector, Savannah, Ga	53,038 55
J. T. Collins, collector, Brunswick, Ga	19,189 58
J. Shepard, late collector, Saint Mary's, Ga	210 60
T. M. Blodgett, collector, Saint Mary's, Ga	822 30
J. W. Howells, collector, Fernandina, Fla.	5,907 90
F. N. Wicker, collector, Key West, Fla	189,219 09
C. Hopkins, collector, Saint John's Fla	556 87
F. C. Humphreys, collector, Pensacola, Fla	61,750 21
H. Potter, late collector, Pensacola, Fla.	500 00
Carried forward	173,238,174 25

STATEMENT of the RECEIPTS of the UNITED STATES, &c.—Continued.

FROM CUSTOMS—Continued.

Brought forward	$173, 238, 174 25
T. F. House, collector, Saint Augustine, Fla	178 83
J. M. Currie, collector, Saint Mark's, Fla	9, 115 22
A. J. Murat, collector, Apalachicola, Fla	292 50
R. T. Smith, collector, Mobile, Ala	49, 615 73
W. G. Henderson, collector, Pearl River, Miss	4, 929 30
A. S. Badger, collector, New Orleans, La	2, 180, 339 73
J. R. Jolley, collector, Teche, La	29 87
N. Patton, late collector, Galveston, Tex	167 28
C. K. Hall, late collector, Galveston, Tex	251 54
E. M. Pearce, collector, Galveston, Tex	321, 165 68
S. C. Slade, collector, Pass del Norte, Tex	38, 859 55
C. R. Prouty, collector, Saluria, Tex	8, 304 14
S. M. Johnson, collector, Corpus Christi, Tex	43, 223 43
N. Plat, late collector, Corpus Christi, Tex	401 98
J. L. Haynes, collector, Brazos, Tex	20, 039 18
W. J. Smith, collector, Memphis, Tenn	14, 757 69
A. Woolf, collector, Nashville, Tenn	319 20
T. O. Shackelford, collector, Louisville, Ky	'52, 921 70
T. G. Pool, collector, Sandusky, Ohio	670 68
J. W. Fuller, collector, Miami, Ohio	23, 767 19
G. W. Howe, collector, Cuyahoga, Ohio	179, 919 90
R. H. Stephenson, collector, Cincinnati, Ohio	464, 200 00
D. V. Bell, collector, Detroit, Mich	231, 035 80
C. Y. Osborn, collector, Superior, Mich	5, 486 10
H. C. Akeley, collector, Michigan, Mich	2 70
J. P. Sanborn, collector, Huron, Mich	209, 973 18
J. Gildersit, collector, Wheeling, W. Va	1, 299 11
W. H. Smith, collector, Chicago, Ill	2, 238, 916 02
J. C. Jewell, collector, Evansville, Ind	229 78
G. St. Gem, collector, St. Louis, Mo	1, 143, 738 50
V. Smith, collector, Duluth, Minn	1, 564 01
E. McMurtrie, collector, Minnesota, Minn	19, 397 72
D. E. Lyon, collector, Dubuque, Iowa	220 75
Geo. Frasee, collector, Burlington, Iowa	73 56
J. Nazro, collector, Milwaukee, Wis	142, 303 75
T. A. Cummings, collector, Montana and Idaho	4, 000 00
J. Campbell, collector, Omaha, Nebr	1, 534 08
M. D. Ball, collector, Alaska	1, 950 50
J. Kelly, collector, Willamette, Oreg	85, 413 07
W. D. Hare, collector, Oregon, Oreg	26, 998 46
H. A. Webster, collector, Puget Sound, Wash	6, 470 99
W. H. Bowers, collector, San Diego, Cal	24, 012 58
T. P. Shannon, collector, San Francisco, Cal	5, 720, 747 37
	$186, 522, 064 60

FROM SALES OF PUBLIC LANDS.

Commissioner of General Land Office	200 00	
Commissioner of general land office, Michigan	54 88	
Commissioner of general land office, Missouri	50 00	
Commissioner of general land office, Kansas	200 00	
Commissioner of general land office, Arizona	194 80	
Commissioner of general land office, Wisconsin	50 00	
J. M. Wilkinson, receiver of public moneys, Marquette, Mich	106, 875 89	
J. M. Farland, receiver of public moneys, Detroit, Mich	799 75	
W. H. H. Mitchell, receiver of public moneys, Reed City, Mich	6, 184 79	
F. J. Burton, receiver of public moneys, East Saginaw, Mich	4, 629 00	
D. L. Quaw, receiver of public moneys, Warsaw, Wis	4, 275 27	
William Callan, receiver of public moneys, Warsaw Wir	2, 559 50	
J. E. Wing, receiver of public moneys, Bayfield, Wis	14, 963 10	
J. F. Nason, receiver of public moneys, Falls Saint Croix, Wis	2, 274 01	
V. W. Bayless, receiver of public moneys, Eau Claire, Wis	4, 247 40	
J. M. Brackett, late receiver of public moneys, Eau Claire, Wis	248 24	
J. Ulrich, receiver of public moneys, La Crosse, Wis	6, 347 56	
N. Thatcher, receiver of public moneys, Menasha, Wis	36, 804 88	
W. B. Mitchell, receiver of public moneys, Saint Cloud, Wis	12, 040 90	
H. W. Stone, receiver of public moneys, Benson, Minn	5, 360 54	
P. C. Stettin, receiver of public moneys, Crookston, Minn	11, 561 96	
T. H. Presnell, receiver of public moneys, Duluth, Minn	19, 057 77	
C. C. Goodnow, receiver of public moneys, New Ulm, Minn	6, 172 44	
G. B. Folsom, receiver of public moneys, Taylor's Falls, Minn	5, 375 63	
J. E. Allen, receiver of public moneys, Fergus Falls, Minn	7, 448 95	
W. B. Herrott, receiver of public moneys, Redwood Falls, Minn	5, 380 31	
J. P. Moulton, receiver of public moneys, Worthington, Minn	4, 771 65	
T. Boles, receiver of public moneys, Dardanelle, Ark	6, 046 07	
M. M. Freed, late receiver of public moneys, Dardanelle, Ark	5, 921 91	
R. S. Armitage, receiver of public moneys, Harrison, Ark	8, 965 89	
J. F. Fagan, receiver of public moneys, Little Rock, Ark	5, 024 73	
A. A. Tufts, receiver of public moneys, Camden, Ark	4, 033 00	
H. H. Griffiths, receiver of public moneys, Des Moines, Iowa	1, 556 92	
J. Dumars, receiver of public moneys, Springfield, Mo	1, 595 58	
Carried forward	301, 931 16	186, 522, 064 60

STATEMENT of the RECEIPTS of the UNITED STATES, &c.—Continued.

FROM SALES OF PUBLIC LANDS—Continued.

Brought forward	$301, 931 16	$186, 522, 064 60
W. J. Bodenhamer, late receiver of public moneys, Springfield, Mo	4, 600 00	
O. Ritchey, receiver of public moneys, Boonville, Mo	4, 134 36	
L. Davis, receiver of public moneys, Ironton, Mo	2, 449 65	
J. A. Somerville, receiver of public moneys, Mobile, Ala	23 00	
F. J. Kaufman, receiver of public moneys, Huntsville, Ala	4, 003 07	
William H. Tancre, receiver of public moneys, Huntsville, Ala	1, 301 93	
P. J. Strobach, receiver of public moneys, Montgomery, Ala	47, 482 78	
E. M. Hastings, late receiver of public moneys, Montgomery, Ala	120 82	
J. Varnum, late receiver of public moneys, Gainesville, Fla	399 70	
J. F. Rollins, receiver of public moneys, Gainesville, Fla	11, 037 72	
R. J. Alcorn, receiver of public moneys, Jackson, Miss	9, 241 67	
A. E. Lamee, receiver of public moneys, Natchitoches, La	4, 584 01	
G. Baldy, receiver of public moneys, New Orleans, La	9, 112 48	
J. Neville, late receiver of public moneys, New Orleans, La	1, 351 46	
C. J. Jenkins, receiver of public moneys, Concordia, Kans	7, 673 64	
L. J. Best, receiver of public moneys, Kirwin, Kans	18, 335 85	
W. J. Hunter, receiver of public moneys, Hays City, Kans	870 28	
W. J. Hunter, receiver of public moneys, Wakeeny, Kans	3, 544 73	
A. Booth, receiver of public moneys, Larned, Kans	3, 396 15	
D. R. Wagstaff, receiver of public moneys, Salina, Kans	610 44	
L. Hauback, receiver of public moneys, Salina, Kans	4, 700 53	
J. L. Dyer, receiver of public moneys, Wichita, Kans	4, 034 44	
H. M. Waters, receiver of public moneys, Independence, Kans	135 99	
Thomas May, receiver of public moneys, Independence, Kans	797 17	
G. W. Watson, late receiver of public moneys, Topeka, Kans	3, 304 29	
H. Kelly, receiver of public moneys, Topeka, Kans	1, 014 59	
J. Stott, receiver of public moneys, Niobrara, Nebr	4, 933 76	
C. N. Baird, receiver of public moneys, Lincoln, Nebr	1, 456 37	
G. W. Dorsey, receiver of public moneys, Bloomington, Nebr	5, 304 07	
J. S. McClary, receiver of public moneys, Norfolk, Nebr	1, 129 94	
W. B. Lambert, receiver of public moneys, Norfolk, Nebr	1, 073 66	
W. Auryn, receiver of public moneys, Grand Island, Nebr	4, 790 53	
John Taffe, late receiver of public moneys, North Platte, Nebr	3, 686 41	
R. B. Harrington, receiver of public moneys, Beatrice, Nebr	765 82	
J. Stout, receiver of public moneys, Boise City, Idaho	3, 669 27	
R. J. Monroe, receiver of public moneys, Lewiston, Idaho	17, 692 81	
T. T. Singiser, receiver of public moneys, Oxford, Idaho	30, 050 43	
J. F. McKenna, receiver of public moneys, Deadwood, Dak	3, 968 43	
J. M. Washburn, receiver of public moneys, Sioux Falls, Dak	24, 490 83	
L. D. F. Poor, receiver of public moneys, Springfield, Dak	7, 738 51	
L. S. Bayless, receiver of public moneys, Yankton, Dak	14, 222 02	
T. M. Pugh, receiver of public moneys, Fargo, Dak	20, 841 72	
E. M. Brown, receiver of public moneys, Bismarck, Dak	3, 117 90	
W. J. Anderson, receiver of public moneys, Grand Forks, Dak	8, 367 43	
C. A. Benstow, receiver of public moneys, Del Norte, Colo	1, 024 00	
C. B. Hickman, receiver of public moneys, Lake City, Colo	11, 812 12	
S. T. Thompson, receiver of public moneys, Denver, Colo	6, 627 40	
E. W. Henderson, receiver of public moneys, Central City, Colo	7, 795 94	
M. H. Fitch, receiver of public moneys, Pueblo, Colo	7, 011 29	
James L. Mitchell, late receiver of public moneys, Pueblo, Colo	2, 200 00	
W. K. Burchinell, receiver of public moneys, Leadville, Colo	29, 651 25	
M. M. Bane, receiver of public moneys, Salt Lake City, Utah	25, 514 24	
L. S. Hills, receiver of public moneys, Salt Lake City, Utah	965 28	
G. B. Overton, late receiver of public moneys, Salt Lake City, Utah	2, 100 00	
F. P. Sterling, receiver of public moneys, Helena, Mont	37, 280 70	
J. V. Bogart, receiver of public moneys, Bozeman, Mont	3, 646 94	
E. Brevoort, receiver of public moneys, Santa Fé, N. Mex	10, 359 40	
M. Barela, receiver of public moneys, La Mesilla, N. Mex	3, 280 80	
Samuel W. Sherfey, receiver of public moneys, La Mesilla, N. Mex	762 75	
S. C. Wright, receiver of public moneys, Carson City, Nev	19, 056 17	
H. Carpenter, receiver of public moneys, Eureka, Nev	9, 450 00	
J. C. Fullerton, receiver of public moneys, Roseburg, Oreg	5, 977 19	
D. Chaplin, receiver of public moneys, Le Grande, Oreg	9, 841 96	
G. Conn, receiver of public moneys, Lake View, Oreg	2, 774 61	
T. R. Harrison, late receiver of public moneys, Oregon City, Oreg	920 81	
J. W. Watts, receiver of public moneys, Oregon City, Oreg	4, 607 35	
C. N. Thornburg, receiver of public moneys, The Dalles, Oreg	3, 171 61	
R. G. Stuart, receiver of public moneys, Olympia, Wash	30, 150 73	
E. N. Sweet, receiver of public moneys, Colfax, Wash	12, 904 36	
S. W. Brown, receiver of public moneys, Vancouver, Wash	5, 202 69	
A. Reed, receiver of public moneys, Walla Walla, Wash	13, 575 95	
W. C. Painter, late receiver of public moneys, Walla Walla, Wash	5 49	
L. Ruggles, receiver of public moneys, Florence, Ariz	13, 867 00	
George Lount, receiver of public moneys, Prescott, Ariz	1, 794 91	
I. C. Whipple, receiver of public moneys, Cheyenne, Wyo	7, 013 14	
William M. Cozzey, receiver of public moneys, Cheyenne, Wyo	3, 190 72	
E. S. Crocker, receiver of public moneys, Evanston, Wyo	1, 768 63	
H. Fellows, late receiver of public moneys, Sacramento, Cal	716 00	
H. C. Beatty, receiver of public moneys, Sacramento, Cal	15, 507 84	
A. Dolrowski, receiver of public moneys, Shasta, Cal	9, 597 92	
T. Lindsey, receiver of public moneys, Visalia, Cal	5, 905 26	
J. W. Haverstick, receiver of public moneys, Los Angeles, Cal	3, 883 17	
Carried forward	916, 166 34	186, 52?, 064 60

STATEMENT of the RECEIPTS of the UNITED STATES, &c.—Continued.

FROM SALES OF PUBLIC LANDS—Continued.

Brought forward...	$916, 168 34	$186, 032, 064 60
H. Z. Osborn, receiver of public moneys, Bodie, Cal......................	23, 397 67	
S. Cooper, receiver of public moneys, Humboldt, Cal..................	19, 240 33	
A. Miller, receiver of public moneys, Susanville, Cal..................	14, 664 93	
O. Perrin, receiver of public moneys, Stockton, Cal......................	14, 955 46	
L. T. Crane, receiver of public moneys, Marysville, Cal................	18, 131 90	
C. H. Chamberlain, receiver of public moneys, San Francisco, Cal	9, 747 97	
		1, 016, 506 6

FROM INTERNAL REVENUE.

Commissioner of Internal Revenue	7, 131, 452 99
Treasurer United States	167 16
L. H. Mayer, collector 1st district, Alabama	60, 914 26
J. T. Rapier, collector 2d district, Alabama	72, 633 97
T. Cordis, collector, Arizona	27, 515 40
E. Wheeler, collector, Arkansas	128, 876 22
W. Higby, collector 1st district, California............................	2, 437, 661 02
A. L. Frost, collector 4th district, California...........................	347, 029 00
J. S. Wolfe, collector, Colorado.......................................	108, 259 54
James Selden, collector 1st district, Connecticut	224, 291 09
D. F. Hollister, collector 2d district, Connecticut	248, 323 80
J. L. Pennington, collector, Dakota....................................	41, 642 91
J. McIntyre, collector, Delaware	304, 398 21
A. A. Knight, late collector, Florida	5, 275 72
D. Eagan, collector, Florida...	197, 663 46
A. Clark, collector 2d district, Georgia	220, 257 51
E. C. Wade, collector 3d district, Georgia	98, 137 74
A. Savage, collector, Idaho	22, 846 74
A. C. Gier, late collector, Idaho	2, 567 70
J. Cummings, collector, Idaho	241 05
J. D. Harvey, collector 1st district, Illinois	8, 936, 614 85
W. B. Allen, late collector 2d district, Illinois	83, 065 55
L. B. Crocker, late collector 2d district, Illinois.......................	149, 032 40
A. Nase, late collector 2d district, Illinois	222, 613 25
A. M. Jones, late collector 3d district, Illinois	480, 472 02
J. Tillson, collector 4th district, Illinois	961, 693 32
H. Knowles, collector 5th district, Illinois	10, 307, 343 28
J. W. Hill, collector 7th district, Illinois	57, 166 33
J. Merriam, collector 8th district, Illinois	810, 267 72
J. C. Willis, collector 13th district, Illinois	262, 233 68
J. C. Veatch, collector 1st district, Indiana	271, 093 08
W. Cumback, collector 4th district, Indiana	3, 291, 150 18
F. Baggs, collector 6th district, Indiana	877, 608 50
D. W. Minshall, collector 7th district, Indiana	1, 528, 977 01
George Moon, collector 10th district, Indiana..........................	161, 302 65
J. F. Wildman, collector 11th district, Indiana.........................	83, 844 45
S. S. Farwell, collector 2d district, Iowa	300, 418 69
J. E. Simpson, collector 3d district, Iowa	267, 713 19
J. Connell, collector 4th district, Iowa................................	164, 567 80
L. F. Sherman, collector 5th district, Iowa	117, 047 95
J. C. Carpenter, collector, Kansas	252, 734 01
J. D Kelly, late collector 1st district, Kentucky	1, 996 98
W. A. Stuart, collector 2d district, Kentucky	621, 266 33
J. F. Buckner, collector 5th district, Kentucky	3, 583, 114 63
W. S. Holden, collector 6th district, Kentucky.........................	3, 290, 411 62
A. M. Swope, collector 7th district, Kentucky	1, 018, 072 28
W. T. Landrum, collector 8th district, Kentucky	278, 304 96
J. E. Blaine, collector 9th district, Kentucky	151, 087 28
M. Marks, collector 1st district, Louisiana.............................	711, 835 05
B. T. Beauregard, late collector 2d district, Louisiana.................	1, 578 69
O. A. Rice, late collector 2d district, Louisiana	765 85
F. J. Rollins, collector, Maine	76, 707 56
R. M. Proud, collector 3d district, Maryland	2, 263, 283 80
D. C. Bruce, collector 4th district, Maryland	131, 658 46
James Hill, collector, Mississippi	91, 088 76
C. W. Slack, collector 3d district, Massachusetts.......................	1, 396, 983 80
C. C. Dame, collector 5th district, Massachusetts	850, 147 57
R. R. Tinker, collector 10th district, Massachusetts....................	386, 521 93
L. S. Trowbridge, collector 1st district, Michigan	1, 000, 764 17
H. B. Rowland, collector 3d district, Michigan	227, 141 95
L. S. Bailey, collector 4th district, Michigan	131, 769 29
C. V. De Land, collector 6th district, Michigan	152, 617 65
A. C. Smith, collector 1st district, Minnesota	106, 431 58
W. Bickel, collector 2d district, Minnesota	257, 900 13
J. H. Sturgeon, collector 1st district, Missouri	4, 680, 266 14
A. B. Carroll, collector 2d district, Missouri	62, 723 51
A. C. Stewart, late collector 4th district, Missouri	263, 134 04
R. E. Lawder, collector 4th district, Missouri	69, 365 34
D. H. Budlong, collector 5th district, Missouri	117, 566 94
R. T. Van Horn, collector 6th district, Missouri	256, 726 85
T. P. Fuller, collector, Montana	33, 714 17
F. C. Lord, collector, Nevada	61, 279 30
Carried forward......................................	64, 400, 214 74 187, 538, 571 20

STATEMENT of the RECEIPTS of the UNITED STATES, &c.—Continued.

FROM INTERNAL REVENUE—Continued.

Brought forward	$64,400,214 74	$187,538,571 20
L. Cronese, collector, Nebraska	912,802 37	
A. H. Young, collector, New Hampshire	273,902 60	
W. P. Tatum, collector 1st district, New Jersey	213,519 48	
C. Barcalow, collector 3d district, New Jersey	267,820 19	
R. B. Hathorn, collector 5th district, New Jersey	3,726,969 19	
G. A. Smith, collector, New Mexico	31,423 56	
C. Blummer, late collector, New Mexico	101 85	
James Freeland, late collector 1st district, New York	1,632,794 49	
R. C. Ward, collector 1st district, New York	1,631,606 17	
M. B. Blake, collector 2d district, New York	3,199,990 87	
Max Weber, collector 3d district, New York	5,063,836 54	
M. D. Stivers, collector 11th district, New York	131,732 48	
J. M. Johnson, collector 13th district, New York	515,671 03	
R. P. Lathrop, collector 14th district, New York	571,102 07	
T. Stevenson, collector 15th district, New York	259,026 63	
J. C. P. Kincaid, collector 21st district, New York	309,577 27	
J. B. Strong, collector 24th district, New York	422,409 34	
B. De Voe, collector 26th district, New York	274,243 91	
B. Van Horn, collector 28th district, New York	946,574 87	
F. Buell, collector 30th district, New York	1,287,481 54	
T. Powers, late collector 2d district, North Carolina	4,716 87	
E. A. White, collector 2d district, North Carolina	52,992 87	
I. J. Young, collector 4th district, North Carolina	925,463 19	
W. H. Wheeler, collector 5th district, North Carolina	920,687 93	
J. J. Mott, collector 6th district, North Carolina	455,457 86	
A. Smith, jr., collector 1st district, Ohio	11,556,849 75	
R. Williams, collector 3d district, Ohio	1,359,348 23	
R. P. Kennedy, collector 4th district, Ohio	511,154 48	
James Purcell, collector 6th district, Ohio	684,351 96	
C. C. Walcutt, collector 7th district, Ohio	475,976 33	
C. Waggoner, collector 10th district, Ohio	1,092,855 40	
B. F. Coates, collector 11th district, Ohio	1,434,313 13	
J. Palmer, collector 15th district, Ohio	211,342 62	
C. B. Pettengell, late collector 18th district, Ohio	435,396 46	
W. S. Streater, collector 18th district, Ohio	322,426 61	
J. C. Cartwright, collector, Oregon	77,063 43	
J. Ashworth, collector 1st district, Pennsylvania	2,523,444 87	
J. T. Valentine, collector 9th district, Pennsylvania	552,179 93	
T. A. Wiley, collector 9th district, Pennsylvania	1,064,042 45	
E. H. Chase, collector 12th district, Pennsylvania	924,207 74	
C. J. Bruner, collector 14th district, Pennsylvania	191,880 54	
E. Scull, collector 16th district, Pennsylvania	191,420 10	
C. M. Lynch, collector 19th district, Pennsylvania	115,337 58	
J. C. Brown, collector 20th district, Pennsylvania	92,567 40	
T. W. Davis, collector 22d district, Pennsylvania	1,184,418 98	
J. M. Sullivan, collector 23d district, Pennsylvania	685,056 85	
E. H. Rhodes, collector, Rhode Island	210,883 98	
F. A. Sawyer, late collector, South Carolina	5,219 15	
E. M. Brayton, collector, South Carolina	112,033 53	
J. K. Miller, late collector 1st district, Tennessee	1,087 98	
J. A. Cooper, late collector 2d district, Tennessee	1,788 72	
J. M. Melton, collector 3d district, Tennessee	86,309 99	
James Mullins, late collector 4th district, Tennessee	810 99	
H. L. Norvell, late collector 5th district, Tennessee	1,511 33	
D. B. Cliffe, late collector 5th district, Tennessee	65 74	
W. M. Woodcock, collector 5th district, Tennessee	805,308 52	
R. S. Patterson, collector 8th district, Tennessee	100,184 55	
W. E. Sinclair, collector 1st district, Texas	99,256 86	
M. N. Brewster, late collector 3d district, Texas	427 50	
B. C. Ludlow, collector 3d district, Texas	74,342 84	
A. G. Mollay, collector 4th district, Texas	61,176 40	
O. J. Hollister, collector, Utah	75,894 83	
C. S. Dana, collector, Vermont	40,618 04	
J. D. Brady, collector 2d district, Virginia	867,567 06	
O. P. Russell, collector 3d district, Virginia	2,054,557 71	
W. L. Fernald, collector 4th district, Virginia	1,002,952 34	
J. H. Rives, collector 4th district, Virginia	1,617,102 70	
B. B. Botts, collector 6th district, Virginia	282,687 54	
J. R. Hayden, collector, Washington Territory	27,205 87	
J. H. Duvall, collector 1st district, West Virginia	313,054 19	
George W. Brown, collector 3d district, West Virginia	61,699 31	
J. M. Bean, collector 1st district, Wisconsin	2,212,083 35	
H. Harnden, collector 2d district, Wisconsin	155,505 99	
A. K. Osborn, late collector 3d district, Wisconsin	25,322 50	
C. A. Galloway, collector 3d district, Wisconsin	5,815 47	
H. M. Hutchins, late collector 3d district, Wisconsin	181,294 80	
H. E. Kelly, collector 6th district, Wisconsin	115,921 72	
E. P. Snow, collector, Wyoming	15,388 89	
		124,609,373 92
Carried forward		311,547,945 12

STATEMENT of the RECEIPTS of the UNITED STATES, &c.—Continued.

FROM CONSULAR FEES.

Brought forward	$311,547,945 12
D. Atwater, consul, Tahiti.............	$516 35
T. Adamson, consul, Pernambuco....................................	7,876 04
L. T. Adams, consul, Geneva	689 50
C. M. Allen, consul, Bermuda	1,797 04
A. Badeau, consul-general, London	16,303 06
J. A. Bridgland, consul, Havre.....................................	5,593 87
S. P. Bayley, consul, Palermo	4,903 16
L. Burckhardt, consular-agent, Stettin.............................	654 27
E. L. Baker, consul, Buenos Ayres.......................\.......	4,394 35
G. E. Bullock, consul, Cologne....................................	1,368 50
S. S. Blodgett, consul, Prescott	682 50
B. H. Barrows, consul, Dublin......................................	1,568 90
D. H. Bailey, consul, Hong-Kong	11,037 55
S. H. M. Byers, consul, Zurich	3,503 40
W. C. Borchard, consul, Omoa and Truxillo........................	223 66
C. P. Brooks, consul, Cork	128 91
F. Crocker, consul, Montevideo...................................	445 01
W. Crosby, consul, Talcahuano..................................	550 56
S. F. Cooper, consul, Glasgow	4,061 95
R. S. Clayton, consul, Callao	1,886 82
A. J. Cassard, consul, Tampico	445 86
R. S. Chilton, consul, Clifton	377 50
T. Canisans, consul, Bristol	986 24
W. W. Cross, vice-consul, Cienfuego.............................	432 99
A. Cone, consul, Para..	1,547 04
E. Conroy, consul, San Juan, P. B	463 26
J. S. Crosby, consul, Florence	2,253 68
J. A. Campbell, consul, Basle	815 00
N. Crano, consul, Manchester	337 00
J. C. S. Colby, consul, Chin-Kiang	200 99
J. M. Donnan, consul, Belfast...................................	7,950 44
S. W. Dabney, consul, Fayal.....................................	613 69
D. M. Dunn, consul, Prince Edward Island	987 50
H. W. Diman, consul, Lisbon	766 32
L. E. Dyer, consul, Odessa	252 50
A. J. Tuffie, consul, Cadiz	1,344 50
B. A. Duncan, consul, Naples....................................	1,350 12
C. W. Drury, consul, Lauthala....................................	10 47
A. V. Dockery, consul, Leeds....................................	1,380 15
O. N. Denny, consul, Tien Tsin	227 86
T. M. Dawson, consul, Apia	80 80
M. M. DeLano, consul, Foo-Choo..................................	732 01
R. L. Doerr, vice-consul, Basle..................................	2,899 07
A. J. DeZeyk, consul, Lyons	104 71
W. W. Douglass, consul, Bradford	296 72
D. Eckstein, consul, Victoria	1,350 59
R. A. Edes, consul, Bahia	762 62
P. M. Eder, consul, Guayaquil	393 68
W. W. Edgecomb, consul, Cape Town	747 86
W. H. Edwards, consul-general, St. Petersburg	358 00
J. T. Edgar, consul, Beirut	74 70
J. C. Eckert, commercial agent, Laguayra	2,136 70
E. E. Farnsan, consul-general, Cairo	424 75
L. Fairchild, consul, Liverpool	20,273 26
P. Figyelmesy, consul, Demarara.................................	1,689 70
J. L. Frisbie, consul, Rio Grande do Sul.........................	579 44
L. H. Foote, consul, Valparaiso	1,543 71
T. E. Frye, consul, Omoa and Truxillo...........................	147 70
G. W. Fish, consul, Tunis	2 50
W. H. Garfield, consul, Martinique	2,308 38
Geo. Gifford, commercial agent, Nantes..........................	289 01
N. K. Grigge, consul, Chemnitz	9,145 65
S. Goutier, consul, Cape Haytien	761 66
J. B. Gould, consul, Birmingham	3,903 55
George Gerard, consul, Port Stanley.............................	5 00
B. Garrish, jr., consul, Bordeaux	3,263 92
W. E. Goldsborough, consul, Amoy	1,402 93
William F. Grunnell, consul, Bremen	3,069 00
G. Grant, vice-consul, Leghorn	166 25
M. Gavin, consul, Leghorn	174 76
D. K. Hobart, consul, Windsor	600 44
H. C. Hall, consul, Havana......................................	16,872 25
J. F. Haselton, consul, Genoa	1,338 47
G. E. Haskinson, consul, Kingston	2,007 80
G. H. Horstmann, consul, Munich	928 75
J. Hibbard, commercial agent, Goderich..........................	420 80
W. H. Hathorne, consul, Zanzibar................................	433 12
J. Harris, vice-consul, Venice	636 82
J. H. Heap, consul, Tunis	728 50
W. C. Howells, consul, Quebec	3,990 48
F. P. Hastings, consul, Honolulu	1,300 13
Carried forward....................................	180,926 53 311,547,945 12

STATEMENT of the RECEIPTS of the UNITED STATES, &c.—Continued.

FROM CONSULAR FEES—Continued.

Brought forward..	$180, 928 53	$311, 547, 945 12
R. Y. Holley, consul, Barbadoes....................................	75 00	
R. M. Hooper, vice-consul, Paris....................................	954 10	
A. Jones, consul, St. Domingo.....................................	998 86	
J. H. Jenks, commercial agent, Windsor.............................	1, 351 18	
E. R. Jones, consul, Newcastle.....................................	744 50	
M. M. Jackson, consul, Halifax.....................................	2, 474 36	
E. Johnson, consul, Tampico.......................................	490 95	
C. B. Jones, consul, Tripoli.......................................	6 84	
W. King, consul, Bremen..	2, 386 71	
H. Kreismann, consul-general, Berlin...............................	7, 145 09	
J. C. Kretchener, commercial agent, San Juan del Norte..............	258 22	
H. Kingan, vice-consul, La Grange..................................	86 00	
A. C. Litchfield, consul-general, Calcutta...........................	7, 319 00	
E. C. Lord, consul, Ningpo..	100 28	
J. M. Lucas, consul, Tunstall......................................	1, 121 25	
O. M. Long, consul, Panama.......................................	1, 335 00	
F. Leland, consul, Hamilton.......................................	1, 687 29	
A. E. Lee, consul-general, Frankfort...............................	4, 905 33	
A. Lacombe, consul, Porto Cabello..................................	482 08	
H. D. Lawrence, commercial agent, Sherbrooke......................	1, 180 08	
H. S. Loring, vice-consul, Hong-Kong..............................	6, 289 12	
C. P. Lincoln, consul, Canton......................................	562 65	
J. C. Landram, consul, Santiago de Cuba...........................	1, 252 34	
H. S. Laaar, commercial agent, San Juan del Norte..................	11 01	
E. E. Lane, consul, Tunstall.......................................	3, 511 43	
H. C. Marston, consul, Port Louis..................................	755 70	
P. A. McKellar, consul, Valparaiso.................................	172 37	
C. McMillen, consul-general, Rome................................	353 00	
T. J. McLain, jr., consul, Nassau..................................	1, 733 19	
W. P. Mangun, consul, Nagasaki..................................	870 66	
J. T. Mason, consul, Dresden......................................	5, 171 60	
J. S. Mosby, consul, Hong-Kong...................................	3, 370 85	
William Morey, consul, Ceylon.....................................	858 30	
M. McDougall, consul, Dundee....................................	2, 597 45	
J. M. Morton, consul, Honolulu....................................	289 80	
Morton, Rose & Co., bankers, London...............................	166, 920 68	
O. Malmros, consul, Picton..	231 70	
F. A. Mathews, consul, Tangier....................................	33 47	
A. McLain, consul, Guayaquil.....................................	832 58	
J. E. Montgomery, consul, Genoa..................................	363 53	
E. Masi, vice-consul, Leghorn......................................	464 27	
R. S. Newton, commercial agent, St. Paul de Loando.................	42 67	
Norse American Line..	6, 447 60	
G. H. Owen, consul, Messina.......................................	2, 901 88	
E. P. Pellet, consul, Sabanilla.....................................	2, 275 51	
S. D. Pace, consul, Port Sarnia....................................	1, 805 50	
P. S. Post, consul, Vienna...	1, 170 02	
J. B. Payno, vice-consul, Manchester...............................	2, 021 21	
S. B. Packard, consul, Liverpool...................................	14, 360 53	
B. F. Peixotto, consul, Lyons......................................	6, 883 89	
J. S. Potter, consul, Stuttgardt....................................	1, 079 75	
A. C. Phillips, consul, Port Erie...................................	773 25	
P. Pela, vice-consul, Batavia......................................	586 10	
T. S. Prentiss, consul, Seychelles..................................	23 38	
W. H. Polleys, consul, Barbadoes..................................	2, 262 83	
A. C. Prindle, consul, Para..	2, 094 78	
C. A. Phelps, consul, Prague......................................	2, 683 82	
F. W. Potter, consul, Marseilles...................................	1, 098 81	
W. N. Pethick, consul, Tien-Tsin..................................	30 00	
J. F. Quarles, consul, Malaga.....................................	1, 288 76	
W. W. Robinson, consul, Tamatine.................................	146 60	
G. W. Roosevelt, consul, Auckland.................................	638 64	
L. Richmond, consul, Cork...	956 19	
T. B. Reid, consul, Funchal..	177 59	
A. L. Russell, consul, Montevideo..................................	1, 608 51	
J. T. Robeson, consul, Leith.......................................	1, 511 08	
H. B. Ryder, consul, Copenhagen..................................	190 00	
J. W. Steele, consul, Matanzas....................................	3, 011 45	
O. M. Spencer, consul, Genoa......................................	2, 434 50	
W. E. Sibell, commercial agent, San Juan del Norte.................	267 75	
A. D. Shaw, consul, Toronto.......................................	8, 530 99	
J. H. Stewart, consul, Leipsic.....................................	3, 230 13	
W. W. Sikes, consul, Cardiff......................................	3, 867 55	
D. B. Sickels, consul, Bangkok....................................	388 99	
H. J. Sprague, consul, Gibraltar...................................	1, 379 07	
C. O. Shepard, consul, Bradford...................................	5, 664 68	
D. Stearns, consul, Trinidad.......................................	2, 151 13	
F. H. Schenck, consul, Barcelona..................................	417 44	
J. W. Siler, consul, St. Helena....................................	279 45	
J. A. Sutter, consul, Acapulco.....................................	588 26	
R. J. Saxe, consul, St. Johns......................................	1, 319 62	
Carried forward..	501, 529 79	311, 547, 945 12

STATEMENT of the RECEIPTS of the UNITED STATES, &c.—Continued.

FROM CONSULAR FEES—Continued.

Brought forward	$501,520 79	$311,547,945 12
B. Stanton, consul, Barmen	2,842 34	
J. Q. Smith, consul-general, Montreal	4,990 68	
J. Stobel, consul, Osaka and Hiogo	3,356 96	
N. C. Stevens, vice consul, Amoy	1,009 14	
D. H. Strother, consul, Mexico	69 90	
W. P. Sutton, commercial agent, Matamoras	523 46	
A. G. Studer, consul, Singapore	2,508 00	
J. F. Shepard, consul, Hankow	1,549 93	
V. V. Smith, consul, St. Thomas	1,907 99	
E. J. Smithers, consul, Smyrna	1,639 34	
E. M. Smith, consul, Maranham	1,650 75	
E. Schuyler, consul, Birmingham	4,076 31	
A. A. Shipley, consul, Auckland	184 78	
W. L. Scruggs, consul, Chin Kiang	400 25	
George Scroggs, consul, Hamburg	3,189 79	
A. W. Thayer, consul, Trieste	2,367 64	
T. M. Terry, consul, Santiago, Cape Verde	105 49	
M. H. Twitchell, consul, Kingston	769 00	
J. W. Taylor, consul, Winnipeg	216 50	
S. T. Trowbridge, consul, Vera Cruz	2,510 73	
William Thomson, consul, Southampton	173 00	
A. T. A. Torbert, consul-general, Paris	955 48	
J. Thurington, consul, Aspinwall	3,191 04	
J. C. Tanner, consul, Verviers and Liege	1,265 00	
G. F. Upton, consul, Geneva	13 55	
T. B. Van Buren, commercial agent, Kanagawa	11,597 14	
W. H. Vesey, consul, Nice	328 50	
E. Vaughan, consul, Coaticook	2,897 66	
H. Van Arsdale, vice-consul, Leipsic	803 05	
J. M. Wilson, consul, Hamburg	8,037 41	
John Wilson, consul, Brussels	2,267 50	
J. F. Winter, consul, Rotterdam	3,082 27	
J. R. Weaver, consul, Antwerp	4,957 45	
H. J. Winsor, consul, Sonneberg	5,201 04	
A. Willard, consul, Guaymas	492 47	
D. B. Warner, consul, St. John's, New Brunswick	2,568 16	
J. S. Willson, consul, Jerusalem	94 00	
J. N. Wasson, consul, Quebec	791 49	
C. B. Webster, consul, Sheffield	4,076 90	
G. L. Washington, consul, Matanzas	944 85	
T. F. Wilson, commercial agent, Cardenas	1,075 52	
		502,161 81

FROM STEAMBOAT FEES.

J. Atkins, collector, Savannah, Ga	3,815 35	
J. A. P. Allen, collector, New Bedford, Mass	520 75	
H. C. Akeley, collector, Muskegan, Mich	4,855 10	
W. L. Ashmore, collector, Burlington, N. J	273 80	
D. V. Bell, collector, Detroit, Mich	7,328 70	
W. A. Baldwin, collector, Newark, N. J	549 85	
C. H. Baldwin, collector, Charleston, S. C	2,622 00	
J. S. Braxton, collector, Norfolk, Va	734 20	
A. W. Beard, collector, Boston, Mass	6,684 60	
A. S. Badger, collector, New Orleans, La	17,477 00	
J. Brady, jr., collector, Fall River, Mass	498 85	
H. L. Brown, collector, Erie, Pa	528 95	
P. J. Babson, collector, Gloucester, Mass	125 00	
W. W. Bowers, collector, San Diego, Cal	264 10	
G. E. Bowden, collector, Norfolk, Va	3,414 35	
T. M. Blodgett, collector, Saint Mary's Ga	25 00	
J. H. Bartlett, collector, Little Egg Harbor, N. J	28 30	
J. T. Collins, collector, Brunswick, Ga	266 25	
W. P. Canaday, collector, Wilmington, N. C	516 65	
J. Campbell, collector, Omaha, Neb	842 40	
E. J. Costello, collector, Natchez, Miss	50 00	
D. G. Carr, collector, Petersburg, Va	75 00	
J. Collins, collector, Bristol, R. I	150 00	
J. M. Currie, collector, Saint Mark's, Fla	253 40	
F. Dodge, collector, Georgetown, D. C	922 85	
W. H. Daniels, collector, Oswegatchie, N. Y	104 05	
A. S. De Wolf, collector, Bristol, R. I	150 00	
J. H. Elmer, collector, Bridgetown, N. J	119 45	
D. G. Fort, collector, Oswego, N. Y	1,227 10	
J. W. Fuller, collector, Miami, Ohio	548 55	
G. Fisher, collector, Cairo, Ill	740 05	
B. Flagler, collector, Niagara, N. Y	25 00	
George Fraser, collector, Burlington, Iowa	715 15	
J. Gilchrist, collector, Wheeling, W. Va	4,425 70	
J. S. Branover, collector, Fairfield, Conn	356 60	
W. H. Huse, collector, Newburyport, Mass	339 26	
A. F. Howard, collector, Portsmouth, N. H	150 00	
W. S. Havens, collector, Sag Harbor, N. Y	350 70	
G. W. Howe, collector, Cuyahoga, Ohio	5,828 70	
Carried forward	67,997 76	312,140,106 93

STATEMENT of the RECEIPTS of the UNITED STATES, &c.—Continued.

FROM STEAMBOAT FEES—Continued.

Brought forward	$67, 907 76 $312, 40, 106 93
W. D. Hare, collector, Oregon, Oreg	534 95
J. A. Hall, collector, Waldoborough, Me	369 40
C. Harris, collector, Providence, R. I	1, 348 15
E. Hopkins, collector, Saint John's, Fla	896 25
G. Hubbard, collector, Stonington, Conn	520 85
C. H. Houghton, collector, Perth Amboy, N. J	1, 118 10
J. L. Haynes, collector, Brazos, Tex	193 05
I. Hacker, collector, Southern Oregon	325 25
George Holmes, collector, Beaufort, S. C	100 00
T. A. Henry, collector, Pamlico, N. C	176 00
J. W. Howell, collector, Fernandina, Fla	63 20
F. C. Hall, collector, Vicksburg, Miss	179 55
T. S. Hodson, collector, Eastern Maryland	25 00
H. F. Heriot, collector, Georgetown, S. C	201 50
J. D. Hopkins, collector, Frenchman's Bay, Me	25 00
F. C. Humphreys, collector, Pensacola, Fla	275 50
T. F. House, collector, Saint Augustine, Fla	50 00
W. P. Miller, collector, Nantucket, Mass	48 90
J. C. Jewell, collector, Evansville, Ind	3, 923 10
J. E. Jolly, collector, Teche, La	567 50
J. T. K. Jones, collector, Annapolis, Md	25 60
J. Kelley, collector, Willametta, Oreg	4, 594 90
I. Lord, collector, Saco, Me	50 00
Charles Lehman, collector, Vicksburg, Miss	254 14
G. Leavett, collector, Machias, Me	75 10
D. E. Lyon, collector, Dubuque, Iowa	688 20
C. S. Mills, collector, Richmond, Va	450 00
L. M. Morrill, collector, Portland, Me	3, 439 20
E. McMurtrie, collector, Minnesota, Minn	2, 083 85
I. H. Moulton, collector, La Crosse, Wis	1, 077 10
A. J. Mural, collector, Apalachicola, Fla	963 80
E. A. Merritt, collector, New York, N. Y	39, 205 85
O. McFadden, collector, Wiscasset, Me	100 00
C. G. Manning, collector, Albemarle, N. C	364 35
W. C. Marshall, collector, Belfast, Me	50 00
J. Nazro, collector, Milwaukee, Wis	6, 939 00
E. S. J. Nealley, collector, Bath, Me	617 00
N. B. Nutt, collector, Passamaquoddy, Me	178 70
C. Northrup, collector, New Haven, Conn	770 50
C. T. Osburn, collector, Superior, Mich	2, 631 10
C. H. Odell, collector, Salem, Mass	50 00
A. Putnam, collector, Middletown, Conn	972 85
J. G. Pool, collector, Miami, Ohio	701 75
F. A. Pratt, collector, Newport, R. I	1, 183 51
E. M. Pease, collector, Galveston, Tex	2, 296 95
J. S. Rutan, collector, Pittsburgh, Pa	9, 840 95
S. P. Remington, collector, Oswegatchie, N. Y	184 35
T. O. Shackelford, collector, Louisville, Ky	4, 151 35
J. L. Smith, collector, Bangor, Me	152 95
J. P. Sanborn, collector, Huron, Mich	5, 004 35
W. N. S. Sanders, collector, Albany, N. Y	7, 942 05
W. J. Smith, collector, Memphis, Tenn	4, 711 80
W. T. Simpson, collector, Geneva, N. Y	175 00
R. H. Stephenson, collector, Cincinnati, Ohio	10, 529 95
W. H. Smith, collector, Chicago, Ill	6, 707 60
G. St. Gem, collector, St. Louis, Mo	14, 369 70
R. T. Smith, collector, Mobile, Ala	3, 184 85
V. Smith, collector, Duluth, Minn	150 00
J. Shepard, collector, Saint Mary's, Ga	53 90
W. H. Sargent, collector, Castine, Me	25 00
T. B. Shannon, collector, San Francisco, Cal	12, 129 20
L. Thompson, collector, Wilmington, Del	1, 216 05
J. Tyler, collector, Buffalo, N. Y	10, 857 80
J. L. Thomas, jr., collector, Baltimore, Md	11, 040 60
George Tay, collector, Cherrystone, Va	50 00
J. A. Tibbetts, collector, New London, Conn	4, 310 70
A. P. Tutton, collector, Philadelphia, Pa	15, 290 24
A. Woolf, collector, Nashville, Tenn	2, 158 30
W. Wells, collector, Vermont, Vt	978 65
A. A. Warfield, collector, Alexandria, Va	259 85
F. N. Wicker, collector, Key West, Fla	95 85
G. W. Warren, collector, Cape Vincent, N. Y	600 70
D. Wann, collector, Galena, Ill	4, 914 40
H. A. Webster, collector, Puget Sound, Wash	1, 822 46
	282, 468 96

FROM REGISTERS' AND RECEIVERS' FEES.

R. J. Alcorn, receiver of public moneys, Jackson, Miss	6, 632 77
R. S. Armitage, receiver of public moneys, Harrison, Ark	10, 194 95
W. J. Anderson, receiver of public moneys, Grand Forks, Dak	18, 240 19
J. H. Allen, receiver of public moneys, Alexandria, Minn	18, 596 59
Carried forward	52, 663 80 312, 422, 575 89

STATEMENT of the RECEIPTS of the UNITED STATES, &c.—Continued.

FROM REGISTERS' AND RECEIVERS' FEES—Continued.

Brought forward	$32, 663 60	$312, 422, 575 89
William Anyan, receiver of public moneys, Grand Island, Nebr	32, 092 59	
H. A. Beatty, receiver of public moneys, Sacramento, Cal	6, 434 06	
G. Baldy, receiver of public moneys, New Orleans, La	6, 100 08	
E. M. Brown, receiver of public moneys, Bismarck, Dak	1, 013 10	
I. J. Best, receiver of public moneys, Kerwin, Kans	89, 975 83	
T. Boles, receiver of public moneys, Dardanelle, Ark	7, 862 64	
C. A. Brastow, receiver of public moneys, Del Norte, Colo	3, 098 63	
L. L. Bayless, receiver of public moneys, Yankton, Dak	20, 707 24	
H. Hook, receiver of public moneys, Larned, Kans	20, 396 74	
J. V. Bogert, receiver of public moneys, Bozeman, Mont	1, 770 90	
C. N. Baird, receiver of public moneys, Lincoln, Nebr	6, 759 49	
E. Brevoort, receiver of public moneys, Santa Fé, N. Mex	1, 769 63	
S. W. Brown, receiver of public moneys, Vancouver, Wyo	5, 451 55	
V. W. Bayless, receiver of public moneys, Eau Claire, Wis	3, 709 14	
W. K. Burchenell, receiver of public moneys, Fair Play, Colo	10, 165 00	
M. M. Bane, receiver of public moneys, Salt Lake, Utah	10, 353 34	
F. J. Burton, receiver of public moneys, East Saginaw, Mich	3, 971 00	
S. Cooper, receiver of public moneys, Humboldt, Cal	3, 030 71	
L. T. Crane, receiver of public moneys, Marysville, Cal	6, 943 76	
C. H. Chamberlain, receiver of public moneys, San Francisco, Cal	11, 213 08	
E. S. Crocker, receiver of public moneys, Evanston, Wyo	382 20	
D. Chaplain, receiver of public moneys, Le Grand, Oreg	9, 945 57	
G. Coon, receiver of public moneys, Linkville, Oreg	4, 637 06	
H. Carpenter, receiver of public moneys, Eureka, Nev	1, 300 90	
W. Callon, receiver of public moneys, Wausau, Wis	1, 001 52	
A. Dabrowsky, receiver of public moneys, Susata, Cal	4, 287 53	
J. Dumars, receiver of public moneys, Springfield, Mo	4, 723 00	
G. W. Dorsey, receiver of public moneys, Bloomington, Nebr	31, 395 09	
J. L. Dyer, receiver of public moneys, Wichita, Kans	9, 765 35	
L. Davis, receiver of public moneys, Ironton, Mo	4, 052 06	
J. C. Fullerton, receiver of public moneys, Roseburg, Oreg	5, 198 54	
J. M. Farland, receiver of public moneys, Detroit, Mich	1, 415 43	
J. F. Fagan, receiver of public moneys, Little Rock, Ark	10, 078 96	
M. H. Fitch, receiver of public moneys, Pueblo, Colo	7, 807 53	
G. B. Folsom, receiver of public moneys, Taylor's Falls, Minn	1, 105 73	
M. H. Griffiths, receiver of public moneys, Des Moines, Iowa	3, 667 30	
C. C. Goodnow, receiver of public moneys, New Ulm, Minn	12, 298 28	
W. M. Garvey, receiver of public moneys, Cheyenne, Wyo	274 00	
J. W. Haverstick, receiver of public moneys, Los Angeles, Cal	3, 379 77	
C. B. Hickman, receiver of public moneys, Lake City, Colo	1, 721 50	
E. W. Henderson, receiver of public moneys, Central City, Colo	3, 518 23	
W. J. Hunter, receiver of public moneys, Hays City, Kans	25, 148 00	
W. B. Harlott, receiver of public moneys, Redwood Falls, Minn	7, 203 80	
L. Hanback, receiver of public moneys, Salina, Kans	13, 643 47	
R. B. Harrington, receiver of public moneys, Beatrice, Nebr	4, 100 47	
T. R. Harrison, receiver of public moneys, Oregon City, Oreg	318 32	
E. J. Jenkins, receiver of public moneys, Concordia, Kans	15, 562 36	
P. J. Kaufman, receiver of public moneys, Huntsville, Ala	12, 640 00	
A. R. Lenoz, receiver of public moneys, Natchitoches, La	2, 681 49	
George Lount, receiver of public moneys, Prescott, Ariz	417 79	
T. Lindsey, receiver of public moneys, Visalia, Cal	2, 976 71	
William S. Lambert, receiver of public moneys, Norfolk, Nebr	3, 311 81	
A. Miller, receiver of public moneys, Susanville, Cal	2, 986 07	
J. F. McKenna, receiver of public moneys, Deadwood, Dak	4, 213 43	
W. H. C. Mitchell, receiver of public moneys, Reed City, Mich	6, 354 01	
J. P. Moulton, receiver of public moneys, Worthington, Minn	6, 130 10	
J. S. McClary, receiver of public moneys, Norfolk, Nebr	7, 223 04	
R. J. Monroe, receiver of public moneys, Lewiston, Idaho	4, 464 22	
W. B. Mitchell, receiver of public moneys, Saint Cloud, Minn	9, 000 00	
J. F. Nason, receiver of public moneys, Falls Saint Croix, Wis	3, 027 89	
H. Z. Osborne, receiver of public moneys, Bodie, Cal	2, 341 00	
O. Pearin, receiver of public moneys, Stockton, Cal	4, 362 10	
L. D. F. Poore, receiver of public moneys, Springfield, Dak	40, 582 21	
T. M. Pugh, receiver of public moneys, Fargo, Dak	77, 251 68	
T. H. Presnell, receiver of public moneys, Du Luth, Minn	1, 510 32	
D. L. Quaw, receiver of public moneys, Wausau, Wis	2, 976 02	
L. Ruggles, receiver of public moneys, Florence, Ariz	1, 412 27	
G. Ritchey, receiver of public moneys, Booneville, Mo	3, 230 00	
A. Reed, receiver of public moneys, Walla Walla, Wash	13, 965 05	
J. F. Rollins, receiver of public moneys, Gainesville, Fla	7, 878 29	
J. A. Somerville, receiver of public moneys, Mobile, Ala	455 10	
R. G. Stuart, receiver of public moneys, Olympia, Wash	9, 373 79	
J. Stott, receiver of public moneys, Niobrara, Nebr	26, 177 50	
H. W. Stone, receiver of public moneys, Benson, Minn	12, 193 07	
P. C. Stettin, receiver of public moneys, Detroit, Minn	43, 114 77	
F. P. Stirling, receiver of public moneys, Helena, Mont	8, 505 50	
J. Stout, receiver of public moneys, Boise City, Idaho	3, 509 56	
R. N. Sweet, receiver of public moneys, Colfax, Wash	27, 052 48	
J. F. Simpson, receiver of public moneys, Oxford, Idaho	4, 060 14	
P. J. Strobach, receiver of public moneys, Montgomery, Ala	18, 573 36	
S. W. Sharfoy, receiver of public moneys, Mesilla, N. Mex	168 39	
Carried forward	877, 727 68	313, 422, 575 89

382

REPORT ON THE FINANCES.

STATEMENT of the RECEIPTS of the UNITED STATES, &c.—Continued.

FROM REGISTERS' AND RECEIVERS' FEES—Continued.

Brought forward	$877,727 63	$312,429, 575 89
A. A. Tufts, receiver of public moneys, Camden, Ark	11, 626 90	
S. T. Thompson, receiver of public moneys, Denver, Colo	10, 576 77	
J. Tafe, receiver of public moneys, North Platte, Nebr	28, 011 07	
C. N. Thornburg, receiver of public moneys, The Dalles, Oreg	8, 335 61	
William H. Taucre, receiver of public moneys, Huntsville, Ala	3, 078 07	
N. Thatcher, receiver of public moneys, Menasha, Wis	3, 102 58	
J. Ulrich, receiver of public moneys, La Crosse, Wis	2, 396 57	
J. Varnum, receiver of public moneys, Gainesville, Fla	707 35	
J. M. Wilkinson, receiver of public moneys, Marquette, Mich	5, 232 70	
J. M. Washburn, receiver of public moneys, Sioux Falls, Dak	47, 387 69	
J. H. Wing, receiver of public moneys, Bayfield, Wis	854 12	
H. M. Waters, receiver of public moneys, Independence, Kans	2, 748 41	
D. R. Wagstaff, receiver of public moneys, Salina, Kans	4, 966 31	
G. W. Watson, receiver of public moneys, Topeka, Kans	2, 765 44	
J. W. Watts, receiver of public moneys, Oregon City, Oreg	7, 088 27	
J. A. Williamson, receiver of public moneys, Commissioner General Land Office	7 00	
J. C. Whipple, receiver of public moneys, Cheyenne, Wyo	786 32	
S. C. Wright, receiver of public moneys, Carson City, Nebr	703 50	
		1, 019, 174 61

FROM MARINE HOSPITAL TAX.

J. Atkins, collector, Savannah, Ga	2, 968 95
H. C. Akeley, collector, Michigan, Ga	3, 409 35
W. L. Ashmore, collector, Burlington, N. J	645 18
I. S. Adams, collector, Great Egg Harbor, N. J	1, 179 87
J. A. P. Allen, collector, New Bedford, Mass	1, 177 74
F. J. Babson, collector, Gloucester, Mass	869 41
D. V. Bell, collector, Detroit, Mich	5, 434 26
W. A. Baldwin, collector, Newark, N. J	1, 062 94
H. L. Brown, collector, Erie, Pa	1, 643 53
C. H. Baldwin, collector, Charleston, S. C	3, 754 41
J. S. Braxton, collector, Norfolk, Va	515 68
A. W. Beard, collector, Boston, Mass	16, 920 74
A. S. Badger, collector, New Orleans, La	15, 681 60
W. W. Bowers, collector, San Diego, Cal	266 20
James Brady, jr., collector, Fall River, Mass	2, 995 03
J. W. Bartlett, collector, Little Egg Harbor, N. J	223 93
E. A. Bragdon, collector, York, Me	15 73
M. D. Ball, collector, Alaska	382 56
G. E. Bowden, collector, Norfolk, Va	4, 753 35
T. M. Blodgett, collector, Saint Mary's, Ga	52 75
G. F. Bayles, collector, Port Jefferson, N. Y	2 71
J. T. Collins, collector, Brunswick, Ga	709 06
John Collins, collector, Bristol, R. I	106 57
J. M. Currie, collector, Saint Mark's, Fla	490 37
D. G. Carr, collector, Petersburg, Va	145 34
J. Campbell, collector, Omaha, Nebr	550 73
W. P. Canaday, collector, Wilmington, N. C	1, 483 74
G. T. Craumer, collector, Little Egg Harbor, N. J	236 17
E. J. Costello, collector, Natchez, Miss	159 40
F. Dodge, collector, Georgetown, D. C	3, 042 70
A. C. Davis, collector, Beaufort, N. C	529 44
S. K. Davis, collector, Port Jefferson, N. Y	630 87
S. Dodge, collector, Marblehead, Mass	100 85
W. H. Daniels, collector, Oswegatchie, N. Y	104 05
S. H. Doten, collector, Plymouth, Mass	81 33
A. S. DeWolf, collector, Bristol, R. I	82 30
J. H. Elmer, collector, Bridgeton, N. J	2, 744 67
G. Fisher, collector, Cairo, Ill	991 81
E. T. Fox, collector, Bangor, Me	31 47
B. Flagler, collector, Niagara, N. Y	250 69
J. W. Fuller, collector, Miami, Ohio	683 11
G. Frazee, collector, Burlington, Iowa	441 47
D. G. Fort, collector, Oswego, N. Y	1, 231 17
F. B. Goss, collector, Barnstable, Mass	2, 006 30
J. Gilchrist, collector, Wheeling, W. Va	2, 899 27
J. S. Hanover, collector, Fairfield, Conn	1, 975 78
W. H. Huse, collector, Newburyport, Mass	210 25
A. S. Howard, collector, Portsmouth, N. H	360 33
W. S. Havens, collector, Sag Harbor, N. Y	862 23
G. W. Howe, collector, Cuyahoga, Ohio	3, 553 92
W. D. Hare, collector, Oregon, Oreg	1, 099 33
P. C. Hall, collector, Vicksburg, Miss	733 65
C. Harris, collector, Providence, R. I	2, 596 29
J. T. Hoskins, collector, Tappahannock, Va	1, 033 09
E. Hopkins, collector, Saint John's, Fla	1, 619 48
G. Holmes, collector, Beaufort, S. C	358 44
T. S. Hodson, collector, Eastern, Maryland	4, 609 95
J. W. Howell, collector, Fernandina, Fla	664 30
Carried forward	102, 452 45	313, 441, 750 50

STATEMENT of the RECEIPTS of the UNITED STATES, &c.—Continued.

FROM MARINE HOSPITAL TAX—Continued.

Brought forward	$102,452 45	$313,441,750 50
G. Hubbard, collector, Stonington, Conn	793 05	
J. A. Hall, collector, Waldoboro', Me	2,552 04	
F. C. Humphreys, collector, Pensacola, Fla	1,908 89	
J. D. Hopkins, collector, Frenchman's Bay, Me	1,647 44	
W. G. Henderson, collector, Pearl River, Miss	1,509 41	
J. L. Haynes, collector, Brazos, Tex	218 96	
I. Hacker, colloctor, Southern Oregon	108 86	
T. A. Henry, collector, Pamlico, N. C	1,052 10	
C. H. Houghton, collector, Perth Amboy, N. J	3,191 60	
T. F. House, collector, Saint Augustine, Fla	11 97	
W. P. Hiller, collector, Nantucket, Mass	138 03	
H. F. Heriot, collector, Georgetown, S. C	415 21	
J. A. Henriques, collector and disbursing agent, New Orleans, La	171 11	
T. Ireland, collector, Annapolis, Md	241 43	
J. C. Jewell, collector, Evansville, Ind	2,399 93	
J. R. Jolley, collector, Teche, La	1,340 93	
S. M. Johnson, collector, Corpus Christi, Tex	247 63	
T. J. K. Jones, collector, Annapolis, Md	802 00	
P. P. Kidder, collector, Dunkirk, N. Y	14 19	
J. Kelley, collector, Willamette, Oreg	3,377 09	
I. Lord, collector, Saco, Me	90 31	
Charles Lehman, collector, Vicksburg, Miss	105 41	
George Leavett, collector, Machias, Me	1,368 22	
D. E. Lyon, collector, Dubuque, Iowa	717 62	
L. M. Morrell, collector, Portland, Me	3,150 89	
S. Moffett, collector, Champlain, N. Y	267 10	
E. McMurtrie, collector, Minnesota, Minn	2,032 49	
C. S. Mills, collector, Richmond, Va	1,102 84	
J. B. Mitchell, collector, Yorktown, Va	1,056 26	
C. G. Manning, collector, Albemarle, N. C	860 04	
J. H. Moulton, collector, La Crosse, Wis	1,056 34	
A. J. Murat, collector, Apalachicola, Fla	805 17	
E. A. Merritt, collector, New York, N. Y	73,311 40	
E. T. Moore, collector, Patchogue, N. Y	747 35	
W. C. Marshall, collector, Belfast, Mo	833 36	
O. McFadden, collector, Wiscasset, Me	475 82	
C. H. Marchant, collector, Edgartown, Mass	516 83	
J. Naaro, collector, Milwaukee, Wis	5,178 44	
E. S. J. Neally, collector, Bath, Me	2,197 57	
N. B. Nutt, collector, Passamaquoddy, Me	2,194 43	
C. Northrup, collector, New Haven, Conn	2,344 08	
C. Y. Osburn, collector, Superior, Mich	800 28	
C. H. Odell, collector, Salem, Mass	160 81	
A. Putnam, collector, Middletown, Conn	1,865 03	
J. G. Pool, collector, Miami, Ohio	985 56	
F. A. Pratt, collector, Newport, R. I	773 04	
E. M. Pease, collector, Galveston, Tex	2,762 83	
C. R. Prouty, collector, Saluria, Tex	506 28	
J. S. Rutan, collector, Pittsburgh, Pa	4,421 49	
S. P. Remington, collector, Oswegatchie, N. Y	202 68	
W. T. Simpson, collector, Genesee, N. Y	291 80	
T. O. Shackelford, collector, Louisville, Ky	1,775 54	
J. S. Smith, collector, Bangor, Me	1,285 81	
J. P. Sanborn, collector, Huron, Mich	4,544 29	
W. N. S. Sanders, collector, Albany, N. Y	4,445 69	
W. J. Smith, collector, Memphis, Tenn	2,955 28	
W. H. Sargent, collector, Castine, Me	1,114 82	
R. H. Stephenson, collector, Cincinnati, Ohio	7,792 65	
V. Smith, collector, Duluth, Minn	72 79	
W. H. Smith, collector, Chicago, Ill	7,529 20	
G. St. Gem, collector, Saint Louis, Mo	13,080 92	
R. T. Smith, collector, Mobile, Ala	3,090 03	
T. B. Shannon, collector, San Francisco, Cal	33,437 07	
J. Shepard, collector, Saint Mary's, Ga	51 80	
J. W. Sargent, collector, Kennebunk, Me	91 76	
S. C. Slade, collector, Paso del Norte, Tex	140 09	
I. Thompson, collector, Delaware, Del	2,584 38	
J. Tyler, collector, Buffalo, N. Y	6,444 60	
G. Toy, collector, Cherrystone, Va	2,099 37	
J. L. Thomas, jr., collector, Baltimore, Md	23,548 92	
J. A. Tebbetts, collector, New London, Conn	2,425 81	
A. P. Tutton, collector, Philadelphia, Pa	21,494 56	
A. Woolf, collector, Nashville, Tenn	1,192 07	
Wm. Wells, collector, Vermont, Vt	197 61	
A. A. Warfield, collector, Alexandria, Va	750 71	
F. N. Wicker, collector, Key West, Fla	3,499 37	
G. W. Warren, collector, Cape Vincent, N. Y	397 21	
D. Wann, collector, Galena, Ill	368 88	
H. A. Webster, collector, Puget Sound, Wash	4,321 39	
		386,973 33
Carried forward		313,828,723 83

STATEMENT of the RECEIPTS of the UNITED STATES, &c.—Continued.

FROM LABOR, DRAYAGE, ETC.

Brought forward..		$313,836,723 83
J. A. P. Allen, collector, New Bedford, Mass............................	$20 98	
J. Atkins, collector, Savannah, Ga.....................................	103 95	
A. W. Beard, collector, Boston, Mass....................................	14,869 81	
D. V. Bell, collector, Detroit, Mich....................................	1,098 00	
A. S. Badger, collector, New Orleans, La................................	350 08	
C. H. Baldwin, collector, Charleston, S. C..............................	1,021 05	
W. P. Canaday, collector, Wilmington, N. C..............................	368 36	
W. H. Daniels, collector, Oswegatchie, N. Y.............................	16 00	
D. G. Fort, collector, Oswego, N. Y.....................................	2,346 00	
J. L. Haynes, collector, Brazos, Tex...................................	650 00	
C. Harris, collector, Providence, R. I.................................	206 08	
E. A. Merritt, collector, New York, N. Y...............................	15,405 43	
L. M. Morrill, collector, Portland, Me.................................	3,311 17	
E. McMurtrie, collector, Minnesota, Minn...............................	46 10	
E. S. J. Nealley, collector, Bath, Me..................................	85 50	
E. M. Pease, collector, Galveston, Tex.................................	530 15	
A. Putnam, collector, Middletown, Conn.................................	189 00	
S. P. Remington, collector, Oswegatchie, N. Y..........................	64 00	
R. H. Stephenson, collector, Cincinnati, Ohio..........................	1,610 80	
G. St. Gem, collector, Saint Louis, Mo.................................	1,465 69	
T. O. Shackelford, collector, Louisville, Ky...........................	74 40	
R. T. Smith, collector, Mobile, Ala....................................	19 30	
T. B. Shannon, collector, San Francisco, Cal...........................	586 29	
V. Smith, collector, Duluth, Minn.....................................	771 00	
A. P. Tutton, collector, Philadelphia, Pa..............................	4,819 23	
J. L. Thomas, jr., collector, Baltimore................................	3,399 22	
J. Tyler, collector, Buffalo, N. Y.....................................	204 76	
Wm. Wells, collector, Vermont, Vt......................................	2 74	
		53,706 10

FROM SERVICES OF UNITED STATES OFFICERS.

F. J. Babson, collector, Gloucester, Mass...............................	780 00	
A. W. Beard, collector, Boston, Mass...................................	29,872 32	
A. S. Badger, collector, New Orleans, La...............................	6,817 49	
D. V. Bell, collector, Detroit, Mich..................................	1,312 20	
C. H. Baldwin, collector, Charleston, S. C.............................	36 00	
G. E. Bowden, collector, Norfolk, Va..................................	12 00	
W. W. Bowers, collector, San Diego, Cal................................	231 00	
W. H. Daniels, collector, Oswegatchie, N. Y............................	368 00	
B. Flagler, collector, Niagara, N. Y..................................	6,860 00	
J. W. Fuller, collector, Miami, Ohio..................................	12 00	
F. B. Goss, collector, Barnstable, Mass...............................	560 00	
W. H. Huse, collector, Newburyport, Mass..............................	18 00	
C. Harris, collector, Providence, R. I...............................	730 00	
J. D. Hopkins, collector, Frenchman's Bay, Me.........................	504 00	
W. C. Marshall, collector, Belfast, Me................................	200 00	
E. A. Merritt, collector, New York, N. Y..............................	139,440 00	
L. M. Morrill, collector, Portland, Me................................	2,024 60	
E. McMurtrie, collector, Minnesota, Minn..............................	1,859 00	
C. Northrop, collector, New London, Conn..............................	200 60	
E. M. Pease, collector, Galveston, Tex................................	840 75	
C. K. Prouty, collector, Saluria, Tex.................................	255 00	
S. P. Remington, collector, Oswegatchie, N. Y.........................	547 00	
J. P. Sanborn, collector, Huron, Mich.................................	9,591 00	
W. H. Smith, collector, Chicago, Ill.................................	3,684 40	
W. J. Smith, collector, Memphis, Tenn................................	1,200 00	
T. B. Shannon, collector, San Francisco, Cal..........................	17,393 84	
V. Smith, collector, Duluth, Minn....................................	465 08	
R. T. Smith, collector, Mobile, Ala..................................	2 40	
J. A. Tibbetts, collector, New London, Conn..........................	30 00	
L. Thompson, collector, Delaware, Del................................	5 90	
A. P. Tutton, collector, Philadelphia, Pa............................	14,476 18	
J. L. Thomas, jr., collector, Baltimore, Md..........................	10,739 70	
J. Tyler, collector, Buffalo, N. Y..................................	8,245 00	
F. N. Wicker, collector, Key West, Fla..............................	2,362 00	
Wm. Wells, collector, Vermont, Vt..................................	6,166 88	
		257,802 11

FROM WEIGHING FEES.

F. J. Babson, collector, Gloucester, Mass..............................	5,540 79	
A. W. Beard, collector, Boston, Mass.................................	11,857 07	
A. S. Badger, collector, New Orleans, La.............................	1,351 09	
C. H. Baldwin, collector, Charleston, S. C...........................	62 55	
F. B. Goss, collector, Barnstable, Mass.............................	261 43	
W. H. Huse, collector, Newburyport, Mass............................	12 29	
C. Harris, collector, Providence, R. I.............................	46 79	
J. W. Howell, collector, Fernandina, Fla............................	2 90	
O. McFadden, collector, Wiscasset, Me...............................	169 48	
E. A. Merritt, collector, New York, N. Y............................	42,348 20	
L. M. Morrill, collector, Portland, Me..............................	1,718 49	
Carried forward..	63,393 08	314,140,232 04

*STATEMENT of the RECEIPTS of the UNITED STATES, &c.—*Continued.

FROM WEIGHING FEES—Continued.

Brought forward	$63/393 08	$314,140,232 04
W. C. Marshall, collector, Belfast, Me	238 01	
C. R. Prouty, collector, Saluria, Tex	24	
W. H. Sargent, collector, Castine, Me	10 02	
T. B. Shannon, collector, San Francisco, Cal	1,879 24	
W. H. Smith, collector, Chicago, Ill	3 00	
J. Tyler, collector, Buffalo, N. Y	1 20	
A. F. Tuttou, collector, Philadelphia, Pa	1,576 58	
J. L. Thomas, jr., collector, Baltimore, Md	283 43	
		67,375 50

FROM CUSTOMS-OFFICERS' FEES.

A. R. Beard, collector, Boston, Mass	56,358 60	
A. S. Badger, collector, New Orleans, La	15,489 02	
W. W. Bowers, collector, San Diego, Cal	323 65	
I. H. Moulton, collector, La Crosse, Wis	119 85	
L. M. Morrill, collector, Portland, Me	13,539 02	
E. A. Merritt, collector, New York, N. Y	286,453 95	
T. B. Shannon, collector, San Francisco, Cal	26,883 63	
A. P. Tutton, collector, Philadelphia, Pa	34,747 64	
J. L. Thomas, jr., collector, Baltimore, Md	27,081 11	
		461,896 56

FROM FINES, PENALTIES, AND FORFEITURES—CUSTOMS.

H. C. Akeley, collector, Michigan, Mich	209 00	
J. S. Adams, collector, Great Egg Harbor, N. J	10 00	
J. Atkins, collector, Savannah, Ga	250 00	
A. S. Badger, collector, New Orleans, La	3,144 70	
A. W. Beard. collector, Boston, Mass	4,929 79	
W. A. Baldwin, collector, Newark, N. J	10 25	
H. L. Brown, collector, Erie, Pa	315 00	
C. H. Baldwin, collector, Charleston, S. C	173 80	
D. V. Bell, collector, Detroit, Mich	2,521 59	
G. E. Bowden, collector, Norfolk, Va	149 00	
F. J. Babson, collector, Gloucester, Mass	100 00	
W. W. Bowers, collector, San Diego, Cal	2,070 34	
J. Campbell, collector, Omaha, Neb	13 10	
J. T. Collins, collector, Brunswick, Ga	70 00	
John Collins, collector, Bristol, R. I	13 00	
W. P. Canaday, collector, Wilmington, N. C	266 40	
J. M. Currie, collector, Saint Mark's, Fla	373 09	
F. Dodge, collector, Georgetown, D. C	30 00	
W. H. Daniels, collector, Oswegatchie, N. Y	295 79	
E. T. Fox, collector, Bangor, Me	51 95	
B. Flagler, collector, Niagara, N. Y	764 67	
J. W. Fuller, collector, Miami, Ohio	100 00	
D. G. Fort, collector, Oswego, N. Y	1,310 00	
F. B. Goss, collector, Barnstable, Mass	812 64	
J. L. Haynes, collector, Brazos, Tex	867 56	
C. H. Houghton, collector, Perth Amboy, N. J	5 00	
T. A. Henry, collector, Pamlico, N. C	5 00	
W. H. Huse, collector, Newburyport, Mass	55 00	
G. W. Howe, collector, Cuyahoga, Ohio	65 64	
E. Hopkins, collector, Saint John's, Fla	595 00	
J. W. Howell, collector, Fernandina, Fla	1 69	
A. F. Howard, collector, Portsmouth, N. H	793 65	
J. A. Hall, collector, Waldeboro', Me	106 57	
C. Harris, collector, Providence, R. I	20 00	
S. M. Johnson, collector, Corpus Christi, Tex	3,932 65	
J. B. Jolley, collector, Teche, La	100 00	
J. Kelly, collector, Willamette, Oreg	480 63	
E. A. Merritt, collector, New York, N. Y	61,004 74	
S. Moffett, collector, Champlain, N. Y	3,411 56	
C. G. Manning, collector, Albemarle, N. C	75 15	
E. McMurtle, collector, Minnesota, Minn	778 37	
L. M. Morrill, collector, Portland, Me	142 75	
J. B. Mitchell, collector, Yorktown, Va	5 00	
N. B. Nutt, collector, Passamaquoddy, Me	1,650 95	
C. Northrup, collector, New Haven, Conn	218 51	
C. Y. Osburn, collector, Superior, Mich	145 02	
C. K. Prouty, collector, Saluria, Tex	1,273 36	
A. Putnam, collector, Middletown, Conn	220 00	
B. M. Pease, collector, Galveston, Tex	217 50	
F. A. Pratt, collector, Newport, R. I	544 40	
J. G. Pool, collector, Miami, Ohio	25 00	
S. P. Remington, collector, Oswegatchie, N. Y	1,365 37	
J. S. Ralston, collector, Pittsburgh, Pa	200 00	
T. B. Shannon, collector, San Francisco, Cal	9,138 44	
William H. Smith, collector, Chicago, Ill	634 50	
G. St. Gem, collector, Saint Louis, Mo	331 97	
Carried forward	106,320 51	314,669,504 10

25 F

386 REPORT ON THE FINANCES.

STATEMENT of the RECEIPTS of the UNITED STATES, &c.—Continued.

FROM FINES, PENALTIES, AND FORFEITURES—CUSTOMS—Continued.

Brought forward	$106,320 51	$314,669,504 16
S. C. Slade, collector, Paso Del Norte, Tex	840 70	
J. S. Smith, collector, Bangor, Me	98 53	
V. Smith, collector, Duluth, Minn	11 75	
J. P. Sanborn, collector, Huron, Mich	2,141 22	
R. T. Smith, collector, Mobile, Ala	212 45	
R. H. Stephenson, collector, Cincinnati, Ohio	477 31	
W. T. Simpson, collector, Genesee, N. Y	23 00	
J. Tyler, collector, Buffalo, N. Y	241 12	
A. P. Tutton, collector, Philadelphia, Pa	1,373 50	
J. L. Thomas, jr., collector, Baltimore, Md	1,528 25	
J. A. Tibbetts, collector, New London, Conn	30 00	
George Tay, collector, Cherrystone, Va	25 00	
A. Vending, collector, Aroostook, Me	2,103 71	
F. N. Wicker, collector, Key West, Fla	1,642 90	
William Wells, collector, Vermont, Vt	6,277 34	
H. A. Webster, collector, Puget Sound, Wash	390 25	
A. Woolf, collector, Nashville, Tenn	25 00	
G. W. Warren, collector, Cape Vincent, N. Y	8 65	
		123,786 26

FROM FINES, PENALTIES, AND FORFEITURES—COURTS.

T. Ambrose, clerk southern district Ohio	191 39
A. R. Ayres, clerk district Wyoming	466 55
E. T. Bishop, clerk district Colorado	244 84
A. E. Buck, clerk northern district Georgia	192 50
W. S. Bellville, clerk district New Jersey	863 49
L. S. Baxter, clerk middle district Tennessee	471 44
C. T. Barry, clerk eastern district Virginia	50 00
W. H. Bradley, clerk northern district Illinois	1,711 25
J. D. Bates, clerk district Massachusetts	1 00
C. Blummer, collector internal revenue, New Mexico	25 00
N. C. Butler, clerk district Indiana	1,254 50
E. Bull, clerk northern district Ohio	1,629 40
B. L. Benedict, clerk eastern district New York	1 00
W. H. Bliss, attorney eastern district Missouri	20 00
J. W. Chew, clerk district Maryland	84 60
A. Clark, collector internal revenue, 2d district, Georgia	96 79
M. B. Converse, clerk southern district Illinois	16 95
J. H. Clark, clerk eastern district Missouri	577 30
S. B. Crail, clerk district Kentucky	495 00
John I. Davenport, clerk southern district New York	181 18
C. Dart, clerk western district Texas	148 75
J. W. Dimmick, clerk middle district Alabama	731 84
F. Douglass, marshal District of Columbia	72 75
B. W. Etheridge, clerk western district Tennessee	201 35
H. Fink, marshal eastern district Wisconsin	138 70
J. H. Finks, clerk northern district Texas	56 70
A. J. Faulk, clerk district Dakota	60 00
G. I. Foster, clerk district Dakota	1,108 00
M. M. Freed, receiver public moneys, Dardanelle, Ark	87 43
R. G. Goodrich, clerk eastern district Arkansas	1,239 78
C. H. Hill, clerk district Massachusetts	1,268 31
A. R. Hunes, clerk eastern district Tennessee	619 77
W. H. Hackett, clerk district New Hampshire	484 36
T. Hillhouse, assistant United States treasurer, New York	1,567 72
W. C. Howard, clerk southern district Ohio	158 79
C. B. Hinsdill, clerk western district Michigan	600 00
E. M. Hinsdill, clerk western district Michigan	10 56
S. Hoffman, clerk district California	30 00
A. Q. Keasby, attorney district New Jersey	10,018 85
E. Kurtz, clerk eastern district Wisconsin	293 40
R. H. Lawson, clerk district Oregon	1,211 26
W. Larkins, clerk eastern district North Carolina	149 32
E. O. Locke, clerk southern district Florida	282 96
A. McGehie, clerk eastern district Mississippi	154 80
A. W. McCullough, clerk northern district Alabama	1,136 53
S. P. Martin, clerk western district Tennessee	1 00
J. W. McKee, clerk southern district Mississippi	222 54
E. E. Marvin, clerk district Connecticut	1,012 42
H. E. Mann, clerk district Minnesota	93 30
S. C. McCandless, clerk western district Pennsylvania	418 32
J. Neville, receiver public moneys, New Orleans, La	69 20
G. B. Overton, receiver public moneys, Salt Lake, Utah	25 00
R. G. O'Brien, clerk district Washington Territory	68 72
S. Patterson, clerk western district Virginia	250 00
A. W. Pool, marshal district California	86 32
S. C. Parks, clerk district New Mexico	36 30
N. B. Prentice, marshal northern district Ohio	1,625 50
G. P. Pottor, receiver public moneys, Pembina, Dak	38 48
W. P. Preble, clerk district Maine	403 50
Carried forward	34,511 89 314,793,290 38

STATEMENT of the RECEIPTS of the UNITED STATES, &c.—Continued.

FROM FINES, PENALTIES, AND FORFEITURES—COURTS—Continued.

Brought forward...	$34,511 89	$314,793,290 88
M. F. Pleasants, clerk eastern district Virginia..............................	25 00	
M. M. Price, clerk eastern district Missouri.................................	6 30	
R. M. Reynolds, First Auditor United States Treasury..........................	37 22	
N. J. Reddick, clerk eastern district North Carolina...........................	51 46	
W. Robbins, clerk northern district New York..............................	50 00	
G. C. Rives, clerk eastern district Texas	124 25	
K. Rayner, Solicitor United States Treasury	5,954 06	
W. C. Robards, clerk western district Texas...............................	23 61	
L. S. B. Sawyer, clerk district California	463 54	
J. G. Stetson, clerk district Massachusetts	561 75	
W. B. Smith, clerk district Nebraska.....................................	2,425 27	
F. M. Stewart, clerk western district Wisconsin	575 00	
W. A. Spencer, clerk district Minnesota	610 00	
T. L. Sanborn, collector internal revenue, 7th district, Virginia	39 05	
E. M. Seabrook, clerk district South Carolina..............................	110 00	
Secretary United States Treasury	1,151 85	
N. W. Trimble, clerk southern district Alabama............................	92 10	
United States courts	2,510 50	
J. K. Valentine, attorney eastern district Pennsylvania	223 95	
S. Wheeler, clerk western district Arkansas...............................	313 75	
J. C. Wilson, clerk district Kansas	125 85	
P. Walter, clerk northern district Florida	207 50	
S. L. Woodford, attorney southern district New York	1,012 00	
J. F. Washabaugh, clerk district Dakota	3 50	
F. A. Woolfley, clerk district Louisiana	11 00	
		50,398 90

FROM EMOLUMENT-FEES—CUSTOMS.

H. C. Akeley, collector, Michigan, Mich	4,588 70	
J. C. Abbott, collector, Wilmington, N. C	284 08	
F. J. Babson, collector, Gloucester, Mass.................................	1,040 05	
C. H. Baldwin, collector, Charleston, S. C	118 19	
J. S. Braxton, collector, Norfolk, Va	502 13	
G. E. Bowden, collector, Norfolk, Va	754 58	
T. M. Blodgett, collector, Saint Mary's, Ga...............................	15 00	
D. V. Bell, collector, Detroit, Mich	1,181 20	
W. P. Canaday, collector, Wilmington, N. C...............................	2,573 15	
D. N. Couch, late collector, Boston, Mass	423 67	
A. C. Davis, collector, Beaufort, N. C....................................	1 05	
D. G. Fort, collector, Oswego, N. Y......................................	15,196 78	
B. Piaglar, collector, Niagara, N. Y	16,568 24	
J. Frankenfield, collector, Minnesota, Minn	1,689 16	
F. C. Humphreys, collector, Pensacola, Fla................................	572 26	
J. L. Haynes, collector, Brazos, Tex	1,475 35	
G. W. Howe, collector, Cuyahoga, Ohio	307 46	
C. K. Hall, collector, Galveston, Tex	120 49	
S. M. Johnson, collector, Corpus Christi, Tex	106 15	
J. Kelly, collector, Willamette, Oreg.....................................	2,462 09	
S. Moffitt, collector, Champlain, N. Y	10,801 95	
E. McMurtrie, collector, Minnesota, Minn	650 76	
N. B. Nutt, collector, Passamaquoddy, Me	490 00	
J. Nasro, collector, Milwaukee, Wis	1,615 01	
C. Northrop, collector, New Haven, Conn.................................	939 16	
E. M. Pease, collector, Galveston, Tex	1,552 47	
N. Plato, late collector, Corpus Christi, Tex...............................	36 56	
N. Patten, late collector, Galveston, Tex	125 20	
S. P. Remington, collector, Oswegatchie, N. Y.............................	600 90	
V. Smith, collector, Duluth, Minn	201 62	
J. P. Sanborn, collector, Huron, Mich	11,982 40	
W. H. Smith, collector, Chicago, Ill	56,276 11	
G. St. Gem, collector, Saint Louis, Mo....................................	13,150 47	
R. H. Stephenson, collector, Cincinnati, Ohio	4,853 77	
J. Tyler, collector, Buffalo, N. Y	12,408 27	
A. Vandine, collector, Aroostook, Me	1,322 56	
D. L. Watson, collector, Southern Oregon	250 00	
J. C. Whitney, collector, Albany, N. Y...................................	317 54	
W. Wells, collector, Vermont, Vt	15,772 37	
H. A. Webster, collector, Puget Sound, W. T	19 01	
		183,150 91

FROM EMOLUMENT-FEES—JUDICIARY.

C. C. Allen, marshal western district Missouri	181 09	
W. H. Bradley, clerk northern district Illinois	7,744 75	
S. Bell, clerk eastern district Pennsylvania	1,064 45	
E. Bill, clerk northern district Ohio.....................................	328 60	
N. C. Butler, clerk northern district Indiana	61 84	
B. H. Campbell, marshal northern district Illinois	1,856 00	
W. H. Clayton, attorney western district Arkansas	1 90	
F. Douglass, marshal District of Columbia.................................	29 72	
Carried forward..	11,258 10	315,026,840 19

STATEMENT of the RECEIPTS of the UNITED STATES, &c.—Continued.

FROM EMOLUMENT-FEES—JUDICIARY—Continued.

Brought forward..................................	$11, 258 41	$315, 026, 840 19
E. Dexter, clerk district Massachusetts	9, 549 63	
John I. Davenport, clerk southern district New York.................	86 20	
William P. Fishback, clerk district Indiana.....................	286 55	
H. C. Goisburg, clerk western district Missouri....................	166 00	
J. S. Hildrup, marshal northern district Illinois	4, 350 66	
C. S. Lincoln, clerk eastern district Pennsylvania.................	2, 623 56	
S. H. Lyman, clerk eastern district New York.................	4, 907 01	
A. V. Lusk, attorney district North Carolina	1, 277 80	
C. E. Mayer, attorney northern district Alabama	1, 009 65	
A. W. McCullough, clerk northern district Alabama	113 10	
William P. Preble, clerk district Maine...........................	152 49	
E. R. Roo, marshal, southern district Illinois......................	449 14	
A. J. Ricks, clerk northern district Ohio..........................	480 77	
A. W. Waters, marshal district Oregon	242 08	
		37, 020 06

PROCEEDS OF GOVERNMENT PROPERTY.

Treasury Department..	27, 158 00	
War Department:		
Quartermaster's	191, 148 76	
Medical..	1, 256 61	
Ordnance.......................................	14, 016 48	
Signal Office	20 05	
Military Academy	3 20	
Engineers......................................	1, 481 03	
Navy Department:		
Yards and Docks..............................	821 02	
Provisions and Clothing	12, 258 24	
Equipment and Recruiting......................	65 63	
Construction and Repair ;......................	11, 647 21	
Medicine and Surgery..........................	69 10	
Marine...	1, 032 30	
Steam Engineering.............................	196 50	
Civil Establishment............................	375 85	
Interior Department..	1, 363 84	
Indian Office	11, 560 68	
Lands...	371 74	
Miscellaneous:		
House of Representatives.......................	2, 283 00	
Public Printer	1, 568 72	
State Department..............................	3, 963 45	
		282, 816 60

Reimbursements of interest paid on bonds to Central Pacific Railroad Company; section 2, act May 7, 1878	252, 736 09	
Sinking fund Central Pacific Railroad Company; section 2, act May 7, 1878	442, 892 49	
Reimbursements of interest paid on bonds to Union Pacific Railroad Company; section 2, act May 7, 1878	331, 694 37	
Sinking fund Union Pacific Railroad Company; section 2, act May 7, 1878............	343, 728 73	
Central Pacific Railroad Company; withheld under section 5260 Revised Statutes......	176, 234 32	
Union Pacific Railroad Company; withheld under section 5260 Revised Statutes.......	154, 731 02	
Kansas Pacific Railroad Company; withheld under section 5260 Revised Statutes......	122, 486 73	
Sioux City and Pacific Railroad Company; withheld under section 5260 Revised Statutes.	14, 285 18	
Central Pacific Railroad Company, 5 per cent. net earnings; act July 1, 1862, &c	616, 907 60	
Reimbursements of interest to Central Pacific Railroad Company (balance due 5 per cent. net earnings; acts July 1, 1862, and May 7, 1878)..........................	39, 191 27	
United States notes	81, 302, 563 00	
Refunding certificates	614, 640 00	
Silver certificates	10, 091, 000 00	
Certificates of deposit...	47, 355, 000 00	
Funded loan of 1907..	72, 450, 900 00	
Premium on funded loan of 1907..	5 00	
Interest, &c., on Indian trust-fund stocks...............................	819, 960 03	
Proceeds of Otoe Missourias Indian lands, act August 15, 1876	60, 489 12	
Reimbursements on appropriations to meet interest on non-paying Indian trust-fund stocks..	16, 368 21	
Proceeds Cherokee school lands...	100 09	
Reimbursements by Chickasaw Nation.....................................	5, 820 00	
Proceeds Cherokee Indian lands, acts May 11, 1872, and February 28, 1877..........	78, 950 55	
Proceeds Sacs and Foxes of Missouri Indian lands, act August 15, 1876 :..........	10, 372 19	
Proceeds Osage Indian lands, act July 15, 1870............................	411, 006 74	
Interest on deferred payments, sale of Indian lands	9, 458 77	
Proceeds Osage ceded lands, act August 11, 1876	77, 456 93	
Proceeds Sioux reservations in Minnesota and Dakota......................	44, 715 61	
Proceeds Pawnee Indian lands, act April 10, 1876..........................	85, 632 05	
Proceeds Kansas Indian lands, acts May 8, 1872, and June 23, 1874	48, 604 19	
Reimbursements for appropriations for Otoe and Missourias	49, 000 00	
Carried forward..................................		531, 384, 207 52

STATEMENT of the RECEIPTS of the UNITED STATES, &c.—Continued.

FROM MISCELLANEOUS—Continued.

Brought forward	$531,384,207 82
Reimbursements for appropriations for surveying Otoe and Missourias reservations in Kansas and Nebraska	12,167 68
Reimbursements, &c.; expenses surveying Osage lands, acts July 26, 1866, July 21, 1868, and March 3, 1871	146,953 60
Mileage of examiners	1,062 70
Reimbursements by national bank redemption agency, salaries office Treasurer (1879)	26,182 35
Reimbursements by national bank redemption agency, salaries office Treasurer (1880)	63,006 88
Reimbursements by national bank redemption agency, salaries office Comptroller of the Currency (1879)	5,565 00
Reimbursements by national bank redemption agency, salaries office Comptroller of the Currency (1880)	16,665 00
Reimbursements to United States contingent expenses national currency, office of the Treasurer (1879)	106,993 68
Conscience fund	8,667 80
Rebate of interest	96 97
Passport fees	15,095 00
Copyright fees	15,353 40
Revenue, District of Columbia:	
General fund	1,569,225 75
Water fund	190,343 61
Redemption-tax-lien certificates	3,459 08
Washington special-tax fund	8,058 82
Washington redemption fund	8,297 33
Pennsylvania avenue paving-certificates	3,561 04
Pennsylvania avenue paving-scrip	584 09
Sales of ordnance:	
War Department	131,110 10
Navy Department	15,280 25
Forfeitures by contractors	588 27
Interest on Nashville and Chattanooga Railroad bonds	66,000 00
Interest on Nashville and Decatur Railroad bonds	3,300 00
Interest on East Tennessee, Virginia, and Georgia Railroad bonds	7,800 00
Copying fees General Land Office	7,957 50
Proceeds of captured and abandoned property	41,926 82
Premium on refunding-certificates	105 00
Trust-fund, interest for support of free schools South Carolina	2,630 49
Profits on coinage	389,517 97
Deductions on bullion deposits	6,400 93
Profits on coinage of standard silver dollars	2,592,982 49
Assays and chemical examinations	3,285 39
Water-rents, Hot Springs, Arkansas	1,488 87
Ground-rents, Hot Springs, Arkansas	1,285 16
Sales of captured Indian stock	911 30
Miscellaneous items	1,692 08
Rent of public buildings	22,990 71
Interest on debts due the United States	25,709 74
Depredations on public lands	43,438 28
Tax on seal skins	303,400 25
Rent for taking seals	55,000 00
Rent of property acquired under internal-revenue laws	661 50
Sale of property acquired under internal-revenue laws	1,561 70
Assessments upon owners for deaths on shipboard	170 00
Tax on circulation of national banks	7,014,971 44
Fees on letters patent	736,692 58
Deposits by individuals for expenses of surveys	474,556 70
Premium on transfer drafts	3,118 55
Reimbursements for appropriation for relief of Josiah Morris	3,135 52
Cost of printing record in Supreme Court cases	11,865 50
Relief of sick and disabled seamen	1,519 54
Surplus fees of shipping-commissioners	1,227 12
Property devised to the United States by John Gardner, deceased	6,035 16
Reimbursements salaries of storekeepers internal-revenue bonded warehouses	742 53
Direct tax	30 85
Moneys recovered from Government of Mexico on claim of S. A. Belden & Co	2,616 82
Redemption of property, act June 8, 1872	394 50
Internal and coastwise intercourse fees	2,905 72
Proceeds of property decreed to United States by the Supreme Court	1,363 37
Total receipts	545,340,713 98

STATEMENT exhibiting the BALANCES of APPROPRIATIONS UNEXPENDED CARRIED to the SURPLUS FUND during the fiscal year ending June 30, 1880, together the next annual statement.

Specific objects of appropriations.	Year.	Statutes.		Balances of appropriations, July 1, 1879.
		Vol.	Page or section.	
CIVIL.				
Salaries and mileage of Senators	1878			$6, 847 60
Do	1879			
Do	1880	21	23	
Salaries officers and employés Senate	1878			376 60
Do	1879	20	251	
		21	56	
Do	1880	21	23, 56, 150, 308	
		20	251	
Contingent expenses Senate:				
Clerks to committees and pages	1878			1, 049 50
Do	1879	21	251	
Do	1880	21	23, 56, 69	
Stationery and newspapers	1878			351 81
Do	1879	21	252	
Do	1880	21	23	
Horses and wagons	1878			88 25
Do	1879			
Do	1880	21	23	
Fuel for heating apparatus	1878			3, 944 66
Do	1879			
Do	1880	21	23	
Furniture and repairs	1878			1, 793 71
Do	1879	21	65	
Do	1880	21	23	
Pay of folders	1878			85 18
Do	1879	21	56, 251	
Do	1880	21	23–71	
Materials for folding	1880	21	23	
Packing-boxes	1880	21	23	
Cartage	1878			132 30
Do	1879			16 50
Do	1880	21	23	
Miscellaneous items	1878			392 45
Do	1879			257 50
Do	1880	21	23, 65, 150, 306	
Salaries of Capitol police	1879			
Do	1880	21	23, 69	
Capitol police, contingent fund	1880	21	23	
Postage of the Senate	1880	21	23	
Reporting proceedings and debates, Senate	1880	21	23	
Expenses of compiling and preparing Congressional Directory	1880	21	23	
Joint Committee on Transfer of Indian Bureau to War Department				80 85
Investigation of epidemic diseases, Senate joint resolution, December 21, 1878				10, 515 75
Contingent expenses Senate, Select Committee on Alleged Frauds in late Presidential Election				10, 000 00
One month's pay discharged employés of the Senate, joint resolution June 24, 1879		21	53, 251	
		20	489	
One month's compensation to certain employés Senate		21	310	
To pay Chester R. Faulkner for services as messenger	1879	21	251	
	1880			
Salaries and mileage of members and delegates House of Representatives	1878			73, 827 74
Do	1879			11, 285 65
Do	1880	21	23	
Salaries officers and employés House of Representatives	1877	21	5	
Do	1878	21	71, 252, 280	844 72
Do	1879	21	52, 53, 56	1, 154 71
			252, 280	
Do	1880	21	23, 56, 52	
		20	280, 480	
Contingent expenses House:				
Clerks to committees	1878	21	252	516 00
Do	1879	21	53	
Do	1879	21	280	
	1880			
Do	1880	21	24, 56	
Pages	1878	21	252	144 13
Do	1879	21	53	

June 30, 1879, *and of the APPROPRIATIONS, EXPENDITURES, and the AMOUNTS with the UNEXPENDED BALANCES on June* 30, 1880, *which are to be accounted for in*

Appropriations for the fiscal year ending June 30, 1880.	Repayments made during the fiscal year 1880.	Aggregate available for the fiscal year ending June 30, 1880.	Payments during the fiscal year ending June 30, 1880.	Amounts carried to the surplus fund June 30, 1880.	Balances of appropriations, June 30, 1880
....	....	$6, 847 60	....	$6, 847 60	....
....	$6, 754 30	6, 754 30	$315 01	....	$6, 438 39
$416, 000 00	....	416, 000 00	416, 000 00	....	....
....	....	376 60	....	376 60	....
696 75	....	696 75	696 75	....	....
154, 932 93	......A...........	104, 932 93	193, 593 87	....	1, 339 06
....	....	1, 049 50	.......!..........	1, 049 50	....
319 30	2, 870 69	3, 189 99	319 30	....	2, 870 69
45, 295 00	....	45, 295 00	45, 295 00	....	....
....	....	351 81	....	351 81	....
9, 500 00	62 97	9, 562 97	9, 500 00	....	62 97
14, 500 00	....	14, 500 00	14, 500 00	....	....
....	....	38 25	....	38 25	....
....	520 62	520 62	....	....	520 62
3, 500 00	....	8, 500 00	3, 500 00	....	....
....	....	3, 944 66	....	3, 944 66	....
....	9 92	9 92	....	....	9 92
7, 000 00	....	7, 000 00	7, 000 00	.............т......	....
12 00	....	1, 793 71	....	1, 793 71	....
7, 000 00	....	12 00	12 00	....	....
....	....	7, 000 00	7, 000 00	....	....
190 00	....	85 18	....	85 18	....
5, 000 00	....	190 00	42 00	....	148 00
4, 000 00	....	5, 000 00	5, 000 00	....	....
600 00	....	4, 000 00	4, 000 00	....	....
....	....	600 00	600 00	....	....
....	....	132 30	....	132 30	....
....	....	16 50	....	....	16 50
600 00	....	600 00	600 00	....	....
....	....	392 45	3 00	389 45	....
....	4, 366 97	4, 624 47	51 25	....	4, 573 22
95, 000 00	....	95, 000 00	95, 000 00	....	....
....	24 16	24 16	....	....	24 16
17, 806 25	....	17, 806 25	17, 806 25	....	....
50 00	....	50 00	50 00	....	....
200 00	....	200 00	200 00	....	....
25, 000 00	....	25, 000 00	25, 000 00	....	....
1, 200 00	....	1, 200 00	1, 200 00	....	....
....	....	80 85	....	....	80 85
'	4, 358 00	14, 873 75	186 00	....	14, 687 75
....	....	10, 000 00	10, 000 00	....	.
3, 415 00	.	3, 415 00	3, 298 14	....	121 86
8, 215 00	....	8, 215 00	8, 215 00	....	....
360 00	................✔.	360 00	360 00	...................'	....
....	37 20	73, 864 94	73, 827 74	37 20	....
....	37 20	11, 322 85	11, 285 65	....	37 20
1, 618, 000 00	180 00	1, 618, 180 00	1, 492, 918 43	....	125, 261 57
1, 250 00	....	1, 250 00	1, 250 00	....	....
.2, 144 93	....	2, 989 65	1, 709 93	844 72	375 00
4, 327 02	61 00	5, 582 72	3, 681 02	....	1, 901 71
238, 008 02	....	238, 008 02	235, 560 73	....	2, 447 29
1, 434 00	....	1, 050 00	1, 434 00	516 00	....
8, 258 00	....	8, 258 00	8, 258 00	....	....
1, 242 00	....	1, 242 00	1, 242 00	....	....
47, 790 00	....	47, 790 00	46, 790 00	....	1, 000 00
87 00	....	231 12	87 00	144 12	....
3, 082 50	....	3, 082 50	3, 082 50	....	....
2, 785, 995 70	19, 283 03	2, 928, 934 33	2, 750, 466 47	16, 551 10	161, 916 76

STATEMENT *exhibiting the BALANCES of APPRO*

Specific objects of appropriations.	Year.	Vol.	Page or section.	Balances of appropriations, July 1, 1879.
Civil—Continued.				
Brought forward				$123, 655 60
Contingent expenses House—Continued:				
Pages	1880	21	24, 56	
Pay of folders	1877	}		22 94
	1878	}		
Do	1878			4, 527 84
Do	1879			
Do	1880	21	24	
Materials for folding	1879			
Do	1880	21	24, 252	
Fuel for heating apparatus	1878			4, 512 95
Do	1879			1, 939 79
Do	1880	21	24, 280	
Horses and wagons	1880	21	24	
Stationery and newspapers	1878			3, 197 61
Do	1879	21	56, 252	
Do	1880	21	23	
Furniture and repairs	1878			828 76
Do	1879			
Do	1880	21	24; 65, 252	
Packing-boxes	1880	21	24	
Cartage	1878			35 00
Do	1879			
Do	1880	21	24	
Miscellaneous items	1878*			
Do	1878	21	252, 281	56 23
Do	1879			3
Do	1880	21	25, 281, 252	
Salaries of Capitol police	1878			17
Do	1879			16
Do	1880	21	23	
Capitol police, contingent fund	1879			
Do	1880	21	23	
Postage House of Representatives	1880	21	23	
Reporting testimony before committees House of Representatives	1878			495 40
Do	1879			69 60
Payment for contesting seats Forty-sixth Congress, act June 16, 1880		21	279 }	
Payment for services rendered under Doorkeeper and Sergeant-at-Arms	1878			983 79
Payment to widow of A. M. Lay, deceased		21	279	
Payment to C. H. Reisinger, John A. Travis, and others	1877	}		689 99
	1878	}		
Investigation of epidemic diseases House of Representatives				15, 500 00
Cleaning Statuary Hall	1879	}		720 00
	1880	} 21	280	
Reimburse N. G. Ordway, late Sergeant-at-Arms				36 52
Summary reports of the Commissioners of Claims, House of Representatives	1879	}		1, 000 00
	1880	}		
One month's extra pay to annual employés House of Representatives, joint resolution July 1	1879	21	53	
Payment to widow and heirs of Hon. Rush Clark, deceased		21	52	
Engraving and printing portraits of the late Representatives Leonard, Quinn, Welch, Williams, Douglas, Hartridge, and Schleicher		21	399	
Salaries Office of Public Printer		21	23	
Contingent expenses Office of Public Printer	1878			8 83
Do	1879			200 00
Do	1880	21	23	
Public Printing and Binding	1878			128, 245 15
Do	1879			25, 962 78
Do	1880	{ 20	{ 23, 70, 72 }	
		21	134, 242 }	
Printing and binding 1st and 2d vols. Catalogue of Library Surgeon-General's Office		21	23	
Telephonic connection between the Capitol and Government Printing Office	1879	21	252	2 14
Do	1880	20	400	
Fire-escape ladders Government Printing Office	1879			756 00
Fire extinguishers Government Printing Office	1880	20	399	
Printing Reports of Commissioner of Agriculture	1878			32, 543 57
Salaries Library of Congress	1878			
Carried forward				348, 505 79

*And prior years.

PRIATIONS UNEXPENDED June 30, 1879, *&c.*—Continued.

Appropriations for the fiscal year ending June 30, 1880.	Repayments made during the fiscal year 1880.	Aggregate available for the fiscal year ending June 30, 1880.	Payments during the fiscal year ending June 30, 1880.	Amounts carried to the surplus fund June 30, 1880.	Balances of appropriations, June 30, 1880.
$2,785,995 70	$19,283 03	$2,928,934 33	$2,750,466 47	$16,551 10	$161,916 76
17,030 00		17,030 00	17,030 00		
		22 94		22 94	
		4,527 84		4,527 84	
	19 53	19 53			19 53
19,200 00		19,200 00	19,188 31		11 69
	37 02	37 02			37 02
17,000 00		17,000 00	14,000 00		3,000 00
		4,512 95		4,512 95	
	519 48	2,459 27			2,459 27
10,016 00		10,016 00	8,200 00		1,816 00
5,000 00		5,000 00	5,000 00		
	211 58	3,409 19		3,409 19	
38,550 00	139 44	38,689 44	26,952 67		11,736 77
43,300 00	874 12	44,174 12	43,300 00		874 12
		323 70		323 70	
	1,988 56	1,988 56			1,988 56
12,500 00		12,500 00	11,000 00		1,500 00
2,200 00		2,200 00	2,200 00		
		35 00		35 00	
	16 90	16 90			16 90
700 00		700 00	700 00		
	759 81	759 81			759 81
		914 23		56 23	
858 00		858 00	858 00		
	3,465 49	2,465 52	185 52		2,280 00
70,580 00	473 17	71,053 17	52,999 76		18,053 41
		17		17	
		16			16
17,750 00		17,750 00	17,704 20		45 80
	30 73	30 73			30 73
50 00		50 00	50 00		
600 00		600 00	600 00		
		495 40			495 40
		69 60			69 60
7,000 00		7,000 00	1,500 00		5,500 00
		983 79		983 79	
6,000 00		6,000 00	6,000 00		
		689 99		689 99	
	1,506 93	17,006 93			17,006 93
400 00		1,130 00	1,130 00		
		36 52			36 52
	165 00	1,165 00	1,000 00		165 00
19,465 49	83 33	19,548 82	19,548 82		
6,000 00		6,000 00	6,000 00		
3,466 00		3,466 00	3,460 00		
13,600 00		13,600 00	13,600 00		
		8 83	8 25	58	
		200 00	156 05		43 95
2,000 00		2,000 00	1,500 00		500 00
		128,245 15	4,846 00	118,245 15	5,154 00
	26,271 82	52,254 60	51,579 05		675 55
1,911,000 00	165,427 64	2,076,427 64	2,011,722 96		64,704 68
20,000 00		20,000 00	9,718 32		10,281 68
37 50		39 64			39 64
300 00		300 00	200 00		100 00
		756 00	503 30		252 70
1,000 00		1,000 00	1,000 00		
		32,543 57		32,543 57	
	84 78	84 78			84 78
5,031,596 69	220,308 36	5,597,412 84	5,103,903 68	181,936 98	311,572 18

394

STATEMENT *exhibiting the BALANCES of APPRO*

Specific objects of appropriations.	Year.	Statutes. Vol.	Page or section.	Balances of appropriations, July 1, 1879.
CIVIL—Continued.				
Brought forward				$345,505 79
Salaries Library of Congress	1880	21	4, 26	
Increase Library of Congress	1880	21	23	
Contingent expenses Library of Congress	1879			
Do	1880	21	23	
Works of art for the Capitol	1876			604 57
Do		21	26	
Salaries Botanic Garden	1878			35 16
Do	1880	21	23	
Improving Botanic Garden	1880	21	23, 236	
Improving buildings Botanic Garden	1878			1 19
Do	1880	20	370	
Salaries judges, &c., Court of Claims	1878			244 67
Do	1880	21	23	
Reporting decisions, &c., Court of Claims	1880	21	23	
Contingent expenses Court of Claims	1880	21	23	
Payment of judgments of Court of Claims		21	41, 252	2,418 91
Salaries Southern Claims Commission	1879			1,777 74
Do	1880	21	29	
Salaries and expenses of agents Southern Claims Commission.	1880	21	29	
Salaries and expenses of agents Southern Claims Commission (reappropriated)		21	244	
Salaries and expenses of agents and clerks Southern Claims Commission	1879			1,890 00
Do				594 76
Contingent expenses Southern Claims Commission	1879			17,000 00
Do	1880	21	29	
Salary of the President United States		21	23	
Salary of the Vice-President United States		21	23	
Salaries Executive Office	1880	21	23	
Contingent expenses Executive Office	1878			19
Do	1879			
Do	1880	21	23, 236	
Salaries Department of State	1878			2,562 25
Do	1879			1,173 10
Do	1880	21	23, 230	
Proof-reading, Department of State	1878			991 50
Do	1879			550 00
Do	1880	21	23	
Stationery, furniture, &c., Department of State	1878			427 48
Do	1879			1,500 00
Do	1880	21	23	
Books and maps, Department of State	1880	21	23	
Lithographing, Department of State	1878			416 00
Do	1879			100 00
Do	1880	21	23	
Rent of stable and wagon-shed, Department of State	1880	21	23	
Postage, Department of State	1877	21	239	
Editing, publishing, and distributing Revised and Annual Statutes, Department of State	1878			27,321 99
Do	1879			3,150 00
Do	1880	21	23	
Contingent expenses Department of State	1878			5,243 60
Do	1879			3,100 00
Do	1880	21	23	
International Remonetization of Silver	1879	21	26	
International Bureau of Weights and Measures	1879			19
Do	1880	20	382	
Expenses of foreign missions and under the neutrality act	1879			10,000 00
Cumming's edition of Hickey's Constitution of the United States				50
North American Ethnology, Smithsonian Institution	1880	20	397	
International Exposition at Paris	1878			9,972 69
International Exposition at Vienna				2,961 34
Smithsonian Institution				446,356 49
Expenses of Smithsonian Institution			R. S. 3689	
Purchase of the stereotype plates of final reports of Centennial Exhibition of 1876, joint resolution June 27, 1879		21	54	
Portrait of the late Professor Joseph Henry		21	46	
International Exhibition at Sydney and Melbourne, Australia	1879	} 21	49, 239	
	1880			
Berlin Fishery Exhibition, joint resolution February 16, 1880		21	301	
Revising and editing consular regulations		20	274	
Carried forward				890,579 51

PRIATIONS UNEXPENDED June 30, 1879, &c.—Continued.

Appropriations for the fiscal year ending June 30, 1880.	Repayments made during the fiscal year 1880.	Aggregate available for the fiscal year ending June 30, 1880.	Payments during the fiscal year ending June 30, 1880.	Amounts carried to the surplus fund June 30, 1880.	Balances of appropriations, June 30, 1880.
$5,031,598 60	$220,308 36	$5,597,412 84	$5,103,903 68	$181,936 98	$311,572 18
36,840 00	....	36,840 00	35,700 00	....	1,140 00
14,000 00	....	14,000 00	14,000 00	....	....
....	1 00	1 00	....	....	1 00
1,500 00	....	1,500 00	1,500 00	....	....
....	....	694 57	....	694 57	....
5,000 00	....	5,000 00	5,000 00	....	....
....	....	35 16	....	35 16	....
10,000 00	9 00	10,009 00	10,000 00	....	9 00
4,850 00	....	4,850 00	4,850 00	....	....
....	....	1 19	....	1 19	....
5,495 00	....	5,495 00	5,495 00	....	....
....	....	244 67	....	244 67	....
29,840 00	....	29,840 00	29,840 00	....	....
1,000 00	....	1,000 00	1,000 00	....	....
2,500 00	....	2,500 00	2,500 00	....	....
285,803 54	....	288,217 45	137,062 24	....	151,155 21
....	....	1,777 74	....	....	1,777 74
17,169 21	....	17,169 21	16,739 65	429 56	....
6,508 24	79 88	6,678 12	6,000 00	79 88	598 24
24 60	....	24 60	....	....	24 60
....	492 19	2,382 19	....	2,382 19	....
....	....	594 76	....	594 76	....
....	422 63	17,422 63	....	17,422 63	....
3,401 76	98 24	3,500 00	3,500 00	....	....
50,000 00	....	50,000 00	50,000 00	....	....
8,000 00	....	8,000 00	8,000 00	....	....
31,464 00	....	31,464 00	31,464 00	....	....
....	....	19	....	19	....
....	7 24	7 24	....	....	7 24
7,000 00	....	7,000 00	7,000 00	....	....
....	....	2,552 25	....	2,552 25	....
....	9 07	1,182 17	207 25	....	974 92
113,340 00	....	113,340 00	111,201 02	....	2,138 98
....	....	991 60	....	991 60	....
2,000 00	112 15	662 15	....	....	662 15
....	....	2,000 00	1,800 00	....	200 00
....	317 33	744 81	317 33	427 48	....
....	....	1,500 00	641 67	....	858 33
5,000 00	....	5,000 00	4,000 00	....	1,000 00
2,000 00	....	2,000 00	1,500 00	....	500 00
....	....	416 00	....	416 00	....
....	27 50	127 50	....	....	127 50
1,200 00	....	1,200 00	1,200 00	....	....
600 00	....	600 00	600 00	....	....
9 68	....	9 68	....	....	9 68
....	....	27,321 09	....	27,321 09	....
....	....	3,150 00	250 00	....	2,900 00
5,000 00	....	5,000 00	....	....	5,000 00
....	....	8,243 60	....	8,243 60	....
....	....	3,100 00	....	....	3,100 00
11,200 00	....	11,200 00	10,000 00	....	1,200 00
20,000 00	....	20,000 00	9,080 00	....	10,920 00
....	....	19	....	....	19
1,900 00	....	1,000 00	1,000 00	....	....
....	....	10,000 00	....	....	10,000 00
....	....	80	....	....	80
*20,000 00	....	20,000 00	20,000 00	....	....
....	....	9,972 80	5,000 00	....	4,972 69
....	....	2,863 34	....	....	2,863 34
....	....	448,358 49	....	....	448,358 49
39,060 00	....	39,060 00	39,060 00	....	....
8,600 00	....	8,600 00	8,600 00	....	....
500 00	....	500 00	491 00	....	9 00
28,000 00	....	28,000 00	15,786 40	....	12,213 60
20,000 00	....	20,000 00	18,306 50	....	1,693 50
3,000 00	....	3,000 00	3,000 00	....	....
5,833,494 72	221,884 59	6,046,258 82	5,726,555 74	243,774 70	975,928 36

* Transferred from Interior Civil Ledger.

STATEMENT exhibiting the BALANCES of APPRO

Specific objects of appropriations.	Year.	Statutes. Vol.	Page or section.	Balances of appropriations, July 1, 1879.
CIVIL—Continued.				
Brought forward				$690,879 51
Salaries of ministers	1878			3,598 57
Do	1879			41,179 02
Do	1880	20	297	
Salaries secretaries of legations	1879			4,421 53
Do	1879			5,142 62
Do	1880	20	268	
Contingent expenses foreign missions	*1871			17 56
Do	*1877			
Do	1878			27,551 51
Do	1879			11,774 21
Do	1880	20	266	
Salaries consular service	*1871			178 57
Do	1872			336 63
Do	1873			2,419 35
Do	1874			2,355 99
Do	1875			5,130 56
Do	*1877			
Do	1878			13,466 74
Do	1879	21	239	114,147 82
Do	1880	20	266	
Allowance for consular clerks	1879			30,257 55
Do	1880	20	273	
Shipping and discharging seamen	1879			3,041 61
Do	1880	20	273	
Salaries interpreters to consulates in China, Japan, and Siam	*1871			542 87
Do	1878			4,291 90
Do	1879			8,752 30
Do	1880	20	273	
Salaries consular officers not citizens	1878			5,322 61
Do	1879			1,781 65
Do	1880	20	273	
Salaries of marshals for consular courts	1878			986 04
Do	1879			2,939 81
Do	1880	20	273	
Expenses interpreters, guards, &c., Turkish Dominions	1878			44 76
Do	1879			708 56
Do	1880	20	273	
Loss on bills of exchange, consular service	1878			6,496 50
Do	1879			8,000 00
Do	1880	20	273	
Contingent expenses United States consulates	1872			420 95
Do	1874			308 02
Do	1875			182 34
Do	1876			1,484 20
Do	1877			1,392 34
Do	*1877	21	283	
Do	1878	21	239	
Do	1879	21	239	13,625 48
Do	1880	20	273	
Salaries United States and Spanish Claims Commission	1878			275 78
Do	1880	20	274	
Contingent expenses United States and Spanish Claims Commission	1878			240 78
Do	1879			84 00
Do	1880	20	274	
Rent of prison for American convicts in China	1879			1,127 78
Do	1880	20	274	
Wages of keepers, &c., for American convicts in China	1879			5,317 85
Do	1880	20	274	
Rent of prisons, wages of keepers, &c., for American convicts in Siam and Turkey	1879			1,000 82
Do	1880	20	274	
Rent of prisons for American convicts in Japan	1879			450 00
Do	1880	20	274	
Wages of keepers, &c., prison for American convicts in Japan	1879			3,108 19
Do	1880	20	274	
Rent of court-house and jail in Japan	1878			150 00
Do	1879			450 00
Do	1880	20	274	
Prisons for American convicts	1878			6,587 50
Buildings and grounds United States legation in China	1878			100 00
Do	1879			850 00
Do	1880	20	274	
Carried forward				1,232,988 98

*And prior years.

PRIATIONS UNEXPENDED June 30, 1879, &c.—Continued.

Appropriations for the fiscal year ending June 30, 1880.	Repayments made during the fiscal year 1880.	Aggregate available for the fiscal year ending June 30, 1880.	Payments during the fiscal year ending June 30, 1880.	Amounts carried to the surplus fund June 30, 1880.	Balances of appropriations, June 30, 1880.
$5,833,494 72	$221,884 59	$5,946,258 82	$5,728,555 74	$243,774 70	$975,928 38
		3,598 57	1,267 15	2,331 42	
280,500 00		41,179 62	29,529 36		11,650 26
		280,500 00	257,509 41		22,990 59
		4,421 53	56 47	4,365 06	
		5,142 62	5,142 62		
39,700 00	......@....	39,700 00	31,650 00		8,050 00
		17 56		17 56	
	597 12	507 12		597 12	
		27,551 51	13,750 00	13,801 51	
		11,774 21	5,526 35		6,247 86
80,000 00		80,000 00	73,054 82		6,945 18
	....r....	178 57			178 57
		336 63			336 63
		2,419 35			2,419 35
		2,355 99			2,355 99
		5,130 56			5,130 58
	138 25	138 25		138 26	
12,121 25	609 90	14,076 64	5,321 41	8,755 23	
381,180 00	13,194 40	139,463 47	137,949 78		1,513 69
	5,332 15	368,432 15	274,930 81		111,501 34
		30,257 55	17,244 69		13,012 86
52,500 00		52,500 00	26,470 45		26,029 55
6,000 00		3,041 61	2,685 00		356 61
		6,000 00	2,610 68		3,389 32
		542 87			542 87
		4,291 90		4,291 90	
		8,752 30	5,567 31		3,184 99
15,500 00	249 50	15,749 50	8,598 92		7,150 58
		5,322 61		5,322 61	
		1,781 65	322 61		1,459 04
3,000 00		3,000 00	554 21		2,445 79
		986 04		986 04	
7,000 00	82 00	2,999 81	2,676 24		283 57
		7,082 00	5,611 72		1,470 28
		44 76		44 76	
	206 87	914 93	909 63		5 30
8,000 00		3,000 00	2,375 55		624 45
		6,496 50		6,496 50	
		8,000 00	3,032 60		4,967 40
8,000 00		8,000 00	11 18		7,968 82
		428 95		428 95	
		308 02			308 02
		182 34			182 34
		1,484 20			1,484 20
		1,392 34			1,392 34
1,619 86	563 99	2,183 85	1,595 86	563 99	27 00
17,637 17		17,637 17	13,996 39		3,640 78
21,929 80	9,796 54	45,350 82	44,029 26		421 80
115,000 00	750 00	115,750 00	114,642 35		1,107 65
		275 78		275 78	
7,200 00		7,200 00	6,318 13		881 87
		240 78		240 78	
		84 00			84 00
750 00		750 00	750 00		
		1,127 78	1,116 66		11 12
1,500 00		1,500 00	744 44		755 56
	1,476 66	6,794 51	4,158 65		2,635 86
9,500 00	864 44	10,364 44	5,594 84		4,769 60
		1,060 82	319 44		741 38
2,000 00		2,000 00	1,015 39		984 61
		450 00	300 00		150 00
750 00		750 00	450 00		300 00
5,000 00		3,108 19	1,215 30		1,892 89
		5,030 00	2,196 22		2,803 78
		150 00		150 00	
		450 00			450 00
3,850 00		3,850 00	3,400 00		450 00
		6,587 50		6,587 50	
		100 00			100 00
		850 00	557 47		292 53
3,100 00		3,100 00	2,250 00		850 00
6,911,752 80	255,744 91	6,400,486 69	6,846,462 11	299,287 68	1,254,756 98

STATEMENT *exhibiting the BALANCES of APPRO*

Specific objects of appropriations.	Year.	Statutes.		Balances of appropriations, July 1, 1879.
		Vol.	Page or section.	

CIVIL—Continued.

Specific objects of appropriations.	Year.	Vol.	Page or section.	Balances of appropriations, July 1, 1879.
Brought forward				$1,232,388 98
Bringing home criminals	1878			4,237 60
Do	1879			3,442 76
Do	1880	20	274	
Relief and protection of American seamen	1877*	21	253	
Do	1878			37,501 88
Do	1879			20,622 63
Do	1880	20	274	
Rescuing shipwrecked American seamen	1878			1,845 45
Do	1879			2,148 00
Do	1880	20	274	
Annual expenses of Cape Spartel light on coast of Morocco	1880	20	274	
Allowance to widows or heirs of diplomatic officers who die abroad	1878			4,707 57
Do	1879			3,597 04
Do	1880	20	274	
Expenses under the neutrality act	1878			6,930 35
Do	1879			4,450 00
Do	1880	20	274	
Commissioner to international penitentiary congress at Stockholm (reappropriated)				726 78
Survey of boundary between United States and British Possessions				7,013 87
Tribunal of arbitration at Geneva				5,184 60
Estates of decedents, trust fund				43,236 81
Payment for certain lands ceded by the United States to Great Britain under treaty of Washington, July 9, 1842; act March 3, 1877, section 2				6,912 50
Compensation and expenses of commissioners to China.... {	1880 1881	} 21	133	
Reimbursement to Charles Dougherty for expenses of consulate, Londonderry		21	29	
Reimbursement to B. R. Lewis, consular agent at China		21	253	
Salaries office Secretary of the Treasury	1878			
Do	1879			
Do	1880	21	23	
Salaries temporary clerks Treasury Department	1878			
Do	1879			
Salaries office Secretary of the Treasury (loans and currency)	1878			
Do	1879			
Do	1880	21	23	
Salaries office Supervising Architect	1878			
Do	1879			
Do	1880	21	23	
Salaries office First Comptroller	1878			16 88
Do	1879			
Do	1880	21	23, 26	
Salaries office Second Comptroller	1878			12 90
Do	1880	21	23	
Salaries office Commissioner of Customs	1878			9 19
Do	1880	21	23	
Salaries office First Auditor	1878			48 69
Do	1879			
Do	1880	21	23, 26	
Salaries office First Auditor (loans)	1878			
Do	1880	21	23	
Salaries office Second Auditor	1878			
Do	1879			
Do	1880	21	23, 68	
Salaries office Third Auditor	1877*	21	254	76 44
Do	1878			
Do	1879			
Do	1880	21	23	
Salaries office Fourth Auditor	1878			9 85
Do	1879			
Do	1880	21	23	
Salaries office Fifth Auditor	1878			22 52
Do	1879			
Do	1880	21	23	
Salaries office Sixth Auditor	1878			64 70
Do	1879			
Do	1880	21	23, 26	
Salaries office Treasurer	1878			182 15
Do	1879			
Carried forward				1,385,986 14

* And prior years.

PRIATIONS UNEXPENDED June 30, 1879, &c.—Continued.

Appropriations for the fiscal year ending June 30, 1880.	Repayments made during the fiscal year 1880.	Aggregate available for the fiscal year ending June 30, 1880.	Payments during the fiscal year ending June 30, 1880.	Amounts carried to the surplus fund June 30, 1880.	Balances of appropriations, June 30, 1880.
$0,911,752 80	$255,744 91	$8,400,426 89	$6,846,402 11	$299,267 86	$1,254,756 92
....	....	4,237 60	....	4,237 60	....
....	....	3,442 76	1,639 71	....	1,803 05
5,000 00	....	5,000 00	....	....	5,000 00
150 00	....	150 00	150 00	....	....
....	41 23	37,543 11	930 23	36,612 88	....
....	2,569 80	23,192 43	21,040 23	....	2,152 20
50,000 00	2,620 44	52,020 44	33,244 16	....	19,376 28
....	....	1,845 45	760 02	1,845 45	....
....	....	2,148 00	....	....	1,387 98
4,500 00	....	4,500 00	1,162 00	....	3,338 00
285 00	....	285 00	285 00	....	....
....	....	4,707 57	....	4,707 57	....
....	....	3,507 04	....	....	3,507 04
5,000 00	....	5,000 00	....	....	5,000 00
....	....	6,930 35	....	6,930 35	....
....	....	4,450 00	....	....	4,450 00
5,000 00	....	5,000 00	....	....	5,000 00
....	....	726 78	....	....	726 78
....	....	7,013 87	....	....	7,013 87
....	....	5,134 60	3,952 21	....	1,232 39
....	11,125 15	54,361 96	10,015 44	....	44,346 52
....	....	6,912 50	283 25	....	6,899 25
37,000 00	....	37,000 00	6,656 00	....	30,344 00
1,000 00	....	1,000 00	1,000 00	....	....
550 00	....	550 00	550 00	....	....
....	17 35	17 35	....	17 35	....
....	13 15	13 15	....	....	13 15
278,600 00	....	278,600 00	278,600 00	....	....
....	109 80	109 80	....	109 80	....
....	1 78	1 78	....	....	1 78
....	98 90	98 90	10	98 80	....
....	15 50	15 50	....	....	15 50
83,800 00	....	83,800 00	83,800 00	....	....
....	8 94	8 94	....	8 94	....
....	35 54	35 54	....	....	35 54
19,420 00	....	19,420 00	13,420 00	....	....
....	....	16 88	....	16 88	....
....	2 72	2 72	....	....	2 72
64,400 00	....	64,400 00	64,400 00	....	....
....	....	12 90	....	12 90	....
88,000 00	....	88,000 00	88,000 00	....	....
....	....	9 19	....	9 19	....
49,630 00	....	49,630 00	49,630 00	....	....
....	....	48 69	....	48 69	....
53,610 00	2 01	53,610 00	53,610 00	....	2 01
....	15 38	15 38	....	15 38	....
14,800 00	213 94	14,800 00	14,800 00	213 94	....
....	1 77	1 77	....	....	1 77
204,603 00	....	204,603 00	204,603 00	....	....
210 00	....	210 00	210 00	....	....
....	....	78 44	....	78 44	....
....	3 15	3 15	....	....	3 15
191,370 00	....	191,370 00	191,370 00	....	....
....	....	5 85	....	5 85	....
....	15 28	15 28	....	....	15 28
66,390 00	....	66,390 00	66,390 00	....	....
....	....	22 52	....	22 52	....
....	1 42	1 42	....	....	1 42
40,450 00	....	40,450 00	40,450 00	....	....
....	....	64 70	....	64 70	....
....	7 28	7 28	....	....	7 28
323,010 00	....	323,010 00	323,010 00	....	....
....	....	182 15	....	182 15	....
....	133 24	133 24	....	....	133 24
8,501,530 80	273,798 63	10,160,315 57	8,409,423 46	354,505 04	1,396,387 07

400

REPORT ON THE FINANCES.

STATEMENT *exhibiting the BALANCES of APPRO*

Specific objects of appropriations.	Year.	Vol.	Page or section.	Balances of appropriations, July 1, 1879.
CIVIL—Continued.				
Brought forward				$1,385,986 14
Salaries office Treasurer	1880	21	23	
Salaries office Treasurer (loans)	1878			
Salaries office Treasurer (national currency reimbursable)	1878			3,453 25
Do	1879			
Do	1880	21	23	
Salaries office Register	1878			2 18
Do	1879			
Do	1880	21	23	
Salaries office Register (loans)	1878			66
Do	1879			
Do	1880	21	23	
Salaries office Comptroller of the Currency	1878			512 14
Do	1879			
Do	1880	21	23	
Salaries office Comptroller of the Currency (national currency, reimbursable)	1878			42 12
Do	1879			
Do	1880	21	23	
Salaries office Commissioner of Internal Revenue	1878			2 10
Do	1879			
Do	1880	21	23	
Salaries office Light-House Board	1880	21	23	
Salaries office Bureau of Statistics	1878			39
Do	1879			
Do	1880	21	23	
Salaries office Life-Saving Service	1880	21	27	
Examination of national banks and bank plates	1880	21	23	
Stationery for Treasury Department	1878			1,089 99
Do	1879			3,021 88
Do	1880	21	23	
Postage for Treasury Department	1878			100 00
Do	1879			138 83
Do	1880	21	23	
Contingent expenses Treasury Department, binding, newspapers, &c	1878			
Do	1880	21	23, 242	
Contingent expenses Treasury Department, investigation of accounts, traveling expenses	1878			1,029 77
Do	1879			
Do	1880	21	23	
Contingent expenses Treasury Department, freight, telegrams, &c	1877*	21	254	
Do	1878			
Do	1879			76
Do	1880	21	23	
Contingent expenses Treasury Department, rent	1878			8,825 00
Do	1880	21	23	
Contingent expenses Treasury Department, horses, wagons, &c	1880	21	23	
Contingent expenses Treasury Department, ice	1880	21	23, 242	
Contingent expenses Treasury Department, fuel, &c	1880	21	23, 242	
Contingent expenses Treasury Department, gas, &c	1879			
Do	1880	21	23, 242	
Contingent expenses Treasury Department, carpets and repairs	1880	21	23	
Contingent expenses Treasury Department, furniture, &c	1879			796 01
Do	1880	21	23, 242	
Contingent expenses Treasury Department, miscellaneous items	1879			
Do	1880	21	23, 242	309 48
Collecting statistics relating to commerce	1878			
Do	1879			
Do	1880	21	23	
Illustration for report on food-fishes	1880	20	383	
Expenses of inquiry respecting food-fishes	1880	20	383	
Propagation of food-fishes	1877*	21	254	
Do	1878			5,221 00
Do	1879			
Do	1879	21	150	62,000 00
Do	1880			
Do	1880	21	264	
Do	1881			
Carried forward				1,467,531 73

* And prior years.

PRIATIONS UNEXPENDED June 30, 1879, &c.—Continued.

Appropriations for the fiscal year ending June 30, 1880.	Repayments made during the fiscal year 1880.	Aggregate available for the fiscal year ending June 30, 1880.	Payments during the fiscal year ending June 30, 1880.	Amounts carried to the surplus fund June 30, 1880.	Balances of appropriations, June 30, 1880.
$8, 501, 530 80	$272, 798 63	$10, 160, 315 57	$8, 406, 423 46	$354, 505 04	$1, 396, 387 07
273, 600 00	....	273, 600 00	273, 600 00	....	....
....	87 83	87 83	....	87 83	....
....	....	3, 453 25	....	3, 453 25	....
....	5, 447 70	5, 447 70	....	....	5, 447 70
101, 584 00	....	101, 584 00	83, 980 00	....	17, 604 00
....	....	2 18	....	2 18	....
....	8 40	8 40	....	....	8 40
57, 750 00	....	57, 750 00	57, 750 00	....	....
....	....	66	....	66	....
....	21 01	21 01	....	....	21 01
100, 840 00	....	100, 840 00	100, 840 00	....	....
....	....	512 14	....	512 14	....
....	1, 698 25	1, 698 25	....	....	1, 698 25
101, 400 00	....	101, 400 00	101, 400 00	....	....
....	....	42 12	....	42 12	....
....	03	03	....	....	03
22, 220 00	....	22, 220 00	22, 220 00	....	....
....	....	2 10	....	2 10	....
....	2 07	2 07	....	....	2 07
253, 330 00	....	253, 330 00	253, 330 00	....	....
14, 080 00	....	14, 080 00	14, 080 00	....	....
....	....	39	....	39	....
40, 760 00	118 61	118 61	....	....	118 61
19, 420 00	....	40, 760 00	40, 760 00	....	....
2, 000 00	....	19, 420 00	19, 420 00	....	....
....	....	2, 000 00	1, 000 00	....	1, 000 00
....	....	1, 089 99	....	1, 089 99	....
40, 000 00	3, 815 25	6, 837 13	5, 537 50	....	1, 299 63
....	44, 585 04	84, 585 04	84, 285 96	....	249 08
....	....	100 00	....	100 00	....
....	....	138 83	111 55	....	27 28
201, 500 00	....	201, 500 00	1, 338 50	....	200, 161 50
....	1 82	1 82	....	1 82	....
12, 000 00	....	12, 000 00	12, 000 00	....	....
....	71 57	1, 101 34	....	1, 101 34	....
....	154 94	154 94	....	....	154 94
2, 500 00	1 60	2, 501 60	2, 500 00	....	1 60
101 40	....	101 40	....	....	101 40
....	704 81	704 81	....	794 81	....
....	....	78	....	....	78
4, 000 00	50	4, 000 50	4, 000 00	....	50
....	....	3, 825 00	....	3, 825 00	....
7, 800 00	....	7, 800 00	7, 800 00	....	....
6, 000 00	....	6, 000 00	6, 000 00	....	....
8, 700 00	....	8, 700 00	8, 700 00	....	....
10, 250 00	....	10, 250 00	10, 250 00	....	....
17, 500 00	856 35	856 35	17, 500 00	....	....
7, 000 00	....	7, 000 00	7, 000 00	....	....
....	333 97	1, 129 98	1, 129 98	....	....
30, 000 00	970 96	30, 970 96	30, 820 40	....	150 56
....	79 91	79 91	79 91	....	....
25, 000 00	....	25, 000 00	25, 000 00	....	....
....	....	309 48	....	309 48	....
....	....	43	....	....	43
8, 800 00	700 00	9, 500 00	9, 500 00	....	....
1, 000 00	....	1, 000 00	1, 000 00	....	....
3, 500 00	....	3, 500 00	3, 500 00	....	....
45 00	....	45 00	....	....	45 00
....	11 78	5, 232 78	5, 232 78	....	....
15, 000 00	....	77, 000 00	69, 067 83	....	7, 932 17
105, 000 00	....	105, 000 00	....	....	105, 000 00
9, 994, 211 30	332, 511 46	11, 794, 254 38	9, 091, 016 24	365, 828 15	1, 737, 411 99

26 F

STATEMENT *exhibiting the* BALANCES *of* APPRO

Specific objects of appropriations.	Year.	Statutes.		Balance of appropriations, July 1, 1879.
		Vol.	Page or section.	
CIVIL—Continued.				
Brought forward				$1,467,531 72
Steam vessels for food-fishes	1879 1880	} 21	150	45,000 00
Expenses of national currency	1873			10
Do	1877*	21	254	
Do	1878			1,903 39
Do	1879			27,470 78
Do	1880	20	383	
Transportation of United States securities	1876			14,005 05
Do	1877*	21	254	
Do	1878			10,171 75
Do	1879			38,307 83
Do	1880	20	383	
Vaults, safes, and locks public buildings	1877*	21	254	
Do	1878			
Do	1879			10,000 00
Do	1880	{ 20 { 21	384 241	}
Salaries Bureau of Engraving and Printing	1878			409 80
Do	1879			
Do	1880	21	23	
Labor and expenses Bureau of Engraving and Printing	1878			323,686 42
Do	1879			13,906 85
Do	1880	20	379	
Extra compensation to discharged employés Bureau of Engraving and Printing				896 10
Building for Bureau of Engraving and Printing		21	360	156,014 46
Plans for public buildings	1879			
Do	1880	20	384	
Suppressing counterfeiting and other crimes	1880	{ 20 { 21	384 241	}
Suppressing counterfeiting and fraud	1878			6,611 40
Do	1879			4,843.37
Examination of rebel archives and records of captured and abandoned property	1878			2 26
Do	1879			434 46
Do	1880	20	384	
Contingent expenses national currency, reimbursable, office Treasurer		18	399	
Lands and other property of the United States	1879			2,500 00
Do	1880	20	384	
Library Treasury Department	1880	20	385	
One month's pay to discharged employés Treasury Departm't	1880	21	56	
Export services relating to the metric system		21	62	
Removal of Bureau of Engraving and Printing	1880	20	379	
Postage-stamps, Executive Departments	1879 1880	}		10,030 40
Purchase and management of Louisville and Portland Canal				590,045 09
Inquiries into causes of steam-boiler explosions (reappropriated)				183 79
Revision and consolidation of statutes, act June 27, 1866				
Trust-fund interest for support of free schools in South Carolina		R. S.	3680	1,480 00
Payment to James Flynn, attorney for Benjamin N. Disbrow		21	250	
Hayt's United States duties on imports, joint resolution July 1, 1879		21	56	
Polaris Report, Smithsonian Institution		21	239	
Coast and Geodetic Survey, Eastern Division	1880	{ 20 { 21	383 150	{
Coast and Geodetic Survey, Western Division	1880	{ 20 { 21	383 150	{
Repairs of vessels, Coast Survey	1878			
Do	1880	{ 20 { 21	382 150	{
Publishing observations, Coast Survey	1878			
General expenses, Coast Survey	1880	20	382	
Do	1878			
Do	1880	20	382	
Vessels for Coast Survey	1878			
Survey western coast United States	1878			
Payment to C. H. Evans for book on imports and duties		21	281	
Refunding national debt, 4 per cent		R. S.	3689	
Refunding national debt, 4½ per cent				8,952 46
Refunding national debt, 5 per cent				5,890 05
Carried forward				2,741,330 18

*And prior years.

PRIATIONS UNEXPENDED June 30, 1879, &c.—Continued.

Appropriations for the fiscal year ending June 30, 1880.	Repayments made during the fiscal year 1880.	Aggregate available for the fiscal year ending June 30, 1880.	Payments during the fiscal year ending June 30, 1880.	Amounts carried to the surplus fund June 30, 1880.	Balances of appropriations, June 30, 1880.
$9,994,211 20	$332,511 46	$11,794,254 38	$9,691,014 24	$365,826 15	$1,737,411 99
12,500 00	....	57,500 00	57,500 00	....	....
....	....	10	....	10	....
105 90	....	105 90	....	....	105 90
....	....	1,903 39	....	1,903 39	....
....	800 00	26,270 78	5,913 72	....	22,357 06
120,000 00	7,000 00	127,000 00	102,284 91	....	24,715 09
....	....	14,005 05	....	14,005 05	....
6 00	....	6 00	6 00	....	....
....	....	10,171 75	....	10,171 75	....
....	708 76	40,076 59	14,260 49	....	25,816 10
60,000 00	623 05	60,623 05	36,274 18	....	24,348 87
35 25	....	35 25	....	....	35 25
....	2,305 56	2,305 56	....	2,305 56	....
....	40 00	10,040 00	10,040 00	....	....
51,000 00	....	51,000 00	50,000 00	....	1,000 00
....	....	409 80	....	409 80	....
....	37	37	....	....	37
25,930 00	....	25,930 00	25,930 00	....	....
....	....	323,686 42	35 80	323,650 62	....
....	31,973 05	45,881 90	12,217 88	....	33,664 02
350,000 00	489,101 26	839,101 26	829,883 44	....	9,217 82
....	....	886 10	....	886 10	....
35,732 70	4,994 63	196,741 79	161,009 09	....	35,732 70
....	874 24	874 24	863 50	....	10 74
1,500 00	1,473 75	2,973 75	2,973 75	....	....
65,000 00	....	65,000 00	60,002 26	....	4,997 74
....	....	6,611 40	110 00	6,501 40	....
....	2,253 77	7,097 14	1,034 56	....	6,062 58
....	....	2 26	....	2 26	....
....	....	434 46	395 50	....	38 96
5,000 00	....	5,000 00	5,000 00	....	....
58,186 78	....	58,186 78	58,186 78	....	....
....	274 45	2,774 45	2 25	....	2,772 20
5,000 00	....	5,000 00	3,739 00	....	1,261 00
1,000 00	....	1,000 00	1,000 00	....	....
1,275 00	....	1,275 00	1,275 00	....	....
350 00	....	350 00	350 00	....	....
50,000 00	....	50,000 00	46,976 80	....	3,023 20
....	405 09	10,435 49	7,516 00	....	2,919 49
....	....	590,045 69	71,910 00	....	518,135 69
....	....	183 79	....	....	183 79
....	150 00	150 00	....	150 00	....
2,830 49	08	4,310 57	2,800 00	....	1,510 57
4,253 63	....	4,253 63	4,253 63	....	....
1,250 00	....	1,250 00	1,250 00	....	....
8,000 00	....	8,000 00	8,000 00	....	....
307,500 00	....	307,500 00	300,000 00	....	7,500 00
187,500 00	....	187,500 00	182,251 75	....	5,248 25
....	265 26	265 26	....	265 26	....
40,000 00	....	40,000 00	40,000 00	....	....
....	99 90	99 90	....	99 90	....
6,000 00	....	6,000 00	6,000 00	....	....
32,000 00	317 80	317 80	....	317 80	....
....	....	32,000 00	32,000 00	....	....
....	94 22	94 23	....	94 22	....
....	4 99	4 99	....	4 99	....
2,000 00	....	2,000 00	....	....	2,000 00
1,619,593 49	3,863 75	1,623,457 24	522,746 46	1,000,000 00	100,710 78
....	....	8,963 46	150 00	....	8,802 46
....	110 22	6,000 22	....	....	6,000 22
_3,047,760 44	889,245 67	16,669,336 24	12,367,156 99	1,726,595 35	2,588,583 90

STATEMENT exhibiting the BALANCES of APPRO

Specific objects of appropriations.	Year.	Statutes.		Balances of appropriations, July 1, 1879.
		Vol.	Page or section.	
CIVIL—Continued.				
Brought forward ...				$2,741,330 13
Refunding taxes illegally collected under direct tax laws, prior to July 1, 1875 ...				796 36
Refunding moneys erroneously received and covered into the Treasury ...		R. S.	3689	
Repayment for lands sold for direct taxes prior to July 1, 1875				1,300 00
Return of proceeds of captured and abandoned property		R. S.	3689	
Sinking fund Union Pacific Railroad Company		{ 20 21 }	{ 58 56 }	37 36
Sinking fund Central Pacific Railroad Company		{ 20 21 }	{ 58 56 }	32 92
Monument to mark the birth-place of George Washington ..		21	90	
Completion of the Washington Monument				144,016 93
Outstanding liabilities				331,231 13
Mail transportation Pacific Railroads.....................	1876	21	420	....
Do.................................	1877	21	420	....
Do.................................	1878	21	420	....
Do.................................	1879	21	420	....
Do.................................	1880	21	420	....
Refunding national banking associations excess of duty, prior to July 1, 1877		21	254	....
Preparation of receipts, expenditures, and appropriations of the government		21	243	....
Salaries office assistant United States treasurer, New York .	1878			1,200 55
Do..	1879			1,874 00
Do..	1880	21	23	....
Salaries office assistant United States treasurer, Boston......	1878			71 87
Do..	1879			275 80
Do..	1880	21	23	....
Salaries office assistant United States treasurer, San Francisco	1880	21	23	....
Salaries office assistant United States treasurer, Philadelphia	1879			....
Do..	1880	21	23	....
Salaries office assistant United States treasurer, Baltimore ..	1878			18 19
Do..	1880	21	23	....
Salaries office assistant United States treasurer, Saint Louis .	1878			24 70
Do..	1880	21	23	....
Salaries office assistant United States treasurer, Chicago ..	1880	21	23	....
Salaries office assistant United States treasurer, Cincinnati .	1880	21	23	....
Salaries office assistant United States treasurer, New Orleans	1880	21	23	....
Salaries office United States depositary, Tucson	1880	21	23	....
Checks and certificates of deposit, independent treasury.....	1878			467 19
Do..	1879	21	240	365 75
Do..	1880	21	23, 239	....
Salaries special agents, independent treasury	1878			....
Do..	1879			2,552 00
Do..	1880	21	23	....
Contingent expenses, independent treasury.................	1878			21,077 93
Do..	1879			7,557 71
Do..	1880	21	23	....
Salaries office Director of the Mint...................	1878			50
Do..	1879			....
Do..	1880	21	23	....
Contingent expenses, mints and assay offices	1878			5 99
Do..	1879			379 36
Do..	1880	21	23	....
Recoinage of gold and silver coins.....................	1877*	21	230	....
Do..	1878			970 50
Do..	1879			4,851 11
Do..	1880	21	23, 240	....
Coinage of standard silver dollar		20	25	....
Salaries United States mint at Philadelphia..............	1880	21	23	....
Wages of workmen United States mint at Philadelphia......	1878			427 69
Do..	1879			....
Do..	1880	21	23, 240	....
Contingent expenses United States mint at Philadelphia ...	1878			3,816 43
Do..	1879			....
Do..	1880	21	23, 240	....
Freight on bullion United States mint at Philadelphia......	1878			4,083 73
Do..	1879			2,480 75
Do..	1880	21	23	....
Salaries United States mint at San Francisco	1880	21	23	....
Wages of workmen United States mint at San Francisco ...	1878			8 19
Do..	1879			10,000 00
Do..	1880	21	23	....
Carried forward				3,281,189 77

*And prior years.

PRIATIONS UNEXPENDED June 30, 1879, &c.—Continued.

Appropriations for the fiscal year ending June 30, 1880.	Repayments made during the fiscal year 1880.	Aggregate available for the fiscal year ending June 30, 1880.	Payments during the fiscal year ending June 30, 1880.	Amounts carried to the surplus fund June 30, 1880.	Balances of appropriations, June 30, 1880.
$13,047,780 44	$880,245 67	$16,689,336 24	$12,357,156 99	$1,726,596 35	$2,585,582 90
....	....	796 36	....	796 36	....
400 00	....	400 00	400 00	....	....
....	....	1,300 00	....	1,300 00	....
75,454 50	....	75,454 50	75,454 50	....	....
343,728 73	....	343,760 09	192,230 63	....	151,545 46
442,892 49	....	442,925 41	287,790 49	....	155,134 92
3,000 00	....	3,000 00	500 00	....	2,500 00
....	....	144,016 93	124,016 93	....	20,000 00
....	13,547 44	344,778 57	11,724 58	....	333,053 99
19,751 79	....	19,751 79	19,751 79	....	....
46,913 90	....	46,913 90	46,913 90	....	....
46,913 90	....	46,913 90	46,913 90	....	....
203,573 84	....	203,573 84	202,573 84	....	....
621,203 85	....	621,203 85	621,203 85	....	....
1,518 92	....	1,518 92	....	....	1,518 92
5,000 00	....	5,000 00	....	....	5,000 00
....	....	1,200 55	....	1,200 55	....
....	438 16	2,302 25	350 00	....	1,952 25
149,070 00	....	149,070 00	147,570 00	....	1,500 00
....	....	71 87	....	71 87	....
....	....	275 80	....	....	275 80
35,560 00	....	35,560 00	35,362 15	....	197 85
22,080 00	....	22,080 00	22,080 00	....	....
....	65 22	65 22	....	....	65 22
33,700 00	....	33,700 00	33,700 00	....	....
....	....	13 19	....	13 19	....
20,600 00	....	20,600 00	20,600 00	....	....
....	....	24 70	....	24 70	....
15,380 00	....	15,380 00	15,386 00	....	....
15,760 00	....	15,760 00	15,760 00	....	....
14,760 00	....	14,760 00	14,760 00	....	....
13,090 00	....	13,090 00	13,090 00	....	....
800 00	....	800 00	800 00	....	....
....	....	467 10	....	467 10	....
248 15	....	553 90	553 90	....	....
16,000 00	....	16,000 00	15,415 34	....	564 66
....	350 50	350 50	....	350 50	....
....	10 57	2,562 57	1,100 00	....	1,462 57
4,000 00	....	4,000 00	3,000 00	....	1,000 00
....	668 24	21,749 17	....	21,749 17	....
....	776 14	8,333 85	5,138 13	....	3,195 72
40,000 00	....	40,000 00	39,147 00	....	853 00
....	....	50	....	50	....
....	343 55	343 53	337 50	....	6 05
17,280 00	....	17,280 00	17,280 00	....	....
....	....	5 99	....	5 99	....
....	....	379 36	258 22	....	121 14
1,200 00	....	1,200 00	826 58	....	373 42
90 94	....	90 94	90 94	....	....
....	....	970 50	....	970 50	....
....	146 77	4,997 68	893 32	....	4,104 56
5,499 49	86 83	5,586 32	5,499 49	....	86 83
114,082 13	....	114,082 13	114,082 13	....	....
34,850 00	....	34,850 00	34,850 00	....	....
....	235 90	427 69	235 90	427 69	235 90
300,000 00	....	300,000 00	300,000 00	....	....
....	4 86	3,816 43	49	3,816 43	4 37
87,500 00	....	87,500 00	87,500 00	....	....
....	....	4,063 73	....	4,063 73	....
....	....	2,480 75	171 75	....	2,309 00
5,000 00	....	5,000 00	4,116 00	....	884 00
24,900 00	....	24,900 00	24,906 00	....	....
....	....	8 19	....	8 19	....
....	4,009 16	14,009 16	....	....	14,009 16
275,000 00	....	275,000 00	253,560 00	....	21,500 00
16,104,563 07	900,919 01	20,286,071 85	15,215,734 44	1,761,879 82	3,309,067 59

STATEMENT exhibiting the BALANCES of APPRO-

Specific objects of appropriations.	Year.	Statutes.		Balances of appropriations, July 1, 1879.
		Vol.	Page or section.	
CIVIL—Continued.				
Brought forward				$3,281,189 77
Contingent expenses United States mint at San Francisco ..	1877*			
Do...	1878			229 31
Do...	1879			13,169 70
Do...	1880	21	23	
Salaries United States mint at Carson....................	1879			
Do...	1880	21	23	
Wages of workmen United States mint at Carson..........	1877*			
Do...	1879			
Do...	1880	21	23	
Contingent expenses United States mint at Carson.........	1877	21	264	
Do...	1879			11,525 07
Do...	1880	21	23	
Salaries United States mint at Denver....................	1880	21	23, 27	
Wages of workmen United States mint at Denver.........	1878			41 00
Do...	1880	21	23, 27	
Contingent expenses United States mint at Denver........	1879			
Do...	1880	21	23, 27	
Salaries United States mint at New Orleans...............	1878			1,292 06
Do...	1879			3,245 00
Do...	1880	21	23	
Wages of workmen United States mint at New Orleans	1878			31 65
Do...	1879			1,227 75
Do...	1880	21	23, 27, 340	
Contingent expenses United States mint at New Orleans...	1878			3,545 34
Do...	1879			8,737 80
Do...	1880	21	23	
Repairs and machinery United States mint at New Orleans.	1879			12,110 11
Do...	1880	21	27	
Salaries United States assay office at New York..........	1879			
Do...	1880	21	23	
Wages of workmen United States assay office at New York.	1878			3,011 00
Do...	1879			1,300 00
Do...	1880	21	23	
Contingent expenses United States assay office at New York.	1878			856 92
Do...	1879			272 23
Do...	1880	21	23	
Salaries United States assay office at Helena.............	1879			
Do...	1880	21	23	
Wages of workmen United States assay office at Helena....	1879			1,623 50
Do...	1880	21	23, 27	
Contingent expenses United States assay office at Helena..	1878	21	340	
Do...	1879			1,330 59
Do...	1880	21	23, 27	
Salaries United States assay office at Boise City.........	1877*			
Do...	1880	21	23	
Wages and contingent expenses United States assay office at Boise City...................................	1877*			
Do...	1878			14 35
Do...	1878			1,806 37
Do...	1880	21	23, 27	
Salaries United States assay office at Charlotte..........	1880	21	23	
Wages and contingent expenses United States assay office at Charlotte..	1879			1 19
Do...	1880	21	23, 27, 340	
Transportation of coin and bullion.......................		20	275	
Storage of silver dollars................................		21	242	5,000 00
Parting and refining bullion.............................				55,113 98
Assay laboratory office Director of the Mint.............	1878			480 50
Do...	1880	21	340	
Salaries governor, &c., Territory of Arizona.............	1879			1,950 00
Do...	1880	21	23	
Legislative expenses Territory of Arizona................	1880	21	23	
Contingent expenses Territory of Arizona................	1880	21	23	
Salaries governor, &c., Territory of Dakota.............	1879	21	52	1,300 00
Do...	1880	21	23, 27	
Legislative expenses Territory of Dakota................	1878			1 21
Do...	1879			
Do...	1880	21	23	
Contingent expenses Territory of Dakota................	1880	21	23	
Salaries governor, &c., Territory of Idaho...............	1878			257 14
Do...	1879			2,540 08
Do...	1880	21	23	
Legislative expenses Territory of Idaho.................	1879			
Carried forward				3,413,293 78

* And prior years.

PRIATIONS UNEXPENDED June 30, 1879, &c.—Continued

Appropriations for the fiscal year ending June 30, 1880.	Repayments made during the fiscal year 1880.	Aggregate available for the fiscal year ending June 30, 1880.	Payments during the fiscal year ending June 30, 1880.	Amounts carried to the surplus fund June 30, 1880.	Balances of appropriations, June 30, 1880.
$16,104,563 07	$906,919 01	$39,286,671 85	$15,215,734 44	$1,761,879 82	$3,309,057 59
....	19 89	19 89	....	19 89	....
....	....	229 37	....	229 37	....
....	6,151 61	21,321 31	9,666 24	....	11,655 07
87,500 00	....	87,500 00	53,286 68	....	34,213 32
....	10	10	....	....	10
23,550 00	....	23,550 00	23,550 00	....	....
....	71	71	....	71	....
....	62	62	....	....	62
80,000 00	....	80,000 00	64,000 00	....	16,000 00
15 42	....	15 42	....	....	15 42
42,500 00	9,926 02	21,841 09	....	24	21,440 85
42,500 00	....	42,500 00	20,151 46	....	22,348 54
10,750 00	....	10,750 00	10,620 70	....	129 30
....	....	41 00	....	41 00	....
10,000 00	....	10,000 00	10,000 00	....	....
....	354 83	354 83	....	24	354 59
6,000 00	....	6,000 00	5,653 12	....	346 88
....	....	1,292 08	....	1,292 08	....
....	21 52	3,266 52	....	....	3,266 52
21,400 00	1,891 90	23,291 90	23,080 60	....	211 30
....	....	31 65	....	31 65	....
....	1,620 83	3,848 58	2,147 49	....	701 09
80,000 00	5,399 65	85,399 65	83,000 00	....	2,399 65
....	....	3,545 34	....	3,545 34	....
....	6,091 88	13,829 68	5,306 09	....	8,523 54
30,000 00	8 96	30,008 96	29,947 50	....	61 46
....	1,427 31	13,537 43	11,379 88	....	2,167 54
5,000 00	5 94	5,005 94	5,000 00	....	5 94
33,150 00	1,000 00	1,000 00	1,000 00	....	1,000 00
....	....	33,150 00	33,150 00	....	....
....	....	3,011 00	....	3,011 00	....
....	355 50	1,650 50	....	....	1,656 50
22,500 00	....	22,500 00	21,000 00	....	1,500 00
....	....	856 92	....	856 92	....
....	922 63	1,294 86	49	....	1,294 37
9,000 00	....	9,000 00	8,882 72	....	117 28
....	22 86	22 86	....	....	22 86
5,700 00	....	5,700 00	5,700 00	....	....
....	272 24	1,895 74	....	....	1,895 74
12,000 00	....	12,000 00	9,042 00	....	2,958 00
10 93	....	10 93	....	....	10 93
....	549 08	1,869 67	1,175 79	....	693 88
15,000 00	1,340 06	15,000 00	10,949 73	....	4,050 27
....	....	1,340 06	....	1,340 06	....
3,000 00	....	3,000 00	3,000 00	....	....
....	500 00	500 00	....	500 00	....
....	....	14 35	....	14 35	....
....	5 98	1,812 30	696,58	....	1,115 72
6,000 00	....	6,000 00	5,644 76	....	355 24
2,500 00	....	2,500 00	2,500 00	....	....
....	33	1 52	1 43	....	09
1,000 00	....	1,000 00	1,000 00	....	....
60,000 00	....	60,000 00	40,769 06	....	19,230 94
20,000 00	....	25,000 00	5,000 00	....	20,000 00
....	263,122 58	318,236 56	236,981 72	....	81,254 84
....	....	480 50	....	480 50	....
480 50	....	480 50	....	....	480 50
....	....	1,950 00	1,950 00	....	....
12,700 00	....	12,700 00	10,750 00	....	1,950 00
2,000 00	....	2,000 00	2,000 00	....	....
500 00	....	500 00	500 00	....	....
680 00	550 00	2,530 00	2,485 70	....	44 30
14,800 00	....	14,800 00	11,550 00	....	3,250 00
....	....	1 21	....	1 21	....
....	502 58	502 58	....	....	502 58
2,000 00	....	2,000 00	2,000 00	....	....
500 00	....	500 00	375 40	....	124 60
....	....	257 14	....	257 14	....
....	....	2,540 08	1,750 00	....	790 08
12,200 00	....	12,200 00	9,058 15	....	3,141 85
....	1,000 00	1,000 00	....	....	1,000 00
16,736,999 92	1,204,975 52	21,355,269 14	16,000,436 21	1,773,501 04	3,581,329 89

. *STATEMENT exhibiting the BALANCES of APPRO*

Specific objects of appropriations.	Year.	Statutes.		Balances of appropriations, July 1, 1879.
		Vol.	Page or section.	
CIVIL—Continued.				
Brought forward..............................				$3,413,293 70
Legislative expenses Territory of Idaho.................	1880	21	23	....
Contingent expenses Territory of Idaho	1878*	21	253	....
Do......................................	1880	21	23	....
Salaries governor, &c., Territory of Montana............	1879			3,050 00
Do......................................	1880	21	23	....
Legislative expenses Territory of Montana...............	1877*	21	253	....
Do......................................	1878			51 87
Do......................................	1879			....
Do......................................	1880	21	23, 240	....
Contingent expenses Territory of Montana...............	1880	21	23	....
Salaries governor, &c., Territory of New Mexico.........	1878			1,293 43
Do......................................	1879			4,025 82
Do......................................	1880	21	23	....
Legislative expenses Territory of New Mexico...........	1880	21	23, 27, 240	....
Contingent expenses Territory of New Mexico...........	1879			190 20
Do......................................	1880	21	23	....
Salaries governor, &c., Territory of Utah..............	1877			50 00
Do......................................	1879			951 70
Do......................................	1880	21	23	....
Legislative expenses Territory of Utah..............	1877*			....
Do......................................	1880	21	23, 27, 240	....
Contingent expenses Territory of Utah..............	1880	21	23	....
Salaries governor, &c., Territory of Washington........	1879			3,040 97
Do......................................	1880	21	23	....
Legislative expenses Territory of Washington..........	1880	21	23, 27, 240	....
Contingent expenses Territory of Washington..........	1877*			....
Do......................................	1880	21	23	....
Salaries governor, &c., Territory of Wyoming	1878			7 06
Do......................................	1879			1,750 00
Do......................................	1880	21	23	....
Legislative expenses Territory of Wyoming	1877			61 50
Do......................................	1878			....
Do......................................	1879			11 50
Do......................................	1880	21	23, 27, 240	....
Contingent expenses Territory of Wyoming	1880	21	23	....
Legislative expenses Territory of Colorado (1875)........				....
Improvements and repairs District of Columbia..........	1880	20	104, 403	....
Do..............................	1880 / 1881	} 21	156	....
Constructing, repairing, and maintaining bridges, District of Columbia...........................	1880	20	104, 404	....
Washington Asylum, District of Columbia..............	1880	20	104, 404	....
Georgetown Almshouse, District of Columbia..........	1880	20	104, 404	....
Hospital for the Insane, District of Columbia...........	1880	20	104, 404	....
Transportation of paupers and prisoners, District of Columbia..........................	1880	{ 20 21	104, 404 302	} ....
Reform School, District of Columbia	1880	20	104, 404	....
Columbia Hospital for Women and Lying-in-Asylum, District of Columbia	1880	20	104, 404	....
Children's Hospital, District of Columbia	1880	20	104, 404	....
Saint Ann's Infant Asylum, District of Columbia........	1880	20	104, 404	....
Industrial Home School, District of Columbia	1880	20	104, 404	....
National Association for Colored Women and Children, District of Columbia..........................	1880	20	104, 404	....
Women's Christian Association, District of Columbia......	1880	20	104, 404	....
Relief of the poor, District of Columbia..............	1880	20	104, 404	....
Howard University, District of Columbia..............	1880	20	104, 404	....
Washington Aqueduct, District of Columbia..........	1880	20	104, 404	....
Salaries and contingent expenses offices District of Columbia	1880	20	104, 404, 407	....
Public schools, District of Columbia	1880	20	104, 407, 408	....
Metropolitan police, District of Columbia..............	1880	20	104, 408	....
Fire department, District of Columbia	1880	20	104, 409	....
Courts, District of Columbia	1880	{ 20 21	104, 409 253	} ....
Streets, District of Columbia	1880	20	104, 409	....
Water supply, Capitol Hill, District of Columbia (reimbursable)		21	9	....
Health department, District of Columbia...............	1880	{ 20 21	104, 410 253	} ....
Interest and sinking-fund, District of Columbia.........	1880	20	104, 410	....
Miscellaneous and contingent expenses District of Columbia...........................	1880	20	104, 409, 410	....
Carried forward..............................				3,427,732 75

*And prior years.

PRIATIONS UNEXPENDED June 30 1879, &c.—Continued.

Appropriations for the fiscal year ending June 30, 1880.	Repayments made during the fiscal year 1880.	Aggregate available for the fiscal year ending June 30, 1880.	Payments during the fiscal year ending June 30, 1880.	Amounts carried to the surplus fund June 30, 1880.	Balances of appropriations June 30, 1880
$10,736,999 92	$1,204,975 52	$21,355,266 14	$16,000,438 21	$1,773,501 04	$3,581,326 89
2,000 00	....	2,000 00	1,000 00	....	1,000 00
60 00	....	60 00	60 00	....	....
500 00	....	500 00	500 00	....	....
....	....	3,050 00	3,050 00	....	....
12,200 00	....	12,200 00	10,900 00	....	1,300 00
3,076 94	....	3,076 94	....	....	3,676 94
....	....	51 87	....	51 87	....
....	5,001 33	5,001 33	....	....	5,001 33
10,040 31	....	10,040 31	2,000 00	....	8,040 31
500 00	....	500 00	500 00	....	....
....	....	1,223 43	....	1,223 43	....
....	....	4,025 82	3,300 00	....	725 82
12,700 00	....	12,700 00	9,400 00	....	3,300 00
24,783 90	....	24,783 90	17,000 00	....	7,783 90
....	....	106 20	....	....	106 20
500 00	....	500 00	250 00	....	250 00
....	....	50 00	....	50 00	....
....	....	951 70	892 31	....	59 39
12,200 00	....	12,200 00	12,200 00	....	....
....	1,021 29	1,021 29	....	1,021 29	....
22,400 00	....	22,400 00	13,500 00	....	8,900 00
500 00	....	500 00	500 00	....	....
....	....	3,049 97	3,049 97	....	....
12,200 00	....	12,200 00	10,450 00	....	1,750 00
21,600 00	....	21,600 00	15,500 00	....	6,100 00
....	10	10	....	10	....
500 00	....	500 00	500 00	....	....
....	....	7 06	....	7 06	....
....	....	1,750 00	1,750 00	....	....
12,200 00	....	12,200 00	11,624 15	....	575 85
....	....	61 50	....	....	61 50
....	15 01	15 01	....	....	15 01
....	300 17	320 67	....	....	320 67
20,820 00	23 93	20,843 90	17,483 53	....	3,360 00
500 00	....	500 00	500 00	....	....
....	546 13	546 13	....	546 13	....
480,000 00	1,355 18	481,355 18	450,000 00	....	31,355 18
288,300 00	....	288,300 00	10,000 00	....	278,300 00
10,200 00	....	10,200 00	9,200 00	....	1,000 00
45,160 00	....	45,160 00	44,000 00	....	1,160 00
1,800 00	....	1,800 00	1,800 00	....	....
17,000 00	....	17,000 00	15,492 99	....	1,507 01
2,500 00	54 75	2,554 75	2,495 24	....	59 51
34,204 28	....	34,204 28	34,204 28	....	....
12,000 00	....	12,000 00	12,000 00	....	....
5,000 00	....	5,000 00	5,000 00	....	....
5,000 00	....	5,000 00	5,000 00	....	....
5,000 00	....	5,000 00	5,000 00	....	....
6,500 00	....	6,500 00	6,500 00	....	....
5,000 00	....	5,000 00	5,000 00	....	....
15,000 00	....	15,000 00	9,700 00	....	5,300 00
10,000 00	....	10,000 00	10,000 00	....	....
20,000 00	....	20,000 00	20,000 00	....	....
163,407 44	....	163,407 44	153,300 00	....	10,107 44
478,750 00	108 99	478,858 99	441,282 57	....	37,576 42
302,859 00	15 00	302,874 00	299,200 18	....	3,673 82
107,300 00	....	107,300 00	102,000 00	....	5,300 00
20,256 00	....	20,256 00	17,600 00	....	2,656 00
294,125 00	....	294,125 00	274,000 00	....	20,125 00
25,000 00	647 28	25,647 28	647 28	....	25,000 00
24,850 50	200 00	25,050 50	24,244 38	....	806 12
1,155,583 56	2,350 48	1,157,934 04	1,157,934 03	....	01
50,375 00	274 20	50,649 20	30,500 00	....	20,149 20
20,402,651 85	1,216,896 36	28,137,272 96	19,262,440 52	1,776,400 92	4,078,422 52

STATEMENT *exhibiting the BALANCES of APPRO*

Specific objects of appropriations.	Year.	Statutes.		Balances of appropriations, July 1, 1879.
		Vol.	Page or section.	
CIVIL—Continued.				
Brought forward				$3, 427, 722 75
General expenses District of Columbia	1879	21	253	188, 284 19
Payment to workingmen employed under late board of public works, District of Columbia				37, 500 00
Water fund, District of Columbia		20	104	5, 319 20
Salaries board of health, District of Columbia	1878			7 84
Expenses board of health, District of Columbia	1878			39 34
Employment of poor of District of Columbia in filling up grounds		21	300	295 00
Salaries and expenses National Board of Health		21	7	14, 088 50
Washington redemption-fund, District of Columbia		20	104	1, 748 82
Redemption of tax-lien certificates, District of Columbia		20	104	299 45
Washington special-tax fund, District of Columbia		20	104	494 14
Fire-proof building for the National Museum, District of Columbia		21	272	190, 000 90
To promote the education of the blind, District of Columbia				
Redemption Pennsylvania avenue paving-certificates, District of Columbia		20	104	
Redemption of Pennsylvania avenue paving-scrip, District of Columbia		20	104	
Redemption of certain funded indebtedness of the District of Columbia				
Interest and sinking-fund water-tax (reimbursable), District of Columbia	1880			
Benefit of the penny lunch house, Washington, D. C		20	175	
Refunding taxes, District of Columbia		20	104	
Judgments, District of Columbia	1880 1881	} 21	253	
Salaries office Secretary of War	1878			58 87
Do	1879			
Do	1880	21	22, 27	
Contingent expenses office Secretary of War	1880	21	23	
Salaries office Adjutant-General	1878			208 98
Do	1879			
Do	1880	21	23, 68	
Salaries office Adjutant-General, old Navy Department building	1880	21	28	
Contingent expenses office Adjutant-General, old Navy Department building	1880	21	28, 345	
Do	1880	21	23	
Salaries office Inspector-General	1880	21	23	
Salaries office Military Justice	1880	21	23	
Contingent expenses office Military Justice	1880	21	23	
Salaries office Quartermaster-General	1876			45 49
Do	1879			
Do	1880	21	23	
Contingent expenses office Quartermaster-General	1880	21	23	
Salaries office Commissary-General	1879			
Do	1880	21	23	
Contingent expenses office Commissary-General	1880	21	23	
Salaries office Surgeon-General	1878			2, 008 47
Do	1879			
Do	1880	21	23, 68	
Contingent expenses office Surgeon-General	1880	21	23, 68	
Salaries office Chief of Ordnance	1880	21	23	
Contingent expenses office Chief of Ordnance	1878			44
Do	1880	21	23	
Salaries office Paymaster-General	1879			
Do	1880	21	23	
Contingent expenses office Paymaster-General	1879			
Do	1880	21	23	
Salaries office Chief of Engineers	1878			28 90
Do	1879			
Do	1880	21	23	
Contingent expenses office Chief of Engineers	1880	21	23	
Salaries Signal-Office	1880	21	23	
Salaries superintendent, &c., War Department building	1880	21	23	
Contingent expenses War Department building	1880	21	23, 344	
Salary superintendent building corner Pennsylvania avenue and Fifteenth street	1880	21	23	
Rent of building corner Pennsylvania avenue and Fifteenth street	1880	21	23	
Salaries superintendent, &c., building on F street	1880	21	23	
Contingent expenses building on F street	1878			746 60
Carried forward				3, 868, 810 38

PRIATIONS UNEXPENDED June 30, 1879, &c.—Continued.

Appropriations for the fiscal year ending June 30, 1880.	Repayments made during the fiscal year 1880.	Aggregate available for the fiscal year ending June 30, 1880.	Payments during the fiscal year ending June 30, 1880.	Amounts carried to the surplus fund June 30, 1880.	Balances of appropriations, June 30, 1880.
$20, 493, 651 85	$1, 216, 898 36	$25, 197, 272 96	$19, 282, 449 52	$1, 776, 400 92	$4, 078, 422 52
1, 073 65	29, 979 71	219, 307 55	136, 945 56	....	80, 361 99
....	....	37, 500 00	21, 323 71	....	16, 176 29
196, 343 61	119 71	201, 782 52	181, 108 61	....	20, 673 91
....	....	7 64	....	7 64	....
....	....	39 24	....	39 24	....
20, 000 00	....	20, 295 00	20, 000 00	....	295 00
500, 000 20	10, 853 59	524, 892 09	215, 035 64	....	309, 856 45
8, 297 33	....	10, 045 95	4, 726 14	....	5, 319 81
3, 459 06	....	3, 758 51	3, 757 66	....	85
8, 058 82	....	8, 552 96	8, 549 79	....	3 17
38, 500 00	....	228, 500 00	190 000 00	....	38, 500 00
....	10, 704 52	10, 794 52	8, 294 52	....	2, 500 00
3, 501 04	....	3, 501 04	3, 092 73	....	408 31
584 09	....	584 09	....	....	584 09
....	1, 092, 300 00	1, 092, 300 00	1, 092, 300 00	....	....
....	20, 610 00	29, 610 00	29, 610 00	....	....
1, 500 00	....	1, 500 00	1, 000 00	....	500 00
5, 753 31	....	5, 753 31	5, 753 31	....	....
20, 000 00	....	20, 000 00	....	....	20, 000 00
....	30 23	53 87	....	53 87	....
....	....	30 23	....	....	30 23
75, 000 00	....	75, 000 00	75, 000 00	....	....
8, 000 00	....	8, 000 00	8, 000 00	....	....
....	110 63	208 98	....	208 98	....
....	....	110 63	....	....	110 63
301, 542 50	....	301, 542 50	301, 542 50	....	....
4, 980 00	....	4, 980 00	4, 980 00	....	....
2, 500 00	....	2, 500 00	2, 500 00	....	....
8, 000 00	....	8, 000 00	8, 000 00	....	....
2, 520 00	....	2, 520 00	2, 520 00	....	....
5, 320 00	....	5, 320 00	5, 320 00	....	....
250 00	....	250 00	250 00	....	....
....	....	45 49	....	45 49	....
....	22 96	22 96	....	....	22 96
152, 120 00	....	152, 120 00	152, 120 00	....	....
8, 000 00	....	8, 000 00	8, 000 00	....	....
....	1 83	1 83	....	....	1 83
31, 680 00	....	31, 680 00	31, 680 00	....	....
5, 500 00	....	5, 500 00	5, 500 00	....	....
....	....	2, 008 47	....	2, 008 47	....
....	68 49	68 49	....	....	68 49
210, 398 40	....	210, 398 40	210, 398 40	....	....
7, 500 00	....	7, 500 00	7, 500 00	....	....
20, 380 00	....	20, 380 00	20, 380 00	....	....
....	....	44	....	44	....
1, 000 00	....	1, 000 00	1, 000 00	....	....
....	17 95	17 95	....	....	17 95
57, 140 00	....	57, 140 00	57, 140 00	....	....
....	132 87	132 87	....	....	132 87
2, 500 00	....	2, 500 00	2, 500 00	....	....
....	....	28 00	....	28 00	....
....	43 48	43 48	....	....	43 48
23, 240 00	....	23, 240 00	23, 240 00	....	....
2, 500 00	....	2, 500 00	2, 500 00	....	....
4, 320 00	....	4, 320 00	4, 320 00	....	....
7, 090 00	....	7, 090 00	7, 090 00	....	....
8, 000 00	....	8, 000 00	8, 000 00	....	....
250 00	....	250 00	250 00	....	....
10, 000 00	....	10, 000 00	10, 000 00	....	....
5, 170 00	....	5, 170 00	5, 170 00	....	....
....	....	746 40	....	746 40	....
22, 265, 223 66	2, 390, 994 13	28, 525, 018 17	22, 171, 448 09	1, 779, 539 45	4, 574, 030 63

STATEMENT *exhibiting the BALANCES of APPRO*

Specific objects of appropriations.	Year.	Statutes. Vol.	Page or section.	Balances of appropriations, July 1, 1879.
CIVIL—Continued.				
Brought forward				$3,868,810 38
Contingent expenses building on F street	1880	21	23	
Rent of building on F street	1880	21	23	
Salaries superintendent building corner Seventeenth and F streets	1880	21	23	
Contingent expenses building corner Seventeenth and F streets	1879			
Do	1880	21	23	
Salary superintendent building on Tenth street	1880	21	23	
Salary superintendent building occupied by Commissary-General	1880	21	23	
Salaries employés public buildings and grounds under Chief Engineer	1878			123 44
Do	1879			
Do	1880	21	23	
Contingent expenses public buildings and grounds under Chief Engineer	1878			19
Do	1880	21	23	
Postage War Department	1878			10
Do	1879			60,014 30
Do	1880	21	23	
Improvement and care of public grounds	1878			866 37
Do	1879			
Do	1880	20	387–8	
Lighting, &c., the Executive Mansion, &c	1878			278 68
Do	1879			
Do	1880	20	388	
Repairs, fuel, &c., Executive Mansion	1878			34 13
Do {	1879			25,000 00
	1880			
Repairs of water-pipes and fire-plugs	1878			1,385 93
Do	1879			
Do	1880	20	388	
Telegraph to connect the Capitol with the departments and Government Printing Office	1878			2 52
Do	1879			
Do	1880	20	388	
Support and medical treatment of transient paupers	1879			1,250 00
Do	1880	20	390	
Repairs of navy yard and upper bridges	1878			251 12
Pedestal for statue of General George H. Thomas				
Rent office Public Buildings and Grounds	1879			
Salaries office Secretary of the Navy	1880	21	23	
Contingent expenses office Secretary of the Navy	1880	21	23	
Salaries Bureau of Yards and Docks	1880	21	23	
Contingent expenses Bureau of Yards and Docks	1878			32 36
Do	1880	21	23	
Salaries Bureau Equipment and Recruiting	1880	21	23	
Contingent expenses Bureau Equipment and Recruiting	1880	21	23	
Salaries Bureau Navigation	1880	21	23	
Contingent expenses Bureau Navigation	1880	21	23	
Salaries Bureau Ordnance	1880	21	23	
Contingent expenses Bureau Ordnance	1880	21	23	
Salaries Bureau Construction and Repairs	1879			60
Contingent expenses Bureau Construction and Repairs	1880	21	23	
Salaries Bureau Steam-Engineering	1880	21	23	
Contingent expenses Bureau Steam-Engineering	1880	21	23	
Salaries Bureau Provisions and Clothing	1880	21	25	
Contingent expenses Bureau Provisions and Clothing	1880	21	23	
Salaries Bureau Medicine and Surgery	1880	21	23	
Contingent expenses Bureau Medicine and Surgery	1880	21	23	
Salaries superintendent, &c., Navy Department building	1879			
Do	1880	21	23, 28	
Contingent expenses Navy Department	1880	21	23, 28, 245	
Postage Navy Department	1877			5,547 57
Do	1878			13,530 28
Do	1879			14,944 18
Do	1880	21	23	
Salaries Post-Office Department	1878			13 95
Do	1879			
Do	1880	21	23, 240	
Contingent expenses Post-Office Department	1878			38
Contingent expenses, stationery, Post-Office Department	1880	21	23	
Carried forward				3,992,086 38

PRIATIONS UNEXPENDED June 30, 1879, &c.—Continued.

Appropriations for the fiscal year ending June 30, 1880.	Repayments made during the fiscal year 1880.	Aggregate available for the fiscal year ending June 30, 1880.	Payments during the fiscal year ending June 30, 1880.	Amounts carried to the surplus fund June 30, 1880.	Balances of appropriations, June 30, 1880.
$22,265,223 66	$2,390,964 13	$28,525,018 17	$22,171,448 09	$1,779,539 45	$4,574,030 63
3,500 00		3,500 00	3,500 00		
4,500 00		4,500 00	4,500 00		
4,450 00		4,450 00	4,450 00		
	229 31	229 31			229 31
6,000 00		6,000 00	6,000 00		
250 00		250 00	250 00		
250 00		250 00	250 00		
		123 44		123 44	
	82	82			82
34,560 00		34,500 00	34,500 00		
500 00		500 00	500 00		
		19		19	
		10		10	
165,000 00		60,014 20	36,512 00		23,502 20
		165,000 00	67,263 22		77,716 78
		866 37		866 37	
	373 27	373 27			373 27
42,500 00		42,500 00	42,500 00		
		278 68		278 68	
	31 88	31 88			31 88
15,000 00		15,000 00	15,000 00		
		34 13		34 13	
		25,000 00	25,000 00		
		1,385 93		1,385 93	
	12 07	12 07			12 07
2,500 00		2,500 00	2,500 00		
		2 52		2 52	
	67	67			67
1,000 00		1,000 00	1,000 00		
		1,250 00	1,250 00		
15,000 00		15,000 00	13,750 00		1,250 00
		251 12		251 12	
	206 20	206 20		206 20	
	75 00	75 00			75 00
36,700 00		36,700 00	36,700 00		
2,500 00		2,500 00	2,500 00		
11,980 00		11,980 00	11,980 00		
		32 36		32 36	
600 00		600 00	600 00		
11,780 00		11,780 00	11,780 00		
500 00		500 00	500 00		
6,180 00		6,180 00	6,180 00		
400 00		400 00	400 00		
7,980 00		7,980 00	7,980 00		
400 00		400 00	400 00		
		64			68
10,980 00		10,980 00	10,980 00		
400 00		400 00	400 00		
10,180 00		10,180 00	10,180 00		
		700 00	700 00		
14,580 00		14,580 00	14,580 00		
400 00		400 00	400 00		
5,780 00		5,780 00	5,780 00		
100 00		100 00	100 00		
	96 98	96 98			96 98
15,890 00		15,890 00	15,890 00		
9,000 00		9,000 00	9,000 00		
		5,547 57		5,547 57	
		13,530 28		13,530 28	
		14,944 18	1,920 00		13,024 18
20,000 00		20,000 00	890 00		19,110 00
		13 95		13 95	
	241 37	241 37			241 37
499,465 00		499,465 00	499,465 00		
		38		38	
9,000 00		9,000 00	9,000 00		
23,235,728 86	2,392,251 10	28,620,066 14	23,108,558 31	1,801,812 07	4,709,695 16

STATEMENT *exhibiting the BALANCES of APPRO*

Specific objects of appropriations.	Year.	Statutes.		Balances of appropriations, July 1, 1879.
		Vol.	Page or section.	
CIVIL—Continued.				
Brought forward				$3, 992, 086 38
Contingent expenses, stationery, Post-Office Department	1879			
Contingent expenses, fuel, Post-Office Department	1879			
Do	1880	21	23	
Contingent expenses, gas, Post-Office Department	1879			
Do	1880	21	23	
Contingent expenses, plumbing and gas-fixtures, Post-Office Department	1879			
Do	1880	21	23	
Contingent expenses, telegraphing, Post-Office Department	1879			
Do	1880	21	23	
Contingent expenses, printing, Post-Office Department	1879			
Do	1880	21	23	
Contingent expenses, carpets, Post-Office Department	1879			
Do	1880	21	23	
Contingent expenses, furniture, Post-Office Department	1879			
Do	1880	21	23	
Contingent expenses, horses and wagons, Post-Office Department	1879			
Do	1880	21	23, 249	
Contingent expenses, hardware, Post-Office Department	1879			
Do	1880	21	23	
Contingent expenses, rent, Post-Office Department	1880	21	23	
Contingent expenses Post-Office Department, miscellaneous items	1879			
Do	1880	21	23, 249	
Publication of Official Postal Guide	1879			
Do	1880	21	23, 249	
Deficiencies in the postal revenues	{ 1876	}		397, 397 91
	1877			
Do	1877*	21	258	
Do	1878	21	249	
Do	1879	21	40, 249	1, 672, 274 72
Do	{ 1880	{ 20	358	}
		21	40, 72, 249	
International Postal Congress, Paris				176 52
General Post-Office Building, Washington, D. C				
Postage stamps, Post-Office Department	{ 1879	} 21	249	
	1880			
Salaries Department of Agriculture	1880	21	23	
Collecting agricultural statistics	1880	21	23	
Purchase and distribution of valuable seeds	1878			420 67
Do	1880	21	23	
Investigating the history of insects injurious to agriculture	1880	21	23	
Contingent expenses, Department of Agriculture	1880	21	23	
Postage Department of Agriculture	1878			554 39
Do	1880	21	23	
Experimental garden Department of Agriculture	1880	21	23	
Museum Department of Agriculture	1880	21	23	
Furniture, cases, and repairs, Department of Agriculture	1880	21	23	
Library Department of Agriculture	1880	21	23	
Laboratory Department of Agriculture	1880	21	23	
Improvement of grounds Department of Agriculture	1880	20	392	
Building Department of Agriculture	1880	20	392	
Investigating diseases of swine and other domesticated animals	1880	21	30	
Salaries Department of Justice	1878			1, 370 05
Do	1879			
Do	1880	21	23	
Rent of building Department of Justice	1880	21	23	
Contingent expenses, furniture and repairs, Department of Justice	1879			
Do	1880	21	23	
Contingent expenses, books for library, Department of Justice	1880	21	23	
Contingent expenses, books for office of Solicitor Department of Justice	1880	21	23	
Do	1879			
Contingent expenses, stationery, Department of Justice	1880	21	23	
Contingent expenses, horses and wagons, Department of Justice	1879			
Do	1880	21	23	
Contingent expenses, miscellaneous, Department of Justice	1879	21	250	
Do	1880	21	23	
Contingent expenses Department of Justice	1878			1, 228 12
Carried forward				6, 065, 508 76

* And prior years.

PRIATIONS UNEXPENDED June 30, 1879, &c.—Coutinued.

Appropriations for the fiscal year ending June 30, 1880.	Repayments made during the fiscal year 1880.	Aggregate available for the fiscal year ending June 30, 1880.	Payments during the fiscal year ending June 30, 1880.	Amounts carried to the surplus fund June 30, 1880.	Balances of appropriations, June 30, 1880.
$23, 235, 738 66	$2, 392, 251 10	$39, 620, 066 14	$23, 108, 556 31	$1, 801, 812 87	$4, 709, 695 16
	47	47			47
	919 57	919 57			919 57
4, 400 00		4, 400 00	4, 400 00		
	20 96	20 96			20 96
5, 000 00		5, 000 00	5, 000 00		
	63	63			63
4, 000 00		4, 000 00	4, 000 00		
	729 26	729 26			729 26
3, 000 00		3, 000 00	3, 000 00		
	20	20			20
8, 000 00		8, 000 00	8, 000 00		
	2 57	2 57			2 57
5, 000 00		5, 000 00	5, 000 00		
	55	55			55
5, 000 00		5, 000 00	5, 000 00		
	22	22			22
1, 500 00		1, 500 00	1, 500 00		
	08	08			08
1, 500 00		1, 500 00	1, 500 00		
1, 500 00		1, 500 00	1, 500 00		
	I 61	1 61			1 61
10, 000 00		10, 000 00	10, 000 00		
	4 24	4 24			4 24
21, 800 00		21, 800 00	21, 800 00		
		897, 397 91		897, 397 91	
97, 717 20		97, 717 20			97, 717 20
75, 700 79		75, 700 79			75, 700 79
91, 467 74	51, 075 80	1, 814, 618 26	122, 075 50		1, 692, 742 46
7, 109, 876 10	102, 610 72	7, 212, 486 82	3, 102, 610 73		4, 109, 876 10
		176 52			176 52
	217 86	217 86		217 86	
1, 000 00		1, 000 00			1, 000 00
66, 900 00		66, 900 00	66, 900 00		
10, 000 00		10, 000 00	10, 000 00		
		420 67		420 67	
75, 000 00		75, 000 00	75, 000 00		
5, 000 00		5, 000 00	5, 000 00		
8, 000 00		8, 000 00	8, 000 00		
		554 39		554 39	
4, 000 00		4, 000 00	4, 000 00		
6, 600 00		6, 600 00	6, 600 00		
1, 000 00		1, 000 00	1, 000 00		
4, 000 00		4, 000 00	4, 000 00		
1, 000 00		1, 000 00	1, 000 00		
1, 500 00		1, 500 00	1, 500 00		
6, 500 00		6, 500 00	6, 500 00		
1, 500 00		1, 500 00	1, 500 00		
10, 000 00		10, 000 00	8, 000 00		2, 000 00
		1, 370 05		1, 370 05	
	770 70	770 70	329 70		441 00
101, 480 00	1, 082 05	102, 562 05	102, 562 05		
10, 000 00		10, 000 00	10, 000 00		
	98 75	98 75			98 75
1, 000 00	196 87	1, 196 87	1, 196 87		
1, 500 00	458 50	1, 958 50	1, 958 50		
500 00	31	500 31	500 00		31
	3 00	3 00			3 00
1, 500 00	5 55	1, 505 55	1, 505 55		
	106 02	106 02			106 02
1, 200 00	280 37	1, 480 37	1, 480 37		
505 50		505 50			505 50
6, 000 00	74 35	6, 074 35	6, 074 35		
		1, 228 12		1, 228 12	
31, 006, 875 09	2, 550, 912 31	39, 623, 297 06	26, 728, 052 22	2, 203, 001 67	10, 691, 743 17

STATEMENT *exhibiting the BALANCES of APPRO*

Specific objects of appropriations.	Year	Statutes.		Balances of appropriations, July 1, 1879.
		Vol.	Page or section.	
CIVIL—Continued.				
Brought forward				$6,065,508 76
Postage, Department of Justice	1878			2,530 00
Do	1879			1,380 00
Do	1880	21	23	
Salary of warden of jail, District of Columbia	1880	21	23	
Defending suits and claims for seizure of captured and abandoned property	1878			95 25
Do	1879			472 75
Do	1880	20	396	
Prosecution and collection of claims	1879			866 00
Do	1880	20	396	
Punishing violations of intercourse acts and frauds	1878			7,052 00
Do	1879			3,878 19
Do	1880	20	396	
Prosecution of crimes	1878			9,438 10
Do	1879			1,121 36
Do	1880	20	396	
Support of convicts	1879			5,617 70
Do	1880	20	396	
Editing 15th volume of Opinions of Attorney-General	1880	20	396	
Expenses Territorial courts of Utah	1875	}		24,465 35
	1876	}		
Do	1877	21	255	
Do	1878			1,748 32
Do	1879			1,252 31
Do	1880	{ 20	} 396, 250	
		21		
Court-house, Washington, D. C		{ 20	} 302, 246	
		21		
Payment to Elmer S. Dundy, United States judge, while holding court in Colorado				281 40
Law library, Territory of Dakota				170 00
Law library, Territory of Wyoming				145 00
Detecting and punishing crime under alleged frauds in late Presidential election				10,000 00
Fees of supervisors of elections		R. S.	3689	4,103 25
Salaries justices, &c., Supreme Court	1878	{ 21	} 23, 682	
		R. S.		
Do	1880	21	23	
Salaries retired United States judges	1880			3,987 65
Salaries circuit judges	1878			2,807 24
Do	1879			
Do	1880	21	23	
Salaries district judges	1878			513 42
Do	1879			3,219 46
Do	1880	21	23	
Salaries district attorneys	1878			456 47
Do	1879			556 36
Do	1880	21	23, 250	
Salaries district marshals	1878	21	250	67 37
Do	1879			95 78
Do	1880	21	23, 250	
Salaries justices and judges supreme court District of Columbia	1879	21	41	155 56
Do	1880	21	23	
Fees of district attorneys United States courts	1880	21	43	
Fees of clerks United States courts	1880	21	43	
Fees of commissioners United States courts	1880	21	43	
Fees of jurors United States courts	1880	21	43, 250	
Fees and expenses of marshals United States courts	1880	21	250	
Fees of witnesses United States courts	1880	21	43, 250	
Support of prisoners United States courts	1880	21	43, 250	
Rent of court-rooms United States courts	1880	21	43	
Miscellaneous expenses United States courts	1880	21	43, 250	
Expenses	1879	21	250	10,137 68
Do	1878	21	250	30,357 35
Do	1877*	21	250, 255	
Contingent expenses Steamboat Inspection Service, prior to July 1, 1877		21	254	
Do		R. S.	3689	168,568 58
Salaries Steamboat Inspection Service		R. S.	3689	302,160 74
Building for State, War, and Navy Departments, south wing				3,762 50
Do		21	268	400,000 00
Carried forward				7,087,012 90

* And prior years.

PRIATIONS UNEXPENDED June 30, 1879, &c.—Continued.

Appropriations for the fiscal year ending June 30, 1880.	Repayments made during the fiscal year 1880.	Aggregate available for the fiscal year ending June 30, 1880.	Payments during the fiscal year ending June 30, 1880.	Amounts carried to the surplus fund June 30, 1880.	Balances of appropriations, June 30, 1880.
$31, 606, 875 99	$2, 550, 912 31	$39, 623, 227 06	$36, 728, 552 22	$2, 203, 091 67	$10, 691, 743 17
....	....	2, 530 00	....	2, 530 00	....
....	....	1, 380 00	....	....	1, 380 00
5, 000 00	....	5, 000 00	....	....	5, 000 00
1, 800 00	....	1, 800 00	1, 800 00	....	....
....	....	95 25	87 00	8 25	....
....	1, 645 64	2, 115 39	....	....	2, 115 39
25, 000 00	500 22	25, 500 22	25, 500 22	....	....
....	....	886 00	300 00	....	586 00
2, 500 00	....	2, 500 00	1, 050 00	....	1, 450 00
....	....	7, 053 00	281 00	6, 772 00	....
....	....	3, 878 19	1, 475 58	....	2, 402 61
3, 000 00	....	3, 000 00	2, 905 76	....	94 34
....	....	9, 438 10	....	9, 438 10	....
....	2, 386 63	3, 510 19	1, 231 75	....	2, 278 44
20, 000 00	89 50	20, 089 50	14, 312 20	....	5, 777 30
....	....	5, 617 70	1, 937 50	....	3, 680 20
15, 000 00	....	15, 000 00	5, 204 77	....	9, 795 23
1, 000 00	....	1, 000 00	....	....	1, 000 00
....	....	24, 485 35	12, 916 08	....	11, 549 27
1, 349 95	....	1, 349 95	....	....	1, 349 95
....	....	1, 748 32	1, 748 32	....	....
....	....	1, 352 31	1, 127 05	....	135 26
26, 000 00	....	26, 000 00	23, 283 25	....	2, 716 75
1, 500 00	80 75	1, 580 75	1, 580 75	....	....
....	....	281 40	....	....	281 40
....	....	170 00	....	....	170 00
....	....	145 00	....	....	145 00
....	....	10, 000 00	....	....	10, 000 00
44, 952 27	745 00	45, 697 27	45, 697 27	....	....
....	....	4, 103 25	....	4, 103 25	....
97, 500 00	....	97, 500 00	97, 500 00	....	....
13, 000 00	....	13, 000 00	13, 000 00	....	....
....	....	3, 987 65	....	3, 987 65	....
....	....	2, 807 24	....	....	2, 807 24
54, 000 00	....	54, 000 00	52, 353 19	....	1, 646 81
....	....	513 42	....	513 42	....
....	....	3, 219 46	1, 952 35	....	1, 267 11
193, 500 00	....	193, 500 00	189, 937 79	....	3, 562 21
....	....	456 47	....	456 47	....
....	....	556 36	226 14	....	330 22
19, 500 00	....	19, 500 00	19, 157 07	....	332 93
12 93	....	100 / 0	87 37	....	12 93
....	....	95 /8	51 51	....	44 27
12, 300 00	....	12, 300 00	11, 935 16	....	364 84
1, 122 22	....	1, 277 78	1, 277 78	....	....
24, 500 00	....	24, 500 00	24, 326 04	....	173 96
305, 000 00	....	300, 000 00	246, 234 30	....	53, 765 70
160, 000 00	....	160, 000 00	110, 480 65	....	49, 519 35
140, 000 00	....	140, 000 00	82, 546 32	....	57, 453 68
440, 000 00	16, 679 45	456, 679 45	427, 355 75	....	29, 323 70
600, 000 00	....	600, 000 00	321, 300 00	....	278, 700 00
610, 000 00	10, 541 46	620, 541 46	553, 684 38	....	66, 657 08
318, 000 00	9, 555 59	327, 555 59	230, 541 40	....	97, 014 19
67, 000 00	....	67, 000 00	44, 885 17	....	22, 114 83
305, 000 00	2, 391 78	307, 391 78	289, 997 44	....	17, 394 34
375, 000 00	21, 310 42	406, 448 10	114, 683 24	....	291, 764 86
26, 000 00	5, 290 77	61, 648 12	32, 141 71	....	29, 506 41
16, 755 27	21, 811 52	32, 566 79	....	17, 846 06	14, 720 73
719 59	....	719 59	719 59	....	....
82, 468 96	....	271, 037 54	82, 349 88	....	238, 687 66
300, 000 00	....	502, 160 74	180, 500 00	....	321, 660 74
....	....	3, 762 50	....	....	3, 762 50
456, 000 00	....	850, 000 00	500, 000 00	....	350, 000 00
55, 054, 356 88	2, 643, 943 24	45, 385, 313 62	30, 450, 324 95	2, 248, 656 87	12, 686, 331 28

27 F

STATEMENT *exhibiting the BALANCES of APPRO*

Specific objects of appropriations.	Year.	Statutes.		Balances of appropriations, July 1, 1879.
		Vol.	Page or section.	
CIVIL—Continued.				
Brought forward				$7, 087, 012 90
Furniture for new building War Department	1879 1880			25, 000 00
Furniture for new building Navy Department	1879 1880			19, 150 00
Treasury building, Washington, D. C		21	260	5, 016 62
Subtreasury building, New York				10, 600 00
Post-office and subtreasury, Boston, Mass		21	259	333, 842 65
Post-office, Harrisburg, Pa		21	259	111, 516 10
Post-office and court-house, Philadelphia, Pa		21	259	207, 180 65
Assay-office building, Helena, Mont				2, 991 42
Court-house and post-office, Atlanta, Ga		21	259	48, 612 81
Court-house and post-office, Austin, Tex		21	259	71, 813 21
Court-house and post-office, Grand Rapids, Mich				28, 680 71
Court-house and post-office, Lincoln, Nobr		21	260	10, 922 53
Court-house and post-office, Little Rock, Ark		21	259	41, 910 76
Court-house and post-office, Parkersburg, W. Va				475 56
Court-house and post-office, Raleigh, N. C				5, 108 28
Court-house and post-office, Topeka, Kans		21	259	68, 906 13
Court-house and post-office, Trenton, N. J				807 48
Court-house and post-office, Utica, N. Y		21	259	56, 116 86
Post-office, Dover, Del				462 82
Court-house and post-office, New York		21	241	42, 464 28
Court-house and post-office, Columbia, S. C				3 46
Court-house and post-office, Covington, Ky				46, 576 90
Post-office, Jersey City, N. J				139 80
Court-house and post-office, Indianapolis, Ind				1, 970 13
Court-house and post-office, Omaha, Nebr				805 56
Court-house and post-office, Pittsburgh, Pa		21	259	
Branch mint building, San Francisco, Cal				3, 680 22
Subtreasury building, San Francisco, Cal				3, 089 87
Relief of the widow of Gustave Schleicher		21	52	
Relief of the bark Grapeshot		21	14	
Relief of the estate of Henry Conrad		21	4	
Relief of M. M. Herr, joint resolution Feb. 25, 1880		21	280	
Relief of Gibbs & Co		21	11	
Relief of Capt. J. B. Campbell		21	10	
Relief of J. P. Zimmerman and H. P. Snow, of Clinton Co., Ky		21	11	
Relief of Miss B. A. Hinks, Cohasset, Mass		21	279	
Relief of George Eyster		21	29	
Relief of Samuel Kimbro and E. V. Kimbro, deceased				
Payment to Samuel Lord, jr., of State Bank of Charleston, S. C.		21	6	
Total				8, 236, 177 00
CUSTOMS.				
Collecting revenue from customs prior to July 1, 1877		21	255	
Collecting revenue from customs (no limit)		R. S.	3687	1, 906, 621 00
Expenses revenue-cutter service		21	255	
Do	1877*			66, 631 99
Do	1878			35, 197 30
Do	1879			
Do	1880	20	379	
Supplies of light-houses	1877*	21	255	51, 968 94
Do	1878			13, 735 96
Do	1879			
Do	1880	20	380	
Repairs and incidental expenses light-houses	1877*	21	255	
Do	1878			5, 778 62
Do	1879			18, 686 29
Do	1880	20	380	
Salaries of keepers of light-houses	1877*			
Do	1878			70, 707 39
Do	1879			20, 219 29
Do	1880	20	379	
Salaries of keepers of light-houses, act June 16, 1880		21	243	
Inspecting lights	1878			586 33
Do	1879			
Do	1880	20	380	
Expenses of light-vessels	1878			292 99
Do	1879			166 58
Do	1880	20	379	
Expenses of fog-signals	1878			725 06
Carried forward				2, 191, 716 84

* And prior years.

PRIATIONS UNEXPENDED June 30, 1879, &c.—Continued.

Appropriations for the fiscal year ending June 30, 1880.	Repayments made during the fiscal year 1880.	Aggregate available for the fiscal year ending June 30, 1880.	Payments during the fiscal year ending June 30, 1880.	Amounts carried to the surplus fund June 30, 1880.	Balances of appropriations, June 30, 1880.
$35,654,356 88	$2,643,943 24	$45,385,313 02	$30,450,324 95	$3,248,656 87	$13,586,331 20
		25,000 00	25,000 00		
	5,539 58	24,689 58	24,689 58		
40,000 00		45,016 62	5,016 62		40,000 00
		10,000 00	6,000 00		4,000 00
350,000 00		683,842 55	232,428 82		451,413 73
50,000 00		161,516 10	54,356 20		107,159 90
350,000 00	324 40	557,180 55	307,180 55	250,000 00	
		3,315 82	1,862 00		1,453 82
15,000 00		63,612 81	48,612 81		15,000 00
13,000 00		84,813 23	48,265 82		36,547 39
		29,680 71	21,096 00		8,584 71
5,000 00	852 38	16,774 91	11,543 69		5,231 22
30,000 00		71,910 76	34,192 38		37,718 38
		475 05	43 00		432 05
50,000 00		5,108 28	2,216 10		2,892 18
		118,966 13	35,815 60		83,150 53
	442 36	1,249 84	8 03		1,241 81
81,000 00	171 81	110,116 86	36,845 09		82,271 77
		624 63	435 05		189 58
15,000 00		57,464 28	42,000 88		15,463 40
		3 46		3 46	
		46,975 90	15,106 08		31,380 82
		139 80	10 38	129 42	
	435 67	2,305 80	9 00		2,296 80
		805 56		805 56	
75,000 00	111 87	75,000 00			75,000 00
		3,792 09		3,792 09	
		2,059 87	2,032 92		26 05
6,000 00		6,000 00	6,000 00		
15,861 50		15,861 50	15,861 50		
7,000 00		7,000 00	7,000 00		
		605 00	605 00		
4,576 92		4,576 92	4,576 92		
2,591 27	8 73	2,600 00	2,600 00		
		98 00	98 00		
5,000 00		5,000 00	5,000 00		
882 50		882 50	882 50		
	800 00	800 00	800 00		
479 00		479 00	479 00		
36,751,451 07	2,652,630 04	47,640,256 11	31,448,284 47	2,254,187 40	13,937,780 24
47,369 79		47,369 79	47,369 79		
6,548,800 16	18,058 50	8,474,374 66	5,994,837 24	2,090,900 00	479,537 42
79 78	33 98	113 76	79 78	33 98	
	1,300 50	68,122 49	1,431 55	66,700 94	
	34,174 61	69,371 91	32,391 79		36,980 12
860,000 00	3,230 76	863,230 76	850,170 47		13,060 29
31 69	569 13	600 82	31 69	569 13	
	5 08	51,973 12	689 06	51,284 06	
	5,968 92	19,609 88	19,651 67		48 21
375,000 00	4,441 11	379,441 11	346,673 15		32,767 96
4 22	1,593 42	1,597 64	4 22	1,593 42	
	686 79	-5,465 41	1,592 42	4,872 99	
	8,084 76	26,971 05	21,642 58		5,328 47
275,000 00	702 30	275,702 30	258,200 90		17,501 40
	5 72	5 72		5 72	
	9 58	70,716 97	4 60	70,712 37	
585,000 00	12,818 32	82,537 61	9,004 68		23,533 53
362 22	784 53	585,784 53	528,005 77		57,778 76
		362 22			362 22
		586 33		586 33	
	2,018 22	2,018 22			2,018 22
4,000 00		4,000 00	2,300 00		1,700 00
		252 99	252 99		
	5,929 08	6,095 66	6,004 66		91 00
230,000 00	20,000 00	250,000 00	244,549 25		5,450 75
	15	735 21	350 00	375 21	
8,935,647 86	120,805 46	11,238,170 16	8,365,277 66	2,196,734 15	576,158 35

420   REPORT ON THE FINANCES.

STATEMENT exhibiting the BALANCES of APPRO

Specific objects of appropriations.	Year.	Vol.	Page or section.	Balances of appropriations, July 1, 1879.
CUSTOMS—Continued.				
Brought forward				$2,191,716 84
Expenses of fog-signals	1879			10,592 14
Do	1880	20	879	
Expenses of buoyage	1878			11,851 18
Do	1879			5,782 00
Do	1880	20	879	
Repairs and preservation of public buildings	1877*	21	255	
Do	1878	21	255	1,544 08
Do	1879			5,521 53
Do	1880	21	255	
Furniture and repairs of same for public buildings	1878*			1,638 69
Do	1879			5,266 07
Do	1880	{ 20 21	{ 384 241 }	
Do	1877*	21	255	
Fuel, lights, and water for public buildings	1878			16,144 02
Do	1879			12,725 56
Do	1880	{ 20 21	{ 383 241 }	
Heating apparatus for public buildings	1877*	21	255	
Do	1878			1,024 82
Do	1879			10,000 00
Do	1880	{ 20 21	{ 384 255 }	
Pay of custodians and janitors	1878			3,972 00
Do	1879			3,500 00
Do	1880	20	384	
Commissioners to superintendents of lights	1878*	21	243	
Do	1879			6,959 93
Do	1880	20	380	
Marine Hospital Service, prior to July 1, 1877*		21	255	
Marine Hospital Service (no limit)		R.S.	3689,4803	265,711 60
Life-Saving Service	1877*			
Do	1878			11,110 31
Do	1879			11,703 73
Do	1880	20	378	
Life-Saving Service, contingent expenses	1877*	21	255	
Do	1878			244 15
Do	1879			5,278 57
Do	1880	{ 20 21	{ 378 241 }	
Establishing life-saving stations (no limit)				107,656 36
Rebuilding and improving life-saving stations				76 80
Building or purchase of such vessels as may be required for the revenue service				6,707 85
Compensation in lieu of moieties, 1877 and prior years, transfer account				
Do	1877*	21	255	
Do	1878			73,064 89
Do	1879			14,096 03
Do	1880	20	384	
Salaries and traveling expenses of agents at seal fisheries in Alaska	1877*			
Do	1878			1,200 00
Do	1879			4,009 51
Do	1880	20	384	
Standard weights and measures	1879			3,271 15
Do	1880	20	383	
Protection of sea-otter hunting grounds and seal fisheries in Alaska	1878			1,260 48
Do	1879			23,522 00
Do	1880	20	386	
Custom-house, Boston, Mass				10,000 00
Custom-house and post-office, Fall River, Mass				76,182 41
Custom-house and post-office, Hartford, Conn				17,951 69
Custom-house and post-office, Albany, N.Y				134,431 03
Barge-office building, New York				204,578 90
Marine Hospital, Pittsburgh, Pa				7,015 24
Custom-house, Norfolk, Va		21	255	
Custom-house, Charleston, S.C				1,125 62
Custom-house, New Orleans, La				36,341 66
Custom-house and post-office, Cincinnati, O				237,630 94
Custom-house and post-office, Evansville, Ind				8,169 28
Custom-house and subtreasury, &c., Chicago, Ill		21	240	697,414 59
Carried forward				4,246,093 45

* And prior years.

PRIATIONS UNEXPENDED June 30, 1879, &c.—Continued.

Appropriations for the fiscal year ending June 30, 1880.	Repayments made during the fiscal year 1880.	Aggregate available for the fiscal year ending June 30, 1880.	Payments during the fiscal year ending June 30, 1880.	Amounts carried to the surplus fund June 30, 1880.	Balances of appropriations, June 30, 1880.
$8,925,647 86	$120,805 46	$11,238,170 16	$8,365,277 66	$2,196,734 15	$676,158 35
....	475 78	11,067 92	13 18	....	11,054 74
50,000 00	....	50,000 00	47,025 13	....	2,974 87
....	3,897 40	15,748 58	500 55	15,248 03	....
....	11,528 70	17,310 70	13,897 13	....	3,413 57
325,000 00	2,582 99	327,582 99	314,487 33	....	13,075 66
109 89	1,148 76	1,258 65	109 89	1,148 76	....
27 69	9 45	1,281 20	1,271 75	9 45	....
....	2,913 67	8,435 20	5,046 62	....	3,388 58
110,000 00	....	110,000 00	100,900 00	....	9,100 00
....	....	1,838 69	2 80	1,035 89	....
....	278 29	5,504 36	934 84	....	4,629 52
131,500 00	....	131,500 00	125,277 73	....	6,222,27
185 75	385 23	570 98	185 75	385 23	....
....	....	16,144 02	70	16,143 32	....
....	7,560 08	20,294 66	210 33	....	20,084 33
395,000 00	52 50	395,052 50	352,554 47	....	42,498 03
61 60	....	61 60	61 60	....	....
....	....	1,024 82	....	1,024 82	....
....	6,698 01	16,638 01	14,476 10	....	2,161 91
80,000 00	....	80,000 00	80,000 00	....	....
....	111 71	3,083 71	....	3,083 71	....
....	61 35	3,561 35	....	....	3,561 35
90,000 00	4 77	90,004 77	79,500 00	....	10,504 77
31,574 96	....	31,574 96	....	....	31,574 96
....	45 58	7,005 41	4,862 41	....	2,143 00
7,500 00	39 87	7,580 87	3,858 11	....	3,681 78
500 27	....	500 27	500 27	....	....
388,592 27	10,537 03	664,841 50	412,722 52	....	252,118 98
....	26 68	26 68	....	26 68	....
....	25 30	11,135 61	....	11,135 61	....
....	671 72	12,376 45	1,210 14	....	11,165 31
472,860 00	1,056 09	473,916 09	390,501 94	....	83,414 15
5 00	11 00	16 00	5 00	11 00	....
....	11 03	255 18	255 18	....	....
....	1,273 80	6,552 23	5,700 87	....	851 36
52,000 00	75 96	52,075 96	40,383 78	....	11,692 18
....	2,042 84	109,699 20	85,488 45	....	24,210 75
....	18 65	95 45	75 00	....	20 45
....	1,351 14	6,058 99	6 97	....	8,052 02
....	7,500 00	7,500 00	7,500 00	....	....
74 62	....	74 62	74 62	....	....
....	202 44	73,267 33	17,301 16	55,966 17	....
....	....	14,096 03	1,187 78	....	12,908 25
20,000 00	....	20,000 00	13,825 18	....	6,174 82
....	278 25	278 25	....	278 25	....
....	....	1,200 00	....	1,200 00	....
....	547 50	4,557 01	3,583 51	....	973 50
13,350 00	....	13,350 00	6,813 26	....	6,536 74
....	....	3,271 15	3,271 15	....	....
7,000 00	....	7,000 00	3,045 75	....	3,954 25
....	....	1,250 48	....	1,250 48	....
....	....	23,522 00	22,902 88	....	619 12
20,000 00	....	20,000 00	....	....	20,000 00
....	221 76	10,221 76	9,517 50	....	704 26
....	....	75,182 41	50,813 35	....	25,369 06
....	....	17,951 69	16,799 50	....	1,152 19
....	....	134,421 03	84,753 34	....	49,667 69
....	....	204,578 80	108,233 30	....	96,345 50
....	....	7,015 24	....	....	7,015 24
5 72	....	5 72	5 72	....	....
....	....	1,125 62	1,125 62	....	....
....	335 53	36,677 19	36,677 19	....	....
....	....	237,630 94	235,422 40	....	2,208 54
....	....	8,169 28	8,034 67	....	134 61
125,000 00	27 00	822,442 19	658,309 09	....	164,133 10
11,945,996 23	184,742 78	15,077,432 46	11,736,501 17	2,305,281 55	1,638,640 74

STATEMENT *exhibiting the* BALANCES *of* APPRO

Specific objects of appropriations.	Year.	Statutes.		Balances of appropriations July 1, 1879.
		Vol.	Page or section.	
CUSTOMS—Continued.				
Brought forward				$4, 246, 693 45
Marine Hospital, Chicago, Ill				98 97
Marine Hospital, Memphis, Tenn		21	109	
Custom-house, court-house, and post-office, Memphis, Tenn				116, 584 54
Custom-house, court-house, and post-office, Nashville, Tenn				69, 746 22
Custom-house, &c., St. Louis, Mo				381, 686 01
Custom-house, post-office, &c., Kansas City, Mo				114, 237 07
Appraisers' stores, San Francisco, Cal				40, 936 24
Marine Hospital, San Francisco, Cal				354 36
Nubble Head light-station, Maine				
Whale's Back fog-signal, New Hampshire				
Day beacons, Maine, New Hampshire, and Massachusetts				10, 000 00
Boat-landing at light-stations, Maine, New Hampshire, and Massachusetts				
Ipswich light-station, Massachusetts				10, 000 00
Cape Poge light-station, Massachusetts				5, 000 00
Stage Harbor light-station, Massachusetts				10, 000 00
Isle La Motte light-station, Vermont				5, 000 00
Bullock's Point Shoals light-station, Rhode Island				1, 500 00
Bullock's Point Shoals light-station, Rhode Island (act June 16, 1880)		21	243	
Feller's Rock and Sassafras Point light-station, Rhode Island				4, 500 00
Castle Hill fog-signal, Rhode Island				10, 000 00
Falkner's Island fog-signal, New York				5, 000 00
Execution Rocks fog-signal, New York				15, 000 00
Steam Mill Point light-station, New York				300 00
Cumberland Head, New York				250 00
Staten Island Depot, New York				10, 000 00
Cold Spring Harbor light-station, New York				20, 000 00
Thirty-mile Point light-station, New York				5, 000 00
Barnegat light-station, New Jersey				9, 000 00
Absecom light-station, New Jersey				20, 000 00
Great Beds light-station, New Jersey				23, 000 00
Wreck of the Scotland light-ship, New York Harbor, New Jersey				
Lights on the Delaware River, Delaware				60, 000 00
Harper's Straits light-station, Maryland				14, 000 00
Jones' Island light-station, Maryland				22, 000 00
Cape Henry light-station, Virginia				73, 068 30
Laurel Point light-station, North Carolina				18, 000 00
Beacon lights in Currituck and Albemarle Sounds, North Carolina				7, 000 00
Paris Island light-station, South Carolina				15, 000 00
Hilton Head and Bay Point light-station, South Carolina				20, 000 00
Fort Ripley light-station, South Carolina				
Fog Island light-station, Georgia				3, 000 00
American Shoal light-station, Florida				81, 968 30
Fowey Rocks light-station, Florida				18, 676 81
Dry Tortugas light-station, Florida				75, 000 00
Cape San Blas light-station, Florida				2, 000 00
Northwest Passage light-station, Florida				
Repairs of iron light-house, Florida				3, 150 00
Fort Point light-station, Texas				12, 500 00
Re-establishment of light-houses, Texas				20, 000 00
South Pass lights, Mississippi River, Louisiana				9, 189 25
Trinity Shoal light-ship, Louisiana				50, 000 00
South Pass light-station, Louisiana				50, 000 00
Calcasieu Range light-station, Louisiana				1, 500 00
Maumee Bay light-station, Ohio				4, 000 00
Sandusky Bay light-station, Ohio				7, 000 00
Pierhead beacon-lights on the lakes, Michigan				54, 916 49
Stannard's Rock light-station, Michigan				78, 000 00
Fort Austin light-station, Michigan				4, 676 80
Passage Island light-station, Michigan				18, 000 00
Frying Pan Island light-station, Michigan				2, 000 00
Cheboygan River light-station, Michigan				7, 000 00
Racine Point light-station, Wisconsin				34, 500 00
Point Wilson light-station, Washington Territory				5, 000 00
Point No Point light-station, Washington Territory				11, 037 77
Tillamook Head light-station, Oregon				49, 000 00
Saint Helen's Bar light-station, Oregon				787 21
Columbia River light-station, Oregon				
Oakland Harbor light-station, California				5, 000 00
Point Fermin light-station, California				900 00
Carried forward				5, 982, 141 79

PRIATIONS UNEXPENDED June 30, 1879, &c.—Continued.

Appropriations for the fiscal year ending June 30, 1880.	Repayments made during the fiscal year 1880.	Aggregate available for the fiscal year ending June 30, 1880.	Payments during the fiscal year ending June 30, 1880.	Amounts carried to the surplus fund June 30, 1880.	Balances of appropriations, June 30, 1880.
$11,245,996 28	$184,742 78	$18,677,432 46	$11,736,561 17	$2,305,361 55	$1,635,649 74
		98 97			98 97
30,000 00		30,000 00	300 00		29,700 00
	878 52	117,583 06	19,808 11		97,754 95
		89,788 22	42,922 22		46,866 00
	80,273 20	461,359 21	286,549 15		174,810 06
		114,227 07	31,554 80		82,672 27
	172 95	41,111 19	40,535 57		575 62
	68 27	422 63			422 63
	4,530 56	4,530 55	1,650 00	2,880 55	
	1,781 74	1,781 74			1,781 74
		10,000 00	4,600 00		5,400 00
	2,000 00	2,000 00	2,000 00		
		10,000 00	10,000 00		
		5,000 00	5,000 00		
		10,000 00	10,000 00		
		5,000 00	5,000 00		
		1,500 00		1,500 00	
146 40		146 40			146 40
		4,500 00			4,500 00
		10,000 00			10,000 00
		5,000 00	5,000 00		
		15,000 00	15,000 00		
		300 00	300 00		
		250 00			250 00
		10,000 00	10,000 00		
		20,000 00	10,000 00		10,000 00
		5,000 00			5,000 00
		9,000 00			9,000 00
		20,000 00			20,000 00
		23,000 00	10,000 00		13,000 00
	1 00	1 00		1 00	
		60,000 00	20,000 00		40,000 00
		14,000 00	14,000 00		
		22,000 00	22,000 00		
		73,068 30	35,000 00		38,068 30
		19,000 00	19,000 00		
	3,980 98	7,000 00	7,000 00		
	5,055 60	18,980 98	3,000 00		15,980 98
		25,055 60	16,000 00		9,055 60
		2 00		2 00	
		3,000 00	1,000 00		2,000 00
	12,470 75	93,539 05	65,000 00		28,539 05
	3,307 59	21,984 40	10,000 00	11,984 40	
		75,000 00			75,000 00
		2,000 00			2,000 00
	1,873 84	1,873 84		1,873 84	
		3,100 00			3,100 00
		12,500 00			12,500 00
		20,000 00			20,000 00
		9,189 25			9,189 25
		50,000 00	5,000 00		45,000 00
		50,000 00			50,000 00
		1,500 00			1,500 00
	825 78	4,825 78			4,825 78
	4,007 46	11,007 46	11,007 46		
	606 29	55,522 78	19,733 14		35,789 64
		70,000 00	55,000 00		15,000 00
		4,076 80		4,076 80	
		18,000 00			18,000 00
		2,000 00			2,000 00
		7,000 00	7,000 00		
		34,500 00	27,481 36		7,018 64
		5,000 00	5,000 00		
		11,037 77	11,037 77		
		49,000 00	49,000 00		
		787 21		787 21	
	1 26	1 26		1 26	
		5,000 00			5,000 00
		300 00			300 00
11,276,142 68	306,580 56	17,564,864 98	12,648,980 75	2,328,388 61	2,587,495 62

STATEMENT exhibiting the BALANCES of APPRO

Specific objects of appropriations.	Year.	Statutes.		Balances of appropriations, July 1, 1879.
		Vol.	Page or section.	
CUSTOMS—Continued.				
Brought forward				$5,982,141 79
Point Pinos light-station, California.................				6,000 00
Point Bonita light-station, California................				
Santa Barbara light-station, California...............				
Farallon fog-signal, California......................		21	240	
Steam tenders for the Atlantic coast				5,000 00
Depot for the sixth district........................				10,000 00
Depot for the twelfth district......................				10,000 00
Roadways at stations on Pacific coast				2,991 96
Repairs and protection of light-stations fourth district......				7,400 00
Duplicate fog-signals for the United States coast..........				20,000 00
Steam tender for the western river lights ....(....		21	240	30,000 00
Steam tender for the Pacific coast				
Laboratory of the Light-House Board				8,000 00
Lighting and buoyage of the Mississippi, Missouri, and Ohio Rivers	1877*			
Do	1878			27,016 47
Do	1879			15,669 12
Do	1880	20	380	
Lighting the Ohio River............................	1875*			7,802 98
Repayments to importers, excess of deposits, charges and commissions cases........................		{ 20 21	{ 414 242	} ...
Repayments to importers, excess of deposits, prior to July 1, 1875..				106,975 45
Repayments to importers, excess of deposits; no limit		R. S.	3689	
Repayments to importers, excess of deposits; no limit; act June 16, 1880		21	242, 255	
Debentures, drawbacks, bounties, or allowances, prior to July 1, 1875......................................				27,046 69
Debentures, drawbacks, bounties, or allowances; no limit		R. S.	3689	...
Debentures, drawbacks, bounties, or allowances; act June 16, 1880		21	255	
Debentures and other charges		R. S.	3689	
Salaries and expenses of Treasury Investigating Committees.	1878			400 00
Refunding moneys erroneously received and covered into the Treasury....................................		R. S.	3689	
Unclaimed merchandise.............................		R. S.	3689	
Detection and prevention of frauds upon the customs revenue..	1880	20	378	
Reimbursement of the master of the Verbena..........				33 83
Refunding duties to the University of Notre Dame du Lac, of Saint Joseph County, Indiana		21	31	
Relief of widows and orphans of surfmen who perished at Point Aux Barques, Lake Huron...................		21	258	
Relief of officers and crews of whaling barks Mount Wallaston and Vigilant............................		21	150	
Total customs				6,268,478 29
INTERIOR CIVIL.				
Salaries Office Secretary of the Interior	1878			47 55
Do	1880	21	23, 28	
Contingent expenses Office Secretary of the Interior.......	1878			1 87
Do	1879			
Do	1880	21	23	
Salaries temporary clerks Department of the Interior	1878			18 50
Do	1879			
Do	1880	21	23	
Salaries watchmen Department of the Interior	1878			154 89
Salary Secretary to sign land warrants	1878			1 00
Fuel, lights, &c., Department of the Interior............	1880	21	23	
Rent of buildings Department of the Interior...........	1878			07
Do	1879			
Do	1880	21	23, 28	
Stationery Department of the Interior	1878			113 53
Do	1879			
Do	1880	21	23, 28, 245	
Packing, &c., Congressional documents	1878			13 20
Do	1879			
Do	1880	21	23	
Postage Department of the Interior	1878			101,626 00
Do	1879			12,044 00
Do	1880	21	23	
Salaries General Land Office	1878			1 23
Carried forward..................................				114,821 84

*And prior years.

PRIATIONS UNEXPENDED June 30, 1879, &c.—Continued.

Appropriations for the fiscal year ending June 30, 1880.	Repayments made during the fiscal year 1880.	Aggregate available for the fiscal year ending June 30, 1880.	Payments during the fiscal year ending June 30, 1880.	Amounts carried to the surplus fund June 30, 1880.	Balances of appropriations, June 30, 1880.
$11,276,142 53	$306,580 56	$17,584,854 98	$12,648,980 75	$2,328,388 61	$2,587,455 02
		6,000 00	6,000 00		
	14 02	14 02		14 02	
	200 90	200 90		200 90	
7,000 00		7,000 00	2,450 00		4,550 00
		5,000 00	5,000 00		
		10,000 00	10,000 00		
		10,000 00	10,000 00		
		2,991 96	2,991 96		
		7,400 00	7,400 00		
		20,000 00	19,327 50		672 84
15,000 00	4,054 82	40,054 82	49,054 82		
	7,276 18	7,276 18	7,247 62	28 56	
		8,000 00			8,000 00
	10 79	10 79		10 79	
	80 30	27,096 82		27,096 82	
	2,017 50	17,686 92	46 98		17,639 99
130,000 00		130,000 00	128,123 00		1,877 00
		7,802 96			7,802 96
90,000 00		90,000 00	1,239 96		88,760 02
		108,975 45	108,972 75		2 70
2,517,827 22	16,867 23	2,534,694 45	2,534,694 45		
319,521 61		319,521 61	4,124 49		315,397 32
		27,046 89	5,069 53		21,977 36
1,835,991 23	13,955 83	1,839,947 06	1,839,947 06		
49 74		49 74			49 74
136 91		136 91	136 91		
		400 00		400 00	
127 50		127 50	127 50		
1,750 41		1,750 41	1,750 41		
100,000 00	5 68	100,005 68	20,000 00	...	80,005 68
		33 83			33 83
2,334 07		2,334 07	2,334 07		
1,000 00		1,000 00			1,000 00
6,000 00		6,000 00			6,000 00
16,292,881 32	351,063 86	22,912,423 47	17,415,050 73	2,356,139 70	3,141,224 04
...		47 55		47 55	
118,510 00		118,510 00	118,510 00		
		1 87		1 87	
	209 26	209 26	100 50		108 76
7,000 00		7,000 00	7,000 00		
		18 50		18 50	
	37 05	37 05			37 05
7,000 00		7,000 00	7,000 00		
		154 89		154 89	
		1 00		1 00	
8,000 00		8,000 00	8,000 00		
		97		97	
	83 37	83 37			83 37
29,100 00		29,100 00	29,100 00		
	21 15	21 15		21 15	
	2,389 06	2,502 59	2,502 59		
35,000 00	15,606 44	50,606 44	45,929 85		4,676 59
		13 20		13 20	
	212 92	212 92			212 92
5,000 00		5,000 00	5,000 00		
		101,826 00		101,826 00	
		12,644 00	12,643 86		20
36,000 00		36,000 00	14,437 50		15,562 50
		1 23		1 23	
239,610 00	18,559 25	372,991 09	250,224 24	102,085 46	20,681 39

STATEMENT exhibiting BALANCES of APPRO

Specific objects of appropriations.	Year.	Statutes. Vol.	Statutes. Page or section.	Balances of appropriations, July 1, 1879.
INTERIOR CIVIL—Continued.				
Brought forward				$114,821 84
Salaries General Land Office	1879			
Do	1880	21	23	
Contingent expenses General Land Office	1877*	21	255	
Do	1879			1 55
Do	1879			
Contingent expenses General Land Office (no limit)				50
Contingent expenses General Land Office	1880	21	23	
Salaries temporary clerks General Land Office {	1877	}		1,057 85
	1878			13 84
Do	1880	20	394	
Commission to classify lands and codify land laws {	1880	} 21	245	
	1881			
Adjusting claims for indemnity for swamp lands		21	41, 150	
Reproducing plate of surveys General Land Office	1879			
Do	1880	20, 21	393, 246	
Salaries Office Commissioner of Indian Affairs	1878			145 02
Do	1879			604 37
Do	1880	21	23, 28	
Contingent expenses Office Commissioner of Indian Affairs	1878			1 63
Do	1880	21	23	
Salaries Office Commissioner of Education	1878			7 70
Do	1879			
Do	1880	21	23, 28	
Contingent expenses Office Commissioner of Education	1878			36 27
Do	1879			
Do	1880	21	23	
Distributing documents Bureau of Education	1880	20	395	
Removal of Bureau of Education	1879			
Salaries Office Commissioner of Pensions	1877*			74 30
Do	1878			
Do	1879			
Do	1880	21	23, 28, 68	
Contingent expenses Office Commissioner of Pensions	1877			8,209 50
Do	1878			1,980 90
Do	1879			
Do	1880	21	23, 68	
Investigation of frauds Pension Office	1879			
Do	1880	21	23	
Furniture, contingencies, and rent, Office Commissioner of {	1879	}		1,500 00
Pensions	1880			
Salaries temporary clerks Office Commissioner of Pensions {	1879	}		43,700 00
	1880			
Salaries Office Commissioner of Patents	1878			3 40
Do	1879			
Do	1880	21	23, 28	
Contingent expenses Office Commissioner of Patents	1879			
Do	1880	21	23	
Scientific Library, Patent Office	1880	21	23	
Publishing the Biennial Register		21	245	
Photolithographing Office Commissioner of Patents	1878			137 85
Do	1880	21	23	
Copies of drawings Office Commissioner of Patents	1878			46
Do	1879			
Do	1880	21	22	
Tracings of drawings Office Commissioner of Patents	1879			
Do	1880	21	23	
Plates for Patent Office Official Gazette	1878			96 10
Do	1880	21	23, 150	
Salaries Office Auditor of Railroad Accounts	1879			
Do	1880	21	29	
Contingent expenses Office Auditor of Railroad Accounts	1880	21	29	
Salaries employés under Architect of the Capitol	1880	21	29, 245	
Salary Director Geological Survey	1879	21	245	
Do	1880	20	394	
Salaries office surveyor-general of Arizona	1878	21	247	
Do	1879			1,241 40
Do	1880	21	23	
Contingent expenses office surveyor-general of Arizona	1878			102 40
Do	1879			425 50
Do	1880	20	394	
Salaries office surveyor-general of California	1878	21	247	469 84
Do	1879			3,474 04
Carried forward				179,086 26

PRIATIONS UNEXPENDED June 30, 1879, &c.—Continued.

Appropriations for the fiscal year ending June 30, 1880.	Repayments made during the fiscal year 1880.	Aggregate available for the fiscal year ending June 30, 1880.	Payments during the fiscal year ending June 30, 1880.	Amounts carried to the surplus fund June 30, 1880.	Balances of appropriations, June 30, 1880.
$239,610 00	$18,559 25	$372,991 09	$250,294 24	$102,185 46	$20,681 39
....	28 07	28 07	....	....	28 07
273,220 00	....	273,220 00	273,220 00	....	....
77 50	....	77 50	....	....	77 50
....	....	1 55	....	1 55	....
....	500 00	500 00	499 60	....	40
....	190 76	191 26	....	191 26	....
25,000 00	270 25	25,270 25	23,750 56	....	1,519 69
....	....	1,057 85	....	1,057 85	....
....	....	13 84	....	13 84	....
20,000 00	....	20,000 00	20,000 00	....	....
15,000 00	....	15,000 00	....	....	15,000 00
20,000 00	....	20,000 00	15,000 00	....	5,000 00
....	4 00	4 00	....	....	4 00
24,000 00	....	24,000 00	12,000 00	....	12,000 00
....	....	145 02	....	145 02	....
....	....	604 37	424 82	....	179 55
74,160 00	....	74,160 00	74,160 00	....	....
....	....	1 63	....	1 63	....
3,000 00	....	3,000 00	3,000 00	....	....
....	....	7 70	....	7 70	....
....	1 05	1 05	....	....	1 05
17,320 00	....	17,320 00	17,320 00	....	....
....	....	36 27	36 27	....	....
....	9 77	9 77	....	....	9 77
18,490 00	135 00	18,535 00	18,535 00	....	....
1,000 00	....	1,000 00	1,000 00	....	....
....	3 49	3 49	....	....	3 49
....	26 44	26 44	....	26 44	....
....	....	74 30	....	74 30	....
....	5 72	5 72	....	....	5 72
538,850 00	....	538,850 00	538,850 00	....	....
....	....	9,309 50	9,309 50	....	....
....	....	1,960 90	....	1,960 00	....
....	34 82	34 82	....	....	34 82
20,000 00	....	20,000 00	20,000 00	....	....
....	4,139 50	4,139 50	....	....	4,139 50
40,000 00	....	40,000 00	30,000 00	....	10,000 00
....	....	1,500 00	1,500 00	....	....
....	....	43,700 00	43,700 00	....	....
....	....	3 40	....	3 40	....
....	89	99	....	....	99
407,070 00	....	407,070 00	407,070 00	....	....
....	32 18	33 18	22 10	....	10 08
35,000 00	....	35,000 00	35,000 00	....	....
5,000 00	....	5,000 00	5,000 00	....	....
2,000 00	....	2,000 00	2,000 00	....	....
....	....	137 85	....	137 85	....
35,000 00	....	35,000 00	35,000 00	....	....
....	....	46	....	46	....
....	71	71	....	....	71
25,000 00	....	25,000 00	25,000 00	....	....
....	2 35	2 35	....	....	2 35
5,000 00	....	5,000 00	5,000 00	....	....
....	....	96 10	....	96 10	....
27,299 22	....	27,299 22	27,299 22	....	....
....	130 74	130 74	13 00	....	118 74
12,300 00	....	12,300 00	12,300 00	....	....
2,500 09	....	2,500 00	2,500 00	....	....
7,824 00	....	7,824 00	7,824 00	....	....
626 37	....	626 37	626 37	....	....
6,000 00	....	6,000 00	6,000 00	....	....
478 17	....	478 17	....	....	478 17
....	....	1,241 40	1,171 04	....	70 36
5,759 09	....	5,750 00	5,750 00	....	....
....	....	102 40	....	102 40	....
....	....	425 50	392 40	....	33 10
1,500 00	....	1,500 00	1,500 00	....	....
4,006 69	....	4,476 53	....	469 84	4,006 69
....	....	3,474 04	3,471 91	....	2 13
1,911,991 95	24,075 09	2,115,153 30	1,935,369 03	106,376 00	73,408 27

REPORT ON THE FINANCES.

STATEMENT exhibiting the BALANCES of APPRO ,

Specific objects of appropriations.	Year.	Statutes.		Balances of ap. propriations July 1, 1879.'
		Vol.	Page or section.	
INTERIOR CIVIL—Continued.				
Brought forward				$179,086 26
Salaries office surveyor-general of California	1880	{ 20	393	} ....
		{ 21	23	}
Contingent expenses office surveyor-general of California	1878	21	247	....
Do	1879	......	....	537 82
Do	1880	20	393	....
Safe for Spanish archives office surveyor-general of California	1880	20	393	....
Salaries office surveyor-general of Colorado	1879	......	....	3,262 17
Do	1880	21	23	....
Contingent expenses office surveyor-general of Colorado	1878	21	247	....
Do	1879	......	....	309 35
Do	1880	20	093	....
Salaries office surveyor-general of Dakota	1878	......	....	87
Do	1879	......	....	1,511 67
Do	1880	21	23	....
Contingent expenses office surveyor-general of Dakota	1879	......	....	268 31
Do	1880	20	393	....
Salaries office surveyor-general of Florida	1879	......	....	950 00
Do	1880	21	23	....
Contingent expenses office surveyor-general of Florida	1878	......	....	121 39
Do	1879	......	....	348 57
Do	1880	20	393	....
Salaries office surveyor-general of Idaho	1878	......	....	5 93
Do	1879	......	....	1,197 11
Do	1880	21	23	....
Contingent expenses office surveyor-general of Idaho	1878	......	....	7 50
Do	1879	......	....	344 59
Do	1880	20	393	....
Salaries office surveyor-general of Louisiana	1879	......	....	1,450 00
Do	1880	21	23	....
Contingent expenses office surveyor-general of Louisiana	1879	......	....	417 82
Do	1880	20	393	....
Salaries office surveyor-general of Minnesota	1878	......	....	12
Do	1879	......	....	1,264 79
Do	1880	21	23	....
Contingent expenses office surveyor-general of Minnesota	1878	......	....	549 74
Do	1879	......	....	717 62
Do	1880	20	393	....
Salaries office surveyor-general of Montana	1878	......	....	299 29
Do	1879	......	....	1,257 84
Do	1880	21	23	....
Contingent expenses office surveyor-general of Montana	1878	......	....	05
Do	1879	......	....	284 20
Do	1880	20	393	....
Salaries office surveyor-general of Nebraska and Iowa	1879	......	....	1,175 88
Do	1880	21	23	....
Contingent expenses office surveyor-general of Nebraska and Iowa	1878	......	....	1 11
Do	1879	......	....	277 05
Do	1880	20	393	....
Salaries office surveyor-general of Nevada	*1877	21	254	....
Do	1878	......	....	3 06
Do	1879	......	....	1,364 84
Do	1880	21	23	....
Contingent expenses office surveyor-general of Nevada	*1877	21	255	....
Do	1878	21	247	....
Do	1879	21	247	156 50
Do	1880	20	393	....
Salaries office surveyor-general of New Mexico	1878	......	....	04
Do	1879	......	....	1,876 23
Do	1880	21	23	....
Contingent expenses office surveyor-general of New Mexico	1878	21	247	20 18
Do	1879	21	247	378 48
Do	1880	20	393	....
Salaries office surveyor-general of Oregon	1878	......	....	
Do	1879	......	....	1,825 00
Do	1880	21	23	....
Contingent expenses office surveyor-general of Oregon	1878	......	....	161 90
Do	1879	......	....	622 54
Do	1880	20	393	....
Salaries office surveyor-general of Utah	1878	......	....	6 89
Do	1879	......	....	1,394 70
Do	1880	21	23	....
Contingent expenses office surveyor-general of Utah	1878	......	....	20
Carried forward				201,302 92

PRIATIONS UNEXPENDED June 30, 1879, &c.—Continued.

Appropriations for the fiscal year ending June 30, 1880.	Repayments made during the fiscal year 1880.	Aggregate available for the fiscal year ending June 30, 1880.	Payments during the fiscal year ending June 30, 1880.	Amounts carried to the surplus fund June 30, 1880.	Balances of appropriations, June 30, 1880.
$1,911,991 95	$34,075 09	$2,115,153 30	$1,935,369 03	$106,376 00	$73,408 27
22,750 00	1 10	22,751 10	22,750 00	....	1 10
497 74	....	497 74	....	....	497 74
....	....	537 82	537 80	....	02
3,000 00	124 00	3,124 00	3,000 00	....	124 00
1,000 00	....	1,000 00	983 25	....	16 75
....	....	1,252 17	1,252 17	....	....
6,000 00	544 67	6,544 67	6,456 36	....	88 31
42 71	....	42 71	....	....	42 71
....	....	309 35	309 35	....	....
1,500 00	223 27	1,723 27	1,723 27	....	....
....	....	87	....	87	....
....	....	1,511 67	1,511 67	....	....
6,500 00	....	6,500 00	6,500 00	....	....
....	....	263 31	263 31	....	....
1,500 00	....	1,500 00	1,500 00	....	....
....	....	950 00	950 00	....	....
3,800 00	....	3,800 00	3,800 00	....	....
....	....	121 39	....	121 39	....
....	....	348 57	311 60	....	36 97
1,000 00	....	1,000 00	1,000 00	....	....
....	....	5 03	....	5 03	....
....	....	1,157 11	1,154 83	....	2 58
5,000 00	....	5,000 00	5,000 00	....	....
....	....	7 50	....	7 50	....
....	....	344 99	344 50	....	49
1,500 00	....	1,500 00	1,500 00	....	....
....	....	1,450 00	1,450 00	....	....
5,890 00	....	5,890 00	5,890 00	....	....
....	....	417 80	302 00	....	115 80
1,000 00	....	1,000 00	1,000 00	....	....
....	....	12	....	12	....
....	....	1,264 79	1,264 30	....	49
7,000 00	....	7,000 00	7,000 00	....	....
....	....	549 74	....	549 74	....
....	....	717 62	378 20	....	339 42
1,500 00	....	1,500 00	1,500 00	....	....
....	....	299 29	....	299 29	....
....	....	1,257 84	1,257 01	....	83
5,750 00	....	5,750 00	5,750 00	....	....
....	....	05	....	05	....
....	....	284 20	284 16	....	04
1,500 00	....	1,500 00	1,500 00	....	....
....	....	1,175 98	1,175 90	....	88
5,000 00	....	5,000 00	5,000 00	....	....
....	....	1 11	....	1 11	....
....	....	277 05	277 05	....	....
1,500 00	....	1,500 00	1,500 00	....	....
480 00	....	480 00	....	....	480 00
....	....	2 08	....	2 08	....
....	....	1,364 84	1,363 46	....	1 38
5,500 00	....	5,500 00	5,500 00	....	....
68 75	....	68 75	68 75	....	....
392 10	....	392 10	....	....	392 10
152 31	....	308 81	156 49	....	152 32
1,500 00	....	1,500 00	1,500 00	....	....
....	....	04	....	....	04
....	....	1,876 23	1,876 23	....	....
8,500 00	1 43	8,501 43	8,500 00	....	1 43
61 97	....	82 15	....	20 18	61 97
32 95	....	401 43	352 78	....	48 65
1,500 00	240 06	1,740 06	1,740 00	....	06
....	....	2 20	....	2 20	....
....	....	1,825 00	1,820 60	....	4 40
7,000 00	....	7,000 00	7,000 00	....	....
....	....	181 00	....	181 00	....
....	....	622 54	342 25	....	280 29
1,500 00	....	1,500 00	1,500 00	....	....
....	....	6 80	....	6 80	....
....	....	1,334 70	1,331 15	....	3 55
5,750 00	....	5,750 00	5,750 00	....	....
....	....	20	....	20	....
2,927,500 48	25,209 92	2,254,132 42	2,070,456 57	107,573 60	76,102 36

STATEMENT exhibiting the BALANCES of APPRO

Specific objects of appropriations.	Year.	Statutes.		Balances of appropriations, July 1, 1879.
		Vol.	Page or section.	
INTERIOR CIVIL—Continued.				
Brought forward				$201,362 82
Contingent expenses office surveyor-general of Utah	1870			492 11
Do	1880	20	394	
Salaries office surveyor-general of Washington	1879			1,625 00
Do	1880	21	29	
Contingent expenses office surveyor-general of Washington	1879			301 12
Do	1880	20 21	393 246	
Salaries office surveyor-general of Wyoming	1878			48
Do	1879			1,164 70
Do	1880	21	23	
Contingent expenses office surveyor-general of Wyoming	1878			554 55
Do	1879			657 89
Do	1880	20	394	
Annual repairs of the Capitol	1880	20	391	
Improving the Capitol grounds	1879			20,000 00
Do	1880	20	391	
Lighting the Capitol and grounds	1879	21	246	
Do	1880	20	391	
Heating apparatus, Senate	1880	20	391	
Ventilation of the House of Representatives				25,000 00
Payment to C. Bramidi for frescoing the Capitol				700 00
Payment to George W. Cook for improving Capitol grounds				709 26
Retained percentages, improving Capitol grounds				2,217 94
Arranging Court of Claims rooms, Capitol, as committee rooms	1880	21	55	
Extension of Government Printing Office				33,300 00
Reconstructing Interior Department building		20	392	90,753 00
Jail, District of Columbia				
Repairs of building Interior Department	1878			38
Do	1880	21	23, 38	
Buildings and grounds Government Hospital for Insane	1879 1880			20,000 00
Do	1880	20	305	
Current expenses Government Hospital for Insane	1880	20 21	395 246	
Current expenses Columbia Institution for Deaf and Dumb	1880	20	395	
Support of Freedmen's Hospital and Asylum, Washington, D. C.	1860	20	306	
Support of Children's Hospital, Washington, D. C.	1878			8 67
National Association for Relief of Colored Women and Children, District of Columbia	1878			1 72
Current expenses National Soldiers and Sailors' Orphan Home	1879			5,000 00
Additional security against fire Smithsonian Institution	1880	20	397	
Preservation of collections Smithsonian Institution	1880	20	397	
Preservation of collections Smithsonian Institution, Armory building	1880	20	397	
Salaries and expenses Hot Springs Commission. (Reimbursable)				18,624 30
Protection and improvement Yellowstone National Park	1880	20	393	
Commission to report on depredation of Rocky Mountain locusts	1879	21	246	
Do	1880	20	397	
Investigating the habits of insects injurious to cotton plant and agriculture	1879 1880	21	246	
Do	1880	21	23	
Expenses of the Eighth Census		21	52	537 40
Expenses of the Ninth Census		21	52	
Expenses of the Tenth Census		21	76	246,500 00
Reimbursement to marshals for taking the Ninth Census				96 24
Rooms for Court of Claims		21	55, 248	
Appraisement and sale Fort Reynolds Military Reservation in Colorado	1880	20	393	
Surveying northern boundary of Wyoming	1880	20	392	
Survey of Fort Kearney Military Reservation in Nebraska				456 65
Retracing boundary between Arkansas and Indian Territory	1878			74 52
Survey of boundary between Colorado and Utah				7,000 00
Geological Survey	1880	20	394	
Geological survey of the Territories	1878 1879			219 26
Surveying private land claims	1877*	21	254	
Examination of the public surveys	1880	20	392	
Surveying private land claims in Arizona	1880	20	392	
Surveying private land claims in California	1880	20	392	
Carried forward				678,144 61

* And prior years.

PRIATIONS UNEXPENDED June 30, 1879, &c.—Continued.

Appropriations for the fiscal year ending June 30, 1880.	Repayments made during the fiscal year 1880.	Aggregate available for the fiscal year ending June 30, 1880.	Payments during the fiscal year ending June 30, 1880.	Amounts carried to the surplus fund June 30, 1880.	Balances of appropriations, June 30, 1880.
$2,027,560 48	$25,309 62	$2,254,132 42	$2,070,456 87	$107,573 80	$76,102 25
....	....	492 11	417 95	....	74 16
1,500 00	....	1,500 00	1,500 00	....	....
....	....	1,625 00	1,625 00	....	....
6,500 00	....	6,500 00	6,500 00	....	....
....	....	801 12	801 12	....	....
1,800 00	....	1,800 00	1,800 00	....	....
....	....	48	....	48	....
....	....	1,164 70	1,164 42	....	28
6,250 00	1 95	6,251 95	6,250 00	....	1 95
....	....	554 55	....	554 55	....
....	....	657 39	334 56	....	322 83
1,500 00	2 00	1,502 00	1,500 00	....	2 00
50,000 00	....	50,000 00	50,000 00	....	....
....	....	20,000 00	20,000 00	....	....
60,000 00	....	60,000 00	60,000 00	....	....
2,898 24	....	2,898 24	....	....	2,898 24
32,400 00	....	32,400 00	32,400 00	....	....
4,000 00	....	4,000 00	4,000 00	....	....
....	....	25,000 00	25,000 00	....	....
....	....	700 00	....	....	700 00
....	....	799 26	....	....	799 26
....	....	2,217 94	2,117 31	....	100 63
2,000 00	....	2,000 00	2,000 00	....	....
....	....	33,800 00	33,800 00	....	....
150,000 00	....	240,750 00	210,000 00	....	30,750 00
....	80 71	80 71	....	80 71	....
....	....	38	....	38	....
5,000 00	....	5,000 00	5,000 00	....	....
....	....	20,000 00	20,000 00	....	....
15,000 00	....	15,000 00	15,000 00	....	....
169,806 91	....	169,806 91	169,806 91	....	....
50,000 00	....	50,000 00	50,000 00	....	....
41,736 00	....	41,736 00	41,736 00	....	....
....	....	8 67	....	8 67	....
....	....	1 72	....	1 72	....
....	....	5,000 00	....	....	5,000 00
3,000 00	....	3,000 00	3,000 00	....	....
28,000 00	234 96	28,234 96	28,234 96	....	....
2,500 00	....	2,500 00	2,500 00	....	....
....	....	18,824 80	9,500 00	....	9,324 80
10,000 00	....	10,000 00	10,000 00	....	....
600 00	....	600 00	600 00	....	....
10,000 00	....	10,000 00	10,000 00	....	....
412 46	....	412 46	412 46	....	....
5,000 00	....	5,000 00	5,000 00	....	....
9,000 00	....	9,537 40	2,529 02	....	7,008 38
4,090 69	....	4,090 69	749 54	....	3,341 15
325,000 00	....	371,500 00	267,018 30	....	104,481 70
....	....	96 24	....	....	96 24
5,120 00	....	5,120 00	5,120 00	....	....
5,000 00	....	5,000 00	2,000 00	....	3,000 00
20,000 00	....	20,000 00	....	....	20,000 00
....	....	456 65	....	456 65	....
....	....	74 52	....	74 52	....
....	....	7,000 00	7,000 00	....	....
100,000 00	82 36	100,082 36	100,074 99	....	7 37
....	....	219 36	....	....	219 36
472 83	....	472 83	....	....	472 83
8,000 00	....	8,000 00	3,472 78	....	4,527 22
15,000 00	....	15,000 00	8,473 53	....	6,526 47
7,500 00	....	7,500 00	6,046 82	....	1,453 18
2,986,647 61	25,611 60	3,690,403 82	3,304,442 24	108,751 28	277,210 30

STATEMENT exhibiting the BALANCES of APPRO

Specific objects of appropriations.	Year.	Statutes.		Balances of appropriations July 1, 1879.
		Vol.	Page or section.	
INTERIOR CIVIL—Continued.				
Brought forward				**$678,144 61**
Surveying private land claims in New Mexico...............	1880	20	392	....
Surveying timber lands	1879	21	247	22,269 90
Recovery of an iron monument from the Colorado River West				208 26
Payment to John Cosley, custodian Detroit Arsenal	1879			83 85
Reimbursement to American Photolithographic Company...		21	246	2,000 00
Payment to John Sherman, jr., United States marshal		21	385	....
Relief of Mrs. Mary E. Harrington, executrix of late G. D. Harrington.................		21	248	....
Maryland Institution for Instruction of the Blind		R. S.	3689	....
Five per cent. of the net proceeds of sales of public lands in Nebraska		15	49	....
Five per cent. of the net proceeds of sales of public lands in Nevada		R. S.	3689	....
Five per cent. fund of the net proceeds of sales of public lands in Oregon		R. S.	3689	....
Five per cent. fund of the net proceeds of sales of public lands in Wisconsin.................		R. S.	3689	....
Five per cent. fund of the net proceeds of sales of public lands in Minnesota....................		R. S.	3689	....
Five per cent. fund of the net proceeds of sales of public lands in Michigan....................		R. S.	3689	....
Indemnity for swamp lands purchased by individuals		R. S.	3689	....
Protection and improvement of Hot Springs, Ark..........		{ 19 20	380 258	} 3,096 99
Publishing proclamations relating to sales of lands		19	357	....
Deposits by individuals for surveying public lands		R. S.	3689	113,880 57
Repayment for lands erroneously sold....................		R. S.	3680	....
Repayment for lands erroneously sold prior to July 1, 1877..		21	254	....
Salaries and commissions of registers and receivers	1877*	21	255	....
Do..................	1878	21	248	2,094 03
Do..................	1879			3,036 63
Do..................	1880	{ 20 21	392 248	} ....
Expenses of depositing public moneys	1878			5,050 14
Do..................	1879			5,207 79
Do..................	1880	20	392	....
Contingent expenses land offices	1877*	21	248	121 33
Do..................	1878	21	255	....
Do..................	1879			6,923 33
Do..................	1880	20	392	....
Depredations on public timber	1878	21	247	54
Do..................	{ 1879 1880	21	247	} 36,300 00
Surveying public and private lands	{ 1877 1878	21	247	} 8,795 36
Do..................	1879	21	247	116,884 06
Surveying public lands.................................	1877*	20	392	....
Do..................	1880	21	254	....
Statistical and historical data respecting the Indians of the United States	1875			....
Total Interior civil......................				997,843 11
INTERNAL REVENUE.				
Salaries and expenses of supervisors and subordinate officers internal revenue	1876*			200 00
Do..................	1877*			....
Salaries and expenses of agents and subordinate officers	1878			47,357 14
Do..................	1879			19,662 47
Do..................	1880	21	23	....
Salaries and expenses of collectors of internal revenue.....	1877*	21	254	....
Do..................	1878			38,386 15
Do..................	1879			57,814 45
Do..................	1880	21	23	....
Stamps, paper, and dies....................	1878			17,927 73
Do..................	1879			20,677 78
Do..................	1880	21	23	....
Punishment for violation of internal-revenue laws.........	1877*	21	254	....
Do..................	1878	21	244	....
Do..................	1879			15,868 17
Do..................	1880	21	23	....
Abstracts of real estate acquired under revenue laws........	1878			189 70
Carried forward......................				216,367 69

* And prior years.

PRIATIONS UNEXPENDED June 30, 1879, &c.—Continued.

Appropriations for the fiscal year ending June 30, 1880.	Repayments made during the fiscal year 1880.	Aggregate available for the fiscal year ending June 30, 1880.	Payments during the fiscal year ending June 30, 1880.	Amounts carried to the surplus fund June 30, 1880.	Balances of appropriations, June 30, 1880.
$2,986,647 61	$25,611 60	$3,690,403 82	$3,304,442 34	$108,751 28	$277,210 30
10,000 00	85	10,000 85	3,654 95		6,345 90
332 64		22,692 74	21,623 38		979 36
		205 28	205 28		
	32 85	32 85			32 85
2,000 00		4,000 00	2,000 00		2,000 00
351 93		351 93			351 93
3,303 14		3,303 14			3,303 14
5,775 00		5,775 00	5,775 00		
615 87		615 87	615 87		
675 73		675 73	675 73		
1,762 54		1,762 54	1,762 54		
902 23		902 23	902 23		
4,121 10		4,121 10	4,121 10		
452 27		452 27	452 27		
4,552 60		4,552 60	4,552 60		
2,774 03		5,870 02	2,550 00		3,320 02
583 10		583 10	583 10		
474,556 70	2,002 03	590,448 30	277,091 29		313,357 01
18,119 18		18,119 18	18,119 18		
4,749 08		4,749 08	533 07		4,217 01
2,786 46	4,910 42	7,696 88		4,910 42	2,786 46
8,219 09	1,468 95	11,692 07	3,328 13	144 85	8,219 09
	14,609 18	17,637 81	17,066 95		570 86
443,900 00	2,617 73	446,517 73	396,318 65		48,199 08
		5,050 14		5,050 14	
	81 15	5,288 94	389 70		4,899 24
10,000 00		10,000 00	4,649 20		5,350 80
75		132 08		131 33	75
106 00		106 00			106 00
	8 50	6,931 83	2,941 15		3,990 68
100,000 00	75 00	100,075 00	90,019 47		10,055 53
127 00		127 24		24	127 00
15,531 00	1,184 40	46,915 40	34,384 20		12,531 20
436 78		9,232 14	2,162 07	7,070 07	
8,881 38	4,018 07	129,783 51	119,441 71		10,341 80
300,000 00		300,000 00	237,653 41		62,346 59
6,698 02		6,698 02	394 34		6,303 68
		16 10		16 10	
4,418,961 43	56,603 98	5,473,428 52	4,560,407 81	126,074 43	786,946 28
		200 00			200 00
763 94		763 94	763 94		
	142 95	47,500 09	1,749 31	45,750 76	
	4,734 00	24,386 47	23,777 51		608 96
1,820,000 00	388 00	1,820,388 00	1,812,473 86		7,914 14
1,019 88		1,019 88			1,019 88
	284 39	38,564 54	2,799 87	35,764 67	
	1,130 02	58,444 57	54,573 42		3,871 15
1,825,000 00	481 21	1,825,481 21	1,768,710 37		56,770 84
	1,099 11	17,027 73		17,027 73	
		21,776 89	21,776 89		
426,283 10	3,504 40	429,787 50	423,138 63		6,648 87
9,481 58		9,481 58	7,429 93		2,051 65
7,547 35		7,547 35	2,667 22		4,880 13
	34 69	15,603 06	15,602 75		31
75,000 00		75,000 00	69,923 68		5,076 32
		189 70		189 70	
4,165,095 85	11,798 97	4,393,162 51	4,205,387 38	98,732 86	89,042 25

STATEMENT *exhibiting the* BALANCES *of* APPRO

Specific objects of appropriations.	Year.	Statutes.		Balances of appropriations, July 1, 1879.
		Vol.	Page or section.	
INTERNAL REVENUE—Continued.				
Brought forward				$216, 267 69
Expenses of assessing and collecting internal revenue	1875*	21	254	1, 004 12
Allowance or drawback prior to July 1, 1875				1, 296 03
Allowance or drawback prior to July 1, 1877		21	254	
Allowance or drawback		R. S.	3689	
Redemption of stamps prior to July 1, 1876				95 00
Redemption of stamps prior to July 1, 1877		21	254	
Redemption of stamps		R. S.	3689	
Refunding taxes illegally collected prior to July 1, 1875				43, 694 46
Refunding taxes illegally collected		R. S.	3689	
Refunding taxes illegally collected prior to July 1, 1877, act June 16, 1880		21	254	
Refunding moneys erroneously received and covered into the Treasury		R. S.	3689	
Refunding moneys erroneously received and covered into the Treasury prior to July 1, 1877		21	254	
Alteration of dies and stamps				10, 000 00
Relief of certain citizens of Lynchburg, Va., act June 8, 1880		21	21	
Relief of certain parties for taxes illegally collected on rope and bagging, act June 16, 1880		21	63	
Total internal revenue				272, 357 32
PUBLIC DEBT.				
Redemption:				
Temporary loan		R. S.	3689	
Coin certificates, act March 3, 1863		R. S.	3689	
Silver certificates, act February 28, 1878		R. S.	3689	
Certificates of deposit, act June 8, 1872		R. S.	3689	
Refunding certificates, act February 26, 1879		R. S.	3689	
Old demand notes		R. S.	3689	
Legal tender notes		R. S.	3689	
Fractional currency		R. S.	3689	
One year notes of 1863		R. S.	3689	
Two years notes of 1863		R. S.	3689	
Compound interest notes		R. S.	3689	
Seven-thirties of 1864 and 1865		R. S.	3689	
Bounty land scrip		R. S.	3689	
Loan of 1858		R. S.	3689	
Loan of February, 1861 (1881s)		R. S.	3689	
Oregon war debt		R. S.	3689	
Loan of July and August, 1861 (1881s)		R. S.	3689	
Five-twenties of 1862		R. S.	3689	
Loan of 1863 (1881s)		R. S.	3689	
Ten-forties of 1864		R. S.	3689	
Five-twenties of June, 1864		R. S.	3689	
Five-twenties of 1865		R. S.	3689	
Consols of 1865		R. S.	3689	
Consols of 1867		R. S.	3689	
Consols of 1868		R. S.	3689	
Funded loan of 1881		R. S.	3689	
Funded loan of 1907		R. S.	3689	
Interest:				
Temporary loan		R. S.	3689	
Navy pension fund		R. S.	3689	
One year notes of 1863		R. S.	3689	
Two years notes of 1863		R. S.	3689	
Compound interest notes		R. S.	3689	
Seven-thirties of 1864 and 1865		R. S.	3689	
Loan of 1841		R. S.	3689	
Loan of 1842		R. S.	3689	
Loan of 1847		R. S.	3689	
Bounty land scrip		R. S.	3689	
Loan of 1858		R. S.	3689	
Loan of February, 1861 (1881s)		R. S.	3689	
Oregon war debt		R. S.	3689	
Loan of July and August, 1861 (1881s)		R. S.	3689	
Five-twenties of 1862		R. S.	3689	
Loan of 1863 (1881s)		R. S.	3689	
Ten-forties of 1864		R. S.	3689	
Five-twenties of March, 1864		R. S.	3689	
Five-twenties of June, 1864		R. S.	3689	
Five-twenties of 1865		R. S.	3689	
Carried forward				

* And prior years.

PRIATIONS UNEXPENDED June 30, 1879, &c.—Continued.

Appropriations for the fiscal year ending June 30, 1880.	Repayments made during the fiscal year 1880.	Aggregate available for the fiscal year ending June 30, 1880.	Payments during the fiscal year ending June 30, 1880.	Amounts carried to the surplus fund June 30, 1880.	Balances of appropriations, June 30, 1880.
$4,165,095 85	$11,798 97	$4,393,162 51	$4,205,387 38	$96,732 88	$89,042 25
2,186 73	1,788 07	4,978 92	1,205 46	1,788 07	1,985 39
....	....	1,296 03	1,296 03	....	....
367 86	....	367 80	....	....	367 80
57,012 27	....	57,012 27	57,012 27	....	....
....	....	95 00	95 00	....	95 00
3,403 31	....	3,403 31	....	....	3,403 31
24,972 71	....	24,972 71	24,972 71	....	....
....	....	43,694 48	17,919 98	25,774 50	....
23,154 82	....	23,154 82	23,154 82	....	....
3,029 27	....	3,029 27	3,029 27	....	....
138 35	....	138 35	138 35	....	....
139 63	....	139 63	139 63	....	....
....	1,065 95	11,065 95	2,846 59	....	8,219 36
26,198 60	....	26,198 60	26,196 60	....	....
2,725 56	....	2,725 56	2,725 56	....	....
4,308,422 96	14,652 99	4,595,433 27	4,384,738 62	127,591 48	103,113 17
100 00	....	100 00	100 00	....	....
7,409,100 00	....	7,409,100 00	7,409,100 00	....	....
183,680 00	....	183,680 00	183,680 00	....	....
63,260,000 00	....	63,260,000 00	63,260,000 00	....	....
12,095,850 00	....	12,095,850 00	12,095,850 00	....	....
495 99	....	495 99	495 00	....	....
81,302,563 00	....	81,302,563 00	81,302,563 00	....	....
251,717 41	....	251,717 41	251,717 41	....	....
2,150 00	....	2,150 00	2,150 00	....	....
1,550 00	....	1,550 00	1,550 00	....	....
16,500 00	....	16,500 00	16,500 00	....	....
2,650 00	....	2,650 00	2,650 00	....	....
25 00	....	25 00	25 00	....	....
40,000 00	....	40,000 00	40,000 00	....	....
2,837,000 00	....	2,837,000 00	2,837,000 00	....	....
202,550 00	....	202,550 00	202,550 00	....	....
32,064,250 00	....	32,064,250 00	32,064,250 00	....	....
9,100 00	....	9,100 00	9,100 00	....	....
12,797,150 00	....	12,797,150 00	12,797,150 00	....	....
135,769,750 00	....	135,769,750 00	135,769,750 00	....	....
3,550 00	....	3,550 00	3,550 00	....	....
31,100 00	....	31,100 00	31,100 00	....	....
968,500 00	....	968,500 00	968,500 00	....	....
38,894,250 00	....	38,894,250 00	38,894,250 00	....	....
19,351,250 00	....	19,351,250 00	19,351,250 00	....	....
23,575,450 00	....	23,575,450 00	23,575,400 00	....	....
1,500,000 00	....	1,500,000 00	1,500,000 00	....	....
11 87	....	11 87	11 87	....	....
420,000 00	....	420,000 00	420,000 00	....	....
107 50	....	107 50	107 50	....	....
158 20	....	158 20	158 20	....	....
3,201 03	....	3,201 03	3,201 03	....	....
762 81	....	762 81	762 81	....	....
60 00	....	60 00	60 00	....	....
90 00	....	90 00	90 00	....	....
42 00	....	42 00	42 00	....	....
33	....	33	33	....	....
1,620 55	....	1,620 55	1,620 55	....	....
1,174,217 20	5,940 00	1,179,257 20	1,179,257 20	....	....
60,752 56	....	60,752 56	60,752 56	....	....
11,826,161 29	15,412 50	11,841,513 79	11,841,513 79	....	....
1,831 38	103 50	1,934 88	1,934 88	....	....
4,709,049 29	7,446 00	4,716,495 29	4,716,495 29	....	....
3,541,053 82	13,381 25	3,554,435 07	3,554,435 07	....	....
27 00	....	27 00	27 00	....	....
1,213 79	18 00	1,231 79	1,231 79	....	....
1,441 17	1,065 00	2,506 17	2,506 17	....	....
454,332,022 20	42,406 25	454,374,488 45	454,374,488 45	....	....

STATEMENT exhibiting the BALANCES of APPRO

Specific objects of appropriations.	Year.	Statutes.		Balances of appropriations, July 1, 1879.
		Vol.	Page or section.	
PUBLIC DEBT—Continued.				
Brought forward	......	......	....	....
Interest—Continued.				
Consols of 1865	......	R. S.	3680	....
Consols of 1876	......	R. S.	3689	....
Consols of 1868	......	R. S.	3689	....
Refunding certificates, act February 26, 1879	......	......	....	....
Central Pacific stock	......	R. S.	3689	....
Kansas Pacific stock (U. P., E. D.)	......	R. S.	3689	....
Union Pacific stock	......	R. S.	3689	....
Central Branch Union Pacific stock (A. & P. P.)	......	R. S.	3689	....
Western Pacific Stock	......	R. S.	3689	....
Sioux City and Pacific stock	......	R. S.	3689	....
Funded loan of 1881	......	R. S.	3689	....
Funded loan of 1891	......	R. S.	3689	....
Funded loan of 1907	......	R. S.	3689	....
Premium:				
Loan of February, 1861 (1881s)	......	R. S.	3689	....
Oregon war debt	......	R. S.	3689	....
Loan of July and August, 1861 (1881s)	......	R. S.	3689	....
Loan of 1863 (1881s)	......	R. S.	3689	....
Funded loan of 1881	......	R. S.	3689	....
Funded loan of 1907	......	R. S.	3689	....
Total public debt	......	......	....	....
INTERIOR—INDIANS AND PENSIONS.				
Pay of—				
Indian agents	1877*	21	256	....
Do	1878	......	....	15, 403 03
Do	1879	......	....	24, 773 60
Do	1880	20	295	....
Special agents	1878	......	....	600 00
Interpreters	1877*	......	....	....
Do	1878	......	....	5, 088 57
Do	1879	......	....	3, 425 27
Do	1880	20	296	....
Superintendents of Central Superintendency	1878	......	....	772 22
Clerks for Central Superintendency	1878	......	....	1, 372 90
Indian inspectors	1878	......	....	1, 480 48
Do	1879	......	....	16 48
Do	1880	20	296	....
Traveling expenses of Indian inspectors	1877*	......	....	....
Do	1878	......	....	570 46
Do	1879	......	....	155 14
Do	1880	20	296	....
Pay of superintendents in Dakota	1878	......	....	22 22
Fulfilling treaties with—				
Apaches	1878*	......	....	....
Apaches, Kiowas, and Comanches	1873*	......	....	3, 204 91
Do	1878	......	....	11, 222 16
Do	1879	......	....	8, 272 72
Do	1880	20	297	....
Arapahoes and Cheyennes of Upper Arkansas River....	1873*	......	....	3, 732 93
Blackfeet, Bloods, and Piegans	1878	......	....	19, 100 80
Do	1879	......	....	610 10
Do	1880	20	297	....
Chastas, Scotans, and Umpquas	1873*	......	....	....
Cheyennes and Arapahoes	1878	......	....	1, 487 23
Do	1880	20	298	....
Calapooias, Molallas, and Clackamas of Willamette Valley	1874	......	....	9 51
Cherokees for lands west of Arkansas River	......	21	248	....
Chickasaws	1880	20	298	....
Chippewas, Bois Fort Band	{ (1874) { 1873 }	......	....	738 41
Do	1876	......	....	542 20
Do	1877	......	....	3, 309 37
Do	1878	......	....	3, 304 10
Do	1879	......	....	2, 196 59
Do	1880	20	298	....
Chippewas of Lake Superior	1873*	......	....	7, 092 41
Do	{ (1874) { 1873 }	......	....	582 34
Do	1875	......	....	....
Do	1877	......	....	127 85
Carried forward	......	......	....	118, 326 19

*And prior years.

PRIATIONS UNEXPENDED *June* 30, 1879, &c.—Continued.

Appropriations for the fiscal year ending June 30, 1880.	Repayments made during the fiscal year 1880.	Aggregate available for the fiscal year ending June 30, 1880.	Payments during the fiscal year ending June 30, 1880.	Amounts carried to the surplus fund June 30, 1880.	Balances of appropriations, June 30, 1880.
$454,332,022 20	$42,466 25	$454,374,488 45	$454,374,488 45		
70,012 04	8,362 75	78,374 79	78,374 79		
2,395,455 00	30,652 16	2,426,107 16	2,426,107 16		
1,068,235 01	2,089 50	1,070,324 51	1,070,324 51		
	188,580 77	188,580 77	187,363 31	1,217 46	
1,553,407 20	360 00	1,553,767 20	1,553,767 20		
377,940 00	240 00	378,180 00	378,180 00		
1,635,300 72	1,410 00	1,636,710 72	1,636,710 72		
95,700 00	300 00	96,000 00	96,000 00		
118,203 60	30 00	118,233 60	118,233 60		
97,669 20		97,669 20	97,669 20		
26,442,840 01	7,192 50	26,450,032 51	26,450,032 51		
11,543,031 47	22 50	11,543,053 97	11,543,053 97		
28,619,226 53	438,567 67	29,057,794 20	29,057,794 20		
74,161 95		74,161 95	74,161 95		
8,273 02		8,273 02	8,273 02		
1,376,085 04		1,376,085 04	1,376,085 04		
549,035 18		549,035 18	549,035 18		
662,206 97		662,206 97	662,206 97		
125,558 26		125,558 26	125,558 20		
531,144,393 40	720,274 10	531,864,667 50	531,863,450 04	1,217 46	
4,263 69	709 30	4,992 99	2,598 21	709 30	1,685 48
		15,403 03	1,047 38	14,355 65	
104,000 00	687 16	25,460 96	2,062 83		23,398 13
	514 84	104,514 84	82,245 50		22,269 24
		600 00	51 04	548 96	
	930 61	930 61		930 61	
	109 00	5,188 57	125 00	5,063 57	
	685 41	4,110 08	1,525 46		2,585 22
26,800 00	125 28	26,925 28	24,302 05		2,623 23
		772 22		772 22	
		1,373 90		1,373 90	
		1,489 48		1,489 48	
		16 48			16 48
9,000 00		9,000 00	8,456 04		543 96
	111 42	111 42		111 42	
	20 57	501 63		591 08	
	412 05	567 19	29 05		538 14
4,000 00	401 65	4,401 65	3,792 20		609 45
	22 22	44 44	44 44	44 44	
	226 00	226 00			226 00
		3,204 91			3,204 01
	5 59	11,228 84	7,325 03	8,787 42	116 39
		8,272 72	7,913 59		359 13
52,700 00		52,700 00	43,083 84		9,616 16
	239 21	3,072 14	3,782 93		239 21
	417 59	19,518 30	237 45	19,280 94	
40,000 00	3,544 33	4,154 43	4,154 43		4,386 33
	97	40,000 00	35,613 67		97
		1,487 23		1,487 23	
35,600 00	3,228 11	38,828 11	38,828 11		
		9 51			9 51
300,000 00		300,000 00	300,000 00		
3,000 00		3,000 00	3,000 00		
		738 41			738 41
		642 20			642 20
		2,309 37			2,309 37
		3,304 10			3,304 10
		2,198 59	34 95		2,163 64
14,100 00	2,621 00	14,100 00	10,076 09		4,029 91
		9,713 41	7,668 30		2,045 11
		582 34	582 34		
	57 32	57 32			57 32
		127 85			127 85
593,483 69	15,061 79	726,871 67	588,479 59	50,546 17	87,845 91

STATEMENT *exhibiting the BALANCES of APPRO*

Specific objects of appropriations.	Year.	Statutes. Vol.	Statutes. Page or section.	Balances of appropriations, July 1, 1879.
INTERIOR—INDIANS AND PENSIONS—Continued.				
Brought forward				$118,326 19
Fulfilling treaties with—				
Chippewas of Lake Superior	1878			1,257 01
Do	1879			
Do	1880	20	296	
Chippewas of the Mississippi	1877			50 00
Do	1878			2,639 30
Do	1880	20	296	
Chippewas, Pillager, and Lake Winnebagoshish Bands..	1873*			
Do (transfer account)..	1874*	18	418	
Do	1875			28 61
Do	1877			29 19
Do	1878			
Do	1879			30 72
Do	1860	20	299	
Chippewas of Red Lake and Pembina Tribe of Chippewas	1876			853 63
Do	1877			1,263 90
Do	1878			1,190 48
Do	1879			3,875 81
Chippewas of Saginaw, Swan Creek, and Black River..	1873*			6,938 75
Choctaws	1873*			
Do	1880	20	299	
Confederated tribes and bands in Middle Oregon	1878			859 65
Do	1879			1,000 00
Do	1880	20	299	
Creeks	1873*			
Do	1880	20	300	
Crows	1878			59,644 17
Do	1879			59,043 44
Do	1880	20	301	
Delawares	1873*			9,571 93
Do	1874			1,772 43
Do	1875			1,819 50
D'Wamish and other allied tribes in Washington	1879			590 00
Do	1880	20	301	
Flatheads and other confederated tribes	1875			5 84
Do	1878			1,308 22
Do	1879			3,646 38
Do	1880	20	302	
Iowas	1873*			263 14
Do	1880	20	302	
Kansas	1878			1,015 27
Do	1879			2,634 69
Do	1880	20	302	
Do	1873*			1,474 98
Do	1874			760 00
Do	1877			4,872 19
Kickapoos	1873*			107 98
Do	1875			1,456 75
Do	1877*			
Do	1878			
Do	1879			452 94
Do	1880	20	302	
Klamaths and Modocs	1877			1 87
Do	1878			2,728 15
Do	1879			931 10
Do	1880	20	302	
Makahs	1878			944 12
Do	1879			205 00
Do	1880	20	302	
Menomonees	1873*			58 05
Do	1878			2,696 51
Do	1879			2,696 51
Do	1880	20	303	
Miamies of Eel River	1873*			45 14
Do	1874			10
Do	1875			09
Do	1876			64 80
Do	1878			05
Do	1879			
Do	1860	20	303	
Miamies of Indiana	1873*			2,147 02
Do	1874			99 74
Do	1875			65 61
Carried forward				391,766 95

PRIATIONS UNEXPENDED June 30, 1879, &c.—Continued.

Appropriations for the fiscal year ending June 30, 1880.	Repayments made during the fiscal year 1880.	Aggregate available for the fiscal year ending June 30, 1880.	Payments during the fiscal year ending June 30, 1880.	Amounts carried to the surplus fund June 30, 1880.	Balances of appropriations, June 30, 1880.
$593, 483 69	$15, 061 79	$726, 871 67	$586, 479 50	$50, 546 17	$87, 845 91
		1, 257 01		1, 257 01	
	27 99	27 99			27 99
15, 500 00	12 47	15, 812 47	15, 812 47		
		50 00	50 00		
		2, 639 30	1, 263 36	1, 376 94	
25, 300 00		25, 300 00	25, 183 12		116 88
	2, 379 00	2, 379 00			2, 379 00
253 46		253 46	253 46		
		28 61	28 61		
		29 19	29 19		
	920 66	920 66	920 66		
	87 06	117 76	117 76		
25, 466 66		25, 466 66	25, 466 66		
		853 63	187 20		666 43
		1, 253 90	395 06		888 84
		1, 190 48		300 00	890 48
	395 00	4, 270 87	1, 824 03		2, 446 84
	921 57	7, 860 32	3, 749 24		4, 111 08
	239 13	239 13	239 13		
30, 032 89		30, 032 89	30, 032 89		
		859 65		859 65	
	710 95	1, 710 95			1, 710 05
8, 100 00	7 55	8, 107 55	7, 975 64		131 91
	966 52	966 52	966 52		
69, 968 40		69, 968 40	69, 968 40		
	3, 641 80	53, 285 97	2, 046 06	61, 239 91	
		59, 043 44	2, 538 42		56, 505 02
112, 000 00	1, 479 02	113, 479 02	73, 765 76		39, 713 26
		9, 571 93			9, 571 93
		1, 773 43			1, 773 43
		1, 819 50			1, 819 50
		900 00	900 00		
11, 950 00		11, 950 00	11, 704 19		245 81
		5 84			5 84
	1 63	1, 309 85		1, 309 85	
	174 39	3, 820 77	1, 123 36		2, 697 41
13, 600 00		13, 600 00	12, 730 00		870 00
		263 14	96 18		166 96
2, 875 00		2, 875 00	2, 875 00		
		1, 015 27			1, 015 27
	53 62	2, 688 31	1, 525 84		1, 162 47
10, 000 00		10, 000 00	9, 826 79		173 21
		1, 474 98	48 21		1, 426 77
		760 00			760 00
		4, 872 19			4, 872 19
		107 98			107 98
		1, 456 75			1, 456 75
	1 50	1 50		1 50	
	205 65	205 65		38 00	167 65
	1, 388 22	1, 841 16	1, 204 14		637 02
12, 295 28	392 66	12, 687 94	12, 395 79		292 15
		1 87	1 87		
		2, 728 15	1, 274 94	1, 026 08	427 13
		931 10	295 00		636 10
14, 700 00		14, 700 00	14, 700 00		
		944 12		704 47	239 65
	21 03	226 03			226 03
7, 600 00	6 15	7, 606 15	7, 606 15		
		58 05			58 05
		2, 696 51		2, 696 51	
		2, 696 51			2, 696 51
16, 179 06		16, 179 06	13, 268 85		2, 910 21
		45 14			45 14
		10			10
		09			09
		64 80			64 80
		05			05
	275 00	275 00	206 25		68 75
1, 100 00		1, 100 00			1, 100 00
		2, 147 02			2, 147 02
		99 74			99 74
		65 61			65 61
970, 704 44	29, 370 42	1, 301, 841 81	943, 044 81	121, 356 09	237, 440 91

STATEMENT exhibiting the BALANCES of APPRO-

Specific objects of appropriations.	Year.	Statutes.		Balances of appropriations, July 1, 1879.
		Vol.	Page or section.	
INTERIOR—INDIANS AND PENSIONS—Continued.				
Brought forward				$301,708 95
Fulfilling treaties with—				
Miamies of Indiana	1876			100 29
Do	1877			67 06
Do	1878			98 78
Do	1879			
Do	1880	20	303	
Miamies of Kansas	1873*			64 62
Do	1875			1, 870 57
Do	{ 1875	}		1, 098 11
	1876			
Do	1877			1, 482 20
Do	1880	20	303	
Mixed Shoshones, Bannocks, and Sheepeaters	1878			2, 219 53
Do	1879			4, 748 10
Do	1880	20	304	
Molels	1878			2, 412 24
Do	1879			1, 658 35
Do	1880	20	303	
Navajoes	1878			39, 785 08
Do	1879			41, 047 63
Do	1880	20	304	
Nez Percés	1873*	18	110	17, 490 47
Do	{ (1874)	18	110	76
	1873			
Do	1875	18	110	· 703 36
Do	1876	18	110	837 73
Do	1877			451 56
Do	1878			2, 614 45
Do	1879			
Do	1880	20	304	
Nisqually, Puyallup, and other tribes and bands	1877*	39	256	
Do (transfer account)	1877*	18	418	
Northern Cheyennes and Arapahoes	1878			18, 866 24
Do	1879			1, 392 87
Do	1880	20	305	
Omahas	1873*			331 32
Do	1876			3, 621 41
Do	1877			3, 010 04
Do	1878			3, 249 89
Do	1879			7, 477 46
Do	1880	20	305	
Osages	1873*			500 00
Do	1877			594 68
Do	1878			2, 957 00
Do	1879			
Do	1880	20	305	
Ottawas of Blanchard's Fork and Roche de Bœuf	1873*			38 49
Otoes and Missourias	1876			501 48
Do	1879			749 67
Do	1880	20	305	
Pawnees	1877			850 00
Do	1878			8, 537 24
Do	1879			8, 049 56
Do	1880	{ 20	305	}
		21	67	
Poncas	{ (1874)	}		267 00
	1873			
Do	1875			1 94
Do	1879			14, 973 56
Do	1880	20	306	
Pottawatomies	1873*			792 11
Do	1874			137 23
Do	1875			55 00
Do	1878			
Do	1880	20	306	
Pottawatomies of Huron	1878			12 78
Do	1880	20	306	
Quapaws	1878			760 00
Do	1879			1, 383 79
Do	1880	20	306	
Qui-nai-elts and Quil-leh-utes	1873*			688 54
Do	1875			12 42
Do	1876			46 55
Carried forward				501, 375 56

*And prior years.

PRIATIONS UNEXPENDED June 30, 1879, &c.—Continued.

Appropriations for the fiscal year ending June 30, 1880.	Repayments made during the fiscal year 1880.	Aggregate available for the fiscal year ending June 30, 1880.	Payments during the fiscal year ending June 30, 1880.	Amounts carried to the surplus fund June 30, 1880.	Balances of appropriations, June 30, 1880.
$970,704 44	$29,370 42	$1,301,841 81	$943,044 81	$121,356 09	$237,440 91
		100 29	33 22		67 07
		67 06			67 06
		98 78	31 96		66 82
	1,636 89	1,636 89	188 52		1,448 87
11,062 89		11,062 89			11,062 89
		64 62	64 62		
		1,870 57	766 71		1,103 86
		1,098 11			1,098 11
		1,482 20	519 53		962 67
5,051 01		5,051 01	3,474 42		1,576 59
		3,210 53		3,210 53	
	24 44	4,772 54	3,897 33		875 21
25,000 00	552 16	25,552 16	18,859 50		6,692 66
		2,412 24	675 00	1,797 24	
		1,658 35	750 00		908 35
3,000 00		3,000 00	1,696 00		1,304 00
		39,785 08		39,785 08	
	270 98	41,318 01	4,506 48		36,811 53
58,000 00	219 07	58,219 07	27,218 01		31,001 06
48,956 09		66,417 16	3,541 55		62,905 61
171 13		171 89			171 89
94 11		797 47			707 47
587 30		1,435 03	100 00		1,325 03
		451 56			451 56
		2,614 45		2,614 45	
	2,506 23	2,506 23			2,506 23
19,800 00		19,800 00	19,531 50		268 50
97 13		97 13	97 13		
237 14		237 14	237 14		
		18,866 24		18,866 24	
		1,392 87			1,392 87
53,000 00		53,000 00	46,978 31		6,021 69
	88 38	419 70			419 70
		3,621 41			3,621 41
		3,010 01	1,700 00		1,310 01
		3,249 89		50 00	3,199 89
	850 59	8,328 05	7,578 69		749 36
20,000 00	2 40	20,000 00	16,360 00		3,640 00
		502 40	502 40		
		594 68	236 32		358 36
		2,957 00			2,957 00
	215 01	215 01			215 01
18,456 00		18,456 00	18,000 00		456 00
		38 49			38 49
		501 46	501 46		
		749 67	566 18		183 49
9,000 00		9,000 00	8,700 86		299 14
		850 00			850 00
	118 68	8,685 92		8,655 92	
	503 42	8,553 08	4,263 37		4,289 71
65,000 00		65,000 00	62,207 12		2,792 88
		267 00	267 00		
		1 94	1 94		
	591 01	15,564 57	9,320 80		6,243 77
52,046 81	950 30	52,997 11	39,065 59		13,931 52
		792 11			792 11
		137 23			137 23
		55 00			55 00
	71 06	71 06	69 23		1 83
20,647 65		20,647 65	20,647 65		
		12 78	12 78		
400 00		400 00	400 00		
		760 00		760 00	
		1,383 79	920 00		463 79
2,060 00		2,060 00	1,291 15		768 85
		688 54	688 54		
		12 42	12 42		
		46 55	46 55		
1,883,372 30	37,971 06	1,922,719 52	1,271,571 84	197,044 55	454,103 13

STATEMENT *exhibiting the BALANCES of APPRO*

Specific objects of appropriations.	Year.	Statutes.		Balances of appropriations, July 1, 1879.
		Vol.	Page or section.	
INTERIOR—INDIANS AND PENSIONS—Continued.				
Brought forward				$501,375 56
Fulfilling treaties with—				
Qui-nai-elts and Quil-leh-utes	1878			2,506 27
Do	1879			3,734 49
Do	1880	20	307	
Seminoles	1873*			1 15
Do	1879			
Do	1880	20	307	
Sacs and Foxes of the Mississippi	1873*			2,370 82
Do	1875			
Do	1877			113 29
Do	1878			236 78
Do	1879			12,265 12
Do	1880	20	307	
Sacs and Foxes of the Missouri	1873*			757 44
Do	1877			2 04
Do	1878			49 64
Do	1880	20	307	
Senecas	1879			940 00
Do	1880	20	308	
Senecas of New York	1873*			
Do	1876			45 00
Do	1880	20	308	
Senecas and Shawnees	1879			388 57
Shawnees	1873*			272 96
Do	1880	20	308	
Eastern Shawnees	1880	20	309	
Shoshonees	1875			2,994 97
Do	1876			2,136 52
Do	1877			1,688 64
Do	1878			454 97
Do	1879			1,312 79
Do	1880	20	309	
Shoshonees and Bannocks	1878			6,715 56
Do	1879			8,118 32
Do	1880	{ 20 / 21	309 / 67.	}
Six Nations of New York	1873*			2,220 25
Do	1875			511 06
Do	1878			424 45
Do	1879			718 18
Do	1880	20	309	
Skiallams	1873*			
Do	1878			703 70
Do	1879			209 76
Do	1880	20	311	
Sioux of different tribes, including Santee Sioux of Nebraska	1873*			28,036 00
Do	1877*			
Do	1878			88,312 09
Do	1879			436,518 34
Do	1880	20	310	
Sioux, Yankton tribe	1873*			162 40
Do	1877			3,382 18
Do	1878			5,058 41
Do	1879			15,687 41
Do	1880	20	310	
Sioux of Dakota	1873*			248 83
Sisseton and Wahpeton, and Santee Sioux of Lake Traverse and Devil's Lake	1873*			
Do	1873*		.0.	2,181 69
Do	1877			1,010 68
Do	1878			1,941 01
Do	1879			17,970 77
Do	1880	20	310	
Snakes, Wal-pah-pee tribe	1878			173 37
Do	1879			790 00
Do	1880	20	310	
Tabequache, Muache, Capote, Weeminuche, Yampa, Grand River, and Uintah bands of Utes	1877*			
Do	1878			11,447 93
Do	1879			7,693 71
Do	1880	20	311	
Umpquas, Cow Creek band	1873*			693 96
Carried forward				1,174,407 09

*And prior years.

PRIATIONS UNEXPENDED June 30, 1879, *&c.*—Continued.

Appropriations for the fiscal year ending June 30, 1880.	Repayments made during the fiscal year 1880.	Aggregate available for the fiscal year ending June 30, 1880.	Payments during the fiscal year ending June 30, 1880.	Amounts carried to the surplus fund June 30, 1880.	Balances of appropriations, June 30, 1880.
$1,383,372 30	$37,971 66	$1,922,719 52	$1,271,571 84	$197,044 55	$454,103 13
....	....	2,506 27	200 00	2,306 27	....
....	50 00	3,784 49	2,419 75	....	1,364 74
6,200 00	....	6,200 00	5,486 40	....	713 60
....	1,073 65	1,073 80	1,073 80	....	....
....	454 00	454 00	454 00	....	....
28,500 00	....	28,500 00	28,500 00	....	....
....	....	2,370 82	....	....	2,370 82
....	67 28	67 28	....	....	67 28
....	....	113 29	....	....	113 29
....	9,089 11	9,325 89	....	....	9,325 89
....	925 80	13,190 92	1,917 79	....	11,273 13
50,016 23	7,443 55	56,364 78	46,162 10	....	12,292 68
....	....	757 44	95 00	....	662 44
....	....	2 04	....	....	2 04
....	....	49 64	....	....	49 64
8,070 00	....	8,070 00	8,057 93	....	13 07
....	....	940 00	940 00	....	....
3,690 00	....	3,690 00	3,480 00	....	210 00
....	8 48	8 48	....	....	8 48
....	....	45 09	....	....	45 00
11,902 50	....	11,902 50	11,902 50	....	....
....	....	388 97	388 97	....	....
....	....	273 96	....	....	273 96
5,800 00	480 50	5,480 50	5,480 50	....	....
1,030 00	....	1,030 00	669 02	....	360 98
....	....	2,994 97	2,994 97	....	....
....	....	2,130 52	2,130 52	....	1 00
....	....	1,688 64	405 88	....	1,282 76
....	....	454 97	454 97	....	....
....	75 00	1,387 79	312 79	....	1,075 00
11,000 00	....	11,000 00	10,023 22	....	976 78
....	....	5,715 56	5,715 56	6,715 56	....
....	1,020 31	9,158 63	5,400 96	....	3,737 67
78,427 00	2,738 54	81,175 54	69,661 24	....	11,514 30
....	....	2,220 25	1,000 00	....	1,220 25
....	....	511 98	....	....	511 98
....	....	424 45	....	....	424 45
....	....	718 18	....	....	718 18
4,500 00	....	4,500 00	3,985 86	....	514 14
....	730 41	730 41	....	....	730 41
....	....	702 79	....	702 79	....
....	....	606 34	106 05	....	500 19
8,200 00	396 48	8,200 00	8,200 00	....	....
....	....	28,036 00	....	....	28,036 00
....	8,670 14	8,670 14	....	8,670 14	....
....	5,710 41	94,022 50	10,167 78	83,854 72	....
....	17,394 81	453,913 15	290,617 68	....	163,295 55
1,468,590 94	10,687 10	1,479,278 04	1,173,508 87	....	305,769 17
....	....	162 40	162 40	....	....
....	....	3,282 18	3,282 18	....	....
....	....	5,058 41	5,058 41	....	....
....	1,140 78	16,828 19	8,023 88	....	8,804 31
83,087 88	2,824 27	85,912 15	77,624 50	....	8,287 65
....	....	248 83	....	....	248 83
....	....	2,181 69	2,181 69	....	....
....	....	1,010 66	785 00	....	225 48
....	94 16	2,035 17	1,833 31	....	201 86
....	127 70	18,098 47	6,746 10	....	11,352 37
80,000 00	335 91	80,335 91	80,055 14	....	280 77
....	....	173 37	173 37	....	....
....	....	700 00	700 00	....	....
1,200 00	....	1,200 00	1,200 00	....	....
....	25 98	25 98	....	26 98	25 98
....	....	11,467 93	....	11,467 93	....
....	674 51	8,568 22	6,154 43	....	2,413 79
78,020 00	4,066 10	82,086 10	75,013 09	....	7,073 01
....	....	693 96	693 96	....	693 96
3,311,716 85	114,480 64	4,600,604 56	3,236,313 44	310,787 94	1,053,503 20

STATEMENT *exhibiting the BALANCES of APPRO*

Specific objects of appropriations.	Year.	Statutes.		Balances of appropriations, July 1, 1879.
		Vol.	Page or section.	
INTERIOR—INDIANS AND PENSIONS—Continued.				
Brought forward				$1,174,407 09
Fulfilling treaties with—				
Umpquas and Calapooias of Umpqua Valley, Oregon	1873*			745 50
Utahs, Tabequache band	1873*			12,877 19
Do	1874			2,582 39
Do	1879			369 90
Do	1880	20	311	
Walla Walla, Cayuse, and Umatilla tribes	1873*			
Do	1876			17 69
Do	1878			1,214 52
Do	1879			1,036 10
Do	1880	20	311	
Winnebagoes	1873*			41,012 04
Do	(1874) 1873			392 95
Do	1875			14,625 39
Do	1876			14,618 00
Do	1877			19,320 87
Do	1878			18,472 37
Do	1879			14,940 63
Do	1880	20	312	
Yakamas	1873*			2,835 43
Do	1877*			
Do	1878			7,835 00
Do	1879			
Do	1880	20	312	
Cherokees, proceeds of school lands		R. S.	2093–6	523 62
Cherokees, proceeds of lands		R. S.	2093–6	29,595 85
Cherokees, proceeds fud Osage diminished reserve lands in Kansas (transfer)				721,748 80
Chippewas of Saginaw, proceeds of lands				400 00
Delawares, proceeds of lands				105 64
Iowas, proceeds of lands				28 30
Kansas, proceeds of lands		R. S.	2093–6	7,040 03
Kaskaskias, Peorias, Weas, and Piankeshaws, proceeds of lands				96 78
Kickapoos, proceeds of lands				1 06
Menomonees, proceeds of lands				1,256 84
Miamies of Kansas, proceeds of lands				10,880 23
Omahas, proceeds of lands				712 26
Otoes and Missourias, proceeds of lands		R. S.	2093–6	82,652 02
Ottawas of Blanchard's Fork and Roche de Boeuf, proceeds of lands				43 49
Osages (trust), proceeds of lands		R. S.	2093–6	1,406,332 03
Pottawatomies, proceeds of lands				32,767 63
Sacs and Foxes of the Missouri, proceeds of lands		R. S.	2093–6	10,901 88
Shawnees, proceeds of lands		R. S.	2093–6	27 86
Stockbridges, proceeds of lands				81 56
Winnebagoes, proceeds of lands				20,621 61
Stockbridge o unsolidated funds				75,804 46
Proceeds of Sioux reservations in Minnesota and Dakota		R. S.	2093–6	71,262 11
Proceeds of Winnebago reservation in Minnesota				1,779 25
Proceeds of New York Indian lands in Kansas				4,058 96
Trust-fund interest due—				
Cherokee asylum fund		R. S.	2093–6	1,603 68
Cherokee national fund		R. S.	2093–6	9,034 84
Do	1880	20	315	
Cherokee school fund		R. S.	2093–6	10,188 49
Cherokee orphans' fund		R. S.	2093–6	4,971 12
Cherokee school fund	1880	20	315	
Chickasaw national fund prior to July 1, 1866				11 25
Chicasaw national fund		R. S.	2093–6	31,780 34
Do	1880	20	315	
Chickasaw incoupetents		R. S.	2093–6	1,700 00
Choctaw general fund		R. S.	2093–6	92 22
Do	1880	20	315	
Choctaw school fund		R. S.	2093–8	1,227 65
Chippewa and Christian Indians		R. S.	2093–5	693 38
Creek orphans		R. S.	2093–5	218 49
Do	1879			
Do	1880	20	315	
Delaware general fund		R. S.	2093–6	5,410 18
Do	1898	20	315	
Delaware school fund		R. S.	2093–6	8,178 74
Carried forward				3,881,237 16

* And prior years.

PRIATIONS UNEXPENDED June 30, 1879, &c.—Continued.

Appropriations for the fiscal year ending June 30, 1880.	Repayments made during the fiscal year 1880.	Aggregate available for the fiscal year ending June 30, 1880.	Payments during the fiscal year ending June 30, 1880.	Amounts carried to the surplus fund June 30, 1880.	Balances of appropriations, June 30, 1880.
$3, 311, 710 85	$114, 480 64	$4, 600, 604 58	$3, 236, 313 44	$310, 787 94	$1, 053, 503 20
....	581 35	1, 326 65	....	....	1, 326 65
....	....	12, 877 19	11, 431 65	....	1, 445 54
....	....	2, 582 39	2, 582 39	....	....
....	....	360 00	360 00	....	....
720 00	....	720 00	360 00	....	360 00
....	8 90	8 90	....	....	8 90
....	....	17 69	17 69	....	....
....	....	1, 214 52	....	1, 214 52	....
....	....	1, 036 10	....	....	1, 036 10
14, 500 00	....	14, 500 00	12, 680 00	....	1, 820 00
....	....	41, 012 94	....	....	41, 012 94
....	....	392 95	....	....	392 95
....	174 50	14, 709 89	....	....	14, 709 89
....	....	14, 618 03	....	....	14, 618 03
....	....	19, 320 87	....	....	19, 320 87
....	....	18, 472 37	....	....	18, 472 37
44, 182 47	5, 954 00	20, 894 63	3, 560 00	....	17, 334 63
44, 182 47	....	44, 162 47	28, 465 23	....	15, 697 24
....	....	2, 835 43	2, 835 43	....	....
....	35 22	35 22	....	35 22	....
....	799 55	8, 634 55	889 50	7, 634 55	110 50
....X.......	3, 108 05	3, 108 05	....	....	3, 108 05
19, 600 00	....	19, 600 00	19, 300 00	....	300 00
100 09	....	623 71	....	....	623 71
58, 121 96	....	87, 717 81	68, 861 49	....	18, 856 32
2, 388 61	....	724, 137 41	....	....	724, 137 41
....	....	400 00	....	....	400 00
....	....	105 64	....	....	105 64
....	....	28 30	....	....	28 30
43, 646 10	....	50, 686 13	....	....	50, 686 13
....	....	96 78	....	....	96 78
....	....	1 08	....	....	1 08
....	807 81	2, 166 45	2, 040 76	....	125 69
....	....	10, 880 23	....	....	10, 880 23
....	....	712 26	....	....	712 26
83, 355 11	....	166, 007 13	51, 120 12	....	114, 887 01
....	....	43 49	....	....	43 49
378, 037 71	....	1, 784, 969 72	159, 890 12	....	1, 625, 079 60
....	....	32, 767 63	....	....	32, 767 63
9, 172 92	367 58	20, 442 33	7, 921 00	....	12, 521 33
200 00	....	227 86	186 60	....	41 26
....	....	81 58	....	....	81 58
....	....	20, 621 61	....	....	20, 621 61
....	....	75, 804 46	....	....	75, 804 46
80, 729 48	285 24	102, 256 83	2, 040 72	....	100, 216 11
....	....	1, 779 25	....	....	1, 779 25
....	....	4, 058 06	....	....	4, 058 06
3, 207 36	....	4, 811 04	3, 207 36	....	1, 603 68
201, 045 75	....	210, 080 09	43, 337 70	....	166, 742 39
26, 060 00	....	26, 060 00	26, 060 00	....	....
191, 098 43	....	201, 286 92	34, 460 41	....	166, 826 51
75, 695 48	....	80, 666 60	15, 749 92	....	64, 916 68
2, 410 00	....	2, 410 00	2, 410 00	....	....
....	....	11 25	....	....	11 25
155, 526 07	....	187, 306 41	77, 569 13	....	109, 737 28
19, 820 00	....	19, 820 00	19, 820 00	....	....
100 00	....	1, 800 00	....	....	1, 800 00
184 44	643 50	920 16	184 44	....	735 72
27, 000 00	....	27, 000 00	27, 000 00	....	....
3, 984 96	....	5, 212 61	2, 467 96	....	2, 744 85
30, 256 37	24	30, 949 99	2, 022 76	....	28, 927 23
5, 877 35	385 00	4, 490 84	785 83	....	3, 705 01
....	17 72	17 72	17 72	....	....
4, 048 00	....	4, 048 00	4, 048 00	....	....
36, 046 46	1, 010 68	43, 067 32	24, 739 09	....	18, 328 23
8, 930 00	....	8, 930 00	8, 930 00	....	....
550 00	....	8, 728 74	....	....	8, 728 74
4, 787, 491 97	128, 689 93	8, 797, 369 06	3, 903, 877 71	819, 672 23	4, 573, 819 12

STATEMENT *exhibiting the BALANCES of APPRO*

Specific objects of appropriations.	Year.	Statutes.		Balances of appropriations, July 1, 1879.
		Vol.	Page or section.	
INTERIOR—INDIANS AND PENSIONS—Continued.				
Brought forward				$3,881,227 16
Trust-fund interest due—				
Iowas		R. S.	2093-6	992 28
Do	1880	20	315	
Kansas schools		R. S.	2093-6	8,848 28
Kaskaskias, Peorias, Weas, and Piankeshaws, general fund		R. S.	2093-6	930 26
Do	1880	20	315	
Kaskaskias, Peorias, Weas, and Piankeshaws, school fund		R. S.	2093-6	2,281 70
Do	1880	20	315	
Kickapoos, general fund		R. S.	2093-6	1,607 12
Menomonees		R. S.	2093-6	1,148 45
Do	1880	20	315	
Osage schools		R. S.	2093-6	6,593 41
Ottawas and Chippewas		R. S.	2093-6	33,785 20
Do	1878			280 00
Do	1879			280 00
Do	1880	20	315	
Pottawatomies, education		R. S.	2093-6	4,756 93
Pottawatomies, general fund		R. S.	2093-6	21,236 45
Pottawatomies, mills		R. S.	2093-6	213 33
Sacs and Foxes of the Mississippi		R. S.	2093-6	1,707 04
Sacs and Foxes of the Missouri		R. S.	2093-6	
Senecas		R. S.	2093-6	1,584 17
Senecas, Tonawanda Band		R. S.	2093-6	
Senecas and Shawnees		R. S.	2093-6	893 17
Shawnees		R. S.	2093-6	974 26
Eastern Shawnees		R. S.	2093-6	673 75
Contingencies, trust fund	1878			500 00
Do	1879			500 00
Do	1880	20	315	
Interest due Cherokees on lands sold to Osages		17	538	
Interest due Otoes and Missourias		19	208	
Interest on avails of diminished reserve lands in Kansas	1880	21	41	
Do	1877			300 29
Do	1878			200 72
Do	1879			20,145 52
Interest due Tabequache, Muache, Capote, Weeminuche, Yampa, Grand River, &c		18	37	53,446 15
Interest due Stockbridge consolidated fund		16	404	
Trust-fund stocks redeemed; due—				
Cherokee national fund				45 00
Cherokee school fund				11 50
Cherokee orphans' fund				
Chickasaw national fund				19 59
Ottawas and Chippewas				2,211 25
Pottawatomies, education				46 81
Sacs and Foxes of the Mississippi				
Senecas and Shawnees				
Trust-fund bonds, proceeds of sales of Kickapoos				79
Trust-fund bonds, proceeds of sales of Pottawatomies mills				415 63
Incidental expenses, Indian service in—				
Arizona	1877*	21	256	
Arizona (transfer account)	1877*	18	418	
Arizona	1878			2,074 01
Do	1879			492 44
Do	1880	20	314	
California	1877*	21	256	
Do	1878			212 26
Do	1879			4,940 91
Do	1880	20	314	
Colorado	1877*	21	256	
Do	1878			666 30
Do	1879			1,343 37
Do	1880	20	314	
Dakota	1877*	21	256	
Do	1878			7,038 82
Do	1879			3,820 63
Do	1880	20	314	
Idaho	1877*	21	256	
Do	1878			233 49
Do	1879			1,412 26
Do	1880	20	314	
Carried forward				4,068,973 38

*And prior years.

PRIATIONS UNEXPENDED June 30, 1879, &c.—Continued.

Appropriations for the fiscal year ending June 30, 1880.	Repayments made during the fiscal year 1880.	Aggregate available for the fiscal year ending June 30, 1880.	Payments during the fiscal year ending June 30, 1880.	Amounts carried to the surplus fund June 30, 1880.	Balances of appropriations, June 30, 1880.
$4,787,491 97	$128,639 93	$8,797,369 06	$3,903,877 71	$319,672 23	$4,573,819 12
13,238 40	1,137 83	15,368 51	6,587 15	....	8,781 36
3,520 00	....	3,520 00	3,520 00	....	....
16,639 54	....	25,487 82	260 00	....	25,227 82
884 29	....	1,814 55	1,776 15	....	38 40
4,801 00	....	4,801 00	4,801 00	....	....
1,035 60	....	3,317 30	1,351 03	....	1,966 27
1,449 00	....	1,449 00	471 47	....	977 53
6,428 48	291 67	8,327 27	6,720 15	....	1,607 12
6,701 96	7 50	7,857 91	7,816 30	....	41 61
950 00	....	950 00	950 00	....	....
1,895 56	....	8,588 97	1,090 00	....	7,498 97
737 24	....	34,522 44	....	....	34,522 44
....	....	230 00	....	230 00	....
....	....	230 00	....	....	230 00
230 00	....	230 00	....	....	230 00
3,847 36	1,235 86	9,842 15	6,196 51	....	3,645 64
4,480 92	....	25,717 37	....	....	25,717 37
852 32	....	1,066 65	852 52	....	214 13
60,679 73	3,287 97	65,674 74	7,653 40	....	58,021 34
8,495 62	200 88	8,696 50	759 52	....	7,936 98
2,049 00	....	3,633 17	2,096 42	....	1,536 75
4,347 52	....	4,347 52	4,347 52	....	....
8,985 46	....	9,878 63	....	....	9,878 63
241 76	....	1,216 02	....	....	1,216 02
553 96	....	1,127 71	712 24	....	415 47
....	....	500 00	....	500 00	....
....	....	500 00	....	....	500 00
300 00	....	300 00	....	....	300 00
36,087 44	....	36,087 44	36,087 44	....	....
2,262 24	....	2,262 24	....	....	2,262 24
60,312 86	....	60,312 86	36,005 72	....	24,307 14
....	....	300 29	300 29	....	....
....	....	200 72	200 72	....	....
....	767 51	20,913 03	20,913 03	....	....
25,000 00	3,386 24	81,832 39	31,672 61	....	50,159 78
3,790 22	423 54	4,213 76	4,213 76	....	....
....	....	45 00	45 00	....	....
....	31,200 00	31,211 50	31,211 50	....	....
....	10,000 00	10,000 00	10,000 00	....	....
....	....	19 59	19 59	....	....
....	....	2,211 25	2,211 25	....	....
....	....	46 81	46 81	....	....
....	54,200 00	54,200 00	54,200 00	....	....
....	1,000 00	1,000 00	1,000 00	....	....
....	....	79	79	....	....
....	....	415 63	415 63	....	....
34 25	301 25	335 50	34 25	301 25	....
1,808 81	....	1,866 81	1,866 81	....	....
....	40 44	2,114 45	625 00	1,489 45	....
....	1,188 11	1,680 56	454 71	....	1,225 84
40,000 00	179 28	40,179 28	36,571 90	....	3,607 38
20	719 74	719 94	20	719 74	....
....	....	212 25	....	212 25	....
....	326 52	5,287 42	2,197 95	....	3,069 48
35,000 00	968 01	35,968 01	35,968 01	....	....
7 26	356 05	365 31	7 26	358 05	....
....	....	666 30	167 98	408 32	....
....	260 14	1,004 01	280 31	....	1,843 70
4,000 00	221 00	4,221 00	3,330 42	....	890 58
103 99	62 08	166 07	103 99	62 08	....
....	857 28	7,896 10	52 00	7,844 10	....
....	2,868 39	6,759 22	165 41	....	6,593 81
12,000 00	181 49	12,181 49	11,857 58	....	323 91
423 27	50 00	473 27	433 27	50 00	....
....	....	233 49	....	233 49	....
....	100 28	1,512 53	271 82	....	1,240 71
5,000 00	157 80	5,157 80	3,828 33	....	1,329 47
5,166,806 23	244,616 79	9,481,418 40	4,288,570 43	332,170 96	4,860,677 01

STATEMENT exhibiting the BALANCES of APPRO

Specific objects of appropriations.	Year.	Statutes. Vol.	Page or section.	Balances of appropriations, July 1, 1879.
INTERIOR—INDIANS AND PENSIONS—Continued.				
Brought forward				$4,089,973 38
Incidental expenses, Indian service in—				
Montana	1877*	21	256	
Do	1878			36 82
Do	1879			915 44
Do	1880	20	314	
Nevada	1878			352 61
Do	1879			1,924 36
Do	1880	20	314	
New Mexico	1877*	21	256	
New Mexico (transfer account)	1877*	18	418	
New Mexico	1878			5,770 19
Do	1879			4,465 53
Do	1880	20	314	
Oregon	1877*	21	256	
Do	1878			1,647 36
Do	1879			256 45
Do	1880	20	314	
Washington	1877*			
Do	1878			138 11
Do	1879			1,339 92
Do	1880	20	314	
Utah	1877*	21	256	
Do	1878			1,137 10
Do	1879			1,337 86
Do	1880	20	314	
Wyoming	1877*			
Do	1878			40 64
Do	1879			684 49
Do	1880	20	314	
Central Superintendency	1878			152 47
Buildings for Gros Ventres	1879			500 00
Buildings at agencies, and repairs	1877*			
Do	1878			852 95
Do	1879			
Do	1880	20	207	
Civilization fund		R. S.	2003–6	877,012 72
Civilization of Winnebagoes				513 10
Civilization of Indians				
Contingencies Indian Department	1877*	21	256	
Do	1878			673 22
Do	1879			768 33
Do	1880	20	207	
Claims of settlers on Round Valley Indian Reservation, California, "Restored to public lands"				594 37
Expenses Indian Commissioners	1880	20	315	
Expenses Ute Commission	1877*			
Do	1878			2,985 51
Do	1879			492 13
Do	1880	21	199	
Expenses of holding a general council of Indians in Indian Territory	1875 1876	}		1,132 00
Pay of Indian police	1879			17,412 98
Do	1880	20	315	
Payment to Flatheads removed to Jocko Reservation, Montana (reimbursable)	1880	20	315	
Payment to L'Anse and Vieux de Sert Chippewas for lands		18	196	20,000 00
Payment to North Carolina Cherokees				41,952 38
Payment to Pottawatomies (citizens)				5,269 45
Payment to old settlers, or Western Cherokees	1873*			
Payment to C. C. O'Keefe		21	246	
Presents and provisions to Indians	1875*			
Removal of the Utes in Colorado	1880	20	396	
Commission to negotiate the removal of the Utes in Colorado	1879			350 86
Removal of Utes and Apaches from Cimarron, N. Mex	1879			1,726 96
Removal of Utes from White River, Colorado	1879			4,333 50
Removal of Pawnee Indians (reimbursable)				22,435 97
Removal of Poncas	1879			
Removal of Nez Perces of Joseph's band	1879			4,276 87
Removal and subsistence of Indians in Oregon and Washington	1873*			
Reimbursement to Osages for losses sustained	1878			5,000 00
Restoring and maintaining peace with Indians in Oregon	1877*			
Carried forward				4,599,466 94

* And prior years.

PRIATIONS UNEXPENDED June 30, 1879, &c.—Continued. [1]

Appropriations for the fiscal year ending June 30, 1880.	Repayments made during the fiscal year 1880.	Aggregate available for the fiscal year ending June 30, 1880.	Payments during the fiscal year ending June 30, 1880.	Amounts carried to the surplus fund June 30, 1880.	Balances of appropriations, June 30, 1880.
$5,166,526 23	$344,618 79	$9,481,418 40	$4,288,570 43	$332,170 96	$4,860,677 01
2 00	90 15	92 15	2 00	90 15	......
......	......	36 82	......	36 82	......
......	367 58	1,283 t2	508 21	......	774 81
6,000 00	......	6,000 00	4,852 00	......	1,148 00
......	......	352 61	111 30	241 31	......
......	67 07	1,991 43	852 87	......	1,138 56
15,000 00	10 00	15,010 00	15,010 00	......	......
107 21	218 15	325 36	107 21	218 15	......
350 00	......	350 00	350 00	......	......
......	900 00	6,670 19	......	6,670 19	......
......	963 72	5,429 25	172 10	......	5,257 15
20,000 00	30 31	20,030 31	12,434 30	......	7,595 97
160 00	455 80	615 80	160 00	455 80	......
......	2 00	1,849 36	......	1,649 36	......
......	1,214 22	1,470 67	1,140 67	......	330 00
25,000 00	278 15	25,278 15	25,000 00	......	278 15
......	349 60	349 60	......	349 60	......
......	233 51	371 62	......	371 62	......
......	285 09	1,626 01	723 77	......	902 24
20,000 00	3 45	20,003 45	20,003 45	......	......
150 00	75 70	225 70	150 00	75 70	......
......	......	1,137 10	......	1,137 10	......
......	1,025 00	2,362 86	1,393 89	......	968 17
12,000 00	......	12,000 00	11,364 35	......	635 45
......	152 00	152 00	......	152 00	......
......	......	40 64	......	40 64	......
......	......	684 40	302 40	......	382 00
2,000 00	......	2,000 00	1,948 83	......	51 17
......	......	152 47	40 00	112 47	......
......	......	590 00	590 00	......	......
......	3 75	3 75	......	3 75	......
......	86 00	536 95	......	938 95	......
......	1,379 32	1,379 32	585 02	......	794 30
15,000 00	471 66	15,471 66	15,471 66	......	......
83,104 85	8,545 45	469,563 02	267,663 38	......	201,899 64
......	......	513 10	......	......	513 10
......	5 04	5 04	......	5 04	......
156 02	1,501 51	1,657 53	156 02	1,501 51	......
......	584 17	1,267 39	516 60	740 79	......
......	2,428 08	3,196 41	2,125 73	......	1,070 68
35,000 00	1,646 86	36,646 86	36,507 31	......	139 55
......	......	594 37	......	......	594 37
15,000 00	......	15,000 00	14,001 81	......	998 19
......	4 17	4 17	......	4 17	......
......	154 93	2,985 51	......	2,985 51	......
......	......	647 06	200 00	......	447 06
25,000 00	......	25,000 00	5,500 00	......	19,500 00
......	......	1,132 00	287 00	......	845 00
......	1,117 40	18,590 36	1,393 90	......	17,196 48
60,000 00	142 14	60,142 14	47,849 63	......	12,292 51
5,000 00	......	5,000 00	5,000 00	......	......
......	......	20,000 00	20,000 00	......	......
2,043 70	......	43,997 08	180 00	......	43,817 08
......	......	5,289 45	......	......	5,289 45
......	449 30	449 30	......	......	449 30
800 00	......	800 00	......	......	800 00
......	38 75	38 75	......	38 75	......
20,000 00	82 00	20,000 00	......	......	20,000 00
......	......	382 86	......	......	382 86
......	1,437 65	1,726 96	......	......	5,745 83
......	......	5,771 15	35 52	......	12,237 33
......	939 72	22,435 97	10,198 64	......	939 72
......	......	4,276 87	4,276 87	......	......
......	27 08	27 08	......	27 08	......
......	......	5,000 00	5,000 00	......	......
......	01	01	......	01	......
5,528,700 01	272,334 68	10,400,501 63	4,822,705 91	350,016 83	5,227,778 89

29 F

STATEMENT *exhibiting the BALANCES of APPRO*

Specific objects of appropriations.	Year.	Statutes.		Balances of appropriations, July 1, 1879.
		Vol.	Page or section.	
INTERIOR—INDIANS AND PENSIONS—Continued.				
Brought forward				$4,599,466 94
Salary of Ouray, head chief of the Ute nation	1879			500 00
Do	1880	20	315	
Statistics and historical data respecting Indians of the United States	1878			1 37
Saw-mill, grist-mill, and bridge at Salt Agency	1878			144 55
Insurance, transportation, &c., of annuities, &c., to Indians in Minnesota and Michigan	1876*			
Surveying Sioux Indian lands in Dakota	1880	20	396	
Wagon road for the Ute Reservation, Colorado				1,500 00
Vaccination of Indians	1878			241 75
Do	1879			482 00
Do	1880	20	297	
Telegraphing and purchase of Indian supplies	1877 1878	}		2,176 15
Do	1879			2,400 24
Do	1880	{ 20 { 21	315 67	}
Transportation of Indian supplies	1877*			
Do	1878			28,601 45
Do	1879			49,457 19
Do	1880	20	314	
Maintenance and education of Catharine and Sophia Germain		18	424	
Maintenance and education of Helen and Heloise Lincoln		16	377	5,062 50
Maintenance and education of Adelaide and Julia Gorman		20	100	5,125 00
Support of Assinaboines in Montana	1879			10,000 00
Support of Apaches in Arizona and New Mexico	1877*			
Support of Apaches in Arizona and New Mexico (transfer account)	1877*			
Support of Apaches in Arizona and New Mexico	1878			95,055 55
Do	1879			27,750 58
Do	1880	20	315	
Support of Arapahoes, Cheyennes, Apaches, Kiowas, Comanches, and Wichitas	1879			26,095 93
Do	1880	{ 20 { 21	315 67	}
Subsistence of Arapahoes, Cheyennes, Apaches, Kiowas, Comanches, and Wichitas	1878			23,485 33
Support of Arickarees, Gros Ventres, and Mandans	1879			15,379 93
Do	1880	20	312	
Subsistence and civilization of Arickarees, Gros Ventres, and Mandans	1877*			
Subsistence and civilization of Arickarees, Gros Ventres, and Mandans (transfer account)	1877*	18	418	
Subsistence and civilization of Arickarees, Gros Ventres, and Mandans	1878			23,601 56
Support of Chippewas of Red Lake and Pembina tribe of Chippewas	1880	20	314	
Support of Chippewas on White Earth Reservation	1880	20	313	
Support of Gros Ventres in Montana	1879			10,274 38
Do	1880	20	313	
Support of Indians at Fort Peck Agency	1879			59,896 52
Do	1880	20	313	
Support and civilization of Indians at Fort Peck Agency	1879			5,389 68
Support of Indians in Idaho	1879			11,023 90
Do	1880	20	313	
Support of captive Indians	1876*			
Support of Indians in Southeastern Oregon	1879			4,230 00
Do	1880	20	313	
Support of Indians at Central Superintendency	1877*			
Do	1879			10,657 41
Do	1880	20	313	
Civilization and subsistence of Indians at Central Superintendency	1878			
Civilization and subsistence of Indians on Malheur Reservation	1878			232 12
Support of Indians on Malheur Reservation	1877*			23 90
Do	1879			
Do	1880	20	313	
Support of Kansas Indians	1879			1,200 33
Do	1880	20	313	
Subsistence of Kansas Indians	1878			252 51
Support of Modocs in the Indian Territory	1879			2,781 15
Do	1880	20	313	
Settlement, subsistence, and support of Modocs in the Indian Territory	1878			52 25
Carried forward				5,003,201 83

* And prior years.

PRIATIONS UNEXPENDED June 30, 1879, &c.—Continued.

Appropriations for the fiscal year ending June 30, 1880.	Repayments made during the fiscal year 1880.	Aggregate available for the fiscal year ending June 30, 1880.	Payments during the fiscal year ending June 30, 1880.	Amounts carried to the surplus fund June 30, 1880.	Balances of appropriations, June 30, 1880.
$5,326,700 01	$272,334 08	$10,408,501 03	$4,823,705 91	$356,016 83	$5,227,778 89
1,000 00		500 00	500 00		
		1,000 00	750 00		250 00
		1 37		1 37	....t......
		144 55		144 55	
	891 50	891 50		891 50	
10,000 00		10,000 00	3,147 89		6,852 31
		1,500 00			1,500 00
		241 75	30 00	211 75	
		482 00	81 00		401 00
500 00		500 00	192 00		308 00
	101 25	2,277 40	234 21	2,043 19	
	249 49	2,709 73	2,483 34		226 39
34,041 58	22 17	34,063 75	28,823 38		5,240 37
	7 40	7 40		7 40	
	299 13	24,900 58	1,449 12	27,451 46	
	12,819 06	60,276 25	60,715 51		1,560 74
225,000 00	876 12	225,876 12	215,432 01		10,444 11
5,191 01		5,191 61	2,500 00		2,691 61
250 00		5,312 50	125 00		5,187 50
250 00		5,375 00	250 00		5,125 00
		10,000 00	1,846 04		8,153 96
	112 04	112 04		112 04	
	210 00	210 00	210 00		
		95,065 55	10,139 54	84,925 01	
	2,016 25	29,766 83	29,234 93		531 90
320,000 00	2,325 66	322,325 66	260,742 60		61,583 06
	524 72	27,220 65	26,891 37		329 28
357,869 65	1,445 89	359,315 54	341,132 24		18,183 30
	34 63	23,519 96		23,519 96	
	2,830 65	18,210 58	5,365 79		12,844 79
60,000 00	4,039 65	64,039 65	56,956 78		7,082 87
	30 81	30 81		30 81	
742 00		742 00	742 00		
		23,001 55		23,001 55	
20,000 00		20,000 00	13,925 99		6,074 01
5,000 00		5,000 00	5,000 00		
	193 42	10,487 80	6,208 61		4,259 19
25,000 00	274 32	25,274 32	18,379 06		6,895 26
	213 27	40,109 80	10,508 29		29,601 51
75,000 00	126 42	75,126 42	73,638 56		1,487 86
	728 00	6,117 68	758 00	5,359 88	
		11,023 90	5,548 28		5,475 62
25,000 00	189 00	25,189 00	21,608 90		3,580 10
	6 02	6 02		6 02	
		4,230 00			4,230 00
5,000 00		5,000 00	4,444 65		555 35
	20 00	20 00		20 00	
	2,308 32	12,965 73	12,392 12		573 61
19,617 75	284 88	19,902 63	19,425 40		477 23
	561 50	561 60		561 00	
	2 76	234 88		234 88	
	36 02	36 02		36 02	
	1,095 50	1,118 86			1,118 86
20,000 00	464 93	20,464 93	12,439 66		8,025 27
	298 95	1,499 28	1,074 86		434 42
9,615 21		9,615 21	9,615 21		
		252 51		252 51	
		2,781 15	1,729 33		1,051 82
6,901 57	1 74	6,903 31	6,560 60		342 71
		52 25		52 25	
6,754,679 38	907,976 25	12,005,857 48	6,095,928 98	519,480 58	5,450,447 90

STATEMENT *exhibiting the BALANCES of APPRO*

Specific objects of appropriations.	Year.	Statutes.		Balances of appropriations, July 1, 1879.
		Vol.	Page or section.	
INTERIOR—INDIANS AND PENSIONS—Continued.				
Brought forward.................................				$5,003,201 83
Support of Nez Perces of Joseph's band................	1880	21	67	....
Support of schools for Otoes and Missourias (reimbursable) (transfer account)...........................	1877*	18	418	....
Support of schools for Otoes and Missourias (reimbursable).	1878	......	......	2,400 51
Do..	1879	......	......	3,000 00
Do..	1880	20	305	....
School buildings for Otoes and Missourias in Nebraska (reimbursable) (transfer account)...............	1876*	18	418	....
Support of schools for Sacs and Foxes in Iowa............	1878	......	......	400 00
Support of schools not otherwise provided for............	1877*	......	......	....
Do..	1878	......	......	496 24
Do..	1879	......	......	2,241 91
Do..	1880	20	312	....
Support of Tonkawas at Fort Griffin................	1880	20	313	....
Settlement, subsistence, and support of Shoshones, Bannocks, and other bands in Idaho and Southeastern Oregon.	1878	......	......	5,154 77
Support of Wichitas and other affiliated bands...........	1878	......	......	1,801 57
Do..	1879	......	......	....
Do..	1880	20	314	....
Relief of Henry A. Webster, V. B. McCollam, and A. Colby, of Washington Territory, pre-empters in Makah Indian Reservation...........................	......	......	......	302 90
Relief of Redick McKee................	......	19	541	....
Relief of Henry Warren, of Weatherford, Tex........	......	21	26	....
Relief of persons for damages sustained by certain bands of Sioux Indians...........................	1873*	21	256	....
Arrears of Army pensions................	......	20	469	....
Fees for vouchers, arrears of Army pensions............	......	20	469	....
Arrears of Navy pensions................	......	20	469	....
Fees for vouchers, arrears of Navy pensions............	......	20	469	....
Navy pensions...........................	1880	20	256	....
		21	150	
Do..	1877*	......	......	....
Navy pensions (transfer account)................	1877*	......	......	....
Navy pensions...........................	1878	......	......	15,308 78
Do..	1879	......	......	....
Pay and allowances, Navy pensions...........	1880	20	266	....
Pay and allowances, Army pensions...........	1880	20	266	....
		21	150	
Army pensions...........................	1877*	21	257	....
Army pensions (transfer account)................	1877*	......	......	....
Army pensions...........................	1878	......	......	1,183 274 48
Do..	1879	......	......	....
Do..	1880	20	266	....
		21	150	
Army pensions to widows and others (reappropriated)......	1871	......	......	114 78
Fees for preparing vouchers, Army pensions...........	1878	......	......	20,635 50
Fees of examining surgeons, Army pensions...........	1878	......	......	5,326 59
Do..	1880	20	267	....
Fees of examining surgeons, Navy pensions...........	1878	......	......	103 00
Do..	1880	20	267	....
Fees for preparing vouchers, Navy pensions...........	1878	......	......	298 00
Compensation to agents, Navy pensions...........	1878	......	......	1,858 75
Compensation to agents, Army pensions...........	1878	......	......	130,345 49
Navy pension fund...........................	......	......	......	31,904 49
Printing pension checks................	1879	......	......	1,066 04
Do..	1880	20	379	....
Total...........................				6,409,235 63
MILITARY ESTABLISHMENT.				
Pay of the Army................	1877*	21	256	....
Pay of the Army (transfer account)............	1877*	......	......	....
Pay of the Army................	1878	......	......	671,566 50
Do..	1879	......	......	243,330 19
Pay, traveling, and general expenses of the Army...........	1880	21	31	....
Pay to discharged soldiers for clothing not drawn...........	1871*	......	......	....
Pay of Military Academy................	1878	21	244	31,446 07
Do..	1879	21	244	60 83
Do..	1880	20	260	....
		21	245	
Bounty to volunteers, their widows and legal heirs...........	1871*	21	256	....

PRIATIONS UNEXPENDED June 30, 1879, &c.—Continued.

Appropriations for the fiscal year ending June 30, 1880.	Repayments made during the fiscal year 1880.	Aggregate available for the fiscal year ending June 30, 1880.	Payments during the fiscal year ending June 30, 1880.	Amounts carried to the surplus fund, June 30, 1880.	Balances of appropriations, June 30, 1880.
$6, 754, 679 93	$307, 970 25	$12, 065, 857 46	$6, 096, 928 96	$519, 480 58	$5, 450, 447 90
25, 000 00	790 88	25, 790 88	23, 451 14	....	2, 339 74
1, 621 91	....	1, 621 91	1, 621 91	....	....
....	....	2, 400 51	2, 400 51	....	....
....	572 83	3, 572 83	3, 572 83	....	....
6, 000 00	99 84	6, 099 84	3, 406 01	....	2, 693 83
2, 452 31	....	2, 452 31	2, 452 31	....	....
....	....	400 00	....	400 00	....
....	75 88	75 88	....	75 88	....
....	7 04	503 28	....	503 28	....
....	8, 613 00	10, 854 91	10, 582 57	....	272 34
75, 000 00	10 98	75, 010 98	74, 519 09	....	491 89
4, 800 00	....	4, 800 00	4, 800 00	....	....
....	....	5, 154 77	....	5, 154 77	....
....	275 47	2, 077 04	225 00	1, 852 04	....
....	6, 692 36	6, 692 36	6, 676 48	....	15 88
24, 000 00	....	24, 000 00	23, 911 32	....	88 68
....	....	302 90	....	....	302 90
1, 027 97	....	1, 027 97	1, 027 97	....	....
15, 867 50	....	15, 867 50	15, 867 50	....	....
128 00	....	128 00	128 00	....	....
19, 155, 380 05	291, 319 95	19, 446, 600 00	19, 446, 680 00	....	....
7, 993 60	481 40	8, 475 00	8. 475 00	....	....
177, 627 55	19, 372 45	197, 000 00	197, 000 00	....	....
24 00	16 00	40 00	40 00	....	....
759, 000 00	28, 558 66	787, 558 66	787, 558 66	....	....
....	1, 836 07	1, 836 07	....	1, 836 07	....
....	52 78	52 78	52 78	....	....
....	1, 879 38	17, 188 16	....	17, 188 16	....
....	26, 073 87	26, 073 87	2, 512 13	....	23, 561 54
3, 500 00	299 56	3, 799 56	3, 277 95	....	521 61
239, 000 00	6, 487 64	245, 487 64	238, 900 00	....	6, 587 64
1, 290 59	23, 968 50	25, 259 09	....	23, 968 50	1, 290 59
....	757 55	757 55	757 55	....	....
....	3, 807 98	1, 187, 142 16	1, 804 00	1, 185, 338 16	....
....	590, 365 07	596, 365 07	89, 562 36	....	506, 803 31
36, 900, 000 00	487, 857 53	37, 387, 857 53	37, 387, 500 00	....	357 53
....	....	114 78	....	114 78	....
....	....	26, 695 50	....	26, 695 50	....
....	14 00	5, 340 59	....	5, 340 59	....
202, 000 00	5, 840 00	207, 840 00	96, 500 00	....	111, 340 00
....	....	103 00	....	103 00	....
2, 500 00	16 00	2, 516 00	2, 386 00	....	130 00
....	....	298 00	....	298 00	....
....	....	1, 858 75	....	1, 858 75	....
....	....	130, 345 49	....	130, 345 49	....
....	....	31, 904 49	....	....	31, 904 49
....	....	1, 066 04	118 95	....	947 09
9, 000 00	....	9, 000 00	8, 336 00	....	664 00
64, 367, 892 86	1, 820, 079 92	73, 597, 307 51	64, 541, 953 00	1, 914, 498 55	6, 140, 760 96
9, 042 85	6, 250 97	15, 883 82	....	6, 250 97	9, 042 85
....	605 17	665 17	605 17	....	....
....	34, 468 10	706, 036 60	5, 694 44	706, 342 16	....
....	578, 790 08	822, 129 87	39, 672 54	....	782, 457 33
12, 300, 776 00	196, 097 20	12, 498, 873 20	12, 238, 940 62	....	259, 932 58
....	1 12	1 12	....	1 12	....
562 50	375 00	32, 383 57	73 60	31, 821 07	562 50
477 79	7, 497 44	8, 046 06	....	....	7, 972 46
207, 292 33	....	207, 292 33	206, 000 00	....	1, 292 33
93, 191 17	11, 363 05	104, 554 22	....	11, 363 05	93, 191 17
12, 611, 942 64	835, 498 73	14, 393, 875 96	12, 489, 046 37	749, 778 37	1, 155, 051 22

·"transportation or the Army and its supplies, 1877 and prior years" military ledger.

STATEMENT exhibiting the BALANCES of APPRO

Specific objects of appropriations.	Year.	Statutes.		Balances of appropriations, July 1, 1879.
		Vol.	Page or section.	
MILITARY ESTABLISHMENT—Continued.				
Brought forward				$946,434 59
Bounty to volunteers and regulate	1871*			
Collection and payment of bounty, prize money, and other claims of colored soldiers and sailors	1836	20	403	
Do	1879			1,900 00
Pay, transportation, services, and supplies of Oregon and Washington volunteers in 1855 and 1856	1871*	21	257	
Support of Bureau of Refugees and Abandoned Property	1871*	21	257	
Pay of two and three years' volunteers (transfer account)	1871*			
Pay of two and three years' volunteers	1871*	21	256	
Pay of two and three years' volunteers (colored claims)	1879 1880	} ...		40,800 00
Pay of volunteers	1871*			
Subsistence of the Army	1871*			869 47
Subsistence of the Army (reappropriated)	1877*			72 60
Subsistence of the Army (transfer account)	1877*			
Subsistence of the Army	1877*	21	257	
Do	1878			7,747 99
Do	1879			2,814 42
Do	1880	21	31	
Regular supplies of the Quartermaster's Department	1877*	21	256	
Regular supplies of the Quartermaster's Department (reappropriated)	1877*			864 40
Regular supplies of the Quartermaster's Department	1878			259,356 89
Do	1879			58,836 22
Do	1880	21	32	
Incidental expenses, Quartermaster's Department	1877*	21	257	
Incidental expenses, Quartermaster's Department (transfer account)	1877*			
Incidental expenses, Quartermaster's Department	1878	21	244	142 37
Do	1879			
Do	1880	21	32	
Barracks and quarters	1877*	21	257	
Do	1878			5,102 47
Do	1879			7 50
Do	1880	21	32	
Transportation of the Army and its supplies (reappropriated)	1871*			335 60
Transportation of the Army and its supplies (transfer account)	1877*			
Transportation of the Army and its supplies	1877*	21	256	
Do	1877			245,004 79
Do	1878			22,365 48
Do	1879			90,906 09
Do	1880	21	32	
Transportation of officers and their baggage	1871*	21	257	
Do	1877*			
Horses for cavalry and artillery	1877*	21	257	
Do	1878			23,069 97
Do	1870			2,872 50
Do	1880	21	32	
Clothing, camp and garrison equipage	1877*	21	257	
Do	1878			122,091 13
Do	1879			127,676 67
Do	1880	21	33	
Payment of expenses under reconstruction acts	1871*			
Protection of Confederate cemetery, Johnson's Island	1877*			
National cemeteries	1877*			
Do	1878			48 10
Do	1879			11,401 73
Do	1880	21	32	
Removing remains of officers to National cemeteries	1879			4,900 00
Pay of superintendents of National cemeteries	1878			3,464 09
Do	1870			2,630 68
Do	1880	21	33	
Headstones for graves of soldiers in private cemeteries	1877*			182,027 40
Medical and Hospital Department	1877*	21	256	
Medical and Hospital Department (transfer account)	1877*			
Medical and Hospital Department	1878			8,720 70
Do	1870			6,357 97
Do	1880	21	33	
Artificial limbs (transfer account)	1877*			
Artificial limbs	1878			20 80
Do	1870			10,078 69
Do	1880	20	380	
Appliances for disabled soldiers	1878			2,836 00
Carried forward				2,101,066 05

* And prior years.

PRIATIONS UNEXPENDED June 30, 1879, &c.—Continued.

Appropriations for the fiscal year ending June 30, 1880.	Repayments made during the fiscal year 1880.	Aggregate available for the fiscal year ending June 30, 1880.	Payments during the fiscal year ending June 30, 1880.	Amounts carried to the surplus fund June 30, 1880.	Balances of appropriations, June 30, 1880.
$12, 611, 942 64	$835, 498 73	$14, 398, 875 96	$12, 489, 046 37	$749, 778 37	$1, 155, 051 22
....	120 00	120 00	....	120 00	....
10, 000 00	....	10, 800 00	10, 000 00	....	....
....	2, 190 41	4, 099 41	....	....	4, 099 41
8, 275 56	....	8, 275 56	....	....	8, 275 56
1 00	....	1 00	....	....	1 00
....	27 43	27 43	27 43	....	....
48, 563 51	21, 612 30	70, 175 81	962 49	20, 649 81	48, 563 51
....	....	40, 000 00	40, 000 00	....	....
....	148 20	148 20	....	148 20	....
....	....	800 47	860 47	....	....
....	....	72 60	....	72 60	....
....	2, 692 81	2, 692 81	2, 692 81	....	....
3, 368 95	571 21	3, 940 16	....	571 21	3, 368 95
....	555 41	8, 303 40	944 59	7, 358 81	....
....	27, 399 10	29, 413 92	1, 081 93	....	28, 331 99
2, 300, 000 00	91, 656 06	2, 391, 656 06	2, 390, 576 21	....	1, 081 85
8, 811 11	409 90	9, 221 01	....	409 90	8, 811 11
....	....	864 40	....	864 40	....
....	13, 803 70	273, 063 59	1, 812 23	271, 251 36	....
....	49, 520 27	99, 356 49	20, 240 61	....	79, 115 88
3, 600, 000 00	53, 729 75	3, 653, 729 75	3, 321, 450 88	....	332, 278 87
7, 020 17	656 43	7, 676 60	....	656 43	7, 020 17
....	2 75	2 75	2 75	....	....
21, 298 92	600 26	22, 041 55	742 46	15	31, 298 92
....	13, 968 83	13, 968 83	3, 720 02	....	10, 248 81
1, 000, 000 00	75 32	1, 000, 075 32	966, 799 61	....	13, 275 71
12, 336 68	5, 797 79	18, 684 47	....	5, 797 79	12, 336 68
....	4, 215 87	9, 318 34	2, 946 84	6, 371 50	....
....	9, 115 96	9, 132 56	7, 744 25	....	1, 378 31
880, 000 00	2, 437 41	882, 437 41	872, 499 81	....	9, 937 60
....	....	335 60	....	....	335 60
....	†27 49	27 49	27 49	....	....
61, 121 18	7, 334 91	68, 456 09	....	7, 334 91	61, 121 18
....	999 15	245, 934 04	16, 646 14	229, 308 98	....
....	15, 104 78	37, 470 26	37, 468 32	1 94	....
....	109, 494 36	200, 496 45	159, 469 34	....	41, 021 11
4, 200, 000 00	1, 540 27	4, 201, 540 27	4, 199, 283 01	....	2, 257 26
167 88	....	167 88	....	....	167 88
....	11 40	11 40	....	11 40	....
5, 258 00	140 00	5, 398 00	....	140 00	5, 258 00
....	352 59	24, 342 56	625 00	23, 717 56	....
....	5, 731 99	8, 604 49	....	....	8, 604 49.
200, 000 00	5, 209 63	205, 209 63	198, 965 72	....	6, 243 91
4 15	1, 525 99	1, 530 14	....	1, 525 99	4 15
....	1, 706 89	123, 798 07	4, 372 88	119, 425 19	....
....	73, 598 53	201, 185 20	93, 515 94	....	107, 669 36
900, 000 00	70, 691 06	970, 691 06	970, 648 47	....	42 59
....	280 95	280 95	....	280 95	....
....	1, 500 00	1, 500 00	....	....	1, 500 00
....	2 60	2 60	....	2 60	....
....	....	43 10	2 75	40 35	....
100, 000 00	1, 855 70	13, 257 43	13, 216 17	....	41 26
....	....	100, 000 00	95, 858 90	....	4, 141 10
....	300 00	5, 200 00	300 00	....	4, 900 00
....	....	3, 464 09	....	3, 464 09	....
....	25 00	2, 655 68	196 66	....	2, 459 02
50, 000 00	....	59, 000 00	58, 578 98	....	421 02
....	....	182, 027 49	30, 000 00	....	152, 027 49
1, 020 46	106 91	1, 138 37	....	108 91	1, 029 46
....	11 25	11 25	11 25	....	....
....	2, 922 13	10, 742 83	821 65	9, 921 18	....
....	10, 642 60	16, 999 97	16, 959 34	....	40 63
200, 000 00	24, 188 33	224, 188 33	196, 974 03	....	27, 214 30
....	....	244 03	244 03	....	....
....	4 37	25 17	25 17	....	....
....	500 00	10, 578 69	273 44	....	10, 305 25
100, 000 00	....	100, 000 00	50, 053 00	....	49, 947 00
....	....	2, 836 00	....	2, 836 00	....
26, 338, 189 21	1, 462, 791 31	29, 993, 046 57	26, 298, 696 06	1, 462, 131 00	2, 231, 217 51

† $757.55 transferred to appropriation for "Army pensions." Interior ledger.

STATEMENT exhibiting the BALANCES of APPRO

Specific objects of appropriations	Year	Vol.	Page or section.	Balances of appropriations, July 1, 1879.
MILITARY ESTABLISHMENT—Continued.				
Brought forward				$2,191,066 05
Appliances for disabled soldiers	1879			
Do	1880	20	389	
Construction and repairs of hospitals	1878			1,902 16
Do	1870			3 86
Do	1880	21	33	
Medical and Surgical History				13,657 05
Medical Museum and Library		21	33	
Rebuilding officers' quarters at Madison Barracks, Sacket's Harbor, N. Y		20	389	
Ordnance service	1878			32 42
Do	1879			
Do	1880	21	34	
Ordnance, ordnance stores and supplies	1877*	21	256	
Do	1878			
Do	1879			
Do	1880	21	34	
Ordnance material, proceeds of sale		18	388	245,686 26
Manufacture of arms at national armories	1880	21	34	
Arming and equipping the militia (permanent)		R. S.	1661	118,305 42
Repairs of arsenals	1877*			
Do	1878			55 78
Do	1879			
Do	1880	20	387	
Rock Island Arsenal, Rock Island, Ill	1878			
Do	1879			39,702 50
Do	1880	20	386	
Rock Island bridge, Rock Island, Ill		20	386	
Springfield Arsenal, Springfield, Mass		20	386	
Benicia Arsenal, Benicia, Cal		20	387	
Armament of fortifications	1879			66,719 63
Do	1880	{ 20 / 21	467 / 34	}
Current and ordinary expenses of United States Military Academy	1877*			
Do	1880	20	250	
Miscellaneous items and incidental expenses of United States Military Academy	1878			285 26
Do	1879			
Do	1880	20	262	
Buildings and grounds of United States Military Academy	1878			2 65
Do	1879			
Do	1880	20	262	
Water supply of United States Military Academy		20	261	
Powder depot		21	34	
Fort Scammel, Maine				181 30
Batteries in Portsmouth Harbor, New Hampshire				916 75
Fort at Lazaretto Point, Maryland				13,000 00
Fort Brown, Texas				25,000 00
Fort Duncan, Texas				10,000 00
Ringgold Barracks, Texas				10,000 00
Preservation and repair of fortifications	1878			1 79
Do	1879			
Do	1880	20	467	
Torpedoes for harbor defenses	1880	20	467	
Purchase of sites for sea-coast defenses				45,944 16
Construction of sea-coast mortar-batteries (reappropriated)				301 50
Military post near Neshara River, Northern Nebraska and Dakota		21	33	
Purchase of cemetery grounds near Columbus, Ohio		21	321	
Engineers' depot at Willet's Point, N. Y	1880	21	33	
Contingencies of fortifications				2,642 65
Improving harbor at—				
Portland, Me				41,000 00
Belfast, Me		20	363	
Improving Richmond Island, Me		20	363	
Improving harbor at—				
Portsmouth, N. H		20	372	
Burlington, Vt		20	364	5,000 00
Swanton, Vt		20	364	
Boston, Mass		20	371	20,000 00
Hyannis, Mass		20	364	
Provincetown, Mass		20	363	
Plymouth, Mass		20	363	1,000 00
Wood's Holl, Mass		20	371	
Carried forward				2,851,487 19

PRIATIONS UNEXPENDED *June* 30, 1879, &c.—Continued.

Appropriations for the fiscal year ending June 30, 1880.	Repayments made during the fiscal year 1880.	Aggregate available for the fiscal year ending June 30, 1880.	Payments during the fiscal year ending June 30, 1880.	Amounts carried to the surplus fund June 30, 1880.	Balances of appropriations, June 30, 1880.
$26,338,189 21	$1,462,791 31	$29,992,046 57	$26,298,698 06	$1,462,131 00	$2,231,217 51
	2,887 00	2,887 00			2,887 09
1,000 00		1,000 00	1,000 00		
	1,783 35	2,785 51		2,785 51	
	1,962 06	1,965 94			1,965 94
75,000 00	561 77	75,561 77	75,540 27		21 50
		18,657 05			13,657 05
10,000 00		10,000 00	10,000 00		
25,000 00		25,000 00	25,000 00		
		32 42	15 00	17 42	
	37 89	37 89			37 89
110,000 00	5 90	110,005 90	110,005 90		
66 00	27 40	93 40		27 40	66 00
	123 66	123 66		123 66	
	577 79	677 79	44 50		533 29
320,000 00	280 72	320,280 72	320,280 72		
131,110 10	a 75	376,797 11	75,000 00		301,797 11
250,000 00		250,000 00	250,000 00		
200,000 00	30,072 03	354,977 45	306,113 59		48,863 86
	11 31	11 31	11 31		
		55 78		55 78	
	96 84	96 84			96 84
30,000 00		30,000 00	30,000 00		
	303 64	303 64		303 64	
	55	39,703 05	39,702 50		55
212,000 00		212,000 00	212,000 00		
15,000 00		15,000 00	15,000 00		
15,000 00		15,000 00	15,000 00		
5,000 00		5,000 00	5,000 00		
	202 04	66,921 67	64,910 00		2,011 67
182,500 00		182,500 00	79,500 00		103,000 00
	4,945 37	4,945 37		4,945 37	
45,915 00		45,915 00	45,915 00		
		265 26		265 26	
	365 71	365 71			365 71
12,840 00		12,840 00	12,840 00		
		2 65		2 65	
	1 30	1 30			1 30
14,000 00		14,000 00	14,000 00		
40,000 00		40,000 00	40,000 00		
50,000 00		50,000 00	50,000 00		
		181 30			181 30
		916 75			916 75
		13,000 00			13,000 00
		25,000 00			25,000 00
		10,000 00			10,000 00
		10,000 00			10,000 00
		1 79		1 79	
	558 08	558 08	500 00		58 08
100,000 00	1,299 48	101,299 48	100,994 48		305 00
50,000 00		50,000 00	50,000 00		
		45,944 16		45,944 16	
		301 50		301 50	
50,000 00		50,000 00	50,000 00		
500 00		500 00	500 00		
5,000 00		5,000 00	5,000 00		
		2,642 65	23 66		2,618 99
		41,000 00	1,000 00		40,000 00
5,000 00		5,000 00	5,000 00		
3,000 00		3,000 00	3,000 00		
10,000 00		10,000 00	10,000 00		
15,000 00		20,000 00	15,000 00		5,000 00
6,000 00		6,000 00	6,000 00		
50,000 00		70,000 00	70,000 00		
2,500 00		2,500 00	2,500 00		
1,000 00		1,000 00	1,000 00		
3,500 00		4,500 00	2,000 00		2,500 00
15,000 00		15,000 00	15,000 00		
28,399,120 91	1,515,495 97	32,766,108 47	28,433,080 68	1,516,916 45	2,816,103 34

458   REPORT ON THE FINANCES.

STATEMENT exhibiting the BALANCES of APPRO

Specific objects of appropriations.	Year.	Statutes.		Balances of appropriations, July 1, 1879.
		Vol.	Page or section.	
MILITARY ESTABLISHMENT—Continued.				
Brought forward				$2,851,487 19
Improving Little Narragansett Bay, Rhode Island and Connecticut		20	368	
Improving harbor at—				
Bridgeport, Conn		20	363	
New Haven, Conn		20	363	
Norwalk, Conn		20	363	
Stonington, Conn		20	363	
Port Chester, N. Y				1,950 00
Buffalo, N. Y		20	369	55,000 00
Little Sodus Bay, N. Y		20	370	10,000 00
Great Sodus Bay, N. Y		20	369	5,000 00
Improving Echo Harbor, New Rochelle, N. Y		20	364	10,000 00
Improving Flushing Bay, New York		20	370	
Improving harbor at—				
Roundout, N. Y				5,000 00
Waddington, N. Y				4,000 00
Oak Orchard, N. Y		20	369	2,000 00
Oswego, N. Y		20	370	35,000 00
Plattsburg, N. Y		20	364	
Port Jefferson, N. Y		20	363	
Pultneyville, N. Y		20	369	5,000 00
Dunkirk, N. Y				4 00
Erie, Pa		20	369	22,000 00
Constructing pier in Delaware Bay, near Lewes, Del		20	364	
Improving ice harbor at New Castle, Del		20	364	
Improving harbor at—				
Wilmington, Del		20	364	
Baltimore, Md		20	366	10,000 00
Breton Bay, Leonardtown, Md		20	364	
Cambridge and Pocomoke River, Md		20	371	
Queenstown, Md		20	371	
Washington and Georgetown, D. C		20	364	20,000 00
Norfolk, Va		20	364	20,000 00
Onancock, Va		20	371	
Edenton, N. C		20	365	
Charlotte, N. Y		20	369	
Charleston, S. C		20	365	123,000 00
Savannah, Ga		20	365	45,000 00
Brunswick, Ga		20	372	
Pensacola, Fla		20	365	5,000 00
Cedar Keys, Fla		20	365	
Mobile, Ala		20	370	
Improving harbor and Mississippi River near Vicksburg, Miss		20	366	24,000 00
Improving harbor at—				
New Orleans, La		20	365	15,000 00
Galveston, Tex		20	365	10,000 00
Ashtabula, Ohio		20	369	3,000 00
Cleveland, Ohio		20	369	
Breakwater at Cleveland, Ohio				75,000 00
Improving ice harbor at mouth of Muskingum River, Ohio		20	369	
Improving harbor at Port Clinton, Ohio		20	369	
Harbor of Refuge, near Cincinnati, Ohio				39,878 97
Improving harbor at—				
Sandusky, Ohio		20	368	2,000 00
Toledo, Ohio		20	360	0,000 00
Fairport, Ohio				4,000 00
Michigan City, Ind		20	368	14,500 00
Calumet, Ill		20	368	
Chicago, Ill		20	368	
Improving Galena Harbor and River, Illinois		20	367	
Improving harbor and Mississippi River at Memphis, Tenn		20	366	
Improving Eagle Harbor, Michigan		20	368	2,000 00
Improving harbor at—				
Frankfort, Mich		20	368	2,000 00
Ludington, Mich		20	369	2,000 00
Muskegon, Mich		20	369	1,000 00
Marquette, Mich		20	368	2,000 00
New Buffalo, Mich				5,000 00
Improving harbor of refuge at entrance of Sturgeon Bay Canal, Wisconsin		20	368	7,000 00
Improving harbor at—				
South Haven, Mich		20	369	2,000 00
Thunder Bay, Mich				564 04
Carried forward				3,440,383 90

PRIATIONS UNEXPENDED June 30, 1879, &c.—Continued.

Appropriations for the fiscal year ending June 30, 1880.	Repayments made during the fiscal year 1880.	Aggregate available for the fiscal year ending June 30, 1880.	Payments during the fiscal year ending June 30, 1880.	Amount carried to the surplus fund June 30, 1880.	Balances of appropriations, June 30, 1880.
$28,390,120 31	$1,515,405 97	$32,766,103 47	$28,433,083 68	$1,516,016 45	$2,816,103 34
5,000 00	....	5,000 00	5,000 00	....	....
10,000 00	....	10,000 00	10,000 00	....	....
15,000 00	....	15,000 00	15,000 00	....	....
10,000 00	....	10,000 00	10,000 00	....	....
37,500 00	....	37,500 00	37,000 00	....	500 00
....	....	1,950 00	....	....	1,950 00
100,000 00	....	155,000 00	65,000 00	....	90,000 00
5,000 00	....	15,000 00	15,000 00	....	....
2,000 00	....	7,000 00	7,000 00	....	....
8,000 00	....	13,000 00	11,000 00	....	2,000 00
20,000 00	....	20,000 00	20,000 00	....	....
....	....	5,000 00	5,000 00	....	....
....	....	4,000 00	4,000 00	....	....
....	....	3,000 00	3,000 00	....	....
1,000 00	....	125,000 00	110,000 00	....	15,000 00
90,000 00	....	2,000 00	....	....	2,000 00
2,000 00	....	5,000 00	5,000 00	....	....
5,000 00	....	9,000 00	9,000 00	....	....
4,000 00	....	4 00	....	....	4 00
25,000 00	....	47,000 00	21,000 00	....	26,000 00
10,500 00	....	10,500 00	10,500 00	....	....
5,500 00	....	5,500 00	5,500 00	....	....
3,500 00	....	3,500 00	3,500 00	....	....
160,000 00	....	170,000 00	65,000 00	....	105,000 00
4,000 00	....	4,000 00	4,000 00	....	....
5,000 00	....	5,000 00	2,500 00	....	2,500 00
3,000 00	....	3,000 00	3,000 00	....	....
50,000 00	....	70,000 00	40,000 00	....	30,000 00
75,000 00	....	95,000 00	75,000 00	....	20,000 00
3,000 00	....	3,000 00	3,000 00	....	....
1,000 00	....	1,000 00	1,000 00	....	....
1,000 00	....	1,000 00	1,000 00	....	....
260,000 00	....	323,000 00	115,000 00	....	208,000 00
100,000 00	....	145,000 00	55,000 00	....	90,000 00
20,000 00	....	20,000 00	1,000 00	/.	19,000 00
10,000 00	....	13,000 00	2,000 00	....	18,000 00
15,000 00	....	15,000 00	10,000 00	....	5,000 00
100,000 00	....	100,000 00	5,000 00	....	95,000 00
50,000 00	....	74,000 00	74,000 00	....	....
60,000 00	....	75,000 00	17,500 00	....	57,500 00
100,000 00	....	110,000 00	95,000 00	....	15,000 00
5,000 00	....	12,000 00	5,200 00	....	6,800 00
100,000 00	....	100,000 00	9,000 00	....	91,000 00
....	....	75,000 00	75,000 00	....	....
30,000 00	....	30,000 00	15,000 00	....	15,000 00
10,000 00	....	10,000 00	4,600 00	....	5,400 00
....	....	39,878 07	30,000 00	....	9,878 07
1,000 00	....	3,000 00	3,000 00	....	....
20,000 00	....	29,000 00	23,300 00	....	5,700 00
....	....	4,000 00	4,000 00	....	....
46,000 00	....	54,500 00	54,500 00	....	....
12,000 00	....	12,000 00	12,000 00	....	....
75,000 00	....	75,000 00	75,000 00	....	....
12,000 00	....	12,000 00	12,000 00	....	....
37,000 00	....	37,000 00	25,000 00	....	12,000 00
2,000 00	....	4,000 00	....	....	4,000 00
4,000 00	....	6,000 00	) 6,000 00	....	....
5,000 00	....	7,000 00	5,000 00	....	2,000 00
5,000 00	....	6,000 00	3,500 00	....	2,500 00
1,500 00	....	3,500 00	....	....	3,500 00
....	....	5,000 00	....	....	5,000 00
30,000 00	....	37,000 00	20,000 00	....	17,000 00
7,500 00	....	9,500 00	7,500 00	....	2,000 00
....	....	564 64	564 64	....	....
30,111,120 31	1,515,405 97	35,076,000 18	29,763,748 83	1,516,016 45	3,795,835 41

STATEMENT *exhibiting the* BALANCES *of* APPRO

Specific objects of appropriations.	Year.	Statutes.		Balances of appropriations, July 1, 1879.
		Vol.	Page or section.	
MILITARY ESTABLISHMENT—Continued.				
Brought forward				$3,449,383 90
Improving harbor at—				
Au Sable, Mich		20	369	
Black Lake, Mich		20	369	
Charlevoix, Mich		20	368	
Cheboygan, Mich		20	369	
Grand Haven, Mich		20	369	
Improving harbor of refuge, Lake Huron, Michigan		20	369	40,000 00
Improving harbor at—				
Manistee, Mich		20	369	
Monroe, Mich		20	369	
Ontonagon, Mich		20	368	
Pentwater, Mich		20	369	
Harbor of refuge at Portage Lake, Mich		20	371	
Improving harbor at—				
Saint Joseph, Mich		20	369	
Saugatuck, Mich		20	369	
White River, Mich		20	369	
Port Washington, Wis				5,500 00
Ahnapee, Wis		20	368	
Green Bay, Wis		20	368	
Kenosha, Wis		20	368	
Manitowoc, Wis		20	368	
Menomonee, Wis		20	368	
Milwaukee, Wis		20	368	
Racine, Wis		20	368	
Sheboygan, Wis		20	368	
Dredging Superior Bay, Wisconsin		20	364	
Improving harbor at—				
Two Rivers, Wis		20	368	
Burlington, Iowa		20	367	2,000 00
Fort Madison, Iowa		20	367	
Muscatine, Iowa		20	371	
Duluth, Minn		20	364	
Grand Marias, Minn		20	371	
Oakland, Cal		20	369	94,000 00
San Francisco, Cal				1,500 25
San Diego, Cal		20	370	
Wilmington, Cal		20	370	
Improving entrance to Coos Bay and harbor, Oregon		20	370	
Improving the Gut, opposite Bath, Me				6,000 00
Improving Saint Croix River, Maine				34,000 00
Improving Lubic Channel, Maine		20	371	
Improving Kennebunk River, Maine		20	363	
Improving Penobscot River, Maine		20	363	
Improving Otter Creek, Vermont		20	364	
Improving Merrimac River, Massachusetts		20	363	
Improving Taunton River, Massachusetts		20	363	
Improving Providence River, Rhode Island				5,000 00
Improving Providence River and Narragansett Bay, Rhode Island		20	363	30,000 00
Improving Connecticut River. Connecticut		20	363	15,000 00
Breakwater, New Haven, Conn		20	371	
Improving Thames River, Connecticut		20	363	
Removing obstructions in East River and Hell Gate, New York		20	364	195,000 00
Improving Harlem River, New York		20	372	360,000 00
Improving East Chester Creek, New York		20	364	
Improving Hudson River, New York		20	363	45,000 00
Improving channel between Staten Island and New Jersey				25,000 00
Improving Cohansey Creek, New Jersey		20	364	
Improving Elizabeth River, New Jersey		20	370	
Improving Manasquan River, New Jersey		20	371	
Improving Passaic River, New Jersey		20	364	
Improving Rahway River, New Jersey		20	370	
Improving Raritan River, New Jersey		20	364	125,500 00
Improving Shrewsbury River, New Jersey		20	372	9,000 00
Improving Woodbridge Creek, New Jersey		20	370	
Improving Alleghany River, Pennsylvania		20	364	
Improving Schuylkill River, Pennsylvania		20	364	
Improving Delaware River below Bridesburg, Pa		20	364	55,000 00
Improving Delaware River between Trenton and White Hill, N.J		20	364	
Carried forward				4,436,884 15

PRIATIONS UNEXPENDED June 30, 1879, &c.—Continued.

Appropriations for the fiscal year ending June 30, 1880.	Repayments made during the fiscal year 1880.	Aggregate available for the fiscal year ending June 30, 1880.	Payments during the fiscal year ending June 30, 1880.	Amounts carried to the surplus fund June 30, 1880.	Balances of appropriations, June 30, 1880.
$30,111,120 31	$1,515,495 97	$35,076,000 18	$29,763,748 32	$1,516,916 45	$3,795,335 41
7,000 00	....	7,000 00	5,000 00	....	2,000 00
6,000 00	....	6,000 00	6,000 00	....	....
9,000 00	....	9,000 00	9,000 00	....	....
3,000 00	....	3,000 00	3,000 00	....	....
9,000 00	....	9,000 00	9,000 00	....	....
75,000 00	....	115,000 00	60,000 00	....	55,000 00
10,000 00	....	10,000 00	4,000 00	....	6,000 00
2,000 00	....	2,000 00	2,000 00	....	....
17,000 00	....	37,000 00	12,000 00	....	5,000 00
6,000 00	....	6,000 00	6,000 00	....	....
10,000 00	....	10,000 00	10,000 00	....	....
6,000 00	....	6,000 00	5,000 00	....	1,000 00
5,000 00	....	5,000 00	5,000 00	....	....
7,500 00	....	7,500 00	6,500 00	....	1,000 00
....	....	5,500 00	5,500 00	....	....
7,000 00	....	7,000 00	5,000 00	....	2,000 00
4,000 00	....	4,000 00	4,000 00	....	....
5,000 00	....	5,000 00	5,000 00	....	....
6,500 00	....	6,500 00	3,000 00	....	3,500 00
10,000 00	....	10,000 00	10,000 00	....	....
7,500 00	....	7,500 00	7,500 00	....	....
6,000 00	....	6,000 00	6,000 00	....	....
3,000 00	....	3,000 00	2,000 00	....	1,000 00
5,000 00	....	5,000 00	1,000 00	....	4,000 00
20,000 00	....	20,000 00	15,000 00	....	5,000 00
5,000 00	....	7,000 00	....	....	7,000 00
3,600 00	....	3,600 00	3,600 00	....	....
7,500 00	....	7,500 00	7,500 00	....	....
25,000 00	....	25,000 00	20,000 00	....	5,000 00
10,000 00	....	10,000 00	8,000 00	....	2,000 00
60,000 00	....	154,000 00	2,000 00	....	152,000 00
....	....	1,500 25	....	....	1,500 25
1,000 00	....	1,000 00	1,000 00	....	....
12,000 00	....	12,000 00	12,000 00	....	....
40,000 00	....	40,000 00	40,000 00	....	....
....	....	6,000 00	6,000 00	....	....
....	....	34,000 00	....	....	34,000 00
10,000 00	....	10,000 00	10,000 00	....	....
2,000 00	....	2,000 00	2,000 00	....	....
6,000 00	....	6,000 00	6,000 00	....	....
5,000 00	....	5,000 00	....	....	5,000 00
5,000 00	....	5,000 00	5,000 00	....	....
1,000 00	....	1,000 00	1,000 00	....	....
....	....	5,000 00	5,000 00	....	....
60,000 00	48 00	90,048 00	40,000 00	....	50,048 00
10,000 00	....	25,000 00	10,000 00	....	15,000 00
30,000 00	....	30,000 00	5,000 00	....	25,000 00
12,000 00	....	12,000 00	12,000 00	....	....
250,000 00	....	445,000 00	280,000 00	....	165,000 00
100,000 00	....	400,000 00	....	....	400,000 00
3,500 00	....	3,500 00	....	....	3,500 00
30,000 00	....	75,000 00	45,000 00	....	30,000 00
....	....	25,000 00	4,000 00	....	21,000 00
4,500 00	....	4,500 00	4,500 00	....	....
7,500 00	....	7,500 00	7,500 00	....	....
12,000 00	....	12,000 00	5,000 00	....	7,000 00
2,000 00	....	2,000 00	2,000 00	....	....
10,000 00	....	10,000 00	8,000 00	....	2,000 00
60,000 00	....	185,500 00	180,000 00	....	5,500 00
10,000 00	....	10,000 00	10,000 00	....	....
4,000 00	....	4,000 00	4,000 00	....	....
10,000 00	....	10,000 00	10,000 00	....	....
25,000 00	....	25,000 00	25,000 00	....	....
45,000 00	....	100,000 00	100,000 00	....	....
6,000 00	....	6,000 00	6,000 00	....	....
31,242,220 31	1,515,543 97	37,194,648 43	30,866,348 32	1,516,916 45	4,811,383 66

462 REPORT ON THE FINANCES.

STATEMENT exhibiting the BALANCES of APPRO

Specific objects of appropriation.	Year.	Statutes.		Balances of appropriations, July 1, 1879.
		Vol.	Page or section.	
MILITARY ESTABLISHMENT—Continued.				
Brought forward				$4,436,884 15
Improving Delaware River at Schooner Lodge, New Jersey		20	372	
Improving Delaware River near Cherry Island Flats		20	370	
Improving Mispillion River, Delaware		20	370	
Improving Chester River, Maryland				3,000 00
Improving Wicomico River, Maryland		20	364	
Improving Pocomoke River, Maryland				5,000 00
Improving Potomac River at Mount Vernon, Virginia		20	372	
Improving Blackwater River, Virginia		20	364	
Improving Chickahominy River, Virginia		20	365	
Improving Hampton River, Virginia		20	365	4,000 00
Improving James River, Virginia		20	364	
Improving Appomattox River, Virginia		20	364	
Improving New River, Virginia		20	365	
Improving Nomoni Creek, Virginia		20	364	
Improving North Landing River, Virginia and North Carolina		20	371	
Improving Rappahannock River, Virginia		20	364	
Improving Staunton River, Virginia		20	371	
Improving Nansemond River, Virginia				1,000 00
Improving Urbana Creek, Virginia		20	371	
Improving Occoquan River, Virginia				4,000 00
Improving Great Kanawha River, West Virginia		20	364	267,000 00
Improving Guyandotte River, West Virginia		20	368	
Improving Little Kanawha River, West Virginia		20	368	8,000 00
Improving Monongahela River, West Virginia and Pennsylvania		20	371	
Improving Elk River, West Virginia				2,250 00
Improving Currituck Sound and North River Bar, North Carolina		20	372	
Improving French Broad River, North Carolina		20	365	6,000 00
Improving Neuse River, North Carolina		20	365	
Improving Cape Fear River, North Carolina		20	364	35,000 00
Improving Scuppernong River, North Carolina		20	370	1,800 00
Improving Pamlico River, North Carolina		20	365	
Improving Tar River, North Carolina		20	371	
Improving Trent River, North Carolina		20	371	
Improving Yadkin River, North Carolina		20	372	
Improving Etowah River, Georgia				9,000 00
Improving Ocmulgee River, Georgia		20	368	2,000 00
Improving Chattahoochie River, Georgia		20	365	
Improving Chattahoochie River, Georgia and Alabama				3,000 00
Improving Oostenaula and Coosawattee Rivers, Georgia		20	368	2,000 00
Improving Saint Augustine Creek, Georgia		20	365	
Improving Cooss River, Georgia and Florida		20	368	42,000 00
Improving Flint River, Georgia and Alabama		20	365	
Improving Oconee River, Georgia		20	368	5,000 00
Improving Apalachicola River, Florida		20	365	
Improving Choctawhatchee River, Florida and Alabama		20	365	
Improving inside passage between Fernandina and Saint John's, Florida		20	365	
Improving Alabama River, Alabama		20	365	
Improving Warrior and Tombigbee Rivers, Alabama and Mississippi		20	365	7,000 00
Improving Big Sunflower River, Mississippi		20	370	
Improving Coldwater River, Mississippi		20	370	
Improving Pascagoula River, Mississippi		20	372	8,000 00
Improving Yazoo River, Mississippi		20	366	5,000 00
Improving Pearl River, Mississippi		20	372	
Improving Tallahatchie River, Mississippi		20	370	
Improving Bayou La Fourche, Louisiana		20	371	3,000 00
Improving mouth of Red River, Louisiana		20	366	115,000 00
Removing snags in Red River, Louisiana		20	366	
Removing raft in Red River, Louisiana		20	366	
Improving Aransas Pass and Bay, Texas		20	371	
Improving Neches River, Texas		20	365	7,500 88
Improving Passo Cavallo, Texas		20	365	38,500 00
Improving Cypress Bayou, Texas and Louisiana		20	366	
Protection of river bank at Fort Brown, Texas		20	370	
Improving ship channel in Galveston Bay, Texas		20	367	143,092 62
Improving Sabine River, Texas		20	365	88
Improving Sabine Pass, Texas		20	365	91 00
Improving Trinity River, Texas		20	365	9,500 87
Improving Arkansas River, Arkansas and Kansas		20	366	
Improving Fourche Le Fevre River, Arkansas		20	367	
Carried forward				5,163,530 40

PRIATIONS UNEXPENDED June 30, 1879, &c.—Continued.

Appropriations for the fiscal year ending June 30, 1880.	Repayments made during the fiscal year 1880.	Aggregate available for the fiscal year ending June 30, 1880.	Payments during the fiscal year ending June 30, 1880.	Amounts carried to the surplus fund June 30, 1880.	Balances of appropriations, June 30, 1880.
$31, 342, 220 31	$1, 515, 543 97	$37, 104, 643 43	$30, 866, 348 32	$1, 516, 916-45	$4, 811, 383 66
50, 000 00	....	50, 000 00	50, 000 00	....	....
100, 000 00	....	100, 000 00	90, 000 00	....	10, 000 00
3, 000 00	....	3, 000 00	3, 000 00	....	....
....	....	3, 000 00	500 00	....	2, 500 00
3, 000 00	....	3, 000 00	3, 000 00	....	....
....	....	5, 000 00	5, 000 00	....	....
4, 000 00	....	4, 000 00	4, 000 00	....	....
2, 500 00	....	2, 500 00	2, 500 00	....	....
1, 000 00	....	1, 000 00	....	....	1, 000 00
2, 000 00	....	6, 000 00	6, 000 00	....	....
75, 000 00	....	75, 000 00	65, 000 00	....	10, 000 00
20, 000 00	....	20, 000 00	20, 000 00	....	....
12, 000 00	....	12, 000 00	12, 000 00	....	....
2, 500 00	....	2, 500 00	2, 500 00	....	....
25, 000 00	....	25, 000 00	25, 000 00	....	....
10, 000 00	....	10, 000 00	5, 000 00	....	5, 000 00
5, 000 00	....	5, 000 00	5, 000 00	....	....
....	....	1, 000 00	1, 000 00	....	....
5, 000 00	....	5, 000 00	5, 000 00	....	....
....	....	4, 000 00	4, 000 00	....	....
150, 000 00	....	417, 000 00	365, 000 00	....	52, 000 00
1, 000 00	....	1, 000 00	1, 000 00	....	....
18, 000 00	....	20, 000 00	20, 000 00	....	....
24, 000 00	....	24, 000 00	24, 000 00	....	....
....	....	2, 250 00	2, 250 00	....	....
25, 000 00	....	25, 000 00	10, 000 00	....	15, 000 00
5, 000 00	....	11, 000 00	11, 000 00	....	....
45, 000 00	....	45, 000 00	30, 000 00	....	15, 000 00
100, 000 00	....	125, 000 00	110, 000 00	....	15, 000 00
2, 000 00	....	3, 800 00	3, 800 00	....	....
3, 000 00	....	3, 000 00	3, 000 00	....	....
3, 000 00	....	3, 000 00	3, 000 00	....	....
7, 000 00	....	7, 000 00	7, 000 00	....	....
20, 000 00	....	20, 000 00	....	....	20, 000 00
....	....	9, 000 00	....	....	9, 000 00
7, 000 00	....	9, 000 00	9, 000 00	....	....
15, 000 00	....	15, 000 00	2, 000 00	....	13, 000 00
....	....	3, 000 00	3, 000 00	....	....
3, 000 00	....	5, 000 00	5, 000 00	....	....
5, 000 00	....	5, 000 00	....	....	5, 000 00
45, 000 00	....	87, 000 00	87, 000 00	....	....
7, 000 00	....	7, 000 00	5, 000 00	....	2, 000 00
1, 500 00	....	6, 500 00	6, 500 00	....	....
5, 000 00	....	5, 000 00	5, 000 00	....	....
5, 000 00	....	5, 000 00	5, 000 00	....	....
7, 000 00	....	7, 000 00	7, 000 00	....	....
30, 000 00	....	30, 000 00	20, 000 00	....	10, 000 00
30, 000 00	....	37, 000 00	27, 000 00	....	10, 000 00
20, 000 00	....	20, 000 00	10, 000 00	....	10, 000 00
7, 000 00	....	7, 000 00	7, 000 00	....	....
14, 000 00	....	22, 000 00	....	....	22, 000 00
15, 000 00	....	20, 000 00	20, 000 00	....	....
6, 000 00	....	6, 000 00	1, 000 00	....	5, 000 00
6, 000 00	....	6, 500 00	6, 000 00	....	....
10, 000 00	....	13, 000 00	6, 000 00	....	7, 000 00
40, 000 00	....	155, 000 00	....	....	155, 000 00
22, 500 00	....	22, 500 00	22, 500 00	....	....
15, 000 00	....	15, 000 00	15, 000 00	....	....
35, 000 00	....	35, 000 00	20, 000 00	....	15, 000 00
5, 000 00	....	12, 500 00	12, 500 88	....	....
25, 000 00	....	63, 500 00	....	....	63, 500 00
6, 000 00	....	6, 000 00	3, 000 00	....	3, 000 00
7, 000 00	....	7, 000 00	7, 000 00	....	....
80, 000 00	....	223, 002 62	131, 002 62	....	92, 000 00
6, 000 00	....	6, 000 88	4, 000 00	....	2, 000 88
25, 000 00	....	25, 091 00	11, 509 00	....	13, 582 00
2, 000 00	....	12, 000 87	6, 000 87	....	6, 000 00
20, 000 00	....	20, 000 00	20, 000 00	....	....
10, 000 00	....	10, 000 00	10, 000 00	....	....
32, 502, 720 31	1, 515, 543 97	39, 181, 794 68	33, 264, 911 69	1, 516, 916 45	5, 399, 966 5

STATEMENT exhibiting the BALANCES of APPRO

Specific objects of appropriation.	Year.	Statutes.		Balances of appropriations, July 1, 1879.
		Vol.	Page or section.	
MILITARY ESTABLISHMENT—Continued.				
Brought forward				$5, 163, 530 40
Improving L'Aquille River, Arkansas		20	371	
Improving Ouachita River, Arkansas and Louisiana		20	366	
Improving White River, Arkansas		20	366	
Improving White and Saint Francis Rivers, Arkansas		20	371	
Improving Fall of the Ohio River and Louisville Canal				25, 000 00
Improving Cumberland River above Nashville, Tenn		20	367	7, 000 00
Improving Cumberland River below Nashville, Tenn		20	357	
Improving Tennessee River				140, 000 00
Improving Tennessee River above Chattanooga, Tenn		20	367	
Improving Hiawassee River, Tennessee		20	368	
Improving Tennessee River below Chattanooga, Tenn		20	367	
Improving Big Sandy River, Kentucky		20	368	
Improving Kentucky River, Kentucky		20	370	
Improving Ohio River, Ohio		20	366	88, 800 00
Improving Wabash River, Indiana		20	366	
Improving White River, Indiana		20	371	
Improving Illinois River, Illinois		20	367	15, 000 00
Improving Mississippi, Missouri, and Arkansas Rivers		20	366	
Improving Mississippi River between mouths of Ohio and Illinois Rivers		20	366	....
Improving Mississippi River from—				
Saint Paul to Des Moines Rapids		20	366	39, 000 00
Des Moines Rapids to mouth of Illinois River		20	367	
Improving Mississippi River at Quincy, Ill		20	372	
Removing bar in Mississippi River opposite Dubuque, Iowa		20	367	
Improving Rock Island Rapids, Mississippi River		20	367	
Improving Des Moines Rapids, Mississippi River		20	367	
Preservation of Falls of Saint Anthony and navigation Mississippi River, Minnesota				1, 000 00
Construction of lock and dam on Mississippi River at Meeker's Falls, Minnesota				25, 000 00
Improving Mississippi River from Des Moines to mouth of Ohio River				25, 000 00
Operating Des Moines Canal		20	367	
Improving Des Moines Rapids and operating canal				16, 033 75
Improving Missouri River at—				
Council Bluff, Iowa, and Omaha, Nebr				35, 000 00
Vermillion, Dak				2, 500 00
Eastport, Iowa, and Nebraska City				24, 000 00
Improving Missouri River near Glasgow, Mo				9, 000 00
Improving Missouri River at—				
Atchison, Kans				12, 000 00
Cedar City				5, 000 00
Improving Missouri River near Fort Leavenworth, Kans				7, 000 00
Improving Missouri River at Sioux City, Iowa				5, 000 00
Improving Missouri River near Kansas City, Mo				24, 000 00
Improving Missouri River above mouth of Yellowstone River		20	366	
Survey of Missouri River from its mouth to Fort Benton, Mont		20	366	
Ganging the water of Lower Mississippi and its tributaries		20	366	
Improving Upper Mississippi River		20	367	
Improving Osage River, Missouri and Kansas		20	372	
Improving Missouri River near Saint Joseph, Mo				4, 000 00
Improving Detroit River, Michigan		20	369	54, 000 00
Improving Au Sable River, Michigan				1, 000 00
Improving Saginaw River, Michigan		20	369	5, 000 00
Improving Saint Clair Flats, Michigan		20	369	
Improving Saint Mary's River and Saint Mary's Canal, Michigan		20	369	65, 000 00
Improving Fox and Wisconsin Rivers, Wisconsin		20	368	75, 000 00
Improving Chippewa River, Wisconsin		20	372	
Surveys for reservoir at sources of the Mississippi, Saint Croix, Chippewa, and Wisconsin Rivers		20	370	
Improving Red River of the North, Minnesota and Dakota		20	367	15, 000 00
Improving Red River of the North, Minnesota				
Improving Saint Anthony's Falls, Minnesota		20	372	
Improving Saint Croix River below Taylor's Falls, Minnesota		20	367	
Improving Upper Red River		20	371	
Improving Yellowstone River		20	370	
Improving Lower Clearwater River, Idaho		20	370	
Improving Mouth of Columbia River, Oregon		20	370	
Improving Upper Columbia River, Oregon		20	370	
Carried forward				5, 881, 864 15

PRIATIONS UNEXPENDED June 30, 1879, &c.—Continued.

Appropriations for the fiscal year ending June 30, 1880.	Repayments made during the fiscal year 1880.	Aggregate available for the fiscal year ending June 30, 1880.	Payments during the fiscal year ending June 30, 1880.	Amounts carried to the surplus fund June 30, 1880.	Balances of appropriations, June 30, 1880.
$32,502,720 31	$1,515,543 97	$39,181,794 68	$32,264,911 69	$1,516,916 45	$5,399,966 54
5,000 00	....	5,000 00	2,500 00	....	2,500 00
10,000 00	....	10,000 00	5,000 00	....	5,000 00
10,000 00	....	10,000 00	10,000 00	....	....
12,000 00	....	12,000 00	12,000 00	....	....
....	....	25,000 00	20,000 00	....	5,000 00
39,000 00	....	40,000 00	46,000 00	....	....
40,000 00	....	40,000 00	40,000 00	....	....
....	....	140,000 00	140,000 00	....	....
11,500 00	....	11,500 00	11,500 00	....	....
3,000 00	....	3,000 00	3,000 00	....	....
210,000 00	....	210,000 00	210,000 00	....	....
12,000 00	....	12,000 00	12,000 00	....	....
100,000 00	....	190,000 00	30,000 00	....	64,000 00
250,000 00	....	338,800 00	243,800 00	....	95,000 00
20,000 00	....	20,000 00	20,000 00	....	....
25,000 00	....	25,000 00	20,000 00	....	5,000 00
40,000 00	....	55,000 00	30,000 00	....	25,000 00
190,000 00	....	190,000 00	190,000 00	....	....
200,000 00	....	200,000 00	166,000 00	....	34,000 00
100,000 00	....	139,000 00	104,000 00	....	35,000 00
40,000 00	....	40,000 00	40,000 00	....	....
20,000 00	....	20,000 00	20,000 00	....	....
4,000 00	....	4,000 00	4,000 00	....	....
6,000 00	....	6,000 00	6,000 00	....	....
25,000 00	....	25,000 00	15,000 00	....	10,000 00
....	....	1,000 00	....	....	1,000 00
....	....	25,000 00	....	....	25,000 00
....	....	25,000 00	25,000 00	....	....
40,000 00	....	40,000 00	40,000 00	....	....
....	....	10,033 75	10,033 75	....	....
....	....	35,000 00	35,000 00	....	....
....	....	2,500 00	2,500 00	....	....
....	....	24,000 00	24,000 00	....	....
....	....	9,000 00	9,000 00	....	....
....	....	12,000 00	12,000 00	....	....
....	....	5,000 00	5,000 00	....	....
....	....	7,000 00	7,000 00	....	....
....	....	5,000 00	5,000 00	....	....
....	....	24,000 00	24,000 00	....	....
45,000 00	....	45,000 00	33,000 00	....	12,000 00
30,000 00	....	30,000 00	30,000 00	....	....
5,000 00	....	5,000 00	5,000 00	....	....
20,000 00	....	20,000 00	17,000 00	....	3,000 00
20,000 00	....	20,000 00	20,000 00	....	....
....	....	4,000 00	4,000 00	....	....
50,000 00	....	104,000 00	40,000 00	....	64,000 00
....	....	1,000 00	....	....	1,000 00
8,000 00	....	13,000 00	13,000 00	....	....
3,000 00	....	3,000 00	3,000 00	....	....
300,000 00	....	365,000 00	200,000 00	....	165,000 00
150,000 00	....	225,000 00	225,000 00	....	....
8,000 00	....	8,000 00	8,000 00	....	....
25,000 00	....	25,000 00	25,000 00	....	....
25,000 00	....	25,000 00	17,000 00	....	8,000 00
....	....	15,000 00	8,000 00	....	7,000 00
10,000 00	....	10,000 00	10,000 00	....	....
8,000 00	....	8,000 00	8,000 00	....	....
10,000 00	....	10,000 00	8,000 00	....	2,000 00
25,000 00	....	25,000 00	25,000 00	....	....
5,000 00	....	5,000 00	5,000 00	....	....
5,000 00	....	5,000 00	5,000 00	....	....
20,000 00	....	20,000 00	15,000 00	....	5,000 00
34,087,220 31	1,515,543 97	42,084,628 43	34,594,245 44	1,516,916 45	5,973,466 54

30 F

STATEMENT exhibiting the BALANCES of APPRO

Specific objects of appropriations.	Year.	Statutes. Vol.	Statutes. Page or section.	Balances of appropriations, July 1, 1879.
MILITARY ESTABLISHMENT—Continued.				
Brought forward	......	......	......	$5, 881, 864 15
Constructing canal around Cascades of Columbia, Oregon...	......	20	379	159, 008 00
Improving Lower Willamette and Columbia Rivers, Oregon.	......	. 20	370	20, 000 00
Improving Upper Willamette River, Oregon	......	20	370	....
Improving Umpqua River, Oregon	......	......	......	4, 685 89
Improving Sacramento River, California	......	20	370	....
Breakwater and harbor of refuge between Straits of Fuca and San Francisco, Cal	......	20	373	....
Repairs of harbor on Northern Lakes	......	......	......	1, 314 35
Examinations and surveys of South Pass, Mississippi River.	......	20	365	2, 241 97
Examinations and surveys on Pacific Coast	......	......	......	8, 014 21
Examinations, surveys, and contingencies of rivers and harbors	......	20	375	24, 083 06
Payment to Commissioners to appraise damages to lands in Fond du Lac County, Wisconsin	......	21	248	....
Miller's patent cartridge extractor	1880	21	252	....
Geographical survey of the territory of the United States west of one hundredth meridian	1879 1880	......	......	14, 000 00
Do	......	21	244	....
Removing obstructions from the harbor at Delaware Breakwater	......	21	61	....
Constructing jetties and other works at South Pass, Mississippi River	......	21	4	....
Mississippi River Commission	......	21	37	....
Contingencies of the Army	1877*	......	......	....
Contingencies of the Army (transfer account)	1877*	......	......	....
Contingencies of the Army	1878	......	......	14, 715 58
Do	1879	......	......	....
Do	1880	21	33	....
Expenses of recruiting	1877*	21	256	....
Expenses of recruiting (transfer account)	1877*	......	......	....
Expenses of recruiting	1878	......	......	24, 867 60
Do	1879	......	......	1, 526 79
Do	1880	21	30	....
Expenses of Commanding General's office	1878	......	......	141 43
Do	1879	......	......	....
Do	1880	21	30	....
Contingencies of the Adjutant-General's Department	1878	......	......	68 25
Do	1879	......	......	....
Do	1880	21	31	....
Signal Service	1877*	......	......	....
Do	1878	......	......	30 23
Do	1879	......	......	....
Do	1880	21	31	....
Observation and report of storms	1877*	......	......	....
Do	1878	......	......	15 68
Do	1879	......	......	....
Do	1880	20	386	....
Military road from Alamosa, Colo., to Pagosa Springs	......	20	390	....
Military road from Ojo Caliente, N. Mex., to Pagosa Springs.	......	20	300	....
Military road from Scottsburg to Camp Stewart, Oreg	......	20	390	....
Military road from Ojo Caliente to Fort Wingate, N. Mex.	......	......	......	....
Military post at El Paso, Tex	......	21	281	....
Expenses of military convicts	1878	......	......	2, 581 13
Do	1879	......	......	4, 888 79
Do	1880	20	388	....
Fifty per centum of arrears of Army transportation due certain land grant railroads	......	20	390	....
Telegraphic cable from the main land in Rhode Island to Block Island	......	21	60	....
Allowance for reduction of wages under the eight-hour law prior to July 1, 1877	......	21	256	....
Construction of a bridge across the Mississippi River at Fort Snelling	......	......	......	65, 000 00
Publication of official records of the war of the rebellion ...	1878	......	......	1 02
Do	1880	20	388	....
Providing for the comfort of sick and discharged soldiers ...	1877*	21	256	....
Support of National Home for Disabled Volunteer Soldiers.	1878	......	......	12, 801 60
Do	1880	20	390	....
Support of Soldiers' Home	......	R. S.	3689	....
Construction, maintenance, and repair of military telegraph lines	1877*	......	......	....
Do	1878	......	......	1 98
Do	1880	20	386	....
Carried forward	......	......	......	6, 236, 843 71

*And prior years.

PRIATIONS UNEXPENDED June 30, 1879, &c.—Continued.

Appropriations for the fiscal year ending June 30, 1880.	Repayments made during the fiscal year 1880.	Aggregate available for the fiscal year ending June 30, 1880.	Payments during the fiscal year ending June 30, 1880.	Amounts carried to the surplus fund June 30, 1880.	Balance of appropriations, June 30, 1880.
$34, 087, 220 31	$1, 515, 543 97	$42, 084, 628 43	$34, 594, 245 44	$1, 516, 916 45	$5, 973, 466 54
100, 000 00	....	259, 000 00	196, 000 00	....	63, 000 00
43, 000 00	....	65, 000 00	65, 000 00	....	....
12, 000 00	....	12, 000 00	12, 000 00	....	....
....	....	4, 685 89	....	....	4, 685 89
20, 000 00	....	20, 000 00	12, 000 00	....	8, 000 00
150, 000 00	....	150, 000 00	10, 257 11	....	139, 742 89
....	....	1, 314 35	1, 314 35	....	....
24, 000 00	325 86	26, 567 83	25, 257 07	....	1, 310 76
....	....	3, 014 21	17 50	....	2, 096 71
150, 000 00	....	174, 083 06	128, 124 33	....	45, 958 73
5, 010 00	....	5, 010 00	....	....	5, 010 00
18, 792 52	....	18, 792 52	....	....	18, 792 52
....	....	14, 000 00	14, 000 00	....	....
30, 000 00	....	30, 000 00	....	....	30, 000 00
25, 000 00	....	25, 000 00	9, 500 00	....	15, 500 00
1, 100, 000 00	....	1, 100, 000 00	1, 100, 000 00	....	....
175, 000 00	....	175, 000 00	162, 000 00	....	13, 000 00
....	2, 065 13	2, 065 13	....	2, 065 13	....
....	149 97	149 97	149 97	....	....
....	1 00	14, 716 58	707 50	14, 009 08	....
....	48 94	48 94	....	....	48 94
40, 000 00	....	40, 000 00	40, 000 00	....	....
118 74	584 20	702 94	....	584 20	118 74
....	60 40	60 40	60 40	....	....
....	38 40	34, 906 90	....	34, 906 00	....
....	1, 992 17	3, 118 96	....	....	3, 118 96
75, 000 00	18 45	75, 018 45	68, 688 55	....	6, 329 90
....	....	141 43	....	141 43	....
....	1 69	1 69	....	....	1 69
2, 500 00	1, 122 53	3, 622 53	3, 622 53	....	....
....	....	68 25	....	68 25	....
....	98 75	98 75	....	....	98 75
3, 000 00	....	3, 000 00	3, 000 00	....	....
....	3 37	3 37	....	3 37	....
....	5 48	35 71	....	35 71	....
....	9 83	9 83	1 06	....	8 77
10, 500 00	15 00	10, 515 00	10, 500 00	....	15 00
....	78	78	....	78	....
....	15 68	15 68	....	15 68	....
....	70 83	70 83	26 33	....	44 50
375, 000 00	12 73	375, 012 73	375, 012 73	....	....
10, 000 00	....	10, 000 00	10, 000 00	....	....
5, 000 00	....	5, 000 00	5, 000 00	....	....
10, 000 00	....	10, 000 00	10, 000 00	....	....
....	71	71	....	....	71
40, 000 00	....	40, 000 00	40, 000 00	....	....
....	....	2, 581 13	....	2, 581 13	....
....	....	4, 868 79	2, 044 52	....	2, 844 27
16, 000 00	....	16, 000 00	9, 809 58	....	6, 190 47
300, 000 00	....	300, 000 00	285, 554 09	....	14, 445 91
15, 000 00	....	15, 000 00	15, 000 00	....	....
119 41	3, 615 84	3, 735 25	....	3, 615 84	119 41
....	....	65, 000 00	65, 000 00	....	....
....	....	1 02	....	1 02	....
40, 490 00	....	40, 490 00	40, 490 00	....	....
....	....	5 95	....	....	5 95
....	....	12, 801 60	....	12, 801 60	....
880, 000 00	....	880, 000 00	880, 000 00	....	....
117, 929 33	23 28	117, 943 61	117, 943 61	....	....
....	688 92	688 92	....	688 92	....
....	....	1 98	....	1 98	....
50, 000 00	....	50, 000 00	50, 000 00	....	....
$8, 532, 677 26	1 526, 096 23	$6, 295, 610 30	$8, 363, 326 62	1, 578, 436 37	6, 354, 856 01

STATEMENT *exhibiting the* BALANCES *of* APPRO

Specific objects of appropriations.	Year.	Statutes.		Balances of appropriations, July 1, 1879.
		Vol.	Page or section.	
MILITARY ESTABLISHMENT—Continued.				
Brought forward				$6,236,843 71
Extension of military telegraph lines by way of new post on Milk River	1880	20	336	
Extension of military telegraph lines from Fort Elliott, Tex	1880	20	336	
Construction and operation of a line of telegraph on the frontier settlements of Texas				
Committee to investigate and report plan for reclamation of alluvial basin of Mississippi River				5,000 00
Capture of Jefferson Davis				2,968 38
Removing remains of William E. English, late first lieutenant Seventh United States Infantry		20	387	
Support of military prison at Fort Leavenworth, Kans	1879			11,896 81
Support of military prison at Fort Leavenworth, Kans	1880	20	389	
Artillery school at Fortress Monroe, Va	1880	20	389	
Erection of barracks at Fortress Monroe, Va.	1880	20	389	
Repair of road between Fortress Monroe and Mill Creek, Va.		20	390	
Military post near Pagosa Springs, Colo		20	380	
Military post near the Black Hills				
Buildings for military headquarters at Fort Snelling, Minn.		20	390	
Bounty act, July 28, 1866		R. S.	3696	
Draft and substitute fund	1871*	21	256	
Collecting, drilling, and organizing volunteers	1871*	21	256	
Payment for keeping United States military prisoners		20	290	
Extra pay to officers and men who served in the Mexican War		20	316	
Commutation of rations to prisoners of war in rebel States prior to July 1, 1875		21	257	7 88
Refunding to States expenses incurred in raising volunteers		21	257	
Reimbursing the State of Kentucky for expenses in suppessing the rebellion		21	257	
Horses and other property lost in the military service prior to July 1, 1876				28,370 72
Horses and other property lost in the military service prior to July 1, 1876				
Horses and other property lost in the military service	1877*	21	257	
Horses and other property lost in the military service		R. S.	3483	
Miscellaneous claims audited by Third Auditor				3,274 29
Claims for quartermasters' stores and commissary supplies				3,411 89
Claims of loyal citizens for supplies furnished during the rebellion				10,160 45
Survey of Northern and Northwestern lakes	1880	20	388	
Relief of John A. Shaw		20	108	
Relief of Leonard L. Lancaster		20	110	
Relief of William Bowlin, Second Arkansas Cavalry				
Relief of H. M. Billingsley		20	171	
Relief of Thomas R. Alexander		20	122	
Relief of Martin Clark		20	124	
Relief of legal representatives of John W. Gall		20	171	
Relief of Board of Trustees of Antietam National Cemetery.		19	289	
Relief of Thomas W. Segar		20	115	
Relief of personal representative of M. G. Harman, of Virginia		20	131	
Relief of families of the men who perished on United States dredge-boat McAllister		20	91	
Relief of James M. Barber of Indiana		20	123	
Relief of M. Granery, N. Wax, and M. Lange		21	10	
Relief of George V. Webb		21	16	
Relief of John N. Read		21	24	
Removal of the remains of the late Maj.-Gen. George Sykes, U. S. A		21	10	
Transportation of the Army and its supplies, (Pacific Railroads)	1873	20	420	
Do	1874	20	420	
Do	1875	20	420	
Do	1876	20	420	
Do	1877	20	420	
Do	1878	20	420	
Do	1879	20	420	
Do	1880	20	420	
Total				6,301,925 93
NAVAL ESTABLISHMENT.				
Pay of the Navy				209,819 70
Pay of the Navy prior to July 1, 1877		20	284	
Carried forward				209,819 70

*And prior years.

PRIATIONS UNEXPENDED June 30, 1879, &c.—Continued.

Appropriations for the fiscal year ending June 30, 1880.	Repayments made during the fiscal year 1880.	Aggregate available for the fiscal year ending June 30, 1880.	Payments during the fiscal year ending June 30, 1880.	Amounts carried to the surplus fund June 30, 1880.	Balances of appropriations, June 30, 1880.
$38, 532, 677 26	$1, 826, 098 23	$40, 295, 619 20	$38, 362, 326 62	$1, 578, 436 57	$6, 354, 856 01
20, 000 00	....	20, 000 00	20, 000 00	....	....
20, 000 00	....	20, 000 00	20, 000 00	....	....
....	50	50	....	50	....
....	....	5, 000 00	....	5, 000 00	....
....	....	2, 968 38	....	....	2, 968 38
300 00	....	300 00	300 00	....	....
....	759 97	12, 651 78	....	....	12, 651 78
67, 440 00	....	67, 440 00	67, 440 00	....	....
4, 750 00	100 00	4, 850 00	4, 850 00	....	....
34, 000 00	....	34, 000 00	· 34, 000 00	....	....
6, 500 00	....	6, 500 00	6, 500 00	....	....
40, 000 00	....	40, 000 00	40, 000 00	....	....
....	5 21	5 21	....	....	5 21
100, 000 00	....	100, 000 00	25, 000 00	....	75, 000 00
123, 469 57	11, 630 43	135, 100 00	135, 100 00	....	....
816 86	....	816 86	....	....	816 86
79 29	1, 379 58	1, 458 87	....	1. 379 58	79 29
5, 400 69	....	5, 400 69	5, 400 69	....	....
4, 725 00	....	4, 725 00	4, 725 00	....	....
8, 221 38	....	8, 229 26	7 88	....	8, 221 38
109, 725 39	....	· 109, 725 39	8, 513 06	....	101, 212 33
15, 000 00	....	15, 000 00	....	....	15, 000 00
....	....	28, 370 72	28, 370 72	....	....
....	110 00	110 00	....	....	110 00
43, 878 60	....	43, 878 60	42, 762 69	....	1, 115 91
46, 718 81	350 00	47, 068 81	47, 068 81	....	....
....	....	3, 274 29	989 54	....	2, 284 75
....	167 88	3, 579 57	2, 231 92	....	1, 347 65
....	....	10, 160 45	645 40	....	9, 515 05
85, 000 00	....	85, 000 00	85, 000 00	....	....
309 12	....	309 12	309 12	....	....
507 42	....	507 42	507 42	....	....
110 73	....	110 73	110 73	....	....
865 74	....	˚ 865 74	865 74	....	....
647 33	....	· 454 33	647 33	....	....
454 33	....	454 33	454 33	....	....
1, 077 07	....	1, 077 07	1, 077 07	....	....
12, 806 04	417 37	13, 223 41	13, 223 41	....	....
457 41	....	457 41	457 41	....	....
˚ 354 00	....	354 00	354 00	....	....
1, 080 00	....	1, 080 00	1, 080 00	....	....
886 09	....	886 09	886 09	....	....
1, 500 00	....	1, 500 00	1, 500 00	....	....
136 50	....	136 50	136 50	....	....
4, 124 50	....	4, 124 50	4, 124 50	....	....
1, 000 00	....	1, 000 00	1, 000 00	....	....
1, 901 07	....	1, 901 07	1, 901 07	'	....
13, 523 22	....	13, 523 22	13, 523 22	....	....
41, 849 03	....	41, 849 03	41, 849 03	....	....
37, 684 45	....	37, 684 45	37, 684 45	....	....
26, 467 51	....	26, 467 51	26, 467 51	....	....
123, 560 66	....	123, 560 66	123, 560 66	....	....
333, 262 40	4 72	333, 267 12	333, 267 12	....	....
112, 470 72	....	112, 470 72	112, 470 72	....	....
39, 985, 730 09	1, 541, 016 89	47, 828, 661 91	39, 658, 690 66	1, 584, 816 65	6, 585, 184 60
6, 768, 275 00	790, 209 27	7, 768, 303 97	6, 370, 903 19	....	1, 397, 400 78
1, 077 25	....	1, 977 25	1, 977 25	....	1, 977 25
6, 770, 252 25	790, 209 27	7, 770, 281 22	6, 370, 903 19	....	1, 396, 378 03

STATEMENT exhibiting the BALANCES of APPRO

Specific objects of appropriations.	Year.	Statutes.		Balance of appropriations, July 1, 1879.
		Vol.	Page or section.	
NAVAL ESTABLISHMENT—Continued.				
Brought forward				$209, 819 70
Pay of the Navy (arrearages)				777 06
Pay of the Navy (deficiency, 1877)	1877			1, 056 57
Pay of the Navy (difference of pay)				
Pay, miscellaneous	1880	20	49	
Contingent, Navy	1877*			
	1878			739 01
Do	1879			3, 022 62
Do	1880	20	285	
Pay of Marine Corps prior to July 1, 1877		21	245	
Do	{	20	290–291	} 5, 111 95
		21	245	
Pay of Marine Corps (deficiency)	1877			511 29
Provisions, Marine Corps	1878			9, 863 71
Do	1879			15, 599 51
Do	1880	20	291	
Clothing, Marine Corps	1878			5, 664 14
Do	1879			311 35
Do	1880	20	291	
Fuel, Marine Corps	1878			7, 336 19
Do	1879			4, 976 34
Do	1880	20	291	
Military stores, Marine Corps	1878			6 44
Do	1880	20	291	
Transportation and recruiting, Marine Corps	1879			
Do	1890	20	291	
Repairs of barracks, Marine Corps	1879			
Do	1880	20	292	
Forage for horses, Marine Corps	1878			1, 000 00
Do	1879			3, 500 00
Do	1880	20	292	
Quarters for officers, Marine Corps	1878			1, 313 79
Do	1879			10, 163 05
Contingent, Marine Corps	1878			60 15
Do	1879	21	245	207 26
Do	1879*	21	258	
Do	1880	20	292	
Pay of Naval Academy	1880	20	289	
Do	1878			2, 024 99
Pay of professors and others, Naval Academy	1879			
Pay of watchmen and others, Naval Academy	1880	20	289–290	
Pay of mechanics and others, Naval Academy	1880	20	290	
Pay of steam employee, Naval Academy	1879			
Do	1880	20	290	
Repairs, Naval Academy	1879			
Do	1880	20	290	
Buildings and grounds, Naval Academy	1878			42
Heating and lighting, Naval Academy	1878			2, 662 79
Do	1880	20	290	
Library, Naval Academy	1879			
Do	1880	20	290	
Stationery, Naval Academy	1880	20	290	
Chemistry, Naval Academy	1880	20	290	
Miscellaneous, Naval Academy	1879			32 16
Do	1880	20	290	
Stores, Naval Academy	1879			
Do	1880	20	290	
Materials, Naval Academy	1880	20	290	
Improving Hanover square, Naval Academy	1878			603 98
Board of Visitors, Naval Academy	1879			
Do	1880	20	290	
Contingent, Naval Academy	1878			116 85
Navigation	1878			11 73
Navigation and navigation supplies	1880	20	285–6	
Pilotage, Bureau of Navigation	1879			21, 512 34
Compasses, Bureau of Navigation	1879			908 29
Nautical instruments, Bureau of Navigation	1879			3, 168 66
Libraries, Bureau of Navigation	1879			906 09
Signals, Bureau of Navigation	1879			1, 244 27
Compass fittings, Bureau of Navigation	1879			1, 979 55
Logs, Bureau of Navigation	1879			1, 516 76
Lights, Bureau of Navigation	1879			40 70
Flags, Bureau of Navigation	1879			1, 070 90
Oils, Bureau of Navigation	1879			297 83
Carried forward				319, 249 46

* And prior years.

PRIATIONS UNEXPENDED June 30, 1879, *&c.*—Continued.

Appropriations for the fiscal year ending June 30, 1880.	Repayments made during the fiscal year 1880.	Aggregate available for the fiscal year ending June 30, 1880.	Payments during the fiscal year ending June 30, 1880.	Amounts carried to the surplus fund June 30, 1880.	Balance of appropriations, June 30, 1880.
$6,776,252 25	$790,209 27	$7,770,281 22	$6,376,903 19	....	$1,309,378 03
....	1,641 56	2,418 68	2,387 17	31 45	....
....	6,094 74	7,091 31	7,091 31	....	....
....	3,565 68	3,565 68	....	3,565 68	....
475 000 00	2,446 44	477,446 44	258,908 85	....	218,537 59
....	36 00	36 00	....	36 00	....
....	1,109 20	1,848 31	416 11	1,432 10	....
....	517 66	3,540 23	3,538 96	....	11 36
80,000 00	7,260 74	87,260 74	86,493 94	....	766 80
109 98	....	109 98	....	....	109 98
650,397 00	25,413 77	680,922 72	584,575 83	....	96,346 89
....	....	511 29	511 29	....	....
....	....	9,883 71	1,348 50	8,535 21	....
....	687 11	16,263 62	679 35	....	15,584 27
75,007 50	....	75,007 50	47,538 11	....	27,469 39
....	....	5,664 14	....	5,664 14	....
60,000 00	1,585 67	1,847 02	1,236 39	....	610 63
....	344 53	60,344 53	60,082 96	....	261 07
....	....	7,336 19	....	7,336 19	....
20,009 00	2,076 08	7,032 42	300 0	....	6,752 42
....	768 93	20,768 93	12,500	....	8,268 93
....	....	6 44	....	6 44	....
9,686 50	....	9,686 50	9,686	....	....
....	509 01	509 01	....	....	509 01
7,000 00	....	7,000 00	7,000 00	....	....
....	37 18	37 18	....	....	37 18
13,000 00	....	13,000 00	13,000 00	....	....
....	....	1,000 00	....	1,000 00	....
....	153 19	3,653 19	....	....	3,653 19
500 00	....	500 00	450 00	....	50 00
....	....	1,319 79	....	1,319 79	....
....	....	10,163 05	4,524 41	....	5,638 64
....	....	60 15	....	60 15	....
207 31	1,336 39	1,650 06	1,407 94	....	243 02
862 75	....	862 75	....	....	862 75
20,000 00	....	20,000 00	20,000 00	....	....
53,126 00	....	53,126 00	52,000 00	....	1,126 00
....	....	2,024 99	....	2,024 99	....
....	879 33	879 33	....	....	879 33
24,455 00	....	24,455 00	24,455 00	....	....
16,835 95	....	16,835 95	16,835 95	....	....
....	1 40	1 40	....	....	1 40
8,577 50	....	8,577 50	8,577 50	....	....
....	8 24	8 24	....	....	8 24
21,000 00	....	21,000 00	21,000 00	....	....
....	....	42	....	42	....
....	....	2,662 79	....	2,662 79	....
17,000 00	....	17,000 00	16,000 00	....	1,000 00
....	04	04	....	....	04
2,000 00	....	2,000 00	2,000 00	....	....
2,000 00	....	2,000 00	2,000 00	....	....
2,500 00	....	2,500 00	2,500 00	....	....
....	12 88	45 06	....	....	45 06
34,000 00	....	34,000 00	34,000 00	....	....
....	25	25	....	....	25
800 00	....	800 00	800 00	....	....
1,000 00	....	1,000 00	1,000 00	....	....
....	....	603 98	....	603 98	....
....	6 72	6 72	....	....	6 72
2,600 00	....	2,600 00	2,600 00	....	....
....	....	116 85	....	116 85	....
....	....	* 11 73	....	11 73	....
104,500 00	603 88	105,103 88	99,632 03	....	5,471 85
....	44 72	21,557 06	19,357 44	....	2,199 62
....	54 03	1,052 32	864 12	....	188 20
....	6 57	3,173 23	2,718 90	....	454 33
....	6 31	912 40	220 00	....	692 40
....	95 76	1,340 03	833 53	....	506 50
....	1 50	1,981 05	1,974 50	....	6 55
....	50 51	1,567 27	1,252 13	....	315 14
....	40 95	81 65	42 52	....	39 13
....	6 38	1,077 18	582 04	....	495 14
....	545 84	847 67	817 67	....	30 00
8,473,017 74	847,932 30	9,940,199 50	7,807,233 94	34,407 91	1,796,557 65

STATEMENT *exhibiting the* BALANCES *of* APPRO

Specific objects of appropriations.	Year.	Vol.	Page or section.	Balances of appropriations, July 1, 1879.
NAVAL ESTABLISHMENT—Continued.				
Brought forward				$310,349 46
Stationery, Bureau of Navigation	1879			83 56
Musical instruments, Bureau of Navigation	1879			241 72
Steering signals, Bureau of Navigation	1879			1,200 81
Civil establishment, Navigation	1880	20	266	....
Contingent navigation	1877*	21	258	....
Do	1878			46 86
Do	1879			43 45
Do	1880	20	266	....
Hydrographic work	1878			11,324 04
Do	1879			7,067 96
Do	1880	20	266	....
Contingent, Hydrographic Office	1879			78 38
Rent and repairs, Hydrographic Office	1879			500 00
Naval Observatory	1877*	21	258	....
Do	1878			1 19
Do	1880	20 / 21	266 / 84	} ....
Contingent, Naval Observatory	1879			29
Astronomers, Naval Observatory	1879			280 00
Lathe, Naval Observatory	1879			166 83
Library, Naval Observatory	1879			370 88
Theory of the moon's motion	1879			190 00
New planets	1879			440 00
Velocity of light	1880	20	399	
Observations, Naval Observatory	1879			.. ..
Observations, transit of Mercury	1878			80 93
Observations of solar eclipse				23 86
Observations California eclipse				600 00
Illustrations for solar eclipse				1,500 00
Illustrations transit of Venus, Naval Observatory	1879			956 00
Solar and stellar photography				640 00
Wood-cuts of nebula in Orion				113 00
Nautical Almanac	1878			31 04
Do	1879			3,078 81
Do	1880	20	266	....
Contingent, Nautical Almanac	1879			356 46
Ordnance and ordnance stores, Bureau of Ordnance	1877*	21	258	....
Do	1878			4,569 90
Do	1880	20	266	....
Materials, Bureau of Ordnance	1879			27,905 91
Labor, Bureau of Ordnance	1879			6 12
Repairs, Bureau of Ordnance	1879			3,213 79
Contingent, Ordnance	1878			2 54
Do	1879			68 17
Do	1880	20	287	....
Civil establishment, Bureau of Ordnance	1880	20	287	....
Torpedo Corps	1880	20	287	....
Labor, Torpedo Corps	1879			....
Materials, Torpedo Corps	1879			1,957 15
Freight, Torpedo Corps	1879			66 90
Repairs, Torpedo Corps	1879			790 00
Experiments, Torpedo Corps	1879			3,556 00
Ordnance material, proceeds of sales		20	242	15,142 22
Sales of small-arms				46,401 60
Equipment of vessels	1878			142,716 12
Do	1879			177,487 69
Do	1880	20	287	....
Contingent, Equipment and Recruiting	1877*	21	258	....
Do	1878			5,418 00
Do	1879			5,515 43
Do	1880	20	287	....
Civil establishment, Equipment and Recruiting	1880	20	287	....
Maintenance, Yards and Docks	1877*	21	258	....
Do	1878			3,162 34
Do	1879			23,002 61
Do	1880	20	287	....
Contingent, Yards and Docks	1878			36 33
Do	1879			4,420 21
Civil establishment, navy-yards	1880	20	287	....
Do	1878			7,331 97
Do	1880	20	287	....
Navy-yard, Mare Island	1879			....
Carried forward				330,429 83

*And prior years.

PRIATIONS UNEXPENDED June 30, 1879, *&c.*—Continued.

Appropriations for the fiscal year ending June 30, 1880.	Repayments made during the fiscal year 1880.	Aggregate available for the fiscal year ending June 30, 1880.	Payments during the fiscal year ending June 30, 1880.	Amounts carried to the surplus fund June 30, 1880.	Balances of appropriations, June 30, 1880.
$8,473,017 74	$847,932 30	$9,640,199 50	$7,807,233 94	$34,407 91	$1,796,557 65
	4 28	87 34	85 32		2 02
	50	242 22	233 90		8 32
	3 09	1,503 89	385 66		818 23
10,417 25	1 00	10,418 25	10,418 25		
22 82		22 82			22 82
		46 85		46 85	
	150 85	203 30	147 38		55 92
2,000 00	62 22	2,062 22	2,042 44		19 78
		11,324 04	11,324 00	04	
	1,236 32	6,305 28	5,565 22		2,741 06
46,000 00	2,856 99	48,856 99	40,512 86		8,344 13
	13 68	92 06	79 22		12 84
		500 00	500 00		
416 88		416 88			416 68
		1 19		1 19	
22,336 25	2 70	22,338 95	21,268 00		1,070 95
	4 10	4 30	20		4 10
	44 66	324 66			324 66
		168 83	168 00		83
	5 00	375 88	355 15		20 73
		190 00		190 00	
		440 00	435 00		5 00
5,000 00		5,000 00	413 00		4,587 00
	21 35	21 35			21 35
	60	81 83	11 00	70 83	
		23 66	23 00	86	
	19 64	619 64	492 00		127 64
	1 43	1,500 00	1,500 00		1,500 00
	88	957 43	203 00		784 43
		640 88	640 88		
		113 00	113 00		
		31 04		31 04	
	43 39	3,122 20	3,073 00		49 20
22,500 00	1,016 58	23,516 53	20,315 00		3,201 53
	25 71	384 17	228 97		155 20
37 53		37 58			37 53
	469 84	5,139 74	5,139 74		
225,000 00	2,667 82	227,667 82	177,990 12		49,677 70
	2,384 56	30,290 47	30,290 16		31
	37 15	43 27	28 34		14 93
	475 41	3,689 20	3,684 08		5 12
	1 27	3 81	3 00	81	
	223 04	291 21	284 56		6 65
3,000 00	38 12	3,038 12	2,230 97		807 15
11,886 25		11,886 25	11,885 24		1 61
45,000 00	9 12	45,009 12	40,567 00		4,442 12
	1 56	1 56			1 56
	60 85	2,018 00	1,990 00		28 00
	3 20	70 10	66 00		4 10
	4 77	794 77	792 00		2 77
	32	3,556 32	2,555 53		1,000 79
15,280 25	3 77	30,426 24	26,946 00		4,080 24
		46,401 00	33,837 10		12,563 90
	234 48	142,950 58	142,729 42	221 16	
	4,036 02	161,523 71	180,436 35		1,097 36
800,000 00	6,448 47	806,448 47	685,338 57		121,109 90
204 90		204 90			204 90
	50	5,418 50	28 00	5,390 56	
	1,981 06	7,496 49	7,391 54		104 95
60,000 00	128 61	50,128 61	47,147 72		2,980 89
18,251 75		18,251 75	18,251 75		
37 37	05	37 43		05	37 37
	29 55	2,191 89	48 05	2,143 84	
	207 26	23,209 87	22,440 00		769 87
440,000 00	49 03	440,049 03	416,421 72		23,627 31
		20 33		26 33	
	77				77
		4,420 98	4,420 21		77
30,000 00	195 24	20,195 24	14,145 70		6,019 54
	24 75				24 75
		7,231 97		7,231 97	
37,006 25		37,006 25	37,113 75		792 50
	7 93	7 93			7 93
10,248,315 24	873,173 01	11,941,918 08	9,839,880 51	49,763 38	2,052,274 19

STATEMENT *exhibiting the BALANCES of APPRO*

Specific objects of appropriations.	Year.	Vol.	Page or section.	Balances of appropriations, July 1, 1879.
NAVAL ESTABLISHMENT—Continued.				
Brought forward				$820,429 53
Navy-yard, Mare Island	1880	20	390	
Navy-yard, Boston, repairs of rope-walk	1880	20	391	
Repairs and preservation at navy-yards	1871*			
Do	1878			1,780 42
Do	1879			12,770 58
Do	1880	20	390	
Naval Asylum at Philadelphia	1878			772 37
Do	1879			22,573 47
Do	1880			
Surgeons' necessaries	1878			48 51
Medical Department	1879			991 23
Do	1880	20	288	
Naval hospital fund	1879			1 36
Do	1880	20	288	
Do				27,622 01
Repairs, Bureau of Medicine and Surgery	1878			270 38
Do	1879			11,497 57
Do	1880	20	288	
Contingent, Bureau of Medicine and Surgery	1877*	21	258	
Do	1878			167 41
Do	1879			2,878 87
Do	1880	20	288	
Civil establishment, Bureau of Medicine and Surgery	1878			129 93
Do	1879			1,375 49
Do	1880	20	288	
Bureau Provisions and Clothing				1,603 44
Provisions; Navy	1878			240 51
Do	1879			458,948 75
Do	1880	20	288	
Clothing, Navy				74,777 13
Small stores, Bureau Provisions and Clothing		20	288	57 96
Water for ships, Bureau Provisions and Clothing	1879			13,159 43
Contingent, Bureau Provisions and Clothing	1878*	21	258	
Do	1878			40 88
Do	1879			2,847 17
Do	1880	20	288	
Civil establishment, Bureau Provisions and Clothing	1880	20	288	
Bureau of Construction and Repair				259,947 04
Do	1880	20	289	
Construction and Repair	1878			5,337 87
Do	1879			17,513 51
Do	1880	20	288	
Repairs United States steamship Antietam	1880	20	391	
Site for new Naval Observatory		21	65	
Miscellaneous expenses new Naval Observatory		21	65	
Bureau of Steam Engineering				86,490 31
Contingent, Bureau of Steam Engineering	1880	20	289	
Steam machinery, Bureau of Steam Engineering	1877*	21	258	
Do	1878			197 17
Do	1879			37,266 54
Do	1880	20	289	
Civil establishment, Bureau of Steam Engineering	1880	20	289	
Statue of Admiral Farragut		21	245	
Machinery for testing iron	1880	20	289	
New propeller for United States steamship Alarm		21	3	
Completing torpedo-boat experiments United States steamship Alarm		21	85	
Bounty for destruction of enemies' vessels prior to July 1, 1877		21	258	
Bounty for destruction of enemies' vessels				
Enlistment bounties to seamen				
Enlistment bounties to seamen prior to July 1, 1877		21	258	
Bounty, gratuity, and mileage to seamen prior to July 1, 1876				15 52
Prize-money to captors				579,805 45
Narrative of Hall's second arctic expedition				15 17
Expedition to the North Pole				
Preservation of Chevalier de Ternay monument at Newport, R. I.				800 00
Erection of Naval Monument				222 84
Medals of honor				500 00
Navy pension fund				
Transfer of lands in Florida not needed for naval purposes				2,267 19
Carried forward				2,447,441 48

* And prior years.

PRIATIONS UNEXPENDED June 30, 1879, &c.—Continued.

Appropriations for the fiscal year ending June 30, 1880.	Repayments made during the fiscal year 1880.	Aggregate available for the fiscal year ending June 30, 1880.	Payments during the fiscal year ending June 30, 1880.	Amounts carried to the surplus fund June 30, 1880.	Balances of appropriations, June 30, 1880.
$10,246,315 24	$873,173 01	$11,941,918 06	$9,839,880 51	$49,783 38	$2,052,274 19
75,000 00	4 38	75,004 38	75,004 38		
20,000 00	1 67	20,001 67	19,999 00		2 67
	6 66	6 66		6 66	
	1 00	1,781 42	120 00	1,661 42	
	742 16	13,513 04	10,293 00		3,220 04
300,000 00	33 69	300,033 69	286,387 00		13,646 69
		772 37		772 37	
	139 48	22,712 95	9,138 00		13,574 95
	50,316 94	59,316 94	40,975 00		18,341 94
		48 51	45 00	3 51	
	5,177 51	6,168 74	5,736 62		432 12
45,000 00	6,696 05	51,696 05	42,798 31		8,897 74
	37 22	38 58	2 96		35 62
50,000 00	24 25	50,024 25	48,705 91		1,318 34
	55,604 30	83,226 31	42,839 85		40,386 46
		270 25		270 25	
	52 45	11,580 02	10,928 00		622 02
30,000 00	13 19	30,013 19	16,307 00		13,706 19
22 82		22 82			22 82
		157 41	155 00	2 41	
15,000 00	382 55	3,259 42	3,257 02		2 40
	26 02	15,026 02	13,150 16		1,875 86
		129 93		129 93	
40,000 00	3 37	1,378 86	1,362 92		15 94
	1,590 00	41,590 00	41,015 00		575 00
		1,693 44		1,693 44	
	420 76	661 27	204 00	457 27	
	2,994 06	461,942 81	375,824 10		86,118 71
1,025,000 00	181 68	1,025,181 68	901,965 70		123,215 98
	308,494 53	383,271 66	129,949 17		253,322 49
100,000 00	43,447 84	143,505 80	45,414 08		98,091 72
	108 85	13,268 28	5,947 82		7,320 46
5,220 35		5,220 35			5,220 35
	98	41 86		41 86	
	988 58	3,835 75	3,460 77		374 98
60,000 00	69 53	60,069 53	53,586 50		6,483 03
11,394 25	1 89	11,396 14	11,394 25		1 89
	26	269,947 30	129,252 99		130,694 31
40,105 75		40,105 75	39,721 00		384 75
	160 37	5,498 24	179 10	5,319 14	
	3,565 27	21,978 78	19,592 98		1,485 80
1,500,000 00	4,514 58	1,504,514 58	1,404,603 90		99,910 68
7,525 00	182 67	7,707 67	7,700 00		7 67
70,000 00		70,000 00	70,000 00		70,000 00
5,000 00		5,000 00	5,000 00		
		88,490 31	25,902 39	26,856 24	35,731 68
1,000 00	70	1,000 70	1,000 70		20
45 81		45 81			45 81
	763 75	980 92	770 44	190 48	
	2,391 33	39,657 97	36,747 03		2,910 84
800,000 00	199,355 97	b 999,355 97	814,483 47		184,872 50
20,038 00		20,038 00	20,037 99		01
10,000 00		10,000 00	10,000 00		10,000 00
3,000 00		3,000 00	3,000 00		3,000 00
3,000 00		3,000 00		11,616 97	3,383 03
20,000 00		20,000 00	20,000 00		20,000 00
1,072 09		1,072 09			1,072 09
	113 82	113 82		102 35	11 47
	1,990 91	1,990 91		1,990 91	
3,809 17		3,809 17			3,809 17
		15 52			15 52
	6,172 97	585,978 42	12,066 08		573,922 34
		15 17	9 98	5 10	
	87 04	87 04		87 04	
		800 00			800 00
		222 84		222 84	
		500 00	55 50		444 50
	420,000 00	420,000 00	59,309 00		360,691 00
	46 89	2,314 08	1,000 00		1,314 08
14,536,549 08	1,999,081 13	18,973,071 69	14,624,886 35	80,576 69	4,258,008 65

STATEMENT exhibiting the BALANCES of APPRO

Specific objects of appropriations.	Year.	Statutes.		Balances of appropriations, July 1, 1879.
		Vol.	Page or section.	
NAVAL ESTABLISHMENT—Continued.				
Brought forward				$2, 447, 441 48
Payment to officers and crew of United States steamship Kearsarge for destruction of the Alabama				
Extra pay to officers and men who served in the Mexican war		20	316	
Indemnity for lost clothing prior to July 1, 1876				120 00
Indemnity for lost clothing prior to July 1, 1877		21	297	
Indemnity for lost clothing				
Burial of officers and others; United States steamship Huron				3 75
Relief of sufferers by wreck of United States steamship Huron		20	423	
Payment to T. C. Basshoo & Co., for ship knees		21	245	
Relief of the children of Otway H. Berryman and others				12, 657 15
Relief of the administrators of John D. McGill		21	12	
Relief of Peter Meagher		21	16	
Relief of Mrs. R. A. Kennedy				732 00
Relief of the widows and orphans of officers, &c., of the Levant		21	257	
Destruction of clothing and bedding for sanitary reasons				1, 178 00
General account for advances				219, 491 37
Totals				2, 681, 630 75

RECAPITU

Specific objects of appropriations.	Balances of appropriations, July 1, 1879.
Civil	$6, 236, 177 00
Customs	6, 268, 478 29
Interior—civil	997, 663 11
Internal revenue	272, 357 32
Public debt	
Department of the Interior (Indians and pensions)	6, 409, 235 63
Military establishment	6, 301, 935 93
Naval establishment	2, 681, 630 75
Total recapitulation	31, 167, 678 03

PRIATIONS UNEXPENDED June 30, 1879, *&c.*—Continued.

Appropriations for the fiscal year ending June 30, 1880.	Repayments made during the fiscal year 1880.	Aggregate available for the fiscal year ending June 30, 1880.	Payments during the fiscal year ending June 30, 1880.	Amounts carried to the surplus fund June 30, 1880.	Balances of appropriations, June 30, 1880.
$14, 526, 549 08	$1, 999, 081 13	$18, 978, 071 89	$14, 624, 886 35	$89, 576 89	$4, 258, 608 65
....	2, 000 00	2, 000 00	1, 000 00	....	1, 000 00
18, 981 28	0, 000 00	27, 981 28	27, 981 28	....	....
....	....	120 00	60 00	....	60 00
1, 197 62	....	1, 197 62	....	....	1, 197 62
....	905 15	905 15	104 66	800 49	....
....	....	3 75	....	3 75	....
504 00	....	504 00	504 00	....	....
22, 692 00	....	22, 692 00	....	....	22, 692 00
....	....	13, 657 15	289 31	....	13, 367 84
102 00	....	102 00	102 00	....	....
170 00	....	170 00	170 00	....	....
....	....	739 00	....	739 00	....
240 00	....	240 00	....	....	240 00
....	....	1, 178 00	258 59	....	919 41
....	4, 529, 918 73	4, 749, 410 10	5, 422, 593 56	....	(*673, 183 46)
14, 570, 435 98	6, 540, 965 01	23, 793, 031 74	20, 077, 949 75	91, 179 93	3, 623, 902 06

* Debit balance.

LATION.

Appropriations for the fiscal year ending June 30, 1880.	Repayments made during the fiscal year 1880.	Aggregate available for the fiscal year ending June 30, 1880.	Payments during the fiscal year ending June 30, 1880.	Amounts carried to the surplus fund June 30, 1880.	Balances of appropriations, June 30, 1880.
$36, 751, 451 07	$2, 652, 630 04	$47, 540, 258 11	$31, 448, 284 47	$2, 254, 187 40	$13, 937, 786 24
16, 292, 361 32	351, 063 86	22, 912, 423 47	17, 415, 059 73	2, 356, 139 70	3, 141, 224 04
4, 418, 961 43	56, 503 98	5, 473, 428 52	4, 560, 407 81	126, 074 43	786, 946 28
4, 308, 422 96	14, 052 99	4, 595, 433 27	4, 364, 758 62	127, 591 48	103, 113 17
531, 144, 393 40	720, 274 10	531, 864, 667 50	531, 863, 450 04	1, 217 46	....
64, 367, 892 86	1, 820, 079 02	72, 397, 207 51	64, 541, 953 00	1, 914, 498 55	6, 140, 760 98
39, 985, 739 09	1, 541, 016 89	47, 828, 691 91	39, 658, 690 66	1, 584, 816 65	6, 585, 184 60
14, 570, 435 98	6, 540, 965 01	23, 793, 031 74	20, 077, 949 75	91, 179 93	3, 623, 902 06
711, 840, 178 11	13, 697, 285 89	756, 705, 142 03	713, 930, 524 08	8, 455, 790 60	$4, 318, 917 35

STATEMENT of OUTSTANDING PRINCIPAL of the PUBLIC DEBT of the UNITED STATES on the 1st of January of each year from 1791 to 1842, inclusive; and on the 1st of July of each year from 1843 to 1880, inclusive.

January 1, 1791	$75,463,476 52		January 1, 1836		$336,957 83
1792	77,227,924 66		1837		3,308,124 07
1793	80,352,634 04		1838		10,434,221 14
1794	78,427,404 77		1839		3,573,343 82
1795	80,747,587 39		1840		5,250,875 54
1796	83,762,172 07		1841		13,594,480 73
1797	82,064,479 33		1842		20,601,226 28
1798	79,228,529 12		July 1, 1843		32,742,922 00
1799	78,408,669 77		1844		23,461,652 50
1800	82,976,294 35		1845		15,925,303 01
1801	83,038,050 80		1846		15,550,202 97
1802	86,712,632 25		1847		38,826,534 77
1803	77,054,680 30		1848		47,044,862 23
1804	86,427,120 88		1849		63,061,858 69
1805	82,312,150 50		1850		63,452,773 55
1806	75,723,270 66		1851		68,304,796 02
1807	69,218,398 64		1852		66,199,341 71
1808	65,196,317 97		1853		59,803,117 70
1809	57,023,192 09		1854		42,242,222 42
1810	53,173,217 52		1855		35,586,858 56
1811	48,005,587 76		1856		31,972,537 90
1812	45,209,737 90		1857		28,699,831 85
1813	55,962,827 57		1858		44,911,881 03
1814	81,487,846 24		1859		58,496,837 88
1815	99,833,660 15		1860		64,842,287 88
1816	127,334,933 74		1861		90,580,873 72
1817	123,491,965 16		1862		524,176,412 13
1818	103,466,633 83		1863		1,119,772,138 63
1819	95,529,648 28		1864		1,815,784,370 57
1820	91,015,566 15		1865		2,680,647,869 74
1821	89,987,427 66		1866		2,773,236,173 69
1822	93,546,676 98		1867		2,678,126,103 87
1823	90,875,877 28		1868		2,611,687,851 19
1824	90,269,777 77		1869		2,588,452,213 94
1825	83,748,432 71		1870		2,480,672,427 81
1826	81,054,059 99		1871		2,353,211,332 32
1827	73,987,357 20		1872		2,253,251,078 78
1828	67,475,043 87		1873		2,234,482,743 20
1829	58,421,413 67		1874		2,251,690,318 43
1830	48,565,406 50		1875		2,232,284,281 95
1831	39,123,191 68		1876		2,180,894,517 15
1832	24,322,235 18		1877		2,205,301,142 10
1833	7,001,698 83		1878		2,256,205,398 20
1834	4,760,082 08		1879		2,349,567,232 04
1835	37,513 05		1880		*2,120,415,120 63

* The amount outstanding July 1, 1880, according to the books of the Register's Office, was $2,126,791,054 63
From which deduct the amount held for the redemption of fractional currency, applied to the payment of arrears of pensions, act June 21, 1879 .... 8,375,934 00

2,120,415,120 63

CUSTOMS.

STATEMENT of EXPENSES for COLLECTING the REVENUE from CUSTOMS, by DISTRICTS, for the fiscal year ending June 30, 1880.

York, Me	$247 69
Bangor, Me	7,155 80
Waldoborough, Me	6,842 84
Frenchman's Bay, Me	4,680 00
Portland, Me	71,437 85
Saco, Me	809 00
Machias, Me	3,072 61
Belfast, Me	3,685 34
Wiscasset, Me	3,648 00
Passamaquoddy, Me	18,858 36
Bath, Me	5,719 00
Castine, Me	4,804 72
Kennebec, Me	748 75
Aroostook, Me	8,697 40
Portsmouth, N. H	6,140 00
Vermont, Vt	57,240 38
New Bedford, Mass	6,164 00
Carried forward	209,941 74

*STATEMENT of EXPENSES for COLLECTING the REVENUE from CUSTOMS,
by DISTRICTS, &c.—Continued.*

Brought forward	$209,941 74
Boston, Mass	665,890 85
Fall River, Mass	3,693 92
Gloucester, Mass	12,487 00
Plymouth, Mass	1,980 00
Marblehead, Mass	1,466 00
Barnstable, Mass	7,141 00
Newburyport, Mass	3,478 00
Nantucket, Mass	1,581 05
Edgartown, Mass	4,828 60
Salem, Mass	6,944 62
Providence, R. I	25,847 84
Newport, R. I	3,699 37
Bristol, R. I	400 71
Stonington, Conn	1,469 69
Fairfield, Conn	2,339 00
New Haven, Conn	19,276 00
Middletown, Conn	4,046 00
New London, Conn	6,196 00
Oswegatchie, N. Y	16,137 35
Niagara, N. Y	44,687 53
Oswego, N. Y	34,055 10
Sag Harbor, N. Y	1,063 00
Dunkirk, N. Y	2,448 00
Champlain, N. Y	29,146 13
New York, N. Y	2,404,660 38
Albany, N. Y	11,201 90
Buffalo, N. Y	39,192 27
Cape Vincent, N. Y	13,154 85
Genesee, N. Y	22,241 00
Burlington, N. J	216 00
Great Egg Harbor, N. J	2,478 70
Newark, N. J	2,952 00
Little Egg Harbor, N. J	2,443 75
Bridgeton, N. J	370 00
Perth Amboy, N. J	6,763 47
Erie, Pa	4,574 00
Pittsburgh, Pa	16,731 00
Philadelphia, Pa	322,946 39
Delaware, Del	7,350 00
Eastern, Md	3,037 22
Annapolis, Md	2,247 00
Baltimore, Md	330,851 00
Georgetown, D. C	4,205 00
Norfolk, Va	14,386 42
Petersburg, Va	3,071 70
Tappahannock, Va	965 00
Yorktown, Va	987 00
Richmond, Va	6,686 44
Cherrystone, Va	2,800 00
Alexandria, Va	2,328 00
Wheeling, W. Va	1,053 00
Wilmington, N. C	15,812 74
Beaufort, N. C	2,031 51
Pamlico, N. C	4,447 00
Albemarle, N. C	1,943 13
Charleston, S. C	20,283 90
Beaufort, S. C	4,420 88
Georgetown, S. C	1,151 00
Savannah, Ga	18,525 01
Saint Mary's, Ga	1,130 19
Brunswick, Ga	8,127 00
Saint Mark's, Fla	6,152 00
Pensacola, Fla	16,390 26
Saint John's, Fla	2,700 00
Saint Augustine, Fla	1,749 00
Fernandina, Fla	4,272 25
Carried forward	4,449,273 86

STATEMENT of EXPENSES for COLLECTING the REVENUE from CUSTOMS, by DISTRICTS, &c.—Continued.

Brought forward	$4,449,273 86
Apalachicola, Fla	962 00
Key West, Fla	24,344 36
Natchez, Miss	625 00
Pearl River, Miss	5,204 90
Vicksburg, Miss	317 51
New Orleans, La	241,607 00
Teche, La	6,911 00
Mobile, Ala	18,756 59
Brazos Santiago, Tex	43,585 28
Corpus Christi, Tex	20,120 67
Saluria, Tex	12,497 99
Galveston, Tex	38,995 83
Paso del Norte, Tex	15,423 12
Memphis, Tenn	5,133 00
Nashville, Tenn	691 00
Louisville, Ky	8,699 00
Miami, Ohio	6,654 25
Cuyahoga, Ohio	15,224 44
Cincinnati, Ohio	29,629 84
Detroit, Mich	33,112 00
Michigan, Mich	2,848 53
Superior, Mich	8,153 74
Huron, Mich	32,622 50
Evansville, Ind	877 00
Cairo, Ill	1,149 23
Chicago, Ill	119,682 50
Galena, Ill	852 00
La Crosse, Wis	1,706 40
Milwaukee, Wis	7,185 48
Minnesota, Minn	18,482 98
Duluth, Minn	6,113 46
Burlington, Iowa	571 62
Dubuque, Iowa	333 56
Saint Louis, Mo	52,297 72
Montana and Idaho	2,353 00
Omaha, Nebr	1,510 00
Alaska, Alaska	11,930 00
Oregon, Oreg	7,043 34
Southern Oregon	2,521 31
Willamette, Oreg	27,712 28
Puget Sound, Wash	24,495 05
San Diego, Cal	8,527 15
San Francisco, Cal	344,105 00
	5,666,843 09
Contingent expenses and fees in customs cases $14,008 79	o
Transportation 1,150 23	
Amount paid by disbursing agents for salaries, &c 184,534 55	
Miscellaneous, stationery, &c 156,716 87	
	356,410 44
Total net expenditures	6,023,253 53

STATEMENT of EXPENDITURES for ASSESSING and COLLECTING the INTER-NAL REVENUE for the fiscal year ending June 30, 1866; embracing SALARIES and EXPENSES of COLLECTORS and SALARIES and EXPENSES of SUPERVIS-ORS and SUBORDINATE OFFICERS.

Alabama, first district	$10,644 13	
second district	17,251 30	
		$27,895 43
Arkansas		26,190 29
Arizona		5,114 61
Colorado		12,722 86
Connecticut, first district	12,654 82	
second district	12,844 94	
		25,499 76

STATEMENT of EXPENDITURES for ASSESSING and COLLECTING the INTERNAL REVENUE, &c.—Continued.

Brought forward..		$97,422 95
California, first district	$56,793 60	
fourth district................................	26,195 73	
		82,989 33
Dakota		7,725 54
Delaware		11,438 88
Florida		10,322 16
Georgia, second district....................................	48,413 50	
third district	22,392 45	
		70,805 95
Idaho..		6,902 18
Illinois, first district......................................	57,602 23	
second district	8,846 16	
third district	14,538 10	
fourth district	21,674 98	
fifth district	65,469 33	
seventh district	5,064 42	
eighth district	27,042 90	
thirteenth district	19,540 24	
		219,778 36
Indiana, first district	13,387 65	
fourth district	32,829 67	
sixth district	15,476 70	
seventh district.............................	23,621 22	
tenth district................................	8,936 16	
eleventh district............................	7,605 05	
		101,856 45
Iowa, second district	12,732 35	
third district..................................	13,919 91	
fourth district................................	11,374 26	
fifth district	10,101 27	
		48,127 79
Kansas...		13,158 51
Kentucky, second district..................................	45,151 80	
fifth district..............................	113,844 51	
sixth district	48,464 34	
seventh district..........................	72,073 60	
eighth district............................	32,651 31	
ninth district	14,362 90	
		326,548 46
Louisiana		27,050 88
Maine		8,738 78
Massachusetts, third district.............................	27,093 07	
fifth district..............................	26,687 31	
tenth district..............................	14,000 52	
		67,720 90
Maryland, third district	50,024 92	
fourth district	20,060 93	
		70,085 85
Montana...		8,444 00
Missouri, first district......................................	42,491 75	
second district	12,548 35	
fourth district	15,162 01	
fifth district	12,044 80	
sixth district................................	21,691 27	
		103,938 18
Minnesota, first district....................................	8,174 15	
second district..............................	9,905 25	
		18,079 40
Michigan, first district.....................................	15,788 86	
third district...............................	9,589 16	
fourth district..............................	6,414 55	
sixth district................................	8,516 92	
		40,309 49
Mississippi		18,929 60
Carried forward..		1,360,433

482 REPORT ON THE FINANCES.

STATEMENT of EXPENDITURES for ASSESSING and COLLECTING the INTERNAL REVENUE, &c.—Continued.

Brought forward		$1,360,433 64
New York, first district	$42,019 54	
second district	35,265 66	
third district	39,687 92	
eleventh district	9,314 53	
twelth district	14,686 14	
fourteenth district	12,273 26	
fifteenth district	7,916 23	
twenty-first district	10,499 04	
twenty-fourth district	15,056 98	
twenty-sixth district	9,123 14	
twenty-eighth district	16,369 50	
thirtieth district	23,678 89	
		235,880 83
New Jersey, first district	10,570 29	
third district	11,852 15	
fifth district	25,261 44	
		47,683 88
Nevada		7,726 70
Nebraska		17,167 28
New Mexico		7,050 85
New Hampshire		10,172 42
North Carolina, first district	17,843 76	
fourth district	41,371 27	
fifth district	76,869 23	
sixth district	182,192 70	
		318,276 96
Ohio, first district	69,823 86	
third district	21,447 21	
fourth district	12,889 94	
sixth district	13,973 97	
seventh district	14,813 69	
tenth district	17,756 51	
eleventh district	15,095 24	
fifteenth district	12,449 25	
eighteenth district	25,045 12	
		203,294 79
Oregon		7,126 18
Pennsylvania, first district	44,598 70	
eighth district	18,379 42	
ninth district	26,104 20	
twelfth district	15,968 34	
fourteenth district	24,108 58	
sixteenth district	28,632 02	
nineteenth district	6,416 85	
twentieth district	10,958 61	
twenty-second district	52,900 56	
twenty-third district	21,680 92	
		251,747 80
Rhode Island		9,144 09
South Carolina		44,486 66
Tennessee, second district	25,278 11	
fifth district	69,269 19	
eighth district	10,993 28	
		105,540 58
Texas, first district	17,242 29	
third district	14,266 64	
fourth district	9,619 80	
		41,128 73
Utah		6,051 05
Vermont		5,216 49
Virginia, second district	23,122 42	
third district	22,193 43	
fourth district	17,021 45	
fifth district	26,172 43	
Carried forward	86,509 73	2,678,128 92

STATEMENT of EXPENDITURES for ASSESSING and COLLECTING the INTER-
NAL REVENUE, &c.—Continued.

Brought forward	$88,509 73	$2,678,128 92
Virginia—Continued.		
sixth district	42,581 23	
		131,090 96
West Virginia, first district	12,526 26	
second district	9,009 04	
		21,535 30
Wisconsin, first district	24,455 71	
second district	8,169 62	
third district	10,640 83	
sixth district	7,491 33	
		50,757 49
Washington Territory		5,742 50
Wyoming Territory		5,294 94
		2,892,550 11
Amount disbursed by F. J. Hobbs for salaries of supervisors, &c.	657,529 73	
Amount paid for salaries of surveyors, &c. (unclassified by districts)	59,190 45	
Amount paid for transportation and expenses	10,156 96	
Amount paid for telegraphing	1,528 46	
Miscellaneous	36,149 39	
		764,554 99
Total net expenditures		3,657,105 10

STATEMENT of EXPENDITURES for MARINE HOSPITAL SERVICE, by DIS-
TRICTS, for the year ending June 30, 1880.

Bangor, Me	$2,017 07
Frenchman's Bay, Me	1,215 37
Waldoborough, Me	603 96
Machias, Me	720 83
Portland, Me	6,388 09
Wiscasset, Me	256 35
Belfast, Me	357 11
Bath, Me	321 22
Passamaquoddy, Me	431 75
Castine, Me	414 00
Portsmouth, N. H	150 40
Vermont, Vt	106 50
New Bedford, Mass	1,066 68
Boston, Mass	13,783 62
Gloucester, Mass	14 00
Fall River, Mass	44 85
Plymouth, Mass	904 25
Barnstable, Mass	6,730 00
Edgartown, Mass	3,998 43
Salem, Mass	202 00
Providence, R. I	2,610 96
Newport, R. I	363 20
New Haven, Conn	920 79
Middletown, Conn	452 02
New London, Conn	987 26
Oswegatchie, N. Y	162 60
Sag Harbor, N. Y	110 00
New York, N. Y	57,500 00
Champlain, N. Y	330 00
Albany, N. Y	90 88
Genesee, N. Y	2 47
Buffalo, N. Y	6,626 61
Cape Vincent, N. Y	32 50
Oswego, N. Y	747 60
Great Egg Harbor, N. J	264 15
Little Egg Harbor, N. J	620 23
Carried forward	110,847 75

STATEMENT of EXPENDITURES for MARINE HOSPITAL SERVICE, &c.—Continued.

Brought forward	$110,847 75
Perth Amboy, N. J	42 00
Erie, Pa	464 92
Pittsburgh, Pa	4,812 51
Philadelphia, Pa	19,950 90
Eastern, Md	225 80
Baltimore, Md	14,086 32
Georgetown, D. C	25,945 04
Norfolk, Va	8,632 24
Tappahannock, Va	115 10
Richmond, Va	2,176 30
Yorktown, Va	11 15
Wheeling, W. Va	270 20
Wilmington, N. C	1,406 71
Beaufort, N. C	21 00
Paulico, N. C	1,496 58
Albemarle, N. C	975 00
Charleston, S. C	5,455 44
Beaufort, S. C	13 50
Georgetown, S. C	62 30
Savannah, Ga	4,998 06
Brunswick, Ga	83 00
Saint Mark's, Fla	249 16
Saint John's, Fla	934 15
Pensacola, Fla	3,401 82
Fernandina, Fla	591 84
Apalachicola, Fla	701 86
Key West, Fla	3,621 07
Mobile, Ala	4,757 38
Pearl River, Miss	119 00
Vicksburg, Miss	3,159 25
New Orleans, La	20,639 46
Teche, La	10 00
Brazos, Tex	159 00
Corpus Christi, Tex	564 50
Saluria, Tex	17 50
Galveston, Tex	7,276 18
Louisville, Ky	11,955 72
Miami, Ohio	1,315 23
Cuyahoga, Ohio	4,059 94
Cincinnati, Ohio	9,328 89
Memphis, Tenn	3,948 50
Nashville, Tenn	743 73
Michigan, Mich	214 85
Detroit, Mich	7,088 32
Superior, Mich	360 92
Huron, Mich	42 60
Evansville, Ind	4,880 10
Cairo, Ill	5,740 22
Chicago, Ill	20,564 64
La Crosse, Wis	959 82
Milwaukee, Wis	3,952 41
Minnesota, Minn	2,637 50
Duluth, Minn	582 10
Dubuque, Iowa	1,269 62
Saint Louis, Mo	14,481 62
Puget Sound, Wash	6,965 00
Oregon, Oreg	40 75
Willamette, Oreg	2,107 18
Southern Oregon	27 20
San Diego, Cal	88 75
San Francisco, Cal	19,795 36
Transportation	179 90
Disbursing agent	28,500 00
Miscellaneous	2,571 90
	402,685 76

STATEMENT of the NUMBER of PERSONS EMPLOYED in each DISTRICT of the UNITED STATES for the COLLECTION of CUSTOMS for the fiscal year ending June 30, 1880, with their OCCUPATIONS and COMPENSATION.

Districts, number of persons, and occupation.	Compensation.
AROOSTOOK, ME.	
1 collector	$1,500 00
1 deputy collector and inspector	729 00
3 deputy collectors and inspectors	3,294 00
1 special deputy collector	1,464 00
1 inspector (railroad)	1,098 00
PASSAMAQUODDY, ME.	
1 collector	3,000 00
1 deputy collector	1,742 30
1 deputy collector	1,600 00
1 deputy collector	1,249 00
5 inspectors	5,490 00
4 inspectors	3,660 00
4 inspectors	2,928 00
1 deputy collector	21 00
1 inspector	00 00
1 inspector	45 00
1 night watchman	915 00
2 night watchmen	1,464 00
MACHIAS, ME.	
1 collector	2,087 07
1 special deputy collector and inspector	1,098 00
2 deputy collectors	1,640 00
FRENCHMAN'S BAY, ME.	
1 collector	1,662 27
1 deputy collector	1,200 00
1 deputy collector	12 00
1 deputy collector and inspector	1,098 00
2 deputy collectors and inspectors	1,200 00
BANGOR, ME.	
1 collector	1,138 69
1 special deputy collector	1,600 00
1 deputy collector	700 00
1 inspector	1,098 00
1 inspector	810 00
1 clerk	742 30
1 weigher, gauger, &c	273 00
CASTINE, ME.	
1 collector	988 80
2 deputy collectors and inspectors	2,190 00
3 deputy collectors and inspectors	2,463 75
BELFAST, ME.	
1 collector	1,105 17
1 deputy collector	300 00
1 deputy collector	490 00
1 deputy collector	100 00
2 inspectors	200 00
1 inspector	100 00
1 storekeeper	100 00
2 storekeepers	100 00
WISCASSET, ME.	
1 collector	644 30
3 deputy collectors	2,190 00
1 temporary inspector	1,095 00
WALDOBOROUGH, ME.	
1 collector	1,838 91
2 deputy collectors	2,920 00
1 deputy collector	912 00
1 deputy collector	1,005 00
1 deputy collector	730 00
1 deputy collector	700 00
1 janitor	240 00

Districts, number of persons, and occupation.	Compensation.
BATH, ME.	
1 collector	$2,480 16
1 deputy collector	650 00
1 deputy collector	265 90
1 inspector, &c	1,281 00
2 inspectors, &c	2,196 00
2 inspectors, &c	498 00
PORTLAND AND FALMOUTH, ME.	
1 collector	6,000 00
2 deputy collectors	6,000 00
4 clerks	4,800 00
2 clerks	2,200 00
3 clerks	3,000 00
1 surveyor	4,500 00
1 deputy surveyor	2,500 00
1 superintendent, warehouse clerks	1,500 00
3 storekeepers	3,285 00
1 appraiser	3,000 00
1 examiner	1,800 00
1 laborer	720 00
2 weighers and gaugers	4,000 00
20 inspectors	21,648 00
1 marker	730 00
2 boatmen	1,095 00
1 messenger	650 00
1 watchman	730 00
SACO, ME.	
1 collector	348 24
1 deputy collector	450 00
KENNEBUNK, ME.	
1 collector	138 55
1 deputy collector and inspector, &c	600 00
2 inspectors	156 00
YORK, ME.	
1 collector	268 17
PORTSMOUTH, N. H.	
1 collector	773 04
1 deputy collector and inspector	1,281 00
1 deputy collector and inspector	1,098 00
1 inspector, weigher, gauger, and measurer	1,143 50
2 inspectors	2,287 00
1 boatman	135 10
VERMONT, VT.	
1 collector	2,581 59
1 deputy collector	2,500 00
2 deputy collectors, at $1,800	3,690 00
2 deputy collectors, at $1,600	3,200 00
3 deputy collectors, at $1,400	4,200 00
5 deputy collectors, at $1,200	6,000 00
2 deputy collectors, at $1,000	2,000 00
1 clerk	1,000 00
1 clerk	36 00
5 deputy collectors, at $600	3,000 00
3 deputy collectors, at $1,098	3,294 00
1 deputy collector	1,074 00
1 deputy collector	1,072 00
2 deputy collectors, at $1,029	2,058 00
1 deputy collector	999 00
3 deputy collector, at $693	2,079 00
1 deputy collector	927 00
1 deputy collector	165 90
3 inspectors, at $1,464	4,892 00
1 inspector	1,174 00
4 inspectors, at $1,098	4,392 00
1 inspector	1,074 00
4 inspectors, at $1,020	4,080 00

STATEMENT of the NUMBER of PERSONS EMPLOYED in each DISTRICT, &c.—
Continued.

Districts, number of persons, and occupation.	Compensation.	Districts, number of persons, and occupation.	Compensation.
VERMONT, VT.—Continued.		**BOSTON AND CHARLESTOWN, MASS.—** Continued.	
1 inspector	$1,017 00	1 assistant deputy naval officer, &c ..	$3,000 00
1 inspector	1,011 00	6 clerks, at $1,800	10,800 00
3 inspectors, at $999	2,997 00	5 clerks, at $1,600	8,000 00
1 inspector	990 00	1 clerk	1,400 00
1 inspector	768 00	2 clerks, at $1,200	2,400 00
1 inspector	189 00	1 clerk and messenger	1,000 00
1 inspector	183 00	1 surveyor	5,000 00
1 tally clerk	481 00	1 deputy surveyor	2,500 00
3 tally clerks, at $215	645 00	1 assistant surveyor	1,800 00
1 tally clerk	210 00	1 clerk	1,600 00
1 tally clerk	26 00	1 clerk and admeasurer	1,300 00
1 night-watchman	750 00	1 clerk	1,200 00
1 night-watchman	524 00	1 clerk	1,000 00
1 boatman	500 00	2 messengers, at $840	1,680 00
		4 inspectors, at $1,460	5,840 00
NEWBURYPORT, MASS.		86 inspectors, at $1,277.50	109,865 00
1 collector	418 14	1 inspector of marble	480 00
1 deputy collector and inspector	1,095 00	1 inspectress	201 00
1 inspector, weigher, and gauger	1,095 00	1 captain night-watch	1,460 00
1 inspector, weigher, and gauger.....	600 00	2 lieutenants night-watch	2,400 00
1 storekeeper	18 00	40 night inspectors, at $912.50	36,500 00
1 janitor	540 00	8 night watchmen, at $730	5,840 00
		1 day watchman, at $730	730 00
GLOUCESTER, MASS.		8 weighers, gaugers, &c., at $2,000	6,000 00
1 collector	3,752 00	1 gauger	2,000 00
1 deputy collector	1,500 00	2 assistant gaugers, at $1,277.50	2,555 00
1 clerk	1,300 00	3 assistant weighers, at $1,460	4,380 00
1 clerk	56 00	17 assistant weighers, at $1,277.50	21,717 50
4 inspectors	4,380 00	16 assistant weighers, at $1,095	17,520 00
1 inspector	300 00	1 general appraiser	3,000 00
1 inspector	588 00	2 appraisers	6,000 00
1 inspector	1,144 00	2 assistant appraisers, at $2,500	5,000 00
1 inspector	1,296 00	1 clerk	1,400 00
1 inspector	28 00	1 examiner of drugs	1,900 00
1 boatman	750 00	2 examiners, at $2,000	4,000 00
		6 examiners, at $1,800	10,800 00
SALEM AND BEVERLY, MASS.		1 examiner	1,600 00
1 collector	869 16	1 examiner	1,500 00
1 deputy collector and inspector	1,800 00	1 examiner	1,400 00
1 inspector, weigher, and gauger	1,095 00	2 examiners, at $1,200	2,400 00
2 inspectors	2,190 00	1 clerk, at $1,800	1,800 00
2 inspectors	1,920 00	2 clerks, at $1,600	3,200 00
1 janitor	540 00	1 clerk	1,400 00
		1 clerk	1,200 00
MARBLEHEAD, MASS.		1 clerk and messenger	1,400 00
1 collector	343 62	3 samplers, at $1,200	3,600 00
1 special deputy collector, &c	1,075 03	3 assistant samplers, at $800	2,400 00
1 deputy collector and weigher	273 50	3 markers, at $800	2,400 00
		9 openers and packers, at $1,003.75	9,033 75
BOSTON AND CHARLESTOWN, MASS.		2 foremen, at $1,095	2,190 00
1 collector	8,000 00	46 laborers, at $730	33,580 00
1 comptroller, &c	4,000 00	1 porter and messenger	950 00
3 deputy collectors, at $3,000	9,000 00	1 ware-house superintendent	2,000 00
1 deputy collector	900 00	11 storekeepers, at $1,277.50	14,052 50
1 auditor, &c	3,000 00	7 storekeepers, at $800	5,600 00
1 cashier	3,000 00	4 boatmen, at $821.25	3,285 00
1 assistant cashier	2,000 00		
1 storekeeper and clerk	2,000 00	**PLYMOUTH, MASS.**	
1 clerk, &c	2,500 00	1 collector	826 78
5 clerks, at $2,000	10,000 00	1 deputy collector	800 00
6 clerks, at $1,800	10,800 00	2 deputy collectors	600 00
16 clerks, at $1,600	25,600 00		
28 clerks, at $1,400	39,200 00	**BARNSTABLE, MASS.**	
21 clerks, at $1,200	25,200 00	1 collector	2,244 00
11 clerks, at $1,000	11,000 00	1 deputy collector	1,095 00
1 clerk	800 00	1 deputy collector	900 00
1 clerk and storekeeper	1,800 00	1 deputy collector	800 00
1 clerk and storekeeper	1,277 50	2 deputy collectors	1,500 00
1 messenger and clerk	1,000 00	2 deputy collectors	1,000 00
8 messengers, at $840	6,720 00	1 deputy collector	400 00
6 messengers, at $720	5,760 00	1 clerk	308 00
1 naval officer	5,000 00	1 boatman	60 00
1 deputy naval officer	2,500 00	1 janitor	350 00
		11 storekeepers	550 00

STATEMENT of the NUMBER of PERSONS EMPLOYED in each DISTRICT, &c.—
Continued.

Districts, number of persons, and occupation.	Compensation.	Districts, number of persons, and occupation.	Compensation.
FALL RIVER, MASS.		**NEW LONDON, CONN.—Continued.**	
1 collector	$1,600 34	1 janitor	$591 60
1 deputy collector and inspector	1,281 00	1 inspector	48 00
1 inspector, weigher and measurer	1,096 00	1 boatman and messenger	40 40
1 temporary inspector, &c	60 00		
1 boatman	300 00	**MIDDLETOWN, CONN.**	
		1 collector	2,419 10
NEW BEDFORD, MASS.		1 special deputy collector	1,200 00
1 collector	2,049 83	1 special deputy collector	641 07
1 deputy collector	1,500 00	1 clerk	582 02
1 clerk	900 00	1 storekeeper	100 00
1 inspector, weigher, &c	1,095 00	1 janitor	500 00
1 inspector	1,095 00	1 temporary inspector	15 00
EDGARTOWN, MASS.		**NEW HAVEN, CONN.**	
1 collector	806 15	1 collector	3,000 00
1 special deputy collector, &c	1,095 00	1 deputy collector	1,600 00
1 deputy collector	900 00	1 inspector and clerk	1,200 00
1 inspector	600 00	1 inspector and clerk	1,095 00
1 inspector	495 00	1 clerk	600 00
1 inspector	495 00	2 weighers and gaugers	2,190 00
1 night-watchman	600 00	4 inspectors	4,380 00
1 boatman	300 00	1 night inspector	912 50
		1 messenger and porter	500 00
NANTUCKET, MASS.		1 janitor	500 00
1 collector	616 55	1 fireman	690 00
1 deputy collector	800 00	1 inspector	72 00
1 deputy collector	450 00	1 inspector	48 00
		1 boatman, &c	400 00
PROVIDENCE, R. I.			
1 collector	3,996 08	**FAIRFIELD, CONN.**	
1 deputy collector and cashier	2,000 00	1 collector	1,383 99
1 deputy collector and clerk	2,000 00	1 deputy collector, inspector, &c	1,200 00
6 inspectors, weigher, &c	6,090 00	1 inspector	225 00
2 inspectors (coastwise)	2,190 00	1 inspector	198 00
1 inspector	1,095 00		
1 inspector	498 00	**SAG HARBOR, N. Y.**	
1 boatman	549 90		
1 messenger	895 00	1 collector	628 81
1 storekeeper	730 00	1 surveyor	561 96
1 night-watchman	547 50	1 deputy collector	300 00
1 appraiser	3,000 00	1 deputy collector	180 00
1 clerk	1,012 20		
1 janitor	825 20	**NEW YORK, N. Y.**	
		1 collector	12,000 00
BRISTOL AND WARREN, R. I.		1 chief clerk	3,500 00
1 collector	104 22	9 deputy collectors	27,000 00
1 deputy collector, inspector, &c	1,095 00	1 assistant collector	2,000 00
1 deputy collector and inspector	249 00	1 auditor	5,000 00
1 boatman	216 00	1 assistant auditor	3,500 00
		1 cashier	5,000 00
NEWPORT, R. I.		1 clerk	2,700 00
1 collector	1,276 74	10 clerks	25,000 00
1 deputy collector	1,000 00	2 clerks	4,800 00
1 inspector	620 00	14 clerks	30,800 00
1 inspector	300 00	34 clerks	68,000 00
1 inspector	1,095 00	19 clerks	34,200 00
1 inspector (occasional)	246 00	45 clerks	72,000 00
1 boatman	400 00	67 clerks	93,800 00
		98 clerks	114,090 00
STONINGTON, CONN.		1 clerk	1,095 00
1 collector	668 14	12 clerks	12,000 00
2 deputy collectors	600 00	2 clerks	1,800 00
1 deputy collector	400 00	1 detective	1,200 00
1 boatman	144 00	1 carpenter	1,150 00
		2 carpenters	2,196 00
NEW LONDON, CONN.		1 telegraph operator	900 00
1 collector	2,586 42	1 janitor	900 00
1 deputy collector and clerk	1,600 00	1 scrubber	540 00
2 inspectors	2,190 00	1 scrubber	300 00
inspector	990 00	1 engineer	1,500 00
		1 engineer	1,000 00
		4 firemen	2,880 00
		6 watchmen	6,000 00
		25 watchmen	27,450 00

STATEMENT of the NUMBER of PERSONS EMPLOYED in each DISTRICT, &c.—Continued.

Districts, number of persons, and occupation.	Compensation.	Districts, number of persons, and occupation.	Compensation.
NEW YORK, N. Y.—Continued.		**ALBANY, N. Y.**	
1 watchman	$915 00	1 surveyor	$5,000 00
4 Sunday watchmen	520 00	1 deputy surveyor	1,464 00
15 porters	10,800 00	4 inspectors	4,392 00
1 engineer	1,200 00	1 temporary inspector	51 00
36 messengers	30,240 00		
6 messengers	4,320 00	**CHAMPLAIN, N. Y.**	
8 messengers	4,000 00		
2 ushers	2,400 00	1 collector	2,500 00
1 usher	1,800 00	1 special deputy collector	1,760 50
1 inspector at Troy	1,038 00	1 deputy collector and clerk	1,400 00
250 inspectors	366,000 00	1 deputy collector and clerk	1,316 50
15 inspectors	7,020 00	1 deputy collector and clerk	1,116 00
4 inspectors (coast)	730 00	1 deputy collector and clerk	59 15
8 inspectresses	8,784 00	8 deputy collectors	6,369 99
1 detective	1,464 00	1 deputy collector	600 00
110 night inspectors	100,650 00	5 deputy collectors	3,510 14
4 weighers	10,090 00	3 special inspectors	4,802 00
66 assistant weighers	82,696 00	7 deputy collectors and inspectors	4,107 00
3 gaugers	6,000 00	1 janitor	480 00
12 assistant gaugers	15,072 00		
1 measurer of marble	2,080 00	**OSWEGATCHIE, N. Y.**	
5 weighers' janitors	3,140 00		
68 storekeepers	84,912 00	1 collector	2,500 00
1 storekeeper	1,464 00	1 special deputy collector	1,600 00
1 assistant storekeeper	1,090 00	1 deputy collector	1,500 00
3 assistant storekeepers	3,660 00	2 deputy collectors	2,400 00
1 general appraiser	3,000 00	1 deputy collector	1,000 00
1 appraiser	4,000 00	2 deputy collectors	1,600 00
10 assistant appraisers	30,000 00	3 deputy collectors	1,800 00
1 clerk	2,500 00	2 deputy collectors	2,190 00
1 clerk	2,000 00	3 inspectors	3,285 00
22 examiners	55,000 00	2 inspectors	1,800 00
8 examiners	17,600 00	1 inspectress	360 00
15 examiners	30,000 00	1 inspector (paid by railroad)	1,460 00
24 examiners	25,200 00		
1 clerk	2,240 00	**CAPE VINCENT, N. Y.**	
8 clerks	5,400 00		
10 clerks	16,000 00	1 collector	2,500 00
1 clerk	1,440 00	1 special deputy collector	1,500 00
1 clerk	1,200 00	1 deputy collector and clerk	1,200 00
1 clerk and stenographer	1,800 00	2 deputy collectors	1,800 00
1 clerk and stenographer	1,000 00	1 deputy collector	276 00
1 examiner of marble	1,500 00	7 deputy collectors	3,137 00
1 stenographer	1,200 00	6 inspectors	3,801 00
1 clerk to general appraiser	1,600 00		
2 clerks to general appraiser	2,400 00	**OSWEGO, N. Y.**	
1 clerk to general appraiser	1,700 00		
8 clerks to verifiers	11,200 00	1 collector	4,500 00
17 clerks to verifiers	20,400 00	1 special deputy collector	1,600 00
24 samplers	28,800 00	1 deputy collector and cashier	1,500 00
10 samplers	10,000 00	1 deputy collector	1,000 00
4 foremen to openers, &c	4,710 00	1 deputy collector	800 00
68 openers and packers	63,896 00	1 deputy collector	661 54
18 messengers	15,120 00	3 deputy collectors and clerks	8,000 00
1 messenger	720 00	1 deputy collector and clerk	789 00
1 naval officer	8,000 00	1 deputy collector and clerk	735 00
1 deputy naval officer	2,500 00	1 deputy collector and clerk	732 00
4 clerks	10,800 00	1 deputy collector and inspector	900 00
5 clerks	11,000 00	1 deputy collector and inspector	720 00
20 clerks	40,000 00	2 inspectors	1,488 00
5 clerks	9,000 00	2 inspectors	1,470 00
18 clerks	29,300 00	1 inspector	792 00
11 clerks	15,400 00	1 inspector	810 00
5 clerks	6,000 00	1 inspector	681 00
1 clerk and messenger	1,000 00	1 inspector	228 00
4 messengers	3,300 00	6 storekeepers	285 50
1 messenger	500 00	1 janitor	454 00
1 surveyor	8,000 00		
1 auditor	5,000 00	**GENESEE, N. Y.**	
1 deputy surveyor	2,500 00		
1 superintendent of weighers	3,500 00	1 collector	2,500 00
1 superintendent barge office	2,500 00	1 deputy collector	1,600 00
8 clerks	8,000 00	1 deputy collector	1,400 00
8 clerks	7,200 00	2 deputy collectors	2,000 00
1 clerk	1,800 00	1 clerk	900 00
1 clerk	1,200 00	5 deputy collectors and inspectors	4,083 00
2 messengers	1,800 00	12 inspectors	9,027 00
5 messengers	3,600 00		

STATEMENT of the NUMBER of PERSONS EMPLOYED in each DISTRICT, &c.—
Continued.

Districts, number of persons, and occupation.	Compensation.	Districts, number of persons, and occupation.	Compensation.
NIAGARA, N. Y.		**BRIDGTON, N. J.**	
1 collector	$2,500 00	1 collector	$727 33
1 deputy collector	2,500 00	1 deputy collector	76 50
1 deputy collector and clerk	1,800 00	1 deputy collector	82 25
1 deputy collector and clerk	1,500 00		
1 deputy collector and clerk	1,400 00	**BURLINGTON, N. J.**	
1 deputy collector and cashier	1,400 00		
1 special inspector	1,340 00	1 collector	150 00
1 special inspector	856 00		
2 storekeepers	2,928 80	**PHILADELPHIA, PA.**	
1 deputy collector and inspector	1,215 00		
14 deputy collectors and inspectors	15,372 00	1 collector	8,000 00
1 deputy collector and inspector	789 00	1 deputy collector and auditor	3,000 00
1 deputy collector and inspector	785 00	1 deputy collector	2,991 87
1 deputy collector and inspector	777 00	1 assistant auditor	2,000 00
1 deputy collector and inspector	699 00	2 clerks	3,973 31
3 deputy collectors and inspectors	2,196 00	1 assistant collector	1,500 00
3 inspectors	3,204 00	1 cashier	2,500 00
1 inspector	732 00	1 assistant cashier	2,000 00
1 inspector	183 00	2 clerks, at $1,800	3,599 94
1 inspectress	728 00	15 clerks, at $1,680	22,404 43
1 messenger	660 14	10 clerks, at $1,400	13,160 59
		5 clerks, at $1,200	4,875 62
BUFFALO CREEK, N. Y.		4 messengers, at $720	2,746 80
		2 watchmen	1,622 50
1 collector	2,500 00	1 naval officer	5,000 00
1 appraiser	3,000 00	1 clerk, at $2,000	1,331 50
1 deputy collector	2,500 00	2 clerks, at $1,800	2,996 40
2 deputy collectors	2,926 00	1 clerk, at $1,600	534 80
3 deputy collectors	3,354 00	2 clerks, at $1,400	2,100 00
2 clerks	2,800 00	3 clerks, at $1,200	2,152 30
3 clerks	2,400 00	1 messenger	720 00
1 cashier	1,200 00	1 surveyor	5,000 00
1 clerk	600 00	1 deputy surveyor	2,500 00
1 clerk	300 00	2 clerks, at $1,400	2,217 50
1 clerk	583 00	1 clerk	1,200 00
1 clerk	174 00	1 messenger	720 00
1 inspector	552 00	1 general appraiser	3,000 00
1 inspector	128 00	1 clerk	1,300 00
1 inspector	915 00	1 appraiser	3,000 00
1 inspector	610 00	2 assistant appraisers	5,000 00
1 inspector	366 00	6 examiners, at $1,700	8,609 77
16 inspectors	17,568 00	1 examiner of drugs	1,000 00
		1 clerk	1,500 00
DUNKIRK, N. Y.		2 clerks, at $1,300	2,600 00
		1 clerk, at $900	489 13
1 collector	3,091 69	14 packers, at $990	11,020 08
1 deputy collector and inspector	1,342 00	1 messenger	700 00
		2 watchmen, at $2.50 per day	835 00
NEWARK, N. J.		4 watchmen, at $730	2,031 69
		1 watchman	700 00
1 collector	996 51	1 foreman of laborers	800 00
1 deputy collector and inspector	1,200 00	8 laborers	3,643 25
1 inspector	1,098 00	1 marker	720 00
		1 weigher	2,000 00
PERTH AMBOY, N. J.		27 assistant weighers, at $1,100	16,094 19
		1 clerk	1,200 00
1 collector	2,126 55	2 foremen, at $2.50 per day	1,830 00
1 special deputy collector	1,200 00	2 gaugers, at $2,000	2,402 22
1 deputy collector	600 00	1 assistant gauger, at $1,200	938 79
1 inspector	1,095 00	1 measurer	1,281 08
2 inspectors	1,200 00	4 inspectors, special, at $4 per day	5,676 00
1 inspector (temporary)	135 00	60 inspectors, at $3.50 per day	60,434 50
1 watchman (temporary)	90 00	2 inspectors, at $3 per day	1,580 00
		29 inspectors, at $2.50 per day	26,505 00
GREAT EGG HARBOR, N. J.		1 inspector, at $600	600 00
		2 bargemen, at $720	1,304 98
1 collector	734 16	1 carpenter	800 00
1 deputy collector	600 00	17 laborers, at $700	11,871 36
1 inspector	438 00	1 night inspector	360 00
1 inspector	540 00	1 storekeeper, at $1,000	250 00
LITTLE EGG HARBOR, N. J.		**ERIE, PA.**	
1 collector	476 58	1 collector	1,843 49
1 deputy collector	600 00	1 deputy collector and inspector	1,600 00
1 inspector	600 00	1 inspector	840 00
1 inspector	180 00	1 inspector	840 00

STATEMENT of the NUMBER of PERSONS EMPLOYED in each DISTRICT, &c.—Continued.

Districts, number of persons, and occupation.	Compensation.	Districts, number of persons, and occupation.	Compensation.
PITTSBURGH, PA.		**BALTIMORE—Continued.**	
1 surveyor	$5,000 00	1 deputy naval officer	$2,500 00
1 special deputy surveyor	1,600 00	2 clerks, at $1,800	3,600 00
1 deputy surveyor	1,400 00	2 clerks, at $1,600	3,200 00
1 clerk	1,200 00	3 clerks, at $1,400	2,800 00
1 inspector	1,460 00	3 clerks, at $1,200	3,600 00
1 inspector	1,095 00	1 messenger	720 00
1 messenger	600 00	1 surveyor	4,500 00
		1 deputy surveyor	2,500 00
DELAWARE, DEL.		1 clerk	1,800 00
		1 clerk	1,075 30
1 collector	2,368 37	1 messenger	720 00
1 special deputy collector	1,800 00	1 special inspector	157 50
1 deputy collector	800 00		
2 deputy collectors	1,000 00	**ANNAPOLIS, MD.**	
2 inspectors	1,986 00		
5 boatmen	1,500 00	1 collector	410 00
		1 deputy collector	300 00
BALTIMORE, MD.		1 inspector	1,095 00
		1 boatman	180 00
1 collector	7,000 00		
2 deputy collectors	6,000 00	**EASTERN, MD.**	
1 deputy collector	800 00		
1 auditor	2,500 00	1 collector	2,312 42
1 assistant auditor	1,800 00	1 deputy collector and inspector	1,098 09
1 cashier	2,500 00		
1 assistant cashier	1,800 00	**GEORGETOWN, D. C.**	
6 clerks, at $1,800	10,800 00		
7 clerks, at $1,600	11,200 00	1 collector	1,621 74
9 clerks, at $1,400	1,588 42	1 special deputy collector	1,490 00
5 clerks, at $1,200	6,000 00	1 deputy collector	1,095 00
1 clerk	1,000 00	1 inspector	220 00
1 messenger and copyist	1,000 00	1 inspector	468 00
2 messengers and copyists	1,800 00		
4 messengers	2,880 00	**ALEXANDRIA, VA.**	
1 captain of watch	1,000 00		
4 watchmen	3,360 00	1 collector	515 01
2 laborers	1,408 27	1 deputy collector	1,200 00
46 day inspectors .C	58,278 50	1 inspector	1,095 00
10 day inspectors (temporary)	6,240 00		
1 captain of night inspectors	1,281 00	**TAPPAHANNOCK, VA.**	
1 lieutenant of night inspectors	1,098 00		
38 night inspectors	29,275 00	1 collector	640 18
10 night inspectors (temporary)	5,740 50	1 deputy collector	600 00
Night service of inspectors	2,971 50		
Night service of inspectors (temporary)	462 00	**YORKTOWN, VA.**	
1 fireman on steam launch	540 00	1 collector	663 73
1 boatman on steam launch	540 00	1 deputy collector	191 16
2 boatmen on steam launch	900 00	1 special deputy collector	260 00
1 female examiner	600 00		
2 debenture markers	1,680 00	**CHERRYSTONE, VA.**	
1 general appraiser	3,000 00		
2 local appraisers	6,000 00	1 collector	283 27
3 examiners, at $1,800	5,400 00	1 deputy collector and inspector	1,277 50
3 examiners, at $1,500	4,500 00	1 deputy collector	365 00
2 clerks at $1,000	3,200 00	2 boatmen	200 00
1 foreman of laborers	1,000 00		
6 laborers, at $840	5,040 00	**RICHMOND, VA.**	
5 laborers, at $720	3,599 92		
1 messenger	720 00	1 collector	1,929 78
1 chief weigher	2,000 00	1 deputy collector	1,600 00
3 clerks, at $1,200	2,871 43	3 inspectors	3,285 00
14 assistant weighers	13,819 88	3 inspectors (temporary)	237 36
1 gauger	1,300 00	1 boatman	375 00
1 messenger	720 00	1 watchman	730 00
5 assistant weighers (temporary)	4,971 59		
Laborers on scales	28,302 11	**PETERSBURG, VA.**	
1 storekeeper	1,800 00		
1 clerk	1,600 00	1 collector	292 12
4 porters, at $820	3,280 00	1 deputy collector and clerk	1,166 20
4 laborers, at $720	1,916 68	1 deputy collector and inspector	1,098 00
1 engineer	1,200 00	1 messenger and watchman	732 00
1 fireman	1,095 00	1 boatman	3 96
5 storekeepers	5,971 00		
1 assistant storekeeper	191 40	**NORFOLK AND PORTSMOUTH, VA.**	
1 temporary storekeeper	336 00		
Night service of storekeepers	497 00	1 collector	3,000 00
1 naval officer	5,000 00	1 deputy collector	1,600 00

STATEMENT of the NUMBER of PERSONS EMPLOYED in each DISTRICT, &c.—
Continued.

Districts, number of persons, and occupation.	Compensation.	Districts, number of persons, and occupation.	Compensation.
NORFOLK AND PORTSMOUTH, VA.— Continued.		**BEAUFORT, S. C.—Continued.**	
2 clerks	$2,600 00	1 boatman	$240 00
1 inspector	1,450 00	1 clerk	360 00
3 inspectors	3,285 00		
1 inspector and clerk	1,095 00	**SAVANNAH, GA.**	
1 watchman	900 00		
1 boatman	510 00	1 collector	3,552 64
3 boatmen	900 00	1 deputy collector	2,200 00
3 inspectors (temporary)	1,250 00	3 clerks at $1,500	4,500 00
		1 messenger	730 00
WHEELING, W. VA.		1 inspector	1,460 00
		3 inspectors at $1,095	3,285 00
1 surveyor	1,225 25	3 boatmen at $520	1,560 00
		1 boatman	368 00
ALBEMARLE, N. C.		3 night inspectors	730 00
		1 temporary inspector	815 00
1 collector	1,281 69		
1 special deputy collector	300 00	**BRUNSWICK, GA.**	
1 deputy collector	1,095 00		
1 inspector (temporary)	270 00	1 collector	2,988 78
1 deputy collector (temporary)	270 00	2 deputy collectors and inspectors	2,190 00
		1 inspector	1,095 00
PAMLICO, N. C.		6 boatmen	1,800 00
1 collector	1,821 11	**SAINT MARY'S, GA.**	
1 deputy collector	1,000 00		
1 deputy collector	700 00	1 collector	688 64
2 deputy collectors	720 00	1 deputy collector	900 00
1 messenger	320 00	1 clerk	300 00
4 boatmen (temporary)	120 00	1 laborer	300 00
BEAUFORT, N. C.		**FERNANDINA, FLA.**	
1 collector	1,178 14	1 collector	1,664 66
1 deputy collector	18 31	1 deputy collector	1,095 00
1 deputy collector	270 00	1 inspector	369 00
1 temporary inspector	186 00	1 inspector	531 00
1 boatman	240 00	1 inspector	720 00
		2 boatmen	480 00
WILMINGTON, N. C.			
		SAINT AUGUSTINE, FLA.	
1 collector	2,653 46		
1 special deputy collector	1,883 00	1 collector	523 50
1 deputy collector and clerk	1,283 00	1 special deputy collector	24 00
1 deputy collector (temporary)	540 00	1 deputy collector	300 00
1 clerk (temporary)	500 00	2 deputy collectors	480 00
1 inspector	1,454 00	2 boatmen	480 00
4 inspectors at $1,098	4,392 00		
1 inspector (temporary)	957 00	**SAINT JOHN'S FLA.**	
4 boatmen at $240	960 00		
1 watchman	139 76	1 collector	1,412 59
		1 deputy collector and inspector	1,093 00
GEORGETOWN, S. C.		1 deputy collector	500 00
		1 special inspector	20 66
1 collector	499 46	1 messenger	50 66
2 boatmen	600 00	1 boatman	120 00
CHARLESTON, S. C.		**KEY WEST, FLA.**	
1 collector	3,796 00	1 collector	5,000 00
1 deputy collector and clerk	2,200 00	1 special deputy collector	2,000 00
3 clerks at $1,500	4,500 00	1 chief clerk	1,600 00
1 chief inspector at $1,460	972 00	3 clerks at $1,200	3,029 35
5 inspectors at $1,095	5,475 00	1 clerk at $1,000	586 10
1 inspector (temporary)	273 00	1 chief inspector	1,189 00
2 night-watchmen at $730	1,460 00	3 inspectors at $1,098	2,676 00
1 night-watchman (temporary)	186 00	1 chief night inspector	762 50
1 watchman	600 00	3 night-inspectors at $732	1,632 00
4 boatmen at $360	1,440 00	2 deputy collectors at $730	1,460 00
1 messenger	730 00	1 inspector	300 00
1 janitor	720 00	1 inspector	476 00
1 janitor	450 00	1 watchman	730 00
		1 messenger	730 00
BEAUFORT, S. C.		2 storekeepers at $1,093	2,196 00
		4 boatmen at $400	1,600 00
1 collector	1,875 55	4 boatmen at $590	1,290 00
2 deputy collectors	2,190 00	1 janitor	500 00
1 special deputy collector	25 69		
2 boatmen	600 00		

STATEMENT of the NUMBER of PERSONS EMPLOYED in each DISTRICT, &c.—
Continued.

Districts, number of persons, and occupation.	Compensation.	Districts, number of persons, and occupation.	Compensation.
SAINT MARK'S, FLA.		**NEW ORLEANS, LA.—Continued.**	
1 collector	$1,577 15	1 clerk and storekeeper	$2,000 00
1 deputy collector	750 00	4 storekeepers at $1,460	5,840 02
1 inspector (temporary)	270 00	1 appraiser	3,000 00
2 inspectors	2,190 00	1 assistant appraiser	2,500 00
1 inspector and deputy collector	1,460 00	5 examiners at $1,800	7,464 19
2 boatmen	600 00	1 special examiner of drugs	1,000 00
		2 openers and packers at $720	1,440 00
APALACHICOLA, FLA.		1 weigher	2,600 00
		10 assistant weighers at $1,200	8,444 52
1 collector	781 13	1 gauger	1,500 00
1 deputy collector	85 66	1 marker	600 00
1 inspector	72 00	1 captain night watch	800 00
4 boatmen	78 00	5 night-watchmen	2,981 98
		10 boatmen at $600	9,575 44
PENSACOLA, FLA.		1 chief laborer	720 00
		13 laborers at $600	7,793 57
1 collector	3,000 00	2 inspectors at $4 per day	1,304 00
1 special deputy collector	1,600 00	37 inspectors at $3 per day	35,613 00
1 clerk and deputy collector	1,200 00	25 night-inspectors at $3.50 per day	18,482 50
1 clerk	1,000 00	1 naval officer	5,000 00
1 deputy collector	360 00	1 deputy naval officer	2,500 00
1 deputy collector	1,095 00	1 clerk	1,800 00
5 inspectors at $1,095	5,475 00	1 clerk	1,600 00
2 inspectors (temporary)	870 00	2 clerks at $1,400	2,800 00
1 inspector (temporary)	582 00	1 messenger	600 00
5 inspectors (temporary)	480 00	1 surveyor	3,429 96
2 night watchmen at $730	1,460 00	1 deputy surveyor	2,500 00
1 night watchman (temporary)	426 00	1 clerk	1,600 00
1 messenger	600 00	1 clerk	1,400 00
4 boatmen at $300	1,200 00	1 clerk	1,200 00
3 boatmen (temporary)	476 67	2 messengers at $600	1,200 00
1 janitor	500 00		
		TECHE, LA.	
MOBILE, ALA.		1 collector	1,456 75
1 collector	3,000 00	2 deputy collectors and inspectors	2,196 00
1 special deputy collector and cashier	1,600 00	2 inspectors	2,184 00
1 deputy collector and clerk	1,500 00	2 boatmen	954 70
1 clerk	1,300 00		
2 special inspectors	2,920 00	**GALVESTON, TEX.**	
5 inspectors	5,475 00	1 collector	3,790 12
2 night-inspectors	1,460 00	1 special deputy collector	2,000 00
1 messenger	730 00	1 chief clerk	1,700 00
5 boatmen	2,400 00	3 clerks at $1,600	4,800 00
2 janitors	1,000 00	1 weigher, gauger, &c	1,394 00
		1 special inspector	1,464 00
PEARL RIVER, MISS.		5 inspectors at $3.50 per day	5,124 00
1 collector	1,450 00	1 inspector	836 50
2 deputy collectors	2,195 00	1 storekeeper	1,159 00
1 deputy collector and inspector	1,098 00	1 storekeeper	143 33
1 inspector (temporary)	183 00	2 deputy collectors and inspectors	3,582 00
2 boatmen	900 00	1 deputy collector and inspector	424 00
		1 inspector (mounted)	1,059 00
VICKSBURG, MISS.		1 inspector	1,174 50
1 collector	524 00	6 night-inspectors	5,490 00
		2 boatmen	1,464 00
NATCHEZ, MISS.		1 messenger and porter	732 00
1 collector	500 00	1 assistant porter	500 00
		1 laborer	220 68
NEW ORLEANS, LA.		6 temporary inspectors	180 00
1 collector	7,000 00	1 assistant weigher, &c	92 00
2 deputy collectors	6,000 00		
1 deputy collector	460 00	**SALURIA, TEX.**	
1 clerk and auditor	2,500 00	1 collector	2,557 74
1 clerk and cashier	2,432 07	1 special deputy collector	1,350 00
1 chief clerk	2,200 00	1 deputy collector	1,342 69
1 entry clerk	2,000 00	1 deputy collector and mounted inspector	1,277 50
9 clerks at $1,600	11,885 96	1 deputy collector and inspector	1,095 00
11 clerks at $1,400	14,026 66	1 inspector	450 00
10 clerks at $1,200	9,700 00	1 inspector (mounted)	1,095 00
2 clerks at $1,000	1,354 20	1 inspector (mounted)	931 00
2 clerks at $600	99 00	1 inspector (mounted)	441 00
6 messengers at $600	3,600 00	1 inspector (temporary)	98 00
1 warehouse superintendent, &c	2,500 00	1 inspector (temporary)	408 00
		2 boatmen	382 50
		1 porter and messenger	360 00

STATEMENT of the NUMBER of PERSONS EMPLOYED in each DISTRICT, &c.—Continued.

Districts, number of persons, and occupation.	Compensation.	Districts, number of persons, and occupation.	Compensation.
CORPUS CHRISTI, TEX.		**CINCINNATI, OHIO—Continued.**	
1 collector	$2,679 00	1 porter	$720 00
2 deputy collectors	3,300 00	1 weigher, gauger, &c	1,095 00
1 deputy collector	1,400 00	4 inspectors	4,380 00
1 deputy collector	1,281 00	1 inspector	172 00
1 deputy collector	1,176 00	1 storekeeper	1,095 00
2 inspectors	2,562 00	1 messenger	480 00
1 inspector and clerk	1,281 00	1 night-watchman	60 00
2 inspectors, mounted	2,562 00	1 janitor	600 00
1 inspector, mounted	1,172 50	1 examiner of drugs	35 00
1 inspector, mounted	126 90	**CUYAHOGA, OHIO.**	
1 storekeeper	108 50	1 collector	2,500 00
1 boatman	702 00	1 appraiser	3,000 00
1 porter	420 00	1 special deputy collector	1,700 00
1 temporary inspector	17 00	1 deputy collector	1,200 00
1 temporary inspector	45 00	1 deputy collector and clerk	1,050 00
1 temporary inspector	21 00	1 clerk	1,100 00
BRAZOS DE SANTIAGO, TEX.		2 deputy collectors and inspectors	2,190 00
1 collector	4,500 00	1 deputy collector and night-inspector	823 00
1 special deputy collector and cashier	2,000 00	2 inspectors	2,190 00
1 deputy collector and clerk	1,800 00	1 night-watchman	1,055 00
1 deputy collector and inspector	1,600 00	1 opener and packer	650 00
3 clerks, at $1,000	4,764 84	2 deputy collectors	960 00
1 storekeeper, &c	1,460 00	2 deputy collectors	800 00
1 watchman	747 98	1 deputy collector	25 00
1 messenger	750 00	**SANDUSKY, OHIO.**	
1 inspector	912 00	1 collector	2,500 00
1 inspectress	1,095 00	1 deputy collector	1,000 00
3 deputy collectors and inspectors	3,832 50	2 deputy collectors	800 00
5 inspectors	5,337 50	2 deputy collectors	400 00
11 inspectors, mounted	15,912 00	2 deputy collectors	240 00
PASO DEL NORTE, TEX.		1 deputy collector	112 50
1 collector	2,000 00	**MIAMI, OHIO.**	
1 special deputy collector	1,500 00	1 collector	2,595 50
1 deputy collector	1,200 00	1 special deputy collector	1,400 00
3 deputy collectors	3,000 00	1 deputy collector	1,000 00
1 deputy collector	600 00	1 night deputy collector	753 00
1 deputy collector	500 00	1 inspector	1,098 00
2 deputy collectors and inspectors	2,100 00	**DETROIT, MICH.**	
3 mounted inspectors	3,285 00	1 collector	3,595 00
1 night-watchman	600 00	1 special deputy collector	2,000 00
MEMPHIS, TENN.		1 deputy collector and clerk	1,600 00
1 surveyor	1,068 81	1 cashier	1,500 00
1 deputy surveyor	1,000 00	3 deputy collectors and clerk	3,600 00
1 messenger	600 00	2 deputy collectors and clerk	2,125 00
1 porter	90 00	5 deputy collectors and clerk	4,500 00
NASHVILLE, TENN.		3 deputy collectors and clerk	3,089 00
1 surveyor	710 90	3 deputy collectors and clerk	2,190 00
LOUISVILLE, KY.		2 deputy collectors and clerk	730 00
1 surveyor	2,884 68	3 deputy collectors and clerk	720 00
1 special deputy surveyor and clerk	1,600 00	6 deputy collectors and inspectors	6,287 50
1 clerk	1,200 00	13 deputy collectors	5,407 73
1 clerk	1,008 00	2 special inspectors	2,920 00
1 inspector and examiner	1,008 00	11 inspectors	9,900 00
1 deputy surveyor and inspector	822 00	1 storekeeper	1,095 00
1 deputy surveyor and bookkeeper	350 00	1 messenger	500 00
1 messenger	549 00	1 janitor	600 00
CINCINNATI, OHIO.		1 assistant janitor	500 00
1 surveyor	5,000 00	**HURON, MICH.**	
1 special deputy surveyor	2,000 00	1 collector	2,978 53
1 assistant bookkeeper	1,200 00	1 special deputy collector	1,700 00
1 invoice clerk	1,000 00	1 deputy collector and cashier	1,400 00
1 admeasurer	1,095 00	1 deputy collector and clerk	1,200 00
1 clerk	900 00	2 deputy collectors and clerk	2,000 00
1 warehouse clerk	900 00	1 deputy collector and clerk	800 00
1 appraiser	3,000 00	1 deputy collector	1,000 00
1 examiner	1,500 00	1 deputy collector	787 50
		1 messenger	600 00
		1 watchman	730 00

STATEMENT of the NUMBER of PERSONS EMPLOYED in each DISTRICT, &c.—
Continued.

Districts, number of persons, and occupation.	Compensation.	Districts, number of persons, and occupation.	Compensation.
HURON, MICH.—Continued.		CHICAGO, ILL.—Continued.	
1 deputy collector	$400 00	1 examiner	$1,675 20
3 deputy collectors	1,260 00	1 examiner	1,558 40
1 deputy collector	1,200 00	1 clerk	1,200 00
4 deputy collectors	800 00	1 messenger	915 00
1 deputy collector	150 00	1 opener and packer	915 00
2 deputy collectors	240 00		
2 deputy collectors and inspectors	2,562 00	GALENA, ILL.	
4 deputy collectors and inspectors	3,648 00		
1 deputy collector and inspector	729 00	1 surveyor	431 80
1 deputy collector and inspector and weigher	610 00	1 deputy surveyor and clerks	500 00
6 deputy collectors and inspectors	6,588 00	CAIRO, ILL.	
1 special inspector	736 00		
2 inspectors	3,166 00	1 surveyor	920 89
1 inspector	807 00	1 deputy surveyor	600 00
6 inspectors	5,472 00		
2 inspectors	1,468 00	MILWAUKEE, WIS.	
1 inspector	240 00		
		1 collector	2,500 00
SUPERIOR, MICH.		1 special deputy collector	1,933 10
		1 deputy collector	1,500 00
1 collector	2,500 00	2 inspectors	2,190 00
1 special deputy collector	1,400 00	1 inspector	270 00
10 deputy collectors	4,012 00	1 deputy collector	360 00
2 inspectors	2,190 00	1 deputy collector	225 00
		1 deputy collector	315 00
MICHIGAN, MICH.		1 deputy collector	300 00
1 collector	2,000 00	1 deputy collector	180 00
1 deputy collector	1,200 00		
2 deputy collectors and inspectors	1,200 00	LA CROSSE, WIS.	
3 deputy collectors	1,344 69		
3 deputy collectors	830 43	1 surveyor	1,200 00
1 deputy collector	275 00		
2 deputy collectors	469 68	DULUTH, MINN.	
3 deputy collectors	554 58		
1 deputy collector	137 91	1 collector	2,500 00
1 deputy collector	120 00	1 special deputy collector	1,400 00
1 clerk	54 00	1 deputy collector	1,095 00
		1 inspector	1,095 00
EVANSVILLE, IND.		1 inspector	693 00
		1 clerk and inspector	735 00
1 surveyor	350 00		
1 deputy surveyor	500 00	MINNESOTA, MINN.	
		1 collector	2,500 00
CHICAGO, ILL.		1 special deputy collector	1,460 00
		1 deputy collector	2,000 00
1 collector	4,500 00	2 deputy collectors	2,190 00
1 deputy collector and clerk	2,800 00	1 clerk and inspector	1,460 00
2 deputy collectors and clerk	4,000 00	1 examiner and inspector	1,460 00
1 deputy collector and clerk	1,500 00	2 mounted inspectors	2,555 00
1 deputy collector and clerk	1,460 00	3 inspectors	3,285 00
1 deputy collector	175 83	1 storekeeper	300 00
1 surveyor	350 00		
1 auditor	2,200 00	DUBUQUE, IOWA.	
1 assistant auditor	1,600 00		
1 cashier	2,000 00	1 surveyor	523 34
1 clerk	2,000 00		
2 clerks, at $1,600	3,200 00	BURLINGTON, IOWA.	
1 clerk	1,441 50		
2 clerks at $1,400	2,800 00	1 surveyor	455 33
1 clerk	1,300 00		
2 clerks, at $1,200	2,400 00		
12 inspectors, at $1,098	13,176 00		
1 inspector	957 00		

STATEMENT of the NUMBER of PERSONS EMPLOYED in each DITSRICT, &c.—
Continued.

Districts, number of persons, and occupation.	Compensation.	Districts, number of persons, and occupation.	Compensation.
SAINT LOUIS, MO.—Continued.		**SAN FRANCISCO, CAL.—Continued.**	
1 storekeeper	$912 50	4 clerks, at $1,600	$6,400 00
1 watchman	913 50	2 clerks, at $1,200	2,400 00
1 messenger	720 00	3 watchmen, at $900	2,700 00
1 messenger	480 00	2 messengers, at $900	1,800 00
1 laborer	720 00	1 messenger	600 00
		1 deputy collector and storekeeper	3,625 00
OMAHA, NEBR.		1 clerk	2,000 00
1 surveyor	414 50	4 clerks, at $1,800	7,200 00
1 inspector	1,095 00	1 superintendent of warehouses	1,800 00
		3 clerks, at $1,600	4,800 00
MONTANA AND IDAHO.		1 clerk, at $1,200	435 17
1 collector	1,263 80	1 assistant storekeeper	1,647 00
1 mounted deputy collector	422 00	10 assistant storekeepers, at $4 per day	13,460 00
		1 engineer	1,200 00
PUGET SOUND, WASH.		1 superintendent of laborers	1,200 00
1 collector	3,000 00	11 laborers, at $900	8,058 74
2 deputy collectors and clerks	4,300 00	1 corder and sealer	900 00
1 clerk and inspector	1,206 00	3 watchmen, at $900	2,700 00
3 inspectors, at $1,460	4,380 00	1 messenger	900 00
5 inspectors, at $1,200	6,000 00	2 appraisers, at $3,625	7,250 00
1 inspector, at $1,095	1,095 00	2 assistant appraisers, at $2,500	5,000 00
1 watchman	730 00	4 examiners, at $2,000	8,000 00
4 boatmen	2,400 00	1 examiner	1,600 00
		1 clerk	1,800 00
OREGON, OREG.		4 samplers, at $1,200	4,800 00
1 collector	3,000 00	12 laborers, at $900	7,842 76
1 deputy collector	1,800 00	1 messenger	900 00
1 inspectress	1,200 00	35 inspectors, at $4 per day	51,240 00
1 inspector	1,095 00	1 inspectress, at $3 per day	1,098 00
2 boatmen	960 00	1 night-inspector, at $4 per day	1,464 00
		2 night-inspectors, at $3.50 per day	2,502 00
WILLAMETTE, OREG.		45 night-inspectors, at $2.50 per day	41,175 00
1 collector	3,000 00	2 boatmen, at $900	1,800 00
1 deputy collector	2,400 00	3 weighers, at $2,000	6,000 00
1 deputy collector	2,200 00	12 assistant weighers, at $1,200	14,400 00
1 clerk	1,500 00	1 gauger	2,000 00
1 appraiser	3,000 00	1 assistant gauger	900 00
3 inspectors	4,382 00	1 naval officer	5,000 00
3 inspectors, night	2,497 50	1 deputy naval officer	3,000 00
1 weigher and gauger	1,464 00	6 clerks, at $1,800	10,800 00
1 opener and packer	1,250 00	1 clerk	1,600 00
1 storekeeper	1,200 00	1 clerk	1,400 00
		1 messenger	1,000 00
SOUTHERN OREGON.		1 surveyor	5,000 00
1 collector	1,059 49	1 deputy surveyor	3,286 34
1 deputy collector	800 00	1 clerk	3,000 00
1 special deputy collector	200 00	1 clerk	1,800 00
		1 messenger	900 00
SAN FRANCISCO, CAL.			
		SAN DIEGO, CAL.	
1 collector	7,000 00	1 collector	3,000 00
1 deputy collector	3,625 00	1 deputy collector	1,180 00
2 deputy collectors, at $1,500	3,000 00	1 mounted inspector	1,095 00
1 auditor	4,500 00	2 inspectors, at $1,000	2,000 00
1 adjuster of duties	3,000 00	1 inspector, temporary	15 00
1 cashier	3,000 00	1 inspector, temporary	804 00
1 secretary	2,500 00		
3 clerks, at $2,000	6,000 00	**ALASKA, ALASKA.**	
13 clerks, at $1,800	23,400 00	1 collector	3,422 55
		1 deputy collector and inspector	1,500 00
		4 deputy collectors and inspector	4,800 00
		1 temporary inspector	108 00
		1 janitor	72 00

STATEMENT showing the NUMBER and TONNAGE of REGISTERED, ENROLLED, and LICENSED VESSELS of the UNITED STATES on June 30, 1880.

States and Territories in which documented.	Registered.		Enrolled.		Licensed.		Total.	
	No.	Tons.	No.	Tons.	No.	Tons.	No.	Tons.
Maine	443	335,420.38	1,658	160,034.60	542	6,665.20	2,643	506,729.18
New Hampshire	7	5,391.66	52	4,106.09	15	180.84	74	9,688.49
Vermont			20	2,671.47	1	6.00	27	2,677.47
Massachusetts	502	237,217.48	1,351	188,006.71	446	4,806.01	2,220	430,183.20
Rhode Island	7	1,263.16	150	38,415.40	143	1,437.03	300	41,105.59
Connecticut	36	2,600.48	482	69,860.85	305	3,354.61	823	82,875.94
New York	648	472,144.18	3,913	668,553.16	886	9,524.44	5,447	1,150,221.78
New Jersey	59	6,068.28	835	96,546.95	409	4,846.35	1,303	108,961.53
Pennsylvania	68	54,410.27	1,473	311,104.05	157	1,976.40	1,698	367,490.72
Delaware	2	657.78	142	15,183.22	38	446.20	183	16,287.20
Maryland	76	28,127.39	1,010	84,821.27	603	8,072.38	1,738	121,021.04
District of Columbia			52	8,277.81	39	403.15	91	8,770.96
Virginia	21	6,507.75	371	19,624.06	758	7,332.12	1,150	33,553.93
North Carolina	13	2,806.30	103	7,493.78	214	2,308.71	330	12,968.80
South Carolina	1	814.10	89	9,096.16	133	1,572.10	223	11,482.48
Georgia	16	6,150.74	58	14,519.20	45	448.18	119	21,118.12
Florida	86	14,032.66	137	17,882.24	172	1,846.34	395	33,761.44
Alabama	23	6,826.97	57	7,994.48	41	356.12	121	15,290.57
Mississippi	5	436.97	100	7,252.47	76	902.66	181	8,594.30
Louisiana	64	29,707.51	205	58,278.04	311	3,753.92	670	91,738.57
Texas	22	3,638.45	91	7,501.89	151	1,508.23	264	12,738.57
Tennessee			85	14,290.75	7	110.27	92	14,401.02
Kentucky			50	17,721.74	3	27.94	53	17,749.68
Missouri			307	141,831.36	12	143.58	319	141,974.94
Iowa			55	6,040.13	5	70.91	60	6,111.04
Nebraska			29	5,887.17			29	5,887.17
Minnesota			85	8,025.29	2	20.67	87	8,045.96
Wisconsin	1	666.60	386	73,467.21	1	8.97	388	74,089.78
Illinois	15	5,294.85	419	81,128.18	16	210.98	450	86,634.01
Indiana			67	6,493.87			67	6,493.87
Michigan	6	2,001.95	905	150,303.35	68	890.48	979	169,195.78
Ohio	2	68.06	445	138,969.15	38	476.24	485	139,509.05
West Virginia			409	43,130.58	23	288.52	432	43,419.05
Arizona	4	834.46	4	554.20			8	1,388.66
California	180	180,021.74	572	90,788.31	132	1,704.25	884	202,114.30
Oregon	10	6,027.86	99	32,762.58	26	267.19	135	39,057.63
Washington Territory	52	15,060.42	39	13,821.30	14	148.10	105	29,029.82
Alaska	9	149.96			2	20.96	11	170.92
Total	2,378	1,352,810.31	16,410	2,640,352.84	5,924	65,871.41	24,712	4,068,034.56

SUMMARY.

Atlantic and Gulf coasts	2,094	1,219,905.75	10,585	1,436,021.23	5,518	60,852.09	18,147	2,716,779.07
Pacific coast	255	123,204.44	714	146,926.30	174	2,140.50	1,143	272,361.33
Northern lakes	28	9,378.23	2,904	594,109.19	135	1,614.71	3,127	605,102.13
Western rivers	1	231.80	2,197	472,296.03	97	1,264.11	2,295	473,792.03
Grand total	2,378	1,352,810.31	16,410	2,649,352.84	5,924	65,871.41	24,712	4,068,034.56

STATEMENT showing the NUMBER and TONNAGE of SAILING VESSELS, STEAM VESSELS, CANAL-BOATS, and BARGES of the UNITED STATES, June 30, 1880.

States and Territories in which documented.	Sailing vessels.		Steam vessels.		Canal-boats.		Barges.		Total.	
	No.	Tons.	No.	Tons.	No.	Tons.	No.	Tons.	No.	Tons.
Maine	2,556	491,348.45	85	16,974.54			2	406.19	2,643	508,729.18
New Hampshire	69	9,482.14	5	206.35					74	9,688.49
Vermont	17	937.96	7	1,531.02	3	208.59			27	2,677.47
Massachusetts	2,136	378,333.99	152	48,687.40			11	3,161.71	2,299	430,182.30
Rhode Island	341	16,587.91	59	24,517.68					300	41,105.59
Connecticut	641	44,299.17	106	30,046.33	1	134.71	73	8,395.73	823	82,875.94
New York	2,984	623,680.97	1,948	357,805.88	971	78,951.28	444	89,783.65	5,447	1,150,221.78
New Jersey	906	58,122.35	113	17,742.40	216	21,406.63	68	11,689.75	1,303	108,961.53
Pennsylvania	655	137,199.80	460	130,026.89	44	5,888.46	539	94,305.57	1,698	367,490.72
Delaware	159	12,127.56	21	4,042.27			2	117.37	182	16,287.20
Maryland	1,645	81,855.77	139	38,741.93			4	423.34	1,788	121,021.04
District of Columbia	58	1,920.45	33	6,850.51					91	8,770.96
Virginia	1,061	26,638.28	86	6,716.99			3	198.66	1,150	33,553.93
North Carolina	289	9,197.87	41	3,510.93					330	12,668.80
South Carolina	173	5,017.46	49	6,414.38			1	50.64	223	11,482.48
Georgia	86	9,354.07	33	11,764.05					119	21,118.12
Florida	323	25,322.56	72	8,422.88					395	33,761.44
Alabama	73	7,936.83	44	7,004.86			4	348.88	121	15,290.57
Mississippi	119	2,969.99	42	3,970.91			20	1,653.40	181	8,594.30
Louisiana	447	31,958.49	215	58,980.33			8	799.75	670	91,738.57
Texas	230	7,712.50	32	4,439.16			2	586.91	264	12,738.57
Tennessee			92	14,401.02					92	14,401.02
Kentucky			53	17,749.68					53	17,749.68
Missouri			162	59,699.13			157	82,275.81	319	141,974.94
Iowa			60	6,111.04					60	6,111.04
Nebraska			20	5,887.17					29	5,887.17
Minnesota	1	49.63	54	6,027.61			32	2,268.72	87	8,345.96
Wisconsin	258	60,800.11	128	23,181.84			2	100.83	388	74,082.78
Illinois	275	66,528.27	162	16,540.52			13	3,565.22	450	86,634.01
Indiana			66	5,708.97			1	694.90	67	6,403.87
Michigan	470	62,105.15	393	70,426.17			116	29,646.46	979	162,193.78
Ohio	196	56,275.32	222	89,404.71			67	13,829.02	485	139,509.05
West Virginia			142	16,711.88			296	26,707.17	432	43,419.05
Arizona			4	834.46			4	554.20	8	1,388.66
California	652	117,970.52	171	75,965.35			61	8,178.43	884	202,114.30
Oregon	38	7,041.33	91	28,808.00			6	3,808.30	135	39,657.63
Washington Territory	62	23,388.56	43	5,641.26					105	29,029.82
Alaska	10	125.07	1	45.85					11	170.92
Total	16,830	2,366,258.03	4,717	1,211,558.35	1,235	106,589.57	1,930	383,628.61	24,712	4,068,034.56

STATEMENT *showing the NUMBER and TONNAGE of SAILING VESSELS, STEAM VESSELS, CANAL-BOATS, and BARGES, &c.*—Continued.

SUMMARY.

States and Territories in which documented.	Sailing vessels.		Steam vessels.		Canal-boats.		Barges.		Total.	
	No.	Tons.	No.	Tons.	No.	Tons.	No.	Tons.	No.	Tons.
Atlantic and Gulf coasts	14,600	1,912,800.23	2,251	631,302.14	663	59,430.32	624	112,246.38	18,147	2,716,779.07
Pacific coast	762	148,525.48	310	111,294.02	....	....	71	12,540.93	1,143	272,361.33
Northern lakes	1,459	304,932.32	931	212,045.30	572	47,159.25	165	40,965.26	3,127	605,102.13
Western rivers	....	....	1,225	256,915.99	....	....	1,070	216,876.04	2,295	473,792.03
Total United States	16,830	2,366,258.03	4,717	1,211,556.35	1,235	106,589.57	1,930	383,628.61	24,712	4,068,034.56

STATEMENT showing the NUMBER and TONNAGE of VESSELS of the UNITED
STATES EMPLOYED in the COD and MACKEREL FISHERIES June 30, 1880.

States and customs districts in which documented.	Vessels above 20 tons.		Vessels under 20 tons.		Total.	
	No.	Tons.	No.	Tons.	No.	Tons.
MAINE.						
Passamaquoddy	16	604.11	14	152.04	30	756.15
Machias	6	180.07	11	142.13	17	332.20
Frenchman's Bay	22	1,178.65	27	305.84	49	1,484.49
Castine	48	2,409.60	52	612.03	100	3,021.63
Bangor			3	32.88	3	32.88
Belfast	27	1,061.23	36	385.80	63	1,447.03
Waldoborough	71	2,776.47	77	992.81	148	3,769.28
Wiscasset	46	2,444.05	33	376.19	79	2,820.24
Bath	4	114.38	18	206.37	22	320.75
Portland and Falmouth	79	8,797.07	44	559.86	123	4,356.93
Saco	1	31.30	11	95.66	12	126.96
Kennebunk	2	56.62	15	198.70	17	255.32
York	1	30.84	3	30.28	4	60.92
Total	323	14,694.19	344	4,090.59	667	18,784.78
NEW HAMPSHIRE.						
Portsmouth	19	1,008.94	11	129.28	30	1,138.22
MASSACHUSETTS.						
Newburyport	14	569.14	9	95.27	23	664.41
Gloucester	296	17,462.66	79	893.06	375	18,355.72
Salem and Beverly	24	1,615.13	13	149.28	37	1,764.41
Marblehead	21	969.21	28	276.83	49	1,246.04
Boston and Charlestown	67	3,634.60	17	170.75	84	3,805.35
Plymouth	19	1,042.08	10	96.90	29	1,138.98
Barnstable	146	10,215.87	43	473.12	189	10,688.99
Nantucket	1	28.23	5	32.69	6	60.92
Edgartown			6	50.31	6	50.31
New Bedford	18	895.66	52	522.39	70	1,417.95
Fall River	7	323.87	22	248.69	29	572.56
Total	613	36,756.45	284	3,009.19	897	39,765.64
RHODE ISLAND.						
Providence			25	206.33	25	206.33
Newport	23	1,429.82	60	633.76	83	2,063.58
Bristol and Warren			5	36.18	5	36.18
Total	23	1,429.82	90	876.27	113	2,306.09
CONNECTICUT.						
Stonington	40	1,570.04	43	494.72	83	2,064.76
New London	40	1,910.09	50	593.71	90	2,503.80
Middletown			2	15.72	2	15.72
Total	80	3,480.13	95	1,104.15	175	4,584.28
NEW YORK.						
New York	17	428.17	235	2,216.33	252	2,644.50
Sag Harbor	51	5,037.30	96	954.35	147	5,991.65
Total	68	5,465.47	331	3,170.68	399	8,636.15
NEW JERSEY.						
Great Egg Harbor	1	24.59			1	24.59
VIRGINIA.						
Tappahannock	2	65.72	7	61.83	9	127.55
CALIFORNIA.						
San Francisco	15	1,888.98	6	69.78	21	1,958.76
San Diego	2	50.51	8	91.70	10	142.21
Total	17	1,939.49	14	161.48	31	2,100.97
OREGON.						
Astoria	1	70.46			1	70.46

STATEMENT showing the NUMBER and TONNAGE of VESSELS of the UNITED STATES, &c.—Continued.

SUMMARY.

States and customs districts in which documented.	Vessels above 20 tons.		Vessels under 20 tons.		Total.	
	No.	Tons.	No.	Tons.	No.	Tons.
Maine	323	14, 694. 19	344	4, 090. 59	667	18, 784. 78
New Hampshire	19	1, 008. 94	11	129. 28	30	1, 138. 22
Massachusetts	613	36, 756. 45	284	3, 009. 19	897	39, 765. 64
Rhode Island	23	1, 420. 83	90	876. 27	113	2, 306. 09
Connecticut	80	3, 480. 13	95	1, 104. 15	175	4, 584. 28
New York	68	5, 465. 47	331	3, 170. 68	399	8, 636. 15
New Jersey	1	24. 59			1	24. 59
Virginia	2	65. 72	7	61. 83	9	127. 55
California	17	1, 939. 49	14	161. 48	31	2, 100. 97
Oregon	1	70. 46			1	70. 46
Grand total	1, 147	64, 905. 26	1, 176	12, 603. 47	2, 323	77, 536. 73

STATEMENT showing the NUMBER and TONNAGE of VESSELS of the UNITED STATES EMPLOYED in the WHALE FISHERIES June 30, 1880.

Customs districts in which documented.	No.	Tons.
Boston, Mass	5	531. 64
Barnstable, Mass	19	1, 817. 15
Edgartown, Mass	6	1, 123. 62
New Bedford, Mass	134	33, 337. 28
New London, Conn	10	1, 598. 43
Total	174	38, 408. 12

CONSOLIDATED STATEMENT showing the CLASS, NUMBER, and TONNAGE of VESSELS BUILT in the UNITED STATES during the year ended June 30, 1880.

States and Territories in which built.	Sailing vessels.		Steam vessels.		Canal-boats.		Barges.		Total.	
	No.	Tons.	No.	Tons.	No.	Tons.	No.	Tons.	No.	Tons.
THE ATLANTIC AND GULF COASTS.										
Maine	78	36, 009. 97	12	1, 155. 18					90	37, 165. 15
Massachusetts	29	2, 545. 48	7	1, 278. 49					36	3, 818. 97
Rhode Island	10	103. 50	4	205. 63					14	309. 13
Connecticut	10	1, 276. 15	3	653. 49			31	3, 150. 71	44	5, 080. 35
New York	59	3, 106. 45	41	3, 842. 27	1	96. 94	9	1, 683. 70	110	8, 729. 36
New Jersey	32	1, 628. 03	5	707. 19			6	1, 925. 93	43	4, 458. 22
Pennsylvania	15	4, 337. 06	28	16, 957. 71					43	21, 294. 77
Delaware	10	1, 356. 94	12	7, 116. 33					22	8, 473. 27
Maryland	48	615. 90	7	221. 94			1	49. 65	57	887. 49
District of Columbia	4	45. 35	1	32. 84					5	78. 19
Virginia	30	308. 16	1	40. 48					31	436. 64
North Carolina	5	121. 90	10	812.23					15	434. 13
South Carolina	10	113. 09	3	98. 65					13	211. 74
Georgia	5	69. 67	2	44. 66					7	114. 33
Florida	15	249. 79	2	112. 28					17	362. 07
Alabama	3	28. 34	2	112. 85					5	141. 19
Mississippi	6	82. 55	1	91. 56			2	184. 21	9	358. 32
Louisiana	18	238. 61					1	38. 75	19	277. 36
Texas	10	145. 66							10	145. 66
Total	397	52, 672. 60	141	32, 973. 78	1	96. 94	50	7, 033. 61	589	92, 776. 33
THE PACIFIC COAST.										
California	11	846. 31	7	4, 948. 85					18	5, 795. 16
Oregon	2	75. 17	13	2, 027. 40			1	362. 99	16	2, 465. 56
Washington Territory	2	15. 96	5	666. 36					7	682. 32
Total	15	937. 44	25	7, 642. 61			1	362. 99	41	8, 943. 04

CONSOLIDATED STATEMENT showing the NUMBER and TONNAGE of VESSELS BUILT, &c.—Continued.

States and Territories in which built	Sailing vessels.		Steam vessels.		Canal-boats.		Barges.		Total.	
	No.	Tons.	No.	Tons.	No.	Tons.	No.	Tons.	No.	Tons.
THE NORTHERN LAKES.										
New York	9	696.12	14	2,806.07	16	1,790.10	2	157.94	41	5,450.23
Ohio	2	42.77	11	4,656.91	...	...	1	316.68	14	5,016.36
Michigan	33	3,910.50	26	5,475.97	...	...	4	362.82	65	9,763.89
Illinois	...	...	1	37.04	...	...	...	...	1	37.04
Wisconsin	4	797.76	11	1,330.80	...	...	1	498.14	16	2,626.70
Total	48	5,447.15	65	14,306.39	16	1,790.10	8	1,355.58	137	22,890.22
THE WESTERN RIVERS.										
Louisiana	...	...	7	448.09	...	...	...	...	7	448.09
Tennessee	...	...	9	834.86	...	...	...	...	9	834.86
Kentucky	...	...	17	5,302.11	...	...	4	3,651.82	21	8,953.93
Missouri	...	...	18	2,023.52	...	...	4	1,731.75	22	3,755.27
Iowa	...	...	4	612.57	...	...	...	...	4	612.57
Nebraska	...	...	1	78.08	...	...	...	...	1	78.08
Wisconsin	...	...	4	277.70	...	...	...	...	4	277.70
Minnesota	...	...	6	581.03	...	...	1	71.56	7	652.59
Illinois	...	...	3	1,529.48	...	...	...	...	3	1,529.48
Indiana	...	...	8	355.96	...	...	...	...	8	355.96
Ohio	...	...	18	6,484.08	...	...	6	1,399.50	24	7,883.67
West Virginia	...	...	12	1,083.70	...	...	...	...	12	1,083.70
Pennsylvania	...	...	10	4,329.74	...	...	3	2,005.67	13	6,335.41
Total	...	...	117	33,930.92	...	...	18	8,860.39	135	32,791.31
SUMMARY.										
Atlantic and Gulf coasts	397	52,672.60	141	32,973.78	1	96.94	50	7,033.01	589	92,776.33
Pacific coast	15	937.44	25	7,642.61	...	...	1	962.99	41	8,943.04
Northern Lakes	48	5,447.15	65	14,306.39	16	1,790.10	8	1,355.58	137	22,890.22
Western Rivers	...	...	117	33,930.92	...	...	18	8,860.39	135	32,791.31
Grand total	460	59,057.19	348	78,853.70	17	1,887.04	77	17,611.97	902	157,409.90

SUMMARY STATEMENT of SAILING VESSELS BUILT in the UNITED STATES during the year ended June 30, 1880.

Class of vessels.	Number.	Tons.
Ships	7	13,456.90
Barks	10	8,058.43
Barkentines	6	3,113.89
Brigs	2	521.00
Schooners	286	33,106.88
Sloops	149	1,798.09
Total	460	59,057.19

SUMMARY STATEMENT of STEAM VESSELS BUILT in the UNITED STATES during the year ended June 30, 1880.

Class of vessels.	Number.	Tons.
River steamers, side-wheel	70	27,049.15
River steamers, stern-wheel	95	14,322.57
River steamers, propellers	134	7,599.81
Lake steamers, side-wheel	1	208.77
Lake steamers, propellers	37	11,662.06
Ocean steamers, propellers	11	18,011.34
Total	348	78,853.70

SUMMARY STATEMENT of CANAL-BOATS and BARGES BUILT in the UNITED STATES during the year ended June 30, 1880.

Class of vessels.	Number.	Tons.
Canal-boats	17	1,887.04
Barges	77	17,611.97
Total	94	19,499.01

STATEMENT showing the CLASS, NUMBER, and TONNAGE of IRON VESSELS BUILT in the UNITED STATES during the year ended June 30, 1880.

Ports.	Sailing vessels.		Steam vessels.		Total.	
	Number.	Tons.	Number.	Tons.	Number.	Tons.
Philadelphia, Pa.			15	15,190.44	15	15,190.44
Wilmington, Del.	1	43.83	12	7,116.33	13	7,160.16
Detroit, Mich.			2	2,816.91	2	2,816.91
Portland, Oreg.			1	414.82	1	414.82
Total	1	43.82	30	25,538.50	31	25,582.32

STATEMENT showing the CLASS, NUMBER, and TONNAGE of VESSELS BUILT in the UNITED STATES from 1803 to 1880, inclusive.

Year ended—	Ships and barks.	Brigs.	Schooners.	Sloops, canal-boats, and barges.	Steamers.	Total number vessels built.	Total tonnage.
Dec. 31, 1803							68,448.40
1804							103,753.91
1805							128,507.03
1806							120,093.29
1807							99,783.92
1808							31,755.34
1809							91,397.55
1810							127,575.86
1811							146,691.82
1812							84,691.42
1813							31,153.40
1814							29,039.90
1815	136	224	680	284		1,324	154,624.39
1816	76	183	781	424		1,414	131,667.86
1817	34	86	859	394		1,073	86,393.37
1818	53	85	428	332		898	82,421.20
1819	53	82	473	242		850	79,817.96
1820	21	60	301	152		534	47,784.01
1821	43	80	248	127		507	55,856.01
1822	64	131	260	168		623	75,346.93
1823	55	127	260	165	15	622	75,097.57
1824	56	156	377	166	26	781	90,939.00
1825	56	197	538	166	35	994	114,997.25
1826	71	187	482	227	45	1,012	126,438.35
1827	58	136	364	141	38	737	104,342.67
1828	73	108	474	197	33	885	98,375.58
1829	44	68	485	145	43	785	77,098.65
1830	25	56	403	116	37	637	58,084.24
1831	72	95	416	94	34	711	85,962.68
1832	132	143	568	122	100	1,065	144,539.16
1833	144	169	625	185	65	1,188	161,626.36
1834	98	94	407	180	88	957	118,309.37
Sept. 30, 1835 (nine months)	25	50	301	100	30	506	46,238.52
1836	93	65	444	164	124	890	113,627.40
1837	67	72	507	168	135	949	122,987.22

STATEMENT showing the CLASS, NUMBER, and TONNAGE of VESSELS BUILT, &c.—Continued.

Year ended—	Ships and barks.	Brigs.	Schooners.	Sloops, canal-boats, and barges.	Steamers.	Total number vessels built.	Total tonnage.
Sept. 30, 1839	83	89	439	122	125	858	120,988.34
1840	97	109	378	224	63	871	118,309.28
1841	114	101	311	157	78	761	118,893.71
1842	116	91	273	404	137	1,021	129,083.64
June 30, 1843 (nine months)	58	34	138	173	79	482	63,617.77
1844	73	47	204	279	163	766	103,537.29
1845	124	87	322	342	163	1,038	146,018.02
1846	100	164	576	356	225	1,430	188,203.93
1847	151	168	689	392	196	1,596	243,732.87
1848	154	174	701	547	175	1,851	318,075.54
1849	198	148	623	370	208	1,547	256,577.47
1850	247	117	547	290	159	1,360	272,218.54
1851	211	65	522	326	233	1,357	298,203.50
1852	255	79	584	267	259	1,444	351,493.41
1853	269	95	681	394	271	1,710	425,572.49
1854	334	112	661	386	281	1,774	535,636.01
1855	381	126	605	689	243	2,024	583,450.04
1856	306	103	594	479	221	1,703	469,393.73
1857	251	58	504	358	263	1,434	378,804.70
1858	122	46	431	400	226	1,225	242,286.69
1859	89	26	297	284	172	870	156,602.33
1860	110	36	372	280	264	1,071	212,892.48
1861	110	36	360	371	264	1,143	233,194.35
1862	60	17	207	397	183	864	175,075.84
1863	97	34	212	1,113	367	1,823	310,884.34
1864	112	45	322	1,389	498	2,366	415,740.64
1865	109	46	360	853	411	1,788	383,805.40
1866	96	61	457	926	348	1,888	336,146.56
1867	95	70	517	657	180	1,519	303,528.66
1868	80	48	590	848	236	1,802	285,304.73
1869	91	36	506	816	277	1,726	275,280.05
1870	73	27	519	709	290	1,618	276,953.31
1871	40	14	498	901	302	1,755	273,226.51
1872	15	10	426	900	292	1,643	309,052.22
1873	28	9	611	1,221	402	2,271	358,245.76
1874	71	22	855	995	404	2,147	432,725.17
1875	114	23	502	340	323	1,301	297,638.79
1876	78	5	424	269	338	1,112	203,585.63
1877	71	4	337	352	265	1,029	176,591.96
1878	81	7	279	557	334	1,258	235,503.57
1879	27	10	256	494	335	1,122	193,030.60
1880	23	2	286	243	348	902	157,400.90

LIABILITIES OF THE UNITED STATES TO INDIAN TRIBES UNDER TREATY STIPULATIONS.

LIABILITIES

UNITED STATES TO INDIAN TRIBES UNDER TREATY STIPULATIONS.

DEPARTMENT OF THE INTERIOR,
Washington, September 28, 1880.

SIR: In compliance with your request of the 15th instant I have the honor to transmit herewith "statement of liabilities to various Indian tribes under treaty stipulations," &c., also a copy of the letter from the Office of Indian Affairs, dated the 24th instant, accompanying said statement.

I am, sir, very respectfully,

C. SCHURZ, *Secretary.*

The honorable the SECRETARY OF THE TREASURY.

DEPARTMENT OF THE INTERIOR,
OFFICE OF INDIAN AFFAIRS,
Washington, September 24, 1880.

SIR: I have the honor to acknowledge the receipt, by your reference of the 16th instant, of a communication addressed to you by the honorable Secretary of the Treasury, dated the 15th September, requesting to be furnished with the statement prepared annually by this Office, showing the liabilities of the United States to Indian tribes under treaty stipulations.

In compliance with the request contained therein, I inclose herewith said statement in sheets, numbered from one to seven, inclusive.

Very respectfully,

E. M. MARBLE,
Acting Commissioner.

The honorable the SECRETARY OF THE INTERIOR.

STATEMENT showing the PRESENT LIABILITIES of the UNITED STATES to INDIAN TRIBES under TREATY STIPULATIONS.

Names of treaties.	Description of annuities, &c.	Number of installments yet unappropriated, explanations, &c.	Reference to laws, Statutes at Large.	Annual amount necessary to meet stipulations, indefinite as to time, now allowed, but liable to be discontinued.	Aggregate of future appropriations that will be required during a limited number of years to pay limited annuities incidentally necessary to effect the payment.	Amount of annual liabilities of a permanent character.	Amount held in trust by the United States on which 5 per cent. is annually paid, and amounts which, invested at 5 per cent., produce permanent annuities.
Apaches, Kiowas, and Comanches.	Thirty installments, provided to be expended under the tenth article treaty of October 21, 1867.	Seventeen installments, unappropriated, at $30,000 each.	Vol. 15, p. 584, §10		$510,000 00		
Do	Purchase of clothing	Tenth article treaty of October 21, 1867.	....do	$15,000 00			
Do	Pay of carpenter, farmer, blacksmith, miller, and engineer.	Fourteenth article treaty of October 21, 1867.	Vol. 15, p. 585, §14	5,200 00			
Do	Pay of physician and teacher	......do	...do	2,500 00			
Do	Three installments, for seed and agricultural implements.	Two installments of $2,500 each due.	Vol. 15, p. 583, §8.		5,000 00		
Do	Pay of a second blacksmith, iron and steel	Eighth article treaty of October 21, 1867.	Vol. 15, p. 584, §8.	2,000 00			
Arickarees, Gros Ventres, and Mandans.	Amount to be expended in such goods, &c., as the President may from time to time determine.	Seventh article treaty of July 27, 1866.	Treaty not published.	50,000 00			
Assinaboines	......do	...do	...do	30,000 00			
Blackfeet, Bloods, and Piegans.	......do	Eighth article treaty of September 1, 1868.	...do	40,000 00			
Cheyennes and Arapahoes.	Thirty installments, provided to be expended under tenth article treaty of October 28, 1867.	Seventeen installments, unappropriated, at $20,000 each.	Vol. 15, p. 596, §10		340,000 00		
Do	Purchase of clothing, same article		...do	14,000 00			
Do	Pay of physician, carpenter, farmer, blacksmith, miller, engineer, and teacher.		...do	7,700 00			
Do	Three installments, for the purchase of seeds and of agricultural implements.	Two installments, of $2,500 each, due.	Vol. 15, p. 595, §8.		5,000 00		
Do	Pay of second blacksmith, iron and steel		Vol. 15, p. 597, §8.	2,000 00			
Chickasaws	Permanent annuity in goods		Vol. 1, p. 619			$3,000 00	
Chippewas, Boise Forte band.	Twenty installments, for blacksmith, assistants, iron, tools, &c.	Five installments, at $1,500 each, unappropriated.	Vol. 14, p. 766, §3.		7,500 00		

Do............	Twenty installments of annuity, in money, goods, or other articles, provisions, ammunition, and tobacco.	Annuity, $3,500; goods, &c., $6,500; provisions, &c., $1,000; five installments unappropriated.	...do		55,000 00	
Chippewas of Lake Superior.	Support of smith and shop, and pay of two farmers, during the pleasure of the President.	Estimated at.......................	Vol. 10, p. 1112...	1,500 00		
Chippewas of the Mississippi.	Ten installments in money, at $20,000 each, third article treaty of February 22, 1855, and third article treaty of May 7, 1864.	Four installments, of $20,000 each, due.	Vol. 13, p. 694, §3.		80,000 00	
Do............	Forty-six installments, to be paid to the chiefs of the Mississippi Indians.	Twelve installments, of $1,000 each, due.	Vol. 9, p. 904, §3.		12,000 00	
Chippewas, Pillagers, and Lake Winnebagoshish band.	Forty installments: in money, $10,666.66; goods, $8,000, and for purposes of utility, $4,000.	Fourteen installments, of $22,666.66 each, due.	Vol. 10, p. 1168, §3; vol. 13, p. 694, §3.		317,333 24	
Do............	Ten installments, for purposes of education, per third article treaty of May 7, 1864.	Four installments, of $3,000 each, due.	Vol. 13, p. 694, §3.		12,000 00	
Choctaws........	Permanent annuities.......................	Second article treaty of November 16, 1805, $3,000; thirteenth article treaty of October 18, 1820, $600; second article treaty of January 20, 1825, $6,000.	Vol. 7, p. 99, §2; vol. 11, p. 614, §13; vol. 7, p. 213, §13; vol. 7, p. 235, §2.		9,600 00	....
Do............	Provisions for smiths, &c	Sixth article treaty of October 18, 1820; ninth article treaty of January 20, 1825.	Vol. 7, p. 212, §6; vol. 7, p. 236, §9; vol.7, p. 614, §13.		920 00	
Do............	Interest on $390,257.92, articles ten and thirteen, treaty of January 22, 1855.	....	Vol. 11, p. 614, §13.		19,512 89	$390,257 92
Creeks........	Permanent annuities	Treaty of August 7, 1790...........	Vol. 7, p. 36, §4..		1,500 00	
Do............	......do	Treaty of June 16, 1802	Vol. 7, p. 69, §2..		3,000 00	
Do............	......do	Treaty of January 24, 1826......	Vol. 7, p. 287, §4..		20,000 00	490,000 00
Do............	Smiths, shops, &c	Treaty of January 24, 1826	Vol. 7, p. 287, §8..		1,110 00	22,200 00
Do............	Wheelwright, permanent	Treaty of January 24, 1826, and August 7, 1856.	Vol. 7, p. 287, §8; vol. 11, p.700,§5.		600 00	12,000 00
Do............	Allowance during the pleasure of the President for blacksmiths, assistants, shops and tools, iron and steel, wagon-maker, education, and assistance in agricultural operations, &c.	Treaty of February 14, 1833, and treaty of August 7, 1856.	Vol. 7, p. 419, §5; vol. 11, p. 700,§5.	840 00 / 270 00 / 600 00 / 2,000 00		
Do............	Interest on $200,000 held in trust, sixth article treaty August 7, 1856.	Treaty of August 7, 1856...........	Vol. 11, p. 700, §6.		10,000 00	200,000 00
Do............	Interest on $675,168 held in trust, fourth article treaty June 14, 1866, to be expended under the direction of the Secretary of the Interior.	Expended under the direction of Secretary of the Interior.	Vol. 14, p.786, §3.		33,758 40	675,168 00
Crows	For supplying male persons over fourteen years of age with a suit of good, substantial woolen clothing; females over twelve years of age a flannel skirt or goods to make the same, a pair of woolen hose, calico and domestic; and boys and girls under the ages named such flannel and cotton goods as their necessities may require.	Treaty of May 7, 1868; eighteen installments, of $19,000 each, due, estimated.	Vol. 15, p. 551, §9.		342,000 00	

STATEMENT showing the PRESENT LIABILITIES of the UNITED STATES to INDIAN TRIBES under TREATY STIPULATIONS—Continued.

Names of treaties.	Description of annuities, &c.	Number of installments yet unappropriated, explanations, &c.	Reference to laws, Statutes at Large.	Annual amount necessary to meet stipulations, indefinite as to time, have allowed, but liable to be discontinued.	Aggregate of future appropriations that will be required during a limited number of years to pay limited annuities incidentally necessary to effect the payment.	Amount of annual liabilities of a permanent character.	Amount held in trust by the United States on which 5 per cent. is annually paid, and amount which, invested at 5 per cent., produce permanent annuities.
Crows	For pay of physician, carpenter, miller, engineer, farmer, and blacksmith.	Treaty of May 7, 1868	Vol. 15, p. 651, §9.	$4,500 00			
Do	Twenty installments, for pay of teacher and for books and stationery.	Nine installments, of $1,500 each, due.	Vol. 15, p. 651, §7.		$13,500 00		
Do	Blacksmith, iron and steel, and for seeds and agricultural implements.	Estimated at	Vol. 15, p. 651; §8.	2,000 00			
Gros Ventres	Amount to be expended in such goods, provisions, &c., as the President may from time to time determine as necessary.	Treaty not published (eighth article, July 13, 1868).			35,000 00		
Iowas	Interest on $57,500, being the balance on $157,500.		Vol. 10, p. 1071, §9			$2,875 00	$57,500 00
Kansas	Interest on $200,000, at 5 per cent.		Vol. 9, p. 842, §2.			10,000 00	200,000 00
Kickapoos	Interest on $93,581.00, at 5 per cent.		Vol. 10. p. 1079, §2			4,679 05	93,581 09
Klamaths and Modocs	Twenty installments, for repairing saw-mill, and buildings for blacksmith, carpenter, wagon and plow maker, manual-labor school, and hospital.	Six installments, of $1,000 each, due.	Vol. 16, p. 708, §2		6,000 00		
Do	For tools and materials for saw and flour mills, carpenter's, blacksmith's, wagon and plow makers' shops, books and stationery for manual-labor school.	Five installments, of $1,500 each, due.	...do		7,500 00		
Do	Pay of physician, miller, and two teachers, for twenty years.	Five installments, of $3,600 each, due.	Vol. 16, p. 709, §5.		18,000 00		
Miamies of Kansas	Permanent provision for smith's shops and miller, &c.	Say $411.43 for shop and $262.62 for miller.	Vol. 7, p. 191, §5			674 05	13,481 00
Do	Interest on $21,884.81, at the rate of 5 per cent., as per third article treaty of June 5, 1854.		Vol. 10, p. 1094, §3			1,094 24	21,864 81
Miamies of Indiana	Interest on $221,257.86, at 5 per cent. per annum. June 5, 1854.		Vol. 10, p. 1099, §4			11,062 89	221,257 86
Miamies of Eel	Permanent annuities.	Fourth article treaty of 1795; third	Vol. 7, p. 51, §4			1,100 00	22,000 00

Tribe	Object	Reference to treaty	Citation				
Molels	Pay of teacher to manual-labor school, and subsistence of pupils, &c.	Treaty of December 21, 1855	Vol. 12, p. 982, §2.	3,000 00			
Nez Percés	Sixteen installments, for boarding and clothing children who attend school, providing schools, &c., with necessary furniture, purchase of wagons, teams, tools, &c.	One installment of $2,000 due	Vol. 14, p. 649, §4.		2,000 00		
Do	Fifteen installments, for repairs of houses, mills, shops, &c.	One installment, of $1,000, due	Vol. 14, p.649, §5.		1,000 00		
Do	Salary of two matrons for schools, two assistant teachers, farmer, carpenter, and two millers.	Treaty of June 9, 1863	Vol. 14, p. 650, §5.	8,500 00			
Northern Cheyennes and Arapahoos.	Thirty installments, for purchase of clothing, as per sixth article treaty May 10, 1868.	Eighteen installments, of $12,000 each, due.	Vol. 15, p. 657, §6.		216,000 00		
Do	Ten installments, to be expended by the Secretary of the Interior, for Indians engaged in agriculture.	Eight installments, of $37,500 each, due.	....do		300,000 00		
Do	Pay of teacher, farmer, carpenter, miller, blacksmith, engineer, and physician.	Estimated at	Vol. 15, p.658, §7.	6,000 00			
Omahas	Fifteen installments, third series, in money or otherwise.	Two installments, of $20,000 each, due.	Vol. 10, p.1044, §4		40,000 00		
Do	Twelve installments, fourth series, in money or otherwise.	Twelve installments, fourth series, of $10,000 each, due.	....do		120,000 00		
Osages	Interest on $69,120, at 5 per cent., for educational purposes.	Resolution of the Senate to treaty, January 2, 1825.	Vol. 7, p. 242, §6.			3,456 00	69,120 00
Do	Interest on $300,000, at 5 per cent., to be paid semi-annually, in money or such articles as the Secretary of the Interior may direct.	Treaty of September 29, 1865	Vol. 14, p. 687, §1.			15,000 00	300,000 00
Ottoes and Missourias.	Fifteen installments, third series, in money or otherwise.	Two installments, of $9,000 each, due.	Vol. 10, p.1039, §4		18,000 00		
Do	Twelve installments, last series, in money or otherwise.	Twelve installments, of $5,000 each, due.	....do		60,000 00		
Pawnees	Annuity goods, and such articles as may be necessary.	Treaty of September 24, 1857	Vol. 11, p.729, §2.		30,000 00		
Do	Support of two manual-labor schools and pay of teachers.	......do	Vol. 11, p.729, §3.	10,000 00			
Do	For iron and steel and other necessary articles for shops, and pay of two blacksmiths, one of whom is to be tin and gun smith, and compensation of two strikers and apprentices.	Estimated, for iron and steel, $500; two blacksmiths, $1,200; and two strikers, $480.	Vol. 11, p.729, §4.	2,180 00			
Do	Farming utensils and stock, pay of farmer, miller, and engineer, and compensation of apprentices, to assist in working in the mill, and keeping in repair grist and saw mill.	Estimated	Vol. 11, p. 730, §4.	$4,400 00			
Poncas	Fifteen installments, last series, to be paid to them or expended for their benefit.	Eight installments, of $8,000 each, due.	Vol. 12, p. 997, §2.		$64,000 00		
Do	Amount to be expended during the pleasure of the President for purposes of civilization.	Treaty of March 12, 1868	Vol. 12, p. 998, §2.	10,000 00			
Pottawatomics	Permanent annuity in money	August 3, 1795	Vol. 7, p. 51, §4.			357 80	7,156 00
Do	do	September 30, 1809	Vol. 7, p. 114, §3.			178 90	3,578 00
Do	do	October 3, 1818	Vol. 7, p. 185, §3.			894 50	17,890 00

STATEMENT showing the PRESENT LIABILITIES of the UNITED STATES to INDIAN TRIBES under TREATY STIPULATIONS—Continued.

Names of treaties.	Description of annuities, &c.	Number of installments yet unappropriated, explanations, &c,	Reference to laws, Statutes at Large.	Annual amount necessary to meet stipulation, indefinite as to time, now allowed, but liable to be discontinued.	Aggregate of future appropriations that will be required during a limited number of years to pay limited annuities incidentally necessary to effect the payment.	Amount of annual liabilities of a permanent character.	Amount held in trust by the United States on which 5 per cent is annually paid, and amounts which, invested at 5 per cent, produce permanent annuities.
Pottawatomies	Permanent annuity in money	September 20, 1828	Vol. 7, p. 317, §2 ..			$715 00	$14,312 00
Do..............	......do	July 29, 1829	Vol. 7, p. 320, §2 ..			5,724 77	114,495 40
Do..............	For educational purposes, during the pleasure of the President.	September 20, 1828	Vol. 7, p. 318, §2 ..	$5,000 00			
Do..............	Permanent provision for three blacksmiths and assistants, iron and steel.	October 16, 1826; September 20, 1828; July 29, 1829.	Vol. 7, p. 296, §3; vol. 7, p. 318, §2; vol. 7, p. 321, §2.			1,008 99	20,179 80
Do..............	Permanent provision for furnishing salt	July 29, 1829	Vol. 7, p. 320, §2..			156 54	3,130 80
Do..............	Permanent provision for payment of money in lieu of tobacco, iron, and steel.	September 20, 1828; June 5 and 17, 1846.	Vol. 7, p. 318, §2; vol. 9, p.855, §10.			107 34	2,146 80
Do..............	For interest on $230,064.20, at 5 per cent.......	June 5 and 17, 1846	Vol. 9, p. 855, §7..			11,503 21	230,064 20
Pottawatomies of Huron.	Permanent annuities........................	November 17, 1808	Vol. 7, p. 106, §2..			400 00	8,000 00
Quapaws	For education, smith, farmer, and smith-shop during the pleasure of the President.	$1,000 for education, $1,060 for smith, &c.	Vol. 7, p. 425, §3..	2,060 00			
Sacs and Foxes of Mississippi.	Permanent annuity.........................	Treaty of November 3, 1804.......	Vol. 7, p. 85, §3.,.			1,000 00	20,000 00
Do..............	Interest on $200,000, at 5 per cent.............	Treaty of October 21, 1837	Vol. 7, p. 541, §2..			10,000 00	200,000 00
Do..............	Interest on $800,000, at 5 per cent.............	Treaty of October 21, 1842	Vol. 7, p. 596, §2..			40,000 00	800,000 00
Sacs and Foxes of Missouri.	Interest on $157,400, at 5 per cent.............	Treaty of October 21, 1837...........	Vol. 7, p. 543, §2..			7,870 00	157,400 00
Do..............	For support of school.......	Treaty of March 6, 1861	Vol. 12, p. 1172, §5		$200 00		
Seminoles..........	Interest on $500,000, eighth article of treaty of August 7, 1856.	$25,000 annual annuity.............	Vol. 11, p. 702, §8.			25,000 00	500,000 00
Do..............	Interest on $70,000, at 5 per cent	Support of schools, &c...........	Vol. 14, p. 757, §3..			3,590 00	70,000 00
Senecas...........	Permanent annuity	September 9 and 17, 1817......	Vol. 7, p. 161, §4; vol. 7, p. 179, §4.			1,000 00	20,000 00
Do	Smith and smith-shop and miller, permanent..	February 28, 1831.................	Vol. 7, p. 349, §4..			1,660 00	33,200 00

Do	Interest on $43,050, transferred from the Ontario Bank to the United States Treasury.	...do...	Vol. 9, p. 35, § 3			2,152 50	43,050 00
Senecas and Shawnees.	Permanent annuity	Treaty of September 17, 1818	Vol. 7, p. 179, § 4			1,000 00	20,000 00
Do	Support of smith and smiths' shops	Treaty of July 20, 1831	Vol. 7, p. 352, § 4	1,080 00			
Shawnees	Permanent annuity for education	August 3, 1795; September 29, 1817	Vol. 7, p. 51, § 4			3,000 00	60,000 00
Do	Interest on $40,000, at 5 per cent	August 3, 1795; May 10, 1854	Vol. 10, p. 1056, § 3			2,000 00	40,000 00
Shoshones, western band.	Twenty installments of $5,000 each, under the direction of the President.	Three installments to be appropriated.	Vol. 18, p. 690, § 7		15,000 00		
Shoshones, north-western band.	...do...	...do...	Vol. 13, p. 663, § 3		15,000 00		
Shoshones, Goship band.	Twenty installments of $1,000 each, under direction of the President.	...do...	Vol. 13, p. 652, § 7		3,000 00		
Shoshones and Bannocks: Shoshones	For the purchase of clothing for men, women, and children, thirty installments.	Nineteen installments due, estimated at $11,500 each.	Vol. 15, p. 676, § 9		218,500 00		
Do	For pay of physician, carpenter, teacher, engineer, farmer, and blacksmith.	Estimated	Vol. 15, p. 676, § 10	5,000 00			
Do	Blacksmith and for iron and steel for shops	...do...	Vol. 15, p. 676, § 8	1,000 00			
Bannocks	For the purchase of clothing for men, women, and children, thirty installments.	Nineteen installments due, estimated at $6,937 each.	Vol. 15, p. 676, § 9		131,803 00		
Do	Pay of physician, carpenter, miller, teacher, engineer, farmer, and blacksmith.	Estimated	Vol. 15, p. 676, § 10	5,000			
Six Nations of New York.	Permanent annuities in clothing, &c	Treaty, November 11, 1794	Vol. 7, p. 64, § 6			4,500 00	90,000 00
Sioux, Sisseton, and Wahpeton of Lake Traverse and Devil's Lake.	Amount to be expended in such goods and other articles as the President may from time to time determine, $800,000 in ten installments, per agreement February 19, 1867	Two installments, of $80,000 each, due.	Revised Treaties, p. 1051, § 2.		160,000 00		
Sioux of different tribes, including Santee Sioux of Nebraska.	Purchase of clothing for men, women, and children.	Nineteen installments, of $130,000 each, due; estimated.	Vol. 15, p. 638, § 10		2,470,000 00		
Do	Blacksmith, and for iron and steel	Estimated	...do...	2,000 00			
Do	For such articles as may be considered necessary by the Secretary of the Interior for persons roaming	Nineteen installments, of $200,000 each, due; estimated.	...do...		3,800,000 00		
Do	Physician, five teachers, carpenter, miller, engineer, farmer, and blacksmith.	Estimated	Vol. 15, p. 638, § 13	10,400 00			
Sioux of different tribes, including Santee Sioux of Nebraska.	Purchase of rations, &c., as per article 5, agreement of September 26, 1876.	...do...	Vol. 19, p. 256, § 5.	1,100,000 00			
Tabequache band of Utes.	Pay of blacksmith	...do...	Vol. 13, p. 675, § 10	720 00			
Tabequache, Muache, Capote, Weeminuche, Yampa, Grand River, and Uintah bands of Utes.	For iron and steel and necessary tools for blacksmith-shop.	...do...	Vol. 15, p. 621, § 9	220 00			

STATEMENT *showing the* PRESENT LIABILITIES *of the* UNITED STATES *to* INDIAN TRIBES *under treaty* STIPULATIONS—Continued.

Names of treaties.	Description of annuities, &c.	Number of installments yet unappropriated, explanations, &c.	Reference to laws, Statutes at Large.	Annual amount necessary to meet stipulations, indefinite as to time, now allowed, but liable to be discontinued.	Aggregate of future appropriations that will be required during a limited number of years to pay limited annuities incidentally necessary to effect the payment.	Amount of annual liabilities of a permanent character.	Amount held in trust by the United States on which 5 per cent. is annually paid, and amounts which, invested at 5 per cent., produce permanent annuities.
Tabequache, Muache, Capote, Weeminuche, Yampa, Grand River, and Uintah bands of Utes.	Two carpenters, two millers, two farmers, one blacksmith, and two teachers.	Estimated....................	Vol. 15, p. 622, § 15	$7,800 00			
Do.............	Thirty installments of $30,000 each, to be expended under the direction of the Secretary of the Interior, for clothing, blankets, &c.	Eighteen installments, each $30,000, due.	Vol. 15, p. 622, § 11		$540,000 00		
Do.............	Annual amount to be expended under the direction of the Secretary of the Interior, in supplying said Indians with beef, mutton, wheat, flour, beans, &c.	....	Vol. 15, p. 622, § 12	30,000 00			
Winnebagoes......	Interest on $804,909.17, at 5 per cent. per annum.	November 1, 1837, and Senate amendment, July 17, 1862.	Vol. 7, p. 546, § 4; vol. 12, p. 628, § 4.			$40,245 45	$804,909 17
Do.............	Interest on $78,340.41, at 5 per cent. per annum, to be expended under the direction of the Secretary of the Interior.	July 15, 1870....................	Vol. 16, p. 355, § 1.			3,917 02	78,340 41
Walpahpe tribe of Snakes.	Ten installments, second series, under the direction of the President.	One installment of $1,200 due.....	Vol. 14, p. 684, § 7.			1,200 00	
Yankton tribe of Sioux.	Ten installments, of $25,000 each, being third series, to be paid to them, or expended for their benefit.	Eight installments due, of $25,000 each.	Vol. 11, p. 744, § 4.			200,000 00	
Do.............	Twenty installments, of $15,000 each, fourth series, to be paid to them, or expended for their benefit.	Twenty installments, of $15,000 each, due.	....do			300,000 00	
Total......				1,435,780 00	10,414,536 24	360,585 16	6,341,303 26

INDEX.

I.—REPORT OF THE SECRETARY OF THE TREASURY.

Page.

AGRICULTURE, DEPARTMENT OF, estimated expenditures on account of, for the fiscal year ended June 30, 1882.. VIII

ALASKA:
  Alaska Commercial Company, seals taken by, during the fiscal year ended June 30, 1880.. XLVII
  a peaceful condition of affairs has prevailed in, during the past year, and why...... XLVI, XLVII
  a steam-vessel adapted to cruising in waters of, necessary to protect the interests of the Territory.. XLVII
  cruise of the revenue steamer Corwin in waters of, and result.......................... XLV
  death of natives by starvation... XLVII
  furs, the traffic in, the dependence of most of the inhabitants for a livelihood.......... XLVII
  government for, the adoption of some simple form of, desirable........................... XLVI
  seals, increased number of at the islands during the past year........................... XLVII

ANIMALS, LIVE, increase in exports of, during the fiscal year ended June 30, 1880, compared with the previous year... XXXII

ARREARS OF PENSIONS. (See Pensions.)

BANKS AND BANKERS:
  receipts from tax on, during the fiscal year ended June 30, 1880......................... XXX
  increase in receipts from tax on, during the fiscal year ended June 30, 1880, compared with the previous year... XXXI
  taxes on, proposed repeal of.. XXXI

BANKS, NATIONAL. (See National banks.)

BANKS, STATE, SAVINGS, and PRIVATE, average amount of capital invested by, for the six months ended May 31, 1880... XXV

BARGES. (See Vessels, merchant, of the United States.)

BOARD OF HEALTH. (See National Board of Health.)

BONDS:
  coupon, loss through the issue of duplicates of...................................XXV, XXVI
  expenditures on account of payment of premium on purchases of, during the fiscal year ended June 30, 1880... IV
  increase in expenditures on account of payment of premium on purchases of, during the fiscal year ended June 30, 1880, compared with the previous year........................ V
  for the sinking-fund, amount of surplus revenue applied to the redemption of, during the fiscal year ended June 30, 1880.. IV
  four-per-cent., amount of authorized and available for the redemption of five and six-per-cents... X, XI
  five-per-cent., maturing May 1, 1881, legislation required to enable the Department to avail itself of the option of redeeming... X
  five and six per-cent., bear a higher rate of interest than now ones can be sold at...... X
    delay in their redemption disadvantageous to the Government........................ X
    new legislation desirable authorizing the sale of other securities sufficient to redeem the whole sum of, soon to be redeemable.. XI
    redeemable at the pleasure of the United States, at maturity........................ X
    redemption of all of outstanding within a year feasible, with a consequent reduction of the interest on the public debt of $12,000,000 per annum................................ XII
    suggestions in regard to providing for the purchase of, by the issue of Treasury notes... XI, XII
    surplus revenue accruing prior to July 1, 1881, to be applied to purchase of......... X
  3.65, the issue of recommended to be applied to the payment of five and six-per-cents., redeemable on or before July 1, 1881.. XII
  held by national banks... XXV
  not due, the payment of premiums on purchases of, can, it is believed, be avoided by the issue of Treasury notes running from one to ten years.............................. XI
  the power granted to sell, will, in a supreme emergency, supply any possible deficiency of coin... XIV

BOUNTY-LAND SCRIP, amount of surplus revenue applied to the redemption of, during the fiscal year ended June 30, 1880.. IV

BUILDINGS. (See Public buildings.)

BULLION. (See Coins and coinage.)

BUREAU OF ENGRAVING AND PRINTING:
  established in its new quarters without any material delay to business.................. XXXVIII
  all the work of engraving and plate-printing required by the Department to be performed in the.. XXXVIII
  has peculiar facilities for executing work.. XXXVIII
  work can be executed in the with more safety and economy than elsewhere..XXXVIII, XXXIX

Page.

CANAL-BOATS. (*See* Vessels, merchant, of the United States.)
CATTLE, NEAT:
  exports of rapidly increasing... XXXIII
  pleuro-pneumonia among, a commission recommended to investigate reports of the ex-
    istence of..XXXIII, XXXIV
  remarks regarding the exportation of, and legislation on the subject of the prevalence
    of disease among recommended..XXXIII, XXXIV
CERTIFICATES, SILVER. (*See* Silver certificates.)
CIVIL EXPENSES:
  during the fiscal year ended June 30, 1880................................... III
  decrease of, during the fiscal year ended June 30, 1880, compared with the previous year.   V
  actual and estimated, for the fiscal year ending June 30, 1881.................... VI
CLAIMS, attention of Congress called to former recommendations of the Secretary in regard
  to the necessity of legislation for the proper adjudication of..............XXXVII, XXXVIII
COAST AND GEODETIC SURVEY:
  charts of, demand for greatly increased..................................... XL
  Coast Pilot, progress of the publication of................................ XL
  co-operation of with the Mississippi River Commission..................... XL
  information gathered by a comprehensive system............................ XL
  its work steadily advanced.. XL
  tide-tables printed for the use of navigators............................. XL
COINS AND COINAGE:
  bullion, amount of held for coinage in the mints and assay-offices on November 1, 1880..   XVIII
  gold, amount of remaining in the mints and New York assay-office, uncoined, at
    the close of the year.. XVI
  impracticability, a modification of the law, so as to authorize a charge for melting, re-
    commended.. XVI
  and coin, amount of deposited, and how paid for, during one year prior to No-
    vember 1, 1880.. XIII
  coin, decrease in receipts on account of premium on sales of, during the fiscal year ended
    June 30, 1860, compared with the previous year........................... V
  amount of in circulation in the country....................................XVII, XVIII
  the Treasury, in the banks, and in the hands of the people, on Novem-
    ber 1, 1880... XXIV
  available for the redemption of United States notes, dur-
    ing the year.. XIII
  gold, amount of deposits of, during the fiscal year......................... XVI
  circulation in the country on January 1, 1879...........................XVII, XVIII
  enters largely into general circulation.................................. XIII
  excess of imports over exports of....................................... XVII
  increase in amount of held by national banks since the day of resumption...   XXIV
  per cent. of customs receipts at the port of New York paid in, for one year
    prior to November 1, 1880... XIII
  many of the current payments from the Treasury necessarily made in.......... XIII
  reserve, in case of an adverse balance of trade, or a sudden panic, becomes the safe-
    guard of resumption... XXIV
  silver, excess of imports over exports of................................. XVII
  circulation in the country on January 1, 1879...........................XVII, XVIII
  increase of, and cause... XIII
  per cent. of customs receipts at the port of New York paid in, for one year
    prior to November 1, 1880... XIII
  total amount of in the Treasury at the close of business on November 1, 1880....   XIII
coinage, receipts from profits on, during the fiscal year ended June 30, 1880............   III
  decrease in receipts from profits, on during the fiscal year ended June 30, 1880,
    compared with the previous year.. V
  actual and estimated receipts from profits on, for the fiscal year ending June
    30, 1881.. V
  estimated receipts from profits on, for the fiscal year ending June 30, 1882..... VII
  amount of executed at the mints, during the fiscal year ended June 30, 1880..XV, XVI, XVII
  gold, made subordinate to that of silver, at the Philadelphia mint, and why....   XVI
  coin and bullion, amount of deposited, and how paid for, during one year prior to Novem-
    ber 1, 1880... XIII
  gold coin and bullion, amount of deposits of, during the fiscal year............ XVI
  excess in deposits of, during the fiscal year ended June 30, 1880,
    compared with the previous year.. XVI
  imports of, at the port of New York..................................... XVI
COIN RESERVE, suggestion that it be set apart for purposes of resumption.............. XIV
COLLISIONS AT SEA, the acceptance by statute of the regulations adopted by other nations for
  the prevention of, recommended.. XXXVI
COLOR-BLINDNESS:
  adoption of a rule for the examination of pilots for........................ XLVI
  number of pilots examined for, during the fiscal year ended June 30, 1880........ XLI
COMMERCE. (*See* Internal commerce.)
CONSULAR FEES. (*See* Fees, &c.)
CORN, increase in exports of, during the fiscal year ended June 30, 1880, compared with the
  previous year.. XXXII
COTTON, increase in exports of, during the fiscal year ended June 30, 1880, compared with
  the previous year.. XXXII
CURRENCY:
  amount of in the Treasury, in the banks, and in the hands of the people, on November
    1, 1880.. XXIV
  our present system of the best ever devised............................... XV
CURRENCY, FRACTIONAL, amount of surplus revenue applied to the redemption of, for the sinking-fund, during the fiscal year ended June 30, 1880........................ IV
CUSTOMS-REVENUE:
  receipts from, during the fiscal year ended June 30, 1880...................III, XXVIII
  increase of receipts from, during the fiscal year ended June 30, 1880, compared with the
    previous year..IV, XXVIII

	Page.

CUSTOMS REVENUE.—Continued.
expenses of collecting the, during the fiscal year ended June 30, 1880............................. IV
increase of expenses on account of collecting the, during the fiscal year ended June 30, 1880, compared with the previous year, and cause........................... XXVIII
actual and estimated receipts from, for the fiscal year ending June 30, 1881................ V
estimated receipts from, for the fiscal year ending June 30, 1882.................. VII
estimated expenses on account of collecting the, for the fiscal year ending June 30, 1882. VIII
fees, fines, penalties, &c., receipts from, during the fiscal year ended June 30, 1880...... III
discriminating duty on tea and coffee produced in the possessions of the Netherlands should be removed... XXIX
imposed by section 2501, Revised Statutes, on certain goods produced east of the Cape of Good Hope, when imported from west of that cape, might be removed...........................XXIX, XXX
duties ad valorem might be converted into specific............................ XXIX
frauds upon the have not, during the past year, been so extensive as formerly, by reason, it is believed, of the vigilance of the customs officers................ XXVIII
free-list, articles that might be added to............................ XXIX
principal articles from which the was derived, during the fiscal year ended June 30, 1880............................... XXVIII
New York, two-thirds of the business pertaining to transacted at the port of.......... XXXVIII
sugar, necessary legislation regarding the collection of duties on urged upon Congress. XXVIII
suits, great delay in their decision, owing to the multiplicity of cases............. XXXVIII
their speedy decision of great importance to both the Government and importers. XXXVIII
a special tribunal should be created for the trial of at the port of New York..... XXXVIII
tariff laws, suggestions regarding............................XXVIII, XXIX
DEBT. (See Public debt.)
DEPARTMENTS. (See Executive Departments.)
DISTINCTIVE PAPER:
adoption and manufacture of.................................... XXXIX
answers the requirements of the Government in every respect...................... XXXIX
its adoption a measure of economy as well as safety.......................... XXXIX
estimated saving on account of reduction in price of below that paid for the paper heretofore used...................................... XXXIX
DISTRICT OF COLUMBIA:
receipts from revenues of the, during the fiscal year ended June 30, 1880............. III
actual and estimated receipts from revenues of the, for the fiscal year ending June 30, 1881.. V
estimated receipts from revenues of the, for the fiscal year ending June 30, 1882...... VII
expenditures on account of the, during the fiscal year ended June 30, 1880........... IV
actual and estimated expenditures on account of the, for the fiscal year ending June 30, 1881.. VI
estimated expenditures on account of the, for the fiscal year ending June 30, 1882..... VIII
DUTIES UPON IMPORTS. (See Customs revenue.)
ENGRAVING AND PRINTING. (See Bureau of Engraving and Printing.)
EXECUTIVE DEPARTMENTS, estimated, itemized, expenditures on account of the, for the fiscal year ending June 30, 1882..................................... VII, VIII
EXPENDITURES:
ordinary, itemized, during the fiscal year ended June 30, 1880................ III, IV
items which show an increase in, during the fiscal year ended June 30, 1880, compared with the previous year............................ V
items which show a decrease in, during the fiscal year ended June 30, 1880, compared with the previous year........................... V
actual and estimated, for the fiscal year ending June 30, 1881...................... VI
estimated, itemized, for the several Executive Departments, for the fiscal year ending June 30, 1882.. VII, VIII
on account of the District of Columbia, during the fiscal year ended June 30, 1880..... IV
Indians, during the fiscal year ended June 30, 1880.................. III
payment of interest on the public debt, during the fiscal year ended June 30, 1880................................... IV
payment of premium on bonds purchased, during the fiscal year ended June 30, 1880.................................. IV
pensions, during the fiscal year ended June 30, 1880................ III
for miscellaneous objects, during the fiscal year ended June 30, 1880.......... IV
decrease in, during the fiscal year ended June 30, 1880, compared with the previous year.............................. VI
actual and estimated, for the fiscal year ending June 30, 1881............... VI
estimated, for the fiscal year ending June 30, 1882............. VII
EXPORTS OF MERCHANDISE:
during the fiscal year ended June 30, 1880.................. XXXI, XXXII.
articles which show an increase in, during the fiscal year ended June 30, 1880, compared with the previous year.......................... XXXI, XXXII
excess over imports of, for the fiscal year ended June 30, 1880............ XXXI, XXXII
excess over imports of, for the last five years..................... XXXII
proportion of, carried in American and foreign vessels, respectively, during the fiscal year ended June 30, 1880................... XXXV
FEES, &c.:
consular, increase in receipts from, during the fiscal year ended June 30, 1880, compared with the previous year................... V
letters patent, and lands, receipts from, during the fiscal year ended June 30, 1880............................ III
actual and estimated receipts from, for the fiscal year ending June 30, 1881......... V
estimated receipts from, for the fiscal year ending June 30, 1882............. VII
customs, receipts from, during the fiscal year ended June 30, 1880................. III
increase in receipts from, during the fiscal year ended June 30, 1880, compared with the previous year.................. V

Page.

FEES, &C.—Continued.
  customs, actual and estimated receipts from, for the fiscal year ending June 30, 1881...   V
    estimated receipts from, for the fiscal year ending June 30, 1882..............   VII
  steamboat, increase in receipts from, during the fiscal year ended June 30, 1880, compared with the previous year   V
FINES, &C., CUSTOMS:
  receipts from, during the fiscal year ended June 30, 1880   III
  decrease in receipts from, during the fiscal year ended June 30, 1880, compared with the previous year   V
FOREIGN INTERCOURSE:
  expenditures on account of, during the fiscal year ended June 30, 1880..............   III
  estimated expenditures on account of, for the fiscal year ending June 30, 1882.........   VII
FRACTIONAL CURRENCY. (See Currency, fractional.)
FRACTIONAL SILVER COIN. (See Minor coins.)
GOVERNMENT PROPERTY:
  receipts from proceeds of sales of, during the fiscal year ended June 30, 1880...........   III
  increase in receipts from proceeds of sales of, during the fiscal year ended June 30, 1880, compared with the previous year..   IV
  actual and estimated receipts from proceeds of sales of, for the fiscal year ending June 30, 1881...   V
  estimated receipts from proceeds of sales of, for the fiscal year ending June 30, 1882   VII
HARBOR AND RIVER IMPROVEMENTS. (See Military establishment.)
IMPORTS, DUTIES ON. (See Customs-revenue.)
IMPORTS OF GOLD AND SILVER, excess over exports of, during the fiscal year ended June 30, 1880   XVII
IMPORTS OF MERCHANDISE:
  during the fiscal year ended June 30, 1880 ....XXXI, XXXII
  increase in, during the fiscal year ended June 30, 1880, compared with the previous year...XXXI, XXXII
  excess over exports of, for the ten years previous to June 30, 1873 ....XXXI, XXXII
  proportion of, carried in American and foreign vessels, respectively, during the fiscal year ended June 30, 1880   XXXV
INDEPENDENT-TREASURY, amount of public moneys deposited, disbursed, and held by officers of, during the fiscal year ended June 30, 1880 ....XXV, XXVII, XXVIII
INDIAN AFFAIRS:
  expenditures on account of, during the fiscal year ended June 30, 1880..............   III
  increase in expenditures on account of, during the fiscal year ended June 30, 1880, compared with the previous year..   VI
  actual and estimated expenditures on account of, for the fiscal year ending June 30, 1881.   VI
  estimated expenditures on account of, for the fiscal year ending June 30, 1882..........   VII
INDIAN LANDS, increase in receipts from sales of, during the fiscal year ended June 30, 1880, compared with the previous year..   V
INDIAN TRUST-FUNDS, increase in receipts from interest on, during the fiscal year ended June 30, 1880, compared with the previous year...................................   V
INTEREST, PUBLIC DEBT:
  expenditures on account of payment of, during the fiscal year ended June 30, 1880   IV
  decrease in expenditures on account of payment of, during the fiscal year ended June 30, 1880, compared with the previous year.......................................   V
  actual and estimated expenditures on account of payment of, for the fiscal year ending June 30, 1881..   VI
  estimated expenditures on account of payment of, for the fiscal year ending June 30, 1882.   VIII
  reduction of, and cause   IX
  annual saving of $12,000,000 in payment of, feasible, and how   XII
INTEREST, PACIFIC RAILWAY COMPANIES:
  receipts from repayment of, during the fiscal year ended June 30, 1880   III
  decrease in receipts from repayment of, during the fiscal year ended June 30, 1880, compared with the previous year..   V
  actual and estimated receipts from repayment of, for the fiscal year ending June 30, 1881   V
  estimated receipts from repayment of, for the fiscal year ending June 30, 1882   VII
INTERIOR DEPARTMENT:
  increase in expenditures on account of the, during the fiscal year ended June 30, 1880, compared with the previous year..   V
  estimated expenditures on account of the, for the fiscal year ending June 30, 1882   VIII
INTERNAL COMMERCE:
  all the principal cities of the country brought into direct competition with each other, and cause of   XXXVI
  exceeds many times in value our foreign commerce.................................   XXXVII
  rapid increase in, would justify a liberal appropriation for the collection of information in regard to ....XXXVI, XXXVII
INTERNAL-REVENUE:
  receipts from, during the fiscal year ended June 30, 1880 ....III, XXX, XXXI
  increase in receipts from, during the fiscal year ended June 30, 1880, compared with the previous year..   IV, XXX, XXXI
  actual and estimated receipts from, for the fiscal year ending June 30, 1881..........   VII
  estimated receipts from, for the fiscal year ending June 30, 1882   VII
  items which show an increase and decrease in receipts, during the fiscal year ended June 30, 1880, compared with the previous year.............................XXX, XXXI
  taxes on certain articles, suggestions regarding the repeal of   XXXI
  tax rates imposed on spirits, tobacco, and fermented liquors, stability urged in the   XXXI
LANDS, PUBLIC. (See Public lands.)
LEGISLATION RECOMMENDED:
  bonds; that authority be given to sell at par an amount not exceeding $400,000,000 of, of the character of the four-per-cents now outstanding, but bearing a rate of interest of 3.65 per cent. per annum   XII
  books of the Treasury Department; that authority be given to reimburse the Treasury for certain unavailable amounts carried on the...................................   XXVII
  bullion, imported; that the law be so modified as to authorize a charge for the melting of.   XVI

Page.

LEGISLATION RECOMMENDED—Continued.
claims; that it be provided that no claim pending in any of the Executive Departments
shall be allowed unless presented for payment within six years after such claim first
accrued, with the usual exception in favor of those disqualified by age or otherwise
from presenting the claim within such time.. XXXVII
coins, minor silver; for the proper accommodation of in the several sub-treasuries .... XXVI,
collisions at sea; to accept by statute the regulations already adopted by other nations
for the prevention of.. XXXVI
customs, classification of duty; that, for the purpose of securing a greater uniformity in
the collection of duties on imports, the Secretary of the Treasury be authorized, in cases of variance between the appraised value or classification for
duty of similar merchandise at two or more ports in the United States, to
prescribe regulations under which the board of general appraisers, or a majority of them, shall decide upon the true dutiable value or classification of
such imports.. XXXVIII
discriminating duty; on certain goods produced east of the Cape of Good Hope,
when imported from west of that cape, section 2501
Revised Statutes, imposing such duty, might be re-
pealed... XXIX, XXX
on tea and coffee produced in the possessions of the Neth-
erlands should be removed.. XXIX
suits; that a special tribunal be created by law for the trial of at the port of
New York.. XXXVIII
sugar; for the more faithful collection of the duties on XXVIII
expenditures of the Government; that a permanent organization of an appropriation
committee for each House of Congress be established to examine.................... VIII
marine-hospital service; that provision be made for return to the marine-hospital fund
of the proceeds of sales of property purchased for or
produced from such fund... XLI
statutory provision be made for examinations for appoint-
ment and promotion in the medical corps of.................... XLI
section 4569 Revised Statutes, which requires a medicine-
chest to be kept on merchant vessels, be amended, by
providing that each vessel, before clearing, shall present
to the collector of customs a certificate of an officer of
the service that the medicine-chest is properly supplied XLII
a National Snug Harbor or Sailors' Home be established
for the reception of destitute American seamen .... XLI, XLII
the sale of effects of deceased seamen be authorized, and
that the proceeds of such sales, and the unclaimed money
of such deceased seamen, be carried to the credit of the
marine-hospital fund.. XLI
an appropriation be made for the relief of seamen ship-
wrecked in places beyond the reach of the life-saving
service.. XLII
to repeal section 1, act of March 3, 1875, directing the Secretary
of the Treasury to cause to be prepared a schedule of the
number of seamen required in the navigation of vessels of the
United States.. XLI
the "advance wages," authorised by section 4582, Revised
Statutes be abolished, and the form of "articles of agreement" in section 4612 Revised Statutes be amended accord-
ingly.. XLII
plouro-pneumonia; for the creation of a commission to investigate reports of the existence of among neat cattle.. XXXIII, XXXIV
public buildings; that Congress, having fixed upon such an amount as it may deem best
to expend upon, shall cut of that sum appropriate sufficient to complete those now in course of construction, and make a liberal appropriation for the work on those in certain cities named....................... XLIV
in authorising the erection of new buildings, consideration be given
only to those for localities where the rental paid for accommodations for Government offices represents a fair percentage on the cost
of the construction of suitable buildings.................................... XLIV
public moneys; to authorize the refund of moneys paid into the Treasury, in excess, by
receivers... XXVI
revenue-marine service; that an appropriation be made for the construction of two revenue-vessels to be stationed on the southern coast, and for the rebuilding of the
steamer Fessenden.. XLV
Treasury notes; that provision be made for the issue of $400,000,000 of, in denominations
not less than $10, bearing interest not to exceed four per cent. per annum, &c........ XII
LIFE-SAVING SERVICE:
assistance rendered to, by vessels of the revenue-marine service, during the fiscal year
ended June 30, 1880... XLV
attention called to recommendations in the report of the general superintendent, in relation to increasing the number of stations, &c................................... XLIII
casualties to shipping, and lives endangered and saved .... XLII, XLIII
estimated value of property involved in disasters to vessels, during the fiscal year ended
June 30, 1880, and percentage of saved and lost............................... XLIII
new stations put in operation during the year, and new districts organised............ XLIII
number of reported disasters to vessels, during the fiscal year ended June 30, 1880 ... XLII, XLIII
persons on board vessels shipwrecked during the fiscal year ended June 30,
1880, and percentage of lost and saved................................... XLII, XLIII
days' relief afforded shipwrecked persons, during the fiscal year ended June
30, 1880... XLIII
vessels totally lost, during the fiscal year ended June 30, 1880............... XLIII
operations of, during the past year, remarkable............................... XLII, XLIII

Page.

LIFE-SAVING SERVICE—Continued.
   recommended that the general superintendent be allowed to fix the compensation of surf-
     men, and why.. XLIII
   special attention called to crew at Point aux Barques XLIII
   the success of, during the past year, has excited attention abroad XLIII
LIGHT-HOUSE ESTABLISHMENT:
   expenditures for the, during the fiscal year ended June 30, 1880 IV
   assistance rendered to, by vessels of the revenue-marine service, during the fiscal year
     ended June 30, 1880 XLV
   continues in its usual satisfactory condition XXXIX
   electric light, experiments with, as an illuminant XL
   laws of sound, when acting through fog and snow, experiments to ascertain............... XL
   mineral-oil substituted for lard-oil as an illuminant XXXIX
   number of light-houses, river-lights, fog-signals, and buoys put in operation during the
     year XXXIX
   lights discontinued and changed during the year XXXIX
LIQUOR, FERMENTED:
   receipts from tax on, during the fiscal year ended June 30, 1880......................... XXX
   increase in receipts from tax on, during the fiscal year ended June 30, 1880, compared
     with the previous year.. XXXI
   tax imposed on, stability urged in the rate of... XXXI
LOANS:
   amount of surplus revenue applied to the redemption of, during the fiscal year ended
     June 30, 1880 IV
   decrease in receipts from premium on, during the fiscal year ended June 30, 1880, com-
     pared with the previous year V
MACHINERY AND IMPROVEMENTS AT NAVY-YARDS. (See Naval establishment.)
MARINE-HOSPITAL SERVICE:
   increase in amount of tax received, during the fiscal year ended June 30, 1880, com-
     pared with the previous year.. V
   expenditures on account of the, during the fiscal year ended June 30, 1880.............. XLI
   medicine-chest, provision of law relating to recommended to be amended XLII
   National Snug Harbor or Sailors' Home recommended to be established by law for the
     reception of destitute American seamen .... XLI, XLII
   pilots, examination of, for color-blindness, by surgeons of the service, during the fiscal
     year ended June 30, 1880 .... XLI, XLVI
   repeal of first section of act of March 3, 1875, regarding the preparation of a schedule of
     the average number of seamen required in the navigation of vessels of the United
     States, &c., recommended XLI
   sales of property, recommended that provision be made for return to the marine-hos-
     pital fund proceeds of covered into the Treasury XLI
   seamen, "advance wages" of recommended to be abolished XLII
     American, number of diminished from year to year, and remedy for suggested............. XLII
     increase in number of, treated during the fiscal year ended June 30, 1880, com-
       pared with the previous year.. XLI
     number of receiving relief, during the fiscal year ended June 30, 1880.................. XLI
     reduction of cost per capita in treatment of, during the fiscal year ended June
       30, 1880, compared with the previous year.. XLI
     renewal of recommendation made in last report relative to statutory provisions
       for appointment and promotion in the medical corps of the service XLI
     shipwrecked in places beyond the reach of the life-saving service, an appropria-
       tion for the relief of recommended.. XLII
     deceased, unclaimed money and effects of, sale of recommended to be author-
       ized, and proceeds of carried to the credit of the marine-hospital fund XLI
MERCHANDISE.
   exports and imports of, during the fiscal year ended June 30, 1880..................... XXXI, XXXII
   increase in exports and imports of, during the fiscal year ended June 30, 1880, compared
     with the previous year.. XXXI, XXXII
   exports, excess over imports of, during the fiscal year ended June 30, 1880 .... XXXI, XXXII
     for the last five years XXXII
   imports, excess over exports of, for the ten years previous to June 30, 1873 XXXII
     during the last year greater than any previous year.................................... XXXII
   articles which show an increase in the value of exports of, during the fiscal year ended
     June 30, 1880, compared with the previous year .. XXXII
     imports of, during the fiscal year ended June 30, 1880,
       compared with the previous year XXXII
   comparative value of exports and imports of, in American and foreign vessels, respect-
     ively, during the fiscal year ended June 30, 1880 XXXV
   specie, increase in exports over imports of, during the years from 1862 to 1879 XXXII
     excess of imports over exports of, during the fiscal year ended June 30, 1880 XXXII
MILITARY ESTABLISHMENT:
   expenditures on account of the, during the fiscal year ended June 30, 1880 III
   actual and estimated expenditures on account of the, for the fiscal year ending June 30,
     1881 VI
   estimated expenditures on account of the, for the fiscal year ending June 30, 1882 VII
MINOR COINS:
   amount of executed at the mints, during the fiscal year ended June 30, 1880 XVII
     coined previous to November 1, 1880.. XXII
     redeemed with lawful money XXII
   accumulated in the several sub-treasuries, legislation recommended for the proper dis-
     position of XXVI
   a legal tender only in sums not exceeding ten dollars XXII
   attention of Congress called to act of July 9, 1879, requiring the redemption of in law-
     ful money, and its repeal suggested .... XXI, XXII
   if classed as money to be redeemed, should be supported by a reserve.................. XXII
   intrinsic value of, compared with the standard silver dollar .... XXI, XXII
   old, probable amount of in circulation XXII

Page.

MINOR COINS—Continued.
should contain silver of approximate value to the standard coin XXII
the excess of, not needed for change, should be coined into standard dollars............ XXII
MISCELLANEOUS EXPENDITURES, estimated, for the fiscal year ending June 30, 1882.......... VIII
NATIONAL BANKS:
receipts from tax on circulation and deposits of, during the fiscal year ended June 30,
1880 III
increase in receipts from tax on circulation and deposits of, during the fiscal year ended
June 30, 1880, compared with the previous year IV
actual and estimated receipts from tax on circulation and deposits of, for the fiscal year
ending June 30, 1881... V
estimated receipts from tax on circulation and deposits of, for the fiscal year ending
June 30, 1882... VII
amount of public moneys deposited in, during the fiscal year ended June 30, 1880 XXV
average monthly amount of public moneys held by, during the fiscal year ended
June 30, 1880... XXVII, XXVIII
bonds held by.. XXV
capital stock of, on October 1, 1880 XXIII
circulation of, outstanding on October 1, 1880.. XXIII
deposits of .... XXIII, XXIV
doing business upon a specie basis XXIV
gold coin, increase in amount of held by, since the day of resumption XXIV
loans of .... XXIII, XXIV
number in operation XXIII
profit upon circulation of.. XXV
system of its fully realized the expectations of its founders XXV
taxes paid by, during the fiscal year ended June 30, 1880.................... XXV, XXX, XXXI
on, and proposed repeal of...................................IX, XXV, XXXI
NATIONAL BOARD OF HEALTH:
annual report of operations of, submitted to the Secretary of the Treasury XLIII
expenditures of, for the year ended September 30, 1880, and how used XLIII
disbursement of appropriation for, duty devolved upon the Secretary of the Treasury
in regard to..XLIII, XLIV
NAVAL ESTABLISHMENT
expenditures on account of the, during the fiscal year ended June 30, 1880 III
actual and estimated expenditures on account of the, for the fiscal year ending June
30, 1881... VI
estimated expenditures on account of the, for the fiscal year ending June 30, 1882 VII
NAVY DEPARTMENT:
decrease in expenditures on account of the, during the fiscal year ended June 30, 1880,
compared with the previous year V
estimated expenditures on account of the, for the fiscal year ending June 30, 1882...... VIII
NAVY YARDS. (See Naval establishment.)
NEAT CATTLE. (See Cattle, neat.)
NOTES, UNITED STATES. (See United States notes.)
OIL, MINERAL, substituted for lard-oil as an illuminant in the light-house service............ XXXIX
PACIFIC RAILWAY COMPANIES:
receipts from repayment of interest by, during the fiscal year ended June 30, 1880...... III
decrease in receipts on account of repayment of interest by, during the fiscal year ended
June 30, 1880, compared with the previous year V
actual and estimated receipts on account of repayment of interest by, for the fiscal year
ending June 30, 1881... V
estimated receipts on account of repayment of interest by, for the fiscal year ending
June 30, 1882.. VII
sinking-fund for, receipts on account of, during the fiscal year ended June 30, 1880 III
estimated receipts on account of, for the fiscal year ending June 30, 1882...... VII
PAPER. (See Distinctive paper.)
PENALTIES (internal revenue), receipts from, during the fiscal year ended June 30, 1880..... XXX
PENSIONS:
expenditures on account of, during the fiscal year ended June 30, 1880 III
increase in expenditures on account of, during the fiscal year ended June 30, 1880, compared with the previous year.. V
actual and estimated expenditures on account of, for the fiscal year ending June 30, 1881. VII
estimated expenditures on account of, for the fiscal year ending June 30, 1882............ VII
PILOTS, examination of for color-blindness ....XLI, XLVI
POST-OFFICE DEPARTMENT, estimated expenditures on account of the, for the fiscal year ending June 30, 1882.. VIII
PREMIUM ON BONDS PURCHASED, expenditures on account of payment of, during the fiscal
year ended June 30, 1880... IV
PROPERTY, GOVERNMENT. (See Government property.)
PROVISIONS, increase in exports of, during the fiscal year ended June 30, 1880, compared with
the previous year XXXII
PUBLIC BUILDINGS:
expenditures on account of, during the fiscal year ended June 30, 1880 IV
number of in process of construction, and estimated amount of appropriation available
for their completion..XLIV, XLV
progress of work on, during the fiscal year ended June 30, 1880.................XLIV, XLV
recommendations in regard to the completion of buildings now in process of construction, and also as to the erection of new ones XLIV
PUBLIC DEBT:
expenditures on account of payment of interest on the, during the fiscal year ended June
30, 1880.. IV
decrease in expenditures on account of payment of interest on the, during the fiscal year
ended June 30, 1880, compared with the previous year V
amount of reduction of the, during the fiscal year ended June 30, 1880.................. IV
actual and estimated expenditures on account of payment of interest on the, for the fiscal
year ending June 30 1881... VI

522 INDEX.

PUBLIC DEBT—Continued.

Page.

estimated expenditures on account of payment of interest on the, for the fiscal year ending June 30, 1882 VIII

amount of redeemable on or before July 1, 1881 X

an annual saving of $12,000,000 in interest possible, and how XI

principal, amount of paid since March 1, 1877 IX

should for surplus revenue be applied to the further reduction of the? IX

the redemption of a large portion of the, can be provided for by the issue of Treasury notes, running from one to ten years X

PUBLIC LANDS:

receipts from sales of, during the fiscal year ended June 30, 1880 III

increase in receipts from sales of, during the fiscal year ended June 30, 1880, compared with the previous year IV

actual and estimated receipts from sales of, for the fiscal year ending June 30, 1881 V

estimated receipts from sales of, for the fiscal year ending June 30, 1882 VII

increase in deposits by individuals for surveys of, during the fiscal year ended June 30, 1880, compared with the previous year V

PUBLIC MONEYS:

receipts from all sources, during the fiscal year ended June 30, 1880 XXV

amount of receipts and payments of, since the organization of the Government to the close of the fiscal year ended June 30, 1880 XXVI

defalcations, &c., of, in former years XXVI

monthly average of funds held by independent-treasury officers and national-bank depositaries, during the fiscal year ended June 30, 1880 .... XXVII, XXVIII

collected, held, and disbursed, without loss, during the fiscal year ended June 30, 1880 XXV

deposited with the States, under act of June 23, 1836 .... XXVI, XXVII

fractional silver coins accumulated in the several sub-treasury offices, legislation for the proper disposition of, recommended XXVI

money paid into the Treasury in excess by receivers, additional legislation to authorize the refund of, recommended XXVI

monetary transactions of the Government, officers through whom conducted XXV

proportion of receipts of deposited in independent-treasury offices and national-bank depositories respectively, during the fiscal year ended June 30, 1880 XXV

PUBLIC SERVICE, suggestions in regard to the XLVIII

PUBLIC WORK, estimated expenditures on account of, for the fiscal year ending June 30, 1882 VIII

RAILWAY COMPANIES. (See Pacific railway companies.)

RECEIPTS:

ordinary, itemized, from all sources, during the fiscal year ended June 30, 1880 III

increase of, during the fiscal year ended June 30, 1880, compared with the previous year .... IV, V

actual and estimated, for the fiscal year ending June 30, 1881 V

estimated, for the fiscal year ending June 30, 1882 VII

items which show an increase and decrease in, respectively, and amount of same, for the fiscal year ended June 30, 1880, compared with the previous year .... IV, V

amount of, since the organization of the Government to the close of the fiscal year ended June 30, 1880 XXVI

from customs, during the fiscal year ended June 30, 1880 XXVIII

internal revenue, during the fiscal year ended June 30, 1880 .... XXX, XXXI

miscellaneous sources, during the fiscal year ended June 30, 1880 III

REFUNDING:

bonds, four-per-cent., amount of authorized inadequate to the redemption of all the five and six-per-cents. maturing .... X, XI

five-per-cent. maturing May 1, 1881, legislation required to enable the Department to avail itself of the option of redemption of X

four and five-per-cent., redemption of all of outstanding, within a year, feasible, and how XII

five and six-per-cent. amount of four-per-cents. available for the redemption of bear a higher rate of interest than new bonds can be sold at X

delay in their redemption disadvantageous to the Government X

new legislation authorizing the sale of securities sufficient to redeem the whole sum of, soon to be redeemable, desirable XI

redeemable at the pleasure of the United States, at maturity X

3.65, the issue of recommended, to be applied to the payment of the five and six-per-cents. redeemable on or before July 1, 1881 XII

maturing December 31, 1880, will be paid from accruing revenue X

not due, the payment of premiums on purchases of can, it is believed, be avoided by the issue of Treasury notes running from one to ten years XI

public debt, amount of redeemable on or before July 1, 1881 X

Treasury notes, suggestions regarding the issue of, in payment of five and six-per-cent. bonds .... XI, XII

revenue, surplus, estimated amount of accruing prior to July 1, 1881, and to be applied to the purchase of X

sinking-fund, estimated requirements of the, for the ten fiscal years from 1882 to 1891 .... XI, XII

REFUND OF DUTIES (customs, internal-revenue, lands, &c.), estimated expenditures on account of, for the fiscal year ending June 30, 1882 VIII

RESUMPTION:

bonds, the power granted to sell will, in a supreme emergency, supply any possible deficiency of coin XIV

coin, total amount of in the Treasury at close of business November 1, 1880 XIII

many of the current payments from the Treasury necessarily made in XIII

and bullion, amount of deposited, and how paid for, for one year prior to November 1, 1880 XIII

reserve, suggested that it be set apart as a special fund for purposes of XIV

in case of an adverse balance of trade, or a sudden panic, becomes the sure safeguard of resumption XIV

RESUMPTION—Continued.
    currency of the United States, the present system of the best ever devised   XV
    customs receipts at the port of New York for one year prior to November 1, 1880, per-
        centage of, paid in gold coin, silver coin, silver certificates, and United States notes,
        respectively   XIII
    gold coin now enters largely into general circulation   XIII
    silver certificates paid for coin and bullion deposited   XIII
    specie payments, nothing has occurred since the last annual report to embarrass the
        maintenance of ....   XII XIII
    United States notes, amount of presented for redemption during one year prior to No-
        vember 1, 1880   XIII
                    coin in Treasury available for redemption of, during
                        the year   XIII
                    surplus revenue applied to the redemption of, during
                        the fiscal year ended June 30, 1880   IV
                    a marked preference shown for, in business transactions   XIII
                    legal-tender quality of, suggestions regarding ....   XIV, XV
                    paid for coin and bullion deposited   XIII
                    per cent. of customs receipts at the port of New York paid in, dur-
                        ing one year prior to November 1, 1880   XIII
                    readily taken at par with coin ....   XII, XIII
                    redemption of, in coin, makes them equal to coin, and of easy circu-
                        lation   XV
                    redeemed, should be temporarily held in place of coin paid out ...   XIII, XIV
                    superior convenience of, will make a greater demand for them than
                        for coin   XIV
                    the best circulating medium known   XIV
                    least burdensome form of debt, and why   XIV
                    entire amount of now outstanding can be maintained at par
                        with coin without new legislation   XIII
                    objections made to their issue, and answers to such objections.   XIV, XV.
                    while their redemption in coin is maintained, it is immaterial
                        whether they are a legal tender or not......................   XV
REVENUE:
    receipts from, during the fiscal year ended June 30, 1880...........................   III
    items which show an increase of receipts, and amount of same, during the fiscal year
        ended June 30, 1880, compared with the previous year.........................   IV, V
                    a decrease of receipts, and amount of same, during the fiscal year
                        ended June 30, 1880, compared with the previous year   V
    actual and estimated receipts for the fiscal year ending June 30, 1881..............   V
    estimated receipts, for the fiscal year ending June 30, 1882.........................   VII
    expenditures on account of collecting the, during the fiscal year ended June 30, 1880....   III, IV
    actual and estimated expenditures on account of collecting the, for the fiscal year end-
        ing June 30, 1881   VI
    estimated expenditures on account of collecting the, for the fiscal year ending June 30,
        1882   VIII
REVENUE, CUSTOMS. (See Customs-revenue.)
REVENUE, INTERNAL. (See Internal-revenue.)
REVENUE, SURPLUS:
    amount of, and how applied, during the fiscal year ended June 30, 1880..............   IV
    actual and estimated, provided for the sinking-fund, for each of the fiscal years 1880, 1881,
        and 1882   VIII
    estimated amount of accruing prior to July 1, 1881, and to be applied to the purchase of
        bonds   X
    how caused   IX
    should it be applied to the further reduction of the public debt?...................   IX
REVENUE-MARINE SERVICE:
    operations of, during the fiscal year ended June 30, 1880   XLV
    expenses of, during the fiscal year ended June 30, 1880   XLV
    cruise of the steamer Corwin in the Arctic Ocean, on the northern coast of Alaska, and
        result of   XLV
    merchant vessels, and value of cargoes of, &c., assisted by vessels of, during the fiscal
        year ended June 30, 1880..   XLV
    recommended that an appropriation be made for the construction of two revenue-vessels,
        and for rebuilding the steamer Fessenden......................................   XLV
    vessels boarded and examined by officers of, during the fiscal year ended June 30, 1880 ..   XLV
                    of, number of miles cruised by, during the fiscal year ended June 30, 1880   XLV
RIVER AND HARBOR IMPROVEMENTS. (See Military establishment.)
SAILING-VESSELS. (See Vessels, merchant, of the United States.)
SEAMEN. (See Marine-hospital service.)
SILVER BULLION:
    amount of purchased and coined into standard silver dollars, during the fiscal year ended
        June 30, 1880   XVIII
SILVER CERTIFICATES:
    paid for coin and bullion deposited..   XIII
    per cent. of customs receipts at the port of New York paid in, for one year from No-
        vember 1, 1880   XIII
SILVER COIN:
    excess of imports over exports of..   XVII
    amount of in circulation in the country...   XVIII
    per cent. of customs receipts at the port of New York paid in, for one year prior to
        November 1, 1880   XIII
SILVER DOLLAR. (See Standard silver dollar.)
SINKING-FUND:
    amount due the, for the fiscal year ended June 30, 1880   IV
                    of deficiency on account of the, for each fiscal year from 1874 to 1879 ....   VI, VII

524 INDEX.

SINKING-FUND—Continued.

Page.

estimated expenditures on account of the, for the fiscal year ending June 30, 1882 VIII

estimated amount due the, for the fiscal year ending June 30, 1881 VI

surplus revenue, amount of applied to the redemption of bonds for the, during the fiscal
year ended June 30, 1880 IV

fractional currency for the, during the fiscal year ended June 30, 1880 IV

actual and estimated, provided for the, for anch of the fiscal years 1880, 1881, and 1882 VIII

estimated requirements of, for ten years from 1882 to 1891, by fiscal years .... XI, XII

an amount sufficient to cover the existing deficiency can probably be applied during the fiscal year ending June 30, 1881 VII

provisions of the law relating to substantially complied with VI

SPECIE:

a large increase in the flow of into the country probable XXXII

excess of imports over exports of, during the fiscal year ended June 30, 1880 XXXII

increase of exports over imports of, during the fiscal years from 1862 to 1879 XXXII

SPIRITS:

receipts from tax on, during the fiscal year ended June 30, 1880 XXX

increase in receipts from tax on, during the fiscal year ended June 30, 1880, compared with the previous year XXX

tax on, stability urged in the rate of XXXI

STAMPS, INTERNAL-REVENUE:

receipts from, during the fiscal year ended June 30, 1880 ....XXX, XXXI

printing of transferred to the Bureau of Engraving and Printing ....XXXVIII, XXXIX

adhesive, proposed abolition of XXXI

STANDARD SILVER DOLLAR:

amount of coined, during the fiscal year ended June 30, 1880 XVII

represented by outstanding silver certificates XVIII

average cost of the silver in XX

bullion, amount of purchased and coined into, during the fiscal year ended June 30, 1880 . XVIII

expense of coinage of XX

inducements offered to facilitate the general distribution and circulation of, and result.. XVIII

intrinsic value of, compared with the minor coins ....XXI, XXII

it is found difficult to maintain in circulation more than 25 per cent. of XVIII

minor coins not needed for change should be coined into XIX

popular discrimination against, and reasons for ....XVIII, XIX

ratio for coinage of ....XX, XXI

reluctantly taken by the people XIX

recommended that the compulsory coinage of be suspended, or that the number of grains of silver in be increased XIX

total coinage of up to November 1, 1880 XVIII

STATE BANKS:

failure of to redeem their notes held by the Government ....XXVI, XXVII

tax on, suggestions regarding .... IX, X

STEAMBOAT FEES. (See Fees, &c.)

STEAMBOAT-INSPECTION SERVICE:

receipts from inspection of vessels and licensing of officers, during the fiscal year ended June 30, 1880 XLVI

surplus of receipts over expenditures, during the fiscal year ended June 30, 1880 XLVI

disbursements on account of, during the fiscal year ended June 30, 1880 XLVI

number and tonnage of vessels inspected, and officers licensed, during the fiscal year ended June 30, 1880 XLVI

increase in number and tonnage of vessels inspected, and officers licensed, during the fiscal year ended June 30, 1880, compared with the previous year XLVI

number of passengers carried, and lives lost by casualties, during the fiscal year ended June, 30, 1880 XLVI

pilots, number of examined for color-blindness, during the fiscal year ended June 30, 1880 XLI

rule relative to the examination of for color-blindness XLVI

amendments to the steamboat laws suggested by the supervising inspector-general XLVI

STEAM-VESSELS. (See Vessels, merchant, of the United States.)

SUGAR, legislation in the interest of the more faithful collection of the duties on, urged upon Congress XXVIII

SURPLUS REVENUE. (See Revenue, surplus.)

TAXES:

reduction of .... VIII, IX

internal revenue, arrears of, under repealed laws, receipts from, during the fiscal year ended June 30, 1880 XXX

on banks and bankers, increase in receipts from, during the fiscal year ended June 30, 1880, compared with the previous year XXXI

TAXES, NATIONAL-BANK. (See NATIONAL BANK.

TIDE-TABLES. (See Coast and geodetic survey.)

TOBACCO:

receipts from tax on, during the fiscal year ended June 30, 1880 XXX

decrease in receipts from tax on, during the fiscal year ended June 30, 1880, compared with the previous year, and cause of ....XXX, XXXI

tax imposed on, stability urged in the rate of XXXI

TONNAGE OF VESSELS entered at seaboard ports from foreign countries, during the fiscal year ended June 30, 1880 ....XXXIV, XXXV

increase of, entered at seaboard ports from foreign countries, during the fiscal year ended June 30, 1880, compared with the previous year ....XXXIV, XXXV

of the United States, amount of, at the close of the fiscal year ended June 30, 1880 ....XXXIV, XXXV.

entered at seaboard ports from foreign countries during the fiscal year ended June 30, 1880.... XXXV

Page.

TONNAGE OF VESSELS—Continued.
    of the United States, increase of, entered at seaboard ports from foreign countries, during the fiscal year ended June 30, 1880, compared with the previous year.. XXXV
TREASURY DEPARTMENT, estimated expenditures on account of the, for the fiscal year ending June 30, 1882.. VIII
TREASURY NOTES:
    suggestions regarding the issue of, in payment of five and six-per-cent. bonds.......... XI, XII
    a large portion of the public debt to be redeemed, can be provided for by the issue of.. XI
    the payment of premiums on purchases of bonds not due can be avoided by the issue of. XI
UNITED STATES NOTES;
    amount of presented for redemption, during one year prior to November 1, 1860........ XIII
    coin in Treasury available for redemption of, during the year................ XIII
    surplus revenue applied to the redemption of, during the year............... IV
    a marked preference shown for in business transactions.................... XIII
    legal-tender quality of, suggestions regarding .... XIV, XV
    paid for coin and bullion deposited................................ XIII
    per cent. of customs receipts at the port of New York paid in, during one year prior to November 1, 1880 XIII
    readily taken at par with coin .... XII, XIII
    redemption of, in coin, makes them equal to coin, and of easy circulation........ XV
    redeemed, should be temporarily held in place of coin paid out............. XIII, XIV
    superior convenience of will make a greater demand for them than for coin........... XIV
    the best circulating medium known............................... XIV
    least burdensome form of debt, and why......................... XIV
    entire amount of now outstanding can be maintained at par with coin without new legislation XIII
    objections made to their issue, and answers to such objections................ XIV, XV
    while their redemption in coin is maintained, it is immaterial whether they are a legal tender or not.. XV
VESSELS, MERCHANT, OF THE UNITED STATES:
    number and tonnage of, at the close of the fiscal year ended June 30, 1880 .... XXXIV, XXXV
    decrease in number and tonnage of, during the fiscal year ended June 30, 1880, compared with the previous year, and suggestions as to the policy to be adopted to restore. XXXIV, XXXV
    number and tonnage of, built during the fiscal year ended June 30, 1880 XXXIV
    decrease in the number and tonnage of built, during the fiscal year ended June 30, 1880, compared with the previous year XXXIV
    enrolled and licensed for the coasting trade and fisheries, number and tonnage of, at the close of the fiscal year ended June 30, 1880........................ XXXIV
    registered for the foreign trade, number and tonnage of, at the close of the fiscal year ended June 30, 1880 XXXIV
    entered at seaboard ports from foreign countries, during the fiscal year ended June 30, 1880... XXXIV, XXXV
VESSELS, REVENUE-MARINE, service performed by, during the fiscal year ended June 30, 1880. XLV
VESSELS, NAVAL. (See Naval establishment.)
WAR DEPARTMENT:
    decrease in expenditures on account of the, during the fiscal year ended June 30, 1880, compared with the previous year V
    estimated expenditures on account of the, for the fiscal year ending June 30, 1882..... VIII
WHEAT AND FLOUR, increase in exports of, during the fiscal year ended June 30, 1880, compared with the previous year XXXII
WOOL, increase in exports and imports of, during the fiscal year ended June 30, 1880....... XXXII
WORKS, public. (See Public works.)

TABLES ACCOMPANYING THE REPORT.*

TABLE A.—Statement of the net receipts (by warrants) during the fiscal year ended June 30, 1880.. 3
TABLE B.—Statement of the net disbursements (by warrants) during the fiscal year ended June 30, 1880 4
TABLE C.—Statement of the issue and redemption of loans and Treasury notes (by warrants) for the fiscal year ended June 30, 1880 6
TABLE D.—Statement of the net receipts and disbursements (by warrants) for the quarter ended September 30, 1880................................... 7
TABLE E.—Statement of outstanding principal of the public debt of the United States on the 1st of January of each year from 1791 to 1843, inclusive, and on the 1st of July of each year from 1844 to 1880, inclusive.............................. 8
TABLE F.—Analysis of the principal of the public debt of the United States from July 1, 1856, to July 1, 1880.. 10
TABLE G.—Statement of the receipts of the United States from March 4, 1789, to June 30, 1880, by calendar years to 1843, and by fiscal years (ended June 30) from that time..... 12
TABLE H.—Statement of the expenditures of the United States from March 4, 1789, to June 30, 1880, by calendar years to 1843, and by fiscal years (ended June 30) from that time 16
TABLE I.—Statement showing the condition of the sinking-fund from its institution in May, 1869, to and including June 30, 1880 20
TABLE K.—Statement showing the purchase of bonds on account of the sinking-fund during each fiscal year from its institution in May, 1869, to and including June 30, 1880..... 24
TABLE L.—Statement showing the purchases of bonds on account of the sinking-fund from November, 1879, to October 31, 1880................................. 27
TABLE M.—Statement of the outstanding principal of the public debt of the United States June 30, 1870 33
TABLE N.—Statement of 30-year six-per-cent. bonds (interest payable January and July) issued to the several Pacific railway companies under the acts of July 1, 1862 (12 Statutes, 492), and July 2, 1864 (13 Statutes, 359).................................. 45

526   INDEX.

TABLE O.—Statement showing the amount of notes, silver certificates, and fractional silver coin outstanding at the close of each fiscal year from 1860 to 1880, inclusive 48
TABLE P.—Statement showing the annual appropriations made by Congress for each fiscal year from 1873 to 1881, inclusive, together with the coin value of such appropriations computed upon the average price of gold for each year in question 49
TABLE Q.—Returns (by judgments) of the United States Court of Claims of proceeds of property seized as captured or abandoned, under the act of March 12, 1863, paid from July 1, 1879, to June 30, 1880 50
TABLE R.—Judgments of the United States Court of Claims for proceeds of property seized as captured or abandoned, under the act of March 12, 1863, rendered, but not paid, during the fiscal year ended June 30, 1880 50
TABLE S.—Receipts and disbursements of United States Assistant treasurers, and designated depositary at Tucson, Ariz., during the fiscal year ended June 30, 1880 50

II.—REPORTS OF TREASURY OFFICERS.

Commissioner of Internal Revenue 57–110
Alcohol:
  Bulk of, exported in 1878, 1879, and 1880 was produced in Northern Illinois, shipped at New York, and consigned to Marseilles 90
  Changes of sections 3287 and 3330 Revised Statutes allowing exportation of, in casks or packages of not less than ten gallons capacity, and further change recommended 87
  Exported, shipped to forty-four ports in 1879 and fifty-three ports in 1880 90
  Exportation of, to Bilboa and Palma during 1880 reached nearly 1,000,000 gallons to each port 90
  Exportation of, to Genoa, Gibraltar, and Valencia during 1880 exceeded 1,000,000 gallons to each port 90
  Fine grades of, are produced in distilleries, ready for use, without additional manipulation 93, 94
  Increase (2,036,728 gallons) over previous year in production of 88
  Increase (537,089 gallons) over previous year in quantity of, withdrawn tax-paid .. 91
  Increase (1,313,993 gallons) over previous year, in quantity of exported 90
  Increase (35,056 gallons) over previous year, in quantity of, remaining in warehouse at close of year 94
  No exportation of, during year in tin cans of ten gallons and upwards................ 87
  No foreign demand for, in cans of larger size than five gallons 87
  Withdrawn for scientific purposes and for use of United States, quantities of (23,048 gallons) 92
  Withdrawn for scientific purposes and for use of United States for 1879 and 1880, quantities of, compared (increase in 1880, 5,362 gallons) 92
Alcoholic vaporizing process in manufacture of vinegar:
  Great majority of manufacturers by this process follow a legitimate and honest business 62
  Low wines of 50 or 60 per cent. strength can be easily produced by it 62
  Low wines produced by it can be fraudulently removed and sold as distilled spirits without payment of tax 63
  Many manufacture vinegar by it for the purpose of defrauding the government out of its tax upon distilled spirits 62
Appropriation for salaries of officers, clerks, and employés in the office of Commissioner:
  Increase of $1,550 over appropriation for present year will give deputy commissioner and each head of division the salary to which he is entitled by law 75
Assessments:
  Amount of during the year by States and Territories 110
  Amount of, in each class and in all classes for the fiscal years ended June 30, 1879 and 1880, compared 109
  Reasons for increase or decrease in the amount of, in the several classes named during the past year 109
Banks and bankers, exclusive of national banks and savings banks:
  Average capital of, for twelve months ended May 31, 1877 and 1878 105
  Average capital of, for twelve months ended May 31, 1879 .... 101, 105
  Average capital of, for twelve months ended May 31, 1880 .... 102, 105
  Average capital of, invested in United States bonds for years ended May 31, 1877, 1878, 1879, and 1880 106
  Average deposits of, for twelve months ended May 31, 1877 and 1878 105
  Average deposits of, for twelve months ended May 31, 1879 .... 101, 105
  Average deposits of, for twelve months ended May 31, 1880 .... 102, 105
  Average taxable capital of, for twelve months ended May 31, 1879 101
  Average taxable capital of, for twelve months ended May 31, 1880 102
  Tax assessed on capital of, for twelve months ended May 31, 1879 104
  Tax assessed on capital of, for twelve months ended May 31, 1880 105
  Tax assessed on deposits of, for twelve months ended May 31, 1879 104
  Tax assessed on deposits of, for twelve months ended May 31, 1880 105
Banks and bankers, exclusive of national banks, but including savings banks:
  Average capital of, for twelve months ended May 31, 1880 103
  Average deposits of, for twelve months ended May 31, 1880 103
  Average taxable capital of, for twelve months ended May 31, 1880 103
  Average taxable deposits of, for twelve months ended May 31, 1880 103
Banks, savings:
  Average deposits of, invested in United States bonds, for the years ended May 31, 1877, 1878, 1879, and 1880 106
  Average deposits of, for years ended May 31, 1877 and 1878 105
  Average deposits of, for year ended May 31, 1879 .... 101, 105
  Average deposits of, for year ended May 31, 1880 .... 102, 105
  Average taxable deposits of, for year ended May 31, 1879 101
  Average taxable deposits of, for year ended May 31, 1880 102
  Tax assessed on deposits of, during twelve months ended May 31, 1879 104

Page.

Commissioner of Internal Revenue—Continued.

Banks, savings, having a capital stock:
  Average capital of, for twelve months ended May 31, 1877 and 1878 105
  Average capital of, for twelve months ended May 31, 1879 .... 101, 105
  Average capital of, for twelve months ended May 31, 1880 .... 102, 105
  Average capital of, invested in United States bonds, during years ended May 31,
    1877, 1878, 1879, and 1880 106
  Average taxable capital of, for twelve months ended May 31, 1879 101
  Average taxable capital of, for twelve months ended May 31, 1880 102
  Tax assessed on capital of, during fiscal year ended May 31, 1879 104
  Tax assessed on capital of, during fiscal year ended May 31, 1880 105

Bourbon whisky:
  Decrease (17,563 gallons) from previous year, in quantity of, exported 90
  Increase (7,747,856 gallons) over previous year, in quantity of, remaining in ware-
    house at close of year 94
  Decrease (6,827,067 gallons) over previous year, in production of 88
  Increase (1,601,050 gallons) over previous year, in quantity of withdrawn tax-paid .. 91

Cigarettes:
  Number of, removed for exportation during the year (41,107,360) 85, 96

Cigars:
  Imported during the year weighed 852,402 pounds, of which 41,369 pounds were ex-
    ported 80
  Imported during the year, withdrawn for consumption, weighed 811,073 pounds,
    estimated to be equivalent in number to 45,264,667 cigars 86
  Number of, removed for exportation during the year, 2,340,825 .... 85, 96
  Number of, imported during fiscal years 1879 and 1880 compared 80

Cigars and cigarettes:
  Production of, during fiscal years 1870 and 1880 compared 85
  Production of, during fiscal year 1880 85
  Receipts from, during the year ($14,922,038 68) 85
  Receipts from, during the year, $2,389,636.16 greater than receipts from same
    sources in 1879 85

Cigars and cigarettes in bond:
  Bonds given for exportation of, unaccounted for June 30, 1880, date of 96
  Exported and during the year accounted for, number of (30,372,306) 96
  Exported and unaccounted for June 30, 1880, number of (21,479,880) 96
  Removed for export and unaccounted for July 1, 1879, number of (8,903,875) 96
  Removed for export during the year, number of (43,648,905) 96

Cigars, manufacturers of:
  Distribution of, among the States and Territories 100
  Number of, in special-tax year ended April 30, 1879 (15,206) 100

Clerks, messengers, and janitors in the several collection districts:
  Number of (179) 74
  Schedule of salaries of 74

Collectors:
  All deficiencies in accounts of, occurring during past four fiscal years, have been
    paid 70
  As a body of officers, can hardly be improved upon in respect to integrity, intelli-
    gence, fidelity, and zeal in the performance of duty 70
  Basis of recommendation for salaries of, for current year 73
  Number of (126) 74
  Schedule of salaries of 73, 74

Collectors, deputy:
  Annual allowance for traveling expenses of 69
  Efficiency in work of policing their districts by, how promoted 69
  Manner in which they perform their duties, how ascertained 69
  More thorough system of work by, how secured 69
  Number of (949) 74
  Required to render pay accounts monthly instead of quarterly 69
  Schedule of salaries of 74

Collectors' offices:
  Effect on the service of quarterly examinations of 68
  Examination of, plan adopted in 1877 68
  How graded 69
  Number of, first-class, according to official standard (119) 69
  Object of making quarterly examinations of 58
  Official standard of first-class office 68, 69

Commissioner:
  Aggregate of present force in office of (193) 75
  Condition of the office of 70
  Officers, clerks, and employés in office of, commended for diligence, fidelity, and
    zeal in the performance of their duties 70
  Schedule of present force in office of 75

Commissioner, deputy:
  Salary of, should be increased, reasons why 75
  Compromise offers received and accepted 108
  Compromises after judgment 82

Dealers in leaf tobacco:
  Distribution of, among the States and Territories 100
  Number of, in special-tax year ended April 30, 1880 (3,538) 100

Dealers in leaf tobacco, retail:
  Distribution of, among the States and Territories 100
  Number of, in special-tax year ended April 30, 1880 (7) 100

Dealers in manufactured tobacco:
  Distribution of, among the States and Territories 100
  Number of, in special-tax year ended April 30, 1880 (365,490) 100

Page.

Commissioner of Internal Revenue—Continued.
Dealers, retail liquor:
  Distribution of, among the States and Territories 100
  Number of, in special-tax year ended April 30, 1880 (163,923) 100
Dealers, wholesale liquor:
  Distribution of, among the States and Territories 100
  Number of, in special-tax year ended April 30, 1880 (4,122) 100
Distillation of spirits, illicit:
  Appropriation for suppression of, why asked for 62
  Combined movement made by armed bodies of internal-revenue officers from West
    Virginia southward in January, 1880, for suppression of 61
  Effect of movement in January, 1880, for suppression of 61
  Precautions taken to prevent old offenders from resuming business of 61
  Probable future decrease in number of seizures and arrests for 61
  Statistics relating to operations for suppression of 61, 79, 80
  System adopted to prevent old offenders from resuming business of, has worked
    satisfactorily 61
Distilleries:
  Cost of production of spirits has been reduced in largest 93
  Quality of spirits produced, has been improved, in largest 93
Distilleries, grain:
  Number of, in districts where illicit distilling formerly prevailed—in 1880 (469); in
    1879 (380); in 1878 (177) 62
Distilleries, legal:
  Establishment of, where illicit distillation has prevailed, encouraged 61
  Policy adopted as to establishment of, in illicit distilling districts; reasons for 62
Distillery:
  Largest in United States in process of construction at close of fiscal year 1879, has
    been in operation during past year 92
District attorneys:
  Abstract of reports of 106–108
Drawback:
  Allowed on spirits, tobacco, cigars, fermented liquors, stills, machinery, and propri-
    etary articles during last two fiscal years, amount of 99
  No provision of law for allowance of, on overrun of stills exported 99
  On stills exported, authorized by section 3244 Revised Statutes as amended by sec-
    tion 16, act of March 1, 1879 99
Employés on stamp roll:
  Letter of the Secretary of the Treasury in relation to 63
  Effect of said letter 64
  Selection and employment of, by the officer who is held pecuniarily responsible for
    their conduct; suggestions in relation thereto 64
  Examination of records, and accounts of each collector 70
Ex parte depositions:
  Circular No. 174 changing system of deciding cases upon, quoted 67
  Enforcement of this circular has rendered evidence in certain internal-revenue
    cases more definite and satisfactory 67
  Passage of law providing for taking depositions for use in internal-revenue cases
    recommended in Annual Report for 1876 67
Appointments and removals of storekeepers, gaugers, and tobacco inspectors:
  Circular changing plan of, quoted 64, 65
  Correspondence respecting, is now carried on by the Secretary of the Treasury 65
  Made on recommendation of Commissioner of Internal Revenue for about twelve
    years, under plan adopted by Hon. Hugh McCulloch, Secretary of the Treasury .. 64
  Work of correspondence in relation to, can be better done by Commissioner of In-
    ternal Revenue; reasons stated 65
Fermented liquors:
  Aggregate number of brewers engaged in production of, during the special-tax
    year ended April 30, 1880 (2,741) 100
  Applications for drawback on, during the year more than four times greater than
    during previous year 96
  Deduction of 7½ per cent. on stamps for payment of tax on, allowed to brewers 96
  Distribution of brewers among States and Territories 100
  Distribution of dealers in, among States and Territories 100
  Foreign demand for, increasing 95
  Number of dealers in, during special-tax year ended April 30, 1880 (11,610) ... 100
  Production of, by fiscal years, from 1863 to 1880, table of 94
  Receipts from each source and aggregate receipts from all sources relating to, for
    last two fiscal years compared 94
  Tax on, prior to September 1, 1866, was paid in currency 95
  Tax on, since September 1, 1866, paid by stamps 95
Frauds upon the revenue:
  Accounts of expenditures for discovery of, and punishment for, are filed in Reg-
    ister's Office, are rendered monthly, and pass through all accounting officers of
    the Treasury Department 81
  By vinegar manufacturers, two methods of preventing 62
  Efforts of past four years for suppression of, substantially crowned with success .. 62
  Expenditures for discovery of, and punishment for, by collectors 80, 81
  Similar expenditures, by revenue agents 81
  Expenditures for examination of abstracts of books of dealers in leaf tobacco 81
  Expenditures for rewards for discovery of illicit distilleries 81
  Expenditures under circular No. 99 81
  Miscellaneous expenditures under appropriation 81
  Now confined to few localities 59
  Provision of section 5, act of March 1, 1879, has opened door to 62
  Statement of expenditures from appropriation for discovery of, and punishment
    for, submitted 80
  Total expenditures under appropriation ($74,797.97) 81

Page.

Commissioner of Internal Revenue—Continued.

Gaugers:
Fees of, not to exceed $5 per day... 75
Greater efficiency, uniformity, and accuracy in the work of, how secured.......... 69, 70
Number of (648).. 75

Gin:
Decrease (29,286 gallons) from previous year, in quantity of, remaining in warehouse at close of year.. 94
Increase (21,692 gallons) over previous year, in production of.................. 88
Increase (36,307 gallons) over previous year, in quantity of withdrawn tax-paid.. 91

Grape brandy:
Loss of, by regauge... 98
Quantities of, produced and bonded during fiscal years 1879 and 1880 compared..... 98
Quantities of, withdrawn tax-paid during fiscal years 1879 and 1880 compared...... 98
Quantity of, bonded and withdrawn from bond tax-paid and for export during the
year... 98
Quantity of, removed for export and unaccounted for July 1, 1879, and June 30, 1880.. 98

Heads of division:
Law creating office of, states what salary each shall receive.................... 75
No just ground for discrimination in salaries of........................... 75

High wines:
Decrease (2,693,263 gallons) from previous year in production of............... 88
Decrease (2,515,982 gallons) from previous year, in quantity of, withdrawn tax-paid. 91
Decrease (224,713 gallons) from previous year, in quantity of, remaining in warehouse at close of year... 94
Increase (3,158 gallons) over previous year, in quantity of, exported............ 90

Inspection of officers:
Design of the system of... 69

Interest tax under joint resolution of Congress extending warehousing period to three
years:
Amount of, collected during the year ($158,994.41)........................... 91

Internal revenue:
Amount of, collected and accounted for during last four fiscal years ($467,080,985). 70
Amount of, collected and paid into Treasury during past year ($123,981,916.10).... 70, 72
Amount of, collected and reported to Commissioner by the several collectors during
the year... 71, 72
Cost of collecting, during the year, detailed statement of...................... 73
Estimated expenses of collecting, for fiscal year ending June 30, 1892.......... 73
Estimate of aggregate receipts of, for current fiscal year, under present laws
($135,000,000)... 59
Increase ($3,658,213.48) in aggregate receipts of, during first four months of current fiscal year... 59, 83
Increase ($2,795,458.01) in aggregate receipts of, during fiscal year 1879 over 1878 ... 59
Increase ($40,532,294.72) in aggregate receipts of, during fiscal year 1880 over 1879 .. 59
Officers of, judged by the rule that fidelity in accounting for public funds is one of
the highest tests of efficiency, are entitled to high rank..................... 70
Percentage cost of collecting during the year (3. 63-100)..................... 73
Receipts of, from the several objects of taxation for the first four months of the
fiscal years ending June 30, 1880 and 1881, compared....................... 83
Judgments.. 107, 106

Laws, internal revenue:
Hearty co-operation of officers charged with enforcement of, will soon establish
authority of government for collecting its taxes in all parts of the country 59
Legislation recommended:
Allowing change in the form of cigar stamps 87
Appropriation for the suppression of illicit distilling...................... 62
Appropriating $254,860 for salaries of officers, clerks, and employés in the office of
Commissioner.. 75
Authorizing the exportation of tobacco, snuff and cigars, by railroad or other land
conveyances... 97
For amendment of section 3689 Revised Statutes, so as to provide for the payment
of drawback on all articles exported under provisions of section 3324 and 3329.. 99
For protection of lives and persons of United States officers, in performance of their
official duties... 62
House bill No. 6460 entitled "A bill to regulate the manufacture of vinegar by the
alcoholic vaporizing process"... 62
Providing for drawback on worms exported since March 1, 1879.............. 99
Providing for exportation of alcohol in metallic cans of five gallons and upwards.. 87
Providing for exportation of fermented liquors in bond..................... 95
Providing for sale of real estate belonging to United States after it has been held
eight or ten years... 82
Repealing part of section 17, act of March 1, 1879, which prohibits redemption of
stamps unless presented within three years after purchase from government..... 78
Suggesting, if taxation is to be reduced, the repeal of the tax on matches, patent
medicines, &c., bank capital and deposits and bank checks.................. 60

Manufacturers of matches:
Probably use a few general proprietary stamps 78

Manufacturers of tobacco:
Distribution of, among the States and Territories 100
Number of (1,005)... 100

Manufacturing warehouses:
Amendment by section 14, act May 28, 1880, of section 20, act March 1, 1879, providing for transfer of spirits to, quoted.................................... 91, 92
Effect of the amendment.. 92
Quantity of spirits transferred to, during fiscal year 1879 (13,213 gallons)......... 92
Quantity of spirits transferred to, during fiscal year 1880 (218,212 gallons)........ 92

34 F

Page.

Commissioner of Internal Revenue—Continued.
Manufacturing warehouses—Continued.
Quantity of spirits transferred to, during fiscal years 1879 and 1880, not fair indica-
tion of what will hereafter annually be withdrawn under the act as amended ...   92
Section 14, act of May 28, 1880, provides for transfer of all kinds of distilled spirits to   92
Section 15, act of May 28, 1880, provides for allowance for loss by unavoidable acci-
dent in transfer of spirits to   92
Section 14, act of May 24, 1880, provides for use of spirits in, in all articles author-
ized to be made in such warehouses..   92
Spirits withdrawn from distillery warehouse for transfer to, prior to passage of
act of May 28, 1880, limited to alcohol   92
Medical bitters:
Containing more than 20 per cent. of proof spirits should remain subject to stamp
tax   60
Notes, circulating, of corporations and individuals:
Amount of assessments on, during past fiscal year ($461,597.82)   61
Disposition of individuals and corporations to flood the country with "shinplas-
ter" circulation   61
Motive for issuing...   61
Increase ($453,355.20) of assessments on, over assessments of previous year   61
Laws respecting; should not be repealed   61
Peddlers of tobacco:
Distribution of, among the States and Territories   100
Number of, in special-tax year ended April 30, 1880 (1,680)   100
Ports to which spirits were exported:
Number of, in 1879 (54)..   90
Number of, in 1880 (71)...   90
Proprietary articles in bond:
Amount of tax on, accounted for as exported ($206,412.94)   97
Amount of tax on, bonded during the year ($235,512.48)   97
Amount of tax on, unaccounted for June 30, 1879 ($19,146.24)   97
Amount of tax on, unaccounted for June 30, 1880 ($29,245.76)   97
Amount of tax on, withdrawn for export ($245,658.76)   97
Prosecutions for technical violations of law:
Letter to prevent, addressed to collectors, April 25, 1878   58
Principle of letter for preventing, recently embodied in instructions to district at-
torneys and United States marshals   58
Number of, less than formerly   58
Prosecutions in State courts:
Number of, during the three fiscal years previous to the last (165)   80
Number of, during the last fiscal year (48)   80
Number of, during the last fiscal year, by collection districts   80
Railroad companies:
Amount of taxes accrued under former laws, collected from, during past four fiscal
years, statement of   82
Number of, from which collections were received (20)   82
Real estate belonging to the United States, acquired under internal-revenue laws:
Efforts made to sell   82
Much of, owned by government for a number of years   82
No immediate prospect of sale of, at a fair valuation   82
Suggestion as to providing by law for sale of   82
Value of (about $500,000)   82
Rectifiers:
Distribution of, among the States and Territories   100
Number of, during special-tax year ended April 30, 1880 (1,291)   100
Relatives in office:
Circular letter No. 44 respecting, approved by Hon. R. C. McCormick, Acting Secre-
tary   66
Principle of this letter approved by the public   67
Repeal of taxes upon bank checks, capital, and deposits, friction matches, patent medi-
cines, preparations, &c., suggestions respecting..   60
Revenue agents:
Distribution of   78
Have brought to the discharge of their duties a high order of intelligence, experi-
ence, and zeal   78
Number of, employed during the year (35)   78
Salaries and expenses of, during the year   78
Work performed by, during the year   70
Rum:
Increase (125,846 gallons) over previous year, in production of   88
Increase (108,792 gallons) over previous year, in quantity of withdrawn tax-paid ...   91
Increase (85,861 gallons) over previous year, in quantity of, exported   90
Increase (54,164 gallons) over previous year, in quantity of, remaining in warehouse
at close of year   94
Rye whisky:
Decrease (5,613 gallons) from previous year, in quantity of, exported   90
Increase (3,492,925 gallons) over previous year, in quantity of, remaining in warehouse
at close of year   94
Increase (2,340,943 gallons) over previous year, in production of   88
Increase (750,208 gallons) over previous year, in quantity of, withdrawn tax-paid ...   91
Seizures, abstract of..   100
Service, internal-revenue:
Efforts to improve in six particulars..   66
Enforcement of circular letter No. 44 beneficial to   67
Further improvement in condition of, since last annual report   59
Important part of work of   69
Present condition of   59

	Page.
Commissioner of Internal Revenue—Continued.	
Special bonded warehouses for storage of grape brandy:	
Grape brandy in warehouse June 30, 1880, distribution of, among	98
Names of proprietors of	98
Quantity of grape brandy remaining in, July 1, 1879, and June 30, 1880	98
Special-tax payers:	
Distribution of, among the States and Territories	100
Number of, in the several classes	100
Spirits:	
Acts providing for loss of, during transportation, for removing restriction as to size of exported packages of, and as to the thousand gallons limitation—passed upon recommendation of the Commissioner	90
Allowed for loss by leakage in transportation from December 29, 1879, to close of fiscal year (4,434 gallons)	87
Allowed for loss by leakage or evaporation in warehouse during first four months of current fiscal year (271,169 gallons) and during June, 1880 (75,874 gallons)	93
Amendments of internal-revenue laws, relating to, have aided in securing four results	88
Apparent overproduction of	88
Attention called in last annual report to deficiency taxes on spirits withdrawn for exportation and to complaints of distillers and others as to hardship of paying such taxes	87
Causes of increase in production of	88
Effect of regulation authorizing railroad and other transportation companies to become sureties for exporters of	90
Exportation of, encouraged by the Internal Revenue Office	90
Exporters relieved from deficiency taxes on, in accordance with recommendation of Commissioner, by act of December 20, 1879	87
Exported each year, quantity of, greater than during preceding year	90
Foreign demand for, increasing	90
Production of, during the year (90,355,170 gallons)	89
Production of, during last two fiscal years compared	88
Railroad and other transportation companies authorized to become sureties for exporters of	90
Receipts from each source relating to, for fiscal years 1879 and 1880 compared	89
Removed in bond for export during the year, quantities of (16,765,666 gallons)	89
Removed in bond for export by fiscal years, from 1873 to 1880, percentages of quantities of, to production	89
Removed in bond for export by fiscal years, from 1873 to 1880, quantities of	89
Withdrawn tax-paid during the fiscal years 1879 and 1880, quantities of, compared	90
Spirits, different kinds of:	
Decrease during fiscal year 1880, as compared with 1879, in quantities of, exported	90
Increase during fiscal year 1880, as compared with 1879, in quantities of, exported	90
Increase during fiscal year 1880, as compared with 1879, in quantities of, produced	88
Increase during fiscal year 1880, as compared with 1879, in quantities of, withdrawn from warehouse on payment of the tax	91
Increase in quantities of, in warehouse June 30, 1880, over quantities in warehouse June 30, 1879	94
Spirits exported:	
Bulk of, in fiscal years 1878, 1879, and 1880, was alcohol	90
During the year, quantities of (16,765,666 gallons)	80
Spirits in warehouse:	
Business of selling, since extension of bonded period, has largely increased	93
Greater portion of, owned by dealers in various parts of the country	93
Spirits in warehouse at close of the year:	
Causes of increase in quantities of, in 1880 over 1879, same as referred to in last year's report, illustrated	93
Increase in quantity of, for 1880 over 1879, was mainly on bourbon and rye whiskies	94
Nearly nine-tenths of quantity of, for 1880, was bourbon and rye whiskies	94
Quantity of, for 1880, greater than for any previous year	93
Quantity of each month's production of, for 1880	91
Quantity of each month's production of, withdrawn during the year	91
Quantity of, for 1879 (19,219,470 gallons)	91
Quantity of, from 1869 to 1880, statement of	93
Spirits lost by casualty:	
Percentage of quantity of, to total on deposit during fiscal year 1880, about one seventy-seventh of 1 per cent	92
Quantity of, for fiscal year 1880 (14,231 gallons)	92
Quantity of, less in 1880 than in 1879	92
Quantity of, on which tax was abated during the year (4,276 gallons)	92
Spirits on deposit in distillery warehouses:	
Attention again called to diligence of distillers and government officers in preservation of	92
Fire insurance on, might safely be fixed at the very lowest rate	92
Quantity of, during the year (109,567,740 gallons)	92
Spirits, pure, neutral, or cologne:	
Are produced in distilleries ready for use without additional manipulation	94
Decrease (158,061 gallons) from previous year in quantity of, remaining in warehouse at close of year	94
Increase (548,908 gallons) over previous year in quantity of, exported	90
Increase (7,198,469 gallons) over previous year in production of	88
Increase (8,866,999 gallons) over previous year in quantity of, withdrawn tax-paid	91
Spirits, tobacco, and fermented liquors:	
Estimated annual receipts from	60

Commissioner of Internal Revenue—Continued.   Page.
Stamps, internal-revenue:
    Amount of claims for exchange of, allowed ($30,988.29)   78
    Amount of claims for redemption of, allowed ($32,361.67)   78
    Commissioner charged with all stamps delivered to him and credited with all
        stamps issued and sold   63
    Commissioner of Internal Revenue charged with duty of procuring and issuing....   63
    Commissioner personally liable for safe keeping and proper issue of   63
    Commissioner, prior to June 28, 1880, employed force to perform work of receiving
        and issuing   63
    Face value of, sold to match manufacturers during last five years   78
    Kind of, printed by American Bank-Note Company prior to October 15, 1880.......   77
    Kind of, printed by Bureau of Engraving and Printing   77
    Kind of, printed by Graphic Company   77
    Kind of, printed by Mr. John J. Crooks..   77
    Most of, are issued by Commissioner to collectors, who sell them to tax-payers   63
    Most of, produced by Bureau of Engraving and Printing   63
    Nearly $534,000,000 worth of, have been issued from Internal Revenue Office since
        September, 1877   63
    New contract for furnishing paper for, again awarded to Messrs. S. D. Warren
        & Co. May 24, 1880   77
    No loss of, during the year...   77
    Number of claims for exchange of, allowed (292)   78
    Number of claims for redemption of, allowed (590).................................   78
    Number of, issued during the year ($11,602,614)....................................   77
    Number of packages of, issued to collectors by registered mail (18,547)...........   77
    Number of persons employed in work of receiving, issuing, and salaries paid
        them, fixed by direction of the honorable Secretary of the Treasury............   63
    Orders under contract for furnishing paper for, are executed with promptness   77
    Paper for, furnished, satisfactory as to quality   77
    Prices paid for paper for, under present and previous contracts   77
    Received from printers, and issued to collectors, agents, and purchasers   77
    Sales to match manufacturers on sixty days' credit   76
    Thanks due to officers of Washington City post-office for promptness and fidel-
        ity in handling registered packages of   77
    Thirteen suits pending for recovery of $117,413.01, due on sale of, to match manu-
        facturers   78
    Value of, issued during the year ($134,942,860.17).................................   77
Stamps, spirit, other than tax-paid and export stamps:
    Change to account by repeal of charge for, how made   78
    Collectors, with one exception allowed credit for, in their hands when the act of
        May 28, 1880, took effect...   78
    Repeal of charge of ten cents for, by act of May 28, 1880   78
Statistics relating to seizures, judgments, compromises, criminal actions, civil actions
    in personam, actions in rem, &c.. 106–108
Stills, manufacturers of:
    Distribution of, among the States and Territories   100
    Number of, in special-tax year ended April 30, 1880 (35)..........................   100
Storekeepers:
    Have improved in diligence and efficiency   70
    Number of (543)   75
    Pay of, not over $4 per day..   75
Storekeepers and gaugers:
    Number of (945)   75
    Pay of, not over $4 per day..   75
    Value of, to government service, how estimated   69
Suits commenced, pending, and disposed of 106, 107
Suits against ex-collectors:
    Amount of judgments rendered in cases of..   82
    List of..   82
Tables:
    Titles of, for fiscal year 1880 and years previous................................   110
Taxation, internal-revenue:
    Should be limited as soon as interests of government will allow, to spirits, malt
        liquors, tobacco, snuff, cigars, and special taxes upon manufacturers and dealers
        in these articles   60
Tobacco:
    Estimated receipts from all sources relating to, had there been no reduction in the
        rates under act of March 1, 1879 ($50,000,000)   86
    Receipts from all sources relating to, during last fiscal year ($38,870,140.09)....   84
    Receipts from all sources relating to, during the year $1,264,662.57 less than during
        the year 1879   84
    Receipts from each source and from all sources relating to, during fiscal years 1879
        and 1880 compared   84
Tobacco inspectors:
    Fees of, paid by manufacturers..   75
    Number of (56)   75
Tobacco, leaf:
    Aggregate quantity of, accounted for during the year (439,272,094 pounds)........   86
    Basis of estimate of quantity of, used in manufacture of, tobacco, snuff, cigars, and
        cigarettes, during the year...   86
    Estimate of quantity of, used in the manufacture of cigars and cigarettes during the
        year   86
    Estimate of quantity of, used in the manufacture of tobacco and snuff during the
        year   86
    Quantity of, exported during the year...   86
    Quantity of, imported, used during the year.......................................   86

Page.

Commissioner of Internal Revenue—Continued.
 Tobacco, manufactured, and snuff :
  Consumption of, during year would probably have been about the same had there
   been no reduction in the rate of tax 86
  Decrease in receipts from, in consequence of reduction of the rate of tax on, under
   act of March 1, 1879 86
  Effect of reduction of the rate of tax on, by act of March 1, 1879, how determined . 85, 86
  Estimated receipts from, during the year, had there been no reduction in the rate of
   tax (over $33,000,000) 86
  Increase in consumption of, how accounted for 86
  Quantities of, on which tax was paid during the year (tobacco, 130,309,527 pounds;
   snuff, 3,966,368 pounds) 85
  Production of, during fiscal years 1879 and 1880 compared 85
  Receipts from, on quantities returned for tax would have been $33,023,505.04, had
   there been no reduction in the rate of tax 85
  Receipts from, removed for consumption during the year compared with receipts
   from same source in 1878 and 1879 85
 Tobacco manufactured, snuff and cigars in bond :
  Effect of amendment of section 3385 Revised Statutes, passed June 9, 1880, governing
   exportation of 97
  Part of section 3385, authorizing exportation of, by railroad cars and other land con-
   veyances, inadvertently left out when section was amended June 9, 1880 97
  Provisions of amendment of section 3385 Revised Statutes, governing exportation of . 97
 Tobacco manufactured and snuff in bond :
  Bonds given for exportation of, unaccounted for June 30, 1880, years in which given . 96
  Exported. and during the year accounted for, quantities of (10,125,349 pounds) 95
  Removed for export and unaccounted for July 1, 1879, quantities of (5,358,844½ pounds) 95
  Removed for export and unaccounted for June 30, 1880, quantities of (5,041,704½
   pounds) 95
  Removed for export by fiscal years, from 1873 to 1880, percentages of, to production . 89
  Removed for export by fiscal years, from 1873 to 1880, quantities of 89
  Removed for export during fiscal year 1880, quantities of (9,808,408½ pounds) 95
  Removed for export during fiscal years 1879 and 1880, quantities of, compared 96
 Tobacco, snuff, cigars, and cigarettes:
  Receipts from, during the year ($36,726,852.02) 85
  Receipts from, during the year, $1,411,610.35 less than receipts from same sources
   in 1879 85
 Work :
  Performed by the several divisions in the office of the Commissioner during the
   year, statement of 75–77
Comptroller of the Currency 111–172
 Report submitted for consideration of Congress 113
 National banks organized during the year 113
 National banks failed during the year, and dividends paid to their creditors 113
 National banks which have voluntarily discontinued business during the year........ 113
 Total number of national banks organized, liquidated, and closed, to November 1, 1880. 113
 States in which national banks are located 113
 States which have the largest national-bank capital 113
 Number of national gold banks organized, and number in operation, with their capital
  and circulation 113
 Bill for repeal of provision of law, limiting ratio of circulation authorized to be issued
  to national banks, pending in Congress 114
 Its passage recommended 114
 Resources and liabilities of the national banks on October 1, 1880, classified by reserve
  cities, &c 114
Comparative statements of the national banks for eleven years 115
 Resources and liabilities of the national banks at corresponding dates in each year,
  from 1870 to 1880 115
The banks since resumption 115
 Movement of currency and operations of the banks since resumption 115
 Resumption of coin payments at time fixed by law and its maintenance deemed by
  some almost impossible 115
 United States an exception to the general rule that a convertible paper currency
  cannot be kept at par unless there be among the banks or the people an equal
  amount of coin 115
 Country has been growing richer in coin since resumption 116
 Redemption of paper currency not demanded by the holder................... 116
 Annual withdrawal of currency from banks in New York City 116
 Ebb and flow of currency to 1879 116
 Differences experienced for the last two years 116
 Low rates of interest for the last two years.................................. 116
 Rate of the Bank of England and Bank of France............................. 116
 Advance in price of English consols, and low rates for call loans in London 116
 Low rates in the United States 117
 Prevailing rates for the last year in various places............................ 117
 Borrowing power of the government... 117
 Comparisons of the loans of the national banks in the commercial cities, with their
  means, and of their cash reserve with their deposits 118
 Ratios of the loans of the national banks to their capital, surplus, and net deposits,
  and of their cash to net deposits in New York City, and the other reserve cities,
  at corresponding dates from 1870 to 1880 118
 Means of the banks in the commercial cities closely employed during the last
  eleven years 118
 Loans of the banks in the principal cities, and in the country districts, larger than
  their net deposits 119
 Ratio of the loans of the national banks to their capital, surplus, and net deposits,
  and of their cash to net deposits in the States and Territories, at corresponding
  dates from 1870 to 1880 ....

Comptroller of the Currency—Continued.
THE BANKS SINCE RESUMPTION—Continued.
  Classification of the loans of the national banks, at the date of their reports, in October, 1879 and 1880 1
  Relation of loans to rates of interest 1:
  Losses resulting from excessive loans—before resumption 1:
  Cash reserve close in New York City during the last three years 1:
  Reserve in interior, as a rule, much stronger than in New York City 1:
  Excess of gold imports since resumption 1
  Coin and currency in the country January 1, and November 1, 1879, and November 1, 1880 .... 1:
  Increase in national-bank circulation and gold and silver coin since resumption 1:
  Coin and currency in the Treasury and in the national and State banks, January 1, and November 1, 1879, and November 1, 1880 .... 1:
  Silver certificates in circulation 1:
  Coin and currency in the hands of the people January 1 and November 1, 1879, and November 1, 1880 .... 1:
  Increase of gold; currency released in Treasury and banks 1:
  Amount of silver in circulation 1:
  Additional amount of silver dollars, gold, and paper currency in circulation outside of banks and Treasury since resumption 1:
  Amount of subsidiary silver and trade dollars in circulation 1:
  Highest amount of fractional paper currency outstanding March 23, 1874 ..... 1:
  Increase in price of goods, provisions, and wages 1:
  Disappearance of circulating medium occasioned by hoarding 1:
  Increase in amount of coin held by banks 1:
  Proportion of gold coin held to cash reserve 1:
  Newspaper criticism of small amount of standard silver dollars held by banks—true reason for this 1:
  Silver and gold held by Bank of France 1:
  Relative amount of gold and silver held by the United States Treasury and the Bank of France 1:
  Policy of the national banks in reference to their coin reserves 1:
  National system of immense advantage to the country 1:
  Banks will not necessarily be exempt from losses because on specie basis 1:
  DISTRIBUTION OF LOANS BY BANK OF FRANCE, THE NATIONAL BANKS OF THE UNITED STATES, AND THE IMPERIAL BANK OF GERMANY ....
  Bank of France—capital, branches, circulation, deposits, coin, and loans 1:
  Amount of commercial paper discounted at Bank of France and its branches 1:
  Advances on collaterals and French securities held 1:
  Classification of the Paris bills 1:
  Classification of the commercial bills discounted by the Bank of France in 1878 and 1879 12
  Bank of France discounts commercial paper only for its depositors—sources of the bills 12
NATIONAL BANKS OF THE UNITED STATES 12
  Classification of loans of the national banks, by geographical divisions, on October, 2, 1879 12
  Number and average amount of pieces of paper discounted 12
  Number and average amounts of pieces of paper discounted in various States and cities 12
  Average amount of pieces in New York City 12
  Average amount of small loan in principal cities of the country 12
THE IMPERIAL BANK OF GERMANY 12
  Location and capital of Imperial Bank of Germany 12
  Amount and classification of bills discounted 12
  Classification by locations, Berlin bills, inland and foreign 12
  Time of Berlin bills and of inland 12
STATE BANKS, SAVINGS BANKS, AND TRUST COMPANIES 12
  Attempts to obtain annual statistics of State banks, savings banks, and trust companies—made prior to February, 1873 12
  Act of February 19, 1873, requiring Comptroller to obtain returns 13
  Returns received through courtesy of State officers 13
  Returns made to Commissioner of Internal Revenue 13
STATE BANKS AND TRUST COMPANIES ....
  Resources and liabilities of State banks and trust companies 13
  States from which returns were received 13
  Difference in capital and deposits as returned to Commissioner of Internal Revenue and as returned to State authorities 13
  Number, deposits, and capital, of all description of banks, reporting to Commissioner of Internal Revenue 13
  Number not reporting to any State authority 13
  Number of private bankers reporting to Commissioner of Internal Revenue 13
SAVINGS BANKS ....
  Resources and liabilities of savings banks 13:
  States from which returns are received 13:
  Aggregate number and deposits in Middle and New England States 13:
  Average deposits returned to Commissioner of Internal Revenue 13:
  Savings banks of New England and Middle States 13:
  Savings banks in California 10:
  Savings banks in Philadelphia 10:
  Savings banks in Southern and Western States and Territories, exclusive of California, as shown by reports made to Commissioner, compared with the number in other sections 19:
  Proportion of savings-bank deposits to those of State banks and trust companies, and also to those of national banks 19:

Page.

Comptroller of the Currency—Continued.
SAVINGS BANKS—Continued.
Proportion of savings-bank deposits to national-bank deposits in the New England States.. 132
Number of savings-deposits accounts in New England, proportion to population, and average amount of each account, and amount per capita............... 132
Per capita of savings-bank deposits to population in New York State............. 132
Investments of New England savings banks in United States and other stocks and bonds in 1860 and in 1873 and proportion to deposits....................... 132
Cash on hand in New England savings banks in 1880 and 1873, and proportion to deposits... 133
Investments in United States and other bonds and cash on hand, with proportion of each to deposits in New York savings banks in 1880 and 1873............. 133
Investments in United States and other bonds and cash on hand, with proportion of each to deposits in California savings banks in 1880 and 1877........... 133
Amount due from banks to New England savings banks........................ 133
Investments of New York savings banks in United States bonds................. 133
Investments of New York savings banks in other stocks and bonds.............. 133
Capital, deposits, and investments in United States bonds, of banks other than national, in the Eastern and Middle States, for the six months ending May 31, 1880.. 133
Capital, deposits, and investments in United States bonds, of banks other than national, in the Southern, Western, and Pacific States........................ 134
Capital, deposits, and investments in United States bonds, of banks other than national, in the United States... 134
Number, capital, and deposits of the State banks, private bankers, &c., for the six months ending May 31, 1880, by geographical divisions....................... 135
NUMBER, CAPITAL, AND DEPOSITS OF NATIONAL BANKS, STATE AND SAVINGS BANKS, AND PRIVATE BANKERS.. 135
Net deposits of the national banks and average deposits of all other banks, including those of savings banks.. 135
Increase of the deposits of all classes of banks............................ 135
Number, capital, and deposits of the State banks, private bankers, &c., for the six months ending May 31, 1880, and of the national banks on June 11, 1880........ 135
Number, capital, and deposits of the national banks, State banks, private bankers, &c., at corresponding dates, 1876–1880.................................. 136
Definition of terms "gross deposits," "individual deposits," and "net deposits" (note)... 136
SECURITY OF CIRCULATING NOTES.. 136
Amounts and kinds of United States bonds pledged to secure national-bank circulation, on November 1, 1880.. 136
Amount of five and six per cent. United States bonds pledged to secure national-bank circulation on October 1, 1865, and October 1, 1870.................... 136
Decrease of six per cent. bonds and increase of five per cent. United States bonds to November 1, 1880.. 137
Amount of four and-a-half and four per cent. United States bonds pledged to secure national-bank circulation.. 137
Amount of four per cent. United States bonds withdrawn from, and of five per cent. bonds deposited for security of circulation during the year ending November 1, 1880.. 137
United States bonds pledged to secure circulation on which interest has ceased.... 137
United States bonds pledged to secure circulation, which are redeemable on or before July 1, 1881.. 137
NATIONAL-BANK AND LEGAL-TENDER NOTES BY DENOMINATIONS, CIRCULATING NOTES OF THE BANK OF FRANCE AND IMPERIAL BANK OF GERMANY, BY DENOMINATIONS...... 137
Amount of each denomination of national-bank notes and of legal-tender notes outstanding on November 1, 1880, and of the aggregate amounts outstanding on November 1, 1878 and 1879.. 137
National banks not to be furnished with notes of a less denomination than five dollars after resumption.. 137
No denominations less than five dollars issued since January 1, 1879............ 137
Amount of one and two dollar national-bank notes outstanding on January 1, 1879, and decrease since.. 137
Amount of one and two dollar legal-tender notes outstanding January 1, 1879, and increase since... 138
Proportion of the different denominations of national-bank and legal-tender notes... 138
Circulation of the Imperial Bank of Germany on January 1, 1870 and 1880........ 138
Amount and denominations of the circulation of the Imperial Bank of Germany on January 1, 1880.. 138
Amount and denominations of the circulation of the Bank of France on January 29, 1880.. 138
Circulation of the Bank of France on January 30, 1879........................ 138
Smallest denomination of notes issued by the Imperial Bank of Germany, the Bank of France, and the banks of Ireland and Scotland......................... 139
Paper circulation of the United States in denominations of five dollars and less on November 1, 1880.. 139
Circulation of the lower denominations in foreign countries consist principally of coin.. 139
Present requirements of the law as to signatures of officers of national banks on circulating notes.. 139
Written signatures should be required..................................... 139
Legislation requiring same recommended.................................. 139
UNITED STATES BONDS OUTSTANDING AND THE AMOUNT HELD BY THE NATIONAL BANKS, STATE BANKS, AND PRIVATE BANKERS....................................... 139
Kind and amount of United States bonds outstanding August 31, 1865, July 1, 1865, to 1880, and November 1, 1880... 139

Comptroller of the Currency—Continued.

UNITED STATES BONDS OUTSTANDING—Continued.   Page.
Average amount of bonded debt of the United States held by the national banks
   since 1865, with rates of interest thereon 140
Kinds and amounts of United States bonds owned by the national banks on July 1,
   1865, to 1880, and on November 1, 1880 140
Maturing bonds to be replaced by those bearing interest at a lower rate 140
Amount of United States bonds held by State banks, trust companies, and savings
   banks in various States 140
Investments in United States bonds, of banks other than national, and private bank-
   ers, by geographical divisions, for the six months ending May 31, 1880 141
Amount of United States bonds held by all the banks and bankers in the country .. 141
CLEARING-HOUSE CERTIFICATES 141
Provisions of law relative to 141
Certificates for legal-tender notes first issued in 1873, and amount outstanding at
   various dates 142
Provisions of law relative to gold certificates 142
Gold certificates first issued November 13, 1865, and amounts outstanding at various
   dates 142
Issue of gold certificates discontinued 142
Establishment of depository for gold coin for clearing-house purposes by the banks
   in New York City 142
Amounts of gold certificates issued from such depository outstanding at various
   dates 142
Establishment of similar depositories in Boston, Philadelphia, and Baltimore, and
   amounts of certificates issued by them up to October 1, 1880 142
TRANSACTIONS OF THE NEW YORK CLEARING-HOUSE 142
Organization of the New York Clearing-House Association 142
Exchanges and balances for the year ending October 1, 1880 142
Average daily exchanges and balances 142
Transactions of the New York clearing-house 143
Transactions of the United States assistant treasurer at New York with the clear-
   ing-house for the year ending November 1, 1880 143
Operations of the clearing-house larger during the past year than ever before 143
SPECIE IN BANK AND IN THE TREASURY OF THE UNITED STATES, AND ESTIMATED AMOUNT
   IN THE COUNTRY—SPECIE IN THE BANK OF ENGLAND AND IN THE BANK OF FRANCE.
Specie held by the national banks at the dates of their reports, from October, 1868,
   to October, 1880 144
Specie held by the State banks in various States and in New York City 145
Estimate of the Director of the Mint of the coin and bullion in the country for the
   fiscal year 1880, and total total amount at the close of the year 145
Amount of gold and silver, and proportion of each, in the United States Treasury
   on September 30 from 1876 to 1880, and on November 1, 1880 145
Amount of bullion in the Bank of England in each year from 1870 to 1880 145
Amount of gold and silver held by the Bank of France from 1870 to 1880 146
STATE TAXATION OF NATIONAL BANKS 146
Provisions of law relative to taxation of national-bank shares by States 146
Extract from decision of United States Supreme Court on the powers of States to
   tax national banks 146
Intent of Congress in authorizing State taxation of national banks evaded 147
Provisions of laws of New York and Ohio relative to taxation of national-bank
   shares, and effect thereof 147
National banks in New York and Ohio protected by decisions of United States
   Supreme Court 147
Particulars in which decisions of United States Supreme Court fail to afford relief .. 147
Propriety of fixing by Congressional enactment the maximum limit of taxation of
   national banks by States suggested 148
Extract from decision of United States Supreme Court as to meaning and effect of
   word "rate," as used in the law 148
Amendment of provisions of law relative to taxation of national banks by States
   recommended and form of amendment suggested 148
TABLES OF NATIONAL AND STATE TAXATION 149
Repeal of tax upon capital, deposits, and bank checks recommended 149
Amount of internal revenue for the last fiscal year and sources from which it was
   derived 149
Reasons for tax upon capital, deposits, and bank checks no longer exist, and the
   repeal of the law imposing such taxes recommended 149
Taxes imposed under State laws are as much as the banking interest should be sub-
   jected to 149
Capital and amount and rate of taxation of the national banks, by States, &c., for
   1879 149
Rates of United States taxation on circulation, deposits, and capital 151
Taxes paid to the United States by the national banks yearly, from 1864 to 1880 ... 151
Taxes paid to the United States by banks other than national from 1864 to 1880 151
Large excess of tax collected upon circulation over the cost of the national banking
   system 151
United States and State taxation of the national banks, yearly, from 1865 to 1879 .. 152
Amount and rate of taxation of the national banks, by geographical divisions,
   yearly, from 1875 to 1879 152
Apparent inequality of ratios of United States taxation in different States ex-
   plained 153
Rates of taxation of the national banks in certain cities for 1877, 1878, and 1879 ... 153
Rates of taxation of the national banks in certain States for 1877, 1878, and 1879 ... 154
LOSSES, SURPLUS, EARNINGS, AND DIVIDENDS OF THE NATIONAL BANKS 154
Provisions of law relative to payment of dividends by national banks, reports
   thereof, and charging off losses 154
Losses charged off by the national banks during the year ending September 1, 1880 . 155
Losses of the national banks, by geographical divisions, yearly, 1876 to 1880 156

Comptroller of the Currency—Continued.

Losses, Surplus. Earnings, and Dividends of National Banks—Continued.

Page.

Proportion of losses caused by depreciation of United States bonds—ratio of losses during last five years to capital 156

Losses charged off by the national banks in certain cities, yearly, 1876 to 1880 ... 156

Funds from which losses have been met and impairment of capital prevented 156

Enforcement of provisions of law requiring losses to be charged off before dividends 157

Losses in 1880 less than in previous years 157

Surplus 157

Provisions of law relative to accumulation of surplus 157

Capital and surplus from the working funds of the banks 157

Amount and increase and decrease of surplus fund semi-annually, 1864 to 1880 157

Dividends and Earnings.. 157

Reports of dividends and earnings made according to law since 1869 157

Capital, surplus, dividends, and earnings of the national banks semi-annually, 1869 to 1880 158

Number and capital of the national banks, by geographical divisions, which paid no dividends in 1880, with totals for the four preceding years 158

Proportion of the number and capital of national banks which passed dividends for the last five years 158

Ratios to capital and to capital and surplus of the dividends and earnings of the national banks, by geographical divisions, for 1878, 1879, and 1880 158

United States Legal-Tender Notes and National-Bank Circulation 159

Provision of law authorizing issue of legal-tender notes 159

Limitation of legal-tender notes to $400,000,000 159

Provisions of law relative to retirement of legal-tender notes 159

Further reduction of legal-tender notes prohibited 159

Maximum amount of legal-tender notes fixed 159

Increase of national-bank circulation and proportional retirement of legal-tender notes authorized 159

Repeal of provision of law authorizing retirement of legal tender notes 159

Provisions of law fixing amount of national-bank circulation, and authorizing its retirement by depositing legal-tender notes in the Treasury 159

Effect of the acts authorizing the issue and retirement of national-bank circulation. 160

Proportion of circulation to capital of national banks 160

Bill for repeal of provision of law limiting ratio of circulation authorized to be issued pending in Congress 160

Circulation of the national banks, by geographical divisions, issued and uncalled for, October 1, 1880 160

Legal-tender notes deposited in United States Treasury and national-bank notes retired under act of June 20, 1874 161

Amounts and kinds of outstanding United States and national-bank notes, 1865 to 1880 161

Changes in the amount of national-bank circulation by issue and retirement during the year ending November 1, 1880 161

Amount of legal-tender notes in Treasury for redemption of national-bank notes on November 1, 1880 161

Issue and retirement of national-bank circulation for the year ending November 1, 1880, and the total amount issued and retired since June 20, 1874 162

Lost or Unredeemed Bank Notes 162

Statistics in reference to the percentage of bank notes issued by State banks not presented for redemption 162

Maximum circulation issued, and amount and percentage unredeemed, of banks in various States 163

Circulation issued, and amount and percentage unredeemed of national banks which failed prior to 1870, to 1873, and to 1874 163

Statistics in reference to the percentage of notes of national banks in voluntary liquidation, for various periods, not presented for redemption 164

Estimated percentage of national-bank notes that will not be redeemed 164

Percentage of demand Treasury notes not presented for redemption 164

Percentage of legal-tender notes not presented for redemption 164

Notes lost or destroyed not a source of profit to the bank of issue, but to the government 165

Loans and Rates of Interest of the New York City Banks 165

Classes of loans in the national banks in New York City at the dates of their reports in October, from 1875 to 1880 165

Statements of the average rates of interest in New York and London, yearly, 1874 to 1880 165

Rate of interest in New York City on November 26, 1880 166

Rates of interest at the Bank of England, the Bank of France, and the Imperial Bank of Germany, at various dates 166

Discount rates at Berlin, Hamburg, and Frankfort in October, 1880 166

Redemption of National-Bank Currency 166

Respect in which expense of redemption is oppressive to national banks in operation. 166

Benefit to the Treasury from the use of funds belonging to insolvent and liquidating banks and those reducing circulation 166

Amount of such funds on deposit and amount of currency balance in the Treasury November 1, 1880 166

Estimated gain to the Treasury from loss or destruction of national-bank notes 166

Legislation recommended to effect just distribution of the expense of redemption between the Treasury and the banks 167

Five per cent redemption fund maintained by the national banks and their notes redeemed without expense to the government 167

Redemption of national-bank notes monthly by the Comptroller and at the Treasury agency, for the year ending June 1, 1880, and total since June 20, 1874 167

National bank notes received at the United States Treasury redemption agency since June 20, 1874 167

Maximum amount received in 1877.. 167

Comptroller of the Currency—Continued.
REDEMPTION OF NATIONAL-BANK CURRENCY—Continued.

	Page.
Decrease since	167
Maximum amount received at office of Comptroller of the Currency in 1875	167
Decrease since	167
Proportionate amounts of national-bank notes received at the Treasury for redemption from the principal cities during the year ending November 1, 1880	168
Amounts received by the Comptroller of the Currency from the banks in the principal cities during the year ending November 1, 1880	168
Denominations and amount of national-bank notes issued, redeemed, and outstanding from 1863 to 1880	168
Amount of national-bank notes received and destroyed yearly since the establishment of the system	168
NATIONAL-BANK FAILURES	169
National banks which failed during the year ending November 1, 1880, with their capital	169
List of insolvent national banks, with rates of dividends paid to creditors	169
Dividends to creditors of insolvent national banks during the year ending November 1, 1880	169
Total dividends to creditors of insolvent national banks	169
Assessments upon shareholders of insolvent national banks, and amount collected .	169
Unclaimed dividends, checks, and recommendation relative to their disposition	170
RESERVE	170
Amount required and held by the national banks at the dates of their reports in October from 1875 to 1880	170
Movement of the legal-tender reserve of the national banks in New York City, weekly, in October of each year, from 1873 to 1880	171
Tables, list of:	
[The following tables appear in the report of the Comptroller of the Currency as printed in this volume. The report, as printed separately, contains numerous other tables of which a full list will be found at page 201 of the small bound volume, and at the large volume, at the end of which will also be found an alphabetical list of the cities and towns in which national banks are located.]	
Table of the resources and liabilities of the national banks on October 1, 1880, classified by reserve cities, &c	114
Table of the resources and liabilities of the national banks at corresponding dates in each year, from 1870 to 1880	115
Table showing the ratios of the loans of the national banks to their capital, surplus, and net deposits, and of their cash to net deposits in New York City, and the other reserve cities, at corresponding dates from 1870 to 1880	118
Table showing the ratios of the loans of the national banks to their capital, surplus, and net deposits, and of their cash to net deposits in the States and Territories, at corresponding dates from 1870 to 1880	119
Table showing the classification of the loans of the national banks, at the date of their reports, in October, 1879 and 1880	120
Table showing the amount of coin and currency in the country January 1 and November 1, 1879, and November 1, 1880	121
Table showing the amount of coin and currency in the Treasury and in the national and State banks January 1 and November 1, 1879, and November 1, 1880	122
Table showing the amount of coin and currency in the hands of the people January 1 and November 1, 1879, and November 1, 1880	122
Table showing classification of bills on Paris held by the Bank of France for 1878.	126
Table showing the classification of the commercial bills discounted by the Bank of France in 1878 and 1879	127
Table showing the classification of loans of the national banks, by geographical divisions, on October 2, 1879	127
Estimated number of loans of $2,500 and upwards of national banks in the city of New York in 1880	128
Table showing classification of loans and discounts of Imperial Bank of Germany on December 31, 1879	129
Table of the resources and liabilities of State banks and trust companies...........	130
Table of the resources and liabilities of savings banks	131
Table showing the capital, deposits, and investments in United States bonds, of banks other than national, in the Eastern and Middle States for the six months ending May 31, 1880	133
Table showing the capital, deposits, and investments in United States bonds, of banks other than national, in the Southern, Western, and Pacific States	134
Statement of the capital, deposits, and investments in United States bonds, of banks other than national, in the United States	134
Table showing the number, capital, and deposits of the State banks, private bankers, &c., for the six months ending May 31, 1880, by geographical divisions.......	135
Table showing the number, capital, and deposits of the State banks, private bankers, &c., for the six months ending May 31, 1880, and of the national banks on June 11, 1880	135
Table showing the number, capital, and deposits of the national banks, State banks, private bankers, &c., at corresponding dates, 1876-1880	136
Table showing the amount and kinds of United States bonds pledged to secure national-bank circulation on November 1, 1880	136
Table showing the amount of each denomination of national-bank notes and of legal-tender notes outstanding on November 1, 1880, and of the aggregate amounts outstanding on November 1, 1878 and 1879	137
Table showing the amount and denominations of the circulation of the Imperial Bank of Germany on January 1, 1880	138
Table showing the amount and denominations of the circulation of the Bank of France on January 29, 1880	138
Table showing the kind and amount of United States bonds outstanding August 31, 1865, July 1, 1866, to 1880, and November 1, 1880	139

Page.

Comptroller of the Currency—Continued.
RESERVE—Continued.
Table showing the kinds and amounts of United States bonds owned by the national banks on July 1, 1865, to 1880, and on November 1, 1880 140
Statement of the amount of United States bonds held by State banks, trust companies, and savings banks in various States 140
Table showing the investments in United States bonds, of banks other than national, and private bankers, by geographical divisions, for the six months ending May 31, in the years 1878, 1879, and 1880 141
Statement of the amount of United States bonds held by all the banks and bankers of the country 141
Table showing transactions of the New York Clearing-house 143
Statement showing transactions of the United States assistant treasurer at New York with the clearing-house for the year ending November 1, 1880 143
Table showing amount of specie held by the national banks, at the dates of their reports, from October, 1868, to October, 1880 144
Estimate of the Director of the Mint of the coin and bullion in the country for the fiscal year 1880, and total amount at the close of the year 145
Table showing the amount of gold and silver, and proportion of each, in the United States Treasury on September 30, from 1876 to 1880, and on November 1, 1880.... 145
Table showing the amount of bullion in the Bank of England, in each year, from 1870 to 1880 145
Table showing the amount of gold and silver held by the Bank of France from 1870 to 1880 148
Table showing the capital and amount and rate of taxation of the national banks, by States, &c., for 1879 149
Table showing taxes paid to the United States, by the national banks yearly, from 1864 to 1880 151
Table showing taxes paid to the United States, by banks other than national, from 1864 to 1880 151
Table showing United States and State taxation of the national banks, yearly, from 1866 to 1879 152
Table showing amount and rate of taxation of the national banks, by geographical divisions, yearly, from 1875 to 1879 152
Table showing rates of taxation of the national banks in certain cities for 1877, 1878, and 1879 153
Table showing rates of taxation of the national banks in certain States for 1877, 1878, and 1879 154
Table of the amount of losses charged off by the national banks during the year ending September 1, 1880 155
Table of the amount of losses of the national banks, by geographical divisions, yearly, 1876 to 1880 156
Table of the amount of losses charged off by the national banks in certain cities, yearly, 1876 to 1880 156
Table showing the amount and increase and decrease of surplus fund, semi-annually, 1864 to 1880 157
Table showing the capital, surplus, dividends, and earnings of the national banks, semi-annually, 1869 to 1880 158
Table showing the number and capital of the national banks, by geographical divisions, which paid no dividends in 1880, with totals for the four preceding years.... 158
Table showing the ratios to capital, and to capital and surplus, of the dividends and earnings of the national banks, by geographical divisions, for 1878, 1879, and 1880 .. 159
Table showing amount of circulation of the national banks, by geographical divisions, issued and recalled for October 1, 1880 160
Table showing the amounts and kinds of outstanding United States and national-bank notes, 1865 to 1880 161
Table showing the issue and retirement of national-bank circulation for the year ending November 1, 1880, and the total amount issued and retired since June 30, 1874 162
Table showing the maximum circulation issued, and amount and percentage unredeemed, of banks in various States 163
Table showing the amount of circulation issued and amount and percentage unredeemed of national banks which failed prior to 1870, to 1873, and to 1874 163
Table showing classes of loans in the national banks in New York City at the dates of their reports in October, from 1876 to 1880 165
Statements of the average rates of interest in New York and London, yearly, 1874 to 1880 165
Table showing amount of redemption of national-bank notes monthly, by the Comptroller and at the Treasury agency, for the year ending November 1, 1880, and total since June 20, 1874 107
Table showing the denominations and amount of national-bank notes issued, redeemed, and outstanding from 1863 to 1880 168
Table showing the amount of national-bank notes received and destroyed yearly since the establishment of the system 169
List of national banks which failed during the year ending November 1, 1880, with their capital 169
List of insolvent national banks, with rates of dividends paid to creditors 169
Table showing the amount of reserve required and held by the national banks at the dates of their reports in October, from 1875 to 1880 170
Table showing the movement of the legal-tender reserve of the national banks in New York City, weekly, in October of each year, from 1873 to 1880 171
Director of the Mint 173–232
African states, monetary statistics of 199
Algiers, monetary statistics of 199
Annual settlements and examinations 183, 184
Appropriations, earnings, and expenditures 181, 182
Argentine Republic, monetary statistics of 198

Page.

Director of the Mint—Continued.

Arts and manufactures, gold and silver used in 226
Assay, annual 182
  offices at Boise, Charlotte, Helena, and New York, condition of 186, 187
Australia, monetary statistics of 193
Austria, monetary statistics of 195
Bars manufactured during the fiscal year 177
Boise City assay-office, condition of 187
Bullion, gold and silver deposits 175
  silver, purchases of 178
  price of bullion and coin in British India 179, 221
Canada, monetary statistics of 194
Cape of Good Hope, monetary statistics of 199
Central American states, monetary statistics of 197
Charlotte assay-office, condition of 187
Circulation and coinage of the silver dollar 181
  of the principal countries of the world 200
Coinage executed during the fiscal year 176, 177
  last three calendar years 177, 218
  and medal dies manufactured at the mint at Philadelphia 207
  charge 187, 188
  of foreign countries 199, 200
  total, from organization of the mint 212–217
Coins, foreign, estimation of the value of 183, 219, 220
Coin, circulation of the United States 191, 192
  and paper circulation of the principal countries of the world 200
Condition of the mints and assay-offices 184, 187
Consumption of the precious metals in the United States 190, 191
  specie in France from 1850 to 1878 230
Course of prices 200, 201
Cuba and Hayti, monetary statistics of 198
Deposits and purchases during the fiscal year 175, 176
Denver mint, condition of 187
Dies and medals manufactured during the fiscal year 178
Disposition of gold and silver received at the mints and assay-offices, estimate of .. 227
Distribution of standard silver dollars 180, 181, 218
Domestic coin and bullion, exports of 223
  commodities exported from the United States, average and comparative price
  of 228, 229
  production, total deposited at the mint since its organization 211
Earnings, expenditures, and appropriations 181
  and expenditures, detailed statement of 216
Egypt, monetary statistics of 199
Estimated disposition made of gold and silver received at the mints 227
Estimation of the value of foreign coins 183, 219, 220
Examinations and annual settlements 183, 184
Exchange on London, average price of, at New York 221
Exports and imports of specie 222–224
  of domestic coin and bullion 223
  foreign coin and bullion 224
  domestic, comparative price of 228, 229
Foreign coins, estimation of the value of 183, 219, 220
  countries, monetary statistics of 193–200
  coinages of 199, 200
  coin circular, estimating and proclaiming value of 220
  and bullion, exports of 224
France, monetary statistics of 194, 195
  movement of specie, production, consumption, and increase of precious metals
  in, from 1850 to 1878 230
  specie and paper circulation in, with comparative price of exports and imports
  from 1850 to 1878 231
Germany, monetary statistics of 194
Great Britain, monetary statistics of 193
Gold and silver production of the United States 189, 190
  in the world 199
  total deposits at the mint of domestic, since its organization 211
  imports and exports of 202–224
  exports of domestic 223
  foreign 224
  used in the arts and manufactures 226
  bullion and coin on hand at the mints and assay-offices, years ending
  June 30, 1879 and 1880 227
Helena assay-office, condition of 187
Imports and exports of specie 222–224
  of American silver coin 53
India, monetary statistics of 193, 194
Indebtedness of the San Francisco mint to the Treasury 186
Italy, monetary statistics of 193, 194
Japan, monetary statistics of 195
Legislation suggested 187–189
Manufactures and the arts, gold and silver used in 226
Medals and dies manufactured during the year 178
  manufactured, list of 206
  and proof sets sold 209
Melting charge 187
Mexico, monetary statistics of 197

Page.

Director of the Mint—Continued.
Minor coins redeemed, reissued, and exchanged 209
Mints, condition of 185–187
Monetary statistics of the United States.. 189–192
foreign countries, summary of.................................. 193–200
Morocco, monetary statistics of 199
Movement, coinage, and circulation of the silver dollar................................... 181
of specie in France, production, consumption, and increase from 1850 to 1878. 230
Netherlands, monetary statistics of.. 196
New Orleans mint, condition of.. 185, 186
New York assay-office, condition of 187
Paper and specie circulation in France from 1850 to 1878, with comparative price of exports and imports 231
Parting and refining at the mints and assay office at New York......................... 177, 178
Peru, monetary statistics of 198
Portugal, monetary statistics of 196
Precious metals, consumption of, in the United States 190, 191
Prices, course of 200, 201
Price of silver at London and New York (average)....................................... 179, 221
exchange on London at New York...................................... 221
Prices of domestic commodities exported... 228, 229
Purchase of silver bullion.. 178, 179
Refinery earnings and expenditures... 162
Regulations for distribution of standard silver dollars.................................... 218
Relative market value of gold to silver.. 221
Reynolds patent.. 188, 189
Russia, monetary statistics of 197
San Francisco mint, condition of 184
indebtedness to the Treasury................................... 189
Settlements, annual 183
Silver bullion, purchases of... 178, 179
price of, at London and New York.................................... 221
Silver coin and bullion, domestic exports of.. 223
foreign exports of... 224
American, imports of.. 225
dollars, distribution of.. 180, 181
coinage and circulation of.. 180, 181
regulations for distribution of..................................... 218
Silver and gold used in the arts and manufactures....................................... 226
imports and exports of 222–224
coin and bullion on hand at the mints and assay-office at New York June 30, 1879 to 1880 227
South American States, monetary statistics of.. 168
Specie, imports and exports of 222–224
in France, movement of.. 230
and specie circulation in France, with comparative price of exports and imports 231
Statistics of the production, consumption, coinage, and circulation of the precious metals. 189–200
monetary, of the United States.. 189–191
foreign countries 193–200
Sweeps, loss in sale of.. 211
Switzerland, monetary statistics of 196
Table of deposits and purchases of gold and silver bullion............................... 202
gold of domestic production 203
silver of domestic production.. 204
coinage during the year.. 205
bars manufactured during the year..................................... 206
dies manufactured during the year..................................... 207
medals manufactured during the year.................................. 208
proof sets sold during the year.. 209
minor coins redeemed during the year................................. 209
earnings and expenditures during the year............................. 210
wastage and loss on sweeps during the year............................ 211
deposits of domestic gold and silver deposited at the mint since its organization. 211
coinage at the mint since its organization.............................. 212–217
coinage for calendar years 1878, '79, '80............................... 218
price of silver bullion 221
market value of gold and silver 221
United States imports and exports of gold and silver.................. 222–224
imports of silver, by countries.. 225
gold and silver used in the manufactures and arts in the United States 225
disposition of gold and silver in the mints and assay-office at New York....... 227
gold and silver in the mints and assay-office at New York at close of years 1879 and 1880.. 227
comparative prices of United States exports............................ 228–229
movement of specie in France.. 230
paper and coin circulation in France................................... 231
Total coinage from organization of Mint 212–217
deposits from organization of Mint 211
Turkey, monetary statistics of 197
Value of foreign coins, estimation of... 183, 219–220
Venezuela, monetary statistics of 198
Wastages and loss on sale of sweeps 211
World, circulation of principal countries of... 200
coinage and paper circulation of.................................... 200
production of gold and silver of..................................... 199

	Page.
First Comptroller	233–242
Accountable and settlement warrants received, examined, and countersigned by	235
amounts covered by	235
Accounts received, revised, and certified by	236–238
of United States marshals	236
of inspectors of hulls and boilers	236
of Territorial officers	236
of Congressional officers and employés	237
of Public Printer	247
of Treasurer for receipts and expenditures	237
of Treasurer for redemption of, and interest upon, the public debt	236
of Assistant treasurers, for salaries and contingent expenses of offices	237
of internal-revenue collectors	237
of internal-revenue stamp agents	237
of internal-revenue disbursing agents	237
of surveyors-general, etc	238
of receivers of public moneys	238
of receivers acting as disbursing agents	238
of deputy surveyors	238
for coinage, &c	236
for expenses of United States courts	236
for payment of outstanding checks	237
for transportation, &c	236, 238
for salaries, etc., of foreign ministers, consuls, etc	237
for relief and protection of American seamen	237
miscellaneous	237
copies of, made and transmitted by	239
Advances to disbursing officers, requisitions for, approved by	238, 239
Affidavits before Treasury Department, corrupt false swearing in, should be punishable	241
Appropriation warrants received, examined, and countersigned by	235
Appropriation to pay balance upon accounts for collection of revenue requested by	242
Assay, mint and, accounts revised and certified by	236
Assistant treasurers, accounts of, for salaries and contingent expenses of offices	237
Auditor, First, accounts from, revised by	236–238
Auditor, Fifth, accounts from, revised by	237, 238
Balances upon accounts for collection of revenue should be paid	242
Bonds of indemnity, sureties upon	241
lost or destroyed government, investigation of facts concerning	239
lost or destroyed, practice of Treasury in claims for issue of duplicate	240
official, registered and filed in First Comptroller's Office	239
Buildings, public, accounts for construction of, revised by	236
Bullion deposits and transfers, accounts for	236
Checks, accounts for the payment of outstanding, revised by	237
Commissioner General Land Office, accounts from, revised by	238
Congressional accounts revised by	237
Consular and diplomatic accounts revised by	237
Contingent expenses—	
of Patent Office, accounts for	236
of State Department	236
of inspectors of hulls and boilers	236
of Territorial governments	236
of mints	236
of United States Senate and House of Representatives	237
of Government Printing Office	237
of offices of assistant treasurers	237
of executive departments	237
of National Board of Health	237
of legations and consulates	237
of offices of surveyors-general	238
of examination of surveys	238
Court of Claims, judgments of, ordered paid by	236
Covering warrants countersigned by	235
Decisions of	241
Defaulters, suits instituted against, by	238, 239
Diplomatic and consular accounts revised by	237
miscellaneous expenses, accounts of disbursing clerk, Department of State, for	237
District of Columbia, accounts relating to, revised by	237
Duplicate bonds, recommendation of, concerning issue of	240
Duplicate bonds, practice of Treasury in claims for issue of	240
Expense, saving of which would be effected by directing local officers to make investigations	239
Expenses, accounts for contingent, of State Department, revised by	236
contingent, of Territorial governments	236
of Government Printing Office, accounts for	237
of executive departments	237
of National Board of Health	237
of legations and consulates	237
of offices of surveyors-general	238
incidental, of Patent Office, accounts for	236
of inspectors of hulls and boilers	236
of assistant treasurers' offices	237
of examination of surveys	238
of United States courts, accounts for	236
of mints and assay-offices	236
of United States Senate and House of Representatives	237
of tenth census	237
of international exhibitions of 1875, 1876, and 1878	237

Page.

First Comptroller—Continued.

Expenses—Continued.

of detecting and suppressing violations of internal-revenue laws 237

of prisons in China and Japan 237

of mixed commissions 237

miscellaneous diplomatic, accounts of disbursing clerk, Department of State for .. 237

False swearing in affidavits before Treasury Department should be punishable 241

Fees of United States marshals, accounts for, revised by................................ 236

First Auditor, accounts from, revised by 236–238

Fifth Auditor, accounts from, revised by 237, 238

First Comptroller, decisions of 241

report of 235–242

recommendations of, for additional legislation 239–242

General Land Office, accounts from Commissioner of, revised by 238

Indemnity, sufficiency of sureties upon bonds of....................................... 241

Internal-revenue accounts revised by 237

stamp books counted and certified by 239

suits against collectors of 238

internal-revenue stamp agents... 239

copies of internal-revenue accounts transmitted by................................ 239

Investigations of transactions and accounts of officers under the Treasury Department .. 239

Judgments of Court of Claims ordered paid... 236

Judiciary accounts revised by.. 236

Lands, public, accounts revised by 238

copies of accounts transmitted by 239

suits against defaulting officers of, instituted by 238

Law clerk for 241

Lottery, official, received by 239

written by 239

Liabilities outstanding, accounts for, revised by....................................... 237

Mint and assay accounts revised by 238

Miscellaneous accounts, revised by 237

Official letters received by.. 239

written by 239

Official bonds registered and filed in First Comptroller's Office 239

Outstanding liabilities, accounts for, revised by....................................... 237

Perjury in affidavits before Treasury Department should be punishable............... 241

Printing, public, accounts revised by... 237

Public buildings, accounts for construction of, revised by............................. 236

Public debt accounts revised by 236

Public land accounts revised by 238

copies of, transmitted by 239

Public lands, suits against defaulting officers of, instituted by 238

Public Printer, accounts of, revised by 237

Receipts of government as shown by covering warrants countersigned by............. 235

Receipts and expenditures, accounts of Treasurer for.................................. 237

Redemption of lost and destroyed bonds, recommendation of.......................... 240

Requisitions for advances to disbursing officers approved by 238, 239

Relief and protection of American seamen, accounts for, revised by 237

Repayment of purchase money paid for lands erroneously sold, accounts for........... 238

Salaries—

of United States commissioners 236

of district attorneys 237

of clerks of United States courts 236

of inspectors of hulls and boilers 236

of Territorial officers 236

of officers and employés of mints 236

of officers and employés of United States Senate and House of Representatives 237

of employés of Government Printing Office 237

of employés of assistant treasurers' offices... 237

of officers and employés of executive departments 237

of Senators and Representatives in Congress.. 237

of judges of United States courts.. 237

of National Board of Health... 237

of Office of Internal Revenue 237

of ministers, chargés d'affaires, consuls, etc 237

of legations and consulates 237

of mixed commissions 237

of surveyors-general and employés in their offices 238

of registers of local land offices not paid by receivers.............................. 238

of agents for examination of surveys.. 238

in State Department.. 236

Steamboat accounts revised by... 236

Stenographer for 241

Suits against defaulters instituted by 238, 239

Sureties upon bonds of indemnity, sufficiency of 241

Swearing falsely in affidavits before Treasury Department should be punishable....... 241

Territorial accounts revised by 236

Transportation accounts revised by 236, 238

Treasurer, accounts of, for receipts and expenditures, revised by 237

for redemption of, and interest upon, the public debt, revised by.................. 236

Unpaid balances upon revenue accounts should be paid.............................. 242

Warrants revised, examined, and countersigned by.................................... 235

Workingmen, claims of, under act of June 20, 1878, approved by 237

Second Comptroller 243–246

Commissioner of Customs 247–254

First Auditor 255–266

	Page.
Second Auditor	267–276
Third Auditor	277–290
Fourth Auditor	291–304
Fifth Auditor	305–308
Sixth Auditor	309–312
Treasurer of the United States	314–362
American Printing House for the Blind:	
United States bonds held in trust for	328
Assay-offices of the United States:	
balances and movement of bullion fund in, for, fiscal year	338
Assets of the Treasury:	
amount of, September 30, 1877, '78, '79, '80	317
note, decrease of, during last four years	317
amount of, November 1, 1879, '80	318
Balances:	
subject to draft, June 30, 1879, '80	315
in Treasury, September 30, 1877, '78, '79, '80	317
in national-bank depositaries, November 1, 1880	318
in national-bank depositaries at close of fiscal years from 1864 to 1880	325
of covered moneys, June 30, 1879	336
June 30, 1880	337
of moneys of General Treasury, June 30, 1879	338
June 30, 1880	339
comparative statement of, at close of fiscal years 1879 and 1880	340
explanation of differences in, on June 30, 1880	341
to credit of disbursing officers, June 30, 1880	341
of moneys of Post-Office Department, June 30, 1879	341, 343
June 30, 1880	341, 343
as shown by warrant ledger	342
Bounty-land scrip:	
redemptions of, by warrant, during fiscal year	337
"Called" bonds:	
and interest in Treasury September 30, 1877, '78, '79, '80	317
matured and in Treasury November 1, 1879, '80	318, 319
redeemed for year ending October 31, 1879	320
Certificates of deposit (act of June 8, 1872):	
fund for redemption of, September 30, 1877, '78, '79, '80	316
decrease in outstanding	317–318, 325
redeemed, in Treasury September 30, 1878, '79, '80	317
outstanding and in Treasury November 1, 1879, '80	318, 319
issued, redeemed, and outstanding to close of fiscal years from 1873 to 1880	325
redemptions of, by warrant, during fiscal year	336, 340
redemptions of, by warrant, during fiscal year	337, 340
Compound-interest notes:	
redemptions of, by warrant, during fiscal year	337
outstanding at close of fiscal years from 1864 to 1879	348
redemptions of, for fiscal year, and total redemptions	348
issued, redeemed, and outstanding at close of fiscal years 1879, '80	351
Consols of 1865:	
redemptions of, by warrant, during fiscal year	337
coupons from, paid during fiscal year	354
total retired for sinking fund	355
total retired by purchase, conversion, and redemption	356
Consols of 1867:	
redemptions of, by warrant, during fiscal year	337
amount of, held in trust for national banks	347
coupons from, paid during fiscal year	354
total retired for sinking fund	355
total retired by purchase, conversion, redemption, and exchange	356
Consols of 1868:	
redemptions of, by warrant, during fiscal year	337
amount of, held in trust for national banks	347
coupons from, paid during fiscal year	354
total retired for sinking fund	355
total retired by purchase, conversion, redemption, and exchange	356
Counterfeits:	
amount of, on United States currency and national-bank notes rejected during fiscal year	326
dangerous, on $100 bank notes	336
Coupons:	
from United States bonds, aggregate amount of, paid during fiscal year	316
paid during fiscal year, by loans	354
from 3.65 bonds of District of Columbia, paid during fiscal year	357
Customs:	
receipts from, by warrant, during fiscal year	326
Customs, light-houses, public buildings, &c.:	
expenditures from appropriations for, by warrant, during fiscal year	336
Deficits:	
amount of, in Treasury, September 30, 1877, '78, '79, '80	317
Depositaries, national bank:	
deposits held by, September 30, 1877, '78, '79, '80	317
November 1, 1880	318
average daily balances of, and securities held for deposits in	325
number of, at close of fiscal year	325
receipts and disbursements by, and balances in, by fiscal years, from 1864 to 1880	325
balances and movement of moneys held by, for fiscal year	338–339
disbursing officers' balances with, June 30, 1880	341
balances and movement of moneys of Post-Office Department held by, for fiscal year	343

Treasurer of the United States—Continued.
Depositories of the United States:
  balances and movement of moneys in, for fiscal year 338–339
  disbursing officers' balances in, June 30, 1880. 341
  balances and movement of moneys of Post-Office Department in, for fiscal year 343
Diplomatic appropriations :
  repayments to, during fiscal year 336
  expenditures from, by warrant, during fiscal year 336
Disbursing officers :
  balances of, in Treasury, June 30, 1880 315
    September 30, 1877, '78, '79, '80 316
    November 1, 1879, '80 .... 318, 319
  by offices, June 30, 1880 341
District of Columbia :
  interest on 3.65 bonds of, included in assets of September 30, 1876, '77, '78, '79 316
  paid during fiscal year 357
Drafts :
  amount of, outstanding September 30, 1877, '78, '79, '80 317
    November 1, 1879, '80 .... 318, 319
  number of, drawn on warrants of the Secretary of the Treasury and of the Post-
  Office Department during fiscal year 326
Employés of the Treasurer's Office :
  changes in, during fiscal year 361
  salaries paid to, during fiscal year 361
Exchange :
  in Treasury, September 30, 1877, '78, '79, '80 317
  sales of, at New Orleans, San Francisco, and Tucson, during fiscal year 325–326
Expenditures :
  increase of, as compared with 1879 315
  by warrant, during fiscal year 336–337
    comparative statement of, for fiscal years 1879 and 1880 340
  by Treasurer on post-office warrants, during fiscal year 341
  by postmasters, during fiscal year 341–343
Five per cent. redemption fund :
  amount of, September 30, 1877, '78, '79, '80 316
    November 1, 1879, '80 .... 318, 319
  credits to, during fiscal year 360
Five-twenties of 1862 :
  redemptions of, by warrant, during fiscal year 337
  coupons from, paid during fiscal year 354
  total retired for sinking fund 355
  total retired by purchase, conversion, and redemption 356
Five-twenties of 1864 :
  redemptions of, by warrant, during fiscal year 337
  coupons from, paid during fiscal year 354
  total retired for sinking fund 355
  total retired by purchase, conversion, and redemption 356
Five-twenties of 1865 :
  redemptions of, by warrant, during fiscal year 337
  coupons from, paid during fiscal year 354
  total retired from sinking fund 355
  total retired by purchase, conversion, and redemption 356
Fractional currency :
  special fund for redemption of, September 30, 1877, '78 317
  in Treasury September 30, 1877, '78, '79, '80 317
  in circulation, April 17, 1876, and redemption of, to October, 1879, and since 324
  redeemed and outstanding, by months, from November, 1879, to October, 1880 324
  counterfeit, rejected during fiscal year 326
  deductions from face value of, on account of mutilations 327, 348
  redemptions of, by warrant, during fiscal year 337, 340
  amount of, outstanding at close of fiscal years from 1863 to 1880 348
  redemptions of, for fiscal year and total redemptions 348
  issued, redeemed, and outstanding at close of fiscal years 1879, '80 352–353
Fractional silver coin :
  in Treasury September 30, 1877, '78, '79, '80 317
  increase of, in fiscal year 317
    November 1, 1879, '80 318
  total amount issued under act of April 17, 1876 323
  exchange of, for lawful money, under act of June 9, 1879 323
  in Treasury, decrease of, since July 31, 1880 324
  number of packages of, sent by registered mail 324
  returned for national-bank notes redeemed during fiscal year 357
Funded loan of 1881 :
  total receipts on account of 320
  bonds of, held for Pacific Railroad sinking fund 327
    for Indian trust fund 327, 346
    in trust for national banks 347
  redemptions of, by warrant, during fiscal year 337
  coupons from bonds of, paid during fiscal year 354
  checks for quarterly interest on, issued, paid, and outstanding 354
  purchased for sinking fund during fiscal year 355
  total retired by purchase and redemption 356
Funded loan of 1891 :
  total receipts on account of 320
  bonds of, held in trust for Pennsylvania Company 358
  held in trust for national banks 347
  coupons from, paid during fiscal year 354
  checks for quarterly interest on, issued, paid, and outstanding 354

35 F

Treasurer of the United States—Continued.   Page.
Funded loan of 1907:
  total receipts on account of 329
  bonds of, held for Pacific Railroad sinking funds.................................. 329
    for American Printing House for the Blind........................ 329
    in trust for national banks.. 347
  receipts on account of, by warrant, during fiscal year 329, 339
  redemptions of, by warrant, during fiscal year.................................... 337
  coupons from bonds of, paid during fiscal year................................... 354
  checks for quarterly interest on, issued, paid, and outstanding 354
  purchased for sinking fund during fiscal year.................................... 355, 356
Gold:
  in Treasury, September 30, 1877, '78, '79, '80 317
    decrease of, in fiscal year..................................... 317
  in Treasury and mints November 1, 1879, '80.................................... 318
    increase of, since resumption.............................. 316
  redemptions of United States notes in 316
Gold certificates:
  outstanding and in Treasury September 30, 1877, '78, '79, '80 317
    November 1, 1879, '80 .... 318, 319
  issue of, discontinued December 1, 1878 326
  issued, redeemed, and outstanding, by fiscal years, from 1866 to 1880............ 326
  redemptions of, by warrant, during fiscal years................................. 337, 340
Indian trust fund:
  bonds and stocks of, held June 30, 1880 .... 327, 346
    changes in, during fiscal year............................ 327, 328
Interest:
  due and unpaid September 30, 1877, '78, '79, '80................................. 317
  due and on hand November 1, 1879, '80... 318
Interior civil appropriations:
  repayments to, during fiscal year.. 336
  expenditures from, by warrant, during fiscal year 336
Interior Department appropriations:
  repayments to, during fiscal year.. 336, 337
  expenditures from, by warrant, during fiscal year 337
Internal revenue:
  receipts from, by warrant, during fiscal year................................... 336
  repayments to appropriations for, during fiscal year 336
  expenditures from appropriations for, by warrant, during fiscal year 336
Judiciary appropriations:
  repayments to, during fiscal year.. 336, 337
  expenditures from, by warrant, during fiscal year 337
Lands:
  receipts from, by warrant, during fiscal year................................... 336
Letters:
  received and sent during fiscal year 360
Liabilities of the Treasury:
  amount of, September 30, 1877, '78, '79, '80..................................... 316–317
    November 1, 1879, '80 .... 318, 319
Loan of 1858:
  redemptions of, by warrant, during fiscal year 337
  total retired by conversion and redemption..................................... 356
Loan of February, 1861:
  redemptions of, by warrant, during fiscal year 337
  bonds of, held in trust for national banks 347
  coupons from, paid during fiscal year 354
  purchased for sinking fund during fiscal year................................... 355, 356
Loan of July and August, 1861:
  redemptions of, by warrant, during fiscal year.................................. 337
  bonds of, held for Indian trust fund 327, 346
    held in trust for national banks........................ 347
  coupons from, paid during fiscal year... 354
  purchased for sinking fund during fiscal year................................... 355, 356
Loan of 1863 (81s):
  redemptions of, by warrant, during fiscal year 337
  bonds of, held in trust for national banks 347
  coupons from, paid during fiscal year 354
  purchased for sinking fund during fiscal year................................... 355, 356
Manhattan Savings Institution:
  duplicate registered United States bonds held in trust for.................... 328
Mexican silver dollars:
  demonetization of, in South and West 323
Minor coin:
  in Treasury September 30, 1877, '78, '79, '80 317
  decrease since September 30, 1880, in amount of, on hand, adverted to......... 324
  on hand, by denominations, September 30, 1880 324
Mints of the United States:
  balances and movement of bullion funds and minor coin accounts of, for fiscal year. 338–339
Money packages:
  received and sent during fiscal year... 360
National-bank notes:
  redeemed during fiscal year, and total redeemed to June 30, 1880............... 316
  in Treasury September 30, 1877, '78, '79, '80 317
  stolen, pieced, and fragmentary, rejected during fiscal year 326
  the redemption of 328–331
  fit and unfit, redeemed during fiscal year as compared with preceding.......... 328, 329
  number of, assorted during fiscal year.. 329

Page.

Treasurer of the United States—Continued.
National-bank notes—Continued.
causes of decrease in redemptions considered 329–330
suggestion that all transportation charges on, be paid from five per cent. fund 330
expenses of assorting 330, 331, 360
persons employed in redeeming 331
total expenses of redemption of, decreased, as compared with previous year .... · 331, 360
redemption of notes of failed, liquidating, and reducing banks, and deductions on
account of mutilations 348
number of packages and amount of, received for redemption during fiscal year, by
months 357
mode of payment for, during fiscal year 357
received for redemption from principal cities, by months, during fiscal year 358
number and amount of each denomination of, assorted during fiscal year 358
average denomination of, assorted during fiscal year 358
balanced statements of receipts and deliveries of 359
disposition made of, during fiscal year 360
credited to national banks in five-per-cent. account during fiscal year 360
number of packages of, received and delivered during fiscal year 360
comparative statement of expenses of redemption of, for fiscal years 1879, '80 360

National banks:
number of, organized, failed, and in voluntary liquidation to June 30, 1880 .... 315, 316, 345
increase and reduction of circulation of, under act of June 20, 1874, discussed 331–334
proportion of bonds of, to capital 334–335
list of, which failed during fiscal year 345
went into voluntary liquidation during fiscal year 345
statement, by loans, of United States bonds held in trust for 347
credits to, in five-per-cent. account during fiscal year 360

Navy Department appropriations:
repayments to, during fiscal year 336, 337
expenditures from, by warrant, during fiscal year 337

Old debt:
outstanding September 30, 1877, '78, '79, '80 317
and in Treasury November 1, 1880 319

Old demand notes:
redemptions of, by warrant during fiscal year 337
outstanding at close of each fiscal year from 1862 to 1880 348
redemptions of, for fiscal year, total redemptions, and deductions on account of mutilations 348
issued, redeemed, and outstanding at close of fiscal years 1879, '80 349

One and two year notes of 1863:
in Treasury September 30, 1877, '78, '79, '80 317
redemptions of, by warrant, during fiscal year 337
outstanding at close of each fiscal year from 1864 to 1880 348
redemptions of, for fiscal year, total redemptions, and deductions on account of mutilations 348
issued, redeemed, and outstanding at close of fiscal years 1879, '80 351

Oregon war debt:
redemptions of, by warrant, during fiscal year 337
bonds of, held in trust for national banks 347
coupons from, paid during fiscal year 354
purchased for sinking fund during fiscal year 355
total retired by purchase and redemption 356

Pacific Railroad sinking funds:
funds held for, September 30, 1879 317
bonds held on account of 327
change in provision for investment of, recommended 327

Pacific Railway bonds:
amount of, held for Indian trust fund 327, 346
Pacific Railroad sinking funds 327
in trust for national banks 347

Pennsylvania Company:
United States bonds held in trust for 328

Personal bonds:
deposited by national banks as security for public deposits 347

Postmasters:
receipts and expenditures by, covered by warrants of Postmaster-General 341, 343

Post-Office Department:
balance of account of, September 30, 1877, '78, '79, '80 316
November 1, 1879, '80 .... 318, 319
summary of Treasurer's quarterly account for service of, for fiscal year 341
balances and movement of moneys of, for fiscal year 343

Public debt:
receipts on account of, by warrant for fiscal year 336
repayments to appropriations for interest on, during fiscal year 336, 337
expenditures by warrant for interest on, during fiscal year 337
expenditures by warrant for redemption of, during fiscal year 337

Quarterly account of Treasurer United States:
summary of, for Post-Office Department for fiscal year 341
as rendered to First Auditor for fiscal year 342

Quarterly interest checks:
number and amount of, drawn during fiscal year 316, 326
amount and number of, issued, paid, and outstanding for each funded loan 354

Quarterly salaries appropriations:
expenditures from, by warrant, during fiscal year 337

Treasurer of the United States—Continued.   Page.

Receipts:
increase of, as compared with 1879 315
on account of funded loans, total, by offices 320
as shown by warrants during fiscal year 336
of general Treasury during fiscal year 338, 339
comparative statement of, for fiscal years 1878 and 1879 340
covered in by warrant on account of Post-Office Department 341
by postmasters 341, 343
of moneys of Post-Office Department for fiscal year 341, 343
Refunding certificates:
in Treasury September 30, 1879 317
conversions of 320
issued, converted, and outstanding 320
issues of, by warrant, during fiscal year 336, 340
redemptions of, by warrant, during fiscal year 337, 340
Refunding operations:
cessation of 320
Reassumption:
balance available for, November 1, 1879, '80 .... 318, 319
Salaries:
of force employed in Treasurer's office, paid during fiscal year 361
Semi-annual duty:
assessed and collected for fiscal year 1880, and total from beginning 316, 328
itemized statement of, by fiscal years from 1864 to 1879 346
Seven-thirty notes:
redemptions of, by warrant, during fiscal year 337
issued, redeemed, and outstanding at the close of the fiscal year 354
Silver bullion:
in Treasury September 30, 1878, '79, '80 317
November 1, 1879, '80 318
Silver certificates:
outstanding and in Treasury September 30, 1878, '79, '80 317
outstanding and on hand November 1, 1879, '80 .... 318, 319
issues of, at various offices to September 30, 1880 323
exchanged for gold 323
issued, redeemed, and outstanding, by denominations 323, 353
issues of, by warrant, during fiscal year 336, 340
redemptions of, by warrant, during fiscal year 337, 340
redemptions of, during fiscal year, and total redemptions 348
issued, redeemed, and outstanding at the several offices of issue 355
Silver coin and bullion:
in Treasury, increase of, in fiscal year 317
Standard silver dollars:
in Treasury September 30, 1878, '79, '80 317
November 1, 1879, '80 318
coinage and distribution of 322
coined, on hand, and outstanding, by months, from March, 1878, to October, 1880 322
amount of, returned for national-bank notes redeemed during fiscal year 357
State of the Treasury, the 316-319
States:
amounts of deposit with, under act of June 23, 1836 344
Sub-treasuries of the United States:
balances and movement of moneys in, for fiscal year 338, 339
disbursing officers' balances in, June 30, 1880 341
balances and movement of moneys of Post-Office Department in, for fiscal year 343
quarterly-interest checks paid by, during fiscal year 364
Telegrams:
received and sent during fiscal year 360
Temporary loan:
redemptions of, by warrant, during fiscal year 337
Ten-forties of 1864:
redemptions of, by warrant, during fiscal year 337
amount of, held in trust for national banks 347
coupons from, paid during fiscal year 354
total retired for sinking fund 355
total retired by redemption and exchange 356
Texas indemnity stock:
total redeemed 356
Trade dollars:
speculation in, by bullion dealers 328
Transfer checks:
amount of, outstanding September 30, 1877, '78, '79, '80 316
number of, drawn during fiscal year 326
amount of, issued in redemption of national-bank notes during fiscal year 357
Transfers of funds:
amount of, during fiscal year 315
Treasury of the United States:
balances and movement of general Treasury moneys in, during fiscal year 338-339
disbursing officers' balances in, June 30, 1880 341
balances and movement of moneys of Post-Office Department in, during fiscal
year 343
Treasury proper appropriations:
repayments to, during fiscal year 336
expenditures by warrant from, during fiscal year 336
Unavailable funds:
amount of, unchanged during fiscal year 315
detailed statement of, June 30, 1880 344

Page.

'reasurer of the United States—Continued.

United States bonds:

held in trust for national banks 326
    Pacific Railroad sinking funds 327
    Indian trust fund 327–346
    American Printing House for the Blind 328
    Pennsylvania Company 328
    Manhattan Savings Institution 328
total amount of, retired from March 11, 1862, to June 30, 1880 316
and interest in Treasury September 30, 1879, '80 317
redeemed from November 1, 1879, to November 1, 1880 320
purchased on account of sinking fund in same period 320
issues of, by warrant, during fiscal year 336, 340
redemptions of, by warrant, during fiscal year 337, 340
held in trust for national banks, classified by loans 347
purchased for sinking fund during fiscal year 355
total retired for sinking fund 355
total retired by purchase, conversion, redemption, and exchange 356–357

United States currency:

total amount redeemed and outstanding June 30, 1880 316
amount of each issue of, outstanding at close of each fiscal year from 1862 to 1880 .. 348
redemptions of, for fiscal year, total redemptions, and deductions on account of mutilations ... 348
issued, redeemed, and outstanding at close of fiscal years 1879, '80 .. 349–353

United States notes:

in Treasury September 30, 1877, '78, '79, '80 317
    November 1, 1879, '80 318
redemptions of, in gold, by months, since resumption 319
receipts of, for customs, by months, since resumption 319
outstanding, by denominations, at close of fiscal years 1877, '78, '79, '80 .. 320, 321
decrease of, of denominations of $5,000 and $10,000 outstanding 321
increase of small and increase of large denominations of, outstanding . 321
issues and redemption of, by denominations, for fiscal years 1878, '79, '80 .. 321
deductions from face value of, on account of mutilations 326–327, 348
counterfeit, rejected during fiscal year 326
issues of, by warrant, during fiscal year 336, 340
redemptions of, by warrant, during fiscal year 337, 340
outstanding at close of each fiscal year from 1862 to 1880 348
redemptions of, for fiscal year, total redemptions, and deductions on account of mutilations ... 348
issued, redeemed, and outstanding at close of fiscal years 1879, '80 .. 349–350
retired for national-bank notes redeemed 357
for credit of 5 per cent. accounts of national banks 360

War Department appropriations:

repayments to, during fiscal year 336, 337
expenditures from, by warrant, during fiscal year 337

Register of the Treasury 363–504

Accounts received 371
Bonds issued and canceled 365, 366
Bonds received and on hand 365, 366
Bonds converted into registered 365, 366
Bonds transferred 365
Bonds redeemed 365
Bonds destroyed 365
Balances of appropriations, June 30, 1880 390–476
Barges, number and tonnage 368
Census, 8th, 9th, and 10th 430
Coin checks 367
Certificates, currency and gold 367
Coupons received, examined, &c 367
Certificates of accounts issued 371
Compound-interest notes redeemed 368
Custom-houses, &c 416–474
Customs, number of persons employed in collection 486–495
Drafts registered 371
Expenditures 390–476
  Legislative 390–394
    Senate 390
    House of Representatives 390–392
    Public Printer 392
    Library 394
    Botanic Garden 394
    Court of Claims 394
    Claims commissions 394
  Executive 394
    State Department 394
    Foreign intercourse 394–398
    Smithsonian Institution 394
    Treasury Department 398–404
    Independent Treasury 404
    Mint 404
    Territorial government 406
    District of Columbia 403–409
    Coast Survey 402
    Public buildings 402
    Refunding national debt 402
    War Department 410–412, 452–468

Register of the Treasury—Continued.

Page

Expenditures—Continued.

Navy Department 412, 468–47;
Post-Office Department 412–41;
Department of Agriculture 41;
Department of Justice 414–41;
Judicial 416–41;
Customs Service 418–422, 478–48;
Steamboat Inspection Service 41;
Marine Hospital Service 422, 483, 48;
Internal Revenue 432–434, 480–48;
Light-House Establishment 42;
Interior (civil) 424
Interior Department 436–45;
Public debt 434
Collecting revenue from customs, by districts. 475
Fractional currency counted, &c 368
Fisheries, tonnage employed in 370, 499, 500
Iron vessels built 369
Legal-tender notes counted, &c 368
Public debt, 1791 to 1842 478
Persons employed in customs service 485
Receipts from:
  customs 372
  public lands 373
  internal revenue 375
  consular fees 377
  steamboat fees 379
  registers' and receivers' fees 380
  Marine Hospital tax 382
  labor, drayage, &c 384
  services of United States officers 354
  weighing fees 384
  customs officers' fees 385
  fines, penalties, and forfeitures—customs 385
  fines, penalties, and forfeitures—courts 386
  emolument fees—customs 387
  emolument fees—judiciary 387
  proceeds of government property 388
  proceeds of captured and abandoned property 389
  Pacific Railroad Companies 388
  bonds, notes, &c 388
  Indian trust funds, &c 388, 389
  mileage of examiners 389
  reimbursements by national banks 389
  conscience fund 380
  District of Columbia 389
  sales of ordnance 388
  interest from certain railroads 389
  trust fund interest schools of South Carolina 389
  profits on coinage 389
  Hot Springs of Arkansas 389
  rents of public buildings 389
  interest on debts due United States 389
  depredations on public lands 389
  seals and tax for taking 389
  sales and rent of property under internal-revenue laws 389
  tax on circulation of national banks 389
  patents 389
  deposits for surveys 389
  premiums on drafts 389
  forfeitures 389
  land office copying fees 389
  reimbursements and reliefs 389
  John Gardner's property 389
  S. A. Belden & Co., moneys from Mexico 389
  miscellaneous 389
Ship-building 369, 500
Surveying public lands 426, 490
Treasury notes counted, &c 368
Tonnage, decrease of 368
Vessels, tonnage, number, and kind employed 389, 496–501
Vessels, tonnage, number, and kind built in 1880 .... 369, 501, 502
Vessels, tonnage, number, and kind built from 1803 to 1880, inclusive ... 502, 503
Warrants, number of 370
Liabilities to Indian Tribes 505–516

www.ingramcontent.com/pod-product-compliance
Lightning Source LLC
Chambersburg PA
CBHW022125020426
42334CB00015B/762